The Routledge Handbook of Language and Identity

The Routledge Handbook of Language and Identity provides a clear and comprehensive survey of the field of language and identity from an applied linguistics perspective. Authored by specialists from around the world, each chapter introduces a topic in language and identity studies and provides a concise, critical survey in which the importance and relevance to applied linguists is explained.

Thirty-seven chapters are organised into five sections covering:

- theoretical perspectives informing language and identity studies
- categories and dimensions of identity
- key issues for researchers in language and identity studies
- topical case studies in areas of interest to applied linguistics
- future directions for language and identity studies in applied linguistics.

With further reading included in each chapter, *The Routledge Handbook of Language and Identity* is an essential reference for all students, teachers and researchers working in the areas of Applied Linguistics, Linguistics, Education and TESOL.

Advisory board: David Block (Institució Catalana de Recerca i Estudis Avançats/Universitat de Lleida, Spain), John E. Joseph (University of Edinburgh, UK) and Bonny Norton (University of British Columbia, Canada).

Siân Preece is Senior Lecturer in Applied Linguistics and TESOL at the UCL Institute of Education. She is the author of *Posh Talk: Language and Identity in Higher Education* (2009) and a co-author of *Language, Society and Power*, 3rd edn (2011).

Routledge Handbooks in Applied Linguistics

Routledge Handbooks in Applied Linguistics provide comprehensive overviews of the key topics in applied linguistics. All entries for the handbooks are specially commissioned and written by leading scholars in the field. Clear, accessible and carefully edited, *Routledge Handbooks in Applied Linguistics* are the ideal resource for both advanced undergraduates and postgraduate students.

The Routledge Handbook of Language and Identity

Edited by Siân Preece

LONDON AND NEW YORK

First published 2016
by Routledge
2 Park Square, Milton Park, Abingdon, Oxon OX14 4RN

and by Routledge
711 Third Avenue, New York, NY 10017

Routledge is an imprint of the Taylor & Francis Group, an informa business

British Library Cataloguing-in-Publication Data
A catalogue record for this book is available from the British Library

Library of Congress Cataloging-in-Publication Data
Names: Preece, Siân, 1960- editor.
Title: The Routledge Handbook of language and identity / edited by Siân
Preece.
Other titles: Handbook of language and identity
Description: Milton Park, Abingdon, Oxon ; New York, NY : Routledge, [2016] |
Series: Routledge Handbooks in Applied Linguistics | Includes
bibliographical references and index.
Identifiers: LCCN 2015039256| ISBN 9781138774728(hbk) | ISBN
9781315669819(ebk)
Subjects: LCSH: Language and languages--Study and teaching. | Group identity.
| Identity (Psychology) | Interdisciplinary approach in education. |
Language and culture. | Language and education. | Multicultural education.
| Psycholinguistics.
Classification: LCC P53.7 .R68 2016 | DDC 400--dc23
LC record available at http://lccn.loc.gov/2015039256

ISBN: 978-1-138-77472-8 (hbk)
ISBN: 978-1-315-66981-6 (ebk)

Typeset in Bembo
by GreenGate Publishing Services, Tonbridge, Kent

MIX
Paper from
responsible sources
FSC
www.fsc.org   FSC® C013056

Printed and bound in Great Britain by
TJ International Ltd, Padstow, Cornwall

For John and Gloria

Contents

Contents

Contents

Figures, tables and boxes

Figures

Tables

Boxes

Contributors

Patricia Andrew is Professor of Applied Linguistics, Sociolinguistics and EFL at the National University of Mexico. Her research interests include identity construction, sociocultural perspectives on second language acquisition, and age studies. She is the author of *The Social construction of age: Adult foreign language learners* (Multilingual Matters 2012).

Judith Baxter is Professor of Applied Linguistics at Aston University, UK. Her areas of research specialism include gender and language, discourses of leadership and feminist poststructuralist discourse analysis. She has written numerous journal articles on these topics as well as three acclaimed monographs, *Double-voicing at work* (2014), *The language of female leadership* (2010) and *Positioning gender in discourse* (2003), all published by Palgrave Macmillan.

Bettina Beinhoff is Senior Lecturer in English and Applied Linguistics at Anglia Ruskin University. Her main research interests are at the crossroads of sociolinguistics, second language acquisition and speech perception and production. Her publications include journal articles and a co-edited volume, *Scribes as agents of language change* (Mouton de Gruyter 2013).

John Bellamy is a researcher at the Centre for Luxembourg Studies at the University of Sheffield. He has carried out a number of projects investigating people's perceptions of language usage and local spoken varieties, published as *Language attitudes in England and Austria* (Franz Steiner 2012). His latest publication is 'Language attitudes in spoken interaction: A case study in the Ruhrgebiet' in G. Rutten and K. Horner (eds) *Metalanguage, language ideologies and standardization* (Peter Lang 2015).

Bethan Benwell is Senior Lecturer in Language and Linguistics at the University of Stirling. She has published extensively on discourse and identity, discursive approaches to reception and popular representations of masculinity. Her latest book (co-authored with J. Proctor) is *Reading across worlds: Transnational book groups and the reception of difference* (Macmillan 2015). Her most recent research involves the analysis of health-care communication.

Adrian Blackledge is Professor of Bilingualism and Director of the MOSAIC Centre for Research on Multilingualism at the University of Birmingham, UK. He is the author of numerous articles and books based on his research on multilingualism in education and wider society. His latest books include *Heteroglossia as practice and pedagogy* (2014), *The Routledge handbook of multilingualism* (2012) and *Multilingualism: A critical perspective* (2010). He is currently engaged in research funded through the Arts and Humanities Research Council's Translating Cultures theme, *Translation and translanguaging: Investigating linguistic and cultural transformations in superdiverse wards in four UK cities*.

David Block is ICREA Research Professor in Sociolinguistics at the University of Lleida (Spain). He is interested in the impact of political economic and social phenomena on multimodal identity-making practices of all kinds (including social movements, multiculturalism, bi/multilingualism and the acquisition and use of languages). In recent years he has focused specifically on neoliberalism as the dominant ideology in contemporary societies and social class as a key dimension of identity. He has published extensively, and his books include *The social turn in second language acquisition* (2003), *Second language identities* (2007/2014) and *Social class in applied linguistics* (2014). He is the editor of the Routledge book series *Language, society and political economy*.

Qumrul Hasan Chowdhury is Assistant Professor at the Institute of Modern Languages, University of Dhaka, Bangladesh. He is currently a doctoral student at King's College London. His research interests include language and identity and the sociology of language education.

Christian W. Chun is Lecturer in the School of Education, University of New South Wales. He has published two books, *Power and meaning making in an EAP classroom: Engaging with the everyday* (Multilingual Matters 2015) and *The discourses of capitalism* (Routledge 2016). A longtime activist, he participated in the 2011 Occupy movement in the United States. His workshop on language and the media for Occupy Los Angeles, entitled *Critical language in action*, can be viewed on YouTube.

Eva Codó is Associate Professor of English and Linguistics at Universitat Autònoma de Barcelona, Catalonia (Spain). Her research focuses on multilingualism from a critical sociolinguistic and ethnographic perspective, on which she has published several journal articles and book chapters. She is currently investigating the indexicalities of English in the Catalan/Spanish educational system.

Victor Corona is a postdoc researcher at the École Normale Supériure de Lyon (ASLAN-ICAR Laboratory). He is interested in ethnographic research from a sociolinguistics perspective and he is currently working on a project which examines the language practices of young people in vocational schools in Lyon and Barcelona. He obtained his PhD in 2012 from the Universitat Autònoma de Barcelona with a thesis entitled *Globalización, Identidades y escuela: Lo latino en Barcelona*.

Angela Creese is Professor of Educational Linguistics at the School of Education, University of Birmingham, and Principal Investigator of AHRC grant *Translation and translanguaging: Investigating linguistic and cultural transformations in superdiverse wards in four UK cities* (AH/L007096/1). Her research interests are in linguistic ethnography, language ecologies, multilingualism in society and multilingual classroom pedagogy. She has published extensively, and her latest books include *Linguistic ethnography* (with Fiona Copland, 2015, SAGE), *Heteroglossia as practice and pedagogy* (edited with Adrian Blackledge, 2014, Springer) and *The Routledge handbook of multilingualism* (edited with Marilyn Martin-Jones and Adrian Blackledge, 2012).

Ron Darvin is a doctoral candidate and Vanier scholar of the University of British Columbia. His areas of interest include digital literacies and issues of identity, social class, and transnationalism. His recent research examines the inequalities of digital access and use among adolescent learners of different class positions, and the impact of these inequalities on their investment in learning and their social and educational trajectories. He has published articles in *Annual Review of Applied Linguistics*, *Journal of Language, Identity, and Education* and *TESOL Quarterly*.

Peter De Costa is Assistant Professor in the Department of Linguistics and Languages at Michigan State University. His primary area of research is the role of identity and ideology in second language acquisition. Much of his current work focuses on conducting ethically applied linguistic research, English as a lingua franca, scalar approaches to language learning, and language learning and emotions, on which he has published several journal articles.

Anna De Fina is Professor of Italian Language and Linguistics in the Italian Department and Affiliated Faculty with the Linguistics Department at Georgetown University, USA. Her interests and publications focus on identity, narrative, migration and diversity. Her books include *Identity in narrative: A study of immigrant discourse* (2003, John Benjamins), *Analyzing narratives* (2012, Cambridge University Press, written with Alexandra Georgakopoulou) and *Discourse and identity* (2006, Cambridge University Press, edited with D. Schiffrin and M. Bamberg).

Myrrh Domingo is Lecturer in Contemporary Literacy at the UCL Institute of Education, University College London. Her projects and publications are focused on social media practices; language and literacy research; technology-mediated teaching and learning; and multimodal and ethnographic methodologies for online research. She has published several articles and and is co-editor of *The SAGE handbook of digital dissertations and theses* (SAGE 2012) with Richard Andrews, Erik Borg, Stephen Boyd Davis and Jude England.

Rob Drummond is Senior Lecturer in Linguistics at Manchester Metropolitan University, teaching sociolinguistics, language variation, and phonetics and phonology. Having previously spent time researching dialect acquisition in a second language, his main focus now is on the speech of adolescents in urban environments and the ways in which they use language to construct and perform identities. He has published a number of journal articles and book chapters. He is the principal investigator on the Leverhulme Trust-funded UrBEn-ID project *Expressing inner-city youth identity through multicultural urban British English.*

John Edwards is Professor of Psychology at St Francis Xavier University. He is a fellow of the British Psychological Society, the Canadian Psychological Association and the Royal Society of Canada. His main research interest is the maintenance and continuity of group identity, with particular reference to language in both its communicative and symbolic aspects. He is also the editor of a *Multilingual Matters* book series. He has published extensively, and his latest books include *Language and identity* (Cambridge University Press 2009), *Multilingualism: Understanding linguistic diversity* (Continuum 2012) and *Sociolinguistics: A very short introduction* (Oxford University Press 2013).

Eva Duran Eppler is Reader/Associate Professor of English Language and Linguistics at the University of Roehampton, London, UK. She is interested in structural and processing aspects of bilingual language and the processes and outcomes of language and culture contact, including identity. She has published a number of books, including *Gender and spoken interaction* (with Pia Pichler) (Palgrave Macmillan 2009), *Emigranto: The syntax of a German/English mixed code* (Braumuller 2010) and *English words and sentences* (with Gabriel Ozon) (Cambridge University Press 2013).

Elizabeth J. Erling is Lecturer in English Language Teaching in the Centre for International Development and Teacher Education at the Open University, UK. Her research focuses on the impact that English language education has on individuals' lives in terms of their identity and social, economic and cultural capital. She is particularly interested in the relationship between

English language skills and economic development in low-income countries. She has published several journal articles, book chapters and reports.

Ann-Carita Evaldsson is Professor in Education, Uppsala University, Sweden. Her area of expertise is children's peer language practices and adult–child interaction, addressing topics such as play, morality, multilingualism, bullying and identity work (gender, class, ethnicity and disability) as socially situated phenomena. The research draws on a peer language socialisation approach and ethnomethodology (membership categorisation analysis and conversation analysis). She has published several journal articles and book chapters and co-edited, with Jacob Cromdal, *An everyday life with multiple languages: Children and young people in interaction in multilingual school environments* (Liber 2004).

Frances Giampapa is Senior Lecturer in Education at the University of Bristol, specialising in Critical Sociolinguistics and Applied Linguistics. Her research and publications focus on the migration, language/literacies and identities nexus across multilingual contexts. More recently, she has published on researcher identities in the process of conducting multilingual critical ethnographic research.

John Gray is Reader in Languages in Education at the UCL Institute of Education, University College London. His interests include the global spread of English; neoliberal ideology in language teaching and language teacher education; the marketisation of language teacher education and language teacher identity; and issues of gender and sexuality in language teaching. He is the author of *The construction of English* (2010), co-author with David Block and Marnie Holborow of *Neoliberalism and applied linguistics* (2012), and the editor of *Critical perspectives on language teaching materials* (2013).

Christina Higgins is Professor at the University of Hawai'i at Mānoa where she teaches in the Department of Second Language Studies. Her research explores the sociolinguistics of multilingual practices in East Africa and Hawai'i across a range of domains, including workplaces, public health education and popular culture. Her books include *English as a local language* (Multilingual Matters 2009), *Language and HIV/AIDS* (co-edited with Bonny Norton, Multilingual Matters 2009), *Identity formation in globalizing contexts* (Mouton 2011) and *Enriching practice in linguistically and culturally diverse classrooms* (with Eva Ponte, Caslon 2015).

Eva Hjörne is Professor in Education at the University of Gothenburg, Sweden. Her research interests are in the analysis of learning and social interaction, processes of marginalisation and mediated action, with special a focus on categorising and identity formation of pupils in school. She has written several articles and book chapters and is one of the co-editors of *Assessing children in the Nordic countries: Framing, diversity and matters of inclusion and exclusion in a school for all* (Springer 2014).

Kristine Horner is Reader in Luxembourg Studies and Multilingualism at the University of Sheffield. Her research interests focus on language politics and language ideologies, particularly in relation to multilingualism. Recent publications include *Introducing multilingualism: A social approach* (with J-J. Weber, Routledge 2012) and *Multilingualism and mobility in Europe: Policies and practices* (with I. de Saint-Georges and J-J. Weber, Peter Lang 2014).

Anna Kristina Hultgren is Lecturer in Applied Linguistics and English Language at the Open University, UK. She works at the intersection of sociolinguistics and globalisation and currently conducts research on issues surrounding English as a medium of instruction and knowledge production in non-English-dominant contexts. She has published several book chapters and journal articles.

Lucy Jones is Assistant Professor in Sociolinguistics at the University of Nottingham. Her research makes use of ethnography and discourse analysis, and is concerned with the construction and representation of gender and sexual identities. Her published work to date has focused mainly on lesbian identities. She is the author of *Dyke/girl: Language and identities in a lesbian group* (Palgrave Macmillan 2012).

John E. Joseph is Professor of Applied Linguistics at the University of Edinburgh, and co-editor of the journals *Language and Communication* and *Historiographia Linguistica*. His books include *Language and identity* (Palgrave 2004), *Language and politics* (Edinburgh University Press 2006) and *Saussure* (Oxford University Press 2012).

Vally Lytra is Lecturer in Languages in Education in the Department of Educational Studies at Goldsmiths, University of London. She uses ethnography to study language and literacy practices, language ideologies and social identities in schools, homes and communities in cross-cultural urban contexts. She co-edited (with Peter Martin) *Sites of multilingualism: Complementary schools in Britain today* (Trentham Books 2010).

Jean McAvoy is Lecturer in Psychology at the Open University, UK. From the perspective of critical social psychology, her work focuses on processes of subjectification and the production of subjectivities, with a particular interest in the ways in which moralities and transgressions are constructed in ideological discursive and affective practices. She is also pursuing the potentials and challenges of inter- and transdisciplinary methods of study. She has published a number of journal articles and book chapters.

Tommaso M. Milani is Associate Professor of Linguistics at the University of the Witwatersrand, Johannesburg, South Africa. He is the co-editor of the journals *African Studies* (Taylor & Francis) and *Gender and Language* (Equinox); he is also the editor of the book series *Advances in Sociolinguistics* (Bloomsbury). He has published several journal articles and is the editor of the book *Language and masculinities: Performances, intersections, dislocations* (Routledge 2015).

Tom Morton is an Honorary Research Fellow in the Department of Applied Linguistics at Birkbeck, University of London, and a Visiting Academic at the University of Southampton. His interests include L2 development in Content and Language Integrated Learning (CLIL), classroom discourse and interaction in CLIL and TESOL, and language teacher knowledge and identity. He has published several journal articles and book chapters and is the co-author of *The roles of language in CLIL* (with Ana Llinares and Rachel Whittaker) (Cambridge University Press 2012).

Louise Mullany is Associate Professor of Sociolinguistics at the University of Nottingham. She has published widely on the topics of the sociolinguistics of work and language and gender research, focusing in particular on communication in professional settings. Key publications include *Language, gender and feminism: Theory, methodology and practice* (with Sara Mills)

(Routledge 2011) and *Gendered discourse in the professional workplace* (Palgrave 2007). She is currently Associate Editor of *Gender and Language*.

Cynthia D. Nelson is an Honorary Associate at the University of Sydney. Her research projects focus on three main areas: research writing practices and pedagogies; social identities in education contexts and texts; and narrative and performance writing, including research-based theatre and performance. She is the author of *Sexual identities in English language education: Classroom conversations* (Routledge 2009) and is on the editorial board of the *Journal of Language and Sexuality*.

Bonny Norton is Professor and Distinguished University Scholar in the Department of Language and Literacy Education, University of British Columbia, Canada. Her primary research interests are identity and language learning, critical literacy and international development. In 2010, she was the inaugural recipient of the Senior Research Leadership Award by the Second Language Research SIG of the American Educational Research Association, and in 2012 was inducted as an AERA Fellow. She has published extensively; her latest book is *Identity and language learning: Extending the conversation*, 2nd edn. (2000, 1st edn.) (Multilingual Matters 2014).

John P. O'Regan is Senior Lecturer in Applied Linguistics at the UCL Institute of Education, University College London, where he leads the MA in Applied Linguistics. His research interests include the political economy of global English, intercultural communication theory, identity politics and critical discourse analysis. He is the author of articles covering a wide range of topics in applied linguistics and cultural studies.

Tope Omoniyi has a chair in Sociolinguistics in the Department of Media, Culture and Language at the University of Roehampton in London. His research interest is in language and identity with a focus on youth. His interest also covers language and development in Sub-Sahara Africa. He has published extensively, and his latest books include *Contending with globalisation in world Englishes* (co-edited with Mukul Saxena) (Multilingual Matters 2010) and *The sociology of language and religion: Change, conflict and accommodation* (ed.) (Palgrave Macmillan 2010).

Miguel Pérez-Milans is Senior Lecturer in Applied Linguistics at the UCL Institute of Education, University College London. He is interested in interactional sociolinguistics; linguistic ethnography; language and identity; and language-in-education policy. He has published several journal articles and authored a book on language education and identity in late modern China, in the *Routledge Critical Series in Multilingualism* (2013). He is the co-editor of the *Oxford Handbook of language policy and planning* (forthcoming).

Siân Preece is Senior Lecturer in Applied Linguistics and TESOL at the UCL Institute of Education, Universtiy College London. Her research examines the relationship between language and identity, particularly the intersection of gender, ethnicity and social class with linguistic minority students in higher education. She is the author of *Posh talk: Language and identity in higher education* (Palgrave Macmillan 2009), editor of *The Routledge handbook of language and identity* (Routledge 2016) and one of the co-authors of *Language, society and power*, 3rd edn. (Routledge 2011). She is Principal Investigator for the ESRC seminar series *The multilingual university: The impact of linguistic diversity on higher education in English-dominant and English medium instructional contexts*.

Ben Rampton is Professor of Applied and Sociolinguistics and Director of the Centre for Language Discourse and Communication at King's College London. He does interactional sociolinguistics, and his interests cover urban multilingualism, ethnicity, class, youth and education. He has published extensively, and his latest books include *Crossing: Language and ethnicity among adolescents* (Longman 1995/St Jerome 2005) and *Language in late modernity: Interaction in an urban school* (Cambridge University Press 2006). He co-edited *Language and superdiversity* (Routledge 2015) and edits *Working Papers in Urban Language and Literacy*. He was founding convener of the UK Linguistic Ethnography Forum.

Sebastian M. Rasinger is Principal Lecturer in Applied Linguistics at Anglia Ruskin University. He is interested in language and migration, ethnic and cultural identities, and the representation of minority groups in public and media discourse, using methods derived from both corpus linguistics and critical discourse analysis. He is the author of *Quantitative research in linguistics: An introduction,* 2nd edn. (Bloomsbury 2013).

Frances Rock is a Senior Lecturer at the Centre for Language and Communication Research at Cardiff University. Her research has examined language and policing in a variety of settings, and recommendations from her work have been taken up by police forces around England and Wales. Her publications include the book *Communicating rights: The language of arrest and detention* and the edited collection *Legal–lay communication: Textual travels in the law*. She is one of the editors of the *International Journal of Speech, Language and the Law*.

Priti Sandhu is Assistant Professor in the English Department at the University of Washington. She works with interview-based narratives. Her research interests include gendered identities in patriarchal societies, the medium of education in postcolonial contexts, the accomplishment or destabilisation of social hierarchies in interactional data and the creation of empowered and disempowered identities in interactional narratives. She has published a number of book chapters and journal articles and is currently working on a book about narratives of the medium of education, Indian women and identity formation.

Erik Schleef is Professor of English Linguistics at the University of Salzburg, Austria. His research focuses on discourse, phonetic and phonological variation and change in dialects of the British Isles, the acquisition of variation, sociolinguistics and perception, and language and gender in educational settings. He has lived and taught in the US, Great Britain, Germany, Austria and Switzerland, and he is the co-editor of the *Routledge sociolinguistics reader* and co-author of *Doing sociolinguistics: A practical guide to data collection and analysis*.

Ana Souza is Senior Lecturer in TESOL and Applied Linguistics at Oxford Brookes University, where she contributes to the MA in TESOL, the BA in English Language and Communication and the PG Cert in Teaching English as an Additional Language. Her research interests include bilingualism, language planning in families and in migrant churches and the teaching of Portuguese as a Heritage Language. She has published a number of journal articles and book chapters.

Elizabeth Stokoe is Professor of Social Interaction in the Department of Social Sciences at Loughborough University. She has published extensively in the fields of conversation and membership categorisation analysis, focusing most recently on applications and translating empirical research into real world impact. Her books include *Discourse and identity* (with Bethan Benwell) (Edinburgh University Press 2006), *Conversation and gender* (with S. Speer) (Cambridge University Press 2011) and *Discursive psychology: Classic and contemporary issues* (with C. Tileaga) (Routledge 2015).

Melissa Yoong is the Director of the Arts and Education Foundation Programme at the University of Nottingham Malaysia Campus. She is currently pursuing her PhD with the University of Nottingham's School of English, UK. Her research focuses on how language is used to construct gender identities and perpetuate discourses of femininity in the mass media. She is particularly interested in how media discourses both celebrate and undermine professional women.

Karin Zotzmann is Lecturer in Applied Linguistics at the University of Southampton. Her main research interests include genre and discourse theory and analysis, language teaching and learning within the framework of transnational or globalisation processes, and the implications of the internationalisation and marketisation of higher education on academic practices and inclusivity. She has published a number of journal articles and book chapters.

Preface

In his Preface to the *Oxford Handbook of Applied Linguistics*, published in 2002, the editor Robert Kaplan argued that applied linguistics, as distinct from autonomous linguistics, has a view of language that considers language use and language users as centrally important in the study of language, and focuses attention on language problems in the 'real world'. With the publication in that collection of a chapter on 'Identity and Language Learning' (Norton and Toohey 2002), the topic of identity was recognised for the first time as an area of interest to an encyclopaedia of applied linguistics. In this chapter, Kelleen Toohey and I argued that language learning engages the identities of learners because language is not only a linguistic system of signs and symbols, but also a complex social practice in which the value and meaning of a given utterance – whether oral or written – is partly determined by the value ascribed to a particular speaker or writer. This value, in turn, is best understood with reference to complex social and cultural practices, and negotiated in the context of shifting relations of power.

In defending this set of claims, Toohey and I drew on diverse theories of language, learning and the learner, to make the case that post-Saussurean theories of language and identity have much to offer the field of applied linguistics. Scholars such as Mikhail Bakhtin, Pierre Bourdieu, Stuart Hall and Christine Weedon take the position that the linguistic system itself cannot guarantee the meaning of linguistic signs, given the heterogeneous and unequal nature of linguistic communities. Further, humanist conceptions of the self as unified and coherent do not do justice to the complex, multiple and changing identities of social beings. In making this case, we also drew on an emerging body of research on language and identity, including journal special issues in *Linguistics and Education* (Martin-Jones and Heller 1996), *Language and Education* (Sarangi and Baynham 1996) and *TESOL Quarterly* (Norton 1997). We noted that the introduction in 2002 of the new *Journal of Language, Identity, and Education*, edited by Tom Ricento and Terrence Wiley, would increase the momentum of interest in language and identity, which has indeed proved prescient.

Fast-forward a decade to the 2011 *Routledge Handbook of Applied Linguistics*, in which the editor, James Simpson, identifies 'Language, Culture and Identity' as one of the major sections in this more recent encyclopaedia. As Simpson notes, 'the applied linguistic concern with language in the social world entails an exploration of phenomena, connections and relationships from the micro to the macro scale – from language related issues of individual identity to those of the global society' (Simpson 2011: 4). This section includes chapters on topics such as language and culture (Kramsch), gender (Baxter), ethnicity (Harris), linguistic imperialism (Canagarajah and Said) and identity (Norton). By 2015, 'identity' was the theme of the state-of-the-art *Annual Review of Applied Linguistics* (Mackey 2015), with 14 articles on topics ranging from issues of class (Block), translanguaging (Creese and Blackledge), and investment (Darvin and Norton) to technology (Thorne, Sauro and Smith), ethnicity (Trofimovich and Turuševa) and migration (Wodak and Boukala). The Douglas Fir Group, which has worked at length to develop a collaborative, transdisciplinary framework of second language acquisition, also incorporates identity as a central component of its ground-breaking model of language learning and teaching (Douglas Fir Group in press, 2016). And now, with Siân Preece's current volume (Preece 2016), the field has its own comprehensive handbook on language and identity. With 37 cutting-edge chapters, *The Routledge Handbook of Language and Identity* is a fitting tribute to a well-established, vibrant area of applied linguistics.

This exciting trajectory has not always been linear, however. While applied linguistics as a field has embraced new conceptions of language, and its relationship to an increasingly wide range of users, settings and problems, it continues to grapple with the investments of diverse stakeholders in particular visions of applied linguistics. In the 2002 *Oxford Handbook*, for example, Kaplan notes that 'the editorial group spent quite a bit of time debating whether research on critical (applied) linguistics/critical pedagogy/critical discourse analysis should be included' (p. vi) in the encyclo-paedia, but ultimately took the decision to omit this dynamic area of work from the collection. Similarly, while de Bot (2015: 78) acknowledges that identity is 'one of the main trends' in applied linguistics, he gives the topic only cursory treatment in his history of the field. It is in fact ironic that the very theories and publications excluded from such texts can help to explain that academic fields, much like learners, have identities that are multiple and often sites of struggle.

The extensive planning and thoughtful organisation of *The Routledge Handbook of Language and Identity* has resulted in a compelling collection of chapters that make an irrefutable case for the salience and resilience of identity research in the field of applied linguistics. Topics include not only multiple perspectives on language and identity, including the previously neglected area of critical discourse analysis, but also the associated challenges of undertaking both innovative and rigorous research on identity. The section on the social categories of identity is particularly extensive: research on race and ethnicity, a primary focus of earlier research on identity in the social sciences, remains robust; however, other social categories such as gender, religion, age and sexuality further enrich debates on language and identity, complementing the increasing interest in intersectionality. Case studies of identity, from Mexico to the UK and from South Africa to Sweden, illustrate how particular configurations of time and space enhance our understanding of language and identity, while the digital age presents new challenges for future research in this area. As the 'real world' of language use and language users grows increasingly complex and often unequal, authors in *The Routledge Handbook of Language and Identity* highlight the ways in which identity research can help navigate this challenging terrain, and contribute to an applied linguistic vision of a more just and hopeful world.

Bonny Norton, University of British Columbia, Vancouver

References

de Bot, K. (2015). *A history of applied linguistics: from 1980 to the present*. London and New York: Routledge.

Douglas Fir Group (in press, 2016). 'A transdisciplinary framework for SLA in a multilingual world', *The Modern Language Journal*, 100.

Kaplan, R. (2002). *The Oxford handbook of applied linguistics*. New York: Oxford University Press.

Mackey, A. (ed.) (2015). 'Identity in applied linguistics', *Annual Review of Applied Linguistics*, 35.

Martin-Jones, M. and Heller, M. (guest eds) (1996). 'Special issue. Education in multilingual settings: discourse, identities, and power', *Linguistics and Education*, 8(1–2).

Norton, B (guest ed.) (1997). 'Special issue. Language and identity', *TESOL Quarterly*, 31(3).

Norton, B. and Toohey, K. (2002). Identity and language learning, in R. Kaplan (ed.) *The Oxford handbook of applied linguistics*. New York: Oxford University Press, pp. 115–124.

Preece, S. (ed.) (2016). *The Routledge handbook of language and identity*. Abingdon: Routledge.

Sarangi, S. and Baynham, M. (guest eds) (1996). 'Special issue. Discursive construction of educational identities: alternative readings', *Language and Education*, 10(2–3).

Simpson, J. (ed.) (2011). *The Routledge handbook of applied linguistics*. Abingdon: Routledge.

Acknowledgements

There are many people to whom I will be eternally grateful for helping to bring this volume into being. First and foremost I would like to thank the contributors for their participation and for tolerating my editing. I would also like to give my sincere thanks to the members of my Editorial Advisory Board: Bonny Norton, David Block and John Joseph. You were all truly superb and I deeply appreciate the amount of time and energy that you invested in this volume. My thanks are also extended to the following, who generously devoted their time to reading and reviewing draft chapters for this volume: Patricia Andrew, Mike Bayham, Bethan Benwell, David Block, Ron Darvin, John Joseph, Claudia Lapping, Constant Leung, Vally Lytra, Li Wei, Steve Marshall, Marilyn Martin-Jones, Tom Morton, Bonny Norton, Phan Le Ha, James Simpson, Jane Sunderland, Elaine Unterhalter and Cathie Wallace. Many apologies if I have missed any of the reviewers off this list. I would also like to thank Pia Pichler, Tope Omoniyi and Angel Lin for help and advice in the early stages of the volume. My colleagues in the Applied Linguistics TESOL team at the UCL Institute of Education have provided much appreciated support to ensure that I could devote time to getting the volume finished. Many thanks go to Alyse Dar, who provided a keen eye for proof reading and editing the chapters and helped me to sort out numerous issues with the English language. Many thanks also go to Louisa Semlyen and Laura Sandford at Routledge for all their help and advice. Finally, I am indebted to Phoebus for all his support and encouragement over the many months it took to complete this volume.

Introduction
Language and identity
in applied linguistics

Siân Preece

I do not remember paying much attention to the question of 'my identity', at least the national part of it, before the brutal awakening of March 1968 when my Polishness was publicly cast in doubt. I guess that until then I expected, matter-of-factly, and without any soul-searching or calculating, to retire when the time came from the University of Warsaw, and be buried when the time came in one of Warsaw's cemeteries. But since March 1968 I have been and still am expected by everyone around to self-define and I am supposed to have a considered, carefully balanced, keenly argued view of my identity. Why? Because once set in motion, pulled out from wherever I could pass for my 'natural habitat', there was no place where I could be seen as fitting in, as they say, one hundred per cent. In each and every place I was – sometimes slightly, at some other times blatantly, 'out of place'.

(Bauman 2004: 12)

I applied for asylum on 20 April. I feel isolated, a man in deep despair. Even if France gives me asylum, can I integrate here? Do they see me as a human being? I need some care. At least in Britain even if I was homeless, I could learn the language. Here is hard and the language is so difficult.

(Fadhel, The Guardian online, 27 July 2015)

This *Handbook* is about identity and its relationship with language. It aims to give readers a comprehensive overview of key topics in the study of language and identity and illustrate how the phenomenon of identity is related to a variety of 'real world problems in which language is a central issue' (Brumfit 1995: 27), Christopher Brumfit's oft-cited definition of applied linguistics. The volume complements *The Routledge Handbook of Applied Linguistics* (Simpson 2013 [2011]) and is part of the Routledge Handbooks in Applied Linguistics series.

The opening quotes illustrate how identity can become 'a real world problem' and also point to how language comes into the picture. Both are narratives that form part of the rich tapestry of migrant stories on displacement, disjuncture, the search for a new place to belong, the learning of a new language and an identity transformation in which the culture, languages, religion, politics, customs and practices of what was left behind enter into a fluid mix with what is and what is to come. Here then we have two migrant narratives invoking identity. The first comes from Zygmunt Bauman's (2004) classic sociological text, *Identity*. Bauman tells the story of his migration from Poland to the UK in order to make a point for his audience. As Bauman tells us, those who feel that they belong have no need to worry about their identities. Identity only becomes an issue when a person's sense of belonging is disrupted. For migrants forced to flee, identity disruption is likely to be severe. Bauman's story shows us that once dislocated from his 'natural habitat' of Poland, he always felt (or was made to feel by others) 'out of place'. As we will see in this *Handbook*, it is this 'out of place' feeling that gives rise to identity work and creates opportunities for new subjectivities through the interaction of the 'old' and the 'new'.

The 'out of place-ness' also looms large in Fadhel's narrative. After thousands of miles of migration, Fadhel has become trapped in 'The Jungle', the name given to a makeshift camp in the port of Calais in France, which, at the time of writing, is sheltering 3,000 dispossessed and stateless migrants from the poorest and most war-torn regions of the world (Taylor *et al.* 2015). Fadhel's words (translated into English and placed in subtitles) come from a short film, 'Life in the Jungle' (ibid.), posted online by *The Guardian*. In putting his story into cyberspace, Fadhel asserts his identity as a refugee seeking asylum in France, a man and a human being. In so doing, he gains a fleeting moment of agency in which he is able to tell viewers about his anxieties, particularly his worries about learning French and fitting into French society. He also constructs a future 'imagined self' in Britain, which he believes will afford him the opportunities to learn English even if homeless. In his plea 'I need some care', Fadhel appeals to a common humanity that indexes a global human identity transcending the nation state, in which migrants such as Fadhel are ensnared as:

> the '*sans-papiers*' – the non-territorials [who live] in a world of territorially grounded sovereignty. While sharing the predicament of the underclass,[1] they are, on top of all the other deprivations, denied the right to a physical presence within the territory under sovereign rule except in specially designed 'non-places', labelled as refugee or asylum-seeker camps to distinguish them from the space where the rest, the 'normal', the 'complete' people live and move.
>
> *(Bauman 2004: 39)*

In both narratives, we see Bonny Norton's (2013: 45) contention that identity refers to 'how a person understands his or her relationship to the world, how that relationship is constructed across time and space, and how the person understands possibilities for the future'. Bauman shows us his ability to relate identity as a theoretical concept to lived experience, to chart the moment of rupture that made him conscious of his identity and how his identity has developed over time and space. He seems to imagine the possibilities for the future as more of the same, i.e. the need to continue maintaining his identity due to feeling 'out of place'. In Bauman's case, however, his future possibilities appear brighter than Fadhel's given the material circumstances of his life and his social status as Emeritus Professor of Sociology at the University of Leeds. Fadhel, on the other hand, has no material comforts or resources to fall back on. His relationship to the world is of a stateless person who is forced to live a precarious and liminal existence in 'The Jungle' while he waits to see whether or not he will be granted asylum in France. The time and space continuum for Fadhel has been compressed into daily survival, and when he imagines possibilities for the future, his best case scenario is homelessness in Britain.

One of the points that we can take from Bauman and Fadhel's stories is that identity is not a free-for-all in which individuals are at liberty to mix and match designer identities of their choosing. As we will see in this volume, the identities that people 'inhabit' (that is, choose for themselves) (Blommaert 2006) are constrained, among other things, by their:

- Access to the types of social spaces and relations (or discursive spaces) in which identities are constructed, constituted, negotiated, accomplished and/or performed;
- 'Ascribed' identities (that is, the identities that individuals are given by others (ibid.). Ascribed identities often position individuals as non-normative and limit their rights to participation);
- Access to material resources, including the income, property and employment status derived from their social class positioning in society. David Block (2014, this volume) gives us a timely reminder that we need to pay closer attention to social class in research on identity, particularly when investigating 'migrants as bilinguals' (2014: 126).

As Block (2007) tells us in his book *Second Language Identities*, identity has long been of interest in the social sciences. Social scientists are interested in identity because it enables the gap between the micro level of the individual and the macro level of the social order to be bridged. It allows for the investigation of an individual's membership of particular groups, affiliations to cultural customs and practices and representations of self and others. Block (ibid.) explains how social scientists have come to see identity as fluid, multidimensional (including e.g. gender, sexuality, class, race, ethnicity, age, religion, culture, etc.) and socially constructed; these views have taken hold in applied linguistics.

In this volume, we will see the shift in applied linguistics from viewing identity as a set of fixed characteristics that are learned or biologically based to seeing identity as a social construct. This shift reflects the way that identity has become an altogether more complex phenomenon as a result of the mobility and diversity that has arisen in the social worlds of the physical and digital due to the processes of globalisation in late modernity. As we will see, this change in thinking is often discussed in terms of 'essentialism' and 'non-essentialism'. Mary Bucholtz (2003: 400) points out that essentialism rests on the assumption that:

> the attributes and behavior of socially defined groups can be determined and explained by reference to cultural and/or biological characteristics believed to be inherent to the group. As an ideology, essentialism rests on two assumptions: (1) that groups can be clearly delimited; and (2) that group members are more or less alike.

In contrast, non-essentialism chimes with Stuart Hall's (1996: 4) oft-cited definition of identities as:

> about questions of using the resources of history, language and culture in the process of becoming rather than being: not 'who we are' or 'where we came from', so much as what we might become, how we have been represented and how that bears on how we might represent ourselves.

Non-essentialised views of identity, such as Hall's, are shaped by poststructuralist and social constructivist theoretical perspectives. These perspectives are discussed in detail in Part I of this volume and inform the chapters in the rest of the *Handbook*.

Since Norton's (1995, 2013 [2000]) pioneering work to inject a social view of identity into second language acquisition (SLA), there has been a surge of interest in identity and its relationship with language in applied linguistics. As Norton points out in the preface to this volume, this has resulted in a considerable number of books, journal articles and special issues devoted to the subject of identity in the field. Zotzmann and O'Regan (this volume) discuss how identity is of particular interest to applied linguists not only because it connects the individual to the social world but also because it frames the use of language as a social, rather than cognitive, enterprise. They put this neatly:

> The concept [of identity] sensitises us to think about the reasons for and the conditions under which people use language, the way they are perceived by others as users of language, the meanings they want to convey in particular situations and the resources they draw upon in order to do so.
>
> *(p. 113)*

If we apply the above to Fadhel's narrative, we can start to draw some tentative conclusions about a number of points as follows. First, Fadhel's reasons for learning French seem likely to be in anticipation of a new life in France should his claim for asylum be granted. As Fadhel tells us, this will require him 'to integrate' with French people, and hopefully give him the chance to return to a normal life in which he has gainful employment, an income and decent housing. Should Fadhel stay in France, French will enable him to inhabit identities that are not currently available to him as a non-French speaker. Second, the conditions under which Fadhel uses French appear constrained by the very limited access to interactions that he is likely to have with French people. However, he may be able to use French with Francophone migrants in 'The Jungle' and, as there are volunteer teachers giving French classes in the camp, perhaps he has access to French lessons. With regard to the ways in which Fadhel is perceived by others as a user of language, he is likely to be ascribed the identity of a second language learner, at least by French people. When it comes to the meanings that Fadhel wants to convey, we know from what he has told viewers that he wishes to convey the difficulties of his current life and how to go about resolving these. As he has stated that he is 'in despair', we can infer that he wishes to communicate more than functional and transactional messages. Finally, with respect to the resources that Fadhel has to draw on for language learning, while we do not know anything about his level of education or country of origin, it is likely that Fadhel has a bi/multilingual linguistic repertoire at his disposal as well as other multimodal resources, such as signing and gesture.

To the points given by Zotzmann and O'Regan, we could also add perceptions about language. In Fadhel's case, his narrative invokes the commonly held view of languages as entities that are (1) named (French, English, etc.); (2) distinct from each other, suggesting a commonly held view that languages should be kept separate; (3) learned in a particular order (L1, L2, L3, etc.); and (4) attached to particular groups of people as markers of national, ethnic and/or cultural identity. Fadhel's statement about French being 'difficult', his life in France being 'hard' and his question of whether French people view him 'as a human being' suggests ambivalence about inhabiting a French or Francophone identity.

Following Norton (2013 [2000]), we begin to get a sense of how language plays a role in Fadhel's identity as a language learner. The argument that Norton puts forward about language appears particularly pertinent to Fadhel's situation:

it is through language that a person negotiates a sense of self within and across different sites at different points in time, and it is through language that a person gains access to – or is denied access to – powerful social networks that give learners the opportunity to speak. Thus language is not conceived of as a neutral medium of communication, but is understood with reference to its social meaning.

(Ibid.: 45)

Language is foregrounded in this *Handbook*. As we will see, there has been a move from seeing language as discrete entities that mark the ethnic, cultural and/or national identities of particular groups of people in an unproblematic way to viewing language as part of a repertoire consisting of linguistic and other multimodal resources for communicative and identity work (Rymes 2010). Many of the contributors to this volume draw on the principles synthesised by Bucholtz and Hall (2010 [2005]: 19–26) for locating identity in language. These can be summarised as follows. (1) 'The emergence principle': Identity is seen as emerging in interaction. While Bucholtz and Hall refer to talk, this could be extended to interaction between a reader and text. (2) 'The positionality principle': This involves speakers temporarily inhabiting particular roles and stances in the unfolding interaction along with locally situated cultural positions and social order identity categories. (3) 'The indexicality principle': Bucholtz and Hall discuss how identities are 'indexed' in interaction by speakers making overt references to particular identity roles and inscriptions or through covert suggestions about self and others. Indexing can also involve making evaluations about what identities are considered to be normative and non-normative as well as using language associated with a particular group identity or persona. (4) 'The relationality principle': This relates to the claim that identities are always constructed in relation to other identity positions and involve a number of overlapping binaries such as self–other, authenticity–inauthenticity and legitimate–illegitimate speaker. (5) 'The partialness principle': This is the idea that as identities are always in a process of becoming, they can only ever be partial.

So far, I have introduced identity and its relationship with language. In what follows we turn to the scope of this volume and a summary of the chapters.

The scope of this volume

This *Handbook* is aimed at a diverse audience, including graduate students, early career researchers, established academics, policymakers and practitioners, although the contributions have been written with relative newcomers in mind. The volume brings together a body of work on language and identity in applied linguistics and associated work in sociolinguistics. As might be expected, bi/multilingual and transnational individuals; second/foreign language learners and teachers; and ethnicity, culture and migration feature regularly. However, the volume also includes other areas of interest in applied linguistics, including gender, sexuality, social class, age and disability; professional settings other than the classroom; and the digital world and multimodality.

The contributors demonstrate the interest in applied linguistics with theorising practice, particularly what the examination of linguistic practices and perceptions about language can tell us about identity. Several chapters suggest how studies of identity in applied linguistics and sociolinguistics could usefully be applied to practice in professional life, in areas ranging from (language) teacher education, the development of postgraduate and early career researchers and the continuing professional development of practitioners, such as mediators.

Other contributors approach application through the lens of social justice. These chapters deal with the identities of marginalised or liminal individuals, such as Fadhel. Here the theory/practice link is seen as a matter of:

1   Identity politics (increasing the recognition of and respect for the identity of an individual or group);
2   The redistribution of wealth (developing policies and practices that seek to redistribute institutional and societal resources to those that are materially disadvantaged in society).

(Fraser 1995; Fraser and Honneth 2003)

Block (2014, this volume) gives us a timely reminder that applied linguistics has given more attention to the former than the latter and invites us to focus more fully on the redistribution issue in future work.

Other contributors are concerned with problematising commonly held views in applied linguistics that inform work on language and identity, such as the idea of languages as discrete entities (as expressed in L1 and L2), the privileging of language as a mode of communication and the focus on the 'real' world. These contributors invite us to consider how 'heteroglossia' (Bakhtin 1984), multimodality and the inclusion of the digital world could transform our understanding of language, identity and their interrelationship, particularly in the superdiverse contexts in which many language and identity studies take place.

While broad in scope, the *Handbook* is not designed to be exhaustive and there are inevitably some gaps and shortcomings. For instance, while the contributors to this volume represent scholars at all stages of their careers (from first-year doctoral students to world-renowned professors) and include more female than male authors, the number of contributors based in universities in the English-dominant world (here taken to be the United States, the United Kingdom, Anglophone Canada, Australia and New Zealand) outweigh those from institutions in non-English-dominant contexts; there is also greater reference to language and identity work within the Anglophone 'centre' than outside it and within 'first world' rather than 'third world' contexts. Nonetheless, the five parts of the volume cover a considerable amount of ground, highlighting a wealth of language and identity research in applied linguistics and sociolinguistics in a diverse range of settings. An outline of the five parts of the volume follows.

Part I: Perspectives on language and identity

The first part of the *Handbook* consists of seven chapters that present readers with a range of theoretical perspectives on identity and the nature of its relationship with language. The purpose of this part is to give an indication of the diversity of theoretical perspectives available for theorising identity along with a detailed overview of some of these. The chapters in this part of the volume follow a similar format: introduction; overview of the theoretical perspective under examination; and discussion of issues and ongoing debates in relation to applied linguistics. Similarly to all the chapters in the volume, each chapter concludes with a summary; a list of related topics (indicating other related chapters in the volume that readers may find useful to read); an annotated bibliography of further reading for readers to consult for more detailed treatment of the topic; and a list of chapter references.

In the opening chapter of the volume, *Historical perspectives on language and identity*, John Joseph sets the scene for readers by providing a detailed account of how contemporary views of identity, along with the ways in which language is used to index identity, are rooted in historical narratives. Joseph discusses how these narratives are revealed through the beliefs that individuals espouse about languages and the ways in which beliefs about languages are used to signal membership in a collective identity. Joseph charts the shift in the social sciences (and applied linguistics) from structuralist views of identity (in which, as mentioned above, identity was seen as a set of genetically inherent and/or learned characteristics that were possessed by the individual in a stable and bounded inner core) to social constructionist perspectives on identity (in which identity has come to be viewed as fluid and emerging in interaction).

The idea of fluidity is taken up by Judith Baxter in her chapter, *Positioning language and identity: Poststructuralist perspectives*, in which the reader is given a comprehensive overview of the ways in which poststructuralism approaches identity and its relationship with language. Baxter shows us that despite there being no one simple definition of poststructuralism, nor a unified poststructuralist perspective on identity, poststructuralist perspectives on identity have become highly influential in the field. She details how Michel Foucault's (e.g. 1980, 1984) seminal theory of discourse has given rise to a discursive view of identity, in which individuals are viewed as taking up 'subject positions', or 'ways of being an individual' (Weedon 1997), in the discourses to which they have access. As Baxter points out, discourses are viewed as a means by which particular ways of viewing the world get into circulation. By adopting a particular subject position, the individual is therefore not just doing identity work, but also playing an instrumental role in maintaining and reproducing discourse, and its attendant ideologies, in society.

The shift from relatively fixed views of identity to those that are more fluid is also charted in *Identity in variationist sociolinguistics*. Here Rob Drummond and Erik Schleef document the changing views of identity in three waves of variationist sociolinguistics, from the initial correlation of language variety with broad demographic identity categories, such as gender and social class, to the idea of language variation being reflective of insider identities in local social networks, to the notion of language variation, such as 'styling', being a resource for identity work in spoken interaction.

Concern with fine-grained analyses of identity in everyday talk is taken up in three related chapters: *Ethnomethodological and conversation analytic approaches to identity, Language and identity in linguistic ethnography* and *Discursive psychology and the production of identity in language practices*. In the first of these chapters, Bethan Benwell and Elizabeth Stokoe point out that ethnomethodological approaches view identity as of relevance only insofar as individuals in their everyday activities 'orient to and describe, classify, or assess each other as particular kinds of people, as members (or not) of identity-relevant categories' (p. 66). As they point out, this is at odds with the perception of identity as the acculturation of an individual into socially constructed identity categories or with Foucauldian-inspired ideas of identity in poststructuralist accounts. Benwell and Stokoe explain how conversation analysis and membership category analysis, informed by ethnomethodology, have developed linguistic tools for fine-grained analysis of talk. As the reader will see, unlike poststructuralist approaches to identity, ethnomethodological ones require that any claims about identity must be rooted in overt references in the data; the researcher is not permitted to impose identity categories if these are not made salient by the participants themselves.

In the following chapter, Miguel Pérez-Milans argues that linguistic ethnography offers a way of moving beyond the impasse that has arisen in the field between ethnomethodology/CA and poststructuralist, particularly Foucauldian-inspired, approaches to identity. Pérez-Milans explains how linguistic ethnography views a person's activities in terms of social practices, in which individuals are viewed as participating with some degree of agency and reflexivity. From this perspective, language comes to constitute social practices and also '[serve] as a terrain for working out struggles that are fundamentally about other things' (Heller 2011: 49). Pérez-Milans sets out how linguistic ethnographers combine the linguistic tools of ethnomethodology with ethnographic approaches to examine identity in the situated practices of everyday life.

A similar stance is taken by Jean McAvoy in her chapter. Similarly to CA and linguistic ethnography, McAvoy explains the importance of an explicit focus on language practices and 'what is accomplished in language-in-use' (p. 98) for the study of language and identity in discursive psychology. Identity is viewed as emerging from talk as it unfolds and also as a resource that individuals draw on to position themselves as particular kinds of people. McAvoy discusses how discursive psychology draws on ethnomethodology and the linguistic tools of CA to see how identity is accomplished in talk; linguistic ethnography, with its notion of identity as emerging from participation in situated practice; and various psychological paradigms related to 'personality, beliefs, attitudes, emotions and ... understandings of self, others and relationships' (p. 98). As McAvoy points out, discursive psychology allows applied linguists to draw on psycho-social frameworks for making sense of identity.

Part I is brought to a close with *Critical discourse analysis and identity*. In this chapter, Karin Zotzmann and John O'Regan set out, by now, a number of familiar ideas about identity, discussing how CDA views identity as located in the social world, as fluid and emergent and as situated in social practices in discourse; however, unlike poststructuralist perspectives, CDA also brings in the material world. Similarly to the other chapters in this part, they point out the role of language as a semiotic resource for doing identity work and the need for a set of linguistic tools that not only allow for the analysis of identity in talk but also how identity is represented in multimodal texts. Unlike the other perspectives discussed so far, which have privileged talk and interaction, CDA places more emphasis on the analysis of written (and multimodal) texts. However, as Zotzmann and O'Regan argue, it is CDA's 'explicit commitment to a critique of problematic social practices with a view of transforming them for the better' (p. 114) that distinguishes CDA from the other theoretical perspectives discussed in this part of the volume. A commitment to the transformation of the social world is therefore uppermost in CDA-inspired studies of language and identity.

Part II: Categories and dimensions of identity

Part II of the *Handbook* develops the discussion set out in Part I by focusing on the view of identity as 'multidimensional'. This part consists of eight chapters, with each focusing on a particular identity inscription. The chapters follow a similar format: introduction; an account of the category or dimension of identity under examination; ongoing issues and debates with regard to applied linguistics; summary; related topics; further reading; and references. The first five chapters in Part II are broadly concerned with race, ethnicity, culture and religion as dimensions of identity for bi/multilingual individuals, groups and communities in the global world. In *Language and ethnic identity*, Vally Lytra shows how ethnicity continues to be an important dimension of identity in contemporary life. Tracing shifts in thinking about ethnicity in the social sciences, Lytra examines the role that language plays in marking ethnic identities. Picking up on themes introduced by Joseph in Part I of the volume, Lytra compares essentialist and constructionist views of ethnic identity. She shows how essentialised views of identity approach languages as separate entities that are used to mark particular ethnic and cultural identities, whereas constructionist perspectives view language and ethnicity as having porous borders that allow for the negotiation of more fluid, and hybrid, ethnic identities, which, as Lytra points out, are characterised by linguistic diversity and multilingual repertoires.

In *Language, race and identity*, Tope Omoniyi presents a discussion of the arguments in various disciplines on race, examining problems with definitions of race that rely on stereotypes to views of race as a complex social construct. Omoniyi shows how interest in race in sociolinguistics and applied linguistics goes beyond the study of racism discourses and argues that the interface of race, language and identity affords opportunities for issues related to social justice to be addressed by applied linguists.

In *Linguistic practices and transnational identities*, Anna De Fina develops the discussion on ethnicity, culture and language by examining transnationalism as a dimension of identity in contexts of migration and mobility. As De Fina points out, transnational identities are not bound to one nation state, ethnicity, culture or language but emerge in the social networks created by migrants to link their ancestral homelands with their place of settlement. Similarly to Lytra, De Fina puts forward a view of identity as fluid and emerging from the culturally and linguistically diverse practices of migrant communities. For De Fina, this allows for a view of migrants as agentive and reflexive transnational individuals rather than as assimilating or resisting the practices and identities of 'people who are firmly grounded in one place' (p. 164).

Similar themes are picked up on in *Identity in post-colonial contexts*. In this chapter, Priti Sandhu and Christina Higgins discuss the relationship between identity and language in postcolonial settings, showing how a 'centre–periphery' binary has come to shape understandings of identity inscriptions, such as class, ethnicity, language and gender. Drawing on Edward Said's (1978) seminal text *Orientalism*, Sandhu and Higgins explain the development of two important binaries in post-colonial studies – 'Self–Other' and 'Occident–Orient' – that have been used to construct a normative Western identity in opposition to a non-normative eastern other. As Sandhu and Higgins point out, these binaries have become increasingly problematic for theorising identity in contemporary post-colonial settings. In a similar vein to De Fina, Sandhu and Higgins argue that identity studies need to start with the transcultural and multilingual language practices that are a feature of the setting under examination, including the use of the language of the colonial legacy, such as English, and consider how these index coloniser–colonised relations, ideologies and identities.

Language and religious identities examines religion as a dimension of identity, focusing on migrant faith communities. Ana Souza gives a detailed overview of the development of 'language and religion' as a major area of interest in sociolinguistics. For Souza, language and religion have a symbiotic relationship. She shows not only how in the context of faith communities heritage and community languages are an important resource for maintaining religious practices and for establishing religion as a dimension of identity, but also how religious practices play an important role in the maintenance of community and heritage languages and identities.

The following two chapters turn to gender, sex and sexuality as dimensions of identity. In *Language and gender identities*, Lucy Jones presents a detailed overview of how the relationship between language and gender identity has developed in applied linguistics and sociolinguistics since the 1970s. She points out how early scholarship was based on the idea of sex and gender binaries that linked biological sex (the male/female body) with learned gender (masculine/feminine identity); language was viewed as reflective of gender socialisation and gender identity as a 'man' or 'woman'. As Jones shows us, this binary was used to construct the 'gender order' (Connell 1987) and the associated idea of 'heteronormativity' (Cameron and Kulick 2003), in which heterosexuality within monogamous relationships and marriage are presented as norms. Jones discusses how Judith Butler's (1990) seminal work on 'performativity' problematised normative views of gender and sexuality, allowing for a range of masculinities, femininities and transgender identities. As she comments, performativity allows for a view of language as a resource for performing gender identities and for representing gender identities in texts.

Sexuality as a dimension of identity is developed in John Gray's chapter, *Language and non-normative sexual identities*. Gray charts the development of non-normative LGBTQI (lesbian, gay, bisexual, transgender, transsexual, queer and intersex) identities and the role of language in representing and expressing non-normative sexual identities through three periods: the work of sexologists in the nineteenth century; the rise of lesbian and gay studies in the late twentieth century; and the development of contemporary queer theory. For Gray, non-normative sexualities, as a dimension of identity, represent a challenge to the gender order along with its heteronormative ideology and essentialised perceptions of identity.

Part II closes with *Class in language and identity research*, in which social class is examined as an identity inscription. David Block presents a detailed discussion of social class, examining its origins in the work of Karl Marx and its subsequent development as a multidimensional and multilevelled construct in the work of Pierre Bourdieu and other scholars. Block challenges the lack of attention to class in language and identity studies in the field. Drawing on Nancy Fraser (1995), Block puts forward the argument that class is different from other identity inscriptions in that it attends to the distribution of material resources rather than the recognition of cultural differences. Block argues that language and identity studies would be enriched by greater attention to distribution issues as well as cultural recognition.

Part III: Researching the language and identity relationship

Part III of the *Handbook* acts as a bridge between the theoretical discussion in Parts I and II and the discussion in Parts IV and V on past and current research and possible future directions for language and identity work. Part III consists of five chapters that address some of the problems and dilemmas that language and identity researchers face. The chapters follow a similar format: introduction; account of the issue; commentary on ways of addressing the issue; summary; related topics; further reading; and references.

Anna Hultgren, Elizabeth Erling and Qumrul Chowdhury open this part of the *Handbook* with *Ethics in language and identity research*, in which they put the question of ethics in the spotlight. Hultgren, Erling and Chowdhury invite us not to approach ethical questions as a checklist to be signed off by an ethics committee, but as an opportunity to develop 'ethical literacy' (Wiles and Boddy 2013), in which ethics becomes an intrinsic part of the research process. For Hultgren, Erling and Chowdhury, ethical literacy enables researchers to become more accountable to their participants along with others who are directly and indirectly involved in their research projects. This is illustrated by a reflection on their own ethical dilemmas on an English language-learning project in rural Bangladesh.

The next chapter, *A linguistic ethnography of identity: Adopting a heteroglossic frame*, invites language and identity researchers to adopt a 'heteroglossic' (Bakhtin 1984) perspective when researching in bi/multilingual contexts. Adrian Blackledge and Angela Creese argue that heteroglossia allows the researcher to problematise the commonly held perception of bi/multilingualism in applied linguistics as two-plus named languages that exist discretely in people's lives. Picking up on the discussion of language presented so far in the volume, Blackledge and Creese make the case for adopting a linguistic ethnographic approach to language and identity studies in which researchers start by examining the linguistic practices of the participants in the setting, considering how these index identities for the participants themselves and drawing on a heteroglossic frame to consider the language ideologies informing the participants' perceptions. They argue that this will allow for a more critical stance towards the classification of research participants in language and identity studies in contexts of superdiversity (Vertovec 2006) and a more nuanced discussion when it comes to using research findings to influence policy and practice in professional domains.

In *The politics of researcher identities: Opportunities and challenges in identities research*, Frances Giampapa gives a detailed account of the role of the researcher in language and identity studies in language learning contexts. She argues that researchers are positioned socially, politically and historically in their research and 'inextricably intertwined with the lives and everyday practices of their research participants' (p. 289). Giampapa invites language and identity researchers to think reflexively in order to bring to light the ways in which researcher identities shape the research. This is illustrated by a reflective account of her own research.

Challenges for language and identity researchers in the collection and transcription of spoken interaction examines common issues that are encountered when collecting and transcribing talk. Eva Eppler and Eva Codó present a detailed discussion of the type of decisions that researchers embarking on a language and identity study need to make. They put forward helpful observations for applied linguists to bear in mind on the sorts of spoken interaction that are useful for answering research questions; the kinds of speakers, contexts and interactions that are likely to generate useful data; different ways of collecting spoken interaction; and the variety of approaches to transcription.

The final chapter in this part of the *Handbook*, *Beyond the micro–macro interface in language and identity research*, focuses on the problems related to linking everyday instances of language with institutional practices and the social order. Kristine Horner and John Bellamy give readers a thorough account of the debate that has taken place in the social sciences on the relationship between two binaries: 'micro–macro' and 'structure–agency'. Horner and Bellamy critique these binaries and illustrate how researchers in applied linguistics and sociolinguistics have attempted to bridge the lifeworlds of their research participants with a bigger picture related to the functioning of broader social, political and economic structures. For Horner and Bellamy, ethnographically oriented studies of language and identity that employ discourse analytic methods offer the best chance of addressing the micro–macro dilemma.

Part IV: Language and identity case studies

Part IV of the *Handbook* addresses the interest in applied linguistics with theorising practice. This part consists of 11 chapters, in which the contributors present their own case studies of language and identity research. These showcase the range of work that is taking place in the field, bring theoretical discussion to life, by illustrating how identity and its relationship with language has been realised in research, and act as a model for novice researchers contemplating their own language and identity research. The chapter format in this part of the volume broadly follows that of a journal article: introduction (scene setting and outline of the main argument); literature review (brief overview of the theoretical perspectives on language and identity informing the study); methodology (a reasonably detailed account of the research process); data presentation (examples of the data showing approaches to data presentation and analysis); discussion (what the data tell us about the overall argument); and issues arising for applied linguistics (some indication of what the field can learn from the study).

As applied linguistics has long been concerned with education, the first five chapters present language and identity case studies undertaken in a variety of educational settings in different parts of the world. In the opening chapter, *Constructing age identity: The case of Mexican EFL learners*, Patricia Andrew focuses on age as a dimension of English language learner identities in Mexico. In her nuanced study, Andrew shows that age as a social construct, rather than a biological characteristic, is a significant dimension of identity for language learners and illustrates how age intersects with other identity inscriptions, such as gender in the EFL classroom. Andrew argues that SLA researchers and language teachers need to take greater account of age as a social phenomenon and a more critical stance towards ageist discourses that mark older learners as non-normative.

The next two chapters – *The significance of sexual identity to language learning and teaching* and *An identity transformation? Social class, language prejudice and the erasure of multilingual capital in higher education* – pick up on the theme of marginalisation and the marking of particular groups of language learners as non-normative. In the first, Cynthia Nelson discusses the importance of sexuality as a dimension of language learners and teachers' identities, drawing on data from her case study of English language classrooms in the United States. Nelson demonstrates how heteronormativity still regulates much of the interaction in the language classroom, thus closing down space for the emergence and recognition of LGTBQI identities. Nelson provides readers with powerful evidence of why sexual identity is not peripheral but integral to the language learning and teaching enterprise and suggestions for language teachers on how to approach sexuality as a dimension of language learners' identities. The following chapter presents my own case study into the identities of linguistic minority undergraduate students on an academic writing programme in a university in London. In this chapter, I discuss social class as both an ascribed identity, arising from the participants' positioning in the British social class system, and an inhabited identity that shapes the participants' perceptions and use of language and linguistic practices in the context of the university. I show how the participants experience language prejudice in the domain of higher education as a result of institutional practices that stigmatised their linguistic practices and erased their multilingual capital. I conclude by discussing how shifts in institutional culture and resources are required to enable working-class students from bi/multilingual migrant communities to achieve the identity transformation on offer in higher education.

In the following two chapters we move out of the language classroom and into other educational settings. In the first of these chapters, *Being a language teacher in the content classroom: Teacher identity and content and language integrated learning (CLIL)*, Tom Morton presents data from the Bilingual Education Project, a large-scale case study in Spain into the acquisition of bilingual Spanish and English through an integrated content-based curriculum. Morton examines the impact of CLIL on the identities of subject teachers as they grapple with teaching their subject in English. Morton illustrates how identity issues emerge in interactions between the teacher and school pupils and in reflective talk on teaching practice. Morton argues that attending to teacher identities in CLIL contexts bridges the worlds of applied linguists and language educators in the field of bilingual education and opens up possibilities for collaborative research. Following this, we move to a case study set in a special school in Sweden for children with learning disabilities. In this chapter, *Disability identities and category work in institutional practices: The case of a 'typical ADHD girl'*, Eva Hjörne and Ann-Carita Evaldsson examine disability as a dimension of identity. Employing an ethnomethodological framework, they show how attention deficit hyperactivity disorder as a disability category is accomplished in talk at school and in interactions between the school and parents. Hjörne and Evaldsson illustrate the intersection of disability with gender through examining how the school uses disability and gender categories to explain and address behaviour that is deemed to be problematic. They make a powerful case for the way in which the identity of a 'typical ADHD girl' is accomplished by the school and how this comes to stigmatise and marginalise the pre-adolescent girl concerned.

In the next two chapters, we turn to case studies set in other professional and institutional domains. In the first of these, *'Comes with the territory': Expert–novice and insider–outsider identities in police interviews*, Frances Rock shows how witness identities are constructed in interviews between police officers and witnesses to crimes in England and Wales. Through analysis of talk in the interview setting, Rock illustrates how witnesses who adopt an expert–insider witness identity rather than a novice–outsider identity can challenge conventional asymmetries in the interview setting. The following chapter, *Language, gender and identities in political life: A case study from Malaysia*, takes us to Malaysia and a case study concerned with the under-representation of women in political life. In this chapter, Louise Mullany and Melissa Yoong examine gender as a dimension of identity in the case of Dyana Sofya Mohd Daud, a female candidate who stood for parliament in a by-election in Malaysia. By contrasting digital texts written by Daud with online articles written by journalists, Mullany and Yoong show how a cocktail of identity inscriptions was created in the mass media intersecting gender with profession, age, race, religion and sexuality and how this cocktail served to reproduce the gender order.

The following chapter, *Straight-acting: Discursive negotiations of a homomasculine identity*, also picks up on gender and sexual identities in digital contexts. In this chapter, Tommaso Milani takes us to the online world of 'meetmarket', a social networking site in South Africa for men looking for other men. In his case study, Milani examines sexuality as a dimension of identity and its intersection with gender and race in the South African context. Through a detailed linguistic analysis of online corpora and interviews with men advertising on meetmarket, Milani shows how 'straight-acting' has become an important practice among non-heterosexual white middle-class men as a way of countering homophobia in the South African context and resisting exclusion from domains of hegemonic masculinity. However, Milani suggests that, in so doing, 'straight-acting' serves to reinforce the 'same old gender script' (Cameron 2001).

The following two chapters turn to the ethnic and cultural identities of adult migrants in Anglophone settings in home and community domains. In the first of these, *Styling and identity in a second language*, Ben Rampton presents a case study drawn from a large ESRC-funded project called *Dialect development and style in a diaspora community*, which investigated the use and development of dialectal varieties of English in families with Indian ancestry in London. Through a detailed linguistic analysis of the style-shifting and L2 variants used by an adult male migrant from the Punjab, Rampton examines the fluidity of identity and the intersection of a range of identity inscriptions for members of migrant communities in London. Rampton argues that applied linguists would do well to start with 'the total linguistic fact' (Silverstein 1985) when doing language and identity studies. For Rampton, an analysis of the relationship between linguistic form, situated discourse and ideology facilitates a more rounded analysis of migrant identities that avoids 'the romantic celebration of difference or creative agency that has been so common in sociolinguistics, and for the presumption of deficit and remedial need in SLA' (p. 472). In a related chapter, *Construction of heritage language and cultural identities: a case study of two young British-Bangladeshis in London*, Qumrul Chowdhury examines the intersection of ethnicity with culture, gender, religion and social class for two female British Asians in London whose families originated from Bangladesh. The interjection of class enables Chowdhury to show the development of asymmetrical class-based relations within the South Asian community based in the UK. For Chowdhury, however, religion emerged as the key dimension of identity, which, he suggests, was a response to Islamophobia in the UK context.

In the final chapter in this part, we turn to minoritised languages and their role in maintaining ethnic and national identities. In his chapter *Minority languages and group identity: Scottish Gaelic in the Old World and the New*, John Edwards examines the role of Gaelic in constructing Scottish identity in Scotland and Nova Scotia. Edwards presents a detailed discussion of a number of case studies that have surveyed attitudes to Gaelic in these locations. Picking up on the issues discussed by several contributors regarding the nature of the relationship between language and ethnic identity, Edwards argues that Gaelic occupies a largely symbolic role when it comes to ethnic and national identity for both the Scots in Scotland and Scottish migrants to Nova Scotia. For Edwards, 'language shift – and a lack of general interest in revival efforts – has come to sit quite easily with a strongly continuing sense of Scottish identity' (p. 501).

Part V: Future directions

Part V concludes the volume with a series of chapters examining the directions for future work on language and identity in applied linguistics. Part V comprises six chapters, with each giving an account of an issue for development in current work and how this could be addressed in future studies. In the opening chapter, *Intersectionality in language and identity research*, David Block and Victor Corona examine identity as a multidimensional phenomenon in which identity inscriptions are viewed as intersecting and shaping each other rather than as discrete and bounded categories. They argue that intersectionality has normally been dealt with by default in language and identity studies and contend that the field would benefit from theorising intersectionality and addressing it more fully as a methodological practice. Block and Corona examine data from Corona's research on the identities of young Latinos in Barcelona to show how an intersectional analysis can be developed.

The following two chapters, *Language and identity in the digital age* and *Language and identity research in online environments: A multimodal ethnographic perspective*, consider closely related topics. In the first of these chapters, Ron Darvin examines how advances in technology have made a dramatic impact on applied linguistics terrain. Darvin points out that the 'real world' in which applied linguistics has traditionally operated has been radically altered by ongoing developments in the digital domain. Darvin examines changes to the applied linguistics landscape brought about by the virtual world and argues that applied linguistics is well placed to investigate the affordances and constraints for the construction of online identities and the ways in which access to technology is positioning language learners as insiders or outsiders. In the following chapter, Myrrh Domingo questions the preoccupation with language in applied linguistics in her examination of multimodality. Domingo argues that, by privileging language as a mode of communication, applied linguists run the risk of not only missing other modes (non-verbal resources) that are brought to bear in the construction of identities, but also how these intersect with language. Domingo illustrates the affordances that multimodality creates for investigating language and identity in online environments by presenting data from her ethnographic study of the Pinoys, a Filipino British rap group.

In the following chapter we turn to neoliberalism. *Exploring neoliberal language, discourses and identities* presents a critique of the neoliberal policies and practices that have come to shape much of what goes on in institutions around the globe. Christian Chun examines the ways in which identities are co-constructed within a neoliberal discursive field and how neoliberalism is maintained through neoliberal policies and practices. Chun invites applied linguists to counter the dominance of neoliberal discourses in future language and identity studies by inhabiting identities that are more concerned with 'community-based notions of social justice and freedom' (p. 559) and examining how identities are 'branded' in the neoliberal order.

The *Handbook* closes with two chapters that provide comprehensive agendas for research in language and identity in sociolinguistics and applied linguistics. In *The future of identity research: Impact and new developments in sociolinguistics*, Bettina Beinhoff and Sebastian Rasinger identify three issues for future work: authenticity, fluidity of identities, and the role of the researcher and research ethics. For Beinhoff and Rasinger, researchers need to pay close attention to the authenticity of data and participants in future language and identity projects; continue to treat identity as fluid rather than static and bounded; and consider the identity of the researcher more closely and how researcher identities impact on language and identity research, particularly with regard to research ethics. The final chapter, *Identity in language learning and teaching: Research agendas for the future*, devotes itself to familiar terrain in applied linguistics – language learning and teaching. Peter De Costa and Bonny Norton examine four broad strands for future work in language and identity: theoretical developments, interdisciplinarity, research populations and methodological innovations. De Costa and Norton make the case that theoretical perspectives on identity in applied linguistics would be enriched by further consideration of globalisation, investment and research in post-colonial settings. Language and identity researchers are invited to continue developing interdisciplinary links, diversify the research populations in their studies and revisit prevailing methodologies in language and identity projects to consider how 'the methodological toolkit' (p. 595) could be developed. Similarly to other contributors, De Costa and Norton also identify researcher identities as an important area for development, particularly in future work in online settings.

Note

1   Bauman (2004: 39) uses the underclass to refer to people on the very margins of society (such as drug addicts, beggars, the homeless, street prostitutes, etc.) who are viewed as 'undesirable'. Bauman argues that the underclass have 'an absence of identity', in that they are denied access to the material resources and type of social spaces in which identities that are coveted are constructed.

References

Bakhtin, M.M. (1984). *Problems of Dostoevsky's poetics*. C. Emerson (ed.) [Trans. C. Emerson]. Manchester: Manchester University Press.

Bauman, Z. (2004). *Identity: conversations with Benedetto Vecchi*. Cambridge: Polity Press.

Blommaert, J. (2006). Language policy and national identity, in T. Ricento (ed.) *Language policy: theory and method*. Oxford: Blackwell, pp. 238–254.

Bucholtz, M. (2003). 'Sociolinguistic nostalgia and authentification of identity', *Journal of Sociolinguistics*, 7(3): 398–416.

Bucholtz, M. and Hall, K. (2010 [2005]). Locating identity in language, in C. Llamas and D. Watt (eds) *Language and identities*. Edinburgh: Edinburgh University Press, pp. 18–28.

Butler, J. (1990). *Gender trouble: feminism and the subversion of identity*. London: Routledge.

Block, D. (2007). *Second language identities*. London: Continuum.

Block, D. (2014). *Social class in applied linguistics*. Abingdon: Routledge.

Block, D. (this volume). Class in language and identity research, in S. Preece (ed.) *The Routledge handbook of language and identity*. London: Routledge, pp. 241–254.

Brumfit, C.J. (1995). Teacher professionalism and research, in G. Cook and B. Seidlhofer (eds) *Principles and practice in applied linguistics: studies in honour of H.G. Widdowson*. Oxford: Oxford University Press, pp. 27–41.

Cameron, D. (2001). *Working with spoken discourse*. London: SAGE.

Cameron, D. and Kulick, D. (2003). *Language and sexuality*. Cambridge: Cambridge University Press.

Connell, R.W. (1987). *Gender and power: sexuality, the person and sexual politics*. Cambridge: Polity Press.

Foucault, M. (1980). *Power/knowledge: selected interviews and other writings 1972–1977*. New York: Pantheon.

Foucault, M. (1984). What is enlightenment?, in P. Rabinow (ed.) *The Foucault reader*. London: Penguin, pp. 32–50.

Fraser, N. (1995). 'From redistribution to recognition? Dilemmas of justice in a "postsocialist" age', *New Left Review*, 212: 68–93.

Fraser, N. and Honneth, A. (2003). *Redistribution or recognition? A political-philosophical exchange*. London: Verso.

Hall, S. (1996). Introduction: who needs 'identity'?, in S. Hall and P. du Gay (eds) *Questions of cultural identity*. London: SAGE, pp. 1–17.

Heller, M. (2011). *Paths to post-nationalism: a critical ethnography of language and identity*. Oxford: Oxford University Press.

Norton (Peirce), B. (1995). 'Social identity, investment, and language learning', *TESOL Quarterly*, 29(1): 9–31.

Norton, B. (2013 [2000]). *Identity and language learning: extending the conversation*. 2nd edn. Bristol: Multilingual Matters.

Rymes, B.R. (2010). Classroom discourse analysis: a focus on communicative repertoires, in N. Hornberger and S. McKay (eds) *Sociolinguistics and language education*. Avon: Multilingual Matters, pp. 528–546.

Said, E. (1978). *Orientalism*. New York: Vintage.

Silverstein, M. (1985). Language and the culture of gender, in E. Mertz and R. Parmentier (eds) *Semiotic mediation*. New York: Academic Press, pp. 219–259.

Simpson, J. (ed.) (2013 [2011]). *The Routledge handbook of applied linguistics*. Abingdon: Routledge.

Taylor, M., Topping, A., Domokos, J. and Mahmood, M. (2015). 'Fortress Calais: fleeting fixtures and precarious lives in the migrant camp', *The Guardian*, 27 July [Online]. Available at www.theguardian.com/world/2015/jul/27/migrant-camp-fortress-calais-jungle

Vertovec, S. (2006). 'The emergence of super-diversity in Britain', *Centre on Migration, Policy and Study, Working Paper 25*, University of Oxford [Online]. Available at www.compas.ox.ac.uk/2006/wp-2006-025-vertovec_super-diversity_britain

Weedon, C. (1997). *Feminist practice and poststructuralist theory*. 2nd edn. Oxford: Blackwell.

Wiles, R. and Boddy, J. (2013). 'Introduction to the special issue: research ethics in challenging contexts', *Methodological Innovations Online*, 8(2): 1–5.

Zotzmann, K. and O'Regan, J.P. (this volume). Critical discourse analysis and identity, in S. Preece (ed.) *The Routledge handbook of language and identity*. London: Routledge, pp. 113–128.

Part I

Perspectives on language and identity

1

Historical perspectives on language and identity

John E. Joseph

Introduction

Language and identity is a topic in which contemporary perspectives cannot be neatly separated from historical ones. Identity, even in the here and now, is grounded in beliefs about the past: about heritage and ancestry, and about belonging to a people, a place, a set of beliefs and a way of life. Of the many ways in which such belonging is signified, what language a person speaks, and how he or she speaks it, rank among the most powerful, because it is through language that people and places are named, heritage and ancestry recorded and passed on, and beliefs developed and ritualised.

No language exists in a homogeneous or unchanging form. It is through variation that the identity of individuals is indexed and interpreted: who they are, what they care about and like, and what they aspire to. Such indexing can have both positive and negative consequences. The evolution of sounds, words and grammatical forms has been a history of changes that started small, in some particular town or village, and spread out through contact with people from other towns and villages. Even now, the development of mass communication has not put an end to local differences in language use, so that how people speak indexes where they are from. Even in a given locale, different generations speak somewhat differently; and other cultural differences, including religious or sectarian ones, and those associated with gender, occupation or education, are indexed as well. Because change does not occur in wholesale fashion, it results in something like layers of time in a language. Any members of the younger generation who resist some new word or pronunciation or intonation used by their age mates, sticking instead to the way their grandparents speak, are likely to have this difference interpreted by others as signifying something deeper about their identity.

This chapter aims to consider historical perspectives in two senses: the perspectives that are embodied within identity itself and the conceptual history of their study. Besides approaching language and identity theoretically and historically, the chapter will focus on how such an approach relates to issues of concern to applied linguistics.

Identities are manifested in language as, first, the categories and labels that people attach to themselves and others to signal their belonging; second, as the indexed ways of speaking and behaving through which they perform their belonging; and third, as the interpretations that others make of those indices. The ability to perceive and interpret the indices is itself part of shared culture. No group can be culturally homogeneous. The urge to tribalise is too deeply rooted in human nature, indeed in animal behaviour generally, which testifies to how deep it runs in our evolutionary heritage. So, for instance, within Christian or Muslim religious identity, there are various ways of 'being Christian' and 'being Muslim'; in other words, a variety of Christian and Islamic cultural identities. They are subsumed under the umbrella of a religious identity that itself admits of variants, Orthodox, Catholic and Protestant, Sunni and Shia, and within the latter, Sufis, each with their distinctive practices and texts, even if most of their central beliefs are shared.

Cultural identities rarely carry great imaginative power unless they are textualised as national or racial/ethnic identities. Religious identities can be forceful, but they tend as well to take on a national or quasi-national dimension, as is currently the case with Islamic State. People do not go to war for other aspects of their culture the way they willingly die for their fatherland or their people, or other 'imagined communities' which they perceive as being *naturally* constituted, rather than just arbitrary, contingent cultural constructs (Anderson 1991). And yet, it is not provable that any race or nation is a 'natural' entity; all are at least partly constructed, and at the same time, as Bateson (1995) has pointed out, 'Everything is natural.' Gender identities might seem to be directly linked to the physical configuration of reproductive organs; and yet, people are readier to accept that an individual is a woman trapped in a man's body, or vice versa, than they are that someone is a Japanese trapped in an Ethiopian's body.

Overview

From earliest recorded history to the present day, reflection on language has included (and has at times been dominated by) ideas concerning the link between a particular language and the people who speak it. These ideas form an initial dichotomy:

1 That the language a people speaks is not connected in any significant way to the nature of the people who speak it;
2 That the language a people speaks plays a crucial role in making them a people.

Idea (1) had its most powerful champion in Aristotle, who believed that all human beings share the same mental experiences, which get coded differently in the words of different languages but without affecting the experiences themselves. Already in Antiquity however a version of (2) was maintained by Epicurus, who argued that the shapes of people's bodies, varying by their ethnicity, caused them to expel air differently, and that this combined with the effects of their environment shaped their languages in profoundly distinct ways. It was the revival of Platonic and Epicurean thought from the fifteenth to the seventeenth century, removing Aristotle from his unique position as 'The Philosopher', that brought about what is known as the Renaissance, and gave rise to modern versions of (2), which, graded from weakest to strongest, include:

2a That the language plays a purely pragmatic role: the simple fact of its being *shared* binds a people together, regardless of the internal form of the language;
2b That the particular form or 'genius' of their shared language *reflects* what distinguishes the people who speak it from other people;
2c That the particular form or genius of their shared language *has endowed them* with their distinct nature or genius as a people.

The difference between (2b) and (2c) is that 'reflecting' implies that something physical or spiritual in the people's nature, other than their language, is the *cause*, and the genius of the language is the *effect* (this would include Epicurus's view); whereas 'endowing' means that the genius of the language is the cause, and the nature of the people is the effect.

When linguistics was established as an academic discipline in the nineteenth century, it was built over a fault line between the Enlightenment conception of a language as a system of rational signs (compatible with 1 and 2a), and the Romantic conception of a language as a *Weltanschauung*, a deep, spiritual vision of the universe that embodies the essence of a particular nation or race (compatible with 2b and 2c). The Enlightenment took linguistic signs to be grounded in the senses, and hence to have a universal basis, but with the signs of particular languages being ultimately arbitrary. For the Romantics, language originates in the senses, as they are directed by the national soul, to which it remains bound.

Idea (2a) in the list above has been referred to by Sériot (2014) as the 'Jacobin' approach, since its most overtly worked-out theorisation and application has been in France, from the seventeenth century through the French Revolution and down to the present day. The Jacobin outlook assumes that creating a shared language is the necessary and sufficient condition for producing a nation out of the sometimes distantly related peoples who live in a contiguous landscape.

Idea (2c) in the list is what Sériot calls the 'Romantic' approach, in which the nation comes first, in the form of a shared soul, out of which the language is projected. Neither the Jacobin nor the Romantic approach lacks precedents from before the eighteenth century; they have an ancient heritage. But the lands that would come in 1871 to form Germany were, a hundred years earlier, a nation without a state. This was in stark contrast to France, which had become a relatively united kingdom in the seventeenth century. It was when Napoleonic France began its imperial drive eastward that the concept of German nationhood came to be aggressively asserted, with the shared German language as its cornerstone. As Sériot (2014: 258) writes, 'For German romantics, language was the essence of the nation, while for French revolutionaries, it was a means to achieve national unity.'

The Romantic view of language was dominant by the time modern linguistics began to crystallise as an academic discipline in the first half of the nineteenth century, though the Jacobin alternative continued to be the principle on which French language policy was formed, both domestically and overseas. Nor did the Jacobin view ever disappear from public discourse about language, even in countries where policy was more Romantically inclined. The Enlightenment/Jacobin concern with signs was reincorporated into modern linguistics with the highly influential Saussure (1916).

These two diametrically opposed views encapsulate the tension and ambivalence inherent in how we think about language and identity. Although no polls have been taken, it seems likely that most of us espouse one or the other view depending on the circumstances. If we believe it is important for the chance to learn a second language to be part of every child's education, it may be for a combination of Jacobin reasons (civic coherence in a multilingual country, for example) and Romantic ones (the belief that you cannot understand how other people think without learning their language, or that you cannot understand your own thought without the perspective on your mother tongue a second language affords).

All this leaves idea (2b) in the list above with a peculiar status. It is very widespread, perhaps more than any of the others, yet it is ambiguous. For some it represents a strong version of (2a), for others a weak version of (2c). It is also bound up with the role of what can broadly be called the 'literary' in national identity. Until universal education became widespread, starting in the second half of the nineteenth century, the linguistic dimension of national identity was already important, but, figuratively speaking, it floated above the daily life and concerns of the vast majority. Across Europe and Western Asia, the commonly inhabited linguistic reality was that of local vernacular dialect plus liturgical language. Either might be distantly related to the national language, if there was one, or even unrelated, as will be discussed in the next section.

Language and identity research has tended to take the links between the two to be *constructed intersubjectively and context-contingently*. Each of these terms requires some unpacking. 'Constructed' stands in opposition to 'essential': the identities a person has (or occupies) are understood not as unchanging, inescapable, determinate categories, but as categories which are potentially fluid and fuzzy, and which the person occupying them does not control. Rather, they are constructed 'intersubjectively', which is to say among the participants in a linguistic encounter. I am having a linguistic encounter at this moment with you, my reader; I cannot control the version of me that you construct in your mind based on how I write. There are as many versions of my identity as there are readers of my text, and the same is true of people with whom I have face-to-face linguistic encounters. There, however, my way of speaking is likely to adjust based on the cues I am getting from them moment by moment, whereas in writing I have to imagine an ideal reader. The '-subjectively' part means that you, as reader, are not an object, passively having my message poured into you. You are actively co-constructing the meaning of this text, as a subject.

'Context-contingently' means that the same people will co-construct different identities for one another depending on the circumstances, even if the linguistic indices are (abstracted from the circumstances) the same. Forensic linguists have to perform that sort of abstraction; for them it is a problem that 'context' is potentially limitless. Researchers in language and identity, while not denying that forensic linguistics has its uses, will worry that such 'objective' data as it purports to turn up will always be dependent on that abstracting, which removes the data from the reality of context.

Modern linguistics has moved slowly but steadily toward embracing the identity function as central to language (for an overview, see Joseph 2004). The impediment has been the dominance of the traditional outlook, which takes representation alone to be essential, with even communication relegated to a secondary place. This outlook was never the only one available, however, and when early twentieth-century linguists such as Jespersen (1925) and Sapir (1927, 1933) came to investigate how language functions to define and regulate the role of the individual within the social unit at the same time as it helps to constitute that unit, they were not without predecessors. It was just that mainstream linguistics as it had developed within the nineteenth century was not inclined to see such questions as falling within its purview.

An important study by Labov (1963) looked at the dialect of English on Martha's Vineyard, an island off the coast of Massachusetts, where the diphthongs in words like *right* and *house* are pronounced as [əy] and [əw] rather than the standard [ay] and [aw]. This feature is not found in the dialects of the mainlanders who 'summer' on Martha's Vineyard, and with whom the Vineyarders (year-round residents) have a complex relationship of dependency and resentment. 'It is apparent that the immediate meaning of this phonetic feature is "Vineyarder". When a man says [rəyt] or [həws], he is unconsciously establishing the fact that he belongs to the island: that he is one of the natives to whom the island really belongs' (Labov 1963: 307). This is very much the sort of analysis of the effect of linguistic identity on language form that would characterise work in the 1990s and since, though it would be sidelined in the mid-1960s by the statistical charting of variation and change.

In the meantime, one particular identity focus – gender – led the way in directing attention to the reading of identity in language (discussed further in the next section). As the notion of separate men's and women's language was accepted, the more general notion of the language–identity link was let in through the back door, leaving the way open for the study of group identities of all sorts beyond those national and ethnic ones traditionally associated with language difference. This was a challenge to a sociolinguistics that had been primarily concerned with class differences (see Block, this volume). By the mid-1980s, this shift was under way in the work of, for example, Gumperz (1982), Edwards (1985) and Le Page and Tabouret-Keller (1985), though it was really in the 1990s that it would come to occupy the mainstream of work in sociolinguistics and linguistic anthropology. (For a small but representational sample of studies see, on the sociological end, Fishman 1999; on the anthropological, Schieffelin *et al.* 1998; in discourse analysis, Benwell and Stokoe 2006; Wodak *et al.* 2009; and in applied linguistics, Block 2009; Norton 2013.)

This work also received significant input from social psychology, where one approach in particular needs to be singled out: Social Identity Theory, developed in the early 1970s by Henri Tajfel. In the years following his death in 1982, it came to be the single most influential model for analysing linguistic identity. Tajfel (1978) defined social identity as 'that part of an individual's self-concept which derives from his knowledge of his membership of a social group (or groups) together with the value and emotional significance attached to that membership'. Within this simple definition are embedded at least five positions which in their time were quite revolutionary: that social identity pertains to an individual rather than to a social group; that it is a matter of *self-concept*, rather than of social categories into which one simply falls; that the fact of *membership* is the essential thing, rather than anything having to do with the nature of the group itself; that an individual's own knowledge of the membership, and the particular value they attach to it – completely 'subjective' factors – are what count; and that emotional significance is not some trivial side effect of the identity belonging but an integral part of it.

Partly under the influence of such work, sociolinguists were beginning to reorient their own object of investigation. Milroy (1980) reported data from studies she conducted in Belfast showing that the 'social class' of an individual did not appear to be the key variable allowing one to make predictions about which forms of particular linguistic variables the person would use. Rather, the key variable was the nature of the person's 'social network', a concept borrowed from sociology which Milroy defined as 'the informal social relationships contracted by an individual' (Milroy 1980: 174). Where close-knit localised network structures existed, there was a strong tendency to maintain non-standard vernacular forms of speech, a tendency difficult to explain in a model such as Labov's (1966), based on a scale of 'class' belonging where following norms of standard usage marked one as higher on the hierarchy and entitled to benefits that most people desire. Labov's early work on Martha's Vineyard had suggested that the answer lay in identity, specifically in the value of belonging to a group who, although not highly placed in socio-economic terms, could nevertheless claim something valuable for themselves (in the Martha's Vineyard case, authenticity). Milroy's book provided statistical backing for such an explanation.

Although the inner workings of the social network depend somewhat on amount of personal contact, the essential thing is that its members share *norms*. As attention turned to understanding the nature of these norms, two much publicised views had an impact. Fish (1980) had devised the concept of the 'interpretive community' to account for the norms of reading whereby people evaluate different readings of the same text as valid or absurd. An interpretive community is a group sharing such a set of norms; its members may never come into direct physical contact with one another, yet share norms spread by the educational system, books or the media. Soon after, Anderson (1991 [1983]) proposed a new understanding of the 'nation' as an 'imagined community', whose members, like that of the interpretive community, will never all meet one another let alone have the sort of regular intercourse that creates a 'network'. What binds them together is the shared belief in the membership in the community.

Notably with the work of Eckert, sociolinguistic investigation of groups ideologically bound to one another shifted from statistically based examination of social networks to more interpretative examination of 'communities of practice', defined as 'an aggregate of people who come together around mutual engagement in an endeavor' (Eckert and McConnell-Ginet 1992: 464). In the course of this endeavour there emerge shared beliefs, norms and ideologies, including though not limited to linguistic and communicative behaviour. The advantage of the community-of-practice concept is its openness – any aggregate of people can be held to constitute one, so long as the analyst can point convincingly to behaviour that implies shared norms, or, better still, elicit expression of the underlying ideologies from members of the community. This line of research is thus continuous with another one that has focused more directly on the normative beliefs or ideologies by which national and other group identities are maintained. Some early work along these lines was published in Wodak (1989) and Joseph and Taylor (1990), and subsequently a great deal more has appeared, e.g. in Brice-Heath and McLaughlin (1993), Blommaert (1999), Verschueren (1999) and Kroskrity (2000).

Other features of recent work on language and identity include the view that identity is something constructed rather than essential, and performed rather than possessed – features which the term 'identity' itself tends to mask, suggesting as it does something singular, objective and reified. Each of us performs a repertoire of identities that are constantly shifting, and that we negotiate and renegotiate according to the circumstances. Very influential in this respect was the Canadian sociologist Erving Goffman, whose doctoral research in the Shetland Islands in the late 1940s led him to the view that

> The human tendency to use signs and symbols means that evidence of social worth and of mutual evaluations will be conveyed by very minor things, and these things will be witnessed, as will the fact that they have been witnessed. An unguarded glance, a momentary change in tone of voice, an ecological position taken or not taken, can drench a talk with judgmental significance. Therefore, just as there is no occasion of talk in which improper impressions could not intentionally or unintentionally arise, so there is no occasion of talk so trivial as not to require each participant to show serious concern with the way he handles himself and the others present.
>
> *(Goffman 1955: 225)*

The 'structure of the self' as presented in speech, the persona, was what Goffman was developing the analytical tools to describe in a way that would be acceptable within the scientific rhetoric of sociologists. He found that the concept of 'face', which Western cultures generally associated with those of East Asia, was actually necessary for understanding human interaction in any culture. Identity and face have much in common. Each is an imagining of the self, or of another, within a public sphere involving multiple actors. Yet they have come into language and discourse research from different directions, and this difference in their origins has led researchers to frame them in such a way that they seem no more than tangentially related to one another.

Identity relates classically to who individuals are, understood in terms of the groups to which they belong, including nationality, ethnicity, religion, gender, generation, sexual orientation, social class and an unlimited number of other possibilities. Face, on the other hand, relates classically to exchanges between or among individuals; more specifically, in the view of Goffman (1967: 5), 'during a particular contact'. There has been, in other words, a fundamental distinction drawn between how the two concepts relate to time, with face as a punctual phenomenon and identity as a durative one. This is not to say that an individual's behaviour in terms of face is devoid of consistency, or that face work does not have enduring consequences, but simply that we tend to think of face as something that becomes relevant in interactions. By the same token, a person's awareness of his or her identity may lie below the surface until a particular contact creates a tension that brings it to the fore; yet it has classically been conceived of as a property of the person. The definitions of both face and identity have however been problematised in work of the last decade (see Joseph 2013a).

It is important not to lose sight of the dual sense of identity as something we take to have an essential (but ungraspable) reality, yet recognise as being constructed based on perceptions that are only partial. The temptation to assume that all identity is always freely constructed is strong, but deceptive. Blommaert, taking inspiration from Wallerstein's (1998) world-systems approach, has argued for applying the metaphor of 'scales' in relation to sociolinguistic agency, where the metaphor refers to maps drawn at different scales (see Blommaert 2007, 2010). An act of identity that may feel like wholly a matter of free choice on the individual scale can appear quite different when viewed on the broader institutional or cultural scale, where the social structures that may have guided the choice are rendered more visible than on the scale of the individual act.

So far, I have given an overview of the historical perspectives of language and identity. The next section samples five areas of current research on language and identity that impinge upon the concerns of applied linguistics, and considers their historical background.

Issues and ongoing debates

The five areas in this section have significant overlaps: it is impossible to consider language standardisation, for instance, separately from mother tongue, or to divide religious language neatly from heritage. But distinct lines of research are identifiable for each of the areas. They are by no means the only ones that might have been chosen. It would be difficult to find an aspect of applied linguistics in which no identity issues arise; and every aspect of applied linguistics, indeed of linguistics generally, gains in richness and insight when examined in a time-depth perspective.

Gender and sexual orientation identity

Besides national, racial/ethnic, religious and social-class identities, gender and sexual orientation are powerfully indexed in language. In many instances, they interact with social-class identity in a way that is related to historical change. Since the 1970s, it has been a regular finding in sociolinguistic research that women are more linguistically conservative than men. In that same period, certain characteristic features of 'women's language' were identified as indexing powerlessness. Lakoff (1973) argued that, in both structure and use, languages mark out an inferior social role for women and bind them to it. Gender politics is incorporated directly into the pronoun systems of English and many other languages, through the use of the masculine as the 'unmarked' gender (as in 'Everyone take his seat'). Lakoff points to features that occur more frequently in women's than in men's English, such as tag questions, hedges, intensifiers and pause markers, which as marks of insecurity and of the role women are expected to occupy are fundamental to maintaining the status quo in gender politics.

Yet in the four decades since, those features have become a regular part of both men's and women's speech. This suggests that in fact the women studied in the earlier reports were being linguistically innovative – the opposite of conservative. It may nevertheless be true that their innovative features were being interpreted by other speakers as indexing powerlessness; but whether this was a direct indexation, or indirect via education, socio-economic status, etc., is not known.

Over these same four decades the study of gender identity in language has meanwhile moved on, as witnessed in the work of such scholars as Cameron (1992) and Butler (1997), who shifted the perspective to a more radically feminist direction. Within sociolinguistics, the studies collected in Erlich *et al.* (2014) present a good range of second-generation gender identity research. Investigations of sexual-orientation identity in language have flourished in parallel with gender studies. Gay identities have tended to be interpreted in terms of the indices established for male and female heterosexual identities and, since male homosexual acts were illegal for much of history and remain so in parts of the world, these identities are also linked to 'secret' codes and indices meant to be interpretable by insiders to the identity but indecipherable to outsiders (see Baker 2002). Here again, this area has been developing more autonomy in its methodology and conceptual modelling in recent years (see Cameron and Kulick 2003; Bucholtz and Hall 2004; Erlich *et al.* 2014).

Religious identity

Religious identity has been second only to national identity in shaping modern history, as civil wars from Ireland to the former Yugoslavia to the Middle East have shown all too bloodily (for good representative studies see Omoniyi and Fishman 2006; Omoniyi 2010). To complete the picture that Sériot has sketched of the national language as an administrative or a cultural concept, we need to add what were the liturgical languages, and the everyday vernaculars, in use at a particular place and time. So for example in parts of the Holy Roman Empire the liturgical language was Latin and the 'national' language German, while the people spoke Hungarian dialects with no historical affinity to either. In the part of the Ottoman Empire that my paternal family inhabited, the vernacular was a local form of Arabic and the 'national' language was a multilingual complex involving Turkish, Persian and a type of Arabic that my relatives might not need to have translated but at least mediated for them. The liturgical language situation was very complex indeed, given the presence of some 20 Christian sects and a smaller number of Muslim ones. For the majority the liturgical language was Syriac, distantly related to Arabic, but substantial segments of the population used Greek, Aramaic, Latin and other tongues. Muslims were united by their liturgical use of Koranic Arabic, within the Ottoman Empire and beyond, across India to China and Indonesia. In areas of the highlands of Scotland where the vernacular was Gaelic, the 'national' language was English, so distantly related to Gaelic that the relationship was not agreed on by linguists until about 1840, and the liturgical language was Latin for Roman Catholics, Gaelic for some Protestants and English for others. In all these cases, each of the languages served an identity function, in terms of social caste, sectarian commitment and education.

Language standardisation

With few exceptions, the liturgical languages discussed in the preceding section have been either languages of the distant past, or living languages used in a conservative form, often preserving archaic features such as the *thy* and *art* of the Lord's Prayer in English. In this way, the history of the language is incorporated into its contemporary use. The same is true, if to a lesser degree, of the 'standard' language, that version of the national language that is taught and examined in schools. Its purpose is essentially to resist innovation, or at least to slow it down; and to allow students to be hierarchised according to their ability and willingness to master the largely arbitrary rules controlling which aspects of their everyday speech are not acceptable in the standard language, written or spoken. Here again the resistance to innovation means that it is the past of the language being incorporated into its present (standard) state, and indexing users of the standard form as educated and – although this is entirely fallacious – as more intelligent than non-standard speakers. This applies as much to mother-tongue speakers of the language in question as to those for whom it is a second language; Joseph (1987) details why it is that the standard language, as an artefact of writing and education, is no one's 'native language'.

Use of the standard language is especially bound up with social-class identity, which is inherently historical in the sense that it is built on a recognition of the fact that we read (correctly or incorrectly) each other's pedigrees and personal histories from the indices that we perceive and interpret in other people's language. It was a concern with social class that was behind the research of the 1960s and 70s that brought sociolinguistics to prominence as an academic field. In those days, when academic linguistics, even in the USA, was heavily dominated by Marxist thought, it was taken as read that pre-revolutionary societies were divided into a capitalist ruling class and the workers, with the various intermediate *bourgeois* layers all serving the interests of the ruling class, although despised and ridiculed by them for their inclination to climb the social ladder. Ross's (1954) division of U and non-U was that between the aristocracy and the middle class, providing each with a catalogue of linguistic features to avoid or adopt. His categories mirrored the concerns of a particular segment of the British reading public of the time. In the USA, inherited aristocracy might be identified with a few families, but there was a considerable class of descendants of men who had earned great fortunes, and who might be called 'upper class', except that their standing did not accord with that of the European aristocrats – so 'upper-middle class' seemed more appropriate to them.

Labov's (1966) analyses were based on a four-way division into lower class, working class, lower-middle and upper-middle class; by the 1970s, he would rebrand the first two as lower-lower and upper-lower, and would shift his focus from class to race. From the start he recognised the difficulty of determining where class boundaries lay, and put considerable effort into developing a 'socio-economic scale' which however could capture only part of what 'class' was about, since a penniless aristocrat still belongs to his class, and a factory worker who wins the lottery might give up his job and rise to middle-class status, but without wishing or being able to shed the linguistic and other behavioural indices of his working-class belonging. Labov's interests were always very much focused on historical linguistics, and he demonstrated how change over time is synchronically visible in variation within the language at any given point in time, with such variation being systematic and predictable by social class and comparable factors. For current views on social class identity and language see Block (this volume) and Preece (this volume).

John E. Joseph

Heritage languages, diaspora and the ethics of identity

Heritage languages is a relatively recent term that gets applied to two kinds of minority languages: on the one hand, the language of an immigrant minority in a diaspora setting (for example, Cantonese in the South Chinese community of Cardiff), and on the other, the traditional language of a place that has become a minority language there, its place taken over by some more widely spoken language (for example, Welsh in Cardiff). Heritage languages possess for their speakers and partisans the ability to form a connection to the past, to origins and to ancestors both real and imagined (the philologist and novelist J.R.R. Tolkien considered Welsh to be his 'native language' even though he could not speak it and had no Welsh family background – just a spiritual connection that he felt to the language).

A number of prominent applied linguists have picked up on the idea of 'translanguaging' (Li Wei and Zhu Ha 2013) within 'super-diversity'. The latter term was introduced by Vertovec (2007) in an attempt to capture the

> tremendous increase in the categories of migrants, not only in terms of nationality, ethnicity, language and religion, but also in terms of motives, patterns and itineraries of migration, processes of insertion into the labour and housing markets of the host societies.
>
> *(Blommaert and Rampton 2011: 1)*

In historical perspective, it is not clear how new or unprecedented this situation actually is. Certainly the Chicago described by Buck (1903) was as linguistically and ethnically diverse as the city is today, and probably even more religiously diverse than now. Nevertheless, Blommaert and Rampton argue that the linguistic indexicality of identity needs to be reconfigured to take account of a context that has shifted historically from the recent past, when stronger restrictions on immigration (and indeed on emigration in the Communist bloc) were the order of the day, and when the emigrating populations were far less likely to have the advanced degrees and specialised skills that would give them high-level access to the labour market.

There is also an ethical dimension to heritage: as Appiah (2005) has shown, it has the potential to be oppressive. Immigrant parents sometimes try to force a heritage identity on children who identify more with the new country in which they were brought up. A good study of how this tension plays out in heritage language classes is Blackledge, Creese *et al.* (2008; see also Spotti 2008; Kramsch 2012). Appiah distinguishes between 'hard' and 'soft' pluralism, the former taking seriously the ethical imperative for allowing dissenters to opt out of the group culture into which they were born. The soft type instead sees the group as the most important unit where autonomy is concerned, and insists that individuals cannot have real autonomy except as part of their group belonging. Appiah objects to Kymlicka's (1995) stress on recognising and preserving identity groups and cultures, which contributes more to reifying them, constraining the individual's rights, than to liberation.

> [W]hen multiculturalists like Kymlicka say that there are so many 'cultures' in this or that country, what drops out of the picture is that every 'culture' represents not only difference but the elimination of difference: the group represents a clump of relative homogeneity, and that homogeneity is perpetuated and enforced by regulative mechanisms designed to marginalize and silence dissent from its basic norms and mores.
>
> *(Appiah 2005: 152)*

We should not, Appiah (2005: 268) says, 'ask other people to maintain the diversity of the species at the price of their individual autonomy. We can't require others to provide us with a cultural museum to tour through.'

Native language/mother tongue

The 'native speaker' is a modern idea, not appearing in the sense in which we use it until the last third of the nineteenth century. Arguably, it named something that was implicit in earlier thought. But the concept of native speaker is historically bound up with that of the standard language, which likewise began to appear in the last third of the nineteenth century, though again having earlier roots. The rise of the standard European national languages, ousting Latin from progressively more of its functions, enabled the illusion that everyone is a native speaker of the language of whichever nation they belong to. On the other hand, insofar as the standard language occupies functions bound up with institutional learning at an advanced level, no one is a native speaker of any standard language – it is a quasi-second language for all its users (for a contemporary view see Preece 2010).

The spread of these languages throughout the wider population in the last part of the nineteenth century occurred in tandem with the spread of universal education and, coincidentally perhaps, with the explosion of attention to the 'Neogrammarian' principles proclaimed at the University of Leipzig. These established a scientific consensus that the history of languages is determined by forces lying outside the conscious, rational dimension. Although other aspects of Neogrammarian linguistics have not endured, this one has; and so has the concept of native speaker that may be partly its corollary. It figures centrally in our understanding of language and identity, because of a strong cultural belief that one's 'native' way of speaking is one's true, genuine, authentic way of speaking, and that any deviation from it represents something inauthentic, an attempt to be what one is not.

For Davies (2013), the native speaker is a myth with dangerous and destructive consequences for language teaching and above all for language testing. It is mythical because in reality there is no clear boundary between native and non-native speakers. There are people who, even starting well after puberty, learn a language to such a level of competence that they are scarcely distinguishable from native speakers. Whatever fine differences in grammaticality judgements psycholinguists may detect belong to the research laboratory, and not to everyday life. In Davies's view, the native-speaker myth is destructive because it gives learners the message that, however strong their motivation and however great their efforts, they can never reach the ultimate goal of foreign-language teaching, by virtue of their birth and other conditions beyond their control. It is thus an unjustifiable form of social exclusion, which applied linguistics should combat rather than reinforce.

If we accept with Davies that the concept of native speaker is neither well defined nor ethically desirable, why does it seem nonetheless that native speakers are different from non-native speakers in most cases? The answer to this has a historical dimension, in this case that of each speaker's *personal* history. The acquisition of our first language was a long apprenticeship, which occupied nearly all our waking moments during the first three or four years of our lives and which has continued since. In the course of this childhood apprenticeship, the knowledge we acquire becomes part not only of our memory but also of our entire nervous system – our 'extended mind' – which is to say part of our bodies. The brain is not a separate organ in our bodies but continues down through the spinal cord and out via the nerves to our sense organs, including the skin. The brain is not the centre of all actions: reflexes, notably, go just to the spinal cord. There is no evidence that the fine-grained muscular movements that produce my 'accent' and all the phonetic indices that people interpret to determine where I am from, what sort of background I have and what I am like are represented as knowledge in the brain, rather than the sort of muscular aptitude developed through practice that a pianist has in her fingers, or that keeps us breathing and digesting and our heart pumping in sleep, or even when 'brain-dead' (see Joseph 2013b).

My knowledge of English is a combination of mental knowledge plus something that connects to what Bourdieu (1991) called *habitus*, a term revived from medieval thought. My first language does not set limits on what I am capable of thinking or doing, but makes some things come more easily than others and makes certain inclinations more natural, while others require greater effort. To be a native speaker is a historical fact concerning the formation of one's *habitus*, the set of dispositions, schemata of action and perception that individuals acquire and incorporate through their social experience. One can, with difficulty, attain later in life a competence indistinguishable from that of a native speaker, without going through the whole apprenticeship that produces the native speaker's *habitus*. But so long as second language learners do not display the entire *habitus* that one expects as the accompaniment of native competence, they remain 'native-like' in the judgement of others.

Summary

Our identities are indexed in the languages we speak and write and in how we speak and write them. This indexicality does not need to be intentional; people will interpret our identities based on our language whether we want them to or not. Their interpretations will be grounded, to a surprisingly large degree, in the 'layers of time' that steady linguistic evolution has produced in every language. Education is concerned with managing these layers of time, through teaching of the standard language, as well as with expanding students' language repertoires, which also has a direct effect on their linguistic identity and how it is interpreted. Such interpretation takes place within a broad cultural tension concerning how the structure of a language relates to the 'genius' of the people who speak it, as well as to what degree individual speakers partake of that genius, all of which again has a deep historical dimension.

George Orwell (1987 [1949]: 37) famously wrote in *Nineteen Eighty-Four*, 'Who controls the past controls the future: who controls the present controls the past.' To which may be added: Who controls the schools controls the past, through the teaching of history; structures the present, through the powerful hierarchisation of individuals and communities entailed by language choice and the enforcement of language standards; and shapes the future, by shaping, or even by failing to shape, those who will inhabit it. So too the future study of language and identity stands to benefit by taking account of history, within individuals, within languages and within our paradigms of investigation.

Related topics

Positioning language and identity: poststructuralist perspectives; Discursive psychology and the production of identity in language practices; Language and ethnic identity; Language, race and identity; Identity in post-colonial contexts; Language and religious identities; Language and gender identities; Language and non-normative sexual identities; A linguistic ethnography of identity: adopting a heteroglossic frame; Minority languages and group identity: Scottish Gaelic in the Old World and the New.

Further reading

Bucholtz, M. and Hall, K. (2005). 'Identity and interaction: a sociocultural linguistic approach', *Discourse Studies*, 7(4–5): 585–614. (A good, compact introduction to the study of language and identity.)

Edwards, J. (2009). *Language and identity: an introduction*. Cambridge: Cambridge University Press. (Includes an account of the development of research in the area.)

Joseph, J.E. (2002). *From Whitney to Chomsky: essays in the history of American linguistics*. Amsterdam and Philadelphia: John Benjamins. Chapter 5, 'The origins of American sociolinguistics'. (Covers many of the key developments in greater historical detail.)

Joseph, J.E. (2006). *Language and politics*. Edinburgh: Edinburgh University Press. (Connects the historical perspective on language and identity to key issues in applied linguistics.)

Joseph, J.E. (2014). 'History of linguistics.' *Oxford Bibliographies* [Online]. Available at www.oxfordbibliographies.com/view/document/obo-9780199772810/obo-9780199772810-0186.xml. (An up-to-date guide to work covering the history of the discipline.)

References

Anderson, B. (1991[1983]). *Imagined communities: reflections on the origin and spread of nationalism*. 2nd edn. London and New York: Verso.

Appiah, K.A. (2005). *The ethics of identity*. Princeton: Princeton University Press.

Baker, P. (2002). *Polari: the lost language of gay men*. London and New York: Routledge.

Bateson, M.C. (1995). On the naturalness of things, in J. Brockman and K. Matson (eds) *How things are: a science tool-kit for the mind*. New York: William Morrow and Co.; London: Weidenfeld and Nicolson, pp. 9–16.

Benwell, B. and Stokoe, E. (2006). *Discourse and identity*. Edinburgh: Edinburgh University Press.

Block, D. (2009). *Second language identities*. London: Continuum.

Block, D. (this volume). Class in language and identity research, in S. Preece (ed.) *The Routledge handbook of language and identity*. London: Routledge, pp. 241–54.

Blackledge, A., Creese, A. *et al.* (2008). 'Contesting "language" as "heritage": negotiation of identities in late modernity', *Applied Linguistics*, 29(4): 533–554.

Blommaert, J. (ed.) (1999). *Language ideological debates*. Berlin: Mouton de Gruyter.

Blommaert, J. (2007). 'Sociolinguistic scales', *Intercultural Pragmatics*, 4(1): 1–19.

Blommaert, J. (2010). *The sociolinguistics of globalization*. Cambridge: Cambridge University Press.

Blommaert, J. and Rampton, B. (2011). 'Language and superdiversity', *Diversities*, 13(2): 1–21.

Bourdieu, P. (1991). *Language and symbolic power: the economy of linguistic exchanges*. J.B. Thompson (ed.) [Trans. G. Raymond and M. Adamson]. Cambridge: Polity, in association with Blackwell.

Brice-Heath, S. and McLaughlin, M.W. (eds) (1993). *Identity and inner-city youth: beyond ethnicity and gender*. New York: Teachers College Press.

Bucholtz, M. and Hall, K. (2004). 'Theorizing identity in language and sexuality research', *Language in Society*, 33(4): 501–47.

Buck, C.D. (1903). 'A sketch of the linguistic conditions of Chicago', *The University of Chicago Decennial Publications*, First Series, vol. 6: 97–114.

Butler, J. (1997). *Excitable speech: a politics of the performative*. London and New York: Routledge.

Cameron, D. (1992). *Feminism and linguistic theory*. 2nd edn. Houndmills, Basingstoke and New York: Palgrave Macmillan.

Cameron, D. and Kulick, D. (2003). *Language and sexuality*. Cambridge: Cambridge University Press.

Davies, A. (2013). *Native speakers and native users*. Cambridge: Cambridge University Press.

Eckert, P. and McConnell-Ginet, S. (1992). 'Think practically and look locally: language and gender as community-based practice', *Annual Review of Anthropology*, 21: 461–490.

Edwards, J. (1985). *Language, society and identity*. Oxford and New York: Basil Blackwell.

Erlich, S., Meyerhoff, M. and Holmes, J. (eds) (2014). *The handbook of language, gender and sexuality.* Malden, MA, and Oxford: Wiley-Blackwell.

Fish, S. (1980). *Is there a text in this class?* Cambridge, MA: Harvard University Press.

Fishman, J. (ed.) (1999) *Handbook of language and ethnic identity.* Oxford: Oxford University Press.

Goffman, E. (1955). 'On face-work: an analysis of ritual elements in social interaction', *Psychiatry*, 18: 213–231.

Goffman, E. (1967). *Interaction ritual.* New York: Doubleday Anchor.

Gumperz, J. (ed.) (1982). *Language and social identity.* Cambridge: Cambridge University Press.

Jespersen, O. (1925). *Mankind, nation, and individual from a linguistic point of view.* Cambridge, MA: Harvard University Press.

Joseph, J.E. (1987). *Eloquence and power: the rise of language standards and standard languages.* London: Frances Pinter; New York: Blackwell.

Joseph, J.E. (2004). *Language and identity: national, ethnic, religious.* Houndmills, Basingstoke and New York: Palgrave Macmillan.

Joseph, J.E. (2013a). 'Identity work and face work across linguistic and cultural boundaries', *Journal of Politeness Research*, 9: 35–54.

Joseph, J.E. (2013b). 'Le corps du locuteur natif: discipline, habitus, identité', *Histoire – Epistemologie – Langage*, 35(2): 29–45.

Joseph, J.E. and Taylor, T.J. (eds) (1990). *Ideologies of language.* London and New York: Routledge.

Kramsch, C. (2012). 'Imposture: a late modern notion in poststructuralist SLA research', *Applied Linguistics*, 33(5): 483–502.

Kroskrity, P.V. (ed.) (2000). *Regimes of language: ideologies, polities, and identities.* Santa Fe, NM: School of American Research Press.

Kymlicka, W. (1995). *Multicultural citizenship: a liberal theory of minority rights.* Oxford: Oxford University Press.

Labov, W. (1963). 'The social motivation of a sound change', *Word*, 19: 273–309.

Labov, W. (1966). *The social stratification of English in New York City.* Washington, DC: Center for Applied Linguistics.

Lakoff, R. (1973). 'Language and woman's place', *Language in Society*, 2: 45–80 (repr. as *Language and woman's place*, New York: Harper and Row, 1975).

Le Page, R.B. and Tabouret-Keller, A. (1985). *Acts of identity: creole-based approaches to language and ethnicity.* Cambridge: Cambridge University Press.

Li Wei and Zhu Ha (2013). 'Translanguaging identities and ideologies: creating transnational space through flexible multilingual practices amongst Chinese university students in the UK', *Applied Linguistics*, 34(5): 516–535.

Milroy, L. (1980). *Language and social networks.* Oxford and New York: Blackwell.

Norton, B. (2013). *Identity and language learning: extending the conversation.* 2nd edn. Bristol: Multilingual Matters.

Omoniyi, T. (ed.) (2010). *The sociology of language and religion: change, conflict and accommodation.* Houndmills, Basingstoke and New York: Palgrave Macmillan.

Omoniyi, T. and Fishman, J.A. (eds) (2006). *Explorations in the sociology of language and religion.* Amsterdam and New York: John Benjamins.

Orwell, G. (1987 [1949]). *Nineteen eighty-four.* New edn. Harmondsworth: Penguin Twentieth Century Classics, in association with Martin Secker and Warburg.

Preece, S. (2010). 'Multilingual identities in higher education: negotiating the "mother tongue", "posh" and "slang"', *Language and Education*, 24(1): 21–39.

Preece, S. (this volume). An identity transformation? Social class, language prejudice and the erasure of multilingual capital in higher education, in S. Preece (ed.) *The Routledge handbook of language and identity.* London: Routledge, pp. 366–81.

Ross, A.S.C. (1954). 'Linguistic class indicators in present-day English', *Neophilologische Mitteilungen*, 55: 20–56.

Sapir, E. (1927). 'Speech as a personality trait', *American Journal of Sociology*, 32: 892–905.

Sapir, E. (1933). 'Language', *Encyclopaedia of the Social Sciences*, 9: 155–169.

Saussure, F. de (1916). *Cours de linguistique générale*. Ed. by C. Bally and A. Sechehaye, with the collaboration of A. Riedlinger. Paris and Lausanne: Payot.

Schieffelin, B.B., Woolard, K.A. and Kroskrity, P. (eds) (1998). *Language ideologies: practice and theory*. New York and Oxford: Oxford University Press.

Sériot, P. (2014). Language and nation: two models, in V.A. Vihman and K. Praakli (eds), *Negotiating linguistic identity: language and belonging in Europe*. Oxford and Bern: Peter Lang, pp. 255–274.

Spotti, M. (2008). 'Exploring the construction of immigrant minority pupils' identities in a Flemish primary classroom', *Linguistics and Education*, 19(1): 20–36.

Tajfel, H. (1978). Social categorization, social identity and social comparison, in H. Tajfel (ed.) *Differentiation between social groups: studies in the social psychology of intergroup relations*. London: Academic Press, pp. 61–76.

Verschueren, J. (ed.) (1999). *Language and ideology: selected papers from the 6th International Pragmatics Conference*. Antwerp: International Pragmatics Association.

Vertovec, S. (2007). 'Super-diversity and its implications', *Ethnic and Racial Studies*, 30(6): 1024–1054.

Wallerstein, I. (1998). 'The time of space and the space of time: the future of social science', *Political Geography*, 17(1): 71–82.

Wodak, R. (ed.) (1989). *Language, power and ideology*. Amsterdam and Philadelphia: John Benjamins.

Wodak, R., de Cillia, R., Reisigl, M. and Liebhart, R. (2009). *The discursive construction of national identity*. Transl. by A. Hirsch, R. Mitten and J.W. Unger. 2nd edn. Edinburgh: Edinburgh University Press.

2

Positioning language and identity
Poststructuralist perspectives

Judith Baxter

Introduction

Applied linguistics now offers a rich diversity of theoretical and analytical approaches to conceptualise the relationship between language and identity; one of the more recent of these can be loosely described as 'poststructuralist'. While this is not easily defined, the poststructuralist approach offers a set of radical, pragmatic and transformative perspectives that challenge and/or supplement dominant paradigms such as ethnomethodology and critical linguistics. Poststructuralist perspectives contest the conventional dichotomies in applied linguistics between subject and object, discourse and materiality, structure and agency, conformity and resistance, power and apoliticism, and micro- and macro-analysis, proposing that such abstractions are always interdependent and mutually contesting. Thus, reciprocally, identities are constructed by and through language but they also produce and reproduce innovative forms of language.

Poststructuralism does not have one fixed definition but is generally applied to a range of theoretical positions developed from such thinkers as Althusser (1984), Bakhtin (1981), Derrida (1987), Foucault (1980), Kristeva (1984) and Lacan (2006 [1977]). Each of these scholars was working more or less independently within the same couple of decades and therefore their collective works did not produce a unified poststructuralist perspective. Rather, there were a range of diverse and competing perspectives on the relationship between language, meaning and identity. Different forms of poststructuralism theorise the relationship between language and identity in contrasting ways. Psychoanalytic forms of poststructuralism look to a fixed psychosexual order in which male identity is generally viewed as 'unmarked' and the female identity as marked; deconstruction considers the ever-shifting relationships between different texts and discourses; and Foucauldian theory, which is the most relevant to this chapter, explores the relationship between historically specific discourses and the construction of social identities. While these different forms of poststructuralism vary in their interests, emphases and practices, they share certain fundamental assumptions about language, meaning and identity. This chapter explores the leading viewpoints in the area, and then reviews some of the debates within applied linguistics about how the relationship between language and identity can be best described, analysed, interpreted and explained.

Overview

At least three points of connection are evident between the various poststructuralist positions above:

1 Philosophical origins in postmodernism;
2 Language and the construction of meaning; and
3 The discursive construction of identities.

Philosophical origins in postmodernism

Postmodernism could be said to encompass and incorporate poststructuralism, which owes its philosophical and discursive stance to this antecedent. Arguably, a poststructualist scholar such as Foucault might be described as postmodernist, but not all postmodernist thinkers would be viewed as poststructuralists.

Postmodernism is a broad movement encompassing a range of fields and disciplines beyond linguistics including philosophy, politics, architecture, art, literature and the social sciences. It is a philosophical stance that underlies much current thinking about how identities are conceived, constructed and enacted in the modern world. Postmodernism challenges the view that there is a determinate, material world that can be definitively known and explained (Lyotard 1984). A postmodernist perspective considers that it is impossible to know the world by dissecting it through apparently objective methods of inquiry. Rather, knowledge is socially constructed, not discovered; contextual, not foundational; singular, localised and perspectival rather than totalising or universal; and egalitarian rather than hierarchical. How we come to 'know the world' is very much bound up with issues of power relations in societies, communities and organisations that, in turn, interact with individual identities and actions.

Foucault (1980, 1984) was particularly interested in theorising the relationship between knowledge and power and how this constructs individual speech and behaviour. He argues that Western knowledge is organised according to irreconcilable binary opposites that are not natural but realised through 'discourses'. He questions the way that modernist theories of knowledge are encoded into binary or hierarchical oppositions such as mind/body, masculinity/femininity, theory/practice and public/private. In every case, knowledge is constructed to ensure that one pole of opposites is privileged over the other (e.g. masculinity over femininity; rationality over emotion; science over art). This polarising and hierarchical ordering of constructs contributes to the formation of meta-narratives that are excluding in principle and normalising in character. Postmodernist thinkers such as Foucault and Lyotard were therefore sceptical of the universal claims and exclusive rights traditionally put forward by most fields of knowledge such as science, politics or religion. This is because, in Foucault's (1980: 109–133) memorable terms, the humanist concern with the 'will to truth' always becomes a 'will to power'. That is, any strong belief or field of knowledge, however well intentioned, inevitably systematises itself into a 'regime of truth'. In other words, it is like saying that my superior knowledge of the world enables me to hold power over you and your inferior knowledge.

Conversely, a postmodernist perspective is sceptical of all universal claims and causes and expresses a profound loss of certainty about the existence of absolute truth. For example, religious or political beliefs that purport to hold the ultimate answers to human problems, such as Christianity or modernist feminism, are viewed as potentially harmful because they attempt to fix meanings and knowledge within a given version of truth and reality. So, a political movement that intends to 'do good', such as Marxist-inspired political thought or action aimed at liberating the popular classes from the negative conditions of capitalism, is valid as long as it is a force for resistance against dominant ways of thinking. However, once it becomes systematised as normative belief or practice, it too could become a means of oppression. This is because postmodernists consider the attempt to fix knowledge permanently as an expression of coercive power. Alternatively they advocate the fluid interplay of multiple but competing theoretical positions, where one form of knowledge is free to enrich, complement, supplement, challenge, contest or overturn any other. In the context of language and identity, individuals have continually to make sense of conflicting 'ways of knowing' and, hence, competing 'ways of being', which are constructed and performed through language and discourses.

Language and the construction of meaning

Whereas postmodernism is a broad, cross-disciplinary movement that has influenced many spheres of intellectual life, poststructuralism is primarily a linguistic movement associated with the development of literary, cultural and discourse theories from the 1960s onwards. Poststructuralist thinkers consider that language is the place where our sense of self and our identity or 'subjectivity' is constructed and performed. The founding insight of poststructuralism, taken from the structuralist linguist Ferdinand de Saussure (1974), is that language, far from reflecting an already given social reality, constitutes social reality for us. Meaning is produced *within* language rather than reflected *by* language. The system of language is composed of signs, which are divided into 'signifiers' (e.g. words, sounds, visual images) and 'signifieds' (concepts). Individual signs (whether in speech, writing or multimodal forms of text) do not have intrinsic meaning but acquire meanings through their relationship with and *difference from* other signs. While meaning is always arbitrary and relational, the language that an individual acquires and understands is the result of an already-existing social contract to which all language users are subject. Thus the meaning of language is to an extent fixed, and individuals are inculcated into this pre-existing 'structuralist' language system that partially shapes their identities.

A poststructuralist perspective of language, while strongly building on Saussure's theory, radically modifies and transforms some of its important aspects. Derrida's (1987) concept of '*différance*', in which meaning is produced through the dual notions of *difference* and *deferral*, has helped theorists to understand language as operating in a perpetual state of flux. According to Derrida, the meaning of signs emerges not only in their *difference* from other words, sounds or images, but also from the way signs are subject to an endless *deferral*. By this he means that any representation of meaning can only be fixed temporarily as it depends upon its discursive context. Signifiers are always located within a discursive context so that the temporary fixing of meaning, which comes from the reading of an image, word or text, will be dependent upon that particular context. Texts are constantly open to rereading and reinterpretation both within the particular context and, of course, when/if they are shifted to other contexts. Thus, the meaning of texts can never be fixed finally as knowable and immutable but is always a 'site' for contestation and redefinition by different readings within varying contexts. Derrida places a particular emphasis upon the way any text, by virtue of the range of readings to which it is subject, becomes the medium for *struggle* among different power interests to fix meaning permanently.

Derrida's (1987) theories of deconstructive criticism – which attend to the plurality and non-fixity of meaning – are a useful perspective on language and identity. This is because 'standard' identity categories such as woman, teacher, mother, wife, friend, scholar, writer and so forth are only temporarily agreed by social contracts to which individual speakers are usually compliant. Such terms are always open to contestation and redefinition as the struggle for the 'true' meaning of each term takes place between social groups with different power interests. So for example, for a modernist feminist, the term 'woman' encapsulates a universal 'female' nature that can be clearly differentiated from an essential male nature, whereas for a postmodernist feminist, 'woman' is viewed as a fluid subject position that only becomes salient within certain discursive contexts but not in others.

Like Derrida, Foucault (1984) considers that language and the range of subject positions it offers always exist within *discourses*. Foucault's view is that language as a system does not represent human experience in a transparent and neutral way but always exists within historically specific discourses. These discourses are often competing, offering alternative versions of reality and serving different and conflicting power interests. Such interests usually reside within large-scale institutional systems such as law, justice, government, the media, education and the family. Thus, a range of institutional discourses provide the network by which dominant forms of social knowledge are produced, reinforced, contested or resisted. As discourses always represent and constitute different political interests, these are constantly vying with each other for status and power. As we have seen above, Foucault (1984: 100) resists a modernist conceptualisation of discourse in terms of dualities or opposites, preferring a more fluid, dynamic, strategic interpretation:

> We must not imagine a world of discourse divided between accepted discourse and excluded discourse, or between the dominant discourse and the dominated one; but as a multiplicity of discursive elements that can come into play in various strategies … Discourse transmits and produces power; it reinforces it, but also undermines and exposes it, renders it fragile and makes it possible to thwart it.

According to Foucault, discourses are responsible for the ways in which individual identities are recognised, constructed and regulated. This process of identity construction is reciprocally achieved through the *agency* of individual language users who are subjectively motivated to take up particular positions within multiple discourses and through the ways they are variously *positioned* as subjects by the social, normalising power of discourses.

The discursive construction of identities

As noted above, a modernist or liberal-humanist perspective of identity presupposes an *essence* at the core of the individual, which is unique, fixed and coherent, and which makes a person recognisably possess a character or personality. Conversely, a poststructuralist perspective posits that individuals are never outside cultural forces or discursive practices but always 'subject' to them. Their identities are governed by a range of 'subject positions' ('ways of being'), approved by their community or culture, and made available to them by means of the particular discourses operating within a given social context. If people do not conform to these approved discourses in terms of how they speak, act and behave, they may be stigmatised by others with labels such as 'weird', 'a misfit', 'a freak' or 'an outsider'. This is now a particular phenomenon on social media networks such as Facebook and Twitter where the capacity to construct identities (and attack the identities of others) through naming, labelling and membership categorisation (see Darvin, this volume) has become particularly stark. Language therefore acts as a regulatory force to pressurise individuals to conform to socially approved patterns of speech and behaviour.

The regulatory effects of discourse upon identity construction can be observed within institutional settings. For example, within a classroom context, students are subject to a range of institutional discourses offering knowledge about 'approved ways to be' in terms of their speech, behaviour, their learning and teacher–student relationships. But of course, not all discourses are institutionally approved or regulated. Competing or resistant discourses will also be constituted by peer value systems and will partly govern peer identities and relationships both in and out of the classroom. These discourses will be interwoven with broader societal discourses, embracing competing perspectives, on age, gender, ethnicity, class and the like. Thus a female student may be subject to various competing discourses within the classroom offering sets of positions relating to her age, gender, race, ethnicity and so on, as well as her participation as a student and membership of a peer group. On the one hand she may feel a pressure by her school and parents to conform to be a 'good' student who achieves high grades, but on another, she may sense that her peers consider that it is not 'cool' to work hard and thus aim to give off the appearance of indifference to her studies (Baxter 2003). Both identities pertain to her and can be invoked or resisted within different contexts by the student herself or by her associates. This does not make her inconsistent, but rather a complex, multifaceted individual with unique yet reasonably predictable ways of being.

Linguists have utilised the 'discursive construction of identity' concept within a wide range of applied contexts. For example, in the field of second language acquisition, Ibrahim's (1999) research on being constructed as Black within certain language learning communities is informed by the poststructuralist notion of being multiply positioned by assumptions about racial identity. Similarly, Moffatt and Norton's (2008) work on sexual orientation shows how language learning practices can naturalise heteronormative sexual identities as well as challenge them. With respect to gender, Pavlenko's (2004) work has revealed that cultural assumptions about female–male dichotomies may lead to inequalities among particular groups of language learners such as women, minorities, the elderly and the disabled, but crucially, they can also be contested. Finally, in multilingual studies, Blommaert and Rampton (2011) propose the poststructuralist notion of 'superdiversity': that is, the increasing access speakers have to plural discursive resources such as 'translanguaging', due to migration, increased mobility, the prevalence of social media and so on.

In all these contexts, individuals are shaped by the possibility of multiple (though not limitless) subject positions within and across different and competing discourses. Furthermore, the formation and reformation of identity is a continuous process, accomplished through actions and words rather than through some fundamental essence of character. Belsey (1980: 132) has suggested that individuals must be thought of as 'unfixed, unsatisfied ... not a unity, not autonomous, but a process, perpetually in construction, perpetually contradictory, perpetually open to change'. Given this understanding of identity/ies as a fluid network of subject positions, many feminist poststructuralists such as Weedon (1997) prefer the term 'subjectivity/ies', which has three defining characteristics: the plural, non-unitary aspects of the subject; subjectivity as a site of struggle; and subjectivity as changing over time. In this chapter, identity is used as the overarching term for a generic, cross-disciplinary concept, and 'subjectivity' is used where it pertains to poststructuralist conceptualisations.

Begging the question within this discussion is the extent to which poststructuralist theory accepts the concept of 'agency': a measure of individual awareness or control over the means by which subjects are 'interpellated' or called into existence (Althusser 1984) to a range of subject positions made available by different discursive contexts. What *is* the relationship between discourse and the individual as implied by poststructuralist theory? How much 'control' does an individual have over their ways of being in the world? In a sense, this is a question inspired by modernist critique that our identity exists at best in some sort of compliance with or resistance to discourses. At worst, identity becomes simply a function or an 'effect' of discourses, seen to be barely relevant to the ways in which meanings are produced through social practices. Indeed, Foucault suggests that the theorist's task is not to address the complexity of the world as experienced by the 'human subject'. Moreover, in his discussion of the question 'What is an author?' in terms of written texts, Foucault explicitly urges theorists that 'it is a matter of depriving the subject (or its substitute) of its role as originator, and of analysing the subject as a variable and complex function of discourse' (1984: 118).

Poststructuralists have argued that individuals are not uniquely positioned, but are produced as a 'nexus of subjectivities' (e.g. Davies and Harré 1990), in relations of power that are constantly shifting, rendering them at times powerful and at other times powerless. However, this notion of identity as little more than a form of interconnection or 'mobility' between different subject positions has not satisfied all poststructuralist theorists. To sum up the range of poststructuralist perspectives on identity, they can be characterised along a *spectrum* between the more radical thinkers, who perceive the concept simply in terms of discursive functions or effects, and the more moderate, who consider that identity embraces psychological elements such as the consciousness and memory of the individual, physical and material aspects such as bodily expressions of pain and pleasure (filtered through discourse) and semiotic expressions that index wider cultural identities.

I will now consider in more detail four key poststructuralist perspectives on the relationship between language and identity:

1   Performativity;
2   Positioning;
3   Feminist poststructuralist; and
4   Enunciative pragmatics.

The performativity perspective

At the more radical end of the poststructuralist spectrum is the view that the materiality of life, and specifically the body, is discursively constructed, and that life itself can only ever be experienced and conceptualised through the lens of competing discourses. Famously, the philosopher Jean Baudrillard (1995) published a book entitled *The Gulf war did not take place* in which he argued that the Gulf War was not really a war but rather an atrocity that masqueraded as a war. He suggested that the American military forces, using mainly air-power, did not directly engage in combat with the Iraqi army and suffered few casualties. Almost nothing was made known about Iraqi deaths. Thus, the fighting 'did not really take place' from the point of view of the Western world. Moreover, spectators only learnt about the war through propaganda imagery. Media representations made it impossible to distinguish between the experience of what materially happened in the conflict and its stylised, selective (mis)representation through Western discourses of war or, in Baudrillard's terms, 'simulacra'.

The poststructuralist linguist Judith Butler (1990 [2007]) has extensively debated the issue of whether or not the materiality of life is fully constructed, characterised by her theory of 'performativity' in relation to aspects of identity such as gender and sexuality. For Butler, such apparently genetic aspects are always achieved through performative acts: that is, 'constituting the identity it is purported to be' (1990: 33). This view links directly with Austin's (1962) speech act theory, which argues that illocutions such as 'I swear' or 'I promise' do not describe pre-existing states but literally *call* them into being. Accordingly, Butler claims that aspects of gender identity such as 'feminine' or 'masculine' behaviour are not what we are, nor traits we have, but effects we produce by way of particular actions we perform. She famously argued that '[g]ender is the repeated stylisation of the body, a set of repeated acts within a rigid regulatory frame which congeal over time to produce the appearance of substance, of a natural kind of being' (1990: 33).

According to Butler, aspects of identity such as gender have to be constantly reaffirmed and publicly displayed by repeatedly performing particular acts in accordance with cultural norms, which themselves are historically and socially constructed and in perpetual flux. Thus, perceived characteristics of a person such as their masculinity or femininity are nothing of the sort; they are symbolic enactments that are semiotically indexed through (for example) speech, body language, dress, appearance and possessions. Spoken language in particular has an influential part to play in that it too is a 'repeated stylisation of the body' and produces the notion that women and men have different speech styles and norms of interaction. Cameron (1997: 49) suggests that Butler's theories of performativity are revelatory for studies in language and identity because:

> This shifts the focus away from a simple cataloguing of differences between men and women to a subtler and more complex inquiry into how people use linguistic resources to produce gender differentiation ... it acknowledges the instability of identities and therefore of the behaviour in which those identities are performed.

Butler primarily illustrates her views of the discursive construction of gender identities by means of the example of drag artists. She argues that the performance of drag plays upon the distinction between the anatomy of the performer and the gender of the performed. She suggests that there are three contingent dimensions at work: anatomical sex, gender identity and gender performance, all of which are in some sort of parodic interplay. Butler uses drag acts to show that the concepts of biological sex and the social construct of gender are revealed to be dissonant. In other words, a drag artist may have the body of a man and perform the gendered identity of a woman in everyday life, but in a drag act perform a transvestite's view of a female identity. In this self-conscious playing with different gendered identities, which are themselves regulated by a discourse of 'compulsory heterosexuality' (Rich 1976), drag artists reveal the irrelevance to human identities of the materiality of biological sex:

> As much as drag creates a unified picture of 'woman' ... it also reveals the distinctness of those aspects of gendered experience which are falsely naturalised as a unity through the regulatory fiction of heterosexual coherence. In imitating gender, drag implicitly reveals the imitative structure of gender itself – as well as its contingency.
>
> *(Butler 1990: 187)*

I suggest that Butler's perspective on gender identity is radical not least because of the way she has also contested the category of biological sex as 'natural'. Butler explicitly challenges biological accounts of binary sex, reconceiving the sexed body as itself culturally constructed by regulatory discourses. The supposed obviousness of sex as a natural biological fact attests to how deeply its production in discourse is hidden. The sexed body, once established as a 'natural' and unquestioned 'fact', is seen as the alibi for constructions of gender and sexuality, inevitably more cultural in their appearance, which can purport to be the seemingly natural expressions or consequences of a more fundamental biological sex. According to Butler, it is on the basis of the construction of natural binary sex that gender identities, and hence normative heterosexuality, are likewise constructed as natural.

In sum, Butler's perspective on the relationship between language and identity is that certain elements such as sex and gender that we take to be 'internal' features of our psyche are actually ones that we anticipate and produce through certain bodily acts and, at an extreme, 'an hallucinatory effect of naturalised gestures' (Butler 2007: xvi). Despite such assertions, Cameron (1997: 49–50) points out that Butler does not reduce women and men to 'automata programmed by their early socialisation to repeat forever the appropriate gendered behaviour, but treats them as conscious agents who may – albeit often at some social cost – engage in acts of transgression, subversion and resistance'. Drag acts are a case in point, demonstrating that individuals are active producers of discourses rather than passively positioned by such discourses, without which an understanding of discursive provenance would always remain unclear. I now consider poststructuralist perspectives on language and identity that bestow rather more agency upon the concept of 'personhood'.

The positioning perspective

Rather more moderate than performativity is the positioning perspective. This views language and identity in terms of a balance between the ways in which discourses position participants as 'subjects' in competing ways and the ways participants make their own and other people's actions socially determinate. Here, there *is* a place for agency as more than simply individual acts of resistance or compliance to discursive practices, but rather as recognition that people are capable of exercising choice in relation to those practices.

Positioning theory emerged from the work of linguistically orientated social psychologists in the 1990s who wished to better understand the socially constructed yet dynamic aspects of linguistic encounters. Two such theorists were Bronwyn Davies and Rom Harré (1990), who adopted the poststructuralist paradigm to make better sense of the psychology of 'personhood' and to address the ambiguity of the question 'Who am I?'. Their discussions are based on poststructuralist principles that acknowledge both the constitutive force of discourse and, in particular, 'discursive practices', yet at the same time recognise that an individual emerges through the processes of social interaction, not as a relatively fixed end product but as one who actively helps to constitute the discourses of which they are a part:

> Accordingly, who one is [must always be] an open question with a shifting answer depending upon the positions made available within one's own and others' discursive practices and within those practices, the stories through which we make sense of our own and other people's lives.
>
> *(Davies and Harré 1990: 46)*

According to the authors, 'positioning' is the discursive process whereby identities or 'selves' are located in conversations as observably and subjectively coherent participants in 'jointly produced story-lines' (1990: 47). In speaking and acting from a position, people are bringing to the particular situation their history as a subjective being. This is not the history of accumulated experience in a liberal-humanist sense but rather the history of one who has been in multiple subject positions and engaged in different forms of discourse. Davies and Harré suggest that there are two types of position within which participants routinely find themselves: *interactive* positioning, in which the utterances of one person position their interlocutor through the process of turn-taking, and *reflexive* positioning, in which one has some agency to position oneself. Neither type of positioning should be viewed as intentional, according to the authors, but rather as part of the ongoing process of reproducing oneself within existing and emerging discourses.

The positioning perspective evolved by Davies and Harré is linked closely to the idea that we (re)produce ourselves through our lived autobiographies. In other words, in order to produce some form of consistency and coherence between our multiple subject positions, we tell ourselves and others stories about how we have lived and how we intend to live our lives. This need to develop storylines involving events, characters and moral dilemmas is an attempt to resolve the ways in which we are continuously positioned by discursive practices in contradictory ways that disrupt the sense of sustaining a coherent identity. According to the authors, appearing to be historically continuous and unitary is how being an 'authentic' person is 'done' in Western culture.

The positioning perspective has since been taken up by discursive psychologists with an interest in ethnomethodology, which views everyday conversation as a resource through which speakers and hearers can intersubjectively negotiate their identities and construct a specific social order. For example, Wetherell (1998: 388) has traversed different schools of linguistic thought to argue that 'a stance which reads [poststructuralism] in terms of [ethnomethodology] continues to provide the most productive basis for discourse work in social psychology'. She argues that the way a subject position emerges within conversation is only partly the consequence of the discourse it is assigned to. Much more significant are the ways in which participants orient to turn-taking procedures in conversation, which serves to reveal the formation and contestation of multiple subject positions. What clearly initiates and sustains one or more subject positions in conversation is 'accountability, or participants' orientations to their setting and the emergent conversational activities' (ibid.: 401).

Wetherell (ibid.: 395) argues that poststructualist theory is almost always discussed in the abstract, on the basis of implicit assumptions of language and identity, and is rarely applied to 'what is happening right now, on the ground, in this very conversation'. She demonstrates the value of interplay between poststructuralist and ethnomethodological approaches by means of a research study involving three young, white, male sixth form students in the UK discussing a sexual encounter. Wetherell (ibid.) analyses how one young man, Aaron, moves between different subject positions within the course of a single conversation, trying to account for these inconsistent positions in varying ways. In talking about how he starts a casual relationship with a young woman, both Aaron and his friends variously position him as drunk, lucky, 'on the pull', having a good month, on the moral low ground, not intentionally 'going for it', displaying impressive conduct and so on. Wetherell explains that the question of how to evaluate these conflicting subject positions remains unresolved within the conversation itself. However, Wetherell suggests that 'this portfolio of positions remains available to be carried forward to other contexts and conversations making up the "long conversation" which is the sixth form common room culture' (ibid.: 400). In other words, these participant orientations do not emerge uniquely from a single conversation but fit within broader, culturally recognisable 'interpretive repertoires' about male sexuality available to young men. In sum, the creative potential of these young men to negotiate who they are and how they relate to others is available as a resource, but always constrained by the culturally governed range of subject positions available to them, and the discursive tension between such positions.

The feminist poststructuralist perspective

This perspective and its analytical version as feminist poststructuralist discourse analysis (FPDA) combines aspects of positioning theory and performativity theory but differs in holding a rather more dynamic, agentic and fluid approach to identity, or what Chris Weedon (1997) calls 'subjectivity'. There is also a focus upon critiquing gender relations, although this is not based upon a simple, binary conceptualisation of gender.

While a feminist poststructuralist perspective recognises identity categories such as 'woman' to be permeable, it does not go along with the view that individuals are just the passive, unstable, fragmented effects of competing discourses. Although 'the subject' in poststructuralism is always socially constructed *within* discourses, Weedon (1997: 102) argues that s/he 'none the less exists as a thinking, feeling subject and social agent, capable of resistance and innovations produced out of the clash between contradictory subject positions and practices'.

In other words, feminist poststructuralism believes in women's lived, embodied reality and their subjective, emotional and cognitive experiences, since the ways in which individuals make sense of their lives is a necessary starting point for understanding the ways in which gendered discourses continue to structure social relations. However, it is in the conceptualisation of a woman's consciousness, agency or ability to act for herself that feminist poststructuralism differs from both modernist and social constructionist versions of identity by centralising her subjectivity as a site contested in discourse. According to this conceptualisation, individuals neither conform to the liberal-humanist conception of the free individual in control of their destiny, nor to the notion of a passively positioned subject. So, female (and male) speakers are positioned in a fluid, dynamic, contextual relation with competing constructs of gender. Notions of 'femininity' and 'masculinity' are continuously being contested by dominant social discourses that vie with each other to fix the meaning of these constructs permanently. Rather than viewing individuals as being at the mercy of these competing discourses, speakers are multiply positioned in terms of their agency to adapt to, negotiate, contest or overturn dominant subject positions. More proactively, people can take up subject positions within oppositional discourses, and this is how substantive social and material changes can occur.

Thus, an FPDA approach aims to describe and critique competing versions of subjectivity available to a person. In a recent paper (Baxter 2014), I showed how women political leaders are often constructed in negative or demonised ways in the news media because women as a social category are still not socially accepted within a male-dominated political world. However, I argued that there is enough 'wriggle room' for the readers/audience to read such articles 'against the grain' and thereby to produce more positive and life-enhancing versions of female subjectivity from these articles. Such critical readings can offer an explanation of where our experiences have come from; why these are often contradictory or inconsistent; and how versions of reality can be 'read against the grain' or changed if necessary. In other words, knowing that subjectivities are discursively constructed does not limit or prescribe a person's agency but simply becomes a precondition for understanding the possibilities for 'breakthrough' action and change.

One radical element of the feminist poststructuralist perspective on subjectivity is its refusal to accept the modernist view that all women are necessarily victims of patriarchy. This refusal is predicated on the broader poststructuralist perspective that subjectivities should not be conceptualised in binary terms as male/female, young/old, villains/victims and so on. This is because feminist poststructuralism appreciates the unevenness and ambiguities of power relations between males and females. Indeed, FPDA questions the way biological sex is classified as a binary, reconceptualising this as a powerful gendered discourse among others. Individuals identifying as female are perceived to be multiply positioned as powerful or powerless within and across a range of competing discourses. During the course of a conversation, for example, they might shift between subject positions of power or powerlessness according to the discourses circulating within that context. This mobility offers women/girls some agency to escape victimhood because they are rarely trapped permanently within a powerless subject position.

The feminist poststructuralist perspective does not consider males and females to be equivalently positioned in terms of the ways in which power is negotiated through gender relations. Its focus is upon the pervasiveness of gendered discourses (Sunderland 2004), which often conspire with other institutional discourses to 'fix' women/girls in positions of relative powerlessness, despite breakthrough moments of resistance. FPDA is thus concerned to equip analysts with the thinking to 'see through' the ambiguities and confusions of particular discursive contexts where females are located as simultaneously powerful and powerless. For example, in my study of a student classroom (Baxter 2003), I show that classroom discourses provide a range of quite powerful subject positions for girls (such as 'peer and teacher approval' and 'collaborative talk'), but yet, at the same time, a discourse of 'gender difference' is constantly working to undermine the possibilities of greater girl power. An FPDA approach can highlight and critique the contradictions and tensions girls experience as subjects/speakers in the classroom. It can also foreground the ways in which girls take up (or can be encouraged to take up) subject/speaking positions that allow them to contest or resist more powerless ways of being.

Discourse analysts such as Kamada (2010) have used FPDA to analyse the relationship between language and identity from a poststructuralist perspective. Kamada explores the intersectional, linguistic construction of ethnic identities among six Japanese-Caucasian girlfriends. She includes ethnicity alongside gender in her exploration of how these multi-ethnic girls are simultaneously positioned as relatively powerful and powerless within a range of dominant discourses. She demonstrates how, on the one hand, the girls feel disempowered because they stand out at school as different and consequently experience isolation, marginalisation and bullying. On the other hand, they are able to take up empowering positions within a discourse of 'foreigner attractiveness' or 'a white-Western female beauty' discourse, which provide them with a certain *cachet* among their Japanese-only peers. They thus achieve an agency that enables them to overcome negative social constructions by others of their identities as only 'half-Japanese'.

The enunciative pragmatics (EP) perspective

This relatively recent approach to poststructuralist discourse analysis provides a tangential yet illuminating perspective on the relationship between language and identity. Rather than directly considering how identity is theorised as it is associated with living, breathing human beings, the EP perspective focuses on the multitude of voices to be found within written texts and considers how such texts orient readers to identify and interpret these voices. Written texts offer an array of competing voices, or identity positions that the reader is required to disentangle and interpret. In simpler terms, we cannot speak or write without mobilising a range of different voices or points of view, some of which appear very 'close' to us and others much further away. A text never expresses a single, obvious meaning; it always says more than the author means to say. Rather than drawing on a unified source of meaning, texts unintentionally let many voices speak, which means that interpreting discourse is often a finely judged process.

The EP perspective has its roots in theories of discursive polyphony (e.g. Bakhtin 1981), which posits that a discourse mobilises many different voices, even in the case of a single author or in statements made by a single speaker or writer. For Bakhtin (1981), the literary work, especially, consists of a plurality of voices, social styles and languages. Through language, the subject of the text is constantly producing and reproducing itself in different forms and occupying ever-changing positions.

Angermuller (2012) has developed the EP method of discourse analysis inspired by the poststructuralist critique of the speaking subject who is presumed to be self-contained, unique, relatively predictable and consistent in speech and action. He advocates a method whereby the analyst scans the text for markers reflecting 'discursive heterogeneity' (2012: 118). Angermuller's method coheres with the poststructuralist perspective on agency outlined above: namely, individuals (speakers, readers, writers, characters) can simultaneously act upon discursive practices while being subject-positioned by those same practices. Rather than a text delivering its meaning in a direct and transparent way, which the reader then decodes, Angermuller (ibid.: 120) argues that:

> the text allows the reader to attribute its various contents to different 'subject positions' such as the author (locutor) and the Other (allocator or addressee) of discourse. The locutor and allocator are not physical individuals; they are communicative instances which allow the reader to reduce the many voices of discourse to a limited number of discursive positions.

Further to this, Angermuller suggests that texts provide 'enunciative markers' that enable readers to spot 'markers of polyphony' such as negators (e.g. *not, un-*) and argumentative devices (*but, however* ...), both of which trigger at least two voices (the play between the allocator and the locutor). This is not a structuralist perspective 'by the back door'; Angermuller argues that readers are crucial to the process of interpreting such enunciative markers as guided by the circumstances of their immediate, local context. He understands the reading of the competing voices within a text as 'the product of active readers trying to understand the message by contextualising the text according to its formal instructions' (ibid.: 119). Angermuller exemplifies his approach in a range of different ways including a complex, multi-staged analysis of the unintentionally conveyed, competing voices within works by Foucault, Derrida, Lacan and others. He also shows how in a radio broadcast of a speech by Russian President Vladmir Putin that a range of anonymous voices, beings and speakers populate the spoken words. Readers can produce two conflicting discourses from the speech – 'internationalist' on the one hand and 'sovereignist' on the other – which do not necessarily presuppose that Putin is offering an ambiguous message. Rather, the use of such multi-voiced speech is that 'readers understand that Putin understands' that he can reach listeners/readers with contrasting values and agendas and allow them to produce either or both readings within the same moment. Identity according to this perspective is understood in terms of the ways in which listeners/readers can resist the impetus of monological discourse and discover the voices in a text that produce alternative or resistant meanings.

Issues and ongoing debates

In this section, I will explore one of the central debates within applied linguistics, which questions how the relationship between language and identity can best be described, analysed, interpreted and explained. While there is a diversity of applied linguistic approaches to the topic, three of the most influential are: (1) ethnomethodological, which underpins discourse analytical approaches such as conversation analysis (CA); (2) critical, which supports approaches such as critical discourse analysis (CDA); and, of course, (3) poststructuralist, in the form of poststructuralist discourse analysis (PDA), encompassing in principle all four perspectives discussed in the previous section. There has been very little agreement over the last three decades about which analytical approach most fittingly explains the relationship between language and identity, and on the whole, applied linguists agree to differ. Drawing on my own work, I will now explore the differences (and points of intersection) between the three analytical approaches, arguing what advantages the poststructuralist position might offer over the other two.

In many ways, PDA is closer to CDA than CA, but there are a number of quite obvious differences. All three approaches are social constructionist in spirit and question the essentialist view that human identity is unique, fixed and coherent. They all assume that identities are constructed through the dynamic process of linguistic interaction. However, unlike CA, both CDA and PDA are explicitly interested in the discursive contexts in which identities are constructed, although each approach conceptualises this rather differently. CDA assumes language and discourse to interact dialectically with the material world (e.g. Fairclough and Wodak 1997). So for example, a discursive event such as a student demonstration may ultimately impact on material practices such as an increase in student grants, but the nature of student demonstrations may also change as a consequence of such material effects. In contrast, PDA tends to adopt an anti-materialist stance to context in its view that social 'realities' are discursively produced, so students' identities as actors and demonstrators are produced through discourse, and rarely outside it. So if students go out into the world to try and change material conditions, those 'material conditions' are principally understood through discourses on student protest and government policy. PDA acknowledges that real material conditions exist and affect people physically and emotionally (Weedon 1997), but such conditions are also a function and effect of discursively formed viewpoints. The extent to which discursive effects interact with the material world is a point of strong debate between critical and poststructuralist thinkers (see Block, this volume). Norton (2006) is one scholar who has bridged the critical/poststructuralist gap by arguing that material hardship does impinge upon discursive identity construction and that it should be acknowledged as such.

Another point of difference between the three approaches is in relation to power. A CA approach relies closely upon analysing the meanings and interpretations of the participants and draws upon the 'common sense' narratives cropping up in naturally occurring data, aiming to interpret the participants' expressions of their identities in their own terms. For CA, with its bottom-up approach, power relations are therefore never assumed, although they may be constructed through the process of linguistic interaction (Benwell and Stokoe 2006). For CDA and PDA, in contrast, power relations are inscribed within social or institutional discourses, which permeate every linguistic interaction. While CA exponents argue that power relations between individuals, if they exist, will emerge 'naturally' from data analysis, both CDA and PDA consider such a data-centred approach to be methodologically 'naive' (Billig 2000). Working from the opposite pole to CA, CDA starts from 'the experiences and opinions of members of [dominated groups] and supports their struggle against inequality' (van Dijk 2001: 96). In contrast, PDA does not support this type of emancipatory approach to discourse analysis because (as discussed in the previous section) 'a will to truth' leads to 'a will to power', which will ultimately transmute into its own 'grand narrative' (Foucault 1980). However, PDA is not apolitical, but rather tends to back small-scale, bottom-up, localised social transformations that are vital in order to challenge and contest 'grand narratives' that oppress people. So Kamada's (2010) analysis based on a small, ethnographic case study of six half-Japanese girls enabled her participants to challenge the negative perceptions that they and others shared of their ethnic and gendered identities.

To illustrate this difference between CDA and PDA, CDA linguists might locate a group whom they had identified as victims of oppressive power, such as stay-at-home mothers, and deconstruct the ways in which this group is perceived to be victimised through institutional language. PDA linguists would analyse how mothers are multiply located in a stretch of data, and cannot be dichotomously cast as powerless and disadvantaged or as victims. The value of PDA over CDA, in my view, is that identities are constructed as multiple, dynamic, fluid and ever-changing, and these are not perceived as fixed within a single, static, powerless position. PDA therefore restores a sense of agency to those individuals or social groups considered to be disadvantaged or disempowered. They are never permanently positioned within a dichotomous villain–victim relationship, but can self-reflexively transform their identity position through acts of negotiation, challenge, self-reflexivity and resistance. This was illustrated by a recent case in the British news media where a woman, Judith Tebbut, who was kidnapped while on holiday in Somalia, described her six-month ordeal thus:

> Everything was conspiring to turn me into a woman without an identity, without freedom, without co-ordinates, and no comprehension of what might happen to her. It was a very frightening place to be, a very disturbing present tense. In spite of it all, I still believed I was Jude the social worker, wife, mother, and this saved me.

> *(Tebbut 2013: 69)*

Finally, PDA is arguably a necessary antidote to CA and CDA, in that it offers a supplementary approach, simultaneously complementing and undermining other discourse-analytical methods. It does not claim to be a complete method or the best method, but simply one that might be fit for purpose. Within applied linguistics, there is much value to be gained from a multi-perspectival approach that combines different methodological tools in a functional way as befits the task in hand. The textual interplay between competing terms, methods and sets of ideas allows for more multiple, open-ended readings of language and identity data. Thus while CDA in principle seeks to deconstruct how hegemonic power relations position individuals or groups, and in so doing may produce a single, oppositional reading that may eventually become authoritative, a poststructuralist, supplementary approach encourages the possibility of several competing readings. This means that no single reading of a text is regarded as fixed, but that every reading can be reviewed and perhaps contested in the light of competing voices, perspectives or methods of analysis.

Summary

In this chapter, I have discussed poststructuralist perspectives of language and identity that all share similar philosophical origins in postmodernism; language and the construction of meaning; and the discursive construction of identities. The chapter explicates four diverse poststructuralist perspectives of language and identity: performativity; positioning; feminist poststructuralist; and enunciative pragmatics. I touch on some of the criticisms levelled against poststructuralism, such as its focus on discursivity, its anti-materialism and its apoliticism. By comparing three methods of analysis, ethnomethodological, critical and poststructuralist, the chapter concludes by arguing that PDA has much to offer the study of language and identity in the future – both as a stand-alone and as a supplementary methodology.

Related topics

Ethnomethodological and conversation analytic approaches to identity; Discursive psychology and the production of identity in language practices; Critical discourse analysis and identity; Language and gender identities; Language and non-normative sexual identities; Beyond the micro–macro interface in language and identity research; Language, gender and identities in political life: a case study from Malaysia; Intersectionality in language and identity research.

Further reading

Angermuller, J., Maingueneau, D. and Wodak, R. (eds) (2014). *The discourse studies reader: main currents in theory and analysis*. Amsterdam and Philadelphia: John Benjamins. (An overview of the main currents in discourse studies including chapters on poststructuralism and its later developments.)

Howarth, D. (2000). *Discourse*. Buckingham, UK: Open University Press. (A clear and readable overview of structuralism and poststructuralist approaches to discourse studies.)

Laclau, E. and Mouffe, C. (1985). *Hegemony and socialist strategy: towards a radical democratic politics*. London and New York: Verso. (A classic text that has adapted post-Marxist approaches to poststructuralism.)

Norton, B. (2013 [2000]). *Identity and language learning: extending the conversation*. 2nd edn. Bristol: Multilingual Matters. (A poststructuralist perspective on the relationship between identity construction and second language learning.)

References

Althusser, L. (1984). *Essays on intertextuality*. London: Verso.

Angermuller, J. (2012). Fixing meaning: the many voices of the post-liberal hegemony in Russia, *Journal of Language and Politics*, 11(1): 115–134.

Austin, J.J. (1962). *How to do things with words*. Oxford: Clarendon Press.

Bakhtin, M. (1981). *The dialogic imagination: four essays*. Texas: University of Texas.

Baudrillard, J. (1995). *The Gulf War did not take place*. Bloomington: Indiana University Press.

Baxter, J. (2003). *Positioning gender in discourse: a feminist methodology*. Basingstoke: Palgrave Macmillan.

Baxter, J. (2014). 'Containing femininity? Reading against sexualised constructions of women leaders in the news media', Paper presented to the British Association of Applied Linguists (BAAL), University of Warwick, UK, April 2014.

Belsey, C. (1980). *Critical practice*. London: Methuen.

Benwell, B. and Stokoe, E. (2006). *Discourse and identity*. Edinburgh: Edinburgh University Press.

Billig, M. (2000). Towards a critique of the critical, *Discourse and Society*, 11(3): 291–292.

Block, D. (this volume). Class in language and identity research, in S. Preece (ed.) *The Routledge handbook of language and identity*. London: Routledge, pp. 241–254.

Blommaert, J. and Rampton, B. (2011). 'Language and superdiversity', *Diversities*, 13(2) [Online]. Available at www.unesco.org/shs/diversities/vol13/issue2/art1

Butler, J. (1990 [2007]). *Gender trouble: feminism and the subversion of identity*. New York: Routledge.

Cameron, D. (1997). Performing gender identity: young men's talk and the construction of heterosexual identity, in S. Johnson and U.H. Meinhof (eds) *Language and masculinity*. Oxford: Blackwell, pp. 47–64.

Darvin, R. (this volume). Language and identity in the digital age, in S. Preece (ed.) *The Routledge handbook of language and identity*. London: Routledge, pp. 523–540.

Davies, B. and Harré, R. (1990). 'Positioning: the discursive production of selves', *Journal for the Theory of Social Behaviour*, 20(1): 43–63.

Derrida, J. (1987). *A Derrida reader: between the blinds*. Brighton: Harvester Wheatsheaf.

Fairclough, N. and Wodak, R. (1997). Critical discourse analysis, in T. van Dijk (ed.) *Discourse as social interaction*. London: SAGE, pp. 258–284.

Foucault, M. (1980). *Power/knowledge: selected interviews and other writings 1972–1977*. New York: Pantheon.

Foucault, M. (1984). What is enlightenment?, in P. Rabinow (ed.) *The Foucault reader*. London: Penguin, pp. 32–50.

Ibrahim, A. (1999). 'Becoming Black: rap and hip-hop, race, gender, identity, and the politics of ESL learning', *TESOL Quarterly*, 33(3): 349–369.

Kamada, L. (2010). *Hybrid identities and adolescent girls*. Bristol: Multilingual Matters.

Kristeva, J. (1984). Woman can never be defined, in E. Marks and I. de Coutivron (eds) *New French feminisms*. New York: Schocken, pp. 137–141.

Lacan, J. (2006 [1977]). *Écrits: a selection* [Trans. A. Sheridan]. New York: W.W. Norton and Co.

Lyotard, J. (1984). *The postmodern condition*. Manchester: Manchester University Press.

Moffatt, L. and Norton, B. (2008). 'Reading gender relations and sexuality: preteens speak out', *Canadian Journal of Education*, 31(1): 102–123.

Norton, B. (2006). 'Identity as a socio-cultural construct in second language education', TESOL in Context Special Edition 1: *Tales out of School* [Online]. Available at www.tesol.org.au/Publications/Special-Editions

Pavlenko, A. (2004). Gender and sexuality in foreign and second language education: critical and feminist approaches, in B. Norton and K. Toohey (eds) *Critical pedagogies and language learning*. New York: Cambridge University Press, pp. 53–71.

Rich, A. (1976). *Of women born: motherhood as experience and institution*. New York: W.W. Norton.

Saussure, F. de (1974). *A course in general linguistics*. London: Fontana.

Sunderland, J. (2004). *Gendered discourses*. London: Palgrave Macmillan.

Tebbut, J. (2013). *A long walk home*. London: Monday Books.

van Dijk, T. (2001). Multi-disciplinary CDA: a plea for diversity, in R. Wodak and M. Meyer (eds) *Methods of critical discourse analysis*. London and Thousand Oaks, CA: SAGE, pp. 95–120.

Weedon, C. (1997). *Feminist practice and poststructuralist theory*. Oxford: Blackwell.

Wetherell, M. (1998). 'Positioning and interpretative repertoires: conversation analysis and poststructuralism in dialogue', *Discourse and Society*, 9: 387–412.

3

Identity in variationist sociolinguistics

Rob Drummond and Erik Schleef

Introduction

This chapter provides an overview of the different perspectives on identity within variationist sociolinguistics (henceforth VS). It also discusses some of the central issues within the field pertaining to applied linguistics; in particular, language discrimination and the recent expansion of VS into second language acquisition. VS is a branch of sociolinguistics that focuses on language variation and change. Variationist sociolinguists may investigate variable linguistic features, such as saying *fink* instead of *think*, or the variable use of different varieties, which may be dialects, languages, accents, styles and so on. VS has much to offer applied linguistics as it takes as axiomatic that, in order to understand language *fully*, we must develop a thorough understanding of categorical, *as well as* variable, processes.

VS focuses strongly on the use of inferential statistics, the use of recorded speech, and the investigation of social factors in addition to linguistic factors. Variationist sociolinguists share the assumption that variation is not random; it is systematic and structured. Patterns can be found in variation, and it is the goal of VS to determine and describe these patterns and the ways in which they are acquired and used. While a large degree of variation is linguistically constrained, a significant proportion of variation can be attributed to social reasons, and identity may play a crucial role in how language varies and changes. Thus, VS focuses not only on language variation in order to determine how it is structured linguistically and socially and how it is put to use and acquired, but also on what variation may mean to speakers and hearers. This makes it particularly relevant to issues of identity within applied linguistics.

Overview

The review contained within the first section of this chapter will be structured using Eckert's (2012) three waves of VS. These waves are loosely ordered; therefore, while one is built chronologically onto the other, all three remain very much alive. What makes these three waves interesting to us is that they all differ somewhat in how they view and use the concept of identity; partly as a logical repercussion of their research focus and the level at which they investigate social meaning. Identity has been a concern in VS since the inception of the field in the early 1960s (Labov 1963). However, the role played by identity in explaining language variation and change, and, most importantly, how identity is defined, has changed throughout the decades and continues to be at the very centre of contention in VS. To an extent, it has come to highlight and symbolise divisions within the field. Conceptualising these differences as variances of scale is helpful, as relevant theories now exist that allow us to link these different levels of meaning.

The first wave

First-wave variationist sociolinguists focus on documenting language variation and change in communities. They identify variation, determine the linguistic and social constraints of this variation and whether or not the variation is a reflection of language change. The social factors that this type of research may investigate tend to be of a relatively broad, census-type macro-sociological nature, such as speaker sex, social class, age and ethnicity. This line of research has laid the conceptual and methodological groundwork that defines VS today. It is based on large-scale surveys of populations, conducted with the goal of statistical representativeness, objectivity and replicability, that result in stratified models of the speech of populations. Seminal studies from this wave focus in particular on urban areas, such as New York (Labov 1966), Detroit (Wolfram 1969), Norwich (Trudgill 1974), Glasgow (Macauley 1977), Sydney (Horvath 1985), Montreal (Thibault and Sankoff 1993) and York (Tagliamonte 1999). Such studies provide us with a bird's-eye view of variation and information on the social and linguistic spread of language change. However, these studies do not simply give a general impression of variation; they filter their view of it through a particular perspective on social space, focusing on socioeconomic hierarchies and, secondarily, other visible census-type categories (see Eckert 2012: 90; Block, this volume, for more detail on the primacy of socioeconomic status).

Identity is seldom theorised in these studies, and usually not mentioned. The closest we may get to identity are the social categories used as factors in statistical testing. If we were to conceive of these macro-sociological labels as identity labels, they would be *reflections* of language use, identities that are stable, unified and essential, as they would be based on membership of individuals in specific social categories. Arguments about identity are sometimes made *indirectly*. That such claims are, in fact, about identity is disputable, but some of the explanations provided for the linguistic behaviour of certain social groups, e.g. individuals in these groups aiming for 'prestige', 'status' or 'solidarity', certainly make assumptions about the kind of people who hold these attitudes. For example, Trudgill (1972) argued that the speech of women in his sample was consistently more standard because of their strong desire for upward mobility and their more pronounced sensitivity to standard pressures. Similarly, he stated that middle-class speakers may adopt working-class innovations because of their association with masculinity. Occasionally, identity concepts are evoked directly; for example, Labov (1972: 70–109) talks about New York City identity in relation to *one* of his participants. However, it is rare for identity to be linked directly to the kind of large category labels used in these studies. There are very good reasons for this, of which sociolinguists working in a quantitative tradition are normally aware.

Significant results in a statistical model often explain only a portion of all variation. In addition, statisticians warn against making unsubstantiated claims about cause and effect. We must not engage in statistically motivated speculations in our quest to uncover identity; our explanation must be based on a principled linguistic or social theory and additional evidence, which may often be found in individual interactions. This is particularly the case since many social categories used are composite indices based on a variety of different factors; for example, when determining the social class of an individual, occupation, income, educational background and a variety of other factors are often combined. Most importantly, individuals within descriptive categories do not have *one* unified, stable identity that has an essential link to language. Specific methods would be refined in the second and third waves of VS to home in on whether identity is relevant in a particular data set and, if so, which dimensions of identity are of salience.

The second wave

While the second wave of variationist sociolinguistics also focuses on documenting language variation and change in communities, the focus shifts from macro-sociological categories and interview data to locally relevant groupings and naturally occurring speech. Nonetheless, because studies in this tradition often share the quantitative interest in language with first-wave research in VS, the underlying assumption about identity is one of fixedness and stability. Similarly to the first wave, variable linguistic features are examined as making up and defining varieties, and as marking certain social groups. However, the focus differs in scale. While the underlying concept of identity has not changed considerably from first- to second-wave VS, identity moves to centre stage in the second wave. Second-wave researchers began attributing social agency to the use of vernacular and standard features. The vernacular was often regarded as an expression of identity, particularly local or class identity. This strand received important input from ethnography and, to a lesser extent, social psychology – in particular, Social Identity Theory (Tajfel 1978), which considers *any* social group relevant to social identity construction, not limiting itself to macro-sociological categories (see Joseph, this volume). Sociolinguists who make use of ethnography examine how certain linguistic forms are locally meaningful to social groupings that emerge in the fieldwork. These social categories are based on participant observation, rather than pre-formulated frameworks of analysis; they are participant-defined. Thus, rather than imposing identity categories on speakers, ethnographic observation enables us to work with identity categories that emerge from the data and that we know are salient to the speakers themselves at the local level.

For example, Milroy (1980) investigated working-class neighbourhoods in Belfast, Cheshire (1982) researched language variation on an adventure playground in Reading, England, and Gal (1979) investigated language shift in a Hungarian-German bilingual community in Austria. In these studies, the identity labels used are not the traditional macro-sociological categories with which we are so familiar. On the contrary, concepts such as social class and ethnicity were often deconstructed, abandoned or glossed over in favour of exploring the research participants' social networks. Yet, this research strand left much unspoken about the identities that exist or develop in these networks, and the relationship between identity, social network and the norms and ideologies that were argued to be shared by members of a social network.

The investigation of communities of practice (Lave and Wenger 1991) is another qualitative step in discovering norms and ideologies that relate to the social lives of research participants. It represents a shift towards more qualitative examinations of communities, although quantitative statistics often continue to play a role in such research. Drawing on Lave and Wenger's seminal text, Eckert and McConnell-Ginet (1992: 464) consider a community of practice to be 'an aggregate of people who come together around mutual engagement in an endeavour. Ways of doing things, ways of talking, beliefs, values, power relations – in short, practices – emerge in the course of this mutual endeavour.'

Thus, this approach focuses on how people use language in different contexts to construct different identities by investigating shared repertoires, values and practices. For example, Eckert

(1989) studied the use of language at a high school in suburban Detroit, where the social order involved two mutually opposed social categories, 'jocks' and 'burnouts', and whose members behaved linguistically in different ways. Uncovering shared norms and beliefs, regarded as crucial in the construction and expression of identities, through observation or direct elicitation is at the very heart of this practice-based approach.

The third wave

Social meaning, style and stance

While linguistic features index social categories in waves one and two, in third-wave variationist sociolinguistics, linguistic features index social meanings. Moore and Podesva (2009: 448–450) conceptualise social meanings as stances, personal characteristics, personae (e.g. 'nerd', 'jock') and social types (e.g. 'middle class'). For example, variation in (ing) has been shown to index specific social meanings, such that *singing* (rather than *singin'*) may express articulateness, intelligence, etc. (Campbell-Kibler 2009). Research within the third wave of variation regards language use as not reflecting identities, but rather constituting them through stylistic practice (Eckert 2012: 94), thereby putting a focus on the social meaning of variable features (e.g. Ochs 1992; Agha 2005; Podesva 2007; Eckert 2008; Kiesling 2009). Exploring the social meaning of a feature can help us understand the role language plays in identity construction. Eckert (2012) provides a very telling example of the variety of different meanings of a single feature. In the US, aspiration of /t/ in intervocalic contexts has been found to be relevant in a variety of different enregistered styles; those of 'geek' girls (Bucholtz 1996), Orthodox Jews (Benor 2001) and gay men (Podesva 2007). The social meaning of aspirated intervocalic /t/ cannot possibly be related specifically to any of these groups or identities. Instead, the meaning of the feature must relate to something shared by all these; they all exploit indexical values linked to hyperarticulation (i.e. extremely articulate and clear speech).

Third-wave variationist sociolinguistics (henceforth TWVS) aims to discover the social meanings of a particular variable in context and how this comes about. This requires us to go beyond the social categories to which we linked variation in the first two waves and also beyond the exploration of identity as the reflection of such categories. For the identity concept to be of value to TWVS, it has to be reconceptualised. In TWVS, identities are regarded as being constructed and reconstructed; they are dynamic and changeable. Language and identity cannot be separated or correlated; they are co-constitutive. Agency continues to matter, which Bucholtz and Hall (2010) consider to go beyond individual choice and deliberate action. Identity emerges in a variety of ways, ranging from deliberate action to habitual practice and as the result of interactional processes. Bucholtz and Hall discuss five principles in the study of identity, summarised below:

- Identity emerges in discourse, rather than preceding it.
- Identity includes not only census-type macro-sociological categories, but also local ethnographic and interactional positionings.
- Identity is constituted by means of a variety of indexical processes.
- Identity is not located with the individual; identities are constructed inter-subjectively through a variety of relations.

- Identity is partial. It is 'produced through contextually situated and ideologically informed configurations of self and other' (ibid.: 25). It shifts continually within interactions and across contexts.

The view that language, along with other social practices, is used to constitute identities, rather than being a reflection of social identities, moves attention away from the study of a single linguistic feature to someone's language use in combination with other social practices. We can only understand what a single variable feature means by investigating how it is used in identity construction. This also means that a linguistic variable need not always have the same meaning and, equally, that a change in someone's identity may result in a change in someone's (linguistic) practice. These assumptions necessitate an important attention shift in TWVS: in order to study and understand identity, we cannot focus solely on one particular linguistic feature. We have to focus on something larger and, for many variationists, this means examining style (Eckert 2000; Moore 2011). For others, the focus is on stance (Ochs 1992; Rauniomaa 2003; Kiesling 2009); that is, 'evaluative, affective and epistemic orientations in discourse' (Bucholtz and Hall 2010: 22). Scholars who favour stance focus on conversational acts and how their display of evaluation, affect and epistemic orientation constitute resources in identity construction, while those who prefer to work with the concept of style *tend to* investigate phonological, grammatical and lexical features below the discourse level (Bucholtz and Hall 2010: 22). Certainly, both traditions are cross-fertilising. In the following, we will focus on style.

In TWVS, styles are often viewed as 'a socially meaningful clustering of features within and across linguistic levels and modalities' (Campbell-Kibler *et al.* 2006). This is important because a clustering of features may be associated with identities – in a broad sense of the word (more on this below). Third-wave research starts frequently with an investigation of styles, rather than individual features. As a result of the association of social meaning with a style, third-wave variationists have extended significantly the scope of investigation to include any kind of linguistic material that helps in the construction of styles, rather than focusing only on changing or stable variable features. An example is Podesva's (2007) research on white, middle-class gay men, which investigated not only variation in segmental phonology, but also voice and vowel quality, intonation and discourse context. Ethnographic methods and the social-organisational structure of the community of practice continue to represent crucial elements of the study of variation, as does the use of quantitative methods. Yet TWVS has also made increased use of experimental perception methods. Not only does experimental work document the potential social meanings of a particular linguistic feature, it has also demonstrated how social meaning may depend on our perceptions of speakers, listener background and listener language use, context and topic (see e.g. Johnstone and Kiesling 2008; Campbell-Kibler 2009).

Levels of identity and indexicality

Identity in TWVS is a relatively broad concept that can be seen to relate to a variety of different levels. This is a useful view to highlight as it allows us to create a link between the three variationist waves, the first two of which show a tendency to focus on one specific identity level. Coupland (2007: 27) argues for macro-, meso- and micro-identity frames, very much in line with Bucholtz and Hall (2005: 592; 2010: 21), whose concept of identity includes '(a) macro-level demographic categories; (b) local ethnographically specific cultural positions; and (c) temporary and interactionally-specific stances and participant roles'. Similarly Kiesling (2013: 452) views this particular issue as one of scale: 'as the scale changes from that of a conversation to an entire nation, so do the relevant identities'. He offers a similar division into (a) large 'census' groups; (b) institutional roles; and (c) stances or positions in interaction. The latter may include stances such as being knowledgeable, nice and confrontational – notions that, due to their temporary nature, are not usually regarded as identities.

Yet, what this broad conception of identity does not make immediately clear is how (different levels of) identity and variable features are linked. This is where the notion of indexicality comes in. Indexicality is a mechanism by which semiotic links are created between linguistic forms and social meanings (Ochs 1992; Silverstein 1985), such that *–ing* can express intelligence and articulateness whereas *–in* expresses casualness. Indexicalities of variants are vague, complex and contestable. Once a variable has acquired social meanings, speakers can use associations of these social meanings to create new ones. For example, if a speaker is perceived as casual, she may also be assumed to be laidback, as the two are ideologically related. However, linguistic and non-linguistic practices can only create a link for both speaker and hearer if they share a belief system and recognise its relevance to a particular interaction.

To understand indexicality, we must explore how social meanings come to be associated with particular linguistic forms, and how indexicality may constitute identities (on a more permanent basis). This occurs through a variety of different processes (see Bucholtz and Hall's indexicality principle), some of which are discussed below. Of course, it is possible to express identity overtly, simply by referring to an identity category and saying 'I am English' or 'Dropping your aitches is sooo working class'. Moreover, identities can be referred to indirectly, for example through implicature and presupposition. The sentence 'You know, she wears a track suit and she's all like 'urricanes 'ardly ever 'appen' may be considered a statement about the speaker's own social class and that of the person to whom they are referring, which is indicated through stereotypical clothing and h-dropping, a widespread non-standard feature in England associated with working-class speakers, and a phrase of Eliza Doolittle's from *My Fair Lady*. However, much more is happening in this sentence: (1) the speaker adopts a certain stance and assumes that the person to whom they are referring also adopts a particular stance on an habitual basis, and (2) the speaker links certain linguistic and other practices to specific personae and groups. These are two indexical processes, which we will examine more closely below.

When identity is expressed indirectly, indexicality plays a crucial role in how this is done. Research that focuses on stance has shed much light on the emergence of indexical links. Many of the indexical distinctions we make today are based on the work by Silverstein (1985, 2003) and Ochs (1992). A very important distinction is that made between direct and indirect indexicality. Ochs (1992) argued that direct indexical links are those between language and stances, social acts and activities. For example, we may use certain language and practice (e.g. by saying *could* and *please* and by smiling: 'Could I have a small latte, please?') and by doing so create and express a particular affective stance, in a specific context. If this stance is ideologically extended to an identity category, for example women, an indirect indexicality has emerged. This does not have to happen, but it can if it is repeated often enough. If individuals within a particular social group repeatedly take a particular stance in particular interactions and contexts, a link may appear between this stance and the social group, and stances may grow into more enduring identity structures – a process also known as stance accretion (DuBois 2002; Rauniomaa 2003).

Kiesling (2009) argues that the process of repeatedly taking the same stance is how styles emerge at individual, local- or macro-group levels. Other researchers use different terminology to refer to similar processes. For example, Johnstone (2010) makes use of Agha's (2005) notion of enregisterment to explain how permanent links emerge between linguistic form and social identity. Johnstone (2010: 34) argued that Agha's concept of a register is similar to what Eckert calls style, with some finer differences: 'a register may be associated with a situation or a set of social relations rather than or in addition to being associated with a social identity like "jock" or "burnout"'. A form is considered enregistered once it has become part of a register, which emerges only once particular indexicalities are seen to be associated with each other. Thus, a form is considered enregistered when it is associated with a particular style, which in turn is associated with a particular identity. Such an identity can then be used for further indexical work.

Similar insights have been made in VS work conducted by Eckert and associates using the concept of style as a repertoire of linguistic forms with specific social meanings. Here, the focus is on a set of linguistic forms becoming associated with specific personae, groups, social characteristics, etc. For example, a particular population may stand out (in a particular context) and one or more linguistic or non-linguistic features of that population may grab people's attention. Once such a link between feature and population is created, the feature can index the population on its own, without the linguistic context. It can then be used to position the population ideologically in a variety of ways; for example, by invoking the attributes or stereotypes of this population or by associating or disassociating oneself with/from the population, similar to the h-dropping example above. Repeating these 'indexical acts' (Eckert 2012: 94) results in conventionalisation of the index; that is, the link between linguistic forms and social meaning. These may be personal characteristics, personae or social types that constitute an identity.

The type of indexical complexity described in the last few paragraphs leads Eckert (2012: 94) to argue that indexical order progresses in multiple directions, rather than in a linear fashion. Meanings comprise what Eckert (2008) refers to as an indexical field: 'a constellation of ideologically linked meanings, any region of which can be invoked in context' (Eckert 2012: 94). Thus, social context always interacts with indexicalities and helps create them: who is uttering what, where, when and to whom influences the particular indexicalities that emerge. The concept of the indexical field is useful because it highlights how speakers and hearers make use of multifaceted social meanings in interaction. The different levels of indexicality are related ideologically, and meanings often involve various levels simultaneously. Variables can index what Kiesling (2013) calls ideological bundles, involving not only macrosociological categories, such as 'man', but also practices and stances, roles and attitudes associated with masculinity in a particular culture. Separating these different meanings does not make much sense, and the indexical field makes this point very well.

Figures 3.1 and 3.2 present examples of such indexical fields for two variants of (t). These fields, which could just as well have been merged into one for the variable (t), indicate many potential social meanings of intervocalic [t] and t-glottalling in Greater Manchester, England. The results are based on data obtained from a perception survey, in which participants heard audio stimuli that were manipulated by cross-splicing to differ only in the occurrence of [t] and [ʔ]. Respondents were then asked to rate stimuli on a series of scales. The fields show the multiplicity of potential meanings of the variable, ranging from social characteristics to social groups. These social meanings may ultimately be exploited by speakers to constitute a variety of different identities, as the variable is used in context-specific styles where meanings are specified and identities are co-constructed.

In the following section, we will explore how the three waves of VS have influenced areas relevant to applied linguistics, and demonstrate that a significant amount of research is situated in the first and second-wave tradition. Occasionally, third-wave concerns are echoed in applied linguistics in that identity may be viewed as dynamic and constructed; however, the complexities of the social meanings of linguistic features, styles or stances are rarely explored in much detail.

more hard-working   more intelligent   more snob-like

more reliable   more correct   more educated   more articulate

more teacher-like   less common

less student-like   less blunt   less sincere

older   [t]   less casual

richer   less down to earth

less urban   less Northern   less laidback

more Chorlton   less outgoing   less confident

less working class   less Moss Side

less Salford   less Manchester

Figure 3.1 Possible indexical field for intervocalic [t]

less hard-working   less intelligent   less snob-like

less reliable   less correct   less educated   less articulate

less teacher-like   more common

more student-like   more blunt   more sincere

younger   [ʔ]   more casual

less rich   more down to earth

more urban   more Northern   more laidback

less Chorlton   more outgoing   more confident

more working class   more Moss Side

more Salford   more Manchester

Figure 3.2 Possible indexical field for intervocalic t-glottalling

Issues and ongoing debates

This section explores the various ways in which research methods and findings from variationist work on identity can inform areas of applied linguistics that do not take language variation and change itself as their primary focus. It will begin by looking at issues of dialect prejudice before moving on to explore second language acquisition (SLA) and language teaching.

Accent and dialect discrimination

An important area of applied linguistics with regard to variationist approaches to identity is that of linguistic prejudice, and accent and dialect discrimination. First and second-wave research in this area has contributed substantially to discredit deficit models of language; specifically, regarding the status of African-American English (Morgan 1994; Rickford 1997), bilingual speech (García 1984; Zentella 1997) and working-class speech (Trudgill 1975). Very positive results have been achieved with programmes that develop language awareness materials for non-linguists in various locations (e.g. Reaser and Adger 2007). However, the two studies to be reviewed here can be regarded as adopting a third-wave variationist approach to identity in the way that identities are seen as being enacted and performed moment by moment, and data are gathered through ethnographic techniques.

Interested in challenging prevailing views of working-class children's non-standard language, Snell (2013) describes an ethnographic research project carried out in two primary schools in Teesside, north-east England. She questions both the deficit approach (that non-standard dialects are inferior to standard English) and the difference approach (that while non-standard dialects are different from standard English, they are just as systematic and logical as standardised varieties) by arguing that trying to delineate boundaries of dialects to enable these descriptions is not an accurate reflection of how language is used in context. Instead, she makes the case for a repertoire approach to the variation at work, examining the use of non-standard first-person objective singular *us* ('give us me shoe back'). She illustrates how the use of the variant can be interpreted not simply as a straightforward alternative to standard *me*; rather, it has indexical meanings related to solidarity, alignment and group identity.

The manner in which Snell is able to make this argument relies largely on the methodology she employs. The use of interactional data, rather than overreliance on abstracted decontextualised linguistic variables, enables her to illustrate the complex mixing of language features in the speakers' repertoire. In doing so, she is able to make a compelling case for viewing the working-class children that she describes as multi-skilled language users. She ends by highlighting the need for further research into issues of linguistic insecurity and identity conflict within education.

The UrBEn-ID project (Drummond and Dray) addresses these issues in an ongoing study into the ways in which identities are performed and negotiated in the speech and social practices of 14 to 16-year-olds in inner-city Manchester, England. In addition to describing the language of a section of twenty-first century urban youth, its aim is to challenge the narratives in British politics and mainstream media, which so often stigmatise some young people as uneducated or unemployable because of the way they speak. At the same time, it allows us to explore with young people the role that language plays in the ways in which they are perceived. Adolescence is a crucial time in the construction of identity, and the project is able to track this process through ethnographic observation, interactional discourse analysis and sociophonetic analysis of the speech of young people, many of whom have been excluded from mainstream school, as they negotiate their way through their educational environment.

At the time of writing this chapter, the project is in its early stages, yet certain aspects of language practice are already becoming apparent. For example, echoing Snell's (2013) argument, it is neither possible nor desirable to identify the linguistic practices of these young people as constituting one or other variety, as the linguistic features are used in ways that simply do not match the patterns expected by those outside these young people's immediate social groups. Most conspicuously, assumed constraints of ethnicity are being challenged by the young people, both in terms of the use and the understanding of what are often thought to be ethnically salient variants. In turn, this challenges widely held views on issues of identity, especially with regard to the notion of authenticity or who 'can' say what.

These two studies (Snell 2013) and the UrBEn-ID project serve as examples of several others that could be mentioned here (see e.g. Rampton 2006; Preece 2010).

Acquisition of variation

Variationist research within second language acquisition (SLA) is usually regarded as addressing two different types of variation: the first looks at linguistic competence, or the acquisition and use of 'correct' L2 variants versus 'incorrect' L1-influenced variants; while the second explores sociolinguistic competence, or the acquisition of native-speaker patterns of variability. Linguistic competence has been referred to as 'the vertical continuum' (e.g. Adamson and Regan 1991) or 'type 1 variation' (Mougeon *et al.* 2004), and sociolinguistic competence as 'the horizontal continuum' or 'type 2 variation'. Whilst the two types are distinct in some respects, it should be borne in mind that the differences are not quite so clear-cut, as the two types of competence are often intertwined. This becomes especially clear when we consider that sociolinguistic competence is simply not possible without some degree of linguistic competence. Here, the focus is very much on research into type 2 variation, as this is where issues of identity are most likely to emerge. In fact, as Figure 3.3 illustrates, the precise focus for this section is on the small overlapping space of SLA research, variationist research and identity research.

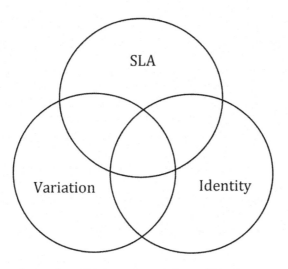

Figure 3.3 Intersections of research on SLA, language variation and identity

As it happens, this overlapping space is somewhat smaller than one might anticipate, given the otherwise social focus of type 2 variation research. Moreover, much of it represents quite a traditional view of identity, which is far more in accordance with first and second-wave variationist work. The focus is on individual linguistic features being seen as representing a particular demographic category, with little attention paid to the possible interaction of other aspects of linguistic or non-linguistic practice in constructing identity. But often these observations can be seen as providing a crucial link to current discussions of identity, by beginning to highlight the agentive nature of the language/identity relationship.

Attitudes towards the locale and the local variety or alignment with the host culture have been identified as important factors that influence the acquisition of variation (Sharma 2005; Drummond 2012; Schleef forthcoming). For example, Sharma (2005) demonstrated that the use of phonological variables among speakers of Indian heritage in the United States did not correlate with proficiency, but rather with their degree of alignment with American culture. We have found similar examples of an attitude–identity connection, which hints at an agentive aspect, in our own studies. For example, Drummond's (2012) study of Polish migrants in Manchester, England, found that those speakers who were planning on returning to Poland were less likely to use the most L2/local-influenced variant [ɪn] than those intent on staying in the UK (when compared with all possible (ing) variants), and more likely to use the most L1-influenced variant [ɪŋk] (when compared with the other non-standard yet local variant [ɪŋg]). Drummond argues that the [ɪŋk] variant could be seen as indexing a degree of allegiance or connection with the L1 culture, albeit in a limited way. The lack of any ethnographic observation and the reliance on traditional sociolinguistic methods meant that further interpretation was impossible, but undoubtedly it is an interesting area for further exploration. Moreover, Schleef (forthcoming) examines the use of a particular variant in the possible performance of identity, by focusing on t-glottalling in the speech of migrant teenagers in London. He finds that, at around the same time (approximately two years), native constraint hierarchies for t-glottalling are acquired by migrants; (t) also begins to become available to be used as a stylistic resource in combination with other features. It is through this stylistic practice that Schleef is able to identify the performance of distinct identities.

Further exploration is required in L2 variation studies on identity. In their recent chapter on 'Sociolinguistics and second language acquisition', Howard et al. (2012: 354) identify one area of interest for future research as being the degree to which acquired gendered variants reflect a 'specific and conscious attempt to "do" gender in the L2, by expressing and creating a sense of gendered identity', thereby suggesting this has not been addressed sufficiently to date. Indeed, increased focus on this agentive aspect of SLA would demonstrate a highly significant step closer to more recent work in (L1) variation and identity. In fact, despite the rather traditional research described by Howard et al., this step has already been taken by some researchers interested in L2 variation and identity, some of which dates back to the early 2000s. This work stems from the understanding that it is simply not the case that SLA is a straightforward process of acquiring 'target language x': how can it be, when, like any language, target language x is inherently variable? Hansen Edwards (2008: 251) emphasises this point, highlighting the fact that L2 learners are socially motivated active agents in their language use, choices and targets for acquisition. Similarly, Ehrlich (1997: 440) accentuates the importance of viewing language learners not as 'idealised, abstract learners', but as individuals responsible for their own social positioning in the target culture.

Both viewpoints resonate strongly with third-wave variationist ideas, where identity is seen as something that can be performed and negotiated in all its fluidity and multiplicity, moment by moment. A further example can be found in the work conducted by Ohara (2001) into the performance of L2 gendered speech by American English speakers learning Japanese. What makes this especially interesting is the fact that the study looked at pitch (a high-pitched voice is a central feature of femininity in Japanese), a linguistic feature that has often been ignored in VS (but see Podesva 2007). Ohara's study is fascinating in that it explores what happens when an aspect of L2 identity that is expected (in the sense of effective sociolinguistic acquisition) to be acquired is resisted on the basis that it represents an undesirable aspect of L1 identity for the individuals in question. In this instance, two English/Japanese bilinguals consciously avoided the use of feminine pitch variation, despite their awareness of its role.

This conscious avoidance of acquisition or use of particular features leads us neatly into questions of the desirability of native-like performance in a second language. Often an assumed goal in language teaching, this degree of proficiency is, in reality, far from straightforward from a social perspective, with issues of identity playing a central role. It is an issue for both variationist and non-variationist L2 research, as achieving native-like competence in a language involves travelling the full extent of both the linguistic and the sociolinguistic competence continuums mentioned above. Here, the focus will be on particular pieces of research that have demonstrated how a variationist-influenced (or variationist-applicable) understanding of L2 proficiency has dealt with issues of identity.

Acquisition of native-like performance

Piller (2002) describes the experiences of expert L2 users (German-English bilingual couples) in relation to the concept of 'passing'; in this context, this refers to the experience of passing as (being believed to be) a native speaker. In doing so, she echoes third-wave variationist interpretations of identity and agency by reporting her participants' views that 'passing is an act, something they do, a performance that may be put on or sustained for a limited period only' (Piller 2002: 191). Indeed, there is such a degree of awareness of passing that several participants report taking pride in the length of time they can sustain the performance. Sociolinguistic competence is key to this practice, with Piller noting the strategic use of stereotypical variants in constructing identities. In some ways, the (over)use of particular variants could be seen as hypercorrection; however, Piller argues that it is precisely these stereotypical markers that help create the insider status. This relates back to the point made earlier about not assuming L2 learners to be passive recipients of the target language/variety. As Piller makes clear in her criticism of previous research into passing, which so often focuses only on L2 users of a standard variety, the reality is that the actual speakers are likely to choose non-standard varieties on which to model their speech; moreover, it is this much more realistic form of passing that 'entails both pronunciation skills and sociolinguistic knowledge' (Piller 2002: 200).

In direct contrast to the practice of passing, another area of variationist-related work into L2 identity is that of individuals who consciously avoid acquiring and/or performing native-like proficiency so as to reinforce and maintain their L1 identities. Gatbonton *et al.* (2005: 492) examined the tension that exists when an individual in an L2 context faces social forces of inclusion and exclusion from both L1 and L2 groups, resulting in the pressure to 'enhance or suppress one of their two identities by manipulating their language'. They reported on two studies: one exploring Francophone learners of English in 1970s Quebec, and the other looking at Chinese learners of English in Montreal in the 2000s. Both studies revealed a relationship between the speakers' accents and their affiliation to their home ethnic group; namely, 'the more learners sound like the speakers of their target language, the less they are perceived by their peers to be loyal to their own group' (ibid.: 504). Gatbonton *et al.* identify three possibilities as speakers balance the 'costs and rewards' of allying with one or other group. Option one is to attempt to achieve as high L2 proficiency as possible, thus gaining access to resources controlled by the target group; option two is the opposite – to aim low in order to maintain and strengthen loyalty to the home group, resulting in a lack of incentive to improve the L2 any further; and option three is somewhere in between, where learners strive for high attainment but 'retain ways of manipulating their pronunciation to clearly signal where their loyalties lie' (p. 506). It is this third option that resonates most strongly with issues of language variation in terms of speakers targeting individual linguistic features, in order to align themselves with one or either social group.

Summary

VS has come a long way since its inception in the 1960s. The field continues to maintain a strong focus on how variation is constrained linguistically and socially, as well as how changes progress in time and space. However, the roles of social meaning and identity have changed dramatically over the decades. Variation is not simply the consequence of a speaker's membership of a social group. Speakers actively create linguistic styles as they construct and reconstruct their identities. There is a general consensus that simple social categories and quantitative work can only tell us so much. Uncovering the social meanings of variable features and styles, in addition to how these are related ideologically, is regarded as an important step in the investigation of language variation and change. This new focus in TWVS is in parallel with an extension of the methods used. Combinations of qualitative and quantitative work, very much in line with the different levels of identity outlined above, is increasingly becoming best practice in sociolinguistic research. With regard to language and identity, the next step in applied sociolinguistics is to find ways to implement these concerns more broadly and harmonise research frameworks with applied linguistics. This will necessarily entail a stronger focus on social meaning. There are ample opportunities for very useful research – in particular, in the area of acquisition of variation. How is social meaning acquired? How does this acquisition progress, and what repercussions do answers to these questions have for theories of language change and language learning? These questions may necessitate quantitative research; but more importantly, they require the detailed exploration of the social meaning of variation in the moment-to-moment development of practices and interaction.

Related topics

Historical perspectives on language and identity; Positioning language and identity: poststructuralist perspectives; Language and identity in linguistic ethnography; Language and gender identities; Class in language and identity research; An identity transformation? Social class, language prejudice and the erasure of multilingual capital in higher education; Styling and identity in a second language; Identity in language learning and teaching: research agendas for the future.

Further reading

Eckert, P. (2012). 'Three waves of variation study: the emergence of meaning in the study of sociolinguistic variation', *Annual Review of Anthropology*, 41: 87–100. (This is an overview of the three waves of VS with a focus on style.)

Kiesling, S.F. (2013). Constructing identity, in J.K. Chambers and N. Schilling (eds) *The handbook of language variation and change*. 2nd edn. Malden, MA: John Wiley and Sons, pp. 448–467. (This is a recent discussion of identity in VS theorising stance.)

Llamas, C. and Watt, D. (eds) (2010). *Language and identities*. Edinburgh: Edinburgh University Press. (This edited collection gives a good overview of identity in sociolinguistics. It includes some new work as well as some foundational texts.)

References

Adamson, H.D. and Regan, V. (1991). 'The acquisition of community speech norms by Asian immigrants learning English as a second language', *Studies in Second Language Acquisition*, 13: 1–22.

Agha, A. (2005). 'Voice, footing, enregisterment', *Journal of Linguistic Anthropology*, 15: 38–59.

Benor, S. (2001). Sounding learned: the gendered use of /t/ in Orthodox Jewish English, in D.E. Johnson and T. Sanchez (eds) *Penn working papers in linguistics: selected papers from NWAV 29*. Philadelphia: University of Pennsylvania, pp. 1–16.

Block, D. (this volume). Class in language and identity research, in S. Preece (ed.) *The Routledge handbook of language and identity*. Abingdon: Routledge, pp. 241–254.

Bucholtz, M. (1996). Geek the girl: language, femininity and female nerds, in N. Warner, J. Ahlers, L. Bilmes, M. Oliver, S. Wertheim and M. Chen (eds) *Gender and belief systems*. Berkeley: Berkeley Women and Language Group, pp. 119–131.

Bucholtz, M. and Hall, K. (2005). 'Identity and interaction: a socio-cultural linguistic approach', *Discourse Studies*, 7: 585–614.

Bucholtz, M. and Hall, K. (2010). Locating identity in language, in C. Llamas and D. Watt (eds) *Language and identities*. Edinburgh: Edinburgh University Press, pp. 18–28.

Campbell-Kibler, K. (2009). 'The nature of sociolinguistic perception', *Language Variation and Change*, 21: 135–156.

Campbell-Kibler, K., Eckert, P., Mendoza-Denton, N. and Moore, E. (2006). *The elements of style*. Poster presented at New Ways of Analyzing Variation 35, The Ohio State University, Columbus, November 2006.

Cheshire, J. (1982). *Variation in an English dialect*. Cambridge: Cambridge University Press.

Coupland, N. (2007). *Style, variation and identity*. Cambridge: Cambridge University Press.

Drummond, R. (2012). 'Aspects of identity in a second language: ING variation in the speech of Polish migrants living in Manchester, UK', *Language Variation and Change*, 24: 107–133.

Drummond, R. and Dray, S. *The UrBEn-ID Project – 'Expressing inner-city youth identity through multicultural urban British English'*. Project funded by The Leverhulme Trust 2014–2016. Project Number: RPG-2014-059.

DuBois, J. (2002). *Stance and consequence*. Paper presented at the Annual Meeting of the American Anthropological Association, New Orleans, November 2002.

Eckert, P. (1989). *Jocks and burnouts: social categories and identity in the High School*. New York: Teachers' College Press.

Eckert, P. (2000). *Linguistic variation as social practice*. Malden and Oxford: Blackwell.

Eckert, P. (2008). 'Variation and the indexical field', *Journal of Sociolinguistics*, 12: 453–476.

Eckert, P. (2012). 'Three waves of variation study: the emergence of meaning in the study of sociolinguistic variation', *Annual Review of Anthropology*, 41: 87–100.

Eckert, P. and McConnell-Ginet, S. (1992). 'Think practically and look locally: language and gender as community-based practice', *Annual Review of Anthropology*, 21: 461–490.

Ehrlich, S. (1997). 'Gender as social practice: implications for second language acquisition', *Studies in Second Language Acquisition*, 19: 421–446.

Gal, S. (1979). *Language shift: social determinants of linguistic change in bilingual Austria*. New York: Academic Press.

García, M. (1984). Parameters of the East Los Angeles speech community, in J. Ornstein-Galicia (ed.) *Form and function in Chicano English.* Rowley: Newbury House, pp. 85–98.

Gatbonton, E., Trofimovich, P. and Magid, M. (2005). 'Learners' ethnic group affiliation and L2 pronunciation accuracy: a sociolinguistic investigation', *TESOL Quarterly*, 39: 421–446.

Hansen Edwards, J.G. (2008). Social factors and variation in production in L2 phonology, in J.G. Hansen Edwards and M.L. Zampini (eds) *Phonology and second language acquisition.* Amsterdam: John Benjamins, pp. 251–282.

Horvath, B. (1985). *Variation in Australian English: the sociolects of Sydney.* Cambridge: Cambridge University Press.

Howard, M., Mougeon, R. and Dewaele, J.M. (2012). Sociolinguistics and second language acquisition, in R. Bayley, R. Cameron and C. Lucas (eds) *The Oxford handbook of sociolinguistics.* Oxford and New York: Oxford University Press, pp. 340–359.

Johnstone, B. (2010). Locating language in identity, in C. Llamas and D. Watt (eds) *Language and identities.* Edinburgh: Edinburgh University Press, pp. 29–36.

Johnstone, B. and Kiesling, S. (2008). 'Indexicality and experience: exploring the meanings of /aw/-monophthongization in Pittsburgh', *Journal of Sociolinguistics*, 12: 5–33.

Joseph, J.E. (this volume). Historical perspectives on language and identity, in S. Preece (ed.) *The Routledge handbook of language and identity.* Abingdon: Routledge, pp. 19–33.

Kiesling, S.F. (2009). Style as stance: stance as the explanation for patterns of sociolinguistic variation, in A. Jaffe (ed.) *Stance: sociolinguistic perspectives.* Oxford: Oxford University Press, pp. 171–194.

Kiesling, S.F. (2013). Constructing identity, in J.K. Chambers and N. Schilling (eds) *The handbook of language variation and change.* 2nd edn. Malden, MA: John Wiley and Sons, pp. 448–467.

Labov, W. (1963). 'The social motivation of a sound change', *Word*, 18: 1–42.

Labov, W. (1966). *The social stratification of English in New York City.* Washington, DC: Cent. Appl. Ling.

Labov, W. (1972). *Sociolinguistic patterns.* Philadelphia: University of Pennsylvania Press.

Lave, J. and Wenger, E. (1991). *Situated learning: legitimate peripheral participation.* Cambridge: Cambridge University Press.

Macaulay, R.K.S. (1977). *Language, social class and education: a Glasgow study.* Edinburgh: Edinburgh University Press.

Milroy, L. (1980). *Language and social network.* Oxford: Blackwell.

Moore, E. (2011). Variation and identity, in W. Maguire and A. McMahon (eds) *Analysing variation in English.* Cambridge: Cambridge University Press, pp. 219–236.

Moore, E. and Podesva, R. (2009). 'Style, indexicality, and the social meaning of tag questions', *Language in Society*, 38: 447–485.

Morgan, M. (1994). 'Theories and politics in African American English', *Annual Review of Anthropology*, 23: 325–345.

Mougeon, R., Rehner, K. and Nadasdi, T. (2004). 'The learning of spoken French variation by immersion students from Toronto, Canada', *Journal of Sociolinguistics*, 8: 408–432.

Ochs, E. (1992) Indexing gender, in A. Duranti and C. Goodwin (eds) *Rethinking context: language as an interactive phenomenon.* Cambridge: Cambridge University Press, pp. 335–358.

Ohara, Y. (2001). Finding one's voice in Japanese: a study of pitch levels of L2 users, in A. Pavlenko, A. Blackledge, I. Piller and M. Teutsch-Dwyer (eds) *Multilingualism, second language learning, and gender.* Berlin: Mouton de Gruyter, pp. 231–254.

Piller, I. (2002). 'Passing for a native speaker: identity and success in second language learning', *Journal of Sociolinguistics*, 6: 179–208.

Podesva, R. (2007). 'Phonation type as a stylistic variable: the use of falsetto in constructing a persona', *Journal of Sociolinguistics*, 11: 478–504.

Preece, S. (2010). 'Multilingual identities in higher education: negotiating the "mother tongue", "posh" and "slang"', *Language and Education*, 24: 21–39.

Rampton, B. (2006). *Language in late modernity: interaction in an urban school.* Cambridge: Cambridge University Press.

Rauniomaa, M. (2003). *Stance accretion*. Paper presented at the Language, Interaction, and Social Organization Research Focus Group, University of California, Santa Barbara, February 2003.

Reaser, J. and Adger, C. (2007). 'Developing language awareness materials for nonlinguists: lessons learned from the do you speak American curriculum development project', *Language and Linguistics Compass*, 3: 155–167.

Rickford, J.R. (1997). 'Unequal partnership: sociolinguistics and the African American speech community', *Language in Society*, 26: 161–197.

Schleef, E. (forthcoming). Developmental sociolinguistics and the acquisition of T-glottalling by immigrant teenagers in London, in G. de Vogelaer and M. Katerbow (eds) *Variation in language acquisition*. Amsterdam: John Benjamins.

Sharma, D. (2005). 'Dialect stabilization and speaker awareness in non-native varieties of English', *Journal of Sociolinguistics*, 9: 194–224.

Silverstein, M. (1985). Language and the culture of gender: at the intersection of structure, usage, and ideology, in E. Mertz and R. Parmentier (eds) *Semiotic mediation: socio-cultural and psychological perspectives*. Orlando, FL: Academic Press, pp. 219–259.

Silverstein, M. (2003). 'Indexical order and the dialectics of sociolinguistic life', *Language and Communication*, 23: 193–229.

Snell, J. (2013). 'Dialect, interaction and class positioning at school: from deficit to different to repertoire', *Language and Education*, 27: 110–128.

Tagliamonte, S. (1999). 'Was–were variation across the generations: view from the city of York', *Language Variation and Change*, 10: 153–191.

Tajfel, H. (1978). Social categorization, social identity and social comparison, in H. Tajfel (ed.) *Differentiation between social groups: studies in the social psychology of intergroup relations*. London: Academic Press, pp. 61–76.

Thibault, P. and Sankoff, G. (1993). 'Diverses facettes de l'insecurité linguistique: vers une analyse comparative des attitudes et du français parlé par des Franco- et des Anglo-Montréalais' [Varying facets of linguistic insecurity: toward a comparative analysis of attitudes and the French spoken by Franco- and Anglo-Montrealers], *Cahiers de l'institut de linguistique de Louvain*, 19: 209–218.

Trudgill, P. (1972). 'Sex, covert prestige and linguistic change in the urban British English of Norwich', *Language in Society*, 1: 179–195.

Trudgill, P. (1974). *The social differentiation of English in Norwich*. Cambridge: Cambridge University Press.

Trudgill, P. (1975). *Accent, dialect and the school*. London: Edward Arnold.

Wolfram, W. (1969). *A sociolinguistic description of Detroit Negro speech*. Washington, DC: Cent. Appl. Ling.

Zentella, A.C. (1997). *Growing up bilingual: Puerto Rican children in New York*. Oxford: Blackwell.

4

Ethnomethodological and conversation analytic approaches to identity

Bethan Benwell and Elizabeth Stokoe

Introduction

This chapter presents an approach to identity grounded in ethnomethodology (EM) and conversation analysis (CA). In contrast to approaches that start with a heavily theorised concept of identity, or with a predetermined set of identity categories, our chapter describes how people themselves, in everyday social life, orient to and describe, classify or assess each other as particular kinds of people, as members (or not) of identity-relevant categories. A key point is that ethnomethodologists and conversation analysts rarely start out with identity as an analytic concept for exploration. Rather, their focus is on the organisation of social life in and through talk and social interaction, in which matters of who we are to one another are members' concerns. While EM and CA are often regarded as 'atheoretical', they simply propose an alternative theory, of social life as grounded in interaction and of language as constitutive of that social life.

We will start by describing EM and CA and the implications of these approaches for understanding identity. We will then explore two interactional sites as a means of illustrating how identities get worked up sequentially and made relevant by conversational participants. The first data set comprises telephone calls made by potential customers to a double-glazing company and focuses particularly on the normative assumptions about relationships and marital status encoded in the sales representative's use of, and negotiation around, categories and titles. The second data set involves telephone calls made to and from an NHS complaints line by or on behalf of patients. What is noteworthy about these calls is the way that a 'legitimate complaining' identity is worked up by the caller (and to an extent collaboratively with the operator) through the use of particular categories and expectable attributes, in ways that seem designed to dispel a lack of entitlement to complain. Such observations also illuminate the meanings of cultural categories and activities and the kinds of obligations, rights and responsibilities that are revealed to be understood by participants in the exchange. We argue that this kind of empirical analysis provides a robust identification of patterns in the way identity matters are made relevant to institutional interaction.

CA has been increasingly deployed for research in applied linguistics (see Kaspar and Wagner 2014) and been used to ground observations of routine, 'good' and 'bad' practice and interactional 'trouble' in professional and institutional settings. More precisely, and as we will demonstrate in the closing section, CA can be used to inform communication training with the practitioners in institutions that comprise the settings under study. We conclude that EM and CA have much to contribute to the 'real world' impact of academic work.

Overview

EM is a discipline that was developed by the sociologist Garfinkel (1967), who was influenced by the phenomenological philosophy of Schütz (e.g. 1962) and Goffman's (e.g. 1959) work on the interaction order. Garfinkel's idea was that the members of a society continuously engage in making sense of the world and, in so doing, methodically display their understandings of it: making their activities 'visibly-rational-and-reportable-for-all-practical-purposes' (1967: vii). Social interaction became central to ethnomethodology's project of explicating members' methods for producing orderly and accountable social activities via CA, which has since developed into an empirical science for understanding everyday life.

CA originates in the work of the American sociologist Sacks and his colleagues Schegloff and Jefferson. Sacks's aim was to develop an alternative to mainstream sociology: an observational science of society and social action that could be grounded in the 'details of actual events' (Sacks 1984a: 26). CA involves the study of transcripts of recorded everyday and institutional talk, focusing on the turn-by-turn organisation of interaction. The aim of CA is, in Sacks's (1984b: 413) words,

> to see how finely the details of actual, naturally occurring conversation can be subjected to analysis that will yield the technology of conversation. The idea is to take singular sequences of conversation and tear them apart in such a way as to find rules, techniques, procedures, methods, maxims ... that can be used to generate the orderly features we find in the conversations we examine. The point is, then, to come back to the singular things we observe in a singular sequence, with some rules that handle those singular features, and also, necessarily, handle lots of other events.

For Schegloff (1996), a key figure in the subsequent development of CA, talk-in-interaction is 'the primordial scene of social life ... through which the work of the constitutive institutions of societies gets done. It is through talking that we live our lives, build and maintain relationships, and establish *who we are to one another*' (Drew 2005: 74, emphasis added).

Related to EM and CA is another approach rooted in Sacks's (1992) lectures on conversation: membership categorisation analysis (MCA). In addition to the CA focus on the sequencing and organisation of talk, MCA also pays attention to the situated and reflexive use of categories in everyday and institutional interaction, as well as in interview, media and other textual data. Sacks focused on the local management of speakers' categorisations of themselves and others, treating talk as 'culture-in-action' (Hester and Eglin 1997). His ideas were based around the membership categorisation device (MCD), which explains how categories may be hearably linked by members of a culture. He provides a now-classic example from a children's story: 'The baby cried. The mommy picked it up' (Sacks 1972). Sacks claimed that we hear links between 'mommy' and 'baby', specifically that the mommy is the mommy of the baby. He provided an explanatory apparatus that allows this 'fact' to occur: the MCD. In this case, the MCD of 'family' allows the categories 'mommy' and 'baby' to be collected together. Categories (including 'members') are therefore linked to particular actions ('category-bound activities') or characteristics ('natural predicates') such that there are conventional expectations about what constitutes a 'mommy's' or 'baby's' normative behaviour, such that absences are accountable. For example, if a mother fails to look after her children, then such things may become the basis of a complaint.

One way in which the categorisation process occurs is via the rich inferential resources carried in categories available to members of a culture. For example, a woman may be categorised as a mother, wife or daughter. Each of these categories carries with it a set of category-bound activities, predicates or 'rights and obligations' that are expectable for a category incumbent to perform or possess (Watson and Weinberg 1982). As Widdicombe (1998: 53) writes:

> the fact that categories are conventionally associated with activities, attributes, motives and so on makes them a powerful cultural resource in warranting, explaining and justifying behaviour. That is, whatever is known about the category can be invoked as being relevant to the person to whom the label is applied and provides a set of inferential resources by which to interpret and account for past or present conduct, or to inform predictions about likely future behaviour.

The analytic interest focuses on the multitude of potential identity ascriptions available to members of a culture and:

> which of those identifications folk actually use, what features those identifications seem to carry, and to what end they are put ... Membership of a category is ascribed (and rejected), avowed (and disavowed), displayed (and ignored) in local places and at certain times, and it does these things as part of the interactional work that constitutes people's lives.
>
> *(Antaki and Widdicombe 1998: 2; see Stokoe 2012)*

If EM and CA adopt a theory on identity, they adopt an indexical, context-bound theory, in which identity is understood as an oriented-to, recipient-designed accomplishment of interaction. Categorical phenomena are studied as phenomena of the sequential organisation of talk and other conduct in interaction. Unlike other approaches in applied linguistics, CA does 'not share the premise of standard social science that interaction varies fundamentally according to sociostructural and cultural context' (Kasper and Wagner 2014: 182). Thus research starts from the basis that an analysis of identity categories should be based on what people do and say in the categories they deploy, rather than on what analysts take to be relevant (e.g. Schegloff 1991, 1997). This is because any person may be categorised in an indefinitely extendable number of ways. To presume that gender, say, rather than any other category (e.g. class, religion and/or occupation, etc.), is the identity inscription that explains behaviour is to rush to explanation ahead of empirical evidence and to close down other potential relevancies (see Benwell and Stokoe 2010). Instead, using CA, ethnomethodologists start with what is demonstrably relevant to participants 'at the moment that whatever we are trying to produce an account for occurs' (Schegloff 1991: 50).

EM and CA are often aligned with constructionism and anti-essentialism, sharing a focus on the investigation of knowledge production (Lynch 1993) and understanding 'the ways in which the world is rendered objectively available and is maintained as such' (Heritage 1984: 220). Ethnomethodologists place reality temporarily in brackets, adopting the position of 'ethnomethodological indifference' (Garfinkel and Sacks 1970: 63) to study how people maintain a sense of a commonly shared, objectively existing world. For EM it is a 'basic mistake' to assume that we need to 'adopt a theoretical stance on "reality" at all' (Francis 1994: 105), partly because preoccupations about ontology inhibit analysis of members' practices (Button and Sharrock 1993). In everyday life, people generally treat identity as a real thing that they know about themselves and others; when people question their own or someone else's membership of an identity category – that is, make it accountable – this is something we can study (Speer and Stokoe 2011).

As noted earlier, this gloss of the theory of EM and CA and their relation in discursive psychology (see Potter and Hepburn 2007) are often criticised for their atheoretical and empiricist practices and lack of interest in social theory. For these reasons, the keenest – often caricatured – debate about identity theory and method has been between two sides (see Schegloff 1997; Wetherell 1998). However, it is also in the EM/CA field that we find a wealth of close analysis of naturally occurring materials that show how identity categories of all kinds figure systematically in, and are consequential for, social action: for example, in institutional care homes for the disabled (Antaki *et al.* 2007), doctor–patient consultations (Kitzinger 2005), neighbour complaints and police interrogation (Stokoe and Edwards 2007; Stokoe 2013a), gender identity clinics (Speer 2011) and classroom interaction (Benwell and Stokoe 2002). In the following section, we provide some empirical examples to show how EM and CA approach the analysis of identity in interaction.

Identifying 'identity' in interaction

In the following extracts, the interactional data are transcribed using Jefferson's (2004) system for CA (see transcription key in Appendix). The Jefferson system does not just attend to what is said, but how it is said, by encoding detailed information about the way talk is delivered. While the data in this chapter are mostly from audio-recorded telephone calls, CA also examines video-recorded interaction and uses a variety of multimodal transcription systems (see e.g. Goodwin 2003; Laurier 2013).

We start by examining telephone calls to a sales organisation, before moving on to an analysis of patient complaints to an NHS telephone line. In everyday life, identifying and analysing identity is something that people regularly attend to, when progressing a particular course of action. In the first five data extracts that follow, which come from a collection of telephone calls from members of the public to a double-glazing sales firm, the call-taker (W) asks the caller (C) their name. Consider Extract 1, in which W is asking C for their surname. Extracts are prefaced with 'WC', which identifies our dataset ('Windows Calls') using standard conventions for doing so in CA.

Extract 1: WC-43

```
 1  W:  And u::m: can I take y'surname please ↑si:r.
 2      (0.4)
 3  C:  Ye:h mister Chu:rchwater.
 4      (0.5)
 5  W:  .hh that's (0.2) cee aitch you are <cee:> double you ay tee ee ↓are.
 6      (0.3)
 7  C:  That's it love,=
 8  W:  =#Lovely.# (0.2) Oka:y,=is- is it just your↑se:lf? or is it mister'n
 9      ↑missu:s? ↓or. .hh
10  C:  Mister an' missus yeh.
11  W:  #Lovely.#
```

Within a series of questions about the caller, W first establishes C's surname. W solicits (line 1), then confirms the spelling (line 5) of the caller. At line 8, W then proceeds to ask a more complex question about C's marital status. W first asks if it is 'just your↑se:lf?', in a yes–no interrogative formatted question. Note the difference between W's first question, which seeks information (W cannot guess at C's name!), and the second substantive question 'is it just your↑se:lf?'. The second question contains a candidate answer; she does not ask 'can I take your marital status?'

Before C responds, W reformulates the question as an alternate interrogative with options ('or is it mister'n ↑missu:s?'), and a further trail-off '↓or.' that C could complete if neither possibility has yet been named by W. W therefore offers, in pursuit of C's 'marital status' category membership, different possibilities to select, confirm or reject. These redesigned questions handle the epistemic asymmetry between C and W; that is, while W displays her normative knowledge about how the world is organised in terms of heterosexual couples living together and buying windows, only C knows about his actual living arrangements and, furthermore, is entitled to do so; W is not entitled to make a best guess. W's subsequent questions both prefer a 'yes' confirmation but the 'or' handles the possibility that C occupies an alternative category. But the questions, and their order of presentation, reveal what W takes to be the most likely category that C is a member of – single or married. In line 10, C confirms that he is 'Mister an' missus yeh'.

In Extract 2, a similar series of questions produces a different response from another male caller.

Extract 2: WC-17

```
1    W:  That's lovely,=is it- ↑is it jus' your↑↑self or is it mister an' ↑missu:s?
2         that we're ↑see[ing or. ]
3    C:                  [It's mister] (it's/just) misterh
4    W:  Just mister Higgins,=[that's great stuff u:m, .hh
5    C                        [Yep.
```

At line 3, C's overlap addresses W's yes–no interrogative question, but rather than providing the preferred response 'yes', he states in full that 'It's mister'. Like many cases of overlapping talk, C then redoes his answer 'in the clear', outside the overlap. Here, he repairs his response by inserting the word 'just'. W's intonation in delivering the first question, 'is it jus' your↑↑self', is hearably 'bright', perhaps conveying that being 'just yourself' is 'no problem' and neither marked nor requiring sympathy. This analysis is supported by W's confirmation of C's answer at line 4: 'Just mister Higgins', which is swiftly followed by an assessment '=that's great stuff'. So the fact that C is 'single' (or widowed, or divorced) is not a problem for W; W has no stake in his answer. Such questions, particularly with the trail-off 'or', are similar to those found in speed-dates in which one dater may ask another, 'have you been married, or ...' (Stokoe 2010b). In this context, it becomes clear that the party asking the question prefers a 'yes (I have been married)' response, but the trail-off handles the preference and positions the questioner as 'happy with either response'.

In Extract 3, the issue of the caller's marital status arises as W makes arrangements to visit the caller.

Extract 3: WC-33

```
1   W:  U:m: so I just need t'have a look on the diary now an' see when I can:
2       arrange for: somebody t- to pop an' see y'both.=obviously measure up
3       an' .hh an' get it quoted.=u:m .hh oh ↑sorry I said both.=is it d- y'said
4       we:. Is it- u- am I right in assuming it's £mister an' missus,£
5       (0.8)
6   C:  Yes.
7   W:  O::h right.=okay.
8       (0.2)
9   W:  °#Mister an' missus.#°
```

Here, W formulates her presupposition that the caller is married, by proposing to see them 'both' (line 2) and then in her subsequent question to W ('Is it- u- am I right in assuming it's £mister an' missus,£'). Note the detail in her question, which is prefaced with an apology for making an assumption and 'is it', which presumably is headed towards the question 'is it mister and missus'. However, she repairs this to ask whether or not her assumption is correct. Here is one crux of the matter. Titles – 'mister' and 'missus' – carry with them particular sorts of information in English. More specifically, the title 'missus' specifies a woman's marital status in a way that 'mister' does not, making such terms highly gendered and the subject of much attention in feminist linguistics. But C is more entitled to know about his marital status than W, and so her presupposition that the company will visit 'both' is problematic. Her subsequent repairs reveal that and how 'speakers are exquisitely sensitive to their epistemic positions relative to addressees, as a condition of developing a turn at talk' (Heritage 2012: 31). The turbulence created by making, then correcting, presuppositions is revealed in the gap that develops at line 5, before C confirms that it is indeed 'mister and missus' at line 6, with a minimal 'yes' response (see Extracts 1 and 2).

In Extracts 1–3, W has addressed these questions to male callers. In Extract 4, W asks a female caller a similar series of questions. The problem here, though, is that 'missus' more directly implies another party in a way that 'mister' does not.

Extract 4: WC-23

```
1   W:  an' is it uh- is it just ↑missus or is it mister an' ↓missus.=o:r [um-
2   C:                                                    [(Only me.
3       (0.2)
4   W:  #U-# ok- ↑so y- is it- i- it's just yourself is it.=[#sorry.#]
5   C:                                          [ (Yeh-) ] I live with
6       my mum.
7       (0.2)
8   W:  ↑↑Oh ↑right okay,.hh
```

W's questions, again built from an assumption about the most likely domestic arrangements of the caller, generates the response 'Only me'. Like Extracts 1 and 2, W starts with the single category, producing a version of 'is it just yourself', but then goes on to propose that it might be 'mister and missus'. Only then do callers begin to answer. Unlike Extract 2, however, in which W repeats 'Just mister' without a glitch, her response to C is delayed (line 4, full of perturbation, hesitations and cut-off sounds) and a formulation of what she takes to be the upshot of C's response '↑so y- is it- i- it's just yourself is it.'. Here, then, W struggles with a 'single' response to a 'missus' caller, which results in C providing an account for her situation: 'Yeh- I live with my mum' (lines 5–6). After another delay, W's response displays a 'change of state' (Heritage 1984), '↑↑Oh ↑right okay,.', indicating that, until now, she has been unable to comprehend C's domestic situation as a 'missus' who is 'just herself' – despite actually living with her mother. In Extract 5, W produces a third option for C to respond to.

Extract 5: WC-2

```
1   W:   ↑Is it- is jus' ↑mi:ster? or is it mister an' mis↑sus? ↑or mister an' a
2        £partner£ [that (we're/we'll) see-]
3   C:          [     No i- ju-     ] no it's just mister. =
4   W:   =Oh it's just- yeah.
```

Note the smile voice as W produces the word '£partner£'. This suggests that, while offering it as an option for C, she does not expect him to be gay and living with a male partner, which is confirmed by C in overlap. Presumably if this was a serious and unmarked option, it would be delivered in the same way as the other items; here it is marked.

Overall, we have seen, much like Kitzinger's (2005) analysis of out-of-hours calls to doctors' surgeries, how matters of identity, in terms of normative assumptions about people's category memberships, may produce turbulence in what are quite banal interactional episodes. This turbulence is different to Kitzinger's, however, who focused on callers' responses to questions that presuppose a heterosexual relationship. In her data, callers are put in the position of having to 'come out' as a lesbian or gay couple and household. In our calls, callers frequently have to reveal their domestic arrangements and relationship statuses to satisfy an organisational 'script'.

In the second data set (Extracts 6–9) representing calls to a 'Patient Relations' complaints line in Scotland, patients and patients' relatives address their complaint to a central operator. While complaining, callers regularly appeal to membership of the implicit category 'reasonable patient', which often involves distancing from the activity of complaining. This pattern supports the observation made by other researchers that there is 'trouble' around the activity of complaining (e.g. Edwards 2005) and that complaining is an accountable, even stigmatised, activity which 'holds powerful negative connotations at the social level' (Dewar 2011: viii). As we will see, membership categorisation activities play a key role in legitimising complaints, either through the announcement of explicit membership of particular kinds of 'reasonable' identity categories; or through attributes or activities tied to the category 'reasonable person'. Through the self-constructions of normative, reasonable identity and behaviour (see also Stokoe and Hepburn 2005), patients' narratives are able 'to express or confirm the continuing integrity and moral virtue of the individual' (Pollock 2005: 23).

Extract 6: CC-17

```
1   C:   The:r (.) there= was a message on the answerphone so we have to go s-
2        go ↓tomorrow=
3   OP:  =Right=
4   C:   =But again she can't drive ah mean i- it's fairly restrictive bu-=
```

5   OP: =Yea:h (.) it's kinda impacting on both of yer=
6   C: =Aye y'know it's there's °nothing°- ↑as ah said it's one of those things
7   and ma I mighta sai- ↑we're not really complaining people but (.) I'm
8   really that the the fact that the sorta >°I've already explained ta yer°<
9   the fact that- .h obviously it was known until we took trouble to find out
10   before they sent us on our way

Here a caller ringing on behalf of his wife is complaining about inadequate and delayed information regarding an appointment. Legitimacy is built into the complaint whereby the caller
justifies the basis of their grievance: delays to his wife's treatment are causing practical inconvenience – the situation is fairly restrictive. OP affiliates to this turn with an assertion of the
caller's probable feelings about the situation, 'it's kinda impacting on both of yer', what Labov
and Fanshel (1977) have described as a B-event (an event about which the recipient knows
more than the speaker). Between lines 7 and 10, the caller develops his complaint, but pref-
aces it with further evidence of the couple's reasonable disposition; 'it's one of those things'
is an idiomatic expression of philosophical resignation, one that reveals a rational appreciation
that some inconveniences are neither intended, personal or rare. Drew and Holt (1988) have
discussed how the figurative character of idiomatic forms acts in a similar way to extreme
case formulations in the contexts of complaints: it avoids empirical detail and has moral force,
acting to secure affiliation. Again an appeal to non-membership of the category 'complainer'
is invoked to enhance and legitimise the grievance: '↑we're not really complaining people'.
Finally the caller verbalises his emotional state 'I'm really annoyed' (see Edwards 1999) to fur-
nish his account with further moral authority.

Extract 7: CC-19

1   C: Ah've been ah've >listen< ah've been ba:shed an'=
2   OP: =Mhmmm
3   C: =bumped all ma days [ah've   ] worked hard >all my days<
4   OP: [Mhmm]
5   OP: Yep
6   C: An' that wuz- (.) but that's nothin' compared tae
7   (0.2)
8   OP: What you went through.

The caller in Extract 7 provides a narrative of his tough working life ('bashed and bumped all
ma days') in order to relativise the more extreme hardship presented by the ordeal he recently
experienced at the hospital. The caller asserts that he does not habitually complain; indeed he is
usually stoical. Like other callers he uses extreme case formulations to enhance the contrast and
emphasise the grievance 'that's nothin' compared tae', a turn completed by the operator reflecting her affiliation to his message. By relativising his suffering in contrast to more normative
hardship, the caller provides more objective yardsticks by which others can assess his suffering
and helps to 'manage [the] complaint's subjectivity' and avoid 'evaluative inferences' about his
own disposition as a complainer (Edwards 2005).

Extract 8: CC-18

```
1   OP: So you had one vodka that [night        ]
2   C:                             [So I felt (.) uh-] hoh I'd only (.) one- had
3       ↑one vodka=I mean that's (0.2) but I'd have ta say (0.1) I think my
4       daughter had said on the phone he had had a drink >or summat like
5       that.<=
6   OP: =Right=
7   C:  =Th- there <wuznae drink involved.>
8       (0.2)
9   OP: M↑huh
10  C:  If there was I wouldn't even be phoning yer.
11  OP: Mhuh
```

The operator's first turn in Extract 8 clarifies a point of information discussed earlier in the patient's narrative, which is that the caller's daughter mentioned that her father had an alcoholic drink prior to his heart attack. The caller's point in topicalising this issue is to stress its irrelevance to his condition, but the operator's turn reveals an ambiguity, whereby her request for confirmation of the drinking of 'one vodka' topicalises it and enhances its relevance. The interactional trouble that this question provokes is revealed in the 'defensive detailing' (Drew 1998) provided by the caller in his next turn, where 'one vodka' is repaired to 'only one vodka'. In line 7, this assertion of the drink's irrelevance is upgraded to 'there <wuznae drink involved>', and in line 10 further moral work is achieved in the claim that if the caller's drinking had been relevant he 'wouldn't even be phoning yer'. This exchange reveals normative understandings about how lifestyle choices such as drinking alcohol are thought to contribute to heart disease. In his repudiation of the identity of excessive or habitual drinker, the caller makes claims to a different kind of identity, that of responsible patient with the entitlement to complain. The implication here is that if a patient were responsible for his own ill-health he would not be able to make a legitimate complaint about his treatment. Again, the appeal to a reasonable and responsible identity, in implicit contrast to other kinds of patient identity, is what underpins and legitimises the grievance.

Extract 9: CC-20

```
1   C:  We waited over an hour to be assessed by a triage nurse which is ↑fine
2       (.) cos (.) ↑you don't mind waiting your ↑turn (.) and (.) and there was
3       just- full of drunk people.=and (.) injured people.=and (.) we were kept
4       waiting a further two ↑hours
5   OP: Right
6   C:  For her to spend almost five minutes with a doctor.
```

In this final extract we see another example of the self-construction of a reasonable patient identity. The caller states that 'we waited over an hour to be assessed by a triage nurse', an utterance that might be thought to represent a complaint; however, this is confounded by her concession that this was '↑fine (.) cos (.) ↑you don't mind waiting your ↑turn'. This utterance reveals the caller to be a reasonable person, one who recognises that hospitals are busy, understaffed and full of equally entitled patients. However, the turn develops to flag up other kinds of patients, whose identities are marked, possibly in contrast to the caller's relative, as 'drunk' and 'injured'. This detail contributes to the impression that the accident and emergency ward was a stressful and unpleasant environment in which to wait and the reasonable hour-long wait is implicitly contrasted with a less reasonable 'further two hours' and the very minimal time actually spent with the doctor: 'almost five minutes'. The category attributes of 'reasonable person' ('↑you don't mind waiting your ↑turn') are strategically established in this account to manage the impression of the actual complaint as reasoned and fair.

In these extracts, we have seen how membership category work operates in the establishment and avoidance of certain kinds of identity. Complaining is a fraught, evaluated and thus accountable activity, and callers to the complaints line must work hard to have their grievances heard as legitimate.

Issues and ongoing debates

In a recent paper, Kasper and Wagner (2014) discuss the relevance of CA in applied linguistics. They point out that application in CA does not mean the same as in applied linguistics. Applied linguistics is interdisciplinary, drawing on a range of theoretical and methodological resources from across the social sciences to investigate 'language-related real-life problems' (ibid.: 186). In contrast, applied CA is transdisciplinary: it does not draw from a range of epistemological or methodological perspectives but instead offers a 'coherent, integrated theory and methodology of interaction, and a large body of research findings, that these researchers can take to investigate their discipline-specific topics and problems' (ibid.).

As we have seen in the data extracts, CA researchers work with ordinary data (comprising talk among friends and family members) as well as applied or institutional data (e.g. talk between colleagues or professionals and laypersons and so on). While there is some debate in CA about the nature of this, there is a substantial literature on institutional interaction, from studies of medical interaction, education, helplines, police and legal settings and other workplace and organisational encounters (e.g. Llewellyn and Hindmarsh 2010). Such studies give rise to potential applications of CA research and the practical uses to which insights may be put by practitioners. This development within CA did not necessarily characterise its initial programme of work, which was more purely focused on the mechanics of sociality as realised in interaction. Recent applied CA research has been anthologised in two significant collections – *Applying conversation analysis* (Richards and Seedhouse 2007) and *Applied conversation analysis: Intervention and change in institutional talk* (Antaki 2011).

Antaki (2011) explains that there is a distinction to be made between applied CA as 'discovery' (a means of shedding light on the institutional character and workings of particular interactional settings) and as 'prescription' (deploying the insights of CA analysis to suggest improvements to the service that an organisation provides). It is this latter interventionist sense that characterises some of the most recent, cutting edge and professionally oriented research in the CA scholarly community and it is to an example of such a programme of research that we now turn.

Applied conversation analysis and identity research

This section presents a case study that showcases how a CA/EM study of identity can lead directly to application. The case study is focused on a particular institutional setting, the community mediation service. These services handle disputes between neighbours, either at the request of one or both parties or at the instigation of organisations, such as the police. In this section, we turn to mediation service encounters between mediators and clients, focusing on cases in which clients say something potentially sexist about their neighbour. That is, clients make identity matters (both their own, as the kind of person who might make sexist remarks and the identity of their neighbour) relevant to their complaint, leaving mediators in the position of having to respond. Mediators respond to sexism (and other '-isms' like racism or ageism) in particular, patterned ways (see Stokoe 2015).

One way in which analytic observations may be turned into practical outcomes for the mediators whose institutional practices are under analytic scrutiny is through CARM. Over the past two years, one of us (Stokoe) has developed a method called the Conversation Analytic Role-play Method (CARM), and delivered over 80 communication skills workshops to mediators funded by the UK ESRC (Stokoe 2011). In contrast to traditional role-play, which is steeped in problems of inauthenticity (see Stokoe 2013b), CARM uses research about actual interaction and identifies practices in the setting under investigation as a basis for training. As the following extracts illustrate, workshops focus on, for example, how to convert callers to services to clients of services, as well as other issues such as 'opening a mediation', 'solution-focused questions' and 'dealing with -isms'. In the context of applied CA, CARM has been described as 'the most significant ... development' (Emmison 2013: 6), and it demonstrates how designedly large-scale qualitative work can impact on professional practice.

Extract 10 comes from an initial meeting between a mediator (M) and four clients who, together, are describing a complaint about one of their neighbours and are 'Party 1' to the dispute. C1, C2 and C3 allege that their neighbour, a single mother with several children, goes out at night leaving her children unattended. M has not met the woman, 'Party 2', and may not, if Party 2 does not agree to participate in mediation.

Extract 10: DM-C02

```
 1  C1: D'y-↑I don't think she ca:res actually she's not spoken to any
 2      of all of us has she in [all the time she['s be]en here[.
 3  C2:                         [No:,       [No, ]        [never
 4      spoke.
 5      (0.8)
 6  C3: Never spoke.
 7      (.)
 8  C3: She jus' dresses up, (1.4) [(What's it,)]
 9  C1:                            [Like a tart.]
10      (0.4)
11  C2: °Ye:[h.°
12  C3:     [Heh hah heh.
13      (0.2)
14  C3: Yeh.
15      (2.4)
16  C3: .hhh ↑but it's::
```

The clients took every opportunity to characterise their neighbour in negative ways, in pursuit of affiliation from mediators, and to attribute blame for the dispute to their neighbour rather than themselves. Extract 10 completes a long discussion (see Stokoe and Edwards 2015) and introduces a category ('tart') to characterise how the neighbour dresses, in ways that fit with, and perhaps formulate as a conclusion, much of what C1, C2 and C3 have been saying about her. Rather than being a person like they imply themselves to be (considerate, civil, responsible, interested in their children's welfare, neighbourly), her interests lie elsewhere, in some kind of wanton and irresponsible self-indulgence. The way she dresses and the category that it invokes are tied to the same range of behaviours in which she goes out at nights, goes on holiday leaving her children at home, and fails to discipline them properly. Her inadequacies are not only behavioural but moral, psychological and generalised: it is her nature.

In CARM workshops, the extract is played to workshop participants, who discuss what sort of response they might make at line 17. Following their discussion, the rest of the extract is played, including what the mediator actually did next.

Extract 10 (contd)

```
17        (0.9)
18  M:   So i- is- is that the same response that everybody- y'know.
19        =I'mean y-y'say that other people (0.2) [in the street, I'mean
20  C2:                                          [Yeh.
21  C3:                                          [( ) talk t'you
22        though.
23  M:   Ri::ght.=an' o(c)- do they say anything he:r.
```

After a delay, M does not orient or respond to C3 and C1's collaborative categorisation of their neighbour as a 'tart'; nor does she join in with their laughter. M does not, therefore, affiliate with their stance towards the woman. Rather, she asks a question about the woman's interactions with other neighbours. As mediation is a process that involves bringing together disputing parties to talk about possible solutions, it is of interest that M asks a mediation-relevant question about the woman's likeliness to participate in mediation.

Consider a final example. Extract 11 comes from an intake call between a mediator and potential client. It is in such calls that problems are first formulated and offers of or requests for mediation are made. The mediator's job is to elicit a summary of the problem from the potential client; explain what mediation is, and offer it to them. C's problem is to do with noise from his female neighbour, which he claims is exacerbated by her visiting boyfriend. We join the call as it comes towards its closing. C has agreed to mediate.

Extract 11: EC-13

```
1  M:   [°Yeh°
2  C:   [.hhh I wouldn't mi:nd the bloke's most probably got a
3        family of his own somewhere else. .hhh
4        (0.8)
5  C:   You kno:w?
6  M:   Mm
7        (0.4)
8  C:   An' 'e's comin' down 'ere for a little bit of fa:ncy bit.
9        (1.0)
10 C:   Heh heh .hhh d'you know what I me:an.
```

C suggests that his neighbour's 'bloke' is already married, thereby implying that she is his 'mistress', or 'fa:ncy bit.' (line 8). After a gap develops in which M says nothing (line 4), C pursues an affiliative, co-member response from M, as if they are friends talking, or as two men, perhaps, rather than as mediator–client (line 5). M responds with a continuer ('mm'), which aligns minimally with C's general project of characterising his neighbour but does not affiliate or take a stance on it (for example, 'oh yes, I know!': see Stivers 2008). At line 10, however, C pursues M's affiliation once more, asking him to display shared knowledge of, and a shared stance towards, what adulterous people are like. Again, in the CARM workshop, participants formulate, discuss and evaluate possible responses. Here is what M actually said in response.

Extract 11 (contd)

```
11      (0.5)
12  M:  Ye:s I [understand] what you're saying yeah:
13  C:         [Y'know?]
14      (0.2)
15  M:  °Yeh°
16      (0.6)
17  C:  Because [that's what she's li:ke.
18  M:          [(Is it cos-)
19      (2.2)
20  M:  Ye:::ah. hh okay.=so .hh w'll- w- [I'm going to contact]=
21  C:                                    [     ((coughs))     ]
22      =um: contact her [...]
```

Like the mediator in Extract 10, M does not display affiliation with C. At line 12, he states that he understands what C is saying, but not that he agrees with what C means. Neither does he reciprocate C's laughter. And, following further pursuit from C (line 17), M returns to procedural issues.

Because mediators are expected to display themselves as impartial, they avoid taking a stance towards the problems described by clients. However, as we see in Extract 11, clients will often pursue affiliation, or displays of stance, and often resist offers of mediation when such affiliation is not forthcoming (see Stokoe 2013c). In CARM workshops about '-isms', participants see mediators doing one of three things in response:

1   Reformulating problems by deleting the prejudicial element;
2   Moving the discussion towards mediation or procedural issues;
3   Occasionally confronting clients.

They therefore get to see mediators dealing with actual interactional problems, as well as potential solutions to the conundrum of avoiding affiliation with problematic stances while keeping the client in mediation.

CARM provides participants with a unique opportunity to scrutinise real recordings of mediation and discuss best practice from actual interactions. The implications of CARM for other workplaces might include recording day-to-day activities, such as meetings. Staff could identify, and scrutinise, practices that may be problematically gendered, or problematic in some other way, as a basis for discussion and as a source of training materials. Crucially, for applied linguistics, we can see how participants and professionals understand and handle issues of identity in real-life settings that matter and ways in which language is central.

Summary

This chapter has outlined an approach to identity grounded in EM and CA. We have explained CA/EM's distinct approach to, and understanding of, language as a site of social action. We have seen how it is in and through social interaction that 'who people are to one another' is a live concern. We have also illustrated the way CA research on identity can have a practical application in the communication training of professionals and, specifically for this chapter, in how to recognise and respond to the lived identity concerns of people in conflict.

Looking ahead, applied CA has much to offer applied linguistics. The success of CARM supports Heritage's (2009) claim that 'the examination of real data using CA is found by many to be a potent experience capable of triggering changes in attitudes and … practices'. But, as Kasper and Wagner (2014) point out, applied linguistics also contributes to applied CA. In particular, 'applied linguistics offers a corrective to classic CA's entrenched monolingualism, a limitation that CA shares with most social sciences outside of linguistic anthropology, sociolinguistics, and applied linguistics' (p. 200). CA, as a designedly large-scale qualitative method, by working with increasingly large datasets and across languages (e.g. Stivers *et al.* 2009), is broadening the set of linguistic questions that applied CA, as part of applied linguistics, can address.

Related topics

Positioning language and identity: poststructuralist perspectives; Discursive psychology and the production of identity in language practices; Critical discourse analysis and identity; Challenges for language and identity researchers in the collection and transcription of spoken interaction; Disability identities and category work in institutional practices: the case of a 'typical ADHD girl'; 'Comes with the territory': expert–novice and insider–outsider identities in police interviews; The future of identity research: impact and new developments in sociolinguistics.

Further reading

Benwell, B. and Stokoe, E. (2006). *Discourse and identity*. Edinburgh: Edinburgh University Press. (A comprehensive overview of discourse analytical approaches to identity with a particular emphasis on ethnomethodology and conversation analytic methods.)

References

Antaki, C. (ed.) (2011). *Applied conversation analysis: intervention and change in institutional talk*. Basingstoke: Palgrave Macmillan.

Antaki, C., Finlay, W.M.L. and Walton, C. (2007). '"The staff are your friends": intellectually disabled identities in official discourse and interactional practice', *British Journal of Social Psychology*, 46(1): 1–18.

Antaki, C. and Widdicombe, S. (eds) (1998). *Identities in talk*. London: SAGE.

Benwell, B. and Stokoe, E. (2002). 'Constructing discussion tasks in university tutorials: shifting dynamics and identities', *Discourse Studies*, 4(4): 429–453.

Benwell, B. and Stokoe, E. (2010). Identity in social action: conversation, narratives and genealogies, in M. Wetherell and C.T. Mohanty (eds) *The SAGE handbook of identities*. London: SAGE, pp. 56–77.

Button, G. and Sharrock, W. (1993). 'A disagreement over agreement and consensus in constructionist sociology', *Journal for the Theory of Social Behaviour*, 23: 1–25.

Dewar, J. (2011). *Calling to complain: an ethnographic and conversation analytic account of complaints to an industry ombudsman*. MSc thesis, Victoria University, Wellington.

Drew, P. (1998). 'Complaints about transgressions and misconduct', *Research on Language and Social Interaction*, 31(3–4): 295–325.

Drew, P. (2005). Conversation analysis, in K.L. Fitch and R.E. Sanders (eds) *Handbook of language and social interaction*. Mahwah, NJ: Lawrence Erlbaum, pp. 71–102.

Drew, P. and Holt, E. (1988). 'Complainable matters: the use of idiomatic expressions in making complaints', *Social Problems*, 35(4): 398–417.

Edwards, D. (1999). 'Emotion discourse', *Culture and Society*, 5(3): 271–291.

Edwards, D. (2005). 'Moaning, whinging and laughing: the subjective side of complaints', *Discourse Studies*, 7(1): 5–29.

Emmison, M. (2013). '"Epistemic engine" versus "role-play method": divergent trajectories in contemporary conversation analysis', *Australian Journal of Communication*, 40(2): 5–7.

Francis, D. (1994). 'The golden dreams of the social constructionist', *Journal of Anthropological Research*, 50(2): 1–22.

Garfinkel, H. (1967). *Studies in ethnomethodology*. Englewood Cliffs, NJ: Prentice-Hall.

Garfinkel, H. and Sacks, H. (1970). On formal structures of practical actions, in J.C. McKinney and E.A. Tiryakian (eds) *Theoretical sociology: perspectives and developments*. New York: Appleton-Century-Crofts, pp. 337–366.

Goffman, E. (1959). *The presentation of self in everyday life*. Harmondsworth: Penguin.

Goodwin, C. (2003). Pointing as situated practice, in S. Kita (ed.) *Pointing: where language, culture and cognition meet*. Mahwah, NJ: Lawrence Erlbaum Associates, pp. 217–241.

Heritage, J. (1984). *Garfinkel and ethnomethodology*. Cambridge: Polity.

Heritage, J. (2009). Conversation analysis as an approach to the medical encounter, in J.B. McKinlay and L. Marceau (eds) *Behavioral and social science research interactive textbook* [Online]. Available at www.esourceresearch.org

Heritage, J. (2012). 'Epistemics in action: action formation and territories of knowledge', *Research on Language and Social Interaction*, 45(1): 1–29.

Hester, S. and Eglin, P. (eds) (1997). *Culture in action: studies in membership categorization analysis*. Boston, MA: International Institute for Ethnomethodology and University Press of America.

Jefferson, G. (2004). Glossary of transcript symbols with an introduction, in G.H. Lerner (ed.) *Conversation analysis: studies from the first generation*. Amsterdam/Philadelphia: John Benjamins, pp. 13–31.

Kaspar, G. and Wagner, J. (2014). 'Conversation analysis in applied linguistics', *Annual Review of Applied Linguistics*, 34: 171–212.

Kitzinger, C. (2005). 'Speaking as a heterosexual: (how) does sexuality matter for talk-in-interaction?', *Research on Language and Social Interaction*, 38(3): 221–265.

Labov, W. and Fanshel, D. (1977). *Therapeutic discourse: psychotherapy as conversation*. New York: Academic Press.

Laurier, E. (2013). Noticing: talk, gestures, movement and objects in video analysis, in R. Lee, N. Castree, R. Kitchen, V. Lawson, A. Paasi and C.W. Withers (eds) *The SAGE handbook of human geography*. London: SAGE, pp. 250–272.

Llewellyn, N. and Hindmarsh, J. (eds) (2010). *Organization, interaction and practice: studies of ethnomethodology and conversation analysis*. Cambridge: Cambridge University Press.

Lynch, M. (1993). *Scientific practice and ordinary action: ethnomethodology and social studies of science*. Cambridge: Cambridge University Press.

Pollock, K. (2005). *Concordance in Medical Consultations: A Critical Review*. Milton Keynes: Radcliffe Publishing Limited.

Potter, J.A. and Hepburn, A. (2007). Discursive psychology, institutions and child protection, in A. Weatherall, B. Watson and C. Gallois (eds) *Language and social psychology*. Basingstoke: Palgrave, pp. 160–181.

Richards, K. and Seedhouse, P. (eds) (2007). *Applying conversation analysis*. Basingstoke: Palgrave Macmillan.

Sacks, H. (1972). On the analysability of stories by children, in J.J. Gumperz and D. Hymes (eds) *Directions in sociolinguistics: the ethnography of communication*. New York: Holt, Rinehart and Winston, pp. 325–345.

Sacks, H. (1984a). On doing 'being ordinary', in J.M. Atkinson and J. Heritage (eds), *Structures of social action: studies in conversation analysis*. Cambridge: Cambridge University Press, pp. 413–429.

Sacks, H. (1984b). Notes on methodology (ed. Gail Jefferson), in J.M. Atkinson and J. Heritage (eds) *Structures of social action: studies in conversation analysis*. Cambridge: Cambridge University Press, pp. 2–27.

Sacks, H. (1992). *Lectures on conversation, Vol. 1*. Oxford: Blackwell.

Schegloff, E.A. (1991). Reflections on talk and social structure, in D. Boden and D. Zimmerman (eds) *Talk and social structure*. Berkeley, CA: University of California Press, pp. 44–70.

Schegloff, E.A. (1996). Issues of relevance for discourse analysis: contingency in action, interaction and co-participant context, in E.H. Hovy and D.R. Scott (eds) *Computational and conversational discourse: burning issues – an interdisciplinary account*. New York: Springer, pp. 3–38.

Schegloff, E.A. (1997). 'Whose text? Whose context?', *Discourse and Society*, 8(2): 165–187.

Schütz, A. (1962). *Collected papers, vol. I: the problem of social reality*. The Hague: Martinus Nijhoff.

Speer, S.A. (2011). On the role of reported, third party compliments in passing as a 'real' woman, in S.A. Speer and E. Stokoe (eds) *Conversation and gender*. Cambridge: Cambridge University Press, pp. 155–182.

Speer, S.A. and Stokoe, E. (eds) (2011). *Conversation and gender*. Cambridge: Cambridge University Press.

Stivers, T. (2008). 'Stance, alignment, and affiliation during storytelling: when nodding is a token of affiliation', *Research on Language and Social Interaction*, 41(1): 31–57.

Stivers, T., Enfield, N.J., Brown, P., Englert, C., Hayahsi, M., Heinemann, T., Hoymann, G., Rossano, F., De Ruiter, J.P., Yoon, K. and Levinson, S.C. (2009). 'Universals and cultural variation in turn-taking in conversation', *Proceedings of the National Academy of Sciences*, 106(26): 10,587–10,592.

Stokoe, E. (2010b). '"Have you been married, or…?" Eliciting and accounting for relationship histories in speed-dating encounters', *Research on Language and Social Interaction*, 43(3): 260–282.

Stokoe, E. (2011). Simulated interaction and communication skills training: the 'Conversation Analytic Role-play Method', in C. Antaki (ed.) *Applied conversation analysis: changing institutional practices*. Basingstoke: Palgrave Macmillan, pp. 119–139.

Stokoe, E. (2012). 'Moving forward with membership categorization analysis: methods for systematic analysis', *Discourse Studies*, 14(3): 277–303.

Stokoe, E. (2013a). 'Overcoming barriers to mediation in intake calls to services: research-based strategies for mediators', *Negotiation Journal*, 29(3): 289–314.

Stokoe, E. (2013b). 'The (in)authenticity of simulated talk: comparing role-played and actual conversation and the implications for communication training', *Research on Language and Social Interaction*, 46(2): 1–21.

Stokoe, E. (2013c). 'Applying findings and creating impact from conversation analytic studies of gender and communication', *Economic and Industrial Democracy*, 34(3): 537–552.

Stokoe, E. (2015). 'Identifying and responding to possible "-isms" in institutional encounters: alignment, impartiality and the implications for communication training', *Journal of Language and Social Psychology*, 34(4): 427–445.

Stokoe, E. and Edwards, D. (2007). '"Black this, black that": racial insults and reported speech in neighbour complaints and police interrogations', *Discourse and Society*, 18(3): 337–372.

Stokoe, E. and Edwards, D. (2015). 'Mundane morality: gender categories and complaints in familial neighbour disputes', *Journal of Applied Linguistics and Professional Practice*, 9(2): 165–192.

Stokoe, E. and Hepburn, A. (2005). '"You can hear a lot through the walls": noise formulations in neighbour complaints', *Discourse and Society*, 16(5): 647–673.

Watson, D.R. and Weinberg, T. (1982). 'Interviews and the interactional construction of accounts of homosexual identity', *Social Analysis*, 11: 56–78.

Wetherell, M. (1998). 'Positioning and interpretative repertoires: doing conversation analysis and post-structuralism in dialogue', *Discourse and Society*, 9(3): 431–456.

Widdicombe, S. (1998). Identity as an analyst's and a participant's resource, in C. Antaki and S. Widdicombe (eds) *Identities in talk*. London: SAGE, pp. 191–206.

Appendix

The system of transcription used is that developed by Gail Jefferson (2004) for conversation analysis, taken from Speer and Stokoe (2011).

Aspects of the relative placement/timing of utterances

= Equals sign indicates immediate latching of successive talk.

(0.8) Time in parentheses shows the length of a pause in tenths of a second.

(.) Period in parentheses indicates a discernible pause that is less than a tenth of a second.

[overlap] Square brackets mark the onset and end of overlapping talk.

// Double obliques in older transcripts mark the onset of overlapping talk.

Aspects of speech delivery

. Period indicates closing, usually falling intonation.

, Comma indicates continuing, slightly upward intonation.

? Question mark marks rising intonation.

¿ Inverted question mark marks rising intonation weaker than that indicated by a question mark.

<u>Underline</u> Underlining indicates talk emphasised by the speaker.

Rea::lly, Colon(s) shows elongation of the prior sound. The more colons, the longer the stretch.

<u>c</u>: Underlining preceding colon indicates that the pitch rises on the underlined letters preceding the colon; the overall contour is 'up-to-down'.

<u>:</u> Underlined colon shows rising pitch on the colon in an overall 'down-to-up' contour.

! Exclamation mark indicates animated tone.

- Hyphen/dash indicates a sharp cut-off just prior to the word or sound.

↑ Upward arrow precedes a marked rise in pitch.

↓ Downward arrow precedes a marked fall in pitch.

< 'Greater than' sign indicates talk that is 'jump-started'.

>faster< 'Lesser than' and 'greater than' signs enclose speeded-up or compressed talk.

<slower> 'Greater than' and 'lesser than' signs enclose slower or elongated talk.

LOUD Upper case marks talk that is noticeably louder than that surrounding it.

°quiet° Degree signs enclose talk that is noticeably quieter than that surrounding it.

huh/hah/heh/hih/hoh indicate various types of laughter taken.

(h) 'h' in parentheses marks audible aspirations within speech (e.g. laughter particles).

.hhh A dot before an h or series of hs marks an in breath (number of hs indicates length).

hhh An h or series of hs marks an outbreath/breathiness (number of hs indicates length).

Hash shows creaky voice.

$ or £ Dollar or pound sign indicates 'smile' voice.

* Asterisk indicates squeaky vocal delivery.

(   ) Empty single parentheses marks non-transcribable segment of talk.

(talk) Word(s) in single parentheses indicates transcriber's possible hearing.

(it)/(at) A slash separating word(s) indicates two alternative transcriber hearings in single parentheses.

((laughs)) Word(s) in double parentheses mark transcriber comments or description of a sound.

Other symbols

→ Arrow placed in the margin of a transcript to point to parts of data the author wishes to draw to the attention of the reader.

5

Language and identity in linguistic ethnography

Miguel Pérez-Milans

Introduction

Linguistic ethnography (LE) is a relatively new term that originated in the United Kingdom (UK). It aims to provide socio- and applied linguists with theoretical and methodological perspectives for studying situated practice vis-à-vis wider sociocultural processes of change. Broadly speaking, this term offers a platform for analysing the ways in which social actors negotiate meaning and identity through language use in the context of large historical configurations that shape (and get shaped by) local instances of language use. In a discussion paper on linguistic ethnography published by the UK Linguistic Ethnography Forum over a decade ago, its general orientation was described as follows:

> Although LE research differs in how far it seeks to make claims about either language, communication or the social world, linguistic ethnography generally holds that to a considerable degree, language and the social world are mutually shaping, and that close analysis of situated language use can provide both fundamental and distinctive insights into the mechanisms and dynamics of social and cultural production in everyday activity.
>
> *(Rampton* et al. *2004)*

A few years after this discussion paper, Creese (2008: 229) pushed LE further by connecting it to new intellectual orientations in applied linguistics. She designated LE as:

> a particular configuration of interests within the broader field of socio- and applied linguistics [which brings] a theoretical and methodological development orientating towards particular, established traditions but defining itself in the new intellectual climate of post-structuralism and late modernity.

While offering a powerful account of what LE is about, these statements open up the door to subsequent questions regarding the very contribution of the term to the existing knowledge that is 'out there' in the social sciences.

In line with the discovery procedures followed by practitioners of conversational analysis, we may raise at this point the fundamental question 'Why that, in this way, right now?' To be more specific we could ask the following questions: 'What are the conditions that have resulted in the emergence and acceptance of this term in applied linguistics?'; 'How is LE different from other traditions across the fields of linguistics and anthropology?'; and 'How does it inform contemporary research on language and identity?' This chapter attempts to respond to these questions by further qualifying the working definition provided by Creese above. I aim to characterise LE through outlining both the established and the new perspectives to which this frame is linked.

I argue that LE allows us to overcome long-standing binaries in the study of language, culture and identity in applied linguistics, such as that of 'micro/macro' or 'local/global', while at the same time bringing about a new sensitivity that places instability, difference and mobility at the centre of the analysis. Although LE originated in the UK, I also show how scholars elsewhere are now drawing LE into a fuller account of political economy, an area of exploration that has not yet been fully integrated in applied linguistics.

The section below begins with an overview of LE, followed by a discussion of the major issues and ongoing debates around this perspective, before concluding with a summary.

Overview

A key issue for applied linguists drawing on LE for the study of language and identity is to identify the ontological and epistemological basis of this theoretical and methodological development. Another issue is to accommodate research of language and identity to the above-mentioned 'new intellectual climate of late modernity'. These two issues will be examined in turn in this section.

Ontologies and epistemologies

LE is built upon specific standpoints that involve certain ontological ways of understanding our social world as well as concrete epistemological decisions about how to approach this world empirically. As regards the understanding of our social world, the analytical focus of this framework rests generally upon the social and linguistic/discursive turns adopted in the social sciences since the mid-twentieth century. In particular, LE has come into existence under the influence of a mélange of traditions across various fields, including philosophy of language (Austin 1962; Searle 1969), linguistic anthropology (Hymes 1968; Gumperz and Hymes 1972; Silverstein 1976; Irvine and Gal 2000), sociolinguistics (Labov 1972; Gumperz 1982; Bernstein 1996), microsociology (Goffman 1981; Erickson 1992), communication studies (Bakhtin 1986) and social theory (Foucault 1970; Bourdieu 1977; Giddens 1982).

Such fields diverge in their conceptions of what counts as, for example, knowledge or as evidence of the social reality to be investigated. However, the combination of these fields leads to a key axiomatic proposition about social reality as being discursively constructed, reproduced, naturalised and sometimes revised in social interaction, in the course of large-scale historical, political and socio-economic configurations. There are two key aspects of this presupposition that need to be highlighted at this point of the discussion, in order to understand some of the theoretical underpinnings that make LE (and similar approaches derived from the above-mentioned traditions) theoretically distinguishable from other approaches in social (linguistic) disciplines.

First, this conceptualisation of social reality understands agency and social structure as mutually constitutive, beyond what is often called the micro/macro dichotomy. Instead of two different realms (i.e. social structure and individual agency) that need distinct analytical tools to be studied, this theoretical standpoint calls our attention to human activities as socially situated practices ordered across space and time. That is to say, human beings are seen as engaging reflexively and agentively in socially situated practices while at the same time reproducing the conditions that make these practices possible (Giddens 1982). Second, such a position addresses language as a domain where social processes are constituted, 'both in the ways that it forms part of the social practices that construct social reality, and in the ways it serves as a terrain for working out struggles that are fundamentally about other things' (Heller 2011: 49).

With respect to the epistemological decisions about how to approach the social world empirically, LE is specifically characterised by the appropriation and combination of both ethnographic and linguistic perspectives. The ethnographic angle of LE has been greatly shaped by the work done in ethnography of communication, where researchers have traditionally been concerned with the organisation of communicative practices within a given community – meaning that linguistic forms are conceptualised as symbolic resources through which people (re)constitute their social organisations (Hymes 1974). The implications of this focus are twofold. On the one hand, the ethnographic perspective implies paying a good deal of attention to people's daily activities and routines so as to derive their meaning and rationality as situated in the local context. On the other, it also involves a focus on how participants' actions at particular moments and in particular spaces are connected and constrained by other interactions across space and time.

While the scope of this approach contributes to counterbalancing highly abstracted and idealised models of communication that come from formal linguistics (i.e. models detached from the social world), the use of participant observation has been regarded as inadequate for the task of giving a full account of the local forms of social action around which people in the social groups under study construct and negotiate meaning in a situated context. This critique points out that since the traditional focus in the ethnography of communication has been to characterise, compare and contrast the communicative events around which a social group constitutes itself, this often leads to a representation of communities as fixed and bounded, and of language as a true reflection of the social order (see Pratt 1987). It is precisely this concern that has formed part of the argument about the capacity of a more linguistically oriented analysis to 'tie ethnography down' (Rampton 2006: 395).

In LE, such a linguistic orientation has been influenced by work in interactional sociolinguistics (Gumperz 1982) and micro-ethnography (Erickson 1992). These analytical perspectives introduce a focus on the routines and patterned usage of language that entail fine-grained methods for the collection, transcription and analysis of spoken interaction (see Eppler and Codó, this volume). By looking closely at audio- and/or video-recorded linguistic and textual data, the researcher is immersed in the moment-to-moment actions of their participants' activities and can follow the process whereby the participants construct frames of common understanding more fully. This procedure requires a commitment from the analyst to suspend all preconceived ideas and general arguments in order to work with the recorded and transcribed activities and to look at them as unique social episodes in which meaning making and context are interactionally constructed in a situated action.

At such moments of immersion, LE researchers explore in detail the linguistic/communicative (verbal and non-verbal) conventions through which participants sequentially coordinate their social actions by constructing social relations among themselves and with the surrounding material setting, in the course of recurrent everyday activities. These conventions include turn taking, language choice, lexical choice, proxemics, kinesics and the use of texts in interaction. In particular, attention is paid to those interactional moments in which the meaning is ambiguous. These potentially disruptive moments are considered especially rich for exploring the social processes by which norms and rules that are frequently tacit, unnoticed and taken for granted by the participants are made explicit and salient.

Therefore, this analytical exercise avoids bounded representations of communities due to its strong orientation toward the discovery of the local–uncertain–unpredictable–changeable positioning of the participants. In addition, when ethnographically driven, this type of inquiry is not carried out by permanently putting aside any connection between the data and other activities removed from the context of the research, which is done in other disciplinary traditions (see e.g. Sacks *et al.* 1974). In this regard, LE researchers work with each recorded and transcribed interaction as part of a web of social activities that participants develop in the course of their trajectories, in interaction with the trajectories of other material artefacts and discourses being produced and circulated in the field.

In sum, the idiosyncratic approach to linguistics and ethnography derived from the perspectives described in this section contributes to strengthening the epistemological status of ethnography while sharpening the analytic relevance of linguistics. This is neatly put by Rampton *et al.* (2014: 4), who argue that:

> There is a broad consensus that: i) … meaning takes shape within specific social relations, interactional histories and institutional regimes, produced and construed by agents with expectations and repertoires that have to be grasped ethnographically; ii) analysis of internal organization of verbal (and other kinds of semiotic) data is essential to understanding its significance and position in the world. Meaning is far more than just the 'expression of ideas', and biography, identifications, stance and nuance are extensively signaled in the linguistic and textual fine-grain.

These ontological and epistemological positions are not placed in a vacuum; instead, they are linked to past intellectual debates while pointing towards forward-looking discussions. Looking backwards, such positions are viewed as the historical outcome of the breakdown of positivist approaches in social studies that resulted from a widespread critique of the structuralist search for universal scientific principles. In contrast to previous ideas about language, culture and identity as natural objects that exist in isolation from the social world to which they refer, poststructuralism has led to a reconceptualisation whereby language, culture and identity are seen as linguistic, discursive and cultural products that cannot be detached from the specific local and social conditions that are responsible for them coming into being (see Baxter, this volume).

Looking forward, the ontological and epistemological considerations reviewed in this section also place LE in a privileged position with respect to the study of new processes of sociolinguistic and cultural change. These new processes are now the focus of ongoing research in the social sciences, in the context of a new intellectual shift in which instability, difference and mobility have all been put at the centre of the analysis – in contrast to previous research where they had been largely treated as peripheral. So it is now worth shifting the attention to this new intellectual climate, which is linked to the conditions of late modernity, and to focus on how this climate is informing research on language and identity in applied linguistics from the perspective of LE.

Language and identity in late modernity

During the last decade, research in the social sciences has paid increasing attention to the dilemmas and contradictions that the so-called conditions of 'late modernity' have posed to nationally oriented ideas about language, culture and identity (Appadurai 1990; Giddens 1991; Bauman 1998; Castells 2010). These conditions involve widespread socio-economic, institutional, cultural and linguistic changes. Examples of these changes include the information revolution associated with rapidly changing socio-economic networks; the intensification of cultural and linguistic diversification leading to growing complexity and unpredictability of the way social life is arranged through daily practices; and the global expansion of late capitalism and its associated forms of selective privatisation of public services (Tollefson and Pérez-Milans forthcoming).

In the light of these changes, nation states have had to reposition themselves and adjust the uniform 'one state/one culture/one language' discourses that underpinned the ideological framework of modern nationalism (Anderson 1983; Hobsbawm 1990; Billig 1995; Bauman and Briggs 2003). This is leading to what has been described as an ideological shift from defining languages as bounded/separate entities tied to particular ethno-national communities towards a new emphasis on multilingualism where earlier linguistic ideologies coexist with new discourses in which languages are also seen as technical skills or commodities in the globalised post-industrial/services-based market (Heller 2010; Duchêne and Heller 2012; Codó and Pérez-Milans 2014).

More specifically, this set of institutional, cultural and sociolinguistic changes has been linked to the increasingly fragmented nature of the overlapping and competing identities that are associated with the complexities of language–identity relations and new forms of multilingual language use in contexts of superdiversity. This new panorama is having considerable impact on the social sciences since researchers are shifting their analytical interest away from normative institutional frames of action in fixed space–time locations. These researchers now have greater interest in translocal, transcultural and translingual practices whereby social actors creatively co-construct and negotiate meanings across changing social networks, communicative genres and regional/national boundaries (Blommaert and Rampton 2011; Pennycook 2012; Canagarajah 2013; Márquez Reiter and Martín Rojo 2014).

Linguistic and cultural practices are no longer examined against the background of abstract standard languages, uniform views of speakers and stable group identities. Rather, such practices are investigated with reference to the linguistic repertoires that people acquire, construct and mobilise while positioning themselves and others in ways that have consequences for access to different social spaces (e.g. formal versus informal), symbolic resources (e.g. institutionalised forms of recognition through certificates) and materialities (e.g. jobs) throughout the course of their life trajectories. Indeed, this view has led to the emergence of terms such as 'new speakers' (Pujolar *et al.* 2011), 'transidiomaticity' (Jacquemet 2005), 'polylingualism' (Jørgensen 2008), 'translanguaging' (Garcia 2009) and 'metrolingualism' (Otsuji and Pennycook 2010). Such terms are attempts to describe linguistic practices placed outside the modern ideological framework of the nation state that involve hybrid linguistic repertoires, viewed as encompassing a range of languages, dialects and varieties rather than discrete national languages.

These shifts in focus require an analytical refinement of some of the poststructuralist traditions that became established in the field of applied linguistics in the second half of the twentieth century. This is the case of the socio-critical perspectives in discourse studies in which description of language and identity vis-à-vis wider institutional, socio-political and economic processes of change are often carried out in a 'top-down' fashion. Indeed, such perspectives have been criticised for relying on analytical methods that privilege propositional content of (verbal and written) texts as the empirical foci at the expense of the view of language as social interaction. Another critique is that these perspectives conceptualise context as a set of 'backgrounding facts' that are imposed too rapidly by the researcher onto people's meaning-making practices instead of being viewed as empirically trackable actions, experiences and expectations that are always being enacted and negotiated in situated encounters across space and time (Blommaert and Bulcaen 2000).

The contemporary emphasis on the increasing destabilisation of bounded, stable and consensual communities and identities makes LE even more pertinent as a situated approach to language and identity. Rather than working from presuppositions about fixed mechanisms of power originating in stable and abstract political and economic structures that shape local forms of social life, a combination of linguistic and ethnographic approaches provides a more nuanced angle. In particular, such approaches allow us to document empirically the ways in which social actors negotiate meaning and stance in response to the increasing uncertainty, discontinuity and lack of sharedness that is brought about by the institutional, socio-economic, sociolinguistic and cultural conditions of late modernity.

The importance of analysing local uncertainty and instability so as to capture the wider institutional and socio-economic processes of change tied to late modernity has been particularly evident in linguistic and ethnographic research in educational settings (Rampton 2006; Jaspers 2011; Pérez-Milans 2015). In contrast to views of the classroom as a social space where teachers and students coordinate their actions smoothly and unambiguously, the former acting as the representatives of the institution/state and the latter as social actors who can only resist or comply with the teacher's authority, a close ethnographic and linguistic look has in the last few years revealed a much less continuous, stable and predictable scenario. Contemporary policies require all educational actors to conform to the functioning of a neoliberal management centred upon extensive auditing practices, resulting in increasing anxiety among students and teachers.

In this new cultural setting, teachers no longer represent the authority of the State as their position is not secure and is always under evaluation. Students are made to constantly compete with each other for the available places in higher education, on the basis of mechanisms of testing and streaming that have become key operations for most schools. Thus, interactions among these social actors has emerged as a rich site for examining the dialogic relationship of agency and structure in the context of localised socio-emotional relations. Beyond simplified accounts reporting domination on the part of either the teachers or students, the study of forms of collusion shows how school participants often collaborate with each other in ways that allow them to overcome institutional constraints without necessarily breaking the official rules (see an example of this type of analysis in Pérez-Milans 2013: 88–122).

Thus far, we have seen how late modernity refers to both changes in the 'real' world and a shift of attention in the social sciences. These two dimensions have direct implications for LE's suitability for the study of language and identity in contemporary societies. Given its ontological assumptions (in which social interaction and social structures are seen as mutually constitutive), and given its epistemological approaches (linguistic and ethnographic perspectives are adopted to empirically describe fine-grained situated meaning-making practices), LE allows applied linguists to address instability, differences and mobility as the key elements in the (re)constitution of new ideas/practices about language, culture and community. There are grounds, though, for questioning the apparently autonomous portrayal of LE that has been developed so far in this chapter.

The strengths and possible weaknesses of this approach cannot be properly grasped if other strands of research on language and identity are not brought more clearly into the picture. This is further discussed below, with reference to some of the major issues and ongoing debates around LE.

Issues and ongoing debates

Two issues emerge as particularly important regarding the place of LE with respect to other related areas of research. The first is the self-proclaimed uniqueness of LE vis-à-vis the closely related area of linguistic anthropology (LA, hereafter), and the second involves what I argue is a lack of a political economy approach that still predominates in the field. The following two sections will address each of these issues in detail.

Linguistic ethnography vis-à-vis linguistic anthropology

Among the sub-disciplines that have well-established links with LE, the North American area of LA stands out given its influence in recent publications by UK-based scholars (Rampton *et al.* 2004; Tusting and Maybin 2007; Creese 2008; Maybin and Tusting 2011; Tusting 2013; Rampton *et al.* 2014). Indeed, the traditions that have most clearly shaped the LE epistemological approaches described in the previous sections are all strands of LA (i.e. the ethnography of communication, interactional sociolinguistics and micro-ethnography). Furthermore, LE has drawn heavily on recent theoretical developments in LA that have articulated the relations between 'context' and 'text' and provided technical vocabularies for describing how language use constructs contexts in meaning-making across space and time. Some examples of this technical vocabulary include indexicality, recontextualisation, en-textualisation, multimodality, genre, register and multiple scales.

There has been extensive discussion of the extent to which LE is needed as a new label. Since the UK Linguistic Ethnography Forum was set up in 2001 to propose an umbrella label for scholars across different areas, the label in itself has been recurrently regarded as exploratory. Creese (2008: 238) illustrated this in her account of LE, seven years after this forum was set up:

> It is not yet clear what the future of linguistic ethnography is. In some ways … it already has a long and established history through its connection to LA and other socio and applied linguistic traditions. However, in others, its newness is in the attempt to negotiate and articulate a distinctiveness. As this chapter is written, LE is in the process of negotiating itself into being and its career length and trajectory is not known. The debate about 'what is' and 'what is not' distinctive to linguistic ethnography is of course, like any field of study, an ideologically and interactionally negotiated process.

However, there have been explicit attempts to define the distinctiveness of LE with respect to LA (the most recent in Rampton *et al.* 2014). Compared to LA, LE's uniqueness relies mainly on its different relationship with anthropology. Contrary to the North American context where researchers interested in the study of language, culture and society have been oriented to the anthropological traditions, those with similar interests based in the UK have been socialised into such lines of inquiry within the field of applied linguistics. This, in turn, has had consequences that have set these LE researchers apart, both in the way they approach their objects of study and in how they interact with other disciplines and professionals.

LE researchers have always taken language as an entry point to the study of the interrelations between culture, language and social differences. That is to say, they have placed more emphasis on close analysis of texts and recordings of interactions as primary sites for the playing out and negotiation of socio-economic difference, often with consequences with regard to cultural differentiation. This has also been the case in recent work done in LA. However, in North American anthropology there has been a long-term tendency to emphasise ethnicity and race as the primary categories of social difference, thereby representing cultural difference as the basis of socio-economic inequality. This different approach to the object of study is also evident in research on education as a key site for social, cultural and linguistic analysis.

Different sociocultural theories have emerged since the 1960s, offering explanations of the persistence of school failure among particular social and ethnic groups in modern societies. Among these theories, the study of the interactional processes of socialisation through which different social groups build their cultural conventions of communication occupied a central position in North American anthropology during the twentieth century. From this perspective, school failure is viewed as the consequence of minority groups having to adjust themselves to the cultural conventions of the group(s) controlling the institutional spaces of the State.

This empirical work has been related to the organisation of everyday routines of schooling, which according to this view are based on the cultural conventions and assumptions of the dominant group. In this way, the social construction of students as competent or incompetent depends on the (majority and minority) students' degree of knowledge about these conventions (see e.g. Gumperz 1982; Heath 1983). This stance represented an attempt to overcome previous historical explanations in which the marginalised groups were represented as culturally deficit, although it has often been pointed out that it is necessary to incorporate power relations more explicitly into the processes that cause school failure to be unequally distributed (Meeuwis and Sarangi 1994; Heller and Martin-Jones 2001).

Meanwhile, sociological explanations that had great impact on British applied linguistics (also French and Canadian sociolinguistics) emphasised a different interrelationship between cultural differences and social inequality where the former is not represented as the basis of the latter; rather, it is seen as the consequence in many cases. In other words, cultural difference is problematised and placed at the centre of wider social processes involving economic structures, collective identities and strategies of contestation/cultural reproduction through daily interactions. In this view, formal education is tied to a social structure of unequally distributed economic opportunities, which leads to the situated production and negotiation of differentiated cultural identities and social strategies in the school life, in ways that contribute to reinforcement of class-based societal structures (see e.g. Willis 1977).

Another reason for the influence of applied linguistics in LE, and for the way it has been differentiated from LA, lies in the specific types of interaction that LE researchers have established with other disciplines and professionals. Under university programmes where most research attention is paid to literacy, ethnicity and identity, ideology, classroom discourse and language teaching, LE researchers have intended 'to use discourse analytic tools in creative ways to extend our understanding of the role language plays in social life' (Creese 2008: 235). In so doing, they have developed an eclectic attitude that contrasts with a stronger sense of a well-defined genealogy in LA. In LE, there is room for cross-collaboration among highly diversified traditions, including conversational analysis, new literacy studies, critical discourse analysis, neo-Vygotskian research on language and cognitive development, classroom discourse studies, urban sociology, US linguistic anthropology of education, interpretative applied linguistics for language teaching or studies of ethnicity, language and inequality in education and in the workplace.

Most importantly, LE has devoted a great deal of attention to further extending communication with non-university professionals, in what Rampton et al. (2014: 16) denominate as a 'commitment to practical intervention in real-world processes'. Oriented to enabling educators and health professionals to become LE researchers, on the one hand, and to set up collaborative projects, on the other, this line of action has paved the way to fruitful and meaningful pro-grammes where professionals have a chance to problematise pervasive ideological frameworks that dominate major public policies. The setting up of a collaborative space with educational and health professionals has not only helped to destabilise taken-for-granted assumptions about language, bi/multilingualism and language learning and teaching in these settings but also pro-vided tools for addressing issues related to professional practice.

So far, the discussion has been centred on the distinction between LE and LA. Although this is a simplified account, my goal has been to provide a flavour of the arguments that UK-based researchers have put forward over the last decade about the nature of LE and its interests. Moreover, it is important to note that in line with its original intention of opening up an intel-lectual space where different strands of work can be gathered under the common ground of ethnographic and discourse-based research (Rampton *et al.* 2004), LE has in the last few years expanded to other geographical areas beyond the UK.

Many of the LE researchers based outside the UK have not just taken up the UK-based developments. They are in many cases young scholars who have been trained in a complex mix of disciplinary traditions where the influence of British LE researchers has been combined with that of sociolinguistic and applied linguistic scholars in other European countries and North America via research networks based in universities in Belgium, Cyprus, Denmark, Finland, the Netherlands, Spain or Sweden, among others (for a range of examples published by young scholars based in different European universities see *King's College London Working Papers in Urban Language and Literacies*).

It is now the case that the uncertainty about LE's future, manifest in the statement that 'whether LE will emerge in the macro-socio and applied linguistic "order" as determinant will depend on the interdiscursive possibilities of micro-interactions and their reconfiguration' (Creese 2008: 238), has been overcome given the flourishing body of LE literature. Important issues are likely to arise from the de-territorialisation of LE and there are likely to be dilemmas regarding the ways of ensuring meaningful appropriation, productive hybridisation, recognis-able contribution and legitimate shaping of the area. The following section illustrates the need for a stronger connection with other strands of research on language and identity in applied lin-guistics, for which I draw on my own academic trajectory across different universities in Spain, Canada, the UK and Hong Kong.

Political economy under the spotlight

Although the pioneers of LE in the UK have always pointed out the necessity of connecting with other traditions in sociology, history, cultural studies or economics, most attention to date has been devoted to integrating linguistic analytical constructs from LA. As mentioned in the previous sections, this has entailed meticulous work that has provided a linguistic-based technical vocabulary to describe empirical work that seeks to make links between situated meaning-making practices and translocal discursive processes. Yet, little analytical base has been offered to describe the ways in which such translocal mechanisms effectively contribute to the wider notion of structuration that is often borrowed from Giddens (1982). The appropriation of Bakhtin's (1986) concept of genre in LE is a good example.

Driven by the principle of providing more mid-level theory, Rampton (2006) has argued for the usefulness of genre as it prevents researchers from jumping carelessly into grand narratives that do little justice to the lived situated experience of participants in the field. Broadly defined as recognisable (and usually institutionalised) types of activity linked to specific configurations of expected goals, sequences of action, forms of participation and social relationships among involved participants, this concept allows practitioners of LE to describe social and communicative patterns upon which institutionally recognised activities are reproduced, negotiated or even resisted. In other words, this notion connects 'the larger bearings that orient our moment-to-moment micro-scale actions … [with the] smallest units in the structural organisation of large-scale institutions' (Rampton *et al.* 2014: 9–10).

This type of mid-level theorisation exemplifies the strong orientation of LE to fill the gap between the so-called 'micro' and 'macro' societal levels, though it does not address the fundamental question of how local interactions lead to unequal distribution of resources. Thus, more work is required to deal with this fundamental question, which is at the core of social structuration processes. The area of political economy presents itself as a relevant candidate at this point, and indeed this area has also been very influential in certain strands of North American LA and other European and Asian socio- and applied linguistic traditions (see Gal 1989; Lin and Martin 2005; Heller 2011; Duchêne and Heller 2012). Block, who has recently emphasised the importance of incorporating a political economy approach into applied linguistics more seriously and directly, provides the following definition:

> Political economy is understood here as an area of inquiry and thought with roots in a Marxist critique of classical economics and society in general. It focuses on and analyses the relationship between the individual and society and between the market and the state, and it seeks to understand how social institutions, their activities and capitalism interrelate.
>
> *(2014: 14)*

There have been already substantial theoretical developments regarding the interrelations between the individual and the society and between the market and the state. Some of these well-known developments include the work done by Bourdieu and Foucault, who proposed notions such as 'symbolic capital' (Bourdieu 1982), 'legitimate language' (Bourdieu 1977) and 'power' (Foucault 1984). These notions conceptualise language, culture and identity as 'fields', 'markets' or 'discursive spaces' that are traversed by historical processes of socioeconomic organisation. In other words, language, culture and identity are conceived of as socially and discursively produced resources that are unequally distributed, resulting in people having different degrees of control over the very processes of attribution of value and circulation as well as over their discursive legitimisation.

While such theoretical constructs have been widely acknowledged in sociolinguistic and applied linguistic literature, they are difficult to operationalise analytically in a bottom-up LE. However, Rampton's (2006) call for more mid-level theory in LE can be more fully realised by stretching the analytical scope in order to include, in a more explicit way than is often done, the work done by sociologists, such as Cicourel, who have engaged with wider theories of language, identity and power in close-up description of communicative practice in institutional settings. Indeed, Cicourel's notion of 'ecological validity' (1996), as well as his previous work during the 1960s and 1970s, always dealt with detailed ethno-methodological analysis of recordings without losing sight of the broader context that multi-sited ethnographic research brings into view by placing a given encounter in a wider context of institutional practices, texts and trajectories of interactions and in the social networks that shape it (see also Cicourel 1992).

Anticipating later developments in the social sciences, Cicourel took sociology away from an understanding of the social world as independent of human action, towards the vision of social reality as produced and transformed through social interaction (Cicourel 1964). But beyond doing so, the most relevant contribution of Cicourel (for the purpose of the study of language and identity in LE research) has been his empirical work describing the ways in which normative forms of knowledge (i.e. what counts as appropriate forms of contribution) and categories (i.e. how participants position themselves and others by reference to which institutional types of persona) get constructed and negotiated in daily communicative arrangements discursively (and textually) through the particular organisational logic of a given institution.

Cicourel provides a classical analysis of socio-institutional genres, showing how such genres are connected to a logic of institutional practice that has to be empirically tracked down. This analytical direction also has more socio-economic direction since description of meaning-making practices addresses the fundamental sociological question of 'Who gets to decide what counts, how, when, where and with what socio-institutional consequences for whom?' The link between Cicourel's work, on the one hand, and the wider accounts by Bourdieu and Foucault, on the other, has been developed by Monica Heller in particular (Heller 2007). Heller relies on Cicourel when she calls for an analysis of the web-like trajectories of linguistic, social and moral orders to understand how and why institutional spaces get discursively configured in specific ways. Description of the normative forms of knowledge and categories by Cicourel allows LE researchers to account for the discursive processes whereby situated communicative and linguistic practices produce moral categories about actors, situations, forms of participation, and linguistic and cultural repertoires (i.e. 'good' or 'bad' participant, form of participation and/or language). All of these categories become institutionalised and have social consequences for participants in the course of their interactions (which are describable through interactional analysis) and in these participants' access (or lack of access) to future interactions throughout their individual trajectories in a given institution and beyond (which is describable through ethnographic analysis of the linkages between the different interactions).

In sum, these notions, dimensions and guiding questions constitute a bridge between analysis of local interactions, institutional genres and the abstract sociological concepts of 'symbolic capital', 'legitimate language' or 'power'; they shed light on the processes whereby certain participants and their (linguistic and/or cultural) repertoires get undervalued through a given organisational arrangement that, if followed up through linguistic and ethnographic inquiry, opens up a window on participants' differential access to institutional spaces and on the associated materialities in their life trajectories. In addition, this integrated analysis of linguistic practices, institutionally produced/negotiated moral categories and trajectories of social inclusion/exclusion allows us to trace the emergence and the changing configuration of ideas of identity, nation and State in a given location at a particular point of time in history.

Ethnographically and discourse-based research on educational institutions gives us, once again, an illustrative example. Based on description of practices and institutional forms of social/discursive organisation, the study of who gets constructed as a 'good student' in a given school, within a certain national educational system, is a good case for pinpointing wider ideological discourses about citizenship or moral education that connect regional, national and international policies of economic reform. In my own study in the People's Republic of China, I devoted special attention to show how the arrangement of daily interactions inside and outside the classroom contributed to a definition of the 'good student' in the local context in which the blending of ideas about academic internationalism, Chinese socialism and Asian cultural traditionalism featured as particularly relevant (Pérez-Milans 2013).

To be considered as a 'good student' required having high marks in all academic subjects and also a good performance in moral education activities involving community service, collectivist physical exercises and patriotic events. This analysis provided me with a basis for further historisation, in line with those linguists who have called for more historical approaches in the field (Pujolar 2007). In particular, the ideas on identity, nation and state discursively associated with the emerging moral categories in the schools that I studied are connected with those mobilised in the wider Chinese national policies that have historically shaped the organisational logic of the educational field since the open-doors economic reforms carried out by Deng Xiaoping in the 1980s.

More collaborative work is needed in this direction. While maintaining the key sensitivities that set LE apart from other traditions in linguistic and anthropological disciplines, stretching the analytical scope in order to reach less-explored lines of study (without necessarily sacrificing empirical scrutiny) may be one way (among many) of pushing fertile inter-institutional and international hybridisation in the future.

Summary

This chapter has traced the origins of LE in its geographical, disciplinary and intellectual contexts. Derived from poststructural developments in the social sciences, LE is characterised by specific ethnographic and discourse-based analytical perspectives that have become deeply established in the UK-based tradition of applied linguistics. Closely linked to the work done in the North American area of LA, such an approach is characterised by a linguistically oriented analysis of situated meaning-making practices which are taken as an entry point to exploring wider institutional, sociocultural and ideological processes. In this sense, culture is not a taken-for-granted entity but rather is conceived of as the outcome of processes of social differentiation that are enacted and negotiated (and therefore empirically trackable) in daily interactions.

This sensitivity to fine-grained description of practices makes LE research of particular relevance to the study of language and identity under contemporary conditions of late modernity since it takes account of both intellectual shifts of attention and ongoing transformations in the 'real' world. In particular, LE allows the placing of mobility, instability and uncertainty at the centre of the picture in that bounded notions of language and community are never conceived of as a starting point for data interpretation; instead, these notions are examined as possible emerging constructs that are interactionally constructed, negotiated and transformed by social actors in situated encounters, in the course of large-scale institutional and societal processes.

It has also been argued that while making sense within this specific context, LE is being shaped by researchers with inter-institutional and transnational trajectories, who have been influenced by UK-based advocates of LE and by other scholars based in other linguistic and anthropological traditions across different geographical regions. To conclude, the case for more explicitly socio-economically oriented accounts has been made. I have argued that certain sociological constructs from the field of political economy can be better integrated analytically in LE without necessarily jeopardising the analytical perspectives that set this approach apart from others in applied linguistics.

Related topics

Positioning language and identity: poststructuralist perspectives; Linguistic practices and transnational identities; A linguistic ethnography of identity: adopting a heteroglossic frame; Challenges for language and identity researchers in the collection and transcription of spoken interaction; Beyond the micro–macro interface in language and identity research; An identity transformation? Social class, language prejudice and the erasure of multilingual capital in higher education; Styling and identity in a second language; Exploring neoliberal language, discourses and identities.

Further reading

Copland, F. and Creese, A. (2015). *Linguistic ethnography: collecting, analysing and presenting data.* London: SAGE. (The book includes both philosophical and methodological discussions, and case studies illustrating the themes discussed.)

Linguistic Ethnography Forum [www.lingethnog.org]. (This website offers a wide range of resources, including the foundational history of LE, examples of definitions, and news on LE-related events and publications.)

References

Anderson, B. (1983). *Imagined communities.* London and New York: Verso.

Appadurai, A. (1990). Disjuncture and difference in the global cultural economy, in M. Featherstone (ed.) *Global culture.* London: SAGE, pp. 295–310.

Austin, J. (1962). *How to do things with words.* Oxford: Oxford University Press.

Bakhtin, M. (1986). *Speech genres and other late essays.* Austin, TX: University of Texas Press.

Bauman, R. and Briggs, C. (2003). *Voices of modernity: language ideologies and the politics of inequality.* Cambridge: Cambridge University Press.

Bauman, Z. (1998). *Work, consumerism and the new poor.* Cambridge: Polity Press.

Baxter, J. (this volume). Positioning language and identity: poststructuralist perspectives, in S. Preece (ed.) *The Routledge handbook of language and identity.* London: Routledge, pp. 34–49.

Bernstein, B. (1996). *Pedagogy, symbolic control and identity.* London: Taylor and Francis.

Billig, M. (1995). *Banal nationalism.* London: SAGE.

Block, D. (2014). *Social class in applied linguistics.* New York and London: Routledge.

Blommaert, J. and Bulcaen, C. (2000). 'Critical discourse analysis', *Annual Review of Anthropology*, 29: 447–466.

Blommaert, J. and Rampton, B. (2011). 'Language and superdiversity', *Diversities*, 13(2): 1–23.

Bourdieu, P. (1977). *Outline of a theory of practice.* Cambridge and New York: Cambridge University Press.

Bourdieu, P. (1982). *Ce que parler veut dire. L'économie des échanges linguistiques.* París: Fayard. [Modified translation published as *Language and symbolic power*, J. Thompson (ed.), Cambridge, UK: Polity Press.]

Canagarajah, S. (2013). *Translingual practice: global Englishes and cosmopolitan relations.* New York: Routledge.

Castells, M. (2010). *The information age: economy, society and culture. Vol. 1: the rise of the network society.* 2nd edn. Oxford: Wiley Blackwell.

Cicourel, A.V. (1964). *Method and measurement in sociology.* New York: The Free Press.

Cicourel, A.V. (1992). The interpenetration of communicative contexts: examples from medical encounters, in C. Goodwin and A. Duranti (eds) *Rethinking context: language as an interactive phenomenon.* Cambridge: Cambridge University Press, pp. 291–310.

Cicourel, A.V. (1996). 'Ecological validity and white room effects: the interaction of cognitive and cultural models in the pragmatic analysis of elicited narrative from children', *Pragmatics and Cognition*, 4(2): 221–264.

Codó, E. and Pérez-Milans, M. (2014). 'Multilingual discursive practices and processes of social change in globalizing institutional spaces: a critical ethnographic perspective', *International Journal of Multilingualism*, 11(4): 1–8.

Creese, A. (2008). Linguistic ethnography, in K.A. King and N.H. Hornberger (eds) *Encyclopedia of language and education*. 2nd edn. *Vol. 10: research methods in language and education*. New York: Springer, pp. 229–241.

Duchêne, A. and Heller, M. (eds) (2012). *Language in late capitalism: pride and profit*. New York: Routledge.

Eppler, E.D. and Codó, E. (this volume). Challenges for language and identity researchers in the collection and transcription of spoken interaction, in S. Preece (ed.) *The Routledge handbook of language and identity*. Abingdon: Routledge, pp. 304–319.

Erickson, F. (1992). Ethnographic microanalysis of interaction, in M. LeCompte, W. Millroy and J. Preissle (eds) *The handbook of qualitative research in education*. New York: Academic Press, pp. 201–225.

Foucault, M. (1970). *The order of things: an archaeology of the human sciences*. London: Tavistock.

Foucault, M. (1984). Space, knowledge, and power, in P. Rabinow (ed.) *The Foucault reader*. New York: Pantheon, pp. 239–256.

Gal, S. (1989). 'Language and political economy', *Annual Review of Anthropology*, 18: 345–367.

García, O. (2009). *Bilingual education in the 21st century: a global perspective*. Oxford: Wiley-Blackwell.

Giddens, A. (1982). *The constitution of society*. Berkeley, Los Angeles: University of California Press.

Giddens, A. (1991). *Modernity and self-identity: self and society in the late modern age*. Stanford: Stanford University Press.

Goffman, E. (1981). *Forms of talk*. Philadelphia: University of Pennsylvania Press.

Gumperz, J. (1982). *Discourse strategies*. Cambridge: Cambridge University Press.

Gumperz, J. and Hymes, D. (eds) (1972). *Directions in sociolinguistics: the ethnography of communication*. New York: Holt, Rhinehart and Winston.

Heath, S.B. (1983). *Ways with words*. New York: Cambridge University Press.

Heller, M. (2007). 'Distributed knowledge, distributed power: a sociolinguistics of structuration', *Text and Talk*, 27(5–6): 633–653.

Heller, M. (2010). 'Linguistic commodification', *Annual Review of Anthropology*, 39: 101–114.

Heller, M. (2011). *Paths to post-nationalism: a critical ethnography of language and identity*. Oxford: Oxford University Press.

Heller, M. and Martin-Jones, M. (eds) (2001). *Voices of authority: education and linguistic difference*. Westport, CT, and London: Ablex Publishing.

Hobsbawm, E. (1990). *Nations and nationalism since 1760*. Cambridge: Cambridge University Press.

Hymes, D. (1968). The ethnography of speaking, in J. Fishman (ed.) *Readings in the sociology of language*. The Hague: Mouton, pp. 99–138.

Hymes, D. (1974). *Foundations in sociolinguistics: an ethnographic approach*. Philadelphia: University of Pennsylvania Press.

Irvine, J.T. and Gal, S. (2000). Language ideology and linguistic differentiation, in P.V. Kroskrity (ed.) *Regimes of language*. Santa Fe, NM: School of American Research Press, pp. 35–83.

Jacquemet, M. (2005). The registration interview: restricting refugees' narrative performances, in M. Baynham and A. De Fina (eds) *Dislocations/relocations: narratives of displacement*. Manchester: St Jerome, pp. 197–218.

Jaspers, J. (2011). 'Talking like a "zerolingual": ambiguous linguistic caricatures at an urban secondary school', *Journal of Pragmatics*, 43: 1264–1278.

Jørgensen, J.N. (2008). 'Polylingual languaging around and among children and adolescents', *International Journal of Multilingualism*, 5: 161–176.

King's College London Working Papers in Urban Language and Literacies [Online]. Available at www.kcl.ac.uk/sspp/departments/education/research/ldc/publications/workingpapers/search.aspx

Labov, W. (1972). *Sociolinguistic patterns*. Philadelphia, PA: University of Pennsylvania Press.

Lin, A. and Martin, P. (eds) (2005). *Decolonisation, globalisation: language-in-education policy and practice*. Clevedon: Multilingual Matters.

Márquez Reiter, R. and Martín Rojo, L. (eds) (2014). *A sociolinguistics of diaspora: Latino practices, identities and ideologies*. Abingdon: Routledge, pp. 102–121.

Maybin, J. and Tusting, K. (2011). Linguistic ethnography, in J. Simpson (ed.) *Routledge handbook of applied linguistics*. Abingdon: Routledge, pp. 515–528.

Meeuwis, M. and Sarangi, S. (1994). 'Perspectives on intercultural communication: a critical reading', *Pragmatics*, 4(3): 309–313.

Otsuji, E. and Pennycook, A. (2010). 'Metrolingualism: fixity, fluidity and language in flux', *International Journal of Multilingualism*, 7: 240–254.

Pennycook, A. (2012). *Language and mobility*. London: Multilingual Matters.

Pérez-Milans, M. (2013). *Urban schools and English language education in late modern China: a critical sociolinguistic ethnography*. New York and London: Routledge.

Pérez-Milans, M. (2015). 'Language education policy in late modernity: (socio) linguistic ethnographies in the European Union', *Language Policy*, 14(2): 99–109.

Pratt, M.L. (1987). Linguistic utopias, in N. Fabb, D. Attridge, A. Durant and C. MacCabe (eds) *The linguistics of writing: arguments between language and literature*. Manchester: Manchester University Press, pp. 48–66.

Pujolar, J. (2007). Bilingualism and the nation-state in the post-national era, in M. Heller (ed.) *Bilingualism: a social approach*. London: Palgrave, pp. 71–95.

Pujolar, J., Fernàndez, J. A. and Subirana, J. (2011). 'Llengua, cultura i identitat en l'era global' [Language, culture and identity in the global era], *Journal of DigitHum*, 13: 55–61.

Rampton, B. (2006). *Language in late modernity: interaction in an urban school*. Cambridge: Cambridge University Press.

Rampton, B., Maybin, J. and Roberts, C. (2014). Methodological foundations in linguistic ethnography. *Working Papers in Urban Language and Literacies* (Paper 125), King's College London.

Rampton, B., Tusting, K., Maybin, J., Barwell, R., Creese, A. and Lytra, V. (2004). 'UK linguistic ethnography: a discussion paper' [Online]. Available at www.lingethnog.org/docs/rampton-et-al-2004-uk-linguistic-ethnography-a-discussion-paper

Sacks, H., Schegloff, E. and Jefferson, G. (1974). 'A simplest systematics for the organization of turn-taking for conversation', *Language*, 50: 696–735.

Searle, J. (1969). *Speech acts*. Cambridge: Cambridge University Press.

Silverstein, M. (1976). Shifters, linguistic categories, and cultural description, in K.H. Basso and H.A. Selby (eds), *Meaning in anthropology*. Albuquerque: University of New Mexico Press, pp. 11–56.

Tollefson, J.W. and Pérez-Milans, M. (eds) (forthcoming). *Oxford handbook of language policy and planning*. Oxford: Oxford University Press.

Tusting, K. (2013). 'Literacy studies as linguistic ethnography', *Working Papers in Urban Language and Literacies*, Paper 105, King's College London.

Tusting, K. and Maybin, J. (2007). 'Linguistic ethnography and interdisciplinarity: opening the discussion', *Journal of Sociolinguistics*, 11(5): 575–583.

Willis, P.E. (1977). *Learning to labour: how working class kids get working class jobs*. Aldershot, UK: Gower.

6

Discursive psychology and the production of identity in language practices

Jean McAvoy

Introduction

Discursive psychology speaks directly to the theoretical and practical concerns of contemporary applied linguistics, particularly the concern with the relationship between language and identity. This is because analysis in discursive psychology places a focus explicitly on language practices and what is accomplished in language-in-use. In the context of discursive psychology, identity is understood to be both produced in the moments of talk and a resource used in talk. Identity is thereby situated in the language-in-use in a particular setting. Consequently the discursive psychology of identity is closely aligned with functional linguistics and linguistic ethnography where the analysts' concerns are with communication in context.

Just as applied linguistics frequently looks to sociology for understanding the relationship between language and society, it also looks to psychology, implicitly or explicitly, for insights into the relationship between psychological concepts of mind, brain and language behaviours. The particular focus of a psychologically orientated analysis has considerable relevance for applied linguistics, with its concern for what people do with language and, indeed, what language does with people (Potter and Wetherell 1987; Davies and Harré 1990; Edwards and Potter 1992; Billig 1996). However, applied linguistics can be disposed to imagine and theorise people, albeit sometimes implicitly, as particular kinds of language users who have particular kinds of psychological characteristics, such as emotions, cognitions, expectations and agency (Wetherell 2007). However, these are potentially problematic assumptions. The kind of psychological subject that gets imagined can often be far removed from that proposed in contemporary psychological debate and risks a naivety in its formulation. Consequently, where linguistic analysis makes use of the psychological as an explanatory or even descriptive tool, it should also make explicit the theorisations of the psychological on which it draws. Discursive psychology is particularly well aligned with the interests of applied linguistics to aid this.

Because of its location within the broader discipline of psychology, discursive psychology is attentive to the focus and theoretical nuances of its parent discipline, that is, to topics such as personality, beliefs, attitudes, emotions and, of course, understandings of self, others and relationships. These topics, typical of professional and indeed lay psychology, are core to understanding identity practices and the theorisation of identity. They are also topics that routinely get picked up and employed outside the discipline of psychology. But, they are frequently applied loosely and uncritically. Because discursive psychology understands and interprets these concepts through examination of language practices, it is well placed to offer an understanding of the psychological that fits well with those branches of applied linguistics concerned with language-in-use and implications for understanding the production and enactment of identity.

What discursive psychology affords the applied linguist is an epistemological framework for recognising when 'psychologisation' is being done, that is, when psychological concepts are being drawn on and how the notion of a psychological actor is presumed to infiltrate social action, both in the language-in-use and in the theoretical account of that language-in-use. It allows the applied linguist to recognise the ubiquity and importance of psychological concepts for understanding identity practices. Importantly, what discursive psychology does not do is to claim some special insight into the workings of the mind. Generally, most discursive psychologists explicitly resist claims to saying anything about interiority and what goes on in the head. The orientation is instead to function; that is, to what is accomplished in the language-in-use and, for some discursive psychologists but certainly not all, to what the implications might be for human subjectivity.

Whether discursive psychology is a helpful theoretical and practical approach for an applied linguist investigating language and identity depends on the kind of claims that the linguist might want to make. Discursive psychology is grounded upon a theorisation of language as situated social action and language users as constructed and constituted in language use. As we will see, this has major consequences for understanding how psychological concepts might be applied to analyses of human actors, to theories of the person and to understandings of identity and some of the limits on that application. Discursive psychology is also grounded in a particular set of epistemological commitments, which restrict the analyst's claims to what can be shown in the data, rather than inferred beyond the data. However, the theoretical and epistemological commitments that enable discursive psychology to make such a valuable contribution to the study of human language use also give rise to a particular set of critiques of discursive psychology in regard to the limits of what it can and cannot deliver.

This introduction to contemporary discursive psychology outlines the emergence and development of discursive psychology, and its characteristic features, but also some of the tensions in and around discursive psychology. These issues are discussed in the light of a sample of interview talk discussing body size. This talk is flooded with implicit and explicit psychologisation as it enacts identity in a discussion of weight control. First though, in order to recognise the contribution that discursive psychology might make to the study of language and identity within applied linguistics and to understand the issues at stake, it is important to know something of the history of the discursive turn in psychology. This sets in context what discursive psychology offers applied linguistics and how this is quite a different project to other versions of psychology more typically assumed in applied linguistics.

Overview

Discursive psychology emerged out of two broad movements: anti-positivism developing in the 1960s, which gained purchase in psychology in the 1970s through social constructionist theories, and the 'turn to language' in the 1980s (Gergen 1985; Harré 2001). The concept of anti-positivism is now a familiar one. It is the argument that the social sciences (in the broadest sense) are such different objects of knowledge in comparison to the natural sciences that the positivistic natural science model of experimentation is not an appropriate means to develop understanding of complex and shifting social behaviours. Anti-positivism urged an interrogation of taken-for-granted hegemonic knowledge and a hermeneutic, interpretivist approach to building knowledge about the world (Harré 2001).

The move away from positivism had a particular significance in psychology, which, since its early roots in the late eighteenth century, had precisely pursued a natural science model. The laboratories of Wundt in Germany and Galton in the UK, for instance, were devised to control and measure psychological phenomena. Early psychology sought authority and influence through a natural science model. Even Freud (1950 [1895]), the founder of psychoanalysis with its emphasis on the largely inaccessible unconscious motivations behind behaviour, maintained the ambition that psychoanalysis would be a scientific project. Many university psychology departments pursued an almost exclusively positivist paradigm. Indeed, many continue to do so today. Against this backdrop, the development of anti-positivism was not simply a way of opening up new ways of understanding behaviour; it was an attack on much that had been accomplished in psychology. Hence some of the bitter debate that has flowed throughout psychology. Nevertheless, it is often this positivist reading of the psychological that is imported into applied linguistics through the narratives of neuroscience and cognitive processing systems.

Coming out of anti-positivism, the articulation of social constructionist theory had profound implications for psychology in general and social psychology in particular. Social constructionism urged a rethink of the apparently 'essential' qualities of being human, qualities such as gender, emotions and even the notion of being a unitary, bounded individual. Instead, a social constructionist stance held that:

> The terms in which the world is understood are social artifacts, products of historically situated interchanges among people. From the constructionist position the process of understanding is not automatically driven by forces of nature, but is the result of an active, cooperative enterprise of persons in relationship.
>
> *(Gergen 1985: 267)*

From this perspective, the notion of an individual, with internal, agentic, autonomous thoughts, feelings and desires, is also a social artefact. In the light of this argument it followed that the processes of this 'enterprise of persons in relationship' should become a primary site for investigation. Moreover, given the centrality of language to people's cooperative enterprises, language and how it produces social artefacts such as 'identity' becomes a focal point for this inquiry.

The antagonism from social constructionist theory to claims that objective knowledge of the world is possible provided an impetus for the development of reflexive, qualitative subjective methods. But, qualitative methods were, and still are, heavily dependent on the use of language data, particularly interview-based methods of data production. While anti-positivism encouraged a commitment to prioritising the voice of the research participants, social constructionism problematised what could be derived from such data. The assumption inherent in wanting to prioritise participants' voices tended to be that people were both willing and able to report accurately on their own behaviours, processes, thoughts, feelings and motivations. The turn to language in the 1980s brought a much-needed critical edge to this assumption and challenged the idea that what people say can be taken to be a straightforward, representational route to some other topic of study such as thoughts, feelings, experience and so on (Wetherell 2007). Rather, language could be better theorised as social action. Language was understood to construct social worlds, including the people within those worlds and, moreover, their understandings of themselves and others. What people did with language, and how it was used and what was accomplished in its use, became the topic of study. This move away from imagining language as neutral, to understanding it as constitutive, also led to a move away from understanding identity as something personally held, something which was internal and simply expressed in language and other practices, to something socially, intersubjectively produced. This also implied that, if the individual was no longer considered the source of identity, then identity must be explored within language practices instead. With this came new questions about how to theorise and analyse speech, speakers and those spoken about and to. And with this, a new rigour in analysing the discursive was called for.

Discursive psychology grew directly out of this intellectual trajectory, drawing on, among others, Wittgenstein (1953/2001), Goffman (1957), Sacks (1992) and a particularly influential analysis by Gilbert and Mulkay (1984) exploring the way scientists used particular patterns of talk to claim expertise and assert scientific authority and scientific identity. There are distinct and contested accounts of the emergence of discursive psychology that followed (e.g. Wetherell 2007; Kent and Potter 2014); these are further entangled by the wide range of different discourse analytic approaches used in psychology. But, one key moment in the development came in the groundbreaking text by Potter and Wetherell (1987) that outlined the argument that what people say is social business and not neutral representations of internal cognitions. Whereas psychology had traditionally taken such things as attitudes, opinions, beliefs and so on as evidence of internal cognitions, this new approach treated these quite differently, as situated, versioned, social accomplishments constructing people in unavoidably non-neutral ways. This interpretation of language as action and not by-product of independent cognitions became the foundation for the development of discursive psychology. The term itself was coined by Edwards and Potter (1992), who explicitly positioned discursive psychology as an oppositional argument to cognitivist information-processing models of language and language users. For applied linguistics then, discursive psychology is explicitly an alternative to the cognitive science models more typically, but not uncontroversially, taken up in SLA, for example.

As discursive psychology began to develop, it diverged into two quite different styles (Wetherell 2007): a micro level of analysis influenced by conversation analysis, focusing on immediate talk and participants' orientations to that talk (see Benwell and Stokoe, this volume), and a macro analysis, sometimes referred to as critical discursive psychology (see Horner and Bellamy, this volume), which added a broader focus, incorporating, for example, analyses of ideologies reproduced in talk. While these two strands have sometimes found themselves at odds with each other (Wetherell 2007; Potter 2010; Kent and Potter 2014), they shared a common project. Both brought close critical attention to the ways the psychological is recruited by speakers to achieve particular kinds of interactional business. Of central concern, for instance, are the ways in which concepts such as remembering and forgetting, and rationality and emotion, are presented in talk. Deploying these kinds of psychological attributes in talk constructs people as certain kinds of individuals possessing certain kinds of psychological qualities and characteristics and capacities and interiorities. This is not to say that discursive psychology concerns itself with 'actual' interiorities. Rather, it is concerned with what gets done when such constructs are deployed. The nature of this project is best summarised by Wetherell:

> Discursive psychologists study discourse as a practical, social activity, located in settings, occurring between people and used in practices. We usually take discursive practices, rather than the individual, as our unit of analysis. And, because we are psychologists, we are interested in studying how people do psychological things – emotions, memory, gender,

identity, knowledge – in talk and texts, as discourse. Some of us are also arguing that the way in which the psychological is organised in discourse is not inconsequential. Rather, these practices are profoundly constitutive of people's subjectivity, of the possibilities for being human and for being a social actor.

(Wetherell 2007: 665)

So, while Wetherell makes it clear that discursive psychology is a psychological project, she brings into focus an important quality of discursive psychology. It is the situated, interactional, discursive practice that is the unit of analysis, not the individual. This is because the theory of the human actor underpinning discursive psychology is of a speaker situated in a particular activity, recruiting socially available, intersubjective, discursive resources. The practices on show are co-produced, by virtue of being located in a social world. They are not theorised as personal, individualised productions. Consequently, they are not explored as individualised productions, but as a particular jointly produced practice. In the process of joining in with these socially available discursive resources, speakers are constituted as particular kinds of persons. This argument, that speakers and identity are produced *in* the talk, has led to a criticism that discursive psychology proposes an 'empty vessel' model of the person: that there is no interiority, no personal continuity, no personal order. This is a fundamental misunderstanding. Discursive psychology, in its most extreme formulation, is agnostic as to interiority – not in denial. The argument is that language-in-use accomplishes social business; but that it is not a pathway to study internal states. Identity resides in practices, it is maintained, challenged or reinvented in practices, and it is made relevant and recognisable in practices. It is in this sense that identity resides in language practices and not 'in the head'. This is not an argument that there is nothing 'in the head'. But that what is externalised does not seamlessly map on to some internalised independent structure.

The shift in perspective from internal, individualised processes to social business can be illustrated by looking at a short extract of material. This fragment comes from a series of interviews in which I asked women in mid-life what they considered to be markers of success and failure for women of their age in contemporary society. The project assumed a socially constituted subject, one constructed and maintained in ongoing practices of neoliberal, accountable self-making (see McAvoy 2009). Typically, participants negotiated complex identities which embraced, resisted and troubled the processes of inhabiting contemporary feminine subjectivities. I have discussed a section of this particular extract elsewhere to draw out an analytic approach synthesising discourse, ideology and affect (McAvoy 2015). Here, I will be focusing on a discursive psychology reading of the extract in order to foreground the local, situated, interactional production of identity and the way in which psychological concerns construct identities in particular ways.

Prior to this segment, the interview had ranged across topics such as family, relationships, career, money and material possessions. At the point where this exchange occurs, the participant Sally (a pseudonym) had been describing the importance to her of home and material possessions for her sense of self. She goes on to introduce the topic of weight, which, she explained, had been a difficult issue for her to deal with. (See Appendix for transcription conventions.)

Extract 1

1 Sally   I mean (.) I really pride myself in (.) y'know nice things and (.)
2 Jean   mm
3 Sally   strive (.) for more (.)

4	Jean	mm
5	Sally	and this is where the money comes into it you see (.) if I was earning
6		more (.) I could spend more (.) I could buy more expensive things (.) or
7		whatever (.) they're all material (.) things I think (.)
8	Jean	mm
9	Sally	but they're things that I I felt that (.) I lacked (.)
10	Jean	er like what
11	Sally	so (.) that was the thing (.) y'know because I didn't like myself that I don't
12		think anybody else (.)
13	Jean	right
14	Sally	necessarily (.) would like me
15	Jean	yeah
16	Sally	d'y'know what I mean I'm very conscious of being fatter (.) now and (.) it
17		it's an absolute (.) erm (.) I make fun of myself d'y'know what I mean
18		and
19	Jean	yeah
20	Sally	er (.) try and laugh it off and and do an' and (.) ((—)) I'm going
21		<you see> ((*gestures towards face as eyes fill with tears*)) I'm going to
22		get emotional now (.) because I really it's y'know it it's erm (.) for me (.)
23		it's a really big thing (.) it is (.) and I think that because (.) I have other
24		things that I am able to control (.) but I can't control my eating (.)
25	Jean	right
26	Sally	and that for me is a real disappointment (.) it is (.) erm (.) y'know I try
27		and (.) y'know whether it be keeping my house in order or whatever else
28		(.) erm (.) and that's why I feel a failure (.) because I'm I allow myself to
29		overeat (.)
30	Jean	right
31	Sally	and I allow myself to put this weight on (.) I do (.)

This is an interesting bit of material for making sense of discursive psychology. On the one hand, this fragment is packed with concepts that have immediate relevance to traditional psychological interests. For example, one could approach this talk from a cognitive psychology perspective by discussing how Sally *rationalises* her current understanding of her weight, explains her *thought processes*, her concern that people would not like her and her explanation of her *internal states* of disappointment and feeling a failure. We might look at how she *attributes* cause for her weight – she places the locus of control entirely within herself and her inability to control her eating. If a researcher was influenced by psychoanalytic psychology they might consider the inner *unconscious tensions* that prevent Sally from achieving her stated desire to control her weight. If a researcher brought a phenomenological psychology interpretation to this data they might begin by looking at Sally's report of her *experience* of herself in her lifeworld. Psychologists interested in *personality* might approach this data as evidence of an internal set of *characteristics* and *dispositions* revealed in the utterances made. Clearly I have glossed what these approaches might make of this data and it is not the intention to imply that detailed careful analysis would not take place. But, what these approaches (or the gloss that I have provided here) have in common is an assumption that the words speakers use reflect some internal, individualised, agentic and actual state of mind (and body).

Discursive psychology makes a different set of assumptions. First is the epistemological commitment that it must focus on what can be seen in the language-in-use, as it is deployed in interaction, rather than what the language might supposedly tell us about other, internal, in-the-head processes of an individual speaker. Second is the assumption that language-in-use accomplishes social business in that it constructs and reproduces social worlds, including the identities that can be worked up. Third is a recognition of the interactional intersubjective situated and versioned qualities of language-in-use. Fourth, and finally, is the particular interest discursive psychology brings to those aspects of talk in which the psychological becomes relevant. So with these assumptions in mind, what might a discursive psychology make of this extract in terms of understanding the relationship between language and identity?

Crucially, there is not just one identity being worked up here. For a start, there are two speakers who are both taking up particular speaking positions: Sally as the interviewee and me, Jean, the interviewer. In discursive psychology I can make this *analytic* claim to a particular position not because I am an insider to the interview and have privileged knowledge, but because these positions are apparent in the question and answer format of the exchange. Sally is the one to hold the floor, to give information to me; I take up the position of receptive listener. But, of course, in this site, a research interview, there is considerable power in the position of interviewer who directs the subject of the talk, despite appearing to give ground to the interviewee. Beyond the position of interviewee though, what is jointly constructed within this situated moment is a multifaceted identity for Sally: one that is both psychological and material; a self-aware, reflective, responsible being, with physical, visceral qualities. The speakers achieve this together. When Sally speaks of 'pride' (line 1) and says 'I'm very conscious' (of being fatter now) (line 16), this invokes a set of psychological qualities including affective self-knowing. Moreover, signalling self-knowledge leads the speaker to take a position on that knowledge: to explain her response to that knowledge; which is to 'make fun of' herself (line 17), to 'try and laugh it off' (line 20). What is worked up here is not just the idea that a person is self-aware, but also that being a self involves at least some agentic capacity for, and expectation of, self-management. The notion of the responsible agent is reinforced through the concept of control: 'I have other things that I am able to control (.) but I can't control my eating' (lines 23–24). Furthermore, 'I allow myself to overeat' (lines 28–29) reinforces the speaker as a being who is responsible for the physical, bodily self and one who is in possession of the wherewithal to change it: Sally, in this construction, *allows* this to happen.

The repetition of 'y'know' is informative here. It appears several times, but is repeated more emphatically as 'd'y'know what I mean' (line 16 and again in line 17). This is a typical way of inviting acknowledgement and I responded affirmatively: 'yeah' (line 19). What particular statements my 'yeah' is affirming is ambiguous, but it works to allow Sally to continue. In so doing it facilitates and colludes in the production of Sally as a particular kind of person; one in possession of certain psychological and indeed bodily qualities. Note that there is no resistance to this formation from me, Jean, in my interviewer role. It may not be an enthusiastic endorsement, but it nevertheless allows this construction to stand. It is tempting for me to offer here an explanation of what I was thinking at this point and what additional analysis I might provide with the benefit of an insider perspective on this interview. But that is precisely what discursive psychology does not do. Where the focus of attention is on the language-in-use, a discursive psychology approach maintains that I am no more in a position to claim special privileged knowledge of what lies behind a response I have made any more than to claim knowledge of what lies behind Sally's responses. Rather, the task is to show in the interactional sequence how this talk unfolds and what it constructs in the process. It is core to the principles of discursive psychology, and the conversation analytic technology on which it draws, that it is the speakers' interactional orientations in talk which warrant the analysts' claims (Benwell and Stokoe, this volume). If an analyst wants to argue, for example, that body weight is a significant and consequential issue, that must be because it is visible in the interaction. It must be the speakers who orientate to importance, not the analyst who decides weight is important. However, when weight is clearly made important, as it is here, the scholarly analysis that Wetherell (1998) and Billig (1999a, 1999b) speak of may follow (see e.g. Bordo 1993; McAvoy 2015). This is not without controversy though, and I will come back to this below.

I said above that this talk of the body brings the material, the physical, into being. It constructs a particular kind of body in this instance, one held deficient. This bodily deficiency is produced in the extract in numerous ways, central to which is the construction of psychological qualities. It is the psychology that is invoked here that signals that the 'fatter' body is a deficient one. Making fun of the self and trying to laugh it off are presented as appropriate things to do in the face of being fatter, and my 'yeah' supports Sally's orientation to this. These are behavioural responses in that they are (reports of) action. But they are also psychologised responses, in that they are mobilised as activities to undertake to manage not just the body, but the psychological responses to the body: the self-awareness of its physical properties. Moreover, the cause of these physical properties are laid at the door of the psychological: failed self-control, allowing the self to overeat – an act which is clearly orientated to as unacceptable. These are qualities which bring into focus further psychological qualities of disappointment, not simply disappointment in the body, but disappointment in the psychologised self, a self that allows this to happen.

There is another notable element in this extract that arrests attention and that is the presence of emotion, both as something referred to and on display. One of the common criticisms of discursive psychology is that, because it refuses to speculate on interiorities, it fails to address emotion and experience (e.g. Frosh 1999). This has certainly been a fair point: discursive psychology has been rigorous about not assuming in-the-head states that cannot be pointed to empirically. However, this does not mean that discursive psychology is oblivious to any concept of emotion (see e.g. Edwards 1999). This extract is flooded with the talk of, and the doing of, emotion, and moreover the significance of emotion in constructing identities. Emotion is brought to bear on what is constructed; this concept of being fatter is something that – in this sequence – is accompanied by this emotion; it constructs a person experiencing emotion in the moment. The gestures and the tears that accompany indexical utterances such as 'I'm going <you see>' and 'I'm going to get emotional now' (lines 20–22) are made significant in the interaction. Further, they are orientated to as requiring explanation: 'for me (.) it's a really big thing' (lines 22–23) *accounts* for the emotion on show. The 'for me' constructs the particular importance this holds for Sally and indeed contributes to making Sally an autonomous person with her own take on being fatter, her own experience of what it means to be fatter.

This talk has constructed an identity for Sally as a psychologised, responsibilised, autonomous, agentic, thinking, feeling and material being, with a body that is fatter (than an unstated standard) and thereby potentially unlikeable; a being who is consciously aware, a being distressed and disturbed by her size, but a being who makes an attempt to manage that distress; a being that exercises physical and psychological control over some things, but not others, who takes entirely to herself the responsibility of her body size, presented as a failure of the self in terms of control (again, the psychological). This is a person who castigates herself for not controlling her eating and yet at the same time does claim control over her eating in that she allows it – she permits this to happen. Overall, what is constructed in this talk is a person who holds herself entirely responsible for who and what she is, both bodily and psychologically and the 'failings' it signifies. This is constituted and enacted as emotionally burdensome; a thing engendering distress. Note that this does not originate with Sally; it is not (ontologically) Sally who burdens herself with her own self-evaluations; but the resources which she mobilises in the construction of herself both to herself and to/with her interlocutor. This identity emerges from the language-in-use, not from the material qualities of the body. What is constructed here is a way of doing being fatter: disliking the (fatter) self, being disappointed by the (fatter) self, feeling responsible for the (fatter) self and feeling a failure on managing the (fatter) self.

This brief illustration allows us to point to what is made relevant for speakers, a psychological identity as well as a physical material identity, without us making arbitrary leaps to what else, or what also, may be happening in some internalised space in the head to which we do not have unmediated access. It draws out a number of possible strands that a discursive psychology analysis might attend to and develop in this kind of data. But, it also lends itself to illustrating some of the tensions that arise out of different ways of conducting discursive psychology. In the next section I will explore some of the contested positions within and around discursive psychology.

Issues and ongoing debates

Discursive psychology is a contested site both in relation to the range of possible ways of conducting discourse analyses (see Benwell and Stokoe, this volume; Zotzmann and O'Regan, this volume) and because of the perceived constraints on what it can or cannot deliver for theorising psychological phenomena and what falls outside of its capacities or elective foci. The extensive (and sometimes hostile) debates in psychology in general about how research should be conducted have led to accusations in the discipline of 'methodolatry', that is, an extreme preoccupation with method over topic (Curt 1994). This preoccupation is as evident in the contests around discursive psychology as in any other branch of psychology. The debates are both epistemological in nature and ontological, in that they are concerned with how knowledge can be claimed and what can be known. But, these are not simply debates about method: they are debates about what this sub-discipline of discursive psychology purports to be studying – whether it is offering a theory of language, or a theory of what it is to be a person. This is a question that is raised both within discursive psychology and from outside.

The debates from within discursive psychology tend to focus on how to maintain an epistemological commitment to building knowledge claims based on what can be shown in the data and avoiding making inferences that go beyond the data, particularly about internal psychological states and processes such as intentions and motivations. In other words, one should not claim that speakers have a particular set of concerns, unless those concerns are made explicit in the talk. Even then, one cannot claim that talk of these concerns demonstrates an 'in-the-head' concern on the part of the speakers. Rather, that the speakers organise their talk in such a way that constructs something as a concern, as something that one should be concerned about. This is a question of the pre-eminence of participants' orientations and to what extent analysts' orientations must be reined in.

For those discursive psychologists influenced strongly by a conversation analytic approach, focusing on members' categories – that is, only those categories invoked by the participants – makes up the legitimate components of an analysis. Researchers should avoid importing their own orientations. Those analysts influenced by critical discourse analysis, for instance (see Zotzmann and O'Regan, this volume), will want, as part of their analysis, to situate the participants' utterances in the broader cultural, ideological context. This debate is explicated in a short series of papers by Schegloff (1997, 1999a, 1999b), Wetherell (1998) and Billig (1999a, 1999b). At the heart of the debate is what one can do as an analyst with one's own local, cultural knowledge; whether one should seek to bracket out what one knows about the culture and context of utterances. For Schegloff, a rigorous analysis must not import the analysts' categories as relevant to the talk, categories such as gender in relation to the above extract perhaps, unless speakers can be shown doing so themselves in the talk. Billig and Wetherell argue that analysts should aim for a scholarly analysis which makes use of their cultural knowledge, rather than pretending to not know what they know. In this latter argument, an analyst's knowledge of the pervasive moralised discourse of overweightness prevalent in Sally's culture and particularly an issue for women (Bordo 1993; McAvoy 2015) is a legitimate referent for making sense of what is happening. For some discursive psychology analysts this goes too far because it risks too free an interpretation – the imposition of the analyst's concerns rather than the explication of participants' concerns.

The issue of whose categories are being privileged underpins a second debate, one around the use of researcher-led interview-generated data, in contrast to naturally occurring data. For Kent and Potter (2014), this issue of focusing on naturally occurring data, such as child telephone helplines, or even what they describe as 'naturalistic' data, such as recorded family mealtimes, as opposed to interview data got-up for the research, is central to contemporary discursive psychology. Indeed, they go so far as to say that this is what marks out the distinction between earlier work in discourse analysis in psychology, which frequently drew on interviews and the tradition that developed in the 1990s. However, this overstates the case. It may be an ideal that discursive psychology uses naturally occurring data. But much work firmly identifying itself as discursive psychology has been conducted using interview data. The differences between naturally occurring data and interview data do matter insofar as the site, the context and the interaction are shaped by the event in question. But, that one is discursive psychology and one is not discursive psychology is not coherent. This is because both forms of material are theorised as, and approachable as, situated, contingent, social action. Both assume social worlds are constructed in particular ways in discursive practices. Both recognise that language use is variable. Both are concerned with social business that takes place, with the meaning-making made possible, with the co-production in interaction and with the recruitment of psychological concepts that (re)produce speakers as beings with particular kinds of inner lives and inner processes. However, following Kent and Potter's argument, the interview data in the extract above would have questionable legitimacy (see also Potter and Hepburn 2005). The complaint, in brief, is that if discursive psychology is committed to understanding the situated social business of talk, then it should study what people do in actual real-world sites and situations that would occur anyway regardless of the research. To study talk generated in researcher-led interviews, where people are taken out of real-world sites of interest into made-for-research sites, is to study the wrong object of knowledge. The counter-argument is that interview talk is worth studying because it reproduces the culturally available discursive resources for making sense of particular meaning-making moments. In the extract above, for instance, this talk is a product of a social sciences research interview and both speakers orientate to it in that way. We cannot say that this precise talk would occur in other situations, but the discursive resources deployed here are drawn from prior encounters with the social world; the topic is comprehensible to both speakers and the conversation unfolds in a way that is understandable.

This chapter has been careful to insist that discursive psychology cannot go beyond language-in-use to infer internal in-the-head processes. Unfortunately, this is often misinterpreted and it is all too frequently claimed that discursive psychologists somehow do not believe there is anything going on in the head. This is nonsense. It is not a position maintained in discursive psychology. People do indeed have rich inner lives populated with internal reflexive meaning-making, influenced by conscious and unconscious motivations and harbouring personal investments and commitments. However, the position that is generally held by discursive psychologists is that what is said and done in interaction cannot be treated as a simple representation of internal thoughts and/or cognitive processes. This is not to suggest there are no such things as thoughts, simply that we have no reason to be confident that the words people use on a topic at any one moment will seamlessly match any of the diverse and changing thoughts and beliefs that a speaker might hold in the head about that topic at any other particular moment.

This does not mean that discursive psychology can say nothing of an ontological quality about thinking. Billig (1996) points out that when people are talking all the words and phrases that are deployed and the concepts that are worked up – the things we do have direct access to – are precisely the tools and resources of thinking. So, when people are using language, these are also the words and concepts people have available for thinking. Consequently, we might not be able to say what people are thinking, but we can say something about the tools – the words, the patterns of talk – that they have available for thinking. Contrast this with the sociocognitive critical discourse analysis of Teun van Dijk (2009), for instance, for whom internal cognitive processes are an essential mediator of the social and the ideological and are therefore an essential component of a discursive model of the subject. For van Dijk, a theory of language as social action must also encompass a set of theories about internal cognitive processes. For discursive psychologists the leap to proposing particular models of interiority is too big a leap. It is an epistemological strength of discursive psychology that it avoids claims to knowing what is in the head, not an ontological claim that there is nothing to know.

However, an extension of this debate is the critique that this epistemological commitment means discursive psychology struggles to contribute to core aspects of human psychology. Much has been written about the way in which discursive psychology needs to find a means to say something more about the processes of self-making and ontology of the self – in other words, to say something about subjectivity, interiority, personal history, the body, affectivity and so on – and how these interact with language and meaning-making. One core aspect of selfhood which gives rise to criticisms of discursive psychology is the quality of 'continuity'. Any study of identity must take seriously the issue of continuity simply because the *construct* of ongoing identity is a consequential one in human social relations. Following the social constructionist antecedents, discursive psychologists tend to suggest that the self is made in the fragmented moments of situated and contingent utterances. That premise might be taken to mean that there is no personal continuity, that discursive psychology cannot, or will not, say anything about personal continuity. But people are clearly located in meaning-making histories. In the extract, Sally's talk of being fatter, of trying to laugh it off, does not come from nowhere. These are mobilisations that Sally has at her disposal. Clearly they have come from somewhere, from some personalised discursive history. Her talk is embedded in a longer set of conversations that precede this conversation in some way. Previous moments of *something* are available to be carried into this exchange now. Wetherell talks about this process as one of personal order, meaning that '[o]ver time particular routines, repetitions, procedures and modes of practice build up to form personal style, psycho-biography and life history and become a guide for how to go on in the present' (Wetherell 2007: 668). In effect, just as social action takes place in sites and institutions, people are their own site, in interaction with others, around which meanings accrue. This interpretation lends itself to extension into a notion of interpersonal, intersubjective order, further repeating patterns of behaviours between subjects who share some history, the kinds of habits of engagement that occur in families, for instance (McAvoy 2009). Personal order and interpersonal order go some way to explaining the ordinary, mundane experience we have of ourselves as individuals existing through time as continuous ongoing coherent selves. It is ordinary and common, but nevertheless made up of many moments of repeating patterns in discursive deployments.

A further challenge to the capacities of discursive psychology has come from the criticism that it fetishises language, prioritising it above all else. This criticism is not unfounded. It is a commonly held view among discourse analysts working in a social constructionist tradition that discourse does indeed mediate all of our engagements with the world. So while on the one hand the accusation is fair, recent developments indicate that discursive psychology could go beyond its roots to engage more fruitfully with the body, the material and the affective (Wetherell 2012; McAvoy 2015). Other future directions also beckon, in terms of site epistemology and ontology. For Kent and Potter (2014), the focus is on site and the potential to move into an expanding field, developing areas of study such as online social media and the construction there of authentic identity. For Wetherell (2012), the challenge to discursive psychology is perhaps greater in that she suggests the next step is to take the analytic insights and resources from discursive psychology into new areas and in particular to the study of affective practices which currently are under-theorised and lack empirical explication. Wetherell argues that the challenge for discursive psychology is to maintain a rigorous attention to the practices that make up social life, while at the same time looking at new areas of analysis that have thus far been considered beyond the scope of discursive psychology, such as affective-discursive practice (Wetherell 2012; see also McAvoy 2015). Whether this means staying within the orthodoxy of discursive psychology, or moving on, is a debate now unfolding.

Summary

The shared agenda for discursive psychology and applied linguistics in the study of identity is extensive. Both recognise that identity is not solely a practice in the sphere of the personal or private, but flows through relational and institutional practices, shaping the way persons in those settings are categorised and the way in which resources are mobilised or constrained accordingly. Both focus on language-in-use, in context, acknowledging that the situated and the contingent is relevant to how speakers orientate to and make sense of encounters. The distinctive contribution that applied linguistics can take from discursive psychology is to interrogate more closely the deployment in such practices of the psychological. Speakers employ psychological concepts to work up particular kinds of identity, for selves and others, such as the thinking, feeling, rational, self-aware person and the emotional, out-of-control other. But, this does not reflect seamlessly onto psychological processes or ontologies. Psychological constructs accomplish social business in these deployments. Discursive psychology draws attention to the taken-for-granted qualities of the person that might be assumed in this process, by speakers, by interlocutors and by analysts. Primary among these is the concept of the person behind the utterance and the psychological qualities supposed to reside therein. What discursive psychology seeks to show is that the psychological concepts are made relevant for social business, including the social business of identity making; but that the individual and the internal cannot be held to be the site of those concepts-in-action. Rather, the psychological, that apparently most 'internal facing' of the human science disciplines, is actually situated and produced, variably and contingently, in the social, intersubjective world. Discursive psychology pays attention to how psychological attributes are worked up and the kinds of inescapably psychologised identities that are thereby produced and which are so ubiquitous as to be almost unremarkable. For the applied linguist studying identity this approach provides a useful alert. What are the psychological and psychologised assumptions in play? What are the consequences for identity of imagining such psychologies? Moreover, if the psychological constructs being imagined are contested within psychology and they are, there is a strong argument for caution about seamlessly importing them into applied linguistics. In essence, a discursive psychology allows the analyst to recognise the prevalence of the psychological in identity construction and performance, without having to favour one version of interiority over another. Moreover, it means that the analyst informed by discursive psychology can maintain an ethically sound agnosticism about different versions of interiority while exploring the use and implications of the psychological for identity practices.

Related topics

Positioning language and identity: poststructuralist perspectives; Ethnomethodological and conversation analytic approaches to identity; Language and identity in linguistic ethnography; Critical discourse analysis and identity; Challenges for language and identity researchers in the collection and transcription of spoken interaction; Beyond the micro–macro interface in language and identity research; Being a language teacher in the content classroom: teacher identity and content and language integrated learning (CLIL); Disability identities and category work in institutional practices: the case of a 'typical ADHD girl'; The future of identity research: impact and new developments in sociolinguistics.

Further reading

Edwards, D. and Potter, J. (1992). *Discursive psychology*. London: SAGE. (This text outlines the way in which analysing talk and text as social action generates a radical rethinking of key concepts from psychology.)

Gergen, K.J. (1985). 'The social constructionist movement in modern psychology', *American Psychologist*, 40(3): 266–275. (Gergen outlines the move from 'old paradigm' positivist psychology, where language is a neutral cognitive phenomenon, to a social constructionist understanding of psychology, which sees language as producing that of which it speaks.)

Potter, J. and Wetherell, M. (1987). *Discourse and social psychology: beyond attitudes and behaviour*. London: SAGE. (This is the foundational text in psychology which introduced and explicated the notion of language as non-neutral social action. It has often been read as a 'methods' text, but it also provides a theoretical basis for understanding language as constitutive social action rather than a neutral representation of inner cognitive processes.)

Taylor, S. (2013). *What is discourse analysis?* London: Bloomsbury. (An excellent introductory text outlining some of the different traditions in discourse analysis. It is suitable for an interdisciplinary audience but also explains the particular significance of discourse analyses in psychology.)

References

Benwell, B. and Stokoe, E. (this volume). Ethnomethodological and conversation analytic approaches to identity, in S. Preece (ed.) *The Routledge handbook of language and identity*. Abingdon: Routledge, pp. 66–82.

Billig, M. (1996). *Arguing and thinking: a rhetorical approach to social psychology*. 2nd edn. Cambridge: Cambridge University Press and Maison des Sciences de l'Homme.

Billig, M. (1999a). 'Whose terms? Whose ordinariness? Rhetoric and ideology in conversation analysis', *Discourse and Society*, 10(4): 543–558.

Billig, M. (1999b). 'Conversation analysis and the claims of naivety', *Discourse and Society*, 10(4): 572–576.

Bordo, S. (1993). *Unbearable weight: feminism, Western culture, and the body*. Berkeley, CA: University of California Press.

Curt, B.C. (1994). *Textuality and tectonics: troubling social and psychological science*. Buckingham: Open University Press.

Davies, B. and Harré, R. (1990). 'Positioning: the discursive production of selves', *Journal of the Theory of Social Behaviour*, 20: 43–65.

Edwards, D. (1999). 'Emotion discourse', *Culture and Psychology*, 5(3): 271–291.

Edwards, D. and Potter, J. (1992). *Discursive psychology*. London: SAGE.

Freud, S. (1950 [1895]). *The complete psychological works of Sigmund Freud, Vol. 1 (1886–1899), Pre-psycho-analytic publications and unpublished drafts*. London: Hogarth Press, 1966.

Frosh, S. (1999). 'What is outside discourse?', *Psychoanalytic Studies*, 1(4): 381–390.

Gergen, K.J. (1985). 'The social constructionist movement in modern psychology', *American Psychologist*, 40(3): 266–275.

Gilbert, N. and Mulkay, M. (1984). *Opening up Pandora's box*. Cambridge: Cambridge University Press.

Goffman, E. (1957). *The presentation of self in everyday life*. New York: Doubleday.

Harré, R. (2001). The discursive turn in social psychology, in D. Schiffrin, D. Tannen and H.E. Hamilton (eds) *The handbook of discourse analysis*. Oxford: Blackwell Publishers Ltd, pp. 688–706.

Horner, K. and Bellamy, J. (this volume). Beyond the micro–macro interface in language and identity research, in S. Preece (ed.) *The Routledge handbook of language and identity*. Abingdon: Routledge, pp. 320–334.

Kent, A. and Potter, J. (2014). Discursive social psychology, in T.M. Holtgraves (ed.) *The Oxford handbook of language and social psychology*. Oxford: Oxford University Press, pp. 295–313.

McAvoy, J. (2009). *Negotiating constructions of success and failure: women in mid-life and formations of subject subjectivity and identity*. PhD thesis, The Open University [Online]. Available at http://oro.open.ac.uk/view/person/jm6769.html

McAvoy, J. (2015). 'From ideology to feeling: discourse, emotion, and an analytic synthesis', *Qualitative Research in Psychology*, 12(1): 22–33.

Potter, J. (2010). 'Contemporary discursive psychology: issues, prospects, and Corcoran's awkward ontology', *British Journal of Social Psychology*, 49: 657–678.

Potter, J. and Hepburn, A. (2005). 'Qualitative interviews in psychology: problems and possibilities', *Qualitative Research in Psychology*, 2(4): 281–307.

Potter, J. and Wetherell, M. (1987). *Discourse and social psychology: beyond attitudes and behaviour*. London: SAGE.

Sacks, H. (1992). *Lectures on conversation*. 2 vols [ed. G. Jefferson]. Oxford: Blackwell.

Schegloff, E.A. (1997). 'Whose text? Whose context?', *Discourse and Society*, 8(2): 165–187.

Schegloff, E.A. (1999a). '"Schegloff's texts" as "Billig's data": a critical reply', *Discourse and Society*, 10(4): 558–572.

Schegloff, E.A. (1999b). 'Naivete vs sophistication or discipline vs self-indulgence', *Discourse and Society*, 10(4): 577–582.

van Dijk, T.A. (2009). 'Critical discourse studies: a sociocognitive approach', *Methods of Critical Discourse Analysis*, 2(1): 62–86.

Wetherell, M. (1998). 'Positioning and interpretative repertoires: conversation analysis and post-structuralism in dialogue', *Discourse and Society*, 9(3): 387–412.

Wetherell, M. (2007). 'A step too far? Discursive psychology, linguistic ethnography and questions of identity', *Journal of Sociolinguistics*, 11(5): 661–681.

Wetherell, M. (2012). *Affect and emotion: a new social science understanding*. London: SAGE.

Wittgenstein, L. (1953/2001). *Philosophical investigations* [Trans. G.E.M. Anscombe]. 3rd edn. Oxford: Blackwell.

Zotzmann, K. and O'Regan, J.P. (this volume). Critical discourse analysis and identity, in S. Preece (ed.) *The Routledge handbook of language and identity*. Abingdon: Routledge, pp. 113–128.

Appendix

The following transcription-light conventions are adopted:

(.) indicates a pause
< > encloses talk which is noticeably quieter than surrounding talk
((*gestures towards face*)) italicised text in double brackets indicates an observation from the interviewer-analyst

7

Critical discourse analysis and identity

Karin Zotzmann and John P. O'Regan

Introduction

The concept of identity is of interest to applied linguistics for a variety of reasons. It links the level of the individual with the social and thus allows us to capture the processes by which individuals affiliate with or distance themselves from particular communities, what kind of information they aim to convey about themselves and how this information in turn resonates with the ideas others hold about them. Identity is hence, as Anna De Fina (2006: 263) describes it, 'crucially, about conveying to one another what kind of people we are; which geographical, ethnic, social communities we belong to; where we stand in relation to ethical and moral questions; or where our loyalties are in political terms'.

More specifically, and closer to one of the central concerns in applied linguistics, the concept of identity ties in with the view that language use is not only a cognitive endeavour but likewise an immanently social one. The concept sensitises us to think about the reasons for and the conditions under which people use language, the way they are perceived by others as users of language, the meanings they want to convey in particular situations and the resources they draw upon in order to do so.

Identity is to a large extent a discursive phenomenon, as representations of self and other are co-constructed through language and other semiotic resources. It is also a material phenomenon in being enacted in time and space, in real settings (including when online), and as a consequence of actual events: individuals do not take up identities context free. It involves acts of embodiment as individuals perform and display their identities (e.g. through fashion, cosmetics or their latest car or avatar). Individuals, however, do not enter these subjectivities on equal terms. Apart from inter-individual differences in capabilities, they vary in terms of their social position and concomitant access to linguistic, cultural, economic and other resources – social and material – that grant them different degrees of recognition. More importantly, though, classifications of self and other are largely influenced by discourses about social groups that are produced and re-produced at different levels of society and in different social spheres, e.g. the media, education and politics. These discourses, in turn, are influenced by and impact on social structures and divisions in a variety of ways.

As identity constructions are imbued with power relations and ideology, critical discourse analysis (henceforth CDA) seems to be an appropriate choice for the conceptualisation and analysis of these processes. CDA, like poststructuralist discourse analysis (PDA), is predicated on the idea that discursive and social processes are intricately related (see Baxter, this volume). CDA, however, aligns not only with poststructuralist but also other sociolinguistic perspectives that do not focus upon 'language or the use of language in and for themselves, but upon the partially linguistic character of social and cultural processes and structures' (Fairclough and Wodak 1997: 271). What makes CDA distinctive is its explicit commitment to a critique of problematic social practices with a view of transforming them for the better (Fairclough and Wodak 1997; Titscher *et al.* 2000). Analyses conducted in this transdisciplinary field hence usually contain a normative component. In this vein, respective authors in CDA aim to open up alternative viewpoints on and explanations of particular social phenomena, which in turn are a pre-condition for alternative courses of action. CDA is based on the conviction that there is no neutral and value-free social science, and claims about the apolitical nature of linguistic analysis are regarded to be themselves ideological, i.e. they conceal their own political interests (Fairclough 1996; de Beaugrande 2001).

This, however, is as far as commonality across approaches to CDA reaches. Although the field incorporates a range of shared fundamental assumptions and research interests, it is neither constituted by a homogeneous theoretical framework, nor by a set of fixed methodological tools. Instead, each individual research project fine-tunes its theoretical and conceptual framework as well as its methodology to its object of investigation, among them the formation, representation and enactment of identity. While this diversity of approach shows that CDA is multiperspectival and not wedded to one-dimensional interpretations of reality and truth, it generates a challenge when writing about identity and language from a CDA perspective. Given the limited space available, we have therefore decided to concentrate our attention on the work of two prominent representatives of the field of CDA: the discourse-historical approach developed by Ruth Wodak and her collaborators (Wodak *et al.* 1990, 2009; Wodak and Meyer 2009), and the dialectical-relational approach of Norman Fairclough (2003, 2010, 2014; Fairclough *et al.* 2004).

We begin by describing the motivation behind the emergence of CDA, the research interests it has and the key constructs it employs; prominent among these are discourse, power and ideology. All three concepts are in need of conceptual clarity as they are not only core to this field but have also enjoyed widespread use and a concomitant range of understandings in other areas of the social sciences and humanities. These theoretical constructs, in turn, depend upon particular epistemological and ontological positions that differ across authors and which also need to be elaborated and explained. In the second part of the chapter we draw upon the existing body of research and theorisation of the discourse-historical and the dialectical-relational approaches in order to give an account of the kinds of questions that are asked, the theoretical perspectives involved and the methodological tools employed in the analysis of objects of research in these two varieties of CDA, and how these could be of assistance for language and identity research in applied linguistics.

Overview

Historical emergence, research interests and transdisciplinarity

CDA is not a discipline but a problem-oriented field with a specific transdisciplinary research programme – i.e. applied social science – that develops its own theoretical frameworks and methodologies in relation to concrete objects of research (Chouliaraki and Fairclough 1999; Titscher *et al.* 2000; O'Regan 2014). Historically, CDA emerged out of the field of critical linguistics, which was formulated by a group of scholars in the 1970s – Roger Fowler, Robert Hodge, Gunther Kress and Tony Trew – who wanted to overcome what they saw as the artificial disciplinary boundaries between linguistics and social theory (Fowler *et al.* 1979). The authors were interested in how the social influences the way we use language and how language in turn contributes to the organisation and transformation of the social. Critical discourse analysts continue to elaborate and refine theories at this disciplinary interface and have engaged with and incorporated influences from, for example, systemic functional linguistics, pragmatics, conversation analysis and sociolinguistics, as well as the following:

- Michel Foucault's (1972, 1980) perspective on discourse;
- Karl Marx's (1977) critique of capitalism;
- Mikhail Bakhtin's (1981, 1986) view of genre, dialogicality and intertextuality;
- Louis Althusser's (1971) approach to ideology;
- Antonio Gramsci's (1971) theory of hegemony;
- The Frankfurt School's (Horkheimer 1976; Habermas 1984, 1987) Critical Theory;
- Pierre Bourdieu's (1984, 1988) concept of habitus and field;
- Roy Bhaskar's (1986, 1989, 1998, 2008) philosophy of Critical Realism.

Differences in theoretical alignments with these and other sources as well as differences in concrete research interests have also generated a variety of strands of CDA, including the:

- Discourse-historical (Reisigl and Wodak 2009 [2001]);
- Socio-cognitive (Chilton 2004; van Dijk 2008);
- Social semiotic (Kress and van Leeuwen 2001; Kress 2010);
- Dialectical-relational (Fairclough 2001, 2010, 2014).

Key concepts: discourse, power and ideology

The term discourse and the notion of critique are not only core to CDA but also many other research areas in the social sciences and humanities. As these terms carry a wide range of vague and sometimes even contradictory understandings (Poole 2010), it is essential to clarify the specific meanings of discourse and critique in CDA. For the term discourse we proceed from the general to the specific, beginning with a common distinction drawn between discourse as an abstract noun and as a countable noun, over particular features attributed to discourse, to the theoretical underpinnings of the concept. In relation to critique, under the account of the dialectical-relational approach, we outline the difference between a normative and an explanatory function that will lead us into a wider understanding of the social ontology underlying the perspectives reviewed here.

Discourse as an abstract noun can be understood as 'language in use', or 'talk and text in context' (van Dijk 1997: 3), a perspective that acknowledges that the contexts of production, distribution and reception influence the make-up of concrete textual instances and that these texts, in turn, have an effect on social reality. Discourse – or more generally semiosis as meaning-making processes and the resources that are used for making meaning – is hence always socially embedded, i.e. it is produced, distributed and interpreted by individuals, groups or institutions in concrete historical and situational contexts. It is also inherently dialogical and intertextual, i.e. agents draw upon and mix a variety of existing linguistic and other semiotic resources in order to make meaning and to position themselves in ongoing conversations, of both an oral and a written nature. In sum, discourse is something that people do, i.e. a form of social practice. Discourse as a countable noun, in contrast, refers to either the use of language in different social domains (media discourse, political discourse, academic discourse) or ways of representing a part of the world from a particular perspective, for instance neoliberal, racist or sexist discourse (Fairclough 2003: 26). As there are potentially infinite representations of the world, there is an equally infinite number of ways of classifying and naming discourse perspectives.

The notion of discourse is profoundly influenced by the work of the French philosopher Foucault (1972). Foucault developed his theory of discourse in response to an orthodox version of Marxism that regarded economic relations as prior to any cultural formation. From an orthodox Marxist perspective, unjust economic relations ('structure') generate an ideological belief system ('superstructure') that helps to sustain the conditions that gave rise to it. Foucault rejected the dualist Marxist representation of ideology as a 'false consciousness' which could be made to stand in contrast to a hidden 'truth', and viewed the conception of truth itself as misleading – in a manner similar to other poststructuralist writers such as Jean-François Lyotard (1984) and Jacques Derrida (1976) – because truth by implication promotes to the level of universality what is in effect simply a claim. Moreover, the universalising pretensions of such claims are viewed as potentially oppressive and totalising as they close down and efface alternative claims (see Baxter, this volume). Foucault (1972) posited instead that truth was relative to discourse, which he understood to be a body of statements and social practices that have been organised in regular, systematic ways. These discursive formations, or 'regimes of truth', are governed by their own internal rules and cut across social divisions. They are complex and distributed in objects (i.e. buildings for particular institutions such as psychiatric hospitals), relations (i.e. the separation between the 'mad' and the 'normal' or 'rational') and texts (i.e. administrative forms and regulations); they are also embodied and enacted by agents occupying identity-inscribed subject positions.

From this perspective individuals are never entirely dominated or oppressed by economic exploitation and a concomitant alienating ideology. Instead, they are objects and agents of discourse as discourse operates through their forms of being, valuing and acting, a process Foucault (1988 [1982]) called 'subjectification'. Consequently, there is no escape from power as 'it is always already present, constituting that very thing which one attempts to counter it with' (Foucault 1980: 82). Conceptually, this means that the term discourse is preferred over the concept of ideology, as analysis along these lines is not so much interested in how power is enacted through discourse but rather how it is enacted in discourse as the actual site of contestation.

While the idea that discourse is imbricated with power relations is accepted by CDA researchers, the idea that reality may be reduced to discourse is not, and many continue to see language as having a referential as well as a representational function in relation to a non-discursive reality. In addition to this, they hold onto the idea of truth and to the concept of ideology as a deviation from it. Ideology is regarded as a collection of historically contingent claims to truth that are presented as 'common sense' and therefore as taken-for-granted or uncontested ideas.

Without determining people's thinking or acting in a mechanistic way, ideological assumptions nevertheless encourage individuals to act in specific, albeit constrained, ways that benefit dominant social groups. In the concrete historical moment we find ourselves in, social justice, democracy and ecology are for instance under threat because the interests of wealthy individuals and groups are advanced while the interests of the majority are marginalised and the common good neglected. Revealing the often opaque workings of power in, but also through, discourse is hence one of the main goals of CDA: 'CDA is not, as one might assume, just a critique of discourse, it is a critique of the existing social reality (including its discourse) which begins with a critique of discourse' (Fairclough 2014 [1989]: 5; see also Gee 2005; Reisigl and Wodak 2009 [2001]).

Two approaches to CDA

The discourse-historical approach

The discourse-historical approach (henceforth DHA) is, as with all other CDA variants, trans-disciplinary and critical. This means that it attempts to unravel contradictions, dilemmas and manipulations in concrete oral or written textual instances with the ultimate aim to contrib-ute to an improvement of ethically and politically problematic situations. DHA is hence not interested in how individuals construct their identity *per se* but in discourses – as part of wider socio-historical processes – that are problematic in the way they represent groups of people such as, for instance, immigrants or women. It is distinctive in its emphasis on detailed linguistic (rhetorical, argumentative, pragmatic and semantic) analysis of empirical genre-texts.

In relation to the topic at hand Wodak and her colleagues depart from the assumption that identity processes revolve around the creation of sameness and difference through concrete discursive strategies. In their work on national identity, for example, they follow Benedict Anderson's (1983) view that the nation is an 'imagined community', i.e. a construct based on mythicised recollections and narratives that suggest a common origin and set of beliefs, tradi-tions and values. In other words, nationalist discourse projects an image of people as being of the same kind (nationals) and different from another kind (citizens of other nation states, for-eigners or immigrants). What is essentially a relational process and hence always in the making is presented here as static and fixed. The construction of nationhood is viewed by the DHA as an ideological strategy that is employed politically in order to create boundaries and to justify practices of inclusion and exclusion: it overemphasises cultural similarity within nation states and differences with other national 'peoples' while at the same time downplaying shared similarities among human beings as well as heterogeneity within national borders. The differences are usu-ally linked to positive evaluations of the in-group and negative evaluations of the out-group:

> Difference which is linguistically constructed through strategies of dissimilation, and which in reference to marginalised groups of others is frequently portrayed as deviance from a pre-ferred norm, here does not usually introduce subtle distinctions, but, on the contrary, implies the affixing of undifferentiated and usually derogatory labels on the group concerned.
>
> *(Wodak et al. 2009 [1999]: 33)*

Wodak *et al.*'s (1990, 2009 [1999]) research on Austrian national identity, for example, analy-ses contemporary constructions of the past at the service of political action in the present and future. Being Austrian is regarded, from this perspective, as historically and socially consti-tuted; it is reinforced through a variety of social practices, from elite to lifeworld discourses, and constantly reinterpreted and rearticulated in relation to contemporary political occasions and (geo)political transformations, such as, for instance, the fall of the Iron Curtain and sub-sequent immigration from East European countries, the commemoration of the Nazi past, Europeanisation and globalisation. Although the construction of Austrian national identity is an object of investigation in itself, it also serves as an example of how similarity and difference are generally constructed through discourse. On the basis of a close-knit analysis of empirical texts that moves between data and theory in a hermeneutic circle, analysts usually draw upon different but interrelated genre-texts that revolve around the same content. For the case of migration (and hence the representation of migrants) these can include, for example, media reports, policy papers, legislation and election campaign materials (Wodak 2014). In order to relate texts to the particular socio-historical context they respond to and in which they are situated, analysts draw upon a layered four-level model that includes an account of the socio-political/historical context (e.g. the historical development of migration policies in a particular nation state), the current context (discussions dominating the public debate), the co-text (text-internal elements and relations), the intertextual context (links to other texts and voices) and interdiscursive relations (the links established between different discourses and genres). This layered contextualisation of particular genre-texts provides, according to Angel Lin (2014: 217), 'a powerful methodology to explain why macrostructures of inequality are persistent and pervasive and can get reinforced and perpetuated via discursive processes across multiple sites and multiple texts over a sustained period of time'.

Wodak and her team provide a detailed methodological and conceptual framework that can be employed and amended through other empirical studies on identity at different historical junctures and in different contexts. They have compiled, for instance, a taxonomy of discursive macro-strategies and sub-strategies that are employed together with particular argumentation patterns in the discursive formation of national identity. Strategies are understood as actions in pursuit of particular objectives, but these actions do not have to be 'planned to the last detail, or [be] strictly instrumentalist; strategies can also be applied automatically' (Wodak *et al.* 2009: 32). Instead, intentionality depends on a variety of factors, among them the particular genre and contexts agents engage with and in. Political speeches are, for instance, usually prepared ahead of the event and with more strategic objectives in mind than participation in a conversation. The macro-strategies Wodak *et al.* identify include strategies of:

- *Construction*: The nation is constructed as a unified entity that is associated with particular characteristics (usually superior to those of the out-group) and positive values such as, for instance, solidarity. The sub-strategy of *justification* helps to present problematic historic events in less problematic, or sanitised, ways that are in accordance with the positive image of the in-group;
- *Transformation*: Modifications and adaptions of an established identity construct in response to the particularities of the situation;
- *Deconstruction*: The dismantling of parts of an existing identity construct without the provision of new elements.

These can occur separately or in diverse combinations in concrete textual instances and are supported by broader sub-strategies like the emphasis or presupposition of sameness (the construction of temporal, interpersonal or territorial similarity in relation to the above) and the emphasis of difference (the construction of temporal, interpersonal or territorial dissimilarity).

As Lin (2014: 217) points out, this elaborated methodological framework is a definite strength of DHA. The difficulty it generates especially for novice researchers is that the 'largely linguistic analytical focus … does not also equip the analyst with the social theoretical frameworks to connect the linguistic analysis to the analysis of social practice'. Fairclough's approach to CDA, in contrast, is characterised by elaborate theorisation of the links between the social and discursive analysis. For the same reason it can also be more difficult to operationalise in terms of micro-linguistic analysis. It is principally for this reason that we dedicate a longer section to the theoretical conceptualisation and methodological procedures of this variant of CDA.

The dialectical-relational approach

The dialectical-relational approach (henceforth DRA) is principally associated with Fairclough's more recent work (2010, 2014; Fairclough *et al.* 2004; Fairclough and Fairclough 2012). His approach is probably most clearly distinct from poststructuralism as it is based on the fundamental idea that even though we apprehend reality to a large extent discursively, not all elements of the social are discursive in nature. While many poststructuralists probably would not deny this, the explicit focus on the construction of the social through discourse marginalises elements and causal relationships that are not manifested in discourse:

> the problematic methodological implication of this line of thinking when translating these abstract arguments to research is that structural issues tend to be analyzed primarily in terms of individual experiences and related understanding of them, to the detriment of the analysis of unrecognized structural impediments and their relationship with individual agency.
>
> *(Martinez* et al. *2014: 454–455)*

Fairclough derives his present perspective largely from the critical realist ontology of Bhaskar (1986, 1989, 1998, 2008). Critical Realism (CR) assumes – in contrast to social constructionism – that the world exists independently of our knowledge of it, hence we might 'construe' but we do not 'construct' the world: 'natural systems endure and act outside the conditions that enable us to identify them' (Bhaskar 2008: 13). This also applies to the social world. Even though social reality is mediated through discourse, there are other elements of the social that are causally effective but distinct from discourse, for example social structures and relations, values, desires and material conditions (Chouliaraki and Fairclough 1999). These elements of social life are dialectically related, i.e. each moment 'internalizes the others without being reducible to them' (Fairclough 2001: 232). Technological systems such as, for example, an urban transportation system are both semiotic and material, i.e. they have a material base but they are also designed on the basis of knowledge that is available at a specific point in time. Transportation systems are, however, more material than, for example, identities, which tend towards the more semiotic or discursive end of the spectrum. This does not mean though that identities can be reduced to discourse alone. Their articulation depends, on the one hand, on the embodied self and agency of an individual and, on the other hand, on material reality and structures as 'the enduring, affording and constraining influences of the social order' (Sealey and Carter 2004: xiii). From a CR perspective, people and pre-existent structures interact with each other on the basis of their distinctive powers. The results of this interaction might not be predictable but they can be causally effective and thus, potentially, explicable (ibid.: 12).

In order to account for causality, CR distinguishes between the 'real', the 'actual' and the 'empirical' as 'three overlapping domains of reality' (Bhaskar 2008: 56). The real consists in naturally existing and enduring objects, including not only material objects such as means of transportation and buildings, but also institutional structures, human agents or partly enduring and institutionalised discourses, such as racism or sexism. Their common characteristic is that they are endowed with causal powers, i.e. 'generative mechanisms underlying empirically observable phenomena' (Sealey and Carter 2004: 68) that exist independently of the observer. This does not necessarily mean that they are always causally effective. A car, for instance, has real powers, but these are actualised only when it is turned on and moving. The real is thus different from the actual – the activation of powers in events that make a difference (such as driving), which in turn is different from the empirical – the domain in which experiences are apprehended (Fairclough *et al.* 2004; Bhaskar 2008). The real, the actual and the empirical therefore exist in a nested relationship with one another.

This stratified ontology allows the analyst to capture causally effective powers that might/might not be actualised in actual events and might/might not be recognised by agents and made salient in their discourse. To remind us, if we focused our analysis on the discursive construction of reality, i.e. on what is present, it would be difficult to capture 'the unsaid, the unknown, the absent and what may lie in potential' (Martinez *et al.* 2014: 456). The same authors provide an example:

> an institution or organization may have an implicit culture of sexism and racism in relation to career progression and the allocation of financial rewards, yet these mechanisms may not be perceived by those benefiting from them, and unacknowledged by those perpetuating them. However, the transfactuality [i.e. the absence at the empirical level] of mechanisms of privilege and discrimination means that they operate whether or not they are acknowledged to exist. It also explains why, within the same organisation, individual women and people of colour might advance, but the demographic composition of the management structure remains predominantly white and male. Though the overall tendency of the structure is governed by the dominant mechanisms of sexism and racism, discriminatory mechanisms may not be actualized in all cases, and other mechanisms – say, a corporate call for diversity or an equal opportunities policy – may potentially provide some countervailing forces.
>
> *(Ibid.: 457)*

CR's stratified ontology draws attention to contextual constraints and affordances that potentially could, and those that actually do, influence individuals and their projected or ascribed identities. It effectively links the concept of identity with discourse, as well as agency and structure, and can thus sensitise the analyst to the unequal distribution of linguistic, cultural and economic resources, as well as locate semiotic processes 'within the practical engagement of embodied and socially organised persons with the material world' (Fairclough *et al.* 2001: 7).

For Fairclough, an account of the relational and stratified whole within which social problems are nested is crucial, as he aims to move beyond 'normative critique' – the critical analysis of discourse and texts – to 'explanatory critique' (Bhaskar 1998) – i.e. critique that attempts to account for causality, which in turn is a precondition for transformative social action. Whereas normative critique deconstructs ideological assumptions and false beliefs, explanatory critique tries to explain the fact that, despite their inherent shortcomings, a respective representation is still in place or false belief is still held. In other words, 'it involves […] an explanation of the reproduction of the account as an accepted and "lived" body of beliefs, which necessitates a mode of substantive *sociological* explanation' (ibid.: 121).

The concept of 'interdiscursivity' (Chouliaraki and Fairclough 1999; Fairclough 2010) is essential in this context. Interdiscursivity refers to the dialectical relations between discourses (as ways of representing), genres (as ways of acting and interacting) and styles (as ways of being). When power relations shift, relations between discourses, genres and styles change and are differently drawn upon. Discourses in this sense are seen as responsible for enacting new genres that may then be inculcated as new styles – i.e. as identities in their semiotic aspect: 'as new ways of being, new identities, including both new styles and new bodily dispositions' (Fairclough *et al.* 2004: 34). It is therefore at the dialectical nexus of discourses, genres and styles that identity becomes a salient object of analysis in itself, because it is as a result of changing discourses that new genres and therefore new identities may come into play. To take an example, 9/11 as a generative event set in train a whole series of discursive changes (e.g. in the form of new discourses of security and public hypervigilance) that have enacted new ways of (inter)acting and inculcated new identities and subjectivities. These can be found in heightened airport security protocols, stricter border controls, revised immigration laws, reformulated attitudes to freedom of speech, newly promulgated policies on multicultural relations and 'deradicalisation'. In each of these circumstances new genres are set in motion that set up a range of new subject positions, or identities, by which individuals are expected to act and interact. In identity terms – but not only these – it matters a good deal that individuals engage with these new genres as they are expected to. For example, in the panopticon of security hypervigilance, which many of us live in today, individuals are being required to take up particular subject positions, often – as in the case of airport security protocols and border controls – with the threat of coercion and even punishment if they do not. The process of changes in discourses leading to new genres and styles is what Fairclough refers to as the 'operationalisation' of discourse, in which discourses are 'put into practice' (Fairclough 2010: 232). The new genres and styles which result may then be physically materialised in space as, for instance, buildings, sections, departments and centres of various kinds, i.e. as physical spaces in which genres and styles may be performed. The institutional and spatial operationalisation of discourses, genres and styles thus correspond to orders of discourse as 'the social structuring of semiotic variation' (Fairclough *et al.* 2004: 33). The different levels of social processes and their semiotic relations are illustrated in Figure 7.1.

Between the levels of structures, practices and events and their respective fields and codes, a dialectic is in play. Therefore, no level is discrete; it is in a constant process of flowing into and between the other elements in each of the levels. Interdiscursivity is the mediating 'inter-level' between the micro-level linguistic analysis of the text (in conjunction with relevant social analysis) and the analysis of social structures (O'Regan and Betzel forthcoming). In other words, relations of interdiscursivity via orders of discourse are what connect the analysis of the text with an analysis of social structures.

Fairclough conceives of DRA as a methodology and not just a method to be applied. Methodology is understood as theory in combination with method in the construction and analysis of an object of research (Bourdieu and Wacquant 1992; Fairclough 2010). In this sense

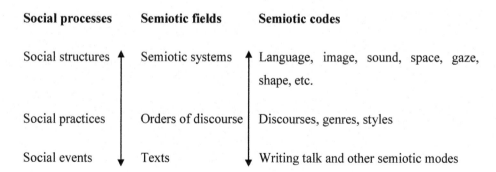

Social processes	Semiotic fields	Semiotic codes
Social structures	Semiotic systems	Language, image, sound, space, gaze, shape, etc.
Social practices	Orders of discourse	Discourses, genres, styles
Social events	Texts	Writing talk and other semiotic modes

Figure 7.1 Dialectic of social processes and semiotic relations

it is not simply a matter of taking a method and applying it to an object of research. The object first has to be theorised itself, drawing upon relevant social theories in a 'transdisciplinary way', 'either in research teams which bring together specialists in relevant disciplines, or by engaging with literature in such disciplines' (Fairclough 2010: 236). Hence, 'not only are research questions essential to research, but there is also the need of a thorough understanding of the reality on which research acts' (David Block, personal communication, 26.03.2015). In this process the object of research is constructed. Having done this, the task is to seek a 'semiotic point of entry' into what are usually the written or spoken texts which circulate as social practices within the order of discourse that corresponds to them and which act as interdiscursive cues. The principal purpose is to identify and discuss the linguistic features of texts that appear to act as cues to interdiscursive relations. The emancipatory agenda of the DRA aims at the righting of social wrongs and involves the following four stages:

1   Focus upon a social wrong, in its semiotic aspect.
2   Identify obstacles to addressing the social wrong.
3   Consider whether the social order 'needs' the social wrong.
4   Identify possible ways past the obstacles.

Space does not permit that these stages can be elucidated in detail (see Fairclough 2003, 2010). DRA is oriented to the research of topics that may be said to have significant implications for human well-being. Topics such as immigration, terrorism, globalisation, environmentalism, neoliberalism, nuclear power, global warming, racism, sexism and war all suggest themselves. Identity in one form or another arguably cuts across them all as these phenomena set discourses in motion leading to the enactment of genres and the inculcation of styles. Stage 1 asks that we focus upon a social phenomenon in its semiotic aspect. This involves seeking out a semiotic point of entry. In DRA, social structures and institutions are not wholly discursive but considered to be comprised of discursive and non-discursive elements. The semiotic point of entry therefore pertains to social practices and events in their semiotic aspect as orders of discourse and texts (see Figure 7.1). Once the topic is selected, the second step is to bring relevant theories to bear upon it: to theorise the phenomenon in a transdisciplinary way. In the context of this chapter and this handbook, theories of identity and possibly others within a sociological, political and economic frame would be deemed suitable. In relation to the topic of the politics of multiculturalism, for example, one or more theories of identity, migration, interculturalism, race or human rights, among others, will be salient.

In the next stage (Stage 2) the point is to discuss the origins and causes of the phenomenon (and if a social wrong, the possible obstacles to changing it). In the topic of the politics of multiculturalism, for example, the history of multicultural relations in the context under discussion will be significant, as will the social and institutional contexts – orders of discourse – in which such a politics operates (e.g. political, police, legal, race relations, ethnic and religious, immigration, etc.) and their associated social events and texts (e.g. political speeches and press briefings, communiqués and policing protocols, official announcements and reports, policy procedures and documents, mission statements, news broadcasts, etc.). The next step in this stage is to select texts and the categories for their analysis, and then to carry it out. For the purposes of undertaking an analysis of texts, linguistic analysis is essential. For example, issues of foregrounding and backgrounding of agents, modality, coordination and subordination, personal deixis (e.g. we vs. they), tense, textual structure and argumentation may each be relevant (see Fairclough 2003 and 2010 for more detailed accounts). It is important to note that this is not simply a tick box exercise; what linguistic features are of import, and why, will need to be argued. CDA – and not just DRA – also requires that we attempt to demonstrate warrant for the interpretations that we make. If the settled assumptions of the text are to be disturbed and possibly dismantled, it must be from within the 'texturing' of the text that this occurs. Opposing the arguments and assumptions of the text may be part of the reason for wanting to critique the text, but is not in itself CDA. The move to interdiscursive analysis comes through linking textual interpretation to the theoretical frame elaborated in Stage 1, as well as through consideration of relevant discursive cues to genres and styles in a dialectical movement between events and social practices, texts and the order of discourse.

Stages 3 and 4 take us further into the domain of explanatory critique in DRA. Stage 3 asks whether the existing social order – e.g. structures of capitalism, race and gender discrimination, nationalism, immigration controls, patriarchal relations, etc. – needs the phenomenon to be the way that it is. An example is that since the 2007–2008 financial crisis the UK government has imposed an austerity regime on the public finances in order to recoup the billions of pounds of public money used to rescue the British (and London-based international) banking system from collapse. Arguments proliferated about what the right response to the crisis should be, but for many, including the authors of the present chapter, the crisis showed that the financialised model of neoliberal capitalism ushered in some 30 years previously under the auspices of the Conservative governments of prime minister Margaret Thatcher had been an abject failure and ought to be dismantled. Since this was – and still is – deemed politically, economically and ideologically unacceptable – i.e. the existing social order needs the system to stay the way it is – the solution to a crisis wrought by that failure has been the even greater dogmatic application of the neoliberal strictures that brought the crisis about. To dismantle the neoliberal hegemony directly threatens the interests of those who have gained most from it – the bankers, hedge funds, brokers, market speculators and investors in whose personal interest it is that the system is maintained – as well as the state apparatuses of political, social and coercive power that administer it – parliament, the mass media, the church, the police, the armed forces and the judiciary. Most problematically, such is the power of the neoliberal hegemony that the long-term interests of the great majority of the UK population have been made to appear ineluctably tied to the shoring up of the entire rotten edifice. Identities are of course at stake too, as people wedded to the notion of being property owners, for example, fixate on the fluctuations of the housing market, while those less fortunate, such as the socially marginalised and the unemployed, are systematically discriminated against and excluded. This all places considerable obstacles in the way of transformative action and change. In sum, while the dominant discourse may be contested (Stage 4), it is by no means a foregone conclusion that it can readily be overcome.

So far we have presented an overview of the key tenets of CDA and how these might be related to identity. In the following section, we turn to how CDA can assist with the study of language and identity in applied linguistics.

Issues and ongoing debates

In recent decades the focus of attention in applied linguistics has gravitated to the concept of identity in all its multifacetedness (Block 2012). According to De Fina (2006: 262), this research on identity has been strongly influenced by a 'shift towards a social constructionist, interactionist paradigm', a concomitant anti-essentialist view of the self and attention to the micro-level of interaction and meaning-making. The idea that identities are socially construed, discursively mediated, dynamic, context dependent and relational is generally embraced by the two versions of CDA reviewed here. They differ, however, both in focus and ontology. In terms of focus, they go beyond analysis of how others are represented or how people generally negotiate and construct their identity in cooperation with others. The concept of identity is of interest to CDA because it is an essential part of a social situation that is problematic, for instance when individuals or groups of people are under threat from discrimination, marginalisation and exclusion. One core strategy in these power-imbued processes is to discursively unify one's in-group, construct differences between groups, frame and polarise representation and categorise others in a derogatory way, as captured by the DHA framework reviewed above.

In terms of ontology, we have already outlined that the DHA variant of CDA does not subscribe to postmodern anti-essentialism and social constructionism. However, authors writing from both CDA perspectives do not assume that there are static essences lying behind social categories but that life is a process of change, whether in body, mind or subjectivity. Like the social constructionists, their objective is to critique discourses that label groups of people in ways that suppress difference and thus contribute to marginalisation, exclusion and violence. The critique, however, does not target essentialism as the core of all social ills (Friedman 2002). The problem, as Andrew Sayer (2011) has pointed out, is not the assertion of sameness or difference, but the mistaken attribution or denial of particular characteristics. Racism, for instance, is wrong on both counts, as it is based on the one hand on 'spurious claims about differences which actually have no significance, and on the other denial of differences – through the stereotyping characteristic of cultural essentialism – which are significant' (p. 457). Conversely, denying sameness and 'asserting instead difference to the point of implosion into "de-differentiation"' (McLennan 1995 in Sayer 2011: 455) runs into the danger of overlooking durable structures and power relations that influence individuals. Social relations are socially constructed, but that does not mean that they can be changed through voluntary individual action. To the contrary, social structure is often not only durable but also resistant to social change since people do not often reflect consciously on its existence. What makes social structure particularly stable is its relation with extra-discursive patterns and elements and the fact that the social structure, 'in so far as it is appropriated by human beings, is always *already made*' (Bhaskar 1998: 33). But although social structure is something that individuals do not make, 'it exists only in virtue of their activity' (ibid.). As Fairclough (1992: 65) argues, discourse is thus 'firmly rooted in and oriented to real, material social structures'. Evaluations and (mis)representations of others are thus – from a CDA perspective – not exclusively based on essentialist categories in people's minds; they are linked to social, economic and political differences and injustices, which in turn are mediated, maintained or resisted through discourse. Structural marginalisation interrelates with discourse in a number of complex ways and impacts crucially upon the amount and quality of recognition people receive from others.

Engaging with discourse as well as social and political-economic theories seems ever more important in the current political and economic climate where inequalities are deepening in and across nation states. Over the last three decades the gap between the rich and the poor globally has widened to such an extent that the richest 85 people on the planet have accumulated the same wealth as the poorest 3.5 billion (Oxfam 2014). One strategy of wealth transfer from the public to small financial elites is to privatise and marketise public services such as health, education and transport. This redistribution of resources is accompanied by an ideology that presents society as an aggregate of individuals pursuing their private purposes according to their own private means in a context of hyper-competition (see Chun, this volume). Paradoxically, the concept of identity and meaning-making processes have thus come to the forefront of academic research and debate at a time when socio-economic and political problems are increasing and identities in the late modern world are in a state of profound crisis. It is our assertion that through its engagement with discourse as well as with social, political and economic theory, CDA can play a key role in applied linguistics research on identity by relating identity processes to other elements of socio-material reality so that obstacles to ameliorative transformative action may be confronted and in time overcome.

Summary

This chapter engages with two versions of CDA – the discourse-historical approach developed by Ruth Wodak and her collaborators and the dialectical-relational approach of Norman Fairclough – and how these may be utilised in language and identity research in applied linguistics. It explores the normative as well as the underlying epistemological and ontological assumptions of CDA, and gives an account of the kinds of questions that are asked, the theoretical perspectives involved, and the methodological tools employed in the analysis of objects of research in these two approaches.

Related topics

Positioning language and identity: poststructuralist perspectives; Language, race and identity; Class in language and identity research; Beyond the micro–macro interface in language and identity research; Exploring neoliberal language, discourses and identities.

Further reading

Chouliaraki, L. and Fairclough, N. (1999). *Discourse in late modernity*. Edinburgh: Edinburgh University Press. (This book provides the theoretical basis for CDA as a transdisciplinary approach to social research.)

Fairclough, N. (2003). *Analysing discourse: textual analysis for social research*. London: Routledge. (This book serves as a handbook for doing CDA with textual data in social scientific research.)

Fairclough, N. (2010). *Critical discourse analysis: the critical study of language*. 2nd edn. London: Longman. (This book is a collection of key papers by Norman Fairclough covering the period 1983–2008. It traces the evolution of CDA in its theoretical and practical dimensions.)

Fairclough, N. (2014). *Language and power*. 3rd edn. London: Longman. (Originally published in 1989, this is the text in which Fairclough's version of CDA was first properly formulated. This edition contains a revised introduction offering a state-of-the-art overview of the field as well as responses to critiques that have been made.)

Wodak, R. and Meyer, M. (eds) (2009). *Methods of critical discourse analysis*. 2nd edn. London: SAGE. (This collection includes contributions from a range of key perspectives in CDA, including discourse-historical, dialectical-relational and multimodal.)

References

Althusser, L. (1971). Ideology and ideological state apparatuses, in L. Althusser (ed.) *Lenin and philosophy and other essays*. New York: New Left Books, pp. 121–176.

Anderson, B. (1983). *Imagined communities: reflections on the origin and spread of nationalism*. London: Verso.

Bakhtin, M.M. (1981). *The dialogic imagination*. Austin: University of Texas Press.

Bakhtin, M.M. (1986). *Speech genres and other late essays*. Austin: University of Texas Press.

Baxter, J. (this volume). Positioning language and identity: poststructuralist perspectives, in S. Preece (ed.) *The Routledge handbook of language and identity*. London: Routledge, pp. 34–49.

Bhaskar, R. (1986). *Scientific realism and human emancipation*. London: Verso.

Bhaskar, R. (1989). *Reclaiming reality: a critical introduction to contemporary philosophy*. London: Verso.

Bhaskar, R. (1998). *The possibility of naturalism: a philosophical critique of the contemporary human sciences*. 3rd edn. London: Routledge.

Bhaskar, R. (2008). *A realist theory of science*. London: Verso.

Block, D. (2012). Economising globalisation and identity in applied linguistics in neoliberal times, in D. Block, J. Gray and M. Holborow, *Neoliberalism and applied linguistics*. London: Routledge, pp. 56–83.

Bourdieu, P. (1984). *Homo academicus*. Paris, France: Minuit.

Bourdieu, P. (1988). *Language and symbolic power*. Cambridge: Polity Press.

Bourdieu, P. and Wacquant, L. (1992). *An invitation to reflexive sociology*. Cambridge: Polity Press.

Chilton, P. (2004). *Analysing political discourse: theory and practice*. London: Routledge.

Chouliaraki, L. and Fairclough, N. (1999). *Discourse in late modernity: rethinking critical discourse analysis*. Edinburgh: Edinburgh University Press.

Chun, C.W. (this volume). Exploring neoliberal language, discourses and identities, in S. Preece (ed.) *The Routledge handbook of language and identity*. London: Routledge, pp. 558–571.

de Beaugrande, R. (2001). 'Interpreting the discourse of H.G. Widdowson: a corpus-based critical discourse analysis', *Applied Linguistics*, 22(1): 104–121.

De Fina, A. (2006). Discourse and identity, in A. De Fina, D. Schiffrin and M. Bamberg (eds) *Discourse and identity*. Cambridge: Cambridge University Press, pp. 263–282.

Derrida, J. (1976). *Of grammatology* [Trans. G.C. Spivak]. Baltimore and London: Johns Hopkins University Press.

Fairclough, I. and Fairclough, N. (2012). *Political discourse analysis: a method for advanced students*. London: Routledge.

Fairclough, N. (1992). *Discourse and social change*. Cambridge: Polity Press.

Fairclough, N. (1996). 'A reply to Henry Widdowson's discourse analysis: a critical view', *Language and Literature*, 5: 1–8.

Fairclough, N. (2001). 'The dialectics of discourse', *Textus*, 14: 231–242.

Fairclough, N. (2003). *Analysing discourse: textual analysis for social research*. London: Routledge.

Fairclough, N. (2010). A dialectical-relational approach to critical discourse analysis in social research, in N. Fairclough (ed.) *Critical discourse analysis: the critical study of language*. London: Longman, pp. 230–254.

Fairclough, N. (2014 [1989]). *Language and power*. 3rd edn. London: Routledge.

Fairclough, N., Jessop, B. and Sayer, A. (2001). *Critical realism and semiosis* [Online]. Paper presented to the International Association for Critical Realism annual conference, Roskilde, Denmark (17–19 August). Available at www.criticalrealism.com/archive/iacr_conference_2001/nfairclough_scsrt.pdf

Fairclough, N., Jessop, B. and Sayer, A. (2004). Critical realism and semiosis, in J. Joseph and J. Roberts (eds) *Realism discourse and deconstruction*. London: Routledge, pp. 20–42.

Fairclough, N. and Wodak, R. (1997). Critical discourse analysis: an overview, in T. van Dijk (ed.) *Discourse and interaction*. London: SAGE, pp. 67–97.

Foucault, M. (1972). *The archaeology of knowledge*. London: Tavistock Publications.

Foucault, M. (1980). *The history of sexuality, vol. I* [Trans. R. Hurley]. New York: Vintage.

Foucault, M. (1988 [1982]). Technologies of the self, in L.H. Martin, H. Gutman and P.H. Hutton (eds) *Technologies of the self: a seminar with Michel Foucault*. Amherst: The University of Massachusetts Press, pp. 16–49.

Fowler, R., Hodge, B., Kress, G. and Trew, T. (1979). *Language and control*. London: Routledge and Kegan Paul.

Friedman, J. (2002). 'From roots to routes: tropes for trippers', *Anthropological Theory*, 2: 21–36.

Gee, J.P. (2005). *An introduction to discourse analysis: theory and method*. London: Routledge.

Gramsci, A. (1971). *Selections from the prison notebooks*. London: Lawrence and Wishart.

Habermas, J. (1984). *The theory of communicative action 1*. London: Heinemann.

Habermas, J. (1987). *The theory of communicative action 2*. Cambridge: Polity.

Horkheimer, M. (1976). Traditional and critical theory, in P. Connerton (ed.) *Critical sociology: selected readings*. Harmondsworth: Penguin, pp. 206–224.

Kress, G. (2010). *Multimodality: a social semiotic approach to contemporary communication*. London: Routledge.

Kress, G. and van Leeuwen, T. (2001). *Multimodal discourse: the modes and media of contemporary communication*. London: Arnold.

Lin, A. (2014). 'Critical discourse analysis in applied linguistics', *Annual Review of Applied Linguistics*, 34: 213–232.

Lyotard, J.-F. (1984). *The postmodern condition: a report on knowledge*. Manchester: Manchester University Press.

Martinez, A., Martin, L. and Marlow, S. (2014). 'Developing a Critical Realist positional approach to intersectionality', *Journal of Critical Realism*, 13(5): 447–466.

Marx, K. (1977). *Capital*. Vol. I [Trans. B. Fowkes]. New York: Vintage.

O'Regan, J.P. (2014). 'English as a lingua franca: an immanent critique', *Applied Linguistics*, 35(5): 533–552.

O'Regan, J.P. and Betzel, A. (2016). Critical discourse analysis: a sample study of extremism, in Zhu Hua (ed.) *Research methods in intercultural communication*. London: Blackwell.

Oxfam (2014). *Even it up: time to end extreme inequality* [Online]. Available at http://policy-practice. oxfam.org.uk/publications/even-it-up-time-to-end-extreme-inequality-333012

Poole, B. (2010). 'Commitment and criticality: Fairclough's critical discourse analysis evaluated', *International Journal of Applied Linguistics*, 20(2): 137–155.

Reisigl, M. and Wodak, R. (2009 [2001]). The discourse-historical approach (DHA), in R. Wodak and M. Meyer (eds) *Methods for critical discourse analysis*. 2nd edn. London: SAGE, pp. 87–121.

Sayer, A. (2011). *Why things matter to people: social science, values and ethical life*. Cambridge: Cambridge University Press.

Sealey, A. and Carter, B. (2004). *Applied linguistics as social science*. London: Continuum.

Titscher, S., Meyer, M., Wodak, R. and Vetter, E. (2000). *Methods of text and discourse analysis*. London: SAGE.

van Dijk, T.A. (ed.) (1997). *Discourse as structure and process 1*. London: SAGE.

van Dijk, T.A. (2008). *Discourse and context: a sociocognitive approach*. Cambridge: Cambridge University Press.

Wodak, R. (2014). 'The discursive construction of strangers: analyzing discourses about migrants and migration from a discourse-historical perspective', *Migration and Citizenship* (Newsletter of the American Political Science Association Organized Section on Migration and Citizenship), 3(1): 6–10.

Wodak, R., de Cillia, R., Reisigl, M. and Liebhart, K. (2009 [1999]). *The discursive construction of national identity*. 2nd edn. Edinburgh: Edinburgh University Press.

Wodak, R. and Meyer, M. (eds) (2009). *Methods for critical discourse analysis*. 2nd edn. London: SAGE.

Wodak, R., Pelikan, J., Nowak, P., Gruber, H., de Cillia, R. and Mitten, R. (1990). *„Wir sind alle unschuldige Täter!" Diskurshistorische Studien zum Nachkriegsantisemitismus*. Frankfurt/Main: Suhrkamp.

Part II

Categories and dimensions of identity

8

Language and ethnic identity

Vally Lytra

Introduction

In his introductory remarks to *Ethnicity and Nationalism*, Eriksen (1993: 2) argues that 'ethnicity and nationalism ... have become so visible in many societies that it is impossible to ignore them'. He opens his subsequent brief historical account by stating how 'in the early twentieth century, many social theorists held that ethnicity and nationalism would decrease in importance and eventually vanish as a result of modernisation, industrialisation and individualism' (ibid.). Yet, subsequent decades saw the emergence and proliferation of internal and external ethnic conflicts, processes of nation-building in former colonies and the political mobilisation of territorial indigenous minorities, hitherto largely marginalised, demanding that their ethnic identity be recognised by nation states. More recently, ethnic identities have come to the forefront of political debate due to the rapidly changing conditions of late modernity. Processes of globalisation involve flows of people, goods, services and ideas within and across international borders at an unprecedented scale. While such global movements are neither a new nor a unique phenomenon in human history, what is new is that they have reached previously unimagined levels enabled by profound developments in communication technologies. These global flows are creating 'global interactions of a new order of intensity' (Appadurai 1996: 27), leading to new degrees of connectedness and opening up new possibilities for contact, communication and social identification. They bring to the forefront several questions about the relationship between language and ethnic identity in a globalised world, such as: How is ethnic identity imagined and performed but also imposed in discourse and social activity? What is the role of the nation state and its institutions, such as schools and the media, in the social reproduction of ethnic categorisation? Whose linguistic and identity practices are considered authentic and whose are not, and who decides?

I was alerted to some of these questions during my own doctoral research in the late 1990s. In 2007, I reflected on some of my early encounters as an ethnographer with the children I came to work with (Lytra 2007). The research site was a state primary school in a socio-economically deprived neighbourhood in the city centre of Athens, Greece, with an unusually high percentage of children with diverse linguistic, cultural and ethnic backgrounds. Almost half of the children spoke a language other than Greek at home. The overwhelming majority of these children were of Roma heritage and spoke a variety of Turkish originating from the region of Western Thrace, which borders Bulgaria and Turkey in the north east of the country. Historically, the members of this Turkish-speaking community are part of an indigenous religious minority officially called the 'Muslim minority of Western Thrace' whose origins can be traced back to the Ottoman conquest of Greece (1354–1715) (Asimakopoulou and Christidou-Lionaraki 2002). The legal status and linguistic, cultural, educational and religious rights of minority members are protected by the Lausanne Treaty signed by Greece and Turkey in 1923. The Muslim minority of Western Thrace consists of ethnic Turks as well as Muslims of Pomak and Roma descent, some of the latter being Turkish-speaking and others Romani-speaking. Economic migration from Western Thrace to Athens in the 1970s and early 1980s led to the settlement of this Turkish-speaking minority community of Roma heritage in the city centre. Being a beginner learner of standard Turkish at the time, I often asked the children about the meaning of words and expressions I heard them use in the playground and at lunchtime. In the early days of my fieldwork children would come up to me and invariably ask the following set of questions in quick succession in Turkish: *'Adın ne?'* <what's your name?>, *'kaç yaşında?'* <how old are you?> and *'nerelisin?'* <where are you from?>. My swift responses in Turkish would generate surprise and delight on the children's part: 'κυρία μιλάς Τουρκικά!' <Miss you speak Turkish!> they repeatedly said, switching to Greek. One day, at the end of a long day of observations in the grade 6 classroom, Bahar, an outspoken 12-year-old bilingual Turkish-Greek girl, came up to me and asked me: 'κυρία, *Türk mü Rum mu?'* <(in Greek) Miss (switching to Turkish), are you Turkish or Greek?>. Possibly reflecting regional Turkish language use, Bahar employed the ethno-religious label *'Rum'*, which was used in the Ottoman period to refer to the Greek Orthodox Christian populations of the Empire, rather than *'Yunan'*, which is currently used in standard Turkish for a Greek national. Without much hesitation, I responded in Turkish, *'Rum'* <Greek>.

My encounters in the field illustrated how a focus on the relationship between language and ethnic identity can provide a lens for the investigation of processes of social categorisation and boundary demarcation. The examination of language practices such as language choice or the use of the ethnic labels Greek and Turk enables us to explore how language users define and perceive ethnic membership, and how they construct, maintain and police ethnic group boundaries and exclude those who are not seen as belonging to the group. At the same time, an attention to language practices allows us to investigate how ethnic boundaries may not be given once and for all but may be negotiated, resisted and contested. As Pavlenko and Blackledge (2004: 4) aptly put it, 'languages may not only be "markers of identity" but also sites of resistance, empowerment, solidarity and discrimination'. In addition, the examination of the relationship between language and ethnic identity demonstrates how language use is intrinsically linked to societal and individual beliefs about languages (influenced by political and historical conditions); to asymmetrical relations of power; and to language users' own views of how they see themselves and each other. Furthermore, as García argues, the co-focus on language and ethnic identity 'illuminates processes of cultural change and continuity' (2010: 519) in that it highlights not only how individuals and groups construct group membership through language practices, but also how group membership has changed or stayed the same and the role of language practices in these processes.

In this chapter, I take an applied linguistics perspective to the investigation of language and ethnic identity. According to Brumfit (1995: 27), applied linguistics is defined as 'the theoretical and empirical investigation of real-world problems in which languages is a central issue'. This widely quoted definition reveals the broad scope and coverage of the field of applied linguistics from well-established areas of language study such as language teaching and learning to the media, language and the law, and language and ageing, to mention a few (see the collection of papers in Simpson 2011). Ethnicity from an applied linguistics perspective has been less studied (Harris 2011); however, as I argue in this chapter, in today's globalised world, ethnic identity is still a salient category for self- and other-ascription and it continues to matter for many people. More specifically, in this chapter, I trace how our understanding of the term ethnicity has changed in the social sciences and how language has developed as a primary marker of group identity. I consider two views of language and ethnic identity, broadly defined as essentialist and constructionist. The first acknowledges that language and ethnic identity are fixed and bounded categories preimposed on individuals and groups in a given interaction. Language is, thus, understood as a marker of an inherited ethnic identity. The second regards language and ethnic identity as social constructs and how these seemingly natural categories are relational and negotiable. In this sense, language and ethnic identity are recognised as historically, contextually, socially and discursively constructed in discourse. While these views have been presented as being exclusive of one another, in practice the conceptual boundaries are not distinct and the relationship between the two views is more nuanced (Harris and Rampton 2003). I discuss key studies that have examined the intersection of language and ethnic identity across different contexts and conditions and highlight some of the main concepts that have informed these studies. Finally, I review some major areas of past and ongoing investigation.

Overview

The word ethnic is derived from the Greek *ethnos*. Originally meaning 'number of people living together, company, body of men, band of comrades', later in antiquity the word came to refer to 'nation, people', and in its plural form, *ethnē*, it was used to denote 'foreign, barbarous nations' as opposed to 'Greeks' (Liddell and Scott 1940). Influenced by the etymology of the word, ethnic groups have been viewed traditionally as internally consistent with clearly defined boundaries delineated by language, culture, heredity and other attributes. Although the meanings of ethnicity and ethnic groups may appear clear and unambiguously reflecting an objective self-evident social reality, they are in fact complex and emotionally charged concepts (Nash 1989). Fishman (2010: xxv–xxvi) critically reflects on the 'polysemic' role of the term ethnicity in the English language and discusses how ethnicity is understood in terms of binary oppositions: i.e. in 'self-perceived positive and self-perceived negative poles', between 'us' and 'them'. He alerts us to the centrality of power in self- and other-ascriptions by asserting that 'ethnicity is a characteristic that can only be attributed to certain others, the contextually more powerful party taking the lead ... because its main desideratum power, is by no means consensually allocated or commended'.

Anthropological work has been influential in the ways we have come to think about ethnicity and ethnic groups. Earlier anthropologists saw cultures as independent, bounded units and ethnic groups neatly mapping onto distinct cultures (Levine and Campbell 1972). However, studies by Leach (1977 [1954]) among the Kachin and Shan of Northeast Burma and Moerman (1965, 1974) among the Lue in Thailand, for instance, shifted analytical attention from identifying objective criteria for ethnic affiliation to the importance of the labelling practices of the groups themselves. As Barth (1969: 14) further argued in his seminal introduction to the edited volume *Ethnic Groups and Boundaries*, 'the features that are taken into account are not the sum of "objective" differences, but only those which the actors themselves regard as significant'. Barth's

(1969) investigation of ethnic groups and their place in society focuses on group boundaries and the processes by which ethnic groups are generated and maintained. He emphasised that the object of inquiry is 'the ethnic boundary that defines the group, not the cultural stuff that it encloses' (ibid.: 15). In this respect, ethnic boundaries organise social life. When interacting with others, ethnic groups maintain their identity by developing criteria that determine membership and exclusion; in other words, who is granted and who is denied membership in the group and by whom. Ethnic identity becomes a matter of self- and other-ascription in social interaction. Ethnic boundaries are viewed as constructed and negotiated by individuals and groups 'not only by a once-and-for-all recruitment but by continual expression and validation' (Barth 1969: 15). In this respect, ethnicity is understood as a process, and the boundaries created by ethnicity as porous and flexible and not as fixed by birth. Moreover, rather than being regarded as the essence of the group, certain symbols, including language, are used to distinguish and signal ethnic affiliation.

In the Introduction to *The Language, Ethnicity and Race Reader*, Harris and Rampton (2003) critically discuss essentialist and constructionist views with regard to ethnicity. They consider the former view, which conceptualises 'ethnicity-as-fixed-and-formative-inheritance', and the later 'strategic' view, which 'gives more credit to free will and active agency' and is often referred to 'as a "roUtes" rather than a "roOts" conception of ethnicity' (ibid.: 5). However, they contend that the 'strategic' view of ethnicity bears traces of the 'ethnicity-as-inheritance' view in that it allows individuals and groups one of three sets of possibilities for self-identification: '(a) embracing and cultivating their ethno-cultural/linguistic legacy, (b) trying to downplay and drop it as a category that is relevant to them, or (c) drawing attention to the different ethnicities of other people (most often in negative stereotyping)'. They argue for the relevance of a fourth option, '(d) taking on someone else's ethnicity, or creating a new one', which draws on recent research on hybridity and new ethnicities. Rather than making ethnicity as a social category cease to exist, this fourth option emphasises 'processes of mixing, blurring and cross-identification' and brings forth 'issues like authenticity, entitlement and expropriation' (ibid.). For instance, Harris's (2006: 1) examination of language use and ethnicity among British-born South Asian youth illustrates how many of the young people he worked with, 'while retaining both diasporic and local links with a variety of traditions derived from the Indian subcontinent, are nevertheless fundamentally shaped by an everyday low-key Britishness with new inflections'. He proposes the combined category 'Brasian' to highlight the coexistence of both British and South Asian elements in the young people's meaning-making practices and identity performances (ibid.: 1–2).

Historically, the pre-eminence of language as a primary marker of group identity is closely associated with the rise of the ideology of nationalism in the late eighteenth and early nineteenth centuries. Similar to ethnicity, nationalism has been perceived in essentialist terms. The idea of a nation understood as natural and fixed to a particular territory and a particular people who speak a particular language has been attributed to the German Romantics and in particular to the work of the German philosopher Johann Herder. In 1783, Herder outlined the close connection between language and nationality as follows:

> Has a nationality anything dearer than the speech of its father? In its speech resides its whole thought domain, its tradition, history, religion and basis of life, all its heart and soul. To deprive a people of its speech is to deprive it of its eternal good ... With language is created the heart of the people.
>
> *(Herder in Fishman 1989: 105)*

Nationalism is, thus, based on the one nation–one language paradigm where a language is seen as a whole and bounded system that indexes peoplehood. The understanding of a language as the marker of an inherited national identity and allegiance is reinforced by states and their representatives through language policy and language planning efforts. A case in point is the Turkish language reform that was initiated in the aftermath of the dismemberment of the Ottoman Empire and the establishment of the modern Turkish state in the late 1920s. It sought to replace Ottoman Turkish (*Osmanlıca*), which was saturated by Turkish, Arabic and Persian vocabulary and grammatical structures, with *Öztürkçe* (Pure Turkish, where '*öz*' means both pure and own). Ottoman Turkish had developed into the administrative and literary language of the Ottoman Empire; however, ordinary people did not use it in their everyday speech (Lewis 1999). While the basis of the new standard was the vocabulary, morphology and the phonology of the Turkish variety of Istanbul, it incorporated elements from other Turkish varieties as well as invented new words. The declared aim of the state and its representatives was to rid the Turkish language of the yoke of foreign languages (Arabic and Persian) and break away from its Ottoman heritage by creating a new standard that was designed to function as the language of education, the media and the government as well as constructing a new modern, Western and secular Turkish national identity.

In the Introduction to the *Handbook of Language and Ethnic Identity*, Fishman (1999: 4) reflects on the link between language and ethnic identity thus: 'Although language has rarely been equated with the totality of ethnicity, it has, in certain historical, regional and disciplinary contexts, been accorded priority within that totality.'

Due to the context-dependency of language and ethnic identity, Fishman continues, it becomes pertinent to examine 'how and when the link between language and ethnic identity comes about, its saliency and potency, its waxing and waning, its inevitability and the possibility of its sundering' (ibid.). A focus on different contexts, conditions and perspectives allows us to understand how the dialogic relationship between language and ethnic identity is (re)produced, contested or modified. García (2010: 519) employs the terms 'languaging' and 'ethnifying' for language and ethnicity respectively. She contends that the use of these terms draws analytical attention to 'people – individuals and groups – who use discursive and ethnic practices to signify what it is they want to be' (ibid.), that is, how individuals and groups construct and perform their identities through language in social interaction.

The shift from code and community as bounded units to language users and their languaging and ethnifying practices is premised on the conception of language as a social construction. Makoni and Pennycook (2007: 1) persuasively argue that languages are inventions and that their naming and development has been the outcome of social and semiotic processes. This assertion resonates with Heller's (2007: 2) view that language is seen as 'a set of resources which circulate in unequal ways in social networks and discursive spaces, and whose meaning and value are socially constructed within the constraints of social organisational processes, under specific historical conditions'.

Central to this view is a focus on language ideologies as 'sets of beliefs about language articulated by users as a rationalization or justification of perceived language structure and use' (Silverstein 1979: 193). Beliefs about language are never neutral; rather, they provide a window to investigating how individuals and groups make sense of their own language activity, how some languages, language varieties or linguistic forms are more valued than others and how ascribed values may be accepted or resisted. Acknowledging that language and ethnicity are social and cultural constructions allows us to explore how individuals and groups mobilise linguistic resources and beliefs about languages to define themselves and others in ethnic terms in social interaction.

At the same time, it is equally important to acknowledge that individuals bring their past histories and stereotypes into social encounters which may inform their thought and action. For instance, Callahan (2012) documented how service workers identified physical appearance, i.e. 'looking Spanish', as one of the main criteria for addressing their customers in Spanish, pointing to the salience of a priori ethnic and racial categories in short one-time service encounters.

Issues and ongoing debates

Key concepts

The relationship between language and ethnic identity has been examined from a range of fields, theoretical approaches and disciplinary traditions (see the collection of papers in Fishman and García 2010, 2011). In this section, I take an applied linguistics perspective and discuss key studies at the intersection of language and ethnic identity, focusing on different contexts and conditions, and highlight some of the main analytic concepts that have informed these studies.

Early studies on language and the negotiation of ethnic identity focused on code-switching (see e.g. Blom and Gumperz 1972; Gumperz 1982; Auer 1984). As Gumperz and Cook-Gumperz (1982: 1) have argued, 'to understand issues of identity and how they affect and are affected by social, political and ethnic divisions we need to gain insights into the communicative processes by which they arise'. In their classic study of a bi-dialectal community in Hemnesberget, Norway, Blom and Gumperz (1972) observed the everyday language use of individual speakers across different interactional contexts and identified two types of code-switching practices, namely situational and metaphorical. The former refers to a switch from one language to another as the outcome of a change in the situational context, such as a change in participant, setting or activity type. The latter refers to a change in language in order to achieve a particular communicative effect (e.g. to indicate co-membership in a local social network or to emphasise status). Gumperz (1982) further developed the social symbolism of metaphorical code-switching by distinguishing between 'we code' and 'they code' to represent the in-group and out-group respectively. He explained that 'the tendency is for the ethnically specific, minority language to be regarded as the "we code" and become associated with in-group and informal activities, and for the majority language to serve as the "they code" associated with the more formal, stiffer and less personal out-group relations' (Gumperz 1982: 66).

Although Gumperz's distinction between the we code and the they code is interactionally produced through participants' language choice and code-switching practices, a common critique is that it assumes a more or less homogeneous speech community and a stable relationship between language and ethnic identity (De Fina 2007). However, early work by LePage and Tabouret-Keller (1985) on language and ethnic identity in the Caribbean highlighted that this relationship is neither stable nor easily predicted. More recently, work on 'crossing' has shown that interactants may move across social or ethnic boundaries and negotiate identities drawing on linguistic resources of groups to which they are not thought to belong (Rampton 1995; Cutler 1999; Lo 1999; Lytra 2007; Rampton and Charalambous 2012). Even though interactants are seen to be using linguistic resources associated with distinct codes, studies on 'crossing' have raised issues of legitimacy and authenticity and have shown how boundaries, including ethnic boundaries, are permeable and ambiguous. Moreover, they have further highlighted the complexity of speakers' communicative repertoires and language practices as well as the different ways these language practices are embedded in broader social, historical, political and economic contexts.

In addition, the assumed stable link between language and ethnic identity has been further disrupted by research on multilingual language use in conditions of superdiversity. This line of inquiry has shown how speakers draw on the full range of their linguistic repertoires for communicative and identificational purposes (Blommaert and Backus 2011). For instance, García (2009: 45) proposes the term 'translanguaging', defined as 'multiple discursive practices in which bilinguals engage in order to make sense of their bilingual worlds'. She views translanguaging as 'go[ing] beyond what has been termed code-switching, although it includes it, as well as other kinds of bilingual use and bilingual contact' (ibid.). In a similar vein, Blackledge and Creese (2010) employ the term 'flexible bilingualism', while, following Bakhtin (1986), Bailey (2007: 257) uses the concept of 'heteroglossia' to show '(a) the simultaneous use of different kinds of forms or signs and (b) the tensions and conflicts among those signs, based on the sociohistorical associations they carry with them'. Otsuji and Pennycook (2010: 244) put forth the term 'metrolingualism' to 'describe the ways in which people of different and mixed backgrounds use, play with and negotiate identities through language', and Saxena (2014) coined the notion of 'lifestyle diglossia' to examine how the language choices (such as language change or shift) people make are closely connected to chosen lifestyles. These concepts provide lenses to theorise how language users move fluidly and flexibly across languages in social contexts. By redefining what counts as language competence, 'ranging from fully formal language learning to entirely "informal" encounters with language' (Blommaert and Backus 2011: 2), they question the assumed stable relationship between language, community and ethnicity on which much of the earlier code-switching research was predicated.

In applied linguistics, social constructionist and poststructuralist perspectives have been influential in the study of language and ethnic identity. These theoretical approaches emphasise the multiplicity and fragmentation of language and identity practices as they are affected by local and global contexts (see Baxter, this volume). Studies drawing on social constructionism and employing approaches to discourse such as conversation analysis, interactional sociolinguistics and ethnographic discourse analysis conceptualise identities as performed, negotiated and interpreted in discourse. These studies have shown that identity categories and their social meanings are not taken for granted, nor are they located in the individual or the group. They are locally constructed in discourse and through the interactants' social and embodied behaviour in everyday interactions. Central to the social constructionist paradigm are the interactants' language practices and the linguistic strategies they deploy in order to make identity claims. As Benwell and Stokoe (2006: 4) argue, 'rather than being *reflected* in discourse, identity is actively, ongoingly, dynamically *constituted* in discourse' (italics in the original). A social constructionist perspective emphasises interactants as social actors who align or distance themselves from social categories of belonging in different discursive environments. This means that in doing identity work participants may foreground particular identity categories, or they may downplay and ignore others. The role of the analyst is not to presuppose which social categories the interactants will orient to or are relevant in a given discourse context, but rather to examine the interactants' own identity claims as 'who we are to each other, then, is accomplished, disputed, ascribed, resisted, managed and negotiated in discourse' (Benwell and Stokoe 2006: 4; also see Benwell and Stokoe, this volume). The context-dependency of identities has been aptly captured by Moerman (1974: 62) in his study of Lue ethnic identity in the following remark: 'The question is not "Who are the Lue?" but rather when and how and why the identification of "Lue" is preferred.'

Language and identity studies drawing on poststructuralism and employing approaches to discourse such as Foucauldian discourse analysis and feminist poststructuralist discourse analysis have emphasised the role of power and inequality in processes of social identification. As

Pavlenko and Blackledge (2004: 10) maintain, 'poststructuralist theory recognizes the sociohistorically shaped partiality, contestability, instability, and mutability of ways in which language ideologies and identities are linked to relations of power and political arrangements in communities and societies'.

Studies drawing on poststructuralism have foregrounded the uneven distribution of linguistic resources and the structural constraints within which speakers have to act. According to Block (2007: 13), poststructuralist approaches allow for 'more nuanced, multileveled and complicated framings of the world around us'. This resonates with Kroskrity's (2001: 108) caution 'against any approach to identity, or identities, that does not recognize both the communicative freedom potentially available at the microlevel and the political economic constraints imposed on processes of identity-making'. For instance, Heller's (1992, 1999) ethnographic explorations of the use of French and English in Ontario and Quebec, Canada, at a time of socio-political and economic transformations, demonstrated that access to linguistic resources is linked to access to material resources and that language choice can no longer be unproblematically linked to a particular ethnic identity. Heller illustrated how language can act as a mechanism for social inclusion and exclusion. In the context of her study, mastery of the valued variety of French and English became a marker of elite status in the new economy. Heller illustrates how this placed some individuals at an advantage over others when it came to gaining access to learning the two codes (French and English) and to maintaining and/or establishing networks that open doors to positions of privilege and power.

In addition, social constructionist and poststructuralist paradigms have enabled language and identity researchers to investigate the interanimation of different identity aspects and how participants may take up, highlight or downplay particular identity categories. Scholars have been able to acknowledge that while some identity aspects may be subject to negotiation in given situations, others may be found to be non-negotiable because individuals and groups may be positioned in ways they do not choose by more powerful groups in society. In this context, individuals and groups may question, resist or transform accepted identity options and may draw upon their linguistic resources more or less strategically to negotiate a 'third space' (Bhabha 1994) where new and hybrid identities can be performed and maintained. As such, ethnicity is not examined on its own but as it intersects with and is shaped by other social categories, such as gender, age, social class, religion, geographical location and so on (see Block and Corona, this volume, for a discussion on intersection). For example, Doran (2004) showed how young people used Verlan (a code characterised by syllabic inversion, borrowings from minority languages and prosodic and phonemic differences from standard French, spoken by young people of different ethnic backgrounds in suburban Paris) as a resource to perform hybrid identities that diverged from dominant discourses available to mainstream French society. Doran (2004: 95) maintained that 'speakers' choices to use, or not to use, Verlan in particular settings were tied to various aspects of identity, including ethnicity, class, cultural values, and the relation to the stereotypical figure of the suburban youth street culture, *la racaille*'.

Many scholars investigating the intersection of language and identity draw on both social constructionist and poststructuralist perspectives. Pavlenko and Blackledge (2004: 13) cogently argue that such an analytical framework brings together 'the social constructionist focus on discursive construction of identities' and 'the poststructuralist emphasis on the role of power relations'. Both perspectives on language and identity presuppose that ethnicity is negotiated, fluid and malleable. However, May *et al.* (2004: 13), in their introduction to the edited collection *Ethnicity, Nationalism and Minority Rights*, remind us that these conceptualisations of language and ethnicity may not resonate with the personal and collective experiences of many people and identify the following disjunction between theory and the reality on the ground that 'there is something strange going on when theorists proclaim that ethnicity is invented and set out to "decentre" it, while at the same time the news is full of ethnic cleansing and genocide'. In a similar vein, Edwards (2009: 48) maintains that '[f]or most societies throughout history, ethnocentrism, hostility and prejudice towards "out-groups" have been the norm'. In this context, May *et al.* (2004) caution that it is important 'to explain why ethnicity does seem to continue to mean something to so many people' (ibid.).

The stability of ethnic boundaries and ethnic classifications in the lives of many people can be witnessed in the multifarious roles played by heritage language or complementary schools (Blackledge and Creese 2010; Lytra and Martin 2010; Lytra 2014), ethnic churches (Han 2011; Souza *et al.* 2012) and ethnic community associations (De Fina 2007; Angouri 2012) for individuals' self-identity and their group membership. This line of research has foregrounded the importance of not simply dismissing essentialist views of ethnic identity, but rather making them the focus of analysis and examining them synchronically as they emerge in social interaction as well as diachronically by charting, for instance, how they may vary within and across groups in a diaspora commuity or how they may have developed and changed over time and across countries, continents and generations. Joseph (2004), for instance, examined the interplay of ethnic and religious identities in Lebanon and historically traced the ebbs and flows of Arab-French bilingualism as a key signifier of Lebanese (mainly Maronite and Catholic) Christian identity, suggesting that during periods of political upheaval French-speaking Christians expressed a weak connection to the Arabic language to demarcate themselves from the Arabic-speaking Muslims.

Key areas of investigation

Research on language and ethnicity centres on indigenous and language minority contexts. Fishman (1999: 4) refers to the last third of the twentieth century as a period of 'ethnic revival' where language has played a key role in ethnic mobilisations around the world. Indigenous and language minority movements have often drawn implicitly or explicitly upon a structuralist–functionalist paradigm (Ferguson 1964; Fishman 1968) where languages and language varieties neatly map onto separate domains of language use connected to social activities, such as education, the family, work and religion, to safeguard and demand linguistic minority rights and autonomy (see Jaffe 2007; Patrick 2007). This paradigm has also been used to inform studies on language assimilation, language shift and language loss or endangerment (see studies in Fishman and García 2011) and nation-state efforts for language policy and language planning (see studies in Spolsky 2004).

While the structuralist–functionalist paradigm has been productive for studies of language and ethnic identity in indigenous and ethnic minority contexts, it is based on the assumption of languages and communities as whole, bounded systems and of a one-to-one relationship between language and ethnic identity. More recent research in indigenous and language minority contexts has emphasised the negotiation of multiple, hybrid or ambiguous affiliations and the recognition of historical, social, cultural, political and economic forces in shaping language practices, language ideologies and forms of individual and collective identification. For instance, taking the French island of Corsica in the Mediterranean Sea as an example, Jaffe traces historical shifts in the discourse of Corsican language revitalisation: from Corsican monolingualism, premised on the belief that only one language can be the legitimate marker of ethnic affiliation, to recognising 'French not just as a language of past domination, but as a permanent part of the

Corsican communicative repertoire'. Jaffe also illustrated the shift in the view of bilingual competence as 'added value' through minority language bilingual education (2007: 55–56) to more recent views in which bilingual competence is linked 'to values of tolerance, inclusion, cultural relativity that are the prerequisites for global, not just European, citizenship' (ibid.: 63). By focusing on the process of becoming bilingual, Jaffe (ibid.: 67) claims that these new discourses 'carry far fewer risks of alienating or undermining the cultural legitimacy of Corsicans who are not native speakers of the Corsican language'. They highlight the internal differentiation in what might be considered as a single ethnic community and reposition the link between the Corsican language and Corsican ethnic identity.

Also focusing on indigenous and language minority contexts, García explores the link between language, ethnic identity and language policy and planning efforts. García asserts that for language maintenance and revitalisation efforts to succeed a group must have developed what Fishman (1977) calls a strong 'ethnolinguistic identity' as well as strong language practices, language ideologies and language management arrangements that support the effort (García 2012: 88). By juxtaposing case studies of different ethnolinguistic groups, García illustrates how the interplay of these components shape the outcome of language planning efforts, leading in some cases to language maintenance and development and in other cases to language endangerment and language shift.

For instance, García contrasts the case of Luxembourgish in the Grand-Duchy of Luxembourg to the case of Gallo in France. The author identifies how the link between Luxembourgish and a Luxembourgish national identity was established and how it was strengthened due to specific socio-economic conditions (e.g. Luxembourg's privileged position as a centre for private banking worldwide and the seat of several European Union organisations). While Luxembourgish coexists alongside French and German in home and institutional settings, this multilingualism has not threatened its preservation and development. Citing a recent study by Fehlen and Giles (2009), García (2012) argues that it is because of the country's multilingual tradition and its non-diaglossic relationship with French and German that a Luxembourgish ethnolinguistic identity remains dominant and language management efforts have been successful. In the case of Gallo (a Romance language and one of the two regional languages in Brittany, in France), recent language management efforts, such as developing a standard orthography and introducing it as an optional subject in schools, have been unsuccessful in reversing the rapid language shift to standard French. The small number of Gallo speakers, coupled with the lack of official recognition of Gallo by the French state as a language in its own right because of its closeness to French and its perceived competition with the other regional language, Breton (seen by Breton activists as the quintessential marker of Breton identity), have positioned Gallo as an 'extremely threatened' language and Gallo ethnolinguistic identity as severely weakened (García 2012: 99). Both examples highlight the role of what García (2012: 88) refers to as 'external authoritative powers', often advanced through education, in supporting or disrupting language management efforts.

Studies on ethnicity and language use have also been concerned with immigrant and transnational communities and how ethnic co-membership is negotiated and constructed through socially meaningful practices. For instance, De Fina (2007: 378) examines how the members of an all-male card-playing club uniting Italian-born and US-born adults of varying ages in the Washington DC area 'construct the club as essentially Italian and frame a great deal of its activities as responding to Italian traditions'. Through the close analysis of the negotiation of ethnicity among club members, the author illustrates how among group members who are dominant English speakers and have varying competences in and preferences to Italian (the standard and its regional varieties) language alternation is in general highly negotiable. However, De Fina (ibid.: 384–385) argues that certain types of code-switching to Italian are enforced:

> players establish a strict association between card-playing and speaking some Italian, so that it is tacitly understood that a good card-player in the club needs to be able to speak at least the basic words of the game in the native language. As a result, when neophytes learn the game they are also taught some of the terms for the cards and moves that characterize the game, and are expected to learn them.

De Fina shows how the situational identity of 'card-player' is continually associated with the collective Italian identity through code-switching to Italian. Elsewhere, in *Multilingual Identities in a Global City: London Stories*, Block (2006) puts multilingualism, multiculturalism, migration and the global flow of people at the centre of his analysis as he explores the stories of four immigrant/ethnolinguistic groups living, working and learning in twenty-first-century London, namely Japanese graduate students, French foreign language teachers, Spanish-speaking Latinos from South America and Caribbean and British Asian students (Preece 2006). He situates the stories in the socio-historical context of each immigrant community and examines how individual members negotiate different subject positions, including their ethnic, racial, social class and language identities as well as 'how they "do being" a Londoner' in a global city like London (2006: ix).

Other studies of immigrant and transnational communities have emphasised how ethnic identities are relationally produced and how participants conform to or resist dominant positionings, racial and ethnic dichotomies and stereotypes circulating in society at large. In the introduction to a special issue on the discursive construction of Asian Pacific American identities, Lo and Reyes (2004: 118) argue that:

> there is no Asian Pacific American without Caucasian American, no African American without Latino, no self without the other. This focus on the situated and relational unfolding of identity reveals how participants position themselves with regard not only to each other, but also to the ways in which they are defined by discourses of race and ethnicity which circulate through mass media, institutions and everyday contexts.

Quoting Tuan (1998), Lo and Reyes (2004) claim that dominant discourses appear to represent Asian Pacific Americans as either 'forever foreigners' or as 'honorary whites' (Tuan 1998 in Lo and Reyes 2004: 116). Both discourses are equally problematic. On the one hand, they emphasise heritage language use, which is often compared to an idealised native speaker norm, and code-switching practices that ignore the fact that frequently English is the primary means of communication. On the other hand, they imply an assimilation to white middle-class American norms that erases the experience of non-middle-class Asian Pacific Americans. These representations are further complicated by the fact that, unlike other ethnic groups, Asian Pacific Americans do not speak a distinct form of English, such as African American Vernacular English (AAVE) or Chicano English, but rather speak with 'some kind of "accent" which is seen as the product of foreign language interference' (ibid.: 117).

The findings of studies such as these challenge the mapping of language onto ethnicity and race in a binary fashion. For instance, Bucholtz (2004: 127) discusses how two Laotian American girls in a multiethnic high school in California exploit linguistic resources from AAVE and youth slang 'to produce linguistic and cultural styles that position them partly inside and partly outside of the school's binary black/white racial ideology'. By employing divergent linguistic and youth cultural practices, they partly align with or distance themselves from 'two contrasting stereotypes of South Asian Americans: the model minority nerd and the dangerous gangster' (ibid.). The ideological power of stereotypes is also exemplified in the use of stereotypical discourse to explicitly mark ethnic or racial difference. Examples of such discourse include what Hill (1998) has called 'Mock Spanish' and Chun (2004) refers to as 'Mock Asian' to index a stereotypical Spanish and Asian identity respectively. However, Chun (2004: 263) shows how a Korean American comedian turns the tables, so to speak, by appropriating 'Mock Asian' to challenge 'the ideologies that legitimate this racializing style'.

To conclude, the studies discussed in this chapter have sought to highlight the relationship between language and ethnic identity across different contexts and conditions. They have showed that while applied linguistics draws on theoretical perspectives of ethnicity that regard ethnic identities as an ongoing process, negotiated and constructed in discourse and emphasising the multiplicity and fragmentation of language and identity practices as they are affected by local and global contexts, there has not been a full-scale replacement of essentialist views of ethnicity – at least in practice. In the face of the increasing mobility of people and languages as a result of globalisation, ethnic boundaries and ethnic classifications linked to essentialist notions of authenticity continue to persist in people's lives. Rather than viewing them in binary opposition, future studies at the intersection of language and ethnic identity will benefit from examining further the interplay between fixed and fluid ethnicity categories.

Related topics

Historical perspectives on language and identity; Positioning language and identity: poststructuralist perspectives; Language, race and identity; Linguistic practices and transnational identities; A linguistic ethnography of identity: adopting a heteroglossic frame; Styling and identity in a second language; Construction of heritage language and cultural identities: a case study of two young British-Bangladeshis in London; Minority languages and group identity: Scottish Gaelic in the Old World and the New.

Further reading

Fishman, J.A. and García, O. (eds) (2010). *Handbook of language and ethnic identity. Vol. 1 Disciplinary and regional perspectives.* Oxford: Oxford University Press. (Volume 1 of the Handbook examines language and ethnic identity from a variety of approaches and through a regional perspective.)
Fishman, J.A. and García, O. (eds) (2011). *Handbook of language and ethnic identity. Vol. 2 The success–failure continuum in language and ethnic identity.* Oxford: Oxford University Press. (Volume 2 of the Handbook focuses on different language and ethnic identity efforts and the reasons for their successes and failures.)
Harris, R. and Rampton, B. (2003). *The language, ethnicity and race reader.* London: Routledge. (The Reader discusses key texts in the field of language, ethnicity and race.)

References

Angouri, J. (2012). '"I'm a Greek Kiwi": constructing Greekness in discourse', *Journal of Language, Identity, and Education,* 11(2): 96–108.
Appadurai, A. (1996). *Modernity at large: cultural dimensions of globalisation.* Minneapolis: University of Minnesota Press.

Asimakopoulou, F. and Christidou-Lionaraki, S. (2002). *Η Μουσουλμανική μειονότητα και οι Ελληνοτουρκικές σχέσεις* [*The Muslim minority of Thrace and Greek–Turkish relations*]. Athens: Livanis.

Auer, P. (ed.) (1984). *Bilingual conversation*. Amsterdam: Benjamins.

Bailey, B. (2007). Heteroglossia and boundaries, in M. Heller (ed.) *Bilingualism: a social approach*. Basingstoke: Palgrave, pp. 257–274.

Bakhtin, M.M. (1986). *Speech genres and other late essays*. [eds C. Emerson and M. Holquist]. Manchester: Manchester University Press.

Barth, F. (1969). Introduction, in F. Barth (ed.) *Ethnic groups and boundaries: the social organisation of ethnic difference*. Long Grove: Waveland Press, pp. 9–38.

Baxter, J. (this volume). Positioning language and identity: poststructuralist perspectives, in S. Preece (ed.) *The Routledge handbook of language and identity*. London: Routledge, pp. 34–49.

Benwell, B. and Stokoe, E. (2006). *Discourse and identity*. Edinburgh: Edinburgh University Press.

Benwell, B. and Stokoe, E. (this volume). Ethnomethodological and conversation analytic approaches to identity, in S. Preece (ed.) *The Routledge handbook of language and identity*. London: Routledge, pp. 66–82.

Bhabha, H. (1994). *The location of culture*. London: Routledge.

Blackledge, A. and Creese, A. (2010). *Multilingualism: a critical perspective*. Clevedon: Multilingual Matters.

Block, D. (2006). *Multilingual identities in a global city: London stories*. Basingstoke: Palgrave Macmillan.

Block, D. (2007). *Second language identities*. London: Continuum.

Block, D. and Corona, V. (this volume). Intersectionality in language and identity research, in S. Preece (ed.) *The Routledge handbook of language and identity*. London: Routledge, pp. 507–522.

Blom, J.P. and Gumperz, J. (1972). Social meaning in linguistic structures: code-switching in Norway, in J. Gumperz and D. Hymes (eds) *Directions in sociolinguistics: the ethnography of communication*. New York: Holt, Rinehart and Winston, pp. 407–434.

Blommaert, J. and Backus, A. (2011). 'Repertoires revisited: "knowing language" in superdiversity', *Working Papers in Urban Language and Literacies*, Paper 67 [Online]. Available at www.kcl.ac.uk/sspp/departments/education/research/ldc/publications/workingpapers/the-papers/67.pdf

Brumfit, C.J. (1995). Teacher professionalism and research, in J. Cook and B. Seidlhofer (eds) *Principles and practice in applied linguistics: studies in Honor of H.G. Widdowson*. Oxford: Oxford University Press, pp. 27–41.

Bucholtz, M. (2004). 'Styles and stereotypes: the linguistic negotiation of identity among Latin American youth', *Pragmatics*, 14(2–3): 127–147.

Callahan, L. (2012). 'Pre-imposition vs. in situ negotiation of group and individual identities: Spanish and English in US service encounters', *Critical Multilingualism Studies*, 1(1): 57–73.

Chun, E. (2004). 'Ideologies of legitimate mockery: Margaret Cho's revoicing of mock Asian', *Pragmatics*, 14(2–3): 263–289.

Cutler, A. (1999). 'Yorkville crossing: white teens, hip hop, and African American English', *Journal of Sociolinguistics*, 3(4): 428–442.

De Fina, A. (2007). 'Code switching and the construction of ethnic identity in a community of practice', *Language in Society*, 36: 371–392.

Doran, M. (2004). Negotiating between bourge and racaille: Verlan as youth identity practice in suburban Paris, in A. Pavlenko and A. Blackledge (eds) *Negotiation of identities in multilingual contexts*. Clevedon: Multilingual Matters, pp. 93–124.

Edwards, J. (2009). *Language and identity*. Cambridge: Cambridge University Press.

Eriksen, T.H. (1993). *Ethnicity and nationalism: anthropological perspectives*. London: Pluto.

Ferguson, C. (1964). Diglossia, in D. Hymes (ed.) *Language in culture and society*. New York: Harper and Row, pp. 429–439.

Fishman, J.A. (ed.) (1968). *Readings in the sociology of language*. The Hague: Mouton.

Fishman, J.A. (1977). Language and ethnicity, in H. Giles (ed.) *Language, ethnicity, and intergroup relations*. New York: Academic Press, pp. 15–57.

Fishman, J.A. (1989). *Language and ethnicity in minority sociolinguistic perspective.* Clevedon: Multilingual Matters.

Fishman, J.A. (1999). Introduction, in J.A. Fishman (ed.) *Handbook of language and ethnic identity.* Oxford: Oxford University Press, pp. 3–5.

Fishman, J.A. (2010). Introduction, in J.A. Fishman and O. García (eds) *Handbook of language and ethnic identity. Vol. 1 Disciplinary and regional perspectives.* Oxford: Oxford University Press, pp. 3–5.

Fishman, J.A. and García, O. (eds) (2010). *Handbook of language and ethnic identity. Vol. 1 Disciplinary and regional perspectives.* Oxford: Oxford University Press.

Fishman, J.A. and García, O. (eds) (2011). *Handbook of language and ethnic identity. Vol. 2 The success–failure continuum in language and ethnic identity.* Oxford: Oxford University Press.

García, O. (2009). *Bilingual education in the 21st century: a global perspective.* Chichester: Wiley-Blackwell.

García, O. (2010). Languaging and ethnifying, in J.A. Fishman and O. García (eds) *Handbook of language and ethnicity: disciplinary and regional perspectives.* Oxford: Oxford University Press, pp. 519–534.

García, O. (2012). Ethnic identity and language policy, in B. Spolsky (ed.) *The Cambridge handbook of language policy.* Cambridge: Cambridge University Press, pp. 79–99.

Gumperz, J.J. (1982). *Discourse strategies.* Cambridge: Cambridge University Press.

Gumperz, J.J. and Cook-Gumperz, J. (1982). Language and the communication of social identity, in J.J. Gumperz (ed.) *Language and social identity.* Cambridge: Cambridge University Press, pp. 1–21.

Han, H. (2011). 'Social inclusion through multilingual ideologies, policies and practices: a case study of a minority church', *International Journal of Bilingual Education and Bilingualism,* 14(4): 383–398.

Harris, R. (2006). *New ethnicities and language use.* London: Palgrave/Macmillan.

Harris, R. (2011). Ethnicity, in J. Simpson (ed.) *The Routledge handbook of applied linguistics.* Abingdon: Routledge, pp. 344–358.

Harris, R. and Rampton, B. (2003). Introduction, in R. Harris and B. Rampton (eds) *The language, ethnicity and race reader.* London: Routledge, pp. 1–14.

Heller, M. (1992). 'The politics of code-switching and language choice', *Journal of Multilingual and Multicultural Development,* 13(1–2): 123–142.

Heller, M. (1999). *Linguistic minorities and modernity: a sociolinguistic ethnography.* Longman: London.

Heller, M. (2007). Bilingualism as ideology and practice, in M. Heller (ed.) *Bilingualism: a social approach.* London: Palgrave Macmillan, pp. 1–22.

Hill, J. (1998). 'Language, race and white public space', *American Anthropologist,* 100(3): 680–683.

Jaffe, A. (2007). Minority language movements, in M. Heller (ed.) *Bilingualism: a social approach.* London: Palgrave Macmillan, pp. 50–70.

Joseph, J. (2004). *Language and identity: national, ethnic, religious.* Basingstoke: Palgrave Macmillan.

Kroskrity, P.V. (2001). Identity, in A. Duranti (ed.) *Key terms in language and culture.* Malden, MA: Blackwell, pp. 106–109.

Leach, E.R. (1977 [1954]). *Political systems of Highland Burma.* London: London School of Economics and Political Science.

LePage, R.B. and Tabouret-Keller, A. (1985). *Acts of identity: Creole-based approaches to language and ethnicity.* Cambridge: Cambridge University Press.

Levine, R.A. and Campbell, D.T. (1972). *Ethnocentrism: theories of conflict, ethnic attitudes and group behavior.* New York: Wiley.

Lewis, B. (1999). *The Turkish language reform: a catastrophic success.* Oxford: Oxford University Press.

Liddell, G.H. and Scott, R. (1940). *A Greek-English lexicon* [Revised and augmented throughout by Sir Henry Stuart Jones with the assistance of Roderick McKenzie]. Oxford: Clarendon Press.

Lo, A. (1999). 'Codeswitching, speech community and the construction of ethnic identity', *Journal of Sociolinguistics,* 3(4): 461–479.

Lo, A. and Reyes, A. (2004). 'Language, identity and relationality in Asian Pacific America: an introduction', *Pragmatics,* 14(2–3): 115–125.

Lytra, V. (2007). *Play frames and social identities: contact encounters in a Greek primary school.* Amsterdam/Philadelphia: Benjamins.

Lytra, V. (2014). 'Revisiting discourses of language, identity and community in a transnational context through a commemorative book project', *Multilingua*, 33(5–6): 551–574.

Lytra, V. and Martin, P. (eds) (2010). *Sites of multilingualism: complementary schools in Britain today*. Stoke-on-Trent: Trentham.

Makoni, S. and Pennycook, A. (eds) (2007). *Disinventing and reconstituting languages*. Clevedon: Multilingual Matters.

May, S., Modood, T. and Squires, J. (eds) (2004). *Ethnicity, nationalism and minority rights*. Cambridge: Cambridge University Press.

Moerman, M. (1965). 'Ethnic identification in a complex civilization: who are the Lue?', *American Anthropologist*, 67: 1215–1230.

Moerman, M. (1974). Accomplishing ethnicity, in R. Turner (ed.) *Ethnomethodology*. Harmondsworth: Penguin, pp. 54–68.

Nash, M. (1989). *The cauldron of ethnicity in the modern world*. Chicago: The University of Chicago Press.

Otsuji, E. and Pennycook, A. (2010). 'Metrolingualism: fixity, fluidity and language in flux', *International Journal of Multilingualism*, 7(3): 240–254.

Patrick, D. (2007). Language endangerment, language rights and indigeneity, in M. Heller (ed.) *Bilingualism: a social approach*. London: Palgrave Macmillan, pp. 111–134.

Pavlenko, A. and Blackledge, A. (2004). Introduction: new theoretical approaches to the study of negotiation of identities in multilingual contexts, in A. Pavlenko and A. Blackledge (eds) *Negotiation of identities in multilingual contexts*. Clevedon: Multilingual Matters, pp. 1–33.

Preece, S. (2006). British Asian undergraduate students in London, in D. Block, *Multilingual identities in a global city: London stories*. Basingstoke: Palgrave Macmillan, pp. 171–199.

Rampton, B. (1995). *Crossing: language and ethnicity among adolescents*. London: Longman.

Rampton, B. and Charalambous, C. (2012). Crossing, in M. Martin-Jones, A. Blackledge and A. Creese (eds) *The Routledge handbook of multilingualism*. Abingdon: Routledge, pp. 482–498.

Saxena, M. (2014). '"Critical diglossia" and "lifestyle diglossia": linguistic diversity, national development, English and language change', *International Journal of the Sociology of Language*, 225: 91–112.

Silverstein, M. (1979). Language structure and linguistic ideology, in P. Clyne, W.F. Hanks and C.L. Hofbauer (eds) *The elements: a parasession on linguistic units and levels*. Chicago: Chicago Linguistic Society, pp. 193–247.

Simpson, J. (ed.) (2011). *The Routledge handbook of applied linguistics*. Abingdon: Routledge.

Souza, A., Kwapong, A. and Woodham, M. (2012). 'Pentecostal and Catholic churches in London – the role of ideologies in the language planning of faith lessons', *Current Issues in Language Planning*, 13(2): 105–120.

Spolsky, B. (2004). *Language policy*. Cambridge: Cambridge University Press.

9

Language, race and identity

Tope Omoniyi

... in my experience race reveals itself as plastic, inconstant, and to some extent volitional.

(Haney-López 1994: 10)

Regardless of what evidence exists for race's biological reality, 'race', because it is a linguistic phenomenon – a word, an utterance – becomes a social construct when it enters the world of discourse, which it must do, of course, in order for us to communicate about it.

(Howard 2010: 1)

Introduction

The title of this chapter calls up a fundamental debate that has raged since the rise of philology and the discovery of the Indo-European language family in the late eighteenth century, concerning whether or not language and race are linked. The 'nature versus nurture' debate pitches those who say race is a biological fact and therefore provide genetic arguments to buttress their claim versus those who say race is a social construction in the Boasian tradition. Sapir (2003 [1921]) identifies race and culture as 'settings' for language. In his account, language, race and culture are the three 'rubrics' under which anthropologists study humankind and they are 'not distributed in a parallel fashion' (2003: 29). Rather, their areas of distribution intercross in the most bewildering fashion. He further notes that races intermingle differently from languages and 'languages may spread far beyond their original home, invading the territory of new races and new culture spheres' (ibid.). The link between language, race and identity has been in the spotlight again recently and a new field of inquiry: 'raciolinguistics' is even being proposed in some quarters.[1]

This chapter seeks to examine 'race' as a dimension of identity in relation to language and identity studies in applied linguistics and to consider the relationship of race with language. In what follows, an overview of race is presented, followed by a number of issues and ongoing debates related to race as a construct with regard to sociolinguistics and applied linguistics.

Overview

This section presents highlights of the scholarship on race that show us that its intersections with language and identity are both evident and complex. The definition of race is contested around whether the associative properties are inherent or constructed and performed. The illustration in the subsection on 'racial passing' underlines this complexity as racial stereotypes are the features that are exploited. These stereotypes arose out of unsubstantiated accounts of nineteenth-century explorers and philosophers.

Haney-Lopez (1994: 165) defines race as a 'vast group of people loosely bound together by historically contingent, socially significant elements of their morphology and/or their ancestry'. He goes further to say that it is:

> neither an essence nor an illusion, but rather an on-going contradictory, self-reinforcing plastic process subject to the macro forces of social and political struggle and the micro effects of daily decisions ... the referents of terms like Black and White are social groups, not genetically distinct branches of humankind.
>
> *(Ibid.)*

The view of race as a social construct has been reinforced, for instance, in a number of seminal texts in sociolinguistics and education, such as Hewitt's (1986) *White talk Black talk*, Alim and Baugh's (2007) *Talkin Black talk* and Bucholtz's (2011) *White kids: language, race, and styles of youth identity*.

Hartigan (2010) notes that the ways race is performed, or constructed, vary from one locale to another. This corresponds with the phenomenon that Eckert describes as style-shifting (2000; see also Coupland 1980). Hartigan (2010: 33) argues that the cultural analysis of race as performative involves three interrelated operations viz 'body work, spatializing practices, and the determination of belonging and difference' (Hartigan 2010: 33). All three operations involve language to varying degrees all geared towards the goal of performing race. The position articulated here is not much different from that taken by others on the subject. Howard (2010: para. 6), for instance, observes that:

> Haney Lopez's story introduces the important point that a person can 'choose' – or *construct* – [their] racial identity not only on a census form, but also, more notably, in the wardrobe, in the classroom, and on the streets of American cities. And, as we all know, biracial individuals are not the only ones who must construct their race in this way: a black man must perform whiteness when interviewing for a corporate job, for example, just as a white kid in an urban public school must perform blackness when changing in the locker room for gym class.

These references to performances of race are in fact only the tip of a robust scholarship that transverses a number of subjects in the social sciences, such as film and cinema studies; postcolonial studies; feminist studies; and cultural studies. As Foster (2003: 25) notes, '[w]hiteness as a construct was already in place at the end of the nineteenth century when photography and cinema began their respective histories'.

By 'biracial', we may suppose that Haney-Lopez was referring to the mixed race offspring of parents from two different racial cohorts who, as a consequence of being mixed race, have access to the signifying practices of the races of both their parents and may choose from both repertoires as occasion demands. However, this is not straightforward. There is a subclass of people whose racial constitution involve differing degrees of hybridity. For instance, the off-spring of the union of a biracial person (A+B) and another biracial person (C+D) has the racial constitution of A, B, C and D to varying degrees, and may socially signify as they choose, using repertoires of any or all of these groups. They will also be adjudged socially on an authenticity scale. Of course, we know from Bucholtz (2011) and Rampton (1995) that youths do not need such constitution per se in order to so signify, especially in the context of multilingual and multicultural urban settings. From this brief overview, we can see that the meaning of race is complex and controversial and raises a number of issues and ongoing debates. In the following section, I address a number of these issues and the complexity of settings in relation to linguistic diversity.

Issues and ongoing debates

The first issue to attend to is on the equality of the races. Ashcroft's (2003) more critical treatment of the relationship between language and race is situated in the 'marriage of linguistic hegemony and racial marginalisation' in imperial discourse (2003: 37). He refutes the nineteenth-century categorisations and descriptions of racial types as 'elaborate fictions, invested with an absurd amount of intellectual energy. They are an elaboration of the *fictionality* of language itself, the arbitrary link between signifier and signified' (2003: 42).

The philosopher David Hume (1758) had, for instance, suggested that 'Negroes were inferior to whites', Africa was tagged the 'Dark Continent', and a 'black–white' binary was constructed in which 'black' acquired connotative properties of, among others, ugliness, filth, degradation, night and mourning while 'white' epitomised cleanliness, purity, beauty, virginity and peace.

But Ashcroft imbues language with agency when he asserts that it inscribes rather than describes human difference 'through such chromatic signifiers' (2003: 40) (in other words, colour-based associative properties), which is somewhat unsettling considering that language is a human attribute. Consequently, the preferred focus of this chapter must be on what Ashcroft referred to as 'the reality of racial experience', which according to him 'centres, not in physical typology, or "community of blood" or genetic variation, but in language' (ibid.). This reality manifests either as Renan's linguistic races, that is, races that are only decipherable on the basis of language, exemplified by the Semitic and Aryan races, or what Ashcroft called 'the figurative power of language in which chromatic signifiers performed the cultural work of racial "othering"' (2003: 40). Renan (1855: 80) concluded that 'there is just one criterion for recognising Semites, and that is language'. This distinction is somewhat different from Ashcroft's ideologically inclined discourse-based account, which is aligned to the thought of race as a social construction subscribed to widely in the discourse of resistance in post-colonial writing.

There is a related debate that pertains to the relationship between language and culture. Some prefer to see language as a component of culture among other components by which aggregates of people may be identified. Others prefer to see language as the embodiment of culture so that the latter exists in language. This requires a broad interpretation of language that includes all manner of expressive and communicative practices, whether vocal, visual or signed. The language–culture link is more usually invoked in discussions of ethnic and ethnolinguistic identities (see Joseph, this volume; Lytra, this volume). Ethnicity is however no less problematic than race in relation to language. This point is well articulated by Hewitt (2003 [1992]) in his discussion of the roles of language and youth in the destabilisation of ethnicity. Stable, unchanging folk identities once ascribed to communities by social and cultural anthropologists have been subjected to hybridisation or what Hannerz (1989) and Barth (1989) referred to as 'creolisation'. Both race and ethnicity can be performatively and symbolically constructed and ascribed based on any sustained or mythical group stereotypes and stylisations. Yet, both terms are also institutionally set demographic cohort descriptors for aggregates of people who possess certain physical or physiological attributes and cultural values. For instance, distinguishing between the Masai of Kenya and the Pygmies of the Congo will entail references to the contrastive physical heights of the groups, their activities, which are conditioned by their ecological environments, and the languages they speak.

The two issues presented above are, however, not entirely discontinuous. Distinctions between various human groups (whether defined by race or ethnicity) based on their views of the world (conveyed by language) have become problematic in our increasingly multilingually and multiculturally resourced and globalised lives. If language influences thought and behaviour as linguistic determinism tells us, then exposure to multiple languages must mean exposure to multiple influences. Which perspective is taken impacts on how the link between language and identity is viewed. The dilemma here is that culture is perceived as a variable in multi-ethnic as well as in multiracial societies. So, in the United States, there are references to 'Black culture', and these are set in contrast to the cultural practices of White, Hispanic, Asian and Native Americans. Similarly, in the UK, and increasingly across the nation states of the European Union whose populations have been diversified through post-colonial migration, multiracialism has resulted in the identification of stereotyped language practices for different groups. These stereotypes inform TV programmes like *Desi Rascals* (Sky Living), *My Big Fat Gypsy Grand National* (Channel 4 Television, UK) and so on, and romanticise folk identities. As Haney-Lopez (2000: x) reminds us: 'Human interaction rather than natural differentiation must be seen as the source and the continued basis for racial categorization.' Arguably, the fact that it takes immigrants who cross racial borders a while to shift from invoking ethnic to racial identity supports Haney-Lopez's placement of premium on interaction (see Ibrahim 2003). Next, what are the sociolinguistics' and applied linguistics' stakes in these debates?

Sociolinguistics

Interest in the relationship between language and race in sociolinguistic and applied linguistic scholarship is primarily a consequence of human mobility on a significant scale that has created zones of racial and language contact and pluralism. In contrast, interest in language and race in anthropology had been driven by the desire to identify and describe communities of people as discrete sociocultural groups. Thus, it is not surprising that the departure from folk identification has been championed by sociolinguistics. Perhaps the largest human mobility with visible language impact (i.e. Caribbean creoles and African American Vernacular English) is the slave trade, which moved 11 million Africans through the Middle Passage to the Americas and Europe (BBC 2015).

History may show that inter-racial encounters existed before large-scale slavery, but sociolinguistics as a discipline emerging in the first half of the twentieth century can only engage with that past in retrospection through secondary data. This is possible because language and race constitute an interface for observing the structuring of society. So, for example, the Greco-Roman empires were marked by what today are clearly ethno-national encounters but at the time were conceptualised as racial encounters.

Wolfram's study of social dialects in Detroit English is a classic study that examines the relationship between language and race. Wolfram's (1969: xiii) discussion of the social setting for linguistic diversity in this study isolated three factors – patterns of migration; racial isolation; and social status (all of which are arguably interconnected) – as follows:

1   Patterns of in-migration: Wolfram examined the distribution of residents of Detroit according to whether they were born in or outside Michigan. He made the intriguing observation that 68 per cent of the 10–14-year-olds in the Negro population had been born in Michigan compared to 83 per cent of the same age cohort for the White population. However, among those aged 45–49, only 5 per cent of the Negro population had been born in Michigan compared to 41 per cent of the White population in the same age cohort. Thus, the majority of the adult Negro population had migrated to Michigan having been born in outlying states like Mississippi, Alabama, Georgia, Arkansas and Tennessee, among others.

2   Racial isolation: Detroit City was racially segregated, with people racially marked by what part of the city they lived in – Inner City (East/West), Middle City and Outer City. Wolfram discovered that the Inner City and Middle City had a 75 per cent and 67 per cent Negro population respectively, while the Outer City was a White community with a 1 per cent Negro population. The same pattern of racial isolation was recorded for school enrolment. According to the United States Commission on Civil Rights (cited in Wolfram 1969: 29), in 1965 70 per cent of the Negro children attended schools in which the school population was 90–100 per cent Negro.

3   Social status: four social classes were delineated – Upper-Middle, Lower-Middle, Upper-Working and Lower-Working class – using fairly sophisticated methodological tools that involved calculations based on the variables of educational qualification, income and housing type. Wolfram reported that out of 40 per cent of the city's population that was classified as Upper-Middle and Lower-Middle class, the Negro population represented less than 1.5 per cent.

All three variables taken together enable us to identify non-standard Negro speech as one of 'racial isolation'. According to Wolfram (1969: 21), over a 20-year span Detroit transformed drastically with the exodus of its White population into the suburbs and the in-migration of a slightly larger population of Afro Americans. This movement accounted for the transformation of the sociolinguistic landscape by the time Wolfram and Shuy carried out their studies in the 1960s and 1970s. The confluence of ethnicity and economics-engendered social classification produced a hybrid community. Wolfram distinguished between Non-Standard Negro speech, which had emotive overtones, and Black English, which captured the racial pride in the Black community of the late 1960s.

Another classic study of the relationship between language and race is Hewitt's (1986) study of Black British talk in the United Kingdom. Hewitt's was not the first study of Black talk in the UK, but the others that preceded it were unambiguously tagged West Indian or Jamaican. For instance, Wells (1973) studied West Indians' assimilation of the features of the vernacular variety of London English as a sociolinguistic strategy deployed to reduce the burden of racial difference on the group. Elsewhere, Edwards (1986) adopted a sociolinguistics of literacy educa-tion perspective that ascribed a West Indian racial identity to members of the Black population in the UK. We can safely say mainstream Black identity at the time of Hewitt's and Edwards' studies, and Black Britain as a referential group, were mainly synonymous with people of West Indian (primarily Jamaican/Caribbean) extraction. Edwards (ibid.) devotes a chapter in her book *Language in a black community* to issues like attitudes to 'West Indian speech', 'interference or influence' and 'sociology of language', all from the perspective of a variety of spoken English described by its speakers as 'patwa' or 'patois' (i.e. Jamaican Creole). Here is an exhortation for an illustration of the language: 'Dem a stop me and say, "We bring you over here fi h'educate you, a learn a fi speak better", and all this kind of thing. Well, me used to listen to dem, but after dem gone, me used to speak the same' (ibid.: 105).

Jamaican Creole is represented as central to West Indian identity in the UK before ethnicity accommodated the notion of language 'crossing' (Rampton 1995). The practice of language crossing, and other practices of a linguistically and ethnically diverse youth in urban areas, contributed to the shift in the sociolinguistics of identity that de-emphasised racial binaries like 'White versus Black', 'Black versus Asian' and 'Black British African versus Black British West Indian' and the emergence in its place of a paradigm that suited the multiculturalism project from the mid-1980s onwards – the birth of 'new ethnicities' (Hall 1989; Rampton 1995, 2006; Harris and Rampton 2003; Harris 2006). In what follows, I shall present a number of case studies from the last half-century or so that illustrate this shift in thinking about the relationship between language and race to demonstrate how these dimensions of identity work.

In Hyland and Paltridge's (2011) *The Bloomsbury companion to discourse analysis*, Lin and Kubota contributed a review of a number of analytical paradigms for investigating the role of discourse in the process of racialisation, which put the spotlight on what they identify as 'intellectual milestones' (p. 277). The treatment of language and race in the sociolinguistic literature however is not confined in focus to racism discourses (see Baxter, this volume, for a discussion on discourse). In fact, before the discourse analytic approach became popular in the last quarter of the twentieth century, language and race had been established in anthropological linguistics and linguistic anthropology under what now seems to be a flawed 'one race, one language' precept, in which researchers described language behaviour and constructed cultural grammars of racial groups.

In examining the link between language and race as a dimension of identity, context is a crucial factor. There are several key contexts that a sociolinguistic or applied linguistic paradigm must consider, three of which are immigration, popular culture and education. All three of these can and have been explored through the prism of language and race. There are two additional strands in this discussion:

1 Descriptive analysis of 'speech style' or language behaviour by which Black racial stereotypes were constructed: this was the approach that was preferred in the mid-twentieth century by sociolinguists who were preoccupied with describing the variety of English spoken by Afro Americans. These speech styles were socio-economically and regionally distributed and drew on work in anthropology on 'slave talk'. The focus was on grammar rather than sociolinguistic variables. The contemporary sociolinguistic application of this form of descriptive analysis is in linguistic profiling.
2 In the educational sector, teaching and learning language skills necessitated by migration, and sociolinguistic scales and resources - bilingual education programmes targeted at immigrant communities such as those for children from English as an Additional Language (EAL) and English as a Second Language (ESL) backgrounds.

At the core of the first strand is the conflict and tension generated by the treatment of the language spoken by African Americans as a substandard dialect of English rather than as a language in its own right. In other words, there is an articulation of language and race as a rights issue. Arguably, there is political expediency in extending such recognition to Ebonics, the term for a variety of language used by Afro Americans in the United States. While African American English may be a dialect of mainstream Standard American English, the articulation of Ebonics as indigenous to Black America made the country multiracial and multilingual. Ebonics is no more similar to English than the Scandinavian languages are similar to each other, but the latter are assigned to different nations and tagged as separate languages. The difference is in the parameters of tagging sought for the former: racial rather than national identity. The second strand is closely related to the first but specialised in its focus on the educational sector. This plays out across various contexts of language education and language in education.

In his foreword to Sutcliffe's (1992) *System in Black language*, Figueroa notes that the assignment of race to language suggested by 'Black Language', 'Black English', 'Black English Vernacular' or Hewitt's (1986) seminal text *White talk Black talk* 'sounds unacceptably genetic' as though that kind of language is 'passed down through the genes' (Figueroa 1992: ix). By extension, the edited volume of *Black linguistics* (Makoni *et al.* 2003) similarly suggests a form of gene-based science of language. While the language forms described in these works may not in reality be genetically transmitted, socialisation restricts them to the communities in which they are observed and thus appear to be racially exclusive. In a similar vein, Labov (1972: xiii) differentiates between 'Black English' and 'Black English Vernacular'. The former was synonymous with 'Nonstandard Negro English', which was a stigmatised variety in that it was contrasted with Standard American English and focused on the use of non-standard grammar as the basis of racial identification.

Figueroa remarked that racists of another era operating within the race–language framework had said that 'Black People' could not pronounce certain European phonemes because of the size of their lips. Drawing on Ashcroft's (2003) plea with post-colonial intellectuals, it is important to realise that language in and of itself has no race. As Ashcroft contends:

> It is not just advisable but crucial that post-colonial intellectuals realise that language has no race, for the consequence of this link – when it leads to the rejection of tools of discursive resistance such as the English Language – has been to imprison resistance in an inward looking world. The ultimate consequence of the belief that language embodies race is the deafening silence of a rage that cannot be heard.
>
> *(Ibid.: 51)*

The positions articulated above on the link between language and race have informed extensive scholarship in literary studies and cultural studies, as well as other related disciplines. In sociolinguistics, a version of that discussion has been couched in the debate around Chomskyan linguistic universals and the emergence of dominant propositions of difference and diversity (see Harris and Rampton 2003). Sociolinguistics has introduced more finely defined contexts or configurations of identity into the debate beyond race with a focus on discursive practice rather than on language per se. Along this line, and crucially for the discussion in this chapter, Johnstone (2010: 29) posed a fundamental question: 'How do linguistic forms and patterns come to be associated with identities?' In answering this question we are not only establishing the interconnection between race and language, but, as it were, we are locating language in identity.

There are two dimensions to the relationship between language and race as a dimension of identity. In one dimension, bi/multilingual linguistic resources are used to evoke or construct an individual's identity. In relation to racial identity, Johnstone (2010) lists four language-related concepts: indexicality (signifying), reflexivity (cause and effect), metapragmatics (discourse of language use) and enregisterment (language and social valuation) (see also Agha 2003, 2005). In a second dimension, interest in language and race in sociolinguistics and applied linguistics has also arisen as a consequence of human mobility on a large scale resulting in racial contact and diversity. This interest has focused on describing the linguistic practices of groups as opposed to individuals, which comes to inform the formulation of social policies designed to manage contexts of racial diversity. The dynamics of multiracial societies, especially within the liberal democratic project, foreground issues of equality, social justice, and human rights. 'Difference and Diversity' paradigm in the 'language-has-no-race' camp since 'difference' and 'diversity' are articulated as properties of human society sociologically and politically speaking.

The multidimensional nature of the task of tracking a trajectory like the one above is not in doubt. First, in order to talk about 'language, race and identity', we require a multiracial society frame (Goffman 1967). Multiracial countries may have followed different historical trajectories. For instance, the narratives of multiracialism in the United States, Britain, Brazil, South Africa, Australia, Germany and Sweden, among others, have emerged from different socio-historical processes of displacement resulting from slavery, colonisation, political, ethnic and religious conflicts and natural disasters, as well as general migration. The different experiences in the formation of multiracial societies have arguably caused differences in the nature of the relationship between language, race and identity in the various polities. Second, the relationship is observable in the institutional discourses deployed in the administration of multiracial societies, in inter-group and interpersonal relations.

Following from the two assumptions above, multiracial nation states have evolved as a definite consequence of the acquisitive and expansionist programmes pursued largely by Europeans during the period of colonialism. The expansionist framework included, for instance, the slave trade as a mechanism of Europe's industrial revolution, and other seemingly legitimate trading activities that culminated in colonisation. These processes account for 'Black America', 'Black Britain', 'White Australia' and 'White South Africa'. Perhaps in the forefront of concerns in these societies is racial prejudice; hence a large body of scholarship has emerged on racism discourse (van Dijk 1987), as I indicated earlier. The identity focus of this scholarship concerns representations of racial groups based on constructed stereotypes. The discourse is perpetuated at individual and institutional levels and it perpetuates institutional racism. For example, the 'Stop and Search' policy of the Metropolitan Police Force in London allegedly targets black youths. In addition, the Macpherson Report described as institutional racism the perversion of justice in the trial that followed the stabbing to death of Stephen Lawrence, a Black teenager by five White youths in 1993. The successful management of racial contact is determined more or less by the extent to which prejudice is reduced or eliminated. The sociolinguistic phenomenon of language crossing (Rampton 1995, 2006) and the emergence of Multicultural London English (Kerswill 2011) may be cited as visible sociolinguistic consequences of inter-racial harmony in an urban context.

In the education sector in multilingual and multiracial nations or societies, language policy and planning as instruments of nation-state administration offer contexts for the examination of the language and race interface. In this regard, the conflict resolution that underlies multiple official languages of the South African government is a case in point. Caution must be exercised not to conflate ethnicity and race in this instance. While there is a Black/White/Coloured racial divide in South Africa that allows us to demarcate immigrant European from indigenous African languages, there is also multiethnicity on which basis diversity programmes and projects are fashioned.

So far I have discussed conceptualisations of language and race in old and new scholarship with a focus on the associative characteristics of racial groups. In the next section, I turn to applied linguistics scholarship to explore the issues that arise around language, race and group identities.

Applied linguistics

In this section, I turn to educational and other professional contexts to examine the interaction of language, race and identity and to focus the discussion more fully on applied linguistics. There is an Applied Linguistics strand that focuses on language learning in the X-Language as an Additional Language community (such as English as an Additional Language, French as an Additional Language, German as an Additional Language and, more recently, Mandarin as an Additional Language). Additional language education has arisen in contexts of migration as migrants attempt to settle into their adoptive environments along with issues of identity negotiation, old and new citizenships, belonging and acceptability. While migration does not change the race of those involved, their ethnicities may be redefined in the context of their adoptive nation states. However, within the school context, race and ethnicity seem to coalesce for Black immigrant children in public discourse. By this I mean, for instance, the reference to Black or Asian children in the British school system, which papers over large-scale cultural differences between children of diverse ethnic heritage, such as Indian, Nepalese, Pakistani, Bengali, Jamaican, Cameroonian, Kenyan and South African, to name a few. The following examples illustrate the link between race and language in educational contexts.

Brown versus Board of Education

Following the proposition that racial diversity is the consequence of human mobility, it is only logical that we draw our illustration from the United States of America in this chapter considering its immigrant history. Two landmark court cases are crucially significant here and will serve to elucidate the language and race link in the context of schooling. The desegregation of schools was implemented following the 14 May 1954 *Brown v. Board of Education of Topeka (Kansas)* ruling. Supreme Court Justice Earl Warren ruled that school segregation was a violation of the 14th Amendment and therefore unconstitutional. A quarter of a century later in 1979, the *Martin Luther King Elementary School Children v. Ann Arbor District School Board* case articulated the legitimacy of 'Black English' as a language in terms of equal language rights and also in terms of language support in the TESOL framework.

Ebonics and the Oakland School Board

Perhaps one of the most volatile links of language to race and identity in education was that initially made by the Oakland School Board in California in its Resolution of December 18, 1996. The Resolution was interpreted as granting linguistic independence to the 28,000 African American students for whom Ebonics was a 'predominantly primary language'. The argument was that Ebonics is not a non-standard dialect of English. The controversy was eventually resolved by referendum, culminating in Proposition 226[2] (Baugh 2004: 305).

The Somali community of Minnesota

Bigelow's (2010b: 1) study of the Somali community of Minnesota had the objective to 'connect dimensions of literacy and language learning to gendered, religious, and racialized identity' and, in so doing, 'offer a model for how Applied Linguists can contribute to social justice and advocacy agendas that align with the communities in which they work' (ibid.: 2). Bigelow conducted a longitudinal study of the literacy and language learning experiences of the Somali in the Upper Midwest United States to re-examine existing theories, determine the impact of mainstream identity-marking processes, expose blind spots, and review advocacy and social justice agendas. African migrants from non-English-speaking countries experience racialisation in their attempt to acquire the linguistic survival repertoires necessary to forge a living in the imagined North American or European adopted homeland. Language programmes are specifically packaged and targeted at a racial group or cohort. Ibrahim (2003) referred to the contexts in which Somali youths learn Black English in Ottawa as 'a symbolic site of identification in language learning'. The account of the Somali in Minnesota presented above is similar to that reported for other immigrant and refugee groups for whom language intervention programmes have been set up (see Ibrahim 2003).

Literacy and race in Reading, UK

The relationship between the state and migrant communities shows signs of what Bigelow (2010a) describes as 'minoritization' (the subordination of minority communities in the social order). Funding cuts to the EAL programmes are often articulated as evidence of this. *The School Funding Reform: Arrangements for 2013–2014* (Department of Education, UK) effectively cut funding support for children from an English as an Additional Language background. This is similar to the slash to funds in the Oakland School Board case I referred to above. But our next example of language and race interaction has a slightly different tenor.

The front-page story by Chris Anderson of the *Reading Chronicle* (23 October 2014) in Figure 9.1 reverberates with the race-based concerns that Baratz and Shuy (1969) were contending with in *Teaching Black children to read*. Anderson's story ran with the headline 'White Boys Sinking to Bottom of Class: Pupils Fail to Meet Literacy Standards'. The implication is that whatever the problem may be with literacy education of the children in these studies stems from the fact of their genetic or biological identity. In the article, the Education Leader for the Reading Borough Council, John Ennis, remarked that:

> There are some schools that are really good in Reading whose Key Stage Two results are above the national average. But their phonics results are still low and it is *the white working class boys* that are particularly low. We have to work extra hard to ensure that they are not being negatively affected.

In the same article, Mike Edwards, a former head-teacher and field worker for the literacy charity ABC to Read, was reported as observing that:

> White working class boys have been among the lowest achievers for some time in Reading but what is concerning is that they still are. If children arrive into the educational system with no knowledge of books or stories then teachers face an uphill struggle.

There is however nothing in the *Reading Chronicle*'s story that supports the racial whiteness causality claim. In the United States, a similar problem was addressed by the Center for Applied Linguistics in Washington, DC. It produced several classic texts in the sociolinguistic literature that sought to correct misconceptions about race and language by demonstrating convincingly that what had been represented as racially homogeneous language patterns were as a matter of fact socially mediated. In the Reading story, it is possible that social classification is more complex than the Borough Council recognised. There are ethnic minority families who have

Figure 9.1 Attributing literacy performance to race

been reclassified as working class on the basis of economic indices like income and housing in the UK who may have come from lower-middle-class backgrounds in their countries of origin. They may exhibit middle-class social practices including literacy practices such as learning the rudiments of reading in pre-school years. Thus the phenomenon observed may have been misinterpreted as due to race membership solely rather than a combination of factors that include demographic history. In the United States, so-called features of Non-Standard Negro English were more representative of working-class Black speakers' repertoire since the Black middle class tended to speak standard American English more except for pragmatic intentions in ideological contexts.

Afrikaans as medium of instruction

The next example of the language–race–identity link I want to cite is drawn from the Apartheid era in South Africa. The Bantu Education Act of 1953 had been flawed on a number of fronts, prominent among which was acute disinvestment in the education of Black children by the South African government. Reports show that while the government invested 644 rand on average on each White school child, it only invested 42 rand on each Black child. With increased enrolment in secondary schools in the townships, more and more Black youth were introduced to Black Consciousness philosophies. When the government introduced the incendiary policy of Afrikaans Medium of Instruction in 1974, it was immediately recognised as an attempt by the Apartheid regime to explore the potency of linguistic ideology and hegemony to enforce the continued domination of Black minds and lives. It was resisted vehemently, culminating in the Soweto Uprising of June 1976 in which many lives were lost.[3]

In the post-Apartheid era, the language–race–identity link has changed somewhat, with much more freedom for individuals to choose between languages according to their preferences and vision of life in South Africa. The investment in the 11 official languages of the country still shows evidence of inequality between them, but the difference is not one that is ideologically racially driven. Kamwangamalu's (2003) study of programme-language allocation on the government-owned South African Broadcasting Corporation reveals lop-sidedness in resource distribution and access among the official languages, for instance. This imbalance has an effect on differences in literacy rates not only between the ethnolinguistic groups but also between White and Black South Africa. The crossover of a growing number of Black middle-class people into the English and Afrikaans-speaking-and-utilising networks is gradually eroding discrimination on the basis of race and replacing it with discrimination on the basis of class.

Linguistic profiling

In his seminal research on linguistic profiling which he described as 'the auditory equivalent of visual "racial profiling"', Baugh (2003) provides us with an illustration of the language–race–identity interface. The research revealed America's institutional racism with its findings, which showed both discriminatory and preferential linguistic profiling by public administrators in the decisions by housing departments and other public service units. He demonstrated in his experiments using actors that responses to inquiries about housing availability correlated with the accent/dialect of the speakers.

Similarly, in the case of *Clifford v. Kentucky* (1999), from which the extract below was taken (Baugh 2003: 157), Justice Cooper of the Kentucky Supreme Court in his ruling opinion remarked that 'an opinion that an overheard voice was that of a particular nationality or race has never before been addressed in this jurisdiction'.

Q: Okay, well, how does a Black man sound?
A: Uh, some male Blacks have a, a different sound of, of their voice. Just as if I have a different sound of my voice as Detective Birkenhauer does. I sound different than you.
Q: Okay, can you demonstrate that for the jury?
A: I don't think that would be a fair and accurate description of the, you know, of the way the man sounds.
Q: So not all male Blacks sound alike?
A: That's correct, yes.
Q: Okay. In fact, some of them sound like Whites, don't they?
A: Yes.
Q: Do all Whites sound alike?
A: No sir.
Q: Okay. Do some White people sound like Blacks when they're talking?
A: Possibly, yes.

The cross-examination above completely dislodged the essentialist logic of a language–race–identity link.

Linguistic passing

Racial passing entails complete and permanent renunciation of the lifestyle associated with one's racial group for a lifestyle associated with another group in order to forge membership of the latter. Linguistic passing facilitates racial passing and is different from language crossing (Rampton 1995) or style shifting in general because it is neither temporary nor momentary. While style shifting is a communicative strategy in interpersonal and intra-group relations, the norm in linguistic passing is for members of a less privileged racial group to attempt to acquire membership of a more privileged racial group surreptitiously through permanent style change. Until the case of Rachel Dolezal, Professor of Africana Studies at East Washington University in the United States, dominant racial group members were not known to desire to pass as members of a dominated racial group through the use of signifying practices that included language. To illustrate this case of passing, I have included three extracts from YouTube on the Rachel Dolezal controversy for analysis. Extract 1 is from an interview by KXLY4's Jeff Humphrey on her parentage.[4] The interviewer is trying to get her to substantiate the relationship between her and the African American man she appeared with in a photo whom she had described as her dad.

Extract 1

Interviewer:	Is that your dad?
Rachel:	Yeah, that's, that's my dad.
Interviewer:	This man right here is your father? Right there?
00:10	
Rachel:	Do you have a question about that?
Interviewer:	Yes ma'am, I was wondering if your dad really is an African American man.
Rachel:	That's a very, I mean I don't know what you're implying.
00:21	
Interviewer:	Are you African American?
Rachel:	I don't understand the question of, yeah I did tell you that's my dad
00:31	
Rachel:	and he wasn't able to come in January.
Interviewer:	Are your parents, are they White?

End of interview inaudible, interview ends abruptly.

Note in this interview clip that Rachel does not provide an answer to the direct question 'Are you African American?'; instead, she exits the interview. She affirms that the African American man in the photo is her father in response to the interviewer's question. The dysfluency marked by her repetition of 'that' in that response may be indicative of hesitation to flout the Gricean maxim of quality, which forbids an interlocutor from saying something they know to be false. When the interviewer repeated the question repeating 'right here' to clear any doubts of whom he was requesting her to identify, she counter-challenges him to be bald on record. The interviewer's two final questions are exactly that. Passing is attempted here through initial affirmation, and then daring the interviewer.

The second extract is from the transcript of a lecture that Rachel Dolezal gave at the university on the politics of Black hair. The fact that she is vastly knowledgeable about the subject only indexes her as an academic. What is notable however from the perspective of racial and linguistic passing is the stance she maintains in the narration; 'a younger, pale, blonde-haired, blue-eyed Dolezal who looks much different than the woman with caramel-colored skin now' (Nelson 2015).

Extract 2

01:00

> When it comes to hair, hair is, for Black women, much more, than just an aesthetic, much more than just and it could torment an appearance or a style and so I'm gonna go through a short synopsis, before our beautiful models walk, and then I will actually walk the, down an aisle according to where they fit on this timeline of Black hair.

01:30

> So hair history and privilege, during child slavery, during the transatlantic slave trade hair styles were banned, so anyone who has an African American lineage, has a history of banned Black hairstyles, we're gonna go, before the oppression, but first we kind of need to look at what happened to our hairstyles here in America.

In Extract 2, Rachel Dolezal takes the stance of an insider. By this, I mean that her pronominal choice as well as investment in victimology with reference to the group oppression of African Americans represents her as an insider. The interesting point to note here is that, in addition to the language, the issue that was made about her appearance underlines the essentialism of racial looks. As a White girl in her youth she had straight hair and light skin, whereas as an adult and particularly since she started passing as Black her skin tone has darkened and she wears her hair in curls and braids which she described as 'natural'. In the lecture on Black hair, Dolezal style-shifts in order to reinforce her claim to membership of the group. In a subsequent interview, she seemed to have exploited the contemporary sympathies attracted by the transgender phenomenon to spotlight the possibility of a 'transracial' parallel.

Passing however has not been confined to White–Black and vice versa. White American Andrea Lee Smith, also a professor, passed for Cherokee Indian for years before she was unmasked in May 2015. From the language, race and identity point of view, Shorter (2015), commenting in the online edition of *Indian Country Media Network Today*, noted: 'As all of these various cases point out, identity is in fact a confusing matter, sometimes designated by blood, *other times by language*, or heritage, or cultural performances' (my emphasis). Perhaps his most incisive comment concerned the demands that professional practice may be making on academics. He notes: 'In Indigenous Studies, we were expected to learn and help a particular community, learning language and culture when invited to do, *essentially dance along the border of cultural insider and outsider*' (my emphasis).[5]

Thus passing is not always self-serving but may be a strategy devised for a greater utilitarian purpose. It is buoyed up by the fact that the voice of an insider may be more effective and trusted in indigenous communities.

Summary

This chapter has presented a brief discussion of the controversies in a number of disciplines around the subject of race, from definition based on stereotypes to its complex constructions across various contexts. I have tried to demonstrate that interest in race in sociolinguistics and applied linguistics study stretches beyond racism discourse even though the scholarship shows that the topic has attracted more interest. The interface of race, language and identity is a site for issues of social justice, marginalisation, access and simply being by ascription and by choice among others.

Related topics

Historical perspectives on language and identity; Language and ethnic identity; Identity in post-colonial contexts; A linguistic ethnography of identity: adopting a heteroglossic frame; Language, gender and identities in political life: a case study from Malaysia; Styling and identity in a second language; The future of identity research: impact and new developments in sociolinguistics.

Further reading

Alim, H.S. and Baugh, J. (eds) (2007). *Talkin Black talk: language, education and social change.* New York: Teachers College Press. (The essays in the volume are intended to facilitate African American empowerment through equal education and language rights.)

Ashcroft, B. (2003). Language and race, in R. Harris and B. Rampton (eds) *The language, ethnicity and race reader.* London: Routledge, pp. 37–53. (Ashcroft argues in this essay that language has no race, showing the weaknesses of arguments to the contrary.)

Bucholtz, M. (2011). *White kids language, race, and styles of youth identity.* Cambridge: Cambridge University Press. (The monograph shows youth as a contrastive category to race and for whom identity is definitely a performance.)

Lin, A. and Kubota, R. (2011). Discourse and race, in K. Hyland and B. Paltridge (eds) *The Bloomsbury companion to discourse analysis.* London: Bloomsbury, pp. 277–290. (Lin and Kubota focus on the discourses of race and racism in sociolinguistics scholarship.)

Notes

1 See https://educationallinguist.wordpress.com/2015/06/14/why-we-need-raciolinguistics
2 www.english.illinois.edu/~people~/faculty/debaron/403/403%20mne/ebonics.pdf
3 www.sahistory.org.za/topic/june-16-soweto-youth-uprising
4 www.washingtonpost.com/news/morning-mix/wp/2015/06/12/spokane-naacp-president-rachel-dolezal-may-be-white
5 http://indiancountrytodaymedianetwork.com/2015/07/01/four-words-andrea-smith-im-not-indian

References

Agha, A. (2003). 'The social life of a cultural value', *Language and Communication*, 23: 231–273.

Agha, A. (2005). 'Voice, footing, enregisterment', *Journal of Linguistic Anthropology*, 15(1): 38–59.

Alim, H.S. and Baugh, J. (eds) (2007). *Talkin Black talk: language, education and social change.* New York: Teachers College Press.

Ashcroft, B. (2003). Language and race, in R. Harris and B. Rampton (eds) *The language, ethnicity and race reader.* London: Routledge, pp. 37–53.

Baratz, J.C. and Shuy, R.W. (1969). *Teaching Black children to read.* Washington DC: Center for Applied Linguistics.

Barth, F. (1989). 'The analysis of culture in complex societies', *Ethnos: Journal of Anthropology*, 54(3–4): 120–142.

Baugh, J. (2003). Linguistic profiling, in S. Makoni, G. Smitherman, A. Ball and A. Spears (eds) *Black linguistics: language, society, and politics in Africa and the Americas.* London: Routledge, pp. 155–168.

Baugh, J. (2004). Ebonics and its controversy, in E. Finegan and J.R. Rickford (eds) *Language in the USA: themes for the twenty-first century.* Cambridge: Cambridge University Press, pp. 305–318.

Baxter, J. (this volume). Positioning language and identity: poststructuralist perspectives, in S. Preece (ed.) *The Routledge handbook of language and identity.* London: Routledge, pp. 34–49.

BBC (2015). *How did slave-owners shape Britain?* [Online]. Available at www.bbc.co.uk/guides/zw8dq6f

Bigelow, M. (2010a). *Mogadishu on the Mississippi: language, racialized identity, and education in a new land.* Malden, MA: Blackwell.

Bigelow, M. (2010b). 'Engaged scholarship in the Somali communities of Minnesota', *Language Learning: A Journal of Research in Language Studies* [Online]. Available at www.academia.edu/2897988/Mogadishu_on_the_Mississippi

Bucholtz, M. (2011). *White kids: language, race, and styles of youth identity.* Cambridge: Cambridge University Press.

Coupland, N. (1980). 'Style-shifting in a Cardiff work setting'. *Language in Society*, 9(1): 1–12.

Eckert, P. (2000). *Linguistic variation as social practice.* Malden, MA: Blackwell.

Edwards, V. (1986). *Language in a Black community.* Clevedon, Avon: Multilingual Matters.

Figueroa, J.F. (1992). Foreword, in D. Sutcliffe, *System in Black language.* Clevedon: Multilingual Matters.

Foster, G.A. (2003). *Performing whiteness: postmodern re/constructions in the cinema.* Albany, NY: State of New York Press.

Goffman, E. (1967). *Interactional rituals: essays in face to face behaviour.* Chicago: Aldine Pub. Co.

Hall, S. (1989). *Old and new identities, old and new ethnicities* [Online]. Available at http://missingimage.com/files/mi/hall_identities.pdf

Haney-Lopez, I.F. (1994). 'Social construction of race: some observations on illusion, fabrication, and choice', *The 29 Harv C.R.-C.L. L. Rev.* [Online]. Available at http://scholarship.law.berkeley.edu/facpubs/1815

Haney-Lopez, I.F. (2000). The social construction of race, in R. Del Gado and J. Stefancic (eds) *Critical race theory: the cutting edge.* Philadelphia: Temple University Press, pp. 163–175.

Hannerz, U. (1989). 'Culture between center and periphery: toward a macroanthropology', *Ethnos: Journal of Anthropology*, 54(3–4): 200–216.

Harris, R. (2006). *New ethnicities and language use.* London: Palgrave/Macmillan.

Harris, R. and Rampton, B. (eds) (2003). *The language, ethnicity and race reader.* London: Routledge.

Hartigan, J. (2010). *Race in the 21st century: ethnographic approaches.* New York: Oxford University Press.

Hewitt, R. (1986). *White talk Black talk: inter-racial friendship and communication amongst adolescents.* Cambridge: Cambridge University Press.

Hewitt, R. (2003 [1992]) Language, youth, and the destabilisation of ethnicity, in R. Harris and B. Rampton (eds) *The language, ethnicity and race reader.* London: Routledge, pp. 188–198.

Howard, J. (2010). 'On the social construction of race', *Occidental Quarterly* [Online]. Available at www.toqonline.com/blog/on-the-social-construction-of-race-2

Hume, D. (1758). Of national characters, in *Essays and treatises on several subjects.* London: A. Miller, pp. 119–129.

Hyland, K. and Paltridge, B. (eds) (2011). *The Bloomsbury companion to discourse analysis.* London: Bloomsbury.

Ibrahim, A.E.K. (2003). 'Whassup, homeboy?' Joining the African diaspora: Black English as a symbolic site of identification in language learning, in S. Makoni, G. Smitherman, A. Ball and A. Spears (eds) *Black linguistics: language, society, and politics in Africa and the Americas.* London: Routledge, pp. 169–185.

Johnstone, B. (2010). Locating language in identity, in C. Llamas and D. Watt (eds) *Language and identities.* Edinburgh: Edinburgh University Press, pp. 29–38.

Joseph, J.E. (this volume). Historical perspectives on language and identity, in S. Preece (ed.) *The Routledge handbook of language and identity.* London: Routledge, pp. 19–33.

Kamwangamalu, N. (2003). 'Social change and language shift: South Africa', *Annual Review of Applied Linguistics*, 23: 225–242.

Kerswill, P. (2011). 'Multicultural London English'. Public lecture, 22 March. British Library, London.

Labov, W. (1972). *Language in the inner city: studies in the Black English vernacular.* Philadelphia: University of Pennsylvania Press.

Lin, A. and Kubota, R. (2011). Discourse and race, in K. Hyland and B. Paltridge (eds) *The Bloomsbury companion to discourse analysis*. London: Bloomsbury, pp. 277–290.

Lytra, V. (this volume). Language and ethnic identity, in S. Preece (ed.) *The Routledge handbook of language and identity*. London: Routledge, pp. 131–145.

Makoni, S., Smitherman, G., Ball, A.F. and Spears, A.K. (eds) (2003). *Black linguistics: language, society, and politics in Africa and the Americas*. London: Routledge.

Nelson, S.C. (2015). 'Rachel Dolezal: "Black" civil rights leader "outed as White" by her family', *The Huffingtonpost.com*, 12 June. Available at www.huffingtonpost.co.uk/2015/06/12/rachel-dolezal-black-civil-rights-champion-outed-white-family_n_7568266.html

Rampton, B. (1995). *Crossing: language and ethnicity among adolescents*. London: Longman.

Rampton, B. (2006). *Language in late modernity: interaction in an urban school*. Cambridge: Cambridge University Press.

Renan, E. (1855). Histoire générale at systém comparés des langues Sémetiques, *Oeuvres completes*. Paris: Calmann-Lévy, 1947–1961, 1: 69–97.

Sapir, E. (2003 [1921]). Language, race and culture, in R. Harris and B. Rampton (eds) *The language, ethnicity and race reader*. London: Routledge, pp. 28–36.

Shorter, D. (2015). 'Four words for Andrea Smith: "I'm Not An Indian"'. *Indian Country Today Media Network.Com*, 1 July. Available at http://indiancountrytodaymedianetwork.com/2015/07/01/four-words-andrea-smith-im-not-indian

Sutcliffe, D. (1992). *System in Black language*. Clevedon: Multilingual Matters.

van Dijk, T.A. (1987). *Communicating racism*. Newbury Park, CA: SAGE.

Wells, J.C. (1973). *Jamaican pronunciations in London*. Oxford: Basil Blackwell.

Wolfram, W. (1969). *A sociolinguistic description of Detroit Negro speech*. Washington DC: Center for Applied Linguistics.

10

Linguistic practices and transnational identities

Anna De Fina

Introduction

Identity is a central area of research and theoretical engagement for socio and applied linguists because language use and language variation are deeply intertwined with processes of identity-building and performance. Identities are conveyed, negotiated and regimented through linguistic and discursive means; therefore, linguistic processes are at the core of identity processes. At the same time, perceptions and constructions of identities fundamentally shape the ways linguistic resources are deployed. Thus, for example, battles about language varieties and even about small linguistic differences mark the creation of boundaries of ethnic or territorial belonging among people. Similarly, linguistic elements at different levels – from phonemes to words – shift, change and are born according to the striving of individuals and communities for differentiation.

Identity is, however, a slippery term, as language can be used to convey and construct different types of identities. A person may for example put on a certain accent to index geographical origin; particular linguistic styles may be regarded as conveying personal characteristics, such as aggressiveness or directness; specific linguistic items or expressions may index a person's gender, and so forth. Thus, linguistic analyses of identities have dealt with different kinds of identity categories. For this reason, it is not only useful to distinguish between personal and social identities, but also to differentiate between individual and collective identities. While personal identities capture characteristics and attributes that the individual regards as defining her/himself as a particular and unique kind of person, social identities refer to membership into social groupings that may be based on gender, age, ethnicity, place of origin and so forth. Finally, while a person may use language and linguistic strategies to convey something about who s/he is, language can also be used to construct collective identities, that is, to create images of groups and communities. While these categories are not always clear cut in practice, they are useful to distinguish different dimensions of identities.

In this chapter, I will focus on transnational identities and the way language practices contribute to construct, convey and negotiate them. Transnational individuals can be defined as people who actively 'build social fields that link together their country of origin and their country of settlement' (Glick Schiller *et al.* 1995: 1). Therefore, studying the identities of transnational individuals involves analysing processes and practices that are different from those that are relevant for people who are firmly grounded in one place. This area of research represents a significant point of intersection between socio and applied linguistics as it deals with 'the theoretical and empirical investigation of real world problems in which language is a central issue' (Brumfit 1995: 27).

The chapter starts with an overview that first describes the theoretical background underlying the relatively recent interest in transnationalism in linguistics, focusing on groundbreaking work about migration in the 1990s, particularly by anthropologists, that has paved the way for a new understanding of migrants as transnational individuals. The following two sections go on to discuss how such understandings about migration can be compounded with insights on mobility offered by recent trends in socio and applied linguistics that focus on globalisation phenomena and the changes that they have brought about in symbolic practices and constructions. The next part of the chapter presents a brief review of work on identity in the same fields, discussing the recent paradigmatic shift from a focus on stable social identities and speech communities towards a reconceptualisation of identity as processes and practices. In the second part of the chapter I focus on methodology, areas of investigation and issues and ongoing debates, starting with a section that reviews studies of transnational identities before presenting some concluding reflections.

Transnationalism and migration

The idea that migrants and other mobile and/or de-territorialised groups could be best described as 'transmigrants' and studied within the frame of transnational phenomena was proposed and developed in the 1990s by social scientists, particularly anthropologists, researching immigration. Scholars such as Glick Schiller and Furon (1990), Gupta and Ferguson (1992) and Rouse (2004 [1991]), among others, pointed to contradictions and fallacies in the way immigrants and migration had been conceptualised in the past and used the concept of transnationalism as a lens to understand mobility in the late-modern world. Crucially, they also used transnationalism as a tool for apprehending changes in the way identities are constructed and conveyed in contemporary societies. Thus, they opposed purely structural explanations of migration, for example economic-based accounts, such as the idea that migration could be understood merely as a product of poverty, underdevelopment and, generally, structural conditions that directly cause push–pull phenomena. According to Glick Schiller and Furon (1990), such structural explanations prevent individual agency and wider cultural factors from entering the picture and do not allow for a consideration of the fact that immigrants are 'actors who often consciously elaborate and manipulate multiple identities in response to structural forces of a global scope' (ibid.: 331). Criticism towards traditional views of immigrants, simply as uprooted individuals and communities who struggle to assimilate to their new homeland, was also central to the arguments made by these scholars. Looking at migrants merely as uprooted people means regarding migration as a one-way process of change in which those who arrive are driven to adapt to their country of adoption but essentially do not produce any change there or in their place of origin. Adaptation only happens in one direction: from the immigrant to the host country and culture. Within this view identities and processes are seen as belonging to binary categories such as 'the national and the transnational, the rooted and the routed, the territorial and the deterritorialized' (Jackson *et al.* 2004: 2). Such simple oppositions do not reflect the complexity of the everyday experiences and identities of transmigrant people or the global processes that underlie them.

The point made by scholars of migration was that not only do immigrants belong to different worlds and continue to maintain ties to such realities, but also that they bring into being new forms of identity and new economic and cultural practices that produce changes both in the host and home countries by creating, for example, transnational circuits and by defining new configurations of spaces and places (see Rouse 2004 [1991]).

The critique of binary conceptions of identities and processes was compounded with a problematisation of many of the traditional categories used to understand and study immigrant identities. In particular, Glick Schiller and Furon (1990) argued for the inadequacy of the category of ethnicity to subsume immigrant identities and explain intergroup struggles. They found this construct to be inadequate, in that it erases differences in culture, race, geographical origin and so forth that exist within immigrant communities and neglects the role of other categories, such as race, which have been used as pivotal constructs in transnational power struggles. The alternative proposed by these authors was an anthropology capable of explaining transnational experiences and finding adequate categories for their analysis; this anthropological perspective must be able to account for the development of identities within a perspective that recognises the interconnections between local and global phenomena and historical developments that go beyond the boundaries of individual nation states and that involve wider systems and power struggles.

Globalisation, space and place

These theorisations about transnational identities have flourished in conjunction with the spread of new ideas about the centrality of fragmentation and flow in the late-modern world that have been developed also by anthropologists and by profound re-theorisations about the concepts of space and place and their relations with identities. Space had already been established as a fundamental notion by Rouse in a classic study of Mexican migration to the United States (2004 [1991]: 25), in which he talked about the need to identify new 'cartographies' that could reflect the changes that have occurred in the relationships between communities and places. He noted that immigrants such as the Mexicans he studied develop activities that span borders and involve different places. As the participants in Rouse's study worked and stayed in the United States for periods but often went back to Mexico, Rouse argued that their place of origin got fundamentally transformed to serve the needs related to this way of life. Thus, members of this group 'see their current lives and future possibilities as involving simultaneous engagements in places associated with markedly different forms of experience' (ibid.: 30).

Spatial images define many of these early works; for example, Glick Schiller *et al.* define transnationalism as 'the process by which immigrants build social fields that link together their country of origin and their country of settlement' (1995: 1). And indeed, besides pointing to transnational processes, scholars also talked about how the very notion of space needs to be at the centre of a theoretical rethinking given that transnational processes and forces have redefined relations between centres and peripheries by bringing the peripheries into the centres and by creating dynamic interaction between the local and the global. As Gupta and Ferguson note:

> In a world of diaspora, transnational culture flows, and mass movements of populations, old-fashioned attempts to map the globe as a set of culture regions or homelands are bewildered by a dazzling array of postcolonial simulacra, doublings and redoublings, as India and Pakistan apparently reappear in postcolonial simulation in London, prerevolution Tehran rises from the ashes in Los Angeles, and a thousand similar cultural dreams are played out

in urban and rural settings all across the globe. In this culture play of diaspora, familiar lines between 'here' and 'there', center and periphery, colony and metropole become blurred.

(1992: 10)

These transformations in the way communities use spaces and in their sense of identities have been increasingly linked with the changes that globalisation has brought about in the late-modern world and therefore theorisations about migration have gone hand in hand with efforts by social scientists to understand the cultural and linguistic impact of globalisation. Indeed, many scholars agree about the fact that one of its central characteristics is the enhancement and intensification of global flows not only of people, but also of artefacts, cultural products and practices. While it is true that mass migration and transnational contacts have always existed, it is also true that, as Appadurai notes, our world is witnessing 'global interactions of a new order of intensity' (1996: 27).

Scholars of globalisation (see Vertovec 2009) point to a number of reasons why our societies have become much more interconnected: the economy has become globalised with the growing influence and power of multinational corporations that dictate new market conditions to local economies and with the frequent decentralisation in the production of goods and the variety of services from developed to developing nations. The labour force has itself become largely globalised due to 'deindustrialization and the rise of service industries' (Vertovec 2009: 2). Concurrently, because of mass migration, entire countries have become more and more dependent on remittances from migrants. At the political level, policies are increasingly dictated in a supranational sphere (Robinson 1998), while with the fall of the post-war global equilibrium in the 1990s the map of political influences and alliances is continuously being redrawn.

These transformations would not have been sufficient to redefine the way we live were it not for the fundamental impact and influence of technology and mass-mediated communication, which facilitated the creation of global cultural and information flows that made news and a variety of cultural products and traditions available to people throughout the world. Observers of modernity such as Gupta, Appadurai and Agha have pointed to the immense influence of the media on the way cultural products are created and consumed, on the quality and intensity of political participation, and, crucially, on ways in which communities and identities are created and negotiated. Appadurai (1996: 4) regards the media, particularly electronic media, as one of the signature phenomena of postmodernity. In his words:

> The story of mass migrations (voluntary and forced) is hardly a new feature of human history. But when it is juxtaposed with the rapid flow of mass-mediated images, scripts, and sensations, we have a new order of instability in the production of modern subjectivities.

Indeed media and global exchanges allow for the sharing of cultural phenomena across physical boundaries. These exchanges determine a dynamic production, reproduction and creative reshaping of practices that while originally created in a particular context and place can become appropriated and reshaped in a completely different context. Local phenomena become global but they also often get 'glocalized' – that is, recontextualised within a new local context. This is the case with music trends, fashion, foods and all kinds of products and practices that become available to consumers across the global sphere.

Processes of identity construction and communication and ways in which communities form and maintain contact are centrally influenced by these changes, and that is why work on migration and globalisation constitutes a fundamental frame for understanding analyses and theorisations about transnational identities. But studies of transnational identities can also be inscribed within new trends in socio and applied linguistics. Thus, I will devote the next section to the emergence of new socio and applied linguistic paradigms connected with mobility and diversity.

Sociolinguistic shift: from stability to mobility

In the previous section I described how in migration research and in cultural studies scholars have initiated a theoretical reflection aimed at delineating a new frame for the study of social and cultural phenomena that have been brought about by globalisation. Socio and applied linguistics have experienced a similar shift, as many voices have come together to question traditional categories and methods of analysis that seem wholly inadequate to account for the new ways in which communication takes place and identities are created and managed in late modernity. At the beginning of the twenty-first century, Coupland (2003: 466) called for a sociolinguistics of globalisation, arguing that linguistically mediated experience at the local level cannot be grasped without taking into account the influence of global processes. In a recent contribution that summarises some of these developments in the field, Blommaert (2014) proposes mobility as one of the key terms to capture the shift that has taken place in sociolinguistics. Indeed, sociolinguists have started questioning some of the basic assumptions that dominated the study of language in society until the end of the twentieth century, particularly the dominant metaphor of the stability of identities, communities and linguistic processes. In traditional sociolinguistic accounts of the interactions of languages and identities, such as in Labov's studies on vernacular English (see Labov 1972), the use of specific language variables was connected to social categories such as gender, age and geographic location. Central to sociolinguistic investigation was the notion of the speech community as a linguistically homogeneous, territorially bounded, culturally unified grouping. Even though scholars such as Hymes (1972) recognised the internal linguistic and social diversity in speech communities and even though this construct has undergone substantial criticism and debate (see Romaine 1994; Silverstein 1996), the speech community can still be regarded as the pillar of the view of a fundamentally static relationship between language and identity.

Critiques of the notion of the speech community are by no means new but they have acquired greater strength within a sociolinguistics and an applied linguistics centred on mobility. Indeed, as discussed in the introduction, a presupposition of boundedness and stability cannot account for language variation and identity formation among mobile individuals and communities and, at the same time, access to transnational and global phenomena is so widespread nowadays that even individuals and groups that are firmly grounded in one place may receive innumerable influences deriving from virtual contact with cultural models and language practices that belong to locations that are physically removed. Thus, mobility is a significant notion for the study of processes that relate to identity.

The critique of speech communities as fixed and stable has been extended to a critique of the perspective of languages as rigid conceptions. This is another theme that has significant implications for the study of identities because it is through the manipulation of linguistic resources that identities are indexed and conveyed, and as a consequence the way linguistic resources are analysed greatly influences how identity processes are studied. The increased contact among people and the transformation of urban centres into 'contact zones' (Pratt 1995), which are the hallmark of globalised societies, have brought to the fore the existence of a plethora of linguistic varieties that cannot be easily accommodated within traditional sociolinguistic categories such as those of language, dialect and so forth. Within traditional sociolinguistic studies, contact between two or more languages is seen as producing code-mixing or code-switching, but these notions are based on the idea that such different codes can be more or less clearly recognised and separated. Thus, studies of identity based on the analysis of code-switching look for ways in which alternation between codes is related to acts of identity. However, a great deal of recent research has demonstrated the relevance of 'heteroglossic' (Bakhtin 1986: 89) phenomena, that is, phenomena demonstrating the incorporation of the voice of others into one's utterances, which is a key element in the study of identity.

The idea that discourse incorporates heteroglossia has been developed and enriched by research on style and stylisation (see Auer 2007; Coupland 2007). This work shows how inter-actants use linguistic resources to index particular identities and personae that are often alien to them, either because they are associated with out-groups or because these resources are not part of their usual repertoire. Research on youth language, particularly in multilingual and multicul-tural environments (see Ag and Jørgensen 2013), has also strengthened the point, demonstrating that youngsters convey and negotiate identities in extremely innovative ways through the crea-tive use of resources that leads to varieties that are not easily separable into distinct languages or easy to categorise as such. Such phenomena are better captured by models of language behaviour based on the idea that speakers manipulate sets of linguistic resources that at times can coincide and be conceived of as separate languages but that can also constitute elements of new bricolages. As we will see, transnational identities are often constructed through the use of these different resources. For this reason, linguists attuned to globalisation and mobility have also coined new terms such as 'translanguaging' (García 2009) or 'metrolingualism' (Otsuji and Pennycook 2010) to try to capture these kinds of hybrid language practices. What these notions account for is the incorporation of multilingual resources into everyday talk that follows from the ubiquitous and simultaneous presence of different languages and cultural models in everyday practice. These languages and models are accessed and attuned to through mobile and traditional media, often by people who are themselves mobile.

The kind of approach described above 'shifts the lens from cross-linguistic influence' to how multilinguals 'intermingle linguistic features that have hereto been administratively or linguistically assigned to a particular language or language variety' (García 2009: 51). Recent work on media, such as web advertising (Martin 2013), has extended the inquiry into the use of multimedia hybrid resources such as music and soundtracks in different languages in trans-national practices.

Identities, interactions and social constructionism

Theorisations on globalisation, de-territorialisation processes and the reconfiguration of linguistic resources that underlie the study of transnational identities involve and build on anti-essentialist and social constructionist views of identity (for a discussion see De Fina 2011). Anti-essentialism is a central characteristic of late-modern theories about identities such as the ones proposed by Giddens (1991) or Bauman (2005). These thinkers underscore the fact that the dominant con-ceptions of identity in the West framed the self as characterised by coherence, rationality and continuity. According to Burr (2002: 4–5), who writes from the point of view of psychological theories, within these approaches individual selves are attributed fixed sets of characteristics that encapsulate their personality and describe them as rational in their actions and deliberations as well separated from their environments. All of these presumptions are questioned in postmod-ern thinking, which, on the contrary, underlines how modern identities cannot be equated with coherent selves and how they are often fragmented, multivocal, discontinuous and contradictory (see Baxter, this volume). Such views are compatible with the idea that hybridity is central to modernity.

The notion of hybridity has been developed in connection with post-colonial studies to point to the subversion of power hierarchies, through recognition of the existence of 'third spaces' in which post-colonised populations and minorities can build their own independent cultural practices (Bhabha 1994). However, it has rapidly been adopted as a trope for the construction of in-between and alternative identities in general. Such a notion is particularly important to encompass identity processes that are initiated and negotiated among diasporic, mobile and de-territorialised people (see Baynham and De Fina 2005; De Fina and Perrino 2013) and in transnational spaces, since individuals and communities that belong to those categories and act in those environments are often dealing with a variety of linguistic resources and inventories of identities.

Another theoretical point of reference for the analysis of identity is social constructionism (see Hall 2000). This perspective views identities as socially built in interaction and within social practices from inventories that are deployed according to contextual constraints. From this perspective, identities do not belong to people but are 'done' and performed in that they involve discursive and strategic work. Identity processes are embedded within semiotic practices that involve different rules, roles, presuppositions, etc., and therefore cannot be studied without attending to those contexts.

In the next section I will describe some of the theoretical-methodological tools employed by scholars who work on transnational identities and the areas in which research has been carried out. For each area I will discuss some of the most representative studies.

Studies of transnational identities: methodologies and areas of interest

As can be inferred from the previous summary of theoretical positions and constructs that have come to influence research on transnational phenomena, sociocultural linguistic studies of transnational identities are generally oriented towards qualitative methodologies and close analyses of linguistic and other types of semiotic practices. There is a general sense, among scholars, that in order to understand this new phenomenon it is imperative to get the emic perspective of transnational individuals and communities and to avoid applying etic (analyst)-only generated categories to the data. For these reasons studies are usually based on ethnographic methodologies such as participant observation or action research, often complemented with other data collection tools, such as interviews and focus group discussions, in order to triangulate interpretations. However, there is a general division in terms of focus and methodology between two types of studies. One examines participant presentation and representation of identities in talk, frequently using interviews, particularly oral and written narratives and life stories, as data (see Eppler and Codó, this volume). The other uses data from more varied sources that depend on the kinds of practices that are targeted, which may include for example mediated practices such as digital resources or mass media (see Darvin, this volume; Domingo, this volume).

Researchers examining language and identity use a variety of instruments, going from the study of linguistic landscapes to observation of multilingual practices, to specific discourse analytic tools such as membership categorisation analysis (MCA), the study of indexicalities and positioning, and combinations of those instruments through narrative analysis. I will briefly describe what MCA, indexicality and positioning involve. MCA (Hester and Englin 1997;

Antaki and Widdicombe 1998) is the study of ways in which participants in spoken interaction invoke social categories of belonging (for example, ethnic or national categories) and the meanings that they assign to those categories. The most prominent representatives of this methodology work within the frame of conversation analysis (see Benwell and Stokoe, this volume), but the study of how social categories are applied and understood is widely used by discourse analysts from different orientations such as critical discourse analysts (see Wodak *et al.* 1999) and interactional sociolinguists (De Fina 2006).

Another very popular construct in the study of identities is the concept of 'indexicality' (Silverstein 1976), which refers to the ability of linguistic elements that include single sounds, words and combinations of resources to evoke particular associations with identities, such as groups or social personae, and cultural constructs, such as ways of life, values and so forth, that are characteristic of those groups. Indexicality is central to an understanding of social semiosis as continuously evolving and of meanings as profoundly contextualised, since the assumption is that any linguistic or semiotic element or combination of elements can become socially significant. Research on styles (for an overview see Coupland 2007) has taken indexicality as a fundamental construct.

Finally, 'positioning' is also widely used in the analysis of identities. Positioning has been interpreted as capturing social agents' stances and evaluations of their and others' roles, ideas, actions, etc. The analysis of positioning is based on both indexical processes and on the use of explicit evaluations and categories. Positioning analysis has had specific theoretical developments in the study of narratives as it can capture the relationships that speakers establish with different contexts, such as the story world, the storytelling world and other pertinent contexts (see Bamberg 1997; Deppermann 2013). The studies reviewed here use some or all of these theoretical-methodological instruments.

With regards to areas of analysis, work on transnational identities has focused mainly on transnational individuals as language learners, transnational families, the types of multilingual and mediated practices developed by transnational agents, and ideological constructions of collective identities through transnational practices, particularly by the media. These areas cannot be rigidly separated. Indeed there are many intersections between these foci (for example, work on literacy practices also looks at transnational agents as learners, while collective identities are often constructed by individuals as well as the media); thus, such categories should be seen as convenient groupings rather than clear-cut distinctions.

Review of research on transnational identities

Before presenting an overview of studies of transnational identities, it is useful to discuss their relationship with work on national identities. Indeed, most scholars dealing with transnational phenomena recognise the strength and resiliency of national affiliation categories. Individuals who see themselves as transnational often confront themselves with national belonging both in positive and negative ways. Differences between studies of national and transnational identities reside more in research methodologies and foci than in the categories analysed. At the level of foci, differences are to be found mainly in the fact that researchers on national identities are more interested in top-down processes such as how language policies reflect, construct and support national identities (or even supranational ones) and to what political ends (see Joseph 2004), or how models of identities proposed by the elites are reflected in the discourse of common people (see Wodak *et al.* 1999; Triandafyllidou and Wodak 2003). For example, Wodak's work on national and supranational identities concentrates mostly on institutional processes through which belonging is defined, in particular processes of exclusion and inclusion. In her recent studies about the European Union (Wodak 2013), Wodak looks not only at how such an organisation positions itself with regards to multilingualism, but also at how citizenship and naturalisation policies in individual European states implicitly contribute to delimiting who is deemed to have greater rights to belong and who should be excluded, thus fostering national hierarchies. A second distinction between research on transnational and national identities is that the former tries to capture the ambiguity and plurality of synergies between different scales (see Blommaert 2007) – that is, how local and global scales are related and influence processes of identity formation at various levels. Transnational studies show how in many cases the creation of a transnational identity goes hand in hand with the establishment of the local as a point of reference or, vice versa, how local identities may be strengthened and authenticated through participation in global processes.

Language learners as transnational individuals and communities

Work in this area focuses on migrants as language learners. One strand of research is interested in ways in which transnational experiences and mobility are incorporated into and support self-constructions (Farrell 2008). Another strand, which represents a growing and burgeoning field, deals with literacy practices among transnational individuals and groups and how they affect both learning and the projection and formation of identities (e.g. Warriner 2007; Hornberger and Link 2012; Sánchez and Salazar 2012).

Studies in the first strand use discourse analysis, particularly narrative analysis, to examine how learners draw on their experiences in different countries and on their personal histories of mobility to construct their present identities. For example, Farrell (2008) conducted interviews with 16 highly proficient speakers of English who had migrated to Australia from different countries. She focused on how their ideas about success and failure as language learners shaped their identity constructions and how they negotiated national identities and their sense of belonging in the Australian context. Farrell analysed the positioning of her participants through the use of categories of belonging and ways in which spatial location and personal deixis were employed by the participants as they narrated their stories. She found that transnationalism was highly relevant to her subjects, because being mobile and being from somewhere else brings to the fore, and makes relevant, relationships between place and belonging and therefore, as she argues, leads adult immigrants to always negotiate 'the here and there' (2008: 16).

Studies of literacy practices among learners are more varied in terms of methodologies, although they share the objective of exploring ways in which participating in discourse communities and accessing different types of semiotic resources may shape not only the experience of learners, but also their self-perceptions. In a special issue of *Linguistics and Education* devoted to transnational literacies, Warriner (2007: 202) argues that the contributors' objective is to represent 'the lived experiences, human practices, and "cultural logics" of people whose everyday lives are dramatically shaped by large-scale global and transnational processes' and, by doing so, to 'explore the different social, cultural, political, ideological, and material consequences of literacy'. Thus, transnational literacies interest researchers in education not only because they allow them to appreciate and theorise different forms of learning, but also because they represent a new terrain where interconnections between global and local processes can be investigated in the light of power relations and inequalities. Literacy studies in the field of socio and applied linguistics ask what kinds of linguistic practices immigrants and other transmigrant individuals such as asylum seekers develop; how they use them in both informal and formal contexts in connection with the construction of identities; and how they index different kinds of identities. Studies in this area use various forms of ethnography (for example, multi-sited ethnography or action research), with participant observation being the most common. Data are collected through video and audiotaping, interviews with focal participants and other data collection tools, such as photographs, student assignments and different digital texts. Practices investigated go from the use of resources such as graffiti and poetry (Richardson Bruna 2007) or traditional oral storytelling (Gutiérrez *et al.* 2001), to different kinds of digital instruments such as instant messaging, blog writing, social networking, etc. (McGinnis *et al.* 2007; Lam 2009; Sánchez and Salazar 2012). Findings typically point to the power of alternative and digital literacy practices in producing change in the way learners position themselves with respect to mainstream and ideologically laden categories of belonging and in contributing to the construction of hybrid identities that are inclusive of aspects, categories and values associated with both their places of origin and their new homes. An example of this recent trend is a two-year-long case study by Lam (2009) about the digital literacy practices of a 17-year-old Chinese immigrant to the United States named Kaiyee. Lam carried out ethnographic observations of Kaiyee's literacy activities at school, at home and within other community sites, as well as semi-structured interviews about her literacy activities, and collected screen photos of her instant messenger online interactions with peers. She observed how Kaiyee communicated with different social networks, involving peers from her local school, friends in the United States and childhood peers in China, and described how different linguistic resources contributed not only to build proficiency in the language varieties that were part of her repertoire, but also to create and foster affiliations with both local and translocal communities in which she performed different identities.

Studies of transnational families

Work on transnational families (see Lee 2010; Song 2012; King 2013) has focused on ideologies and practices related to language use and how the latter affects identities. In particular, researchers have studied ways in which families use and foster transnational ties and activities and how these transnational engagements shape and are shaped by family views and desires about identity. Researchers normally use participant observation, recordings of family events and interviews, or interviews only, to ascertain how different members of the family create and develop transnational ties and what kinds of affiliations they develop. For example, King (2013) conducted a 14-month case study of three sisters in an Ecuadorean family living in the United States using interviews, observations and recordings of family interactions. King analysed the dynamics created in the family by the parents' language ideologies (for example, the idea that English should be learned quickly and smoothly and should be practised) as well as how the siblings negotiated identities and family roles through language choices and ideologies. Her research points to how nationality and race identities intertwine with ideologies about language use. As King argues, ideologies about language learning also shape perceptions about identities. This was the case with the less proficient English speaker in her research, who was framed as an unsuccessful learner, and with unrealistic expectations about the children's symmetric bilingualism, which created anxieties in the English-proficient daughter.

Thus, studies of transnational families throw light on how multilingualism is practised inside these units and on how people's sense of self develops in relation to the contact and simultaneous presence of geographically distant referents in everyday life.

Studies of practices and identities among transnational communities

Work in this area does not focus on language learning but investigates different kinds of migrant and transmigrant communities, often defined in terms of ethnicity (Farr 2006; Sabate y Dalmau 2012; Sánchez and Salazar 2012; Li Wei and Zu Hua 2013), nationality (Park and Lo 2012; Perrino 2013), gender (Skandrani *et al.* 2012) and/or age (Giampapa 2004). Sometimes the focus is on communities that are not mobile but who use mobile resources and transnational spaces (Hornberger and Swinehart 2012; Schneider 2013) and/or transnational practices. The questions investigated are not different from those formulated by researchers in the area of language learning, except that in these studies learning is not the centre of attention. Scholars analyse linguistic and cultural practices, for example the creation of hybrid styles both in speech and within new digital practices, or the reproduction of cultural constructs associated with the home country in the host country or ideological constructs related to transnational identities. Some of this research interrogates ways in which semiotic practices associated with transnationalism shape and are shaped by participants' identities focusing on everyday contexts of interaction. In other studies, the analysis centres on the role of different types of media and their audiences in the production and reproduction of transnational identities (see Lo and Kim 2012; Chun 2013; De Fina 2013).

Studies comprised in this category use ethnographic methodologies, participant observation and collection of naturally occurring data. Interview data has less pre-eminence here and, given that most of the studies are recent, there is a greater awareness of the role of multimodal resources and modes of communication. An example of research on transnational communities is the study by Farr (2006) on Mexican ranchero families living in Chicago. Farr conducted a decade-long ethnographic study comprising participant fieldwork, interviews and recordings of conversations of these families, following their networks both in Chicago and San Juanico, a ranch in Michoacán from which they originated. Farr focuses on how ways of speaking that are associated with the ranchero culture are recontextualised in the reality in which Mexicans operate in Chicago to create and configure new identities. For example, ways of speaking that can be characterised as direct and frank are used by speakers to distinguish themselves as a group with a distinct personality within the mass of Hispanic immigrants in the United States. At the same time, the values associated with being a 'ranchero' are selectively assembled as to respond to the needs of this mobile community, so that characteristics such as individualism and entrepreneurship are privileged over other traits associated with the ranchero culture in Mexico.

An example of a study examining the production and reproduction of transnational identities in more formal environments is my own research (De Fina 2013) on a Latin American radio station in Washington DC. My data come from a three-year-long study of the station's broadcasts and from recordings of a variety of radio programmes, including talk shows, news, advertising and interviews with experts. I argue that the radio station constructs a Pan Latino transnational identity for its Latin American audience. Pan Latinos are presented as mobile individuals who have not completely established a home in the United States, who have a preference for speaking Spanish and who belong to a low-income stratum of the American population. I analyse the linguistic and discursive strategies used by the radio station to construct such an image, such as the choice of Spanish as the main language of the radio, the implementation of rituals that highlight national pride within the Latino community, the presentation of achievements by Latinos in the US and the participation of Latinos in pro-immigration campaigns. I also discuss how the identities constructed through such practices are both imposed by economic transnational powers (such as the multinational corporation owning the radio station), who are trying to penetrate the potential market constituted by Latin American immigrants, and ascribed in a top-down fashion through the semiotic practices of the radio station via the interaction between the radio host and their audience.

Summary

As discussed in this chapter, research on transnational identities is a relatively recent but also fast-growing area within socio and applied linguistics. Its merit is to incorporate into the analysis of identities notions of mobility and hybridity and to demonstrate the advantages of considering the intersection of different scales in the investigation of modern migrant, transmigrant and generally mobile populations. It is also clear that much of the existing work focuses on migrants and transmigrants, while neglecting (with few exceptions) other kinds of mobility, such as refugees or asylum seekers. In that sense, the scope of research should be extended. But the fact that researchers have mostly targeted migrants is also due to a problem of ambiguity in the term 'transnational'. Indeed, critics have pointed to the difficulty of delimiting the phenomena that can be called transnational (see Glick Schiller 1997 and Vertovec 2009 for a discussion). Defining which social groups belong to that category has also proven hard because of a lack of clarity on the criteria that make people or activities transnational. One dilemma is for example whether transnationalism involves only people who are in a situation of mobility or not. It seems from the research reviewed here that many scholars agree with Jackson *et al.* (2004: 13) that it would be beneficial to develop 'more encompassing notions of transnationality including those who are not themselves transnational migrants' to include those who are involved in the social field created by transnational flows. Concurrently, it is important to delimit the boundaries for how individuals and communities can be identified as transnational. The field potentially includes not only investigation on migrants, but on study-abroad students, refugees, asylum seekers, members of travellers groups and so forth. Portés (1997: 16) argued, for example, that the notion should only be applied to people who sustain activities that involve transnational contacts on a regular basis and as a part of their occupations. Other scholars (see Cohen 1997) have tried to build taxonomies of diasporic populations in order to distinguish between different cases. Future research will not only have to deal with these definitional issues, but also to be more comprehensive in its scope. It is, however, likely that the field of study of transnational identities within socio and applied linguistics will continue to expand given that it allows researchers to tackle ways in which the semiotic processes of construction and negotiation of identities have changed in late-modern contexts.

Related topics

Positioning language and identity: poststructuralist perspectives; Language and identity in linguistic ethnography; Language and ethnic identity; A linguistic ethnography of identity: adoping a heteroglossic frame; Styling and identity in a second language; Construction of heritage language and cultural identities: a case study of two young British-Bangladeshis in London; Language and identity in the digital age.

Further reading

Jackson, P., Crang, P. and Dwyer, D. (eds) (2004). *Transnational spaces*. London: Routledge. (A collection of works on transnationalism by social scientists.)

Piller, I. and Takashi, K. (2013). At the intersection of gender, language and transnationalism, in N. Coupland (ed.) *The handbook of language and globalization*. Malden, MA: Wiley-Blackwell, pp. 540–554. (A state-of-the-art chapter on transnational identities with a specific focus on gender.)

Rubdy, R. and Alsagoff, L. (eds) (2014). *The global–local interface and hybridity*. Bristol: Multilingual Matters. (A collection of works devoted to connections between identity and hybridity.)

References

Ag, A. and Jørgensen, J.N. (2013). 'Ideologies, norms, and practices in youth poly-languaging', *International Journal of Bilingualism*, 17(4): 525–539.

Antaki, C. and Widdicombe, S. (eds) (1998). *Identities in talk*. London: SAGE.

Appadurai, A. (1996). *Modernity at large: cultural dimensions of globalization*. Minneapolis: University of Minnesota Press.

Auer, P. (ed.) (2007). *Style and social identities: alternative approaches to linguistic heterogeneity*. Berlin: Mouton de Gruyter.

Bakhtin, M. (1986). *Speech genres and other late essays* [Trans. V.W. McGee]. Austin, TX: University of Texas Press.

Bamberg, M. (1997). 'Positioning between structure and performance', *Journal of Narrative and Life History*, 7: 335–342.

Bauman, Z. (2005). *Work, consumerism and the new poor*. London: Open University Press.

Baxter, J. (this volume). Positioning language and identity: poststructuralist perspectives, in S. Preece (ed.) *The Routledge handbook of language and identity*. London: Routledge, pp. 34–49.

Baynham, M. and De Fina, A. (eds) (2005). *Dislocations/relocations: narratives of displacement*. Manchester: St Jerome Publishing.

Benwell, B. and Stokoe, E. (this volume). Ethnomethodological and conversation analytic approaches to identity, in S. Preece (ed.) *The Routledge handbook of language and identity*. London: Routledge, pp. 66–82.

Bhabha, H. (1994). *The location of culture*. London: Routledge.

Blommaert, J. (2007). 'Sociolinguistics and discourse analysis: orders of indexicality and polycentricity', *Journal of Multicultural Discourses*, 2(2): 115–130.

Blommaert, J. (2014). 'From mobility to complexity in sociolinguistic theory and method', *Tilburg Papers in Culture Studies*, Paper 103 [Online]. Available at www.tilburguniversity.edu/upload/5ff19e97-9abc-45d0-8773-d2d8b0a9b0f8_TPCS_103_Blommaert.pdf

Brumfit, C.J. (1995). Teacher professionalism and research, in G. Cook and B. Seidlhofer (eds) *Principle and practice in applied linguistics*. Oxford: Oxford University Press, pp. 27–42.

Burr, V. (2002). *The person in social psychology*. Hove: Psychology Press.

Chun, E. (2013). 'Ironic blackness as masculine cool: Asian American language and authenticity on YouTube', *Applied Linguistics*, 34(5): 592–612.

Cohen, R. (1997). *Global diasporas: an introduction*. London: University College London Press.

Coupland, N. (2003). 'Introduction: sociolinguistics and globalization', *Journal of Sociolinguistics*, 7(4): 465–472.

Coupland, N. (2007). *Style: language variation and identity*. Cambridge: Cambridge University Press.

Darvin, R. (this volume). Language and identity in the digital age, in S. Preece (ed.) *The Routledge handbook of language and identity*. London: Routledge, pp. 523–540.

De Fina, A. (2006). Group identity, narrative and self representations, in A. De Fina, D. Schiffrin and M. Bamberg (eds) *Discourse and identity*. Cambridge: Cambridge University Press, pp. 351–375.

De Fina, A. (2011). Discourse and identity, in T.A. van Dijk (ed.) *Discourse studies: a multidisciplinary introduction*. London: SAGE, pp. 263–282.

De Fina, A. (2013). 'Top-down and bottom-up strategies of identity construction in ethnic media', *Applied Linguistics*, 34(5): 554–573.

De Fina, A. and Perrino, S. (2013). 'Introduction', *Applied Linguistics*, 34(5): 509–515.

Deppermann, A. (2013). 'Positioning in interaction', *Narrative Inquiry*, 23(1): 1–15.

Domingo, M. (this volume). Language and identity research in online environments: a multimodal ethnographic perspective, in S. Preece (ed.) *The Routledge handbook of language and identity*. London: Routledge, pp. 541–557.

Eppler, E.D. and Codó, E. (this volume). Challenges for language and identity researchers in the collection and transcription of spoken interaction, in S. Preece (ed.) *The Routledge handbook of language and identity*. London: Routledge, pp. 304–319.

Farr, M. (2006). *Rancheros in Chicagoacan: language and identity in a transnational community*. Austin, TX: University of Texas Press.

Farrell, E. (2008). *Negotiating identity: discourses of migration and belonging*. PhD thesis, Macquarie University.

García, O. (2009). *Bilingual education in the 21st century: a global perspective*. Malden, MA, and Oxford: Blackwell-Wiley.

Giampapa, F. (2004). The politics of identity, representation, and the discourses of self-identification: negotiating the periphery and the center, in A. Pavlenko and A. Blackledge (eds) *Negotiation of identities in multilingual contexts*. Bristol: Multilingual Matters, pp. 192–218.

Giddens, A. (1991). *Modernity and self-identity: self and society in the late modern age*. Stanford: Stanford University Press.

Glick Schiller, N. (1997). 'The situation of transnational studies. Introduction to a symposium: transnational processes/situated identities', *Identities: Global Studies in Culture and Power*, 4(2): 155–166.

Glick Schiller, N., Basch, L. and Blanc, C.S. (1995). 'From immigrant to transmigrant: theorizing transnational migration', *Anthropological Quarterly*, 68(1): 48–63.

Glick Schiller, N. and Furon, F. (1990). '"Everywhere we go, we are in danger": Ti Manno and the emergence of a Haitian transnational identity', *American Ethnologist*, 17: 329–347.

Gupta, A. and Ferguson, J. (1992). 'Beyond "culture": space, identity and the politics of difference', *Cultural Anthropology*, 7(1): 6–23.

Gutiérrez, K., Baquedano-López, P. and Alvarez, H. (2001). Literacy as hybridity: moving beyond bilingualism in urban classrooms, in M. Reyes and J. Halcon (eds) *The best for our children: Latina/Latino voices in literacy*. New York: Teachers College Press, pp. 122–141.

Hall, S. (2000). Who needs identity?, in P. Du Gay, J. Evans and P. Redman (eds) *Identity: a reader*. London: SAGE and the Open University, pp. 15–30.

Hester, S. and Eglin, P. (1997). Membership categorization analysis: an introduction, in S. Hester and P. Eglin (eds) *Culture in action: studies in membership categorization analysis*. Washington, DC: University Press of America, pp. 1–24.

Hornberger, N. and Link, H. (2012). 'Translanguaging and transnational literacies in multilingual classrooms: a biliteracy lens', *International Journal of Bilingual Education and Bilingualism*, 15(3): 261–278.

Hornberger, N. and Swinehart, K. (2012). 'Bilingual intercultural education and Andean hip hop: transnational sites for indigenous language and identity', *Language in Society*, 41(4): 499–525.

Hymes, D. (1972). Models of the interaction of language and social life, in J. Gumperz and D. Hymes (eds) *Directions in sociolinguistics: the ethnography of communication*. London: Blackwell, pp. 35–71.

Jackson, P., Crang, P. and Dwyer, C. (2004). The spaces of transnationality, in P. Crang, C. Dwyer and P. Jackson (eds) *Transnational spaces*. London: Routledge, pp. 1–23.

Joseph, J.J. (2004). *Language and identity: national, ethnic, religious*. Basingstoke: Palgrave.

King, K. (2013). 'A tale of three sisters: language ideologies, identities, and negotiations in a bilingual, transnational family', *International Multilingual Research Journal*, 7: 49–65.

Labov, W. (1972). *Sociolinguistic patterns*. Philadelphia: University of Pennsylvania Press.

Lam, W.S.E. (2009). 'Multiliteracies on instant messaging in negotiating local, translocal, and transnational affiliations: a case of an adolescent immigrant', *Reading Research Quarterly*, 44: 377–397.

Lee, H. (2010). '"I am a Kirogi mother": education exodus and life transformation among Korean transnational women', *Journal of Language, Identity, and Education*, 9(4): 250–264.

Li Wei and Zu Hua (2013). 'Translanguaging identities and ideologies: creating transnational space through flexible multilingual practices amongst Chinese university students in the UK', *Applied Linguistics*, 34(5): 516–535.

Lo, A. and Kim, J. (2012). 'Linguistic competency and citizenship: contrasting portraits of multilingualism in the South Korean popular media', *Journal of Sociolinguistics*, 16(2): 255–276.

Martin, E. (2013). Linguistic and cultural hybridity in French web advertising, in R. Rubdy and L. Alsagoff (eds) *The global–local interface and hybridity: exploring language and identity*. Bristol: Multilingual Matters, pp. 133–152.

McGinnis, T., Goldenstein-Stolzenberg, E. and Saliani, A. (2007). '"Indnpride": online spaces of transnational youth as sites of creative and sophisticated literacy and identity work', *Linguistics and Education*, 18: 283–304.

Otsuji, E. and Pennycook, A. (2010). 'Metrolingualism: fixity, fluidity and language in flux', *International Journal of Multilingualism*, 7(3): 240–254.

Park, J.S. and Lo, A. (2012). 'Transnational South Korea as a site for a sociolinguistics of globalization: markets, timescales, neoliberalism', *Journal of Sociolinguistics*, 16(2): 147–164.

Perrino, S. (2013). 'Veneto out of Italy? Dialect, migration, and transnational identity', *Applied Linguistics*, 34(5): 574–591.

Portés, A. (1997). 'Globalization from below: the rise of transnational communities', Working Paper Series, University of Oxford. *Transnational Communities: An ESRC Programme*, 98(8).

Pratt, M.L. (1995). 'Arts and the contact zone', *Profession*, 91: 33–40.

Richardson Bruna, K. (2007). 'Traveling tags: the informal literacies of Mexican newcomers in and out of the classroom', *Linguistics and Education*, 18(3–4): 232–257.

Robinson, W.I. (1998). 'Beyond nation state paradigms: globalization, sociology and the challenge of transnational studies', *Sociological Forum*, 13(4): 561–594.

Romaine, S. (1994). *Language in society: an introduction to sociolinguistics*. London: Blackwell.

Rouse, R. (2004 [1991]). Mexican migration and the social space of postmodernism, in P. Crang, C. Dwyer and P. Jackson (eds) *Transnational spaces*. London: Routledge, pp. 24–39.

Sabate y Dalmau, M. (2012). 'A sociolinguistic analysis of transnational SMS practices: non-elite multilingualism, grassroots literacy and social agency among migrant populations in Barcelona', *Lingvisticœ investigationes*, 35(2): 318–340.

Sánchez, P. and Salazar, M. (2012). 'Transnational computer use in urban Latino immigrant communities: implications for schooling', *Urban Education*, 47(1): 90–116.

Schneider, B. (2013). 'Heteronormativity and queerness in transnational heterosexual Salsa communities', *Discourse and Society*, 24(5): 553–571.

Silverstein, M. (1976). Shifters, linguistic categories, and cultural description, in K. Basso and H.A. Selby (eds) *Meaning in anthropology*. Albuquerque: University of New Mexico, pp. 11–55.

Silverstein, M. (1996). Monoglot standard in America: standardization and metaphors of linguistic hegemony, in D. Brenneis and R. Macaulay (eds) *The matrix of language: contemporary linguistic anthropology*. Boulder, CO: Westwood Press, pp. 284–306.

Skandrani, M., Taieb, O. and Moro, M.R. (2012). 'Transnational practices, intergenerational relations and identity construction in a migratory context: the case of young women of Maghrebine origin in France', *Culture and Psychology*, 18(1): 76–98.

Song, Y. (2012). 'The struggle over class, identity, and language: a case study of South Korean transnational families', *Journal of Sociolinguistics*, 16(2): 201–217.

Triandafyllidou, A. and Wodak, R. (2003). 'Conceptual and methodological questions in the study of collective identity: an introduction', *Journal of Language and Politics*, 2(2): 205–223.

Vertovec, S. (2009). *Transnationalism*. London: Routledge.

Warriner, D. (2007). 'Transnational literacies: immigration, language and identity', *Linguistics and Education*, 18(3–4): 201–214.

Wodak, R. (2013). 'Dis-citizenship and migration: a critical discourse-analytical perspective', *Journal of Language, Identity, and Education*, 12(3): 173–178.

Wodak, R., de Cillia, R., Reisigl, M. and Liebhart, K. (1999). *The discursive construction of national identity*. Edinburgh: Edinburgh University Press.

11
Identity in post-colonial contexts

Priti Sandhu and Christina Higgins

Introduction

In August 2014, Hindi-speaking citizens of India aspiring to take the nation's civil service examination protested against the exam's English component, which was first instituted in 2011. Arguing that it discriminated against them and reproduced a class division, they called for the removal of the English aptitude section. The government conceded, and although the English portion of the exam remained, the government decided that it would no longer contribute toward the final score. Observers have argued that the critique of the English portion of the test is about the enduring legacy of colonialism and the division of haves and have-nots along linguistic lines in Indian society. This example shows the continuing relevance of post-colonialism for contemporary contexts, particularly with reference to the significance of English in shaping people's lives.

In this chapter, we discuss the relationship between identity and language in post-colonial contexts. After describing the foundational concepts of post-colonialism and examining the impact that it has had in applied linguistics, we engage with more recent work on the sociopolitics of language and identity, which have emerged largely as a critique of post-colonial theory. While the term post-colonial still has widespread use in scholarship, many other concepts have emerged to complicate and to challenge the underpinnings of this term. In particular, work on translanguaging and translingual practices have challenged the relevance of colonial legacies by foregrounding local, transcultural language practices as the key sites for identity construction (see Pennycook 2010; Canagarajah 2013; Sultana *et al.* 2013; García and Li Wei 2014). This work moves away from the coloniser–colonised dichotomy frequently used in post-colonial approaches and highlights the importance of mobility in the relationship between language and identity, drawing attention to the varied use of language in new forms of cultural production afforded by intersecting scapes of people, media, ideas, technology and capital (Appadurai 1996; Higgins 2011a). Within this body of work, however, discourses tied to the colonial era can still be encountered as speakers themselves enact identities that explicitly index coloniser–colonised relations and ideologies.

Post-colonialism refers to a theoretical lens that is concerned with the legacies of colonial rule, including how the identity dimensions of class, ethnicity, language and gender have been formed in response to centre–periphery political relations. *Centre* is a label used to refer to developed nations which have engaged in the colonisation of much of the world. Post-colonialism is multidisciplinary, though it is most often associated with literary and cultural studies. Usually considered the father of post-colonial theory, Edward Said (1978) was instrumental in producing a framework for post-colonial analysis and critique in his classic work *Orientalism*, which analysed literature as a key site in which representations of the cultural Other are created by the West. Said argued that 'Self–Other' and 'Occident–Orient' dichotomies exist because the West has produced them and it is the post-colonial scholar's task to examine this production and reproduction. Through analysing literary representations of Middle Eastern cultures, Said focused specifically on the ways a Western self is produced through the act of creating an Eastern other. Spivak takes the argument further, asserting that 'Western intellectual production is … complicit with Western international economic interests' (2010 [1988]: 237). Working toward decolonisation, the prominent Kenyan writer Ngũgĩ wa Thiong'o (1986) took the stance that African writers need to express their stories in African languages to escape the bondage of colonialism, including the effects of English as a 'cultural bomb', which he asserted had annihilated pre-colonial histories, literatures and cultures.

Scholarship on English as a global language has raised questions about the effects that English has on languages, schemas and cultures of people who were subjected to colonial rule. Hence, in this chapter we will examine the relationship between language and identity in post-colonial societies by focusing on the ideologies, policies and discourses about English in these settings. We also pay attention to the discursive (re)production of ideologies by examining how bi/multilingual individuals respond to the power of English in their everyday lives. We illustrate these ideas drawing on interview-based narratives, conversational interaction and media representations. While questions concerning post-colonial identities are relevant across a wide range of geographical and linguistic contexts, we frequently refer to settings which we are most familiar with, namely India, Tanzania and Hawai'i, settings that qualify as post-colonial due to their occupation by British or American imperial powers. We then turn to a discussion of ongoing debates in applied and sociolinguistics, focusing on the thorny topic of hybridity and the politics of knowledge production and dissemination. The chapter ends with a discussion of the relationship between individual and societal multilingualism involving English in post-colonial contexts.

Overview

In this section we discuss salient concepts of post-colonial identities in research literature, focusing specifically on how ideologies become visible in varied discursive practices. For each concept within post-colonialism, we present discussions of ideologies (also referred to as big 'D' Discourses) (Gee 2014) that are illustrated by research that draws on studies of language use. We wish to shed light on the relationship between the individual and society in understanding the role of English in post-colonial contexts.

Self and Other

As mentioned in the Introduction, an important concept within post-colonial literature on identity is the notion of 'Self' and 'Other'. Language ideologies can be analysed as the discursive effects of colonialism whereby Self and Other identities have been formed in connection to the West and to English. While the post-colonial project seeks to identify the ways in which

Self and Other relations have been critically re-examined and refuted, it is also the case that self-colonisation in the form of continued subordination can be found. These formations occur regularly in Hawai'i, where Self and Other relations are visible in sentiments expressed about Pidgin, the creole language of the islands, in comparison to what is often called 'proper English', a language associated strongly with the continental United States (Marlow and Giles 2008; Higgins *et al.* 2012). Pidgin is spoken by the majority of local residents of Hawai'i, but due to its plantation roots and the long history of educational authorities treating it as 'broken English', it remains a stigmatised language. Posts in an online newspaper forum from 2008 clearly demonstrate these language ideologies. The posts were made after a legislative bill was proposed to the Hawai'i state legislature that sought funds to examine the role of Pidgin in educational contexts (the bill failed). Though many pro-Pidgin comments were posted, including ones that drew attention to the linguistic status of Pidgin as a 'real' language, other posts attributed low intelligence to Pidgin speakers:

> Stop trying to legitimize [Pidgin]. It sounds like retarded cave people talking to each other because the correct word or pronunciation doesn't come to their simple mind. The people for it are afraid and embarrassed to say that they have been teaching their children how to speak like an imbecile and they learned it from their parents.
>
> *(Balzac, Online post, 21 May 2008)*

The portrayal of Pidgin in this post reproduces Said's dichotomy in that English speakers are portrayed as educated and sophisticated while Pidgin speakers are Othered and presented as backward and uncivilised. Even when Pidgin is defended, it is always with deference to English, as another post reveals: 'I say long live pidgin, speak it well, and speak straight English too. As adults it is our responsibility to demonstrate to the rising generation which is which. (In the classroom generally not, except maybe for creative writing.)' (hoomalimali, Online post, 28 June 2008).

In India, social class and political ideologies are also at work in creating Self and Other categories. As Chand (2011) explains, groups of elites have a range of ideological positions, both in favour of and counter to English. Conservative elites who align with Hindi-based nationalism and right-wing nationalism valorise Hindi and produce a narrative that draws on India's colonial past to support this discourse. In contrast, liberal elites downplay the potential of Hindi to unify the country and explain their Hindi incompetency through references to the failure of Hindi-based nationalism and to years of English-medium schooling that diminished the role of Hindi in their lives.

These same discourses are also articulated in interviews with Hindi-medium educated (HME) women from northern India who construct disempowered identities in their narratives as a consequence of their Hindi-medium education. One of the authors for this chapter, Sandhu (2014a), shows how Aditi, a highly educated woman, reports feelings of significantly diminished self-worth when negatively comparing her past non-proficient-in-English self to fluent English speakers: 'when I used to listen that people who are speaking in English I feel very impressed that wow they are very much intelligent and I am nothing in front of them' (ibid.: 34). Similarly, another HME woman, Sanjana, speaks of feeling highly inadequate in a romantic relationship with an English-medium educated man, imagining the negative positioning his family would ascribe to her as '*Apne-aap ko kya samajhti hai aisa?* [What does she think of herself like this?]' (Sandhu 2014b: 27).

Hybridity

In addition to Self and Other theorisations, another salient concept within post-colonial discussions on identity is the notion of *hybridity* (Rampton 1995; Creese and Blackledge 2010). Hybridity offers space for new identities that are seen as the product of mixing. Many discussions of hybridity invoke Bakhtin's work on 'heteroglossia', used to refer to the multi-voiced nature of language. When post-colonial speakers use English, they voice the language anew, imbuing it with their own meanings and aesthetic qualities. By incorporating others' discourse into their own, speakers constantly engage in Bakhtinian 'double-voicing' since their articulations express novel sentiments and framings while retaining echoes of the previously articulated utterances. In performing hybrid identities, double-voicing is transparent in a number of domains in East Africa, including in the creative use of artistic naming practices among hip hop artists such as E-Sir, a Kenyan rapper whose name simultaneously indexes his given name (Issa Mumar) and his status as a youth icon through affiliation with e-commerce and e-entertainment, and in advertisements, where slogans play off the double meanings in Swahili-English, in ads such as *Longa Longer* [Chat Longer], to relate to young, cosmopolitan consumers (Higgins 2009).

Hybridity is also described by Bhabha (1994: 2) as the process of subverting colonial authority by interrogating 'originary and initial subjectivities', focusing instead on instances and processes where cultural differences are articulated. For him, in-between, interstitial, 'third spaces' of engaging cultural differences are sites where collaborative or contested new identities are performed from the minority viewpoint located in the peripheries of power and privilege. In Sandhu's (2010: 230–231) analysis of North Indian women's narratives, Aditi, who is located in the linguistic peripheries due to her Hindi-medium education, provides an instance of Bhabha's cultural interrogation. She contrasts a narrative of an unsuccessful job interview for a school teaching position where she claims that she is rejected due to her Hindi background with a narrative where she is offered a similar post at a more prestigious school with a higher salary:

> *Rejection narrative*: 'But when they asked me that *ki* [that] "are you from Hindi medium or English medium?" then I ... [said] ... "yeah I am from Hindi medium" ... then they got then they have not shown their interest and they say "yes you can go".'

> *Counter-narrative*: 'I have got selected in CHS <name of school which hired her> ... [the salary is] ... almost double ... even that time uhh our princi- vice-principal has asked me that *ki* [that] "Aditi you now you don't give ... you not need to give any interview in any school ... because our school pays the highest salary in the surrounding area".'

While portraying herself as subject to a social order that elevates English speakers over Hindi ones in the first narrative, Aditi succeeds in discursively constructing a more powerful identity that is capable of overcoming such social hierarchies in her counter-narrative.

In applied linguistics, hybridity has most often been applied to language practices such as code-switching and code-mixing, areas of inquiry that require microanalysis of language data (see e.g. Spitulnik 1998; Woolard 1998; Jaffe 2000; Higgins 2007; Rubdy 2013). Hybridity has also been identified using Bhabha's (1994) notion of a third space, where local linguistic resources mix with global resources to produce new identities. For example, Rubdy (2013: 44) theorises linguistic landscapes in India as third spaces in which language on public signs inscribes a new class identity that is 'simultaneously local and global, traditional and modern, indigenous and cosmopolitan', enacted for and by the English-knowing bilinguals whose identity is dependent on knowing English but who also constantly and creatively rework their multilingual resources.

Similar arguments are made by Stroud and Mpendukana (2009) about Khayelitsha, a township in the Western Cape of South Africa, where hybridity involving isiXhosa and English in signs advertising luxury goods produces consumerist identities for working-class South Africans to aspire toward. In their analysis, the hybrid signage of the linguistic landscape (along with other markers of socio-economic mobility such as brick-built houses) literally puts a better life on display and invites people to desire that lifestyle.

Appropriation

A third concept that has significantly influenced post-colonial work on identity has been the idea of appropriation. An oft-cited sentiment by the late Chinua Achebe summarises the concept of appropriation (1965: 21):

> My answer to the question, Can an African ever learn English well enough to be able to use it effectively in creative writing? is certainly yes. If on the other hand you ask: Can he ever learn to use it like a native speaker? I should say: I hope not. It is neither necessary nor desirable for him to be able to do so. The price a world language must be prepared to pay is submission to many different kinds of use.

Appropriation refers to the act of taking a cultural or linguistic legacy, such as English, and making it one's own through shaping it to fit the local circumstances and to express the local aesthetics and worldview. Ashcroft *et al.* (1989) argue that appropriation is impossible without abrogation, or the rejection of the categories instantiated by the imperial culture. In British post-colonial countries, the presence of English has become an established phenomenon both at the level of national linguistic policymaking as well as in more individualised contexts of everyday language use. Most post-colonial countries have granted some official status to English in their national and educational linguistic policies. For example, English is the associate official language in India and is used for administration and judicial work at the central level as well as being the lingua franca of higher education, urban professional landscapes and upper-class social circles. Similarly, it is one of the four official languages of Singapore. Kachru (1985, 1986) delineates the independent English varieties that proliferate within post-colonial Outer Circle countries. Kirkpatrick (2007: 28), situating the model within contemporary perspectives, points out that it is useful as it pluralises the notion of English by acknowledging the presence of several Englishes without suggesting the linguistic superiority of any one variety. Though the Kachruvian model has been critiqued for inadequately representing the dynamic heterogeneity of highly divergent English-speaking communities, academics have found it useful as a framework for representing 'dominant ideologies that constrain speakers' performativity in English in local contexts' (Park and Wee 2009: 390).

Appropriation underlies much of the World Englishes (WE) research paradigm, an approach that seeks to describe variation in English as an international language. Rather than viewing World Englishes, such as Kenyan or Indian English, as deficient versions of standard British English, unique features of these varieties are identified and the analysis is located within cultural and multilingual contexts.

While the WE paradigm focuses on describing new Englishes, it is often the case that appropriation includes multilingual practices involving English. Canagarajah and Ashraf (2013: 275–277) highlight the 'blurring of identities of language' in communicative language practices within education and society in post-colonial India and Pakistan. Though these countries have adopted a multilingual approach whereby local languages and English are viewed as separate autonomous systems, at the level of communicative practices, what exists is plurilingualism or the meshing of vernacular languages and English to 'form hybrid grammatical and communicative practices'. Scholars have also examined the various appropriations of English where localised performativity has instantiated the role of human agency and resistance, such as the opposition towards Western-centric English language lessons demonstrated by students in Sri Lanka (Canagarajah 1999) and examinations of local post-colonial literatures where authors 'write back' to the Empire by expressing their voice in English (Ashcroft *et al.* 1989; Pennycook 1994). Similarly, Sandhu (2010) examines the identity constructions of North Indian women with a combined Hindi and English-medium education who narrate instances of successfully 'passing' as English-medium educated, thereby appropriating professional and social advantages associated with English education. Another instance of post-colonial appropriation is Yamuna Kachru's (2006: 223) analysis of Hindi Bollywood songs demonstrating the nativisation of English through a blending of English with Hindi and exemplifying a playful 'fun with the language'.

From post-colonial to transnational

In the present era of late modernity, discussions of scholarship on language and identity in post-colonial contexts have benefited from examining the consequences of globalisation and transnationalism. Despite the unequal, patchy influence of globalisation processes, the commodification of language and identities is acknowledged as one of its major consequences (Coupland 2003: 470) and has been widely studied (e.g. Rubdy 2008; Heller 2010; Duchêne and Heller 2012; Park and Wee 2013). The ruptures between past and present wrought by globalisation and partially symbolised through new constructions of imagined selves and worlds (Appadurai 1996: 3) are well established, with the incessant flow of material goods and discourses, images and symbols across borders, cultures, languages and lives examined through the lens of local–global interactions, 'super-diversity' (Vertovec 2007), mobility and the use of new technologies (De Fina and Perrino 2013: 509–510). Such physical mobility has created super-diverse metropolises where myriad cultures and languages become dynamic (and/or) conflicted 'contact zones' (Pratt 2008: 7), impacting identity negotiation and formation. While the value of linguistic repertoires or specific language varieties and discourse practices owned by people/communities are transferable across borders, their local value shifts with such mobility (Blommaert 2005, 2010). For instance, a variety of English viewed as imparting considerable prestige to its owner/speaker in a particular context (especially so in the peripheries of a globalised world) might have the impact of imparting to its speaker a subordinated position in an English-dominant setting. Such local/translocal ascriptions of identities need to be understood in the context of a world order typified by inherent inequalities exemplified at the level of language varieties and discourses (Blommaert 2010).

Within discussions of the impact of globalisation on language and identity research, the ever-increasing impact of transnationalism is particularly significant due to large-scale movement of people across national borders motivated by globalised economic and educational incentives. Such people are no longer permanently displaced from their original countries and cultures either physically (due to ease of travel) or virtually (because of audio/video connectivity, globalised media, the Internet, social networking sites). No longer limited to binaries of 'here' or 'there', but able to participate in multiple cultures and languages, novel identity constructions are available to transnational individuals (De Fina and Perrino 2013). However, this transnationalism, characterised by processes of 'movement, dislocation and uprooting' and often accompanied by the contradictions and ambiguities of inhabiting in-between and hybrid spaces, results in complex 'self–other differentiation, proclamations of sameness, and strategic identity positionings' (ibid.: 512) (also see Baynham and De Fina 2005). Language and identity scholars have examined such nuanced, transnational language and identity interconnections across multiple sites; for example, in an edited volume, Higgins (2011a) explores the impact of phenomena such as transnationalism, intercultural contact zones and globalised media on additional language learning, teaching and learner identity formation across multiple languages and geographical contexts. In this collection, Higgins (2011b) examines how expatriate learners of Swahili adhere to a transnational positionality rather than taking up the opportunity to develop second language identities attached to Tanzanian culture or Swahili pragmatics and norms, largely because of their negative reactions to the gendered identities available to them in the Tanzanian context. Despite positively evaluating Tanzanian culture, they identify themselves most strongly as global citizens who occupy a third space and feel most at home with others who share their global orientation.

Issues and ongoing debates

We now turn to a discussion of debates and controversies that post-colonial thinking has spawned with regard to studies of language and identity. Responses to the role of hybridity in decolonisation and representation have centred on two areas:

1 Arguments about linguistic purism and mixing;
2 The failure of hybridity to overcome enduring economic divisions.

A third area that has received significant attention is the politics of knowledge construction and dissemination. We examine the challenges that these new perspectives have raised, with attention to our own contexts of research.

Questions of ontological purity and the translingual turn

In recent years, hybridity has been the centre of criticism for the assumptions that it carries with it regarding origins. On the face of it, hybridity entails mixing, so the term presumes that languages and cultures must exist in pure forms prior to hybridisation. This is problematic since it is impossible to establish that any language is in fact pure. While interrogating the concept of an English, or any other, language, Makoni and Pennycook (2005: 137) emphasise the 'need to understand the interrelationships among metadiscursive regimes, language inventions, colonial history, language effects, alternative ways of understanding language, and strategies of disinvention and reconstitution'. Moreover, linguistic hybridity is associated with cultural hybridity in that it is assumed that bi/multilingual individuals inhabit a hybrid cultural identity by virtue of translanguaging, or mixing the codes in their linguistic repertoires. Otsuji and Pennycook (2010, 2013) have argued that this is problematic, drawing attention to the 'unmarked' nature of hybridity. Drawing parallels with 'metrosexuality', a gendered identity ascription related to grooming and appearance that is typically attributed to men, they offer up the new term 'metrolingualism', which refers to how people

use, play with and negotiate identities through language; it does not assume connections between language, culture, ethnicity, nationality or geography, but rather seeks to explore how such relations are produced, resisted, defied or rearranged; its focus is not on language systems but on languages as emergent from contexts of interaction.

(Otsuji and Pennycook 2010: 246)

Metrolingualism challenges the very ontology upon which language is based. Just as metrosexuality is not the reallocation of male and female attributes, but instead a questioning of those very attributes, metrolingualism is also a questioning of the countable and separable nature of language in multilingual practices.

Metrolingualism foregrounds a practice-based understanding of language that begins not with identifying codes, but with analysing social practices that are at the heart of identity construction. In examining the localised mixing of English with vernacular languages in South India and the Philippines, Pennycook (2010: 13) argues that language is a practice influenced by the confluences of 'time, place, repetition and relocalization' rather than as a fixed structure. This view enables an examination of the creativity evident in local practices and usages of English rather than an analysis of difference from a 'core of similarity'. It also pushes analysis beyond acritical celebrations of multiplicity, which tend to view hybridity as mere combinations of cultural and linguistic resources. Rather than examining the practices in depth, these 'happy hybridity' (Lo 2000) approaches tend to pluralise languages and to present multiculturalism as Benetton ads instead of considering the complex social practices that are at the forefront of their production.

Other forms of language that reflect a transborder, transcultural influence have been designated as 'polylanguaging' (Jørgensen 2008) and 'translanguaging' (García 2009). Like metrolingualism, these terms reflect an approach to language that avoids compartmentalising linguistic resources into language categories; instead they begin by viewing language as a practice and as an activity rather than a structure. Hence, speakers engage in 'languaging' in the process of meaning-making, and their languaging can draw from different linguistic and semiotic resources, which may or may not be viewed as crossing linguistic boundaries. As Otsuji and Pennycook (2013) note, multilingual speakers move between fixed and fluid identities, and this movement in itself is worth analysing to better understand the ways that they construct social spaces and identities.

In addition to code-switching, code-mixing and borrowing, translanguaging includes 'stylisation', a form of speech that is highly performative, usually exaggerated, and put on for effect (Coupland 2001). Stylisation raises difficult questions about authenticity and the ownership of English when people with more linguistic and cultural capital stylise those with less, and vice versa. A useful example is found in Sandhu's (2015) analysis of stylisation by Gayatri, a transnational, English-medium educated woman, who employs 'mock Hindi-medium English' to critique the English used by the generic HME masses. Her mock language works to reproduce hegemonic linguistic discourses within India as it portrays the masses as unsophisticated because of their lack of proficiency in English. Suhani's stylising of a socially authoritative English-medium educated person through 'Hinglish' (a mixture of Hindi and English) is also an example of translanguaging. However, Sandhu shows that this second instance of stylisation highlights the ambiguous linguistic identities of Hinglish speakers, their equation of social power with English fluency and, in this instance, the narrator's inability to resist subordinate positioning within her narrative. In Hawai'i, similarly ambiguous forms of stylisation are found in local television advertisements targeting local consumers. In 2008, one ad for a local cable company featured a local man dressed in a velvet smoking jacket, reciting poetic verses that praise the company in a stylised upper-class, overly enunciated English (Hiramoto 2011). At the end of his recitation, he turns to the camera and says '*No kæn help. Ai ste ejumakeited!* [I can't help it. I'm educated!]' in Pidgin, thus mocking both the upper class and forms of American English usually associated with the continental U.S., and reproducing the historical class divisions between Pidgin and English-speaking people in Hawai'i, a state with a legacy of linguistic discrimination toward Pidgin.

Enduring economic divisions

Another controversy that hybridity has provoked surrounds the question of social class. Block (2012) argues that hybridity often posits overly romanticised ways of coping with globalisation, drawing on glocalisation models from the business world to account for the ways in which multilinguals have adopted and adapted English for their local purposes. At the same time, he notes that social class remains unexamined within discussions of hybridity, which typically take a culturalist approach to understanding language and identity. Similarly, Kubota (2014) points out that questions of power and language ideologies remain inadequately addressed and asserts that the promotion of translingual practices is ironically similar to the romanticisation of hybridity that translinguists have critiqued. This raises questions for applied linguists with regard to English and language mixing, such as:

- Who gets to mix English with local languages?
- Which segments of society have the facility to move with ease between English (typifying power and prestige) and 'lesser' languages?
- What social groups/individuals project which types of identities when mixing English with local vernaculars?

Investigating these questions has the potential to reveal the roles of power, class, structure and agency in the performance of metrolingual and translingual practices.

Though language blending and meshing of English are considered examples of appropriation by post-colonial thinkers and proponents of translanguaging alike, the elevated cultural and economic capital enjoyed by English speakers in these countries continues, and the resulting linguistic ideologies in turn ensure its insidious connections with social class. In India, English-medium education is widely perceived as leading to social, educational and economic advancement. However, due to its colonial past and post-independence educational language policies, English-medium education is available only to about 6 per cent of the elite (Annamalai 2004) and so is implicated in deepening class-based chasms (Ramanathan 2005, 2013; Sandhu 2010). Vernacular-medium students in Gujarat, India, have been shown to struggle with English curricula at the tertiary level due to the divergent pedagogical practices adopted in K-12 schooling in vernacular and English-medium schools (Ramanathan 2013). Consequently, Rubdy (2008) discusses the commodification of English in India (as elsewhere) as manifested in an ever-increasing demand for English-medium education. It is not surprising that Chaise LaDousa (2014), in his extensive work across mostly Hindi-speaking North India, demonstrates that English acts as an important identity-building category for social structuration.

In Tanzania, discourse analytic studies have for many years demonstrated how class distinction is performed among those who have more access to English, as in the case of professors at the University of Dar es Salaam (Blommaert 1992) and among journalists working at an English-medium newspaper office (Higgins 2007). Both groups use English-infused Swahili, thereby enacting 'elite closure', a concept which Myers-Scotton (1990) used to refer to class-based language choice in Kenya which excludes listeners by virtue of their lack of familiarity with certain types of mixed codes. Similar forms of class distinction are present in Tanzanian beauty pageants, where language mixing is proscribed for the contestants who are expected to produce monolingual, globally intelligible varieties of English in a context where everyone around them is using a hybrid variety (Billings 2013).

Current Indian commercials typically use a mix of Hindi and English (or other local vernaculars and English) to sell a range of high-end products. On the surface, these are encouraging examples of local appropriations, hybrid language use, plurilingualism and translanguaging, but a closer examination reveals that the target audience and potential buyers are the urban socio-economic elite with access to English-medium education, facility with the local vernaculars and ever-increasing disposable incomes. Therefore, in effect, it is the linguistic mobility of this class of people that is catered to. Usually depictions of people from lower socio-economic backgrounds mixing English with local languages in social media or in interpersonal communication show them using marked accents, incorrect grammar or displaying limited English fluency. Recent Indian debates about the mixing of Hindi and English (labelled Hinglish, as mentioned above) call it the 'fashionable language' of the elite of metropolitan India; however, Hinglish is also wielded by Indians relocating from hinterlands to metropolises to gain entry into the imagined sites inhabited by urban denizens (Das *et al.* 2011: 191–196).

If both scenarios are to be believed, then the question arises if such Hindi–English mixings are uniform across both contexts. When attempting an answer, Joshi distinguishes between two such types of fusions (Das *et al.* 2011: 191–192). First is 'Indi', or the language spoken by speakers fully conversant with English grammar, who 'twist Hindi words, for instance *chutnefying* or *rakhoed*'. This is accomplished by adding English inflections or conjugations to Hindi base words to create new, hybrid words and phrases. In these examples, chutney ('a condiment made from a mixture of spices, vegetables and/or fruits') is inflected with the English suffix '-ing' to create a verb signifying a hybrid, innovative mixing of elements. *Rakhoed* inflects the base Hindi verb *rakhna* ('to keep, lay or put') with the English past tense '-ed'. This playfully twisted and contorted language is spoken by English-educated, young, urban Indians who are reportedly rediscovering a sense of pride in their country and roots and is used to index a certain cool, urban identity. It is also now widely used in advertising and popular media where neither only Hindi nor pure English are deemed sufficient to connect to urban markets. The second variety of Hindi–English blending is the more sedate Hinglish, where words/phrases from one language are inserted into the other with no contortions or grammatical innovations. For example, *Mera baap* off *ho gaya* ('My father died'). This, Joshi posits, is the language of work, communication and survival. While Indi symbolises 'experimentation and attitude', Hinglish is used for ease of communication, according to Joshi (Das *et al.* 2011: 197). Both allow what Joshi calls a 'loosen[ing] of the idea of English, especially around the margins', creating spaces for greater inclusion into the various benefits associated with English (Desai *et al.* 2011: 200). But the point remains that they index remarkably different identities, potentially leading to the ascription of divergent social positionings to their speakers. Similar points have been made about Campus Kiswahili and Street Swahili in Dar es Salaam (Blommaert 1992) and the mixed varieties Engsh and Sheng in Nairobi (Meierkord 2009). Perhaps the metaphor of 'cultural omnivores' – or the phenomenon of elite segments increasingly being able to participate in and adopt the cultural practices of the masses and of popular culture (Peterson 1992) – might be modified to explain these phenomena. While being 'linguistic omnivores' is no longer only the privilege of the elite, the shape it takes is significant for identity construction. This is an issue for further language and identity research in applied linguistics.

While these discussions show that in spite of linguistic and cultural hybridity ideologies tied to economic advantage still shape people's lives, English can also be used to enhance the subaltern's (i.e. member of an oppressed group) status and offer alternative, possibly more prestigious, identities to inhabit. From Hong Kong, Lin (2013) reports the success content teachers have experienced in incorporating innovative plurilingual pedagogies that accommodate local sociocultural contexts. This success was achieved despite challenges emanating from firmly entrenched purist language ideologies and dominant TESOL methodologies. In India, Vaish (2005) examines how English works as a tool for decolonisation, enabling urban, socioeconomically disadvantaged students from a dual education school in Delhi to access the global economy through unique workplace literacy practices. It is crucial, however, to recognise that the success of any school in providing economically disadvantaged students with education depends greatly on their linguistic and material resources. Bhattacharya (2013) shows the problematic outcomes of resource-poor institutions that aim for English-medium education but lack the material and literacy resources to achieve it in her study of an English-medium school for orphans. She shows how the children are doubly disadvantaged as they fail to learn content or English in their English-medium school.

Politics of knowledge construction

Another important issue connected to language and identity scholarship for applied linguists concerns the politics of knowledge construction. This is closely connected to the politics of location, both of which can work to exclude and marginalise language and identity scholars (as well as of other areas of applied linguistics) from non-Western periphery countries. While documenting the unequal representation of research conducted outside North America and European contexts in a sample of 33 applied linguistics texts on language learning and teaching written in English, Pakir (2005) identified only one scholar (Braj Kachru) who proposed a non-Western perspective. She then raised the question if this work was 'a Western representation of non-Western societies rather than an Indian representation of Indian society' (ibid.: 720). Explaining such phenomena, Altbach (1998) claims that editors and reviewers of international journals based in North America and Europe are usually oriented towards their own national audiences, which could serve to disadvantage research studies located in non-Western contexts. Adding to this explanation is a study conducted by Flowerdew (2001: 121), who interviewed the editors of 12 leading international journals in applied linguistics and English language teaching, who in turn described the specific characteristics they found problematic in the writing of non-native scholars: surface errors, insularity, the 'absence of authorial voice' and 'nativized' English varieties. The identity of an applied linguistics scholar is therefore another issue that the field could usefully follow up in language and identity studies.

Summary

In this chapter, we examined identity scholarship in post-colonial contexts with a specific focus on India, Tanzania and Hawai'i. Our discussions encompassed the historical and current forms of ideologies, policies and discourses about English impacting the values accorded by people to English and their local languages. We also illustrated how these were experienced in everyday lives.

We first examined Said's (1978) Self–Other concept, focusing on how identities were shaped in relation to English and the West. We then examined the concept of hybridity theorised as Bakhtinian heteroglossia and double-voicing. Hybridity was illustrated through code-switching and code-mixing and as providing a theoretical base for change in institutional practices.

Appropriation, or the act of shaping cultural and linguistic legacies to fit local circumstances, aesthetics and worldviews, was examined with reference to Chinua Achebe's (1965) stance against native-speaker conformity and a rejection of imperialist culture (Ashcroft *et al.* 1989). We then discussed the movement from post-colonialism to transnationalism as a consequence of globalisation and the impact of such mobility on identity construction.

In the section on issues for applied linguistics scholars interested in language and identity, we evaluated the translingual turn in the field, looking at notions of metrolingualism (Otsuji and Pennycook 2013), polylanguaging (Jørgensen 2008) and translanguaging (García 2009) as useful frames to understand languages as practices and activities rather than static structures. Simultaneously, we engaged with issues of authenticity and ownership of English connected to translanguaging exemplified through stylisation, with data from India and Hawai'i. We also discussed the relevance of social class, questioning acritical cultural approaches to linguistic pluralism in language and identity scholarship with inadequate attention to power and language ideologies. Finally, we questioned the politics of knowledge construction and location and the challenges that multilingual scholars, especially those situated in underdeveloped post-colonial contexts, face in getting published in Western-based international journals and the impact this has in marginalising post-colonial scholarship.

Related topics

Positioning language and identity: poststructuralist perspectives; Language and ethnic identity; Linguistic practices and transnational identities; Class in language and identity research; Ethics in language and identity research; A linguistic ethnography of identity: adopting a heteroglossic frame; Beyond the micro–macro interface in language and identity research; Language, gender and identities in political life: a case study from Malaysia; Styling and identity in a second language; Language and identity research in online environments: a multimodal ethnographic perspective.

Further reading

Block, D., Gray, J. and Holborow, M. (2012). *Neoliberalism and applied linguistics*. London: Routledge. (This volume examines the interconnections between neoliberalism and applied linguistics in relation to the political economy and language-related issues across the globe.)

Higgins, C. (2009). *English as a local language: postcolonial identities and multilingual practices*. Bristol: Multilingual Matters. (Utilising the Bakhtinian concept of multivocality, this book shows how multilinguals in East Africa utilise English as a local resource.)

Otsuji, E. and Pennycook, A. (2010). 'Metrolingualism: fixity, fluidity and language in flux', *International Journal of Multilingualism*, 7(3): 240–254. (Moving beyond multicultural and multilingual approaches, this article proposes the concept of metrolingualism as a way to examine contemporary urban language practices.)

Rubdy, R. and Alsagoff, L. (eds) (2013). *The global–local interface and hybridity: exploring language and identity*. Bristol: Multilingual Matters. (This volume examines how linguistic resources and practices are interlinked with re-inscriptions of identity across multiple cultural and geographical contexts.)

Sandhu, P. (2014a) 'Constructing normative and resistant societal discourses about Hindi and English in an interactional narrative', *Applied Linguistics*, 35(1): 29–47. (This article examines a hypothetical narrative of a North Indian Hindi-medium educated woman to demonstrate how the act of narrating can resist discourses elevating English over Hindi.)

References

Achebe, C. (1965). 'English and the African writer', *Transition*, 18: 27–30.

Altbach, P. (1998). *Comparative higher education: knowledge, the university, and development*. Hong Kong: Comparative Education Research Centre.

Annamalai, E. (2004). Medium of power: the question of English in education in India, in J.W. Tollefson and A.B.M. Tsui (eds) *Medium of instruction policies: which agenda? whose agenda?* Mahwah, NJ: Lawrence Erlbaum Associates, pp. 177–194.

Appadurai, A. (1996). *Modernity at large: cultural dimensions of globalization*. Minneapolis and London: University of Minnesota Press.

Ashcroft, B., Griffiths, G. and Tiffin, H. (1989). *The empire writes back*. London: Routledge.

Balzac (2008). 'Pidgin and education forum', *The Honolulu Advertiser*, 21 June [Online]. Available at http://the.honoluluadvertiser.com

Baynham, M. and De Fina, A. (eds) (2005). *Dislocations/relocations: narratives of dislocation*. Manchester: St Jerome Publishing.

Bhabha, H. (1994). *The location of culture*. London and New York: Routledge.

Bhattacharya, U. (2013). 'Mediating inequalities: exploring English-medium instruction in a suburban Indian village school', *Current Issues in Language Planning*, 14(1): 164–184.

Billings, S. (2013). *Language, globalization and the making of a Tanzanian beauty queen*. Bristol: Multilingual Matters.

Block, D. (2012). Economising globalisation and identity in applied linguistics in neoliberal times, in D. Block, J. Gray and M. Holborow (eds) *Neoliberalism and applied linguistics*. London: Routledge, pp. 56–85.

Blommaert, J. (1992). 'Codeswitching and the exclusivity of social identities: some data from Campus Kiswahili', *Journal of Multilingual and Multicultural Development*, 13(1–2): 57–70.

Blommaert, J. (2005). 'Situating language rights: English and Swahili in Tanzania revisited', *Journal of Sociolinguistics*, 9(3): 390–417.

Blommaert, J. (2010). *The sociolinguistics of globalization*. Cambridge: Cambridge University Press.

Canagarajah, S. (1999). *Resisting linguistic imperialism in English teaching*. Oxford: Oxford University Press.

Canagarajah, S. (ed.) (2013). *Literacy as translingual practice: between communities and classrooms*. New York: Routledge.

Canagarajah, S. and Ashraf, H. (2013). 'Multilingualism and education in South Asia: resolving policy/practice dilemmas', *Annual Review of Applied Linguistics*, 33: 258–285.

Chand, V. (2011). 'Elite positionings towards Hindi: language policies, political stances and language competence in India', *Journal of Sociolinguistics*, 15(1): 6–35.

Coupland, N. (2001). 'Dialect stylization in radio talk', *Language in Society*, 30(3): 345–375.

Coupland, N. (2003). 'Introduction: sociolinguistics and globalization', *Journal of Sociolinguistics*, 7(4): 465–472.

Creese, A. and Blackledge, A. (2010). 'Translanguaging in the bilingual classroom: a pedagogy for learning and teaching?', *Modern Language Journal*, 94: 103–115.

Das, G., Joshi, P., Panday, P., Kothari, R., Barocha, C. and Dev, R. (2011). Panel Discussion I: is Hinglish the language of India's future?, in R. Kothari and R. Snell (eds) *Chutnefying English: the phenomenon of Hinglish*. New Delhi: Penguin Books, pp. 190–198.

De Fina, A. and Perrino, S. (2013). 'Transnational identities', *Applied Linguistics*, 34(5): 509–515.

Desai, S., Bhutalia, U., Rao, R.R., Bharathan, K., Sharma, D., Kansal, R. and Tandan, A. (2011). Panel Discussion II: is Hinglish a unifying force?, in R. Kothari and R. Snell (eds) *Chutnefying English: the phenomenon of Hinglish*. New Delhi: Penguin Books, pp. 199–207.

Duchêne, A. and Heller, M. (eds) (2012). *Language in late capitalism: pride and profit*. Vol. 1. New York: Routledge.

Flowerdew, J. (2001). 'Attitudes of journal editors to nonnative speaker contributions', *TESOL Quarterly*, 35(1): 121–150.

García, O. (2009). *Bilingual education in the 21st century: a global perspective*. Malden, MA: Wiley-Blackwell.

García, O. and Li Wei (2014). *Translanguaging: language, bilingualism and education*. New York: Palgrave Macmillan.

Gee, J.P. (2014). *An introduction to discourse analysis: theory and method*. 4th edn. London and New York: Routledge.

Heller, M. (2010). 'The commodification of language', *Annual Review of Anthropology*, 39(20): 101–114.

Higgins, C. (2007). 'Shifting tactics of intersubjectivity to align indexicalities: a case of joking around in Swahinglish', *Language in Society*, 36(1): 1–24.

Higgins, C. (2009). *English as a local language: postcolonial identities and multilingual practices*. Bristol: Multilingual Matters.

Higgins, C. (ed.) (2011a). *Identity formation in globalizing contexts: language learning in the new millennium*. Berlin: Mouton de Gruyter.

Higgins, C. (2011b). 'You're a real Swahili!': Western women's resistance to identity slippage in Tanzania, in C. Higgins (ed.) *Identity formation in globalizing contexts: language learning in the new millennium*. Berlin: Mouton de Gruyter, pp. 147–168.

Higgins, C., Nettell, R., Furukawa, G. and Sakoda, K. (2012). 'Beyond contrastive analysis and codeswitching: student documentary filmmaking as a challenge to linguicism in Hawai'i', *Linguistics and Education*, 23: 49–61.

Hiramoto, M. (2011). 'Consuming the consumers: semiotics of Hawai'i Creole in advertisements', *Journal of Pidgin and Creole Languages*, 26(2): 247–275.

hoomalimali (2008). 'Pidgin and education forum', *The Honolulu Advertiser*, 28 June [Online]. Available at http://the.honoluluadvertiser.com

Jaffe, A. (2000). 'Comic performance and the articulation of hybrid identity', *Pragmatics*, 10(1): 39–59.

Jørgensen, J. (2008). 'Polylingual languaging around and among children and adolescents', *International Journal of Multilingualism*, 5(3): 161–176.

Kachru, B. (1985). Standards, codification, and sociolinguistic realism: the English language in the Outer Circle, in R. Quirk and H.G. Widdowson (eds) *English in the world: teaching and learning the language and literatures*. Cambridge: Cambridge University Press, pp. 11–30.

Kachru, B. (1986). *The alchemy of English: the spread, functions and models of non-native Englishes*. Oxford: Pergamon.

Kachru, Y. (2006). 'Mixers lyricing in Hinglish: blending and fusion in Indian pop culture', *World Englishes*, 25(2): 223–233.

Kirkpatrick, A. (2007). *World Englishes: implications for international communication and English language teaching*. Cambridge: Cambridge University Press.

Kubota, R. (2014). 'The multi/plural turn, postcolonial theory and neoliberal multiculturalism: complicities and implications for applied linguistics', *Applied Linguistics* [Online]. DOI: 10.1093/applin/amu045

LaDousa, C. (2014). *Hindi is our ground, English is our sky: education, language, and social class in contemporary India*. New York and Oxford: Berghahn Books.

Lin, A. (2013). 'Toward paradigmatic change in TESOL methodologies: building plurilingual pedagogies from the ground up', *TESOL Quarterly*, 47(3): 521–545.

Lo, J. (2000). Beyond happy hybridity: performing Asian-Australian identities, in I. Ang, S. Chalmers, L. Law and M. Thomas (eds) *Alter/Asians: Asian-Australian identities in art, media and popular culture*. Annandale, NSW, Australia: Pluto Press, pp. 152–168.

Makoni, S. and Pennycook, A. (2005). 'Disinventing and (re)constituting languages', *Critical Inquiry in Language Studies*, 2(3): 137–156.

Marlow, M. and Giles, H. (2008). '*Who you tink you, talkin propah?* Hawaiian Pidgin demarginalised', *Journal of Multicultural Discourses*, 3(1): 53–68.

Meierkord, C. (2009). 'It's kuloo tu: recent developments in Kenya's Englishes', *English Today*, 25(1): 3–11.

Myers-Scotton, C. (1990). Elite closure as boundary maintenance: the case of Africa, in B. Weinstein (ed.) *Language policy and political development*. Norwood, NJ: Ablex, pp. 25–42.

Ngũgĩ wa Thiong'o (1986). *Decolonising the mind: the politics of language in African literature*. London: James Currey.

Otsuji, E. and Pennycook, A. (2010). 'Metrolingualism: fixity, fluidity and language in flux', *International Journal of Multilingualism*, 7(3): 240–254.

Otsuji, E. and Pennycook, A. (2013). Unremarkable hybridities and metrolingual practices, in R. Rubdy and L. Alsagoff (eds) *The global–local interface and hybridity: exploring language and identity*. Bristol: Multilingual Matters, pp. 83–99.

Pakir, A. (2005). 'Applied linguistics proper? Relocation, reorientation, and realignment', *TESOL Quarterly*, 39(4): 720–723.

Park, J.S. and Wee, L. (2009). 'The three circles redux: a market–theoretic perspective on World Englishes', *Applied Linguistics*, 30(3): 389–406.

Park, J.S. and Wee, L. (2013). *Markets of English: linguistic capital and language policy in a globalizing world*. London: Routledge.

Pennycook, A. (1994). *The cultural politics of English as an international language*. New York and London: Routledge.

Pennycook, A. (2010). *Language as a local practice*. London and New York: Routledge.

Peterson, R.A. (1992). 'Understanding audience segmentation: from elite and mass to omnivore and univore', *Poetics*, 21(4): 243–258.

Pratt, M.L. (2008). *Imperial eyes: travel writing and transculturation*. 2nd edn. New York: Routledge.

Ramanathan, V. (2005). *The English–vernacular divide: postcolonial language politics and practice*. Clevedon, UK: Multilingual Matters.

Ramanathan, V. (2013). A postcolonial perspective in applied linguistics: situating English and the vernaculars, in M. Hawkins (ed.) *Framing languages and literacies: socially situated views and perspectives*. New York: Routledge, pp. 83–104.

Rampton, B. (1995). *Crossing: language and ethnicity among adolescents*. London: Longman.

Rubdy, R. (2008). English in India: the privilege and privileging of social class, in P.K.W. Tan and R. Rubdy (eds) *Language as commodity: global structures, local marketplaces*. London and New York: Continuum, pp. 122–145.

Rubdy, R. (2013). Hybridity in the linguistic landscape: democratizing English in India, in R. Rubdy and L. Alsagoff (eds) *The global–local interface and hybridity: exploring language and identity*. Bristol: Multilingual Matters, pp. 43–65.

Said, E. (1978). *Orientalism*. New York: Vintage.

Sandhu, P. (2010). *Enactments of discursive empowerment in narratives of medium of education by north Indian women*. PhD thesis, University of Hawai'i at Manoa.

Sandhu, P. (2014a). 'Constructing normative and resistant societal discourses about Hindi and English in an interactional narrative', *Applied Linguistics*, 35(1): 29–47.

Sandhu, P. (2014b). '"Who does she think she is?" Vernacular medium and failed romance', *Journal of Language, Identity, and Education*, 13(1): 16–33.

Sandhu, P. (2015). 'Stylizing voices, stances, and identities related to medium of education in India', *Multilingua: Journal of Cross-Cultural and Interlanguage Communication*, 34(2): 211–235.

Spitulnik, D. (1998). 'The language of the city: Town Bemba as urban hybridity', *Journal of Linguistic Anthropology*, 8(1): 30–59.

Spivak, G. (2010 [1988]). Can the subaltern speak?, in R.C. Morris (ed.) *Can the subaltern speak? Reflections on the history of an idea*. New York: Columbia University, pp. 237–292.

Stroud, C. and Mpendukana, S. (2009). 'Towards a material ethnography of linguistic landscape: multilingualism, mobility and space in a South African township', *Journal of Sociolinguistics*, 13(3): 363–386.

Sultana, S., Dovchin, S. and Pennycook, A. (2013). 'Styling the periphery: linguistic and cultural takeup in Bangladesh and Mongolia', *Journal of Sociolinguistics*, 17(5): 687–710.

Vaish, V. (2005). 'A peripherist view of English as a language of decolonization in postcolonial India', *Language Policy*, 4(2): 187–206.

Vertovec, S. (2007). 'Super-diversity and its implications', *Ethnic and Racial Studies*, 30(6): 1024–1054.

Woolard, K.A. (1998). 'Simultaneity and bivalency as strategies in bilingualism', *Journal of Linguistic Anthropology*, 8(1): 3–29.

12
Language and religious identities

Ana Souza

Introduction

The twenty-first century has seen the start of the systematic development of 'language and religion' as a subfield of sociolinguistics (Darquennes and Vandenbussche 2011). Studies in this subfield have pointed to two fundamental issues: first, the importance of language for the maintenance of religion and religious practices and, vice versa, the importance of religious practices for the maintenance of language, and, second, the role of language and religion as markers of identity (Mukherjee 2013). This chapter presents a general view of both these issues, with particular consideration of language and religious identities within the field of applied linguistics.

The publication of Omoniyi and Fishman's (2006) *Explorations in the Sociology of Language and Religion* established the sociology of language and religion as a field of study. Their edited collection had four parts:

1   The effects of religion on language;
2   The mutuality of language and religion;
3   The effects of language on religion; and
4   The effects of language and religion on literacy.

That religious practices may influence the maintenance and the loss of migrants' languages is illustrated in Dzialtuvaite's (2006) study of Lithuanians, published in Part One of Omoniyi and Fishman's volume. The first Lithuanians arrived in Scotland at the end of the nineteenth century and nurtured their identity and culture through the use of the Lithuanian language in Catholic services. However, the present generation is reported to have become more secular. Consequently, the youth of Lithuanian background have become less connected with their language of origin through religious practices. Nevertheless, as noted by Chruszczewski (2006), another study in Omoniyi and Fishman's volume, it is language that sometimes impacts on what happens to religion. He analyses Jewish benedictions (i.e. prayers that ask for divine blessing) and their role in integrating specific Jewish discourse forms. He concludes that it is through these prayers that the religious identity of Jews, a multi-ethnic and multilingual group, is established. Nonetheless, the relationship between language and religion is not necessarily causal.

Reciprocity between language and religion is possible, as is illustrated in Joseph's (2006) study of Lebanon in Part Two of Omoniyi and Fishman's collection. Both Arabic and French are spoken in the region; however, bilingualism in French by the Christian population was increasingly used to highlight their religious identities after Lebanon came under *de facto* control of the Muslim Syrian government in 2000. Indeed language and religion can be so intertwined that they can affect a group's literacy. An example comes in Rosowsky's (2006) explorations of the role of liturgical literacy (i.e. reading exclusively for ritual/devotional practices) in the lives of a Pakistani community in the UK. Despite being multilingual, Koranic Arabic literacy is the one mostly supported and maintained by this community. In other words, this group of Muslims most value literacy in the language that is closely linked to their religious practices.

A number of studies on language and religion have been conducted in various parts of the world since the establishment of the sociology of language and religion. One of the latest publications is Mukherjee's (2013) special edition. The articles in this volume draw on three of the categories used in Omoniyi and Fishman's seminal publication – namely:

1   The mutuality of language and religion;
2   The effects of religion on language; and
3   The effects of language on religion.

Koechert and Pfeiler (2013) display the mutuality of language and religion in their analysis of the ritual speech form of the prayers of the Kaqchikel indigenous group in Guatemala. As a result of Spanish colonisation, Spanish words and notions of Catholicism were incorporated into the Kaqchikel's religious rituals, although indigenous spirituality was maintained in their prayers. Consequently, syncretism (i.e. the symbolic modifications in the cultural practices of the indigeneous Kaqchikel that resulted from their interaction with non-indigenous Spanish *mestizo*) is represented in the Kaqchikel's prayers.

Within the studies that consider the effects of religion on language, Gregory *et al.* (2013a) examine four migrant faith communities in England. They provide examples of how sacred texts are used by teachers and family members from these different groups in order to socialise children into their faiths. Hence, this study also covers the effects of language and religion on literacy. While this was an original category in the work of Omoniyi and Fishman (2006), it was not used by Mukherjee (2013) to structure her special edition. Nevertheless, the descriptions in Gregory *et al.*'s article show the importance of learning heritage languages in providing children with access to the religious and cultural membership of their communities. The effects of language on religion are exemplified by Vajta's (2013) study in Alsace, a region that has alternated repeatedly between being part of Germany and France. In this region, Catholicism is linked to French, and Lutheranism is connected to German. Vajta explains that, although secularisation and the promotion of French in the twentieth century was expected to erase this linguistic division, language and religion have been stronger identity markers for Alsatians than national belonging.

These examples give an indication of the relationship between language and religion generally and in studies of identity in sociolinguistics. In this chapter, I further explore the role of language and religion as markers of identity. I start by presenting an overview of these markers in the next section. This overview is followed by three ongoing debates of salience for applied linguistics: faith literacy, language planning and policy, and faith in English language teaching.

Overview

Religious organisations play a key role in supporting migrants as they settle into a new country. From the perspective of migrants, this role can be summarised as the search for refuge (i.e. stability, sense of belonging, psychological comfort and physical safety), respectability (i.e. status recognition and social mobility within the migrant group) and resources (i.e. practical assistance and access to social networks) (Hirschman 2004). Religious support provided in the form of resources is illustrated in the work of Oosterbaan (2010), which explores the role of religious institutions in giving migrants access to important social networks in their hosting country. He focuses on how evangelical churches use the Internet to make resources available to Brazilian migrants in Barcelona and Amsterdam. These virtual religious communities were observed sharing information on how to plan the trip to Europe and how to settle in the new country, including advice on services and products as well as housing and employment possibilities. The sharing of these pieces of information indicated that the churches in Oosterbaan's study offered members practical assistance as well as providing spiritual services.

Religious organisations are also known for providing migrants with respectability. Han's (2011) study of a Chinese church in Canada illustrates this. She explored how the multilingual policies adopted by the church facilitated the social inclusion of new arrivals. The church delivered services in different languages (i.e. Cantonese, Mandarin and English), and code-switching was a common practice. In addition, the church also offered an English programme for adults that integrated language and the content of Christian practices. This programme served the role of supporting the church members with resources, as improving their English may improve their settlement experiences in the new country, including their employment opportunities. Additionally, the programme enabled the church members to practise their religion in English, and public speeches by speakers with limited English language competence were common practice. Han argues that a 'good Christian' identity secures migrants a respected status within the church, regardless of their language competences.

The studies above indicate that the access migrants have to specific social networks (i.e. resources) and the recognition of their social status (i.e. respectability) within a religious institution can provide them with a positive sense of belonging. Migrants' search for refuge through religion is more specifically exemplified by the work of Peek (2005). Her study indicated that religious identity was the most salient source of personal and social identity (i.e. how individuals see themselves and how they wish to be perceived by others in a specific social context) for the Muslim university students with whom she worked in New York. Peek's analysis of the religious development of her participants revealed three stages: ascription, choice and declaration. The ascribed identity referred to the students' assigned religious identity taken for granted as part of their everyday lives due to their family upbringing. It is interesting to note the difference of meaning in the term 'ascribed' as used by Peek and as used by Blommaert (2006). Peek appears to merge Blommaert's 'ascribed' (i.e. given to someone else) and 'achieved' (i.e. claimed by oneself) identities under 'ascription'. Peek's (2005) participants reported that, as children, they followed their parents' religious identification as Muslim, thus being content to inhabit the religious identity ascribed to them by their parents and heritage community. As they became older, Peek's participants reported viewing religion as their chosen identity – a conscious preference. The third stage in the religious identity development of these Muslim young people, 'declared' identity, took place in response to the events of 9/11. Peek's participants reported experiencing discrimination on the basis of their religion, claiming that, in the search for answers to this discrimination, their religious attachments were reinforced along with the need to assert Muslim identity to retain a positive view of themselves. As this declared identity is articulated by individuals, it can also be considered an achieved identity (Blommaert 2006).

Independently of how an identity is reached, religion has long been considered an important dimension of an individual's identity, whether a migrant or not. Religious identity (i.e. the identification of an individual with a religious tradition) is nowadays described as being fourfold and composed of '(1) affiliation and belonging; (2) behaviours and practices; (3) beliefs and values; and (4) religious and spiritual experiences' (Hemming and Madge 2011: 40). According to Hemming and Madge (2011), the way an individual labels him/herself; how often s/he attends a place of worship; what s/he believes in; and how s/he expresses and experiences his/her beliefs contribute to religious identity. Hemming and Madge developed this description when trying to make sense of the complexity of children's religious lives. They argue that children's agency is an important aspect of the development of religious identity and acknowledge that religious identity, as with any other dimension of identity, is developed through social interactions and linked to specific social contexts. This socially situated view of identity also applies to adults and, thus, is adopted in this chapter. In addition, the fact that language is associated with religious identities and practices is highlighted in the discussions below.

Language, religion and identity

Kouega's (2008) work with 20 Catholic parishes in Yaoundé, Cameroon, shows how linguistic identities may affect linguistic practices within religious organisations. Kouega identified the various parts of the religious services of the parishes in his study and described the languages used for each part of the service. The structural-functional approach adopted by Kouega revealed that the parishes were multilingual congregations that alternated services in the official languages of Cameroon (i.e. French and English) and in a selection of indigenous languages. This approach shed light on the use of language for liturgical practices, with Kouega pointing out the use of French, English, Beti and Basa for the Gospel, the sermon, the offertory and the Eucharist, along with other minority languages for singing and the occasional reading of epistles (i.e. letters written by Jesus's followers with Christian teachings). More importantly, this study demonstrates how individuals with high levels of religious commitment influenced the language choices made in the Catholic services attended by local groups in Cameroon. As Yaoundé is in the francophone part of Cameroon, French is the default language of Catholic services. However, another language was found to be used if at least one priest spoke it. Catechists (i.e. teachers of the Catholic faith) also influenced the language used in the parishes, as they prepared the epistles and helped to select their readers. Moreover, the active participation of a multilingual linguistic community in Mass (i.e. the Catholic communal worship) and their involvement in other parish activities led to the use of a specific language in church.

Chew (2014) raises the point that particular languages in a religious context may favour certain practices and identities. She compared the language choices and religious identities of three weekend madrasahs (i.e. schools for Islamic instruction) in Singapore: a traditional one, where Arabic was the language of instruction; a moderate one, where Malay was the language of instruction; and a liberal one, where English was the language of instruction. As Arabic is the language of the Koran, its status as a liturgical language (here treated as language used for ritual/devotional practices) was maintained in all three madrasahs, where key verses and compulsory prayers of the Koran were learned in Arabic. Nevertheless, the language choices of each of the madrasahs enabled links with specific cultural and pedagogical practices. Arabic as a means of instruction signalled the more traditional position of the first madrasah in relation to religion and language. The use of Malay, the mother tongue of the children attending the madrasah described as moderate, helped to promote a generally more familiar and informal atmosphere. While the third madrasah offered the option of lessons in English or Malay, two-thirds of its attendees opted for English. Chew argues that the language choices of the madrasahs are juxtaposed with a set of distinctive religious and pedagogical approaches. Arabic symbolised a pious religious reverence followed by the adoption of traditional and conservative teaching methodology. Malay allowed for the connection between religious and home domains, and thus reproduced mainstream teaching in Malaysia. English enabled engagement with a globalised world and, as such, offered the possibility of a more critical approach to teaching.

The links between religion and language in educational contexts have also been approached with attention to issues of gender. Jule (2005), for example, investigated the language practices of women in an evangelical theological college in Canada. More specifically, she focused on the use of linguistic space (i.e. amount of talk during formal classroom lessons) by the female students in relation to male students and male lecturers in two groups, one formal and the other more informal, over the course of a term. Jule observed that the lectures were structured in two parts. In the first part, the lecturers delivered the content of their sessions. In the second, the floor was opened for the students to ask questions. Although the lecturers used most of the linguistic space in both groups, there was a clear difference in the use of linguist space by male and female students regardless of group. In the more formal group, only male students asked questions for a whole term; this finding was replicated in the less formal group where there was only one example of a female student asking a question. Jule argues that these patterns may be common in classroom interactions and concludes that 'women [in this Evangelical theological college are] consciously or subconsciously colluding in such patterns' (p. 164). According to Jule, the issue that leads to these female students' silence in public space relates to gender identity norms in Christian discourses that view women as being supportive of others and submissive to male leadership.

Issues and ongoing debates

One perspective used to explore issues of language choice and religious identity in the twenty-first century is that of language socialisation. Language socialisation is the process by which individuals learn how to communicate in a way that is culturally appropriate and effective in the social interactions of a particular group. Participation in language-mediated interactions allows individuals to learn cultural knowledge and ways of using language (Schieffelin and Ochs 1986). Hence, individuals are socialised through language at the same time that they are socialised into the use of language (Ochs and Schieffelin 2008). From this perspective:

> language acquisition is far more than a matter of ... learning to produce well-formed referential utterances; it also entails learning how to use language in socially appropriate ways to co-construct meaningful social contexts and to engage with others in culturally relevant meaning-making activities.
>
> *(Garrett and Baquedano-López 2002: 342)*

Following a language socialisation paradigm, Baquedano-López (2008) names the experiences of faith lesson attendance as 'religious socialisation' and argues that the linguistic practices of these lessons socialise children into the necessary skills and appropriate behaviour of their religion.

With this purpose, Baquedano-López examined how prayers are read in Catholic lessons offered to Mexican migrant children in California, analysing the Act of Contrition, the prayer used by Catholics to tell God that they are sorry for their sins and ask for forgiveness. She argued that in the process of learning the Act of Contrition the children were prepared to participate in the Catholic ritual practice of confession of sins. That is, children were socialised into the appropriate behaviours, the religious language and the cultural facts necessary to participate in the ritual of confession by reading, writing, interpreting and comparing texts and memorising and reciting facts.

There are other contexts in which children and adults participate in religious socialisation. In other to explore these, the following subsections discuss faith literacies, language planning and policy, and faith in ELT.

Faith literacies

The teaching, learning and use of language to read sacred texts has had a number of labels (see e.g. Fishman 1989; Watt and Fairfield 2010; Rosowsky 2013). Yet, language is not the only knowledge necessary for the reading of religious texts (see e.g. Gregory *et al.* 2013a). Indeed, elsewhere I propose (Souza forthcoming) a broadening of the perception of literacy on religion as 'faith literacies', which are defined as:

> practices which involve the reading of written texts (scripts), the use of oral texts (discussions about the faith, interaction with a deity or other members of the faith community), the performance of faith through actions (silent or not), and knowledge (including theological, geographical and historical information about the faith).

Faith literacies may lead individuals to learn a language as a consequence of their interest in becoming members of a specific religion. These literacies may also have a positive impact on secular literacies. For instance, faith literacies can provide language learners with further opportunities to develop their knowledge of sound–letter correspondences in an alphabetic script, a general principle that could be applied to other alphabets (Rosowsky 2013). Faith literacies can also support the meaning-making of secular texts, as demonstrated by Skerrett's (2014) study of a ninth-grade teacher and her students in a school in the United States. One of Skerrett's participants, a Christian Colombian named Carlos, presents an interesting illustration of how religious literacies can be a resource for learning in other contexts. Skerrett observed Carlos reading a book that portrayed the image of a poor man with his arms spread out. Carlos linked this image to the one of Jesus on a cross, which led to a class discussion of the validity of this comparison. Skerrett points out that while the teacher did not critically explore the students' different perspectives, it was clear that the students were drawing on their experiences of religious literacy developed outside school to make sense of their secular literacy experiences in class.

The way in which understanding of meaning in one context may support the learning in another has also been witnessed with younger children. Gregory *et al.* (2013b), for example, present the case of four children in London with links to different religions and explore how these children make sense of their faith and everyday experiences. One of the children in their study is Tanja, a seven-year-old Hindu girl, who was video-recorded as she told a story in English about fairy-tale characters and Hindu gods. Through this story, Tanja displayed an ability to bring together her experiences in two different settings (i.e. temple and school). In addition, Tanja's story revealed her ability to transform the knowledge she had acquired in different settings in a coherent way. This transformation of knowledge is seen as a positive force in the language and literacy learning of multilingual and multicultural children and has been named 'syncretic acts' (ibid.: 3). Through these acts, children combine the experiences they have in different contexts in a creative way, which enables them to develop individual understanding of the world.

Language planning and policy

Language planning and policy (LPP) refers to decisions made about language that may refer to its standardisation, status, acquisition and/or use. Ricento and Hornberger (1996) present LPP as having three layers, namely national, institutional and interpersonal. The national layer, i.e. the macro one, refers to the political processes of a nation in relation to language planning. The institutional layer, i.e. the meso one, represents the ideologies of the different institutions in a society. The interpersonal layer, i.e. the micro one, relates to the language negotiations that take place in spoken interaction. One example of LPP at both the meso and micro layers in faith contexts is Woods' (2004) 'Language–Religion Ideology (LRI) continuum' of ethnic churches. Woods studied a variety of Christian denominations of varied linguistic and ethnic backgrounds in Melbourne. She observed that the role of language was valued differently by each of these denominations, and so developed a framework to explore the links between their language ideologies and language practices.

As Figure 12.1 illustrates, the horizontal axis of the LRI continuum represents the relationship between language and religion. A strong link between language and religion is represented by placing an ethnic church on the left of the continuum. A strong link grants one language the status of being special enough to be used with God. A weak link between language and religion is placed on the right of the continuum. A weak link allows for the use of an individual's everyday

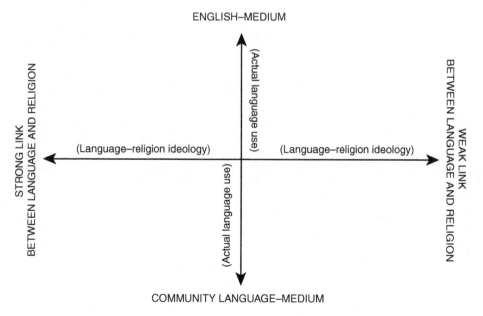

Figure 12.1 The LRI continuum

Source: adapted from Woods (2004).

language practices for a personal relationship with God. The vertical axis represents the language practices of a congregation. The use of English is at the top of this axis and the use of community languages at the bottom. Woods uses this framework to interpret the relationship between the institutional and the interpersonal level of language planning and policy in ethnic churches.

Woods (2006) observed that language ideologies can vary within a single religious institution. In the case of the Latvian Lutheran congregation in her study, the congregation's goal was to preserve their cultural heritage as well as to gather for spiritual reasons. As a consequence, they expected their religious services to be in Latvian, following the Lutheran perspective that everyone has the right to listen to God's Word in their mother tongue. As can be seen in Figure 12.2, Woods placed the Latvian Lutheran congregation on the left of the LRI continuum, where the links between language and religion are perceived to be strong and only one language, in this case Latvian, was considered acceptable. Yet, given the location of the church in Australia, the Latvian minister also considered it necessary to adopt the use of English in communicating the Gospel to Latvian-heritage youth. This ideology represents weak links between language and religion, and as such, Woods placed the Latvian minister's ideologies towards the right of the LRI continuum.

In this later publication, Woods (2006) stressed that the place of language in migrant churches is influenced by two sources: the cultural value system of an ethnic group and the culture of the religious denomination. In fact, the cultural characteristics of a group (i.e. ethnicity) have been considered of relevance to the understanding of the role of language and religion in one's identity formation. Along with Kwapong and Woodham, I have developed the Religion–Ethnicity–Language (REL) triangle (Figure 12.3) (Souza *et al.* 2012), a framework in which each dimension of identity is placed at one of the angles of a triangle with a continuum moving inwards. A move inwards represents weaker identity links with that aspect of identity, whereas a move outwards means stronger links.

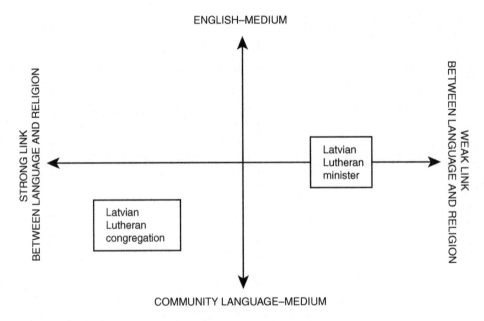

Figure 12.2 The LRI continuum of a Latvian Lutheran church

Source: adapted from Woods (2006).

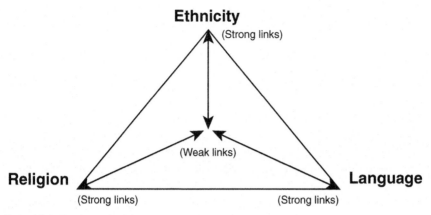

Figure 12.3 The REL triangle

Source: Souza *et al.* (2012).

In the case of the Brazilian Catholic setting in our study, the theological orientation was to support migrants abroad and to offer support in Portuguese as the mother tongue. This concern affected the religious services offered to the adult congregation, such as mass, and the ones offered to their children, such as the catechism (i.e. faith lessons that introduce children to the Catholic sacraments). According to the priest, the decision to deliver the faith lessons in Portuguese was a consequence of the importance the Brazilian Catholic Chaplaincy in London gave to language maintenance and to the children's emotional and cultural links to Brazil. In other words, the study found that the religious, ethnic and linguistic dimensions of identity were reinforced in the Brazilian Catholic lessons. Although the REL triangle is a tentative framework which needs refining, especially in relation to how religion, ethnicity and language can be accounted for (Souza 2015), it is useful in allowing for an understanding of the opportunities children have to develop their cultural, linguistic and religious identities.

Faith and English language teaching

While the sociology of language and religion has developed as a subfield of sociolinguistics, ELT research on language and religion is an emerging subfield of second language acquisition (SLA) and has been developing since the 1990s (Wong *et al.* 2013). It is also relevant to note that a number of English language teachers are 'evangelical Christians for whom faith and professional work are inextricably intertwined' (Varghese and Johnston 2007: 5). Therefore, this section starts with a consideration of how faith may affect the professionalism of ELT teachers and then moves to issues of the ELT curriculum in relation to faith with a focus on teachers of different religious backgrounds. These sections are followed by a discussion on faith from the perspective of the learners.

Faith and the professionalism of ELT teachers

Varghese and Johnston (2007) consider the link between religion and profession to raise moral questions, as the 'prominent view in [the teaching of English to speakers of other languages is] that the teacher should not influence students' beliefs' (p. 16). With this in mind, they interviewed ten trainee teachers at two evangelical colleges in the United States and examined (a) whether their religious beliefs were shared with their students; (b) what their attitudes were toward attempts at converting students; and (c) what they thought about using ELT as a platform for missionary work. Varghese and Johnston highlight that the working context of teachers may influence how much religion can be brought into their teaching. As the trainees were planning to work in the American public educational system, they would not be allowed to discuss religion in their lessons. In fact, the crucial point raised by the trainee teachers in this study was not talking openly about religion nor trying to convert students, but how to be exemplars of their religion. However, Varghese and Johnston interpret the underlying goal of these teachers to be one of conversion to Christianity, especially in the case of ELT programmes run by evangelical groups. Nevertheless, these researchers acknowledge that both evangelical and non-evangelical Christian teachers of English as a foreign language have implicit and explicit agenda, and call upon both to undertake a self-critical, reflective and open dialogue about the effect a teacher's religious identity has on their professionalism.

In contrast, Wong (2013) examines the impact of faith on the professional identity formation of three Christian American English teachers in China and argues that religious identities guarantee the teachers' professional high standards. Five in-depth interviews with each of the teachers were conducted in two studies a decade apart. The data were analysed using the framework of communities of practice (Lave and Wenger 1991). In this way, Wong (2013) looked into the process through which the teachers went from a peripheral to a more engaged participation in three different communities of practice, namely local academic colleagues, church communities and Christian expatriate teachers. One of Wong's participants, Suzanne, who engaged most with her local academic colleagues, chose not to participate in the practice of manipulating students' exam results, claiming that it went against her faith values. Wong found that Jacque, who engaged most with the local academic and church communities, overcame his prejudices against Muslims as he befriended a Muslim colleague. He shifted from 'we Christians vs. those Muslims' to 'we fellow believers of God' (Wong 2013: 24). Another of Wong's participants, Cynthia, who interacted most with the group of Christian expatriate teachers, resisted pressure by this group to cover religious topics in her teaching. In spite of identifying as a missionary, Cynthia felt that religious topics should only be incorporated into her lessons if relevant to the students' learning needs – a faith-informed belief of what teaching with integrity entails.

The relevance of considering whether to incorporate religion as a topic into the teaching of English is not restricted to Christianity. Therefore, the following section further discusses faith in the ELT curriculum from the perspective of Christianity and other religions.

Faith and the ELT curriculum

Lessard-Clouston (2013) examines the integration of faith and learning in an English as a Second Language programme in the United States and in EFL courses at a university in Indonesia, both connected to the American Council for Christian Colleges and Universities. A total of eight teachers, four from each institution, answered a questionnaire on the implementation of the integration of faith into the English language curriculum, the resources used for the integration, the teaching benefits/challenges for the integration and the instructors' previous/desired training in integration. The teachers reported that faith and language learning integration was taking place in their classes, albeit in different ways. Some of the teachers had incorporated prayers as part of the lessons; others had used readings on Christian themes, related textbooks to their faith, developed critical thinking skills about their faith, behaved in favour of their faith and shared life experiences and/or successful stories. Variety was also reported in relation to the materials used: writings and discussions, textbooks, exercise books, readings, lectures, presentations, vocabulary and pronunciation materials, and websites – the same variety of resources used in a regular ELT classroom. The only difference between the two sets of materials (i.e. the one used in regular ELT classrooms and the one used in Christian ELT classrooms) was the content, with the latter explicitly including religious issues while the former did not. The integration of faith topics into language learning was perceived as positive by the teachers for promoting learners' engagement with language learning, stronger teacher–student relationships, faith strengthening and improved classroom dynamics. The teachers however mentioned a number of barriers that they faced in implementing this integration, such as the lack of the necessary background knowledge, time, guidance, training and the neglect of ESL/EFL syllabi in relation to faith and learning integration. As a result, even in the context of Christian universities, the ELT curriculum is dependent on the action of individual teachers.

Considering the topic of religion in language learning more generally, Foye (2014) conducted a survey with 277 teachers, teacher-trainers and materials developers of different religions in 44 countries. The respondents were asked three multiple-choice questions and were invited to comment on them. In response to the first question, whether religion should be totally avoided in English lessons, 60 per cent of the respondents disagreed. Interestingly, 'teachers based in the Middle East were nearly 50 per cent more likely than respondents in general to feel … that religion should be avoided in class' (ibid.: 6–7). The positioning of these teachers may be related to issues of conflict and war, as raised by academics such as Karmani (2005). Nevertheless, the sensitivity of religion as a topic in ELT is highlighted by some of the teachers in Foye's study. In reply to the second question, 85 per cent of respondents agreed that it is acceptable to discuss religion in lessons as long as culture is respected and neutrality is adopted. In relation to the third question, whether it is appropriate to include religious references when focusing on linguistic features, 70 per cent of respondents provided a positive reply. Nevertheless, their written comments pointed to some restrictions in their views: the inclusion of religious references should serve the learning needs of the students and should relate to the teachers' or the learners' daily lives. Overall, religion was acknowledged as having an important role in people's lives and, as such, was deemed to be a legitimate subject for the ELT classroom, as long as it was handled with care.

Faith and the language learner

I start this section by focusing on faith from the perspective of language learners in a study in Sri Lanka. In this study, Liyanage et al. (2010) highlight the importance of understanding the learning strategies linked to specific ethno-religious affiliations in lesson planning and emphasise that language learner strategy should be accommodated in ELT. This observation resulted from the exploration of the learning strategies of almost 1,000 ESL students from three religious groups, Buddhist, Hindu and Muslim, in government schools. It was found that the participants had a strong preference for advance organisation (i.e. skimming the text for its organising principle) as a metacognitive strategy. They liked to learn text-based content sequentially and systematically in the same way they had learned to read religious texts. The three groups also had a preference for note-taking when doing listening activities in class. According to Liyanage et al., the selection of this strategy suggests the importance of memory-building, which is promoted in the learning of the three religions. In reading activities, repetition was a strategy most preferred by Muslims. Nevertheless, both Buddhist and Hindu learners also showed a strong preference for repetition as a reading strategy, which was constantly encouraged in their traditional educational practices too. Although the learners from the three different ethno-religious groups did not strikingly differ in relation to their learning preferences, Liyanage *et al.* make a valid point that pedagogical approaches should reflect the sociocultural contexts of learners.

Religious faith has been taken into consideration in SLA as a possible motivation for language learning. Lepp-Kaethler and Dörnyei (2013), for instance, investigated how the use of a sacred text can motivate learners to learn a language. They selected seven Christian adult participants from different nationalities who demonstrated unusually high motivation to learn languages to access the Bible. Motivation, in Lepp-Kaethler and Dörnyei's (2013: 171) words, is:

> responsible for *why* people decide to do something, *how hard* they work to pursue the activity, and *how long* they are willing to sustain it. Accordingly, investigations into L2 motivation are important because they allow us to tap into the reasons for language-learning success or failure, and a greater understanding of the various sources of motivation may help both students and teachers to reenergize the often dreary and arid terrain of mastering a new language.

While motivation can also be regarded as a social concept (i.e. learners' levels of motivation depend on the social context in which they experience learning and on the opportunities the context offers for access to the target language community) (Norton 2013), learners' self-identity and motivation need to be addressed in relation to decisions made about the topics and the materials used in the L2 curriculum, as highlighted by Lepp-Kaethler and Dörnyei (2013). Their results show that learners welcomed discussions that allowed for their religious identities to be brought to light with the use of texts that had special significance to their religious affiliations. However, Lepp-Kaethler and Dörnyei (2013: 186) acknowledge that 'sacred texts by no means tap into all language learners' motivations'. They also remind us that this is true of any content in ESP courses. In fact, no type of text or topic are considered interesting by all learners in any learning situation. Therefore, there is a need to address the appropriateness of topics and materials with the different groups of learners a teacher may have.

In conclusion, the studies discussed in this chapter highlight the relevance of religion, particularly Christianity and Islam, as a dimension of identity and the relationship of language and religion in identity studies. Countries that are culturally and linguistically diverse would benefit from a better understanding of religion as an identity marker and its role in language maintenance to support the learning of indigenous and migrant children in and out of mainstream schooling. Religious identities are also significant for adults learning foreign or second languages, although the extent to which religion can be or should be integrated into language learning curricula remains a contentious issue. Teachers with strong religious identities also face challenges in relating their faith to pedagogical practices. There is certainly scope for applied linguists to investigate these matters further in future language and identity studies.

Summary

This chapter highlights the literature on language and religion in relation to language and identity studies in applied linguistics and sociolinguistics. With this purpose, the multidisciplinarity (engagement with different disciplines) and the interdisciplinarity (application of the methods and approaches of different disciplines) involved in researching religion as a dimension of identity and the link between language and religion in language and identity studies are covered. These issues are introduced with a discussion of the development of the sociology of language and religion (SLR) as a subfield of sociolinguistics in the twenty-first century. One fundamental issue in the studies of language and religion is that both aspects play an important role as identity markers. An overview of identity and its relationship to language, to religion and to language and religion is presented in the following section. Issues of language and religious identities are then revisited with an examination of ongoing debates in applied linguistics in relation to faith literacies, language planning and policy, and faith and English language teaching. A number of denominations, a variety of contexts and a diversity of ethnic groups were used to illustrate the relevance of language, religion and identity in different parts of the world, although the chapter has in the main focused on studies involving Christian and Muslim participants and/or contexts.

Related topics

Historical perspectives on language and identity; Positioning language and identity: poststructuralist perspectives; Language and ethnic identity; Linguistic practices and transnational identities; The politics of researcher identities: opportunities and challenges in identities research; Being a language teacher in the content classroom: teacher identity and content and language integrated learning (CLIL); Language, gender and identities in political life: a case study from Malaysia; Identity in language learning and teaching: research agendas for the future.

Further reading

Joseph, J. (2004). *Language and identity: national, ethnic, religious.* Basingstoke: Palgrave Macmillan. (This book is an excellent introduction to the study of language and identity with discussions from a wide range of academic fields, including structural linguistics, sociology, social psychology and sociolinguistics.)

Jule, A. (ed.) (2005). *Gender and the language of religion.* Basingstoke: Palgrave Macmillan. (This timely edited collection adds religion to the discussions of language and gender with articles that apply a variety of methods and theoretical frameworks.)

Omoniyi, T. and Fishman, J. (eds) (2006). *Explorations in the sociology of language and religion.* Amsterdam and Philadelphia: John Benjamins. (This is a seminal publication of studies within the sociology of language and religion that covers a variety of religions and countries.)

Wong, M., Kristjánsson, C. and Dörnyei, Z. (eds) (2013). *Christian faith and English language teaching and learning research on the interrelationship of religion and ELT.* Abingdon: Routledge. (This collection is a rich contribution to the exploration of the relationships between faith, pedagogical practices and motivation.)

References

Baquedano-López, P. (2008). 'The pragmatics of reading prayers: learning the act of contrition in Spanish-based religious education classes (doctrina)', *Text and Talk*, 28(5): 581–602.

Blommaert, J. (2006). Language policy and national identity, in T. Ricento (ed.) *Language policy: theory and method.* Oxford: Blackwell, pp. 238–254.

Chew, P. (2014). 'Language choice and religious identities in three Singaporean madrasahs', *International Journal of the Sociology of Language*, 229: 49–65.

Chruszczewski, P. (2006). Prayers as an integrative factor in Jewish religious discourse communities, in T. Omoniyi and J. Fishman (eds) *Explorations in the sociology of language and religion*. Amsterdam and Philadelphia: John Benjamins, pp. 278–290.

Darquennes, J. and Vandenbussche, W. (2011). 'Language and religion as a sociolinguistic field of study: some introductory notes', *Sociolinguistica*, 25: 1–11.

Dzialtuvaite, J. (2006). The role of religion in language choice and identity among Lithuanian immigrants in Scotland, in T. Omoniyi and J. Fishman (eds) *Explorations in the sociology of language and religion*. Amsterdam and Philadelphia: John Benjamins, pp. 79–85.

Fishman, J. (1989). *Language and ethnicity in minority sociolinguistic perspective*. Clevedon: Multilingual Matters.

Foye, K. (2014). 'Religion in the ELT classroom: teachers' perspectives', *Language Teacher*, 38(2): 5–12.

Garrett, P. and Baquedano-López, P. (2002). 'Language socialization: reproduction and continuity, transformation and change', *Annual Review of Anthropology*, 31: 339–361.

Gregory, E., Choudhury, H., Ilankuberan, A., Kwapong, A. and Woodham, M. (2013a). 'Practice, performance and perfection: learning sacred texts in four faith communities in London', *International Journal of the Sociology of Language*, 220: 27–48.

Gregory, E., Lytra, V., Choudhury, H., Ilankuberan, A. and Woodham, M. (2013b). 'Syncretism as a creative act of mind: the narratives of children from four faith communities in London', *Journal of Early Childhood Literacy*, 13(3): 322–347.

Han, H. (2011). 'Social inclusion through multilingual ideologies, policies and practices: a case study of a minority church', *International Journal of Bilingual Education and Bilingualism*, 14(4): 383–398.

Hemming, P. and Madge, N. (2011). 'Researching children, youth and religion: identity, complexity and agency', *Childhood*, 19(1): 38–51.

Hirschman, C. (2004). 'The role of religion in the origins and adaptation of immigrant groups in the United States', *International Migration Review*, 38(3): 1206–1233.

Joseph, J. (2006). The shifting role of languages in Lebanese Christian and Muslim identities, in T. Omoniyi and J. Fishman (eds) *Explorations in the sociology of language and religion*. Amsterdam and Philadelphia: John Benjamins, pp. 165–179.

Jule, A. (2005). Language use and silence as morality: teaching and lecturing at an evangelical theology college, in A. Jule (ed.) *Gender and the language of religion*. Basingstoke: Palgrave Macmillan, pp. 151–166.

Karmani, S. (2005). 'TESOL in a time of terror: toward an Islamic perspective on applied linguistics', *TESOL Quarterly*, 39(4): 738–744.

Koechert, A. and Pfeiler, B. (2013). 'Maintenance of Kaqchikel ritual speech in the confraternities of San Juan Sacatepéquez, Guatemala', *International Journal of the Sociology of Language*, 220: 127–149.

Kouega, J.P. (2008). 'Language, religion and cosmopolitanism: language use in the Catholic Church in Yaoundé, Cameroon', *International Journal of Multilingualism*, 5(2): 140–153.

Lave, J. and Wenger, E. (1991). *Situated learning: legitimate peripheral participation*. Cambridge: Cambridge University Press.

Lepp-Kaethler, E. and Dörnyei, Z. (2013). The role of sacred texts in enhancing motivation and living the vision in second language acquisition, in M. Wong, C. Kristjánsson and Z. Dörnyei (eds) *Christian faith and English language teaching and learning research on the interrelationship of religion and ELT*. Abingdon: Routledge, pp. 171–188.

Lessard-Clouston, M. (2013). Faith and learning integration in ESL/EFL instruction: a preliminary study in America and Indonesia, in M. Wong, C. Kristjánsson and Z. Dörnyei (eds) *Christian faith and English language teaching and learning research on the interrelationship of religion and ELT*. Abingdon: Routledge, pp. 115–135.

Liyanage, I., Bartlett, B. and Grimbeek, P. (2010). 'Religious background and language learning: practical suggestions for deriving best practice in ELT', *Asian EFL Journal*, 46: 1–20.

Mukherjee, S. (2013). 'Reading language and religion together', *International Journal of the Sociology of Language*, 220: 1–6.

Norton, B. (2013 [2000]). *Identity and language learning: extending the conversation.* 2nd edn. London: Longman.

Ochs, E. and Schieffelin, B. (2008). Language socialization: an historical overview, in P. Duff and N. Hornberger (eds) *Encyclopedia of language education,* vol. 8. New York: Springer, pp. 3–15.

Omoniyi, T. and Fishman, J. (eds) (2006). *Explorations in the sociology of language and religion.* Amsterdam and Philadelphia: John Benjamins.

Oosterbaan, M. (2010). Virtual re-evangelization: Brazilian churches, media and the postsecular city, in J. Beaumont, A. Molendijk and C. Jedan (eds) *Exploring the postsecular: the religious, the political, the urban.* Leiden: Brill, pp. 281–308.

Peek, L. (2005). 'Becoming Muslim: the development of a religious identity', *Sociology of Religion,* 66(3): 215–242.

Ricento, T. and Hornberger, N. (1996). 'Unpeeling the onion: language planning and policy and the ELT professional', *TESOL Quarterly,* 30: 401–427.

Rosowsky, A. (2006). The role of liturgical literacy in UK Muslim communities, in T. Omoniyi and J. Fishman (eds) *Explorations in the sociology of language and religion.* Amsterdam and Philadelphia: John Benjamins, pp. 309–324.

Rosowsky, A. (2013). 'Faith, phonics and identity: reading in faith complementary schools', *Literacy,* 47(2): 67–78.

Schieffelin, B. and Ochs, E. (1986). 'Language socialization', *Annual Review of Anthropology,* 15: 163–191.

Skerrett, A. (2014). 'Religious literacies in a secular literacy classroom', *Reading Research Quarterly,* 49(2): 233–250.

Souza, A. (2015). 'Language and faith encounters: bridging language–ethnicity and language–religion studies', *International Journal of Multilingualism* [Online]. DOI: 10.1080/14790718.2015.1040023

Souza, A. (forthcoming). Faith and language maintenance in transnational places of worship: Brazilian Christian settings in London, in T. Omoniyi, R. Pandharipande and M. Ebsworth (eds) *Maintenance and revival in the sociology of language and religion.* Bristol: Multilingual Matters.

Souza, A., Kwapong, A. and Woodham, M. (2012). 'Pentecostal and Catholic migrant churches in London – the role of ideologies in the language planning of faith lessons', *Current Issues in Language Planning,* 13(2): 105–120.

Vajta, K. (2013). 'Linguistic, religious and national loyalties in Alsace', *International Journal of the Sociology of Language,* 220: 109–125.

Varghese, M. and Johnston, B. (2007). 'Evangelical Christians and English language teaching', *TESOL Quarterly,* 41(1): 5–31.

Watt, J. and Fairfield, S. (2010). Religious and sacred literacies, in B. Spolsky and F. Hult (eds) *The handbook of educational linguistics.* Oxford: Wiley-Blackwell, pp. 355–366.

Wong, M. (2013). Called to teach: the impact of faith on professional identity formation of three Western English teachers in China, in M. Wong, C. Kristjánsson and Z. Dörnyei (eds) *Christian faith and English language teaching and learning research on the interrelationship of religion and ELT.* Abingdon: Routledge, pp. 11–30.

Wong, M., Kristjánsson, C. and Dörnyei, Z. (eds) (2013). *Christian faith and English language teaching and learning research on the interrelationship of religion and ELT.* Abingdon: Routledge.

Woods, A. (2004). *Medium or message? Language and faith in ethnic churches.* Clevedon: Multilingual Matters.

Woods, A. (2006). The role of language in some ethnic churches in Melbourne, in T. Omoniyi and J. Fishman (eds) *Explorations in the sociology of language and religion.* Amsterdam and Philadelphia: John Benjamins, pp. 197–212.

13

Language and gender identities

Lucy Jones

Introduction

Research into the relationship between language and gender identity in applied linguistics and sociolinguistics has evolved considerably since its emergence in the 1970s, when it was primarily concerned with two things: demonstrating that power inequalities between the sexes were reflected in the language women were socialised into using, and finding evidence for – and explaining – linguistic differences between the sexes. As will be shown below, a key development in the field – largely since the 1990s – has been a greater emphasis on constructionist approaches to gender. In this chapter, gender is considered as a dimension of identity, both in terms of how gender identities are performed by speakers themselves and in terms of how gender is represented in texts. Before introducing research in this area, however, it is important to define what we mean by the term gender.

Gender concerns cultural norms about what roles and identities are considered to be appropriate for women or men, such as whether something is feminine or masculine. It is important to note that gender in this sense is not a synonym for sex difference. Gender may include the concept of femininity, for example, which may refer to a person's appearance or their personality; they may wear soft, pastel colours in their clothing or makeup and they may be caring, polite or nurturing in their behaviour. At least some of these features are learnt as a result of a person's socialisation as a female, yet they are often taken to be inherent or essential qualities. This essentialist view is popular and pervasive and is used to explain another cultural assumption: that there are two genders naturally attached to two sexes. Labelled by Connell (1987) as 'the gender order', this refers to the dominant idea that men and women are binary opposites; they are fundamentally different from one another (dichotomous) and hold certain characteristics, such as men being strong and women being emotional. Within Western societies, there has historically been no cultural recognition of people who fall outside of this binary system of gender, meaning that a person who identifies differently – the 'effeminate' gay man, 'mannish' lesbian or transsexual person, for instance – has typically been classed as deviant or 'other' (Foucault 1978).

The perceived existence of two clear, fixed and opposing genders is part of an ideological system. Ideologies are prevalent ideas of what is normal or natural and they vary from culture to culture. Our experiences in a given society provide us with particular beliefs, and our position in that society (in terms of our class, gender, ethnicity and so on) informs the ways in which we relate to those beliefs; Bourdieu (1977) terms this 'habitus'. By recognising that what is normal is defined by our habitus and the prevailing ideologies in our society, we may view concepts related to gender, such as the gender order, as socially constructed. In other words, these concepts are created via ideological norms that shape our expectations, such as those relating to the roles and behaviours of women and men. In turn, we may say that these ideologies are produced via salient discourses, or particular 'sets of ideas' which carry weight in society (Eckert and McConnell-Ginet 2013: 28). Language and gender scholars work to uncover these discourses, both in terms of how they are produced by people through the language that they use, but also in terms of how they are invoked and reinforced through the language that is used to talk about women and men. An important aspect of this, discussed below, is the way that particular gender identities are privileged in Western culture as being more (or less) normal than others.

This chapter will begin by exploring this notion of normality by outlining key concepts in relation to gender and identity. It will then provide a discussion of constructionist approaches to language and gender, including both modern and postmodern perspectives, before considering ongoing issues relevant to gender identity for applied linguistics. In particular, this discussion will consider: how gender identities are performed; issues of masculinity, femininity and transgender identities; communities of practice; and representations of gender in written texts. The chapter will conclude with a summary and some observations about key issues in the field to be addressed.

Overview

Gender as a normative system

By viewing gender as a set of ideas or ideologies about what is normal, attention is drawn to the fact that many of the beliefs we have about women and men – such as that women are naturally caring and men are naturally competitive – suit the interests of the most powerful members of society. This draws on the Gramscian (1971) notion of 'cultural hegemony', the theory that most people in society live by certain ideological norms because they seem natural and broadly in the interests of society as a whole, yet may in fact primarily benefit those with cultural, political or economic power. The concept of patriarchy, for instance, whereby men have historically had authority, can be seen to be reflected in many of the everyday norms that are often taken for granted; men are less likely than women to give up their jobs in order to be the primary caretaker to their children (because women are seen to be inherently more caring), and women are less likely than men to hold leadership positions (because they are seen to be less psychologically suited to such a role).

Tied into this is the notion of heteronormativity: the cultural expectation that people not only adhere to the gender order, but that they also naturally desire the 'opposite' sex (see Gray, this volume). Heteronormative ideologies include beliefs about the gendered roles that individuals take up within a (heterosexual) relationship, such as those regarding the family, as well as those regarding dating and sex itself. For example, Eckert and McConnell-Ginet (2013) refer to what they call 'the heterosexual market', a point in a child's life when their social lives begin to be split according to the gender order. Important ideologies that children learn at an early stage include the idea that boys and girls are complementary and that they should eventually be paired up together; children often play out dating games, where 'relationships' will last anything from a few hours to a few days, long before any sort of sexual desire has emerged (ibid.). By engaging in these activities, children are repeating what they see in broader society, and are reproducing and reinforcing fundamentally heteronormative discourses. They are also performing a gender identity.

When thinking about the notion of gender as a performance, language and gender scholars tend to draw on the important work of Butler (1990), who frames femininity and masculinity as identities that are achieved, rather than as aspects of the self which are essential. Butler's concept of 'performativity' demonstrates that gender is produced via cultural acts, including language, dress and other forms of self-presentation. Butler argues that we perform our gender, albeit often unconsciously, through mundane and everyday acts. We engage in these acts – such as putting on makeup or a dress – again and again, until we no longer view them as a performance; they seem to be natural. Scholars of language and gender have made much use of the concept of performativity, as will be discussed later, as it helps to explain the importance of language for reinforcing and projecting gendered identities.

Approaches to studying language and gender identities

Although the prevalent position of sociolinguists and applied linguists who currently study language and gender is to take a constructionist approach, early research in the field was focused less on deconstructing and challenging heteronormative ideologies associated with the gender order and more with the feminist activist concern of highlighting social differences between the language used by women and men. Three main approaches to understanding the relationship between language and gender emerged from the 1970s onwards, now recognised as the 'deficit', 'difference' and 'dominance' approaches. Cameron (2005) refers to research taking these approaches as modern, as opposed to postmodern, the latter term indicating the emphasis on deconstructing binary gender that developed largely from the 1990s, and the former reflecting the research that laid the foundations for this. These approaches to language and gender are outlined in more detail below.

Modern approaches to language and gender

Lakoff's (1975) account of women's and men's language is typically heralded as the beginning of scholarly work into differentiating linguistic styles on the basis of gender, and is widely referred to as the deficit approach. Her work had the explicitly feminist aim of drawing attention to the ways that women were expected to use language. Lakoff argued that women had a subordinate position in a patriarchal society and that one way in which this was perpetuated was by socialising girls into language considered to be 'ladylike'. The features Lakoff identified as part of what she called 'Women's Language', which included the use of tag questions and intensifiers, were thought to be culturally deficient because they indicated, among other qualities, hesitancy and uncertainty; Lakoff argued that this put women at a cultural and social disadvantage to men.

Lakoff's claims led to two alternative approaches to language and gender: difference and dominance. Approaches based on difference argued that women's style of communication was not deficient, but simply different. Women's speech styles were claimed to be valuable and effective for conversation in ways that 'men's language' was not (Bergvall 1999: 277). For example, Tannen (1990) argued that the language women were taught to use was effective in developing relationships and rapport, while men were socialised into using more competitive or technical, 'report-oriented' communicative styles. In order to make such claims, scholars taking a difference approach, such as Maltz and Borker (1982), drew on Gumperz's (1982) work on miscommunication in ethnically diverse cultures by arguing that men and women interact differently due to their socialisation into distinct gender subcultures. Approaches based on dominance, on the other hand, continued to argue that language perpetuated asymmetrical gender relations. Instead of seeing women's language as lacking, however, men's speech styles were seen to be problematic. For example, through an analysis of interruptions and overlaps in spoken interaction in mixed-sex talk, West and Zimmerman (1977) concluded that women's speaking rights were on a par with children. Fishman's (1980) study of spoken interaction among heterosexual couples reached similar conclusions, with Fishman famously coining the phrase 'interactional shitwork' to describe the conversational strategies that women employed to keep the conversation going with their male partners.

In order to make generalisable claims, research taking these approaches relied on certain assumptions of homogeneity. Cameron (2005) argues that much of the work from this time concerned itself with white, straight, middle-class, monolingual speakers, yet it was often taken as being representative of all women or all men. However, even at that time, work that suggested that not all women and men used language in such clear-cut, delineated ways was emerging. In a famous study of courtroom talk, for example, O'Barr and Atkins (1980) found that the features associated with the stereotypical 'Women's Language' identified by Lakoff could reflect a powerless and inferior social position in society. This was based on the finding that men in subordinate occupational roles would also use the features that had been previously identified as feminine when in institutional settings (and vice versa). This demonstrated that language was not exclusively female or male, and was instead suggestive of how gender intersected with other identity inscriptions, such as social class and professional status, in spoken interaction.

While work taking these approaches emphasised the fact that gender was not an inherent quality and was, instead, a consequence of women's (and men's) gendered socialisation, it did continue to rely on the notion of men and women as homogeneous (presumably white, heterosexual) entities. In this sense, such work ran the risk of reproducing essentialist ideologies of gender. By contrast, work taking a more explicitly constructionist focus – that termed postmodern by Cameron (2005) – aimed to deconstruct the binary gender categories of 'woman' and 'man' and sought out the ways in which multiple masculinities or femininities might be constructed among a diverse range of speakers. Such approaches are outlined below.

Postmodern approaches to language and gender

Many studies since the 1990s have aimed to challenge the concept of binary gender and view gender identity as performed. In doing so, they often draw on postmodern critiques of gender and of heteronormativity, which aim to deconstruct seemingly fixed ideological categories. From this perspective, gender is not only learnt according to the sex category a person falls into, but is also brought into being through being performed; gender may, therefore, not always be attached in a normative or expected way to a person based on their sex. In this sense, postmodern approaches to language and gender consider the interaction between gender and sexuality more fully, and are more concerned with liminal gender identities, particularly queer identities (those that are non-normative or non-mainstream [see Gray, this volume]).

A seminal development of postmodern approaches to the study of language and gender identity has been the notion of 'indexicality'. Indexicality concerns the semiotic process that exists within interaction, whereby speakers connect particular linguistic features with representations of the social groups that are stereotyped as using them (Irvine and Gal 2000). The term comes from the word index, meaning 'to point to'; indexicality, then, is the process by which particular ways of using language point towards, or indicate, culturally recognisable identities. This means that a speaker may use language that carries a particular ideological meaning associated with their gender, in turn gendering their identity performance. Ochs's (1990) research with mothers in Samoa, who had a very specific cultural role of caregiving, illustrates this. She found that language seen to have a facilitative or caring function in Samoa was indexical of femaleness; this was because women in that community were associated primarily with nurturing roles and motherhood. Ochs classifies the indexical relationship between the language that the women in her study used and its cultural meaning (of being caring) as 'direct', but the relationship between a given linguistic feature and the category of woman as 'indirect'. This is because the language itself did not directly index womanhood; rather, the language indexed caring, which in turn was something associated with women in this community. The importance of the sociocultural context in which language is being interpreted is therefore emphasised by Ochs and is strengthened by her finding that the same language features do not necessarily index femaleness in cultures where women have less of a primary caregiver role.

Indexicality has an important role to play in bridging modern and postmodern studies of language and gender. Whereas early research highlighted the linguistic features that were stereotypically associated with women or men, including those that carried functions associated with dominance or powerlessness, a postmodern focus allows us to reinterpret those associations in terms of how speakers use language to index a wider range of cultural identities. Importantly, these identities need not be restricted to the generic categories of male and female that were studied in the past; it is possible instead to consider particular kinds of gendered self, which may exist in specific settings, or be realised in unique ways. This is considered below.

Issues and ongoing debates

In the preceding section, we saw how postmodern approaches to language and gender identity take a constructionist approach. This means that gender identity is understood to be formed of cultural ideologies and performed by individuals through their everyday acts, rather than something innately connected to a person's biological sex. In this section, I outline three main issues that have emerged for the study of language and identity with regard to gender as a result of this understanding: first, ways in which speakers have been found to perform gender identities through interaction; second, the construction of community-specific gender identities; third, how gender identities are represented.

Performances of gender identities

'Masculine' identities

Contemporary research into language and gender identity often concerns speakers' use of indexical relationships between linguistic features and cultural ideas about gender in order to perform their identity as a woman or a man. A range of gender identities is now considered but, partly as a result of the fact that women's issues were at the forefront of feminist linguistics from the 1970s onwards, research was largely focused on women's identities until Johnson's (1997) edited collection on language and masculinity brought men's identities firmly into focus.

Typically, studies of language and masculinity have shown that men's identities are constructed via the reproduction of stereotypes and ideologies that are specific to men rather than women, and that index hegemonic, heteronormative masculinity. Coates (2003), for example, found that the white British men in her study indexed their masculinity through talk about topics that are stereotypically male, such as sports, women or technology. Similarly, Kiesling (1997) considered the hierarchical way in which a group of fraternity men organised themselves, analysing their language styles as competitive and arguing that men were likely to draw on discourses of power in order to construct their masculinity. Kiesling's (2002) work with the same group also shows that masculinity can be performed and displayed through claims by the young men to have 'conquered' many women and to be both non-committal and sexually obtainable (even if they are in a long-term relationship). Through telling 'fuck stories', Kiesling argues, these young men were able to index their masculinity; in this way, it is clear that heterosexuality and hegemonic masculinity are culturally intertwined. This is also evident from Cameron's (2001) analysis of conversations between male undergraduate university students in America, whereby a male student was accused of being 'the antithesis of man' (ibid.: 173) due to his poor taste in clothes and women, and was ultimately branded as being gay. Hegemonic masculinity, it is shown, is at least partly based on heterosexuality.

Masculinity does not always manifest itself in this hegemonic, heteronormative way, however. Research into gay men's speech styles, for example, has shown that culturally specific forms of language can enable speakers to index their sexual identity, including coded, metaphorical forms (Leap 1996), a falsetto voice quality to index flamboyance and campness (Podesva 2007), and the use of language ideologically associated with femininity (Graf and Lippa 1995). As outlined earlier, however, an important aspect of postmodern approaches to language and gender includes challenging and deconstructing binary gender. Barrett's (1995) work is an important example of this; he focused on African-American drag queens in order to pick apart essentialist assumptions about sex and gender. The men in his study used language that was indexical of stereotypical white femininity, black masculinity and homosexuality, a combination of which was used to perform an entirely new drag persona. Gender identity can thus be multifaceted and achieved in myriad ways, with indexical meaning shifting and changing according to the sociocultural context.

Similarly, Hall's (1995) research with the operators of a telephone sex line shows how speakers can index 'fantasy' identities that do not necessarily reflect their own sense of self, often through the use of linguistic features ideologically associated with 'bimbos', virgins or nymphomaniacs, depending on what the client desires. An important part of Hall's analysis is that not all those performing these various female roles were women; one was a gay man who could pass as female through his performative language use. This shows how we cannot assume that 'the language of men' necessarily involves the indexing of hegemonic masculinity.

Nonetheless, the understanding of norms of gender afforded to us by this research is extremely useful when applying linguistics to real-life contexts such as the classroom. Preece (2009), for example, identifies discursive strategies used by undergraduate students in a British university, showing that one way that young men from non-traditional backgrounds in higher education (particularly ethnic minorities and those who are working class) save face in an environment in which they feel marginalised is to adopt a laddish persona that indexes an indifference to academic success. In turn, this allows them to draw on ideologies associated with working-class masculinity, such as independence and toughness. By exploring the construction of gender in such contexts, work such as Preece's may help to explain why gendered groups of university students may appear to be less engaged, and may therefore assist practitioners in providing more targeted support.

'Feminine' identities

As with masculinities, there continues to be a rich discussion of language and femininities, though many of the studies taking place in the postmodern period investigate identities outside of the heteronormative gender order. For example, Bucholtz's (1999) important study of self-identified 'nerds' in a US high school showed that not all white, middle-class girls identify with mainstream, heteronormative ideals of femininity. Indeed, rather than reproduce what is typically perceived as 'cool' for high school girls (being pretty and fashionable), the 'nerds' consciously performed an oppositional identity that was focused on academic success. For example, they deliberately wore unfashionable clothing, avoided slang terms and employed high-culture terminology (such as Latin) to demonstrate their intelligence. This allowed them to index a version of girlhood that was salient for them and which disrupted ideals of teenage femininity. Similarly, studies of lesbian identity construction (e.g. Queen 2005; Morrish and Sauntson 2007; Jones 2012) have typically found that gay women often actively dissociate themselves from mainstream ideas of femininity in order to perform a non-heteronormative version of woman, showing again how issues of sexuality are intrinsically tied to questions of gender.

Research into how women's identities are produced can also highlight how social inequalities are perpetuated, such as by looking at public and political contexts. Much emphasis in this area has been placed on examining the language of women in leadership or professional roles that have traditionally been seen as suited to men. Mullany (2011), for example, shows how female managers using language which indexes assertiveness or power – attributes which would classify most male managers as successful – tend to be negatively evaluated; by failing to conform to gendered norms surrounding their speech, they are often judged to be 'scary' or domineering. This harks back to Lakoff's claim that women's speech is evaluated as 'deficient' in the public domain, not only when they conform to 'ladylike' talk, but also when they do not. In this sense, research into language and gender can reveal much about the ways in which women are prevented from being successful as leaders (see also Holmes 2006; Baxter 2009). Work by McElhinny (1995), in contrast, finds that it is possible for women to gain respect and to 'break the glass ceiling', but only if they adapt their way of speaking to construct a new identity relevant to their workplace. Her study of police officers in Pittsburgh, for example, shows that female police officers who altered their voice, language and clothing to index a cool, professional identity were taken more seriously than if they conformed to overtly feminised styles. Despite demonstrating that it is possible for women to have success in what is culturally perceived to be 'men's work', studies such as these also demonstrate that traditional expectations of femininity do not match cultural ideas of success, professionalism or authority.

This work reveals broader ideologies of gender normativity and the ways in which these ideologies not only constrain but also shape the identities it is possible for women to perform. As Litosseliti and Sunderland (2002: 11) outline, assumptions about what women's (and girls') roles will be may constrain the way in which they communicate and behave in educational contexts, by being more quiet or passive than boys. Research such as Swann's (2009) has shown that gender is continually relevant in the classroom, as children engaged in activities that are not obviously gendered will still draw on their prior knowledge of gender norms when interacting in mixed-sex contexts, such as by making reference to heterosexual couplings in order to tease one another. This demonstrates the need for applied linguists doing language and identity studies to carefully consider the role that gender plays in educational, or other institutional, contexts. In classroom contexts, gender norms are likely to play a role in how different children learn or succeed in the classroom and in the identities that they inhabit or are ascribed even in contexts that do not appear to be gendered. For applied linguists, then an understanding of how gender roles are produced and drawn upon is important when trying to understand patterns of language use in real-world contexts.

Trans identities

A less explored area of language and gender research concerns trans identities. The term 'trans', an abbreviation of transgender, is commonly used 'to refer to all individuals who live outside of normative sex/gender relations' (Namaste 2000: 1). Some trans people – but by no means all – take hormones or have surgery in order that their bodies match their gender identity, and the term 'transsexual' is often used in a medical context to refer to these individuals. People whose gender identity matches the biological sex they were assigned at birth may be categorised as being 'cisgender', or simply 'cis'. Perhaps unsurprisingly, given the cultural privilege and dominance of cisgender people, the vast majority of work that has taken place so far into language and gender identity involves speakers who are cisgender, though this aspect of their identity would typically be implicitly presumed. A limited body of work has emerged to combat this, however.

One of the more established approaches to language and trans identities is the exploration of gendered grammar; Kulick (1996) considers how Brazilian transgender prostitutes use feminine gendered grammar to construct their own subjectivity as females, for instance, as does Livia (1995) in her analysis of the writings of a French trans woman. Other work aiming to explain language use outside of a binary gender system includes King's (2015) consideration of an intersex individual and Hall and O'Donovan's (1996) work with the Hijra community in India – eunuchs who are often categorised as 'the third gender'.

Recent research exploring other aspects of trans people's language use includes Zimman's (2012) important study. Using sociophonetics, he shows that trans men do not always use the entire pitch range generally associated with masculinity (though many do); this conflicts with the heteronormative expectation that a trans person would use language to allow them to pass as cisgender. He argues that, once trans men begin to be perceived as men through more outward styles and symbols, some feel less concerned about engaging fully in – and therefore indexing – heteronormative cis masculinity; some trans men may feel more comfortable including aspects of language in their speech that might be said to index femininity. This research is particularly important because it breaks free of the binary gender system; it shows that trans men do not simply 'switch' from a female-sounding to a male-sounding voice. Instead, it reveals that the experiences and identities of an individual will lead to a specific form of identity construction. Again, gender is revealed to be a complex phenomenon.

Communities of practice

What has become increasingly evident in research exploring the performance of gender identities is the fact that groups of speakers, such as 'nerd' girls (Bucholtz 1999) or fraternity men (Kiesling 2002), develop ways of doing things that – within the context of their group – allow them to index a coherent identity specific to that group. Such analyses have been enabled partly by the development of the community of practice (CoP) approach, introduced to sociolinguistics and applied linguistics by Eckert and McConnell-Ginet (1992, 1999). The CoP, first established by Lave and Wenger (1991) as a theory of learning through shared participation, focuses on speakers who interact and engage together in a mutual endeavour, leading to shared practices or 'ways of doing things' (Eckert and McConnell-Ginet 1999: 185), including ways of talking and interacting. The concept of the CoP has been extensively drawn on by Eckert. For example, in her ethnographic study of an American high school, Eckert uses the CoP to examine the practices of two recognisable groups in the school: the Jocks and the Burnouts (Eckert 2000). Eckert analysed their language use in relation to the social structures within the school, most specifically in terms of gender and class. The language practices of the Jocks were intrinsically tied to their social aspirations as middle-class kids, for example, as they used more standard forms of English to index an academically oriented persona. The Burnouts, by contrast, used non-standard forms that allowed them to index an affiliation with their local, working-class roots. Eckert found that there was a clear difference between each CoP in terms of gender; girls in the Jock group used more standard language than the boys, while Burnout girls used more non-standard language than Burnout boys. In both groups, then, the girls seemed to work harder than the boys at indexing their membership of the CoP; this reflects findings in variationist sociolinguistics that women may rely more on symbolic means of articulating their identities than men, who have historically been more able to gain power and prestige through such means as employment (see Labov 1990).

The CoP approach has been used in other studies of gender, including Mendoza-Denton's (2008) research with Chicana girl gangs in California. Through ethnographic fieldwork, Mendoza-Denton learnt that the girls valued skills associated with fighting and qualities associated with loyalty. Because she understood these values from their perspective – a fundamental aim of ethnography – Mendoza-Denton was able to explain the various linguistic and stylistic practices that the girls engaged in; they wore eyeliner in a specific way to symbolise how tough they were and tended not to wear certain items of jewellery, such as earrings, in order to show that they were always ready to fight. These girls identified with some aspects of heteronormative femininity but in specific ways; they adopted or reworked familiar practices (such as wearing makeup) depending on how they suited their needs, enabling them to index a locally salient identity as gang girls. The CoP, then, has made an important contribution to the study of gender identity in sociolinguistics and applied linguistics because it enables us to move beyond predefined structures, such as those associated with binary gender, and encourages us to consider those who do not fit squarely – or normatively – into an ideological category.

Research using the CoP also emphasises the importance of understanding the context in which an identity is produced in order to gain clear insight into the meaning of that identity; this is very important to applied linguists hoping to learn more about how and why, for example, learners of a target language are more or less successful. Norton's (2000) theory of 'investment' demonstrates this; she argues that success in acquiring a new language depends on the extent to which language learners feel invested in acquiring not only the target language but also the cultural advantages that come with it. In this sense, Norton sees language learning as not simply about learning a code, but as developing a new identity; successful learners will be able to imagine themselves benefiting from their use of a new language, such as by becoming a legitimate member of a new CoP. Norton's work with immigrant women in Canada shows the intersection of class, gender and ethnicity for second language learners, as many of the women in her study were more invested in learning English if their role as a primary caregiver meant that they needed to be proficient in the language, or if their status as a single woman meant that they needed to avoid becoming vulnerable due to language weaknesses. Through in-depth research such as this, then, applied linguists can better understand the impact that gender identity has on real-world problems such as those that impact on migrants.

Representations of gender identities

In addition to the analysis of gender identities as they are performed in everyday speech, linguists have considered how identities are represented in texts. By text, we may refer to spoken, written or multimodal forms of language. Many linguists interested in gender and sexuality use a critical discourse analysis approach (Fairclough 1989; also see Zotzmann and O'Regan, this volume) combined with feminist theory to see how texts contribute to the reproduction and maintenance, or even the resistance and transformation, of structural ideologies relating to heteronormativity and the gender order (see Lazar 2005; Benwell and Stokoe 2006). Critical discourse analysts are concerned with identifying, challenging and unpicking instantiations of discourse, with the aim of revealing how those with power and control over the production and distribution of texts push particular ideological discourses. This approach also reveals much about the identities we recognise within society, since they are legitimised through their repeated representation. In this sense, the analysis of texts in language, gender and sexuality research tends to focus on not only the text itself, but the way it has been created, why, by whom and for whom, and what consequences its creation has had (Baker 2008).

For example, by looking at media texts such as magazines, we can see how particular identity categories are represented by analysing assumptions made about a text's audience. Talbot's (1995) analysis of a teenage girls' magazine tells us much about ideological femininity and the normative expectations surrounding girlhood, for instance. Talbot shows how the magazine writers create a 'synthetic sisterhood', using inclusive language that encourages their readers to feel as though they are being directly and personally addressed by an older sister figure, one who can advise them on the things that it is assumed will matter to them (how to wear makeup, for example). Talbot reveals the patriarchal notions present in the text (such as the idea that girls must make themselves look beautiful) but also demonstrates that the media are active in reproducing gender ideologies. These ideologies may be drawn upon by girls when attempting to index a salient feminine identity, one that allows them to fit in with their peers.

Messages that spell out the norms for how women and men should behave have long been present in such media. For instance, Mills and Mullany (2011: 146) provide an example from a British women's magazine in the 1950s where women are advised on how best to prepare for their husband's daily return from work (by making sure the house is tidy, clean and quiet), thus perpetuating the ideology that women's work is domestic and principally concerned with pleasing men. Though such overtly sexist representations may now strike us as shocking, evidence exists to suggest that indirect forms of sexism prevail in media texts today, such as in the depiction of women as either nagging annoyances or sex objects in British 'lad' magazines (Benwell 2003; Mills 2008).

As well as analysing texts where women or men are represented in sexist or heteronormative ways, research in this area can also concern analyses of texts where particular groups are not well represented. Of particular relevance to applied linguists is research that analyses resources used by language teachers, as these may often reveal important stereotypes and ideologies relating to gender. Scholars such as Sunderland (2004), for example, have found that women are often underrepresented in language learning textbooks, with male discourse frequently presented as the norm, or men rather than women being the initiators of conversations. In part, this is because the resources used to teach students a language are expected to represent, in some way, the culture in which that language is spoken; the ideology of men being more dominant than women continues to be salient in many English-speaking contexts. However, stereotypes in textbooks also have the potential to alienate certain readers, potentially impacting on their motivation and investment in learning the target language, and also run the risk of reinforcing negative preconceptions that learners might have about the roles of women or men. In this sense, the study of how women and men are differently represented in such texts is an extremely important aspect of research into the representation of gender identity.

Summary

Research into gender identities is of crucial importance to applied linguistics. Language and gender work demonstrates that there are gender inequalities regarding women and men's experiences, opportunities and representations and can also show how these are perpetuated and reinforced. Whether we look at interactions occurring within institutional settings – workplaces where women are prevented from moving forward at the same pace as men, for instance, or schools where young children engage in a 'heterosexual market' – or whether we consider how ideologies of gender are reproduced in the media around us, we can both shed light on and begin to address real-world problems of structural, culturally ingrained systems of gender inequality by examining language in its context of use and noting how gender is of salience.

However, just as modern approaches to language and gender might have inadvertently reinforced binary, heteronormative notions of gender identity, through its ambition to find evidence of differences between women and men, postmodern approaches with clear feminist intentions can still run the risk of reinforcing notions of normativity by being restrictive in the identities that are researched. For example, the vast majority of studies into gender and sexual identities that have been carried out consider cisgender speakers and there has not, as yet, been a large-scale linguistic study of trans women. It is important that more research into trans identities is developed, not only to prevent a cisgender bias in the field and to further deconstruct the sex/gender binary, but also to develop a much richer and more nuanced understanding of how complex gender identities are indexed and performed in real-world contexts.

Similarly, as argued above, the speakers typically included in many of the earlier studies into language and gender were white, middle-class, heterosexual Westerners. Increasing numbers of studies are taking place in non-Western contexts, such as Milani's (2013; also see Milani, this volume) analysis of queer identity construction in South African online spaces, Ellece's (2011) research into gender identities during marriage ceremonies in Botswana, and Borba and Ostermann's (2007) work with Southern Brazilian trans communities. However, there is also a need to consider gender identity construction as it intersects with other identities beyond sexuality or nation, such as ethnicity, age or social class. As Crenshaw (1989) argues, different factors of a person's subjective experience can combine to marginalise them in a very specific way. As feminist linguists, it is therefore crucial that we explain language use not simply in terms of a speaker's identity as a woman, for example, but as a woman of a particular age, class, ethnicity, sexuality and so on. This means not only considering speakers of a variety of backgrounds and in a range of cultural contexts (though this is extremely important), but also acknowledging that many of the speakers that have been researched to date also had identities which were informed by their race or their social status; those who are white and middle class may be privileged, but their class and ethnicity are not neutral and their gender identity does not sit in isolation from these factors. Applied linguists must take all factors of speakers' sociocultural identities into account in order to more fully explain their linguistic behaviour (see Block and Corona, this volume).

In this chapter, I have provided an account of key issues and debates surrounding language and identity studies in which gender is under examination. This chapter has demonstrated that language produces, as well as reflects, ideological categories associated with heteronormativity and binary notions of gender. Research into language and gender has highlighted the myriad ways in which we index and perform gender and sexual identities in given contexts and the ways in which these identities are culturally represented. This research provides evidence of a cultural reliance on a system of binary gender that assumes speakers' heterosexuality, as well as the diversity that actually exists in terms of the gendered identities that speakers construct.

The field of language and gender has changed enormously since its foundations were laid by feminist linguists in the 1970s, with current work using increasingly varied methods and approaches to study speakers and texts in a range of contexts and communities. As the field continues to evolve, however, it is important to remember its origins: at the heart of all we do when investigating language and gender in applied contexts must be the intention to highlight inequality, raise consciousness, create change and evaluate progress. The study of language and gender identities is, after all, a fundamentally feminist endeavour.

Related topics

Positioning language and identity: poststructuralist perspectives; Identity in variationist socio-linguistics; Language and non-normative sexual identities; The significance of sexual identity to language learning and teaching; Language, gender and identities in political life: a case study from Malaysia; Straight-acting: discursive negotiations of a homomasculine identity; Intersectionality in language and identity research; The future of identity research: impact and new developments in sociolinguistics.

Further reading

Baker, P. (2008). *Sexed texts*. London: Equinox. (This book offers a very good introduction to key issues relating to language and gender, and intrinsic to this discussion is a consideration of sexual identity.)

Bucholtz, M. and Hall, K. (eds) (1995). *Gender articulated: language and the socially constructed self.* Abingdon: Routledge. (This edited volume brings together research using a wide range of methods and analytical tools, studying both gender and sexuality in a variety of cultural contexts. Despite the publication date it remains an enormously useful volume, marking a time of change in the field and reflecting the agenda of language, gender and sexuality scholars today.)

Eckert, P. and McConnell-Ginet, S. (2013). *Language and gender*. 2nd edn. Cambridge: Cambridge University Press. (This textbook provides a very thorough and detailed account of what gender is and how it is researched by linguists, as well as chapters dealing with key areas of inquiry such as politeness, style and assertiveness.)

Mills, S. and Mullany, L. (2011). *Language, gender and feminism*. London: Routledge. (In this textbook, Mills and Mullany show how feminism has been, and must continue to be, central to the methods and approaches used to analyse gendered discourse, while offering an up-to-date account of research in the field of language, gender and sexuality.)

References

Baker, P. (2008). *Sexed texts*. London: Equinox.

Barrett, R. (1995). Supermodels of the world, unite! Political economy and the language of performance among African American drag queens, in W. Leap (ed.) *Beyond the lavender lexicon: authenticity, imagination and appropriation in lesbian and gay languages*. New York: Gordon and Breach Press, pp. 207–226.

Baxter, J. (2009). *The language of female leadership*. Basingstoke: Palgrave Macmillan.

Benwell, B. (2003). *Masculinity and men's lifestyle magazines*. Oxford: Blackwell.

Benwell, B. and Stokoe, E. (2006). *Discourse and identity*. Edinburgh: Edinburgh University Press.

Bergvall, V.L. (1999). 'Toward a comprehensive theory of language and gender', *Language in Society*, 28: 273–293.

Block, D. and Corona, V. (this volume). Intersectionality in language and identity research, in S. Preece (ed.) *The Routledge handbook of language and identity*. Abingdon: Routledge, pp. 507–522.

Borba, R. and Ostermann, A.C. (2007). '"Do bodies matter?" Travestis' embodiment of (trans)gender identity through the manipulation of the Brazilian Portuguese grammatical gender system', *Gender and Language*, 1(1): 131–148.

Bourdieu, P. (1977). *Outline of a theory of practice*. Cambridge: Cambridge University Press.

Bucholtz, M. (1999). '"Why be normal?" Language and identity practices in a community of nerd girls', *Language in Society*, 28(2): 203–223.

Butler, J. (1990). *Gender trouble: feminism and the subversion of identity*. London: Routledge.

Cameron, D. (2001). *Working with spoken discourse*. London: SAGE.

Cameron, D. (2005). 'Language, gender and sexuality: current issues and new directions', *Applied Linguistics*, 26(4): 482–502.

Coates, J. (2003). *Men talk: stories in the making of masculinities*. Oxford: Blackwell.

Connell, R.W. (1987). *Gender and power: sexuality, the person and sexual politics*. Cambridge: Polity Press.

Crenshaw, K. (1989). 'Mapping the margins: intersectionality, identity politics, and violence against women of color', *Stanford Law Review*, 43(6): 1241–1299.

Eckert, P. (2000). *Linguistic variation as social practice: the linguistic construction of identity in Belten High*. Massachusetts: Wiley-Blackwell.

Eckert, P. and McConnell-Ginet, S. (1992). 'Think practically and look locally: language and gender as community-based practice', *Annual Review of Anthropology*, 21(1): 461–488.

Eckert, P. and McConnell-Ginet, S. (1999). 'New generalizations and explanations in language and gender research', *Language in Society*, 28(2): 185–201.

Eckert, P. and McConnell-Ginet, S. (2013). *Language and gender*. 2nd edn. Cambridge: Cambridge University Press.

Ellece, S.E. (2011). '"Be a fool like me": gender construction in the marriage ceremonies in Botswana – a critical discourse analysis', *Agenda*, 25(1): 43–52.

Fairclough, N. (1989). *Language and power*. London: Longman.

Fishman, P.M. (1980). 'Interactional shitwork', *Heresies*, 2: 99–101.

Foucault, M. (1978). *The history of sexuality. Vol. 1, An introduction*. New York: Pantheon.

Graf, R. and Lippa, B. (1995). The Queen's English, in W. Leap (ed.) *Beyond the lavender lexicon: authenticity, imagination and appropriation in lesbian and gay languages*. New York: Gordon and Breach, pp. 227–234.

Gramsci, A. (1971). *Selections from the prison notebooks of Antonio Gramsci*. New York: International Publishers.

Gray, J. (this volume). Language and non-normative sexual identities, in S. Preece (ed.) *The Routledge handbook of language and identity*. Abingdon: Routledge, pp. 225–240.

Gumperz, J.J. (1982). *Discourse strategies*. Cambridge: Cambridge University Press.

Hall, K. (1995). Lip service on the fantasy lines, in M. Bucholtz and K. Hall (eds) *Gender articulated: language and the socially constructed self*. New York: Routledge, pp. 183–216.

Hall, K. and O'Donovan, V. (1996). Shifting gender positions among Hindi-speaking Hijras, in V. Bergvall, J. Bing and A. Freed (eds) *Rethinking language and gender research: theory and practice*. London: Longman, pp. 228–266.

Holmes, J. (2006). Workplace narratives, professional identity and relational practice, in A. De Fina, D. Schiffrin and D. Bamberg (eds) *Discourse and identity*. Cambridge: Cambridge University Press, pp. 166–187.

Irvine, J. and Gal, S. (2000). Language ideology and linguistic differentiation, in P. Kroskrity (ed.) *Regimes of language: ideologies, polities, and identities.* New Mexico: SAR Press, pp. 35–83.

Johnson, S. (1997). Theorizing masculinity: a feminist perspective, in S. Johnson and U.H. Meinhof (eds) *Language and masculinity.* Oxford: Blackwell, pp. 8–26.

Jones, L. (2012). *Dyke/girl: language and identities in a lesbian group.* Basingstoke: Palgrave Macmillan.

Kiesling, S.F. (1997). Power and the language of men, in S. Johnson and U.H. Meinhof (eds) *Language and masculinity.* Oxford: Blackwell, pp. 65–85.

Kiesling, S.F. (2002). Playing the straight man: displaying and maintaining male heterosexuality in discourse, in K. Campbell-Kibler, R. Podesva, S. Roberts and A. Wong (eds) *Language and sexuality: contesting meaning in theory and practice.* Stanford: CSLI Publications, pp. 249–266.

King, B. (2015). Reclaiming masculinity in an account of lived intersex experience: language, desire, and embodied knowledge, in T. Milani (ed.) *Language and masculinities: performances, intersections, dislocations.* London: Routledge, pp. 220–242.

Kulick, D. (1996). 'Causing a commotion: scandal as resistance among Brazilian Travesti prostitutes', *Anthropology Today,* 12(6): 3–7.

Labov, W. (1990). 'The intersection of sex and social class in the course of linguistic change', *Language Variation and Change,* 2: 205–254.

Lakoff, R.T. (1975). *Language and woman's place.* New York: Harper and Row.

Lave, J. and Wenger, E. (1991). *Situated learning: legitimate peripheral participation.* Cambridge: Cambridge University Press.

Lazar, M. (2005). *Feminist critical discourse analysis.* Basingstoke: Palgrave Macmillan.

Leap, W. (1996). *Word's out: gay men's English.* Minnesota: University of Minnesota Press.

Litosseliti, L. and Sunderland, J. (2002). Gender identity and discourse analysis: theoretical and empirical considerations, in L. Litosseliti and J. Sunderland (eds) *Gender identity and discourse analysis.* Amsterdam: John Benjamins, pp. 3–39.

Livia, A. (1995). I ought to throw a Buick at you: fictional representations of butch/femme speech, in M. Bucholtz and K. Hall (eds) *Gender articulated: language and the socially constructed self.* London: Routledge, pp. 245–278.

Maltz, D. and Borker, R. (1982). A cultural approach to male–female miscommunication, in J.J. Gumperz (ed.) *Language and social identity.* Cambridge: Cambridge University Press, pp. 196–216.

McElhinny, B. (1995). Challenging hegemonic masculinities: female and male police officers handling domestic violence, in M. Bucholtz and K. Hall (eds) *Gender articulated: language and the socially constructed self.* London: Routledge, pp. 217–244.

Mendoza-Denton, N. (2008). *Homegirls: language and cultural practice among Latina youth gangs.* Malden: Blackwell.

Milani, T.M. (2013). 'Are "queers" really "queer"? Language, identity and same-sex desire in a South African online community', *Discourse and Society,* 24(5): 615–633.

Milani, T.M. (this volume). Straight-acting: discursive negotiations of a homomasculine identity, in S. Preece (ed.) *The Routledge handbook of language and identity.* Abingdon: Routledge, pp. 443–457.

Mills, S. (2008). *Language and sexism.* Cambridge: Cambridge University Press.

Mills, S. and Mullany, L. (2011). *Language, gender and feminism.* Abingdon: Routledge.

Morrish, E. and Sauntson, H. (2007). *New perspectives on language and sexual identity.* Basingstoke: Palgrave Macmillan.

Mullany, L.J. (2011). Discourse, gender and professional communication, in J. Gee and M. Handford (eds) *The handbook of discourse analysis.* London: Routledge, pp. 509–522.

Namaste, V. (2000). *Invisible lives: the erasure of transsexual and transgendered people.* Chicago: University of Chicago Press.

Norton, B. (2000). *Identity and language learning: gender, ethnicity and educational change.* Harlow: Longman.

O'Barr, W. and Atkins, B. (1980). 'Women's language' or 'powerless language'?, in S. McConnell-Ginet, R. Borker and N. Furman (eds) *Women and language in literature and society.* New York: Praeger, pp. 93–110.

Ochs, E. (1990). Indexicality and socialization, in J. Stigler, R. Shweder and G. Herdt (eds) *Cultural psychology: the Chicago symposia*. Cambridge: Cambridge University Press, pp. 287–308.

Podesva, R.J. (2007). 'Phonation type as a stylistic variable: the use of falsetto in constructing a persona', *Journal of Sociolinguistics*, 11: 478–504.

Preece, S. (2009). 'A group of lads, innit?': performances of laddish masculinity in British higher education, in E. Eppler and P. Pichler (eds) *Gender and spoken interaction*. Basingstoke: Palgrave Macmillan, pp. 115–138.

Queen, R. (2005). 'How many lesbians does it take …: jokes, teasing, and the negotiation of stereotypes about lesbians', *Journal of Linguistic Anthropology*, 15(2): 239–257.

Sunderland, J. (2004). *Gendered discourses*. Basingstoke: Palgrave Macmillan.

Swann, J. (2009). Doing gender against the odds: a sociolinguistic analysis of educational discourse, in E. Eppler and P. Pichler (eds) *Gender and spoken interaction*. Basingstoke: Palgrave Macmillan, pp. 18–41.

Talbot, M. (1995). A synthetic sisterhood: false friends in a teenage magazine, in M. Bucholtz and K. Hall (eds) *Gender articulated: language and the socially constructed self*. London: Routledge, pp. 143–165.

Tannen, D. (1990). *You just don't understand! Women and men in conversation*. New York: William Morrow.

West, C. and Zimmerman, D. (1977). 'Women's place in everyday talk: reflections on parent–child interaction', *Social Problems*, 245: 521–529.

Zimman, L. (2012). *Voices in transition: testosterone, transmasculinity, and the gendered voice among female-to-male transgender people*. PhD thesis, University of Colorado at Boulder.

Zotzmann, K. and O'Regan, J.P. (this volume). Critical discourse analysis and identity, in S. Preece (ed.) *The Routledge handbook of language and identity*. Abingdon: Routledge, pp. 113–128.

14

Language and non-normative sexual identities

John Gray

Introduction

This chapter looks at the way in which language plays a key role in the representation and expression of non-normative sexual identities, all of which tend to be stigmatised to a greater or lesser degree, and the ways in which this relationship has been theorised. By non-normative sexual identities I refer to the identities of lesbians, gay men, bisexuals and those identifying as transgender or transsexual, as well as those identifying as queer (a broad term for a wide range of non-normative sexual and gender identifications) and intersex – hereafter LGBTQI. Collectively these identities represent a challenge to prevailing binary gender norms and the hegemony of heteronormativity, which has been defined as 'those structures, institutions, relations and actions that promote and produce heterosexuality as natural, self-evident, desirable, privileged, and necessary' (Cameron and Kulick 2003: 55).

Given the focus on language and identity in applied linguistics in this volume, it is important to clarify at the outset what an applied linguistics perspective entails. Such a perspective is determined by the twofold nature of the field. On the one hand, there is the general subscription to Christopher Brumfit's (1997: 93) definition of applied linguistics as the 'theoretical and empirical investigation of real-world problems in which language is a central issue'. On the other hand, there is the increasingly wide acceptance of Ben Rampton's (1997: 8) case for the reconceptualisation of the field as an interdisciplinary one that 'brings cultural and social organisation centre-stage, and which construes language in the first instance not as grammar but as a repertoire of ways of speaking shaped through the part it plays in social action and communicative conduct'. This understanding yokes together a problem-focused orientation with a view of language as a set of culturally determined semiotic resources for the making of personal and social meanings. As we shall see later, such a perspective can help shed light on problems that can arise in interactions in settings where speakers' attempts at meaning-making are perceived as culturally unintelligible or otherwise problematic – particularly when ascribed identities are being negotiated or refused.

The chapter begins with the theorisation of non-normative sexuality by a small number of sexologists in the nineteenth century, and the emergence of 'the homosexual' as emblematic of sexual non-normativity in a recognisably modern sense. The chapter then turns to the rise of lesbian and gay studies in the late twentieth century and the emergence of a specific kind of identity politics in which the role of language received a considerable amount of attention. From there I move on to consider more recent queer perspectives, all of which are hostile to essentialised views of identity and some of the uses to which the concept has been put in relation to non-normative sexuality.

Overview

As acronyms such as LGBTQI and terms such as genderqueer, gender fluid and gender questioning suggest, we live at a time in which minority sexual identities are increasingly pluralised. In theorising this development, most scholars recognise the centrality of Michel Foucault who emphasises the power of discourse in the shaping of social life and in the formation of the individual. At its simplest, discourse in the Foucauldian sense refers to:

> a group of statements in any domain which provides a language for talking about a topic and a way of producing a particular kind of knowledge about that topic. The term refers both to the production of knowledge through language and representation and the way that knowledge is institutionalized, shaping social practices and setting new practices into play.
>
> *(Hall 1997: 222)*

But how exactly does this work with regard to sexual identity? Foucault (1978) shows that the pluralisation of non-normative sexualities we are familiar with today began in earnest in the nineteenth century with the identification and the categorisation of certain types of people in terms of their sexual behaviour. This was largely the work of early sexologists, most of whom were sympathetic to the plight of the 'sexually peculiar' whose behaviour placed them outside the law or condemned them as sinful (ibid.: 44). Indeed several of the pioneers were themselves members of sexual minorities. Between them they were responsible for the introduction of a new vocabulary which included terms such as 'transvestite', 'fetishist', 'third sex', 'invert' and 'Uranian' (a nineteenth-century catch-all term for a variety of types of female and male homosexual), along with the concept of a spectrum of 'sexual intermediaries'. Crucially for many early sexologists, non-normative sexual behaviours were conceptualised as natural, indicative of inherent conditions (however unfortunate these might be deemed) and enduring personality types. Magnus Hirschfeld (2006 [1910]: 37–38) is typical of this kind of essentialist thinking when he states that 'sexual individuality as such with respect to body and mind is inborn, dependent upon the inherited mixture of manly and womanly substances, independent of externals'. He is also typical in that his discussion of sexual diversity (generally seen at this time as a form of gender variance) is couched entirely in the new medical discourse in which the bodies of case studies, having been probed and measured in the surgery, are described in detail. This literature has a modern parallel with the medicalised discourse surrounding the surgical and hormonal modification of the transgender body (Borba 2015) and the anatomical atypicality of the intersex body, whereby the latter is currently classified as comprising a range of 'disorders of sexual development' – although this language is increasingly contested by activist intersex organisations (Organisation Intersex International 2012).

Foucault (1978), somewhat humorously, lists a welter of scientific-sounding terms culled from the work of the early sexologists. These include categories such as zoophiles, auto-monosexualists, presbyophiles and sexoesthetic inverts. And indeed their work was the subject of parody in the popular press at the time. Graham Robb (2003) describes a cartoon entitled 'Berlin Census in a Thoroughly Modern Home', which appeared in 1905 in a German weekly arts magazine. The cartoon featured the following exchange between a census taker and a mother:

Census Taker: 'How many children?'
A Mother: 'Two daughters, one boy, three homosexual intermediates, and one Uranian.'

(Ibid.: 190)

Although Robb is not a Foucauldian, the text of the cartoon he reproduces makes an important Foucauldian point about the way in which this new medicalised discourse entered the public domain, often via the media, and thus making new concepts and vocabularies available for wider consumption and use. Ultimately, Foucault's argument, which is critical of these 'scientific' developments, is that non-normative sexualities were pathologised through the production of this discourse. For Foucault, this was representative of what he saw as the problematic incursion of medicine into people's lives – as a way of making them 'knowable' and therefore subject to regulation. However, at the same time he states that those classified (and increasingly self-identifying) as sexually different began to make use of this language to describe themselves and to agitate – if not for recognition, then at least for toleration – precisely in the terms set by these new discourses. This is what Stuart Hall (1996: 6) means when he says that identities 'are the result of a successful articulation or "chaining" of the subject into the flow of discourse' – namely that people can see themselves as interpellated or hailed by the discourses put into circulation and come to 'identify with' and 'invest in' the ways in which they are discursively constructed and represented (see Baxter, this volume). Little wonder then that the 'sexually peculiar' were increasingly willing to self-identify as sexual intermediaries, transvestites, inverts and Uranians (and crucially as members of the putative collectives these identities implied) when their stigmatised behaviours were discursively repackaged as a condition and a way of being.

The clinical view of non-normative sexualities was to go largely unchallenged until well into the second half of the twentieth century. In 1968 Mary McIntosh published what would become a groundbreaking paper in the sociology journal *Social Problems*; this argued that far from being a pathologised condition, homosexuality was best understood as a social role and a type of behaviour. McIntosh (1968) argued that, when looked at historically and geographically, same-sex relations varied hugely in terms of the forms they took and the social meanings attributed to them. She showed that in some settings the homosexual fulfilled a culturally determined and recognised social role, while in other places and at other times, despite the presence of same-sex relations, no such role existed. As McIntosh (ibid.: 187) put it, 'there may be much homosexual behaviour … there are no "homosexuals"'. McIntosh's paper, much as Foucault's work which it prefigured, would function in Britain and the United States as a foundational text for the emerging lesbian and gay liberation movement. Its message that the form sexuality took was socially constructed opened up the possibility for a powerful reimagining of what it meant to be a member of a stigmatised sexual minority. As Jeffrey Weeks (2007: 82), commenting on the influence of McIntosh's paper, explained, 'if the sexual categorizations that were taken for granted were actually human inventions, then they could be reinvented'. In terms of this chapter, McIntosh's paper is also important for another reason, as it refers in passing to studies which suggest that homosexuals used language in very particular ways – and it is to this that I now turn.

Gayspeak and Gay English

Although the early sexologists were largely uninterested in language, McIntosh (1968) cites a number of eighteenth-century sources that drew attention to the way men in Molly Houses (taverns frequented by transvestites and homosexual men) were said to speak:

> [They] adopted all the small vanities natural to the feminine sex to such an extent that they try to speak, walk, chatter, shriek and scold as women do, aping them as well in other respects.
>
> *(Ward 1709, in McIntosh 1968: 188)*

> It would be a pretty scene to behold them in their clubs and cabals, how they assume the air and affect the name of Madam or Miss, Betty or Molly, with a chuck under the chin, and 'Oh, you bold pullet, I'll break your eggs', and then frisk and walk away.
>
> *(Anon 1729, in ibid.)*

Here the assumption is clear that the speech of homosexual men and transvestites is gender inappropriate in terms of the titles and names used to address one another, the variety of stereotypically feminine and camp (see below) forms of talk they engage in, the way they sound, as well as the way in which they move their bodies. McIntosh's point, which is only tangentially concerned with language, is that there was greater overlap between male homosexuality and transvesticism at certain historical moments and that non-normative sexuality (indeed all sexuality) is always historically, geographically and culturally specific. However, the quotations are a reminder that specific ways of using language have been associated with homosexual men and transvestites (much more so than with lesbians and other sexual minorities) at least since the beginning of the early modern period.

Cameron and Kulick (2003) identify four main phases in the study of language and homosexuality that are helpful for the discussion in this chapter:

1   1920s–1940s;
2   1950s–1960s;
3   1970s–mid-1990s;
4   1990s–the present.

Twentieth-century interest in this area parallels the rise of identity studies across the social sciences and the changing role attributed to language as a key feature of identity. With regard to homosexuality, this was a development in which language (and other semiotic activity) was initially seen as reflective of an ascribed, inherent and pathologised condition (Phases 1 and 2); then as reflective of an assumed, essentialised and non-pathologised identity (Phase 3); and finally as a repertoire of culturally shaped semiotic resources for indexing a range of identifications and performatively producing a non-essentialised identity (Phase 4).

Research in the first two phases was limited mainly to the compilation of slang terms used mainly by North American gay men and the ways in which such language functioned as a means of communication and self-identification. By the 1970s, politically motivated lesbian and gay scholars were starting to look at those identifying as lesbian, gay and bisexual (there was little talk of transgender at this time) in terms of community and specifically in terms of a speech community. Although this is a term with a multitude of definitions, speech community at its most general implies a collective with shared knowledge of a particular language or language variety and whose members are familiar with the ways in which that language (or language variety) is used. These scholars (e.g. Chesebro 1981) were influenced by early sociolinguistic studies of

African American speech (Labov 1972), but also by studies of women's language (Lakoff 1975). Richard Mohr (1992: 27) provides a flavour of this lesbian and gay linguistic turn:

> The gay community cannot be thought of as an artifice like, say, a stamp collectors' club or Alcoholics Anonymous … Rather, the gay community is a natural community in a way that English is a natural language but the computer languages Fortran and Cobol are not. If one is born in England of English parents, it is not an option to decide not to speak English as one's mother tongue but to set up linguistic shop instead in some artificial language, in the way one can, if one does not like some computer language, simply make up one's own.

Although the equation of a 'natural' 'gay community' with a 'natural language' is problematic and the notion of community itself was contested, the overall implication was clear – gay people were born gay and spoke the language of the gay community.

In this way, despite the impact of McIntosh and Foucault, whose work suggested the socially and discursively constructed nature of sexual identity, a new kind of essentialism came to typify lesbian and gay theorising. This kind of move has been described by Gayatri Chakravorty Spivak (1988) as 'strategic essentialism' – namely, the politically necessary mobilisation of a collective identity as part of a rights-claiming endeavour on the part of marginalised groups. For Spivak this strategy would ideally be accompanied by the simultaneous critique of the categories invoked. However, such an apparently contradictory approach proved difficult and some scholars were more than happy to make the case for a new non-pathologised lesbian and gay essentialism. Thus, in the third phase of study (now properly inaugurated as lesbian and gay studies), some scholars sought to identify the ways in which language was used in uniquely gay ways. Joseph Hayes (2006 [1981]) and William Leap (1995) drew attention to the ways in which gay men spoke euphemistically or indirectly in settings where the sexual orientation of interlocutors was unknown and in need of checking, or where interlocutors were presumed to be straight and possibly prejudiced. They also drew attention to the ways in which language was used in homo-social settings; in addition, Hayes referred to language as used in what he called the radical-activist setting. These uses of languages went by the name of Gayspeak and/or Gay English. However, as James Darsey (2006 [1981]) pointed out in his response to Hayes, there is nothing particularly gay about the kind of indirect speech a gay man might use (for example, saying 'my friend' instead of 'my boyfriend') on meeting a stranger. All competent users of language make use of such strategies as part of their everyday conversations, and the fact that gay men engage in it does not make it gay *per se*. Similar objections were raised with regard to the use of language in the radical-activist setting. Here Gayspeak referred to the use of politically correct language and the reappropriation of stigmatising terms such as 'dyke' and 'faggot'. But again, as Darsey argued, there is nothing uniquely gay about such practices – reappropriations of terms of abuse are typical of many minority groups.

Initially those making the case for uniquely gay language might seem to be on firmer ground when it came to the social setting. Hayes and Leap saw this as characterised by extensive use of what was termed the lavender lexicon (Leap 1995). This kind of language typically relates to sexual identities, sex roles and sexual preferences. Contemporary examples might include items such as 'butch', 'femme', 'top' and 'bottom', as well as the multiple uses of 'queen' to form compound words indicating (generally male) sexual preferences such as 'rice queen' or 'size queen'. Hayes (2006 [1981]: 70) also identifies camp as a feature of Gayspeak, which he described as the 'the art of the put-down' – although, as we shall see, camp can be understood as being much more than this. At the same time, language as used in the social context was held to go beyond lexis and camp to incorporate a specific interactional style.

Ruth Morgan and Kathleen Wood (1995), in line with earlier analyses of women's speech by feminist scholars such as Jennifer Coates (1988), argued that lesbian speech was typified by a high degree of collaborative co-construction. In the following extract, a group of friends discuss the contents of a lunch pack:

1	Kathy:	What else do you pack in lunches?
2	Mandy:	(laughs)
3	Linda:	Weeell …
4	Kathy:	chips
5	Mandy:	bananas
6	Linda:	fruit
7	Tonya:	and a sandwich.

(Morgan and Wood 1995: 248)

Morgan and Wood suggest that this collective answer to Kathy's initial question is somehow specifically lesbian – indicative of the women's mutual supportiveness and designed to produce a sense of group cohesiveness. However, Cameron and Kulick (2003: 95) suggest that 'an analyst might be hard pressed to identify its specifically lesbian content' and they argue that the reason this kind of speech is identified as lesbian is simply because the speakers are known to be lesbians. Similar extracts and interpretations are found in Leap (2006 [1999]: 86–87) who concluded that 'gay men follow any number of linguistic strategies to ensure that conversations with other gay men are cooperative, not exclusionary or antagonistic'. But speech that is indirect and cooperative is characteristic of *all* human verbal interaction, at least some of the time. And even the lavender lexicon can be and is used by those who do not identify as LGBTQI.

Another kind of Gayspeak is Polari, which comprises a lexicon of about 500 words (Baker 2000). This British variety appears to have flourished in urban centres in the early to mid-twentieth century but was dying out by the late 1960s. One male informant in Matt Houlbrook's (2005: 152) study of early twentieth-century gay London commented on the use of Polari as follows:

> We always said Girl at the end of a sentence … You'd say something like "you all right girl" or "fancy a drink girl" … "ooh will you just vada the bona filiomi ajax" … It was all camp and rather silly. [Translation: 'look at that good-looking young man over there']

As Houlbrook points out, Polari was associated with camp talk, which has been defined by Keith Harvey (2000) as relying on four strategies for effect, not all of which would necessarily be present in any instantiation. These are:

- 'Paradox' – brought about through incongruities of register and mixing of references to high and low culture;
- 'Inversion' – of grammatical gender markers, rhetorical routines or value systems;
- 'Ludicrism' – verbal playfulness of all kinds such as puns and double-entendres;
- 'Parody' – of stereotypical femininity, through the use of exclamations and vocatives such as 'My dear' and of the mannerisms of the upper classes or of those aping them – often through the use of French as a signifier of high culture.

Despite Susan Sontag's (1966) assertion that camp was not political, Harvey argues that camp performances – particularly noticeable in the speech of drag artists – can serve to disrupt, ironise and undermine the prevailing gender and sexual order. That said, campness is not the sole preserve of those identifying as LGBTQI, as scholars such as Pamela Robertson (1996) have argued convincingly. Furthermore, as Houlbrook (2005) notes, Polari was also used by other marginalised groups such as female prostitutes.

Another feature associated with Gayspeak has been termed 'the voice' (Zwicky 1997). This refers to the phenomenon whereby some gay men in particular are said to be identifiable by their voice quality, characterised by wide ranges in pitch, extended vowel production as in 'FAABulous' (Barrett 1997), breathy voice and sibilant duration. However, research in this area, which tends to involve listeners making judgements about the perceived gayness of voices, suggests that listeners are only right some of the time. This leads Cameron and Kulick (2003: 90) to conclude that '[n]ot all gay men have "the voice" and not everyone who has "the voice" is gay' – something which is confirmed by more recent studies (Levon 2007; Piccolo 2008).

What then are we to make of all this? It is clear that some members of sexual minorities can and do use language in particular ways, but that these are not confined to those identifying as LGBTQI. Ultimately, the notion of specifically gay language proved to be a dead end. It was clear that an exploration of the relationship between language and non-normative sexual identities required an altogether different analytical lens. This would be provided in the fourth phase of the study of language and homosexuality by queer linguistics (Bucholtz and Hall 2004). Queer linguistics draws heavily on queer theory and it is to this I now turn.

Queer perspectives on language and non-normative sexual identities

Two foundational texts of queer theory are Eve Kosofsky Sedgwick's (1990) *The epistemology of the closet* and Judith Butler's (1990) *Gender trouble*. It is no coincidence that they both originate in the United States in a historical moment characterised by renewed political activism on the part of sexual minorities against a background of the spiralling AIDS crisis. In many ways the AIDS crisis served to expose gender, class and race divisions within the so-called LGBTQI community, as those living in poverty, in low-paid jobs, with no medical insurance or without appropriate residency documentation found themselves less able to access health care than white, middle-class gay men. Suddenly the 'community' looked less seamless and identity politics less sustainable than had previously been claimed. Although queer theory is hardly a unified project, Sedgwick's and Butler's texts had two targets in their sights that have remained more or less constant in subsequent queer theorising – heteronormativity and the concept of identity (at least as construed in early lesbian and gay identity politics). Reflecting on the unforeseen consequences of strategic essentialism with regard to homosexuality, Sedgwick (1990: 45) writes:

> an unfortunate side effect of this move has been implicitly to underwrite the notion that 'homosexuality as we conceive of it today' itself comprises a coherent definitional field rather than a space of overlapping, contradictory, and conflictual definitional forces.

In such a changing environment, the role of language was also being rethought. Instead of seeing language as reflective of an essentialised identity, many LGBTQI scholars took the view that it was more usefully understood as a set of semiotic resources used in contextually contingent ways to index a range of identifications, which might well be overlapping, contradictory and conflictual. Although queer linguistics retains the concept of identity, as Rusty Barrett (2002: 28) explains, 'identity categories are not accepted as a priori entities, but are recognised as ideological constructs produced by social discourse'. Key to this rethinking was Butler's (1990) appropriation of the concept of the performative utterance from the philosophy of language. John Austin (1962) famously categorised utterances such as 'I now pronounce you man and wife' as performatives – namely linguistic interventions that brought about a new state of affairs in the world. Butler's innovation was to apply this to gender. From this perspective an individual's gender is produced and sustained through its own repeated performance – and what is performed Butler implied is all too often constraining and limiting, given that the blueprint for the prevailing gender norms derive from heteronormativity. Butler's reconceptualisation of gender as performative allows for the possibility of its subversion, which she explores through her interest in drag. Butler sees drag as an agentive and highly political activity in which the fabricated nature of gender is exposed in the performance of the drag king or queen whose exaggerated and patent falseness undermines and mocks the notion of any true or stable gender. Implicit in the drag artist's imitation is the suggestion that gender itself is a form of drag:

> To claim that all gender is like drag, or is drag, is to suggest that 'imitation' is at the heart of the *heterosexual* project and its gender binarisms, that drag is not a secondary imitation that presupposes a prior and original gender, but that hegemonic heterosexuality is itself a constant and repeated effort to imitate its own idealizations ... In this sense, then, drag is subversive to the extent that it reflects on the imitative structure by which hegemonic gender is itself produced and disputes heterosexuality's claim on naturalness and originality.
>
> *(Butler 1993: 85)*

Butler's concept of performativity and her view of language in general would prove attractive to scholars interested in theorising non-normative sexualities. For Butler (1990: 196), '[l]anguage is not an exterior medium or instrument into which I pour myself and from which I glean a reflection of that self' – rather, holding that there is no pre-existing gender or essentialised self to reflect, she sees it as a medium in and through which speakers (to echo Stuart Hall again) locate themselves within particular discourses and in which they index particular identifications or recognisable identities – in some cases ironically, in some cases not – in ways which are influenced by the range of discursive and semiotic resources that are culturally and contextually available. From this perspective, identities can be seen as being 'brought about' in discourse but also, as Mike Baynham (2015) argues, as being 'brought along' – in the sense that repeated performance can lead to more sedimented and enduring senses of self.

Such an understanding informs Robin Queen's (1997) analysis of the language of lesbian comic-book characters who are shown to draw on a contradictory range of styles and Barrett's (2006 [1995]; see also Mann 2011) analysis of Texan African American drag queens' language. Barrett (2006 [1995]) shows that the language used in their performances is typified by a considerable amount of switching between what he calls white woman's style (see women's language in Lakoff 1975), Gay English and specifically southern forms – as well as limited use of African American Vernacular English (AAVE). Such switching, Barrett suggests, is indicative of the complex identity work African American drag queens may engage in. In the following extract a drag queen is introducing a white stripper to a largely white gay audience in a club. At line 7 the performer notices one of the few black men in the audience and, abandoning the higher-pitched white woman's voice she has been using, addresses him directly:

1   Please welcome to the stage, our next dancer,
2   He is a butt-fucking tea, honey.

3   He is hot.
4   Masculine, muscled, and ready to put it ya, baby.
5   Anybody in here (.) hot (.) as (.) fish (.) grease?
6   That's pretty hot, idn't it?
7   (Switch to low pitch) Hey what's up, home boy? (Switches back)
8   I'm sorry that fucking creole always come around when I don't need it.
9   Please, welcome,
10 hot, gorgeous, sexy, very romantic,
11 and he'd like to bend you over and turn you every which way but loose.

(Barrett 2006 [1995]: 156)

Barrett suggests that the utterance at line 7 is an expression of solidarity with the black audience member. However, having signalled an identity at odds with the white woman persona being performed, the performer follows this with an apology to the audience. Barrett argues that the packaging of the apology in line 8, which is delivered in the resumed white woman voice, but with the missing –*s* morpheme typical of AAVE and containing an expletive, creates an ambiguity as to the speaker's sincerity. This ironises the white woman performance and signals the speaker's own complex set of identifications – while simultaneously drawing attention to African American social marginalisation and white privilege.

Although clearly informed by a Butlerian/Sedgwickian perspective, Cameron and Kulick (2003) argue that this kind of research, for all its insightfulness into the ways in which those identifying as LGBTQI index their (multiple) identifications, remains rooted in an identity-based paradigm. They take the view that such an approach has limited the study of language and sexuality to the ways in which speakers index claims to or attitudes towards category membership but which has tended to ignore desire. Cameron and Kulick (ibid.: 4) argue that sexuality (understood broadly as 'the socially constructed expression of erotic desire' and encompassing the irrational and the unconscious) exceeds many such linguistic acts of identity and that desire (as we shall see below) can exist in tension with identity – whether claimed or ascribed.

So far we have considered the emergence of non-normative sexual identities. In the following section we look at three institutional settings in which language and non-normative sexual identities are central and consider the relevance and applicability of the theoretical perspectives considered thus far to the specific real-world problems they raise from an applied linguistics perspective.

Issues and ongoing debates

Identity can certainly appear to be inadequate as a conceptual tool when trying to make sense of some queer speakers' talk about how they see themselves and the ways in which they discuss their sexual desires. One illuminating example of this is provided by David Valentine's (2003) analysis of data gathered in an alternative lifestyles support group in New York. Valentine, who identifies as a gay man, focuses on a series of interactions involving Miss Angel, an African American ex-drug user and sex worker (who some would categorise as a pre-op trans woman). The group was facilitated by Nora, a Latina and ex-drug user who self-identified as a heterosexual transsexual woman. In a series of excerpts, Angel is shown to use a wide range of identity categories to describe herself, often within the same utterance. Throughout the session Angel describes herself variously as one of 'these homosexuals', 'a pre-op transsexual', 'a woman', 'a drug addict woman' and 'a woman with a large clit', as well as saying 'I dunno what I am' (ibid.: 129–132). At one point Angel describes how at the age of 13 she had to make new friends, as she 'turned gay'. Valentine argues 'gay' is an umbrella term among the African American and Latino communities in which he did his fieldwork for sexual orientation *and* transgender identification (thus conflating two categories held to be separate by contemporary sexual identity politics). Valentine explains that it emerged that Angel had had sex with straight and gay men, and that she had also had sex with women and fathered a child. This range of experiences presents the group, and Nora in particular, with a problem. In the following excerpt involving Ben (another group member), Nora attempts to get Angel to give herself a precise identity label:

1	Angel:	I went to bed with my own kind. I tried it once.
2	Ben:	How was it?
3	A:	How was it?
4	B:	Uh huh.
5	Nora:	Now what is your own kind mean by definition, because you're always telling us–
6	A:	I'm a woman, well you know.
7	N:	You're a woman, transsexual, you're gay, you're homosexual.
8	B:	A man.
9	A:	Look, me, like me, someone like me. Someone like me … Someone like me.
10	N:	[who] changes sexuality, uh huh.
11	B:	With breasts.
12	A:	With breasts.
13	N:	OK.
14	A:	I went out with someone like me. Her name was Billie Jean, she lives in Coney Island.

(Ibid.: 131)

Valentine argues that Nora, ventriloquising the identity politics paradigm of social services in which gender is one thing and sexual orientation is another, is here 'attempting to get Angel to channel her expressions (and experiences) of erotic desire – be it desire for a woman, a man, or for "someone like her" – through identity categories that cannot in the end account for them' (ibid.). Although originating in a very different historical moment, Guy Hocquenghem (1993 [1972]: 49–50), whose work anticipates much contemporary queer theory, would have had no problem in understanding Angel – as the following comment suggests:

> 'Homosexual desire' – the expression is meaningless. There is no subdivision of desire into homosexuality and heterosexuality. Properly speaking, desire is no more homosexual than heterosexual. Desire emerges in a multiple form, whose components are only divisible a posteriori, according to how we manipulate it.

Angel's repetition of 'like me' is an indication of the difficulty she experiences in being pushed to self-categorise in any one way, thereby queering the whole notion of stable L, G, B or T identities. In fact when Angel does elaborate on her thoughts on sex and desire, she shows that she prefers to eschew completely the identity categories on offer and to talk in terms simply of enjoyment:

> When it comes down to sex, I don't think … it's two men going to bed with each other, a man and a woman […] or pre-op or nothing like that. I think it's just two people having

sex, making love to each other, enjoying each other's company, enjoying each other's time, when we're together.

(Valentine 2003: 132)

Valentine recounts that a social worker he spoke to took the view that Angel needed to be 'educated into a more enlightened understanding of identity' (ibid.: 136). From this perspective, Angel can be seen as a victim of what has been called the 'coercive force' and the 'terrible singularity' of identity politics (Brubaker and Cooper 2000: 6) that can operate in institutional settings where highly normative understandings of identity hold sway. The very place where she goes for support is unable to make sense of what she says in terms of the discourses within which the group operates. At the same time, identities clearly can be useful and can be claimed in ways which enable us to make sense of our lives and to make them meaningful – but as Valentine's work suggests, they can also be constraining and serve to render some voices unintelligible, particularly to those who are working within the discourse of stable and discrete sexual and gender identities. Valentine's argument is essentially one in favour of paying attention to the way in which desire is expressed and of the need for a Spivakian watchfulness with regard to the mobilisation of identity categories in interpreting what is said. Failure to do so he suggests means that people like Angel are unable to make themselves 'culturally intelligible' (Butler 1990: 23) and thus do not get a hearing.

A similar case of needing to achieve cultural intelligibility in terms of normative institutional understandings of identity (although with considerably higher stakes) is described by Rodrigo Borba (2015). He explains how, in order to qualify for surgery and hormone therapy, Brazilians who seek gender reassignment must first obtain a psychiatric diagnosis confirming that they are 'true transsexuals' – and not 'travestis' (i.e. biological males who, despite feminising their bodies through silicone injection and hormone ingestion, generally retain their male genitals). Borba's (2015: 11) analysis of a series of consultations involving Inês, a psychologist in a gender identity clinic, and Verônica, a pre-op trans woman, reveals the ways in which medical professionals operating on the basis of discrete and non-porous identity categories 'act as evaluators of clients' identities'. From the institutional perspective, a 'true transsexual' has to present as knowing the difference between a transsexual and a travesti and as hating their own genitals (something which was not Verônica's case). Borba's data show how Verônica was coached by Inês over several months until she was able to produce an institutionally acceptable performance of a 'true transsexual'. In the following extract from the first consultation, Inês is shown to be clearly at work performing the role of institutionally sanctioned judge and authorised shaper of Verônica's identity. She begins by asking Verônica to explain the difference between a transsexual and a travesti.

```
 9  Verônica:  ah I think they are : : :- they are different people who
10             have the- they think in different ways right=
11  Inês:      =>exactly<, they feel different things=
12  Verônica:  =right. [they feel-]
13  Inês:             [their <sexua]lity is di[fferen-]
14  Verônica:                               [different] one from the
15             other=
```

Lines omitted

28 Inês: <the transsexual> he- the <u>great</u> majority they
29   <u>don't</u> have (sexual) relations ° with the penis °
30   (0.7)
31 Inês: get it?=
32 Verônica: =uhum
33 Inês: but the travesti don't. they are- they are
34   both top and [bottom]
35 Verônica: [bottom] this I know
36   [they do both]
37 Inês: [so they] U: : :se the penis,
38 Verônica: uhum
39   (0.6)
40 Inês: >understand< the difference?
41 Verônica: ° I do °

(Ibid.: 9–10)

In a series of moves very similar to a language teacher engaged in instructional conversation, Inês elicits, corrects and instructs simultaneously while managing the interaction. Borba shows how Verônica eventually learned to perform the required institutionally recognised identity to receive the treatment she wanted. But he concludes by arguing that such practices force trans clients to ventriloquise the pathologising knowledge systems on which the diagnosis of 'true transsexual' is based – an approach that serves ultimately to deny the complexity of trans experience.

If part of the problem in the case of Angel is a surfeit of the identity categories on offer, none of which fit, and in the case of Verônica it is one of having to learn how to perform an ascribed identity that does not match her experience, in the case of Sam, a gay male student in a Spanish language class analysed by Anthony Liddicoat (2009), the problem is one of the scarcity of identity options available. Much has been written about the pervasive heteronormativity of English and modern foreign language classrooms (Nelson 2010; Coffey 2013; Gray 2013), which, it has been suggested, is such that it tends to silence LGBTQI students. Given that much of the talk that goes on in modern language classrooms revolves around students discussing and sharing personal information about likes and dislikes, leisure time activities and personal relations, LGBTQI students are faced with the problem of whether to come out, lie about their orientation or (thinking back to Hayes and Leap) attempt to dodge the issue by speaking indirectly. However, in languages where gender is marked grammatically, students will have to work harder if they decide on obfuscation. Even if they decide to come out, they may be presented with the problem of having their utterances misunderstood – as the following interaction between Sam and his teacher shows:

T: *Y Sam. (.) ¿Como es tu novia?*
       And Sam. What's your girlfriend like?
Sam: *Mi uhm (0.2) novio es alto y:: delgado.*
       My uhm (0.2) boyfriend is tall (m) and slim (m).
       (0.4)
T: *¿alta y delgada?*
       Tall (f) and slim (f)?

Sam: *¿alta y delgada?*
      Tall (f) and slim (f)?
      (0.3)
      Mi novio (.) uhm es alta y delgada.
      My boyfriend is tall (f) and slim (f).
T: *Tu novia es alta y delgada.*
      Your girlfriend is tall and slim.
Sam: *.hh uhm:: (n-)¿novia?*
      .hh uhm:: (n-) girlfriend?
T: *Sí tu novia e::s::*
      Yes your girlfriend i::s::
Sam: *O::h no es novio. Mi novio es alto y delgado. (0.2) Y tiene barba.*
      O::h no it's boyfriend. My boyfriend is tall and slim. (0.2) And he has a beard.
      (0.7)
T: *Lynn. (.) ¿Como es tu novio?*
      Lynn. (.) What's your boyfriend like?
Sam: *Mi novio es guapo y alto.*
      My boyfriend is handsome and tall.
T: *Muy bien.*
      Very good.

(Liddicoat 2009: 193)

The heteronormative framing of the initial question, which Liddicoat explains is taken from a textbook, means that Sam has already been positioned as straight. However, his first answer in which he changes the gender of the noun from feminine (*novia*) to masculine (*novio*) so that it is true for him is grammatically correct – the adjectives agree in gender and number with the noun. This is taken by the teacher to be a grammatical error (rather than a statement of fact) and the adjectives are echoed back with feminine endings by way of corrective feedback. Sam too appears to think he has made an error as he repairs and repeats the utterance – this time with the masculine noun intact and the adjectives in their (now incorrect) feminine form. The exchange in its entirety shows how hard he has to work to communicate his meaning and how rooted in heteronormativity the classroom is.

It is significant that the opening question originated in a textbook, as published materials tend to be relentlessly heteronormative in terms of their content. In one study of contemporary English language teaching textbooks (which exert a strong influence on the form textbooks for other global languages take) it was shown that there were no reading or listening activities that suggested the existence of sexual diversity and that in none of the activities that students were asked to do was their being LGBTQI or knowing anyone who was LGBTQI in any way implied (Gray 2013). Such practices are a form of erasure that constitute a denial of recognition, which is not necessarily without consequences for those affected. Sociologists such as Nancy Fraser (1998) and Andrew Sayer (2005) have argued persuasively that the denial of recognition to marginalised groups is a kind of harm that can impact negatively on their well-being and ability to function in wider society. Although Sam was able to negotiate his gay identity successfully, not all students have the confidence or the linguistic ability to do so. For them, to borrow a phrase from Sedgwick (1990: 63), the classroom has the potential to become 'the stigma-impregnated space of refused recognition'. Liddicoat does not speculate on how the issue of heteronormativity might be addressed in such settings. However, lesbian and gay teachers I interviewed (Gray 2013) suggested that the solution is necessarily multifaceted. They all felt that there should be greater LGBTQI representation in pedagogical materials, but that classroom discussion was best addressed as a set of discourses rather than in terms of personal experiences and disclosures (see Nelson, this volume).

Summary

This chapter has argued that non-normative sexualities came to be seen at the beginning of the lesbian and gay liberation movement in the late twentieth century as social and discursive constructions and that some early theorists such as Hocquenghem (1993 [1972]: 75) went so far as to assert that identity categories such as homosexual and heterosexual were themselves manipulations that served to silence the 'polyvocality of desire'. But a politics based on desire would prove difficult to implement, and as lesbian and gay activists and scholars began to make the case for their legitimacy they had recourse to identity as a strategy, which in turn led to a focus on community and on language as reflective of community members' identities. The contemporary turn to queer theory marks in many ways a return to an earlier sexual politics in which language remains central but in which essentialised views of identity are repudiated and in some cases identity itself is seen as a limiting lens for the exploration of sexuality (Cameron and Kulick 2003), if not potentially repressive of the non-conforming (Valentine 2003; Borba 2015), at least in its institutional deployment. The stories of Angel, Verônica and Sam, each in their different ways, suggest that despite the proliferation of identity labels in some settings and their complete absence in others, normativities – both old and new – have the power to create (linguistic) problems for speakers who do not conform to expectations, and it is here that the application of an applied linguistics perspective can be particularly useful.

Related topics

Positioning language and identity: poststructuralist perspectives; Language and gender identities; The significance of sexual identity to language learning and teaching; Language, gender and identities in political life: a case study from Malaysia; Straight-acting: discursive negotiations of a homomasculine identity; Intersectionality in language and identity research; Identity in language learning and teaching: research agendas for the future.

Further reading

Cameron, D. and Kulick, D. (eds) (2006). *The language and sexuality reader*. Abingdon: Routledge. (This reader contains a wide selection of key texts on language and sexuality.)

Livia, A. and Hall, K. (eds) (1997). *Queerly phrased: language, gender, and sexuality*. Oxford: Oxford University Press. (This collection remains one of the best introductions to language and sexual identity from a queer/sociolinguistics perspective.)

Nelson, C.D. (2009). *Sexual identities in English language education*. Abingdon: Routledge. (This volume draws on the experiences of LGBT teachers and students in a wide range of educational settings globally and explores queer pedagogy from a broadly applied linguistics perspective.)

References

Austin, J.L. (1962). *How to do things with words*. Oxford: Clarendon Press.

Baker, P. (2000). Bona to vada your dolly old eke! Construction of gay identity in the Julian and Sandy radio sketches [Online]. Available at www.lancaster.ac.uk/fass/groups/clsl/pubs/clsl114.pdf

Barrett, R. (1997). The 'homo-genius' speech community, in A. Livia and K. Hall (eds) *Queerly phrased: language, gender, and sexuality*. Oxford: Oxford University Press, pp. 181–201.

Barrett, R. (2002). Is queer theory important for sociolinguistic theory?, in K. Campbell-Kibler, R.J. Podesva, S.J. Roberts and A. Wong (eds) *Language and sexuality: contesting meaning in theory and practice*. Stanford: CSLI Press, pp. 25–43.

Barrett, R. (2006 [1995]). Supermodels of the world unite! Political economy and the language of performance among African American drag queens, in D. Cameron and D. Kulick (eds) *The language and sexuality reader*. Abingdon: Routledge, pp. 151–163.

Baxter, J. (this volume). Positioning language and identity: poststructuralist perspectives, in S. Preece (ed.) *The Routledge handbook of language and identity*. London: Routledge, pp. 34–49.

Baynham, M. (2015). Identity: brought about or brought along? Narrative as a privileged site for researching intercultural identities, in K. Risager and F. Dervin (eds) *Researching identity and interculturality*. London: Routledge, pp. 67–87.

Borba, R. (2015). How an individual becomes a subject: discourse, interaction and subjectification at a Brazilian gender identity clinic, *Working Papers in Urban Language and Literacies*. London: King's College London.

Brubaker, R. and Cooper, F. (2000). 'Beyond "identity"', *Theory and Society*, 29: 1–47.

Brumfit, C. (1997). 'How applied linguistics is the same as any other science', *International Journal of Applied Linguistics*, 7(1): 86–94.

Bucholtz, M. and Hall, K. (2004). 'Theorizing identity in language and sexuality research', *Language in Society*, 33: 469–515.

Butler, J. (1990). *Gender trouble*. New York: Routledge.

Butler, J. (1993). *Bodies that matter*. Abingdon: Routledge.

Cameron, D. and Kulick, D. (2003). *Language and sexuality*. Cambridge: Cambridge University Press.

Chesebro, J.W. (ed.) (1981). *Gayspeak: gay male and lesbian communication*. New York: Pilgrim Press.

Coates, J. (1988). Gossip revisited: language in all-female groups, in J. Coates and D. Cameron (eds) *Women in their speech communities: new perspectives on language and sex*. London: Longman, pp. 94–122.

Coffey, S. (2013). Communicating constructions of Frenchness through language coursebooks, in J. Gray (ed.) *Critical perspectives on language teaching materials*. Basingstoke: Palgrave Macmillan, pp. 137–160.

Darsey, L. (2006 [1981]). 'Gayspeak': a response, in D. Cameron and D. Kulick (eds) *The language and sexuality reader*. Abingdon: Routledge, pp. 78–85.

Foucault, M. (1978). *The history of sexuality: an introduction*. Harmondsworth: Penguin Books.

Fraser, N. (1998). 'Heterosexism, misrecognition, and capitalism: a response to Judith Butler', *New Left Review*, 1(228): 140–149.

Gray, J. (2013). LGBT invisibility and heteronormativity in ELT materials, in J. Gray (ed.) *Critical perspectives on language teaching materials*. Basingstoke: Palgrave Macmillan, pp. 40–63.

Hall, S. (1996). Introduction: who needs identity?, in S. Hall and P. du Gay (eds) *Questions of cultural identity*. London: SAGE, pp. 1–17.

Hall, S. (1997). The centrality of culture: notes on the cultural revolutions of our time, in K. Thompson (ed.) *Media and cultural regulation*. London: SAGE, pp. 208–238.

Harvey, K. (2000). 'Describing camp talk: language/pragmatics/politics', *Language and Literature*, 9(3): 240–260.

Hayes, J. (2006 [1981]). Gayspeak, in D. Cameron and D. Kulick (eds) *The language and sexuality reader*. Abingdon: Routledge, pp. 68–77.

Hirschfeld, M. (2006 [1910]). The transvestites: the erotic drive to cross-dress, in S. Stryker and S. Whittle (eds) *The transgender studies reader*. New York: Routledge, pp. 28–39.

Hocquenghem, G. (1993 [1972]). *Homosexual desire*. London: Duke University Press.

Houlbrook, M. (2005). *Queer London: perils and pleasures in the sexual metropolis, 1918–1957*. London: University of Chicago Press.

Labov, W. (1972). *Sociolinguistic patterns*. Oxford: Basil Blackwell.

Lakoff, R. (1975). *Language and woman's place*. New York: Harper & Row.

Leap, W. (1995). *Beyond the lavender lexicon: authenticity, imagination, and appropriation in lesbian and gay languages*. Trenton, NJ: Gordon and Breach.

Leap, W. (2006 [1999]). Can there be gay discourse without gay language?, in D. Cameron and D. Kulick (eds) *The language and sexuality reader*. Abingdon: Routledge, pp. 86–93.

Levon, E. (2007). 'Sexuality in context: variation and the sociolinguistic perception of identity', *Language in Society*, 36: 533–554.

Liddicoat, A. (2009). 'Sexual identity as linguistic failure: trajectories of interaction in the heteronormative language classroom', *Journal of Language, Identity, and Education*, 8: 191–202.

Mann, S.L. (2011). 'Drag queens' use of language and the performance of blurred gendered and racial identities', *Journal of Homosexuality*, 58(6–7): 793–811.

McIntosh, M. (1968). 'The homosexual role', *Social Problems*, 16(2): 182–192.

Mohr, R. (1992). *Gay ideas: outing and other controversies*. Boston, MA: Beacon Press.

Morgan, R. and Wood, K. (1995). Lesbians in the living room, in W. Leap (ed.) *Beyond the lavender lexicon: authenticity, imagination and appropriation in gay and lesbian languages*. Buffalo, NY: Gordon and Breach, pp. 235–248.

Nelson, C.D. (2010). 'A gay immigrant student's perspective: unspeakable acts in the language class', *TESOL Quarterly*, 44(3): 441–464.

Nelson, C.D. (this volume). The significance of sexual identity to language learning and teaching, in S. Preece (ed.) *The Routledge handbook of language and identity*. London: Routledge, pp. 351–365.

Organisation Intersex International (2012). *Brief guide for intersex allies* [Online]. Available at www.oii-usa.org

Piccolo, F. (2008). 'Perceived sexual orientation and attitudes towards sounding gay or straight', *University of Pennsylvania Working Papers in Linguistics*, 14(2): 130–138.

Queen, R. (1997). 'I don't speak spritch': locating lesbian language, in A. Livia and K. Hall (eds) *Queerly phrased: language, gender, and sexuality*. Oxford: Oxford University Press, pp. 233–256.

Rampton, B. (1997). 'Retuning in applied linguistics', *International Journal of Applied Linguistics*, 7(1): 3–25.

Robb, G. (2003). *Strangers: homosexual love in the nineteenth century*. London: Picador.

Robertson, P. (1996). *Guilty pleasures: feminist camp from Mae West to Madonna*. London: Duke University Press.

Sayer, A. (2005). *The moral significance of class*. Cambridge: Cambridge University Press.

Sedgwick, E.K. (1990). *The epistemology of the closet*. London: University of California Press.

Sontag, S. (1966). Notes on camp, in S. Sontag, *Against interpretation and other essays*. London: Penguin Books, pp. 275–292.

Spivak, G.C. (1988). *In other worlds: essays in cultural politics*. London: Routledge.

Valentine, D. (2003). 'I went to bed with my own kind once': the erasure of desire in the name of identity, *Language and Communication*, 23: 123–138.

Weeks, J. (2007). *The world we have won: the remaking of erotic and intimate life*. Abingdon: Routledge.

Zwicky, A.M. (1997). Two lavender issues for linguistics, in A. Livia and K. Hall (eds) *Queerly phrased: language, gender, and sexuality*. Oxford: Oxford University Press, pp. 21–34.

15

Class[1] in language and identity research

David Block

Introduction

Great British Class Survey finds seven social classes in UK.
Old model of working, middle and upper classes makes way for tiers ranging from 'precariat' to 'elite' based on economic, social and cultural indicators.

(Jones 2013)

This is the title and lead of an article appearing in the *Guardian online* in April 2013. The article is about the results of the Great British Class Survey (GBCS), which was launched on the BBC website in January 2011. The survey captured the attention of the public in the UK beyond the 161,400 individuals who eventually participated in it and it was extensively reported on in both print and audio-visual media, Jones's article being just one example. Designed by Savage, Devine and their collaborators (see Savage *et al.* 2013), the GBCS followed several earlier class surveys in Britain, such as the UK National Statistics Socio-Economic Classification (NS-SEC), which distributed the 2001 British population across multiple class positions according to their occupation and employment status, and the more recent Cultural Capital and Social Exclusion (CCSE) survey, which led to the 2009 publication *Culture, class, distinction* (Bennett *et al.* 2009). Like the 2001 NS-SEC survey, the GBCS put respondents into general occupational categories, in this case seven. These categories, along with their estimated proportions in the population at large (this, according to an independent survey carried out in 2011 by GfK, a survey firm), are as follows:

- Elite (e.g. high-level systems managers, lawyers, doctors, dentists) (6 per cent);
- Established middle class (e.g. electrical engineers, occupational therapists, teachers) (25 per cent);
- Technical middle class (e.g. pilots, pharmacists, higher education teachers, natural and social sciences professionals, physical scientists) (6 per cent);
- New affluent workers (e.g. electricians, plumbers, sales and retail assistants, postal workers) (15 per cent);

- Traditional working class (e.g. secretaries, van drivers, electricians, care workers) (14 per cent);
- Emergent service workers (e.g. bar staff, nursing auxiliaries, routine operatives, customer service workers) (19 per cent);
- The precariat (jobs from the previous three categories, but with discontinuities and a lack of security) (15 per cent).

Importantly, the GBCS survey was based on a more ambitious view of what constitutes class, one which draws on and updates Bourdieu's (1984) capitals: economic (income, savings, possessions, property), social (friends, acquaintances, work associates) and cultural (education level and cultural consumption patterns). There will be further discussion of this view of class below.

The work of Savage *et al.* (2013) is also important because it further updates understandings of what constitutes class in Britain, with resonances to societies around the world. Its popularity and the commentary that it inspired in the British media says something about the enduring relevance of class, even in countries where those in power have done their utmost to convince the general public that class is no longer relevant in the so-called 'new economy'. Indeed, there is much in Savage *et al.*'s work that resonates with the current general preoccupation with rising inequality around the world, the success of Piketty's (2014) *Capital in the twenty-first century* and the rise of alter-system parties in countries such as Greece (*Syriza*) and Spain (*Podemos*) being just two examples. Following authors such as Duménil and Lévy (2011) and Harvey (2014), we see how over 30 years of neoliberal policy and practice have constituted a form of class warfare, whereby the top 1 per cent, aided and abetted by the next 2–10 per cent, have accumulated wealth and property on the back of the remaining 90 per cent via the latter's stagnated salaries and wages, bank-induced debt and mortgage defaults (just to mention three emblematic examples of the collateral damage of neoliberalism) (Block forthcoming).

With this backdrop in mind, this chapter aims to explore how class has (and has not) figured as a construct in language and identity research. Specifically, it will examine and make the case for class as a key prism through which researchers in applied linguistics can better understand language and identity issues arising in a broad range of contexts. It will do so based on the premise that class exists in different societies around the world, although it should be noted that it plays itself out as a social phenomenon and mediator of activity in very different ways and is therefore contingent on local circumstances. This premise is based on and supported by a long list of publications focusing on class in societies as diverse as Chile (Han 2012), China (Chen 2013), Egypt (Masoud 2013), India (Ganguly-Scrace and Scrace 2010), Japan (Ishida and Slater 2010) and Spain (Subirats 2012).

The chapter begins with an examination of what is meant by class, exploring the historical development of the construct as well as current understandings that see it as multidimensional and multilevelled. This discussion includes a challenge to the notion that class is somehow not a relevant construct for social scientists today, as well as a consideration of how it is different from other identity dimensions such as gender, ethnicity, race and nationality: in Nancy Fraser's terms, the former is more about distribution issues while the latter are more about recognition issues. The chapter then moves to an examination and critique of how class has (or has not) been a key construct in research on language and identity in recent years, before closing with some future challenges. It should be noted that this chapter does not include a great deal of research that has dealt with class in applied linguistics writ large. Thus it does not cover the early variationist work of Labov (1966), which put class on the map in sociolinguistics; Bernstein's (1971) work on links between class positions and codes; or later ethnographic work such as

Eckert (1989), where social groups in an American high school (the institution and system-oriented 'jocks' and the counter-system 'burnouts') corresponded to broadly middle-class and working-class positions in society at large. These omissions are due primarily to space limitations. However, they are also attributable to my interest in narrowing the focus of this chapter to the specific area of language and identity research. This body of research arguably began with Norton Peirce's (1995) oft-cited call for 'a comprehensive theory of social identity that integrates the language learner and the language learning context' (Norton Peirce 1995: 12), and it has become an important sub-area of applied linguistics over the past two decades. Indeed, so large is language and identity research today that many readers will find the few studies which I am able to include in my critique to be a partial or even poor representation of the field. I refer these readers to Block (2014) for more thorough coverage of a larger sample of studies in which class has been a key construct.

Overview

Marx (1981 [1894], 1990 [1867]) is often looked to as the starting point for any discussion of class, despite the fact that he never provided an explicit definition of the construct in his work. It has therefore been left to scholars who succeeded him to attempt to capture the essence of his view of class. One such scholar in recent times is Wright (2005), who identifies five key concepts in Marxist class analysis that are relevant to Marx's understanding of class and his sense of purpose. These are:

1 Class *interests*, or the material interests that people derive from their lived class experiences;
2 Class *consciousness*, or 'the subjective awareness people have of their class interests and conditions for advancing them' (ibid.: 22);
3 Class *practices*, or the activities people engage in, in pursuit of class interests;
4 Class *formations*, or organisations and associations which serve to defend class interests (e.g. trade unions);
5 Class *struggle*, or the conflicts arising when individuals and collectives pursue divergent class interests.

The first two concepts cited by Wright are vital to any understanding of class as lived materially and lived in the mind and body, respectively. Following this reasoning and with a view to historicising class, Thompson (1980 [1963]) argued that the study of class was not a question of putting individuals into static categories but one of documenting their experiences in the material world – their relationships to the means of production – and then examining how these experiences contributed to the construction of class positions in societies as lived experiences. In this sense, his work parallels that of Polanyi (2001 [1944]), who focused on how human beings fashion history via the social circumstances in which they live. Thompson was interested in what Marx understood as two sides to class: (1) 'class in itself', that is, class as an objective reality independent of the actions or thoughts of individuals, 'as something which in fact happens (and can be shown to have happened) in human relationships' (Thompson 1980 [1963]: 8), and (2) 'class for itself', that is, how people 'as a result of common experiences (inherited or shared), feel and articulate the identity of their interests as between themselves, and as against other … [people] whose interests are different from (and generally opposed to) theirs' (ibid.: 8–9).

A range of more recent scholars have noted that any conceptualisation of the construct must be consonant with the increasing complexification of societies since Marx's death some 130 years ago. Writing in the early twentieth century, Weber (1968 [1922]) believed that the class positions of individuals and groups in industrial societies derived from the economic order in these societies. Also like Marx, he understood class and class positions to be relational phenomena arising during the course of interaction among individuals and groups engaged in social activity. Where Weber differed from Marx was in taking a more culturally sensitive view of society than that formulated by Marx (even if it would be an error to see Marxism as devoid of a cultural dimension; see Block 2014), introducing notions such as status, honour, prestige and style. Drawing on Marx, Weber and other scholars, Bourdieu crafted a version of class attuned to a French society heading towards the end of the twentieth century, a version that has been adapted to many other societies since. He saw class not only in material terms but also as a cultural activity, as he developed a sophisticated collection of metaphors that have become common currency in the discourse of many researchers in the social sciences and humanities today. Central to Bourdieu's theory of class are the capitals cited above in the discussion of the GBSC survey – economic, social and cultural – which can be understood in terms of degrees and volumes, 'as the set of actually usable resources and powers' (Bourdieu 1984: 114) that individuals draw on as they engage in practices in 'fields' or domains of social practices constituted and shaped by particular ways of thinking and acting (e.g. education, football, cinema, etc.). Class is thus framed as a social relation and as emergent in the day-to-day activities of human beings and it becomes embodied in the individual, forming a class 'habitus', which is an ever-evolving set of internalised dispositions, formulated out of engagement in situated social practices taking place in fields and shaped by institutions as well as larger social structures, such as global economic forces. Elsewhere, I sum up this approach as follows:

> [Class] has become a convenient working label in the social sciences (as well as in society in general) for a number of dimensions. These include: wealth (an individual's possessions and disposable money); occupation (manual labour, unskilled service jobs, low-level information based jobs, professional labour, etc.); place of residence (a working class neighbourhood, a middle class neighbourhood, an area in process of gentrification); education (the educational level attained by an individual by early adulthood); social networking (middle class people tend to socialise with middle class people, working class people with working class people, and so on); consumption patterns (buying food at a supermarket that positions itself as 'cost-cutting' vs. buying food at one that sells 'healthy' and organic products); and symbolic behaviour (e.g. how one moves one's body, the clothes one wears, the way one speaks, how one eats, the kinds of pastimes one engages in, etc.).
>
> *(Block 2012: 80–81)*

Whether class is understood in more basic terms (e.g. around income and occupation) or more complex ones (see my definition above), its demise has been a common trope in sociology in the late twentieth century (and now early twenty-first century). This has been the case because societies have changed so much since Marx, Weber, Durkheim and others were writing. And Bourdieu's updated version of class notwithstanding, many authors (e.g. Gorz 1982; Pakulski and Waters 1996; Touraine 2007) have painted a picture whereby the construct simply does not make sense either as 'class in itself', given that society today is very different from what it was 100 years ago, or 'class for itself', given that a large proportion of the population 'dis-identify' with class, preferring recognition markers such as race, ethnicity, nationality, gender, sexuality, religion and so on when talking about themselves (Savage *et al.* 2010). Authors who question the relevance of class in contemporary societies are no doubt right to point out how these societies have become more complex over the last century. However, in my view they exaggerate the extent to which conditions have changed dramatically for the majority of people in the world today. They do not, for example, devote enough attention to the billions of people living outside the digitised economy and society – people living in poverty who do not have mobile phones, CVs showing their flexibility or access to shopping malls full of consumer items. In addition, they fail to take on board how the increasing complexification of life conditions in many parts of the world does not, in and of itself, mean that class and class conflict have disappeared in recent decades. In contexts in which there has been a shift from manufacturing-based economic activity and skilled manual labour, to more service-based activity and digitised labour, inequality has not disappeared, nor have the exploitation and alienation of the workforce (Fuchs 2014).

One final issue that needs to be addressed is the relationship between class and identity. Is class an identity dimension, much like race, gender or nationality? Or is it different? As I note elsewhere (Block 2013), applied linguists have in general followed trends in the social sciences as regards the study of identity and they have therefore adopted what might be termed a culturalist approach. This approach has arisen above all in the economically advanced nation states of the world (and particularly in the Anglophone world) and it is connected with the rise of what some call 'identity politics' and what Fraser (1995; Fraser and Honneth 2003) sees as struggles related to 'recognition', a term she borrows from Taylor (1994). Recognition is about respect for others and 'an ideal reciprocal relationship between subjects in which each sees the other as an equal and also separate from it' (Fraser and Honneth 2003: 10). The focus is generally on key identity markers such as nationality, gender, race, ethnicity, religion and sexuality and the relationship of the individual with society at large, both as an individual and as a member of a community. Recognition may be seen as either in conflict with, or as articulated with, what Fraser (1995) calls 'redistribution', which is concerned with the material bases of the life experiences of 'collective subjects of injustice [who] are classes or class-like collectives, which are defined economically by a distinctive relation to the market or the means of production' (ibid.: 14). Fraser articulates a kind of philosophical dilemma when she laments how '[t]he discourse of social justice, once centered on distribution, is now increasingly divided between claims for distribution, on the one hand, and claims for recognition, on the other' (Fraser and Honneth 2003: 7–8), attributing this shift to developments such as the demise of communism (both as a material and discursive alternative to capitalism), the rise to dominant doxa of neoliberal economic ideology and the aforementioned rise of identity politics.

Fraser's way through the potential conflict between recognition claims and redistribution claims is to explore how the former interrelate with inequalities arising from the material bases of society (i.e. a Marxist perspective). For Fraser, recognition and redistribution claims may be satisfied in very different ways. On the one hand, action taken can be 'affirmative', providing 'remedies aimed at inequitable outcomes of social arrangements without disturbing the underlying framework that generates them' (Fraser 2008: 28). This is what happens when, in response to recognition claims, diversity and difference are supported and even promoted in multicultural societies as a defence against xenophobic, racist, sexist, homophobic and religion-based attacks (anti-Semitic, Islamophobic, anti-Christian, etc.). In response to redistribution claims, this is what happens when the state collects taxes and then provides resources to the most needy. It is worth noting that, in both examples of affirmative action, little or nothing is done to deal with underlying conditions that lead to reactive politics and inequality in the first place. So the question that arises is whether or not affirmation is enough if we wish to explore the roots of these problems in society. For Fraser, the answer is 'no', and she argues that actions taken in favour of recognition and redistribution need to be 'transformative', providing 'remedies aimed at correcting inequitable outcomes precisely by restructuring the underlying generative framework' (ibid.). Transformative recognition means problematising group differentiations, such as black vs. white, or male vs. female, or straight vs. gay/lesbian, and so on. Meanwhile, transformative redistribution means the arrival of socialism, as a deep restructuring of the political economy of a nation state.

The principal point to be derived from Fraser's discussion is, as I stated above, that class is not an identity dimension of the same type as race, ethnicity, gender, nationality or sexuality because it is first and foremost in the realm of distribution and redistribution of material resources and it is not about respect and recognition, at least not in its origins. As Fraser (1995) and Sayer (2002, 2005) note, the solution to societal ills like racism and sexism is for people to stop being racist and sexist, to accept diversity and to respect others as equals. These remedies do not work when it comes to class and class-based inequality, as accepting another's relative poverty, and respecting the position in society that it affords, does not do anything to overturn material-based inequality. This problematised view of the interrelationship between class and identity dimensions like race, gender and nationality will be a running theme in the remainder of this chapter.

Issues and ongoing debates

A close examination of a range of publications on language and identity in sociolinguistics and applied linguistics over the past three decades reveals several approaches to class:

1   Outright erasure (class is not mentioned at all);
2   What we might call 'class in passing' (class is mentioned and discussed only briefly and then disappears);
3   Partial class-based analysis (class is discussed explicitly as a factor but it is not theorised or dealt with in any depth as a concept);
4   Fuller class-based analysis (which entails a discussion of what the construct actually means).

The first approach is typical of the numerous publications dealing with one or more of the traditional (or, following Fraser, recognition-based) identity dimensions: these make no mention whatsoever of class, which therefore undergoes a form of erasure. There is obviously nothing wrong with taking on this topic in this way as researchers are free to focus on whatever aspect or angle on identity serves their research interests and purposes. Thus, in one of the better monographs on the topic to date, Edwards's (2009) *Language and identity*, the author never really brings class into his multi-level and nuanced discussion of the interrelationship between language forms and uses and collective and individual senses of self. The same applies to other excellent monographs on language and identity that have appeared over the past 15 years (e.g. Joseph 2004; Benwell and Stokoe 2006; Riley 2007), to say nothing of the vast majority of journal articles and book chapters on the topic. Of course, if authors who research language and identity in this way are working according to the distinction developed by Fraser, between class (as a redistribution issue) and traditional identity dimensions (as a recognition issue), then perhaps they are only making a choice about what is important in favour of the latter over the former. However, the same researchers who practise class erasure in this way do not seem to be working according to such logic, or in any case they do not position themselves according to Fraser's distinction; rather, it seems more likely the case that class is simply not on their radar.

The second approach to class is to mention it in passing, as just another identity dimension, but with no further discussion. Thus class might appear on the tail end of a list of identity dimensions that are considered important in a given context. In this case, class is considered as a social variable, and even worthy of mention, but not, it would seem, worthy of any kind of discussion.

The third approach is to bring class into a discussion of language and identity fleetingly before letting it fade away. A good example of this approach appears in Doran's (2004) excellent account of the uses of Verlan among the children of working-class immigrants in Paris. Verlan is a variety of French that has arisen among French minority youth, incorporating vocabulary from a wide range of immigrant languages (from Arabic to Romani to English) and other features such as syllabic inversion (the term derives from the inversion of syllables in the French word for backwards, *l'envers*). Doran found that Verlan acted as an important in-group identity marker among immigrant minority youth, and at one point in her analysis she introduces the class position of its speakers as significant. She writes about how:

[f]or many of these minority youths, their sense of difference from 'les Francais' was not simply about a difference in skin color, but also about a relation of alterity to the class status and value system of 'le bourgeois', the idealized figure of the French 'citoyen'.

(Ibid.: 114)

Several quotes taken from her contacts with informants make the point well that the use of more standard (or 'elevated') French not only means selling out to dominant French values, but it also constitutes 'showing off' or 'acting *bourgeois*' (ibid.: 115), and ultimately is a form of class betrayal.

Doran concludes her two-page discussion of class as a factor in the use of Verlan by returning to the notion that the variety serves as 'a means of asserting group identity and solidarity, and simultaneously resisting the authority (and hegemonic ideology) of the dominant ideology' (ibid.). However, she does not delve deeply into the class angle, which means for example that she does not make connections between the working-class behaviour of the young people in her study and the working-class behaviour of young people who might be classified as autochthonous French. The issue is worth exploring because it is difficult to imagine that for the latter group speaking 'elevated French' would be an acceptable option in a conversation. There is thus space for exploring working-class masculinity as a phenomenon that cuts across the minority or non-minority condition of young men in France, and indeed in any other contexts around the world (Block and Corona 2014, this volume).

Elsewhere, in her groundbreaking book *Identity and language learning: gender, ethnicity and educational change*, Norton (2000) exemplifies what might be seen as a fourth approach to class, as she invokes the construct more explicitly and in more detail than Doran and others in her study of five immigrant women in Canada in 1989–1990 and their relative and variable access to English in classroom and naturalistic settings. This occurs above all in two cases discussed in the book: Katarina, a Polish woman in her mid-thirties, and Felicia, a Peruvian woman in her mid-forties. The former had recently immigrated with her husband and, despite having an MA in Biology and self-reported proficiency in Czech, Slovak, Russian and German, she had to take a job as a kitchen help in a German restaurant due to her low English language proficiency. This was a position far below what she had been accustomed to in Poland, where her academic qualifications and multilingualism counted for something. Katarina was all too aware that her effective 'declassing' (and 'reclassing')[2] was to a great extent due to her limited English and, as

Norton notes, 'she was very eager to learn it so that she would become part of a social network of people who would value the professional status she had acquired in Poland' (ibid.: 92). To make matters worse, Katarina's husband was in a similar position, as a professional 'declassed' by his lack of English language competence. In Katarina's recounted experiences we see elements of what Sennett and Cobb (1972) long ago termed the 'hidden injuries of class', that is, the personal anguish, disappointment and shame felt by people who have not achieved as much as they might have in life in terms of material wealth, education, housing and a long list of class indexicals. The difference is that in this case we are talking about the hidden injuries of 'declassing' (and 'reclassing') that come with migration experience.

Meanwhile, Felicia made clear to Norton from the start that she and her family had left behind in Peru a home in an exclusive neighbourhood in Lima, a second home at the beach, extensive holiday travel and private schools for their three children, all of which had been provided by her husband, who was described as 'a successful businessman'. The reason for the family's move to Canada was a fear of 'terrorism' even if, in her contacts with Norton, Felicia often presented her past life in Peru as a relaxing idyll. Indeed, Felicia was a conflicted individual, struggling to establish and maintain a coherent narrative as an upper-class woman in a country and local context in which she worked as a babysitter and delivered newspapers, while her husband struggled to secure a stable job. For Felicia the hidden injuries of declassing made her bitter as she oscillated between trying to present herself to others as someone to be reckoned with, for example by talking about property that she and her husband had in Peru or by criticising the way Canada treated more privileged immigrants like herself who 'lose a lot coming to Canada' (Norton 2000: 56).

Katarina and Felicia were very different people: the former was perhaps more middle class in Poland in educational and occupational terms, while the latter was more upper class in Peru in economic and consumer terms, her class position deriving above all from her husband's occupation and income. However, the two women shared a certain feeling of shame that derived from the feeling of having had income, possessions, status and recognition in their home countries and of having none of these things to a sufficient degree in their adopted home, Canada. It should be added here that Norton does not really explore class along these lines, although she does bring into her discussion the notion of 'legitimacy' derived from her readings of Bourdieu, challenging what she sees as a common assumption in studies of language and identity migration contexts, that 'those who speak regard those who listen as worthy to listen, and that those who listen regard those who speak as worthy to speak' (ibid.: 8).

Such legitimising (and de-legitimising) processes are obviously embedded in relations of power, and Norton in particular follows the Foucauldian notion of micro-level power to complement macro-level institutional power, noting how 'power does not operate only at the macro level of powerful institutions such as legal systems, the education system and the social welfare system, but also at the micro level of everyday social encounters between people with differential access to symbolic and material resources' (ibid.: 7). However, beyond drawing on Bourdieu and Foucault somewhat selectively, Norton only devotes a paragraph to class as a construct (ibid.: 13). It should be noted, however, that Norton's intention was always to focus primarily on ethnicity and gender, as the title of her book suggests.

In research similarly attuned to class (but again, without an in-depth treatment of it as a theoretical construct), Pichler (2009) focuses on the construction of gendered identities among female secondary-school students in London and how these gendered identities intersect with class and race. Drawing on the work of scholars such as Skeggs (e.g. 1997), she focuses on three cohorts: 'cool and socially aware private-school girls'; 'sheltered but independent East End girls';

and 'tough and respectable British–Bangladeshi girls'. While the first group was made up of four distinctly upper middle-class girls, the latter two groups were working class in composition in terms of family income, family dwelling, neighbourhood, parenting at home, the kinds of activities that they engaged in and the kind of talk that they produced.

The private-school girls positioned themselves in multiple domains of activities ranging from their studies to music and sex. Pichler found these girls to be more overtly aware of class than the girls in the other two cohorts as in their talk they made distinctions between state schools and private schools; they talked about university study as a given in their future lives; and they oriented to youth culture from an elite perspective, as nascent cultural omnivores (Warde *et al.* 2007) who could effortlessly consume at 'high', 'middle' and 'low' levels. Meanwhile, the sheltered girls manifested 'an (unexpressed) awareness of a range of pathologizing discourses about working-class adolescents and families, especially about single mothers' (Pichler 2009: 65), which they 'disidentified' with. Instead, they positioned themselves as 'respectable' and, further to this, 'sheltered', that is, as living under the constant vigilance and care of their single mothers (and, as Pichler notes, their absent fathers). Ultimately, they came across as 'responsible with regard to their schooling/education, boyfriends and sexual experiences and as compliant with the mostly strict but loving parenting they experience at home' (ibid.). Finally, the third cohort, the Bangladeshi girls, navigated their ways through family expectations about being 'good' girls and a prototypically working-class toughness via a generally anti-school stance, combined with 'verbal challenges and insults in the form of teasing and boasting' (ibid.: 109), which were 'influenced by ideologies of and norms of British lad(ette)/working class culture' (ibid.: 147).

Still more recently, Shin (2014) discusses her research on the experiences of young Koreans whose families move them to countries such as the Australia, New Zealand, the United States and Canada so that they can receive a part of their primary and secondary education in English. Here we see how her middle-class informants suffered a degree of declassing, along with racism and social exclusion both inside and outside of school. Their reaction was to shift ground, moving to a heightened sense of Korean cosmopolitanism and middle-class entitlement, 'distinguishing themselves from both long-term immigrants in local Korean diasporic communities and Canadians by deploying (as stylistic resources) revalued varieties of Korean language and culture in the globalized new economy' (ibid.: 101). These resources included living in upmarket high-rises in a posh part of Toronto (as opposed to living in Koreatown), keeping up with fashion trends in Korea, frequenting Korean restaurants and karaoke bars, keeping up with K-pop and texting friends using Korean slang.

Shin does a good job of including several of the class indexicals cited in the section above devoted to class. We understand that the Korean families in the study are headed by well-educated professionals with high incomes and that they are accustomed to a certain standard of living in South Korea in terms of housing and consumption patterns. Added to this situation, however, is a very important lifestyle shift for the children of these families, one that relates to social networking, cultural consumption and, above all, symbolic behaviour. In the midst of a hostile English-speaking environment, they find a way to impose cosmopolitanism and Korean-ness onto their otherwise negative and undermining experiences and this allows them to inhabit a higher status and position themselves as superior to their tormentors. They associate with people like themselves (fellow young Korean cosmopolitans) with whom there is a common cultural consumption and above all symbolic behaviour around the body, clothes, speech, food and pastimes. As Shin notes, there is a certain irony in all of this, as the learning of English – the whole point of the family's move in the first place – is relegated to the background. This means that what was to be the acquisition of English as a middle-class marker in South Korea gives way to the display of a Korean-ness as a middle-class marker in Canada.

While Shin's research is certainly a big step towards what I refer to above as fuller class-based analysis, it is really only in Rampton's (2006, 2010) work that we encounter a good example of this approach. In *Language in late modernity*, Rampton (2006) devotes considerable space to an in-depth discussion of class as a construct, and this discussion is intermeshed with his analysis of the everyday interactions of students attending a London secondary school. Rampton's informants speak 'multicultural London English' (Cheshire *et al.* 2011), a dynamic emerging variety that draws on traditional Cockney, as well as the Englishes of the Caribbean, South Asia and the United States, and Rampton focuses on the Cockney features in their speech. He freeze-frames for analysis the instances in which the Cockney is 'mock' (i.e. exaggerated and put on) and stands in contrast to imitations of how middle-class and wealthy people in Britain are supposed to talk – 'mock posh'.

Rampton argues that the production of Cockney, both in unmonitored and 'mock' form, is constitutive of working-class subjectivities, as is 'mock posh', which positions the middle and upper-class 'other' as what these adolescents *are not*. In effect, Rampton is suggesting that the students in his study are doing class in the ways that they use language, an example of 'class in itself' (see discussion above) that contrasts with the same students' reluctance to talk about themselves (and presumably see themselves) as working class in a socio-economically stratified society. Rampton's informants thus display little that could be qualified as 'class for itself' and instead orient to gender, race and ethnicity as markers of who they are, that is, they construct themselves in terms of recognition as opposed to redistribution (Fraser 1995). This occurs despite the fact that the educational equalities wrought by the neoliberal policies enacted by British governments from the early 1980s onwards are clearly in evidence. We thus have the enduring material-based presence of class in contemporary societies, standing in marked contrast to its denial and erasure on the part of those living it. Rampton does not present matters in these exact terms, but it is a strength of his book that it allows the reader to observe how such realities play out and are constructed in the ongoing activity of both teachers and students. Indeed, I am only able to make such a statement because Rampton does the groundwork, combining an in-depth and incisive discussion of class with the careful collection, preparation and presentation of data.

Summary

In this chapter I have attempted to clarify what class means as a construct for language and identity researchers in applied linguistics, covering some of the principal theoretical bases ranging from Marx to Bourdieu. I have also commented on a select few publications (five) that I consider to be representative of different approaches to class in language and identity research over the years, pinpointing what I think they can offer and where I find them lacking. There is, to be sure, a great deal of work to be done. Among other things, researchers would help matters if they actually explained what they mean by class, as we see done in Rampton's work (see also Vandrick 2014). This applies both to applied linguistics as a whole and to research that focuses specifically on language and identity. One problem is that most researchers seem not to have read beyond Bourdieu on the topic and this limits the ways in which they might conceptualise class in their work.

Taking on class in a more explicit manner leads to a second issue: Fraser's important work on the interrelationship between recognition and redistribution. I must say that in recent years when I have spoken to groups of fellow academics and graduate students about class, I have often found a reluctance to engage with the idea that class might be a different sort of aspect of human experience from gender, race, nationality and other dimensions of identity, what Sayer (2005: 87) calls 'identity-neutral' in contrast to 'identity-sensitive' mechanisms (although he does argue for the 'contingent co-presence' of the two). I have also encountered an averseness to the possibility that class might be a central (and indeed, the most important) mediator of people's lives, lest this mean abandoning or lessening the importance of more valued constructs such as race and gender. If we are to move forward with class in language and identity research, scholars in applied linguistics and sociolinguistics will need to think deeply about the issues Fraser raises, which in turn will surely mean a good deal of self-critique and (quite possibly) letting go of some cherished, doxa-like ways of thinking. It should be noted that situating class front and centre in one's research does not mean an abandonment of key identity dimensions such as gender and race; rather, it is an opportunity to explore the ways in which different dimensions of identity, along with class, intersect (see Block and Corona, this volume, for a discussion of intersectionality; see Fraser 2013 for a broader discussion).

Finally, I would like to acknowledge that there are a good number of important issues that I have not been able to cover in this chapter – how to research class in language and identity being a significant one. On the one hand, there is the question of survey-based research on class, such as the work of Savage *et al.* (2013) cited at the beginning of this chapter, which is often juxtaposed to more experientially based research. Researchers need to explore ways of working in a multi-method way when dealing with class, combining surveys with more ideographic methodologies. There is also on the experiential side a certain tension between working at the micro-level of interaction (class emergent in interaction), working with personal narratives of class-based experiences (talk about class) and bringing macro-level political economy perspectives to bear on analysis; for example, examining how the shift from Keynesian economic policies to neoliberal economic policies in Europe over the past four decades has led to a realignment of class politics and practice (Duménil and Levy 2011). Tensions need to be resolved, and the way forward is a multilevelled approach that takes on all of the elements mentioned above (see Buruwoy 2009).

Another issue is the geographical location of research. The five studies highlighted above were based in France (1), Canada (2) and the UK (2). In Block (2014), while I discuss a great deal of work from the Anglophone world, I also manage to include work from India (Ramanathan 2005), South Africa (Blommaert and Makoe 2011), Colombia (de Mejia 2002) and other countries. A key argument in this chapter is that there is a need for a more prominent class angle in language and identity research, and it is worth adding that there is also a need for a more global perspective in this research. As I noted at the beginning of this chapter, the number of publications focusing on class in countries around the world is on the rise. A similar rise is needed in applied linguistics as a whole and specifically in language and identity research.

To conclude, class is a difficult construct, both in conceptual and research terms. However, it holds the promise of helping us develop better understandings of a range of issues related to language and identity in the midst of the current crisis of capitalism, which engulfs and affects us all, albeit in very different and unequal ways. And that is something for all language and identity researchers to bear in mind.

Related topics

Positioning language and identity: poststructuralist perspectives; Critical discourse analysis and identity; An identity transformation? Social class, language prejudice and the erasure of multilingual capital in higher education; Construction of heritage language and cultural identities: a case study of two young British-Bangladeshis in London; Intersectionality in language and identity research; Exploring neoliberal language, discourses and identities; Identity in language learning and teaching: research agendas for the future.

Further reading

Block, D. (2014). *Social class in applied linguistics*. London: Routledge. (This book contains an in-depth theoretical discussion of class: an exploration of the extent to which class has been a key construct in three general areas of applied linguistics – sociolinguistics, bi/multilingualism and second language acquisition and learning research.)

Block, D., Gray, J. and Holborow, M. (2012). *Neoliberalism and applied linguistics*. London: Routledge. (This is the most explicit integration of political economy with applied linguistics to date and it contains multiple references to class, including Chapter 4, which is entirely about class.)

Kanno, Y. (guest ed.) (2014). 'Special issue. Social class in language learning and teaching', *Journal of Language, Identity, and Education*, 13(2). (This forum contains five principal papers plus a commentary piece, all of which focus on class as a mediating construct in research on identity in language learning and teaching.)

Rampton, B. (2006). *Language in late modernity: interaction in an urban school*. Cambridge: Cambridge University Press. (This book is primarily about linguistic ethnographic approaches to interaction taking place in urban school settings in London, but it also contains four lengthy chapters (6–9) on class that constitute the best discussion of the construct for interactional data analysis published to date.)

Notes

1 In this chapter I will use 'class' and not 'social class'. I do so while acknowledging that both terms are used interchangeably in many publications, including Savage *et al.* (2013), cited in the introduction to this chapter, and my own work (e.g. Block 2014). 'Class' has the advantage of being shorter and of working better in adjectival form than 'social class'.

2 'While *declassing* refers to changes in one's life conditions and reference points, specifically the loss of the economic power and prestige and status which previously marked one's class position, *reclassing* is about the reconfiguration and realignment of class position in society due to changes in one's life conditions' (Block 2016: see also Block 2014).

References

Bennett, T., Savage, M., Silva, E., Warde, A., Gayo-Cal, M. and Wright, D. (2009). *Culture, class, distinction*. London: Routledge.

Benwell, B. and Stokoe, L. (2006). *Discourse and identity*. Edinburgh: Edinburgh University Press.

Bernstein, B. (1971). *Class, codes and control. Vol. 1, Theoretical studies towards a sociology of language*. London: Routledge and Kegan Paul.

Block, D. (2012). 'Class and SLA: making connections', *Language Teaching Research*, 16(2): 188–205.

Block, D. (2013). 'Issues in language and identity research in applied linguistics', *ELIA (Estudios de lingüística inglesa aplicada)*, 13: 11–46.

Block, D. (2014). *Social class in applied linguistics*. London: Routledge.

Block, D. (2016). Migration, language and social class, in S. Canagarajah (ed.) *The Routledge handbook on migration and language*. London: Routledge.

Block, D. (forthcoming). The materiality and semiosis of inequality and class struggle and warfare: the case of home evictions, in Spain, in R. Wodak and B. Forchtner (eds) *The Routledge handbook of language and politics*. London: Routledge.

Block, D. and Corona, V. (2014). 'Exploring class-based intersectionality', *Language, Culture and Curriculum*, 27(1): 27–42.

Block, D. and Corona, V. (this volume). Intersectionality in language and identity research, in S. Preece (ed.) *The Routledge handbook of language and identity*. London: Routledge, pp. 507–522.

Blommaert, J. and Makoe, P. (2011). 'Class in class: ideological processes of class in desegregated classrooms in South Africa', *Working Papers in Urban Language and Literacies*, Paper 80. King's College London/Tilburg University.

Bourdieu, P. (1984). *Distinction*. London: Routledge.

Buruwoy, M. (2009). *The extended case method*. Berkeley: University of California Press.

Chen, J. (2013). *A middle class without democracy: economic growth and the prospects for democratization in China*. Oxford: Oxford University Press.

Cheshire, J., Kerswill, P., Fox, S. and Torgersen, T. (2011). 'Contact, the feature pool and the speech community: the emergence of Multicultural London English', *Journal of Sociolinguistics*, 15: 151–196.

de Mejia, A-M. (2002). *Power, prestige and bilingualism*. Clevedon, UK: Multilingual Matters.

Doran, M. (2004). Negotiating between *Bourge* and *Racaille*: 'Verlan' as youth identity practice in suburban Paris, in A. Pavlenko and A. Blackledge (eds) *Negotiation of identities in multilingual contexts*. Clevedon, UK: Multilingual Matters, pp. 93–124.

Duménil, G. and Lévy, D. (2011). *The crisis of neoliberalism*. Cambridge, MA: Harvard University Press.

Eckert, P. (1989). *Jocks and burnouts: social categories and identity in the high school*. New York: Columbia University Press.

Edwards, J. (2009). *Language and identity*. Cambridge: Cambridge University Press.

Fraser, N. (1995). 'From redistribution to recognition? Dilemmas of justice in a "postsocialist" age', *New Left Review*, 212: 68–93.

Fraser, N. (2008). *Adding insult to injury: Nancy Fraser debates her critics* [ed. K. Olsen]. London: Verso.

Fraser, N. (2013). *Fortunes of feminism*. London: Verso.

Fraser, N. and Honneth, A. (2003). *Redistribution or recognition? A political-philosophical exchange*. London: Verso.

Fuchs, C. (2014). *Digital labour and Karl Marx*. London: Routledge.

Ganguly-Scrace, R. and Scrace, T. (2010). *Globalisation and the middle classes in India: the social and cultural impact of neoliberal reforms*. London: Routledge.

Gorz, A. (1982). *Farewell to the working class: an essay on post-industrial socialism*. London: Pluto Press.

Han, C. (2012). *Life in debt: times of care and violence in neoliberal Chile*. Berkeley: University of California Press.

Harvey, D. (2014). *Seventeen contradictions and the end of capitalism*. London: Profile Books.

Ishida, H. and Slater, D.H. (eds) (2010). *Social class in contemporary Japan: structures, sorting and strategies*. London: Routledge.

Jones, S. (2013). 'Great British Class Survey finds seven social classes in UK', *The Guardian*, 3 April [Online]. Available at www.theguardian.com/society/2013/apr/03/great-british-class-survey-seven

Joseph, J.E. (2004). *Language and identity*. London: Palgrave.

Labov, W. (1966). *The social stratification of English in New York City*. Washington, DC: Center for Applied Linguistics.

Marx, K. (1981 [1894]). *Capital. Vol. 3*. Harmondsworth, UK: Penguin.

Marx, K. (1990 [1867]). *Capital. Vol. 1*. Harmondsworth, UK: Penguin.

Masoud, T. (2013). *Counting Islam: religion, class, and elections in Egypt*. Cambridge: Cambridge University Press.

Norton, B. (2000). *Identity and language learning: gender, ethnicity and educational change*. Harlow: Longman/Pearson Education.

Norton Peirce, B. (1995). 'Social identity, investment, and language learning', *TESOL Quarterly*, 29(1): 9–31.

Pakulski, J. and Waters, J. (1996). *The death of class*. London: SAGE.

Pichler, P. (2009). *Talking young femininities*. London: Palgrave.

Piketty, T. (2014). *Capital in the twenty-first century*. Cambridge, MA: Belknap Press.

Polyani, K. (2001 [1944]). *The great transformation: the political and economic origins of our time*. Boston: Beacon Press.

Ramanathan, V. (2005). *The English–vernacular divide: postcolonial language politics and practice*. Clevedon, UK: Multilingual Matters.

Rampton, B. (2006). *Language in late modernity: interaction in an urban school*. Cambridge: Cambridge University Press.

Rampton, B. (2010). 'Social class and sociolinguistics', *Applied Linguistics Review*, 1: 1–21.

Riley, P. (2007). *Language, society and identity*. London: Continuum.

Savage, M., Devine, F., Cunningham, N., Taylor, M., Li, Y., Hjellbrekke, J., Le Roux, B., Friedman, S. and Miles, A. (2013). 'A new model of social class? Findings from the BBC's Great British Class Survey experiment', *Sociology*, 47(22): 219–250.

Savage, M., Silva, E. and Warde, A. (2010). Dis-identification and class identity, in E. Silva and A. Warde (eds) *A cultural analysis and the legacy of Bourdieu*. London: Routledge, pp. 60–74.

Sayer, A. (2002). 'What are you worth? Why class is an embarrassing subject', *Sociological Research* [Online], 7(3). Available at www.socresonline.org.uk/7/3/sayer.html

Sayer, A. (2005). *The moral significance of class*. Cambridge: Cambridge University Press.

Sennett, R. and Cobb, J. (1972). *The hidden injuries of class*. New York: Norton.

Shin, H. (2014). 'Social class, habitus, and language learning: the case of Korean early study-abroad students', *Journal of Language, Identity, and Education*, 13(2): 99–103.

Skeggs, B. (1997). *Formations of class and gender: becoming respectable*. London: SAGE.

Subirats, M. (2012). *Barcelona: de la necesidad a la libertad. Las clases sociales en los albores del siglo XXI* [Barcelona: from necessity to freedom. Social classes at the turn of the 21st century]. Barcelona: Universitat Oberta de Catalunya.

Taylor, C. (1994). The politics of recognition, in A. Gutman (ed.) *Multiculturalism: examining the politics of recognition*. Princeton: Princeton University Press, pp. 25–73.

Thompson, E.P. (1980 [1963]). *The making of the English working class*. Harmondsworth, UK: Penguin.

Touraine, A. (2007). *A new paradigm for understanding today's world*. Cambridge: Polity Press.

Vandrick, S. (2014). 'The role of social class in English language education', *Journal of Language, Identity, and Education*, 13(2): 85–91.

Warde, A., Wright, D. and Gayo-Cal, M. (2007). 'Understanding cultural omnivorousness: or, the myth of the cultural omnivore', *Cultural Sociology*, 1(2): 143–164.

Weber, M. (1968 [1922]). *Economy and society*. Vols 1 and 2. Berkeley: University of California Press.

Wright, E.O. (2005). Foundations of a neo-Marxist class analysis, in E.O. Wright (ed.) *Approaches to class analysis*. Cambridge: Cambridge University Press, pp. 4–30.

Part III

Researching the language and identity relationship

Challenges, issues and puzzles

16

Ethics in language and identity research

Anna Kristina Hultgren, Elizabeth J. Erling and Qumrul Hasan Chowdhury

Introduction

It is unlikely to have escaped anyone's notice that ethics – which we will define initially as 'the "right" thing to do' – is a key part of the research process. There is no shortage of handbooks, edited volumes and dedicated journals devoted to the issue, and most professional organisations, such as the British Association for Applied Linguistics, the Linguistic Society of America, the British Educational Research Association and the British Psychological Society, have ethical frameworks, as do many funding bodies (Oates 2006; Rice 2011). Most universities in an Anglophone research context also have their own ethical guidelines and processes for monitoring adherence to ethical codes. In English-dominant settings at a national level, the United Kingdom and Australia have Human Research Ethics Committees (HRECs); the United States and Canada have Research Ethics Boards (REBs); and New Zealand has Ethics Committees (Wynn 2011). Although ethics codes are probably most elaborated in the field of medicine, few researchers today, irrespective of the discipline in which they work, can avoid reflecting on ethical issues in their research. So for scholars working in applied linguistics, sociolinguistics, TESOL, ELT, applied language studies or a related field, ethics has become an inescapable and intrinsic part of conducting research.

Aimed at applied linguists whose research projects focus on aspects of language and identity, this chapter sets out to encourage researchers to reflect critically and constructively upon ethics when doing language and identity projects. We recommend thinking of ethics, not as a checklist that needs to be completed and never returned to again, but as something that is intrinsic to the research process. The chapter is not meant as a replacement for ethical guidelines offered by institutions or professional organisations, such as the British Association for Applied Linguistics. Such guidelines are certainly relevant to those conducting language and identity research and they should be consulted. Rather, the chapter supplements established guidelines by providing real-world examples of the complexities involved in making 'ethical' decisions in the research process. A key concept is 'ethical literacy', which is

> more than learning how to achieve a favourable opinion from an ethics committee, it is a matter of research quality and integrity. It means encouraging the development of an

attitude to research where ethical issues are foregrounded and one where attention to ethical issues is given throughout the process of conducting research.

(Wiles and Boddy 2013: 1–2)

Becoming 'ethically literate' is a continually evolving process in which there is no end point. No scholar can ever claim to be fully 'ethically literate' as, for every ethical dilemma resolved, new ones will invariably emerge. As a reflection of this, it is becoming increasingly common to establish advisory boards as a condition of funding so that a continuing ethics review can be conducted throughout the project (Hammersley and Traianou 2012). Moreover, in each project, we can try to think of and build on ways to 'do better' in future. In order to do so, we need to continually ask ourselves questions about our research, such as:

Am I making the best use of the data I have gathered? Is my study fairly and accurately representing the participants it has engaged with? What do I need to do besides simply put the results out there? Whom should I be talking to about this research, and how?

(Eckert 2013: 25)

Other questions include: 'Are the people involved in the project being harmed by the research? Are they benefiting from it? Would it be possible/desirable for me to try to enhance that benefit?' (Bond and Tikly 2013: 437). Striving to become 'ethically literate' is a way of making researchers reflect carefully about their responsibilities to everyone who is indirectly or directly involved in or affected by their research: from research participants and collaborators to colleagues, funders, employers, the discipline and society itself.

In what follows, we explore some of the reasons why ethics has become such a crucial issue to researchers today and argue that this should be seen against a backdrop of a wider set of sociopolitical changes as well as intellectual shifts which have taken place in the social sciences, including applied linguistics, over the past decades. We then illustrate some ethical dilemmas in practice through a case study of a research project on attitudes to English language learning in rural Bangladesh before we summarise the chapter. Equipped with the concept of 'ethical literacy' (Wiles and Boddy 2013), we hope the reader will feel empowered to tackle any ethical dilemma that might emerge in the research process. Before we begin, we want to echo the American sociolinguist Penny Eckert that 'no discussion of research ethics can be comprehensive' and that 'all one can hope to do in a chapter on research ethics is raise issues' (2013: 11).

Overview

Ethics: why now?

It is tempting to ask if the increased concern with ethics over the past few decades is a result of humankind generally becoming more 'ethical'. Certainly, there may be some evidence to support this when one considers the rise of transformative and emancipatory projects such as feminism, queer theory and Black Power (Punch 1994) and a general increase in concerns with diversity and equality in many organisations and societal domains. Since the end of the Second World War, there has been a growing consciousness of the rights of the individual (ibid.), with the UN's Universal Declaration of Human Rights adopted in 1948. This came only a year after the drawing up of the Nuremberg Code in 1947, the first research ethics code of conduct, aimed at the medical profession, which had been the source of widespread public condemnation after a revelation that doctors had secretly experimented on inmates in concentration camps in the period around the Second World War (Oates 2006).

However, there are also less altruistic and more critical explanations for the increased concern with ethics. These are to do with the general growth in 'ethical regulation' and the 'audit culture' (Shore 2008; Hammersley and Traianou 2012). Pels suggests that the increased 'legalism' since the 1990s has shifted the emphasis in ethics 'away from research practice to the practice of rulemaking' (2005: 82). More specifically, organisations, including universities and other research institutions, are increasingly obliged to demonstrate that they have protocols and regulations in place and that these are abided by to avoid reproach and litigation. In a questionnaire study exploring academics' perceptions of ethics protocols, only 8 per cent of those who had made an application to their institution's ethics committee believed that the proposed changes would protect informants, while 32 per cent believed that the modifications were 'detrimental to the welfare of the informants or research participants' (Wynn 2011: 99). A common perception among these respondents was that ethics regulations existed more for the purpose of protecting the university than the research participants (Wynn 2011). Critics also argue that ethics codes compromise the researcher's 'sense of personal accountability' (Payne *et al.* 1981: 249), potentially leading to ethical complacency once their project has been formally approved.

Notwithstanding such criticism, it is hard to imagine that some of the research undertaken in the past could be undertaken today. Gone are the days when researchers had carte blanche to treat their research participants as they liked, as in the Milgram human obedience experiment where research participants were led to believe that they would give severe electrical shocks to fellow human beings when pressing a button – and still pressed it. In reality, the person they believed to be subjecting to electric shocks was an actor who only pretended to be in pain. The psychological and sociological impacts on those 'super-obedient' research participants when realising that they were capable of imposing such harm on fellow human beings have been the subject of much discussion. Another example of research that would be unlikely to happen today is the appalling experiments conducted as part of the Tuskegee project undertaken in the southern US from 1932 to 1972 where African-American men with syphilis were withheld treatment and kept unaware of their disease in order for doctors to study its development. In this respect, then, it does seem that some societies have advanced in a positive way – at least as far as human research participants are concerned.

Irrespective of whether societies have become more or less ethical over time, there are other reasons why attention to ethics has increased. An important one is a change in research funding structures. In order to receive funding, researchers must ground their project in an issue that helps solve a key societal issue. For instance, as part of their priority to tackle 'societal challenge', the current Horizon 2020 framework (the European Union's joint framework for research funding) lists among their fundable topics: 'health, demographic change and well-being', 'secure, clean and efficient energy' and 'climate action, environment, resource efficiency and raw materials' (EU 2014). Buzzwords such as 'impact', 'knowledge exchange', 'outreach' and 'public engagement' all reflect this contemporary concern with paying back society for the funding it has invested in research. As far as ethics is concerned, the involvement of additional stakeholders in the research process adds complexity, as there are then more interests at stake.

Another reason, which is particularly relevant to the case study described in this chapter, is globalisation. Transnational research collaboration has become much more widespread over the past decades, and may even be a condition for obtaining funding. The funding for the project described below, for instance, was contingent on building an international research partnership. Such funding structures may privilege projects that are composed of international teams, which raise further challenges of how to conduct research ethically (Robinson-Pant and Singal 2013). We will consider some such issues below.

Epistemology and ethics

The increased concern with ethics is not only a result of sociopolitical changes such as those briefly outlined above, but also of epistemological and ontological shift emanating from within the academy. Epistemology has to do with how claims to knowledge are made and how researchers can be certain that what they are observing is a true and faithful account of their object of study. Ontology, in turn, relates to the nature of things and how concepts should be understood. Of course, the extent to which sociopolitical changes are distinguishable from academic changes is questionable, but we keep them apart here for analytic purposes.

Within the social and linguistic sciences, the concept of ethics has not escaped the post-structuralist turn to complexity, fluidity and relativism which has reconceptualised other key concepts, such as identity, language and gender (for a fuller discussion of such shifts, see Baxter, this volume; Benwell and Stokoe, this volume; Jones, this volume; McAvoy, this volume). As far as ethics is concerned, one outcome of the epistemological shifts which have occurred over the past few decades is an increased realisation that researchers need to move away from thinking of ethics as a set of items to tick off on a checklist, as may happen when they seek ethical clearance for their research project from their institution's ethics committee (a prerequisite in most UK and US universities). Instead ethics is viewed as an intrinsic part of the epistemology, theory and methodology of a research project and is embedded into every step of the research project, from the questions asked to how the findings are reported (e.g. Stutchbury and Fox 2009). There has been a shift from absolutism to relativism and a realisation that this opens up 'a new landscape of ethical dilemmas' (Kubanyiova 2008: 503).

One concrete outcome of the reconceptualisation of ethics within applied linguistics is the well-thought-out guidelines for practice by the professional organisation for applied linguists in the UK: the British Association for Applied Linguistics (BAAL). The guidelines were first published in 1994 because it was felt that applied linguists had specific needs and interests that were not adequately covered by the then-existing guidelines (Rampton, personal communication, 2015; Swann, personal communication, 2015). The guidelines, first produced in 1994 and revised in 2006, are representative of the social turn in the social sciences (Rampton 1994). The aim of the guidelines is declared as such:

> In a changing climate of teaching and research, its suggestions are intended to help applied linguists to maintain high standards and to respond flexibly to new opportunities, acting in the spirit of good equal opportunities practice and showing due respect to all participants, to the values of truth, fairness and open democracy, and to the integrity of applied linguistics as a body of knowledge and a mode of inquiry.
>
> *(BAAL 2006: 2)*

Recognising the multiplicity of stakeholders directly and indirectly involved in a research project, the guidelines are structured around a set of responsibilities that the applied linguistic researcher has to the various stakeholders in research: informants, colleagues, students, applied linguistics scholars in general, sponsors, their institutions and the public.

Another seminal work in ethics which was published around the same time is the book *Researching language: issues of power and method*, co-authored by key figures in applied linguistics including Deborah Cameron and Ben Rampton. Despite it being published more than 20 years ago, this book continues to be relevant because it views ethics as an intrinsic part of methodological choices. Cameron *et al.* (1992) distinguish broadly between 'positivist' and 'non-positivist' epistemologies, and make a further subdivision in 'non-positivism' between 'realist' and 'relativist' epistemologies. Each epistemology is associated with different aims, methodologies and types of relationships between the researcher and the researched upon, and, consequently, with different orientations to ethics. These orientations to ethics are referred to as 'ethics', 'advocacy' and 'empowerment' research, and the accompanying relationships with the researched upon are, respectively, 'research *on*', 'research *on and for*' and 'research *on, for and with*' (Cameron *et al.* 1992: 14–22). Examples of each will be provided below.

A positivist epistemology subscribes to the idea that there is an objectively identifiable truth 'out there' for the researcher to uncover, and the aim is to describe this truth as accurately as possible without it being contaminated by confounding variables. Research in the natural sciences is typically located within this epistemology. An example from linguistic research where a positivist approach might be most appropriate can be drawn from the subdiscipline of phonetics, where physical and acoustic factors shape the object of inquiry. A phonetician would therefore control the study for potentially intervening variables such as speaker sex and age, which distort the pitch and other phonetic factors. The type of ethics associated with such a positivist epistemology is referred to as ethical because the ethical dimension of the work is explicitly acknowledged. There will typically be ethics codes or frameworks in place to protect the anonymity and privacy of participants, to ensure that they are not abused or exploited and to make sure that they are compensated for any inconvenience and discomfort (Cameron *et al.* 1992). However, despite ethical considerations being explicitly acknowledged, the relationship between the researcher and their participants still rests on a model of 'research on' (Cameron *et al.* 1992). In other words, '[h]uman subjects deserve special ethical consideration, but they no more set the researcher's agenda than the bottle of sulphuric acid sets the chemist's agenda' (Cameron *et al.* 1992: 15).

Not all applied linguists and sociolinguists committed to a positivist epistemology subscribe to a 'research on' model. The work of William Labov, who is often credited as the founding father of sociolinguistics, has been cited as an example of an advocacy-oriented positivist conducting 'research on and for' his participants. Labov's positivist commitment is evident in his coinage of the term 'observer's paradox', which captures the idea that sociolinguists' preference for studying naturally occurring speech uncontaminated by the research process is hampered by that very research process. In other words, it rests on an idea that there is an objectively identifiable ontology 'out there' for the researcher to uncover and subsequently report on. Yet, Labov also felt that sociolinguistics had to be socially responsible, a view clearly expressed in his statement on 'Objectivity and commitment in linguistic science' (Labov 1982), which was published as a retrospective account of a lawsuit known as the Ann Arbor case, in which Labov acted as an expert witness. In this case, which was raised by a group of African-American parents in Ann Arbor, Michigan, USA, the parents claimed that their children were being disadvantaged because they were classed as having learning difficulties by the teachers who were unaware of a mismatch between the standard language used in the classroom and the particular linguistic variety AAVE (African American Vernacular English) used by the African-American children. Labov's role in the case was to show how AAVE is just as regular and rule-bound as standard English, contrary to popular belief that it was 'sloppy' and 'lazy'. Labov was also driven by another principle, that of 'debt incurred', which meant that he saw it as his obligation to pay back to the community in return for the data and ensuing knowledge that they had provided him and the science of linguistics with. Cameron *et al.* (1992) refer to this as advocacy research, i.e. the linguistic expert speaks on behalf of a disadvantaged community because they have privileged expert knowledge of things.

The third type of researcher–researched relationship is 'research on, for and with', which would place the researcher under even further obligations. This type of research involves researchers in empowering their participants so that they can speak for themselves. Empowering research is different from an advocacy approach in which an academic expert acts in the interests of a particular community to defend their rights. So, for instance, where an advocacy approach might be adopted by researchers in language documentation and revitalisation who collect data on threatened languages with a view to documenting and preserving them for future generations of speakers (e.g. Rice 2011), empowering research would not assume that such documentation was in the interest of the participants themselves. Some might prefer to bring up their offspring in a non-indigenous language, which will increase their life chances and they might even actively oppose attempts to preserve the indigenous language (e.g. Manatowa-Bailey 2007). As Eckert observes about such cases, '[t]here is an awkward distinction between the interests of speakers and those of science, and it is one that linguists often ignore' (2013: 12). Empowering research is meant to shape every step of the research process from generating a research question, which places the participants' wishes and needs at the heart of its concerns, through to ongoing consultation on analysis and possibly even reporting.

It is probably fair to say that most research conducted in applied linguistics could be described as being 'on and for'. Indeed, it is not entirely surprising that a discipline like applied linguistics is by definition concerned with applying the knowledge it generates to some sort of real-world context. Norton's (2013 [2000]) research on the identities of migrant communities in Canada is an example of this. By shedding light on the narratives of struggle and achievement in learning English both at home and in their workplace, she brings attention to their plight with the hope of improving the experiences of people like them and benefiting the community (see also Andrew 2012, this volume). All the participants involved in these projects could be said to being researched 'on and for', but probably not 'with'. In the report of our own research project below, we will show some of the complexities we encountered in making our research a project 'on, for and with' our participants.

Ethical dilemmas in action

In this section, we will illustrate some ethical issues that can arise in conducting research into language and identity by reflecting on a research project that we were involved in rural Bangladesh. We will consider some ethical dilemmas that arose in practice and how these relate to the frameworks laid out by BAAL and Cameron *et al.* (1992). Before going into the ethical issues that arose, it is first necessary to describe, in brief, the research project.

The research project

The research was designed to investigate the attitudes and aspirations of community members in rural Bangladesh to English language learning and its potential to transform their social prospects, communities and cultural identities (see Erling *et al.* 2012; Seargeant *et al.* forthcoming).[1] The study was conducted in two rural communities (Toke and Shak Char) in Bangladesh, a lower-middle income country that ranks low on the human development index. Two Bangladeshi researchers – one a co-author of this chapter – conducted semi-structured interviews during field visits of five days at each site. In total, 28 people were interviewed, 23 male and 5 female participants, aged between 22 and 62. They were chosen to represent a broad cross-section of people in terms of profession, age, social class, religion and gender. However, despite aiming to have equal participation of women in the study, this was not possible due to familial and social challenges that women face when taking part in research in rural Bangladesh. The participants included a banker, college teacher, politician and religious leader, as well as self-employed workers with roles such as barber, fisherman, farmer, rickshaw driver, cleaner and housewife. There was great variation in the education levels of the participants, with a large number of them reporting very limited formal education and virtually no literacy skills apart from the ability to sign their names.

With regard to English in the research setting, it functions as a foreign language for the majority of the population in Bangladesh, and as a second language only for the elite (Banu and Sussex 2001). English is a compulsory school subject from Grade 1 to 12, and passing of high-stakes assessment in the subject is a requirement for entry into higher education. The language is also strongly perceived as a requirement for employability and economic gain (Seargeant and Erling 2011). Several national curriculum reforms, supported by international development projects, have taken place over the last 20 years to enhance the quality of English language teaching and the proficiency level of the society in English (Hamid and Erling forthcoming). A recent example is the English in Action project, a £50 million English language development project funded by the UK Department for International Development (2008–2017) (see Walsh *et al.* 2013). It was in the context of this project that this research project was conceived.

In a sense, the research was ethically inspired, as it aimed to explore whether there was evidence to support national language education policy discourses, as well as international development discourses, which frame English language skills as having the potential to positively benefit the lives of millions of people (Seargeant and Erling 2011). It was also aligned with aspirations to gain a broader understanding of education in the post-colonial world and to attempt to devise an 'emancipatory, situated and dialogical view of research ethics appropriate for the postcolonial era' (Bond and Tikly 2013: 430). However, given that local communities often have very severe material development needs (e.g. need for clean water, access to the community via reliable roads, and accessible health care), we wanted to explore the extent to which our own ethically driven commitment to the provision of quality ELT in low-income countries cohered with the interests of the communities themselves.

Several ethical dilemmas arose while conducting fieldwork that were not predicted when filling out the required ethical protocol. In the following we will explore some of the most pertinent dilemmas that occurred in three phases of the research project:

1   In developing a research focus;
2   In selecting the research team and collecting the data; and
3   In reporting on the research.

By engaging with these issues honestly, and highlighting the complexity of the decisions we faced in just these three stages of the process (while admitting that there were others that we are not going into detail here), we aim to demonstrate that ethical issues emerge all the time and that no checklist can substitute the need for researchers to be 'ethically literate' in order to manage unforeseen ethical concerns in language and identity research.

Developing the research focus

In a previous section, we outlined BAAL's range of responsibilities to the various stakeholders in applied linguistics research. A multitude of stakeholders with potentially conflicting interests was reflected in our own project. The project was sponsored by the British Council under their English Language Teaching Research Partnership; their mission is to 'create international opportunities for the people of the UK and other countries, and build trust between them worldwide' (British Council 2014). It is no secret that the British Council views the establishment and provision of English language teaching (ELT) programmes as key in creating such 'international opportunities'. As such, it might be said to reinforce hegemonic relations between Western powers and 'developing' nations (e.g. Appleby 2010). Despite their openly declared interests, however, the representatives of the British Council with whom we collaborated were themselves admirably set on fostering honest findings. Like ourselves, they were more than open to the idea that ELT may not be perceived by the communities themselves, particularly in the poorer, rural areas, as enhancing their life opportunities or as a priority for poverty alleviation, and that other issues might be more pertinent to them. We were also aware of the potential unethical idea of perpetuating the hope that learning English will offer unrealistic opportunities for the majority of Bangladeshis to escape poverty (Imam 2005).

As the BAAL (2006) guidelines on good ethical practice in research also point out, relationships between researchers and their sponsors also play a crucial role in how research projects are played out, as our example shows. Although we were uncertain about whether participants would view English as useful, one requirement of the funding was to ensure that the research had practical applications, and this of course put us as researchers under the obligation to come up with something that would be useful for the British Council and, consequently, applicable to ELT. The same situation applied to the Open University, the institution to whom the funding had officially been awarded and with which we are affiliated. The Open University has well-established ELT and teacher trainer projects in several low-income projects around the world, and is funded externally for their work on these. Thus, we felt under obligation not to paint a picture that would be damaging to the funder's – and our employer's – core activities. Luckily the findings complied well with what the funder and our institution would have expected, and do have practical implications for the implementation of ELT initiatives in low-income contexts.

Given our obligations to our funder and employer, it was a challenge for us to also ground our project in the interests of the local community. We had to make an assumption that this research area was worth exploring: the research focus was therefore driven by the researchers and not the participants. Using Cameron *et al.*'s (1992) terminology, the project represented advocacy research, conducting 'research on and for' the community with the assumption that the outcome would benefit the participants, for instance by enhancing opportunities for learning English, or the quality of English language provision provided.

We were also mindful of the fact that any attempt to empower participants by involving them in the project might, in fact, result in a potentially unethical disempowering. The mere fact of taking part in the interview meant a potential loss of income for these participants, several of whom were rickshaw-pullers, fishermen and cleaners, who lived at or below the poverty line. On the other hand, compensating them for taking part in this research might have resulted in participants being overly eager to take part in the research or reproduced common notions about institutions from the Global North (i.e. economically developed nation states, mainly in Europe, North America and Australia) being the benefactors of communities in the Global South (less economically developed countries outside of the aforementioned areas). In an attempt to resolve this dilemma, it was decided that (a) the research would not be participatory (i.e. on and for, but not with), and (b) the participants would be provided with a small, yet significant, token of appreciation in return for being interviewed. The researchers decided that food items would be the most appropriate tokens of appreciation. It remained uncomfortable for the researchers, however, that no matter what they told the participants about them not receiving any direct benefit from taking part in the research project, they were unable to shake the impression that they were creating false hopes and being perceived as potential donors or benefactors. This constituted an ethical dilemma to which there was no easy answer.

Composing the research team and collecting data

Although our research question was grounded in our own and our funder's interests, we did want to involve local people as much as possible in the research project; this intention was also welcomed by the funders. In fact, one of our intentions was to 'bring to the fore the voices and experience of those who have been historically marginalised by the colonial encounter', as suggested by Bond and Tikly (2013: 435). The majority of the funding was therefore used to employ two Bangladeshi researchers, who were to conduct the fieldwork in Bangla, and also transcribe and translate the data into English so that it could be analysed by the non-Bangla-speaking UK-based academics. While this decision may at first seem purely altruistic, it also has its strategic advantages. The funding applied for was rather modest and could not have covered the necessary flights to Bangladesh to conduct the research; it was thus financially necessary to employ local researchers. Furthermore, this decision was beneficial for the research being undertaken: in order to gain access to and develop rapport with the participants, the researchers needed to carry out the research in Bangla, a language in which none of the UK research team had ability. Given that the sites of research were rural areas in Bangladesh that were not easily accessible and rarely receive foreign visitors, it was felt that foreign researchers would significantly disrupt the research environment. While disruption of the research environment cannot be avoided altogether, attempts were made to minimise it by using local researchers.

While attempts were made throughout the project to negotiate its direction with the Bangladeshi researchers and to involve them as much as possible, it was impossible to escape the power asymmetries that arise from this set up: Bangladeshi researchers from a low-income country (albeit affiliated with arguably the most prestigious institute of higher education in Bangladesh) were undertaking research with Bangladeshi, underprivileged communities, under the direction of academics in the UK. So it was the institution in the Global North who conceptualised and defined the research questions and who 'owned' the data, and the researchers from the Global South that were brought into the project to offer, primarily, linguistic and cultural expertise. This highlights that working in a Global South context poses particular challenges because it involves an inherent power asymmetry (see Robinson-Pant and Singal 2013). We attempted to negotiate this asymmetry by 'clarifying the roles, rights and obligations of team members' (BAAL 2006: 8) and by explicitly recognising and discussing the workings of power among the research team (see Bond and Tikly 2013: 437). We also tried to embrace any opportunities for capacity-building and deeper academic collaboration provided through the project – for example, by offering research methods training and exploring further opportunities for research exchanges and co-authoring.

We also recognised that power asymmetries remain even when the relationship between the researcher and the researched does not transcend cultural or ethnic divides. In this project, this was manifested in the fact that the field researchers are both highly educated university employees, living in the capital city of Dhaka, and have high levels of competence in English. While they both have familiarity with and personal connections to the rural contexts they visited, it is very likely that they were viewed by people within the communities they were researching as outsiders with a different social and economic standing, especially in Shak Char, where literacy levels are lower than the national average and poverty levels higher. They thus had to use resources such as local guides and engage in community activities, like participating in cricket matches and drinking tea in the central market place, to establish rapport with participants and gain their trust.

Attempting to embrace the spirit of capacity-building, it was the intention of the directors of this research project to enable opportunities for women, who tend to be underrepresented in Bangladeshi society and academia. Therefore, we wanted women to be both represented in both the research team and the participants, ideally making up at least 50 per cent of the research team and the participants. This, however, turned out to be an unreasonable expectation. The project only had adequate funding for two researchers, who would travel to the research sites together and work as a team. In rural Bangladesh, however, it would have most likely been deemed inappropriate for a woman to travel and work closely with a member of the opposite sex to whom she is not related. Moreover, women might be less inclined to undertake fieldwork that would require them to be away from home for an extended period of time. Thus, we made the choice to engage two male researchers. This posed an ethical dilemma in that our wish to elicit the voices and ultimately improve the prospects of rural women, a marginalised group, had to be overridden by other ethical and more practical considerations to protect our research participants from harm and comply with local norms (in order to navigate this in any subsequent research, we would seek to have a three-person research team made up of two female and one male researcher). The involvement of male researchers also meant that it would be even more difficult to recruit female participants for the research, as women in rural communities generally prefer/are preferred not to interact with men they do not know. In the cases where women were interviewed, the interviews were generally conducted in the women's homes, often with a male family member present, which, again, may have had an impact on the data collected.

Finally, issues arose in this project around obtaining 'informed consent', the process by which participants were made aware of the conditions of their participation in the research. Bryman (2008) identifies informed consent as one of the cornerstones of being ethical, and this consent forms one of the most important aspects of the relationship between researchers and participants (BAAL 2006: 4). It was a goal of this research (and a requirement of the ethics protocol) to obtain informed consent from participants. The BAAL guidelines highlight that participants 'are rarely familiar with the nature of academic activities such as publication or conference presentations, making it difficult for them to give fully informed consent to the use of data' (2006: 4). This concern was exaggerated in this research because many of the participants had very low education and literacy levels. The researchers were concerned that asking participants to sign formal documents would intimidate them from freely expressing their opinions. Moreover, signing or giving a fingerprint is a practice viewed with much suspicion in rural areas, particularly since there is a history of feudal lords taking advantage of people in these areas by asking them to sign documents that they do not understand. Therefore, all statements of informed consent were explained orally, in Bangla, and oral agreement to participate in the research was sought. However, given the educational backgrounds of the participants, and the fact that many of them seemed to be unfamiliar with the concept of research, it cannot be stated with confidence that these participants were fully informed about what they were being asked to be a part of (see Batra 2014). As Shamim and Qureshi (2013) note, there is a need to develop ethical regulations that are appropriate for researchers undertaking research in low-income contexts.

Reporting research: ownership and giving back

An important part of the research process is writing up the results for different audiences, and there can be particular requirements for outputs stipulated by institutions and funders as well as a wish to report back to the community. The power balances that were mentioned above with regards to the composition of our research team became particularly heightened with regards to publication. Being a named author on an internationally recognised publication in English is a highly prestigious accolade for those working in Bangladeshi academia, and can be used to support promotion and build up the status of the academic for further research consultancy, for example. Therefore, the Bangladeshi researchers were both surprised and challenged by the initial assumption of the UK-based researchers that they would be the sole authors of any publications related to the research. This assumption was formed, in part, by training materials on research collaboration that featured in an Open University research leadership course. The guidance on authorship attribution in research collaboration stipulated that 'authors are generally expected to make significant contributions to the design, interpretation and drafting. Contributing to only one of these tasks is sometimes accepted for authorship credit' (Open University 2015: no pagination). It also explicitly states that 'if a collaborator simply collected data – for example, a field worker in another country – that role would normally be acknowledged but would not deserve authorship credit' (ibid.).

However, in projects such as this one that have capacity-building of researchers as part of their ambition, it is unclear how capacity can be built in terms of authoring international, peer-reviewed publications, with all their implicit codes (Lillis and Curry 2010), without having the Global South academics involved in the process of writing. At the same time, this experience of co-authoring (as enacted in this chapter) allowed the Bangladeshi researchers to become more familiar with research norms in the Global North and encouraged them to develop their understanding of intellectual ownership and exercise their critical agency in further projects. The gap in expectations regarding authorship between the Bangladeshi and UK-based researchers highlights the contextually contingent nature of what counts as 'ethical' behaviour. While the training materials on research collaboration had fixed ideas about this – which in itself can be seen as a product of acting 'ethically' and setting out fair and regularised protocols for authorship attribution – the particular context seemed to call for an exception, as otherwise it would arguably have been 'unethical'. As a result, the Bangladeshi researchers have co-authored a number of publications stemming from this work – including this one.

A further ethical dilemma that faced us concerned the research findings and their interpretation. Because of the critical discourses about the spread of English as 'linguistic imperialism' (Phillipson 1992) and established perceptions among the Bangladeshis about English being the displacer of a Bangla-mediated national identity (Imam 2005), we were surprised, when it came to doing the analysis, that the research participants were overwhelmingly positive about English and saw it as an important part of their own, or their children's, potential development. There was virtually no concern expressed that English should be perceived as an imperialist force or a usurper of local identity (Erling *et al.* 2012; Seargeant *et al.* forthcoming). This posed ethical dilemmas in that the findings seemed to have the potential to perpetuate global power divisions between a globally powerful North and a relatively less powerful South. It also caused us to wonder whether the participants were perhaps naive in their perceptions that English had a generally benign presence in their communities, or that by learning it they may be able to change their situation or status for the better. However, at the same time, in wondering this, it also became clear to us that we were imposing a 'we know better' attitude. Ethical literacy forced us to ask ourselves: Who are we to tell people what they do or don't need, or what they should or shouldn't value? If English is part of these people's real or imagined development, who are we to try and quash those dreams?

Other ethical issues arise around liaising with the participants in reporting on the research. In 'empowering research' this is meant to ensure that the participants' voices are accurately represented. However, in this particular context, where participants are of low educational backgrounds and from rural, hard-to-reach areas, keeping up a liaison with them would be logistically challenging – if not impossible. Moreover, as the project data was translated into English, and the findings were also reported solely in English, this would make it virtually impossible for research participants to access. It is perhaps then an ethical weakness of this project – or a failure in the project design – that participants were given no opportunity to assess how they and their views are represented, or attempt made to convert the research into a format or language that the participants could access (presuming that it would be of value or of interest to the community).

Summary

In this chapter, we have given an overview of some of the key issues related to ethics in applied linguistics research that apply to language and identity projects. We have also illustrated some of the ethical dilemmas that applied linguists may come across in the field. The example of the research project highlighted here shows that, despite original intentions, it may become necessary to make changes to how research is conducted due to contextual demands. Similarly, there may be times when, in the process of conducting research, we have to respond in a way that is unforeseen in the planning and ethical guidelines, in order to act more ethically. This requires flexibility and reflexivity. Therefore, the most important conclusion to take away from this chapter is not to think of ethics as a checklist that needs to be completed and never returned to again. Rather, ethics is something that is part of each phase and aspect of language and identity projects, and should inform every decision made. It is also something that is inextricably bound up in the epistemological and ontological choices made from the outset of the project (Cameron *et al.* 1992). To conclude, a researcher needs to demonstrate 'ethical literacy' (Wiles and Boddy 2013) by practising sound judgement, being explicit and reflective about epistemological assumptions, being guided by well-established frameworks, and considering the impact on all stakeholders of each decision made in the research process.

Related topics

Positioning language and identity: poststructuralist perspectives; Ethnomethodological and conversation analytic approaches to identity; Discursive psychology and the production of identity in language practices; The politics of researcher identities: opportunities and challenges in identities research; The significance of sexual identity to language learning and teaching; Disability identities and category work in institutional practices: the case of a 'typical ADHD girl'; Language and identity in the digital age; The future of identity research: impact and new developments in sociolinguistics; Identity in language learning and teaching: research agendas for the future.

Further reading

British Association for Applied Linguistics (BAAL) (2006). *Recommendations on good practice in applied linguistics* [Online]. Available at www.baal.org.uk/dox/goodpractice_full.pdf. (These are the official ethical guidelines set by the British Association for Applied Linguistics.)

Cameron, D., Frazer, E., Harvey, P., Rampton, B. and Richardson, K. (1992). *Researching language: issues of power and method*. London: Routledge. (Published more than two decades ago, this co-authored book by key linguistics scholars remains an accessible must-read for understanding the interrelationship between ethics and epistemology.)

Hammersley, M. and Traianou, A. (2012). *Ethics in qualitative research: controversies and contexts*. London: SAGE. (This book offers a valuable and critical account of the rise of ethics in the modern era.)

Rice, K. (2011). Ethical issues in linguistic fieldwork, in N. Thieberger (ed.) *The Oxford handbook of linguistic fieldwork*. Oxford: Oxford University Press, pp. 407–429. (Rice is a linguistic anthropologist and her fieldwork centres on language documentation. Her chapter discusses some of the ethical issues that abound in linguistic fieldwork.)

Stutchbury, K. and Fox, A. (2009). 'Ethics in educational research: introducing a methodological tool for effective ethical analysis', *Cambridge Journal of Education*, 39(4): 489–504. (Written by educational researchers, this article offers the reader a comprehensive and detailed framework to reflect systematically on ethical issues they are likely to come across in their research.)

Note

1 We gratefully acknowledge the British Council English Language Teaching Research Partnerships for funding this research.

References

Andrew, P. (2012). *The social construction of age identity: the case of Mexican EFL learners*. Bristol: Multilingual Matters.

Andrew, P. (this volume). Constructing age identity: the case of Mexican EFL learners, in S. Preece (ed.) *The Routledge handbook of language and identity*. London: Routledge, pp. 337–350.

Appleby, R. (2010). *ELT, gender and international development*. Bristol: Multilingual Matters.

Banu, R. and Sussex, R. (2001). English in Bangladesh after independence: dynamics of policy and practice, in B. Moore (ed.) *Who's centric now? The present state of post-colonial Englishes*. Melbourne: Oxford University Press, pp. 122–147.

Batra, N. (2014). *Teacher cognitions about the teaching of reading: a case study from a state school in India*. Masters of Research Dissertation, The Open University.

Baxter, J. (this volume). Positioning language and identity: poststructuralist perspectives, in S. Preece (ed.) *The Routledge handbook of language and identity*. London: Routledge, pp. 34–49.

Benwell, B. and Stokoe, E. (this volume). Ethnomethodological and conversation analytic approaches to identity, in S. Preece (ed.) *The Routledge handbook of language and identity*. London: Routledge, pp. 66–82.

Bond, T.N. and Tikly, L.P. (2013). 'Towards a postcolonial research ethics in comparative and international education', *Compare: A Journal of Comparative Education*, 43: 422–442.

British Association for Applied Linguistics (BAAL) (2006). *Recommendations on good practice in applied linguistics* [Online]. Available at www.baal.org.uk/dox/goodpractice_full.pdf

British Council (2014). *ELT Research Partnerships* [Online]. Available at http://englishagenda. britishcouncil.org/elt-research-partnerships

Bryman, A. (2008). *Social research methods.* 3rd edn. Oxford: Oxford University Press.

Cameron, D., Frazer, E., Harvey, P., Rampton, B. and Richardson, K. (1992). *Researching language: issues of power and method.* London: Routledge.

Eckert, P. (2013). Ethics in linguistic research, in R.J. Podesva and D. Sharma (eds) *Research methods in linguistics.* Cambridge: Cambridge University Press, pp. 11–26.

Erling, E.J., Seargeant, P., Solly, M., Chowdhury, Q.H. and Rahman, S. (2012). *Attitudes to English as a language for international development in rural Bangladesh.* ELTRP Report, British Council [Online]. Available at www.teachingenglish.org.uk/publications/attitudes-english-a-language-international-development-rural-bangladesh

European Union (EU) (2014). *The EU framework programme for research and innovation* [Online]. Available at http://ec.europa.eu/programmes/horizon2020

Hamid, M.O. and Erling, E.J. (forthcoming). English-in-education policy and planning in Bangladesh: a critical examination, in R. Kirkpatrick (ed.) *English education policy in Asia and the Middle East.* Dordrecht: Springer.

Hammersley, M. and Traianou, A. (2012). *Ethics in qualitative research: controversies and contexts.* London: SAGE.

Imam, S.R. (2005). 'English as a global language and the question of nation-building education in Bangladesh', *Comparative Education*, 41(4): 471–486.

Jones, L. (this volume). Language and gender identities, in S. Preece (ed.) *The Routledge handbook of language and identity.* London: Routledge, pp. 210–224.

Kubanyiova, M. (2008). 'Rethinking research ethics in contemporary applied linguistics: the tension between macroethical and microethical perspectives in situated research', *Modern Language Journal*, 92(4): 503–518.

Labov, W. (1982). 'Objectivity and commitment in linguistic science: the case of the Black English trial in Ann Arbor', *Language in Society*, 11(2): 165–201.

Lillis, T. and Curry, M.J. (2010). *Academic writing in a global context.* London: Routledge.

Manatowa-Bailey, J. (2007). 'On the brink. An overview of the disappearance of America's first languages: how it happened and what we need to do about it', *Cultural Survival Quarterly*, 31(2): 12–17.

McAvoy, J. (this volume). Discursive psychology and the production of identity in language practices, in S. Preece (ed.) *The Routledge handbook of language and identity.* London: Routledge, pp. 98–112.

Norton, B. (2013). *Identity and language learning: extending the conversation.* 2nd edn. Bristol: Multilingual Matters.

Oates, J. (2006). Ethical frameworks for research with human participants, in S. Potter (ed.) *Doing postgraduate research.* London: SAGE, pp. 200–227.

Open University (2015). *Professional skills for research leaders research collaboration.* Virtual Research Environment (internal online document).

Payne, G., Dingwall, R., Payne, J. and Carter, M. (1981). *Sociology and social research.* London: Routledge.

Pels, P. (2005). 'Where there are no ten commandments': redefining ethics during the *Darkness in El Dorado Scandal*, in L. Meskell and P. Pels (eds) *Embedding ethics.* New York: Berg, pp. 69–99.

Phillipson, R. (1992). *Linguistic imperialism.* Oxford: Oxford University Press.

Punch, M. (1994). Politics and ethics in qualitative research, in N.K. Denzin and Y.S. Lincoln (eds) *Handbook of qualitative research.* Thousand Oaks, CA: SAGE, pp. 83–97.

Rampton, B. (1994). 'Politics and change in research in applied linguistics', *Occasional Papers*, 28. Southampton: University of Southampton.

Rice, K. (2011). Ethical issues in linguistic fieldwork, in N. Thieberger (ed.) *The Oxford handbook of linguistic fieldwork*. Oxford: Oxford University Press, pp. 407–429.

Robinson-Pant, A. and Singal, N. (2013). 'Researching ethically across cultures: issues of knowledge, power and voice', *Compare: a Journal of Comparative Education*, 43(4): 417–421.

Seargeant, P. and Erling, E.J. (2011). The discourse of 'English as a language for international development', in H. Coleman (ed.) *Dreams and realities: developing countries and the English language*. London: British Council, pp. 248–267.

Seargeant, P., Erling, E.J., Solly, M., Chowdhury, Q.H. and Rahman, S. (forthcoming). 'Analysing perceptions of English in rural Bangladesh: insights from postcolonialism and World Englishes', *World Englishes*.

Shamin, F. and Qureshi, R. (2013). 'Informed consent in educational research in the South: tensions and accommodations', *Compare: a Journal of Comparative Education*, 43(4): 464–482.

Shore, C.N. (2008). 'Audit culture and illiberal governance: universities and the politics of accountability', *Anthropological Theory*, 8(3): 278–299.

Stutchbury, K. and Fox, A. (2009). 'Ethics in educational research: introducing a methodological tool for effective ethical analysis', *Cambridge Journal of Education*, 39(4): 489–504.

Walsh, C., Power, T., Khatoon, M., Biswas, S.K., Paul, A., Sarka, B. and Griffiths, M. (2013). 'The "trainer in your pocket": mobile phones within a teacher continuing professional development (CPD) program in Bangladesh', *Professional Development in Education*, 39(2): 186–200.

Wiles, R. and Boddy, J. (2013). 'Introduction to the special issue: research ethics in challenging contexts', *Methodological Innovations Online*, 8(2): 1–5.

Wynn, L.L. (2011). 'Ethnographers' experiences of institutional ethics oversight: results from a quantitative and qualitative survey', *Journal of Policy History*, 23(1): 94–114.

17

A linguistic ethnography of identity
Adopting a heteroglossic frame

Adrian Blackledge and Angela Creese

Introduction

In recent times, scholars in applied linguistics and sociolinguistics have found that language use in late modern societies is changing. Rather than assuming that homogeneity and stability represent the norm, mobility, mixing, political dynamics and historical embedding are now central concerns in the study of communication (Blommaert and Rampton 2011). As large numbers of people migrate across borders and as advances in digital technology make available a greater range of linguistic resources, so communication patterns are changing. In these conditions the notion of separate languages as bounded systems of specific linguistic resources may be insufficient for analysis of language in use and in action (Jørgensen *et al.* 2011). The idea of 'a language' therefore may be important as a social construct but it is not suited as an analytical lens through which to view language practices. In this chapter we discuss the limitations of an approach to understanding language and identity for scholars in applied linguistics that relies on the naming and separation of languages – that is, an approach that relies on the concept of multilingualism to describe the identities of speakers in the context of language contact.

There are implications of research findings into language use in contexts of superdiversity for policymakers in the areas of education, community relations, international affairs and public opinion. Cultural dynamics are intimately bound up with the negotiation and performance of the politics of identity, and the data we present in this chapter bring into question the usefulness of long-held and cherished categories such as 'monolingual', 'bilingual', 'multilingual', 'majority' and 'minority' as classifications of people. These groupings have influenced the organisation of practices in schools and the development of policies in educational, health and other social policy domains. Furthermore, as local, national and federal governments seek to tailor policy to the needs of individuals and groups, we argue that people's identities be considered not in terms of apparent or visible categories, but rather as emic positions which are self-identified. Linguistic ethnography is central to achieving this local perspective. From this view, identities should be understood as shifting rather than stable and subject to contingencies of time and space. Additionally, they should be understood as responses to complex, dynamic societies in which subject positions orient to the old and the new, the permanent and the ephemeral, the local and the global, and the collective and the individual. That is, identities are neither fixed nor unitary but are bound up with overlapping histories and are best understood through an ethnographic lens, as this examines the fine grain of local interaction in the light of these histories and social structures.

In this chapter we argue that applied linguists undertaking language and identity studies have much to learn from Bakhtin's notion of 'heteroglossia'. Bakhtin's (1984) concept of heteroglossia views the utterance as socially, politically and historically 'entangled' with the voices of others. Adopting this perspective foregrounds the complexity of communication and identity in the contemporary world. Heteroglossia is a key approach to interrogating linguistic practice because it goes beyond analysis of the co-occurrence of languages and varieties, to focus on the coexistence of competing ideological points of view that are indexed by language in certain communicative situations (Androutsopoulos 2007).

However, we will argue that it is not sufficient to develop a theoretical orientation to language and social diversity in superdiverse contexts. We must also reflect critically on the means by which we gather evidence of complex communication patterns and the ways in which we may view those communication patterns from the perspective of their authors. There are also significant challenges in describing this complexity. Vertovec (2011: 90) calls for 'fresh and novel ways of understanding and responding to such complex interplays', while Blommaert *et al.* (2012: 9) suggest that new forms of diversity raise methodological issues that cannot be addressed by means of the 'modernist paradigm'. In this chapter we consider the affordances and limitations of a linguistic ethnographic approach to language and identity. The chapter is organised along the following lines. The following section provides an overview of key terminology and theoretical framing that sets up the discussion of empirical data in the final section. This final and substantial segment of the chapter provides a critical reflection on how an ethnographic approach brings data and theory together and illustrates this journey through analysis of four detailed transcripts.

Overview

Heteroglossia

Sociolinguistic study of multilingualism has moved away from a view of languages as separate, bounded entities, to a view of communication in which language users employ the linguistic resources at their disposal to achieve their communicative aims as best they can (Jørgensen *et al.* 2011). Rather than taking the named language as the unit of analysis, Blommaert and Rampton (2011: 1) propose that 'it is far more productive analytically to focus on the very variable ways in which linguistic features with identifiable social and cultural associations get clustered together whenever people communicate'. Makoni and Pennycook (2007) argue for an understanding of the relationships between what people believe about their language (or other people's languages), the situated forms of talk they deploy and the material effects – social, economic, environmental – of such views and use. Recently, a number of terms have emerged, as scholars have sought to describe and analyse linguistic practices in which meaning is made using signs flexibly. These include, among others:

- Flexible bilingualism (Creese and Blackledge 2010);
- Codemeshing (Canagarajah 2011);
- Polylingual languaging (Jørgensen 2010; Madsen 2011);
- Contemporary urban vernaculars (Rampton 2011);
- Metrolingualism (Otsuji and Pennycook 2011);

- Translingual practice (Canagarajah 2013); and
- Translanguaging (García 2009; Creese and Blackledge 2011; García and Li Wei 2014).

The shared perspective represented in these various terms considers that meaning-making is not confined to the use of languages as discrete, enumerable, bounded sets of linguistic resources. Rather, signs are available for meaning-making in communicative repertoires (Rymes 2010) which extend across languages and varieties that have previously been associated with particular national, territorial and social groups. These terms, different from each other yet in many ways similar, represent a view of language as a social resource without clear boundaries in which the speaker is at the heart of the interaction.

Recently sociolinguists have turned to Bakhtin's term 'heteroglossia' to better understand the diversity of linguistic practice in late modern societies (Blackledge and Creese 2014). Bakhtin (1981: 291) argued that language in use and in action represents 'specific points of view on the world, forms for conceptualizing the world in words, specific world views, each characterized by its own objects, meanings and values'. That is, language points to, or 'indexes', a certain point of view, ideology, social class, profession or other social position. Heteroglossia is therefore not only – in fact not principally – about the simultaneous use of languages but rather refers to the coexistence of different competing points of view, whether constituted in a single national language (as Bakhtin proposed) or within the complex communicative repertoires in play in superdiverse, late modern societies. Bakhtin's heteroglossic lens leads to a conceptualisation of language that differs quite radically from the traditional view of language (and language teaching) in applied linguistics. The application of Bakhtin's literary theory in current studies in applied linguistics is explained through the work of contemporary scholars.

Pietikäinen and Dufva (2014) adopt the term 'languaging' in preference to the notion of unitary monolithic language, emphasising the notion of language as 'doing', 'action' or 'activity' and describing language in terms of a dynamic set of interconnecting and shifting, essentially multilingual, language practices. Heteroglossic languaging thus avoids seeing language as singular, and avoids viewing multilingualism in terms of enumeration of languages. Heteroglossia is a concept that highlights the essential variability present in all human languaging, not only in contexts traditionally seen as multilingual. Pietikäinen and Dufva (2014) argue that taking heteroglossia as a default assumption embeds a redefinition of language itself, but also reconceptualises such notions as 'speaker', 'language learning', 'native speaker' and the like. Madsen (2014) refers to Bakhtin's distinction between 'centripetal' and 'centrifugal' forces in discourse. A centripetal force draws features, structures and norms towards a central unified point, while a centrifugal force works in the opposite direction, drawing away from the central unified point towards variation in all directions. This distinction is often understood to refer to centripetal forces that result in language standardisation and centrifugal forces that result in language variation. Madsen notes, however, that both sets of forces are at work in discourse.

Bailey (2012: 508) argues that what is distinctive about heteroglossia 'is not its reference to different kinds of linguistic signs and forms, but rather its focus on social tensions inherent in language'. The use of words in a certain way indexes particular social position(s) because these words are characteristically used by members of a specific group. Wortham (2008) similarly notes that a voice indexes a social position in the stratified world, as presupposed by stratified language. Bakhtin saw that what we talk about most are the words of others, such that our speech is overflowing with other people's words. Any utterance, in addition to its own themes, always responds in one form or another to others' utterances that precede it; speech inevitably becomes the arena where viewpoints, worldviews, trends and theories encounter each other.

Bailey (2012: 504) summarises heteroglossia as 'the simultaneous use of different kinds of forms or signs, and the tensions and conflicts among those signs, on the sociohistorical associations they carry with them'.

These arguments have significant repercussions for applied linguistics. For example, the intensely social and constructed approaches these authors develop clash significantly with much cognitive and psycholinguistic research and their 'within' approaches to understanding language acquisition. In much of the SLA paradigm the human brain is conceptualised as dealing with languages as discrete systems, which researchers subsequently go on to measure in terms of proficiency judged against an idealised native speaker. Such approaches are not interested in the complexity of the social context, social relations and the array of sign types in use. A heteroglossic lens also has significant implications in terms of pedagogy and the L1/L2 divide. For many years scholarship in communicative language teaching, particularly in the field of English as a Foreign Language (EFL) and English as a Second Language (ESL), has argued that the target language and the first language of the language learner (viewed as having a distinct L1) should be kept separate. However, this perception is being increasingly questioned by a range of scholars. Although these issues are significant in the field of applied linguistics, our focus here is on heteroglossia, identity and ethnography rather than specifically on pedagogy or different disciplinary perspectives. For a very helpful overview of these issues see Jørgensen and Møller (2014).

What we propose is an analytic gaze that takes as its focus speakers as social actors deploying heteroglossic linguistic resources to negotiate the social world. Such an analytic gaze 'encourages us to interpret the meanings of talk in terms of the social worlds, past and present, of which words are part-and-parcel, rather than in terms of formal systems, such as "languages", that can veil actual speakers, uses, and contexts' (Bailey 2012: 502).

Heteroglossia and identity

Riley (2007) points to an increasing weight of interdisciplinary evidence that identity is socially constructed and that our sense of self can only emerge as the result of communicative interaction with others; the chapters in this book reinforce this point. Blommaert and Varis (2013: 146) have developed a four-tiered framework for investigating complex and dynamic identity processes, as follows:

1   Identity discourses and practices can be described as discursive orientations towards sets of features viewed as emblematic of particular identities. That is, through our repertoires we take positions in relation to stereotypical identities. This positioning is dynamic, as we at times affiliate with these identities and at times distance ourselves.

2   These features are not randomly distributed in a free-for-all, but are more often presented in specific arrangements and configurations. (We illustrate this below when heavily normative classroom discourse patterns are used by the teacher to play creatively with language and identity positioning.)

3   One has to have enough of the emblematic features in order to be ratified as an authentic member of an identity category, which means that some social actors are held to be inauthentic and lacking legitimacy if the right constellation is not evident.

4   These processes involve conflict and contestation, and are highly dynamic: configurations of features and criteria of authentic membership or belonging can be adjusted, reinvented and amended.

Emblematic features include the way people speak, the way they text (in SMS messages), the way they update their Facebook profile, the way they dress, the food they eat, the beverage they prefer, the music they listen to, the films they enjoy, the novels they read, and so on. Judgements about whether a person has (or performs) enough of the requisite emblematic templates to be accepted as, or endowed with, membership of a particular identity or group is highly nuanced and not always negotiable (Pavlenko and Blackledge 2004). Some may not have access to the necessary resources, while others may be viewed as fake members of an identity category. Moreover, it is likely that in picking our way through the complex and dynamic processes of identity negotiation, we develop a heteroglossic 'identity repertoire' (Blommaert and Varis 2013: 157) which enables us to adapt to the contingencies of social life. In this conception of identity, emblematic features are empirically observable and can be investigated ethnographically. Emblems of identity are not merely psychological, but are corporeal and performed as practice. This is true of the clothes we wear, the music we listen to, the sport we play, and so on. It is also true of the way in which we deploy heteroglossic linguistic resources. Our accents, vocabulary and grammar are material resources that index our individual histories and trajectories.

Gal (2006) points out that in Europe a new elite of multilingual speakers of, for example, French, German and English sustains a breadth of linguistic repertoires that transcends national boundaries. For these elite groups, ethnolinguistic identity may be only an occasional issue. But for multilingual speakers of languages with lower status, language issues are likely to be more salient as they negotiate identities often from relatively powerless positions. Language ideologies are neither simple nor monolithic, however. Notwithstanding the argument that minority language speakers are subject to the pervasive ideology of the dominant language, some speakers who (or whose families) may traditionally have been associated with minority ethnic languages are using language and languages in new ways (Rampton 1995, 1999). While some speakers are either unable to negotiate their identities from inextricably powerless positions, and others in powerful positions have no need to do so, some speakers in modern nation states are using their linguistic skills to negotiate new subject positions (Blackledge and Pavlenko 2001; Pavlenko and Blackledge 2004). In what Gal (2006: 27) describes as 'self-conscious, anti-standardizing moves', such negotiations may include linguistic practices that reframe previous standard varieties, incorporating, inter alia, urban popular cultural forms, minority linguistic forms, hybridities and inventions. Here language practices associated with immigrant groups no longer represent backward-looking traditions but may be linked to global youth culture and urban sophistication. Languages and language practices are not necessarily equated to national identity (but may be so) and are not necessarily dominated by the standardised variety. Despite powerful ideologies of homogeneity, populations in many countries – especially countries with a history of recent immigration – continue to be heterogeneous in their practices.

Jørgensen (2010) points to the fluidity of late modern society, in which identities are not necessarily imposed from above, but may be negotiable within certain social settings. Jørgensen proposes that language users create, construct and negotiate identities on the basis of a range of resources. To the extent that such resources are part of language, identities are constructed and negotiated in linguistic discourse. Identities are performed, constructed, enacted and produced in communication with others. That is, 'identities arise in interaction among people' (ibid.: 4). As such, identities are to a large extent subject to negotiation. García (2010) refers to the role of language diversity in the negotiation and construction of identity and suggests that language choice involves negotiation in every interaction, as particular linguistic resources may provide or prevent access to powerful social networks. That is, multilingual speakers 'decide who they want to be and choose their language practices accordingly' (ibid.: 524). However, it is important to remember that not all linguistic resources are equally available to all speakers at all times (Creese *et al.* 2006). Certain subject positions may either be non-negotiable, or only partly negotiable, in particular places and at particular times, as social contexts prevent individuals from accessing resources (Pavlenko and Blackledge 2004). The relationship between language in use and action and the ascription, performance and negotiation of identities is therefore dynamic and complex.

Researching heteroglossia and identity: an ethnographic approach

What we have argued so far is that when people communicate they position themselves and others in the social world. They do so through the deployment of linguistic (and other semiotic) resources with recognisable associations. Some linguistic resources point to certain types of profession, sets of beliefs or socio-economic categories. However, the relationship between linguistic resources and belonging to social groups is not straightforward or linear. When membership of a group may be (perceived to be) faked and when stylisation, irony, parody, satire, mockery, pastiche and so on are commonplace, it is clear that the ways in which identities are performed linguistically are highly nuanced and may best be understood through detailed and repeated observation. We therefore turn to linguistic ethnography as an approach to the investigation of heteroglossia and identity.

Copland and Creese (2014) point out that linguistic ethnography is equipped to study local and immediate action from the point of view of social actors and to consider how (inter)actions are embedded in wider social contexts and structures (see also Pérez-Milans, this volume). They argue that linguistic ethnography views language as communicative action functioning in social contexts in ongoing routines of people's daily lives. In doing so, a linguistic ethnographic approach is able to investigate how language resources are deployed and what this can tell us about wider social constraints, structures and ideologies. In linguistic ethnography, researchers analyse linguistic and other semiotic signs (that is, appearance, gesture, gaze, etc.) as social phenomena open to interpretation and translation, but also predicated on convention, presupposition and previous patterns of social use and social action. Because the sign is the basic unit of meaning, linguistic ethnographers are keen to understand how it is interpreted within its social context. Through rich description, the recording of audio and video files, a range of interview techniques and the collection of other textual documents, researchers attempt to understand the relevance of signs in ongoing communicative activity and situated multimodal social action.

Blommaert (2007: 682) argues that ethnography does not attempt to reduce the complexity of social events by focusing a priori on a selected range of relevant features, 'but it tries to describe and analyse the complexity of social events *comprehensively'*. It is the comprehensive description and analysis of the complex social world that confronts researchers as a challenge. Blommaert and Rampton (2011: 10) take context as a crucial feature of ethnographic research. They argue that contexts for communication should be investigated rather than assumed. They point out that meaning takes shape within specific places, activities, social relations, interactional histories, text trajectories, institutional regimes and cultural ideologies, produced and construed by people with expectations and repertoires that should be understood ethnographically. Blommaert and Rampton further point out that analysis of meaning should include attention to biography, identifications, stance and nuance as they are signalled in the linguistic and textual fine grain. Blommaert and Rampton propose that it is therefore worth turning to language and discourse to understand how categories and identities are circulated and reproduced in textual representations and communicative encounters. They argue for a combination of linguistics and ethnography, an extension of ethnography into intricate zones of culture and society that might otherwise be missed. An approach that combines linguistics and ethnography and insists on intense scrutiny of textual and discursive detail discloses the ways in which widely distributed ideologies penetrate the world of talk and text. Blommaert and Rampton argue for an ethnography enriched with highly developed heuristic frameworks and procedures for discovering otherwise under-analysed intricacies in social relations. In doing so they propose an approach based in 'ethnographic description of the who, what, where, when, how and why of semiotic practice' (ibid.: 12).

Heller (1984) asked the following key questions, which have been influential in shaping research combining an interest in language and social life and which are helpful for applied linguists doing language and identity studies to keep in mind: 'What is it about the way we use language that has an impact on social processes? What is it about social processes that influences linguistic ones?' (ibid.: 54). In later work, Heller (2008: 250) pointed out that:

> Ethnographies allow us to get at things we would otherwise never be able to discover. They allow us to see how language practices are connected to the very real conditions of people's lives, to discover how and why language matters to people in their own terms, and to watch processes unfold over time.

Heller argued that ethnographies allow us to see complexity and connections and to tell a story that illuminates social processes and generates explanations for why people do and think the things they do. Heller (ibid.) proposed the term 'ethnography of bilingualism' to describe a research process that accepts that 'bilingualism' is a socially and historically produced notion, politically and ideologically embedded and related to identity at global, national and local levels. An ethnography of bilingualism allows the linking of language in everyday life to the trajectories of individuals, the construction of social boundaries and relations of inequality. In more recent work, Heller (2010: 400) further explains that: 'The challenge is to capture the ways in which things unfold in real time, and the ways in which they sediment into constraints that go far beyond the time and place of specific interactions.'

We take up this challenge, proposing an approach that incorporates ethnography of bilingualism, or we should say an ethnography of heteroglossia, that enables us to interpret the meanings of language in use in terms of social worlds past and present.

Linguistic ethnography's strength derives from combining different data collection and analytic processes rather than separating them out. It is in combining approaches that robust and nuanced findings emerge. The generation of knowledge from ethnographic data requires not only that different types of evidence (e.g. field note entries, audio recordings of spoken interaction, SMS messages, interview transcripts, etc.) are analysed in relation to their synchronic and diachronic contexts, but also that they are analysed in relation to each other. That is, rather than remaining decontextualised, they should be linked in the analytic process, so that meanings are produced from the interaction of a number of sources and types of evidence. Analysis of ethnographic data also requires a dynamic interaction between the biographical and historical trajectories of the researcher(s) and the material under scrutiny. A key part of the context of ethnographic material is the collection of that material. Gathering evidential stuff changes it. Field notes, audio recordings, photographs, Facebook updates and so on are not unmodified or raw material. Rather, they are products of the interaction between the researcher(s) and the phenomena under observation. Furthermore, analysing evidential material changes it. As we annotate, code, summarise, link and expand upon the evidence, we bring to bear our own past, present and future. In so doing, we create meanings from the interface between our own experience (including our reading, thinking, talking and listening) and the behaviour and practice (including the linguistic behaviour and practice) of those who have consented to be observed. This is a process that defines ethnography: becoming sufficiently reflexive to recognise that we are not only part of our evidence, but also agentic meaning-makers in the construction of knowledge.

In order to illustrate these points we will briefly offer an example from our recent research. The example is taken from a research project[1] that observed and analysed multilingual practices in different educational sites in four European countries. The UK case study investigated a Panjabi complementary school that was mainly devoted to the teaching of Panjabi. Complementary schools are community-run, often small-scale organisations staffed by community groups. Angela Creese and researcher Jaspreet Kaur Takhi spent nine months observing and writing field notes in all classes in the school. After five months, one class on each of two sites was identified for closer observation, based on the teachers' and students' willingness to participate in the research project. Two students and the teacher and teaching assistant in each class were identified as 'key participants' for focused observation. Key participant students, teachers and teaching assistants were issued with digital voice recorders to audio-record themselves during class time. The key participants were also asked to use the digital voice recorders outside the classroom to record their linguistic repertoires at home and in other environments. The researchers interviewed 15 key stakeholders in the schools, including teachers and administrators, children and their parents. In addition, classroom sessions on each of the sites were video-recorded. In each of two focal classrooms the teacher, teaching assistants and two young people were given audio-recording devices for self-recording. Each week the researchers downloaded the recordings from home and classroom recordings. Interviews were conducted after field visits had ended. Teachers, students, teaching assistants, parents and administrators were interviewed. Here we refer to excerpts from a single interaction that was audio-recorded in one of the classrooms in the Panjabi school.

Extract 1 occurs at the beginning of class. In this interaction, a student, Gopinder (female, aged 15), is audible, along with Komal (aged 17) and the teacher, Gurpal (aged 23).

Extract 1

1	Gurpal:	ok what's a mustachio?
2	Komal:	a moustache
3	Gurpal:	moonsh <i><moustache></i>
4	Gopinder:	mooch mooch is a
5	Komal:	oh moonsh <i><moustache></i>
6	Gurpal:	[laughs]
7	Komal:	moonsh moustache a mustachio what's a mustachio?
8	Gurpal:	[to Gopinder:] not a pistachio
9	Gopinder:	I didn't say mus
10	Gurpal:	mustachio
11	Komal:	mustach
12	Gurpal:	[laughs:] mustachio
13	Gopinder:	what is it?
14	Komal:	what language

15	Gopinder:	can you explain in English? no that's moochaa <*moustache*>
16	Gurpal:	mustachio
17	Gopinder:	is that what Indian people say? No one says mustachio
18	Gurpal:	mustachio
19	Komal:	[laughs:] right
20	Gurpal:	you've learnt a new word, we'll start using mustachio from now on
21	Gopinder:	I said it do you say moochaa <*moustache*> or
22	Komal:	yeah I thought it was moochaa <*moustache*>
23	Gopinder:	I say mooch for English
24	Gurpal:	homework, where's your mustachio man
25	Gopinder:	that sounds like Michelin Man that joke
26	Komal:	right maybe he just can't read

The teacher, Gurpal, introduces the lesson with a question that generically fits the context, asking what appears to be a request for the students to define an unfamiliar word: 'what's a mustachio?' The purpose of the class (and school) is for the students to learn Panjabi. It might therefore be assumed that the teacher would request the meaning of a Panjabi word, or the Panjabi translation of an English word. However, instead, he asks a question that has no readily available 'correct' answer. 'Mustachio' does not appear in the *Oxford English Dictionary*, although 'moustachioed' is listed as deriving from the Spanish *mostacho* and the Italian *mostaccio*. 'Mustachio' has a number of connotations in contemporary popular culture, including a luxurious handlebar moustache, the name of a nightclub in Birmingham and a character in a best-selling video game (Gurpal often referred to the names of video games). While Gurpal's question fits the norms of the language teaching class, it is a parody, or perhaps a pastiche, of the genre. Rampton (2006: 235) distinguishes between 'parody grounded in moral and political criticism of the oppressive distortions of class' and 'pastiche, pleasure in the play of voices'. Komal recognises the 'language teaching' genre and volunteers an answer (line 2). Consistent with the structural norm of Initiation–Response–Feedback (IRF), in line 3, Gurpal offers what appears to be an answer to his question: '*moonsh*'. However, this linguistic feature is straightforwardly associated with neither English nor Panjabi (the norms for this classroom), but Hindi. Gurpal adds to the already heterogeneous nature of the interaction by introducing this word. Gopinder volunteers an answer, '*mooch*' (line 4), an Anglicised version of the Panjabi word *moochaa* (*moustache*). Komal meanwhile, recognising the familiar IRF structure, dutifully accepts her teacher's offer.

In Bakhtin's terms, while the departure from the expected linguistic norms pulls centrifugally, the adherence to structural norms pulls centripetally. The teacher's laughter indicates his amusement at the game, which is neither random nor chaotic, but relies on all participants' shared knowledge of the genre. Komal tries out three of the versions of the word currently in play (line 7) and repeats Gurpal's initial question. However, she does more than merely repeat the question as, in recontextualising it, she portrays and evaluates it. Gurpal keeps up the game, saying to Gopinder 'not a pistachio' (line 8). Gopinder, however, defends herself, again responding within the expected norms. Her refusal to have the 'incorrect' term ascribed to her ('I didn't say' in line 9) indexes her attitude to correctness and academic success, which we saw on many occasions in this class. Gurpal repeats the original term on several occasions (e.g. lines 12, 16, 18), correcting Gopinder's (non-existent) error; again his laughter reveals his amusement. With some exasperation now, Gopinder demands the correct answer – 'what is it?' (line 13) and 'can you explain in English?' (line 15) – while Komal asks 'what language?' (line 14). Gopinder corrects Gurpal, offering the normative Panjabi term '*moochaa*' (line 15). These interjections index the students' orientation to correctness and academic achievement, as they attempt to pull the interaction round to the 'right answer'. The teacher's response is again to merely repeat the original word, prompting Gopinder to ask 'is that what Indian people say?' (line 17). In doing so, she distances herself from 'Indian people', as if they may be so foreign that they use this alien word. Komal, however, seems to tumble the trick, her laughter and intonation in saying 'right' (line 19) expressing both shared amusement and scepticism. Gurpal continues, extending the parody or pastiche of the normative, generic discourse: 'you've learnt a new word, we'll start using mustachio from now on' (line 20) and 'homework, where's your mustachio man' (line 24). Here the informal 'man' provides a signal that the homework task is not serious, but is part of the pastiche. Komal ultimately suggests, in an aside apparently to herself, 'maybe he just can't read' (line 26). This apparent (but not serious) explanation of her teacher's behaviour positions him as the very antithesis of her orientation to academic success.

In Extract 2 Gurpal has turned the focus of the lesson to include discussion of kinship terms, one of the core elements of the curriculum in this school.

Extract 2

1	Sandip:	a brother's wife a brother's wife would call the sister-in-law a nanaan
2		*<husband's sister>* wouldn't they?
3	Gurpal:	[to Simran:] he would call you bhabbi *<brother's wife>* because he's
4		younger than you
5	Simran:	he wouldn't call me bhabbi *<brother's wife>*
6	Gurpal:	no I mean your, no you, his wife would call you bhabbi *<brother's*
7		*wife>* yeah
8	Komal:	yeah yeah because my mum calls my chachi ji *<father's brother's*
9		*wife>* nanaan *<husband's younger brother's wife>* what's dehraani?
10		*<husband's younger brother's wife>*
11	Sandip:	I think it's the same thing isn't it?
12	Komal:	is it?
13	Gurpal:	because he's younger than you; if he's older than you then he
14		wouldn't, then she wouldn't call you bhabbi *<older brother's wife>*
15	Sandip:	why do they make everything so complicated?
16	Komal:	isn't it the oldest wife is bhabbi ji *<older brother's wife>*
17	Shaan:	I am just going to call them by their names
18	Komal:	like the oldest one
19	Gurpal:	yeah nobody uses these words, but they're good to know
20	Sandip:	err no, because my chachi *<father's younger brother's wife>*
21	Gurpal:	because when you go to India that's, these are the words that they use
22		in India, they wouldn't say to you tere phraa di boti kiddha *<how is*
23		*your brother's wife?>* they will say you know teri bhabbi *<older*
24		*brother's wife>* you know they call her bhabbi *<older brother's wife>*

Agha (2007: 342) proposed that analysis of how kinship behaviours are performed and construed in context reveals that much of the complexity of kinship relations derives not from disembodied ideas in the head, 'but from models of social relationship inferable from text-in-context relations among perceivable signs'. Across data sets in this study (field notes, interviews, transcripts of audio-recordings) kinship terms were represented in Panjabi, and were not translated into English. Translation into English appeared to deplete the richness of familial relations available to the speakers. The students and teacher do not appear to have language boundaries in mind as they discuss kinship terms in their families. They have a bank of linguistic resources that they draw on together, sharing a common knowledge (if partial knowledge) of family relations. In Extract 2 Simran contests the teacher's answer ('he wouldn't call me *bhabbi*', line 5), while Sandip ('why do they make everything so complicated?', line 15) and Shaan ('I am just going to call them by their names', line 17) take a stand against the necessity to become familiar with the complex system of kinship terms. Both of these positions appear to be acceptable in the inclusive ecology of this classroom.

Furthermore, in the terms of García and Li Wei (2014), this section of discourse is likely to strengthen the students' metalinguistic awareness and cross-linguistic flexibility. In addition to quick-fire metasemantic negotiations about the labelling of particular kinship terms, language comments on itself metapragmatically (Silverstein 1993) and meaning is made visible through metacommentary – i.e. through comment about language (Rymes 2014: 314) (e.g. 'nobody uses these words, but they're good to know', line 19). Gurpal aligns himself as a member of the same group as the students: somebody with a knowledge of, and proficiency in, kinship terms that might index a greater investment in 'Indianness', or 'Panjabiness'.

Now the lesson turns to the not uncommon task of students composing sentences in the target language (Panjabi) on the theme of 'what I did on my holidays'. Ten-year-old Himmat is the first to present his sentences to the class. Pavan, the 19-year-old teaching assistant, is shocked that Himmat claims to have gone to the cinema to watch a horror film.

Extract 3

1	Himmat:	mair cinema gaya si mair dukaan gaya si <*I went to the cinema, I went*
2		*to the shop*>
3	Pavan:	what did you watch in the cinema?
4	Himmat:	*Little Red Riding Hood*
5	Komal:	[laughs]
6	Pavan:	isn't that a horror film? [laughter] why did you watch it? why do your
7		parents let you watch it?
8	Komal:	you didn't go, your parents, no, no dude
9	Pavan:	Himmy Himmy Himmy your mum would not let you see that, and
10		neither would your dad
11	Himmat:	no I got it on piracy copy
12	Komal:	so you didn't go to the cinema?
13	Gurpal:	ok guys listen, I think we are missing the point here, it's sentence
14		structure that we are looking at
15	Komal:	[ironically]: yeah, but illegal, you know, illegal activities
16	Pavan:	your sentences were good but you watch illegal DVDs [class laughs]
17	Komal:	that's not good
18	Sandip:	I bet it was Chinese man
19	Gurpal:	after you've finished mair vi dekhlunga <*I will see it too*> [class
20		laughs]

Amid some scepticism about Himmat's story from Pavan and the other students, Gurpal points out that this is an academic exercise about practising sentence structure ('I think we are missing the point here', line 13). Komal in particular is willing to gently tease the young student (e.g. line 15), while Pavan is able to simultaneously praise him and tease him ('your sentences were good but you watch illegal DVDs', line 16). Gurpal's second intervention serves to position himself as a member of the youth group interested in the pirated DVD (line 19), while at the same time modelling heteroglossic discourse that calls for comprehension of the mixed code in order to understand his joke ('after you've finished *mair vi dekhlunga*'). Gurpal flattens the distinction between teacher and students, translanguaging for identity investment and cultural engagement.

The prescribed classroom activity prompts a discussion of what Sandip (male, 17 years of age) did during the school holidays. The gurdwara is the local place of worship for members of the Sikh religion:

Extract 4

```
 1  Sandip:   [shouts:] I went to the gurdwara three days in a row
 2  Komal:    did you have an akhand path? <72 hours of continuous
 3            prayer>
 4  Sandip:   and then I got constipation. My days
 5  Komal:    dude, dude
 6  Sandip:   [laughs]
 7  Komal:    I don't want to know about this
 8  Sandip:   the rotiyaan <chapattis> are hard as rock I'm not even joking
 9  Komal:    did you not make them?
10  Gurpal:   listen
11  Sandip:   no, at the gurdwara
12  Gurpal:   don't bad mouth the roti in the gurdwara, those rotiyaan are for people
13            who don't get roti
14  Simran:   yeah, seva <selfless service>
15  Sandip:   no, cos they're usually, they're usually dank, they're usually dank,
16            they're usually dank
17  Komal:    I love the gurdwara food to be fair
18  Gurpal:   there you go
19  Sandip:   no, I do like it, it was just that weekend I think it was cos my thyee
20            <father's older brother's wife> was cooking
21  Komal:    [laughter] don't diss your thyee <father's older brother's wife>
```

In Extract 4, the discussion moves forward confidently, retaining Panjabi for terms associated with Sikhism and kinship. Sandip describes his commitment to the religious practice of undertaking 72 hours of continuous prayer. However, he does so through a mini-narrative that partly usurps this serious cultural-religious practice ('I got constipation', line 4). Gurpal acts as a moderator of cultural values here, intervening in the discussion to insist that there should be no criticism of the emblematic 'roti', bread served at the gurdwara to any poor person who may come looking for a meal (line 12). He finds support from Simran ('yeah, *seva*', line 14) and Komal ('I love the gurdwara food to be fair', line 17), and Sandip concedes with a more emollient 'no, I do like it' (line 19), although in doing so he runs up against Komal's family values (line 21). The exchange provides examples of young people being light-hearted but also serious about their cultural heritages.

However, this is not an example of heteroglossia that merely moves between 'English' and 'Panjabi'. A more nuanced analysis reveals that the young people adopt a discourse that is sharply aware of terms emblematic of certain cultural values and traditions (e.g. '*seva*', '*akhand path*', '*roti*') and kinship ('*thyee*'). Furthermore, this is not a binary discourse. A more helpful lens than language(s) here is that of register, as the young people adopt a discourse that positions them as urban, sophisticated speakers of a repertoire which includes non-standard terms commonly understood (by them at least) to index a youthful, 'cool' positionality: 'my days', 'dude', 'I'm not even joking', 'bad mouth', 'dank', 'to be fair', 'diss'. Such discourse is rapidly mobile, and at the time of writing, a year or two after the interaction itself, these same terms are no doubt as uncool as can be. At the time, however, they served as part of a repertoire that indexed a common identity position for this group of young people.

So how does an analysis based on Bakhtin's notion of 'heteroglossia' illuminate our understanding of the 'identities' of these young people and their families? Certainly we are not able to make arguments based on the very small fragments of material presented in this chapter. However, when we view them alongside similar material gathered ethnographically, that is, repeatedly and in detail, over the course of a year, and, crucially, when we analyse them in relation to each other, Bakhtin's thinking offers valuable insights into the complexity of communication and identity in the contemporary world. In this classroom different ideological points of view coexist and compete in the discourse of the young people.

Facing challenges

What are the challenges for applied linguists of adopting and adapting Bakhtin's analysis of heteroglossic language to ethnographic research in contemporary conditions? While Bakhtin's notion of heteroglossia offers a valuable and elegant tool to understand the dynamic nature of the construction of linguistic identities, Lähteenmäki (2010) suggests that its explanatory potential may nonetheless be limited. In his enthusiasm to describe linguistic diversity as the normal state of a language, Bakhtin tends to 'ignore the fact that within heteroglossia linguistic resources are not equally distributed between individuals and different social groups' (Lähteenmäki 2010: 30). Celebrating diversity does not account for the ways in which linguistic difference often constitutes social inequality. Bakhtin's theoretical apparatus, developed in the context of analysis of Dostoevsky's novels, has the capacity to move us from identification of different languages to an analysis of the coexistence of competing ideological points of view. However, such an apparatus, subject to the contingencies of the time and space of its own production, cannot be imported wholesale as a means to interpret linguistic and social phenomena in the twenty-first century. Instead we take heteroglossia as a point of departure, a powerful lens with which to bring into focus the complexity and mobility of superdiverse societies.

A second challenge for language and identity research in applied linguistics relates to Blommaert's (2007: 682) imperative that social research should 'describe and analyse the complexity of social events *comprehensively*'. If we are interested in social and ideological differentiation in society and the ways in which linguistic forms index various aspects of individuals' and communities' 'social histories, circumstances, and identities' (Bailey 2012: 506), an analysis of heteroglossia is well suited to our aims. However, the practical considerations present a challenge. Comprehensive observation of people communicating in their everyday lives requires considerable investment of time. Whether in institutional or private/semi-private settings, it requires repeated and long-term observation and detailed attention to participants' sensitivities. At a time when other pressures determine that time available for fieldwork is limited, compromises are almost unavoidable.

A third challenge for applied linguistics' scholars is perhaps the most significant. It is the challenge to ensure that we do not move to a position in which heteroglossia and ethnography become detached and separate from each other, with Bakhtin's theoretical ideas providing the analysis, while ethnography gets its hands dirty with the everyday stuff of description. What we propose is perhaps the opposite of this – an 'ethnography of heteroglossia', in which ethnography provides a perspective on language and identity, while heteroglossia is defined as and by sets of practices. The challenge is to develop a programme of research, an ethnography of heteroglossia, which is a theory of practice which is situated *in* practice. When we do so we may make visible the ways in which linguistic diversity indexes and brings into being social diversity.

Summary

In this chapter we have reviewed recent research, which has argued that Bakhtin's notion of heteroglossia has considerable potential as a lens through which to view and better understand the diversity of linguistic practice in late modern societies. Pursuant to scholarship that has demonstrated that language and other semiotic resources are not articulated separately, but are deployed in changing communicative repertoires through which people make meaning, heteroglossia does not focus on which language is in use in a particular interaction, but starts from an understanding of voice. We further argued that a heteroglossic analysis enables us to gain purchase on specific positionings in the social world; that such an analysis engages with social tensions and conflicts; and that discourse is frequently filled with the voices and perspectives of others. We proposed an analytic perspective that takes linguistic diversity to be constitutive of, and constituted by, social diversity.

We further argued that a heteroglossic analysis is equipped to investigate and understand the construction, ascription, performance and negotiation of identities in discourse. We proposed that language users create, construct and negotiate identities on the basis of a range of resources and that identities are constructed and negotiated in linguistic discourse. Identities are performed, constructed, enacted and produced in communication with others. While the deployment in a particular context of certain resources traditionally associated with a language constitutes identity work, a heteroglossic analysis does not end there. Discourse points to social position and enacts social tensions and conflicts, wherever certain signs point to certain (economic, or symbolic) resources, or where particular voices coexist within an utterance. These phenomena are invariably identifiable, whether a single language is in use, or several languages are deployed simultaneously. In these respects a heteroglossic analysis, on which language and identity studies in applied linguistics could draw, illuminates claims and contestations related to identities.

Related topics

Positioning language and identity: poststructuralist perspectives; Language and identity in linguistic ethnography; Language and ethnic identity; Linguistic practices and transnational identities; The politics of researcher identities: opportunities and challenges in identities research; Styling and identity in a second language; Language and identity research in online environments: a multimodal ethnographic perspective; The future of identity research: impact and new developments in sociolinguistics; Identity in language learning and teaching: research agendas for the future.

Further reading

Bailey, B. (2012). Heteroglossia, in M. Martin-Jones, A. Blackledge and A. Creese (eds) *The Routledge handbook of multilingualism*. Abingdon: Routledge, pp. 499–507. (Further reference to key concepts and theoretical orientations discussed in this chapter.)

Blackledge, A. and Creese, A. (eds) *Heteroglossia as practice and pedagogy*. Abingdon: Routledge. (An edited collection of empirical evidence produced through an ethnography of heteroglossia.)

Copland, F. and Creese, A. (2014). *Linguistic ethnography: collecting, analysing and presenting data*. London: SAGE. (Ethnography and language-focused book with a detailed discussion of fieldwork.)

Heller, M. (2008). 'Doing ethnography', in Li Wei and M. Moyer (eds) *Blackwell guide to research methods in bilingualism and multilingualism*. Oxford: Blackwell, pp. 249–262. (Helpful reading on doing ethnographic-oriented research in bi/multilingual settings.)

Lähteenmäki, M. and Vanhala-Aniszewski, M. (eds) (2010). *Language ideologies in transition: multilingualism in Russia and Finland*. Frankfurt: Peter Lang. (An edited collection of empirical evidence produced through an ethnography of heteroglossia.)

Note

1 Adrian Blackledge (PI) with Co-investigators Jan Blommaert, Jens Normann Jorgensen and Jarmo Lainio. Researchers: Angela Creese, Liva Hyttel-Sørensen, Carla Jonsson, Kasper Juffermans, Sjaak Kroon, Jinling Li, Marilyn Martin-Jones, Anu Muhonen, Lamies Nassri and Jaspreet Kaur Takhi. *Investigating discourses of inheritance and identity in four multilingual European settings* (AHRC/Humanities in the European Research Area, 09-HERA-JRP-CD-FP-051). 2010–2012.

References

Agha, A. (2007). *Language and social relations*. Cambridge: Cambridge University Press.

Androutsopoulos, J. (2007). Bilingualism in the mass media and on the Internet, in M. Heller (ed.) *Bilingualism: a social approach*. Basingstoke: Palgrave Macmillan, pp. 207–230.

Bailey, B. (2012). Heteroglossia, in M. Martin-Jones, A. Blackledge and A. Creese (eds) *The Routledge handbook of multilingualism*. Abingdon: Routledge, pp. 499–507.

Bakhtin, M.M. (1981). *The dialogic imagination: four essays* [ed. M. Holquist, trans. C. Emerson and M. Holquist]. Austin: University of Texas Press.

Bakhtin, M.M. (1984). *Problems of Dostoevsky's poetics* [ed. C. Emerson, trans. C. Emerson]. Manchester: Manchester University Press.

Blackledge, A. and Creese, A. (2014). Heteroglossia as practice and pedagogy, in A. Blackledge and A. Creese (eds) *Heteroglossia as practice and pedagogy*. Netherlands: Springer, pp. 1–20.

Blackledge, A. and Pavlenko, A. (2001). 'Negotiation of identities in multilingual contexts', *International Journal of Bilingualism*, 5(3): 243–259.

Blommaert, J. (2007). 'On scope and depth in linguistic ethnography', *Journal of Sociolinguistics*, 'Special Issue: Linguistic Ethnography', 11(5): 682–688.

Blommaert, J., Leppänen, S. and Spotti, M. (2012). Endangering multilingualism, in J. Blommaert, S. Leppänen, P. Pahta and T. Räisänen (eds) *Dangerous multilingualism: northern perspectives on order, purity and normality*. Basingstoke: Palgrave Macmillan, pp. 1–21.

Blommaert, J. and Rampton, B. (2011). 'Language and superdiversity', *Diversities*, 13(2): 1–22.

Blommaert, J. and Varis, P. (2013). Enough is enough: the heuristics of authenticity in superdiversity, in J. Duarte and I. Gogolin (eds) *Linguistic superdiversity in urban areas: research approaches*. Amsterdam/Philadelphia: John Benjamins Publishing Company, pp. 143–160.

Canagarajah, A.S. (2011). 'Codemeshing in academic writing: identifying teachable strategies of translanguaging', *Modern Language Journal*, 95: 401–417.

Canagarajah, A.S. (2013). *Translingual practice: global Englishes and cosmopolitan relations*. Abingdon: Routledge.

Copland, F. and Creese, A. (2014). *Linguistic ethnography: collecting, analysing and presenting data*. London: SAGE.

Creese, A., Bhatt, A., Bhojani, N. and Martin, P. (2006). 'Multicultural, heritage and learner identities in complementary schools', *Language and Education*, 20(1): 23–43.

Creese, A. and Blackledge, A. (2010). 'Translanguaging in the bilingual classroom: a pedagogy for learning and teaching', *Modern Language Journal*, 94: 103–115.

Creese, A. and Blackledge, A. (2011). 'Separate and flexible bilingualism in complementary schools: multiple language practices in interrelationship', *Journal of Pragmatics*, 43(5): 1196–1208.

Gal, S. (2006). Minorities, migration and multilingualism: language ideologies in Europe, in P. Stevenson and C. Mar-Molinaro (eds) *Language ideologies, practices and polices: language and the future of Europe*. Basingstoke: Palgrave, pp. 13–27.

García, O. (2009). *Bilingual education in the 21st century*. Oxford: Wiley-Blackwell.

García, O. (2010). Languaging and ethnifying, in J.A. Fishman and O. García (eds) *Handbook of language and ethnic identity: disciplinary and regional perspectives. Vol. 1*. Oxford: Oxford University Press, pp. 519–534.

García, O. and Li Wei (2014). *Translanguaging: language, bilingualism and education*. Basingstoke: Palgrave Macmillan.

Heller, M. (1984). 'Sociolinguistics: theory', *Annual Review of Applied Linguistics*, 5: 46–58.

Heller, M. (2008). Doing ethnography, in Li Wei and M. Moyer (eds) *Blackwell guide to research methods in bilingualism and multilingualism*. Oxford: Blackwell, pp. 249–262.

Heller, M. (2010). *Paths to post-nationalism: a critical ethnography of language and identity*. Oxford: Oxford University Press.

Jørgensen, J.N. (2010). *Languaging: nine years of poly-lingual development of young Turkish-Danish grade school students*. Copenhagen Studies in Bilingualism. Copenhagen: University of Copenhagen.

Jørgensen, J.N., Karraebæk, M.S., Madsen, L.M. and Møller, J.S. (2011). 'Polylanguaging in superdiversity', *Diversities*, 13(2): 23–38.

Jørgensen, J.N. and Møller, J. (2014). Polylingualism and languaging, in C. Leung and B.V. Street (eds) *The Routledge companion to English studies*. Abingdon: Routledge, pp. 67–83.

Lähteenmäki, M. (2010). Heteroglossia and voice: conceptualizing linguistic diversity from a Bakhtinian perspective, in M. Lähteenmäki and M. Vanhala-Aniszewski (eds) *Language ideologies in transition: multilingualism in Russia and Finland*. Frankfurt: Peter Lang, pp. 17–34.

Madsen, L.M. (2011). 'Social status relations and enregisterment in contemporary Copenhagen', *Working Papers in Urban Languages and Literacies, Paper 72*. London: King's College.

Madsen, L.M. (2014). Heteroglossia, voicing and social categorisation, in A. Blackledge and A. Creese (eds) *Heteroglossia as practice and pedagogy*. Netherlands: Springer, pp. 41–58.

Makoni, S. and Pennycook, A.D. (2007). Disinventing and reconstituting languages, in S. Makoni and A. Pennycook (eds) *Disinventing and reconstituting languages*. Clevedon: Multilingual Matters, pp. 1–41.

Otsuji, E. and Pennycook, A.D. (2011). 'Social inclusion and metrolingual practices', *International Journal of Bilingual Education and Bilingualism*, 14(4): 413–426.

Pavlenko, A. and Blackledge, A. (2004). New theoretical approaches to the study of negotiation of identities in multilingual contexts, in A. Pavlenko and A. Blackledge (eds) *Negotiation of identities in multilingual contexts*. Clevedon: Multilingual Matters, pp. 1–33.

Pérez-Milans, M. (this volume). Language and identity in linguistic ethnography, in S. Preece (ed.) *The Routledge handbook of language and identity*. London: Routledge, pp. 83–97.

Pietikäinen, S. and Dufva, H. (2014). Heteroglossia in action: Sámi children, textbooks and rap, in A. Blackledge and A. Creese (eds) *Heteroglossia as practice and pedagogy*. Netherlands: Springer, pp. 59–74.

Rampton, B. (1995). *Crossing: language and ethnicity among adolescents*. London: Longman.

Rampton, B. (1999). 'Styling the other: introduction', *Journal of Sociolinguistics*, 3(4): 421–427.

Rampton, B. (2006). *Language in late modernity*. Cambridge: Cambridge University Press.

Rampton, B. (2011). 'From "Multi-ethnic adolescent heteroglossia" to "Contemporary urban vernaculars"', *Language and Communication*, 31: 276–294.

Riley, P. (2007). *Language, culture and identity: an ethnolinguistic approach*. London: Continuum.

Rymes, B.R. (2010). Classroom discourse analysis: a focus on communicative repertoires, in N. Hornberger and S. McKay (eds) *Sociolinguistics and language education*. Avon: Multilingual Matters, pp. 528–546.

Rymes, B. (2014). Marking communicative repertoire through metacommentary, in A. Blackledge and A. Creese (eds) *Heteroglossia as practice and pedagogy*. Netherlands: Springer, pp. 301–316.

Silverstein, M. (1993). Metapragmatic discourse and metapragmatic function, in J. Lucy (ed.) *Reflexive language*. Cambridge: Cambridge University Press, pp. 33–58.

Vertovec, S. (2011). 'The cultural politics of nation and migration', *Annual Review of Anthropology*, 40: 241–256.

Wortham, S. (2008). Linguistic anthropology, in B. Spolsky and F. Hult (eds) *The handbook of educational linguistics*. Oxford: Blackwell, pp. 83–97.

18

The politics[1] of researcher identities
Opportunities and challenges in identities research

Frances Giampapa

Introduction

In applied linguistics there is a long tradition of varied routes of methodological inquiry that are grounded within particular epistemological (i.e. ways of knowing) and ontological (i.e. the nature of reality) questions. The paradigm from which a researcher works will impact on the research design, the manner in which data is gathered and analysed. It also affects the way in which a researcher sees his/her role in the field and their relationships in/out of the field.

From traditional quantitative/semi-experimental paradigms to qualitative ones, researchers have addressed issues of trustworthiness and rigour in research design in a variety of ways. What has also been part of these discussions, in varied degrees, is the role of the 'objective' researcher. In fact, in many quantitative pieces of research the role of the researcher is traditionally absent in discussions (or rather is limited with regards to impact on the research), whereas in qualitative research there tends to be greater discussion around the role of the researcher as insider/outsider and how the researcher ensures objectivity and neutrality. There is an abundance of research methods books and journals in applied linguistics that provide good introductory chapters to some of the issues relating to collecting and analysing data within the above-mentioned research positions (see e.g. Paltridge and Phakiti 2010; Mackey and Gass 2012).

Research on language and identity has fallen within a number of methodological traditions. However, for well over a decade there has been the emergence of what Block (2003) has termed the 'social turn' in applied linguistics. That is, the advancement of theoretical frameworks such as sociocultural theory, second language socialisation and learner identity, to name a few. This has opened the door to new methodological forms of inquiry and analyses. What holds these theoretical approaches together is that language learning is seen as a social process and the contexts of learning become important sites of inquiry.

This chapter opens up the debates on the ways in which researchers as socially, politically and historically positioned selves are part of, and inextricably intertwined with, the lives and everyday practices of their research participants. As a critical/linguistic ethnographer, I am challenged to think 'reflexively' and to consider the ways in which my identities, positionalities, values, beliefs and biases come to bear on the research that I do. In the following section, I provide an overview of the shifts in language and identity research in relation to both theoretical and methodological issues. In particular, I will focus on the rise in critical approaches to researching language and identity, which have spotlighted and problematised the role of the researcher and the researcher–researched relationship. This is followed by an account of researcher identities and a critical reflection on the issues faced by researchers investigating language and identity drawn from my own experience.

Overview

An important example of language and identity study with second language learners is Norton's (2013 [2000]) seminal research on migrant ESL women in Canada, which challenged the conceptualisation of English language learners, their motivation and participation in ESL communities in their personal and professional lives. This research and others in the same vein have produced ethnographic cases that have challenged the methodological traditions and tools within traditional applied linguistics research. Norton's research redrew the long trajectory of SLA research that conceptually based its understanding of concepts such as identity, learning and motivation within a psycholinguistic frame that up to the mid-1990s did very little to incorporate the social within its analysis (i.e. social factors and the collective process that impact language learning). As such, it offered a different way of talking about issues of identity at a time when larger social and political processes at play resulted in an unprecedented influx of large-scale migration and mobility in tandem with increased economic and cultural change.

As Norton reminds us, the question of 'Who am I?' is reframed within a politics of identity, and the struggle for recognition and representation within a globalising world. As such, the identity politics of the young immigrant women in Norton's research show not only the struggle for legitimacy and authority to be heard within and across various contexts, but also the ways in which they invested and repositioned themselves in resistance to the dominant discourses reproduced in Canadian society that labelled them as immigrants and English language learners. Instead, their choices and investment in language and culture as well as the resistance to identity positions showed the way in which these participants' language practices and desires to reimagine themselves would open up possibilities for the future, and access to symbolic capital (e.g. prestige, social networks) and material resources (e.g. employment and monetary gains).

From Norton's research, three important concepts in second language acquisition have been challenged and retraced – 'investment', 'identity' and 'imagined communities' (Kramsch in Norton 2013). For Norton (2013: 50), the notion of investment 'conceives of the language learner as having a complex social history and multiple desires'. This stood as a direct challenge at that time to the fixed and static notion of motivation in SLA, which dominated SLA research for decades. Investment is strongly embedded within a Bourdieusian approach to the economics of linguistic practice (see Bourdieu 1991; Norton Peirce 1995), bringing into frame the language learner's commitment and choice as well as his/her desire to learn. The benefits and return of this investment rests on the learner exercising his/her agency in order to be heard and claim legitimacy and authority as an English language speaker. This shifts the English language learner into the 'driver's seat' in challenging institutional and societal discourses of passiveness, disengagement and inability to speak with authority because s/he does not fit the native speaker mould.

Norton's theorisation of identity moved applied linguistics researchers further along from traditional concepts of identity (singular) as a fixed, immutable characteristic of a language learner. Drawing from Weedon's (1997) theory of subjectivity (identity), Norton's research brought into frame issues of power and the multiple identities that social agents perform discursively to access social networks and in turn material and symbolic resources. As Norton (2010: 350) notes, 'Every time we speak, we are negotiating and renegotiating our sense of self in relation to the larger social world, and reorganizing that relationship across time and space.'

This brings me to the concept of 'imagined communities'. Coined by Anderson (1983: 49) in his discussion about the construct of the nation, he states:

> I propose the following definition of the nation: it is an imagined political community ... It is *imagined* because the members of even the smallest nation will never know most of their fellow members, meet them, or even hear of them, yet in the minds of each lives the image of their communion.

In Norton's research and her work with other scholars (e.g. Kanno and Norton 2003), imagined communities take on a powerful conceptual role, signalling that as social agents the possible communicative realities and social affiliations are beyond the current conditions of people's lives. Identities are also linked to the desire and aspiration of language learners to be part of communities in which their linguistic and cultural forms of capital are legitimised.

The influence of Norton's original work in scoping the conceptual roadmap noted above and the theoretical shifts in the development of critical approaches in applied linguistics and sociolinguistics has also had an impact on the methodological positioning and tools for language and identity research. Researching language, identities and power in the field of critical applied linguistics and critical sociolinguistics has pushed forward in new directions, and with it has come new ways of thinking about the methodologies and methods that we use.[2]

We have also seen the advancement of critical approaches in applied linguistics (and sociolinguistics) that has opened up further both theoretical and methodological routes into researching language and identity, such as the use of a range of qualitative and ethnographically oriented methods that include, for example, the use of diaries, interviews and participant observation for data collection and the use of discourse analysis. What is meant by critical in the field relates to critical theories underpinned in the traditions of Marx, the Frankfurt School, Gramsci, Freire, Bernstein, Bourdieu and many others. The strength of critical approaches also comes from the plurality of synergies that results from linking critical theories together with other areas such as post-colonial and cultural studies, postmodernism and poststructuralist approaches to language research. Talmy (2010: 128) notes a number of key features of critical research, stating that it signals

> a conception of *society* as stratified and marked by inequality, with differential structural access to material and symbolic resources, power, opportunity, mobility and education. Accordingly society is characterized by asymmetries in *power* arrangements ... there is a reciprocal, mutually constitutive relationship between social structures and human *agency*. That is, social structures shape or mediate social practices, but do not determine them (Giddens 1979; also see Ahearn 2001). This means that *social reproduction* (i.e. the reproduction of unjust social relations) is never 'guaranteed' since power is not uni-directional or top/down.

In addition to Talmy's incisive explanation, it is important to keep in mind that concepts such as society, power, agency and culture are socially and historically situated across space and time. Furthermore, critical research is action driven, that is, it aims to do more than merely describe conditions but aims to push for change and the dismantling of inequalities through emancipatory measures of critique and direct action by the very participants involved. Further development in the field has led to the critiquing of such positions; however, this is part of the ongoing dialogue within the critical applied linguistic field to search for more collaborative, inclusive and reflexive ways of doing research.

As I have noted in previous writings (Giampapa 2011: 134), 'research should be a process of democratisation ... where attention is focused on issues of power within the research process'. I connect this with Cameron et al.'s (1992) call for a move away from research 'on' or 'for' participants to research that is 'with' participants. I would go further in the advancement of research that is co-produced and community driven that sees participants as co-researchers and drivers of the research in tandem with the researchers themselves (e.g. in the field of education) and the social sciences more broadly where there is a shift towards co-produced research. This has also opened up discussions around voice and ethics of co-production (see Banks 2012).

In framing critical research in this way, what is also questioned is the statement that research is value-free (Lather 1986). As Lather (1986: 64) argues, 'scientific "neutrality" and "objectivity" serve to mystify the inherently ideological nature of research'. She offers alternative forms of validity as part of the development of data credibility checks that are necessary to 'protect our research and theory construction from our enthusiasms' as part of 'our efforts to create a self-reflexive human science' (1986: 67). Such concerns are not simply for those researchers who are bound to critical methodological approaches or working from critical theories to investigate language, power and identity. SLA researchers such as Ortega (2005: 433) also remind us that 'an ethical lens on ... research would make us view research as always value-laden', regardless of which methodological paradigm one favours. She raises a number of questions that push researchers to think about the social responsibility and the impact of their research (even within quantitative paradigms).

This certainly puts the researcher into the frame not as an invisible and ideologically neutral being but rather as part of the research narrative in terms of what stories get told and how they are interpreted and told. An expanded notion of the researcher as social being with multiple identities that impact on the process and analysis of research is taken up in the work of critical sociolinguistics (see Cameron et al. 1992; Copland et al. 2015).

The development of critical sociolinguistic approaches has also drawn from similar sets of theoretical frameworks as critical applied linguistics. Martin-Jones and Gardner (2012) highlight that, by the end of the 1980s to this day, influences and developments in critical theory, poststructuralism and postmodernism have had long-lasting effects on the development of a particular movement in sociolinguistic research. From this, a critical sociolinguistic approach was born, laying the foundations for a trajectory of research that brought together ethnographic and discourse analytic frameworks to investigate linguistic ideologies, identities and practices through discourse across time and space (Norton Peirce 1995; Giampapa 2004a, 2004b; Pavlenko and Blackledge 2004; Block 2007).

This has also led researchers in the pursuit of qualitative methodologies and methods that offer new ways of capturing social and linguistic processes of everyday life, for example ethnography of communication (Gumperz and Hymes 1972; Duff and Uchida 1997; Watson-Gegeo 1997; Duff 2002; Hymes 2003), critical ethnography (Canagarajah 1993; May 1997; Ibrahim 1999; Giampapa 2004a; Talmy 2012) and linguistic ethnography (Rampton et al. 2004; Creese 2008; Maybin and Tusting 2011), to name a few. Many of these approaches draw from the traditions of linguistic and cultural anthropology, interactional sociolinguistics, language and literacies studies and cultural studies.

Within such methodological approaches, the researcher's role and the reflexive[3] stance of the researcher are a key consideration within the research process. Discussions around the role of the researcher as insider/outsider have often been discussed in relationship to the research participants and the ethics of maintaining the role of the 'objective' researcher who will reflect on the researcher–researched relationship (see Hultgren *et al.*, this volume). However, reflection does not generally involve problematising the researcher–researched relationship reflexively. Being critically reflexive is part of a much broader debate around methodological rigour and knowledge production. In her discussion about quality in critical ethnography, Lather (1986: 65) describes this pursuit of guaranteeing trustworthiness in data as being 'between a rock and a soft place'; on the one hand, the unquestioned pursuit of trustworthiness in research by alternative paradigms, and the other being the imposition of positivist claims for objectivity and neutrality. Alongside the reconceptualisation and introduction of data checks such as triangulation and reflexivity (i.e. the capacity to become the 'other' and 'turn back on oneself') (Davies 2003: 4), Lather (1986) proposes 'catalytic validity' as a way of understanding the degree to which the research puts in motion conscious-raising and what might be in Freirian terms 'conscientisation', that is, developing a critical awareness of one's social reality through reflection and action (Freire 2000). Researchers continue to push forward these agendas as well as the redefinition of the researcher in the research process, as can be seen within critical sociolinguistics and, in particular, linguistic ethnography (Creese 2008).

Two decades of social, political, economic and technological change as a result of globalisation has led to shifts in migration flows that have been described as 'super-diversity' (Vertovec 2007). That is a description of contemporary migration that is far more transitory and multiple in movement, as well as far more diversified in terms of migrants' social markers (e.g. nationality, ethnicity, linguistic, religious and so forth) and multiple objectives for migration. This has also led to a shift from seeing language as a structured form of communication to a view of language as sets of linguistic resources that agents carry with them and use creatively and, in combination with other modes, to make meaning as part of everyday life. This has led a number of researchers to investigate these new and complex multilingual realities, social orders and communicative processes across transnational discursive spaces and scales (Blommaert and Rampton 2011; Creese and Blackledge 2012; Duchêne and Heller 2012).

This new linguistic landscape offers both opportunities and challenges to researchers in the documenting, analysing and representation of multiple voices across multiple discursive terrains. These multiple voices are not only those of participants (as co-researchers, collaborators and so forth), but also intertwined are the voices of the researchers themselves walking alongside participants and engaging in complex, multilayered and mutable relationships of power, positioning (self/other), representation and identities (Creese *et al.* 2009; Giampapa 2011; Giampapa and Lamoureux 2011).

The extensive body of research from the Mosaic Centre for Research on Multilingualism at the University of Birmingham (see e.g. Creese 2008; Creese *et al.* 2009; Blackledge and Creese 2010; Blackledge *et al.* 2013) has made a considerable contribution to our understanding of multilingualism in contemporary Britain, especially the linguistic and cultural practices of ethnic minority youth in complementary schools. The legacy of Blackledge and Creese's research as part of the Mosaic Centre (which also includes the work of Marilyn-Martin Jones, Sheena Gardner and Deidre Martin) has contributed to an expanded understanding of the process and product of linguistic ethnography. Creese and Blackledge have shed light on ethnographic team work, raising pertinent questions about the role of multilingual researcher identities within the research, as well as the representation of data, voice and meaning-making in doing research. In laying bare the process of conducting ethnographic research in multilingual teams, Creese *et al.* (2009: 215) aimed to not only demystify the process of conducting research across multilingual educational settings but also develop 'innovative forms of ethnographic team methodologies'. Thus in order to capture the multiple voices, languages and cultures represented across educational settings, researchers investigating language and identity need to grapple with the same types of issues and seek new ways of researching identities and language practices in contemporary life.

As Eisenhart (2001) reminds us, while ethnographers are responding to the changing conditions and experiences of contemporary life through conceptual adjustments and theoretical expansion, they are not moving forward as quickly with the methodological shifts necessary to robustly investigate them. Eishenhart argues for 'various reflexive practices as one way to respond methodologically to new theorising of social life' (in Creese *et al.* 2009: 219).

Reconsidering the tools for research, Creese *et al.* (2009) challenge us to think of the ways in which we are representing the diversity and multivocality of the communities we study. They highlight the importance for 'multiple approaches that explicitly address how diversity shapes data collection, analysis and final written accounts' (ibid.: 281). This also raises questions about how we think, write and teach ethnographic methods that would lead to addressing the new issues and aspects of linguistic and social practices and events of late modernity. Through a process of researcher vignettes, the multilingual team in Creese *et al.*'s research addressed questions about their relationships to participants and also how they negotiated their research identities within the team. What this highlighted was a number of interlocking themes related to the insider/outsider research roles and the importance of language and culture among the team members. In the first instance, what Creese *et al.* (2009) show is the fuzziness of the insider/outsider dichotomy and how fluid and mutable these categories are with respect to the research participants and the team itself. That is, they show how researchers will 'move in and out of insider and outsider' (ibid.: 228) positions in order to perform particular identities in order to maintain distance or gain access into particular settings. The same insider/outsider performances are discussed in terms of the team itself. What this shows are the tensions of 'ongoing identity work of researcher performance' (ibid.: 229). The positioning of particular team members as linguistic and cultural experts as a constructed identity also signals the importance of language (i.e. both English and the community languages) in building rapport and trust within the field.

In Creese and Blackledge (2012: 306), we are taken further into the workings of ethnographic teams and the process of ethnography by exploring 'how teams of researchers negotiate and come to (dis)agreements in the process of making "meaning" out of "data"'. Creese and Blackledge offer a window into this process by audio-recording team discussions of data analyses. As Creese and Blackledge indicate, this becomes more than simply negotiating, arguing and listening to different team perspectives. Rather it is about representation – a key component in ethnographic research. It is also about voice – the researcher's voice in the construction of the stories from the research data. It is the multiple voices – researchers', participants' and research team's – all coming together to make meaning out of data and out of experiences in the field. What is particularly pertinent here is that issues of interpretation and representation of data cut across all types of qualitative research, not just ethnographic research. This is what is important about the methodological work that Creese and Blackledge have explored, as it offers insights into all qualitative research into language and identity.

What has also become more pertinent is an understanding of the ways in which researchers themselves are implicated in the process of research. Part of this process is the reporting of research; the traditional genre of research reporting does very little to bring in researcher identities, values and 'partial' knowledge. These are not simply issues pertaining to a particular methodology for language and identity research – the point here is that these are debates that challenge thinking about the very nature of research and its impact.

As I have shown in the discussion so far, critically driven research has sought to deconstruct the researcher in the research. Within qualitative research, there are a number of well-written 'how-to' authored texts (e.g. Coffey 1999; Davies 2003) that have led the call for reflexive practices. This is particularly the case within the traditions of critical and/or linguistic ethnography, which will be the focus of the following sections. Within critical approaches to researching language, methodologically a number of challenges remain, including:

1 What does it mean to be and become a reflexive researcher?
2 How do researcher identities and positionalities play into the research process?
3 What does it mean 'to be in the field' and how is the 'field' itself mutable?
4 How do researchers and participants engage in a tango of positionalities, power plays and representations that are not always brought to bear on the process of doing research?

In many cases, some of these reflexive musings, collective stories and hybrid storylines have been left at the margins of research diaries. Challenging the ongoing beliefs that 'reflexive epistemological and narrative practices ... might [be considered] subjective and unscientific' (Foley 2002: 469), I will bring to the forefront some of the challenges and opportunities that I have grappled and engaged with as a researcher, advocating that these reflexive moments, the discussions with participants and the 'self', be taken from the margins and brought centre stage as part of the messiness and detailed practices of the research process in applied linguistics research into language and identities.

In the following section, I will begin by considering what has led researchers, like myself, towards a vocalised outward thinking of our own researcher identities, relationships of power and positionalities. This process is ongoing across my research trajectory and begins within my own epistemological and ontological engagement with researching the politics of language, identities and power.

Researcher identities – extending the dialogue

As part of becoming a reflexive and critical researcher, one must unpack and strip away researcher beliefs, values and experiences that construct the ways in which we define our points of departure – that is, the questions we pose and the analytical lens we take. Working from emancipatory, critical approaches to research, Cameron et al. (1992: 5) state: 'Researchers cannot help being socially located persons. We inevitably bring our biographies and our subjectivities to every stage of the research process and this influences the questions we ask and the ways in which we try to find answers.'

As I have mentioned in Giampapa (2011), casting a reflexive gaze on who we are as socially constructed draws attention to what we research and the way we research it. Being and becoming researchers is shaped by our multiple histories and social and linguistic capital. Our multiple identities position us as researchers in specific ways, crafting particular relationships to participants, communities and the contexts in which we work. These identities continue to be of importance at every level of the research process. At the pre–during–post field stages, the interplay of researcher identities positions the researcher in particular ways in relation to participants.

Rampton *et al.* (2004) suggest that unpacking the complex situatedness of the everyday practices of our participants takes time and close engagement. Part of the researcher's own interpretive capacity to understand these practices is also coloured by his/her own experiences. These experiences, positions and identities can open up and shut down opportunities for enriching the research. These relationships are also subject to participants' control when in the field. That is, participants' interpretations of researchers' roles, and their positioning of researchers as 'insiders/outsiders/both and neither' (Creese *et al.* 2009: 221). However, our interpretive capacity and what we can 'know' about whom and what we study is only ever partial.

As discussed in the previous section, issues of methodological rigour, reflexivity and also ethical mindedness have been part of ongoing discussions, in particular, within (critical) ethnographic research (Cameron *et al.* 1992; Rampton *et al.* 2004; Hammersley 2007). Relationships within the field are paramount in enabling a 'close up and personal' view into the lives of participants and the phenomena under investigation. Discussions on what it means to take on an insider/outsider role are key to any 'how-to guide' to designing an ethnographic research.

The role of the researcher and his/her positionality in traditional ethnographic accounts is one of objective observer, taking field notes and producing the types of ethnographic diaries/journals that have also raised questions about 'field relationships … ethical and political questions' (Foley 2002: 474). These have long been at the heart of an ethnographer's research journey. However, drawing on Tedlock, Foley (2002) points out that while the practice of 'confessional reflexivity' pre-dates postmodernism (e.g. Malinowski's diary accounts), these reflexive diary accounts were always separate from the business of writing 'formal, scientific realist ethnography' (Tedlock in Foley 2002: 474). Others have agitated against this schism between what is made visible and what is kept at the margins. In particular, Foley (2002) reminds us of the ways in which auto-ethnographers' works (such as Ruth Behar's) openly argue against the 'grandiose authorial claims of speaking in a rational, value-free, objective, universalizing voice' (ibid.).

Canagarajah (1996) also criticised the lack of researcher identity and voice in research accounts even within critically grounded research. Canagarajah (ibid.: 324) argued that:

> For all practical purposes, the researcher is absent from the report, looming behind the text as an omniscient, transcendental, all knowing figure. This convention hides the manner in which the subjectivity of the researchers – with their complex values, ideologies, and experiences – shapes the research activity and findings. In turn, how the research activity shapes the researchers' subjectivity is not explored – even though research activity can sometimes profoundly affect the researchers' sense of the world and themselves.

While he singled out Norton's extensive research on identity, because of its significant contribution to the field, it is certainly an aspect of the research process that has given researchers pause and reflection. Norton and Early (2011) responded to the critical questions posed by Canagarajah over a decade earlier by addressing the ways in which researcher narratives and the multiplicities of research identities impact on and are incorporated into their language-teaching research. Norton and Early highlight the importance of 'small stories' (Georgakopoulou 2006) co-constructed by them and the teachers in their research in order to understand how their use of narrative inquiry sheds light on the ways in which researcher identities were negotiated. These small stories or 'stories in action' (Norton and Early 2011: 421) offer significant insights into the diverse identity positions that are negotiated and co-constructed in daily interactions.

In my own fieldwork, I have recognised the importance of both field notes and a research journal as a way of looking back over and into the interpretative accounts that I develop in my research. These 'scribbles' on the page or within the margins raise questions about my role and the relationships I forge within the field; they also help me to consider issues of power and positionality as raised by the participants. That is, the positioning of the researcher and the power that participants can hold also has an impact on the beginning, middle and end of the research process, as will be discussed in the following sections. Furthermore, in the analysis and writing up of research, I have also struggled with the idea that my interpretations are in fact only one part of the stories I document. Questions of voice and power resonate within my own reflexive pauses.

To illustrate these issues, I draw from a series of experiences across several years of being a researcher: from doctoral and postdoctoral research to more recent experiences of research and teaching. As Bourdieu and Wacquant (1992) highlight (drawing on the work of Barnard), to 're-flectere' is about making the field itself the subject of reflexivity and 'subjecting the position of the observer to the same critical analysis as that of the constructed object at hand' (Barnard in Bourdieu and Wacquant 1992: 41).

Being and becoming a researcher: tales from an incomplete journey

Our identities and multiple points of reflexivity as a dynamic process of being and becoming a researcher are negotiated, managed and resisted across time and space within the process of doing research (i.e. pre–in–post field). As England (1994: 81) highlights:

> '[T]he field' is constantly changing and researchers may find that they have to manoeuvre around unexpected circumstances … this in turn ignites the need for a broader, less rigid conception of the 'appropriate' method that allows the researcher the flexibility to be more open to the challenges of field work.

At the doctoral stage of being/becoming a researcher I was inducted into the academy through a programme of work that was to focus in on the epistemological and ontological questions in my field. The making of a researcher was constructed in ways that quickly positioned me as the novice, locating me within the research in relation to institutional ethical expectations about what it means to do research and go into the field. The research training tied to the doctoral process was built around understanding research in applied linguistics and sociolinguistics and the expansive methodologies and methods (e.g. critical ethnography) that would arm me with the expertise to undertake my doctoral investigation into what it meant to be and become Italian Canadian across space and time and the discourses and ideologies attached to speaking the right language and reproducing the right forms of cultural capital to access symbolic and material resources in Toronto.

As such I asked research questions that focused on:

1. What are the discourses on identities and what does it mean to be and become Italian Canadian within the Italian Canadian world?
   a. Who produces these discourses and how do these discourses function to include some and exclude others and in what ways is this accomplished?
2. How do Italian Canadian youth define what it means to be and become Italian Canadian?
   a. How do participants self-identify and perform their identities socially and discursively?
   b. How are identities negotiated across and within worlds?
   c. Which identities are negotiated in which spaces and which identities are non-negotiable?

3   In what ways do Italian Canadian youth manage, resist and challenge the discourses on
     identities from within the Italian Canadian community as well as from the Canadian and
     Italian worlds?

Over 18 months, I conducted fieldwork that crossed multiple worlds and spaces (Italian
Canadian, Canadian and Italian worlds – as represented by participants' discourses and the
university, home, workplace and social spaces). I used diverse methods[4] and broadened the participant baseline to include unheard 'voices'[5] within the Italian Canadian community in order
to situate and engage with discourses of Italianness (e.g. Italian Canadian youth groups, Italian
Canadian media representatives, a lesbian, gay, bisexual, transgendered (LGBT) group called
FUORI, to name a few). I documented, challenged, analysed and engaged with the production
of discourses of Italianness and those of the eight Italian Canadian youths, who were participants
in my study, negotiation, resistance and management of their multiple identities (see Giampapa
2004a, 2011).

As a critical ethnographer, I recognise how my identities are socially constructed and historically and politically embedded across time and space. The past, present and future identities are
inculcated in my discursive performances as a Canadian-born, Australian-raised straight female
of immigrant Italian heritage. My family's histories and experiences of multiple transnational
immigration in Italy, Canada, Australia and back to Canada, spanning the 1950s, 1970s and
1990s, socialised and coloured my identities. The personal trajectory intertwining with the professional (i.e. moving from Australia to Canada to pursue my doctorate and then postdoctoral
studies) led to a complex layering of identities that would create points of tension and also open
up dialogue with the participants in my doctoral research (as well as my future research that
unfolded in my postdoctoral and mid-career programme as an assistant/associate professor).

The fruitfulness of these possible and multiple dialogues were countered by a less flexible
and more rigid understanding of the researcher and research conduct constructed by institutional structures and reproduced through ethical hoops that all researchers are required to jump
through. Instead, a conflictual relationship was constructed by ethical processes that require
researchers to fill out mandatory forms, submit multiple copies of tools and discuss possible
ethical issues in ways that fulfilled the guise that research can be sanitised of subjectivities, one-
way power relationships and possible 'harmful effect' to participants. The tick-box approach to
ethics satisfied the ethics committee at the time, which also recommended the swift destruction
of data post-research. For most researchers, particularly novice ones embarking on doctoral
research, I was intimidated by this unknown committee of ethical elites who would have the
power to challenge and possibly restrict and halt my progress into the field. However, I do not
wish to suggest that ethics committees are not important or productive. From later experiences
as a departmental and faculty ethics representative, I have seen how members of ethics committees see their role not only as risk management, but as supporting and enhancing the reflexive
dialogue in research.

As a departmental ethics coordinator, the role of dialogue in producing and exploring ethical
mindedness have become key for all researchers – from the early career to the professoriate. This
dialogic process opens up the possibilities for researchers and doctoral supervisors and students
to engage in the consideration of opportunities and possible tensions of doing research. As
Guillemin and Gillam (2004) suggest, our understanding of ethics should be reframed as an 'ethics in practice' moment where research and real life collide, offering important pauses for critical
reflection. This realigns the process as ongoing and shifting as the research evolves and relationships with participants hopefully develop towards trust and openness. However, as indicated so

far, my research training did not lead to the deconstruction of my researcher identities and how these might be experienced once in the field.

Experiences later on in the field were important for reflecting on the importance of researcher identities. One was in my postdoctoral research[6] on the Multiliteracy Project (see www.multiliteracies.ca; Cummins and Early 2011), and another was in a project with an early years teaching school partnership; these highlighted that the construction of the role of the researcher as conceptualised by the participants can create potential tension and conflict. In both contexts, I was challenged as a researcher to unpack and explain the ways in which I work. While for me research is both collaborative and co-produced, I realised that the participants' experiences of researchers was more along the lines of 'enter, take what they need and leave' and never be heard from again. In the case of the Multiliteracies Project, one of the project teachers had had experiences where she felt her own intellectual property had been transgressed. Equally, in the early years teaching school context, I was interrogated on my research practices and whether I co-authored with participants and collaborated in ways that were mutually beneficial. In both these instances, the tensions that were created at the outset made it possible for a trusting relationship to evolve and to negotiate a set of principles and embedded practices that set out data ownership. As Guillemin and Gillam (2004: 265) purport:

> There can be all sorts of ethically important moments: when participants indicate discomfort with their answer, or reveal a vulnerability; when a research participant states that he or she does not want to be assigned a pseudonym in the writing up of the research but wants to have his or her real name reported.

The representation of the researcher as experienced by participants made entering field sites such as the school settings, as noted above, a negotiated process. Looking back at my doctoral journey, I have written openly about the ways in which my own identity as 'Italian' Canadian was troubled and negotiated (Giampapa 2011). In the case of two participants in my doctoral research, Salvatore and Paolo, both had rather fixed and static views of what it meant to be Italian Canadian and who could legitimately belong. While similar in denying their 'Canadianness', even though they were both born in Toronto, each produced identities that were locked into the production of particular varieties of Italian (e.g. Salvatore valuing the institutionalised national language – a standard form of Italian; Paolo demarcating his Calabrese dialect as a more valued form of capital within his social and family networks). Each positioned me as an outsider as I did not 'sound' Italian (Canadian) – indeed my English is marked by an Australian accent. However, at the same time I was legitimised through the fact that I spoke standard Italian and had the cultural markers that both Salvatore and Paolo saw as valuable – someone who they presumed to be engaged with their cultural identity and language, reinforced by travel to Italy and by periods of living there as well. The unpacking of my cultural and ethnic identities also challenged these participants' production of discourses of Italianness, which in fact divided rather than contributed to what they saw as the Italian Canadian world.

My relationship with FUORI[7] (the LGBT group in my research) also created interesting points of engagement. These were both productive and reflective in the ways in which I was positioned: as an Italian Canadian female and lesbian. The assumption was that my interest in investigating the representations and performances of being Italian Canadian and gay equated for FUORI that I had a personal link to the research. While I felt committed to working with an activist group that sought to shift the dominant discourses of Italianness, rooted for them within a heterosexual macho male image, I found myself intertwined within their agenda. Thus the research relationship was coloured by my attempts to open up a different set of discourses that challenged their construction of being Italian Canadian and gay. I needed to go further in my attempts for self-positioning and critical reflexive pauses to unpack the ways in which our relationship would unfold and how this would in turn impact on the analysis and representation of voices within the group. This highlights the point that being critically reflexive is an ongoing process, and that there are moments within the research where leaving my sexual identity outside the research was not enough and that through my actions (e.g. attending specific LGBT events that were open to friends and family) I could reposition in terms of my own researcher identities.

Summary

This chapter has explored the theoretical and methodological trajectories of identity and language research. Norton's (2013) seminal research has led the way in understanding the links between the language-learning process and a learner's social identities. In particular, the social turn in applied linguistics and the advancement of critical theoretical approaches in the field have shed further light on understanding contemporary communicative practices across transnational spaces and time. This can be seen through the contribution of key researchers who have pushed our understanding of the impact of globalisation on the multilingual practices and discursive performances of identities across urban settings (e.g. Blackledge and Creese 2010).

The methodological challenges and tensions that have come out of researching language and identities cuts across qualitative research – researcher role, field relationships, insider/outsider positioning, reflexivity and ethical mindedness, to name a few. Of particular importance in this dialogue has been the work of critical and linguistic ethnographers, who have advanced the work on researcher identities, positioning, voice and representation as part of the demystification of the research process and product.

My research is situated within the multiple methodological conversations that I have sketched and my work continues to engage with issues of identity, language and power. Through narratives and research stories I continue to deconstruct the processes and affordances that come from being and becoming a researcher. The process of challenging the researcher's identities and positionalities, in the field as well as outside it, is complex. Participants can exercise their own power through personal and political agendas that can at the same time open up new and interesting spaces for dialogue. My research experiences raise questions about the way researchers are trained and given opportunities to think differently about the methodological tools used to negotiate the spaces in which we observe, interpret and investigate. These all become the 'methodological rich points' (Hornberger 2006: 221) where the potential for co-construction and co-production of knowledge provides greater potential for the critical reflexive work that is necessary within our field.

Related topics

Language and identity in linguistic ethnography; Linguistic practices and transnational identities; Ethics in language and identity research; A linguistic ethnography of identity: adopting a heteroglossic frame; The future of identity research: impact and new developments in sociolinguistics; Identity in language learning and teaching: research agendas for the future.

Further reading

Byrd Clark, J.S. and Dervin, F. (eds) (2014). *Reflexivity in language and intercultural education: rethinking multilingualism and interculturality*. New York: Routledge. (Offering a historical route into the field of multilingualism and intercultural research, the reader will find the untangling of the concept of 'reflexivity' and its theoretical underpinnings very helpful.)

Copland, F., Creese, A., Rock, F. and Shaw, S. (2015). *Linguistic ethnography*. London: SAGE. (This is an important read for not only linguistic ethnographers but for all interested and working with language data, qualitative and of course ethnographic approaches to research.)

Giampapa, F. and Lamoureux, S. (guest eds) (2011). 'Special issue. Voices from the field: identity, language and power in multilingual research settings', *Journal of Language, Identity, and Education*, 10(3). (This special issue offers a range of important insights into the reconceptualisation of the researcher and the research process.)

Paltridge, B. and Phakiti, A. (eds) (2010). *Continuum companion to research methods in applied linguistics*. London: Continuum. (This edited volume provides a particularly insightful understanding of key methodological issues in current applied linguistic research.)

Notes

1 I use 'politics' in this chapter to signal the micro-politics of relationships and cultures in doing field-work. But this also aligns with the theoretical frameworks that I draw on as a critical researcher, which highlights power and inequalities within social life.

2 In Norton's (2013 [2000]) 2nd edition of *Identity and language learning*, she signals new themes in identity research – one of which is examining researcher identities (see also Norton and Early 2011).

3 For me being critically reflexive is a process that engages with an internal dialogue as researcher as 'self' (i.e. one's identities and positionalities which are influx) alongside participants' positionings of themselves and of the researcher, which are also shifting.

4 These methods included: (1) interviews (individual and focus group interviews, and special themed interviews around work, religion, sexuality and travelling to Italy); (2) the shadowing of core participants across different spaces such as the home, university classrooms, social spaces and workplaces; (3) auto-ethnography where the core participants became the ethnographer by audio-recording their interactions across diverse settings; (4) questionnaires; (5) participant identity narratives and travel diaries reflecting on the 'trip to Italy' as a transnational experience; (6) newspaper documents; and (7) researcher diaries.

5 Similarly my use of 'voice/voices' relates to Creese (forthcoming) who notes 'voice' in her own team ethnographies as both a descriptive and analytical tool. For me this relates strongly to other concepts of authority and legitimacy – the right to speak and be heard in Bourdieusian (1991) terms.

6 I was a postdoctoral researcher on a Canada-wide research project known as the Multiliteracy Project (www.multiliteracies.ca). Based as part of the Toronto team, I coordinated the collaborative research with the seven project schools as well as being based in one of the primary schools (Coppard Glen) working collaboratively with Perminder the teacher to explore multilingual identities and the production of her students' dual language identity texts.

7 FUORI (translated from Italian as *Out*) is the pseudonym used for the Italian Canadian LGBT group.

References

Anderson, B. (1983). *Imagined communities: reflections on the origin and spread of nationalism*. London: Verso.

Banks, S. (2012). *Community-based participatory research: a guide to ethical principles and practice*. Bristol: National Co-ordinating Centre for Public Engagement.

Blackledge, A. and Creese, A. (2010). *Multilingualism: a critical perspective*. London: Continuum.

Blackledge, A., Creese, A. and Takhi, J.K. (2013). Beyond multilingualism: heteroglossia in practice, in S. May (ed.) *The multilingual turn: implications for SLA, TESOL and bilingual education*. London and New York: Routledge, pp. 191–215.

Block, D. (2003). *The social turn in second language acquisition*. Edinburgh: Edinburgh University Press.

Block, D. (2007). *Second language identities*. London: Continuum.

Blommaert, J. and Rampton, B. (2011). 'Language and superdiversity', *Diversities*, 13(2): 1–22.

Bourdieu, P. (1991). *Language and symbolic power*. Malden: Polity Press.

Bourdieu, P. and Wacquant, L. (1992). *An invitation to reflexive sociology*. Chicago: University of Chicago Press and Polity.

Cameron, D., Frazer, E., Harvey, P., Rampton, M.B.H. and Richardson, K. (1992). *Researching language: issues of power and method*. London: Routledge.

Canagarajah, A.S. (1993). 'Critical ethnography of a Sri Lankan classroom: ambiguities in student opposition to reproduction through ESOL', *TESOL Quarterly*, 27: 601–626.

Canagarajah, A.S. (1996). 'From critical research practice to critical research reporting', *TESOL Quarterly*, 30(2): 321–330.

Coffey, A. (1999). *The ethnographic self*. London: SAGE.

Copland, F., Creese, A., Rock, F. and Shaw, S. (2015). *Linguistic ethnography*. London: SAGE.

Creese, A. (2008). Linguistic ethnography, in K.A. King and N.H. Hornberger (eds) *Encyclopedia of language and education. Vol. 10, Research methods in language and education*. New York: Springer, pp. 229–241.

Creese, A., Bhatt, A. and Martin, P. (2009). Multilingual researcher identities: interpreting linguistically and culturally diverse classrooms, in J. Miller, A. Kostogriz and M. Gearon (eds) *Culturally and linguistically diverse classrooms: new dilemmas for teachers*. Bristol: Multilingual Matters, pp. 215–233.

Creese, A. and Blackledge, B. (2012). 'Voice and meaning-making in team ethnography', *Anthropology and Education Quarterly*, 43(3): 306–324.

Cummins, J. and Early, M. (eds) (2011). *Identity texts: the collaborative creation of power in multilingual schools*. London: Trentham Books.

Davies, A. (2003). *Reflexive ethnography: a guide to researching selves and others*. London: Routledge.

Duchêne, A. and Heller, M. (2012). *Language in late capitalism: pride and profit*. New York: Routledge.

Duff, P. (2002). 'The discursive co-construction of knowledge, identity, and difference: an ethnography of communication in the high school mainstream', *Applied Linguistics*, 23: 289–322.

Duff, P. and Uchida, Y. (1997). 'The negotiation of teachers' sociocultural identities and practices in postsecondary EFL classrooms', *TESOL Quarterly*, 31(3): 451–486.

Eisenhart, M. (2001). 'Educational ethnography past, present and future: ideas to think with', *Educational Researcher*, 30(8): 16–27.

England, K. (1994). 'Getting personal: reflexivity, positionality, and feminist research', *Professional Geographer*, 46(1): 80–89.

Foley, D.E. (2002). 'Critical ethnography: the reflexive turn', *International Journal of Qualitative Studies in Education*, 15(4): 469–490.

Freire, P. (2000). *Pedagogy of the oppressed*. New York: Continuum.

Georgakopoulou, A. (2006). 'Thinking big with small stories in narrative and identity analysis', *Narrative Inquiry*, 16(1): 122–130.

Giampapa, F. (2004a). The politics of identity, representation and the discourses of self-identification: negotiating the periphery and the center, in A. Pavlenko and A. Blackledge (eds) *Negotiation of identities in multilingual contexts*. Clevedon: Multilingual Matters.

Giampapa, F. (2004b). *Italian Canadian youth and the negotiation of identities: the discourse on italianità, language and the spaces of identity*. PhD thesis, OISE University of Toronto, Canada.

Giampapa, F. (2011). 'The politics of "being and becoming" as researcher: identity, language and power in multilingual research settings', *Journal of Language, Identity, and Education*, 10(3): 127–131.

Giampapa, F. and Lamoureux, S. (guest eds) (2011). 'Special issue. Voices from the field: identity, language and power in multilingual research settings', *Journal of Language, Identity, and Education*, 10(3).

Guillemin, M. and Gillam, L. (2004). 'Ethics, reflexivity, and "ethically important moments" in research', *Qualitative Inquiry*, 10(2): 261–280.

Gumperz, J.J. and Hymes, D. (eds) (1972). *Directions in sociolinguistics*. New York: Holt, Rienhart and Winston.

Hammersley, M. (2007). 'Reflections on linguistic ethnography', *Journal of Sociolinguistics*, 11(5): 689–695.

Hornberger, N. (2006). Negotiating methodological rich points in applied linguistics research: an ethnographer's view, in M. Chalhoub-Deville, C. Chapelle and P. Duff (eds) *Inference and generalizability in applied linguistics: multiple perspectives*. Amsterdam: John Benjamins, pp. 221–240.

Hultgren, A.K., Erling, E.J. and Chowdhury, Q.H. (this volume). Ethics in language and identity research, in S. Preece (ed.) *The Routledge handbook of language and identity*. London: Routledge, pp. 257–271.

Hymes, D. (2003). *Foundations in sociolinguistics*. London: Routledge.

Ibrahim, A. (1999). 'Becoming Black: rap and hip-hop, race, gender, identity, and the politics of ESL learning', *TESOL Quarterly*, 33: 349–369.

Kanno, Y. and Norton, B. (eds) (2003). 'Imagined communities and education possibilities: introduction', *Journal of Language, Identity, and Education*, 2(4): 241–249.

Lather, P. (1986). 'Issues of validity in openly ideological research: between a rock and a soft place', *Interchange*, 17(4): 63–84.

Mackey, A. and Gass, S. (eds) (2012). *Research methods in second language acquisition: a practical guide*. Chichester: Blackwell Publishing.

Martin-Jones, M. and Gardner, S. (2012). Introduction: multilingualism, discourse and ethnography, in S. Gardner and M. Martin-Jones (eds) *Multilingualism, discourse and ethnography*. New York: Routledge, pp. 1–15.

May, S. (1997). Critical ethnography, in N.H. Hornberger and D. Corson (eds) *Encyclopedia of language and education. Vol. 8, Research methods in language and education*. Dordrecht, the Netherlands: Kluwer Academic, pp. 197–206.

Maybin, J. and Tusting, K. (2011). Linguistic ethnography, in J. Simpson (ed.) *The Routledge handbook of applied linguistics*. Abingdon: Routledge, pp. 515–528.

Norton, B. (2010). Language and identity, in N. Hornberger and S. McKay (eds) *Sociolinguistics and language education*. Bristol: Multilingual Matters, pp. 349–369.

Norton, B. (2013 [2000]). *Identity and language learning: extending the conversation*. 2nd edn. Bristol: Multilingual Matters.

Norton, B. and Early, M. (2011). 'Researcher identity, narrative inquiry, and language teaching research', *TESOL Quarterly*, 45(3): 415–439.

Norton Peirce, B. (1995). 'Social identity, investment and language learning', *TESOL Quarterly*, 29(1): 9–31.

Ortega, L. (2005). 'For what and for whom is our research? The ethical as transformative lens in instructed SLA', *Modern Language Journal*, 89(3): 427–443.

Paltridge, B. and Phakiti, A. (eds) (2010). *Continuum companion to research methods in applied linguistics*. London: Continuum.

Pavlenko, A. and Blackledge, A. (eds) (2004). *Negotiation of identities in multilingual contexts*. Clevedon: Multilingual Matters.

Rampton, B., Tusting, K., Maybin, J., Barwell, R., Creese, A. and Lytra, V. (2004). 'UK linguistic ethnography: a discussion paper'. Linguistic Ethnography Forum, King's College London.

Talmy, S. (2010). Critical research in applied linguistics, in B. Paltridge and A. Phakiti (eds) *Continuum companion to research methods in applied linguistics*. London: Continuum, pp. 127–142.

Talmy, S. (2012). Critical ethnography, *Encyclopedia of applied linguistics*. DOI: 10.1002/9781405198431. wbeal0279.

Vertovec, S. (2007). 'Super-diversity and its implications', Special issue. New directions in the anthropology of migration and multiculturalism, *Ethnic and Racial Studies*, 30(6): 1024–1054.

Watson-Gegeo, K.A. (1997). Classroom ethnography, in N.H. Hornberger and D. Corson (eds) *Encylopedia of language and education. Vol. 8, Research methods in language and education*. Dordrecht, The Netherlands: Kluwer Academic, pp. 135–144.

Weedon, C. (1997). *Feminist practice and poststructuralist theory*. London: Blackwell.

19

Challenges for language and identity researchers in the collection and transcription of spoken interaction

Eva Duran Eppler and Eva Codó

Introduction

The goal of this chapter is to address some of the complexities involved in the process of choosing, collecting and transcribing empirical data to investigate the relationship between language and identity. It provides less experienced researchers working in the field of applied linguistics with the tools for making informed decisions throughout the research process.

The first thing novice researchers need to have clear from the start is what (broad) definition of identity they adhere to, since identity research may be undertaken from a variety of ontological and epistemological perspectives within linguistics and applied linguistics (henceforth AL). The choice of perspective is of fundamental importance because distinct stances demand not only the gathering of distinct pieces of data, but also a different approach to data collection and transcription. For example, social constructionist researchers who follow ethnomethodological principles (see Benwell and Stokoe, this volume) assume that identity categories are emergent in social interaction. This means that they are generally not interested in obtaining background details on informants or the contexts in which the data was collected, since for them what identities are relevant in a given stretch of talk is an emergent, empirically traceable and locally negotiated matter. One type of data, i.e. talk-in-interaction, is usually enough, although it may be gathered in different sites with the purpose of building a collection or comparing across contexts. Researchers try to adopt fly-on-the-wall roles; some even choose to be totally absent from the field to prevent any unwanted disruptions of the naturalness of the focal interactional data. Additionally, since who speakers claim to be is a discoverable matter, transcription procedures search for neutrality. This is reflected in the use of uninformative speaker codes in transcripts, such as AAA or BBB.

By contrast, poststructuralist, interpretivist approaches, such as linguistic ethnography (see Pérez-Milans, this volume), require the researcher to gather different sorts of data, which may of course include naturally occurring talk-in-interaction but not exclusively. Instead, emphasis is placed on triangulation and dialogism. Claims about unfolding identity processes are usually made on the basis of ethnographic observations, interviews, recorded social interaction and various other types of data. Researchers are required to self-reflect on how their subjectivities have shaped the research process; they are not mere collectors, but active generators of data (Mason 2009). Transcription practices reflect the situated nature of research: participants are only identified by their real names if they want to (otherwise codes or pseudonyms are used), and their personal trajectories are explained in full detail (see Norton 2013 [2000]). So, what this brief comparison illustrates is that there are a number of decisions that applied linguists doing identity and language research must make very early on in their projects.

This chapter thus addresses some of the issues faced by scholars in the field of applied linguistics and sociolinguistics when collecting and transcribing spoken interaction for the investigation of the relationship between language and identity. The following are questions that researchers embarking on an empirical research project in language and identity research are likely to include:

1   Why did I decide to study identity from a (socio)linguistic perspective?
2   Which framework am I going to work in? What approach/perspective am I going to adopt? (See Part I of this volume.)
3   What are the research questions I intend to answer? (See Parts II–V of this volume.)
4   Which types of data will enable me to answer these questions?
5   Which speakers in which kind of contexts/interactions are likely to provide these data?
6   What's the best way of collecting these data? Do I do it myself? Do I use a fieldworker? Do I ask the participants to record themselves?
7   How do I prepare the data so that I can analyse it? How do I transcribe it?

Only researchers themselves can answer the first questions. Parts I–V in this volume offer suggestions for them. This chapter mainly addresses questions 4–7 and provides inexperienced researchers with information, guidance and the tools for making informed decisions throughout the process of data collection and transcription.

This chapter is divided into two main sections. The first discusses the most important considerations to be made in choosing and collecting one or several types of spoken data. The second one addresses the principal aspects involved in transcribing the data collected. Each section first provides an overview of the main issues and subsequently reflects critically on how these issues might be addressed. A brief summary of the key points made follows. The chapter closes with a list of related topics and the further reading section.

Issues in collecting spoken interaction and how to address them: different data types and their critical appraisal

Most research on language and identity in linguistics is based on the examination of spoken interaction, be it casual conversation, institutional talk, interview responses or narrative data. However, it must be borne in mind that powerful insights can also be gained by examining written texts. Sometimes, as with diachronic research, written documents are the only possibility. A case in point is the work by Pavlenko (2004), who analyses the autobiographical memoirs of Russian émigrés to North America at two different historical moments to compare and contrast the ideologies of integration that underpinned these women's language-learning accounts. Another research strand that draws on textual materials for analysis is the critical discursive perspective (see Zotzmann and O'Regan, this volume). An example is Blommaert and Verschueren's (1998) analysis of the construction of national identity in relation to foreign immigration into Belgium by the Belgian progressive press.

Textual and oral materials are not mutually exclusive; they may in fact be conveniently integrated within one single research design. For example, investigating hegemonic (or stereotypical) representations in public discourse of a particular social, ethnic or religious group, whether by mainstream society or by group representatives, is a necessary step to follow in order to understand the practices of self (re)definition of its members, that is, what social categorisations or aspects of it they may be trying to negotiate or simply challenge in their practices/accounts (see Giampapa 2004 for an illuminating case study). Be that as it may, spoken interactive data, whether in combination with other types or on its own, is the most common sort of empirical material used to investigate the relationship between language and identity. This is because it is generally accepted that, on the one hand, identities do not exist independently of language and that, on the other, identity construction is a social matter. In what follows, we shall discuss the most common types of interactional data to be gathered, together with their advantages and limitations.

Naturally occurring interactional data

Various kinds of interactional data may be collected to investigate identities in/through language use. Interactions may involve two or multiple parties; they may occur face to face or be technology mediated; they may be formal or informal; they may have an institutional character or they may not; they may involve social distance and asymmetries of power and knowledge; or they may occur among peers (for a nice collection of studies in a variety of settings, see Antaki and Widdicombe 1998). They may be audio-recorded or video-recorded and used in combination with other types of data or in isolation. As we mentioned earlier, it all depends on the specific questions a researcher wants to answer and the stance s/he takes on what the nature of identity is – where it resides and how it can be best studied. Following common usage, in this section we use the term 'naturally occurring interactional data' to refer to unplanned interactive language use that unfolds – insofar as possible – without researcher intervention. This is to distinguish it from (solicited) interview data. Yet many a researcher would rightly claim that interview data is also a naturally occurring type of data, though produced in a specialist type of communicative event.

The advantage of using naturally occurring interactional data is that it enables researchers to examine identity as social action, as part of the business of getting things accomplished in talk. Identity construction in interaction is situated, relational, empirically traceable and, following poststructuralist positions (see Baxter, this volume), multiple, flexible and dynamic. However, it must be borne in mind that the centrality and methodological treatment accorded to interactional data depends, as we said, on researchers' theoretical point of departure. In fact, what we are dealing with is a continuum of methodological positions rather than discrete, separate choices. From a conversation-analytical perspective, it is fundamental to collect data that is 'untouched' by the researcher's presence. Additionally, conversation analysts depart from the assumption that identity is done in interaction through participants' ongoing self- and other-categorisation processes (see Benwell and Stokoe, this volume). For that reason, they often make a point of not knowing who the participants are so as not to be 'biased' in their analyses by conversationally extraneous identity details. Edwards (1998: 20), for example, claims the following in his analysis of social categories in relationship counselling sessions: 'I know nothing of any of the three participants (and have never met them) outside of what is said on the tape.' By contrast, the researcher's acquaintance with the researched is not to be refrained from in ethnographic approaches to language and identity, which may include the collection of interactional data. In those studies, it is the researcher's long-term involvement with informants rather than his/her absence that facilitates participants being oblivious to the researcher's presence and methods.

As regards the practicalities of data collection, similar considerations must be made when gathering talk for other research purposes (see Cameron 2001). Participants' informed consent must be obtained and their anonymity guaranteed (see Hultgren *et al.*, this volume). If video-recording is involved, participants and researchers must come to an agreement as to what constitutes good informant protection in ways that abide by university regulations for appropriate research conduct. A major source of difficulty with naturally occurring talk is noise. To ensure good quality recordings, external noise must be kept under control insofar as possible. This may be difficult when recordings take place in institutional settings where a number of social activities may be going on at the same time and participants and other individuals may be manipulating different kinds of artefacts. For instance, recording data in classrooms can be particularly hard going if researchers attempt to capture everything. The best way of going about recording in a classroom is to focus on recording specific types of data at different moments in time (e.g. focused teacher–student interaction, small group work, etc.; cf. Norton and Toohey 2011). Further complexity may be added in professional contexts where interconnected but different courses of action may take place in geographically distant spaces. This is the case in Mondada (2007), where analysing a videotaped operation in a major French hospital involves understanding what goes on in the operation theatre but also in an amphitheatre where the image is transmitted for training and advisory purposes.

Interview data

Traditionally, interviews have been considered to be the privileged point of entry into people's life meanings, identities and experiences. For a long time, it was believed that there was no better way of understanding who people believed themselves to be than to ask them. Yet in recent decades there has been thorough questioning of both interviewing as a method to access people's values, ideas and emotions, and of identity as having some pre-existing reality status in people's brains (see Benwell and Stokoe 2006 for a comprehensive critique of this perspective).

Being interviewed is not about telling some inner truth about ourselves; it is a communicative event between two or more interlocutors situated in particular linguistic, socioeconomic, historical and political regimes. This means that interviewees' responses are shaped by perceptions of the interviewer – that is, who s/he is; what his/her values and expectations might be; what s/he might be after, etc. Interviewers may also be concerned about the larger audience/readership for their words, and thus construct their responses accordingly. This does not mean that respondents are not being truthful; it just means that they are producing appropriate answers in keeping with their understandings of the interview situation. Of course, interviewees will try to self-present in a positive (or even negative) light, that's only human, but understanding what constitutes positive or negative self-presentation will provide researchers with valuable information about how they are being positioned as interviewers. This information will then be key for their analytical endeavours. Another source of worry for inexperienced researchers tends to be the veracity of informants' accounts of the past. It must be taken into account that memories are always reconstructions, which are fashioned and refashioned as they are (re)told. This has nothing to do with informants being sincere. As Block (2006) states, the analytical purchase of past narratives is not to get to understand informants' past lives but rather to comprehend their process of self-construction in the present.

The third major pitfall of interviewing as a technique that is still often overlooked is its interactive nature. Responses are shaped by previous questions; they are interactively situated. There is no way in which responses can be rigorously analysed without taking into account the way they were framed by previous interviewer talk, not just the immediately preceding question but the whole (evolving) context of the interaction. With all this, we are not trying to dismiss the interview as a valid research methodology for language and identity research; we just want to make novice researchers aware of its limitations and the ways in which they can be circumvented (for more details on general interviewing procedures see Kvale 2007; Codó 2008).

Talking about one's identity is no easy task, as it goes to the heart of our most intimate beliefs and emotions. It generates discomfort, and in certain politically charged contexts it may cause stress and even anxiety. For this reason, inquiring directly about identity is generally useless. It will only produce short and ready-made responses. The most suitable approach is to try to engage informants in experiential, self-reflective talk through the formulation of open-ended response prompts (they do not have to be phrased as questions; oftentimes they actually work better if they are not). One ideal field for investigating identity is precisely language (see Preece 2009 as an example of language-based interviews), due to the close (ideological) connection that exists between what language(s) we speak and who we believe we are/want to be. In the case of migration, additionally, local language competence is the symbolic terrain over which issues of legitimacy, moral worth and citizenship are constantly fought.

The semi-structured or unstructured interview format allows researchers the flexibility necessary to formulate context-sensitive questions, pursue emergent topic leads and elicit longish pieces of discourse. One of the elements that researchers will have to consider is the language(s) in which to conduct the interviews, taking into account not only individual repertoires and linguistic competences, but also informants' will. This may entail having to search for an interviewer who is proficient in informants' (preferred) language(s) and giving him/her specific training. Researchers will have to decide what to prioritise, taking into account the advantages and disadvantages of each option, whether informants' voice and ease of expression or their own role as interviewees. Another consideration to make is how many interviews to carry out, how separate in time, and their nature. Of course, the number of interviews will be conditioned by access to informants and practical considerations. Yet this is an important aspect to be thought through before embarking on any research project because it will have an impact on the depth and quality of the data collected.

Among interviewing techniques, perhaps the most popular type for understanding processes of self-definition, self-categorisation, (dis)identification and (dis)affiliation is the life-story interview. Atkinson (1998: 8) defines the life story as a 'fairly complete narrating of one's entire experience of life as a whole, highlighting the most important aspects'. One crucial aspect of life stories is that interviewees are in control of the telling. This means that interviewers must deploy a facilitator stance but refrain from trying to steer the narration in particular directions.

Life stories are long interview events, which usually involve (but not necessarily) repeated meetings with informants. The first encounter may be focused on building a relationship of trust, and getting at general details about informants' past and present lives (and possibly future expectations). Subsequent interviews may be more concrete, purporting either to obtain details of specific events/spheres of informants' lives (e.g. work, religious practices, social networks, etc.) or the reasoning behind specific life-changing decisions and their significance. Evaluative questions are more risky to ask and more complex to answer than factual questions, and this is why they tend to be asked later in the research process. One possibility to even out the power asymmetries inherent to any interview situation is to build subsequent encounters around the discussion of transcripts from previous occasions, as in Mills (2004). This is a way of handing control over to informants while simultaneously allowing for the emergence of unexpected foci of interest in interview contexts that may serve to illuminate identity-related issues.

Narrative data

Since the 1980s, the popularity of narratives for identity research has continued to grow. This is linked to a major epistemological shift in the social sciences away from abstract, positivist and rational thinking, and towards valuing situated constructions of meaning and emotions. According to De Fina and Georgakopoulou (2012), narrative has flourished because, as a heuristic tool, it encapsulates the ontological and epistemological principles of postmodernism, which values subjectivity (rather than objective reality) and individual experience (rather than factual events).

The use of narrative in identity research follows from biographical approaches to life which hold that becoming social beings is about developing a (coherent) life story about ourselves (Linde 1993), one that is constantly revisited and retold. Narrative is at the heart of the ways in which we construct ourselves as moral individuals, and it is closely associated with de-essentialist understandings of the self, as socially negotiated and relational.

A great deal of research on language and identity has been based on narratives of various sorts: from the life-story narrative mentioned above to specialist narratives of major illness; divorce; religious, ideological or political conversion; career choice, etc. Particularly interesting for applied linguistics are narratives of language conflict (Relaño-Pastor and De Fina 2005). The analytical purchase of narratives in identity research lies in the assumption that it is in narrative that people make sense and give coherence to their fragmented and situated life experiences, and convey a sense of who they are or want to be. Narratives are pervasive in everyday life. For research purposes, we can either tap naturally occurring narratives in professional, family or peer-group contexts, or simply collect research narratives through unstructured or semi-structured sociolinguistic interviews. Although elicited narratives have often been presented as unnatural and constrained, De Fina (2009) advocates a context-sensitive approach to (elicited) narratives which views them as co-constructed and emergent in interaction in the same way as unelicited narratives are.

Atkinson and Delamont (2006) follow a similar line of thinking in cautioning researchers against assuming that narratives are the most 'authentic route' to the inner self of informants. As they rightly point out, narratives are forms of self-representation, which are interactively, historically, politically and culturally located. Narratives are not discursive renderings of some pre-existing social reality; instead, it is in narrative that reality is constructed. In Atkinson and Delamont's (2006: 166) words, narratives have to be analysed in their dual nature as both 'accounts' and 'performances'. As accounts, they are rhetorical devices by which narrators construct their version of past events, legitimise actions and motives, and evaluate others morally; in sum, they are forms of persuasion. Narratives are also situated performances, that is, pieces of discourse produced with and for a given audience, both present and absent. Narratives are thus social events oriented to achieving certain interpersonal effects, such as moving, instilling pity in one's interlocutors, saving one's face, etc. Dramatic features play a fundamental role in achieving narrative purpose, and as such they must be central to any analytical endeavour.

Over the last two decades, considerable effort has been made at proposing systematic ways of examining narrative genres, e.g. accounts, and at expanding the notion of narrative beyond Labov's canonical narrative form. (De Fina and Georgakopoulou 2012 is an excellent overview of major methodological trends and issues, as well as analytical frameworks in narrative inquiry.) There is increasing recognition of narratives as situated events where tellers do identity. Identity is linked to notions such as 'indexicality', 'positioning' and 'stance'. Identity work is said to happen at various levels, and in particular at the level of the story-world and that of the interaction. Understanding how identity is done through self-presentation in the telling of particular stories (which are conglomerates of form, content and performance), how this level intersects with the unfolding interactional business of relating to the story recipient (whoever it may be) and how both levels index hegemonic imaginaries of particular social groups has been a major accomplishment of interactional approaches to narrative. Even though these approaches draw extensively on conversationalists' attention to detail, they also incorporate analytical principles from various other theoretical paradigms (and, accordingly, also other types of data, such as ethnographic details and discursive representations).

To conclude, this section has discussed different types of data to be collected for identity analysis in applied linguistics. As we mentioned at the beginning, they can be used in isolation or in combination. In any case, all the types of data presented can be complemented by participant observation, whose scope and depth will depend on the epistemological paradigm adopted, not only with regard to the nature of identity but also to the relationship between language and social life (see Blommaert and Jie 2010). Deciding on research questions and broad theoretical positions right away is important, because as we have discussed there are important choices to be made as to how much data to be collected and what type(s) from very early on. The following section will introduce researchers to the main issues with regard to data transcription and coding.

Issues in transcription and how to address them

Transcription is the process of representing spoken interaction in an (ortho)graphic medium. This includes information on who said what to whom and when, and may include information on how and under what circumstances. The most frequent comments on linguistic transcripts by people who have never seen one before tend to focus on the main features of naturally occurring spoken interaction (and consequently transcriptions thereof): there are repetitions, false starts, retracings (with or without repetition of previously said material), pauses, interruptions and overlaps, to name just a few.

The first question we need to address is whether transcription is still a key issue that researchers who wish to use naturally occurring data for their study of language and identity need to get to grips with. The question poses itself because today the data types discussed in the first section of this chapter tend to be gathered, stored and reproduced digitally. This greatly eases accessing them as a whole or in sections/frames. So why do researchers of spoken interaction still embark on the notoriously time-consuming process of transcription? We do so because even multiple replays do not enable us humans to absorb, store and recall a fraction of the impermanent, synchronous, multidimensional details that constitute interaction. Transcription facilitates data analysis by making interaction available for economical and systematic examination. In the long run, transcription saves time, and this is why analyses are often mainly based on transcripts. The process of capturing real-time interaction in a less transient, written and spatial medium advances our understanding of verbal interaction. As one of the foremost authorities on transcription, John Du Bois (1991: 75), puts it, 'through the experience of transcribing the transcriber is constantly learning about discourse'.

Transcription is theory

Although transcription is fundamentally a methodological choice, transcripts are never neutral representations of oral language (Ochs 1979); some researchers even view transcription as a political process (Roberts 1997; Bucholtz 2000).

Transcripts are biased for two main reasons. First, they have to be selective because human interaction is too rich for all of it to be represented (ortho)graphically. If we tried to focus on all aspects of an interactional piece, we could only work on short sections, and it would be virtually impossible to examine one aspect over several interactional episodes. Therefore, researchers/transcribers have to be selective and decide what to transcribe, i.e. what types of information to preserve, which descriptive categories to use, and how to transcribe it (layout and choice of symbols).

Second, decisions made early on in the process of a research project affect later stages. The three main stages of sociolinguistic research projects, adapted from Holmes and Hazen (2013), illustrate that the two activities discussed in this chapter are situated at the later stages.

Table 19.1 Stages of sociolinguistic research projects

Decision stage →	Realisation stage →	Execution stage
Objectives	Participants	**Data collection**
Research questions	Corpora/databases	**Transcription**
Theoretical framework	Data collection instruments/	Coding/tagging
Units of analysis/linguistic level	method	Accountability/reliability
		Analytic method

Adapted from Holmes and Hazen (2013: 181).

The questions identity researchers need to ask themselves (see introduction to this chapter) can now be associated with the three main stages of sociolinguistics research projects. Questions 1–3 ((1) Why did I decide to study identity? (2) Which framework am I going to work in? (3) What are the research questions I intend to answer?) form part of the decision-making process. Questions 4–6 ((4) Which types of data will enable me to answer these questions? (5) Which speakers in which kind of contexts/interactions are likely to provide these data? (6) What's the best way of collecting these data?) relate to the realisation stage. Question 7 (How do I prepare the data so that I can analyse them?) is a crucial process in the execution of an applied linguistics/sociolinguistic research project.

Data collection and transcription are linked to the project's objectives, the research questions, and the theoretical approach chosen at the decision stage. Every theoretical framework has a focus that needs to be addressed in transcripts (for the researcher to be able to draw conclusions within the chosen approach); transcription is shaped by theory. Furthermore, every type of spoken interaction data has characteristics that need to be transcribed/coded. For example, only interactions that involve two or multiple parties involve overlaps and lend themselves to a conversation analytical approach. The type of data collected thus also influences – but does not determine – many aspects of the transcription process.

There is no single, unique, correct method of transcription and no unbiased representation of data. The decision about what to transcribe affects not only the researcher who collects the data, but also all researchers who subsequently use the transcripts (especially if the original audio/video recordings are not made available). Decisions on how to transcribe can furthermore affect less experienced researchers' perception of the data. Elinor Ochs (1979), for example, argues that the speaker represented in the left-most column in a column-based transcription format may be viewed as the principal interactant. We would, however, argue that even fairly novice researchers can see beyond points of data presentation as long as they are aware of the format choices (discussed later in the section on format-based decisions) and reflect on transcription practices. This is what we aim to enable researchers to do with this chapter.

The politics of transcription

Both Celia Roberts and Mary Bucholtz, who work within interactional sociolinguistic and social constructionist approaches respectively, have argued that transcription is a political process. Both of them take up the issue of representing non-standard speech with non-standard orthography (sometimes also called 'eye dialect') with the aim of creating a transcript 'that will look to the eye how it sounds to the ear' (Schenkein 1978: xi). Apart from the fact that not even phonetic transcripts achieve this, Roberts (1997) points out that the use of non-standard orthography can influence the social evaluation the reader makes of the informants. Bucholtz (2000) demonstrates the inaccuracy and inconsistency of the representation of colloquial speech with non-standard spelling, and refers to the work of Jaffe and Walton (2000: 561), who 'found that people uncritically and spontaneously read non-standard orthographies as indices of low socioeconomic status'. We question the generality of this statement but agree with Roberts and Bucholtz in calling for a reflexive transcription practice that shows awareness and acknowledgement of the limitations of transcription choices. Non-standard spellings furthermore create considerable problems for computer-readable corpora (the majority today), because of the inconsistency with which lexical items are represented in such transcripts. The word *of*, for example, has been found to be represented as *of, uff, ohv, awv, off, awf* and *aff* in one transcript (Bucholtz 2000). Automatic searches for this word token are only possible if the various tokens of the word are linked to the type in the transcript, with conversion tables, or files which supplement the standard syntax of automated search programmers. Although phonetic or phonological transcription is generally considered to be too time consuming for most types of language interaction research, it may be more practical to transcribe short relevant sections in the IPA (to preserve phonological variation) than use non-standard spellings.

General principles of transcription

The next sections assume that readers who are about to embark on transcription have already made several decisions: they wish to investigate language and identity, they have clear research questions, and they have collected one of the types of interactional data discussed in the first part of this chapter. In the next sections we will therefore mainly discuss transcription issues that emerge in research projects of this type. We will provide researchers with guidelines for choosing/adapting a system of transcription that will allow them to transcribe the features most relevant to their research questions and method of analysis/theoretical framework. What follows draws on the seminal work by Jane Edwards (2003) and John Du Bois (1991).

Most transcripts contain three types of encoding: transcription, coding and mark-up. The more complex and refined the process of transcription becomes, the more it starts to resemble coding, the classification of units of data into analytical categories (also referred to as annotation or tagging in corpus linguistics). In language and identity projects, researchers may, for example, want to code passages in which the speaker indexes multiple identities. This example illustrates that coding is even more interpretive and closely tied to theoretical approaches than transcribing. Mark-up is the frequently hidden (behind an interface) and therefore neglected formatting information of transcripts (which also includes metadata/text classifications and structural representations). SGML (Standard Generalised Markup Language) and XML (eXtensible Markup Language) are the most widely used mark-up languages in corpus and computational linguistics. Mark-up is essential for data conversion between different formats/systems and thus crucial for data sharing.

Since the mid-1990s many spoken language projects (MARSEC, HCRC, ToBI, Transcriber, SignStream, CHILDES) have developed the ability to link transcripts to audio and video recordings. This is an important development as it allows researchers to verify transcripts and retrieve information from the original interactional data, which has not been transcribed and/or coded.

When selecting, adapting or developing a transcription system that allows researchers to transcribe the features most relevant to their research questions and theoretical framework, they should ensure that the categories within each contrast set (e.g. short and long pause in the contrast set pause length) of the transcription system satisfy three general principles. More specifically, the categories must be:

- Systematically discernible, i.e. it should be clear whether a section of the recording is a pause or not;
- Exhaustive, i.e. the system should contain a transcription convention or code that allows researchers to transcribe or code each relevant aspect of the data, or allows the addition of categories (plus associated symbols);
- Usefully contrastive, i.e. long and short pauses are defined in relation to the type of data.

These are criteria that every transcription system should fulfil because it is impossible to create an accurate and consistent transcript if one does not know how many and what type of categories there are (in a set).

As virtually all transcripts produced today are machine-readable, the single most important design principle of transcripts is that similar instances are encoded in predictably similar ways. If transcription and encoding is unsystematic, a computer will never find all the instances of what data analysts are looking for; consequently results will be unrepresentative and misleading (because they will contain false positives and/or false negatives). The non-standard orthographic representations of 'of' given earlier are an illustrating case in point. Systematic encoding is also important for updating, reformatting and sharing transcripts.

A principle that tends to be particularly important to audiences at the receiving end of research is readability. Readability, however, is not only important for presentation purposes, but also for 'getting a feel for the data', hypothesis generation, minimising error in data entry and error checking. This is why many transcription systems, especially those used in spoken interaction research, draw on conventions employed by playwrights (for example, three dots to mark a pause).

Like most written materials, transcripts frequently make use of two main cues for making sense of data: spatial organisation and visual prominence. The use of these two cues is fairly intuitive, but as systematicity is so important for transcripts, it is worth spelling them out. For example, closely related events/types of information tend to be placed spatially near each other;

temporarily earlier events are presented earlier on the page; and information that helps interpret an utterance or event is placed before the utterance. The representation of qualitatively different types of information (e.g. spoken words vs. researcher comments) in distinctly different ways (e.g. different fonts), and the use of few, short, iconic and straightforwardly interpretable symbols (e.g. the use of a slash (/) to mark rising intonation), facilitate readability.

These are the general design principles of transcripts that have emerged in the approximately 22 centuries since spoken language has been rendered in writing (Parkes 1993 cited in Edwards 2003). Naturally, the transcription of video recordings poses even more challenges, as even more information is available than can be captured (ortho)graphically. (For excellent work on multi-modal transcription see Kress and van Leeuwen 2001; Machin 2007; Jewitt 2011.) Going against the general design principles in the transcription of recorded interactional data is comparable to ignoring a red traffic light. Researchers/transcribers may therefore want to save their energy for the decisions they will have to make. These decisions are important, as the options chosen may affect their own and/or others' perceptions of the interactions presented in the transcript.

Decisions in transcription

The decisions researchers working on interactional data have to make fall into two main categories: format-based and content-based decisions.

Format-based decisions

Format-based decisions involve the format of the transcripts, and the symbols used to represent features of spoken interaction relevant to the research question. In a column-based format, utterances by different speakers are arranged in separate columns (e.g. in carer–child interactions). The most widely used format in the transcription of naturally occurring interactions is the vertical format, in which utterances by individual speakers are arranged one above the other. This format also helps with the issue of translation and/or inter-linear glossing that many AL scholars who collect data in multilingual contexts face (cf. Creese and Blackledge, this volume; Edwards 2003). Partiture notation (also called 'musical score' or 'stave' format) is a version of the vertical format which, as the name suggests, resembles a musical score in that utterances/turns by different speakers are put on different lines and the spatial arrangement (frequently in combination with brackets which indicate overlapping stretches of speech) shows when different speakers come in or drop out of the spoken interaction.

Box 19.1 Partiture notation

```
1   Marion:   I see if it can        (st-)

2   Carole:          ┌ Oh, I have          office hours=
3   Len:             │ Yeah, that's (   ) three of em
4   Rafe:            └ Is that OK? Could we try that

5   Carole:   =but I'm here. I mean office hours doesn't count
```
Source: Edelsky (1993: 193).

Box 19.1, an example of a moderately detailed partiture transcript, which marks overlapping speech ([), truncated words (-), pauses (   ), self-completion (=) and rising intonational contour (?), also illustrates that more detailed interspersed transcription or coding can lead to information overload. This is why many researchers nowadays opt for the multi-linear (or inter-linear) format in which codes are placed on separate lines (called tiers) beneath the line that contains the speaker's utterance (with one-to-one linking between the tiers).

Researchers/transcribers who adopt an existing transcription system will have little choice over the symbols/notations used. How accessible (easily learned), economical, robust and adapt-able the symbols used for discourse transcription are may, however, influence researchers'/transcribers' choice of transcription system. The good news about format-based decisions in a digital day and age is that, with consistent encoding and appropriate software, most formats can be easily translated into others.

Content-based decisions

Content-based decisions relate to the types of information that are preserved in a transcript, and the descriptive categories used. Unlike format-based decisions, content-based decisions cannot be adjusted by machine. For every data type and set, and for every research question, a decision has to be made regarding the number and type of descriptive categories used to encode informa-tion present in interactional data. Content-based choices have to be matched with those made at the decision stage: the categories not only have to fulfil the general principles of category design outlined earlier (systematically discernible, usefully contrastive and exhaustive), but they also need to be compatible with the theoretical framework adopted, and have to enable the researcher to answer his/her research questions; that is, the categories used need to meet the research objectives. Content-based decisions create distinctions between different transcription systems because they most directly reflect the impact of theory on methods.

The most basic content-based decision involves the units of analysis a researcher wants to investigate (this is why 'unit of analysis/linguistics level' is in the first [decision] stage column of Holmes and Hazen's outline of the research process). In language and identity research, possible choices include a speaker turn, an utterance, an intonation unit or an idea unit. The pros and cons of another important content-based decision, whether to transcribe in standard orthogra-phy or eye dialect, has already been discussed. Because language and identity research aims at capturing aspects of interaction as they are perceived by human participants, the categories used in such transcription – just like the transcript itself – are always interpretive. This particularly applies to pause length and prosody. In language and identity research, pause length is consid-ered to be locally negotiated and is therefore more frequently given in terms of interpretive judgements of long and short rather than measured. Similarly it is the researcher's/transcriber's task to determine which prosodic cues (prominence/stress, duration/length of sounds/syllables and intonation) are meaningful within a set of data and theoretical framework, and whether and how to encode them. The rhythm of interaction and coordination among participants also require content-based decisions by the researcher/transcriber. The musical score transcript illustrates one way of encoding this type of information. Conversation analysts are particularly interested in turn transition and wish to encode features of naturally occurring interactions such as latching, overlap and interruption. The amount of detail encoded and the number of categories in each contrast set (e.g. self-interruption vs. other interruption or just interruption; beginning and end of overlap or just beginning of overlap) depends on the research question. Researchers who focus on non-verbal aspects and events accompanying spoken interaction still occasionally encode those aspects that are most relevant to their research questions. Mostly, however, this type of information is nowadays retrieved from time-stamped video recordings that are linked to the transcript. For an illustration and explication of how content- and format-based decisions can lead to quite different transcripts of the same recording by the same researcher (Deborah Tannen), see Mishler (1991: 262–264).

Practicalities

Practicalities are always more appealing than decisions. Researchers who have never transcribed naturally occurring spoken interaction might find it useful to transcribe two to five minutes from their own data before they read on. This will flag up the importance of the general design principles and choices they will be facing when creating representations in writing of the speech events they (or their fieldworkers) recorded. Many practicalities impact on the transcription process: they range from the quality of the recording and the availability of equipment (computers, transcription software, controllers, headsets, etc.), time and space, to the health of the transcriber's back. We will therefore only include a few that seem particularly relevant to us and would like to advise novice transcribers to have a chat with more experienced researchers (on transcription fora such as http://forum.linguisticteam.org or in person) before they start and whenever they encounter practical problems.

The piece of information that those researchers unacquainted with transcription would probably most like to know about is: how time-consuming is transcription? The answer to this question depends on the quality of the recording, the type of interaction (one, two or multiple participants, frequency of overlaps, etc.) and the amount of detail encoded. Of course, the better the quality of the recording, the easier the transcription process will be. In our experience transcription time lies somewhere between 16:1 and 20:1 (16 to 20 hours to transcribe one hour of recorded interaction), that is, without time stamping and checking.

New transcription and encoding projects and associated software reaches the market virtually every year. If you would like to link your work to a bigger project or contribute to a database (this is a question of data storage and sharing), you may want to use transcription software that facilitates this integration. Most of this software is freely available on the web, so all you need to do is search for CAVA, EAGLES, ELAN, HIAT-DOS, Media Tagger, TED, TEI and the CA format in CLAN, to mention just a few. If you want to integrate your transcripts into a bigger project or database and/or use automated analysis tools, you will have to check the syntax of your files and correct it for the file to become readable by automatic analysis programs.

This leads us back to the single most important design principle of modern – i.e. machine-readable – transcripts: they need to be accurate, consistent, reliable and systematic. To avoid transcriber effects (such as category drift; this is when a feature of spoken interaction first gets transcribed/coded as one category but then slips into a different category during the transcription process) and achieve a 'Gold Standard' in transcription, you may want to keep a transcription/coding protocol that records, for example, information on the anonymisation of speakers and the decisions discussed earlier and have the transcript checked by the transcriber after a time interval or, ideally, by another researcher (called inter-rater reliability checks). To achieve the 'Gold Standard', this should involve approximately 10 per cent of randomly selected data (Rietved and van Hout 1993).

Transcription is an open-ended process that can start with a 'rough' transcript that gets more and more refined until the format and categories used match the research objectives and questions.

Summary

This chapter has examined the main issues faced by scholars in the field of applied linguistics and sociolinguistics when collecting and transcribing spoken interaction for language and identity projects. In summary, when collecting data, the following principles should be borne in mind:

- Before starting, it is important to have a clear definition of identity and of the role of language in its constitution. This will shape research questions, and determine choice of data and methods of data collection/generation.
- Spoken interactional data, be it naturally occurring talk-in-interaction, interviews or narratives, is always contextually situated and interactively constructed. This general principle should always inform data collection decisions. In particular, researchers should be reflexive about their own impact on the production of interview responses and solicited narratives.

The most important points about transcribing, the process of representing spoken interaction in an (ortho)graphic medium, are:

- Like the data collected, transcripts must serve the aims of the research project; that is, they must 'fit' the theoretical approach and answer the research questions.
- Transcripts are always interpretive.
- Existing transcription systems/coding schemes should be used and, if necessary, adapted to the specific needs of the research project.
- The transcription should be as accurate, consistent and systematic as possible.

Related topics

Identity in variationist sociolinguistics; Ethnomethodological and conversation analytic approaches to identity; Language and identity in linguistic ethnography; Discursive psychology and the production of identity in language practices; Ethics in language and identities research; The politics of researcher identities: opportunities and challenges in identities research; Constructing age identity: the case of Mexican EFL learners; Being a language teacher in the content classroom: teacher identity and content and language integrated learning (CLIL); Disability identities and category work in institutional practices: the case of a 'typical ADHD girl'; 'Comes with the territory': expert–novice and insider–outsider identities in police interviews; The future of identity research: impact and new developments in sociolinguistics.

Further reading

Barnett, R., Codó, E., Eppler, E., Forcadell, M., Gardner-Chloros, P., van Hout, R., Moyer, M., Torras, M.C., Turell, M.T., Sebba, M., Starren, A. and Wensing, S. (2000). 'The LIDES coding manual: a document for preparing and analyzing language interaction data', *International Journal of Bilingualism*, 4(2): 131–270. (This transcription and coding manual demonstrates and illustrates the steps every transcriber has to take, that is, select an appropriate system and adjust it to their own needs, and provides rationales for these decisions.)

Blommaert, J. and Jie, D. (2010). *Ethnographic fieldwork: a beginner's guide*. Bristol: Multilingual Matters. (This introductory book provides very concrete and practical advice on how to conduct an ethnographically designed research project. Using the authors' examples, it serves to answer most of the questions novice researchers may have. A recommended read before getting into the field.)

Cameron, D. (2001). *Working with spoken discourse*. London: SAGE. (A very accessible introduction to research on interactional discourse and the issues involved therein.)

Du Bois, J.W. (1991). 'Transcription design principles for spoken language research', *Pragmatics*, 1(1): 71–106. (This publication is old but encourages everybody, including upper-level undergraduates, postgraduates and academics, to systematically think through what they want from a transcription and thus helps in choosing the most appropriate system to start with.)

Edwards, J.A. (2003). The transcription of discourse, in D. Schiffrin, D. Tannen and H.E. Hamilton (eds) *The handbook of discourse analysis*. London: Blackwell, pp. 321–348. (This chapter is the most recent, easily accessible publication on the topic by one of the leading international experts, with the added advantage that it focuses on the transcription of discourse.)

References

Antaki, C. and Widdicombe, S. (eds) (1998). *Identities in talk*. London: SAGE.

Atkinson, P. and Delamont, S. (2006). 'Rescuing narrative from qualitative research', *Narrative Inquiry*, 16(1): 164–172.

Atkinson, R. (1998). *The life story interview*. London: SAGE.

Baxter, J. (this volume). Positioning language and identity: poststructuralist perspectives, in S. Preece (ed.) *The Routledge handbook of language and identity*. London: Routledge, pp. 34–49.

Benwell, B. and Stokoe, E. (2006). *Discourse and identity*. Edinburgh: Edinburgh University Press.

Benwell, B. and Stokoe, E. (this volume). Ethnomethodological and conversation analytic approaches to identity, in S. Preece (ed.) *The Routledge handbook of language and identity*. London: Routledge, pp. 66–82.

Block, D. (2006). *Multilingual identities in a global city: London stories*. London: Palgrave.

Blommaert, J. and Jie, D. (2010). *Ethnographic fieldwork: a beginner's guide*. Bristol: Multilingual Matters.

Blommaert, J. and Verschueren, J. (1998). *Debating diversity: analysing the discourse of tolerance*. London: Routledge.

Bucholtz, M. (2000). 'The politics of transcription', *Journal of Pragmatics*, 3: 1439–1465.

Cameron, D. (2001). *Working with spoken discourse*. London: SAGE.

Codó, E. (2008). Interviews and questionnaires, in L. Wei and M.G. Moyer (eds) *The Blackwell guide to research methods in bilingualism and multilingualism*. London: Blackwell, pp. 158–176.

Creese, A. and Blackledge, A. (this volume). A linguistic ethnography of identity: adopting a heteroglossic frame, in S. Preece (ed.) *The Routledge handbook of language and identity*. London: Routledge, pp. 272–288.

De Fina, A. (2009). 'Narratives in interview – the case of accounts: for an interactional approach to narrative genres', *Narrative Inquiry*, 19(2): 233–258.

De Fina, A. and Georgakopoulou, A. (2012). *Analyzing narratives*. Cambridge: Cambridge University Press.

Du Bois, J.W. (1991). 'Transcription design principles for spoken language research', *Pragmatics*, 1(1): 71–106.

Edelsky, C. (1993). Who's got the floor?, in D. Tannen (ed.) *Gender and conversational interaction*. Oxford: Oxford University Press, pp. 189–230.

Edwards, D. (1998). The relevant thing about her: social identity categories in use, in C. Antaki and S. Widdicombe (eds) *Identities in talk*. London: SAGE, pp. 15–33.

Edwards, J.A. (2003). The transcription of discourse, in D. Schiffrin, D. Tannen and H.E. Hamilton (eds) *The handbook of discourse analysis*. London: Blackwell, pp. 321–348.

Giampapa, F. (2004). The politics of identity, representation, and the discourses of self-identification: negotiating the periphery and the center, in A. Pavlenko and A. Blackledge (eds) *Negotiation of identities in multilingual contexts*. Clevedon: Multilingual Matters, pp. 192–218.

Holmes, J. and Hazen, K. (eds) (2013). *Research methods in sociolinguistics*. London: Wiley-Blackwell.

Hultgren, A.K., Erling, E.J. and Chowdhury, Q.H. (this volume). Ethics in language and identity research, in S. Preece (ed.) *The Routledge handbook of language and identity*. London: Routledge, pp. 257–271.

Jaffe, A. and Walton, S. (2000). 'The voices people read: orthography and the representation of non-standard speech', *Journal of Sociolinguistics*, 4(2): 561–587.

Jewitt, C. (ed.) (2011). *The Routledge handbook of multimodal analysis*. London: Routledge.

Kress, G. and van Leeuwen, T. (2001). *Multimodal discourse: the modes and media of contemporary communication*. London: Hodder Arnold.

Kvale, S. (2007). *Doing interviews*. London: SAGE.

Linde, C. (1993). *Life stories: the creation of coherence*. New York: Oxford University Press.

Machin, D. (2007). *Introduction to multimodal analysis*. London: Hodder Arnold.

Mason, J. (2009). *Qualitative research*. 2nd edn. London: SAGE.

Mills, J. (2004). Mothers and mother tongue: perspectives on self-construction by mothers of Pakistani heritage, in A. Pavlenko and A. Blackledge (eds) *Negotiation of identities in multilingual contexts*. Clevedon: Multilingual Matters, pp. 161–191.

Mishler, E.G. (1991). 'Representing discourse: the rhetoric of transcription', *Journal of Narrative and Life History*, 1(4): 255–280.

Mondada, L. (2007). Bilingualism and the analysis of talk at work: code-switching as a resource for the organisation of action and interaction, in M. Heller (ed.) *Bilingualism: a social approach*. London: Palgrave, pp. 297–318.

Norton, B. (2013 [2000]). *Identity and language learning: extending the conversation*. 2nd edn. Bristol: Multilingual Matters.

Norton, B. and Toohey, K. (2011). 'Identity, language learning, and social change', *Language Teaching*, 44(4): 412–446.

Ochs, E. (1979). Transcription as theory, in E. Ochs and B.B. Schieffelin (eds) *Developmental pragmatics*. New York: Academic Press, pp. 43–72.

Pavlenko, A. (2004). 'The making of an American': negotiations of identities at the turn of the twentieth century, in A. Pavlenko and A. Blackledge (eds) *Negotiation of identities in multilingual contexts*. Clevedon: Multilingual Matters, pp. 34–67.

Pérez-Milans, M. (this volume). Language and identity in linguistic ethnography, in S. Preece (ed.) *The Routledge handbook of language and identity*. London: Routledge, pp. 83–97.

Preece, S. (2009). *Posh talk: language and identity in higher education*. London: Palgrave.

Relaño-Pastor, M. and De Fina, A. (2005). Contesting social place: narratives of language conflict, in M. Baynham and A. De Fina (eds) *Dislocations, relocations, narratives of displacement*. Manchester: St Jerome Publishing, pp. 36–60.

Rietveld, T. and van Hout, R. (1993). *Statistical techniques for the study of language and language behaviour*. Berlin: Mouton de Gruyter.

Roberts, C. (1997). 'Transcribing talk: issues of representation', *TESOL Quarterly*, 31(1): 167–172.

Schenkein, J. (ed.) (1978). *Year studies in the organisation of conversational interaction*. New York: Academic Press.

Zotzmann, K. and O'Regan, J.P. (this volume). Critical discourse analysis and identity, in S. Preece (ed.) *The Routledge handbook of language and identity*. London: Routledge, pp. 113–128.

20

Beyond the micro–macro interface in language and identity research

Kristine Horner and John Bellamy

Introduction

The fields of applied linguistics and sociolinguistics developed in the 1960s, at a time when generative linguistics was prominent and linguistic research tended to conceptualise language in a formulaic way. Juxtaposed to this view, research in applied linguistics and sociolinguistics regards language as part and parcel of social life and accordingly has drawn on cognate work in the social sciences, including in particular sociology, anthropology, psychology and education studies. Research in applied linguistics was driven by the goal of finding solutions to real world problems in which language was considered to be a central issue (perceived or real) (Brumfit 1995); initially this focused largely on language policy and planning, second and foreign language education and language in the workplace. In this way, applied linguistics was cast as complementary to theoretical linguistics.

With the boom in identity studies in the 1970s and 80s, work in applied linguistics sought to explore the interface between language and identity and the scope of applied linguistic research broadened. In the 1990s, this research increasingly took on a critical orientation that drew upon social theory and sociological insights (e.g. Pennycook 2001; Tollefson 2001; Block 2003), thus dovetailing even more closely with the field of sociolinguistics (Coupland *et al.* 2001). This research raised the issues of power, access and (in)equality. The subsequent focus on the interface between language, identity and power in applied linguistics and sociolinguistics has served as an impetus for researchers to grapple with links between *micro* and *macro* levels of language use, which are often cast respectively as interactional patterns or language choice and regulatory mechanisms or language policy. In this vein, reference to the micro–macro continuum in applied linguistics has the potential to serve as an analytical device, in that it can orient the focus of research towards interactional discourse, individual actions and speech-events on the one hand, or towards institutions and social structures on the other (Wortham 2012: 129).

In other social sciences, the micro and macro levels of social life are similarly conceptualised as an analytical continuum consisting of a range of small to large-scale phenomena. Definitions vary according to the theory, approach and outlook. In the simplest and most fundamental terms in sociology, the micro level is considered to be that which relates to the individual, whereas the macro level concerns structured organisations. These group dynamics, which are essential to understanding the construction and negotiation of identities, are located between the two end points of the micro–macro continuum. Tickameyer and Li (2000: 1703) state that micro-level research focuses on 'individual thought, action, and interaction, often coinciding with social-psychological theories and models', while macro-level research deals with 'social structures and those forces that organize as well as divide individuals into political, social or religious organizations, ethnic populations, communities, and nation-states'. In terms of approaches, there are two key sociological paradigms: 'symbolic interactionism' and 'structural functionalism'; the former is generally considered to be more micro-oriented, while the latter is regarded as macro-oriented.

The issue of how to conduct comprehensive research that bridges the micro and macro levels of social life has been flagged up as a key concern in the social sciences, in particular over the last three decades. The aim of this chapter is to evaluate the relevance and usefulness in applying a micro–macro framework to research on language and identity, with a focus on sociological, social theoretical and sociolinguistic trends that have shaped these debates. Particular consideration will be given to the fact that the predominantly discourse-based approaches to identity research go beyond strict compartmentalisation into one or the other conceptual sphere, ultimately leading to the issue of whether a micro–macro dichotomy is a suitable analytical device for research in applied linguistics that specifically focuses on the interface between language and identity.

In light of the aforementioned influence of social theory and sociology on research in applied linguistics and sociolinguistics, the following section will present an overview of leading approaches to this issue in sociology, including parallel discussions on agency and structure, and how they have been applied explicitly to research on language and identity. Following this, there will be a discussion of selected studies in applied linguistics and sociolinguistics that have grappled with the relationship between the micro and macro, in particular those that examine in some detail the relationship between language practices and policies; language and context; and/or agency and structure. The final section will sum up key points and highlight points for future language and identity research in applied linguistics.

Overview

Although the terms micro and macro may be useful for succinctly establishing the focus of a study as on a narrower or broader context, attempts have been made to retreat from a strict polarity between the micro and the macro. Debates on this issue gained prominence in the early 1980s. In some cases, the debates focused on how to integrate micro and macro levels of analysis. In other cases, the emphasis centred on the agency–structure interface rather than on the relationship between micro and macro levels.

As a means of bridging the analysis of the micro and macro levels of social life, a number of integrative approaches developed in sociology. One of the most well known is the integrated sociological paradigm developed by Ritzer (1981). He plots two continua that consist of 'micro–macro' and 'objective–subjective' levels of analysis. Ritzer's first continuum bears parallels to work in applied linguistics and sociolinguistics that attempts to link the analysis of linguistic practices (micro) and policies (macro). The second, 'objective–subjective', continuum resonates with work on language attitudes (micro) and ideologies (macro). An additional, highly prominent integrative approach entails the introduction of a middle level of analysis, referred to as the 'meso' level, that allows for the exploration of how structural organisations impact on specific interactions and how these interactions potentially may shape aspects of structural organisations. This is of particular relevance to applied linguistics scholars who examine language and identity in institutional settings, as several of the case studies in Part IV of this volume attest to (see e.g. Andrew; Hjörne and Evaldsson; Morton; Nelson; Preece; Rock, this volume). Approaches that include a meso level have been adapted and fleshed out by various scholars, but the terminological coinage in sociological literature is often credited to Maines (1979).

Rather than concentrating on a perceived gap between micro–macro issues, other paradigms focus on the relationship between agency and structure. The theory of structuration developed by Giddens (1984) is one of the most prominent theories along these lines, although Bourdieu's (1984) conceptualisation of the habitus may also be regarded as mediational between structure and agency. Giddens postulates agency and structure not as discrete poles of a dichotomy but rather as connected components that mutually affect one another. From this outlook, structure is described as being both a restricting and an enabling factor for agency. Individual agency is situated in relation to social structure and is therefore also restricted by it. However, at the same time, it is the social structure that makes the activity possible, which serves to reproduce or potentially challenge structure.

To varying degrees, research on language and identity has been influenced by sociological paradigms that engage with the interface between agency and structure or the micro and macro levels of social life. A paramount example of the former is the ethnographic work carried out by Heller and her team of researchers in a French-medium school, the École Champlain, in the Anglophone province of Ontario, Canada (2006 [1999]). Dealing with tensions and contradictions between the linguistic practices in the school and the official language policies of the state, this study is informed by Giddens's (1984) duality of structure. Through this theoretical lens, human agency and organisational structure are not viewed as distinct entities but rather in a mutually dynamic relationship. Although agency is to some extent restricted (and acted upon) by organisational structures, agency is enabled by these structures and can even ultimately have (not always intentional) structural repercussions.

The École Champlain that constituted the focus of Heller's study had a highly heterogeneous school population that consisted of three main groups: speakers of French as their L1, middle-class Anglophones wanting to become bilingual for instrumental reasons, and new immigrants, including individuals from Somalia and Haiti, who are speakers of French as an L1 or L2. The school offered two streams: a more advanced one, where many of the middle-class Francophone and Anglophone students could be found, and a more vocational or general stream, attended by many working-class French Canadians, as well as new French-speaking immigrants from Somalia and Haiti. In the latter stream, Heller found that a much wider range of vernacular and contact varieties of French was used and there was frequent code-switching into English by both students and teachers. Although teachers were expected to implement a system of linguistic surveillance, promoting the use of standard European French, they were not able to implement this in all cases. In exploring the interface between individual and societal multilingualism, Heller was able to demonstrate how the students' linguistic practices played a role in partially shifting the institutional policy of the school towards increased inclusiveness of linguistic diversity and flexible multilingualism.

Importantly, Heller maintains that regarding language as discourse, or language-in-use, as opposed to an abstraction, as a named language, is pivotal in the relationship between agency and structure. As Heller argues, this is because linguistic practices are the means by which people go about drawing on, reproducing and building new knowledge (ways of organising relationships and building social categories, as well as producing and distributing resources). For this reason, research on language and identity in applied linguistics and sociolinguistics is optimally positioned to grapple with the interface between agency and structure.

While also emphasising the key role of discourse, other research on language and identity has taken an integrative approach to exploring the interface between the micro and macro levels of social life. Based on an analysis of workplace conversations in a travel agency in Cardiff, Wales, Coupland (2007: 112–121) develops a macro-, meso- and micro-level framing model as a theoretical basis to discuss the stylising of social identities. Here, he draws on Goffman's (1974) seminal work on framing in order to look into factors that determine the ways in which specific identities are made relevant or salient. Framing is one of five processes (the others being 'targeting', 'voicing', 'keying' and 'loading'; see Coupland 2007 for an explanation) that Coupland considers useful when looking at how people construct identities in the process of social interaction. The observations of the verbal interactions, social frames of relevance and projections of identity are discussed in relation to their relevance for matters concerning social class, general principles of public discourse and what he calls the Cardiff sociolinguistic ecosystem.

Coupland explains that 'socio-cultural framing ([regarded as] macro-level social frames)' is relevant for the broader evaluation of identity inscriptions, such as social class, gender, sexuality, age and/or ethnicity. 'Genre framing ([seen as] meso-level social frames)' applies to the current context of the genre of talk that is taking place, for example formal versus informal contexts or professional versus casual settings. Participant roles and generic constraints are aspects that are typically relevant in this context. He points out that there may be differences in the way specific linguistic features characterise social identity between the macro-level and meso-level framing, for example a particular linguistic feature that would index a social identity in the sociocultural frame might resonate differently in the generic frame. For 'interpersonal framing ([viewed as] micro-level social frames)', Coupland describes the positioning strategies of the interactants themselves in the course of their talk on a personal and relational plane. In this way, a 'sociolinguistic feature that might otherwise bear, for example, a social class or a participant role significance might do personal identity work in the interpersonal frame' (Coupland 2007: 113–114).

As in the case of sociological research, the above studies explicitly deal with addressing micro–macro issues (Coupland 2007) or with agency and structure (Heller 2006 [1999]). However, unlike the majority of sociological research, Coupland and Heller emphasise the key role of discourse and contextualisation in their respective analyses (also see Blommaert et al. 2001). This emphasis opens pathways for applied linguistics and sociolinguistics to contribute to interdisciplinary research given the predominance of social constructivist approaches to identity in the social sciences, which invoke the importance of discourse and contextualisation. In the following section, we provide an overview of predominantly micro- and macro-oriented areas of research and illustrate how the interface between the micro and macro or agency and structure has been addressed in a number of studies.

Transcending the micro–macro in language and identity research

In this section, we synthesise examples of key studies on language and identity that are often regarded as predominantly micro or macro in their point of orientation. We start by discussing research that is focused on identity in linguistic interaction. This body of work may appear to be micro-oriented due to the focus on the social positioning of the individual as well as the fine-grained details of linguistic utterances. Then, we shift focus to identity in language politics, which may seem to be more macro-oriented in scope due to its focus on the construction of group identity and broader patterns of socio-political organisation. However, we show how certain studies in both of these strands share commonalities in that they prioritise the role of discourse in shaping the interface between linguistic features or named languages and various conceptualisations of identity.

Identity, the individual and linguistic interaction

Studies focused on identity in linguistic interaction and related areas, such as individual multi-lingualism and language attitudes, are often regarded as micro-oriented in that they concentrate on the finer details of the picture rather than the bigger context. However, there have been attempts in this line of research to consider macro as well as micro levels of linguistic interaction with reference to identity and/or structural organisation. Attempts to take a more holistic approach are often expressed in terms of discourse and contextualisation. These attempts reflect the increased interest in applied linguistics and sociolinguistics with the wider socio-political field in which interactional events are situated.

Recognition of the dynamic interface between individuals and broader social structure is instrumental for researchers to achieve a well-rounded understanding and interpretation of the role of identity in interactions. Specific interactions (akin to the micro level) simultaneously shape and are shaped by broader structural aspects of the social world (akin to the macro level). Kiesling (2006) underlines how identity emerges through interactions, while also pointing out that these interactions simultaneously play a reciprocal role in constructing identity:

> Identities are created and re-created when speakers are actually talking to each other, but the way these identities emerge is contingent on the speakers' sociocultural discourses and ideologies ... Because identities are relational, a person has no single fixed identity, only identities constructed and contextualized in interaction (and to the extent that an identity is psychologically real, it is based on the self's conception of its place in psychologically idealized models of interaction).
>
> *(Ibid.: 495–496)*

In their landmark article, Bucholtz and Hall (2005) similarly espouse a holistic approach that is aimed at transcending the dichotomy between micro and macro as well as agency and structure. They discuss five principles for tackling the question of identity from a linguistic interactional perspective: 'emergence', 'positionality', 'indexicality', 'relationality' and 'partialness' (see Bucholtz and Hall 2005 for an explanation of these principles). Bucholtz and Hall use these principles to show how speakers construct identity in discourse. Indeed, the indexical properties of discourse (see Jones, this volume, for a discussion of indexing) play a key role in positioning speakers in relation to certain social groups, stereotypes and cultural phenomena:

> The interactional view that we take here has the added benefit of undoing the false dichotomy between structure and agency that has long plagued social theory (see discussion in Ahearn, 2001). On the one hand, it is only through discursive interaction that large-scale social structures come into being; on the other hand, even the most mundane of everyday conversations are impinged upon by ideological and material constructs that produce relations of power. Thus both structure and agency are intertwined as components of micro as well as macro articulations of identity.
>
> *(Bucholtz and Hall 2005: 607)*

In her research on language varieties spoken in Pittsburgh and their relevance to local identity, Johnstone (2007) looks into positioning, stance-taking and the sources the participants in her study draw on, indirectly or directly, when describing their identity as Pittsburghers. The data consist of interviews conducted in Pittsburgh, during which the participants are encouraged to talk about the local dialect. Relevant details, such as certain phonological variables, particular lexical choices and the way the speakers interact, are taken into consideration and examined within the context of the Pittsburgh dialect and its role in the identity of being a Pittsburgher.

Johnstone (ibid.) observes how the participants in the conversation make references to a variety of local phenomena in order to support their stance in the interaction, including souvenirs, local dictionaries and regional magazines. The objects selected by the informants play a key role in shaping the relationship between the local spoken variety and being from Pittsburgh. Johnstone brings the content of these observed interactions together with the history of Pittsburgh's industrial background, the role of social class and patterns of migration. In so doing, the micro-level analysis of this interactional data is undertaken with reference to the macro-level circumstances surrounding the discussions. This is necessary for evaluating which discourses are informing the participants' positioning with regard to dialect and identity in Pittsburgh. The necessity for analysis on a number of contextual levels is underlined by Johnstone, who discusses the notion of identities as being 'culturally circulating, frequently adduced ways of categorizing groups of people that are often oriented to as being relevant outside of and prior to the interaction as well as inside it' (ibid.: 52).

Analysing interaction within stretches of recorded conversation forms the basis of Liebscher and Dailey-O'Cain's (2009) identity-themed project *(Inter)acting identities in dialect and discourse: migrant western Germans in eastern Germany*, where they investigate the expression of attitudes towards spoken German in Saxony, while looking into how these attitudes develop within the speakers' interactions both with the researchers and with one another. The group interviews undergo a detailed analysis, for which Liebscher and Dailey-O'Cain suggest three levels of investigation. The first level is content-based approaches, which 'have frequently been used to analyse directly-expressed language attitudes as they appear within discourse, often to lend weight to a quantitative analysis' (ibid.: 197). Turn-internal semantic and pragmatic approaches, which constitute the next level of inquiry, 'analyse the same sort of data as can be found in the content-based approaches, but require the researcher to examine the specifics of the linguistic features used in individual expressions of these attitudes' (ibid.: 198). The third level of analysis, interactional approaches, uses concepts from interactional sociolinguistics and conversation analysis to provide further insight into the expression and formation of the observed language attitudes.

The analysis focuses on the ways in which language attitudes arise from and are part of the argument structure in these discussions about local speech. In addition, speakers are shown to position themselves with regard to discursive and social identities through the expression of these attitudes. The analysis also reveals that ideology in the form of the discourse of the stigmatisation of the local Saxon dialect is a factor in the way language attitudes are constructed and negotiated (ibid.: 202). Finer points, such as the use of particular conjunctions, the labels the speakers suggest for the varieties they describe and the flow of the dialogue with each interaction, form the micro-level evaluation of the recorded interviews. The authors frequently relate their findings to the wider macro-level context of language ideologies and the general social context in which the speakers' positionings are situated. They emphasise the importance that the speakers attribute to the conversational context, which includes factors such as where the conversation takes place and how well the speakers know each other, as this can have a large bearing on the ways in which attitudes and stances are formed (ibid.: 201). The authors also find inspiration in discourse analytic approaches (see Blommaert 2005), as these can be related to the ways in which ideologies and social discourses inform the construction of identities, perspectives and attitudes in interaction.

When looking closely at the stylisation of dialect in radio shows and projected identities, Coupland (2001) provides another relevant example for our discussion when he associates the micro-level analysis of radio talk with the macro-level concepts of Welsh cultural practices, rural Welshness and contemporary issues in Wales. Coupland selects snippets of radio shows and explores them for instances of dialect stylisation which contribute to the presenter's projection of being 'audibly a "really Welsh" presenter' (ibid.: 351). Some characteristic ethnolinguistic examples of this that Coupland emphasises are traditional Welsh first names, specific references to Welsh culture and a number of distinctive phonological and prosodic features.

The styles that Coupland detects in these radio shows are on a variety of levels, so that there is not just a stylisation of being Welsh but also styles that transcend different spoken formats, behaviours and genres, such as switching to a gossip genre (where historical events are described in a manner of 'over the garden fence' gossiping) and at other times to a self-stylisation of being 'camp' in line with a lengthy tradition of similar stylised affectations in British radio shows. The detailed breakdown of the transcribed speech of the presenters (in this case the portrayal of history in the form of a gossiping duo) is discussed with reference to the more general themes of long-established radio practices, general performances of dialect and subjects largely familiar to the daily life of most Welsh people. Commenting on such performances and the projected identities, Coupland reaches the conclusion that speakers design their talk according to their awareness of alternative possibilities and likely outcomes and they 'perform identities, targeted at themselves or others, when they have some awareness of how the relevant personas constructed are likely to be perceived through their designs' (ibid.: 146). The social groups, discourses and stereotypes indexed by the speakers' performances, adopted styles and projected identities only become meaningful in relation to the wider social context in which these interactions are situated.

A further study that underlines the importance of grappling with the interface between discourse and context is Deumert's (2010) work on patient–provider interactions in public hospitals in the Western Cape, South Africa, which focuses on linguistic barriers that have arisen between English/Afrikaans-speaking providers and isiXhosa-speaking patients. By monitoring these interactions closely, Deumert recognises the difficulties faced by both patients and medical staff who sometimes do not have sufficient competence of each other's respective language(s), as the following extract from Deumert's fieldnotes illustrates:

> A female doctor in her late 20s steps out of her consulting room into the waiting area of the outpatients department. She looks at the name on the folder in her hand: Ngx.?, Ngx.?, trying to pronounce the African surname of the patient [/ngx/ represents a voiced, unaspirated lateral click preceded by a nasal], Ehm, ehm, ehm, oh here! Kushman [the first European name of the patient], that is better! An old man in his 70s gets up slowly (Hospital A).
>
> *(Ibid.: 57)*

The wider referential repercussions of this interaction are explained by Deumert, who calls attention to the doctor's use of the European-sounding first name of the patient, which is one of two names held by many older black South Africans (i.e. a Europeanised 'name of work' and an African 'name of home'). In South Africa, the 'name of work' used by the doctor 'is strongly associated with out-group contact, labour exploitation/oppression, and the invisibility of African heritage' (ibid.). Such contextualised analysis characterises the manner in which Deumert considers the wider economic, historical and social framework in which the communication between the individuals is embedded, thus enabling her to reach the following conclusion: 'Such everyday practices are profoundly stigmatizing and contribute to the reproduction of the racist legacies of colonialism and apartheid in South Africa's post-1994 health system' (ibid.).

To sum up, in all of the studies discussed in this section, there has been an acknowledgement of the ever-widening spheres of relevance for the interaction at the micro level. Rather than considering the macro and micro levels of analysis as binary opposites, they are interpreted in terms of being interrelated and central to the construction and negotiation of identity, for example through indexical stance-taking and references made by speakers to certain indexed styles and performances. In the following section, we turn to a discussion of identity in relation to nation and language policy, which will elaborate further on ways in which the micro–macro interface has been transcended in recent research on language and identity.

Identity, the nation and language policy

Research dealing with identity in language policy and related areas, such as societal multilingualism and language ideologies, is often regarded as macro-oriented in that the aim is to provide an overview of the bigger picture rather than provide a fine-grained analysis of a particular set of interactions. However, there have been attempts in this area of research to consider the relationship between the micro and macro with reference to identity and/or the interface between agency and structure. Studies that address questions on a macro scale but are nevertheless fine-grained are often conducted by means of ethnography and/or (critical) discourse analysis, enabling so-called top-down language policies to be linked with bottom-up language practices. There has been a broad paradigmatic shift in language policy and planning (LPP) to focus on these interrelated processes, which in turn has led some contemporary researchers in the field to refer to their work as language politics.

LPP research initially prioritised the study of activities at the level of the state and was intended to regulate societal language use, with society frequently conceptualised as synonymous with the (nation-) state. LPP scholarship traditionally encompassed the two prongs of status (i.e. uses of language) and corpus (i.e. forms of language) planning, viewing them as the crux of state language policy and largely perpetuated by means of state-sanctioned language-in-education policy. Although not exclusively the case, it is worth noting that much of the work on identity and language policy has focused on linguistic minorities that have been marginalised by the state or on states that are officially multilingual. On the whole, this research has shown how named languages can function as a symbol of national identity and how this symbolism often becomes increasingly salient in times of societal change or contestation. For all of these reasons, scholarship on language and identity at the more macro level has been bound up with work on LPP and, more recently, language politics and language ideologies.

Ricento's (2000) overview of LPP scholarship is roughly divided into three phases: the 1960s, the 1970s to the late 1980s, and the late 1980s to the present. Ricento underlines the gradual shift away from the dominance of structuralist paradigms based on assumed foundational structures that presupposedly organise social life that characterised the first phase of LPP towards critical approaches foregrounding social processes which were a hallmark of the second phase. Scholarship in the third phase of LPP has been marked by influences from poststructural approaches that engage with the dynamics between structure and agency as well as the discursive construction of identity categories. According to Ricento, the third phase of LPP is marked by the discursive turn and is informed by insights from critical theory. Ricento maintains that it is agency or 'the role(s) of individuals and collectivities in the processes of language use, attitudes and ultimately policies' (ibid.: 208) that distinguishes many recent studies on language policy from previous work in the field.

With the increased emphasis on agency and related interest in the interface between language, identity and power in LPP, Baldauf (2006) flags up the growing acknowledgement among researchers that LPP is operational at multiple levels of social life, which he refers to as the macro, meso and micro levels. Underlining the move away from the predominantly macro-oriented orientation of LPP scholarship, he queries the implications of the shift towards more micro-oriented issues. In this vein, Spolsky (2003) considers the family unit to be the most basic level of LPP. He maintains that research in this domain is fully within the ambit of LPP, and does so without explicitly labelling family language policy as 'micro'.

Broadening the scope of inquiry and taking a more holistic approach to LPP constitutes a priority in the field. Shohamy (2006) prompts us to engage with multiple devices used to implement language policy, which she refers to as language policy 'mechanisms'. On a visual diagram, she situates these mechanisms at mid-level between policies and practices. The mechanisms could perhaps be regarded as situated at the meso level of social life, although they are not labelled in this way, nor are the terms micro and macro used. In considering the role of mechanisms, the goal is to explore the complex interface between language policies and practices, a point that has been taken up in multiple studies. For example, the ethnographic and discourse analytic studies in a special issue of *Language Problems and Language Planning* (Horner 2009) explore compliance and resistance to language policy in a variety of interpersonal, educational and workplace settings in Luxembourg. In her commentary in this issue, Shohamy (2009) stresses the importance of studying language policy in terms of human experiences, especially as this enables us to shed light on the interface between top-down policy and bottom-up practices (see Kaplan and Baldauf 1997). Moreover, Shohamy underlines the potential applications of this kind of research in relation to the implementation of language policy:

> These people, the consumers of policy, who use or resist the languages dictated to them from the top down, have something to say from the bottom up: their voices need to be heard and incorporated in the formulation of policy. There is an urgent need to observe, study and interpret language experiences in various phases of people's lives in multiple domains. Such an effort may lead to a more valid type of language policy.
>
> *(Ibid.: 188)*

Taking a top-down/bottom-up integrativist approach that prioritises discourse allows us to discover nuances, tensions and disjunctures in LPP. With the symbolic function of language often being central to national identity, researchers frequently grapple with the labelling and discursive construction of the status of the language itself, in addition to prescriptivist ideologies concerning what the language ought to be like. In his study on the construction of the Scots language in the context of UK devolution, Unger (2013) analyses official texts (top-down) and transcripts from focus group sessions (bottom-up), in addition to examining political and policy developments. The starting point for his study is the overall low evaluation of Scots, as well as the fact that many people, even Scots speakers themselves, consider it as a dialect rather than a language. Unger finds that Scots has increasingly become part of the political agenda over the last 20 years, although this top-down discourse has not translated into the implementation of language activists' goals, such as the provision of uniform bilingual signage. Unger explains how the discursive 'double-voiced' strategies that are deployed by focus group participants closely resemble those of official discourse, thus presenting myriad challenges for altering language policy. These discourses simultaneously value and devalue Scots, constructing it as part of cultural identity but not necessary for national identity. On a broader level, Unger asserts that the mutually constitutive relationship between discourse and social practices is 'nowhere more apparent than in the area of language policy' (ibid.: 155).

Another study focused on identity and linguistic minorities in Europe is Jaffe's (1999) seminal work on language ideologies on Corsica, which provides a fine-grained ethnographic study of minority language activism. Similar to Unger, Jaffe encounters patterns of 'double discourse' in her fieldwork, with the same speakers sometimes positively and negatively evaluating Corsican. One of the central issues that she explores is the way that the Corsican language itself is discursively and strategically constructed. For example, Jaffe notes how activists construct Corsican as different from Italian so that it can be perceived as a language in its own right and therefore stand up as a valid competitor to the hegemony of French. Her research centres upon issues of material and symbolic linguistic domination, including language-in-education policy and the teaching of Corsican. Jaffe concludes that the promotion of Corsican does not constitute an example of either successful or failed language policy. However, in her subsequent research, she shows how a flexible language-in-education policy is adopted, which in turn appears to support the use of Corsican and allows children to build on their multilingual resources (Jaffe 2011). Central to Jaffe's research on Corsica is the way that agency intersects with structure, with language ideologies playing a key mediational role in the process.

Also taking a language ideological approach, Bokhorst-Heng and Wee (2007) sketch how top-down government policy has to a large extent impacted on linguistic practices in Singapore. Language is regulated on many levels in the small multilingual country whose official discourse constructs national identity as multilingual and recognises four official languages: English, Mandarin, Malay and Tamil. Since the 1980s, bilingual education aims for all students to master English plus their ascribed 'mother tongue'. Each person is assigned to one of three language groups based on their father's ethnicity. In addition to this, there exist further layers to language policy, including the regulation of Chinese itself. The 'Speak Mandarin' campaign has largely homogenised the use of Chinese, with people having switched from other Chinese dialects such as Cantonese, Hokkien and Teochew to speaking Mandarin only, and also to exclusively using Hanyu Pinyin, the Romanised version of Mandarin. However, there has been resistance to this policy with regard to personal names, with individuals continuing to give their children dialect names rather than Hanyu Pinyinised ones, as stipulated by official requests. To illustrate this resistance, Bokhorst-Heng and Wee cite a poem by Tan (1982) published in the *Straits Times*, the last stanza of which reads as follows:

When you determined what language I
should speak,
I complied.
Now, you want me to change my name after
four generations in Singapore …
it's tough, it's real tough!
A proud, a very, very proud Tan.

(Bokhorst-Heng and Wee 2007: 335)

Bokhorst-Heng and Wee maintain that the Hanyu Pinyinising of personal names was regarded as going too far, in that there was no evident purpose to this policy and that it would create a break with ancestral ties. Furthermore, such a change would involve altering pronunciation as well as orthography. They show how the discourses of pragmatism and communitarianism, linked to Confucianism, that had enabled the government's implementation of the shift from other Chinese dialects to Mandarin in nearly all areas of social life, functioned in the opposite way when it came to the practice of personal naming. From this, Bokhorst-Heng and Wee stress the importance of considering language policy in 'the context of the broader discourses operant in a nation, and in its ideological framing' (ibid.: 339). The discursive frame beyond the level of the state facilitates agency on the part of individuals who wish to resist the naming policy that is stipulated by state organisations.

The conclusions drawn by Bokhorst-Heng and Wee in their study, which emphasise the role of discourses beyond the level of the state, resonate with commentary on sociolinguistics and globalisation (see Coupland 2003). Blommaert's (2010: 32) discussion of sociolinguistic scales is particularly illuminating here, as he points out that 'events and processes in globalization occur at different scale-levels, and we see interactions between the different scales as a core feature of understanding such events and processes'. Scales refer not only to spatial but also temporal dimensions and are conceptualised as interlocked 'SpaceTime' that is inherently social and contextualised via semiotic processes. Blommaert's discussion is informed by Wallerstein's (2004) work on world-systems analysis as a means of prompting us to explore the interface between local (micro) and global (macro) scales, with specific reference to issues in applied linguistics and sociolinguistics.

This line of thought takes us full circle back to Heller's work on language, identity and nation, primarily in Canada. In a reflective monograph, Heller (2011) provides a discussion of 30 years of ethnographic work in multiple sites in Canada and beyond, including factories, schools, community associations, Christmas markets and so on, in order to explore the linkages and disjunctures between local and global sociolinguistic phenomena, with the state as the potential intermediary in these processes. With regard to the issue of bridging the macro and micro, Heller cogently lays out her rationale for adopting Giddens's (1984) stance that the macro–micro dichotomy is non-existent and that there are instead:

> Observable processes that tie local forms of social action into durable, institutionalized frames that constrain what can happen along chains or flows of interactions: they constrain the distribution of resources, the mobility of social actors, the shape activities can take and where and when they can unfold.
>
> *(Ibid.: 40)*

Drawing on her extensive ethnographic experience and findings, Heller reminds us that the concepts of language, identity and nation are by no means natural objects but rather are concepts constructed over space and time. This is perhaps becoming all the more obvious in the period of late modernity that is marked by accelerated globalisation, with the centrality of the (nation) state in the organisation of social life and linguistic practices being increasingly challenged. Most importantly, she highlights the need for us to continue to scrutinise the methods and theories of social science. In this way, research on language and identity in applied linguistics and sociolinguistics can play a leading role if scholars – as Heller encourages us to do – take up the challenge to 'break down the false dichotomy of structure and agency to reveal agents involved in the construction of social order, using the resources they find at hand' (ibid.: 193).

Summary

Scholars in the social sciences have long grappled with the perceived gap between the micro and macro levels of social life and the parallel concern of the interface between agency and structure. Debates on this issue have gained in prominence since the 1980s and new paradigms have been developed to address the relationship between the macro and micro and structure and agency. In this context, theoretical models were developed that aimed to bridge the micro–macro levels of analysis, mainly by means of integrative approaches, some of which proposed the introduction of an intermediary, meso level of inquiry. On the other hand, some researchers do not recognise the existence of micro and macro levels of social life. This latter approach is advocated by Anthony Giddens (1984), whose theory of structuration emphasises the mutually constitutive relationship between agency and structure and notably prioritises the role of discourse as pivotal in the dynamics of social life.

In this light, research in applied linguistics and sociolinguistics has considerable capacity to lay bare the ways that agency and structure intersect. As Heller (2011: 34) puts it, studies that focus on issues of language and identity are especially well suited to this purpose due to 'the complex role of language in constructing the social organization of production and distribution of the various forms of symbolic and material resources essential to our lives and to our ability to make sense of the world around us'. This chapter discussed how studies in applied linguistics and sociolinguistics that examine identity in some way have grappled with issues of contextualisation as they relate to the study of specific instances of interactional discourse. We then showed how contemporary research on language policy has been influenced by the discursive turn and discussed the growing emphasis on exploring the interface between top-down policy and bottom-up practices and the identities that are implicated in this interface. We have also observed how studies on language and identity that employ discourse analytic and ethnographic methods are an optimal means of linking fine-grained observations of spoken interaction with the functioning of broader social, political and economic structures.

Related topics

Historical perspectives on language and identity; Language and identity in linguistic ethnography; Language and ethnic identity; Linguistic practices and transnational identities; Class in language and identity research; A linguistic ethnography of identity: adopting a heteroglossic frame; Constructing age identity: the case of Mexican EFL learners; The significance of sexual identity to language learning and teaching; An identity transformation? Social class, language prejudice and the erasure of multilingual capital in higher education; Being a language teacher in the content classroom: teacher identity and content and language integrated learning (CLIL); Disability identities and category work in institutional practices: the case of a 'typical ADHD girl'; 'Comes with the territory': expert–novice and insider–outsider identities in police interviews; The future of identity research: impact and new developments in sociolinguistics.

Further reading

Blommaert, J., Collins, J., Heller, M., Rampton, B., Slembrouck, S. and Verschueren, J. (Contributors) (2001). *Critique of Anthropology*, 21(1&2). (The collection of articles in this special issue grapples with multifaceted theoretical and methodological issues concerning discourse, including contextualisation.)

Bucholtz, M. and Hall, K. (2005). 'Identity and interaction: a sociocultural linguistic approach', *Discourse Studies*, 7(4/5): 585–614. (Bucholtz and Hall present a clear and detailed analysis of identity as it is constructed in interaction, focusing on the importance of micro and macro approaches in identity research, as well as related issues of agency and structure.)

Coupland, N., Sarangi, S. and Candlin, C.N. (eds) (2001). *Sociolinguistics and social theory*. London: Longman. (This volume underlines the need for sociolinguistics to engage with social theory. See the chapters by Coupland and Heller for discussion of the micro–macro interface and related debates on the agency–structure interface.)

Heller, M. (2011). *Paths to post-nationalism: a critical ethnography of language and identity*. Oxford: Oxford University Press. (Heller discusses 30 years of ethnographic fieldwork, primarily conducted in Canada, and underlines the need for researchers to scrutinise the methods and theories of social science. Heller applies Giddens's (1984) theory of structuration, which conceptualises agency and structure as mutually constitutive.)

Ricento, T. (2000). 'Historical and theoretical perspectives in language policy and planning', *Journal of Sociolinguistics*, 4(2): 196–213. (Ricento provides an overview of three phases of language policy and planning scholarship, focusing on the importance of agency, ideology and ecology to the present-day, third phase of research.)

References

Andrew, P. (this volume). Constructing age identity: the case of Mexican EFL learners, in S. Preece (ed.) *The Routledge handbook of language and identity*. Abingdon: Routledge, pp. 337–350.

Baldauf, R.B. (2006). 'Rearticulating the case for micro language planning in a language ecology context', *Current Issues in Language Planning*, 7(2/3): 147–170.

Block, D. (2003). *The social turn in second language acquisition*. Georgetown: Georgetown University Press.

Blommaert, J. (2005). *Discourse: a critical introduction*. Cambridge: Cambridge University Press.

Blommaert, J. (2010). *The sociolinguistics of globalization*. Cambridge: Cambridge University Press.

Blommaert, J., Collins, J., Heller, M., Rampton, B., Slembrouck, S. and Verschueren, J. (2001). 'Discourse and critique. Part one: introduction', *Critique of Anthropology*, 21(1): 5–12.

Bokhorst-Heng, W.D. and Wee, L. (2007). 'Language planning in Singapore: on pragmatism, communitarianism and personal names', *Current Issues in Language Planning*, 8(3): 324–343.

Bourdieu, P. (1984). *Distinction: a social critique of the judgement of taste*. London: Routledge.

Bucholtz, M. and Hall, K. (2005). 'Identity and interaction: a sociocultural linguistic approach', *Discourse Studies*, 7(4/5): 585–614.

Brumfit, C.J. (1995). Teacher professionalism and research, in G. Cook and B. Seidlhofer (eds) *Principles and practice in applied linguistics: studies in honour of H.G. Widdowson*. Oxford: Oxford University Press, pp. 27–42.

Coupland, N. (2001). 'Dialect stylization in radio talk', *Language in Society*, 30(3): 345–375.

Coupland, N. (2003). 'Introduction: sociolinguistics and globalisation', *Journal of Sociolinguistics*, 7(4): 465–472.

Coupland, N. (2007). *Style: language variation and identity*. Cambridge: Cambridge University Press.

Coupland, N., Sarangi, S. and Candlin, C.N. (eds) (2001). *Sociolinguistics and social theory*. London: Longman.

Deumert, A. (2010). '"It would be nice if they could give us more language": serving South Africa's multilingual patient base', *Social Science and Medicine*, 71: 53–61.

Giddens, A. (1984). *The constitution of society: outline of the theory of structuration*. Cambridge: Polity Press.

Goffman, E. (1974). *Frame analysis*. Harmondsworth: Penguin.

Heller, M. (2006 [1999]). *Linguistic minorities and modernity: a sociolinguistic ethnography*. London: Continuum.

Heller, M. (2011). *Paths to post-nationalism: a critical ethnography of language and identity*. Oxford: Oxford University Press.

Hjörne, E. and Evaldsson, A-C. (this volume). Disability identities and category work in institutional practices: the case of a 'typical ADHD girl', in S. Preece (ed.) *The Routledge handbook of language and identity*. Abingdon: Routledge, pp. 396–412.

Horner, K. (ed.) (2009). Luxembourg, *Language Problems and Language Planning*, Special Issue, 33(2).

Jaffe, A. (1999). *Ideologies in action: language politics on Corsica*. Berlin: Mouton de Gruyter.

Jaffe, A. (2011). Critical perspectives on language-in-education policy: the Corsican example, in T. McCarty (ed.) *Ethnography and language policy*. New York: Routledge, pp. 205–229.

Johnstone, B. (2007). Linking identity and dialect through stancetaking, in R. Englebretson (ed.) *Stancetaking in discourse: subjectivity in interaction*. Amsterdam: John Benjamins, pp. 49–68.

Jones, L. (this volume). Language and gender identities, in S. Preece (ed.) *The Routledge handbook of language and identity*. Abingdon: Routledge, pp. 210–224.

Kaplan, R.B. and Baldauf, R.B. (1997). *Language planning: from practice to theory*. London: Routledge.

Kiesling, S. (2006). Language and identity in sociocultural anthropology, in K. Brown (ed.) *Encyclopedia of language and linguistics*, Vol. 5. 2nd edn. Oxford: Elsevier, pp. 495–502.

Liebscher, G. and Dailey-O'Cain, J. (2009). 'Language attitudes in interaction', *Journal of Sociolinguistics*, 13(2): 195–222.

Maines, D.R. (1979). 'Mesostructure and social process', *Contemporary Sociology*, 8: 524–527.

Morton, T. (this volume). Being a language teacher in the content classroom: teacher identity and content and language integrated learning (CLIL), in S. Preece (ed.) *The Routledge handbook of language and identity*. Abingdon: Routledge, pp. 382–395.

Nelson, C.D. (this volume). The significance of sexual identity to language learning and teaching, in S. Preece (ed.) *The Routledge handbook of language and identity*. Abingdon: Routledge, pp. 351–365.

Pennycook, A. (2001). *Critical applied linguistics: a critical introduction*. Mahwah: Lawrence Erlbaum Associates.

Preece, S. (this volume). An identity transformation? Social class, language prejudice and the erasure of multilingual capital in higher education, in S. Preece (ed.) *The Routledge handbook of language and identity*. Abingdon: Routledge, pp. 366–381.

Ricento, T. (2000). 'Historical and theoretical perspectives in language policy and planning', *Journal of Sociolinguistics*, 4(2): 196–213.

Ritzer, G. (1981). *Toward an integrated sociological paradigm*. Boston: Allyn and Bacon.

Rock, F. (this volume). 'Comes with the territory': expert–novice and insider–outsider identities in police interviews, in S. Preece (ed.) *The Routledge handbook of language and identity*. Abingdon: Routledge, pp. 413–427.

Shohamy, E. (2006). *Language policy: hidden agendas and new approaches*. Abingdon: Routledge.

Shohamy, E. (2009). 'Language policy as experiences', *Language Problems and Language Planning*, 33(2): 185–189.

Spolsky, B. (2003). *Language policy*. Cambridge: Cambridge University Press.

Tan (1982). 'It's a difficult thing', *Straits Times*, 14 July 2015, p. 15.

Tickameyer, A.R. and Li, J. (2000). Macrosociology, in E.F. Borgatta (ed.) *Encyclopedia of sociology*, Vol. 3. 2nd edn. New York: Macmillan Reference USA, pp. 1703–1712.

Tollefson, J. (2001). *Language policies in education: critical issues*. Mahwah: Lawrence Erlbaum Associates.

Unger, J.W. (2013). *The discursive construction of the Scots language: education, politics and everyday life*. Amsterdam: John Benjamins.

Wallerstein, I. (2004). *World-systems analysis: an introduction*. Durham: Duke University Press.

Wortham, S. (2012). 'Introduction to the special issue: beyond macro and micro in the linguistic anthropology of education', *Anthropology and Education Quarterly*, 43(3): 128–137.

Part IV
Language and identity case studies

21

Constructing age identity
The case of Mexican EFL learners

Patricia Andrew

Introduction

During my lengthy career teaching EFL (English as a Foreign Language) in Mexico to adults aged 18 to 70, I often wondered what significance the differences in their ages had on my students, not only in terms of success in learning but also on the social interaction in the classroom. In undertaking a case study to explore these issues, I set out to discover what the experience meant to adult students, how they were changed by it and what part age played in the construction of their identities. My goal was to learn about the non-linguistic outcomes of the language learning experience. This is of particular relevance to applied linguists who grapple with interdisciplinary issues involving language, including language acquisition, second language pedagogy, identity and discourse (Block 2013).

The impact of age on second language acquisition (SLA) has long been a concern of SLA researchers. A vast number of studies on the Critical Period Hypothesis (CPH) have attempted to determine the extent to which the biological constraints operating on first language acquisition are transferrable to second language learning. However, the tradition of CPH studies had several drawbacks for the case study discussed in this chapter. First, CPH studies look at child–adult differences but not at variations among adults of different ages. In addition, the research is limited to the possible effects of age on linguistic attainment, thereby leaving out the question of the non-linguistic outcomes of language study. Moreover, CPH research addresses age in strictly chronological terms, an approach which does not coincide with my own understanding of age as socially constructed and as a dimension of identity. Therefore, I found embarking on the study of age and age identity from a social constructionist perspective to be more in line with my research goals. It also made more sense when considering the inherently social nature of language and language learning.

In order to determine the part that the social dimensions of age played in the experience of learning and constructing identities, and in the broader life circumstances of the participants, I aimed to examine four key issues for the case study: how age was co-constructed in the EFL classroom context and in the personal narratives of adult language learners; what beliefs and attitudes the learners had about age and about language learning; how these beliefs and attitudes intersected with the way age was enacted; and how age as a subject position was interlinked with the learners' other subject positions.

I carried out the research at a branch campus of the National University of Mexico (actual name) where foreign language classes are offered to members of the neighbouring community as well as to university students. The findings confirmed the existence of many common characteristics in the construction of age in adulthood in present-day Mexico and in other countries of the West, yet some interesting differences emerged. While the issues are explored in one specific sociohistorical context, it is hoped that what has been learned will resonate with the experience of people in other situations and add to their understanding of the social significance of age and age identity.

Overview

The conceptual foundations

Identity is constructed in our interaction with other people through language, that is, it is 'constructed out of the discourses culturally available to us, and which we draw upon in our communications with other people' (Burr 2003: 106). In order to highlight the fundamental role of discursive interaction in identity construction, I address the issue of age identity from a poststructuralist perspective, as multiple, fragmented, changeable over time and a site of struggle. Different strands of poststructuralism, particularly feminist poststructuralism (Weedon 1997), have provided solid theoretical support for identity studies on gender, ethnicity and other social dimensions (see e.g. Norton 2013 [2000]) and I believe offer an equally sound approach to age identity or 'subjectivity'.

For poststructuralists, identity is not something people have or are, but rather something they perform or do (Butler 1990; Baxter 2003, this volume). This perspective stands in stark contrast to the essentialist portrayal of identity as a single fixed essence pertaining to a unified, conscious, rational subject. The notion of subjectivity, coming from positioning theory (Harré and van Langenhove 1999), can be defined as our sense of ourselves, our conscious and unconscious thoughts and emotions and our ways of understanding our relation to the world (Weedon 1997). It is formed in our relationships with other people through our identification with specific subject positions, or ways of being an individual, within certain discourses, as an ongoing process that is reconstructed in discourse every time we speak or act. The range of subject positions an individual assumes or is assigned by others is of necessity restricted to those available in a particular sociohistorical context, and may be actively taken up, tried out and accepted, rejected or challenged (Harré and van Langenhove 1999). Moreover, subject positions are frequently in conflict with each other, making subjectivity a site of struggle between competing yet interwoven discourses. Consequently, a person may adopt or be allocated multiple positions as part of their age identity, depending on the particular situation.

Poststructuralists maintain that experience has no meaning apart from that constituted in language and is subject to varied and potentially contradictory interpretations. The meaning of age, then, is contingent on the ways individuals interpret the world and on the discourses available to them. Accordingly, the experience of ageing and the construction of age identity can only occur through language and the competing discourses of a particular culture, including gender, ethnicity, social class and other discourses. Furthermore, a person's age identity is in constant flux, readily appreciated if we consider that the very definition of ageing is 'change over time'.

Age identity reveals itself in the stories people tell, availing themselves of the narrative form to make sense of their experiences and to 'present themselves, and others, as actors in a drama' (Harré and van Langenhove 1999: 8) in which they take up different subject positions. Narrative is the primary means individuals use to give meaning to their lives over the course of time and to communicate their experience to others. Thus, the construction of identity may be seen as an ongoing 'narrative' project, in Giddens's (1991) terms, in which we jointly produce stories about ourselves in our interaction with others.

The life-story narrative is necessarily a story of ageing because it gives meaning to our experience of 'change over time' by bringing to light and interpreting the important events in our lives, weaving together our past, present and future. Our age identity – that is, where we position ourselves in the life trajectory – emerges from the narratives we tell and are told through culturally shared discourses.

The cultural discourses of age

The prevalent discourses surrounding age in contemporary Western culture grow out of decline ideology. The view of age and ageing as decrement or deterioration is a pervasive one, shaping 'our expectations of the future, our view of others, our explanatory systems, and then our retrospective judgments' (Gullette 2004: 11). While this is not the case in other parts of the world, such as Africa and the Far East, where age has traditionally been associated with respect and esteem, changes in attitudes towards age are taking place in many of those same societies because of increasing urbanisation and industrialisation. Such is the situation in Mexico, a country only recently industrialised.

The decline narrative is sustained by public and private institutions as well as the market economy. It is readily discernible in displays of societal ageism, understood as a set of adverse attitudes and discriminatory practices that target an age group, reinforce their subordinate and marginal place in society and dispossess them of access to material and social resources. Ageism is supported in large part by stereotypic beliefs that ascribe generally unfavourable characteristics to a person solely on the basis of their belonging to a particular age cohort. Some of the stereotypes conventionally associated with old age are inflexibility, verbosity, egocentrism, irascibility, childishness, disengagement and unproductiveness. Similar stereotypes in Mexico characterise old age as 'a period of poor health, economic instability, loneliness and declining physical and mental capacities' (Franco Saldaña et al. 2010: 989). Other stereotypes target middle-aged adults, focusing on the loss of physical attractiveness, the empty-nest syndrome and the midlife crisis (Shweder 1998). Beliefs about young people often depict them as rebellious, reckless and lazy.

At the same time, positive stereotypes, such as those portraying older adults as exceptionally wise, dignified or kindly grandparent figures, also contribute to ageism by making oversimplifications that do not take into consideration real differences among people in an age group. Both positive and negative stereotypes disregard the fact that people age in very different ways and ageing does not follow a straightforward course of decline. Research evidence suggests that the experience of ageing is variable both over the life span and also among people of the same age cohort (Coupland et al. 1991).

An ageist discourse that stems from the decline narrative is manifested in age behaviour, that is, the way we concern ourselves with age-appropriateness or the tacit rules regulating the proper manner of acting, dressing, talking or behaving at a certain age. Acting older or younger than the accepted norm will ordinarily be sanctioned.

The way we talk about age can also reveal ageist attitudes. Disparaging words and expressions, such as 'old codger', are part of our everyday discourse. So are euphemisms, like 'golden-ager', which endeavour to skirt the taboo theme of old age. In fact, a myriad of examples abound in clichés, humour and the media (Palmore 2005). Equivalent terms in Spanish, such as the derogatory *ruco* or *chocho*, are commonly used in Mexico. Ageist or patronising behaviour is also evident in the way people sometimes simplify their speech by using baby talk or elder speech when talking to young children or older persons (Nelson 2005).

Age-category discourses disclose another source of ageism. The arbitrary separation of the life course into named stages is often linked to social problems. For example, 'old age' became a recognised age category in the early part of the twentieth century because, with urban industrialisation, the latter part of adulthood became problematised as older people were progressively excluded from productive roles in the economy and viewed as a burden to society. These explicit references to age categories are ageist in that they segregate people into groups of 'us and them' (Nelson 2005: 217). Further examples of ageism can be found in biomedical and other discourses relating to the body. In today's world, the norm is indisputably the youthful body and, connected with this, a generalised preoccupation with the loss of attractiveness and other physical changes associated with ageing. Mexico, like most other Western countries, is a target of mass media campaigns by the cosmetic industry, which has capitalised on the fear of bodily ageing prevalent in the female population (Montes de Oca 2001).

At the same time, ageing is considered a 'health problem' and illness to be the natural outcome of biological decline. In response to the widespread fear of sickness and death rampant in Western culture, the medical community has directed its attention primarily to the pathology of ageing and channelled its resources to inhibiting the ageing process and prolonging life rather than focusing on ways to promote lifelong good health (Cruikshank 2003). Yet, it is important to note that, while older people may be more susceptible to illness, ageing does not cause it as such. Furthermore, behind the fear of bodily ageing is the value we place on the ageing process, one necessarily linked to the social context. As Featherstone and Hepworth (1995: 30–31) argue:

> Whilst the biological processes of aging, old age, and death cannot in the last resort be avoided, the meanings which we give to these processes and the evaluations we make of people as they grow physically older are social constructions which reflect the beliefs and values found in a specific culture at a particular period of history.

Two types of successful or positive ageing discourses have emerged in counter-position to decline ideology. The first of these, the quest for eternal youth or agelessness, seeks ways to eradicate the 'negative' manifestations of ageing through, for example, anti-ageing products, health regimes and self-help courses. Such attempts to detain the process of growing old are ageist in that they are based on a decremental vision of ageing. Conversely, a second approach to positive ageing regards the process as one of change or difference rather than decline. These discourses call attention to the range of options offered at each new stage of life, including the freedom to re-evaluate priorities and explore new avenues as we grow older, and the opportunity to live well at every point in the life course by making 'sensible and efficacious lifestyle choices' (Tulle-Winton 1999: 289).

Finally, it is important to point out that the age discourses which frame the enactment of identity are invariably interlaced in different ways with other discourses, such as gender, ethnicity and social class (see Block and Corona, this volume). The result is the construction of a complex and nuanced age identity.

Methodology

In view of the complexities involved in exploring the interconnection between age identity and second language learning, I chose a qualitative research design for the case study discussed in this chapter that utilised features of Layder's (1998) adaptive model in order to underscore the cyclical and emergent nature of the research process, one involving a continuous fine-tuning of both theory and methodology. Adaptive theory is Layder's proposal for linking theory and social research. It is a complement to his theory of social domains and works to interlace the systemic elements with the micro-features of social life in the research process; theory and data mutually influence each other. I opted for a multiple case study (see Robson 2011) with a broadly ethnographic orientation in that I sought to understand and interpret the experience of the participants from their perspective and in light of the larger sociocultural context in which they were immersed.

My goal was to gather stories and identify critical moments or events that would elucidate the meaning the participants gave to their language learning and other life experiences and to ascertain the part age played in the construction of their identities. To accomplish this, I used a combination of narrative inquiry (Clandinin and Connelly 2000), semi-structured interviews (see Brinkmann and Kvale 2015 [1996]), audio-taped narrative accounts and classroom observations.

Participants

From a group of volunteers, I selected seven Mexican adult EFL students for the study on the basis of purposive sampling (Robson 2011), that is, I addressed the specific needs of the project rather than seeking representativeness. I included adults of different ages, course levels and both genders. The participants comprised four women and three men whose ages ranged from 23 to 70, named David (23), Elsa (34), Gilda (36), Adela (48), Berta (59), Felix (68) and Hector (70) (all names are pseudonyms).

Data collection design

The principal source of data consisted of five co-constructed in-depth interviews for each participant, which took place over the course of the four-month school term. The interviews were semi-structured in that I drew up a tentative guide for each interview and adhered to it in very general terms. My purpose was to obtain pertinent information about the participants' language learning experiences, their beliefs about language learning, and how they constructed their age identity. However, as a consequence of the co-constructed or shared nature of the interviews, the participants often took charge and shifted the direction of the conversations in unexpected, and ultimately enriching, ways.

Moreover, because close relationships between the researcher and the participants typically develop in the case of narrative inquiries, the effects – both positive and negative – are potentially greater, and in consequence so is researcher responsibility. Uppermost in my mind during the interviews was the need to respect the privacy of my informants while at the same time opening up a space for them to share their personal stories. This entailed, among other things, being candid and genuine in my relations with them, both as a researcher and as a person (Holliday 2002).

The interviews were complemented by weekly audio-taped narrative accounts the participants made in Spanish, in which they reflected on the experiences of the previous week, their difficulties and achievements, relations with their classmates and teacher, and any noteworthy incidents they wished to share with me. From the beginning of the term, I attended every English language lesson in order to observe the participants' interaction in the language classroom with a view to determining how age identity was enacted and what part it played in the language learning experience of these students. Although certain telling incidents occurred over the course of the months during which I was an observer, the English language classes proved to be more teacher-centred than I had anticipated so that the principal interaction took place between the teachers and the participants. Nevertheless, my regular presence in the classroom helped build rapport with the participants. By utilising these three data collection methods concurrently, I was able to capitalise on the connections between them. This allowed me to reduce researcher bias and strengthen the credibility of the research by incorporating some of the measures Robson (2011) recommends, including prolonged involvement with the participants, persistent observation of the context and participants, and triangulation through the use of multiple data sources and collection techniques.

Organisation and analysis of the data

Because the interviews, which had been audio-taped, provided the most important source of data, I transcribed them in their entirety, using a simplified transcription style. A Spanish speaker then reviewed the transcriptions for accuracy. I translated only the relevant sections needed for the analysis. For the classroom observations, I recorded field notes during each class session, using a straightforward format which included the classroom activities, their duration, the interaction of the participants with the teacher or with their classmates, and any events which occurred of possible interest to the study. In the case of the audio-taped narrative reflections, I made a detailed summary of each, later transcribing and translating only those sections important for the analysis.

I carried out a qualitative content analysis (QCA) (Bryman in Kohlbacher 2006) to enable the core themes to emerge from the data. QCA places particular emphasis on the role of the researcher and of the surrounding context in interpreting the meaning of a text. It was helpful for me, as the researcher, to be able to function both as an insider, someone with a deep-seated knowledge of the country I had lived in for over 40 years, and as an outsider, an academic and a foreigner, positions which afforded me the critical distance needed to interpret the data.

The data

I began the study with few predetermined notions of what the data would reveal, yet it soon became evident that the participants positioned themselves and each other in three clearly delimited age groups: older adults, (midlife) adults and young adults. While this had a certain connection to their chronological age, it turned out that many other factors played a significant role in the construction of these three categories. In what follows, I present a few highlights, taken principally from the interview data, pertaining to each of these categories (see Andrew 2012 for a fuller treatment of the complete data set and the triangulation of the three collection methods).

Age identity in later adulthood

Hector (70) and Felix (68), both retired professionals, identified themselves, and accepted being positioned by others, as older adults. Taking up the study of English in later adulthood responded primarily to their desire to remain active and to keep mental decline at bay. It is a socially acceptable leisure activity and also a means of acquiring cultural capital (Bourdieu 1977), for knowing how to speak English is a source of prestige in Mexico. Yet the spectre of ageism was a constant in our interviews. Hector told me that he was interested in learning the language as fast as possible because if he did not hurry up he might not have time. As he explained:

> Yes, it's not a drama but now at this age ... at my age ... you have to do things more quickly because at this point in time, what for? If I've lived my whole life without the language, I can keep living whatever time I have left.
>
> *(Hector, Interview 2)*

All the participants in the study, young and old, believed that the ability to learn a new language decreases with age throughout adulthood. Felix said that it is more difficult for him to learn and to make progress now because of age-related deficits. Not only did he feel disadvantaged in relation to young people in the classroom but also outside it. He told me:

> No matter what, age is going to win out because just that fact that you are an older person means that it is inevitable that you will lose your capacities.
>
> *(Felix, Interview 3)*

Such ageist beliefs were displayed in Hector and Felix's enactment of age in the classroom, where they tended to self-segregate and self-handicap, that is, they themselves withdrew or set up obstacles to their own success. It also occurred in the world outside the classroom, where they reported often feeling marginalised and disengaged from mainstream society. This was augmented because of retirement, an event that had a major impact on their lives. In many productivity-oriented Western cultures, retirement has both economic and social consequences, including the loss of status. Both men have internalised this widespread ageist discourse. Felix's assessment of his own alleged age-related cognitive deficits is a forceful example of 'internalized ageism' (Cruikshank 2003: 153), in which 'the myth of mental decline becomes a self-fulfilling prophecy – and one that brings active harm to the aged' (Combe and Schmader 1999: 97).

Yet at other times Hector and Felix actively rejected the ageist ideas they encountered and adopted positive ageing attitudes, expressing satisfaction with their lives and the place they now found themselves in the life course. Felix spoke of a recent experience in a job that required both mental and physical abilities, saying, 'I showed myself that I could do it. I can do anything' (Felix, Interview 3). Acceptance and resistance to these competing discourses generated an internal tension between their admiration of youth culture and their life satisfaction as older adults.

Hector and Felix's enactment of age as language learners is closely bound up with their professional, social and gendered identities. The importance of their past professional success is part of their social identity and also characteristic of the identity of the 'traditional Mexican male'. Moreover, Hector's deprecating references to himself as an Indian and other negative remarks about his dark-skinned *mestizo* appearance point to a devaluation of his ethnic heritage and likely explain his lifelong need to attain a prestigious social position. The complex interplay of identities and the competing discourses of age point up the variable and often conflicting ways in which Hector and Felix enact their age as older adults.

Age identity in (middle) adulthood

The four women participants in the study, aged 34 to 59, identified themselves simply as 'adults'. This term designates a mid-range falling between young adulthood and old age. There is no named age category in Mexican Spanish equivalent to what is generally referred to in English as 'middle age'. This marks an important distinction between the construction of age in Mexican and Anglophone cultures, for many of the characteristics of the latter, such as forced early retirement or the empty-nest syndrome, have as yet no appreciable presence in the former.

One of the significant issues which the adult women cited as signalling the distinction between themselves and both younger and older adults was that of responsibility. Elsa, the youngest of the 'adult' participants at 34, remarked that young people 'do not have everyday worries or the responsibilities of a job' (Elsa, Interview 1). The question of responsibility also arose in relation to older adults, who are seen as largely free of their former professional and family responsibilities. When referring to their classmates, the women often utilised 'we' and 'they' to erect an identifiable partition between themselves and the older and younger students.

Their life stories were punctuated with instances of the responsibilities they shoulder at home and in the workplace. This characterised their approach to the study of English, for they took their classes very seriously. Since they all work, they are not seeking a leisure-time activity like Hector and Felix. Learning English at this moment of their lives meets their need to achieve something important to them, in some cases a new goal and in others an unfulfilled one from childhood. While aware of the professional opportunities that come with knowing English, their motives are more strongly linked to the prestige of the language and the identities they are constructing as adult learners.

Decline discourses surfaced on occasion, particularly when the women spoke of their relations with the other students. Berta (59), for instance, mentioned feeling 'out of date' and 'out of place' (Berta, Interview 2) in a world belonging to young people. In an interview with Gilda (36), she expressed her fear of the inevitable physical debility and loss of independence she equates with growing old, a position in keeping with prevailing discourses of age (Gullette 2004). She commented:

> I'd like to get to be a little old lady, but only if I can take care of myself, not have health problems or not be able to move or need to depend on someone.
>
> *(Gilda, Interview 3)*

More often the narratives of the adult women contained subtler manifestations of ageism, as observed in their collective preoccupation with age-appropriacy. Concerns with having finished school, got married, given birth to their children or having reached other goals within a socially acceptable chronological time frame proved to be a major issue with each of them. A tacit time-table mapping the life course effectively controlled their appraisal of their own achievements.

Age identity was interconnected with these participants' other identities. Their gender identity as adult women, which in Mexican culture signifies first and foremost that of wife and mother (López Hernández 2007), often conflicted with their identities as professionals. Until recently the customs and traditions in Mexico have discouraged women from assuming both subject positions. The upshot is that working women have had to demonstrate both at home and in the workplace that they can satisfactorily meet both sets of obligations. If they wish to take on another identity, such as that of a language learner, the result is often the generation of additional conflict. Even though Adela's (48) children are university students, she explained that she still has to make an effort 'to free myself of certain burdens that Mexican society itself makes us feel' (Adela, Interview 3). This complex of identities shaped the experiences of the (midlife) adults both in and out of the classroom.

Age identity in young adulthood

At the time of the study, David (23), the only self-identified young adult among the participants, was living at home while completing his university work. Older than most of his fellow students, he still needed to pass examinations in subjects he had failed, meet the foreign language requirement and write a thesis in order to graduate. He spoke often of how much he was enjoying his present life as a student and seemed in no hurry to finish. While he exercised a great deal of liberty in his personal life, he nonetheless remained completely dependent on his widowed mother to provide for him economically. As is typical of many young adults, he had distanced himself emotionally from his family and adopted the social norms of his peers, who constituted his main source of companionship.

David said that he was taking English classes because it might help him to get a job in the future or offer an opportunity to study abroad. Interestingly, he never mentioned the foreign language requirement that was an immediate necessity for him to obtain his college degree. It seems, then, that English had value for him principally as symbolic or cultural capital (Bourdieu 1977). Studying a language was simply part of the student culture, an additional pursuit, but not one perceived to have any practical usefulness.

When writing about young adults in France, Bourdieu (2003) claimed that young adult workers and their same-age student counterparts have little in common. Students, he maintained, are characterised by a kind of interim irresponsibility; in some ways they are children and in others they are adults. They are given a great deal of latitude during their student years but are expected to take up full adult responsibilities after they have finished. This situation is replicated in Mexico, where urban workers, peasants and members of indigenous communities move effortlessly from childhood to adulthood, unlike students, for whom the transition is extended almost indefinitely over time. Because of the critical economic situation of Mexico, part-time work is not accessible to students, and family traditions dictate that young adults should live at home until they marry (Zermeño 2005).

David fits this pattern, for at the time of the study he was entirely dependent on his mother for financial support and still enjoying a carefree student life while at the same time harbouring a vague desire to be fully independent and established professionally at some future moment. He said, in painting a positive, though remote, scenario for himself, 'By 33 I'd like to be already married and to have at least one child … probably have a stable job and have experience by then … I don't know' (David, Interview 3). Yet he had not taken any concrete steps to make this happen, nor had he defined any tangible career goals. The interplay between the competing discourses of dependence and independence generated a certain amount of tension in his life and that of many young adult students in Mexico.

David's enactment of young adulthood was to a large extent intertwined with his identity as a student. Speaking of the young people in the classroom, he said:

> And it's also kind of funny ... or interesting ... to observe how all of us sit in the back right up against the wall. Sometimes we students have the idea that only show-offs or nerds sit up front, that is, the 'brains' ... and, I don't know, we put them down.
>
> *(David, Narrative account 9)*

Here David gave voice to a deeply entrenched norm of student culture, namely that it is not socially acceptable to show off or perform well in class. Benwell and Stokoe (2005) and Preece (2009) reported similar findings in their studies in the UK.

He also demonstrated the kind of insularity found in young people's tendency to limit their social involvement to their peer group and to avoid interaction with older adults. In fact, David never spoke to any of his midlife or older classmates during the entire term. His perception of them as the 'Other', outside the group of young university students, was reinforced by his belief that old age begins early in the life span. He said, 'I suppose that, like everything, you need to know when to retire in time. So, I imagine that between 40 and 50, I'd better go, if I've been working such a long time' (David, Interview 3). He confirmed this viewpoint in a subsequent interview when he commented, 'Maybe when I'm 50, I won't be able to work because, well, maybe I'll be tired' (David, Interview 4).

David spoke little about his childhood and made only vague references to the future, confirming García Canclini's (2004) contention that young people do not have much of a sense of history or a connection to the past. Like most young adults, David's life and identity were firmly rooted in the present moment.

Discussion

Among the findings to emerge in the course of the research, the following are particularly noteworthy.

The co-construction of age is rooted in the prevailing cultural discourses of age

Decline discourses and ageism in various manifestations provided the framework for the social construction of age for all the participants in the study. This was corroborated by the narratives and stories they told and was reflected in their enactment of age in the classroom (see Andrew 2012 for examples of this). In general, they seem to have internalised ageist discourses and to have adopted the traits they believe to be characteristic of their age group. Yet, this involved some conflict as the participants struggled with potentially competing discourses of dependence and independence, engagement and disengagement and competence and incompetence in the construction of their age identity.

The impact of age on the language learning experience varies according to where each person positions herself/ himself in the lifespan

The participants positioned themselves and were positioned by others in three broad categories: older adults, (merely) adults and young adults. There was complete agreement about this classification, suggesting that both explicit and implicit cultural discourses have a significant effect on the construction of age and that chronological age is only one factor.

A surprising finding was that (middle) adulthood is not a lexicalised category in Mexico, marked only by its separation at one end from later adulthood and at the other end from young adulthood. It corresponds in most respects to the named category of middle age in Anglophone cultures. The (midlife) adults were characterised by their sense of responsibility at home and in the workplace and their concern with issues of age-appropriacy. This distinguished them from young adults, who were seen as yet unencumbered by the economic and emotional responsibilities that come with a job and a family. It also set them apart from the older adults who, having retired, no longer feel the weight of such responsibilities.

The language learning experience varied in accordance with each person's position in the life course and included both linguistic and non-linguistic dimensions. While the motivation for studying English could be defined in every case as the acquisition of cultural capital (Bourdieu 1977), this had a different meaning for the younger adults, older adults and (midlife) adults. Participation in class activities and feelings of inclusion or exclusion were also largely contingent on each person's position in one of the constructed age categories. Moreover, it carried over into their lives in the world beyond the classroom.

Age as a subject position is interlinked with other subject positions in adult language learners

Age identity is inevitably nuanced by other social dimensions, such as gender, profession and ethnicity. As seen in the study, dominant cultural discourses surrounding masculinities and femininities remain especially powerful in Mexico. Professional identity and the analogous student identity were also critical for these adults. Ethnicity and social standing played a role in some cases. The addition of a language learner identity contributed further to the complex of multiple subject positions of these participants.

Issues for applied linguistics

Two areas of applied linguistics impinge directly on the case described in this chapter involving the age identity of second language learners. The first of these areas, second language acquisition (SLA) research, aims to provide the theoretical foundations that illuminate the language acquisition process. By the end of the 1980s, the cognitive or psycholinguistic orientation to applied linguistics and SLA research had begun to share the stage with a social focus, one that highlighted 'language and more general social phenomena and processes' (Rampton 2014 [1995]: 234), including contextualised language use, interactional discourse and the social meaning of language. A growing body of SLA work in the sociocultural tradition embarked on studies of socially constructed dimensions of identity, including gender, social class and ethnicity. Yet, interestingly, age has not been included, traditionally being treated in SLA research only as an isolated biological factor that could account for differential success in language learning. This is a serious oversight. A better option, in my view, is a social constructionist approach to the issue, one that offers a more nuanced understanding of age, takes into consideration the experiential side of language learning and encompasses both linguistic and non-linguistic outcomes. Because age is a fundamental part of the complex of an individual's identities, a comprehensive understanding of a person means taking into account their constructions of age/temporality, and SLA research should reflect this.

The change of focus from the cognitive to the social, embraced by many applied linguists (Block 2003), has been extended to foreign language teaching and learning, historically the area of dominant concern in the field. This is the second and more immediate area of relevance to this study. The social perspective on language learning has brought the social dimension of language use to the fore, language being regarded as a complex social practice, a social and cultural phenomenon learned through interaction. The importance of age as socially constructed to this process has been confirmed by the research findings reported in this chapter. Some of the ramifications of the study for foreign language teaching practices can be summed up in the following reflections:

> Adult learners cannot be treated as a single indistinguishable population. Age-related differences exist among them, yet chronological age does not tell us enough about where a person is in the life course because people age in a variety of different ways. Age is a core part of a person's identity, and the social dimensions of age are particularly significant in a language learning situation. This should be borne in mind by teachers, curriculum planners and textbook designers.

> Teachers should look carefully at their textbooks, teaching materials and classroom activities in order to avoid reinforcing ageist discourses. Global textbooks, which target the young adult market, generally under-represent older people or assign stereotypical roles to them (Gray 2010). Conscientious selection and planning can counterbalance this. At the same time, attitudes and behaviour based on faulty preconceptions about age and language learning may surface in the classroom and inadvertently contribute to ageism.

> Taking a foreign language class may have distinct purposes for adults of different ages, and mastering the language may not be the top priority. More important priorities might include improving self-esteem, developing personal strengths, seeking new intellectual challenges, engaging in social encounters, acquiring cultural capital or creating a new identity. For this reason, it is important for teachers to be aware that their lessons should go beyond the single goal of language mastery and include other rewarding and meaningful experiences for the learners, who are ultimately persons with multiple identities involved in a world extending far beyond the classroom.

Summary

The case study reported in this chapter examines age as discursively constructed in social interaction in the context of English foreign language learning (EFL) in Mexico. It focuses on the dominant discourses and narratives in contemporary Western culture, particularly the discourse of decline, through which age and age identity are enacted, to illustrate how adulthood is constructed in our present-day world. Attention is directed to the specific case of Mexico, which has tended to follow the pattern of contemporary American and European societies in adopting age discourses and categories, yet with some interesting differences.

The study corroborates the prevalence of ageist attitudes on the part of all the participants, as seen in their denigration of the ageing process and corresponding glorification of youth, as they constructed age as a dimension of their identities. This is reflected in their beliefs about the progressive difficulty of learning a second or foreign language in adulthood. What also emerges from the data is a more nuanced understanding of age identity as it is linked fundamentally to other social phenomena, such as gender, ethnicity and social class. In a broader sense, the study suggests that social constructionism can offer a privileged vantage point from which to appreciate the complex nature of identity.

Related topics

Positioning language and identity: poststructuralist perspectives; Language and ethnic identity; The significance of sexual identity to language learning and teaching; Being a language teacher in the content classroom: teacher identity and content and language integrated learning (CLIL); Intersectionality in language and identity research; Identity in language learning and teaching: research agendas for the future.

Further reading

Andrew, P. (2012). *The social construction of age: adult foreign language learners*. Bristol: Multilingual Matters. (This book contains a more detailed description of the study reported in this chapter.)

Bamberg, M., De Fina, A. and Schiffrin, D. (eds) (2007). *Selves and identities in narrative and discourse*. Amsterdam: John Benjamins. (The authors provide a thorough treatment of the three principal traditions in identity studies, sociolinguistic, ethnomethodological and narrative, centring on the role of discursive and narrative practices in the ongoing construction of our identities.)

Gullette, M.M. (2011). *Agewise: fighting the new ageism in America*. Chicago: University of Chicago Press. (In this scholarly, but readable, book, Gullette continues her very cogent discussion of age discourses, bringing new insights to the topic of ageism.)

References

Andrew, P. (2012). *The social construction of age: adult foreign language learners*. Bristol: Multilingual Matters.

Baxter, J. (2003). *Positioning gender in discourse: a feminist methodology*. Basingstoke: Palgrave Macmillan.

Baxter, J. (this volume). Positioning language and identity: poststructuralist perspectives, in S. Preece (ed.) *The Routledge handbook of language and identity*. Abingdon: Routledge, pp. 34–49.

Benwell, B. and Stokoe, E. (2005). University students resisting academic identity, in K. Richards and P. Seedhouse (eds) *Applying conversation analysis*. Basingstoke: Palgrave Macmillan, pp. 124–139.

Block, D. (2003). *The social turn in second language acquisition*. Washington: Georgetown University Press.

Block, D. (2013). 'Issues in language and identity research in applied linguistics', *Estudios de Lingüística Inglesa Aplicada*, 13: 11–46.

Block, D. and Corona, V. (this volume). Intersectionality in language and identity research, in S. Preece (ed.) *The Routledge handbook of language and identity*. Abingdon: Routledge, pp. 507–522.

Bourdieu, P. (1977). *Outline of a theory of practice* [Trans. R. Nice]. Cambridge: Cambridge University Press.

Bourdieu, P. (2003). La juventud es sólo una palabra ['Youth' is just a word], in *Cuestiones de sociología* [*Sociology in question*] [Trans. E. Martín Criado]. Madrid: Istmo, pp. 142–153.

Brinkmann, S. and Kvale, S. (2015 [1996]). *InterViews: learning the craft of qualitative research interviewing*. 3rd edn. London: SAGE.

Burr, V. (2003). *Social constructionism*. 2nd edn. London: Routledge.

Butler, J. (1990). *Gender trouble: feminism and the subversion of identity*. New York: Routledge.

Clandinin, D.J. and Connelly, F.M. (2000). *Narrative inquiry: experience and story in qualitative research*. San Francisco: Jossey-Bass.

Combe, K. and Schmader, K. (1999). 'Naturalizing myths of aging: reading popular culture', *Journal of Aging and Identity*, 4: 79–109.

Coupland, N., Coupland, J. and Giles, H. (1991). *Language, society and the elderly*. Oxford: Basil Blackwell.

Cruikshank, M. (2003). *Learning to be old: gender, culture, and aging*. Lanham, MD: Rowman and Littlefield.

Featherstone, M. and Hepworth, M. (1995). Images of positive aging: a case study of *Retirement Choice* magazine, in M. Featherstone and A. Wernick (eds) *Images of aging: cultural representations of later life*. London: Routledge, pp. 170–196.

Franco Saldaña, M., Villarreal Ríos, E., Vargas Daza, E.R., Martínez González, L. and Galicia Rodríguez, L. (2010). 'Estereotipos negativos de la vejez en personal de salud de un Hospital de la Ciudad de Querétaro, México' [Prevalence of negative stereotypes towards old age among personnel of a general hospital], *Revista Médica de Chile*, 138: 988–993.

García Canclini, N. (2004). 'Culturas juveniles en una época sin respuesta' [Youth cultures in an age with no answers], *Revista de Estudios sobre Juventud*, 20: 43–53.

Giddens, A. (1991). *Modernity and self-identity: self and society in the late modern age*. Cambridge: Polity Press in association with Blackwell.

Gray, J. (2010). *The construction of English: culture, consumerism and promotion in the ELT global coursebook*. Basingstoke: Palgrave Macmillan.

Gullette, M.M. (2004). *Aged by culture*. Chicago: University of Chicago Press.

Harré, R. and van Langenhove, L. (eds) (1999). *Positioning theory: moral contexts of intentional action*. Oxford: Blackwell.

Holliday, A. (2002). *Doing and writing qualitative research*. London: SAGE.

Kohlbacher, F. (2006). 'The use of qualitative content analysis in case study research', *Forum: Qualitative Social Research*, 7(1) [Online]. Available at www.qualitative-research.net/index.php/fqs/article/view/75/153

Layder, D. (1998). *Sociological practice: linking theory and social research*. London: SAGE.

López Hernández, L.J. (2007). 'Historia de la mujer en México' [History of women in Mexico], *Mujeres, Derechos y Sociedad*, 3(5) [Online]. Available at Google.co.uk

Montes de Oca, V. (2001). 'Discourses, voices and visions on the aged in Mexico City', *Indian Journal of Gerontology*, 15: 53–66.

Nelson, T.D. (2005). 'Ageism: prejudice against our feared future self', *Journal of Social Issues*, 61: 207–221.

Norton, B. (2013 [2000]). *Identity and language learning: extending the conversation*. 2nd edn. Bristol: Multilingual Matters.

Palmore, E.B. (2005). 'Three decades of research on ageism', *Generations*, 29: 87–90.

Preece, S. (2009). *Posh talk: language and identity in higher education*. Basingstoke: Palgrave Macmillan.

Rampton, B. (2014 [1995]). *Crossing: language and ethnicity among adolescents*. 2nd edn. Abingdon: Routledge.

Robson, C. (2011). *Real world research: a resource for users of social research methods in applied settings*. 3rd edn. Chichester: John Wiley and Sons.

Shweder, R.A. (ed.) (1998). *Welcome to middle age! (and other cultural fictions)*. Chicago: University of Chicago Press.

Tulle-Winton, E. (1999). 'Growing old and resistance: towards a new cultural economy of old age?', *Ageing and Society*, 19: 281–299.

Weedon, C. (1997). *Feminist practice and poststructuralist theory*. Oxford: Blackwell.

Zermeño, A. (2005). 'La familia en la génesis del siglo XXI' [The family at the beginning of the 21st century], *Razón y Palabra*, 10(45) [Online]. Available at www.redalyc.org/pdf/1995/199520623014.pdf

22

The significance of sexual identity to language learning and teaching

Cynthia D. Nelson

I can remember ... [hearing about] your presentation at TESOL [Teachers of English to Speakers of Other Languages] thinking *why* in the *world*? ... Now I'm embarrassed ... that I had such a narrow view of it. But I kept thinking What does this whole *sex* thing have to do with ESL [English as a Second Language]?

(Janice, a teacher quoted in Nelson 2009: 102)

Introduction

It is perhaps not surprising that a teacher might find it perplexing, as Janice once did, to think that sexuality, in this case sexual identity, could be relevant to language learning or teaching. Janice was referring to a colloquium entitled 'We are your colleagues: lesbians and gays in ESL', which was delivered at an international TESOL Convention in Canada (by myself, Lisa Carscadden and Jim Ward) back in 1992. At that time, there were virtually no discussions of sexual identity at language teaching conferences or in published research. Since then, research on language and identity has evolved substantially, as the current volume attests, but in much of this work the socio-sexual dimensions of identity are still barely acknowledged and rarely investigated in depth. Meanwhile, language and sexuality has become an established research area (Leap and Motschenbacher 2012), but the implications of its findings for language education are rarely considered (Nelson 2012).

Steadily coming into its own as a research area, though, are investigations of sexual identity in language education, which I have elsewhere called 'queer inquiry' (see Nelson 2006). Its key studies can be classified into two main strands. One strand examines sexual identity – most often, lesbian, gay, bisexual and transgender (LGBT) lives and issues – as content in language curricula and as a topic in class conversations. This work includes studies of the following: an ESL class discussion of same-sex affection and the pedagogic value of queer theory (more on that later) (Nelson 1999); language learners' online discussions of homosexuality (Nguyen and Kellogg 2005); the use of local LGBT life-narratives as language learning material in Japan

(O'Móchain 2006); sexuality issues that arise in the teaching of French, Italian and Japanese as foreign languages (de Vincenti *et al.* 2007); LGBT absences and problematic representations in English language teaching materials (Gray 2013), and more.

The other main strand of research focuses on sexual identity as a dimension of language learners' and teachers' lives and interactions, in and beyond the classroom. This work includes studies of: language teachers' intended sexual identity self-presentations versus their students' interpretations (Nelson 2004); a teacher coming out as gay in his Australian ESL class (Curran 2006); gay language learners' pursuit of English in Korea (King 2008) and in Japan (Moore 2013); teacher responses to learners' openly gay stances in foreign language classes in Australia (Liddicoat 2009; see also Kappra and Vandrick 2006); the in-class identity negotiations of a gay Mexican immigrant in the United States (Nelson 2010), and so on.

Concerns pertaining to both research strands were investigated in the first, and to date the only, book-length study on the topic, which was published as *Sexual identities in English language education: classroom conversations* (Nelson 2009). This study investigated the role and significance of sexual identities in language education by analysing over 100 language teachers' and learners' perspectives and classroom talk on the topic. Interweaving empirical data with theory throughout, it addressed the following questions:

- Why and how does sexual identity content arises in English language classes and what teaching/learning challenges and opportunities result?
- What ways of theorising sexual identity are evident in classroom practice and which conceptual-pedagogic approaches are most engaging and effective for learners?
- How can poststructuralist identity theories – especially queer theory – be useful in language teaching?

This chapter is based on that larger study and presents a small sampling of its data and findings (for a full discussion see the original work). In so doing, my larger aim is to provide students and scholars in applied linguistics who study language and identity with a basic understanding of why sexual identity is not peripheral but integral to language learning and teaching. I also suggest that research on the relationship between language learning and sexual identity can enhance investigations in other language and identity arenas in ways that have yet to be explored. Before turning to the data, I provide an overview of some of the key concepts informing the study.

Overview

The focal study was interdisciplinary, drawing from research on identity (e.g. Norton Peirce 1995), sexual identity and queer theory, the latter of which is my focus in this section. Though the term 'queer' can be used as a term of derision or to succinctly summarise an array of non-heterosexual identities (LGBT and more), its usage in queer theory is meant to call into question the solidifying of sexualities into sexual 'identities' by deliberately blurring the boundaries between clear-cut categories and highlighting their constructedness (as opposed to their naturalness) (see Butler 1990; Nelson 1999, 2009; Sedgwick 1990).

Below I briefly outline three of the queer theory concepts that underpinned the study and that pertain to the data presented in this chapter.

Not facts but acts: sexual identities as performative

First, the notion of performativity frames sexual identities as being not 'natural' or inherent but socially constructed, not properties or attributes but processes and practices, and not predetermined but *performative* social actions: in short, not facts but acts (Nelson 1999). This understanding of performativity is informed by Butler's (1990) seminal work in which she drew on Austin's notion that utterances act upon the world rather than merely describe it. It is through the cumulative effect of repeated discursive and semiotic acts that sexual identities become constituted; and these layered acts of identity are not freely chosen but subject to certain social constraints (Butler 2004). Thus, sexual identities are understood to be not inner essences to be suppressed or expressed but rather performative actions that are instantiated, communicated and contested through social interactions (see also Gray, this volume; Jones, this volume).

Beyond the bedroom: sexual identities as an important part of public life

Second, with queer theory the category of sexual identity (much like race and gender) is recognised as having broad social relevance, since the powerful 'hetero–homo' defining binary shapes societal knowledge and institutions (Sedgwick 1990). Thus, the performative acts through which sexual identities are (co-)constituted are not confined to the privacy of the bedroom but infuse public life. Moreover, the ways in which sexual identities are named, enacted, interpreted and negotiated – and the meanings and importance they are accorded – vary widely according to the specific cultural milieu, the confluence of local/global discourses at play, the setting, situation, interlocutors and so on (see Leap and Motschenbacher 2012).

Heteronormativity: sexual identities as unequally valued

Finally, the study engages with the notion of heteronormativity in order to analyse which sexual identity options seem available, allowable and valued in a given setting or situation and which do not. The concept of 'heteronormativity' refers to the normative discourses and practices through which it is heterosexuality – and only heterosexuality – that is made to seem normal or natural and therefore legitimate (Warner 1993; Nelson 2009; Gray, this volume). Powerful social and linguistic norms that constrain sexual identity options and enactments can be upheld, resisted and challenged; these norms are dynamic, not static.

Having offered a brief account of the identity theories that inform the case study for this chapter, in the following sections I turn to the methodology for the study and the data.

Methodology

To address the research questions outlined above, I conducted a multi-site study that involved an international cohort of over 40 English language teachers and over 60 learners. All adults hailed from (or had taught in) various countries in Africa, the Americas, Asia, Europe and Oceania and included international students, migrants and refugees. I focused on a crucial dimension of second/foreign language education: participants' interactions in the language classroom and their reported experiences of these interactions (van Lier 1996).

The study was in two parts. For the first, I collected data via teacher focus groups and individual interviews (all of which I recorded and later transcribed). The focus groups were held at universities in the United States and an international TESOL convention, and participation was voluntary. In each I posed the same question: 'What, if anything, do sexual identities (straight, gay, bisexual, lesbian, transgender, queer, etc.) have to do with teaching or learning English?' (Nelson 2009: 5). For the second part of the study, I observed English language classes at colleges and universities in two American cities over a six-week period and repeatedly interviewed the three participating teachers as well as nearly half of their students (28 in total). In many of the interviews I used the technique of 'stimulated recall', which involved replaying selected excerpts of a recorded class session, showing a rough transcript and asking the participant what they had thought or felt at the time (Nunan 1992: 94).

Through professional affiliations, I was already acquainted with about half of the teachers who took part in my study, which meant we had already established some trust, but also some distance, as I was no longer living in the United States. As both insider and outsider, my combined emic and etic insights about the teachers and their courses proved advantageous to the research (see Watson-Gegeo 1988). I had no prior knowledge of the students. I conducted all interviews in English so that any student who volunteered could be interviewed (rather than targeting those from particular language groups). Being interviewed in a language they were learning most likely limited what some students felt they could say and what I was able to understand of what they said; on the other hand, some may have found it easier to discuss this topic (sexual identities) in English, especially in an education setting (see Extract 3 below).

I collected 150 hours of data in total and took an empirical-conceptual approach to the analysis. This involved a rigorous and iterative, yet invariably subjective, process of listening to the recordings, transcribing the most relevant portions and rereading the transcripts numerous times to identify the emerging thematic issues and to code, categorise and refine these. In analysing the focus group and interview data, I sought to map out the main issues about sexual identities that participants considered significant to language learning or teaching; I also highlighted points of divergence or contention in order to illuminate competing discourses and changing practices at play. With the classroom data, I drew on Lemke (1985), Lather (1991) and others to analyse how participants were theorising sexual identities and how their conceptions were shaping their learning/teaching experiences, as well as how different participants experienced the same classroom interactions (Nelson 2009). In the following section I present ten short extracts of data that are illustrative of the research participants' experiences of, and views on, sexual identities in language education.

The data

For the purposes of this chapter, the data extracts have been separated into two categories (though the categories are, of course, interrelated): first, those pertaining to sexual-identity content and heteronormative discourses; and second, those pertaining to learners' and teachers' sexual identities. It is worth noting that the research participants almost always discussed sexual identities in terms of gay and lesbian identities, with some mention of transgender people but almost no talk of bisexuality; there was also little talk about heterosexuality, with one important exception: straight teachers speaking about negotiating their sexual identities in class. Therefore, this largely lesbian and gay emphasis is reflected in the data extracts. Due to space limitations I have not included detailed transcriptions.

Sexual-identity content and heteronormativity

As Extract 1 illustrates, the practice of vocabulary development was found to be a way in which the subject of sexual identity became foregrounded in the language classroom.

Extract 1: 'Boyfriend'

A male student ... was talking about his boyfriend ... So I had to explain that ... in this culture if you say 'boyfriend' that has a gay overtone to it ... Whereas a woman can say 'girlfriend' and it doesn't have those connotations.

(Mark, a teacher quoted in Nelson 2009: 50)

Due to the likelihood of lexical and grammatical errors in second and foreign language classes, such as with pronouns, it is not always possible to discern whether a student is mistakenly signifying a gay relationship or identity, as Mark believed his student was, or intentionally coming out as gay (see Liddicoat 2009). Thus, in explaining to students the gay connotations of an utterance, as Mark reported here, it would be problematic to imply that gay connotations are undesirable.

I found that sexual-identity content arose in class when defining vocabulary such as 'gay', 'bisexual' and 'transgender', discussing ways of referring to same-sex relationships, debating same-sex marriage, and sharing information about (international) students' host-families. The subject also arose in the course of talking about a number of topics other than family and relationships: for example, television shows, online communities, poetry, anti-racist and feminist activism, local businesses, and more.

Extract 2 is from a class discussion that touched on gender and appearance as part of a lesson on 'community'. The extract shows a student from China, Ping, introducing the topic of sexual identity, and her teacher, who was from France, responding.

Extract 2: 'Lifestyle'

Ping: Wear earring just for woman. But for man, lifestyle.
Gina: Aaah! (laughter) (G smiles) Is *that* what you think? (much laughter).

(Nelson 2009: 153)

The follow-up interviews revealed that this teacher and student had divergent understandings about what this exchange meant. The student was trying to explain to her (international) classmates that, in the United States, earrings on a man are a 'sign' that he is gay (ibid.: 156). However, the teacher believed that Ping was about to out a male classmate as gay, and to do so in a 'nasty' way. To circumvent this, the teacher tried to make the point to the class that 'making assumptions about somebody's sexual orientation because of the way they look' is problematic, as she put it in our interview. Ping did not comprehend this message, though, thinking the problem was her choice of vocabulary: 'I never get it good words' (ibid.). Moreover, not all students picked up on the gay subtext of this classroom exchange.

In analysing the class discussion (necessarily truncated here), I noted the need to sometimes make implicit sexual-identity meanings explicit for language learning purposes, especially given the ambiguities often associated with this identity domain. However, doing so can be challenging, since having open conversations about LGBT identities is not universally practised or condoned. This is illustrated in Extract 3, in which a student explained the situation in his home country of Morocco:

Extract 3: 'We don't talk about that'

Our education system, in the class we don't talk about that ... In Morocco ... *all* the society is prohib to talk about that.

(Neuriden, a student quoted in Nelson 2009: 185)

In some countries homosexuality is not openly discussed, at least not in education contexts, which may help to explain why nearly all of the students interviewed for the study said they had not previously discussed LGBT themes in a classroom. Neuriden's comment also underscores the need for teachers to be cognisant of the likely novelty, for some students, not of this subject matter necessarily, but of openly discussing it in class.

At the same time, Neuriden's comment may also help to explain why engaging with this subject matter is often revelatory and useful for students: in the same interview, we were discussing a class discussion of the cultural variations of lesbian/gay signifiers which Neuriden enjoyed very much, describing it as 'very good ... very helpful ... With this kind of discussion you ... express yourself, you feel very comfortable, you feel happy after that' (ibid.: 187). So even though openly mentioning or discussing LGBT themes may be unfamiliar for some students (and teachers), this does not mean these themes should be banned or avoided (see O'Móchain 2006).

Cultural and institutional norms dissuading open discussions of LGBT themes and perspectives are not restricted to certain countries, of course, but can be found worldwide. As Extract 4 shows, even in countries that are known to have visible LGBT communities and at least some legal rights for this population, LGBT content in classroom talk can be prohibited. In this extract, the teacher was referring to a language centre in the local gay neighbourhood in a city in the United States.

Extract 4: 'A block from a gay bar'

I have friends who teach at [x], and their administrative dictate is This is not to be discussed in the classroom. So the teachers aren't allowed to bring it up as a topic ... [Even though] the students walk outside the door and see men holding hands ... They're a block from a gay bar!

(Mark, a teacher quoted in Nelson 2009: 47)

Other teachers in my study mentioned similar silencing practices and unofficial policies. One told of a group of teachers who had prepared a handout with referrals to assist students who either identified as LGBT or who wanted to learn about LGBT issues, but the teachers were prohibited by their administrator from distributing it to students 'because it was not the kind of thing that we should be talking about in our classes' (ibid.: 46). Another teacher in my study took the view that overtly excluding people on the basis of race is not generally tolerated in language education, whereas excluding people on the basis of sexual identity is: 'By saying Well we don't talk about it' (ibid.: 47).

In the interviews, a number of students spoke about the novelty of encountering openly gay or lesbian people in public and the benefits of being able to talk about this in their second language class. Sara was one such student:

Extract 5: 'In front of your eyes'

I think every people should know it ... Especially if you living here ... Because at first ... I didn't know anything about it ... It just happen in front of your eyes ... When you walking ... you see the gay people they holding the hand ... If you don't know those gay people exist, you would question. But if you know they are gay ... you understand.

(Sara, a student quoted in Nelson 2009: 164–165)

This student told me that back in her home country (Vietnam) she was not aware that gay people existed, so when she first moved to the United States she found it perplexing to see same-sex affection; thus, she was grateful for the gay-themed discussions in her English class because they helped her understand local phenomena.

Such comments underscore the importance of allowing, even inviting, students to talk about day-to-day identity practices that they find unfamiliar and confusing. As one teacher explained it, 'What we're striving to do is teach cultural fluency', and she demonstrated the need for this by explaining that some students had gone to a bar of all men without realising they were in a gay bar (ibid.: 55). Another teacher said that students often tease each other about who is gay and who is not, which gives teachers an opportunity to explain the negative reaction they are likely to get locally if they talk openly about people in that way. Thus, understanding cultural meanings and norms includes understanding those associated with sexual identities and inequities.

With regard to inequities, one common challenge cited by teachers was how to respond to discriminatory, anti-LGBT language in the classroom. This is described in Extract 6 by one of the teachers:

Extract 6: 'Homophobic comments'

Some of the nicest students I know have some of the most ... intense homophobic comments to make. And when that comes up ... little jokes or stuff, I don't know quite how to jump in there and ... challenge that.

(Scott, a teacher quoted in Nelson 2009: 68)

On the one hand, teachers thought their students need to become familiar with the linguistic/cultural meanings associated with sexual identities and inequities, so that they do not unintentionally or unknowingly offend their interlocutors (this concern was also expressed by some students). But on the other hand, many teachers felt unprepared and unsure of how to go about this.

Some teachers would prohibit anti-gay talk in class, but a few took a more analytic approach. This latter approach is evident in Extract 7:

Extract 7: 'Display for one's peers'

If [students] want to write, um, homophobic stuff they have to understand that they're representing a series of values for a community. That these aren't given. [...] I think ... racist and homophobic comments often come from ... a display for one's peers.

(Rachel, a teacher quoted in Nelson 2009: 84–85)

As Rachel noted, when someone takes a homophobic (or racist) stance in their writing or speech, this does not necessarily represent their true views, but can be understood as an attempt to establish an identity and foster a sense of affiliation with a given group. Thus, conceptualising homophobia and heteronormativity as acts of discourse can help language teachers to frame and examine these issues productively. It is also worth mentioning that, while some teachers in my study were disturbed by their students' anti-LGBT comments, the converse was also the case: some students were disturbed by their teachers' anti-LGBT comments.

Sexual identities of language learners and teachers

Though it is rarely acknowledged in applied linguistics research, for some learners the desire for a second language (in this case, English) is directly linked to their sexual identity. In Extract 8 this is demonstrated by Pablo, a student from Mexico:

Extract 8: 'Accepted'

> I decided to come to this country [the United States] because ... I want to ... be in a place where [being gay] is accepted, to– to see what I feel, how I change.
>
> *(Pablo, a student quoted in Nelson 2009: 193)*

Given the anti-gay violence that Pablo said was rampant in the part of Mexico where he was from, 'he considered migration a pathway to gay liberation, and English the passport to a cosmopolitan gay life' (Nelson 2010: 458). At the same time, while learning to be gay in the new environment and language (see Espín 1999), Pablo was finding that the United States was not quite the safe gay haven he had imagined it to be. He did not directly disclose his gay identity in his classes, nor to his teachers, even those he guessed were lesbians (though he did send a coded signal to a classmate; see Nelson 2010). Taking part in just one 15-minute class discussion with lesbian and gay content (within a 100-hour class) was a rare opportunity that this student found extremely meaningful and pleasurable: 'I enjoyed *everything* in that class [discussion] ... every every word' (Nelson 2009: 194).

A few teachers spoke of having students who were openly lesbian, gay or transgender in the classroom, but it was more common for students to come out to teachers privately (some lesbian teachers said this occurs on a regular basis). As Extract 9 shows, having a student come out to them outside class posed some dilemmas for teachers, especially those who felt that they lacked gay/queer knowledge.

Extract 9: 'Take your time'

> I had a student ... who wanted to come out [as gay] here in the United States ... About all I knew was to say Take your time, and take it step by step. But– So I'm trying to learn more about how to support students.
>
> *(Maggie, a teacher quoted in Nelson 2009: 31)*

Since students who identify as LGBT often lack well-established social and community networks in the new locale (family relationships can be problematic too), some turn to their language teachers for learning support and/or community resources and referrals – perhaps especially those students who are being shunned by their classmates, or who lack confidence or competence in their linguistic ability to connect with the local LGBT community (see Nelson 2010). Some straight teachers in my study wanted to be able to refer LGBT students to LGBT teaching colleagues for assistance. However, many of those teachers did not feel they could be open about their sexual identity in their teaching contexts.

On that point, another important issue that emerged for teachers was how they negotiated their own sexual identity in the classroom and how these identity negotiations and enactments shaped their teaching choices and interactions with students. Many varied perspectives emerged, one of which is illustrated in Extract 10.

Extract 10: 'Agenda'

You guys can even say you're straight and that's fine ... But me, if they [students] found out that I was gay ... they would go Oh well he's got an agenda.

(Tony, a teacher quoted in Nelson 2009: 113)

Addressing his straight colleagues in the focus group, Tony pointed out that they could openly enact their sexual identities in class. However, he felt it necessary to hide his sexual identity, believing that knowledge of this would somehow taint students' perceptions of his motives – that he wished to change students' attitudes, perhaps, or even that he was sexually predatory, given the prevalent hypersexualising of homosexuality, especially for men. Nonetheless, while Tony deliberately constructed a straight persona for his classroom, his students were not persuaded (see Nelson 2004).

A number of gay male teachers found it challenging to broach gay topics in class for similar reasons as Tony. On the other hand, a number of lesbian teachers did broach these topics regularly, and some came out in their classes too; one said she wanted her students to know that she was a lesbian because otherwise they might make homophobic comments in class and feel 'really embarrassed if they found out afterwards' that they were 'hurting their teacher' (Nelson 2009: 105). Meanwhile, some straight teachers said they avoided LGBT discussions because they would feel like 'an outsider talking about this' (ibid.: 113), or because they would feel 'uncomfortable' if their students were to make homophobic comments (ibid.: 68). Thus, I found that how teachers present and manage their own sexual identity in class can and does have a shaping effect on their teaching practices.

Discussion

As the small sample of data presented in this chapter from my larger study has shown, language learners can benefit from opportunities to talk explicitly about sexual-identity signals and norms that tend to be communicated implicitly and often ambiguously (Extracts 1 and 2). However, some learners (and teachers) may find it unfamiliar and uncomfortable when LGBT content is introduced, perhaps especially in the globalised classroom (Extract 3), while some may be pressured to avoid such content altogether (Extract 4). Yet learning a second language involves navigating the interpretive demands of the new cultural environment – and learning to decode the sociocultural meanings associated with the performative acts of sexual identity can be an integral part of that process (Extract 5).

Given the social inequities associated with sexual identities, one common challenge facing teachers and students alike is responding to heteronormative discourses, both oral and written, in the language classroom (Extract 6). Teachers in my study who adopted a rhetorical or discourse-oriented view would have their students analyse the cultural and linguistic practices associated with sexual identities and inequities (Extract 7). For example, one teacher in my study asked her class to discuss possible interpretations of same-sex affection in their countries versus the United States (see Chapter 8 of Nelson 2009 for a full discussion); another asked students who were writing anti-gay essays to consider the effect their texts were likely to have on a local reader (ibid.: 84).

The significance of sexual identity in language education extends beyond curricula and pedagogy. It can drive the desire for a second or foreign language. Invariably, some language learners will be in the process of coming out (to themselves or to others) as LGBT, which can be all the more complex in the midst of a new language and country. Indeed, many second-language learners will have moved to a new country and be learning the new language precisely *because* they are seeking a less heteronormative environment (Extract 8; see also Nelson 2010). This raises the question of how willing – and how prepared – teachers are to create learning environments that are supportive of LGBT and questioning students and to identify and address their needs as language learners (Extract 9). Exacerbating the challenge for teachers are the notoriously low levels of LGBT representation in language curricula and materials (Gray 2013).

Some teachers in my study were just beginning to consider how effective their teaching practices and curricula were likely to be with sexually diverse student cohorts. Although LGBT content and perspectives are badly needed in language curricula and pedagogy, it seems ironic that – due to the predominance of heteronormative thinking in the field – teachers who identify as LGBT often feel they cannot be open about their sexual identities in the language classroom, and must contort their teaching accordingly (Extract 10; see also Simon-Maeda 2004).

Pedagogic implications

As intimated in the data shown above, when content and perspectives associated with sexual identities are incorporated into curricula and classroom talk, this is meaningful not only to LGBT students but to all students – in part because understandings and expectations associated with the socio-sexual dimension of identity are not universal but culturally varied. Moreover, sexual-identity enactments and negotiations, both inside and outside the classroom, are subject to social and linguistic norms that constrain what can be said in certain situations and with certain interlocutors, so language learners may benefit from learning to unpack these practices and constraints.

My argument is that practices and dilemmas associated with sexual identities can and should be highlighted in the language classroom to both illuminate and to interrogate identity practices: in other words, for learning purposes the links between language and sexual identity can be examined functionally and critically. While this case is fully elaborated in my book, here I briefly describe some conceptual-pedagogic tools that can help in the classroom.

By examining a range of language teaching practices as well as participants' perspectives on these, I identified and critically evaluated three main pedagogic approaches (often used in combination) to sexual-identity content (primarily, though not exclusively, LGBT content) (see Table 9.1 in Nelson 2009: 210). In brief, these approaches can be summarised as follows.

Counselling approach

The counselling approach conceptualises sexual identities as inner essences. It is concerned with homophobia, i.e. the fear or hatred of those perceived to be LGBT, and seeks to enhance learners' personal growth or social tolerance through a focus on feelings and attitudes about LGBT people. To this end, positive mainstream LGBT representations are included in curricula.

Controversies approach

The controversies approach conceptualises sexual identities as sociohistorical constructs. It is concerned with heterosexism, defined as institutionalised discrimination against those perceived to be LGBT. It seeks to enhance learners' interest in social justice and human rights, focuses on social controversies, prohibits anti-LGBT utterances and involves class debates of issues such as same-sex marriage.

Discourse inquiry approach

The discourse inquiry approach conceptualises sexual identities as performative and is concerned with heteronormative discourses. It seeks to enhance learners' ability to analyse linguistic and cultural acts of sexual identity by engaging in activities that involve unpacking socio-sexual identities and inequities in everyday discourses and public life. It is this third approach, though used the least often, that was found to be most effective with language learners (Nelson 2009).

In line with a discourse inquiry approach, language learners need to develop the capacity to understand and critically engage with the sexual-linguistic dimensions of identity, which are ubiquitous and socially meaningful, yet potentially fraught. Drawing on Alexander and Banks (2004), I argue that language learners (and, thus, their teachers) need to develop 'socio-sexual literacy' (Nelson 2009). This involves becoming adept at recognising, decoding and being able to produce cultural/linguistic meanings and innuendo associated with sexual identities. It also requires skills in identifying, analysing and critically responding to heteronormativity in spoken interactions and written and multimodal texts. It means too that, when addressing and interacting with classmates, colleagues and other interlocutors across school, work and community contexts, students and teachers do not unthinkingly presume that everyone is necessarily heterosexual.

Though anyone can potentially benefit from learning socio-sexual literacy, it should be noted that some LGBT people may have already developed a nuanced awareness of this, having had to 'cloak meanings' within heteronormative environments (Britzman 1997: 193). Accordingly, LGBT-identified people may already bring a well-developed linguistic awareness to their language learning endeavours (Nelson 2010), though this is rarely recognised in most language education research, where the existence of LGBT learners is barely acknowledged.

Issues for applied linguistics

The study presented in this chapter, along with other research into sexual identities, shows some of the reasons why sexual identity is highly salient in language learning and teaching. As this is not yet widely recognised in applied linguistics, several issues warrant serious attention in the future.

Research

There is plenty of scope for new research in applied linguistics on language learning and sexual identities, especially from the perspective of queer theory, as this is still a nascent research area that offers rich opportunities. Investigations set in and across various institutional types, education levels and world regions would enrich the field, as would more investigations that focus specifically on heterosexuality (see Appleby 2014), lesbianism, bisexuality and transgenderality, all of which have received scant attention to date. Also fruitful would be work that draws out the implications for language teaching of language and sexuality studies and queer linguistics, as well as work that explores dimensions of sexuality other than sexual identity.

Given the intersectionality and interplay of identities – which is widely acknowledged in applied linguistics but not yet widely investigated – studies of language and identity should not overlook the sexual dimensions of identity or, for that matter, queer theory (see e.g. Harissi *et al.* 2012). And conversely, sexuality and queer-focused research would benefit from more fully engaging with other identity domains and theories, such as post-colonial, anti-racist or feminist theories, or those pertaining to space and place.

Learner resources and teacher development

The ongoing, overwhelming heterosexualisation of language learning materials and curricula – noted by many teachers in the study presented in this chapter – is an unnecessary hindrance for language learning; thus, language learning materials urgently need updating (see Gray 2013). Also, little is known about how existing sexual identity research is being incorporated into teacher education and development programmes and with what effects. It would be useful for teachers, teacher educators and teachers-in-training to share their accounts. In this, narrative inquiry offers alternatives that may be more broadly accessible than empirical inquiry yet still rigorous (Nelson 2011).

Creative ways of fostering engagement with sexual identity research are needed too. An example is my ethnographic play *Queer as a second language*, which is based on research transcripts from the focal study described in this chapter (Nelson 2013). When performed at universities and conferences internationally, it has generated lively post-play discussions of the issues at hand.

Scholarly networks

Significant advances in research, learning resources and teacher development cannot be made until the field collectively and visibly values this sort of work. Those who wish to develop LGBT-inclusive or queer curricula or pursue sexual identity investigations ought to be encouraged and supported and not dissuaded, harassed or subjected to negative career consequences (the latter is known to occur in applied linguistics, although it is not well documented).

To this end, an invaluable resource is face-to-face and online networks for teachers and researchers to discuss these issues, such as the innovative ESRC-funded seminar series 'Queering ESOL: towards a cultural politics of LGBT issues in the ESOL classroom', organised by John Gray, Michael Baynham and Melanie Cooke (see https://queeringesol.wordpress.com).

Summary

Given the persistent lack of critical engagement with, or even simple acknowledgement of, sexual diversity in many language and identity studies and language learning materials, it surely is not just Janice (the teacher I quoted at the opening of this chapter) left wondering why 'this whole *sex* thing' is worth discussing in language education. But as my focal study and related studies have shown, sexual identity is not irrelevant but integral to language use, language learning and language teaching.

This is showing to be the case across a range of geographic locations, as a raft of recent (and often small-scale) language-education studies, set in Cyprus, Germany, Spain, Thailand and elsewhere, are making clear (see Nelson 2012). Yoshihara (2013), for example, found that English language learners in Japan are more open to LGBT content than are their teachers, which underscores the urgency of incorporating this content into learner resources, teacher development programmes and language education research if the field is to keep up to date with language learners' needs and interests in these changing times.

I hope the study presented in this chapter will spur the field of applied linguistics – particularly students and scholars of language and identity – to consider the socio-sexual dimensions of identity and will encourage language teachers and language teacher educators to develop their students' socio-sexual literacy by experimenting with discourse inquiry approaches. To this end, it may be useful to utilise queer theory concepts, such as performativity and heteronormativity.

Related topics

Positioning language and identity: poststructuralist perspectives; Language and gender identities; Language and non-normative sexual identities; Language, gender and identities in political life: a case study from Malaysia; Straight-acting: discursive negotiations of a homomasculine identity; Intersectionality in language and identity research; Identity in language learning and teaching: research agendas for the future.

Further reading

Hall, K. and Barrett, R. (in press). *The Oxford handbook of language and sexuality*. Oxford: Oxford University Press. (Discusses sociocultural linguistics research, from various sub-disciplines, on language and sexuality, and recommends directions for future research; includes chapters on language learning and literacy education.)

Malinowitz, H. (1995). *Textual orientations: lesbian and gay students and the making of discourse communities*. Portsmouth: Heinemann. (Examines the (first-language) literacy development of lesbian, gay, bisexual and heterosexual college students in New York in a writing class with a lesbian and gay thematic focus.)

Murray, D.A.B. (ed.) (2014). Queering borders: language, sexuality and migration. *Special issue of Journal of Language and Sexuality*, 3(1). (Introduces six studies of the interconnections between language, sexuality and transnational border crossing for queer asylum seekers, refugees and migrants. The focus is queer migration discourses, not education.)

Nelson, C.D. (ed.) (2006). Queer inquiry in language education. *Special issue of Journal of Language, Identity, and Education*, 5(1). (Introduces 'queer inquiry' with five studies that investigate sexual-identity discourses in first-, second- and foreign-language education settings in Australia, Brazil, Canada and Japan.)

Rivers, D. and Zotzmann, K. (eds) (in press). *Isms in language education: oppression, intersectionality and emancipation*. Berlin: Mouton de Gruyter. (Examines different forms of social oppression, including chapters on heterosexism and heteronormativity, within language education contexts.)

Takahashi, K. (2013). *Language learning, gender and desire*. Clevedon: Multilingual Matters. (Explores the English language learning experiences of Japanese women in Australia in relation to their interlinked desires for English, the West and Western-styled masculinity and romance.)

Cynthia D. Nelson

References

Alexander, J. and Banks, W.P. (2004). 'Sexualities, technologies, and the teaching of writing: a critical overview', *Computers and Composition*, 21: 273–293.

Appleby, R. (2014). *Men and masculinities in global English language teaching*. Basingstoke: Palgrave Macmillan.

Britzman, D.P. (1997). What is this thing called love? New discourses for understanding gay and lesbian youth, in S. de Castell and M. Bryson (eds) *Radical in<ter>ventions: identity, politics, and difference/s in educational praxis*. Albany: State University of New York Press, pp. 183–207.

Butler, J. (1990). *Gender trouble*. New York: Routledge.

Butler, J. (2004). *Undoing gender*. New York: Routledge.

Curran, G. (2006). 'Responding to students' normative questions about gays: putting queer theory into practice in an Australian ESL class', *Journal of Language, Identity, and Education*, 5: 85–96.

de Vincenti, G., Giovanangeli, A. and Ward, R. (2007). 'The queer stopover: how queer travels in the language classroom', *Electronic Journal of Foreign Language Teaching*, 4: 58–72.

Espín, O.M. (1999). *Women crossing boundaries: the psychology of immigration and the transformations of sexuality*. New York: Routledge.

Gray, J. (2013). LGBT invisibility and heteronormativity in ELT materials, in J. Gray (ed.) *Critical perspectives on language teaching materials*. Basingstoke: Palgrave Macmillan, pp. 40–63.

Gray, J. (this volume). Language and non-normative sexual identities, in S. Preece (ed.) *The Routledge handbook of language and identity*. Abingdon: Routledge, pp. 225–240.

Gray, J., Baynham, M. and Cooke, M. (No date). *Queering ESOL: towards a cultural politics of LGBT issues in the ESOL classroom* [Online]. Available at https://queeringesol.wordpress.com

Harissi, M., Otsuji, E. and Pennycook, A. (2012). 'The performative fixing and unfixing of subjectivities', *Applied Linguistics*, 33(5): 524–543.

Jones, L. (this volume). Language and gender identities, in S. Preece (ed.) *The Routledge handbook of language and identity*. Abingdon: Routledge, pp. 210–224.

Kappra, R. and Vandrick, S. (2006). 'Silenced voices speak: queer ESL students recount their experiences', *CATESOL Journal*, 18(1): 138–150.

King, B.W. (2008). '"Being gay guy, that is the advantage": queer Korean language learning and identity construction', *Journal of Language, Identity, and Education*, 7(3/4): 230–252.

Lather, P. (1991). *Getting smart: feminist research and pedagogy with/in the postmodern*. London: Routledge.

Leap, W.L. and Motschenbacher, H. (2012). 'Launching a new phase in language and sexuality studies', *Journal of Language and Sexuality*, 1(1): 1–14.

Lemke, J.L. (1985). *Using language in the classroom*. Geelong, Australia: Deakin University Press.

Liddicoat, A.J. (2009). 'Sexual identity as linguistic failure: trajectories of interaction in the heteronormative language classroom', *Journal of Language, Identity, and Education*, 8(2): 191–202.

Moore, A.R. (2013). The ideal sexual self: the motivational investments of Japanese gay male learners of English, in P. Benson and L. Cooker (eds) *The applied linguistic individual: sociocultural approaches to identity, agency and autonomy*. Sheffield, UK: Equinox, pp. 135–151.

Nelson, C.D. (1999). 'Sexual identities in ESL: queer theory and classroom inquiry', *TESOL Quarterly*, 33(3): 371–391.

Nelson, C.D. (2004). 'A queer chaos of meanings: coming out conundrums in globalised classrooms', *Journal of Gay and Lesbian Issues in Education*, 2(1): 27–46.

Nelson, C.D. (2006). 'Queer inquiry in language education', *Journal of Language, Identity, and Education*, 5(1): 1–9.

Nelson, C.D. (2009). *Sexual identities in English language education: classroom conversations*. New York: Routledge.

Nelson, C.D. (2010). 'A gay immigrant student's perspective: unspeakable acts in the language class', *TESOL Quarterly*, 44(3): 441–464.

Nelson, C.D. (2011). 'Narratives of classroom life: changing conceptions of knowledge', *TESOL Quarterly*, 45(3): 463–485.

Nelson, C.D. (2012). 'Emerging queer epistemologies in studies of "gay"-student discourses', *Journal of Language and Sexuality*, 1(1): 79–105.

Nelson, C.D. (2013). From transcript to playscript: dramatizing narrative research, in G. Barkhuizen (ed.) *Narrative research in applied linguistics*. Cambridge: Cambridge University Press, pp. 220–243.

Nguyen, H.T. and Kellogg, G. (2005). 'Emergent identities in on-line discussions for second language learning', *Canadian Modern Language Review/La Revue Canadienne des langues vivants*, 62(1): 111–136.

Norton Peirce, B. (1995). 'Social identity, investment, and language learning', *TESOL Quarterly*, 29(1): 9–31.

Nunan, D. (1992). *Research methods in language learning*. Cambridge: Cambridge University Press.

O'Móchain, R. (2006). 'Discussing gender and sexuality in a context-appropriate way: queer narratives in an EFL college classroom in Japan', *Journal of Language, Identity, and Education*, 5(1): 51–66.

Sedgwick, E.K. (1990). *Epistemology of the closet*. London: Penguin.

Simon-Maeda, A. (2004). 'The complex construction of professional identities: female EFL educators in Japan speak out', *TESOL Quarterly*, 38(3): 405–436.

van Lier, L. (1996). *Interaction in the language curriculum: awareness, autonomy and authenticity*. London: Longman.

Warner, M. (1993). Introduction, in M. Warner (ed.) *Fear of a queer planet: queer politics and social theory*. Minneapolis: University of Minnesota Press, pp. vii–xliv.

Watson-Gegeo, K.A. (1988). 'Ethnography in ESL: defining the essentials', *TESOL Quarterly*, 22(4): 575–592.

Yoshihara, R. (2013). 'Learning and teaching gender and sexuality issues in the EFL classroom: where students and teachers stand', *Language Teacher* [Online]. Available at www.jalt-publications.org/tlt, Sept/Oct 2013: 8–11.

23

An identity transformation?
Social class, language prejudice and the erasure of multilingual capital in higher education[1]

Siân Preece

Introduction

> The fact is, when two or more languages come together, two or more peoples have come together and the result is always about power and identity.
>
> *(Morgan 2002: 12)*

Recent decades have witnessed a steep rise in the numbers of students enrolled in post-compulsory education. Despite disparities between low and high-income countries,[2] tertiary education has grown rapidly across the globe (UIS 2015). Increases in participation have resulted in the massification of the system, including higher education. In England (the location of the case study for this chapter), the number of university students rose from 44,500 in the mid-1960s to over 3 million in 2012, with the number of institutions offering higher education programmes increasing substantially in the same period (Whitty *et al.* 2015).

Increased participation in higher education has been driven in part by government policies on widening participation (WP). WP is focused on changing ratios so that universities recruit a higher proportion of students from societal groups who are under-represented in the sector. WP has led to a more diverse student population, with many more women, ethnic minorities and mature students than previously. However, there has been less progress in the sector when it comes to social class, which is assessed using the NS-SEC (National Statistics Socio-Economic Classification) categorisation of occupation[3] (Office for National Statistics 2010; see Block 2014: 57–58). The ongoing under-representation of working-class students in higher education was highlighted in a recent review, which found that working-class students only accounted for 33.3 per cent of young full-time undergraduate students in English universities (Whitty *et al.* 2015). So, it seems that class continues to 'count' (Wright 2013 [2001]) when it comes to higher education. Following David Block's (2014, this volume) call for applied linguists to pay closer attention to class, classed identities are the focus of this chapter.

Drawing on Christopher Brumfit's (1995: 27) definition of applied linguistics as 'real-world problems in which language is a central issue', this chapter examines what happens to the identities of working-class linguistic minority students when their linguistic practices come into contact with those of the 'academic tribes' (Becher and Trowler 2001) that they seek to join. Illustrated with data from my study of the identities of multilingual undergraduate students on an academic writing programme in a university in London (Preece 2009a), I argue that learning the language and literacy practices of the academic community involves 'power and identity' (Morgan 2002: 12). In the case discussed in this chapter, institutional discourses framed linguistic diversity as a 'problem' to be fixed rather than 'resource' to be used. Informed by 'language-as-problem' (Ruiz 1984), the institution erased the multilingual capital in their midst and positioned those on the academic writing programme as in need of English language remediation. This 'ascribed' identity (Blommaert 2006) troubled the participants' identities, as a person worthy of a place in higher education, by stigmatising their linguistic repertoires and categorising them as in danger of failure. This negative identity ascription was resisted by the adoption of other more powerful identities, not all of which were conducive to the scholarly enterprise (see Preece 2009a, b). These issues will be examined in the following sections following an overview of identity and social class informing the study.

Overview

Identity

The view of identity put forward here is informed by poststructuralist literature (see Baxter, this volume). I view identity as fluid and emergent and coming about as individuals negotiate 'subject positions' in discourses. I subscribe to Chris Weedon's (1997: 32) view of discursive subject positions as 'ways of being an individual', together with a Foucauldian view of discourse (Foucault 1974). Three points about identity are helpful for framing the discussion in this chapter. The first is the idea of identity as 'contextually situated' (Bucholtz and Hall 2005: 605); the context is viewed as a site of power that creates the conditions for particular identities to emerge. Identities are seen as encompassing temporary roles and stances arising from the ongoing interaction (or 'interactional positions') within the context along with locally situated cultural and broad social identity categories. The social relations in the setting are perceived to create affordances for individuals to exercise some degree of agency over their identities.

The second point to highlight is the idea of identity as 'ideologically informed' (Bucholtz and Hall 2005: 605). Bucholtz and Hall explain that over time interactional positions accrue ideological associations that are linked to local and social order identity categories. As they argue, 'once formed [these ideological associations] may shape who does what and how in interaction, though never in a deterministic fashion' (Bucholtz and Hall 2010: 21). From this we can surmise that an examination of the ongoing interaction about language in a particular context, such as an academic writing programme, will enable us to ascertain something about the values, norms and assumptions attached to particular language and literacy practices. This supposition is illustrated in Bonnie Urciuoli's (1996) study of working-class Puerto Ricans in New York. Urciuoli demonstrates how talk about language can be mapped onto classed, raced and gendered norms of what it is to be the 'ideologically unmarked American citizen, the white, Anglo, middle-class, English-speaking male to whom people routinely compare themselves and their kin' (ibid.: 138). Urciuoli argues that what her participants had to say about language pointed to their social stratification in American society as 'marked' (i.e. non-normative) by their social class (as working class), by race (as Puerto Ricans) and by language (as bilingual Spanish-English speakers).

Finally, it is important to highlight the view of identity as multidimensional and intersectional. Dimensions of identity consist of a range of identity inscriptions that are viewed as intersecting and shaping each other. Indeed, as David Block and Victor Corona argue (this volume), one of the challenges for language and identity researchers is to bring intersectionality to light in the analysis of their data. Urciuoli's (1996) study is a case in point. In the next section, an account of class as a dimension of identity will be given.

Social class

In *Social class in applied linguistics*, Block (2014: 2) makes the case for the salience of class for 'those who wish to make sense of the social realities of twenty-first-century societies, and especially for those who wish to do so within the general realm of applied linguistics'. Block makes a compelling argument for considering a Marxist perspective on class 'whereby economic phenomena are seen as the bases of much of what goes on in our lives and our interactions with politics, cultural worlds and institutions like the legal system' (ibid.: 56). Following Block's argument, we cannot afford to ignore the economic foundations of the social order, nor the way in which asymmetrical relations of class are enshrined in institutional settings.

Block points out how Bourdieu's concepts of 'field', 'capital' and 'habitus' have been key to conceptualising class as a lived experience as well as an economic phenomenon. Put simply, the 'field' is a social location in which asymmetrical relationships of class, gender and race are established. 'Capital' relates not only to material wealth, but also 'cultural capital' (e.g. tastes, cultural commodities and institutional qualifications), 'social capital' (networks and group memberships) and 'symbolic capital' (economic, cultural and social capital legitimated by the establishment) (Skeggs 2004; Block 2014). 'Habitus' refers to more permanent embodied cultural experience, or dispositions, such as ways of talking, tastes and so on that become integrated into an individual's psyche over time. Block argues that dispositions are 'backward looking', in that they are learned in social interactions in particular 'fields' and come to structure the habitus. Dispositions are also 'forward looking', in that they shape expectations of the future and influence an individual's actions.

In sum, class is a lived experience that has its roots in the economic base of society and an individual's position within the social order. Block (personal communication, 27 June 2015) puts forward a number of elements that applied linguists can use to index social class, categorising these into: sociocultural resources (e.g. occupation, education); behaviour (e.g. consumption patterns, styles of dressing, walking, etc., pastimes); life conditions (e.g. type of neighbourhood); and spatial conditions (e.g. mobility, type of dwelling and proximity to others in daily activities). As we will see, these are helpful for considering class as a lived experience.

Having given an account of identity and social class, in the next section we come to the study.

Methodology

The participants in the study were 93 first-year undergraduate students (45 women and 48 men) who had been referred to an academic writing programme, set up to improve the prospects of WP students, on the basis of their results in an academic literacy screening administered to first-year undergraduates. Most came from working-class linguistic minority communities resident in London, with a high proportion of South Asian ancestry. The majority were aged 18–20; they had been born in the UK, or arrived at a young age, and had received all, or a substantial part, of their schooling in London. They had grown up in a linguistically diverse environment in which English was used along with one or more of the 350 languages in use among London's school children (Eversley *et al.* 2010).

The study was ethnographically oriented (Blommaert and Jie 2010; also see Creese and Blackledge, this volume, for an account of ethnography) and lasted two years. In year one I was both teacher and researcher. While teaching, I collected field notes of classroom proceedings, audio recordings of classroom interaction, a questionnaire and information from official records. In year two, when I was no longer teaching the participants, I undertook two rounds of audio-recorded interviews to explore issues arising from the classroom data. All the data were collected in English and the audio recordings were transcribed. I examined the data to see what stories the participants told each other and me about language in their everyday lives and in the academic community (see Preece 2006) and what could be inferred from these narratives about the participants' identities. As Pavlenko and Blackledge (2004: 18) tell us, 'identity narratives' impose coherence on 'fragmented, decentered and shifting identities' arising in contexts of migration. For the participants there was not only the 'decentring' of self associated with the family story of migration, but also with being the first generation of their family to enter higher education.

The data

Family backgrounds

Official records indicated that the participants came from humble origins and resided in deprived areas of London. Their parents were unemployed or in unskilled or low-skilled jobs, which resulted in an official categorisation of lower socio-economic status (HESA no date). All had attended state schools, mostly in inner-city London areas, with several experiencing interrupted education as a result of events around their family's application for asylum in the UK. After secondary school, the participants had attended vocational courses of study in further education or taken up paid employment. Very few had stayed at school post-16 to study for A-levels,[4] the traditional route into higher education for students domiciled in the UK. The few that did were awarded low grades. Consequently, the participants mostly had non-traditional qualifications for university entry.

Linguistic repertoires

The participants' linguistic repertoires were typical of the working-class migrant communities in which they resided. Their repertoires encompassed languages and dialects from the Indian subcontinent (e.g. Tamil, Punjabi, Gujarati), Africa (e.g. Swahili), the Caribbean (e.g. Jamaican Creole) and the Middle East (e.g. Arabic), as well as English. Extract 1 typifies self-reports of language practices at home.

Extract 1

[English] all the time. Punjabi I only speak with grandparents.

(Baldeep, questionnaire)

Urdu is spoken with my parents only. I use English in almost every situation, in my studies, at work and at home.

(Kanwal, questionnaire)

As Extract 1 illustrates, the participants reported using English along with heritage languages, the languages associated with their ancestral communities (Blackledge and Creese 2008), while at home. English was portrayed as the dominant language, with heritage languages used in interactions with parents and elders. Extract 2 shows how the participants reported 'mixing' the languages in their repertoires.

Extract 2

I sometimes find it difficult to explain what I'm trying to say in Punjabi so I therefore mix it with English only because I'm not so fluent.

(Baldeep, questionnaire)

The thing is I don't speak very well Punjabi. I tend to mix it with Urdu ... I don't know which is which so I just talk ... My sisters and brothers, we [speak] mixed, innit?

(Tahir, Interview 1)

Creese and Blackledge (2011: 1197) have termed the mixing of languages 'flexible bilingualism', which refers to 'the simultaneous use of different kinds of forms or signs' in the linguistic repertoire of bi/multilingual individuals. Creese and Blackledge point out that flexible bilingualism draws on 'translanguaging' (García and Li Wei 2014) and 'heteroglossia' (Bakhtin 1986) and is rooted in notions of 'language-as-communicative-action' in which interaction reflects and shapes its context of use (Creese and Blackledge 2011: 1198). Despite literature in applied linguistics and sociolinguistics indicating that flexible bilingualism is the norm in bi/multilingual settings, the participants were more inclined to frame this practice as a language deficiency rather than a communicative resource.

The manner in which the participants portrayed their bi/multilingualism was suggestive of an orientation to the dominant discourse of 'separate bilingualism' (ibid.), in which languages are viewed as discrete and bounded cultural entities attached to particular domains of use. Bilingual identity in this discourse has been characterised as 'two monolinguals in one body' (Gravelle 1996: 11), in that bilinguals are required to display high levels of proficiency in two languages and use 'one language only' and 'one language at a time' (Li Wei and Wu 2009). Given that most of the participants had received little sustained education in their heritage language(s), they were not in a position to conform to these norms.

The participants' linguistic repertoires also encompassed two varieties of English: standard British English taught at school and the vernacular variety of English in use in the Thames Estuary. This has been variously termed 'London English' (Harris 2006), 'Multicultural London English' (Cheshire et al. 2011) and 'post-estuary English vernacular' (Block 2014), a variety that has emerged, for the most part, from working-class areas of south London and the East End of London. It incorporates linguistic features from Cockney (the dialect of English associated with traditional white working-class East Enders) and linguistic items from the migrant communities resident in south London and the East End, particularly those from the Caribbean and South Asia (Cheshire et al. 2011). Table 23.1 gives examples of some of the linguistic features of London English found in the classroom data.

Studies of schools in urban settings of the UK demonstrate that school students are well aware of the differential status of standard and vernacular English, with many denoting this relationship as a 'posh–slang' binary (see Rampton 2006). As we will see in the following extracts, the 'posh–slang' binary continued to be of salience in higher education. In the first of these (Extract 3), Tahir (aged 22, British Pakistani) is discussing his experiences of participating in the language and literacy practices of his discipline.

Table 23.1 Linguistic features of London English

T-glottalling
Khaled: so you get like/better [be?er] … English   Dilip: yeah/overall you'll be better [be?er]
TH fronting with /f/ used to replace /θ/ and /v/ to replace /ð/
'I … *think* [fink] of myself as shy and quiet/if there's group work obviously you have to work toge*th*er [to-gever]' (Dilip)
Past participle to replace some irregular past simple tenses
Vritti: I was like THIS CLOSE/to … sitting my Punjabi exams/I can read and write the language   Tahir: I didn't sit none of 'em/I *done* French/ain't *done* Punjabi
Ain't to replace negative present simple use of the verb 'be/have'
'you *ain't* stopped talking yet/have you?' (Richard)
Double negatives in an utterance
'everyone says that's why I've been reading/'cos everyone's English will improve/and I'm just thinking/"okay" and it just *doesn't do nothing*' (Seema)
Innit to replace standard tag questions
'[Let's] see if we can do … the er question, *innit*?' (Lalit)

Extract 3

1   That [subject] is probably the one that we did the most reading on and … it
2   was really good quality English … they ain't using slang, they use proper
3   English so we had to write in [proper] English … so we used to spend most
4   of our time trying to revise the way they've written it and what they've
5   written … but it was hard, that was proper hard.

(Tahir, Interview 2)

In Extract 3 Tahir depicts the English required for his studies as 'really good quality' and as 'proper' (line 2). The reference to quality and correctness indexes standardised English along with its prestigious status, while the reference to 'slang' (line 2) hints at the stigmatisation of the vernacular. Tahir's use of pronouns is suggestive of asymmetric power relations. The 'we/they' binary positions Tahir and his peers in opposition to expert users of standardised English (in this case the authors of scholarly texts) (lines 2–3). The use of 'so we had to' (line 3) shows Tahir's understanding of the power dynamics in higher education, in which students are expected to emulate high-status language and literacy practices. Tahir's final comment (line 5) depicts the difficulty of reproducing these norms. By drawing on his repertoire, Tahir graphically communicates his struggles, telling me that scholars '*ain't* using slang' (line 2) and that he found it '*proper hard*' (line 5). Extracts 2 and 3 suggest how flexible bilingualism was Tahir's customary practice and indicate the effort involved for Tahir in separating the codes in his repertoire (see Snell 2013).

There were some instances where the participants portrayed themselves as more willing to conform to the norms for language/dialect separation. As we will see, this served to draw attention to social status. In Extract 4, Leela (aged 19, British Asian), Biba (aged 22, British Moroccan) and Awino (aged 32, Kenyan) are discussing how code-switching between standard and vernacular English ('posh' and 'slang') has helped them to form friendships in higher education.

Extract 4

L = Leela, A = Awino, B = Biba

```
 1  L:   when we came 'ere [to university] I mean/if I saw a posh person I
 2       actually spoke posh with them/but if I saw somebody who was happy
 3       with their slang/I spoke slang with them and I think that's how you
 4       socialise with them
 5  A:   yeah
 6  B:   it's how you adapt to different people [that's what adapting is about
 7  A:                                          [yeah/you've got to adapt/yeah
 8  L:   yeah
 9  B:   adapting to different people an' their cultures y'know/an' their
10       backgrounds.
```

(Classroom interaction)

Extract 4 shows how the participants portray themselves as switching between standard and vernacular English dependent on the social status of their peers. The conformity to 'separate bidialectalism' (Preece 2011) points to the asymmetrical social relations of higher education; the participants see their job as adapting to their interlocutors (lines 6–10), by switching to standard English with those that they perceive to be of higher social status. The interaction on this matter points to social class, with standard English denoting 'poshness' (i.e. doing being middle class) and the vernacular marking its users as 'not posh' (i.e. doing being working class). The utterance 'when I saw a posh person' (line 1) is indicative of how social class is inscribed on the body (Skeggs 2004) and manifested in bodily behaviours (see Block, above) such as walking, gesture, dressing, grooming and so on.

Literacy practices

What the participants had to say about their preferences when it came to reading and writing was also indicative of how literacy practices are tied up with class. Figure 23.1 illustrates self-reports of reading of choice at home.

Tabloid newspapers, particularly *The Sun*, were the participants' favoured choice of reading along with a variety of popular magazines. The participants also reported reading broadsheet newspapers, such as *The Times*. However, this finding probably resulted from the departmental requirement for undergraduates on the participants' degree programmes to read a broadsheet newspaper on a daily basis. It is questionable whether the participants genuinely read broadsheet newspapers out of choice. Very few reported reading novels, with those that did citing popular writers, such as Jeffrey Archer and John Grisham, as their preferred authors. No one reported

Figure 23.1 Reading of choice at home

reading literary fiction. Some reported reading religious texts, particularly the Bible and the Koran, while a few reported reading in heritage language(s). Some also stated that they read 'nothing' when left to their own devices.

The participants' taste for tabloid newspapers was examined further in the interviews. Extract 5 comes from an interview with Geet (aged 19, British Asian).

Extract 5

```
1    I think the reason [I read The Sun] is because I have seen people around
2    me, they all read the same paper. So I think that is the reason, I have been
3    influenced as well. So I think he is reading that same paper, so I will read
4    the same paper as well. So I think that is the reason I read The Sun.
```
(Geet, Interview 1)

This extract illustrates how Geet was socialised into the literacy practices of the working-class community in which he grew up. Geet starts by populating his social world with tabloid readers, particularly *Sun* readers (lines 1–2), and genders this world by referring to the 'people around [him]' as 'he' (line 3). Finally, he explains how his taste in tabloid newspapers arose from his desire to conform to the literacy practices of the men whom he identifies as his social equals (lines 3–4). Reading tabloid newspapers, such as *The Sun*, is a common practice in the social world of the participants and indexes how this world is classed. Mark Pursehouse's (2007) study of *Sun* readers, for example, found that tabloid newspapers remain a cultural signifier of working-class culture. His observation that archetypal readers of *The Sun* are constructed as 'male, young and "working class"' (ibid.: 298) resonates with Geet's narrative on his disposition for *The Sun* and is indicative of how class and gender interact in the construction of identity.

While expressing a preference for tabloid newspapers, very few of the participants displayed any taste for the bookish practices that symbolise prestige in the academic domain. An example of the lack of appetite for such practices comes in Extract 6, in which Seema (aged 19, British Asian), Maya (aged 19, British Asian) and Deena (aged 20, Mauritian) are discussing their experiences of reading a set undergraduate sociology textbook.

Extract 6

S = Seema, D = Deena, M = Maya

```
1    S    I had to do a sociology module/and the FUCKing/reading/text/
2         was SO HARD/even the whole class said/"we don't understand
3         what the hell the book's going on about/we don't understand at
4         all"/so everyone pulled out A-level books and was doing it/but it
5         was sociology/and he gave us like (1) the chapters were like/THIS
6         BIG/honestly like forty pages/and he made us do two chapters/and
7         everyone got the books/and couldn't understand a word it was
8         saying/
9    D    Yes
10   S    just thought "fuck it"/just leave/just leave it (1.5) but other than
11        that/it's cool
12   M    yeah/it's all right/it's not bad.
```
(Classroom interaction)

Seema starts by trashing the set text through the use of taboo language with raised volume (line 1) and then characterises the text as very difficult, achieved through the raised volume of 'so hard' (line 2); she claims her view is representative of her classmates (lines 2–4). She goes on to cast the lecturer in a coercive role (lines 5–6), although the lecturer's demands to read two chapters of an undergraduate textbook do not seem particularly excessive. The reading is portrayed as alienating on the grounds of length (lines 5–6) and difficulty (lines 6–8). Seema's final statement (line 10) embodies her alienation and suggests that she would prefer to give up than struggle. The pause at this point followed by the statement that everything else is 'cool' (lines 10–11) may be a way of mitigating her distaste for academic literacy practices.

Extracts 5 and 6 point to the gulf in the reading tastes of the participants and the academic community. While a taste for tabloid newspapers and popular magazines is commonplace at home and among peers, once in the institutional space they are faced with a book culture. This disjuncture in dispositions points to habitus and is indicative of the classed gap that these participants had to traverse in higher education.

In the following section, we will consider what the data tell us about the ascribed and inhabited classed identities of the participants within the context of higher education.

Discussion

Social class as an ascribed identity

As mentioned, the participants were ascribed a classed identity on the basis of the NS-SEC categorisation of occupation. The NS-SEC classification conferred lower socioeconomic status, commonly referred to as working class. While ascribing class on the basis of occupation is a blunt instrument, Block (2014) points out that it has the 'advantage of clarity'. In particular, it enables the examination of inequalities between social groups in society.

The WP literature indicates that class continues to play a key role when it comes to inequality in higher education. In a recent overview, Geoff Whitty et al. (2015) cite both quantitative inequalities (related to the under-representation of working-class students in HE) and qualitative inequalities (referring to 'fair access' to different types of institution and degree programme). As they point out, qualitative inequalities are stark, with (upper) middle-class students dominating elite institutions and working-class students clustered in less prestigious universities.

Despite overcoming barriers to accessing higher education, the participants encountered qualitative inequalities arising from their classed status. The participants' families lacked what Block refers to as sociocultural capital (see above) that assists in making informed choices about different types of higher education institutions and programmes of study; they also lacked the economic capital to fund the development of the type of cultural capital valued by elite universities. An example can be seen in the choices made at the end of compulsory schooling. The decision not to do A-levels constrained the participants' choice of higher education institutions to those that recognised vocational or access qualifications. These were primarily 'new' universities (former polytechnics granted university status in 1992) rather than elite higher education institutions, such as those in the Russell Group[5] and other 'old' (i.e. established prior to 1992) universities.

Additionally, the participants were enrolled on vocationally oriented programmes in subjects such as business studies and management. These programmes are marketed to prospective students on the basis of future employability and, for WP students, are considered to be a safer bet in terms of facilitating upward mobility for the family in British society than less utilitarian subjects, such as English literature, or vocationally oriented subjects deemed to be highbrow, such as law and medicine. Such decisions on educational trajectories appear highly unlikely in (upper) middle-class and professional families, in which going to university is viewed as a natural part of a child's biography and in which the family pays attention to the accumulation of cultural and social capital that will facilitate access to prestigious universities and high-status subjects.

The decision to study close to home is also indicative of how spatial conditions – here involving mobility, type of dwelling and physical proximity to others (see Block, above) – index social class. While the cultural traditions of some ethnic minorities encourage enrolment in universities in close proximity to the family home (Farr 2001), it seems likely that the socioeconomic status of the family was a constraint on mobility. Staying at home enabled the participants to limit the financial burden of higher education for the family and to contribute to the family household by taking on paid employment and by acting as carers for siblings and family elders. As the family household was often cramped, several of the participants had no private space for study at home and had to compete for study resources with their school-aged siblings. Living at home also restricted the time that the participants spent participating in social and academic interactions on campus. More time spent on these may have been helpful for their transition into higher education and for their understanding of academic language and literacy practices.

Finally, the physical environment of the university, which bore similarities with Vaidehi Ramanathan's (2005) study of post-compulsory education in India, was also suggestive of the participants' classed ascription. In Ramanathan's study, working-class students were clustered in a vernacular-medium institution in a congested downtown location in a multistorey building with no outdoor space apart from a car park and a few student facilities. This was in marked contrast to the 'upper-middle-class' students, who attended an English-medium institution that was set in grounds in a leafy suburb with abundant facilities.

Physical differences were also evident between the institutional environment in which the participants were situated and that of one of the nearby Russell Group universities. While the predominantly (upper) middle-class students in the nearby Russell Group university had access to neoclassical buildings, tended grounds, state-of-the-art facilities and a wide range of student amenities, the participants in my study were located in a utilitarian block situated on one of the most polluted roads in London. The only outdoor space on campus was a concrete quad with a few benches. Student facilities consisted of a basic canteen, a student bar and a library. The participants were routinely taught in large numbers in packed rooms, some with insufficient seating and desks. At the time of the study, there was major building work on site with scaffolding erected around the classrooms, on which building workers regularly appeared, and continual noise from building activity. To sum up, juxtaposing institutions in this way enables us to see how 'class-related aspects stand out sharply' (ibid.: 64) when it comes to accessing higher education. In the following section, we turn to the 'subjectively experienced cultural side' (Block 2014: 58) of class to consider how class as a lived experience played out in the participants' inhabited identities.

Social class as an inhabited identity

The participants brought the linguistic repertoires and literacy practices acquired in the working-class neighbourhoods in which they had been raised and still resided into higher education. Entering higher education meant crossing a classed boundary between the working-class neighbourhoods of the East End of London, characterised by superdiversity and heteroglossia, in which flexible bilingualism is the norm, and the (upper) middle-class institutional space of higher education. In an English-dominant setting, such as England, higher education is a mono-lingualised site in that the multilingual capital embodied in the staff–student population is rarely acknowledged. For the participants a transformation in identity was equated with 'poshness'. Learning to talk and act 'posh' involved struggling to separate the codes in their linguistic repertoires into their constituent parts, in which English dialects and heritage languages were kept separate and translanguaging was avoided. As Urciuoli (1996) reminds us, as soon as a member of the working class seeks a path to class mobility, the 'correctness' model of language surfaces, which, as she comments, requires:

> the ability to negotiate the language required by status-oriented integration with meta-communicative success. People typify this communicative competence metalinguistically as 'good English' … What … count[s] are the functions referable to dictionaries and grammars: the referential (being clear and exact) and the metalinguistic (knowing the rules and explaining them when tested).

A transformation in the participants' inhabited classed identities involved not only conforming to the norms of 'separate bilingualism', but also struggling with the bookish literacy practices of the academic community, for which they were ill-prepared. Drawing on Tony Bennett *et al.*'s (2009) study of cultural capital and classed dispositions in the UK, the participants' taste for tabloid newspapers and popular magazines points to a working-class habitus. Bennett *et al.* found that reading books was mainly restricted to 'urban, educated and cosmopolitan populations' (ibid.: 110), whereas newspapers and magazines had a much more widespread appeal. They argue that literacy tastes are indicative of classed dispositions, with bookish reading tastes indexing a highbrow professional and middle-class habitus, while taste for tabloid and broadsheet newspapers allow for a broader cross-section of society to do 'identity-work of various kinds' related to social class and political affiliation (ibid.: 111).

When participating in the elite language and literacy practices of the academic community, the participants often appeared ambivalent. This was manifested in behaviour such as denigrating academic literacy practices (Extract 6; also see Preece 2009a), making jokes about bookish practices (Preece 2009a, b, 2010) and displaying lack of interest in academic work (Preece 2009a, 2014). In many ways, this resonated with the 'laddish' identities described by Willis (1977), in his seminal study of working-class school pupils, as well as with a range of studies since Willis that have documented the negotiation of identities in educational settings with adolescents and young people. For the participants in the study, displaying ambivalence to the bookish practices of the academic community indexes the maintenance of a classed identity in which, as Block (2014: 61) points out,

> a lack of academic capital reflects a different kind of class habitus, one which confers onto individuals lower status and prestige in society as a whole while also conferring greater status and prestige in the working class cultures into which they are socialised.

However, it also seems likely that the participants' ambivalence was, in part, a way of managing social identities among peers in the face of an ascribed institutional identity as in need of English language 'remediation'. As Alan Wall (2006) comments, no learners, let alone university students, want to be thought of as 'remedial'. The ascription of a 'remedial' identity cast the academic writing programme as a site for 'fixing' the participants' language 'deficits' and a 'public admission of failure' (ibid.: xii). This was a difficult positioning for the participants to negotiate. While conforming involved accepting the stigma of the remedial label and the potential loss of face among peers, resistance involved occupying roles and stances which, as discussed elsewhere, were generally not conducive to the scholarly enterprise (Preece 2009a, b). Here class comes into the picture, for, as discussed in the previous section, the participants had accrued less of the sort of cultural capital that would have created affordances for them to 'redeem the scholarly enterprise whilst maintaining the social need to orient to other forms of identity' (Benwell and Stokoe 2002: 450).

To summarise, there were particular challenges for the participants in inhabiting the 'posh' and 'bookish' identities on offer in higher education. The task was not made any easier by the 'language prejudice' that they encountered in the institution, which labelled linguistic diversity and the practices of linguistic diversity, such as 'flexible bilingualism' (Creese and Blackledge 2011), as a problem to be fixed rather than an asset to be welcomed. This resulted in the ascription of a 'remedial' English language learner identity and the erasure of the participants' multilingual capital in the institution. The next section will outline some of the issues the study raises for applied linguistics.

Issues for applied linguistics

Bringing class into sharper focus illustrates its importance when it comes to considering the identities of 'migrants as bilinguals' (Block 2014: 126). Social class enables us to see the inequalities among members of linguistic minority communities in accessing higher education. It illustrates how the upwardly mobile middle-class narrative in WP is not easily achievable and requires considerable efforts to accomplish. Focusing on class as economically, as well as culturally, inscribed also enables us to make intra-group differentiations in the bi/multilingual cohort in higher education. This is important for bringing asymmetrical social relations to light among the bi/multilingual student population, for developing an understanding of whose bilingualism is valued and whose is not, and for critiquing language prejudice and reification (see e.g. Ramanathan 2005; Vandrick 2011).

For working-class students from migrant communities to achieve the identity transformation on offer in higher education requires shifts not only in institutional culture, but also in institutional resources. This brings me to Nancy Fraser's (2000) call for identity to be viewed in terms of material economic issues in addition to 'cultural recognition'. Fraser argues that an overemphasis on cultural recognition not only risks imposing an essentialised group identity on individuals, but also fails to address the unequal allocation of resources between individuals in the social and economic sphere. To strengthen the link between the cultural world and the economic and social order in which identity is constituted, Fraser (ibid.: 113) argues for a 'status model' of identity. This involves examining institutional practices to discover which 'actors [are constituted] as inferior, excluded, wholly other, or simply invisible – in other words, as less than full partners in social interaction' (ibid.) and taking appropriate action to redress status subordination. Fraser argues that the status model allows for two 'analytically distinct dimensions' of social justice: 'recognition' and 'distribution'. While recognition involves examining the impact of institutional practices on the status of different groups in the institution in relation to each other, distribution involves allocating resources to redress inequalities in status between groups and that facilitate full participation. In sum, the status model includes addressing both the cultural misrecognition of an individual's identity and the maldistribution of material resources that constrain an individual's participation on an equal footing with their peers in institutional practices. These claims appear pertinent for the kinds of identity studies undertaken by applied linguists and, as such, the 'status model' proposed by Fraser could prove fruitful for future language and identity studies.

Summary

This chapter presented the case of working-class undergraduate students from linguistic minority communities on an academic writing programme at a university in London. Following Block's (2014) call for applied linguists to attend more closely to social class, the data were examined to see how the participants were ascribed and inhabited classed identities. The ascription of classed identities enabled the examination of inequalities that the participants encountered from their social stratification in society, such as being clustered in a less prestigious higher education institution than many of their (upper) middle-class counterparts. The salience of social class as an inhabited identity was indexed by the construction of a 'posh–slang' binary to narrate experiences of higher education. Class was further indexed through the participants' reading tastes and their ambivalence towards the type of bookish practices favoured by the academic community. While the institution devoted some resources to addressing social inequality, their efforts were misdirected by institutional language prejudice, in which it was assumed that the practices associated with linguistic diversity, particularly flexible bilingualism, were incorrect and in need of remediation. This rendered the multilingual capital of the participants as worthless and meant that no efforts were made to discern how this capital could be put to use as a bridge into disciplinary language and literacy practices. This constrained both the participants' efforts to participate in academic life and in their identity transformation as fully fledged undergraduate university students worthy of their place in higher education.

Related topics

Positioning language and identity: poststructuralist perspectives; Class in language and identity research; A linguistic ethnography of identity: adopting a heteroglossic frame; Intersectionality in language and identity research; Identity in language learning and teaching: research agendas for the future.

Further reading

Block, D. (2014). *Social class in applied linguistics*. London: Routledge. (Essential reading for applied linguists interested in language and identity.)

Kanno, Y. and Vandrick, S. (guest eds) (2014). 'Special issue. Social class in language learning and teaching', *Journal of Language, Identity, and Education*, 13(2). (The articles in this special issue examine social class as an identity inscription in various educational settings. There is also a helpful account of social class privilege and its impact on language learning.)

Preece, S. (2009). *Posh talk: language and identity in higher education*. Basingstoke: Palgrave Macmillan. (This book presents a fuller discussion of the study.)

Preece, S. and Martin, P. (guest eds) (2010). 'Special issue. Imagining higher education as a multilingual space', *Language and Education*, 24(1). (The articles in this special issue report on studies that examine bi/multilingual identities of migrant students in college and university education in English-dominant settings.)

The multilingual university: the impact of linguistic diversity on higher education in English-dominant and English-medium instructional contexts, ESRC seminar series 2014–2016, https://multilingualuniversity. wordpress.com. (An ESRC-funded seminar series examining the phenomenon of multilingualism in higher education in Anglophone settings and in EMI programmes in the non-Anglophone world.)

Notes

1 This is a revised version of a paper given on 6 March 2015 as part of the ESRC-funded seminar series 'The multilingual university: the impact of linguistic diversity on higher education in English-dominant and English-medium instructional contexts'. Further details of this seminar series can be found at https://multilingualuniversity.wordpress.com
2 The World Bank classifies countries into low-, lower-middle-, upper-middle- and high-income economies. Low-income countries (Gross National Income $1,045 per capita) include Bangladesh, Kenya and Zimbabwe. High-income economies ($12,746 or more per capita) include most of the EU, OECD members and countries such as Russia, Saudi Arabia and South Korea (World Bank 2015).
3 For students aged under 21, socio-economic status is based on the occupation of the parent (or carer) with the highest income. For students aged 21 and over, socio-economic status is based on the student's occupation (HESA no date).
4 A-levels (advanced levels) are normally taken in the two years following compulsory schooling. Elite universities normally require 3 A-levels at A grade, or A and B grades.
5 The Russell Group comprises 24 elite UK universities; no 'new' universities are members of the Russell Group. See http://en.wikipedia.org/wiki/Russell_Group and www.russellgroup.ac.uk

References

Bakhtin, M.M. (1986). The problem of speech genres, in C. Emerson and M. Holquist (eds) *Speech genres and other late essays*. Austin: University of Austin Press, pp. 60–101.

Baxter, J. (this volume). Positioning language and identity: poststructuralist perspectives, in S. Preece (ed.) *The Routledge handbook of language and identity*. Abingdon: Routledge, pp. 34–49.

Becher, T. and Trowler, P. (2001 [1989]). *Academic tribes and territories*. 2nd edn. Buckingham: Society for Research into Higher Education and Open University Press.

Bennett, T., Savage, M., Silva, E., Warde, A., Gayo-Cal, M. and Wright, D. (2009). *Culture, class, distinction*. London: Routledge.

Benwell, B. and Stokoe, E. (2002). 'Constructing discussion tasks in university tutorials: shifting dynamics and identities', *Discourse Studies*, 4(4): 429–453.

Blackledge, A. and Creese, A. (2008). 'Contesting "language" as "heritage": negotiation of identities in late modernity', *Applied Linguistics*, 29(4): 533–554.

Block, D. (2014). *Social class in applied linguistics*. London: Routledge.

Block, D. (this volume). Class in language and identity research, in S. Preece (ed.) *The Routledge handbook of language and identity*. Abingdon: Routledge, pp. 241–254.

Block, D. and Corona, V. (this volume). Intersectionality in language and identity research, in S. Preece (ed.) *The Routledge handbook of language and identity*. Abingdon: Routledge, pp. 507–522.

Blommaert, J. (2006). Language policy and national identity, in T. Ricento (ed.) *Language policy: theory and method*. Oxford: Blackwell, pp. 238–254.

Blommaert, J. and Jie, D. (2010). *Ethnographic fieldwork: a beginner's guide*. Bristol: Multilingual Matters.

Brumfit, C.J. (1995). Teacher professionalism and research, in G. Cook and B. Seidlhofer (eds) *Principles and practice in applied linguistics: studies in honour of H.G. Widdowson*. Oxford: Oxford University Press, pp. 27–41.

Bucholtz, M. and Hall, K. (2005). 'Identity and interaction: a sociocultural linguistic approach', *Discourse Studies*, 7: 585–614.

Bucholtz, M. and Hall, K. (2010). Locating language in identity, in C. Llamas and D. Watt (eds) *Language and identities*. Edinburgh: Edinburgh University Press, pp. 18–28.

Cheshire, J., Kerswill, P., Fox, S. and Torgersen, E. (2011). 'Contact, the feature pool and the speech community: the emergence of Multicultural London English', *Journal of Sociolinguistics*, 15: 151–196.

Creese, A. and Blackledge, A. (2011). 'Separate and flexible bilingualism in complementary schools: multiple language practices in interrelationship', *Journal of Pragmatics*, 43: 1196–1208.

Creese, A. and Blackledge, A. (this volume). A linguistic ethnography of identity: adopting a heteroglossic frame, in S. Preece (ed.) *The Routledge handbook of language and identity*. Abingdon: Routledge, pp. 272–288.

Eversley, J., Mehmedbegovic, D., Sanderson, A., Tinsley, T., von Ahn, M. and Wiggins, R. (2010). *Language capital: mapping the languages of London's school children*. London: CILT.

Farr, M. (2001). 'Home or away? A study of distance travelled to higher education 1994–1999', *Widening Participation and Lifelong Learning*, 3: 17–25.

Foucault, M. (1974). *The archaeology of knowledge*. London: Tavistock.

Fraser, N. (2000). 'Rethinking recognition', *New Left Review*, 3: 107–120.

García, O. and Li Wei (2014). *Translanguaging: language, bilingualism and education*. Basingstoke: Palgrave Macmillan.

Gravelle, M. (1996). *Supporting bilingual learners in schools*. Stoke-on-Trent: Trentham Books.

Harris, R. (2006). *New ethnicities and language use*. Basingstoke: Palgrave Macmillan.

HESA (no date). *UKPIs: definitions*. Available at www.hesa.ac.uk/index.php?option=com_content&view=article&id=2379#top

Li Wei and Wu, C.-J. (2009). 'Polite Chinese children revisited: creativity and the use of codeswitching in the Chinese complementary school classroom', *International Journal of Bilingual Education and Bilingualism*, 12: 193–211.

Morgan, M. (2002). *Language, discourse and power in African American culture*. Cambridge: Cambridge University Press.

Office for National Statistics (2010). *SOC2010 volume 3: the National Statistics Socio-Economic Classification (NS-SEC rebased on SOC2010)*. Available at www.ons.gov.uk/ons/guide-method/classifications/current-standard-classifications/soc2010/soc2010-volume-3-ns-sec--rebased-on-soc2010--user-manual/index.html?format=print

Pavlenko, A. and Blackledge, A. (2004). Introduction: new theoretical approaches to the study of negotiation of identities in multilingual contexts, in A. Pavlenko and A. Blackledge (eds) *Negotiation of identities in multilingual contexts*. Clevedon: Multilingual Matters, pp. 1–33.

Preece, S. (2006). British Asian undergraduates in London, in D. Block, *Multilingual identities in a global city: London stories*. Basingstoke: Palgrave Macmillan, pp. 171–199.

Preece, S. (2009a). *Posh talk: language and identity in higher education*. Basingstoke: Palgrave Macmillan.

Preece, S. (2009b). 'A group of lads, innit?': performances of laddish masculinity in British higher education, in P. Pichler and E. Eppler (eds) *Gender and spoken interaction*. Basingstoke: Palgrave Macmillan, pp. 115–138.

Preece, S. (2010). 'Multilingual identities in higher education: negotiating the "mother tongue", "posh" and "slang"', *Language and Education*, 24(1): 21–40.

Preece, S. (2011). 'Universities in the Anglophone centre: sites of multilingualism', *Applied Linguistics Review*, 2: 121–145.

Preece, S. (2014). '"They ain't using slang": working class students from linguistic minority communities in higher education', *Linguistics and Education*, doi.org/10.1016/j.linged.2014.10.003

Pursehouse, M. (2007). Looking at '*The Sun*': into the nineties with a tabloid and its readers, in A. Biressi and H. Nunn (eds) *The tabloid culture reader*. Maidenhead: Open University Press, pp. 287–302.

Ramanathan, V. (2005). *The English–vernacular divide: postcolonial language politics and practice*. Clevedon: Multilingual Matters.

Rampton, B. (2006). *Language in late modernity: interaction in an urban school*. Cambridge: Cambridge University Press.

Ruiz, R. (1984). 'Orientations in language planning', *Journal of the National Association for Bilingual Education*, 8(2): 12–34.

Skeggs, B. (2004). *Class, self, culture*. London: Routledge.

Snell, J. (2013). 'Dialect, interaction and class positioning at school: from deficit to difference to repertoire', *Language and Education*, 27(2): 110–128.

UNESCO Institute for Statistics (UIS) (2015). *Education: enrolment by type of institution*. Available at http://data.uis.unesco.org/index.aspx?queryid=130&lang=en

Urciuoli, B. (1996). *Exposing prejudice: Puerto Rican experiences of language, race, and class*. Boulder: Westview Press.

Vandrick, S. (2011). 'Students of the new global elite', *TESOL Quarterly*, 45(1): 160–169.

Wall, A. (2006). Introduction, in S. Davies, D. Swinburne and G. Williams (eds) *Writing matters*. The Royal Literary Fund Report on Student Writing in Higher Education, London, pp. xi–xv.

Weedon, C. (1997). *Feminist practice and poststructuralist theory*. 2nd edn. Oxford: Blackwell.

Whitty, G., Hayton, A. and Tang, S. (2015). 'Who you know, what you know and knowing the ropes: a review of evidence about access to higher education institutions in England', *Review of Education*, DOI: 10.1002/rev3.3038, pp. 1–41.

Willis, P. (1977). *Learning to labour: how working class kids get working class jobs*. London: Saxon House.

World Bank (2015). *Data: country and lending groups*. Available at http://data.worldbank.org/about/country-and-lending-groups#Low_income

Wright, E.O. (2013 [2001]). Foundations of class analysis: a Marxist perspective, in S. Ferguson (ed.) *Race, gender, sexuality and social class: dimensions of inequality*. Los Angeles: SAGE, pp. 104–114.

24

Being a language teacher in the content classroom

Teacher identity and content and language integrated learning (CLIL)

Tom Morton

Introduction

This chapter aims to show how applied linguistic work on identity can contribute to our understanding of a real world issue in language education. In this case, how content teachers charged with teaching their subjects through the medium of English in bilingual education programmes deal with the complexities of integrating content and language in their instructional practices and the identity issues this entails. This is an important issue in social, educational and economic terms, as more and more education systems in the non-Anglophone world are diverting resources to integrating English as a basic skill and medium of instruction, and not just another subject in the curriculum, as predicted by Graddol (2006).

The chapter also aims to contribute to strengthening ties between two related fields: applied linguistics and language education. According to Nicholas and Starks (2014: 4), much of the applied linguistics literature that focuses on issues relevant to language education does not engage with 'the ways of knowing and doing and the talking about knowing and doing of Language Education'. In focusing on how 'ways of knowing and doing and the talking about knowing and doing' are inextricably linked to issues of identity, the chapter draws on applied linguistics work on identity that sees it as a discursive process (e.g. Benwell and Stokoe 2006, this volume; De Fina *et al.* 2006; McAvoy, this volume). As Li Wei (2014a: 6) points out, applied linguists have to be a 'Jack of all trades', drawing on different models and frameworks from linguistics and adjacent fields to address real world problems in which language is a central issue. Thus, the case described in this chapter draws on conversation analysis (CA) as an approach to talk-in-interaction, combining it with two more psychological approaches: discursive psychology and positioning theory.

The chapter is structured as follows. First, there is a brief overview of the background to the language education issue under examination: content and language integrated learning (CLIL) and the challenges CLIL raises for teachers. CLIL refers to bilingual education that aims to integrate the learning of foreign/additional languages with that of academic subjects. This is followed in the same section by a brief introduction to the theoretical framework used: mainly a version of positioning theory linked to discursive psychology. The context of the study, its main participants and the methods used are then described. This leads to a section in which data from one participant, Carlos, are presented, with these data showing how identity issues were played out in how he talked about his 'knowing and doing'. The chapter ends by highlighting the key argument: close attention to how teacher identities are played out in how they talk about their knowing and doing can make a strong contribution to crossing the bridges between the concerns of applied linguists and language educators in the field of bilingual education.

Overview

CLIL and teacher identity

In many parts of the world, there is a growing interest in forms of language education in which participation in subject-matter learning through the medium of an L2 is seen as a means of promoting plurilingual competence. The variety of forms such educational initiatives can take is kaleidoscopic, with terms such as immersion, English-medium instruction, sheltered instruction, content-based language instruction and content and language integrated learning (CLIL) all being used. In a state-of-the-art article on this subject, Cenoz *et al.* (2014) attempted to impose some order by recommending that CLIL be used as a blanket term to incorporate this diversity. In this article, Cenoz *et al.* identify as 'the most important' direction for future research that of finding 'efficient ways to effectively integrate language and content instruction', and they argue that more classroom research is needed in this aspect of CLIL if we are to '*enhance teacher effectiveness*' (ibid.: 258, emphasis added). Thus, the teacher is put at the centre of the CLIL enterprise, but this is not without its challenges, as 'there are many aspects of the integration of language and content instruction that require careful theoretical, empirical, and pedagogical attention' (ibid.: 258–259).

The challenges of CLIL are very apparent in recent studies of teachers in contexts in which they are charged with the task of integrating content and additional language instruction, such as immersion education in the US (Cammarata and Tedick 2012), English-medium instruction in Malaysia (Tan 2011) and vocational CLIL in Austria (Hüttner *et al.* 2013). Cammarata and Tedick (2012) depict the process of these teachers coming to see themselves as content and language teachers as a struggle to establish new identities. Tan (2011) shows how science, mathematics and English language teachers may be entrenched within their disciplinary identities, holding dichotomous beliefs about their respective roles, which may be limiting for their students' learning opportunities. Hüttner *et al.* (2013) found that the Austrian content teachers in their study positioned themselves as having an expert identity in the content they were teaching but oriented to an identity as co-learners with the students in terms of their knowledge of English. What these studies point to is that, while CLIL advocates integration of content and language, based on sound theoretical and pedagogical principles, the field as a whole may not only be underestimating the demands on teachers in bringing this about, but also the extent to which being a content and language teacher is a struggle to establish a new identity. The studies cited here have begun to explore how CLIL teachers construct their identities, with studies like that of Cammarata and Tedick using qualitative data to tap into teachers' lived experiences. However, fewer studies focus on the actual discursive actions by which such teachers do their 'talking about knowing and doing' within CLIL, and CLIL-oriented contexts. This is the gap that the case study described in this chapter attempts to fill: teacher identities, not as fixed and immutable properties, but as emergent in discursive processes.

Theoretical perspectives

The theoretical perspectives on language and identity that inform the case described in this chapter draw on discursive approaches to identity. Benwell and Stokoe (2006: 17–18) point out that discursive approaches to identity can both explicate its 'fixedness', in that it can show consistency in people's accounts of who they and others are, while also showing identity's contingency in unfolding interaction, in the ongoing ways in which people position themselves and others in discourse. Benwell and Stokoe identify three main, and related, strands in discursive approaches to identity: ethnomethodological conversation analysis (CA) (see Benwell and Stokoe, this volume); membership categorisation analysis; and discursive psychology (see McAvoy, this volume).

The case study described in this chapter draws mainly on the third strand, discursive psychology, which grew out of social psychologists' concern with the ways in which discourse was used in social psychological studies to explore such constructs as attitude and memory (Edwards and Potter 1992; Edwards 1997). Their main critique was that discourse was being used as a resource to gain access to 'cognitive' constructs such as attitude or memory, rather than examining the nature of the discourse through which participants in psychological studies (or in everyday life) themselves oriented to psychological matters in their interactions. Thus, in discursive psychological work, identity is not seen as some fixed construct that people have and which can be accessed through their talk, but as something people do as they orient to who they, and others, are in their discursive actions (Antaki and Widdicombe 1998).

The other theoretical perspective informing the case in this chapter is a version of positioning theory, which is very close to discursive psychology both in its theoretical and methodological assumptions. Positioning theory originates in the work of Harré and his colleagues (e.g. Harré and van Langenhove 1999) and is a field of research that sets out to explore how the speakers in a conversation take up, resist or offer 'subject positions' (see McAvoy, this volume). These positions may draw on wider social grand narratives and they may appear in the local domain where interaction occurs as concepts and principles relating to beliefs and practices involving rights and duties. Korobov (2010: 272), in a discursive psychological take on positioning, brings identity explicitly to the fore. For him, a discursive psychological approach sees positioning as 'the identity-relevant force of certain discursive actions'. Thus, positioning theory as informed by discursive psychology allows us to examine how identity work is performed through discursive actions, rather than positions being seen as reflecting some kind of normative moral order or 'rules' that lie behind the interaction. In the case in point here, constructing an identity as a teacher responsible for both content and language instruction is seen as something which emerges in situ as the participant positions himself and relevant others as he reacts to video-recorded examples of his own classroom practices.

Methodology

The context from which the case examined in this chapter is drawn is the Bilingual Education Project (BEP), a large-scale national project jointly run by the Spanish Ministry of Education and the British Council, involving, by 2009, 74 primary schools and 40 secondary schools (Dobson *et al.* 2010). One of the stated goals of the BEP was '[t]o promote the acquisition and learning of both languages (Spanish and English) through an integrated content-based curriculum' (ibid.: 12). In participating schools, around 40 per cent of the curriculum was taught in English, with the main subjects being history, geography and biology. Other subjects, such as technology, could also be taught through English. The participating schools taught an integrated curriculum combining elements from both the Spanish and UK national curricula.

The aim of the study, on which the data in this chapter is drawn, was to investigate the relationship between teacher cognitions (knowledge and beliefs), identities and classroom practices in relation to the integration of content and language (Morton 2012). Specifically, the study focused on how teachers of science, technology, history and geography approached the integration of content and language in their planning, teaching and post-teaching reflection. Four teacher participants were chosen for the study who fulfilled certain key criteria: they were primarily trained as content teachers; they were fluent and competent users of English; and they were relatively experienced in teaching their subjects in English (at least two years each).

The data were collected over a period of six months in the Bilingual Department of a secondary school near Madrid that had begun its participation in the BEP in 2004. Data collection methods included a pre-interview teaching unit preparation task designed to represent teachers' pedagogical content knowledge (Loughran *et al.* 2004), semi-structured interviews, video-recordings of lessons and stimulated recall sessions in which the teachers talked about their practices in attempting to integrate content and language. Other data included documents such as lesson plans, materials used and samples of students' work. I had gained access to this setting through participation in a Comenius teacher education project and had led professional development workshops that three of the four teachers had attended. Thus, I needed to carefully manage my own double identity as teacher educator and researcher and this, in fact, contributed to my choice of discursive psychology as a theoretical framework. In other words, rather than seeing discourse data as a resource to access other stuff, such as knowledge and beliefs, it is seen as a topic in which all aspects of identity can be played out, including the positioning of the researcher in relation to the participants.

The interview, stimulated recall and classroom interaction data were transcribed using the conventions of conversation analysis (see appendix), and the methodological procedure of building collections of interactional sequences in which phenomena of interest appear was followed (see Sidnell 2010 for a full methodological account). Thus, for the current study, the data were examined to find sequences of interaction in which issues relevant to content and language integration were topicalised and in which the teachers were positioning themselves, or others, in relation to this issue, thus making relevant certain identity positions. More specifically, for each such episode the following analytic procedure was followed:

1   Identify which discursive actions such as complaining, criticising, praising, etc. are being brought off in the interactional sequence;
2   Show how speakers use rhetorical devices to carry out these actions, e.g. by accentuating or mitigating them, or by accompanying them with other actions, such as displays of knowledge;
3   Show how doing this positions the speakers, and others, in terms of available relevant identities in the context (in this case relating to integration of content and language in a bilingual education project);
4   Show how certain rules, norms and identities which are relevant to the context are worked up or played down in and through the social interaction as an effect of how speakers rhetorically manage their own positioning with regard to these items.

The resulting collection consisted of sequences drawn from all three interactional settings. However, it was found that the video-stimulated recall sessions were a particularly rich context for such identity and positioning work, and it is two data extracts from one of these sessions that are analysed in the next section.

The interaction in the video-stimulated comments sessions had the following overall pattern: after viewing the short (around a minute) video clip, the interviewer produced an invitation for the teacher to comment, usually in the form of the question 'What was going on here?' This normally produced a 'discourse unit' (DU) response (ten Have 2004). In DU interviews or sections of interviews, the interviewer allows the interviewee to be positioned as an expert on their own experiences, as the questions mark out an 'answering space' indicating broadly what kind of response is expected (ibid.: 64). It is in these spaces, in which teachers produced accounts of their practices, including their aims and intentions, and their views of what was happening, that issues relating to CLIL teacher identities emerged.

While issues related to teacher identities emerged in one way or another for all four participating teachers in the study, in this chapter I present data relating to the technology teacher, Carlos (a pseudonym). This case is chosen as the specific type of teaching represents a challenge that is likely to be present for CLIL teachers more generally, especially in more technical and scientific subjects, where teaching takes place not just in classrooms, but in labs or workshops. Such variety of interactional situations can put pressure on teachers' linguistic competence and raise rich issues for individual reflection. In the stimulated recall session, Carlos comments on clips from two 7th grade (12 to 13 years old) technology lessons, one in the classroom and one in the workshop. The students' task was to work in small groups to design and make a wooden toy with simple, moveable parts. In the first (the classroom) lesson, Carlos introduced the task, calling this the 'theory' part, and he focused a lot of the lesson on how the students were to read instructions and write summaries of the information they had gathered.

In the second lesson (in the workshop), the students began working in small groups to design and make the toy, and Carlos, after setting up the activity, went round helping and orienting groups with their work. The first data extract corresponds to a clip from the first lesson, in which Carlos draws the class's attention to a language item, 'a wide range of facts', in the material they are reading. In the second data extract, Carlos is commenting on a segment of the workshop lesson in which he is orienting a group while they work at their table on designing the toy. The two extracts illustrate ways in which Carlos positioned himself, and others, with regards to two separate issues relating to language instruction in the context of content teaching: explicit focus on language items and the use of the target language in the classroom (both by himself and by his students). The extracts are also chosen because they exemplify how particular social actions (self-criticism and self-justification) can be implicated in such positioning and identity work.

The data

Integrating a language focus in instruction

In the classroom incident Carlos is commenting on (not shown for reasons of space), he mainly relies on translation into Spanish to get across the meaning of 'wide range of facts'. The extract begins with the usual interviewer's question after the viewing of the video clip:

Extract 1: 'Wide range of facts'

208	Tom	okay I'd just like you to comment on ↓this
209		(.) wide range of facts.
210	Carlos	yeah

211	Tom		episode
212	Carlos		yeah the way I try-
213		->	when I am looking at me this way
214		->	I don't like it so much
215			for instance I tell the parents
216			when they come to talk to me
217			my children they don't use
218			or my daughter my son
219			they he she doesn't use the the dictionary
220			I want them to translate
221			and they don't know what they are studying
222			I- I tell them that they don't need to
223			look it up every word in the dictionary so (.)
224			but I translate it into Spanish
225		->	and I don't find it so interesting
226		->	as I'm looking at me myself
227			maybe they should guess I'm telling them
228			guess what the words are
229			from from the rest of the text
230			and maybe that's more interesting
231		->	and hhh I don't know I don't like it so much
232		->	the way I'm translating it
233			or maybe I'm just spending my time
234			trying to trying them
235			to know what I am talking about
236	Tom		is it is this kind of important
237			this piece of vocabulary
238			wide range of facts or
239	Carlos		no actually that's another thing which is-
240			I told them that's simply to read
241		->	that's even not so important
242		->	to spend so much time (on words and so on)
243	Tom		hm
244	Carlos		anyway I want to I want them
245			to focus on English though so

Many of the descriptions and evaluations produced by Carlos in this extract can be seen as formulated so as to bring off the discursive action of 'self-criticism'. This is done explicitly at lines 213, 214, 225, 226, 231 and 232, and perhaps more implicitly at lines 241 and 242. This self-criticism is a positioning activity that makes relevant certain identities pertinent to the activity of bilingual teaching that Carlos can take up or resist. After his first negative evaluation of his own performance at lines 213 and 214, he produces, from lines 215 to 223, a narrative of habitual practice in another context (meetings with parents) to show that what he has done in the classroom contradicts what he tells parents about good practice. Thus, his actions in the classroom can be seen as contradicting a stated belief (at least in interaction with parents) that it is not good practice to rely on translation, for example by looking up words in a bilingual dictionary. But, as he states in line 224, relying on translation is precisely what he has done in the classroom episode. By adopting this position, he orients to a rule or norm, one that is quite familiar in monolingually oriented communicative language teaching, that translation is not an effective practice for getting meaning across, especially if it involves looking up a lot of words in dictionaries. By aligning himself with this denial of the benefits of translation, at least in his reported statements to parents, and implicitly in the position he is taking up in the here and now of the stimulated comment session, he brings off an identity as a methodologically informed language teacher, at least at these moments where language becomes the focus of attention.

After the second explicit negative self-evaluation at lines 225–226, Carlos also positions himself as knowledgeable with regard to the practices of communicative language teaching by suggesting that it might have been a better idea for them to guess the meaning of the expression from the surrounding text (lines 227–230). It is not, then, that Carlos is positioning himself in terms of an identity as an academic subject teacher who has no knowledge or interest in language teaching pedagogy. Indeed, by highlighting his own negative performance with respect to an aspect of language instruction, he highlights a position as a reflective, thinking practitioner, who is well aware of pedagogical alternatives when it comes to dealing with language items, and is capable of critical self-appraisal of his failure to use a more appropriate one on this particular occasion.

However, lines 233–235 point to a deeper underlying tension in the struggle to balance language and content instruction. After another explicit self-criticism in lines 231 and 232, he begins line 233 with 'or', signalling that a different interpretation of the whole scenario that he has just commented on is forthcoming. Rather than seeing what has transpired in the classroom as a piece of intentional language teaching, he reframes its possible intention as simply an attempt to make sure his students could follow what he was talking about. Here, the identity position oriented to is not that of a language teacher, but that of a content teacher who happens to be teaching in another language, and who needs to ensure, as any teacher does, that the students can follow the lesson. However, in lines 239–242, he undermines this interpretation by pointing out that, in fact, the vocabulary focused on was not actually that important and not a particularly good use of time. In lines 244–245 he shifts back to a position more aligned with a language teacher identity by justifying his actions in drawing attention to this vocabulary by the need to get the students to 'focus on English'. Interestingly, if focusing on English is an orientation, but the actual English focused on is not that important (it is just 'English'), this raises questions about how this teacher orients to the task of balancing both types of instruction. It would seem that another available position, that of a content teacher who selects language to focus on motivated by the nature of the content topic, is not picked out. Attention to language, in this orientation, may be a somewhat random and incidental addition to the content teaching, an occasional attempt to get them to 'focus on English'.

Using the target language in the classroom

In the second extract from the same video-stimulated comment session (divided into two parts for ease of analysis), Carlos positions himself and his students with regard to competence and willingness to use the target language, English, in the classroom. In the first part of the extract, he again produces a self-criticism, this time of his own competence in using English in the type of situation seen in the video clip, that is, when he is going round the tables helping and encouraging the students with their work.

Extract 2a: 'I find myself not so prepared to teach in English'

343 Tom   talk about this situation a little bit
344 Carlos   no that's quite often (.)

345		over (1.0) in at the beginning of
346		when they are starting building
347		whatever making whatever they have to make
348		in the workshop .hh
349		they don't know how to get started with the thing
350	Tom	mm
351	Carlos	they don't know where to start from
352		or they don't know
353		so <I (1.8) should help every work
354		every team work> fo- more particularly.
355	->	(1.5) a::m (1.0) I may tell you (.)
356	->	this is where I find myself not so:: (1.8)
357	->	prepared to teach in English
358		= because ↑those kinds of things
359		when you're in the classroom
360		I manage with the language I have to use
361		very very well.
362		but here I find myself
363		that I don't find a certain word
364		that's >°I don't know°< (.)
365		because it's quite quite particular
366		specific language you have to use
367		((quoting voice)) you have to put this thing
368		into this hole and drill this
369		or whatever and this (.)
370	->	a(h)nd I don't find myself (1.5) comfortable
371	->	in the workshop speaking in English.
372		I would like to and that's .hh
373		where I want to to learn more English
374		and to practise more and more true English
375		but that's a thing
376		and it's very difficult (0.5)

In Carlos's long discourse unit (DU) turn from lines 351 to 376, he again brings off the social action of self-criticism in his explicit negative evaluations of his own competence at lines 355–357 and 370–371, and more implicitly throughout the turn. Interestingly, he situates his evaluations of his own competence in the context of responding to the needs of his students, in that they have problems in getting started on the task of building the toy. At lines 353–354, he pinpoints the nature of the problem. The kind of language he needs to use in this context is much more challenging than the language he uses in the classroom, where he manages 'very very well' (lines 359–361). But here, in the workshop, he has to work with individual groups 'more particularly' and he may have problems in finding words due to the fact that very specific technical vocabulary is used. He illustrates the kind of language needed by shifting into performance (lines 367–369) to enact a typical classroom moment where he may have to explain a process to students. He ends the DU by expressing a desire to learn and practise more English for use in this type of situation. Interestingly, he characterises this as 'true' English (line 374), as if, by implication, the kind of language he uses in the classroom is somehow not genuine English but perhaps a restricted classroom variety.

In bringing off this discursive action of self-criticism of his own performance and in the details of the account he produces in the answering space, Carlos positions himself as an English language learner. In terms of English language competence, Carlos depicts himself as needing to improve his English in order to meet the needs of his students in an interactional situation (working in the workshop with small groups), which occurs frequently because of the nature of his subject. There is no sense of a learner identity when it comes to teaching his subject, as we saw in the previous extract where he may have been concerned that the students knew 'what he was talking about'. There can be little doubt, from his construction of that incident, that he himself knew what he was talking about – the doubts only arose in the context of how and why he was focusing on language. In this extract, in the way in which Carlos constructs his first revelation of his lack of competence at line 355, with two long pauses, a stretching of 'a::m', the phrase 'I may tell you' and the micro-pause, we can see that this may be something of a delicate matter for him. It touches on his positioning of self, as a person who may be less than competent in a crucial aspect of his work, attending to the needs of learners in a key interactional context typical of his subject.

In the second part of this extract, Carlos shifts attention from his own use of English to that of his students, and his own pedagogical preferences and responsibilities in this area.

Extract 2b: 'I am supposed to make them speak to each other in English'

377	Carlos	I am meant I am supposed to make them
378		speak to each other in English
379	Tom	hm mm=
380	Carlos	=no way no way for them
381		because they are so enthusiastic
382		and (.) they are very very happy
383		to to make something in the workshop
384		all together and they want to organise them<u>selves</u>
385		and they are kind of arguing with each other
386		because ((quoting voice)) you want to do this
387		but I want to do this and that doesn't work
388		and so on .hh
389		no way to make it
390		and I I've given up [trying to
391	Tom	[heh heh
392	Carlos	no I mean I should but (.)
393		I prefer them to to enjoy the lesson
394		to enjoy the workshop
395		that being so .hhh tightened or tight
396		or how do you say
397		to to speak in English and <u>forced</u> to (1.0)
398		from time to time I tell them just in English
399		and they speak for (.) <u>five</u> seconds
400		in English to each other
401		and then when I'm away
402		they speak again in Spanish.

At lines 377–378 he positions himself as less than agentive in the requirement to get the students to speak to each other in English – it is constructed as an external constraint ('I am meant', 'I am supposed to'). This indexes the wider contexts of the aims of the BEP and of his methodological training, in which there was a focus on communicative L2 use in the classroom. However, in his DU turn beginning at line 380, he describes reality as being in contrast with this require-ment – there is 'no way' the students will use English spontaneously as they are so 'enthusiastic' and 'happy' to be working in the workshop. The inference here (and it is confirmed later at lines 393–397) is that attempts to 'force' them to speak English would destroy this enjoyment and enthusiasm. At lines 384–388 he accentuates this position by providing a vivid description of what goes on in these workshop contexts, again enlivened with performance features (lines 386–387). This lively description prepares the ground effectively for his positioning himself as unable or unwilling to make them talk in English ('I've given up trying to' – line 390). In con-trast to his comments on his attempts to explain 'wide range of facts' or his lack of competence in using English in small group situations, here there is less self-criticism, as his unwillingness to keep on trying to enforce an English space in the workshop is justified by the vivid account of the students' enjoyment and enthusiasm when carrying out workshop activities.

Carlos positions himself as allowing L1 Spanish in spite of external constraints ('no I mean I should but' – line 392). Thus he orients to a kind of resistance identity, as someone who is willing to forego a key aim of the project he is involved in (the acquisition and learning of both languages) in order to maintain his own pedagogic preference for the students to 'enjoy the lesson'. Indeed, in lines 395–397, his characterisation of what it would be like if they had to speak English ('tightened', 'tight', 'forced to') invokes a kind of language policing that would be detrimental to the classroom atmosphere he wants to maintain. His description of what happens when he does insist on their using English (lines 398–402) only serves to highlight the futility of doing so, as they only speak in English for 'five seconds' and go back to Spanish as soon as he leaves the group.

In this second part of the extract, Carlos, rather than bringing off the social action of self-criticism through his evaluations and formulations, produces a self-justification, using lively descriptions of his students' actions to support this. He positions himself with regard to an identity of a subject teacher more concerned with maintaining a lively and positive classroom atmosphere than enforcing the demands of the Bilingual Education Project he is working within. It seems that he is not willing to sacrifice this classroom atmosphere (which presumably is more conducive to achieving subject-related goals) on the altar of achieving another key goal of the BEP, the learning of English. It would seem that there is not a strong enough identifica-tion with the goals and methods of communicative language instruction (in a CLIL context) to push aside, make room beside or merge with a strong subject teacher identity.

Discussion

Studies such as that by Cammarata and Tedick (2012) which document the protracted identity struggles of teachers as they attempt to integrate content and language, or that of Tan (2011) which show the potentially harmful effects on their learners of teachers holding dichotomous beliefs, have contributed much to understanding about what is necessary for the enhancement of teacher effectiveness in bilingual education. The discursive approach to identity adopted in this study contributes to this understanding by documenting the subtle shifts in positioning which occur when a CLIL teacher talks about what he knows and does. Rather than using the discur-sive data to tap into Carlos's lived experiences, the analyses presented here show how identity issues are played out in ongoing interaction as he positions himself and others in relation to the task of integrating content and language. Carlos's discursive actions are not seen as a window onto something real beyond the discourse itself, such as his beliefs, knowledge or identity. By carrying out such discursive acts as self-criticism or justification, Carlos brings into play a set of identity-relevant items that relate to issues of knowledge and competence. In analysing Carlos's identity-relevant discursive actions, we can throw more light on some of the issues that were the focus of the studies on CLIL/immersion teachers and their beliefs and identity struggles.

The analyses support Hüttner *et al.* (2013) findings that CLIL teachers, as opposed to EFL teachers, saw themselves more as 'co-learners' (Li Wei 2014b) in terms of their English language competence, while maintaining their subject matter expertise. Thus, Carlos's readiness to position himself as less than competent in using English in one teaching situation in no way implied any negative assumptions about his competence in teaching technology. Hüttner *et al.* (2013) also found that the CLIL teachers in their study did not at all orient to having explicit language aims in their instruction, and indeed seemed astonished at the idea. They suggest that if schools insisted on the inclusion and enactment of explicit curricular aims for English, this would have 'detrimental effects on the perception of CLIL as a success, as the relaxed atmosphere and positive affect would not realistically be maintained' (ibid.: 278). Although Carlos was not referring to explicit language goals, his comments on how insisting on English use in the workshop would affect the classroom atmosphere very much echo this.

A strength of the discursive approach taken here is that it warns us to be cautious about ascribing to teachers like Carlos fixed beliefs or identities in relation to issues such as their own, or others', competence. We can see that Carlos subtly positioned himself as being aware of his own 'incompetent' behaviour when it came to focusing on a piece of vocabulary. He did not position himself as a content teacher only concerned with technology, but as someone who was aware of language teaching options he had not taken. Thus, this 'incompetence' can be seen as transitory and more easily remedied than the gaps in his competence in interacting with students in the workshop. Findings such as this have implications for work on teachers' knowledge, as what teachers know, rather than being seen as a fixed entity, can be seen as shifting and changing according to the contingencies of interaction and identity positioning.

Issues for applied linguistics

The perspective on language and identity taken in the case study reported in this chapter is closely allied with the ethnomethodological, conversation analytic and discursive psychological approaches (see Benwell and Stokoe, this volume; McAvoy, this volume). It is an approach which does not attempt to read off larger social issues from discourse data, but examines the ways in which actors position themselves, and others, in their discursive actions. For applied linguists interested in such language education topics as teacher beliefs and identity, this approach can avoid the pitfalls of some qualitative research studies, especially those based on interviews, which obviate the co-constructed nature of the discursive events that produce the data from which claims about beliefs and identity are made (see Mann 2011). It can thus allow applied linguists' claims about 'the ways of knowing and doing and the talking about knowing and doing' (Nicholas and Starks 2014: 4) of language educators such as the CLIL teacher in this study to be grounded in the details of the interactions that unfold between participants.

The case in this chapter can be seen as contributing to what Nicholas and Starks (2014) identify as a need to build bridges between the two fields of applied linguistics and language education. Applied linguists can use studies such as this one to engage in dialogue with language educators and researchers beyond the more well-trodden terrain of EFL and ESL, something that has been lacking in the field of CLIL/bilingual education. As Cenoz *et al.* (2014: 258) point out, much CLIL research has focused on L2 attainment (especially in English) to the detriment of 'students' achievement in non-language academic domains, such as mathematics and science'. The case study described in this chapter shows how applied linguists can engage with educational research that focuses on what non-language content teachers know and do and how they construct their practices in talk. Such work can illuminate the ways in which discursive practices both inside and outside the classroom may impact on students' opportunities for learning both non-language content and language.

Language educators can use insights from the ways in which applied linguists draw on a range of models and frameworks from linguistics and communication to see the importance of teacher identity and its discursive negotiation to meeting their aims of enhancing pedagogic practice (in this case, in CLIL/bilingual education). The theoretical and methodological sophistication of applied linguistics perspectives on language, discourse and identity can provide language education researchers with new tools with which to tackle issues that are of key importance to them, such as enhancing teacher effectiveness and strengthening professional identities for teachers who face the task of integrating language and content in bilingual education.

Related topics

Ethnomethodological and conversation analytic approaches to identity; Discursive psychology and the production of identity in language practices; A linguistic ethnography of identity: adopting a heteroglossic frame; Challenges for language and identity researchers in the collection and transcription of spoken interaction; Disability identities and category work in institutional practices: the case of a 'typical ADHD girl'; Identity in language learning and teaching: research agendas for the future.

Further reading

Cammarata, L. and Tedick, D.J. (2012). 'Balancing content and language in instruction: the experience of immersion teachers', *Modern Language Journal*, 96: 251–269. (A different approach to identity to the one in this chapter, but one of the few studies to look at the challenges for teachers in integrating content and language from an identity perspective.)

Korobov, N. (2010). 'A discursive psychological approach to positioning', *Qualitative Research in Psychology*, 7: 263–277. (A thorough treatment of the underlying assumptions of the approach to discourse and identity exemplified in this chapter.)

Wiggins, S. and Potter, J. (2008). Discursive psychology, in C. Willig and W. Stainton Rogers (eds) *The SAGE handbook of qualitative research in psychology*. London: SAGE, pp. 72–89. (A useful, brief introduction to the theory and methodology of discursive psychology.)

References

Antaki, C. and Widdicombe, G. (eds) (1998). *Identities in talk*. London: SAGE.

Benwell, B. and Stokoe, E. (2006). *Discourse and identity*. Edinburgh: Edinburgh University Press.

Benwell, B. and Stokoe, E. (this volume). Ethnomethodological and conversation analytic approaches to identity, in S. Preece (ed.) *The Routledge handbook of language and identity*. Abingdon: Routledge, pp. 66–82.

Cammarata, L. and Tedick, D.J. (2012). 'Balancing content and language in instruction: the experience of immersion teachers', *Modern Language Journal*, 96: 251–269.

Cenoz, J., Genesee, F. and Gorter, D. (2014). 'Critical analysis of CLIL: taking stock and looking forward', *Applied Linguistics*, 35: 243–262.

De Fina, A., Schiffrin, D. and Bamberg, M. (eds) (2006). *Discourse and identity*. Cambridge: Cambridge University Press.

Dobson, A., Pérez Murillo, M.D. and Johnstone, R.M. (2010). *Bilingual Education Project Spain: evaluation report*. Madrid: Gobierno de España Ministerio de Educación and British Council (Spain).

Edwards, D. (1997). *Discourse and cognition*. London: SAGE.

Edwards, D. and Potter, J. (1992). *Discursive psychology*. London: SAGE.

Graddol, D. (2006). *English next: why global English may mean the end of 'English as a Foreign Language'*. London: British Council.

Harré, R. and van Langenhove, L. (1999). *Positioning theory*. Oxford: Blackwell.

Have, P. ten (2004). *Understanding qualitative research and ethnomethodology*. London: SAGE.

Hüttner, J., Dalton-Puffer, C. and Smit, U. (2013). 'The power of beliefs: lay theories and their influence on the implementation of CLIL programmes', *International Journal of Bilingual Education and Bilingualism*, 16: 267–284.

Korobov, N. (2010). 'A discursive psychological approach to positioning', *Qualitative Research in Psychology*, 7: 263–277.

Li Wei (2014a). Introducing applied linguistics, in Li Wei (ed.) *Applied linguistics*. Oxford: Wiley-Blackwell, pp. 1–25.

Li Wei (2014b). Who's teaching whom? Co-learning in multilingual classrooms, in S. May (ed.) *The multilingual turn: implications for SLA, TESOL and bilingual education*. Abingdon: Routledge, pp. 167–190.

Loughran, J., Mulhall, P. and Berry, A. (2004). 'In search of pedagogical content knowledge in science: developing ways of articulating and documenting professional practice', *Journal of Research in Science Teaching*, 41(4): 370–391.

Mann, S. (2011). 'A critical review of qualitative interviews in applied linguistics', *Applied Linguistics*, 32(1): 6–24.

McAvoy, J. (this volume). Discursive psychology and the production of identity in language practices, in S. Preece (ed.) *The Routledge handbook of language and identity*. Abingdon: Routledge, pp. 98–112.

Morton, T. (2012). 'Classroom talk, conceptual change and teacher reflection in bilingual science teaching', *Teaching and Teacher Education*, 28(1): 101–110.

Nicholas, H. and Starks, D. (2014). *Language education and applied linguistics: bridging the two fields*. Abingdon: Routledge.

Sidnell, J. (2010). *Conversation analysis: an introduction*. Chichester: John Wiley and Sons.

Tan, M. (2011). 'Mathematics and science teachers' beliefs and practices regarding the teaching of language in content learning', *Language Teaching Research*, 15: 325–342.

Appendix

Transcription conventions

.	A full-stop indicates a falling, final tone.
?	A question mark indicates rising intonation, not necessarily a question.
,	A comma indicates continuing intonation.
↑↓	Up or down arrows indicate sharply rising or falling intonation, with the arrow placed just before the syllable in which the change in intonation occurs.
:	Colons indicate the stretching or prolongation of the sound preceding them.
[	Square brackets indicate overlapping talk onset.
=	Equal signs indicate latching of immediately previous utterance.
(0.5)	Numbers in brackets indicate silence, represented in tenths of a second.

(.)	A dot in brackets indicates a 'micro-pause' of less than 0.2 of a second.
word	Underlining indicates stress or emphasis.
> <	'More than' and 'less than' signs indicate that the talk between them was speeded up.
< >	'Less than' and 'more than' signs indicate talk is produced noticeably more slowly than surrounding talk.
.hhh	Aspiration is represented by the letter h. A row of hs with a dot indicates an inbreath. Without the dot it indicates an outbreath.
m(h)e	An h or row of hs in brackets within a word indicates aspiration, which may be breathing or laughter.
(( ))	Double parentheses contain the transcriber's descriptions of events.
(word)	Words in parentheses indicate that the transcription is uncertain, but is a likely possibility.
( )	Empty parentheses indicate that something was said but it was not possible to hear it clearly enough for transcription.

(Based on Sidnell 2010: ix–x)

Disability identities and category work in institutional practices

The case of a 'typical ADHD girl'

Eva Hjörne and Ann-Carita Evaldsson

Introduction

In this chapter, we draw on an ethnomethodological framework to examine how shifting forms of disability identities (see Renshaw *et al.* 2014) are accomplished for Annika,[1] a preadolescent girl diagnosed with Attention Deficit Hyperactivity Disorder (ADHD), during her first year in a special educational setting in Sweden. We make this argument by employing membership categorisation analysis (MCA) to investigate how different forms of identity categories are invoked and how the features and category attributes of those identities are negotiated and accumulated over time in everyday interactions (Antaki and Widdicombe 1998; Benwell and Stokoe, this volume). We will analyse everyday interactions to show how Annika becomes identified as a 'typical ADHD girl' by teachers, parents and other pupils.

Schools are significant institutions in the lives of children. The manner in which staff handle school problems will be decisive for the future, not just for the individual child but for the families and the teachers involved. From an applied linguistics perspective, school difficulties can be seen as 'real-world problems in which language is a central issue' (Brumfit 1995: 27), in that the difficulties that children face at school become discursively classified and coded by the institution in order to be able to handle a problematic situation (Roberts 2013). In this process, 'real-world problems', such as children's school problems, are addressed in the more abstract language of institutional discourse that defines the nature of the problem. For example, a pupil in need of support for learning difficulties can be categorised as a 'learning disabled pupil' in order to get educational support (Mehan 1993; Roberts 2013). As Hjörne and Säljö (2004) show, interpreting children's school problems through the use of neuropsychiatric diagnoses, such as ADHD, serves as a resource both for placing children in special classes and for reminding a child of her/his alleged disability within the classroom.

At the moment, learning disabled pupils in most countries are identified predominantly through the deployment of a medical model, where disability is conceived of as the outcome of impairment (Shakespeare 1996). Increasing numbers of school-aged children are categorised as behaviourally and emotionally disordered and diagnosed with ADHD (Hjörne and Säljö 2004; Graham 2010; Velasquez 2012). From a gender perspective, it is worth noting that more boys than girls receive the ADHD diagnosis (Kopp 2010; Velasquez 2012). The gendered differences have been related to the core symptoms that can result in an ADHD diagnosis – namely: inattention, hyperactivity and impulsivity; these symptoms are claimed to be more common among boys than girls (Holmberg 2009; Graham 2010). We want to emphasise that we do not take a stand on the controversial issues of the nature and aetiology of ADHD or whether the diagnosis can be seen as valid and as a reliable indicator of identifiable medical and/or psychological conditions. Our interest lies instead in the in situ use of this diagnosis as a social phenomenon that may be manifestly relevant for 'responding to problems put forward', to use Li Wei's expression (2014: 6). In the case study of Annika presented in this chapter, we treat the ADHD diagnosis as a form of identity category that 'is implicated in real-world decision-making' (Simpson 2013: 2). For example, what is accomplished in various steps of everyday interactions and activities, between teachers and parents and between teachers and pupils in various special educational activities, and how this might be contributing to the identification, recognition and categorisation of particular children as differently abled, are some of the questions this chapter aims to shed light on.

Overview

Ethnomethodological research on disability, framing social identities as accomplished social and situated phenomena, has highlighted the everyday practices through which children and adults become recognised as deviant and disabled. Moreover, studies have demonstrated the need to examine how the identities of the disabled are actively reconstituted in particular institutional and interactional contexts of use (Rapley et al. 1998; Renshaw et al. 2014; Roberts 2013).

An important line of ethnomethodological research on how children become recognised and treated as disabled in the everyday practices of education has been carried out by Mehan and his colleagues (see Mehan et al. 1986; Mehan 1991, 1993). This research demonstrates in great detail how schools locate the problems of the child '[b]eneath the skin and between the ears' (Mehan 1993: 241) in the process of sorting pupils into categories such as 'normal', 'special' or 'educationally handicapped'. A focus on disability from psychological perspectives thus implies that a disabled person will be recognised and treated mainly in the deficient terms associated with the specific disability label (Mehan 1993; Hjörne 2006; Graham 2010; Velasquez 2012; Evaldsson 2014). Identifying children as disabled through the deployment of medical and psychological models, where disability is conceived of mainly as the outcome of individual impairment, is viewed as a necessary condition for addressing and compensating for their shortcomings (see Shakespeare 1996; Hjörne and Säljö 2004; Renshaw et al. 2014). In this sense, categories are part of an 'institutional machinery' (Mehan et al. 1986: 164) through which schools simultaneously (re)produce knowledge and coordinate its daily practices. An example is the creation of special classes for children described as having 'special needs' (Hester 2000) or ADHD (Hjörne 2006; Velasquez 2012). The process of categorising children as disabled thus has material consequences for their social and personal identifications (Bowker and Star 1999; Hjörne and Säljö 2012). For example, diagnoses such as ADHD operate both as tools for excluding children from mainstream classes and as guiding principles for organising teaching and learning practices for children deemed to be in need of specialised educational support (Hjörne 2006; Evaldsson 2014).

Previous ethnomethodological studies have also demonstrated how children who are identified as displaying learning and behavioural difficulties at school are routinely placed in a binary category and contrasted with the 'normal child' (Maynard 1991, 1992; Mehan 1991, 1993; Hester 1998). For example, Hester (1991, 1998) shows in his studies of referral meetings that children who are recognised as disabled are marked out in relation to the non-disabled by reference to a range of activities, attributes and characteristics recognised as deviating from non-disabled norms. 'Such recognitional "work" provided a sense for the participants of their being respondents to an independent or objective set of problems within the school' (Hester 1991: 461). Thus, normalising practices contribute to the construction of disability as facts that, in turn, become the 'grounds for intervention and treatment' (ibid.: 462). Gill and Maynard (1995) also show in their study of professional lay conduct at a clinic for developmental disabilities how categories such as, for example, mental retardation, autism, emotional disabilities, learning disabilities and related conditions are products of the social system rather than inherent deficiencies.

However, as Renshaw et al. (2014: 1) note, a focus on disability as the defining identity category may sometimes hide 'the complexity and subtlety of how diverse disability identities are actually achieved in everyday schooling contexts'. They found, for example, how different versions of the identity of a 'child with a disability' were accomplished through communication books sent between parents and teachers. The analysis revealed how diverse disability identities were deployed variously and strategically by teachers and parents in various special educational contexts, in turn contributing to a view of the disabled child as 'more agentic and self-aware' (ibid.). Hester (1998) also demonstrates in his study of referral meetings how various forms of disability identities were ascribed to pupils, ranging from the identity of a 'pupil with reading difficulties', a 'pupil with behavioural problems' and an 'immature boy', to that of a 'deviant pupil'. Through using categories that indicated different forms of disability, Hester noted how children were ascribed an identity as a 'weak', 'disabled' or 'special' pupil by the institution or, as Thomas and Loxley (2001: 76) express it, 'to be called "special" is to be given a new identity within the schooling system'. In one of our studies, Evaldsson (2014) highlights the complexity of locally accomplished identity practices through considering how boys diagnosed with ADHD exert a considerable degree of agency in using bald imperatives and a sexual language when resisting teacher authority and the categorical conduct of a 'special student' ascribed to them. As Rapley et al. (1998) demonstrate, a person with a learning disability can, like any other, either assert or dismiss his/her institutionally ascribed identity.

Methodology

Drawing on the ethnomethodological outline given above on disability identities as accomplished social and situated phenomena, we argue that an ethnomethodological approach to members' understandings of categorisations (Sacks 1972; Hester and Eglin 1997; Antaki and Widdicombe 1998; Fitzgerald 2012; Benwell and Stokoe, this volume) provides a fruitful way to capture 'the shifting and situated enactments of disabilities' accomplished for children 'in schools and homes' (Renshaw et al. 2014: 48). For this purpose, in this section we will present a case study of Annika, a preadolescent girl aged 10 and diagnosed with ADHD, to illustrate how everyday interactions in which different forms of school problems are ascribed to Annika led to her accumulating a record of disability identities. The data presented here draw mainly on the communication books that were used by Annika's parents and her teachers to inform each other of how she was managing at school. The messages in Annika's communication book over one school year, together with data collected from the observation of classroom activities of a special class organised in a Swedish primary school for children assigned with the diagnosis ADHD, provide the everyday interaction that we analyse in this chapter.

Using ethnomethodological principles of members' understanding of social categories (MCA), we will focus on exchanges in which the participants account for and make relevant forms of category memberships (see Benwell and Stokoe, this volume); in this chapter we are interested in category memberships that contribute to establishing and maintaining disability identities. In Sacks's (1972, 1995) work, the exploration of categories is based on examining the in situ work deployed in the members' organisation of taken-for-granted social categories and their related actions, the so-called category-bound activities characteristic or constitutive of a category. Not only is the conventional connection between categories and activities a sense-making device in that it makes inferences about other people, but the activity itself may be used as a way of implicitly categorising people (Watson 1998). As will be shown, categories such as 'ADHD girl', a 'child with emotional and behavioural disorders' or a 'child with a disability' are seldom used explicitly in the interaction; however, these categories may be inferred in the variety of ways that Annika is described in the course of the interaction. As Antaki and Widdicombe demonstrate, '[m]embership of a category is ascribed (and rejected), avowed (and disavowed), displayed (and ignored) in local places and at certain times, and it does these things as part of the interactional work that constitutes people's lives' (1998: 2). Of interest also is how the activity descriptions and category memberships ascribed to Annika are not only used to describe her actions but also to undercut, realign or discredit the account of these in the interactions between her parents and teachers and between her teachers and fellow students. In our analysis we use the accepted convention of single quotation marks ('problematic pupil') to signify the specific category under investigation.

From an ethnomethodological perspective, members' categories are inference rich, which implies that 'a great deal of knowledge that members of a society have about the society is stored in terms of these categories' (Sacks 1992: 40). The use of categories describes and displays members' understanding of the world and their common sense and routine orientation to category-organised knowledge (Hester and Eglin 1997; Fitzgerald 2012; Stokoe 2012). These understandings may be of broader social phenomena such as disability identities, gender, race or other social identities, but they may also be of how emergent social identities are made operative, relevant and consequential over the course of an interaction (Sacks 1995: 327).

In the presentation and analysis of the data in the following section, we will demonstrate how membership categories and category-bound activities associated with the neuropsychiatric diagnosis ADHD are occasioned and negotiated by the participants in particular instances and are charged with institutionalised agendas, leading to a version of Annika as a 'typical ADHD girl'.

The data

In order to retrospectively track the various steps of everyday interactions and activities in the case study presented in this section, the MCA analysis is here combined with ethnographic knowledge (see Goodwin 2006; Evaldsson 2007). The data draws from an ethnographic study that involved collecting video recordings during the course of one school year in a special educational unit that was integrated into a primary school located in a multi-ethnic, low-income suburban area in Sweden. The study was conducted by Velasquez (2012) as part of her PhD study in the research project *Boys in need of remedial support*.[2] The unit was named 'the ADHD group' after the pupils, who were all diagnosed with ADHD. Six boys and one girl, Annika, attended the special class, which was assigned two teachers. We will focus on the events during the school year that were relevant for ascribing Annika a disability identity and displacing her from mainstream classes. As mentioned in the previous section, the analysis is mainly based on the interactions that took place between Annika's teachers and parents in the communication book that passed between them during the school year. We will demonstrate how Annika's ascribed identity shifts during the course of the year from a 'good pupil' to a 'problematic pupil' and a 'typical ADHD girl'. We also analyse a series of exchanges from classroom interaction at the end of the school year to demonstrate how Annika's fellow students also come to align themselves with Annika's ascribed identity as a 'typical ADHD girl'.

Through the retrospective selection of temporally unfolding events, we want to bring into the foreground how the gradual reconstitution of Annika as a problem child involves assembling observations and accounts of temporally unfolding events in which everyday actions and classroom behaviours become repeatedly evaluated and compared with features associated with ADHD, whether recognised as problematic or not (Wortham 2003, 2004).

Mitigating Annika's school problems

During the first month of school after the summer holidays, the communication book mainly consists of short and more general reports from the teacher of how Annika manages in school. As Hall *et al.* (2006: 90) note in their analysis of category work in social welfare, 'incompleteness and incoherence are intrinsic to case records, because by definition they are selective for the purpose of day-to-day management'. Extract 1 illustrates the type of comments that were typical at the start of the school year. Short comments such as '*a good day*' followed by a star are commonly used in the communication book.

Extract 1 Teacher assessment of Annika during first few weeks of the school year

> En bra vecka för Annika; Det har gått bra idag, hon kämpar på; Vi är sju stycken i gruppen just nu så det är ju inte alltid alldeles tyst; En bra dag!, En bra dag som vanligt, En bra dag för Annika!
>
> ((Annika's lärare))
>
> *A good week for Annika; Today, everything has been just fine, she's keeping it up; There are seven of us in the group right now so it's not always completely quiet; A good day!; A good day as usual; A good day for Annika!*
>
> ((Annika's teacher))

As Extract 1 illustrates in the first entries in the communication book, the teacher uses a series of more general positive assessments to indicate to Annika's parents how well Annika is settling in at school. However, the teacher's repeated and upgraded recyclings of positive assessments also suggest that Annika might have long-term problems that need to be mitigated and accounted for in positive terms. However, during the same period, Extract 2 shows that the teacher also referred to Annika's long-term school difficulties more explicitly in terms of her medication.

Extract 2 Teacher references to Annika's medication

Vi har bara tre tabletter kvar; Annika hade inte tagit sin medicin hemma, det märktes, det var svårt att koncentrera sig, efter lunch bättre koncentration.

((Annika's lärare))

We only have three tablets left; Annika didn't take her medication at home, which was obvious; hard to concentrate, after lunch better concentration.

((Annika's teacher))

Extract 2 indicates the teacher's view that medication would enable Annika to become better disposed to learning and suggests some criticism of the lack of medication at home. The argument displays the teacher's orientation to Annika's school difficulties as unrelated to her classroom situation and the teacher's ability to engage the children in learning, but as strictly biological and so outside teacher expertise (Prosser *et al.* 2002). In this sense, an individuating logic that places school problems within individual children is put forward as a way of addressing Annika's school difficulties (Hester 1998). Simultaneously, the use of the particular category-bound activity '*hard to concentrate*' invokes the category identity of ADHD. As a result, Annika becomes not personally accountable for her school difficulties. Instead, an account of the parents as the ones to be blamed for not following the medical prescriptions is constructed through the use of the predicate '*at home*'. As will be discussed, the teacher's account opens up a series of counter-arguments in which the boys who are Annika's fellow classmates become the ones to be blamed for Annika's school problems.

Extract 3 Parental accounts of the impact of fellow students' conduct

Det är under stor vikt att Kalle låter Annika vara ifred på skoltid (ringde dig om det!). För att hon ska kunna lära sig något så måste hon få lugn och ro, det har jag lämnat intyg på förra året. Med vänliga hälsningar Monika P.

((Annika's mamma))

It's of great importance that Kalle ((a male classmate)) gives Annika peace at school (phoned you about this!). If she's going to learn something she must have peace and quiet, I affirmed this last year. With kind regards Monika P.

((Annika's mother))

Jag har talat med Kalle.

((Lärarens svar))

I have talked to Kalle.

((Teacher's response))

Extract 3 puts forward a counter-explanation for the difficulties that Annika was encountering at school in which Annika's mother relates her daughter's difficulties to the social relations that she is encountering in the classroom. It is the view of Annika's mother that Kalle, one of the boys in Annika's class, is causing Annika trouble. Annika's mother also emphasises the need for a peaceful learning environment for her daughter. Both the social arrangements and the individualised problem are used to understand and remedy Annika's school problems. Tying the particular category-bound activities and the comment '*she must have peace and quiet*' to Annika, affirmed by a doctor, invokes the category identity of 'ADHD' as a reason for intervention.

In these very first entries of the communication book, Annika's teachers and parents establish what they consider relevant with regard to Annika's disability and school situation (Renshaw *et al.* 2014). Although they provide slightly different versions, the accounts given by both the teacher and the parents offer explanations of Annika as not accountable for her school difficulties. The medical diagnosis of ADHD distances the teachers and the parents from any potential blame (see Lloyd and Norris 1999) about Annika's difficulties at school.

Invoking gender as relevant to disability: negotiating a 'problem pupil' identity

During the next few months, the messages from the teacher develop into more detailed accounts invoking both the properties of Annika as a person having emotional and behavioural difficulties and the social arrangements in class. The more detailed descriptions of Annika's everyday school situation, as illustrated in Extract 4 below, allow both the teacher and the parent to reflect on Annika's actions in emotional and behavioural terms and to take a moral stance towards the actions being accounted for.

Extract 4 Teacher orientation to gender

Annika hade huvudvärk på förmiddagen, kände sig lite hängig, annars jobbat bra; Annika blev ledsen i morse, hon la sig på soffan och ville sova innan alla kom. Då kom både Kalle och Noa och skrek i hennes öra att hon skulle vakna. Annars har allting varit bra med skolarbetet.
Annika blev sur och arg idag p.g.a. att hon förlorade i ett mattespel som hon spelade med GUNNEL ((lärarens namn)). Dålig förlorare är hon tyvärr ofta.

((Annika's lärare))

Annika suffered from a headache this morning, felt out of sorts, otherwise has been working well; Annika was sad this morning, she lay down on the sofa and wanted to sleep before everyone arrived. Then both Kalle and Noa came and screamed in her ear that she should wake up. Otherwise everything has been just fine when it comes to schoolwork.
Annika got sore and angry today because she lost a maths-game she was playing with GUNNEL ((name of the other teacher)). Unfortunately, she is often a sore loser.

((Annika's teacher))

Despite describing how Annika is doing well in school when it comes to schoolwork, the teacher provides details about a range of emotional and physical problems deemed noteworthy in the communication book, referring to '*headache*', feeling '*out of sorts*', '*sad*', '*[wanting] to sleep*', feeling '*sore and angry*' and being a '*sore loser*'. Several of the listed emotional problems are linked to the attributes that characterise the disorders described as typical for girls with ADHD (Holmberg 2009; Kopp 2010). The teacher describes the children as acting out their disorders. While the boys, Kalle and Noa, are represented as loud and aggressive, in that they '*came and screamed in [Annika's] ear*', Annika is described as withdrawn and a '*sore loser*'. In this sense, the teacher invokes gender dualism, mapping the girl's versus the boys' classroom conduct into contrastive disability categories on the basis of their sex category (see Evaldsson 2014).

In the response from Annika's mother in Extract 5, the essentialised notions of gender are explicitly referred to Annika's disability identity, which now is made relevant in order to make her difficulties in class understandable.

Extract 5 Mother's defence of her daughter

Det beror ju på hennes funktionsnedsättning att det är svårt att ta vissa saker! Har man ADHD så är man en känslomänniska! M.P.

((Annika's mamma))

It's because of her dysfunction that it's difficult to put up with some things! If you have ADHD you are an emotional person! M.P.

((Annika's mother))

Det vet jag också. Men vi jobbar på att det ska bli bättre.

((Lärarens respons))

I know that too. But we are working on improving this.

((Teacher's response))

Försök få grabbarna att minska retandet på Annika. Hennes form av funktionshinder gör att det är lätt att ta åt sig, typiskt för tjejer. Grabbar är mer aggressiva. Med vänlig hälsning Monika.

((Mammans respons))

Try to make the boys reduce the teasing of Annika. Her kind of disability makes it easier to be hurt, typical for girls. Boys are more aggressive. With kind regards Monika.

((Annika's mother))

The mother's responses can be seen as an open contestation of the teacher's prior depiction of Annika as a '*sore loser*' (see Extract 4), which in turn implies that Annika is partially to be blamed for her conduct in class. In her responses to the teacher in Extract 5, Annika's mother explicitly categorises her daughter as 'dysfunctional'. The implication is that Annika's behaviour is associated with her ADHD diagnosis and so she is to be expected to be 'an emotional person'. The reference made to Annika as displaying introvert emotional behaviours provide an argument for casting Annika as a 'typical girl with ADHD'. This time it is the mother who invokes binary disability categories for girls versus boys on the basis of different gendered forms of emotional instabilities, i.e. 'easily hurt' versus 'more aggressive' (compare with Evaldsson 2014).

One way to understand the different disability identities ascribed to Annika by the teacher and her parents is that this ascription is not 'simply "a product of social interaction"' (Hester 2000: 205); rather, it is part of a negotiation between 'particular categories of people' (ibid.). Belonging to the category of 'mother', Annika's mother speaks up for her daughter as not accountable and capable of handling social relations, defending her behaviour and questioning the interventions made by the school. However, it is interesting to note that it is not the teacher but the mother who makes use of the medical diagnosis to legitimise Annika's school problems (see Mehan *et al.* 1986).

Recognising category attributes associated with ADHD

Medicine, or rather the lack thereof, becomes the topic of the communication book for some weeks at the end of autumn. During this period, the parents do not write in the book at all, while the teacher continues to explain Annika's conduct in school as problematic due to a lack of medication:

Extract 6 Teacher's account of emotional problems

sur på killarna; blev ledsen för att hon kom försent till idrotten och kom inte in först; väldigt irriterad på sina klasskamrater, ibland i onödan; blev arg på Kalle och kastade salt på honom; Varit lite för lättirriterad idag.

((Annika's lärare))

sore at the boys; sad because she arrived too late for physical education and didn't get in as the first one; very annoyed with her peers, sometimes unnecessarily; angry with Kalle and throwing salt at him; A bit difficult concentrating; Been a bit too touchy today.

((Annika's teacher))

As can be noted in Extract 6, the teacher's descriptions of Annika's school performance as '*sore*', '*sad*', '*very annoyed ... sometimes unnecessarily*', '*angry*', '*difficult concentrating*' and '*too touchy*' focus on what may be seen as problematic emotional conduct. The list of negative emotional states ascribed to Annika make available a frame of reference for managing her disruptive conduct and for seeing the emotional disturbances as individual characteristics. The emotional instabilities and disturbances listed above further strengthen the view of Annika as a 'typical ADHD girl' with introvert symptoms. During this period, there are also several messages in which the teacher complains to the parents about the lack of medication. Although the teacher does not specify what the anticipated behaviours are, the problematic behaviours invoked make it likely that Annika's behaviour will be understood mainly in terms of having a specific kind of disability, that of a 'typical ADHD girl'.

Solidifying a typical ADHD identity in everyday classroom interaction

As demonstrated so far, the identity of a 'typical ADHD girl' was gradually accomplished for Annika in the interactions in the communication book that passed between her parents and teachers during almost an entire school year (August–April). By the end of the spring, Annika's ADHD identity was more or less solidified. At this point, her fellow ADHD classmates increasingly oriented to her as disabled in everyday classroom interactions as well. The children's placement in a withdrawal class especially organised for students diagnosed with ADHD played a crucial role both in the reproduction and the resistance of the ADHD identities of the children who were assigned to this group and in the case here to Annika.

We will now analyse a series of classroom activities that took place between the teacher and the pupils, including Annika, at the end of the school year. Extracts 7a and 7b are from a classroom event at the beginning of May, in which some of the boys in class complain to the teacher about Annika's social conduct. As will be demonstrated, the pupils account for Annika's actions by aligning themselves to the teacher's version of events in which Annika's conduct is deemed to be deviant. As Extracts 7a and 7b illustrate, this is achieved through explicit references to Annika's medication.

Extract 7a Teachers and pupils ascribing deviant identity to Annika

1 2	Marcelo:	när hon kom idag sa hon ba "flytta på dig"
		when she came today she just said "move"
3	TEACHER 1:	[Annika?
4	Kalle:	[sa Annika de. de e ba för att ni-
		[did Annika say that. it's only cause-
5	Marcelo:	[NÄ:
		[NO:
6 7	TEACHER 1:	NÄ: för hon har inte tatt sin medicin å då e hon lite kaxigare
		NO: cause she's not been taking her medicine, then she gets more bossy
8 9	Kalle:	FETT ↑SYND (.) alltså ska man slå henne
10		så hon håller käften (.) [den °djävla horan°
		TOO ↑BAD (.) then you have to hit her (.) so she'll shut up [that °fucking whore°
11 12	TEACHER 1:	[du måste ta av dig
13		skorna - ((till Marcelo)) ta av dig skorna
		[you have to take off
13		*your shoes - ((to Marcelo)) take off your shoes*
14 15	Kalle:	↑A:: då ska ja också ta- å va utan min medicin
		↑YEAH:: then I'll also take- be without my medicine
16	Marcelo:	↑JA ska också de, Å BLI MER ↑KAXIGARE
		↑ME: ↑TOO, AND BE MORE ↑BOSSY

As can be noted in Extract 7a, Marcelo and Kalle, two male classmates, justify their offensive behaviour toward Annika by narrating a version of Annika as problematic and deviant; their description aligns with the teacher's stated view of Annika as '*bossy*' (line 7). The fact that the teacher explains Annika's conduct in negative terms can be seen as a sign that the problematic behaviour ascribed to Annika has come to be taken for granted and that her fellow pupils' offensive behaviour toward her may thereby be justified. Thus, as in the communication book, the teacher orients to Annika as a 'disabled pupil with ADHD' who deviates from the classroom norms because of her lack of medicine (line 6), which is expected to mitigate the symptoms (see Renshaw *et al.* 2014). However, the teacher's categorisation of Annika as in need of medication also provides a platform for the two boys to collude in putting forward their own medical recommendations (lines 14–16). The use of bald imperatives such as '*you have to hit her*' and swear words and sexist language like '*so she'll shut up that fucking whore*' (lines 8–10) not only warrants an upgrading of Kalle's recurring offensive conduct towards Annika, but also demonstrates how gender and disability interact in complex ways in constituting Annika as 'a typical ADHD girl'. In Extract 7b (line 2), Kalle again aligns with the teacher's categorisation of Annika as a 'problematic and deviant pupil' who is in need of medicine in order to be less disruptive.

Extract 7b Teachers and pupils accounting for Annika as morally accountable

1	TEACHER 1:	Annika e <u>vä</u>ldigt- *Annika is <u>very</u>-*
2	Kalle:	hon <u>stör</u> (.) ge henne m<u>e</u>dicin *she's di<u>sr</u>uptive (.) give her <u>me</u>dicine*
3 4	TEACHER 2:	↑NÄ (.) de e tur att hon e lite störig (.) som alla andra *↑N<u>O</u> (.) it's a <u>good</u> thing she's a bit d<u>is</u>ruptive (.) as everybody <u>else</u>*
5	TEACHER 1:	hon får del av <u>gra</u>cerna lite *you have to di<u>s</u>tribute one's <u>fa</u>v<u>ou</u>r*
6	TEACHER 2:	↑<u>Ja</u>:: (.) <u>pre</u>cis *↑<u>Yeah</u> (.) <u>ex</u>actly*
7 8	Federico:	↑AH:: då får du inte säga tyst till oss heller *↑<u>YE</u>AH (.) then you may not to t<u>ell</u> us to be q<u>u</u>i<u>e</u>t <u>ei</u>ther*

Annika is present during the interaction in Extract 7b between the teachers and her fellow pupils in which an account of her behaviour as problematic is built up step by step. In line 2 Kalle interrupts one of the teachers to expand on Annika's conduct as disruptive. Kalle also suggests a solution as he directs the teachers to '*give her medicine*' (line 2). In response, teacher 2 defends Annika. Although she echoes Kalle's criticism of Annika as '*disruptive*', instead of criticising her, she evaluates her conduct in positive terms, stating that '*it's a good thing she's a bit disruptive (.) as everybody else*' (lines 3–4). In this interaction, Annika is no longer differentiated from the other pupils in the ADHD class. As a result, the interaction between the teachers and the boys in class present a view of Annika as a morally accountable pupil who can be blamed for her problematic classroom conduct (see Wortham 2003).

A couple of weeks following the classroom interaction in Extracts 7a and 7b, Annika was involved in an argument in class with Amir that escalated to the point that Annika announced her departure and acted on it; she was observed walking away alone into the forest. At this juncture, Amir was observed shouting after Annika, '*DON'T EVER COME BACK!*' Neither of the teachers tried to stop Amir or went after Annika. Extract 8 comes from the following day, when the teacher talks with Annika about what happened in the forest.

Extract 8 Annika accounting for her position as a victim

1 2	TEACHER 2:	↑<u>ALL</u>tså: (.) hur ska vi göra (.) [ja blir ju oroli:g *↑<u>So</u>: (.) what are we going to do [I got worri:<u>ed</u>*
3	Annika:	[men (.)
4		>jag menar- vet du- vet du- ja sa kan du
5		sluta va så elak mot mig-< (.) >å han ba
6		fortsätter- å fortsätter-< jag sa de- ((pratar fort, gråter))
		[but (.) >I m<u>ean</u>- do you know- do you *know- I said can you stop being that nasty* *to me< (.) >and he just continu<u>es</u>- and contin<u>ues</u>-< (.) I* *s<u>ai</u>d so ((talks fast while crying))*

7 8	TEACHER 2:	↑NEJ (.) men du bara försvann (.) Amir har
		gjort [precis som vi har sagt åt honom
		↑NO (.) but you just disappeared (.) Amir has been
		doing [exactly as we told him
9	Annika:	[men –men- men] vet du vad
10		han sa (?) "bra kom aldrig tillbaka"
		[but- but- but] do you know what he said (?)
		'good, don't ever come back'
11 12	TEACHER 2:	De var elakt sagt (.) de kan ja förstå [men
		att du-
		That's mean (.) I understand that [but you-
13	Annika:	[ja vill inte gå här längre
		[I don't want to be here
		any more
14	TEACHER 2:	varför kom du inte å berätta de för mig (.)
15		för att ja känner så här (.) Annika (.) så
16		fort Amir öppnar sin mun (.) så säger du
17		att Amir har gjort så (.) du liksom
18		förstorar upp saker [de blir så stort
		why didn't you come to me and tell me (.)
		cause I feel like this (.) Annika (.) as
		as Amir opens his mouth (.) you say
		Amir has done this (.) you kind of
		exaggerate things [it gets that big
19	Annika:	[men- (.) ja menar- [.] han kommer-
		[but- (.) I mean- [.] I mean he comes-
20	TEACHER 2:	↑NÄ: (.) men du går
		↑NO: (.) but you're leaving

Extract 8 gives another example of the way in which the teacher constructs Annika's conduct as problematic and as causing a disturbance. When the teacher asks Annika how they should proceed following the incident and expresses her worry, Annika begins to cry and defends her actions by describing how Amir is repeatedly '*nasty*' to her (lines 3–6). Although Annika tries to justify her actions in the light of prior victimisation, the teacher does not treat the actions as casting Annika as a victim. Instead, she blames Annika for running away and exaggerating what Amir has done (lines 7–8, 14–18). Annika raises further objections and persistently tries to defend herself by referring to Amir's actions as longstanding and 'always mean', as she continues crying. By doing this, Annika tries to convince the teacher that she is worthy of the category of 'victim', and that she deserves some protection and redress from her classmates' taunts. In a bid to persuade the teacher of her unjust treatment, Annika continues crying and tells the teacher, '*I don't want to be here any more*' (line 13). Matters escalate, as on the following day Annika's mother phones the teacher to inform her that Annika has stated that she wants to commit suicide. This action ultimately resulted in the school finding an alternative class for Annika.

Discussion

The data presented in the preceding section illustrates how shifting forms of disability identities are solidified for Annika during the school year through the interactions between Annika's teachers and parents and between Annika's teachers and peers in the segregated setting for pupils assigned the diagnosis of ADHD. Membership categorisation analysis (MCA) allows for a social view of disability as a shifting category that is deployed variously and strategically by the participants in the study. Through the temporally unfolding events over one school year, the category of disability is accomplished for Annika in order to account for the difficulties that she faces at school that in turn constitute her as a 'typical ADHD girl' in contrast to her male classmates. Both Annika's teachers and parents account for her conduct with emotional terms that are typical for girls diagnosed with ADHD (see Velasquez 2012). For example, there are frequent references in the data to Annika as having a '*headache*', feeling '*out of sorts*', being '*sad*', being '*sore and angry*' or being a '*sore loser*'. While orienting to the membership category of being a 'Teacher', Annika's teachers account for her difficulties as being caused by individual characteristics. The parents, on the other hand, orient to their membership category of being 'Parents' by defending their daughter. They give an account of Annika's difficulties as neuropsychiatric problems, which legitimises the ADHD diagnosis and make her actions understandable in the classroom. This implies that no one is to be blamed for the problems (see Lloyd and Norris 1999).

Moreover, many of the negative category-bound activities and predicates attributed to Annika in the accounts given by the teachers and the parents are symptoms typical of ADHD diagnosis attributed to girls as a group. As has been pointed out elsewhere, the individualistic character of the disability category provides for category-tied institutional activities, which in this case resulted in withdrawal to a special class for children assigned the diagnosis (Hester 2000; Antaki 2007). Furthermore, the character attributes ascribed to Annika make available a frame of reference for legitimising medicalisation and for individualising emotional disturbances.

The data show that, in everyday classroom interaction, the categorisation of the girl as a problem child are occasioned and given shared meanings for the participants at particular instances and are charged with institutionalised agendas, neither of which can be reduced to the other (Wortham 2004). Thus, across a trajectory of selected school events, an inference-rich pattern of accumulated records of disabled behaviours contributes to the development of the girl's disability identity, warranting a particular category membership as an 'ADHD girl', which comes to identify Annika in the end (Sacks 1995).

Issues for applied linguistics

From an applied linguistics perspective, where language is at the core of all activities (Li Wei 2014), teachers, parents, fellow pupils and especially Annika, as the focal participant, are addressing 'real-world problems' that affect their lives in different ways. In this chapter, we have reported on how the attributes of particular disability identities are accomplished in everyday communication practices in the context of a withdrawal class for children categorised as having ADHD. Categorisation is fundamental to institutions and institutional practices (Sarangi and van Leeuwen 2003; Roberts 2013). Through the use of categories, institutions define what the nature of a problem is and what measures are relevant to take. Institutions 'think and act' through categories, as Douglas (1986: 60) puts it. Furthermore, the category, in this case ADHD, operates as a filter through which the school, children, parents, teachers and society more generally interpret and understand different behaviours as problematic (or not); thus marking the identity of children diagnosed with ADHD as non-normative. In this sense, the diagnosis will be 'the relevant thing' (Edwards 1998: 19) about Annika, and this will have consequences for her throughout her education and future life. Insights into how educational, and other, institutions ascribe disability identities, and the intersection of disability with other dimensions such as the gender of individuals' identities, are issues of great relevance for applied linguistics (Simpson 2013) and future language and identity studies.

Summary

In this chapter, we analysed how a specific disability identity was accomplished for a girl in a special class through the interactions of her teachers, parents and classmates, as they accounted for the everyday events of school. We employed an ethnomethodological framework, which, from our perspective, provided an effective way to understand how membership categories and category attributes, here associated with neuropsychological disorders of individuals, are used to explain and address problematic conduct in a special educational school context. The analysis illustrated how, across the trajectory of a school year, the accumulation of inference-rich records of problematic conduct contributes to the development of a preadolescent girl's disability identity as a 'typical ADHD girl'. Over the course of the year, this identity comes to the fore in the school context and is used to stigmatise and marginalise the individual concerned (Sacks 1995).

Related topics

Ethnomethodological and conversation analytic approaches to identity; Discursive psychology and the production of identity in language practices; Language and gender identities; Being a language teacher in the content classroom: teacher identity and content and language integrated learning (CLIL); Intersectionality in language and identity research.

Further reading

Antaki, C. (2007). 'Conversational shaping: staff members' solicitation of talk from people with an intellectual impairment', *Qualitative Health Research*, 17(10): 1403–1414. (In this paper, Antaki investigates aspects of disability identities as constructed in naturally occurring talk-in-interaction.)

Hall, C., Slembrouck, S. and Sarangi, S. (2006). *Language practice in social work: categorisation and accountability in child welfare*. London: Routledge. (The authors demonstrate how social workers categorise and manage problems in a social work context in ways that render understandable, and justify, professional intervention.)

Hester, S. (1998). Describing 'deviance' in school: recognizably educational psychological problems, in C. Antaki and S. Widdicombe (eds) *Identities in talk*. London: SAGE, pp. 133–150. (From an ethnomethodological perspective, Hester examines how children with a disability are marked out as different by placement in special educational programmes and by referring to their failure to live up to the expectations associated with the non-disabled pupil.)

Smith, D. (1978). 'K is mentally ill: the anatomy of a factual account', *Sociology*, 12(1): 23–53. (In this classic paper, Smith makes an ethnomethodological reading of an interview, describing how K comes to be defined as mentally ill by her friends.)

Stokoe, E. (guest ed.) (2012). 'Special issue. Categories and social interaction: current issues in membership categorization', *Discourse Studies*, 14(3). (In this special issue, the authors provide different angles on MCA as a method for investigating culture-in-interaction, reality and society.)

Notes

1 Annika is a pseudonym.
2 The project was financed by the Swedish Research Council.

References

Antaki, C. (2007). 'Mental health practitioners' use of idiomatic expressions in summarising clients' accounts', *Journal of Pragmatics*, 3: 527–541.

Antaki, C. and Widdicombe, S. (1998). Identity as an achievement and as a tool, in C. Antaki and S. Widdicombe (eds) *Identities in talk*. London: SAGE, pp. 1–14.

Benwell, B. and Stokoe, E. (this volume). Ethnomethodological and conversation analytic approaches to identity, in S. Preece (ed.) *The Routledge handbook of language and identity*. Abingdon: Routledge, pp. 66–82.

Bowker, G.C. and Star, S.L. (1999). *Sorting things out: classification and its consequences*. Cambridge, MA: MIT Press.

Brumfit, C.J. (1995). 'Teacher professionalism and research', in G. Cook and B. Seidlhofer (eds) *Principles and practice in applied linguistics: studies in honour of H.G. Widdowson*. Oxford: Oxford University Press, pp. 27–42.

Douglas, M. (1986). *How institutions think*. London: Routledge and Kegan Paul.

Edwards, E. (1998). The relevant thing about her: social identity in use, in C. Antaki and S. Widdicombe (eds) *Identities in talk*. London: SAGE, pp. 87–106.

Evaldsson, A.C. (2007). 'Accounting for friendship: moral ordering and category membership in girls' relational talk', *Research on Language and Social Interaction*, 40(4): 377–404.

Evaldsson, A.C. (2014). 'Doing being boys with ADHD: category memberships and differences in SEN classroom practices', *Emotional and Behavioural Difficulties*, 19(3): 266–283.

Fitzgerald, R. (2012). 'Membership categorization analysis: wild and promiscuous or simply the joy of Sacks?', *Discourse Studies*, 14: 305–311.

Gill, V.T. and Maynard, D.W. (1995). 'On "labeling" in actual interaction: delivering and receiving diagnoses of developmental disabilities', *Social Problems*, 42(1): 11–37.

Goodwin, M.H. (2006). 'Participation, affect, and trajectory in family directive/response sequences', *Text and Talk*, 26(4/5): 513–542.

Graham, L. (ed.) (2010). *(De)constructing ADHD: critical guidance for teachers and teacher educators*. New York: Peter Lang.

Hall, C., Slembrouck, S. and Sarangi, S. (2006). *Language practice in social work: categorisation and accountability in child welfare*. London: Routledge.

Hester, S. (1991). 'The social facts of deviance in school: a study of mundane reason', *British Journal of Sociology of Education*, 42: 443–463.

Hester, S. (1998). Describing 'deviance' in school: recognizably educational psychological problems, in C. Antaki and S. Widdicombe (eds) *Identities in talk*. London: SAGE, pp. 133–150.

Hester, S. (2000). The local order of deviance in school: membership categorisation, motives and morality in referral talk, in S. Hester and D. Francis (eds) *Local educational order: ethnomethodological studies of knowledge in action*. Philadelphia: John Benjamins Publishing, pp. 197–222.

Hester, S. and Eglin, P. (1997). Membership categorisation analysis: an introduction, in S. Hester and P. Eglin (eds) *Culture in action: studies in membership categorisation analysis*. Washington: International Institute for Ethnomethodology and Conversation Analysis and University Press of America, pp. 1–23.

Hjörne, E. (2006). Pedagogy in the ADHD classroom: an exploratory study of the Little Group, in G. Lloyd, D. Cohen and J. Stead (eds) *Critical new perspectives on Attention Deficit/Hyperactivity Disorder*. Oxford: Routledge Falmer, pp. 176–197.

Hjörne, E. and Säljö, R. (2004). '"There is something about Julia" – symptoms, categories, and the process of invoking ADHD in the Swedish school: a case study', *Journal of Language, Identity, and Education*, 3(1): 1–24.

Hjörne, E. and Säljö, R. (2012). Institutional labeling and pupil careers: negotiating identities of children who do not fit in, in T. Cole, H. Daniels and J. Visser (eds) *Routledge international companion to emotional and behavioural difficulties*. London: Routledge, pp. 40–48.

Holmberg, K. (2009). *Health complaints, bullying and predictors of Attention-Deficit/Hyperactivity-Disorder (ADHD) in 10-year-olds in a Swedish community*. Uppsala: Uppsala Universitet.

Kopp, S. (2010). *Girls with social and/or attention impairments*. Göteborg: Intellecta Infolog AB.

Li Wei (2014). Introducing applied linguistics, in Li Wei (ed.) *Applied linguistics*. Oxford: Wiley-Blackwell, pp. 1–26.

Lloyd, G. and Norris, C. (1999). 'Including ADHD?', *Disability and Society*, 14(4): 505–517.

Maynard, D.W. (1991). The perspective-display series and the delivery and receipt of diagnostic news, in D. Boden and D.H. Zimmerman (eds) *Talk and social structure: studies in ethnomethodology and conversation analysis*. Oxford: Polity Press, pp. 77–90.

Maynard, D.W. (1992). On clinicians co-implicating recipients' perspective in the delivery of diagnostic news, in P. Drew and J. Heritage (eds) *Talk at work: interaction in institutional settings*. Cambridge: Cambridge University Press, pp. 331–358.

Mehan, H. (1991). The school's work of sorting pupils, in D. Boden and D.H. Zimmerman (eds) *Talk and social structure: studies in ethnomethodology and conversation analysis*. Cambridge: Polity Press, pp. 71–90.

Mehan, H. (1993). Beneath the skin and between the ears: a case study in the politics of representation, in S. Chaiklin and J. Lave (eds) *Understanding practice: perspectives on activity and context*. Cambridge: Cambridge University Press, pp. 241–269.

Mehan, H., Hertweck, A. and Meihls, J.L. (1986). *Handicapping the handicapped: decision making in pupils' educational careers*. Stanford: Stanford University Press.

Prosser, B., Reid, R., Shute, R. and Atkinson, I. (2002). 'Attention Deficit Hyperactivity Disorder: special education policy and practice in Australia', *Australian Journal of Education*, 46(1): 65–78.

Rapley, M., Kiernan, P. and Antaki, C. (1998). 'Invisible to themselves or negotiating identity? The interactional management of "being intellectually disabled"', *Disability and Society*, 13(5): 807–827.

Renshaw, P., Choo, J. and e. emerald. (2014). 'Diverse disability identities: the accomplishment of "Child with a disability" in everyday interaction between parents and teachers', *International Journal of Educational Research*, 63: 47–58.

Roberts, C. (2013). Institutional discourse, in J. Simpson (ed.) *The Routledge handbook of applied linguistics*. London: Routledge, pp. 81–95.

Sacks, H. (1972). On the analysability of stories by children, in J. Gumperz and D. Hymes (eds) *Directions of sociolinguistics: the ethnography of communication*. New York: Holt, Rinehart & Winston, pp. 325–345.

Sacks, H. (1992). *Lectures on conversation*. Vol. I. Oxford: Blackwell.

Sacks, H. (1995). *Lectures on conversation*. Vols I and II. Oxford: Blackwell.

Sarangi, S. and van Leeuwen, T. (2003). *Applied linguistics and communities of practice*. London: MPG Books.

Shakespeare, T. (1996). Disability, identity and difference, in C. Barnes and G. Mercer (eds) *Exploring the divide*. Leeds: The Disability Press, pp. 94–113.

Simpson, J. (2013). Introduction: applied linguistics in the contemporary world, in J. Simpson (ed.) *The Routledge handbook of applied linguistics*. London: Routledge, pp. 1–8.

Stokoe, E. (2012). 'Categorial systematics', *Discourse Studies*, 14(3): 345–354.

Thomas, G. and Loxley, A. (2001). *Deconstructing special education and constructing inclusion*. Buckingham, England: Open University Press.

Velasquez, A. (2012). *ADHD i skolans praktik: en studie av normativitet och motstånd i en särskild undervisningsgrupp* [ADHD in everyday school practice: a study of normativity and resistance in a special teaching group]. Uppsala: Uppsala Universitet.

Watson, N. (1998). Enabling identity: disability, self and citizenship, in T. Shakespeare (ed.) *The disability reader: social science perspectives*. London: Cassell, pp. 147–162.

Wortham, S. (2003). 'Curriculum as a resource for the development of social identity', *Sociology of Education*, 76: 229–247.

Wortham, S. (2004). 'From good student to outcast: the emergence of a classroom identity', *Ethos*, 32(2): 164–187.

Appendix

[ ]	Overlapping talk.
(.)	A micropause shorter than (0.5).
wo::rd	Prolongation of the sound.
word-	A hyphen after a word indicates a cut-off.
w<u>o</u>rd	Underlining indicates some form of stress or emphasis.
WOrd	Loud talk is demarcated by upper case.
°word°, °°word°°	Talk that is markedly quieter than the surrounding talk.
↑	The up arrow marks a sharp rise in pitch.
> <	The talk is markedly faster than the surrounding talk.
((cries))	Double parentheses mark the transcriber's description of events.
"word"	Citation is used to indicate reported speech.
what	Italics used for translation into English.

(Transcription conventions adopted from Jefferson 2004)

The English translations are as close as possible to the Swedish verbatim records. All names have been changed to ensure the anonymity of the participants, and have been replaced with fictional names, preserving the ethnic backgrounds.

26

'Comes with the territory'
Expert–novice and insider–outsider identities in police interviews

Frances Rock

Introduction

It is a late summer afternoon. A woman in her early twenties is sitting in a quiet bar, talking to a male police officer. She smokes a cigarette, with her chair pushed back from the table. He holds a clipboard. As they talk, he writes on pages clipped to the clipboard, turning to a new sheet periodically. Sometimes they share a joke and sometimes both look serious. At one point they consider a map together. Later she demonstrates movements with her arms and upper body, acting out past events by way of explanation. Scenes like the one just described take place daily,[1] as police officers, in gathering evidence, interview victims and witnesses of crime about what they have experienced. This is done through processes of speaking, listening, reading and writing which construct a written account, a 'statement', on the witness's behalf. Try to picture the language of these encounters. You might imagine descriptions of crime scenes and actions which occurred there. Sure enough, during the interaction described above, the witness talked about an attack in her workplace, explaining who was involved and what happened.

However, we know that interactions in institutional, workplace and professional contexts, like police interviews, are also concerned with presenting, constructing and reconstructing identities, with showing who one is or wants to be and how one affiliates. Many previous studies have indicated that interactions that might be expected to be concerned purely with transacting tasks go well beyond that (e.g. Hobbs 2008; Angouri 2011; Charalambous 2013; Golden and Lanza 2013). In the interview described above, the witness introduced things that appeared completely unconnected to the crime (Rock 2016). For example, while the police officer was noting down the witness's name and contact information, the witness suddenly said, 'I come from a tiny village where nothing ever happens; I come to [city name] and this happens.' Later, when the officer was reading over some text he had just written and beginning to write the next part of the witness's account, the witness began to rub and move her shoulder and said, 'I've been carrying an autistic child around all day and it's caned my shoulder in [i.e. injured my shoulder].' There was no need for the witness to tell the officer about her quiet, uneventful home town and the contrast it offers with the city where she now lives. Likewise the minor shoulder injury happened to be sustained on the day of interview, so subsequent to the crime.

Yet this witness often spoke like this, apparently off-topic, during extended silences. She seemed to want to tell the officer about herself. In doing so she was not simply relating 'facts' or filling what might have seemed like an awkward silence. The details she selected and their delivery cast her in a particular way. In the first example, she categorises herself as being from a small town where crime is rare (Sacks 1972). She highlights that she is not the kind of person usually tangled up in police investigations. In the second example, she refers back to earlier talk, which had introduced her volunteering at a playgroup for children with special needs. By flagging this activity, she presents herself as someone public-spirited and even willing to sustain minor injuries for her cause, highlighted through her gestures. In these two statements she presents herself as a novice interviewee and an outsider to policing and crime.

This example serves to illustrate the subject of this chapter: how witness identities are constructed. Through further data, this chapter will explore in more detail how witnesses say who they are during police interviews. It will consider how police officers respond and what witnesses might achieve through identity talk. It will show that the outsider or novice identity performed in the example illustrated above is not the only option for witnesses and that other witnesses take the opposite tack, constructing an identity of expert or insider. In doing so, the case study illustrates how witnesses blur conventional asymmetries of police interviews, in turn challenging assumptions about institutional interactions. It also shows how presentation of identities in legal settings happens one to one.

The study of language in settings construed as 'workplace', 'professional' or 'institutional', such as those in which police operate, give opportunities to undertake applied linguistics: 'the theoretical and empirical investigation of real world problems in which language is a central issue' (Brumfit 1995: 27). While disagreement remains on the nature of applied linguistics (see e.g. Rampton 1997; Widdowson 2000; McCarthy 2001) and the fit between 'real world', 'problems' and 'theoretical and empirical investigation', Candlin and Sarangi (2004: 2) propose 'cutting through' this 'knot' by renewing a focus not on what applied linguistics is, but what it does, how and why. Through this they recommend an applied linguistics which is reflexive about its principles and practices and which makes itself relevant to practitioners (see Rock 2007; Stokoe 2014). This chapter seeks to show how applied linguistics can be used to gain insights on identities in institutional settings. The police interview exemplifies such settings. It is part of a web of legal contexts where institutions connect with those they claim to serve and where, consequently, the presentation of one's identity can have larger-than-usual consequences.

Overview

This chapter is influenced by a conception of identity which draws on interactional sociolinguistic, constructionist and, to some extent, poststructualist thinking. The position taken here is that that we all inhabit a range of identities as we go about portraying who we are. We can display our inhabited identities in different ways and to different extents at different times of life, or times of day, in different interactions with different individuals, and in different social contexts (see Blommaert 2006). Identities do not just happen. Rather, they are made and remade in and through social interactions. Identity, or 'making faces' (Anazaldúa 1990: xvi), is then social, collaborative and constructed.

Research that examines language and identity in legal systems asks who we are, or are taken to be, when we confront the law and what consequences this has. Studies of interpreters in legal settings, for example, indicate their potential to recast the identities of those who they interpret for, making them seem more or less convinced or convincing (e.g.

Hale 2002; Nakane 2008). Many studies have shown that an individual's ascribed identity can systematically lead to disadvantage in legal setting. This happens, for example, when those whose ethnicity is stigmatised receive negative treatment because of their ascribed ethnic identity (Giles *et al.* 2012), which can be exploited (e.g. Eades 2008; D'hondt 2009). Identity work in legal settings can meet wide-ranging interactional goals, as Stokoe and Edward's (2007) and Stokoe's (2009a, 2009b) concerted studies of ethnicity, categorisation and self-disclosure show. The courtroom has attracted considerable attention from identity scholars. That work has explored how identities can be constructed (Tracy 2009, 2011) and manipulated (e.g. Conley *et al.* 1978) and asked how the presentation of self can be constrained (e.g. Ehrlich 2008), misrepresented (e.g. Hobbs 2008) and misunderstood (e.g. Gumperz 1982: 175).

Two key characteristics are considered in many of these identity studies and are relevant to this chapter: first, the presence of an audience and, second, the existence of power relations. Considering audience first, many legal contexts examined in relation to identity are public: they involve addressees beyond the immediate interlocutor. These addressees may be physically present, as in the courtroom with its juries, public galleries and press areas, or present only through technology, as in the police–suspect interview where audio and video recordings can allow listeners to access the speech event across times and places. Accordingly, work on identity and law often focuses on how one participant manipulates the identity presentation of another in order to influence an audience. This brings us to the second major focus, power. Because of the presence and influence of audiences, power relations are enacted in legal settings, as interactants try to persuade audiences. Usually, an institutional actor has power over a lay person through their position in a hierarchy, their familiarity with the context's conventions and their discursive dominance. The asymmetrical relationship allows the more powerful interactant to ascribe identities to the less powerful speaker, who is left to resist undesired ascribed identities more or less effectively. However, power relations are not always as we might expect in police interviews. Research shows how a police suspect can subvert predictable power structures by resisting police officers' questions (Newbury and Johnson 2006) and challenging and undermining their position (Haworth 2006). Such drama and confrontation does not feature in the interviews I examine here which involve witnesses, rather than suspects, meaning that less is generally at stake. However, the matter of audience and thus interactional asymmetry remains a feature which the witnesses address through identity work.

The data excerpts at the beginning of this chapter indicated that identities flow in and through police interviews. In that instance, the witness presented herself as normally disconnected from the world of police and policing. This involved both being a novice, on the 'periphery' (Vickers 2010) of interviewing practice and expectations, but also having 'outsider identity' (Van De Mieroop 2007), not fitting into the legal world, its activities and its motivations. This is in D'hondt's (2009: 807) terms 'a kind of "otherness of the second order"'. It is not concerned directly with the first-order categories of the legal system, which classify activities as crimes, but rather with assumptions put into play by aspects of identity, but still potentially influential. In the interview we turn to in the following sections, the interviewee presents himself as an expert in being interviewed and an insider to crime and law. An expert is 'someone who can access specific cultural or other knowledge domains and apply this knowledge in daily practice' (Androutsopoulos 1997: 10). It is a useful notion when considering police interviews because it brings together the 'multiple asymmetries of knowing' which are 'necessarily' involved in interactions, with the idea that through interaction 'participants display ... the relevance of the differing amounts or kinds of their knowing as well as their assumptions concerning the knowledge of other participants' (Jacoby and Gonzales 1991: 152). So expertise is a construct, an 'achieved identity' (ibid.: 174), which can be brought to bear by one speaker and ratified, or not, by their interlocutor. An insider will 'blend in', while an outsider will 'keep a distance' (Sarangi and Candlin 2003: 278). These are likewise not discrete and exclusive positions. As Hult (2014: 63) reminds us, an individual can be both simultaneously activating either identity through symbolic competence.

Methodology

The work presented here is part of a suite of studies on language and policing (e.g. Rock 2007, 2013, 2016). All are grounded in discourse analysis and linguistic ethnography. Each study focuses on a particular policing activity such as explaining suspects' rights, handling police complaints and answering telephone calls for police assistance. Each collects naturally occurring data along with as many additional forms of data as possible, such as:

- Photographs of research sites and the people in them;
- Written documents that underpin policing processes, such as scripts that the police recite and leaflets which they distribute;
- Interviews with participants;
- Fieldnotes and research diaries capturing impressions from the field.

The approach to these diverse forms of data has been to consider them in tandem so that each data source can inform examination of the others. The analytic process involves repeatedly visiting and revisiting the data and bringing them into dialogue with theoretical concepts and perspectives. Sometimes the analysis will zoom in to a particular turn; sometimes it will identify patterns across exchanges. Sometimes connections will emerge between interviews, photographs and naturally occurring talk. This methodological framework views language as a resource for meaning-making. It sees this resource necessarily combining with other semiotic resources, practices and artefacts (see Domingo, this volume). This view highlights that when people communicate together they do something complex and 'multi'. For example, their communication has multiple functions, meanings and significances simultaneously. In order to analyse communication, we must not only recognise but also interrogate this multiplicity. The type of discourse analysis used in linguistic ethnography provides for this by allowing a close focus on one thing at a time in order to consider its full significance. This is achieved by asking not only how that thing (a discourse feature or linguistic strategy, for example) looks and sounds on the talk's surface, but also how it interweaves across interactions, operates in a textual and intertextual environment, fits with activities and actions which accompany talk, becomes part of wider structures and how participants orient to it (see e.g. Gumperz 1982; Ivanič 1998; Pérez-Milans, this volume).

I began studying witness interviews because I was interested in how texts 'travel' through them (Rock 2001, 2013). This is a productive topic in its own right, as it enables us to find out more about how people work, alone and together, to transform language, for example from the spoken to written mode (Rock 2007). However, it is also productive from the perspective of applied linguistics because the process of transforming texts is one which can influence events and outcomes in the social world. As Candlin and Sarangi urge (2004: 2), we can usefully ask of textual transformation not just what it *is*, but also what it *does*. The flow of identities alongside other textual flows is the focus of the case study in this chapter. The notion of identities makes it possible to see interpersonal aspects of interviews from different perspectives. In particular, the following sections present data that explore the identity performances that occurred when participants' talk was ostensibly superfluous to the main task of telling and recording a story about a crime – informal asides, for example.

The data are from a set of 25 interviews between police officers and witnesses to crimes from murder to minor vandalism in England and Wales. I audio-recorded the interviews, as witness interviews are not routinely audio-recorded in this jurisdiction. I also attended the interviews, so had opportunities to observe gestures, facial expressions and bodily orientations (Matoesian 2012; Martin *et al.* 2013) as well as the writing practices of the police officers who were tasked with producing a written version of the witness's words, a 'statement' to represent the witness in later legal processes. The police officers allowed me to 'go along' (Kusenbach 2003) with them as they went about their work, which permitted conversations about their interviewing practices in general and about things which happened in particular interviews. Thus the research design gave access to police officers who did interviewing, rather than to specific interviews where police officers were, analytically, incidental.

The two interviews presented here neatly exemplify the type of witness identities that arose in the data set.

The data

The interviewer in the data below is an experienced ex-police officer. He is in his late fifties and had been an officer for 30 years. He very recently retired from the police and now interviews part-time and on a freelance basis. The interviewee is an experienced staff nurse (an entry-level nurse) in his early forties who works shifts. The nurse is giving a witness statement after being attacked in the Accident and Emergency Department of a large hospital in an English city (abbreviated to 'A and E' by the participants) where he works. Accident and Emergency Departments, as the name suggests, handle unexpected medical incidents. Screaming ambulance sirens and blue lights are a trope of A and E. The often fast-paced work is demanding for staff, who cannot easily predict or prepare for what will happen during their shift. Cases can be life-or-death, but at the other extreme some patients are 'time-wasters' or 'worriers'. Emotions can run high in A and E, with patients and their companions often behaving unexpectedly. In many respects, then, the work of the A and E staff nurse can be seen as akin to the work of a police officer, being public-facing, high-stakes and unpredictable, with a need to distinguish trivial from serious incidents. This connection between working lives becomes important to the way that the witness involves himself in the interview. The interview takes place in a hospital staff-room, which periodically becomes busy.

The incident under investigation was an attempted assault on the nurse by the male partner of a female patient. They had come to hospital with their child one evening. The nurse had suggested that while the patient was being treated, the partner and child should go home to 'get some rest' and return to hospital the following day. Despite leaving as requested, they unexpectedly reappeared in the early hours of the morning. It transpired that the female patient's child and male partner had apparently been travelling around the local area in the interim in a taxi, during which time the patient's partner had been trying to obtain drugs. The nurse was concerned about this turn of events and decided to contact Social Services (the UK welfare service) to try to have the child removed from this man's care. When the nurse told the man this, there was an altercation and the man attempted to hit the nurse. Nearby police officers restrained the man. The incident, then, is one in which the nurse's identity as an institutional actor who works in concert with social agencies and police is foregrounded.

All the names in the data are pseudonyms: the witness is named Will as a memory aid for the reader, as 'witness' and 'Will' share a first letter. The interviewer is retired and thus not strictly a civilian. However, I refer to him as 'the police officer' because this is how the reader is likely to understand someone in this role and, crucially, because the nurse oriented to him as a police representative. He also fulfilled his task in a way typical of an officer. He is referred to as Ollie in the following data extracts. All other places and participants are anonymised.

The first set of extracts (1a–c) occurred at the beginning of the interview. The interviewer, Ollie, had been explaining to Will about what will happen during the interview. He then remarks that they are 'doing well', shifting footing (Goffman 1979) from preliminary talk to getting the interview underway.

Extract 1a 'Not the first time'

1	Ollie (Officer)	oh we're doing well
2	Will (Witness)	((Inaudible: three syllables))
3	Ollie	lovely
4	Will	this is not the first time (.) I'm sure it's probably not
5		going to be the last time uh hhhhh

In lines 4–5, the witness, Will, responded to the officer's changed footing by noting his prior experience in giving witness statements about work. The expression 'not the first time' implies that the event described 'should not be taken as an individual incident' nor 'a rare happening' (Bilal *et al.* 2012: 71). 'I'm sure it's not going to be the last' intensifies and enables him to present himself as aware of, and, possibly, resigned to, future workplace risks. These phrases may serve to poke fun at the darker side of his work, which calls to mind Dyer and Keller-Cohen's (2000: 298) observation that self-mockery democratises. These idiomatic phrases, in combination with his exaggerated, melodramatic sigh at the turn's end, suggest that he intends to convey something more than simply the 'fact' that he has been interviewed before. That 'something more' concerns identity. The verb 'identify' and nominalisation 'identification' flag that these are processes through which, as Ivanič (1998: 11) puts it, 'individuals align themselves with groups, communities and/or sets of interests, values, beliefs and practices'. Will's turn enabled him to present himself as having seen it all before. We might infer that he is someone resigned to unpleasant events (values); that he sees these as typifying his work (beliefs); and perhaps that he takes them in his stride (practices). He also hinted, through these expressions and the sigh, at his alignment with particular interests. He identifies as an expert interviewee – an insider to this task and its requirements. He aligns himself with the officer, as someone else experiencing interviews for neither the first nor the last time. This is in contrast to the witness at the beginning of this chapter, who specifically identified herself as not accustomed to similar interests, values, beliefs and practices. Will later reiterated his position when explaining to a colleague that he would be late starting his shift because he was 'doing a police statement'. After a hearty laugh, he declared that this 'comes with the territory really'. Although this formulaic expression connotes resignation to one's fate (see Paikeday 1992), the witness used it with a certain pride.

Returning to the interview opening, Extract 1b follows directly from 1a and shows how the conversation developed:

Extract 1b 'It's a public order offence'

6	Ollie (Officer)	so you were on (.) duty at the A 'n' E (.) [W: yeah] at
7		five ten hours [W: yep] on 12th November when [W:
8		yep] the defendant Waverley [W: yep] er became
9		abusive and threatening towards staff p- (.) [W: yeh] and
10		the police which resulted in his arrest (.) [W: yes] for
11		section fo- a section four public order offence (.) [W:
12		right] er (.) all we need to know is (.) what you (.) you're
13		employed by the (.) [W: yep] [approximate hospital
14		name] whatever it is (.) [W: yeh] hhhh you (.) on such
15		and such a day you reported for duty at such and such a
16		time [W: right] and at such and such a time when you
17		first noticed the person when he came in or whatever
18		[W: yeah] (.) erm (.) and events leading up to [W: yep]
19		the (police) being called (.) [W: right] and then when the
20		police were called probably (.) //reactions//
21	Will (Witness)	//police // actually
22		weren't called they were here
23	Ollie	oh were they okay that's fine (.) and (.) as it's a public
24		order offence [W: yes] were you actually (.) frightened
25		or [W: mm] was anyone else around [W: right] you who
26		in your opinion //might have been frightened//
27		// right right (.) yep yep //
28	Ollie	hhhhhh anything else you want to discuss //with me//
29	Will	// no not // at
30		all
31	Ollie	lovely get it down and- get it done and done (.) and get
32		out to my car before I get it clamped [wheel-locked in
33		place by the authorities as a punishment for overstaying
34		a parking time-limit]

Throughout lines 6–26 the officer appeared to lead the witness, telling him what he expects the statement to contain by reading from a written summary devised from evidence to date. He did prospect an opportunity, later in the interview, for the witness to discuss 'anything else' (line 28), but concluded that this will need to be brief as he was worried about his car being clamped (lines 31–32).

Police officers are trained to encourage witnesses to tell their own stories with minimal interruption (College of Policing 2014). Ollie seems to fail in this. If we examined this extract in isolation, we might identify power as a factor here. We might assume that the officer's talk is designed to steer, constrain or even silence Will. However, by considering the witness's prior turn (Extract 1a), in combination with a focus on identity, we can see that there may be something else going on. Interviewers are given written summaries of crimes but they make their own decisions about whether to mention these summaries to witnesses. In my data, officers variously read them aloud, paraphrased, ignored or emphatically dismissed them. The data suggest that these practices were motivated and situated choices. In this instance, Ollie opted to present a detailed paraphrase. He itemised topics for discussion (lines 6–10) and then clarified what information was required (lines 12–23). While this could be taken to disempower the witness, suggesting that his contribution is perfunctory, it can alternatively be heard as acknowledging the witness as an insider who knows that statements require certain elements and might be expected to take the summary as a reminder or briefing on these elements. From this perspective, 'all we need to know' (line 12), which introduces the reformulation, casts the interview as routine and straightforward. The officer's repeated use of the terminology 'public order offence' in lines 11 and 23–24 contributes to the impression that he is, right from this early stage in the interview, orienting to the witness as an expert, someone who will likely recognise specialist terms. Terminology is central to legal language. It is a hallmark of legal identity, a specialised register through which speakers foreground knowledge (Van De Mieroop 2007: 1126) and an 'in-group language' (Gibbons 2003: 39). Its use here draws the two men together. Ollie's summary was prefaced with 'so' (line 6). Here, 'so' raises the possibility that his summary follows from the witness's expert identity (see Johnson 2002) and thus that Ollie recognised and validated this. Will appeared receptive to being cast as someone who understood the task at hand. Throughout Ollie's summary, he provided minimal feedback (lines 6–20 and 24–25). He also leant forward attentively and nodded frequently. He appears to receive Ollie's summary as informative orientation, not restrictive scripting, and in doing so, he reinforces his position as a professional and expert.

Turning to Ollie's stated intention to 'get it down and- get it done ... and get out to my car before I get it clamped' (lines 31–32), the lens of identity reveals more about the officer's orientation to Will's insider identity. By confessing that he must hurry, the officer implied that he trusted Will to understand the pressures of a hectic job and to understand that he recounted this in good faith. Ollie, a police officer, and Will, a nurse, are both public servants who encounter situations at work that are experienced by few other workers. Both operate in contexts of rules and responsibilities relating to how and why they can interact with members of the public. Both work long, irregular hours in extreme situations, in which one mistake could end their career – or indeed someone's life. While each profession has a distinctive identity (see Candlin and Candlin 2007; Rock 2007), we can see Will's reference to his parking predicament as an opportunity to align their professional worlds, in which both experience haste and compliance. Throughout the interview, these positions developed.

Extract 1c follows soon after 1b. In it, Ollie and Will move into perhaps more generic and familiar identity work, in the form of small talk, 'supposedly minor, informal, unimportant and non-serious modes of talk', in this instance 'time-out talk' (Coupland 2000: 2). They discuss what the officer calls 'the tragedy in India', referring to a severe accident which caused deaths and injuries and had received extensive news coverage.

Extract 1c 'That tragedy in India'

63	Ollie (Officer)	'bout that tragedy in India 've you seen it // on this //
64	Will (Witness)	//ooh I n-//
65		know
66	Ollie	good God hhhh
67	Will	(.) we'd never cope so how the hell they're coping God
68		only knows
69	Ollie	I don't think- I don't think they are going to cope to be
70		// honest //
71	Will	//no they// won't sure //they won't//
72	Ollie	// and // I'm sure half the
73		people that are (.) seriously injured are // going to die//
74	Will	//they're going// to
75		they're not going to make it

In this extract, we see Ollie and Will presenting themselves as amiable people taking an interest in world events. Ollie selected a topic of professional interest to his medic interlocutor, a developing healthcare emergency. However, this is also an example of two emergency workers sharing their professional perspectives on a situation in which they both have workplace expertise. De Fina *et al.* (2006: 4) and Gumperz (1982: 185) have commented on the significance of pronouns to the construction of identity, and the use of 'we' in Will's observation in line 67 that 'we'd never cope' illustrates connection. Here, 'we' could denote Will's workplace affiliation, the medical profession. Alternatively, 'we' might take in emergency response personnel, in which case he includes the officer. Whether this is an exclusive or inclusive use of 'we', he is addressing the officer as an equal and insider.

At one point in the interview, Will became so entrenched in his expert, insider identity that he began to do the officer's job for him. In Extract 2, he had been interrupted from his interview by a colleague passing through the busy staffroom where the interview happened. Will tried to discover, from her, whether she was in the hospital at the time of the attack.

Extract 2 'We lost the track'

1	Will (Witness)	just a sec were you here last Wednesday Carol
2	Carol (Colleague)	what day is it @@
3	Will	did you do a night last Wednesday
4	Carol	I did nights (.) what did I do (.) I did- no Friday Saturday
5		Sunday
6	Will	right fine in which case doesn't matter trying to work out
7		((Inaudible: four syllables)) at the minute
8	Will and Carol	[further discussion of which nursing staff were on duty
9		on the night of the crime. Ollie writes quietly]
10	Will	right so we lost the track a bit there

In Extract 2, Will attempted to open up investigative lines for the officer by identifying new witnesses. At the close of the extract, he displayed his identity as an expert statement-giver once more through a structural move that shifted footing, 'right so we lost the track a bit there', marking the end of his conversation with Carol and his transition back into the interview (line 10). Such shifts in footing are common from police officers, as we saw in Extract 1a. Will's accomplishment of this, and his use of the pronoun 'we', discussed above, is very reminiscent of the officer's talk.

So far we have seen Will, the witness, foreground his expert, insider identity and the officer, Ollie, orienting to him as insider and professional equal. At the close of the interview in Extract 3, Will's insider identity was reinforced by Ollie's nostalgic narrative.

Extract 3 'On more than one occasion'

1	Ollie (Officer)	I've been in the police for thirty years (.) [W: uuhm] (.)
2		on the t- (.) mmp (.) eighteen of those years on the traffic
3		department and uh although I came here (.) with some of
4		the (.) enquiries we had (.) I think the m- majority of my
5		work covered Hospital A and Hospital B being (.) in
6		Cityside [W: yeh] but I got brought in here and was
7		treated very well on more than one occasion @ when I
8		was assaulted @@@@@@ (.) the wife was saying
9		[imitating wife] 'where are you taking him this time'

While this was an amalgam of recollections, it recalls Holmes's (2006) label, workplace anecdotes. These provide a means of not only doing professional and personal identity but also constructing 'professional identities of others as good or poor' (Holmes 2006: 186). We see these processes as Ollie connected his identity to Will's. Ollie flagged his status as a long-serving police officer (line 1) just as Will is a long-serving nurse. He noted that he has visited Will's workplace multiple times during his service (lines 3–4 and 6), a point of connection, if not similarity, with Will. He noted in most detail however that, like Will, he has been a victim of assault during his career (lines 6–8, from his own perspective, and lines 8–9, from his wife's). Just as Will's experience of workplace violence was 'not the first time' and 'comes with the territory', Ollie also experienced violence on 'more than one occasion'. This tying together of their identities as people who encounter danger at work, and do so routinely, initiated in Extract 1b at the beginning of the interview and concluded here, at the interview's close, is integral to getting the work done.

Discussion

This chapter opened with an extract from a witness interview in which the witness foregrounded her outsider identity, as someone distant from law and crime and not at all expert in statement-giving. In contrast, the data presented in the previous section illustrate an alternative witness identity. In the extracts, we saw how Will, the witness, constructed an identity as an expert interviewee, a professional insider, resigned to experiencing and recounting crime. He appeared to relish this identity and used several devices to support it. These included:

- Lexical choices (pronouns which potentially included Ollie in Will's in-group);
- Phrasal selections (using idiomatic expressions such as 'comes with the territory' for implicature, intensification and self-mockery);
- Practices (recruiting other witnesses);
- Discursive activities (responding to and initiating shifts in footing, such as 'lost the track');
- Interactional moves (minimal feedback during expert talk) and physical paralanguage (leaning forward and nodding).

Additionally, the data showed that his identity is not something that he developed single-handedly. Instead the interviewer, Ollie, contributed, co-constructing it (Page 2013). This was done in a number of ways, including:

- Prospection (introducing interview content);
- Topic control (introducing discussion of a medical emergency);
- Changes in footing (when moving between phases of interview);
- Using the discourse marker *so* (taking up Will's themes);
- Lexically (using specialist legal terminology such as offence names).

We might ask whether these self-presentations are anything more than chance, in that witnesses cannot present identities that they cannot support. As Ivanič (1998: 10) cautions, while there is a sense of 'multiplicity, hybridity and fluidity' conveyed by plurals like 'subjectivities' and 'positionings', 'people are not free to take on any identity they choose'. Yet these witnesses did not have to foreground these aspects of themselves but rather chose to do so. I noted at the beginning of this chapter that interactants often work on identity in dramatic ways in legal settings because of the audience. Here, there is no extended audience, so the identities are only constructed between those present. Nonetheless, identity work is crucial here.

Expert-insider and novice-outsider interview identities are not confined to these interviews. Across the data set the expert-insider identity is co-constructed in multiple interviews with public-facing workers including bar staff, public house managers, security guards and also other police officers. Presenting as an expert could be seen as a risky strategy. By doing it, the witness claims to understand the task at hand and sanctions the officer to take knowledge of processes and norms for granted. This has practical advantages, making interviews more speedy and focused, but also offers interpersonal advantages. By acknowledging a witness as an insider, as able to share back-stage humour about public-facing jobs and with common concerns, social distance can be decreased and affiliation achieved. This raises the question of why witnesses would take up the opposite positioning, inhabiting the identity of a naive outsider. Yet this position certainly offers interpersonal advantage. The novice witness is not subject to high expectations. They have outed themselves as likely to need help and thereby invited the officer's interventions. Interpersonally, the witness appeals to the officer's own experiences of being an outsider. Even as they create social distance by differentiating themselves, they also minimise that distance by alluding to the recognisable experience of being outside. Foregrounding a novice identity also appeals to the notion of the innocent bystander, which enables a novice witness to present him/herself as having observed criminal events 'in passing' (Zimmerman 1992) and as an ordinary person (Sacks 1972: 215). The novice-outsider identity was predominantly taken up by women in the wider data set. However, a much larger data set would be needed to establish whether this was a gendered practice.

Where the novice-outsider witness might appear to be a 'good witness' because they bring a fresh view of a crime, untainted by prior experiences, the expert-insider witness brings their expertise – their ability to appraise an incident dispassionately because they have 'seen it all before'. In the 'Overview of theoretical perspectives' section of this chapter, I noted that identity had often been studied in those legal settings which were extremely public. Identities of courtroom participants, for example, are paraded for all to see. In contrast, in witness interviews, identities of interviewees and even interviewers are salient interpersonally (they are about the relationship between the speakers) yet with institutional implications (they can influence the way that the task gets done).

Issues for applied linguistics

The case study presented in this chapter raises a number of issues for applied linguistics. Application of linguistic knowledge to legal settings is an obvious and important form of applied linguistic work. It is obvious because language is so fundamental to all aspects of the operation of law, and important because of the potential value of linguistic work to the just operation of legal processes through measures such as training for practitioners and campaigning about legal issues. Another important issue for applied linguistics is that, in police interviews with witnesses, language and communication accomplish what is intended to be a process of transmission from the witness to the legal system. The linguist is well equipped to comment on the impoverished nature of the metaphor of transmission to such a process and to note ways in which the processes around speech and writing function. Their challenge is, recalling Candlin and Sarangi (2004), to share insights with practitioners in order to contribute not only to what applied linguistics is, but also what it does.

Summary

This chapter sees identity as fluid and negotiable. It explores what this means in a specific social context – that of the police interview with a witness to a crime. Police interviews with witnesses ask those who have seen crimes to recount their experience in order that evidence can be gathered for criminal investigation. While a witness interview, with this purpose, might appear to be an encounter in which the task will be the focus, the chapter shows that the presentation of identity also features. Talk from two witness interviews is examined. In one, the witness presents herself as a novice interviewee who is naive to the experience of crime and an outsider to the activity of being interviewed by a police officer. In the other, the witness presents himself as experienced in being exposed to violent crime, an expert interviewee and someone who is an insider to the world of policing and intense public service. The chapter examines how witnesses construct expert–novice or insider–outsider identities and why they might do so. It suggests that the foregrounding of these identities has interactional functions such as lowering expectations and showing alignment, but also that these identities help with getting the task done in showing whether help is needed or things can be taken for granted.

Related topics

Ethnomethodological and conversation analytic approaches to identity; Language and identity in linguistic ethnography; Ethics in language and identity research; Challenges for language and identity researchers in the collection and transcription of spoken interaction; Being a language teacher in the content classroom: teacher identity and content and language integrated learning (CLIL); The future of identity research: impact and new developments in sociolinguistics.

Further reading

Kjelsvik, B. (2014). '"Winning a battle, but losing the war": contested identities, narratives, and interaction in asylum interviews', *Text and Talk*, 34(1): 89–115. (This journal article examines interviews with asylum seekers which aim to assess their claims to asylum. It suggests that these interviews progress differently depending on how interviewees are framed.)

Matoesian, G. (2001). *Law and the language of identity in the William Kennedy Smith rape trial*. Oxford: Oxford University Press. (This book focuses on courtroom interaction, showing that identity becomes part of the social construction of rape as a fact.)

Ostermann, A. and Comunello, C. (2012). 'Gender and professional identity in three institutional settings in Brazil: the case of responses to assessment turns', *Pragmatics*, 22(2): 203–230. (This journal article considers how professional and gender identities combine in policing and legal advice. The article shows how professionals in each setting respond when victims of violence assess themselves and others.)

Note

1 The most recent statistics for England and Wales reveal around 6.9 million incidents of crime against households and adults (aged over 15) annually (Office of National Statistics 2015).

References

Anazaldúa, G. (ed.) (1990). *Making face, making soul*. San Francisco: Aunt Lute.

Androutsopoulos, J. (1997). 'Fashion, media, and music: adolescents as language experts', *Der Deutschunterricht*, 6: 10–20.

Angouri, J. (2011). '"We are in a masculine profession": constructing gender identities in a consortium of two multinational engineering companies', *Gender and Language*, 5(2): 373–403.

Bilal, H., Zafar, M., Ahmed, I., Tariq, H. and Ishaq, K. (2012). 'Language of news reporting: application of critical discourse analysis', *British Journal of Humanities and Social Sciences*, 6(1): 67–79.

Blommaert, J. (2006). Language policy and national identity, in T. Ricento (ed.) *Language policy: theory and method*. Oxford: Blackwell, pp. 238–254.

Brumfit, C. (1995). Teacher professionalism and research, in G. Cook and B. Seidlhofer (eds) *Principles and practice in applied linguistics: studies in honour of H.G. Widdowson*. Oxford: Oxford University Press, pp. 27–42.

Candlin, C. and Sarangi, S. (2004). 'Making applied linguistics matter', *Journal of Applied Linguistics*, 1(1): 1–8.

Candlin, S. and Candlin, C. (2007). Nursing over time and space: some issues for the construct 'community of practice', in R. Iedema (ed.) *Hospital communication*. London: Palgrave, pp. 244–267.

Charalambous, C. (2013). 'The "burden" of emotions in language teaching: negotiating a troubled past in "other"-language learning classrooms', *Language and Intercultural Communication*, 13(3): 310–329.

College of Policing (2014). *Investigative interviewing* [Online]. Available at www.app.college.police.uk/app-content/investigations/investigative-interviewing

Conley, J., O'Barr, W. and Lind, E. (1978). 'The power of language: presentational style in the courtroom', *Duke Law Journal*, 6: 1375–1399.

Coupland, J. (2000). Introduction, in J. Coupland (ed.) *Small talk*. Harlow: Pearson, pp. 1–26.

D'hondt, S. (2009). 'Others on trial: the construction of cultural otherness in Belgian first instance criminal hearings', *Journal of Pragmatics*, 41(4): 806–828.

De Fina, A., Schiffrin, D. and Bamberg, M. (2006). Introduction, in A. De Fina, D. Schiffrin and M. Bamberg (eds) *Discourse and identity: studies in interactional sociolinguistics*. Cambridge: Cambridge University Press, pp. 1–23.

Domingo, M. (this volume). Language and identity research in online environments: a multimodal ethnographic perspective, in S. Preece (ed.) *The Routledge handbook of language and identity*. Abingdon: Routledge, pp. 541–557.

Dyer, J. and Keller-Cohen, D. (2000). 'The discursive construction of professional self through narratives of personal experience', *Discourse Studies*, 2(3): 283–304.

Eades, D. (2008). *Courtroom talk and neocolonial control*. Berlin: Walter de Gruyter.

Ehrlich, S. (2008). Sexual assault trials, discursive identities and institutional change, in R. Dolón and J. Todolí (eds) *Analysing identities in discourse*. Amsterdam: John Benjamins, pp. 159–178.

Gibbons, J. (2003). *Forensic linguistics: an introduction to language in the justice system*. Oxford: Blackwell.

Giles, H., Linz, D., Bonilla, D. and Gomez, M.L. (2012). 'Police stops of and interactions with Latino and White (Non-Latino) drivers: extensive policing and communication accommodation', *Communication Monographs*, 79(4): 407–427.

Goffman, E. (1979). 'Footing', *Semiotica*, 25(1–2): 1–30.

Golden, A. and Lanza, E. (2013). 'Metaphors of culture: identity construction in migrants' narrative discourse', *Intercultural Pragmatics*, 10(2): 295–314.

Gumperz, J. (1982). *Language and social identity*. Cambridge: Cambridge University Press.

Hale, S. (2002). 'How faithfully do court interpreters render the style of non-English speaking witnesses' testimonies? A data-based study of Spanish–English bilingual proceedings', *Discourse Studies*, 4(1): 25–47.

Haworth, K. (2006). 'The dynamics of power and resistance in police interview discourse', *Discourse and Society*, 17(6): 739–759.

Hobbs, P. (2008). 'It's not what you say but how you say it: the role of personality and identity in trial success', *Critical Discourse Studies*, 5(3): 231–248.

Holmes, J. (2006). 'Workplace narratives, professional identity and relational practice', in A. De Fina, D. Schiffrin and M. Bamberg (eds) *Discourse and identity: studies in interactional sociolinguistics*. Cambridge: Cambridge University Press, pp. 166–187.

Hult, F. (2014). 'Covert bilingualism and symbolic competence: analytical reflections on negotiating insider/outsider positionality in Swedish speech situations', *Applied Linguistics*, 35(1): 63–81.

Ivanič, R. (1998). *Writing and identity: the discoursal construction of identity in academic writing*. Amsterdam: John Benjamins.

Jacoby, S. and Gonzales, P. (1991). 'The constitution of expert–novice in scientific discourse', *Issues in Applied Linguistics*, 2(2): 149–181.

Johnson, A. (2002). So? Pragmatic implications of *so-prefaced questions* in formal police interviews, in J. Cotterill (ed.) *Language in the legal process*. Basingstoke: Palgrave, pp. 91–110.

Kusenbach, M. (2003). 'Street phenomenology: the go-along as ethnographic research tool', *Ethnography*, 4(3): 455–485.

Martin, J.R., Zappavigna, M., Dwyer, P. and Cléirigh, C. (2013). 'Users in uses of language: embodied identity in youth justice conferencing', *Text and Talk*, 33(4–5): 467–496.

Matoesian, G. (2012). 'Gesture's community: social organization in multimodal conduct', *Language in Society*, 41(3): 365–391.

McCarthy, M. (2001). *Issues in applied linguistics*. Cambridge: Cambridge University Press.

Nakane, I. (2008). 'Politeness and gender in interpreted police interviews', *Monash University Linguistics Papers*, 6(1): 29–40.

Newbury, P. and Johnson, A. (2006). 'Suspects' resistance to constraining and coercive questioning strategies in the police interview', *International Journal of Speech, Language and the Law*, 13(2): 213–240.

Office of National Statistics (2015). *Crime in England and Wales, year ending December 2014*. London: Office for National Statistics.

Page, R. (2013). 'From small stories to networked narrative: the evolution of personal narratives in Facebook status updates', *Narrative Inquiry*, 23(1): 192–213.

Paikeday, T. (1992). 'What makes people "peruse"?', *English Today*, 8(3): 33–38.

Pérez-Milans, M. (this volume). Language and identity in linguistic ethnography, in S. Preece (ed.) *The Routledge handbook of language and identity*. Abingdon: Routledge, pp. 83–97.

Rampton, B. (1997). 'Retuning in applied linguistics?', *International Journal of Applied Linguistics*, 7(1): 3–25.

Rock, F. (2001). 'The genesis of a witness statement', *Forensic Linguistics: The International Journal of Speech, Language and the Law*, 8(2): 44–72.

Rock, F. (2007). *Communicating rights: the language of arrest and detention*. Basingstoke: Palgrave Macmillan.

Rock, F. (2013). 'Every link in the chain': the police interview as textual intersection, in C. Heffer, F. Rock and J. Conley (eds) *Legal–lay communication: textual travels in the law*. Oxford: Oxford University Press, pp. 78–103.

Rock, F. (2016). Talking the ethical turn: drawing on tick-box consent in policing, in S. Ehrlich, D. Eades and J. Ainsworth (eds) *Discursive constructions of consent in the legal process*. Oxford: Oxford University Press, pp. 93–117.

Sacks, H. (1972). An initial investigation of the usability of conversational data for doing sociology, in D. Sudnow (ed.) *Studies in social interaction*. New York: Free Press, pp. 31–74.

Sarangi, S. and Candlin, C. (2003). Introduction. Trading between reflexivity and relevance: new challenges for applied linguistics, *Applied Linguistics*, 24(3): 271–285.

Stokoe, E. (2009a). 'Doing actions with identity categories: complaints and denials in neighbour disputes', *Text and Talk*, 29(1): 75–97.

Stokoe, E. (2009b). '"I've got a girlfriend": police officers doing "self-disclosure" in their interrogations of suspects', *Narrative Inquiry*, 19(1): 154–182.

Stokoe, E. (2014). 'The Conversation Analytic Role-play Method (CARM): a method for training communication skills as an alternative to simulated role-play', *Research on Language and Social Interaction*, 47(3): 255–265.

Stokoe, E. and Edwards, D. (2007). '"Black this, black that": racial insults and reported speech in neighbour complaints and police interrogations', *Discourse and Society*, 18(3): 337–372.

Tracy, K. (2009). 'How questioning constructs appellate judge identities: the case of a hearing about same-sex marriage', *Discourse Studies*, 11: 199–221.

Tracy, K. (2011). Identity work in appellate oral argument: ideological identities within a professional one, in J. Angouri and M. Marra (eds) *Constructing identities at work*. Basingstoke: Palgrave, pp. 175–199.

Van De Mieroop, D. (2007). 'The complementarity of two identities and two approaches', *Journal of Pragmatics*, 39(6): 1120–1142.

Vickers, C. (2010). 'Language competencies and the construction of expert–novice in NS-NNS interaction', *Journal of Pragmatics*, 42(1): 116–138.

Widdowson, H. (2000). 'On the limitations of linguistics applied', *Applied Linguistics*, 21: 3–25.

Zimmerman, D.H. (1992). The interactional organization of calls for emergency assistance, in P. Drew and J. Heritage (eds) *Talk at work: interaction in institutional settings*. Cambridge: Cambridge University Press, pp. 418–469.

Appendix

Transcription conventions

@@@	Laughter (each @ indicates 1 second's duration)
@funny@	Enclosed words said while laughing
=	Latching on
((something))	Unclear speech (the 'best guess' at what was said is included; if applicable, otherwise the number of inaudible syllables is noted or approximated)
//speech//	Overlapping talk
[coughs]	'Stage directions' and other extra-linguistic features
[W: yep]	Minimal feedback within extended turns
(.)	A pause of one second or less
(3.4)	A pause of the duration indicated inside the brackets in seconds
hhhhh	Outbreath

27

Language, gender and identities in political life
A case study from Malaysia

Louise Mullany and Melissa Yoong

Introduction

Researchers investigating gender identities in applied linguistics and sociolinguistics have stressed the need for the field to become more diverse by investigating cultural contexts outside the Western world (McElhinny 2008; Mills and Mullany 2011). With the exception of a handful of studies (Kaur 2005; Yoong 2017), there is little work on language and gender identities in Malaysia. Our decision to focus on the Malaysian political domain is motivated by the continued lack of women in positions of political power in the country. Latest figures from the Inter-Parliamentary Union (IPU 2015) show that Malaysia is ranked 113th out of 190 countries for the overall percentage of women in parliament. The current world average is 21.8 per cent – in Malaysia, it is 10.4 per cent.

An applied linguistics analysis can investigate how negative gender identity constructions, created and maintained through the language of the mass media, can be a contributing factor to the complex problem of the lack of women in positions of political power. Researchers have argued that investigations of 'women's media(ted) representation' are needed (Adcock 2010: 136), as the media play such a significant role in shaping and influencing contemporary politics. The UN Secretary-General (2010) reported that voters of both sexes prefer to elect men due to the prevalence of gender stereotypes, including those perpetuated by the media, and deeply ingrained beliefs against the ability of women to lead.

There are clear echoes of the 'double-bind' in such negative findings: researchers have found that women who occupy professional roles are often deemed as unsuitable if they display characteristics that are perceived to be too feminine, but they are also negatively evaluated if they display characteristics that are judged as too stereotypically masculine (see Mullany 2007; Baxter 2011). In Malaysia, 'the widespread stereotyping of women as followers and supporters rather than leaders' has significantly reduced women's opportunities 'to develop their leadership and decision-making skills in the public domain' (Committee on the Elimination of Discrimination against Women 2004: 24); the media continue to be a critical source of these gender stereotypes.

Constitutionally democratic, Malaysia has an ethnicised political system where ethnic considerations dominate political and electoral processes (Saravanamuttu 2001).

Demographically, Malays constitute the majority of the population (63.1 per cent), followed by Chinese (24.6 per cent) and Indian (7.3 per cent) minorities (Department of Statistics Malaysia 2013). Strengthened by ethnic polarisation in a political system which accommodates ethnic-based demands (Ng *et al.* 2006), Barisan Nasional (BN), a 13-member coalition of mostly ethnic-based and regional parties, including the United Malays National Organisation (UMNO), the Malaysian Chinese Association (MCA) and the Malaysian Indian Congress (MIC), has retained parliamentary control since the country gained independence from Britain in 1957.

The alternative to BN during the 13th Malaysian General Election held in 2013 was the multi-ethnic opposition coalition Pakatan Raykat (PR), comprising the Democratic Action Party (DAP), the People's Justice Party (PKR) and the Pan-Malaysian Islamic Party (PAS). Known for a more inclusive approach to politics (Schafer and Holst 2013), it gained 50.9 per cent of the popular vote in the 2013 General Election. However, it lost overall, as it gained only 40 per cent of the parliamentary seats (Boo 2014a).

In this chapter, we focus on a high-profile case from May 2014. Female candidate Dyana Sofya Mohd Daud was elected as the parliamentary candidate for the DAP in a by-election in the constituency of Teluk Intan. She faced male candidate Mah Siew Keong, the president of Gerakan, a non-ethnic-based, though predominantly Chinese, party of the BN coalition. We analyse data from two online media sources published at various stages of the two-week by-election campaign. We examine the ways in which Dyana constructs her own identities in online media sources authored by herself, alongside the manner in which journalists construct her identities. The analysis will demonstrate how gender and professional identity categories intersect with age, race, religion and sexuality to create particularly powerful subject positions, with the overarching aim of influencing the readers of these data sources, some of whom will be part of the voting public.

In the subsequent section, we provide an overview of the theoretical perspectives on language and identity that inform our case study. The methodology section then outlines the significance of Dyana's gender, race, religion and age within the Malaysian socio-political context, before defining the data set and our analytical approach. This is followed by a detailed lexico-grammatical analysis and discussion of the linguistic constructions of Dyana's identity and the influence this plays in her campaign to become an MP.

Overview

Theorising identities

In this chapter, we move away from analysing gender in isolation from other identity categories. Earlier research on language and gender identities has been critiqued for foregrounding gender as the most salient variable, with other potentially relevant social identity categories pushed into the background (see Mills and Mullany 2011). Instead, a much broader analysis of different intersecting identity features, which may be relevant at any one time, are analysed (see Block and Corona, this volume). In particular, we focus on the interplay between gender, age, sexuality, ethnicity and religion.

The approach we take to conceptualising identities is informed by the social constructionist approach to gender, namely that gender relations are socially constructed and upheld by powerful gender ideologies in any given society. These gender ideologies are created and maintained by power relations that have become naturalised – the core idea of Gramsci's (1971) notion of hegemony.

These power relations dictate a set of gendered norms and expectations that govern how women and men are evaluated within the societies in question. This is often referred to as 'the gender order' (see Eckert and McConnell-Ginet 2013; Jones, this volume), where certain ways of talking and acting are associated with cultural capital for women and men (Bourdieu 1999).

We are also influenced by Bucholtz and Hall's (2004, 2010) complementary approach, that identity is manifested through language, rather than pre-existent to language. A key principle in their work is the notion of indexicality, namely that language use is indexicalised with ideological beliefs, structures and values, i.e. the gender order. It is through these deeply ingrained beliefs, structures and values that gender inequality is constructed and maintained. This approach is valuable for identifying and examining how mass media discourses can create and maintain deeply ingrained beliefs, structures and values surrounding gender in the society under scrutiny.

We examine how gendered and professional identities are manifested through online media language, using linguistic analysis to critique discourses that 'systematically privilege men as a social group and disadvantage, exclude and disempower women' (Lazar 2005: 5). Marra and Angouri (2011) point out that Bucholtz and Hall's approach is advantageous when thinking about professional identity construction as it brings together the dynamic relationship between the self and society that has remained central to a constructionist understanding of identity. They cite Goffman to emphasise the important relationship between identity and self; of particular relevance to our case study is their emphasis on ideology, audience and role performance. They argue that the 'credibility of role performance relies on an audience's understanding of the acceptable/expected spectrum of performances and an individual's manner in enacting these' (Marra and Angouri 2011: 4). Arguably, what media producers are attempting during any election campaign is to tap into their intended audiences' understanding of the acceptable and expected spectrum of performances of political candidates and then endorse or critique these, depending upon the media source's ideological stance and the wider sociocultural practices operating where the media texts are produced.

Within language and gender studies, it has become commonly established practice to follow Foucault's (1972: 49) definition of discourse as 'practices that systematically form the objects of which they speak' in order to produce analyses of dominant gendered discourses that operate at an overarching, societal level (Sunderland 2004; Mullany 2007; Baxter 2011). By producing a political critique of gendered social practice and gender relations, the ultimate research goal is to bring about social transformation (Lazar 2005).

Identities, the professions and media discourse

Researchers including Iyer (2009) and Lazar (2009) have conducted feminist work examining gendered identity constructions in the discourses of the mass media in non-Western contexts. Iyer's study examines how the professional identities of successful women entrepreneurs are constructed. She analyses a range of dominant discourses in Indian media sources to highlight multiple subject positions, including the dominant discourses of patriarchy and femininity, as well as resistant discourses signalling that more positive social change is taking place. Lazar (2009) examines a dominant discourse of 'entitled femininity' in Singaporean media texts, emergent from the global neoliberal discourse of post-feminism. She makes a convincing case for the problematised nature of this discourse, which propagates the view that women can 'have it all' by working hard and celebrating being a woman through consumerism of beauty products.

It is well established that dominant discourses of femininity have been increasingly constructed in visual terms, with an ever stronger focus on the body (Jeffries 2007). Professional women often experience a tension between their sense of gendered (sexual) embodiment and their professional identity constructions, and the gendered body can be a significant obstacle for professional women to overcome. This is particularly the case in male-dominated professions such as politics (Mullany forthcoming).

In a review of studies of women's political representation in locations including India, South Africa, North America and Australia, Adcock (2010: 140) reports 'significant similarities in patterns of mediation (albeit inflected by cultural differences). Findings suggest female politicians often receive less coverage and are more likely to be described in gendered, sexualised, sex-stereotyped or negative terms than male counterparts.'

Within Western contexts, researchers, including Walsh (2001) and Shaw (2006), have documented numerous examples of how women politicians are evaluated first and foremost on mass media appraisals of their bodies and physical appearances rather than on their professional identities in terms of job role performance – the norm for their male counterparts and the norm for the successful role construction of being an effective politician. Wodak (2005) examines how gender identities are constructed, achieved and orientated in the European Parliament (EP). She observes three successful role constructions that women politicians can adopt: the 'assertive activist', the 'expert' and 'positive difference'/'special bird' (2005: 106). She argues that the EP provides a flexible political sphere as it is loosely organised, making it more open in comparison with other political systems.

In our analysis, we will focus on dominant and resistant discourses and examine the multiple identity categories that emerge. Drawing on Butler (1993), Jeffries (2007: 21) argues that 'every reference to the body will construct the body in some way'. Identifying dominant discourses of the body presents an effective means of analysing identity constructions and constructions of the self that affect women politicians in the Malaysian political context. By focusing on Dyana Sofya Mohd Daud, we will produce an analysis of how these dominant discourses affect the construction of her professional identity.

Methodology

We take a case study approach to analysing how Dyana was represented by online media outlets during the May 2014 by-election, as well as examining how she constructed her own identities. The analysis demonstrates that gender does not exist in a vacuum. Dyana's gender identity is represented in a way that simultaneously provides evidence of ideological positioning based on other salient aspects of her identity including race, religion, sexuality and age.

Malays who join the DAP, such as Dyana, tend to have their loyalty to their race and religion questioned because of the party's socialist roots, as well as the general perception that the DAP is a Chinese-centric party (Zubaidah 2014) despite its 'Malaysian Malaysia' slogan and the fact that it has fielded non-Chinese candidates in past elections (Lam 2014). If Dyana won, she would have been the DAP's first Malay woman MP and she would have defeated the ethnically Chinese president of a predominantly Chinese party in a Chinese-majority constituency (Chinese 42 per cent; Malay 38 per cent; Indian 19 per cent). This would have been a significant moment in a country with a long history of communal politics.

By standing for political office, Dyana was not adhering to the traditional prescription of female roles taken by Malay women. Since the end of World War II, women have actively participated in Malaysian (then, Malayan) politics, particularly through their involvement in the women's wings of political parties. Nevertheless, in post-independent Malaysia, such wings have occupied a subordinate status. The role of women politicians has mainly been to serve the interests of the parent party (Ng *et al.* 2006). In order to maintain political power, members of the women's wing of UMNO, Wanita UMNO, would engage

> the cultural approach of spreading goodwill through house-to-house visits to build rapport between local party members and the village community. Wanita UMNO members say they have to consistently project a caring face by visiting households for weddings, funerals, births and numerous other social events.
>
> *(Ibid.: 89)*

Islam is the official religion of the state, with Article 160 of the Constitution defining Malays as Muslim. Due to the resurgence of Islam in Malaysia, coupled with the Asian values/anti-Westernisation rhetoric commonly employed since the mid-1990s (Ng *et al.* 2006), women's bodies have become a visible ethno-religious symbol of the Malay-Muslim community: 'the embodied markers of boundaries that ideally guard against the intrusions of other races' (Ong 1995: 159). This includes adopting the veil and covering one's *awrat* (parts of the body required by Islam to be concealed). By not wearing a veil, Dyana does not conform to the 'hyper-ethnicised feminine identity (the veiled, modest, maternal Malay-Muslim woman)' (Ng *et al.* 2006: 23) that has taken pre-eminence over other 'legitimate' socially valued identities among Malay-Muslim women since the global revivalist Islamic movement in the 1970s, so much so that to not adopt this identity has become a limited option for many Malay women.

Nevertheless, Dyana was not the first non-veiled Malay-Muslim woman to stand for election. Her novelty also lay in her age: she was 27, while her male opponent was 53. In Malaysia, young women have been largely overlooked in politics. UMNO's young women's wing, Puteri UMNO, which literally translates as UMNO's Princesses, was formed in 2001 to mobilise Malay women under 40 into the party (Ng *et al.* 2006). However, it is still dubbed the 'baby wing' – it is not taken seriously by the party or the media. Members are evaluated based on their youth and looks and criticised for not 'maintaining a reasonable body weight [which] is important for those in the public eye' (Tan 2014a: 2). Within such a gendered political context, Dyana's candidature was seen as progressive by many media commentators.

In order to examine these issues further, data was collected from two online media sources between 15 and 31 May 2014. Dyana's by-election candidature was officially announced on 17 May 2014 for the by-election on 31 May. However, as rumours that Dyana would be the DAP candidate grew, she became the topic of news stories on online media, so we broadened the start date of the data collection to 15 May.

The decision to examine online media was motivated by the fact that some of the most significant issues relating to Dyana's identity constructions as a suitable professional to stand for political office emerged online. It was also chosen as detailed linguistic analysis of gender identity constructions in online media is an important yet currently under-researched area of investigation. The first data source is *The Star Online*. *The Star* is the most visited Internet news portal in Malaysia across all languages, with 1.07 million visitors a month (Kuppusamy 2013). *The Star*'s print edition and its exact digital replica are the most widely read mainstream English language news source in the country (Mahpar 2014). Therefore, the news articles in *The Star* arguably play an influential role in constructing the identities of women politicians for public consumption. The second data source is *The Rocket*, the official online news portal of the DAP. It contains articles on national issues and events as well as opinion pieces by members of the party, including articles purporting to be written by Dyana. This provided the opportunity to analyse how Dyana constructed her identities during the by-election.

The Star's main shareholder is the Malaysian Chinese Association (*Malaysian Insider* 2010) – one of the largest parties in the ruling BN coalition. The contrast between this media outlet and *The Rocket* provides an opportunity to assess how the two media sources represent Dyana's identities from opposing sides of the political spectrum.

We take a multilayered approach to examining how text producers construct identity categories and subject positions in Malaysian political media texts, by focusing on the following:

1 The media's construction of Dyana's identity through journalists' linguistic representations and evaluations of her;
2 Dyana's self-construction of her own identity via:
    (a) Her personal writing published in *The Rocket*;
    (b) Her reported speech (strategically) selected by media text-producers.

It is highly likely that her entries for *The Rocket* were authored in close conjunction with political script-writers and heavily edited/controlled. However, they are very clearly presented in the public domain as her own 'personal' views and reflections upon her own identity construction; as such, they are valuable data sources to include.

The data

The bikini scandal

We begin our analysis by focusing on the first incident to arise during the 17-day data collection period: the emergence of an online smear campaign. As rumours about Dyana's candidature were circulating (before she had been officially announced as the DAP candidate), this smear campaign began. The campaign and the linguistic strategies that emerged in Dyana's reactions to it raise a series of important issues surrounding dominant discourses of gender, sexuality and the body in Malaysian society, as well as simultaneously commenting on the intersection of the crucially important social identity variables of race and religion.

The smear campaign consisted of a poster with a head and shoulders photograph of Dyana on the left-hand side, juxtaposed with a photograph of a woman in a pink bikini on the right-hand side. No text accompanied the image, but the clear message was that the woman in the bikini, who bears a passing physical resemblance to Dyana, actually was Dyana. The poster first entered the public domain via Facebook, though the identity of the author of the original posting was never found. The poster image quickly went viral on social media. It immediately placed Dyana's character as a Malay-Muslim woman in question, since to wear a bikini – a Western garment that exposes the *awrat* – can be perceived as a rejection of the moral imperative to embody the values of race and religion, and was presumably aimed to discredit her as a suitable candidate to hold political office. The woman in the bikini in the photograph was soon identified as Filipina actress Pauleen Luna (Ng 2014). However, the smear campaign continued, and these photos were found during the campaign at a mosque as well as scattered in two Malay villages in the Teluk Intan constituency (Ahmad Fazlan Shah 2014; Boo 2014b).

Extract 1 documents Dyana's account in *The Rocket* of what happened as rumours of her candidature emerged:

Extract 1

My personal details were misused. My phone number was distributed and I have since been the target of hundreds of lewd messages. Another thing I have realised – Malaysian society is misogynistic!

(Dyana Sofya 2014)

Dyana places herself in the subject position of a victim of harassment and she evaluates this experience using the adjective 'misogynistic'. As this politically loaded term is clearly intertextually linked to resistant, feminist discourses, she is arguably attempting to construct a subject position that aligns her with a feminist identity, potentially building solidarity with women voters by signalling awareness of gender politics and the struggles faced by women across Malaysian society.

Extract 2

To tarnish my image further, there appears to be a photo of me allegedly wearing a bikini. While I think the Pinay actress in question is very attractive, I feel this really displays the level of guttural politics that our opponents would go to, especially against a female. Guys, please grow up.

(Dyana Sofya 2014)

In Extract 2 from later in the same *Rocket* article, Dyana distances herself from the photograph and constructs a 'good Malay-Muslim woman' identity in several ways. The strategic choice of the verb 'appears' and adverb 'allegedly' convey the implicature that she has not seen the photograph, reinforcing that this has nothing to do with her. In addition, this hedged expression – with reference to the photo – is not thematised. Instead, it is the dependent clause containing the claim that she has been a victim that is foregrounded. By explicitly commenting on the attractiveness of the 'Pinay actress', she indirectly establishes that it is the actress and not her in the photograph.

There are multiple issues at play here in terms of her presentation of self for her audience. Even as she dissociates herself from the overt, Westernised sexuality presented in the photo, Dyana seems to be simultaneously constituting a Westernised post-feminist identity via the dependent clause 'While I think the Pinay actress in question is very attractive'. In the West, post-feminist rhetoric represents female sexualisation as 'liberation from repressive societal codes' (Duits and Van Zoonen 2006: 112) and a form of empowerment even when this sexualisation is defined from the perspective of the heterosexual male (Redfern and Aune 2010). In her positive appraisal of Luna's exposed body via the postmodifier 'very attractive', she adopts the male gaze. Lesbianism is illegal in Malaysia, so a reading of same-sex attraction is highly improbable. She participates in the public scrutiny and evaluation of the objectified female body, constructing a self that is not prudish or opposed to bodily display (Attwood 2011; Press 2011).

The experienced 'gentleman' versus 'beauty' and youth

The second area that we focus on is a recurrent theme throughout the rest of the campaign. The identities of the two candidates were polarised by media text producers in terms of the older age and experience of Mah versus Dyana's youth and beauty. This can be observed through the dominant discourses of the body and the dominant discourses of femininity. To demonstrate how these subject positions are constructed, we analyse how journalists create these identity categories through specific linguistic choices and how Dyana responded to the construction of a heteronormative gendered 'beauty' identity.

Extract 3
Age versus looks in bellwether polls

> The camera loves Dyana Sofya. Her photograph was on the front pages of all the Chinese newspapers and she looked good in every single picture. The DAP candidate is definitely the prettiest face to ever appear in DAP … She is only 27, a lawyer and a relative greenhorn.
>
> *(Tan 2014b)*

The headline in *The Star* in Extract 3 immediately polarises 'age' and 'looks', where the two nouns are adopted as terms of reference, drawing on the audience's shared knowledge of Mah and Dyana respectively. Dyana's age is further emphasised by the descriptions of her as 'only 27' and 'a relative greenhorn', a term of reference chosen to indicate directly her lack of experience, despite being a political secretary for a prominent leader of the DAP for a number of years. This gives rise to the implicature that, since experience and youth are in direct opposition with each other, Dyana cannot possess both.

Further, the repeated emphasis on her looks and beauty sets the tone for the rest of the article, which constructs a youthful, pretty – and consequently – inexperienced and heavily feminised position for Dyana. The opening declarative 'The camera loves Dyana Sofya' invites readers to partake in the photographer's gaze of Dyana's body, the object of voyeuristic scrutiny, assessed positively via the verbal phrase 'looked good in every single picture'. This evaluation of her physical appearance, reinforced by the adverb 'definitely' and superlative 'prettiest', is followed by the metonymic use of 'face', constituting Dyana as a disembodied body part rather than a whole person.

Positioning her professional identity as 'a lawyer' between her age and the noun 'greenhorn' downplays her professional status, burying it between descriptors of youth and inexperience. Mah has yet to be mentioned explicitly, but already these strategies work to position him as the stronger candidate.

Extract 4

> Can Mah reverse the tide? Will he be able to persuade the voters to fall in love with him again even as everyone rushes to have a close-up look at his sweet young thing of a rival?
>
> *(Tan 2014b)*

In Extract 4 from later in the same *Star* article, the verbal phrase 'fall in love with him again' infers that voters had fallen in love with Dyana instead. The presupposition that this is due to Dyana's looks rather than her professional capabilities is built into the proposition in the dependent clause 'even as everyone rushes to have a close-up look at his sweet young thing of a rival'. The verb 'rushes' connotes excessive emotionalism, strongly implying that Dyana's popularity is not based on reason. The diminutive 'sweet young thing' further objectifies her and damages her credibility as a worthy opponent.

The title of *The Star* article in Extract 5, with its wordplay on 'huff', 'puff' and 'wolf', makes intertextual reference to a children's fairytale:

Extract 5
Dyana does not huff and puff about wolf whistles

> Although DAP's young and pretty Dyana Sofya gets wolf whistles when she hits the cer-
> amah trail, she is not slighted by this type of attention. 'I think voters are smart enough
> to know what I can deliver rather than to focus on my looks,' said the Teluk Intan parlia-
> mentary candidate.
>
> *(The Star 2014)*

Arguably this opening wordplay trivialises the whole news item, marking it out as humorous 'soft' news (Bell 1991), as opposed to an opportunity for Dyana's political identity to be
discussed through what she actually says in terms of political policies on her *ceramah* trail or an
opportunity to produce a critique of catcalling. Again, the premodifiers 'young' and 'pretty'
objectify her, drawing on dominant discourses of femininity and the body in terms of youth and
beauty. Her gendered body is foregrounded, instead of any focus on a professional identity construction. There is inclusion of a direct quotation from Dyana, which at least gives her a voice.
She attempts to flatter her voting public, describing them as 'smart', and downplays the effect of
the catcalling, claiming that it will have no effect on how seriously she is taken.

In Extract 6, from another article from *The Star*, a range of dominant discourses of femininity
can be observed:

Extract 6

> She used to love hanging out with her friends for a drink after work and going shopping.
> She is eloquent, has a ready smile and, most of all, is a good listener as she went about
> fielding questions from the journalists.
>
> *(Foong and Loh 2014)*

Dyana is first aligned with a stereotypical feminine identity through the verb phrase 'going
shopping', drawing on a discourse of consumer femininity. The next sentence also appears
to evaluate Dyana positively, but both verb phrases 'has a ready smile' and 'is a good listener'
indirectly index gendered discourse styles. They are a key part of the dominant discourse of
femininity, namely that women are stereotypically supportive conversationalists who listen well
and smile at appropriate places. This sits in direct opposition to the interactional expectations of
political discourse, where assertive, competitive, stereotypically masculine speech patterns are
the norm. While it could be argued that being a good listener is a desirable quality for politicians
when communicating with the public, in this case Dyana is complimented for listening well to
questions posed by the media, not for her answers, which are not mentioned. Moreover, the
adjective phrase 'most of all' re-emphasises her listening rather than oratory skills, positioning
her as a passive subject.

The final extract is taken from *The Star* on the day of the by-election:

Extract 7

> Barisan Nasional's 53-year-old Mah, who is also Gerakan president, versus DAP's 26-year-
> old Dyana, in today's Teluk Intan parliamentary by-election, dubbed by some as beauty
> versus gentleman.
>
> *(Foong 2014)*

The first contrastive structure represents Mah as the more experienced candidate: explicit references to their ages place Dyana in a weaker position in terms of professional experience, and the referent 'Gerakan president' highlights Mah's powerful political position, constructing him as an established leader with a strong professional identity. No professional identity category is used for Dyana. Additionally, the dichotomous phrase 'beauty versus gentleman' evaluates Dyana purely on her physical appearance, constituting her within the dominant male view of femininity. Mah is defined by the directly indexicalised gendered term 'gentleman', one with clear connotations of respectability and an entitlement to deference. The pronoun 'some' is a strategic use of vague language, so the author of this asymmetrical dichotomy remains ambiguous. Taken together, these strategies all convey Mah as the stronger contender.

Discussion

Although the by-election results were very close, Dyana lost what had been a safe DAP seat to Mah, who won by 238 votes. Just a year before, when Mah had also stood, the DAP had won by 7,313 votes. The successful DAP candidate on that occasion, Seah Leong Peng (whose death caused the by-election), was male, aged 48 and ethnically Chinese. Given these figures, it seems highly likely that Dyana's gender, age and ethno-religious identity worked against her, and that the mass media's negative construction of Dyana's gendered identity may well have played an influential role in affecting voters' choice in terms of candidate preference. In this section, we will first discuss how Dyana is represented by journalists in online media texts, before evaluating how she herself 'chooses' (we assume, jointly with her political script-writing team) to construct her identity as a young, female, Malay-Muslim lawyer who is aiming to increase her professional identity portfolio by becoming a member of the Malaysian parliament.

Our analysis of the extracts from *The Star* demonstrates how Dyana's gender is consistently foregrounded, in conjunction with a focus on her age, her body/appearance, her inexperience and her heterosexual desirability. In contrast, Mah is portrayed as the reliable, experienced choice, with the most desirable political qualities. His professional qualifications are highlighted, whereas Dyana's status as a lawyer and her previous political experience are either ignored or backgrounded by textual positioning. The male-as-norm discourse is clearly evident (Mullany 2011): Mah is presented as the candidate whose identity corresponds most closely with the expected professional identity construction of a successful politician, whereas Dyana is regarded as a novelty. In relation to the dominant discourses of the body, the representations of Dyana's beauty and attractiveness are, at a superficial level, presented as compliments. However, these are powerful ideological devices that serve to undermine her as a professional while simultaneously drawing attention away from her political policies, focusing instead on the personal, sexual and trivial. These portrayals of Dyana's identity in Malaysia's most popular English language newspaper accord with the broader, worldwide patterns identified by Adcock (2010), that women politicians are described in gendered, sexualised and sex-stereotyped terms compared with their male counterparts.

While the overwhelming focus on Dyana's youth and bodily appearance trivialises her professional identity as a serious candidate, age and sexuality are not the only significant sites of identity construction in this case study. The analysis demonstrates how gender also intersects with ethnicity and religion to create particularly powerful subject positions. The whole by-election was overshadowed by the smear campaign aimed to discredit Dyana's identity as a Malay-Muslim. The online platform of *The Rocket* provided her with space to articulate resistance and conceptualise her identity in alternative ways. As demonstrated in Extracts 1 and 2,

Dyana's linguistically constructed self-identity displays multiple facets, a move which can arguably be interpreted as evidence of political shrewdness.

On the one hand, she distances herself from the overt sexuality in the photograph to manifest a 'good Malay-Muslim woman' identity, which is crucial since there is a large Malay-Muslim population (38 per cent) in Teluk Intan, a fact that very likely motivated the bikini scandal. On the other hand, due to the multiracial composition of Teluk Intan, it is equally important to avoid being perceived as conservative while doing so, which she achieves by drawing on feminist and post-feminist discourses. Despite growing criticism by certain Malay-Muslim groups that feminism is anti-Islam (Zurairi 2013; Syed Jamal 2014), Islamic feminism is a growing political force in Malaysia (Segran 2013), so presenting herself as a Muslim feminist allows Dyana to leverage on the movement's 'progressive' image. However, a great deal of time is spent responding to negative gendered and sexualised portrayals of herself as a young Malay-Muslim woman, instead of constructing a legitimate political identity.

After the by-election, it was argued that religion and race had played a significant role in the DAP's loss. In a generally unpopular move among the country's non-Muslims, the Pan-Malaysian Islamic Party (PAS), which was part of the PR coalition during the by-election, had proposed to implement *hudud*, the Islamic penal code, in Kelantan, a northern state in Malaysia. Dyana's public declaration that she would vote against the implementation of *hudud*, despite being Muslim, may not have lessened the DAP's supporters' increasing discomfort with the party's alliance with PAS. The Islamic party, however, attributed her loss to her ethnicity, claiming that Chinese voters had preferred a Chinese candidate.

Issues for applied linguistics

The approach that we have taken here has a set of emancipatory aims, and this accords well with definitions of applied linguistics as a discipline designed to intervene, in this case in issues of professional identity construction (see Sarangi 2006). We have shown how an analysis of the multiple identity constructions of Dyana can be seen to have played a role in her failure to win a parliamentary seat. An applied linguistics analysis can reveal the specific linguistic mechanisms by which such damaging stereotypes and male-as-norm discourses, where women are seen as interlopers at best, are held in place by powerful ideological assumptions.

We argue that our case study has demonstrated a need for social transformation in terms of a democratisation of linguistic representations of identity in mediated political discourse. The fact that our findings accord with those from numerous countries worldwide (Adcock 2010) highlights that this is not a problem specific to Malaysia, but one that intersects with a more global pattern of complex gender politics. As applied linguists, we can play a role in attempting to bring about social change by raising awareness of these damaging discourses and by arguing that women candidates should not be focalised through their gender, through sexualisation or through the management and presentation of their bodies. Equal space should be given to political candidates of any gender to construct professional credentials and focus instead on political policies.

Summary

In this chapter we addressed the question of whether the language used in media discourse affects the very low numbers of women being elected to political positions in Malaysian politics.

The analysis focused on a recent by-election with two candidates, one female and one male. Analysing data taken from online media texts, we highlighted how constructions of gender identities intersect with a range of other relevant social identity categories including age, sexuality, ethnicity and religion at various points by text-producers.

We produced a detailed analysis of a range of discourses, including dominant discourses of the body, dominant discourses of femininity, and the 'male-as-norm' discourse, as well as resistant discourses, including feminist discourses. Our analysis demonstrated how Mah was constructed as the serious candidate, whereas Dyana's professional identity was diminished by focusing on her body and appearance, alongside dominant discourses of femininity focusing on trivial, non-political topics, including those of consumer femininity. Even where there were resistant discourses invoked by Dyana herself, these were in response to her positioning as a sexualised, gendered object. The usefulness of this analysis in terms of attempting to bring about social transformation via applied linguistics research was also discussed and evaluated.

Related topics

Positioning language and identity: poststructuralist perspectives; Language and ethnic identity; Identity in post-colonial contexts; Language and religious identities; Language and gender identities; Constructing age identity: the case of Mexican EFL learners; Straight-acting: discursive negotiations of a homomasculine identity; Intersectionality in language and identity research; Language and identity research in online environments: a multimodal ethnographic perspective; The future of identity research: impact and new developments in sociolinguistics.

Further reading

Iyer, R. (2009). 'Entrepreneurial identities and the problematic of subjectivity in media-mediated discourses', *Discourse and Society*, 20(2): 241–263. (This article critically examines representations of women entrepreneurs' identities in Indian print media.)

Lazar, M.M. (ed.) (2005). *Feminist critical discourse analysis*. Basingstoke: Palgrave. (This volume brings together empirical studies from a range of countries and institutional settings exploring the complex ways gender hegemony is discursively reinforced and challenged.)

Yoong, M. (forthcoming). 'Men and women on air: gender stereotypes in humour sequences in a Malaysian radio phone-in programme', *Gender and Language*, 11(1). (This article demonstrates how the use of humour in a Malaysian radio phone-in programme can uphold hegemonic power relations as well as repackage traditional stereotypes in innovative ways.)

References

Adcock, C. (2010). 'The politician, the wife, the citizen, and her newspaper', *Feminist Media Studies*, 10(2): 135–159.

Ahmad Fazlan Shah (2014). 'Dyana's "bikini" photos found at mosque', *The Rakyat Post* [Online]. Available at www.therakyatpost.com/news/2014/05/24/dyanas-bikini-photos-found-mosque

Attwood, F. (2011). Through the looking glass? Sexual agency and subjectification online, in R. Gill and C. Scharff (eds) *New femininities: postfeminism, neoliberalism and subjectivity*. Basingstoke: Palgrave Macmillan, pp. 203–214.

Baxter, J. (2011). *The language of female leadership*. Basingstoke: Palgrave.

Bell, A. (1991). *The language of news media*. Oxford: Blackwell.

Block, D. and Corona, V. (this volume). Intersectionality in language and identity research, in S. Preece (ed.) *The Routledge handbook of language and identity*. Abingdon: Routledge, pp. 507–522.

Boo, S. (2014a). 'Election 2013 lacked integrity, study finds', *The Malay Mail* [Online]. Available at www.themalaymailonline.com/malaysia/article/election-2013-lacked-integrity-study-finds

Boo, S. (2014b). 'Teluk Intan Malays denounce bikini smear campaign against Dyana', *The Malay Mail* [Online]. Available at www.themalaymailonline.com/malaysia/article/teluk-intan-malays-denounce-bikini-smear-campaign-against-dyana

Bourdieu, P. (1999). *Language and symbolic power.* Reprint edition. Cambridge: Polity Press.

Bucholtz, M. and Hall, K. (2004). 'Theorizing identity in language and sexuality research', *Language in Society*, 33: 469–515.

Bucholtz, M. and Hall, K. (2010). Locating identity in language, in C. Llamas and D. Watt (eds) *Language and identities.* Edinburgh: Edinburgh University Press, pp. 18–28.

Butler, J. (1993). *Bodies that matter: on the discursive limits of 'sex'.* London: Routledge.

Committee on the Elimination of Discrimination against Women (2004). *Consideration of reports submitted by states parties under article 18 of the Convention on the Elimination of All Forms of Discrimination against Women: combined initial and second periodic reports of states parties, Malaysia* [Online]. Available at www.un.org/womenwatch/daw/cedaw/reports.htm#m

Department of Statistics Malaysia (2013). *Population distribution and basic demographic characteristic report 2010* [Online]. Available at www.statistics.gov.my/index.php?r=column/cthemeByCat&cat=117&bul_id=MDMxdHZjWTk1SjFzTzNkRXYzcVZjdz09&menu_id=L0pheU43NWJwRWVSZklWdzQ4TlhUUT09#

Duits, L. and Van Zoonen, L. (2006). 'Headscarves and porno-chic: disciplining girls' bodies in the European multicultural society', *European Journal of Women's Studies*, 13(2): 103–117.

Dyana Sofya, M.D. (2014). 'They will not break me', *The Rocket*, 16 May [Online]. Available at www.therocket.com.my/en/they-will-not-break-me

Eckert, P. and McConnell-Ginet, S. (2013). *Language and gender.* 2nd edn. Cambridge: Cambridge University Press.

Foong, P.Y. (2014). 'D-day for Teluk Intan', *The Star*, 31 May [Online]. Available at www.thestar.com.my/News/Community/2014/05/31/Dday-for-Teluk-Intan-Daily-routine-of-the-people-will-be-back-to-normal-whether-it-is-Mah-or-Dyana

Foong, P.Y. and Loh, I. (2014). 'Dyana fights for what she believes in', *The Star*, 22 May [Online]. Available at www.thestar.com.my/News/Community/2014/05/22/Dyana-fights-for-what-she-believes-in-She-gives-up-a-career-in-corporate-sector-to-enter-turbulent

Foucault, M. (1972). *The archaeology of knowledge.* London: Tavistock.

Gramsci, A. (1971). *Selections from the prison notebooks* [Trans. Q. Hoare and G. Nowell-Smith]. New York: Lawrence and Wishart.

Inter-Parliamentary Union (IPU) (2015). *Women in national parliaments* [Online]. Available at www.ipu.org/wmn-e/classif.htm

Iyer, R. (2009). 'Entrepreneurial identities and the problematic of subjectivity in media-mediated discourses', *Discourse and Society*, 20(2): 241–263.

Jeffries, L. (2007). *Textual construction of the female body.* Basingstoke: Palgrave Macmillan.

Jones, L. (this volume). Language and gender identities, in S. Preece (ed.) *The Routledge handbook of language and identity.* Abingdon: Routledge, pp. 210–224.

Kaur, S. (2005). The performance of gender in online discussion boards. *BAAL/CUP Seminar: Theoretical and Methodological Approaches to Gender and Language Study*, University of Birmingham, UK, 18–19 November 2005.

Kuppusamy, B. (2013). 'The Star Online is a most visited news portal in Malaysia', *The Star* [Online]. Available at www.thestar.com.my/Business/Business-News/2013/10/17/Mainstream-media-dominates-online-scene-The-Star-Online-is-the-most-visited-news-portal-in-Malaysia/?style=biz

Lam, C.W. (2014). '*Malaysian seats' are the future of DAP and Pakatan.* Available at http://blog.limkitsiang.com/2014/06/02/malaysian-seats-are-the-future-of-dap-and-pakatan

Lazar, M.M. (ed.) (2005). *Feminist critical discourse analysis.* Basingstoke: Palgrave.

Lazar, M.M. (2009). 'Entitled to consume: post-feminist femininity and a culture of post-critique', *Discourse and Communication*, 3(4): 371–400.

Mahpar, M.H. (2014). '*The Star* remains top English daily', *The Star* [Online]. Available at www.thestar. com.my/Business/Business-News/2014/05/30/The-Star-remains-top-English-daily-Circulation-up-24-in-second-half-2013-with-17-rise-in-digital-edi/?style=biz

Malaysian Insider (2010). 'MCA buys *The Star* for RM1.28b from investment arm', *Malaysian Insider* [Online]. Available at www.themalaysianinsider.com/malaysia/article/mca-buys-the-star-for-rm1.28b-from-investment-arm

Marra, M. and Angouri, J. (2011). Investigating the negotiation of identity: a view from the field of workplace discourse, in M. Marra and J. Angouri (eds) *Constructing identities at work*. Basingstoke: Palgrave, pp. 1–16.

McElhinny, B. (ed.) (2008). *Words, worlds and material girls*. Berlin: Mouton.

Mills, S. and Mullany, L. (2011). *Language, gender and feminism: theory, methodology and practice*. Abingdon: Routledge.

Mullany, L. (2007). *Gendered discourse in the professional workplace*. Basingstoke: Palgrave Macmillan.

Mullany, L. (2011). 'Gender, language and leadership in the workplace', *Gender and Language*, 5(2): 1–10.

Mullany, L. (forthcoming). *The sociolinguistics of gender in public life*. Basingstoke: Palgrave.

Ng, C., Mohamad, M. and Tan, B.H. (2006). *Feminism and the women's movement in Malaysia: an unsung (r)evolution*. Abingdon: Routledge.

Ng, E. (2014). 'Bikini smear campaign against DAP's Dyana nothing but "gutter politics", say politicians, analysts', *Malaysian Insider* [Online]. Available at www.themalaysianinsider.com/malaysia/article/bikini-smear-campaign-against-daps-dyana-nothing-but-gutter-politics-say-po

Ong, A. (1995). State versus Islam: Malay families, women's bodies and the body politic in Malaysia, in A. Ong and M. Peletz (eds) *Bewitching women, pious men: gender and body politics in Southeast Asia*. Berkeley: University of California Press, pp. 159–194.

Press, A.L. (2011). 'Feminism? That's so seventies': girls and young women discuss femininity and feminism in *America's Next Top Model*, in R. Gill and C. Scharff (eds) *New femininities: postfeminism, neoliberalism and subjectivity*. Basingstoke: Palgrave Macmillan, pp. 117–133.

Redfern, C. and Aune, K. (2010). *Reclaiming the F word: the new feminist movement*. London: Zed Books.

Sarangi, S. (2006). The conditions and consequences of professional discourse studies, in R. Kiely, P. Rea-Dickens, H. Woodfield and G. Clibbon (eds) *Language, culture and identity in applied linguistics*. London: Equinox, pp. 199–220.

Saravanamuttu, J. (2001). 'The roots and future of the Reformasi Movement', *Communique*, 58(March–August).

Schafer, S. and Holst, F. (2013). 'Us versus them – Othering in the Malaysian elections and beyond (Part 1)', *New Mandala* [Online]. Available at http://asiapacific.anu.edu.au/newmandala/2013/08/26/us-versus-them-othering-in-the-malaysian-elections-and-beyond-part-1

Segran, E. (2013). 'The rise of the Islamic feminists', *Nation* [Online]. Available at www.thenation.com/article/177467/rise-islamic-feminists

Shaw, S. (2006). Governed by the rules? The female voice in parliamentary debates, in J. Baxter (ed.) *Speaking out: the female voice in public contexts*. Basingstoke: Palgrave, pp. 81–102.

Sunderland, J. (2004). *Gendered discourses*. Basingstoke: Palgrave.

Syed Jaymal, Z. (2014). 'Feminism is a facade to dishonour Muslim women, says Isma chief', *Malay Mail*, 27 April [Online]. Available at www.themalaymailonline.com/malaysia/article/feminism-is-a-facade-to-dishonour-muslim-women-says-isma-chief

Tan, J. (2014a). 'Puteri UMNO still learning to fly', *The Star* [Online]. Available at www.thestar.com.my/Opinion/Columnists/Analysis/?c=%7b51CF0A9C-923E-4D42-B2C0-185DA376DC7A%7d

Tan, J. (2014b). 'Age versus looks in bellwether polls', *The Star*, 19 May [Online]. Available at www.thestar.com.my/Opinion/Columnists/Analysis/Profile/Articles/2014/05/19/Age-versus-looks-in-bellwether-polls

The Star (2014). 'Dyana does not huff and puff about wolf whistles', *The Star*, 21 May [Online]. Available at www.thestar.com.my/News/Nation/2014/05/21/Dyana-does-not-huff-and-puff-about-wolf-whistles

United Nations Secretary-General (2010). *Review of the implementation of the Beijing Declaration and Platform for Action, the outcomes of the twenty-third special session of the General Assembly and its contribution to shaping a gender perspective towards the full realization of the Millennium Development Goals* [Online]. Available at http://un.org/ga/search/view_doc.asp?symbol=E/2010/4&Lang=E

Walsh, C. (2001). *Gender and discourse: language and power in politics, the church and organisations*. London: Longman.

Wodak, R. (2005). 'Interdisciplinarity, gender studies and CDA: gender mainstreaming and the European Union', in M. Lazar (ed.) *Feminist critical discourse analysis*. Basingstoke: Palgrave, pp. 90–114.

Yoong, M. (forthcoming). 'Men and women on air: gender stereotypes in humour sequences in a Malaysian radio phone-in programme', *Gender and Language*, 11(1).

Zubaidah, A.B. (2014). 'Malays joining DAP should be of concern to UMNO', *The Rakyat Post* [Online]. Available at www.therakyatpost.com/columnists/2014/10/04/malays-joining-dap-concern-umno

Zurairi, A.R. (2013). '"Allah" row an attempt to gauge Islam's limits, JAKIM officer alleges', *Malay Mail*, 19 October [Online]. Available at www.themalaymailonline.com/malaysia/article/allah-row-an-attempt-to-gauge-islams-limits-jakim-officer-alleges1

28

Straight-acting

Discursive negotiations of a homomasculine identity[1]

Tommaso M. Milani

Introduction

Recent sociological work on masculinity has highlighted how *straight-acting* has become somewhat of an obsession among non-heterosexual men across various sociocultural contexts (Clarkson 2005; Payne 2007; Eguchi 2009). Scholars, however, are in disagreement about how to interpret this phenomenon, which is in many ways reminiscent of those traits of hegemonic masculinity that are prerequisites for a heterosexual man to be viewed as 'normal' (Connell 1995).

What can applied linguistics offer to this debate? As the contributions in this volume illustrate, applied linguistics is a diverse and developing field that intersects with sociology and anthropology, as well as gender and queer studies, contributing to, as well as borrowing from, these associated fields. Through detailed linguistic analysis, this chapter teases out the ambiguous performances of homomasculinity, and thus seeks to offer a rigorous textual analysis of the ways in which gender and sexuality are discursively constructed and negotiated. Because of the hybrid methodology as well as the queer heuristic that underpins it, however, the chapter perhaps represents a challenge to institutional requirements that we produce strictly delimited disciplinary identities within research.

Against this backdrop, the aim of this chapter is to investigate performances of 'straight-acting-ness' both in online and offline environments. More specifically, two data sets will be analysed:

1   A large corpus of profiles downloaded from meetmarket, a South African online community for men who are looking for other men; and
2   In-depth, semi-structured interviews with 10 white, middle-class South African men about their engagement with meetmarket and other social networking sites.

For contextual purposes, it should be highlighted that the choice of meetmarket is not random. This online community is part of a website – Mambaonline – that defines itself as:

> South Africa's premier (and most stylish) gay lifestyle portal. Mambaonline.com is aimed at the 18-to-45-year-old urban and trendsetting Internet connected gay male. It is important to highlight that South Africa constitutes an interesting case in point of social transformation.
>
> *(Mambaonline Facebook page)*

Hyperbolic overtones aside (e.g. 'premier', 'most stylish'), the description of Mambaonline encapsulates the 'politics of aspiration' (Nuttall, 2004), as has been pointed out by scholars in other arenas of South African consumer culture in a time of post-apartheid social transformation (see in particular Stroud and Mpendukana 2009). As Nuttall (2004: 243) explains it, the politics of aspiration refers to

> [h]ow people seek to transform themselves into singular beings, to make their lives into an oeuvre that carries with it certain stylistic criteria [and also refers] to the emergence of explicit forms of selfhood within the public domain and the rise of the first person singular within the work of liberation.

The manifestations of this individualistic project have been illustrated by Stroud and Mpendukana (2009) in a series of analyses of commercial signage in the streets of the township of Khayelitsa outside Cape Town. These public texts, the authors assert, embody forms of consumerist 'stylizations of the self' (Foucault 1989) that promise social betterment through identifications with specific products and the lifestyles associated with them. In this sense, Mambaonline and meetmarket are not particularly dissimilar from the commercial signs in Khayelitsa in that they capitalise on Internet users' aspirations to identify with, and be part of, a 'trendsetting' discourse, which, in this specific case, has overtly gendered and sexual connotations.

In sum, meetmarket is a key discursive space in South Africa where men, irrespective of racial categorisation and social class, can come into mutual contact to express their desire for other men. In order to do so, they mobilise different semiotic resources to style themselves and their desired 'Other' in a particular fashion, giving rise to an array of different identities, which are differentially valued in this virtual marketplace.

The public visibility of same-sex desire on meetmarket needs to be located in a context where, since the end of the state-sanctioned system of discrimination commonly known as apartheid, equality on the grounds of race, gender, sexual orientation and religious beliefs has been enshrined in the South African constitution. However, attitudes to non-normative sexual and gender performances are not unanimously positive throughout the country. Moreover, in its well-meaning attempt to recognise and thus empower all sexual minorities, the constitutional recognition of equal rights on the basis of sexual orientation did not benefit everyone in the same way but followed specific racial and social class patterns. Such intersectional splits appeared most forcefully during Johannesburg Pride in 2012. There the activist group One in Nine performed a die-in protest in order to critique what they saw as the failure on the part of the middle-class white organisers of Pride to acknowledge and critique the phenomenon of so-called corrective rape – the violence against black bodies that do not conform to sexual and gender normativity.

Having offered the social context in which the data under investigation in this chapter has been produced, I want now to move on to give an overview of queer theory, the heuristics that inform this chapter. I then present the methodology through which the data was collected. The chapter finishes with an analysis of both online profiles and interview transcripts, and a discussion of the ambiguous politics of homomasculinity.

Overview

Together with the notions of discourse and ideology, identity has become one of the most discussed concepts in the social sciences (see Preece, this volume). At the risk of falling into undue oversimplifications, identity has been conceptualised mainly in two ways in sociolinguistics and applied linguistics:

1   As a stable, unified core with ontological status that can explain a particular linguistic behaviour (e.g. women use more tag questions; women's speech contains fewer expletives); or
2   As a fluid, multifaceted social construct which is itself in need of explanation (see Joseph, this volume).

Informed by the latter, there is now a vast body of work illustrating the ways in which individuals employ a variety of meaning-making resources (i.e. spoken and written language, gestures and other visual modalities) through which they perform different, competing identities that have specific purposes in particular contexts. Put simply, this research illustrates that identity is not a quality one has but emerges through discursive action. Moreover, identity is never in the singular, but is always a compounded nexus of intersecting social axes.

An interest in teasing out how identities materialise discursively should, however, not make us lose sight of the troubles that come with identity. This argument has been made by queer theorists, for whom 'identity categories tend to be instruments of regulatory regimes, whether as the normalizing categories of oppressive structures or as the rallying points for a liberatory contestation of that very oppression' (Butler 1991: 13–14). Identities then are inevitably caught up in power relations even when they are mobilised for emancipatory purposes, such as in the case of sexual minority movements. This is a type of activism that has used specific identity labels – 'gay' and 'lesbian' – as standpoints for the achievement of legal enfranchisement.

Why is this problematic? Political theorist Nancy Fraser (1995) would argue that the issue lies in the 'affirmative' character of a politics that dispenses benefits to individuals by virtue of belonging to a minority group that share a common and single identity. For affirmation can in the best of cases only produce a temporary recalibration of power inequalities, but does not lead to a more radical transformation of the status quo (Fraser 1995; see also Stroud 2001 for a similar point in the context of linguistic minorities). In brief, through identity politics, power is partially reshuffled, but the system of inter-group divisions remains unchallenged while intra-group divisions are obscured.

Moreover, when minorities seek acknowledgement from dominant institutions, their credibility is measured against the benchmark of norms and values shared by the majority (Munt 2008: 25). So those minority individuals who conform to dominant sensibilities will accrue more symbolic value than those who 'deviate' from them. In this way, differentials within one and the same minority group are created in the name of recognition.

So what to do with such an impasse? Queer theorists do not dismiss identity categories altogether, not least because 'people do self-identify and are labelled by others as male, female, gay, lesbian or heterosexual, etc. These identities "exist" within discourse, shaping the minds, bodies and lives of many people' (Baker 2008: 194). What is advocated is sensitivity to the ambiguities that identity categories bring with them, as well as their complicities in entwining privilege with oppression (Nash 2008: 12).

Partly due to its disciplinary origins within literary and cultural studies, queer theory has not had a breakthrough in sociolinguistics and applied linguistics until relatively recently (see Livia and Hall 1997, Baker 2008 and Motschenbacher 2011 for useful overviews; see also Pennycook 2001; Nelson 2006; Gray, this volume). And perhaps because of the same disciplinary belonging, studies informed by queer theory have been more qualitative in nature, thus 'making quantitative research notable by its absence' (Browne and Nash 2010: 11; see Baker 2008 and Milani 2013 for exceptions). Some scholars would go as far as to endorse a paradigmatic stance according to which

> a queer heuristic [...] *must* qualitatively account for its object of inquiry. This is not because of an implicit phobia of numbers but because any attempt to quantify homosexuals, heterosexuals, etc., assumes a commonality between the individual's desires and lives that is suspect. Qualitative approaches have a better chance of accounting for queer experiences in the same terms as the actual people living these experiences.
>
> *(Warner 2004: 321, emphasis added)*

Indeed, one of the basic tenets of queer theory is that we should be wary of too facile conflations between sexual processes (e.g. a man desiring and/or having sex with another man) and sexual identities (gay). This is because forms of categorisation and enumeration on the basis of sexual mores are the products of historical processes that work in the interest of modern state power (Foucault 1978). Nevertheless, a suspicion of numbers, especially when employed for the purpose of state statistics, does not necessarily entail that 'queer epistemologies, methodologically, require the use of qualitative methods only, or must always contest traditional and conventional techniques' (Browne and Nash 2010: 12). For a categorical dismissal of quantitative methodologies is inherently at variance with the anti-normative attitude of any queer enterprise. A compromise can be reached by recognising that '[j]ust as queer theory aims to deconstruct a range of different identity constructions, so, too, are the range of possible sources of data and analytical methods available to queer theorists' (Baker 2008: 215), including quantitative approaches such as corpus-based discourse analysis, to which I will now turn.

Methodology

In light of the critical deconstructionist agenda of queer theory outlined in the section above, the case study presented in this chapter is informed by the following research questions:

1 How do the members of meetmarket represent themselves and their object of desire?
2 Which identities are valorised and which ones are devalued?
3 How are these identities perceived and understood by other men looking for other men who browse these profiles?

These questions will be answered with the help of an innovative methodology that brings together (1) a corpus-assisted discourse analysis of meetmarket profiles with (2) a discourse analysis of interviews with South African men who desire other men.

Let us begin with explaining how corpus-assisted discourse analysis works. Corpus linguistics 'utilizes bodies of electronically encoded text, implementing a more quantitative methodology' (Baker 2006: 1). The size of corpora can range widely from a few thousand to several billion tokens and can include texts from one or several different genres. When the research project on which this chapter is based started in June 2010, meetmarket contained approximately 14,000 profiles. Because of time and financial constraints, it was impossible to analyse this community in its entirety. Therefore, I decided to concentrate on a sample that included the largest number of profiles in one geographical area, namely the 4,738 profiles registered under the location of Gauteng, Johannesburg. Two research assistants downloaded the textual sections of each profile over a period of three months and saved them as electronic text files (.txt); all screen names were deleted and substituted with a numerical code. This generated a corpus of 428,174 words.

Because of their dimensions, corpora are typically analysed with the help of computer software (e.g. WordSmith Tools) in order to compute the following information:

1   Wordlists – which give frequencies of both function and content words;
2   Concordances – a list of the contexts in which a particular word is used;
3   Collocations – pairs of words that consistently occur near each other; and
4   Keywords – which specific words characterise a corpus versus another, usually larger, corpus.

In the specific case of the data presented in this chapter, the focus is exclusively on concordances (see Milani 2013 for a more comprehensive analysis of wordlists, concordances and collocations). At this juncture, it is also important to highlight that the data was tagged using the identifiers <self>, </self>, <other> and </other> in order to be able to conduct more precise corpus linguistic counts of concordances and collocates related to forms of 'Self- vs Other' identification (Baker 2003).

Why use corpus linguistic tools for discourse analysis? According to Baker (2006), the greatest advantage offered by corpus linguistics is that it helps to reduce researcher bias. This is not to say that the quantitative results generated by corpus-linguistic software speak for themselves. An element of subjectivity is always present because a researcher needs to make sense of numerical information. However, corpus-based investigations can be helpful to triangulate qualitative analyses by adding a quantitative layer that buttresses a researcher's analysis of a specific social phenomenon or a conclusion drawn upon very small data sets (Baker *et al.* 2008).

Critics of quantitative approaches might counter-argue that the benefits of corpus linguistics are limited to facilitating the analysis, but the overall understanding of discourse patterns can be produced with qualitative techniques on their own. However, it would not have been possible in this research project to read through over 4,000 online profiles in the attempt to find recurrent patterns. Furthermore, the technological affordances of corpus-linguistic software flag up certain categories that would not have immediately been obvious to an analyst's eyes. Yet, numbers can hardly reveal anything about discursive nuances in specific contexts of usage. Therefore, it is necessary to look in greater detail at a subset of collocations and concordances.

In sum, quantitative techniques of a large set of written data such as the online profiles analysed in this chapter give us insights into which identities are more or less frequent and which ones are more or less valued in the specific data set. What remains uncharted, however, is how such identities are understood, reproduced and possibly contested by the people who browse those profiles. Hence a textual analysis of a corpus of written data can be enhanced with individual or focus group interviews of website users. In this way, we can achieve a more multifaceted picture of how identities are used, understood and negotiated in a specific context at a particular moment in time.

In such a spirit, in-depth, semi-structured interviews were undertaken with 10 middle-class, white English and/or Afrikaans speaking, South African men about their engagement with meetmarket and other social networking sites. Taken together, the interviews generated approximately 15 hours' recorded material, which was then transcribed using a simplified technique that reflects hesitations, pauses and intonation contours (see Appendix for transcription conventions). The interviews were conducted in English and concentrated on the meaning of some of the main identity categories that had emerged from the quantitative textual analysis. The reasons for the choice of this specific group of participants were manifold. All the participants had formed part of my circle of acquaintances for the last five years. While such a connection could be criticised for bringing a personal bias into the research, it allowed me to gain deeper ethnographic insights into these men's lives and beliefs beyond the relatively limited space of the actual interviews (see Leap 1996). Moreover, all the men whom I interviewed had spent their childhood living under apartheid but had first-hand experience of the transition to a democratic South Africa during adolescence and early adulthood. As such, they can be viewed as 'men of social transformation'. Unlike many of their peers who strongly bemoan post-apartheid conditions, they could be defined as 'liberal' insofar as they all consistently showed positive attitudes towards the main tenets of the new dispensation, embracing a multiracial South Africa. They would also generally not pronounce overt racist utterances, nor would they make easy racist jokes or gaffes (see Hill 2008). When talking about sex, however, nearly all these men strongly disavowed the possibility of engaging in sexual relationships with black men.

The data

Concordance data

The quantitative element of the study revealed that grammatical words occupied the top position in the word list. This is a fairly familiar result in corpus analytical investigations. However, as Baker (2006: 100) notes, function words do 'not always reveal much of interest' because it is difficult to extrapolate discourses from them. Content words are instead the most common entry points for the enterprise of discourse digging. A closer look at content words showed that the lemmas GUY and MAN occupied the first and third place in the top-10 nouns in the corpus. Furthermore, not only were *straight/str8* and its compound *straight/str8-acting* the most common adjectives through which the members of meetmarket presented themselves (N: 218) and described their object of desire (N: 196); these qualifiers also showed a very strong collocation with GUY and MAN.

It goes without saying that the higher frequency of a word does not tell us much about its meaning; nor do frequencies alone reveal whether a word is the carrier of positive or negative connotations in the corpus in question. In order to understand the evaluative aura that words carry, it is important to explore their contexts of use, their collocational patterns with other words, as well as the 'perspectivation strategies' (Wodak 2001: 73) – ironic, serious or otherwise.

So what is the meaning of straight/str8-acting on meetmarket? Is it positively or negatively valued? Is this form of Self and Other-identification in collusion with dominant discourses of masculinities? Or is it a resistance to them? A closer look at the concordances below will help to shed light on these questions.

Table 28.1 Concordances of the straight-acting Self

1	**Str8 acting** Gay couple am 39 my partner is 33. We do enjoy li
2	I am a **straight acting** guy brown hear blue eyes who enjoys a lot of
3	Yung blk **str8 acting** dude Celebrity: JayZ, Anthony Hamilton, Lira. TV
4	Genuine romantic I'm an easy-going, **straight acting** handsome gay guy
5	IM BLK **STRAIGHT ACTING** BOTTOM GUY honest loving caring .NAUGHTY.adve

6   **straight acting** and looking good looking, friendly person who

7   **Straight acting** in the closet. Opreg en eerlik! Celebrity: Opr

8   AM A 23YRS SLIM, TALL GOOD LOOKING BLACK GUY **STR8 ACTING** FUN AND SWEET PERSON AM WHAT YOU SEE

9   w to this world, so still finiding my way around. I'm a **shy straight acting** guy who is brutally honest and i dont take s

10   persuit, My goal is to strive towards it. Where to start?? **Straight acting**, lead a balanced and systematic lifestyle, n

11   mehow I am interested in doing nice things to sexually. I'm **straight** looking & **acting**, versatile, but if you are, then

12   Non-scene, **str8 acting**, good looking, down to earth guy, love the outdoo

13   Goodlooking **straight acting** lad Muscular goodlooking **straight acting** man

14   Instead, I have grown into a down2earth **straight acting**/straight looking closeted metrosexual who paradoxically happ

15   Dinks and dents included I am boringly normal. I'm not **straight acting** … I don't act. What you see is what you get!

Table 28.2 Concordances of the straight-acting Other

1   m not looking for fats, fems or queens. A well looked after **str8 acting** man who will sweep my feet off the ground. Cauca

2   **Straight acting**, straight looking guy, no fems please. Independant. Age betwee

3   Please **straight acting** guys only!! I want a guy who is intelligent a

4   cute or ugly guys, who are intelligent and must be very very str8 looking and **str8 acting** as. 8 looking and str8 acting

5   y around. Not into intense gay activity (no f*cking)!~ into **str8 (acting)** men for clean fun - nothing intense! e!

6   looking for friendly, **straight acting** & looking, down to earth black, coloured or i

7   m all the love in the world. I am looking for a fun loving, **straight acting** and open-minded man. He must also be well-sp

8   BLACK, mature, discrete and a good dose of Wit and humour. **Straight acting** and masculinity is necessary. Strong charact

9   - because then the sex is damn good!! Looking for a decent, **STRAIGHT acting** man who's going to be there for me as I am t

10   ing areas the better.pliz no slims,fems or queens.want very **straight acting** person.da person must be in da closet

11   I am looking for someone that: has the same needs as me **Str8 acting** guy who enjoys feeling his way around my body and

12   Friends Anyone I would love to meet other **straight acting** guys for friendship, and maybe something more

13   thoughtful, respectful, friendly, funny … who accepts me. **Straight acting** please, as I'm attracted to masculinity. to

14   d liaison or whatever we both feel comfortable with. Only **straight** looking & **acting** lean, defined or muscled guys betw

15   your average gay guy, even the ones that claims to be very **str8 acting** … are'nt really, so stop kidding yourselves … a

Lines 1–14 in Tables 28.1 and 28.2 seem to suggest that displaying straight-acting traits carry a positive value-judgement on meetmarket. This evaluative aura is testified further by the collocations of straight-acting with typically positive traits such as 'good-looking' and 'handsome'. Moreover, unlike the case of the gay and lesbian personal advertisements in the UK analysed by Thorne and Coupland (1998: 247) in which the expression '100% straight [...] is identifiable to a gay readership as ironic', the members of meetmarket seem to be generally serious in defining themselves and their object of desire in these terms. There are however a few exceptions to this general trend, to which I will return below.

It is important to clarify that 'straight-acting' is a complex category that has less to do with (heterosexual) identities and practices alone than with a specific nexus of gender and sexuality, namely the kind of 'attributes stereotypically linked with heterosexual men, which might include the equally slippery "masculine", perhaps "manly" and "butch", but also what these attributes are often taken to oppose, such as "feminine", "queeny" and "camp"' (Payne 2007: 526; see also Clarkson 2005; Eguchi 2009). That the valorisation of masculinity goes hand in hand with an overt disavowal of femininity is manifest on meetmarket in the negative connotations surrounding the adjectives *feminine* and *fem/fems*, of which the cluster 'NO FEMS' is an obvious example.

Thus, the promotion of straight-actingness might suggest that meetmarket is characterised by 'hegemonic homosexuality' (Baker 2008: 176) in that 'the most highly-valued identity is traditional heterosexual hegemonic masculinity or an approximation to it'. One could go as far as to suggest that we are witnessing here the manifestation of a form of internalised homophobia, or 'sissyphobia' as Bergling (2001) has called it.

Crucially, it has been pointed out that '[s]traight acting means more than being masculine: it also means to be undetectable as a gay person' (Phua 2002: 186). In this sense, men who desire or identify as 'straight-acting' are drawing upon a heteronormative discourse that implicitly promotes heterosexuality as the acceptable norm in the public space, while devaluing homosexuality as an inappropriate identity not to be displayed (see Eguchi 2009). From a political point of view, the valorisation of a straight-acting identity could be interpreted as a sign of an assimilationist trend through which South African men might seek to aspire to gain acceptance by conforming or approximating to a heterosexual masculine script (see Clarkson 2005). To this, Sonnekus (2009) would add a racial dimension. His analysis of mainstream gay visual culture would suggest that straight-acting homo-masculinity is overlayered with an exclusively white coating.

The appreciation of masculine attributes in meetmarket, with the concomitant stigmatisation of male femininity, however, should not lead us to draw facile conclusions about South African homosexual men's collusion in the workings of male hegemony. Neither should too absolute links be posited between a straight-acting identity and whiteness in South Africa. Analogous to other contexts studied in the literature (see Thorne and Coupland 1998; Chesebro 2001; Baker 2008), the emphasis on masculinity on meetmarket could be read as a way through which South African men desiring other men contest widespread societal discourses that stereotype them as intrinsically effeminate, discourses which also contribute to making the very notion of homo-masculinity a contradiction in terms. Second, the fetishisation of masculinity could be interpreted as a form of objectification that reduces hegemonic masculinity to a commodity to be consumed either virtually (just by reading an advert or profile) or really (by having sex) (see Baker 2008: 177). Third, those macho personas so cherished online might just remain a chimera to long for but do not necessarily coincide with the gender performances of the actual people with whom the men on meetmarket have sex or engage in a long-lasting relationship (see Baker

2005; Eguchi 2011). Fourth, the collocations with both 'white' and 'black' in the corpus do not warrant a reading of 'straight/str8' as a bearer of racially uniform connotations on meetmarket.

Lastly, straight-actingness is not always unambiguously championed on meetmarket. Line 15 in Table 28.1 is one of the few cases (N: 7) indicating an outright rejection of straight-acting as a characteristic of self-identification. This does not mean, however, that masculinity is fully discarded here. Quite the contrary – the writer dismisses a straight-acting identity on the basis of its theatrical nature of a 'performance'. By proxy, the writer's manhood – whatever this might be – is portrayed as a 'real', perceivable and verifiable trait ('What you see is what you get').

By the same token, line 15 in Table 28.2 illustrates another ambivalent relation to the valorisation of masculine attributes – this time, in relation to a prospective partner. Here, the ambivalence is the effect of a humorous 'perspectivation' (Wodak *et al.* 1999; Baker *et al.* 2008), that is, a tongue-in-cheek attitude (e.g. Heywood 1997; Thorne and Coupland 1998) on the part of the writer vis-à-vis the propositional content of the utterance (see Benwell 2004, 2005 and Milani 2013 for a more detailed qualitative analysis).

Interview data

An ambiguous attitude towards straight-acting and masculinity more broadly also emerged very clearly in the interview data. Unlike the online profiles, which tended to be short and therefore did not go into details about what straight-acting entails, in the interviews the participants unpacked more clearly what kind of qualities this identity category encompasses.

While there was no complete agreement among the interviewed men about what being straight-acting involved, certain qualities emerged from the data. Some stated that it was indicative of not 'being out' as a gay man, of still being 'in the closet'. They also indicated that it comprised (1) certain qualities of voice – a dark timbre, and low pitch; (2) specific postures ('standing around with a finger in the pants', 'crossing one's legs'); or (3) *ex negativo* by referring to what it is not, namely through the absence of specific bodily and behavioural traits that are perceived as effeminate ('being flamboyant', 'having limp wrists', 'waving one's hands too much', 'clutching an imaginary pearl necklace around the neck'). Only occasionally was straight-actingness unreservedly espoused or dismissed outright, *inter alia* through a questioning of the 'acting' part of this compound. As Mark[2] puts it:

Extract 1

```
1   Mark:   It's the acting part I don't like about it. It's like you should
2           be comfortable with who you are. And that's how it should
3           proceed from there. If you are like having to put on like a
4           (...) I could, I could also be straight-acting pretty much by
5           pulling my shoulders back, and lower my voice a bit and say
6           'hey dude' ((lowers his voice)) and standing around with
7           my finger in my pants <laughs> that would also make me
8           straight-acting.
```

Similar to what we saw earlier on line 15 in Table 28.2, what is questioned here is the performance aspect of straight-acting. Once again through 'denaturalization' (Bucholtz and Hall 2005), an identity is held up as being inauthentic, and therefore dismissed as unreal (line 1). If one concurs with poststructuralist epistemologies that there is no such thing as an 'inner' identity that an individual has, but all identities are ultimately performances, what we see here is a discursive process whereby some identity performances are presented as more 'authentic' and 'real' than others.

Like Mark, most of the men in the study expressed more or less strong reservations against this category. Unlike him, however, they also at some point showed a fascination with – or even attraction to – the qualities connected to masculinity, recasting femininity into the domain of abjection (Bourdieu 1998). The extract below, taken from an interview with Michael, who identifies himself as 'radically queer', is a representative case in point.

Extract 2

```
 9  Tommaso:  Are you attracted to the qualities which go under the
10            label straight-acting?
11  Michael:  Less than ever, less than than ever. Definitely when I
12            was younger, absolutely. But for me it wasn't
13            straight-acting, it was straight that I was attracted to.
14            For me straight-acting gay men are sort of
15            suspicious to me. I'm like what are you hiding?
              [...]
16            When I was younger I was attracted to straightness
17            not like straight gayness like actual straightness.
18            I still often fall for straight men. I would always pick
19            a straight man over a gay man.
              [...]
20  Tommaso:  Why?
21  Michael:  I don't know. They were the men that didn't love me
22            at school. They were the boys who were more good-looking.
              [...]
23            Straight-acting gay people especially the ones who
24            say about themselves seem to really be trying to
25            produce some really sad copy, some really really sad
26            imitation.
```

What emerges most patently here is how heterosexual masculinity is the utmost object of Michael's desire. Through 'denaturalization' (Bucholtz and Hall 2005), straight-actingness is dismissed as something that is not real (lines 25 and 26); it is portrayed as a copy of, or a bad approximation to, an original, 'authentic' form of masculinity, one that paradoxically can never be really attained because it can only be embodied by heterosexual men (lines 16–19). In a later part of the interview, Michael does acknowledge that he finds male femininity attractive, but he hedges his standpoint by stating:

Extract 3

```
26  Michael:  It depends on how much or how uhm like a sort of
27            comfortableness like you know I have no problems
28            sitting however I want [...] a sort of balance, a sort of
29            natural, uhm, natural. I know don't want to think
30            about effeminate people. Part of me like just like
31            don't find them attractive because they are not
```

32	masculine enough but more than that uhm most of
33	I don't know they also feel like sometime like a cliché
34	like kind of homonormative it's like they are
35	producing themselves as a cartoon maybe I don't
36	know but also I don't underestimate the stress and
37	trauma and the need that some of those people have
38	to do what they have done […]. I don't devalue that
39	some people have found their ways to make the
40	world livable.

The hesitations ('uhm' – lines 26, 29 and 32; 'I don't know' – lines 33 and 35–36) are sympto-matic here of an uneasiness with settling on a definite position on the matter. On the one hand, Michael's self-identification as a 'radical queer' seems to be playing at the back of his mind, reminding him that it is controversial to completely reject femininity. On the other hand, there is a clear acknowledgement that femininity is not attractive because it is the opposite of mas-culinity. For Michael, the problem lies again in a perceived inauthenticity that turns feminine behaviour in gay men into an exaggerated parody of itself ('a cartoon'). That being said, the societal role of those who do not conform to masculine norms is acknowledged.

Having presented the data, in the next section we turn to its relevance for applied linguists who are interested in studies of language and identity.

Discussion

This chapter has illustrated how the men on meetmarket reproduce dominant forms of mas-culine identification for the 'Self' and the desired 'Other'. Thus, they seem to hyper-conform to normative ideas about what counts as a 'real man'. In doing so, however, they might not be paying lip service to heterosexual patriarchy but are actually shaking it by making an oxymoron – homo-masculinity – a visible reality. As Ratele forcefully remarks about homosexual practices in African contexts, '[m]en who are attracted to men (or both), […] *by the mere fact of their exist-ence*, question and potentially mess up the power […] of ruling heterosexual masculinity' (2011: 417, emphasis added). By the same token, the men on meetmarket make male same-sex desire visible and heard. In so doing, they are countering oppressive homophobic forces that seek to silence homosexuality in South Africa; they are also resisting marginalising discourses that attempt to exclude any non-heterosexual man from the domain of the masculine.

At the same time, though, their misogynist attitudes towards feminine traits ultimately reinforce dominant societal discourses that valorise masculinity at the expense of femininity. This complic-ity in the reproduction of hegemonic masculinity allows these men to tap into the privilege that comes with 'passing' as a man's man. Whether conformist or subversive, the straight-acting per-sona – no matter how central it might be on the virtual stage of meetmarket – is not performed alone; it is accompanied by a *doppelgänger* (Rank 1971 [1914]) that, from the fringes, puts a mirror in front of 'straight-actingness', and sneeringly discloses its artificial character of a performance.

It is the performance aspect of straight-acting that constitutes the main object of critique on the part of the South African men interviewed in this study. This is not to say that masculin-ity is downplayed, however. Quite the contrary – these men might be sceptical about what straight-acting entails but they still valorise the traits connected to masculinity at the expense of femininity, although some of them do recognise the role played by gender-non-normative behaviour in making 'the world livable', as Michael puts it.

This is an important concern for applied linguists not least because '[c]hanges in conceptions of gender and sexuality, and the future of research into these areas, are central to our understanding of many real-world problems' (Cook and Kasper 2005: 479). Chauvinism on the grounds on gender – sexism – and prejudices on the basis of sexual identities – heterosexism and homophobia – are well-known social phenomena that have real effects on people's lives. This chapter has illustrated how other, possibly more subtle, but no less tangible forms of in-group inequities – Bogetic (2014: 334) calls it 'recursive marginalization' – are produced by those very people who are otherwise the target of broader societal discrimination. This is, however, a form of marginalisation that is not always straightforward but operates in ambivalent ways.

Summary

In this chapter I examined whether men who desire other men were colluding with hegemonic masculinity through the fetishisation of straight-acting or whether they were instead opposing widespread societal views that essentialise non-heterosexual men as inherently feminine. These are key questions for applied linguistics with its interests in 'the theoretical and empirical investigation of real world problems in which language is a central issue' (Brumfit 1995: 27). These problems include but are not limited to issues of marginalisation and discrimination.

Unlike much scholarly work that has privileged either online or offline interactions, the analysis in this chapter used a multi-pronged methodological approach that sought to capture the on/offline dimension of 'straight-actingness'. Such a dual focus was realised by a mixed methods study that combined textual analysis of a large corpus of online profiles from meetmarket, a South Africa-based website for men who are looking for other men, with audience reception interviews with a sample of South African men who were looking for other men.

The study found that the male participants were countering oppressive homophobic forces that seek to silence homosexuality in South Africa; they were also resisting marginalising discourses that attempt to exclude any non-heterosexual man from the domain of the masculine. At the same time, though, their misogynist attitudes towards feminine traits ultimately reinforced dominant societal discourses that valorise masculinity at the expense of femininity. This complicity in the reproduction of hegemonic masculinity allowed the participants to tap into the privilege that comes with 'passing' as a man's man (i.e. as heterosexual and abiding by the conventions of heteronormativity).

Related topics

Postioning language and identity: poststructuralist perspectives; Language and gender identities; Language and non-normative sexual identities; Beyond the micro–macro interface in language and identity research; The significance of sexual identity to language learning and teaching; Language, gender and identities in political life: a case study from Malaysia; Intersectionality in language and identity research; Language and identity research in online environments: a multimodal ethnographic perspective; The future of identity research: impact and new developments in sociolinguistics.

Further reading

Baker, P. (2003). No effeminates please: a corpus-based analysis of masculinity via personal adverts in *Gay News/Times* 1973–2000, in B. Benwell (ed.) *Masculinity and men's lifestyle magazines*. Oxford: Blackwell, pp. 243–260. (An incisive study that employs quantitative techniques in order to unveil the discursive constructions of masculinity in gay personal ads.)

Bogetic, K. (2013). 'Normal straight gays: lexical collocations and ideologies of masculinity in personal ads of Serbian gay teenagers', *Gender and Language*, 7(3): 333–367. (A recent quantitative investigation of masculinity among gay youth in a non-Anglophone context.)

Payne, R. (2007). 'Str8acting', *Social Semiotics*, 17(4): 525–538. (A social semiotic analysis of the ambiguities of 'straight-acting' on *Gaydar*.)

Pennycook, A. (2001). *Critical applied linguistics: a critical introduction*. Mahwah: Lawrence Erlbaum. Chapter 6. (A lucid introduction to queer theory in applied linguistics.)

Thorne, A. and Coupland, J. (1998). 'Articulations of same-sex desire: lesbian and gay male dating advertisements', *Journal of Sociolinguistics*, 2(2): 233–257. (An important qualitative study that compares the discursive strategies employed in gay and lesbian personal ads in the UK.)

Notes

1 Parts of this chapter have appeared in Milani (2013) and have been reproduced with permission of SAGE.
2 All the names used here are pseudonyms.

References

Baker, P. (2003). No effeminates please: a corpus-based analysis of masculinity via personal adverts in *Gay News/Times* 1973–2000, in B. Benwell (ed.) *Masculinity and men's lifestyle magazines*. Oxford: Blackwell, pp. 243–260.

Baker, P. (2005). *Public discourses of gay men*. London: Routledge.

Baker, P. (2006). *Using corpora in discourse analysis*. London: Continuum.

Baker, P. (2008). *Sexed texts: language, gender and sexuality*. London: Equinox.

Baker, P., Gabrielatos, C., KhosraviNik, M., Krzyżanowski, M., McEnery, T. and Wodak, R. (2008). 'A useful methodological synergy? Combining critical discourse analysis and corpus linguistics to examine discourses of refugees and asylum seekers in the UK', *Discourse and Society*, 19(3): 273–306.

Benwell, B. (2004). 'Ironic discourse: evasive masculinity in men's lifestyle magazines', *Men and Masculinities*, 7(3): 3–21.

Benwell, B. (2005). '"Lucky this is anonymous!" Men's magazines and ethnographies of reading: a textual culture approach', *Discourse and Society*, 16(2): 147–172.

Bergling, T. (2001). *Sissyphobia: gay men and effeminate behavior*. New York: Harrington Park Press.

Bogetic, K. (2013). 'Normal straight gays: lexical collocations and ideologies of masculinity in personal ads of Serbian gay teenagers', *Gender and Language*, 7(3): 333–367.

Bourdieu, P. (1998). *Practical reason*. Cambridge: Polity Press.

Browne, K. and Nash, C.J. (2010). Queer methods and methodologies: an introduction, in K. Browne and C.J. Nash (eds) *Queer methods and methodologies: intersecting queer theories and social science research*. Farnham: Ashgate, pp. 1–24.

Brumfit, C. (1995). Teacher professionalism and research, in G. Cook and B. Seidlhofer (eds) *Principle and practice in applied linguistics: studies in honour of H.G. Widdowson*. Oxford: Oxford University Press, pp. 27–41.

Bucholtz, M. and Hall, K. (2005). 'Identity and interaction: a sociocultural linguistic approach', *Discourse Studies*, 7(4–5): 585–614.

Butler, J. (1991). Imitation and gender insubordination, in D. Fuss (ed.) *Inside/out: lesbian theories, gay theories*. New York: Routledge, pp. 13–31.

Chesebro, J.W. (2001). Gender, masculinities, identities, and interpersonal relationship systems: men in general and gay men in particular, in L.P. Arliss and D.J. Borisoff (eds) *Women and men communicating: challenges and changes*. Long Grove: Wavel and Press, pp. 33–64.

Clarkson, J. (2005). 'Contesting masculinity's makeover: queer eye, consumer masculinity, and "straight-acting" gays', *Journal of Communication Inquiry*, 29(3): 235–255.

Connell, R.W. (1995). *Masculinities*. London: Polity.

Cook, G. and Kasper, G. (2005). 'Editorial', *Applied Linguistics*, 26(4): 479–481.

Eguchi, S. (2009). 'Negotiating hegemonic masculinity: the rhetorical strategy of "straight-acting" among gay men', *Journal of Intercultural Communication Research*, 38(3): 193–209.

Eguchi, S. (2011). 'Negotiating sissyphobia: a critical/interpretive analysis of one "femme" gay Asian body in the heteronormative world', *Journal of Men's Studies*, 19(1): 37–56.

Foucault, M. (1978). *The will to knowledge: the history of sexuality, vol. 1*. London: Penguin.

Foucault, M. (1989). Technologies of the self, in L.H. Martin, H. Gutman and P.H. Hutton (eds) *Technologies of the self: a seminar with Michel Foucault*. Boston: MIT Press, pp. 16–49.

Fraser, N. (1995). 'From redistribution to recognition? Dilemmas of justice in a "post-socialist" age', *New Left Review*, 212: 68–91.

Gray, J. (this volume). Language and non-normative sexual identities, in S. Preece (ed.) *The Routledge handbook of language and identity*. Abingdon: Routledge, pp. 225–240.

Heywood, J. (1997). The object of desire is the object of contempt, in S. Johnson and U.H. Meinhof (eds) *Language and masculinity*. Oxford: Blackwell, pp. 188–207.

Hill, J. (2008). *The everyday life of white racism*. Malden: Wiley-Blackwell.

Joseph, J.E. (this volume). Historical perspectives on language and identity, in S. Preece (ed.) *The Routledge handbook of language and identity*. Abingdon: Routledge, pp. 19–33.

Leap, W. (1996). *Word's out: gay men's English*. Minneapolis: University of Minnesota Press.

Livia, A. and Hall, K. (eds) (1997). *Queerly phrased: language, gender and sexuality*. Oxford: Oxford University Press.

Mambaonline (no date). *Facebook page* [Online]. Available at www.facebook.com/mambaonline?fref=ts

Milani, T.M. (2013). 'Are "queers" really "queer"? Language, identity and same-sex desire in a South African online community', *Discourse and Society*, 24(5): 615–633.

Motschenbacher, H. (2011). 'Taking queer linguistics further: sociolinguistics and critical heteronormativity research', *International Journal of the Sociology of Language*, 212: 149–179.

Munt, S. (2008). *Queer attachments: the cultural politics of shame*. Aldershot: Ashgate.

Nash, J. (2008). 'Re-thinking intersectionality', *Feminist Review*, 89: 1–15.

Nelson, C.D. (2006). 'Queer inquiry in language education', *Journal of Language, Identity, and Education*, 5(1): 1–9.

Nuttall, S. (2004). 'Stylizing the self: the Y generation in Rosebank, Johannesburg', *Public Culture*, 16: 430–452.

Payne, R. (2007). 'Str8acting', *Social Semiotics*, 17(4): 525–538.

Pennycook, A. (2001). *Critical applied linguistics: a critical introduction*. Mahwah: Lawrence Erlbaum.

Phua, V.C. (2002). 'Sex and sexuality in men's personal advertisements', *Men and Masculinities*, 5(2): 178–191.

Preece, S. (this volume). An identity transformation? Social class, language prejudice and the erasure of multilingual capital in higher education, in S. Preece (ed.) *The Routledge handbook of language and identity*. Abingdon: Routledge, pp. 366–381.

Rank, O. (1971) [1914]). *The double: a psychoanalytic study*. Chapel Hill: University of North Carolina Press.

Ratele, K. (2011). Male sexualities and masculinities, in S. Tamale (ed.) *African sexualities: a reader*. Cape Town: Pambazuka Press, pp. 399–419.

Sonnekus, T. (2009). 'Macho men and the queer imaginary: a critique of selected gay "colonial" representations of homomasculinity', *De Arte*, 8: 37–53.

Stroud, C. (2001). 'African mother-tongue programmes and the politics of language: linguistic citizenship versus linguistic human rights', *Journal of Multilingual and Multicultural Development*, 22(4): 339–355.

Stroud, C. and Mpendukana, S. (2009). 'Towards a material ethnography of linguistic landscape: multilingualism, space and mobility in a South African township', *Journal of Sociolinguistics*, 13(3): 363–386.

Thorne, A. and Coupland, J. (1998). 'Articulations of same-sex desire: lesbian and gay male dating advertisements', *Journal of Sociolinguistics*, 2(2): 233–257.

Warner, D. (2004). 'Towards a queer research methodology', *Qualitative Research in Psychology*, 1(4): 321–337.

Wodak, R. (2001). 'The discourse-historical approach', in R. Wodak and M. Meyer (eds) *Methods of critical discourse analysis*. Thousand Oaks: SAGE, pp. 63–94.

Wodak, R., de Cillia, R., Reisigl, M. and Liebhart, K. (1999). *The discursive construction of national identity*. Edinburgh: Edinburgh University Press.

Appendix

The following transcription conventions have been followed:

? ! , .	intonation contours
(...)	long pause
[...]	deleted text not relevant for discussion in this chapter
(( ))	author's comments
< >	paralinguistic features

29

Styling and identity in a second language[1]

Ben Rampton

Introduction

Applied linguistic accounts of identity in conditions of contemporary globalisation are beset by two kinds of bias. On the one hand, second language acquisition research tends to assume that the language it investigates is deficient. On the other, sociolinguistics is inclined to respond to linguistic difference with romantic celebration. To cut a path between these problematic subdisciplinary dispositions, this chapter focuses on the English of an adult migrant who started to speak the language later in life and it examines his speech through the prism of Silverstein's 'total linguistic fact'. The 'total linguistic fact' directs our attention to linguistic form, social interaction and ideology, but rather than simply correlating a couple of these dimensions or treating them separately, it emphasises their 'dynamic interplay'. It insists that claims about a speaker's control of linguistic structure, about their rhetorical effectiveness or about their political position should be grounded in a detailed empirical investigation of how these elements operate together in communicative practice, and in doing so, it reduces the scope for analysts to introduce their own a priori assumptions.

The chapter begins by specifying two linguistic concepts relevant to identity, 'style' and 'second language' ('L2'), and it approaches these from the perspectives of quantitative style-shifting and discursive stylisation. After describing the study that it draws on, the empirical analysis begins with an account of the focal informant's diasporic experience in London and then shows how his style-shifting and some of his L2 speech variants chime with now well-established local patterns. It then turns to stylisation in the performance of character speech in narrative, exploring the complex and not always effective relationship between linguistic form, discursive context and socio-indexical resonance, first in the informant's performance of Anglo vs Indian styles and then in his production of vernacular Anglo. The analysis then moves to a characterisation of the informant's participation in the London sociolinguistic economy, insisting that 'L2 speaker' is an integral (and influential) part of the local landscape.

Overview

Historically, style and second language have not sat easily together in language research. They have often been associated with antagonistic views of non-standard mixed speech data and as an either/or choice of how to look at one's data (e.g. Gumperz 1982; Rampton 1995). L2 research has typically drawn on notions like learning, development, error and interference, while sociolinguistic studies of style speak of social differentiation, identity-projection, sociolinguistic markers and code-switching, but there is surely no necessary incompatibility of style and L2 (Talmy 2008). Kramsch (2009: 5) suggests that 'imagined identities, projected selves, idealisations or stereotypes of the other ... seem to be central to the language-learning experience [even though ...] they are difficult to grasp within the current paradigms of SLA research', and when Eckert (2008: 456) proposes that in 'one way or another, every stylistic move is the result of an interpretation of the social world and of the meanings of elements within it, as well as a positioning of the stylizer with respect to that world', there is no principled reason for excluding the L2 user from analysis. So as someone's grasp of a different language develops, it is worth asking: Which social categories, figures and stances do they (start to) explore through the connotational – the non-referential, socially indexical – possibilities of the language they are using, how, where, with whom and with what kinds of alignment? Indeed, how far do the abilities to distinguish different social types, to recognise the ways of speaking associated with them, and then to reproduce them linguistically, develop in synchrony? To tackle questions like these, we first need to define what we mean by 'style' and 'second language'.

Generally speaking, a 'style' can be seen as a distinctive set of linguistic (and other semiotic) features indexically linked to typifications of the social world, produced and construed in situated interaction. This has been approached in a number of different ways in sociolinguistics (see Auer 2007; Coupland 2007), and in what follows, I will draw on two in particular: 'style-shifting' and 'stylisation'.

1 The notion of style-shifting derives from the tradition of variationist sociolinguistics and it uses quantitative correlation to link patterns of phonological variation to different situations (Labov 1972; see Drummond and Schleef, this volume). There are a number of well-recognised limitations in quantitative style-shifting as a window on interactional processes (e.g. Coupland 2007; also see discussion below), but it does offer a valuable account of formal linguistic variability, and its embedding in survey methods allows us to place the style-shifting of any given individual in a much wider empirical view of speech in the area where s/he lives.

2 Stylisation is reflexive communicative action in which speakers produce specially marked and often exaggerated representations of linguistic varieties that lie outside their habitual repertoire (at least as this is expected within the situation on hand; Rampton 1995, 2006). Stylisation is closely linked to the linguistic anthropological notion of register. But whereas registers/styles are distinctive forms of language, speech and non-linguistic semiosis used as a normal part of social interaction and indexically evoke specific typifications of stance, person or situation in the course of routine conduct (Agha 2004, 2007; Eckert 2008), stylisation involves a degree of self-conscious performance, a second-order meta-representation of varieties and styles (Agha 2007: 187). In what follows, stylisation is central because the focal informant's production of distinctively different varieties of English was far clearer in instances of reported speech of the kind analysed here than in his ordinary oral language use.

Second language is a more contested term than style. Certainly, second-language learning and use are culturally recognisable practices, and there is a basic truth to the idea that adults with different lexico-grammars can be mutually unintelligible. But L2 learning and use are hugely politicised, foregrounded as the focus of government policies, professional specialisations, educational curricula and media reporting, and there is a considerable history of the terms being misapplied, both globally and to people from South Asia, in the UK (see Rampton 1983; Pennycook 1994). To guard against this overextension, claims about L2 status and proficiency need to be properly situated in careful empirical accounts of at least three factors:

1   Focal informants' own linguistic self-classification and classification by local others;
2   The speech of people who inhabit the same environment but have been using English all their lives. As Blommaert *et al.* (2005: 201) note, '[p]rocesses such as diaspora [that] develop over long spans of time ... result in *lasting* ... social, ... sociolinguistic and discursive reconfigurations which have effects across a wide range of situations', and what sounded 'foreign' 30 years ago may now no longer do so; and
3   The situated expectations associated with particular interlocutors, interpreters, analysts, genres, footings, etc., since judgements of proficiency are themselves always relational and socio-ideologically positioned and there are a great many interactions where the fact that one participant learnt to speak the language in use later in life is irrelevant to the encounter (Blommaert 2008; Young 2009).

At the same time, assumptions about shared understanding are especially precarious in the study of L2 style. If one is analysing people who are not particularly proficient in the language in use, it can be particularly difficult to know whether specific speech forms really are being used to evoke particular stances, images, categories or stereotypes. Even if an L2 speaker can discern a particular style receptively (which of course cannot be taken for granted), they may not have the linguistic resources to reproduce it accurately, in spite of their efforts to do so (cf. Preston 1989; Sharma 2005; Agha 2007).

With these perspectives in place, it is now worth moving to investigation of the relationship between style and second language use in the case study.

Methodology

My data come from the 2008–9 ESRC project *Dialect Development and Style in a Diaspora Community*, conducted with Devyani Sharma, Lavanya Sankaran, Pam Knight and Roxy Harris. This set out to examine the use and development of dialectal varieties of English within families of Indian origin in London and it combined the methods of quantitative variationist with qualitative interactional sociolinguistics. The project was based in Southall in West London, where in 2001, according to the UK Census (Wells no date), 48 per cent of the 89,000 inhabitants were ethnically South Asian, 38 per cent were white, 9 per cent were black and, overall, 43 per cent were born outside the UK. Most of the fieldwork involved two 1–2 hour interviews with 75 mostly adult and mainly ethnic Punjabi informants, born both in Britain and abroad, collecting speech data and constructing bilingualism, network, attitudinal and cultural consumption profiles. In addition, 10 individuals were given recorders to record themselves in a range of situations; the focal informant in this chapter – Mandeep (not his real name), who came to London in 2001 aged 28 – was one of these. With Mandeep, our data-collection involved approximately five and a half hours of audio recordings – two interviews with Lavanya Sankaran, and four self-recordings (with a group of colleagues at work (one Anglo and several people born in India); with an Indian-born friend; with a newly arrived relative; on his own in the car) (see also Rampton 2013).

The data

We can start with Mandeep's account of coming to England and engaging with English.

What Mandeep told us in interview

In interview, Mandeep told us he had been a teacher in the Punjab, and he had left India to find a better life. Soon after arriving, he had found work as a newsreader and editor in a local Southall Punjabi-language radio station, but now he was working there only part-time because he wanted to do postgraduate teacher training and first he had to do a year's maths enhancement course. He did not have any family in London when he had arrived, but he had known three or four people from home, and now he had married a health-care professional from India. His cultural taste in music and media had not changed, he said, but 'it's developed … opened up new branches'. Although he did not get any spare time to watch the game, he said he would support England in cricket against India – after all, there were now two Punjabis in each team (Harbhajan and Yuvraj vs Panesar and Bopara).

Mandeep said that he 'wasn't speaking English at all' until he came to England aged 28, but actually, he had had a lot of exposure to the language through study and, among other things, most of his MA in Economics had been in English. Since arriving in the UK, he had done a year's GCSE in English, and he regarded soaps-with-subtitles on British TV as a great resource for language learning. With the British-born English speakers on his maths course, he said, 'it's fine, you always mingle with them, talk with them, joke with them – obviously you don't know every single joke', but that was no reason for feeling 'you are … being excluded'. He did not like it when people with Punjabi backgrounds born in Britain called him a 'freshie', but he was convinced that 'if you are calibre enough, no one can stop you', and his stock reply was that at least he was not 'worn out' and stale like them. With the Anglos in his maths classes, he said he avoided the Punjabi pronunciation of his name, while with people who were weak in English but could not speak Punjabi, he would de-anglicise his pronunciation of English. Lastly, he was conscious of social stratification in English speech:

> accent is to do with … watching telly, talking to the other people … Sometimes, say in English, you're swearing a lot, and 'yo mate yo mate' or something you're doing, and then – you're glorifying yourself, some other people are glorifying you, then you develop that accent for the whole of your life. Then your family says, 'No, that's not the way how you speak.'

And dispositions like these were not just restricted to Anglos:

> the children of Indian subcontinent, [the] third generation … know other things as well – pub culture, these sorts of things – [and] now they are as bad as white partners and as good as white partners – they are now normals … of this country.

So to sum up before moving into an examination of how Mandeep actually used English himself, there are three points to take from all this:

1   Second language learning is not just our own external analytic attribution: learning to speak English as an additional language had been a significant issue for Mandeep in London, even though English had also been important in his education in India.

2   It is worth looking at least two major axes of local sociolinguistic differentiation: not just Indian vs Anglo, or newcomer vs local, but also high vs low and posh vs vulgar.

3   At the same time, it looks as though the stereotypic links between language, ethnicity and class have all been scrambled up and we could go seriously wrong if we just accepted the traditional image of a minority ethnic L2 speaker migrating into a host society dominated by an L1 ethnic majority.

In fact, we will see the significance of Mandeep's residence among born-and-bred Londoners with family links to the Indian subcontinent in the quantitative analysis of stylistic variation in the following section.

Quantitative analysis of style-shifting across contexts

In our analyses of style in Mandeep's English, we first carried out a quantitative variationist analysis of his style-shifting in three settings, conducting an auditory analysis of the use of Punjabi and Anglo variants in his English. Table 29.1 shows what we examined: Ls, Ts and the FACE and GOAT vowels, in three contexts (in self-recorded interaction with an Indian friend who was himself a fluent speaker of standard Indian English; in one of the interviews with Sankaran (brought up in southern India and Singapore, and a non-speaker of Punjabi); and at work, conversing together with an Anglo L1 English-speaking man and several L2 Indian English-speaking women).

What we found was that, yes, there was quantitative style-shifting: Mandeep used most Punjabi variants with his Punjabi friend at home, and fewest at work (in the presence of an Anglo colleague), and this is broadly in line with the findings of other studies of L2 speech (Figure 29.1).

The plot thickens, however, when we bring in other informants and discover that even though these other speakers have been speaking English since early childhood, the patterns are broadly similar. This is illustrated in Figure 29.2, which summarises the distribution of Punjabi and Anglo variants in the speech of Anwar, a British-born 40-year-old who ran a successful local business and travelled a lot between London and Pakistan.

Table 29.1 Linguistic variables used in the analysis of Mandeep's situational style-shifting

Linguistic variable	Punjabi variant	Standard British English variant	Vernacular British English variant
(t) in the environments vt#, #tv and vtv (as in 'eight', 'time', 'thirty')	Retroflex [ʈ]	Alveolar [t]	Glottal [ʔ]
Postvocalic (l) as in 'will' or 'deal'	Light [l]	Dark [ɫ]	
(e) – 'FACE' (e) as in 'say' and 'game'	Monophthong [e]	Diphthong [eɪ]	
(o) – 'GOAT' as in 'don't' and 'road'	Monophthong [o]	Diphthong [əʊ]	

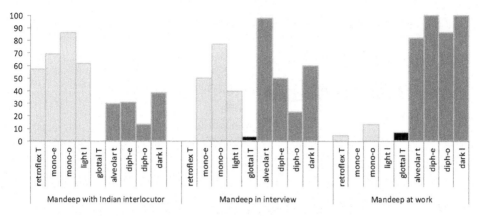

Key: light grey = Punjabi origin; dark grey = Anglo origin; black = vernacular London

Figure 29.1 Distribution of Punjabi and Anglo variants across three settings: Mandeep

Mandeep is obviously different from Anwar in his non-use of glottal T, and I will return to this later. But before that, the comparison suggests that:

1   Nowadays, retroflexion, postvocalic clear Ls and monophthonged 'FACE' and 'GOAT' vowels are not foreign any longer in British-born London speech, so Mandeep would not have to completely erase them in order to sound local;
2   The directionality of Mandeep's stylistic adjustment with these four variants was broadly in line with the directions of shift produced by people who have been speaking English all their lives, so on the Anglo vs Indian axis of social differentiation, Mandeep's socio-stylistic sensibility seemed to be roughly in tune with native residents'.

In interview, Mandeep said that if you come from Punjab to Southall, 'you won't feel like you are living abroad', and there is support for this in these quantitative analyses of style. In addition to the fact that Punjabi itself has a lot of local currency in Southall, the Britain–India link is inscribed in the patternings of local English.

Of course, quantitative measures like this have clear limitations: there is no control for the talk's discursive development – for changes of footing, topic, genre, etc. – and if you just look at only four out of potentially umpteen linguistic variables, you cannot tell whether, overall, Mandeep's speech sounded more Anglo or more Indian at different times with different people. So let's now turn to some discourse.

Styling in narrative discourse

Mandeep told a lot of stories in his interviews with Lavanya Sankaran, and it was in the performance of character speech in stories that his accent became most Anglo. Extract 1 is an example from an account of the difficulties he had finding a job when he first arrived in England, where he found that all the employers were asking for experience, even in basic jobs.

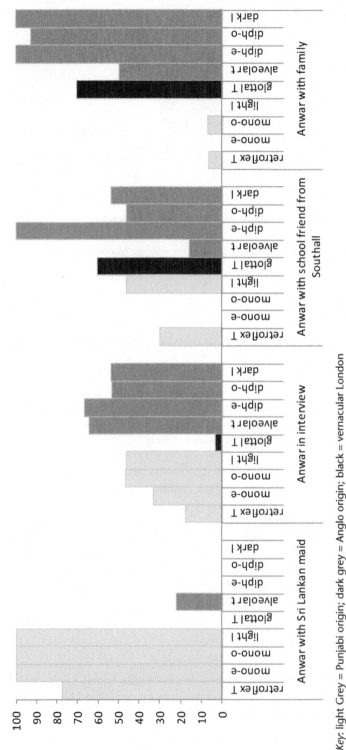

Key: light Grey = Punjabi origin; dark grey = Anglo origin; black = vernacular London

Note: 'family' here refers to his UK born children.

Figure 29.2 Distribution of Punjabi and Anglo variants across four settings: Anwar

Extract 1 'Okay wait wait'

Mandeep in interview with Lavanya Sankaran (female; aged 25–30). (Key: **Anglo variants**; ***Punjabi variants***)

    1   ˍ**th**en I was s**a**ying
          [ðen ɑ wz seɪɪŋ]
    2   "↑ ˈ**no: I do**n have any- ˌ**th***at* sort of exˌperience"
          [nəʊ aɪ dõ hʌv əni ḍæt sɔtɒv əkspiːɹɪəns]
    3   ↑**so** .hhh
          [sɒ]
→ 4   ˌ**th**ey **w**ere giving me "**o:**ˌ**kay:**
          [ḍᵉ   vʌ gɪvɪŋ mɪ əʊkʰeɪ]
→ 5   (0.3) ˌ**wait** ˌ**wait**"
            weɪtʰ weɪtʰ
    6   and **th**en ˉafter- (0.5) ˈ**two**- (0.3) ˈ**two** months
          [ən ḍən ɑftˀə   tˢʰu   tʰu mʌns]

In line 5, Mandeep marks the difference between the narrating and the reported speech with shifts in tempo, becoming much slower in reported speech, and he renders the voice of the employers in exclusively British variants.

So Mandeep could do some pure Anglo, and indeed, the fact that he mixed Anglo and Punjabi features elsewhere in the story – for example, in line 2's '↑ˈ**no: I do**n have any- ˌ**th***at* sort of exˌperience' – does not itself necessarily mark Mandeep as an L2 speaker. Mixing occurred even in the relatively formal English of Punjabis born and raised in the UK, and we can see this, for example, in Anwar's business talk with an RP-speaking barrister (see Rampton 2011 a or b):

> **the reason** why I c**alled** you is e::h I jus wa**nted to let** you **know tha***t* ((*name*)) he came.. and e::h we **decided** *no*t *tu* pursue **h**is case.

Even so, when we looked across our data set more generally, there were very clear differences in the length of the utterances in which Mandeep and Anwar maintained exclusively Anglo-accented character speech: whereas Anwar produced one stretch of almost completely Anglo-sounding multi-clause direct speech that lasted 29 syllables, Mandeep's exclusively Anglo-accented voicing never exceeded 12 and, as we shall see, it was actually rather rare to find a consistent separation of Anglo and Punjabi forms in the speech of the figures in his narratives.

Of course, that itself raises a question: if Mandeep's '**o:**ˌ**kay:** (0.3) ˌ**wait** ˌ**wait**' was actually rather rare in the consistency of its phonological anglicisation, how did he actually manage to style narrative character speech as distinctly Anglo? If his mobilisations of linguistic code resources were somewhat unpredictable, how did he achieve stylistic effects?

To address this, we should now turn to his stylisation of the local Anglo-English vernacular, moving from an Anglo-Indian axis of differentiation to socially stratified class styles. As we do so, we will begin to see how important it is to address linguistic forms, discourse and ideology each in their own right.

Stylising vernacular English

In the interviews, there were signs of Mandeep's class consciousness when he talked about 'pub culture' and linked accent to watching television, swearing and behaving in ways that got you

into trouble with your family. How far did this translate into his own dramatised speech performances, and with what kinds of rhetorical success?

The excerpt below forms part of an argument that people make too much of a fuss about racism and that you should not overgeneralise about racism on the basis of single incidents. In it, Mandeep is presenting the hypothetical scenario of a white man shouting racist abuse:

Extract 2 Sun² reader

Mandeep in interview with Lavanya Sankaran. (Key: **Anglo variants**; *Punjabi variants*)

```
 1   Mndp:   if ˌsomeone just misbeˌhaves wi**th** you
 2            .hh ↑ˈsomeone ˈdrunk ˌwhi**te** ˌperson and uh (.)
 3            .hhhh you are just ˌpassing by or ˌsome**th**ing,
 4            he ˌsaw you
 5            ((pitch step-up and shift to non-modal phonation:))
 →           ↑"you ˈbloody 'Asians ˈwhy you 'come to 'my 'country"
 6            or some**th**ing
 7            ((high pitched:)) ↑↑thats not 'racism-
 8            ⁻**th**at's- he::- .hh m**ay** be 'rea**d**ing 'Su**n** ˈonly (0.5)
 9            ˌso: m- m- he m**ay** be just 'listeni:ng aˌbou:**t** s-som-ˌso:me like
10            ((shift in voice quality similar to line 5:))
11            ((non-modal phonation on first three words:))
             " ˈwhy '**th**ey 'c**a**me to our 'country"
12            e- 'he 'm**ay** 'no**t** ˈkn**ow** (.)
13            ((faster:)) **what th**e e'conomy is
14            wha**t th**e **c**ontribution of .hhh
15   LS:     [As-
15   Mndp:   [ˈmig**r**ant 'peo**pl**e to 'Bri**d**ish e'conomy is-
16            so 'he d**o**n know ↑↑any↓ˈthing
17            ˈh:e jus ↑ˈshouting a ˈ'y**ou** and **th**en ˈˈswearing ˌeven
```

Mandeep describes the character as ignorant, drunk, uncouth and informed only by the (very lowbrow) popular press – in effect, as a stereotypical lower-class white racist – and there are two things worth noting. First, Mandeep locates the white British lower class in a global economy, and he portrays this group as the ignorant victim of restricted mobility and very limiting national horizons. Second, the segmental phonology used to enact the man's speech in line 5 sounds more Anglo than Indian – ↑ˈyou ˈbloody |Asians |why you |come to |my |country'. But does it sound more *vernacular*? Here it is again in a more detailed transcript:

Extract 3

((pitch step-up with shift to tense muscular phonation)):

↑"you ˈbloody 'Asians ˈwhy you 'come to 'my 'country"
[ju   bᵘɬʌdiː eɪʃɳz waɪ jʊ kʰʌm tʊ maɪ kʼʌntɹiː]

Segmentally, the onsets of the diphthongs in 'Asian' and 'why' sounded RP, as they lacked the backed vowel quality of traditional working-class London – [eɪ], not [ʌɪ], and [aɪ], not [ɒɪ] – and in fact there was also a detectably Punjabi influence in *country*'s unaspirated word-initial consonant. Even so, there are lots of semiotic cues showing that Mandeep was aiming for more than just ordinary British:

- Segmentally, the onset of the diphthong in 'my' was relatively backed, as in popular London speech ([ɑɪ], not [aɪ]);
- 'You bloody Asians' is also very marked supra-segmentally with abruptly raised pitch and tenser muscular non-modal phonation. This gives the impression of shouting without actually doing so, and when this is linked to swearing it is often typed as vulgar;
- In addition, of course, Mandeep used an explicit metalanguage of social types to characterise the speech/speaker both before and after ('drunk', 'white', 'reading *Sun*').

So even though the segmental phonetics were not especially vernacular, this was not rhetorically incapacitating. Yes, if you extracted this impersonation of a 'white London lout' from its narrative context, it probably would not carry very far, and the groups and networks where it would be rated, or even recognised for what is intended, might be limited. But within the specific narrative world and narrating event in which it was produced, the social typification worked reasonably well, and the voice can be heard as Anglo vernacular English.

So even though Mandeep was not terribly good at doing traditional London vernacular vowels and consonants, he knew that they sounded different and he did not mind trying to impersonate it. In fact, there is other evidence that he was aware of vernacular London features without accurately reproducing them, and here we can also see that his apprehension of the vernacular's connotational potential extended beyond social group stereotypes to typifications of stance.

In his interview comments on accent, Mandeep linked 'swearing a lot' to saying 'yo mate yo mate', and in fact he pronounced 'mate' as 'yo [meɪ] yo [meɪ]'. In contemporary vernacular London, the postvocalic T in 'mate' is a glottal, not an alveolar stop, and it looks as though Mandeep got halfway – he removed the alveolar, but did not replace it with the glottal, doing a zero realisation instead. In fact, the quantitative style-shifting analysis showed that he hardly ever produced glottal Ts – 3 out of 88 possible realisations (Tables 29.2–29.4), and Sharma and Sankaran's (2011) survey showed that he was very similar in this to a great many other informants born in India. But this did not stop Mandeep using zero T strategically in constructed dialogue.

Table 29.2 Mandeep's English with an Indian friend

	retro-flex ʈ	monophthong e	monophthong o	light l	glottal ʔ	t	diphthong e	diphthong o	dark l
%	57.5	69.2	86.7	61.5	0	30	30.8	13.3	38.5
Tokens	23	9	13	8	0	12	4	2	5
Total	40	13	15	13	28	40	13	15	13

Table 29.3 Mandeep's English in interview

	retro-flex ʈ	monophthong e	monophthong o	light l	glottal ʔ	t	diphthong e	diphthong o	dark l
%	0	50	76.9	40	3.3	97.8	50	23.1	60
Tokens	0	7	10	6	1	44	7	3	9
Total	45	14	13	15	30	45	14	13	15

Table 29.4 Mandeep's English in mixed white and Indian company at work

	retro-flex ʈ	monophthong e	monophthong o	light l	glottal ʔ	t	diphthong e	diphthong o	dark l
%	4.4	0	13.3	0	6.7	82.2	100	86.7	100
Tokens	2	0	2	0	2	37	15	13	15
Total	45	15	15	15	30	45	15	15	15

In the excerpt below, Mandeep is continuing the argument that accusations of racism are often exaggerated. He has just been talking about the notorious Shilpa Shetty episode in *Celebrity Big Brother*,[3] and he has taken the line that when the other contestants criticised Shilpa for touching some food they were not being racist – the complaint was 'just normal talk'. He now follows this up with a story about being ticked off by his mum when he was small, the overall point being that there is very little to distinguish these two episodes.

Extract 4 Spoiled carrots

Mandeep in interview with Lavanya Sankaran. (Key: **Anglo variants**; *Punjabi variants*)

```
        33      one ˌday (.)
                .hh I was 'very ˈlittle (.)
                    [ɑ]    [w]    [t]
        34      and er my mum ˌbought some ˌcarrots (.)
                                  [t]              [t]
        35      an I put 'all the ˈcarrits in::- (.)
                [aɪ] [t][ə̪ɫ ḍə]  [ɾ][t]
        36      er- as 'outside in- on the ˈsand
                            [t]
        37      so I 'spoiled ˈeverything
                            [d]        [t̪ʰ]
        38      so 'she 'sla:pped ˈme (.)
        39  L:  ((very quiet laugh:)) hehe
        40  M:  ((half-laughing in 'bought' and 'that':))
→       41      that "'I 'bough 'tha fo 'us              1.04
                [ḍætʰ aɪ  bᵊhɔ:ø ḍæø ɸɔ:ʷ ʌs]
        42      (0.2)
→       43      a:nd 'you pu the  'everything aˌway" (.)
                [ænd ɟɪu pʊø̞_ḍəʔ evɹɪt̪ʰɪŋ    ʔəweɪ]
        44      hh -so
                    [əʊ]
        45      th- th- th- ↑tha s not ˈracism (.)
                            [ḍæøs]  [ø]
        46      ⁻tha s 'simple 'talk as ˌwell
                    [ø]
        47      ⁻and that was the-                       (0.2)
        48      and 'other thing is
                ((Mandeep continues about another aspect))
```

The distribution of alveolar and zero Ts is shown in Table 29.5.

Table 29.5 Realisation of the postvocalic Ts in Mandeep's 'spoiled carrots' story

Environments	The setting, events and actions leading up to the reprimand (lines 33–38)			The reprimand in direct reported speech (lines 41–43)			The evaluation (lines 44–46)		
	[t]	[?]	[ø]	[t]	[?]	[ø]	[t]	[?]	[ø]
V_#C, V_#V, V_C	7/7	0	0	0	0	3/3	0	0	3/3

In the part leading up to the reprimand (lines 33–38), there are seven potentially variable T sounds, and all of them are alveolar ('li[t]le', 'bough[t]', 'carro[t]s', 'pu[t]', 'carro[t]s', 'ou[t]side', 'tha[t]'). But in the direct reported reprimand in lines 41–43, all three Ts are zero realisations ('bough[ø]', 'tha[ø]', 'pu[ø]'), and after that, the zero realisations are carried into the evaluation in lines 45–46 ('tha[ø]', 'no[ø]', 'tha[ø]').

Now in the quoted utterance in lines 41 and 43, Mandeep's approximations of vernacular London contribute to a character portrait that is very different from the white working-class figure in the *Sun*-reader episode. Here, the speaker is Mandeep's mum; she is saying the kind of thing that Mandeep approves of ('simple talk' that only the misguided would read as racism); and indeed in its incorporation of zero Ts in the evaluation, there is a 'fusion' of the narrating and the quoted voices (Bakhtin 1984: 199). So if it is not just unruly working-class types that Mandeep is trying to index with the concentration of zero-Ts in lines 41–43, what is it? If we turn back to Anwar and look back at the quantitative data on Anwar's style-shifting, T-glottalling increased with family and friends (Figure 29.2), and of course this pattern is repeated not just with other locally born individuals in our survey, but in British society much more generally. Vernacular forms often index not only types of person but also types of stance and relationship, and in the quoted speech in the carrots story, the glottal-T approximations seem designed to evoke the intimacy or informality of a mother–son relationship, a relationship which Mandeep seemed quite happy to inhabit (Mandeep's mum had always lived in India and apparently only spoke to him in Punjabi, so this is unlikely to be an accurate copy of her speech). So yes, Mandeep's reproduction of the linguistic specifics of emblematic vernacular English forms is only partial, but his grasp of the social meaning is not restricted to the stereotypes of people and groups that you might expect with speech styles seen from afar.

Which is not to say that the partiality of this approximation was itself cost-free, or that the impersonation was as effective as it had been with the white lout in Extract 2. Compared with Extract 2, there is very little supplementary characterisation of Mandeep's mum in the tale of spoiled carrots, and the sociolinguistic iconography associated with 'mums' is generally much more indeterminate. Admittedly, low levels of T-glottalling are common in the English of local people born in India, so local people born in India might well constitute a social network where the social indexicality of the zero-Ts in the carrots narrative could be easily appreciated. But beyond those networks – and maybe even within – Mandeep's stylised performance of his mum sounds odd rather than indexically resonant, and it certainly took our research team quite a lot of time and analysis to generate a plausible interpretation of the social typification being attempted.

Let's now move to a more general discussion.

Discussion

So how does this case study of Mandeep's sociolinguistic styling help us to rethink second language identity in contemporary urban settings? I shall take this in two stages, focusing first on London as a sociolinguistic space (see Block 2006; Harris 2006), and second on Mandeep's position in London as an L2 speaker.

At a number of points in the account, I have referred to traditional imageries being scrambled: you do not feel like you are living abroad if you come to London from the Punjab; retroflexion and other traditionally Indian immigrant features now form part of the local London vernacular; children of the Indian subcontinent are fully incorporated into pub culture; and Punjabis play cricket for England. But this mixture does not end up in kaleidoscopic chaos – the analysis has not descended into what Wimmer and Glick-Schiller (2002: 326) call 'fluidism', in which 'structures are replaced with fluidity [and researchers spend their time] breathlessly hunting after signifiers shooting around the globe, driven by new techniques of communication and globalised markets'. Our analyses of style have shown Mandeep positions himself within a quite well-defined sociolinguistic space – a space formed at the historical intersection of socio-economic stratification within the UK on the one hand, and migration and movement between Britain and the India subcontinent on the other. In this space, class and ethnic processes have drawn different sets of linguistic forms, practices and evaluations into the environment, and over time these sociolinguistic forms and practices have been configured in a series of conventionalised contrasts – Punjabi vs English, vernacular vs standard English and high vs low (Rampton 2011a).

What about Mandeep's position as a second language speaker? When compared with people who had grown up in the neighbourhood such as Anwar, Mandeep's English appeared more limited in a number of ways: in the range of English phonological variants that he commanded; in the number of identifiably distinct English styles that he performed; in the duration of the speech in which he sustained artful stylisations; and in the discursive actions achieved with switches of style. By contrast, Anwar's English style repertoire included Cockney, standard Indian English, Indian English foreigner talk and London multi-ethnic vernacular (which included elements of Jamaican; Rampton 2011b). Additionally, his shifts of style occurred with a far wider range of footing changes, contributing to the management of non-stylised, non-artful, routine interaction as this moved between business and personal matters, between greeting and reason-for-call in telephone conversations, and so forth (Gumperz 1982; Rampton 2011b). Nevertheless, in spite of the relative limitations in his English, it would be wrong to locate Mandeep as an L2 speaker outside the London sociolinguistic economy, aspirationally looking in. Mandeep insisted that, in his maths class, 'I am perfectly fine', and in the interview stories he presented himself as a now-established citizen of multi-ethnic London, among other things siding with the Anglos criticising Shilpa Shetty and dismissing white racism as just parochial lower-class ignorance. Beyond this explicit self-placement, there were a number of similarities between Mandeep's stylistic practices and Anwar's, which invited us to treat both of them together as active participants in broadly the same sociolinguistic space. Anwar was more fully engaged with the stylistically differentiated positions in the local sociolinguistic economy, but Mandeep also actively oriented to these schemata. He referred to high/low and Anglo/Indian contrasts explicitly and he performed them in narrative stylisations. In the quantitative analysis, several of the context-sensitive variables in Mandeep's speech were similar to others', and the directionalities of shift were also broadly similar (more Punjabi variants with speakers of English brought up in South Asia, and more Anglo ones with people brought up in England). His reproduction of the high–low, standard–vernacular binary traditional in Anglo English had its limitations, but he could exploit the contrast between Punjabi- and Anglo-accented English, and far from being simply confined to people born abroad, this Punjabi–Anglo contrast was itself widespread and well established as a local practice. Indeed, Sharma and Sankaran (2011) have shown that, over time, the presence of people like Mandeep has made a major contribution to the development of this.

So even though Mandeep only started to speak the language as an adult, he displayed a practical sensitivity to key dimensions of local English sociolinguistic structure, and it is obvious that a label like 'immigrant learner of English' does not do justice to his position in the local London speech economy.

Finally, what of the analytic moves that have led to this conclusion?

Issues for applied linguistics

First and most obviously, we consciously avoided the a priori separation of L1 and L2 English speakers in our variationist survey and discovered that L1 speakers do not talk quite as we might have expected. So plainly, if anyone wants to talk about a target language, it is essential to be rather careful, both in a specification of the forms that compose the 'target' and in an assessment of the linguistic distance that newcomers would need to travel to reach it.

But at a more fundamental level, it is important to work with a properly rounded view of language itself, and in linguistic anthropology Gumperz and Silverstein provide guidance on what this might mean. Gumperz (1982: 29) argued early on that 'we need to begin with a closer understanding of how linguistic signs interact with social knowledge in discourse'. Silverstein (1985: 220) subsequently formalised this as the 'total linguistic fact':

> The total linguistic fact, the datum for a science of language, is irreducibly dialectic in nature. It is an unstable mutual interaction of meaningful sign forms, contextualised to situations of interested human use and mediated by the fact of cultural ideology.

Both propose that linguistic forms, situated discourse and ideology need to be analysed together, but this has certainly not been standard practice in the study of language. Variationist sociolinguistics, for example, engages with linguistic form and ideology (in work on attitudes and evaluation) but has only turned towards interaction rather recently. Conversation analysis focuses on interaction and attends to linguistic form, but generally neglects ideology. In critical discourse analysis, there is form and ideology, but often not enough on situated interactional processing. In second language research, Young (2009: 1) seeks a similar perspective to Gumperz and Silverstein's, attending to the 'construction and reflection of social realities through actions that invoke identity, ideology, belief and power'. But Young also suggests that

> [i]n studies [of L2 discursive practice], rich descriptions of context are illustrated with superficial analyses of language, whereas in other studies, a close analysis of a newcomer's developing utilization of verbal, non-verbal, and interactional skills is explained by a rather thin description of context.

> *(Ibid.: 230)*

But why does this matter? What are the consequences of failing to investigate form, discourse and ideology together? The problem is that, when analysts engage empirically with only two of the elements in the 'total linguistic fact', they tend to fall back on the default common-sense assumptions characteristic of their subdisciplines in order to fill the gap left by their failure to explore the third. This gap then becomes the point of entry for the romantic celebration of difference or creative agency that has been so common in sociolinguistics, and for the presumption of deficit and remedial need in SLA. And when this happens, potentially crucial aspects of their informants' actual political, rhetorical or linguistic positioning are obscured.

In my attempt to counter this, I have examined stylistic moves individually, breaking them down into the forms, the discursive acts and the socio–ideological typifications that compose them, considering each of these in turn and then looking at the effects of their combination. As a result, we have developed a rather nuanced picture of Mandeep's L2 English, showing how it forms part of larger sociolinguistic structures and processes, without, I hope, either romanticising or remedialising him by erasing or exaggerating the differences and limitations. So with Extract 4, we have seen that a grasp of the indexical relationship between stance and vernacular style need not be matched by accurate reproduction of the canonical structural forms, and this could make the interpretation quite tricky. At the same time, Extract 2 showed that an imperfect grasp of vernacular Anglo forms was not automatically an expressive handicap in the impersonation of a lower-class white man.

When it comes to humanising migrants, seeing them in their embedded complexity as mothers, brothers, uncles, friends and workmates who also make agentive contributions to local sociolinguistic processes, linguistics is not always especially effective. Yes, it is quite easy to focus on the structural details of second language speech or, alternatively, to study the impact of newcomers as ideological emblems, uniting long-term residents in opposition. But the old categories and distinctions cannot account for the generative splits and alignments emerging in contemporary urban environments, and we need to be very careful about the a priori distinctions we build into our research (Gumperz 1982; Blommaert and Backus 2011; Blommaert and Rampton 2011). But there is a route past these premature reifications, celebrations and exclusions in the 'total linguistic fact'.

Summary

If sociolinguistics and second language research are treated as separate fields, linguistics cannot do justice to contemporary urban environments. To provide a rounded account of urban L2 speech, rhetorical acts, ideological positioning and limitations in the structural linguistic repertoire need to be analysed together, as the description of Mandeep's English styling presented in this chapter has set out to do.

Related topics

Identity in variationist sociolinguistics; Language and identity in linguistic ethnography; Challenges for language and identity researchers in the collection and transcription of spoken interaction; Language and ethnic identity; Class in language and identity research; Beyond the micro–macro interface in language and identity research; An identity transformation? Social class, language prejudice and the erasure of multilingual capital in higher education; Construction of heritage language and cultural identities: a case study of two young British-Bangladeshis in London; The future of identity research: impact and new developments in sociolinguistics.

Further reading

Agha, A. (2004). Registers of language, in A. Duranti (ed.) *A companion to linguistic anthropology*. Oxford: Blackwell, pp. 23–45. (A succinct statement of Agha's ground-breaking approach to style.)

Blommaert, J. and Backus, A. (2011). 'Repertoires revisited: "knowing language" in superdiversity', *Working Papers in Urban Language and Literacies*, Paper 67 [Online]. Available at www.academia. edu/6365319/WP67_Blommaert_and_Backus_2011._Repertoires_revisited_Knowing_language_ in_superdiversity. (A lucid and original approach to repertoire.)

Kramsch, C. (2009). *The multilingual subject*. Oxford: Oxford University Press. (Outlines an approach capable of overcoming the traditional separation of sociolinguistics and second language research.)

Notes

1 This chapter draws on material first published in B. Rampton (2013). 'Styling in a language learned later in life', *Modern Language Journal*, 97(2): 360–382.

2 The *Sun* is a national tabloid newspaper in the UK, where tabloid newspapers are traditionally associated with working-class culture.

3 In this series of the *Big Brother* reality TV show, a number of contestants were accused of racism for the way they commented on the Bollywood film star Shilpa Shetty. See http://en.wikipedia.org/wiki/Celebrity_Big_Brother_racism_controversy

References

Agha, A. (2004). Registers of language, in A. Duranti (ed.) *A companion to linguistic anthropology*. Oxford: Blackwell, pp. 23–45.

Agha, A. (2007). *Language and social relations*. Cambridge: Cambridge University Press.

Auer, P. (ed.) (2007). *Style and social identities*. Berlin: Mouton de Gruyter.

Bakhtin, M. (1984). *Problems in Dostoevsky's poetics*. Minneapolis, MN: University of Minnesota Press.

Block, D. (2006). *Multilingual identities in a global city*. Basingstoke: Palgrave.

Blommaert, J. (2008). *Grassroots literacy: writing, identity and voice in central Africa*. London: Routledge.

Blommaert, J. and Backus, A. (2011). 'Repertoires revisited: "knowing language" in superdiversity', *Working Papers in Urban Language and Literacies*, Paper 67 [Online]. Available at www.academia. edu/6365319/WP67_Blommaert_and_Backus_2011._Repertoires_revisited_Knowing_language_ in_superdiversity

Blommaert, J., Collins, J. and Slembrouck, S. (2005). 'Spaces of multilingualism', *Language and Communication*, 25: 197–216.

Blommaert, J. and Rampton, B. (2011). 'Language and superdiversity', *Diversities*, 13(2). UNESCO [Online]. Available at www.unesco.org/shs/diversities/vol13/issue2/art1

Coupland, N. (2007). *Style*. Cambridge: Cambridge University Press.

Drummond, R. and Schleef, E. (this volume). Identity in variationist sociolinguistics, in S. Preece (ed.) *The Routledge handbook of language and identity*. London: Routledge, pp. 50–65.

Eckert, P. (2008). 'Variation and the indexical field', *Journal of Sociolinguistics*, 12: 453–476.

Gumperz, J. (1982). *Discourse strategies*. Cambridge: Cambridge University Press.

Harris, R. (2006). *New ethnicities and language use*. Basingstoke: Palgrave.

Kramsch, C. (2009). *The multilingual subject*. Oxford: Oxford University Press.

Labov, W. (1972). *Sociolinguistic patterns*. Philadelphia: University of Pennsylvania Press.

Pennycook, A. (1994). *The cultural politics of English as an international language*. London: Longman.

Preston, D. (1989). *Sociolinguistics and second language acquisition*. Oxford: Blackwell.

Rampton, B. (1983). 'Some flaws in educational discussion of the English of Asian schoolchildren in Britain', *Journal of Multilingual and Multicultural Development*, 4: 15–28.

Rampton, B. (1995). *Crossing: language and ethnicity among adolescents*. London: Longman.

Rampton, B. (2006). *Language in late modernity: interaction in an urban school*. Cambridge: Cambridge University Press.

Rampton, B. (2011a). 'Style contrasts, migration and social class', *Journal of Pragmatics*, 43: 1236–1250.

Rampton, B. (2011b). 'From "multi-ethnic adolescent heteroglossia" to "contemporary urban vernaculars"', *Language and Communication*, 31: 276–294.

Rampton, B. (2013). 'Styling in a language learned later in life', *Modern Language Journal*, 97(2): 360–382.

Sharma, D. (2005). 'Dialect stabilization and speaker awareness in nonnative varieties of English', *Journal of Sociolinguistics*, 9: 194–224.

Sharma, D. and Sankaran, L. (2011). 'Cognitive and social forces in dialect shift: gradual change in London Asian speech', *Language Variation and Change*, 23: 399–428.

Silverstein, M. (1985). Language and the culture of gender, in E. Mertz and R. Parmentier (eds) *Semiotic mediation*. New York: Academic Press, pp. 219–259.

Talmy, S. (2008). 'The cultural productions of the ESL student at Tradewinds: contingency, multidirectionality, and identity in L2 socialization', *Applied Linguistics*, 29: 619–644.

Wells, A. (no date). *UK polling report: survey and polling news from YouGov* [Online]. Available at http://ukpollingreport.co.uk/guide/seat-profiles/ealingsouthall

Wimmer, A. and Glick Schiller, N. (2002). 'Methodological nationalism and beyond: nation-state building, migration and the social sciences', *Global Networks*, 2(4): 301–334.

Young, R. (2009). *Discursive practice in language learning and teaching*. Oxford: Wiley-Blackwell.

Appendix

Transcription conventions

Segmental phonology

[ ] IPA phonetic transcription

text English pronounced with Anglo variants

text English pronounced with Punjabi variants

Intonation

\ low fall

/ low rise

\ high fall

/ high rise

∨ fall rise

∧ rise fall

| high stress

⁻ high unaccented prenuclear syllable

↑ pitch step-up

↓ pitch step-down

Conversational features

(.)	micro-pause
(1.5)	approximate length of pause in seconds
[	overlapping turns
[	
CAPITALS	loud
.hh	in-breath
>text<	more rapid speech
°text°	quietly spoken
( )	speech inaudible
(text)	speech hard to discern; the analyst's guess
((text:))	'stage directions'
"text"	direct reported speech
→	words and utterances of particular interest to the analysis

30

Construction of heritage language and cultural identities

A case study of two young British-Bangladeshis in London

Qumrul Hasan Chowdhury

Introduction

The construction of ancestral language and cultural identities for the children of migrants is intricately embedded in their lived experiences and discursive positions in the host society. The level of identification with their heritage language(s) and culture varies depending on how minority ethnic youth participate in the social networks available to them and is influenced by other identity inscriptions, such as gender, ethnicity and social class. In this chapter, I present the case of two young British-Bangladeshi women in London, who are representative of educated middle-class Bangladeshis. By British-Bangladeshi, I refer to young people of Bangladeshi origin who have lived in Britain for a considerable period and attained British citizenship. I argue that identification with heritage language for the young British-Bangladeshi women in this case is significantly shaped by their gendered identity. By heritage language I mean 'nonsocietal' and 'nonmajority' languages which are spoken by linguistic minority communities, including migrant communities (Valdés 2005: 411). Cultural identity, on the other hand, is more sociopolitically loaded in that social class and religious positioning, along with their gender roles in the family, play important roles. Social class as an identity construct is complex and relevant in the context of globalisation, increased migration and the neoliberal political economy (see Block 2014, this volume). Gender identity in relation to language has increasingly been viewed 'performatively' (Butler 1990), meaning how we perform our gender, rather than deterministically, meaning male or female attributes as a result of biology or socialisation (see Cameron 2005; Jones, this volume). I argue in this chapter that there is a need to deconstruct elements of ancestral culture and examine cultural difference within the family to understand the intersection of gender with culture in South Asian culture. Before I present the case study, I provide some general comments on the Bangladeshi community and discourses of multilingualism and multiculturalism in Britain as a means to orient readers with the context.

The Bangladeshi community in Britain is the fastest-growing and third-largest immigrant group from South Asia (Gardner 2009). Fifty-five per cent live in London, with half of these London-based Bangladeshis living in Tower Hamlets (Piggott 2004). Ninety per cent of the total Bangladeshi population in Britain have their origin in the Sylhet region of Bangladesh. Despite the large size of this community in the UK, it struggles with poverty, unemployment, unskilled job experience, lack of formal education and poor housing and health conditions (Eade and Garbin 2006). A large number of the Bangladeshis are known to work in the clothing industry and in restaurants (Lawson and Sachdev 2004).

The two heritage languages spoken in the Bangladeshi community are Bangla and Sylheti. As Bangla, the official language of Bangladesh, played an important part in the political history of Bangladesh (Thompson 2007), it is deeply integrated with building the secular, national and cultural identities of the people of Bangladesh. Sylheti is arguably a regional variety of Bangla or a separate language which is spoken in the north-eastern Sylhet region of Bangladesh (Lawson and Sachdev 2004). In the case study presented in this chapter, Bangla is the two participants' heritage language in the sense that it is the language of their parents and their grandparents (Ovando *et al.* 2005), while Sylheti is the heritage language spoken by the Sylhet-originated British-Bangladeshi community.

As the majority of the population is Muslim, Bangladesh follows many Islamic traditions and rituals. Simultaneously, the country also has a long history of fighting against Muslim invaders that has contributed to the development of a cultural spirit that is secular in nature (Riaz 2003). Therefore, in the cultural space of the Bangladeshis, both in Bangladesh and also in Britain, there is an underlying tension between secular nationalist and Islamic culture (Eade and Garbin 2006).

To date, applied linguistics research into the Bangladeshi community in Britain has mostly been limited to the working-class Bangladeshi communities situated in East London. The case study presented in this chapter makes an effort to shed light on educated professional Bangladeshis who have largely been under-represented in research. To understand how the two participants discussed in this chapter identify and perform ancestral language and cultural identities, it is important to take account of the context of multilingualism and cultural diversity in Britain. Multilingualism, even though a reality in Britain, challenges the country's national ideological discourse of a monolingual and homogeneous Britain (Moyer and Martin Rojo 2007). Bilingual communities have been seen as a threat to the 'cultural unification' of Britain, and the spread of multilingualism has been viewed with suspicion (Blackledge and Creese 2010). In comparison to multilingualism, multiculturalism in Britain was the 'scene of passive, even complacent, satisfaction' (Wood *et al.* 2006: 2). The scene started to change at the beginning of the twenty-first century with the rise of the power of the European Union and the 9/11 terrorist attack in the United States. As Modood (2005) asserts, the 7/7 bomb attacks in London in 2005 by four British Muslim youths made the Muslim community, including those of Bangladeshi origin, an 'undesirable Other' to British mainstream society even in the time of a pluralist society. The changed multicultural context of Britain connects with the case study presented in the chapter to understand the dynamics between Bangladeshi cultural identity and Islam.

After setting the scene by providing some background, I now move on to the theorisation of language and cultural identity in this chapter. This done, I discuss the methodological framework undertaken for doing this research. I then present the findings of the research and discuss the findings in light of the adapted theoretical framework. Finally, the chapter identifies some issues of interest for applied linguistics regarding the heritage language and cultural identities of the children of South Asian migrants.

Overview

Poststructuralism: identity, discourse and positioning

The study is theoretically framed by the poststructuralist view of identity that regards identity as fluid, multiple and dynamic rather than fixed and essential (Bhabha 1986; Hall 1990). Poststructuralism argues that the relationships of individuals with groups are not neat and constant, but rather situated and shifting (Brah *et al.* 1999; also see Baxter, this volume). This ambivalence of human relationships with group affiliations foregrounds the multidimensionality of social categories and creates scope for exercising individual agency within the macro structures. Closely intertwined with the poststructuralist approaches to identity and also relevant in this chapter are the notions of discourse and positioning. Paul du Gay (1996: 43) considers discourse as the linguistic manifestation of a 'particular kind of knowledge about a topic' that also institutionalises such knowledge in social settings and practices. 'Positioning' has been perceived by Pavlenko and Blackledge (2004) as a 'perpetual tension' between how discursive practices position us and how we want to position ourselves. Weedon (1997: 3) sees this perpetual tension as 'negotiation' of 'ways of being an individual', which she calls 'subject position'. Having given a brief overview of a poststructuralist framework of identity, I now turn to the two main dimensions of identity for this chapter: culture and language.

Cultural identity

Culture can be perceived from 'essentialised' and 'unitary' views that consider culture as an ancestrally shared finished product (Baumann 1999). A 'processual' view, in contrast to an essentialised view, perceives culture 'to exist in the act of being performed', which 'can never stand still or repeat itself without changing its meaning' (ibid.: 26). Culture, according to this view, is not neatly divided in terms of nationality or religion; it is rather dynamic, fluid and emergent (Holliday 2009). Hall similarly takes on board the fluidity of culture and says this about cultural identity:

> [...] as well as the many points of similarity, there are also critical points of deep and significant *difference* which constitute 'what we really are'; or rather – since history has intervened – 'what we have become'. [...] Cultural identity, in this second sense, is a matter of 'becoming' as well as of 'being'.
>
> *(Hall 1990: 225)*

Drawing on Hall, cultural identity is the juxtaposition of an imagined unitary ancestral heritage and the adoption of different subject positions in the discourses available to migrants. In this case study, cultural identity refers to ways in which culture is performed in lifestyle, dress, food, festivals, relationships, etc. (Adaskou *et al.* 1990), and also takes into account ways in which culture intersects with other dimensions of identity such as ethnicity, nationality, gender, social class and religion in a more holistic sense (Ferdman and Horenczyk 2000; Mathews 2000).

Language identity

Poststructuralist theory perceives language to be reciprocally connected with subjectivity as it helps one to construct and negotiate the self across a diverse range of space and time (Norton and Toohey 2011). Language identity, if seen through the lens of hereditary endowment or by belonging to a particular community only, is restricting in scope as it undermines the possibility of choice or agency in shaping one's language identity. Rampton's (1990) formulation of language identity as 'language expertise', 'language inheritance' and 'language affiliation' is useful in this regard to take account of choice-driven possibilities. Language expertise suggests the level of proficiency that a person has obtained; expertise can be seen through the prism of objective measures. Importantly, expertise in a language is always developed (i.e. it is not inherited) and, as Rampton (1990) argues, someone can be expert in a language without feeling close to it. Language inheritance relates to the language(s) that are passed on to children by virtue of their family's heritage. Finally, language affiliation refers to our 'sense of attachment' or bonding to any language. As Rampton (1990) argues, we cannot assume that just because a language is inherited that there is a strong affiliation to it. Additionally, language affiliation is influenced by social contexts and by societal and governmental discourses about heritage languages. Taking the theoretical insight of language and cultural identity, I now contextualise the discussion to migrant youths.

Language and cultural identity of the migrant youth

The relationship between heritage languages and the cultural identity of minority ethnic youth has been widely taken up in applied linguistics in the context of education (e.g. Lambert 1975; Cummins 2000). Four decades ago, Wallace Lambert (1975), in the Canadian educational context, proposed four possible modes of how immigrant children accommodate to the dominant society: the children of migrants may become completely anomic and forsake the ancestral language and culture; they may disregard the language and culture of the dominant society; they may show indifference to both societies; and, finally, they may show balance by becoming bilingual and bicultural. Lambert's formulation of heritage language and cultural identity adjustments of the children of immigrants, even though it was offered a long time ago, is probably still useful to draw upon to explain the identity constructions of the two young British-Bangladeshis in this chapter, particularly in relation to their degree of participation in the host society.

Heritage language and cultural identity constructions among young South Asian minorities can be influenced by their membership in the social categories of gender and social class among other factors. Young South Asian British Muslim women's diasporic cultural identities have been documented as being shaped by their gender roles in the family and in the community (Dwyer 2000; Talbani and Hasanali 2000). In research conducted among young Mirpuri Pakistanis in the UK, Dwyer (2000) shows that young Muslim women are expected to be the custodians of cultural and religious honour and are held responsible for transferring cultural heritage, Islamic values and heritage language from the mother to the daughter. Talbani and Hasanali (2000), in their research on young South Asian immigrants in Canada, similarly show that ancestral religion-culture inspired a male-dominated gendered hierarchy that influences the socialisation and identity of young women in the family. Gender continues to be a significant factor in the maintenance of heritage language and the construction of cultural and language identity among South Asians (Mills 2004; Preece 2008). Preece (2008) shows with the case of Sita, a young British Sri Lankan Tamil woman, that the intersection of gender and language identity can be influenced by the political as well as the cultural contexts of migrants. While Sita has less competence in Tamil, her heritage language, than English, she shows high affiliation with Tamil, relating her responsibility to maintain the heritage language of the Tamil diaspora in the UK to the political instability of the Tamil community in Sri Lanka and her role as a future imagined wife and mother. Construction of heritage language identities is in some cases linked with the social class of the minority individuals. In Ogbu's (1999) study, his participants' responses manifest the close link between higher social class and linguistic assimilation (i.e. integration to the other language even though risking own language). Having fairly discussed the theoretical foundation of language and cultural identity and some research studies on heritage language and cultural identities of minority youth, I now turn to the research framework of this study.

Methodology

The case study that I present in this chapter comes from my MA dissertation project at a London-based British university (Chowdhury 2010). The project researched British-Bangladeshis in London with the aim of examining how they identified with Bangla language and Bangladeshi culture. Six participants took part in the study, who I contacted based on my networks and acquaintances with Bangladeshis in London. In this chapter, I present a case study of two of my British-Bangladeshi participants: Nitu and Saima (pseudonyms) (see Table 30.1). These two participants were young (aged 19 and 22 respectively), female and middle class. The fact that I ascribe a middle-class positioning to these participants is broadly based on the social status of their families with regard to income, education and occupation (see Block 2014, this volume). Moreover, during the research process, I became familiar with the classed positioning of the families through commonly referred indicators of social class such as neighbourhood, mobility, taste and symbolic behaviour. I will also draw on data from Renu, Saima's mother, another participant in my study.

The overall questions that guided the research to build the case study were:

1   Where do the young British-Bangladeshis stand in terms of their identification with Bangla language and culture?
2   What are the different factors that influence their identifications?

The data for this research was collected in two phases. The first phase comprised audio-recorded semi-structured interviews (Gray 2009), where the participants were asked questions concerning their identification with Bangla language and Bangladeshiness. These interviews were primarily carried out in Bangla, with Nitu's interview lasting for 58 minutes and Saima's for 94 minutes. The second phase had two stages, starting with short follow-up interviews to clarify some of the interview responses of the participants. Following this, in order to supplement the self-reported identity positions, participants were engaged in audio-recorded conversations with their family members in the absence of the researcher. I supplied the participants with a number of photographs that represented Bangladeshi culture (e.g. photos of Bangla new year, Eid festival); Bangla language (e.g. photo of the national language martyr monument in Bangladesh); Britishness (e.g. photo of Westminster); and the Bangladeshi community in London (e.g. photo of Brick Lane in London, known for Bangladeshi curry restaurants). I asked the participants to

Table 30.1 Participant profile

Name	Age	Sex	Education	Religion	Linguistic repertoire
Nitu	19	Female	Undergraduate student	Islam	Bangla, English, Hindi, Spanish
Saima	22	Female	Graduate	Islam	Bangla, English, German

pick two photos on the basis of their affiliation to the themes in the photos and talk about those to the interlocutors. My purpose was to see how the participants positioned themselves in connection to culture and language during their interaction.

Given the nature of the research and the participants involved, it is important to talk about the relationship between the researcher and the participants and the role of this relationship on the research process. I was fairly familiar to Nitu as I had met her twice in community events, but I was unknown to Saima as we had never met before. To ensure that the two young women participants felt comfortable in the presence of a male researcher, the research process was carried out at the residences of the participants. My status of being a Bangla-speaking Bangladeshi academic doing an MA in the UK had two possible positional dimensions. First, it gave me a certain degree of authority and legitimacy, with the possible effect of increasing the seriousness of the research process for the participants. Second, it accorded me the status of 'insider' on the grounds of education, social class and the ethnolinguistic background of the participants. However, this was offset by the fact that I was also a young male researcher who was not familiar with the lives of young female children of migrants in the UK, in particular their everyday experiences, concerns and ways of living and doing things in present-day Britain. This mixed status of mine influenced the questions that I asked, the responses that the interviewees gave and the interpretations that I have made of the data.

Good ethical practice has been maintained throughout the research process, which included among other measures using a consent form to obtain permission from the participants and identifying the participants with pseudonyms. The family group discussions were transcribed based on the transcription conventions devised by Coates (2003) (see Appendix). For a nuanced understanding of participants' positions across the interaction, the family interactional data were transcribed showing conversational features, such as overlapping, false starts, variation in volume of the participants, etc. As the data includes the use of Bangla, the extracts that have been used in this chapter have been translated into English with an effort to keep the translation as close as possible to the original. English words used by the interviewees have been kept unchanged. To make a clear distinction between English in the original data and my translation, all the English in the original data have been bold faced in the excerpts. However, since the interview data were primarily analysed in terms of its semantic content, they have been presented with standardised grammar and punctuation. The data were then analysed for the themes of language and cultural identity, drawing on Lave and Wenger's (1991) notion of 'community of practice'. Lave and Wenger argue that social relations are constructed, reconstructed and further developed through participation in the practices of different communities. It is through participation that we become active in the 'practices of social communities' and 'construct identities in relation to these communities' (Wenger 1998: 3). This notion shaped the way that I analysed how the participants construct Bangla language and Bangladeshi cultural identity, in that I looked at their participation in different communities, predominantly their family and their peer groups. In the following section, I present the findings.

The data

Nitu

Nitu was born in Dhaka, Bangladesh, in a Bangla-speaking Bangladeshi family. The family migrated to London in 1999 as Nitu's father was transferred to the London office of his company. Nitu's father, Belal, is an electrical engineer who works at a leading multinational tobacco company in London, and her mother, Shaila, is a practising gynaecologist. When Nitu was interviewed, she was doing a Bachelor's degree in Graphic Design and New Media in a university specialising in creative arts. The professional occupations of Nitu's parents and the trend of mobility in the family, as evidenced by Nitu's undergraduate study, are indicative of the family's middle-class positioning (Block 2014).

Bangladeshi cultural identity

In Extract 1, Nitu and I are discussing what she likes wearing. The extract indicates a strong sense of identification with Bangladeshi culture in that she likes wearing Bangladeshi dress. However, performance of the Bangladeshi cultural identity, in her case, seems to be guided by her perceived appropriateness of the expectations and norms of the Bangladeshi community in Britain and the community of friends and classmates located at the British university that she attends. This is illustrated in what she says about wearing *salwar-kameez*, a common Bangladeshi dress.

Extract 1 Part of my identity

> When I go to a Bangladeshi party, I wear salwar-kameez or *fotua*. When I go to **university**, I wear **skirt–tops–pants** ... **personally** I like the thing *salwar-kameez* so much. I think ... **part of my identity**. When I wear salwar-kameez, I feel **at home**.
>
> *(Nitu, Interview 1)*

Dress is often considered to be the strongest marker of cultural identity for young South Asian women (Dwyer 2000). Nitu, by wearing salwar-kameez at the Bangladeshi parties, makes herself culturally intelligible (Butler 1990) as a traditional Bangladeshi girl with her Bangladeshi relatives and friends. On the other hand, her choice of Western attire at university can be interpreted as an attempt to conform to the dressing pattern norms of young women in British higher education institutes. Nitu, by wearing salwar-kameez at the Bangladeshi parties and skirts–tops–pants at the university, is probably trying to make her a 'legitimate participant' in the community of practice of Bangladeshi friends and relatives and the British academic institution-based peer group community of practice (Lave and Wenger 1991).

Bangla language identity

Nitu's relationship with Bangla appears to intersect with gender and her family emotions. She reported speaking in Bangla with her father on topics such as daily activities, the weekend plan or household matters. However, when they talk about sports, politics or academic subjects, they switch to English. Despite the fact that she reported the practice of 'separate bilingualism' with her father, determined by topic (Holmes 2013), there is scope to view this sceptically. It seems plausible that evidence of English–Bangla code-switching would be found if their interaction was audio-recorded over a period of time. What Nitu reported about her language choice with her father is probably suggestive, among other possible explanations, of the perceived impurity of mixing two languages. In addition, there may be an idealised home diglossic situation in that Nitu and her father preserve the 'prestige' variety English for higher-level topics and functions, while they allocate Bangla for mundane domestic matters. However, such assumptions do not greatly problematise the possible fact that English–Bangla flexibility is likely to help

Nitu perform the subject position of an everyday traditional British-Bangladeshi daughter to her father. Extract 2 illustrates what Nitu reported about the language choice with her mother.

Extract 2 It is physically impossible to speak in English with ma

I just can't speak in **English** with ma … if I want to speak in **English** with ma, I would translate Bangla into English (laughing). It is **physically impossible** to speak in **English** with ma. I just CAN'T do it.

(Nitu, Interview 1)

Nitu presents her use of Bangla with her mother as effortless and 'natural', claiming that translating to English would require conscious effort. The seeming automaticity of using Bangla with her mother and her perceived absurdity of translating Bangla into English in interactions with her mother is highly suggestive of a gender-mediated heritage language identity. Speaking Bangla with her mother enables her to nurture a spontaneous and intimate mother–daughter relationship (Preece 2008). The laughter in Extract 2 probably is indicative of the merriness and playfulness of this relationship, and the raised volume of 'can't' suggests that English would provide a different type of relationship with her mother.

Thus far, I have presented data related to Nitu. In the next part of this section, we turn to Saima.

Saima

Saima came to the UK when she was four years old; she is the youngest child of a Bangla-speaking Bangladeshi family. Saima's father is an electrical engineer and her mother is a homemaker. Saima's father came to the UK in 1973 to pursue higher study. Saima's mother is a history graduate from a prestigious Bangladeshi university. When she was interviewed, Saima had just finished her undergraduate degree in English Literature from a British university and was working as a support teacher in a school. The family status of Saima is exemplified by her academic capital and decent occupational start; the academic refinement of her mother and her father's professional career in a lucrative engineering profession after he had earned a British higher degree qualifies the family as occupying a middle-class status.

Bangladeshi cultural identity

Saima positions herself as having less emotional affiliation to the Bangladeshi community than Nitu. The position that she adopts in the interviews about the Bangladeshi community appears shaped by the class identity of her parents, as Saima's mother, in a separate interview, reported that she and her husband had carefully distanced the children from Bangladeshi culture by living in a white British neighbourhood so that the children could 'concentrate' on their education and compete with the 'Whites'. As can be seen in Extract 3, her reading about Bangladesh and the Bangladeshi community in London while she was growing up also seemed to have contributed to some negative stereotypes of Bangladeshiness.

Extract 3 Everything seems to be tabloid news

Actually while I was growing up, I used to think of the negatives of being brought up in the Asian community. Everything seems to be tabloid news

and [you are] **more vulnerable to picking up the bad as well as the good from fellow Asians ... there's a possibility that there may be Bengalis who can have bad influence on you.**

(Saima, Interview 1)

By using 'Bengali' in Extract 3 (and also in the rest of the interview) instead of the more common 'Bangladeshi' or 'Bangali' to refer to the people of Bangladesh, Saima appears to alienate herself from the Bangladeshis. 'Bengali' here works to distance Saima from the local working-class-dominated Bangladeshi community that she does not admire. Saima's mention of the Asians making 'tabloid news' of 'everything' prompts her to essentialise the South Asians as shallow and gossip lovers.

Saima distances herself from a Bangladeshi identity and also rejects a possible British identity on religious grounds. The identity position that she embraces is her religious identity as a practising Muslim, despite her mother's secular view of religion. Extract 4, which consists of a conversation between Saima and her mother Renu regarding the Eid festival, sheds light on the intersection of Saima's cultural and religious identities.

Extract 4 Practising Muslim

Saima = S; Renu = R

1   S: Eid I was saying to her that <laughing>/ I erm we started to celebrate Eid from **2005**/ from the day (.) erm (.) I have become (1) you know **practising Muslim**/ before that (.) I just had heard slightly about Eid/ I did not know or understand much about Eid ((xxx))/ when I went to university, I noticed that <low voice> this is a **community event**/ specially the one that comes after the fasting is the **most meaningful** to me/ moreover (.) you have given me **broader perspective on religion**/ I could somewhat (1) **discuss-judge** with you/ I could **evaluate** with you the other Eid/ the Eid ul Adha/ the one where **animals** are **sacrificed**/

2   R: Eid ul Adha/

3   S: that=

4   R: =that is called sacrificing Eid/

5   S: yes sacrificing/ then I thought (2) ok **how right is this to slaughter** erm **sacrifice an animal**=

6   R: =on the **excuse of sacrifice**=

7   S: =**as part of a celebration? something did not ring right about that**/ but because of you I could **evaluate** that/ because you have taught me (.) to ask **questions** regarding-**religion-anything**/ **well not anything but specially religion**/

8   R: but but the **funny** thing is that this **sacrifice** is also in **Hindu religion**/ I could never accept this/ (.) the *kurbaani* (.) never (.) from my **childhood** (.) **from childhood** this **is the most cruel thing I have seen**/ on the **excuse of religion**- from there **jealousy** and **CRUELTY** develop in human/ because of this human beings kill another human/ they don't **care**/ because (.) they **already** have the **practice**/

9   S: **that is in the context of religion**/ [**but also**

10 R: [**I don't know**=

11 S: =**there is good side**=

12 R: =**good side (.) well**

(Saima and Renu, Family conversation)

In Extract 4 Saima and her mother Renu discuss their perceptions of Eid. In turn 1, Saima starts the conversation by saying that she had not celebrated the Eid festival before she started to practise

Islam. When Saima says that she has become a practising Muslim (turn 1), she takes a pause, hesitates and also uses hedging like 'you know'. Saima's hesitation and use of hedging here may indicate that she is trying to maintain a good relationship with her mother, who has a secular orientation to religion, given that hedging is frequently used when interlocutors want to be 'sensitive' to 'topics which are controversial in some way' (Coates 1996: 162). In the interview data, Saima reported that she does not disclose that she is a Muslim to people, as saying to people that she is a Muslim may result in a 'new sense of insecurity'. Saima's hesitation about her religious positioning is indicative that she is aware of the social and political discourses about Islam in the post 9/11 context of Britain. Saima then says that she finds the Eid which comes after fasting (turn 1) 'most meaningful', while she questions the ritual of animal sacrifice on Eid-ul-Adha (turn 1). Tension arises when Renu sees the ritual of animal sacrifice as an 'excuse' for brutality, claiming an extreme standpoint that it creates cruelty, jealousy and homicide in society (turn 8). This is the point when Saima disagrees with Renu and tries to restrict the conversation to the context of religion. She also wants her mother to see the good side of such a ritual. The mother's subsequent use of hedging in turns 10 and 12, especially the use of 'well', suggests that what she would say on the issue is in conflict with her daughter (Schiffrin 1987). This conversation suggests two important things about the intersection of Saima's cultural and religious identities. One, she is trying to achieve a Muslim identity by balancing it with the secular viewpoints of her mother in the context of post 9/11 and 7/7 discourses of Islam in Britain. Two, she identifies with Bangladeshi Muslim culture as it also conforms to her religious identity, but distances herself from a secular Bangladeshi culture, as represented by her mother, when it is in conflict with her Muslim identity.

Bangla language identity

In the community of practice of her family, Saima speaks Bangla only with her mother, and her mother is the only one in the family who speaks Bangla with her. Saima's mother says that, when she and her husband brought up the children, they always spoke English with them to help them have enough exposure to English. It is Saima's mother who later considered it her responsibility to teach the children Bangla. Mills's (2004) study of Pakistani mothers in Britain shows that, while emphasising the role of English in their children's lives as the means of becoming successful in UK society, they also consider it their responsibility to transmit the heritage language to their children. Saima in this way learned Bangla from her mother. Extract 5 shows how Saima's relationship with Bangla is primarily through her mother.

Extract 5 I speak a lot with my mum

I do listen to song but not by myself ... through by my mum. I don't listen to Bangladeshi music by myself. My mum tells me to read. I learned how to read but I don't always understand a lot. I can read the things that my mum writes to bring down.

(Saima, Interview 1)

Saima's main experience of Bangla as her heritage language is mediated by her mother. Although there is a risk of overgeneralisation concerning gender, Coates's (1996) argument that talk helps to establish rapport among women may be salient here. Saima's repetitive use of 'my mum' indicates her intimacy and affection with her mother and, by speaking a lot of Bangla with her mother, Saima fosters this affectionate relationship. Saima's case here resonates with Nitu in this study and the Tamil participant of Preece's (2008) study, both of whom identify heritage language with intimacy with their mothers. In the next section I discuss the findings and then highlight some key issues for applied linguistics.

Discussion

The research shows that identification with heritage language and Bangladeshi culture for the two young British-Bangladeshi women is closely interlinked with the identity inscriptions of gender and religion in their lives with some influence of their classed upbringings. Construction of what cultural identity is for Saima is not based on her social experience of coming across the community first hand, but rather from her reading and from the negative and safe-distanced representation of the Bangladeshi community through her middle-class-educated parents. Blommaert (1999) explains that if the cultural identity of a group is perceived negatively in society, members of the group are also likely to perceive their cultural identity negatively. In the case of Saima, cultural and social capital-based essentialism received via her parents about Bangladeshis in the UK shapes her reading of Bangladeshiness in British newspapers and magazines, particularly the negative discourses about the East London-based British-Bangladeshis. Despite this alienation from Bangladeshiness based on her social class, we see a possible mother-mediated avenue of identification with less social class-conflicting forms of Bangladeshi culture such as listening to Bangla songs, for example Rabindranath Tagore's song, as she reported elsewhere in the interview, and reading popular Bangla literature. However, such a possible identification is not easily constructed as we can see in Extract 4, where Saima's Muslim identity is contested by her mother's counter-narrative about the ritual of animal sacrifice in Islam. Saima, however, appears to keep her Muslim identity safe and humble by not risking her intimate relationship with her mother. The care with which she positions her Muslim identity is also indicative of her awareness of the negative discourses of South Asian Muslim identity in present-day Britain (Modood 2005).

Nitu's identification with Bangladeshiness is mediated by how she makes sense of performing her gender in line with the expected practices of the communities of practice she encounters in her life. Nitu's choice of salwar-kameez in the communities of British-Bangladeshis and her family can be interpreted, along with her feminine comfort, as a reproduction of the discourses of gender roles and expectations of South Asian immigrant communities (Dwyer 2000). Her choice of Western dress in British academic institution-based communities of practice probably can be interpreted as an attempt to conform to the unified cultural expectations of minorities in present-day Britain.

This research shows that gender, as a dimension of identity, intersects with language identity for British-Bangladeshis such as Nitu and Saima. Even though Nitu and Saima have varying expertise in Bangla (Rampton 1990), both of them associate their use of Bangla with an affectionate relationship with their mother. This research shows that even though motivation among middle-class South Asian parents to enable their children to achieve success in British society may result in limited use of heritage language in the family (Ogbu 1999), the language is still transferred as part of the gendered role of the mother (Mills 2004; Preece 2008). Finally, speaking the language is necessitated by the filial roles of Nitu and Saima, as both of them use the language to maintain a unique and intimate relationship with their mother.

Finally, where do these cases stand in terms of Lambert's (1975) four modes of language and cultural identification among minority children? Saima's case illustrates Lambert's mode of minority children having anomic distance from both communities. In Saima's case, she does not feel close to the Bangladeshi culture based on her negative perception about Bangladeshiness effectuated by her classed upbringing. Moreover, her religious identity is in conflict with the representation of Bangladeshi culture by her mother, who is secular minded. She also appears ambivalent about British cultural identity as she associates Britishness with a free and open life-style which Islam does not favour. Nitu's case, however, provides support for Lambert's mode that minority children identify with both cultures. Nitu, partly driven by her gendered identity, attempts to gain legitimacy in both the Bangladeshi and the British society by attending to the cultural norms of these two societies. In addition to positioning minority ethnic children in terms of broad categories as Lambert proposed, this small case study sheds light on the processes of identification by showing how identification with language and culture forms a complex relationship with other social categories.

Issues for applied linguistics

The research provides support for the role of gender in construction of the cultural identity of young South Asian women (Dwyer 2000; Talbani and Hasanali 2000). However, rather than framing national/ethnic culture together with religion to understand South Asian Muslim culture, it is important to deconstruct the elements of ancestral culture, particularly with the case of Bangladeshi culture where there is a mixed element of secularism and Islamism (Eade and Garbin 2006). Moreover, the commonplace mother–daughter transference nature of South Asian immigrant communities can be troubled and questioned if the mother and daughter do not share a common cultural platform, for example, as this research shows in the case of religious viewpoints. This research sheds light on how social class positioning influences the process of identification with the heritage language and heritage culture. Social class-based alienation from the mainstream home-country community by middle-class South Asian parents in pursuit of academic success of the children may result in potential 'othering' of the community among the children. Depressing discourses that are available about the working-class majority ancestral community in the host country may solidify already negative discursive positioning about the community among ethnic minority children.

The research echoes some previous assumptions that heritage language is maintained in South Asian families mostly as part of maternal responsibility. Male parents in South Asian middle-class families, as it appeared in this study, associate English with upward mobility and high-level thinking in the Anglophone British society and show conservatism in using the heritage language. The mothers, on the other hand, identify with the heritage language to a greater extent and want to transfer it to the female children in the family. As we have seen with both the participants, speaking Bangla fosters gendered affection and a closer bond between the mother and daughter.

Finally, this research shows the emergence of a religious identity trumping both Britishness and Bangladeshiness. However, the making of this identity is in tension with the increasingly strong Islamophobic discourses in Britain and the resulting insecurity within the family about the performance of this identity.

Summary

This chapter provides a snapshot of heritage language and cultural identity constructions of two young middle-class British-Bangladeshi women in Britain. The two participants have their own trajectories and breadth of identification with Bangla language and Bangladeshiness that are intricately embedded in the structures surrounding them. While they make cases of exercising their agency by trying to negotiate identities, as we saw Saima do in the question of achieving her Muslim identity, their negotiations do not cloud the fact that their identity positioning is also significantly shaped by the structures of family, home and host country communities. The research shows the fluidity and overlapping of social categories of religion, social class and gender in the process of ethnolinguistic and cultural identifications of these young British-Bangladeshis. This research provides support for the roles of gender in constructing South Asian cultural identity. It also raises the need for careful analysis of the dynamics of cultural-religious commonalities and differences between the mother and the daughter to have a nuanced understanding of the gender-mediated transference nature of South Asian culture. Given the emergence of social class as a very important construct in influencing the identity positioning of the participants in this study and the general lack of attention it has received in similar contexts (see Block, this volume), this research raises the need for more identity research into social class and its intersection with culture and language among South Asians. Moreover, the performance of Muslim identity and how this may contest secular discourses in Bangladeshi families, along with negative discourses of Islam in wider society, needs to be examined in greater depth and in diverse contexts. Overall, this research shows the multifaceted intersections of gender, social class and religion in heritage language and cultural identity constructions of the two young Bangladeshis in my study. Moreover, it documents the need for building a macro understanding of ancestral culture; the cultural political dimension of dominant society discourses where minority identities are positioned; and a micro analysis of cultural socialisation within the family to understand the possibilities of South Asian identities.

Related topics

Positioning language and identity: poststructuralist perspectives; Language and ethnic identity; Language and religious identities; Language and gender identities; Class in language and identity research; Language, gender and identities in political life: a case study from Bangladesh; Styling and identity in a second language; Intersectionality in language and identity research; The future of identity research: impact and new developments in sociolinguistics.

Further reading

Eade, J. and Garbin, D. (2006). 'Competing visions of identity and space: Bangladeshi Muslims in Britain', *Contemporary South Asia*, 14(2): 181–193. (This journal article is useful to gain understanding about cultural and religious tension among the Bangladeshi community in Britain.)

Pavlenko, A. and Blackledge, A. (ed.) (2004). *Negotiation of identities in multilingual contexts*. Clevedon: Multilingual Matters. (This edited book provides valuable insights about the varied dimensions of multilingual identities in diverse contexts.)

References

Adaskou, K., Britten, D. and Fahsi, B. (1990). 'Design decisions on the cultural content of a secondary English course for Morocco', *ELT Journal*, 44(1): 3–10.

Baumann, G. (1999). *The multicultural riddle: rethinking national, ethnic and religious identities*. New York: Routledge.

Baxter, J. (this volume). Positioning language and identity: poststructuralist perspectives, in S. Preece (ed.) *The Routledge handbook of language and identity*. Abingdon: Routledge, pp. 34–49.

Bhabha, H. (1986). Foreword: remembering Fanon. Self, psyche and the colonial condition, in F. Fanon. (ed.) *Black skin, white masks*. London: Pluto Press, pp. vii–xxvi.

Blackledge, A. and Creese, A. (2010). *Multilingualism: a critical perspective*. London: Continuum.

Block, D. (2014). *Social class in applied linguistics*. London: Routledge.

Block, D. (this volume). Class in language and identity research, in S. Preece (ed.) *The Routledge handbook of language and identity*. Abingdon: Routledge, pp. 241–254.

Blommaert, J. (1999). The debate is open, in J. Blommaert (ed.) *Language ideological debates*. Berlin: Mouton de Gruyter, pp. 1–38.

Brah, A., Mac, M. and Hickman, G.M. (1999). *Thinking identities: ethnicity, racism and culture*. London: Macmillan.

Butler, J. (1990). *Gender trouble: feminism and the subversion of identity*. New York: Routledge.

Cameron, D. (2005). 'Language, gender, and sexuality: current issues and new directions', *Applied Linguistics*, 26(4): 482–502.

Chowdhury, Q.H. (2010). *Construction, performance and/or negotiations of Bangla language identities and Bangladeshi cultural identities of the Bangladeshis in London*. MA dissertation. Institute of Education, University of London.

Coates, J. (1996). *Women talk*. Oxford: Blackwell.

Coates, J. (2003). *Men talk*. Oxford: Blackwell.

Cummins, J. (2000). *Language, power and pedagogy: bilingual children in the crossfire*. Clevedon: Multilingual Matters.

du Gay, P. (1996). *Consumption and identity at work*. London: SAGE.

Dwyer, C. (2000). 'Negotiating diasporic identities: young British South Asian Muslim women', *Young Women's International Forum*, 23(4): 475–486.

Eade, J. and Garbin, D. (2006). 'Competing visions of identity and space: Bangladeshi Muslims in Britain', *Contemporary South Asia*, 14(2): 181–193.

Ferdman, B. and Horenczyk, G. (2000). Cultural identity and immigration: reconstructing the group during cultural transition, in E. Olshtain and G. Horenczyk (eds) *Language, identity and immigration*. Jerusalem: The Hebrew University Magnes Press, pp. 81–103.

Gardner, K. (2009). 'Lives in motion: the life-course, movement and migration in Bangladesh', *Journal of South Asian Development*, 4(2): 229–251.

Gray, D. (2009). *Doing research in the real world*. 2nd edn. London: SAGE.

Hall, S. (1990). Cultural identity and diaspora, in J. Rutherford (ed.) *Identity: community, culture, difference*. London: Lawrence and Wishart, pp. 222–237.

Holliday, A. (2009). 'The role of culture in English language education: key challenges', *Language and Intercultural Education*, 9(3): 144–155.

Holmes, J. (2013). *An introduction to sociolinguistics*. 4th edn. Essex: Pearson Education Ltd.

Jones, L. (this volume). Language and gender identities, in S. Preece (ed.) *The Routledge handbook of language and identity*. Abingdon: Routledge, pp. 210–224.

Lambert, W.E. (1975). Culture and language as factors in learning and education, in A. Wolfgang (ed.) *Education of immigrant students*. Toronto: Ontario Institute for Studies in Education, pp. 55–83.

Lave, J. and Wenger, E. (1991). *Situated learning: legitimate peripheral participation*. Cambridge: Cambridge University Press.

Lawson, S. and Sachdev, I. (2004). 'Identity, language use, and attitudes: some Sylheti Bangladeshi data from London, UK', *Journal of Language and Social Psychology*, 23(1): 49–69.

Mathews, G. (2000). *Global culture/individual identity: searching for home in the cultural supermarket*. New York: Routledge.

Mills, J. (2004). Mothers and mother tongue: perspectives on self-construction by mothers of Pakistani heritage, in A. Pavlenko and A. Blackledge (eds) *Negotiation of identities in multilingual contexts*. Clevedon: Multilingual Matters, pp. 161–191.

Modood, T. (2005). *Multicultural politics: racism, ethnicity, and Muslims in Britain*. Minneapolis: University of Minnesota Press.

Moyer, M. and Martin Rojo, L. (2007). Language, migration and citizenship: new challenges in the regulation of bilingualism, in M. Heller (ed.) *Bilingualism: a social approach*. Basingstoke: Palgrave, pp. 137–160.

Norton, B. and Toohey, K. (2011). 'Identity, language learning, and social change', *Language Teaching*, 44: 412–446.

Ogbu, J. (1999). 'Beyond language: Ebonics, proper English, and identity in a Black-American speech community', *American Educational Research Journal*, 36(2): 147–184.

Ovando, C.J., Combs, M.C. and Collier, V.P. (2005). *Bilingual and ESL classrooms: teaching in multicultural contexts*. New York: McGraw-Hill.

Pavlenko, A. and Blackledge, A. (2004). Introduction: new theoretical approaches to the study of negotiation of identities in multilingual contexts, in A. Pavlenko and A. Blackledge (eds) *Negotiation of identities in multilingual contexts*. Clevedon: Multilingual Matters, pp. 1–33.

Piggott, G. (2004). *2001 Census Profiles: Bangladeshis in London DMAG Briefing 2006/16*. London: Greater London Authority, Data Management and Analysis Group.

Preece, S. (2008). 'Multilingual gendered identities: female undergraduate students in London talk about heritage languages', *Journal of Language, Identity, and Education*, 7: 41–60.

Rampton, B. (1990). 'Displacing the "native speaker": expertise, affiliation, and inheritance', *ELT Journal*, 44(2): 97–101.

Riaz, A. (2003). 'Nations, nation-state and politics of Muslim identity in South Asia', *Comparative Studies of South Asia, Africa and the Middle East*, XXII: 53–58.

Schiffrin, D. (1987). *Discourse markers*. Cambridge: Cambridge University Press.

Talbani, A. and Hasanali, P. (2000). 'Adolescent females between tradition and modernity: gender role socialisation in South Asian immigrant culture', *Journal of Adolescence*, 23(5): 615–627.

Thompson, H. (2007). Bangladesh, in A. Simpson (ed.) *Language and national identity in Asia*. Oxford: Oxford University Press, pp. 33–54.

Valdés, G. (2005). 'Bilingualism, heritage language learners, and SLA research: opportunities lost or seized?', *Modern Language Journal*, 89(3): 410–426.

Weedon, C. (1997). *Feminist practice and poststructuralist theory*. 2nd edn. Oxford: Blackwell.

Wenger, E. (1998). *Communities of practice: learning, meaning and identity*. Cambridge: Cambridge University Press.

Wood, P., Landry, C. and Bloomfield, J. (2006). *Cultural diversity in Britain: a toolkit for cross-cultural co-operation*. York: Joseph Rowntree Foundation.

Appendix

Transcription conventions

X means an unidentified speaker

A slash – / – shows the end of a chunk of talk

A hyphen – - - – illustrates an incomplete word or utterance

A question mark – ? – indicates question intonation

Pauses of less than one second are shown with a full stop inside brackets – (.)

Pauses of one second and longer are timed to the nearest second and the number of seconds is put in brackets – (3)

[square brackets on top of each other indicates the point where [speakers overlap

An equals sign – = – at the end of one utterance and the start of the next speaker's utterance shows that there was no audible gap between speakers

Double brackets around a word or phrase shows that there is ((doubt about the transcription))

Double brackets around xs – ((xxx)) – shows that the speaker's utterance is inaudible or can't be made out

<phrases or words in angled brackets> is an additional comment by the transcriber on what is
  happening at the time or the way in which something is said
WORDS or Syllables in CAPital letters are spoken with extra emphasis
% words % or phrases enclosed by percentage symbols are spoken very quietly, almost like an
  aside
: means an elongated vowel (e.g. no:o)

(Coates 2003)

Bold means English in original, not translation

31

Minority languages and group identity
Scottish Gaelic in the Old World and the New

John Edwards

Introduction

This chapter examines the relationship between a minoritised language, Scottish Gaelic, and Scottish identity in two English-dominant settings: Scotland and Anglophone Canada. Some historical contextualisation is clearly necessary, and that – together with the geographical scope of the discussion – has suggested that an overview of several case studies is preferable to an emphasis upon only one. Given the focus, the organisation of this chapter departs somewhat from that of the other contributions. Such an overview, combining historical analysis and contemporary research, reveals that the vicissitudes of Gaelic are particularly illuminating when we concern ourselves with matters of language, identity and their relationship. For we have a unique opportunity here to consider the fortunes of a variety that is both an indigenous and an immigrant minority language, and both a European and a North American variety – each of them once having considerable strength. One of the chief findings is, simply, that very similar pressures were (and are) brought to bear on both, that the trajectories of language maintenance, decline and shift are essentially the same in each, that the important factors on one side of the Atlantic are mirrored on the other, and that the story of Gaelic is a rich chapter in the story of endangered languages everywhere. Can one imagine a fully fleshed treatment of applied linguistics, of sociolinguistics or of the sociology/social psychology of language that does not have a consideration of 'small' languages at its core?

There are longstanding relationships, in many parts of the world, among language, nationalism and the desire for self-government. Nationalists, especially where the relevant language is 'small' or threatened, have long endorsed the words of John Stuart Mill (1964 [1861]: 363): 'it is in general a necessary condition of free institutions that the boundaries of governments should coincide in the main with those of nationalities'. A recent study by Paterson *et al.* (2014: 15) found – within an overall population that generally sees Gaelic as a symbolically important part of Scottish identity – 'strong evidence that, all other things being equal, people who want there to be more Gaelic speakers tend to want full [political] powers'. One might, then, have reasonably expected that current Gaelic speakers would have endorsed the 'yes' option more strongly in the 2014 referendum on Scottish independence.

Unlike the situation in Ireland (and Wales, to some extent), Gaelic in Scotland has not figured prominently in nationalist politics. McLeod (2001: 7) says simply that 'the Gaelic language does not serve as a talisman of Scottish national identity'. At the end of his recent attitudinal survey (see below), MacCaluim (2002: 335) added that the language is 'rather peripheral to Scottish life', that it is not a major political issue, that it is 'rarely seen or heard by most Scots' and that the connection between Gaelic and a sense of Scottishness 'tends to be weak, or even non-existent, in the mind of most Scots'. Not surprising, then, that eight years before the referendum McLeod (2006: 6) observed that 'support for Scottish independence by no means signals a commitment to Gaelic, and speaking Gaelic by no means signals support for Scottish independence'. (More nuanced analyses, as well as the findings of Paterson *et al.* 2014, suggest of course that, as a symbolic quantity, the language is or has become rather less peripheral; see also Market Research UK 2003.) The reasons for what some have seen as a Scottish anomaly have historical roots, of course. The upshot is that the rise of the nationalist effort coincides with a severely diminished Gaelic-speaking population.

The issues surrounding 'small' and endangered languages have become important in recent years and, within academia, two basic stances coexist. Both scholar-activism, on the one hand, and committed but more detached application of expertise, on the other, are united in their concern for minority or 'at-risk' languages.

More is at stake here than a communication system *tout court*. All languages also have very powerful symbolic significance as bearers of culture, as vehicles of group myth and narrative, and as markers of ethnic or nationalist belonging – in short, as carriers and indicators of identity. It might be argued that this looms larger among activists than among linguistic recorders and archivists – and it is certainly true, of course, that language promoters and activists outside the academic cloisters are animated largely by a concern for vernacular continuity that rests quite solidly upon conceptions of group identity. While there are many things that can act as markers of identity, and many things that can galvanise and give focus to action, the influence of language is often important. Language-as-communication is certainly relevant, but it is when powerful allegiances involving language-as-symbol are added that people are more willing to go to the barricades, as it were. This is what gives minority-language contexts their particular significance: it is not that communicative and symbolic facets of language are unique to these settings, but that their parlous nature throws matters into starker relief. While minority-language dynamics are always of intrinsic interest, then, they can also illuminate features of much wider occurrence or application and, to repeat, the broadest of these always centres upon group identity.

To examine the relationship of Gaelic, as a minority language, with identity, the following sections will first give an historical overview of Gaelic in Scotland and Nova Scotia and then examine key large-scale case studies examining attitudes to Gaelic in these settings. This will be followed by a discussion of what conclusions we can draw about the role of Gaelic in Scottish identity.

Overview

Gaelic in Scotland

The pattern of Gaelic in Scotland is a familiar one: a language that once had considerable regional dominance was forced into steady retreat, pushed into ever more remote regions as a shrinking 'Celtic fringe' resulted from the policies of 'internal colonialism' (Hechter 1999). As

Gregor (1980), Durkacz (1983), Withers (1984) and many others have noted, the overall picture of Gaelic in Scotland has been one of decline for some time. Its gradual demise can be dated to the late fourteenth century, when it began to lose its position as both a national variety and one broadly acceptable in the corridors of influence. The hardening of the division between Highlands and Lowlands contributed to the increasing isolation of Gaelic and its association with an alien and 'troublesome' population. But then, as the Highlands became better known and more travelled, 'civilising' and anglicising thrusts further accelerated the language shift. Reliable data are hard to come by before the mid-nineteenth century, but Withers (1984: 253) tables a decline from the 50 per cent of the population who were Gaelic speakers in 1500 to only about 2 per cent five centuries later. From the 1881 census – the first to ask about Gaelic fluency – to that of 2001, the number recorded as Gaelic speakers dropped from about 250,000 to about 59,000. Gaelic monolingualism is now 'vestigial, prevalent only among pre-school infants and the oldest women' (Withers and MacKinnon 1983: 113). Most speakers of the language now live outwith the traditional areas – the largest concentration, of about 11,000 people, is found in and around Glasgow. The reduced heartland, in the Western Isles, still has a population of whom 60 per cent can speak Gaelic, but it is not immune to broader trends. The latest census suggests that only about one-quarter of the youngest children now speak it. And, while two-thirds of speakers say that they can read Gaelic, and half that they can write it, McLeod (2006: 5) observes that many 'do not necessarily do so frequently or comfortably'.

Today, more than 98 per cent of Scots do not speak Gaelic, and McLeod (2006: 7) writes that more of them 'would know the French words *petit* and *rouge* than their Gaelic counterparts, *beag* or *dearg*'. He claims that the most common attitude towards Gaelic is of 'mild support … shallow and vague … and does not necessarily translate into backing for proactive language revitalisation measures' (ibid.: 5). It is possible to understand the new Gaelic Language Act of 2005 as part of this mild and vague support, this time at the level of officialdom. The legislation grants official status to the language for the first time, but – as with many such nods in the direction of minority-language communities that one finds around the world – the phrasing is rather weaker than activists would like: Gaelic is described as 'an official language of Scotland commanding equal *respect* with the English language' (my italics) – and McLeod (2006) notes that the word has no clear and obvious legal meaning.

A brief note on education: McLeod (2006) provides some general notes on the growth of Gaelic in education – essentially, no room for it at all when state schools were established in 1872 and some very limited introduction by the close of the twentieth century. Earlier (2001), he reported that 60 schools (or 'units') were providing Gaelic-medium education to about 1,900 primary-school pupils. These 'units' are classrooms within English-medium schools, which means children receiving their education in Gaelic surrounded by English speakers; there are only a couple of all-Gaelic primary schools. (See also Bòrd na Gàidhlig 2007 for further information on education.)

Gaelic in Nova Scotia

Following the 'clearances' of the eighteenth and nineteenth centuries, large numbers of Gaelic speakers were either directly or indirectly forced from their land. Many moved to the urban Lowlands and soon there were sizeable groups of Gaelic speakers in Edinburgh, Glasgow and other towns and cities; by the end of the nineteenth century, indeed, the *Oban Times* was calling Glasgow the 'capital of the Highlands' (see Withers 1991, 1998). But many went much further afield, to Australia, New Zealand and, most notably, to the United States and Canada.

The first major destinations in the United States were Georgia, New York and North Carolina. By the middle of the nineteenth century, however, Gaelic had lost its place as a community language. In Canada, on the other hand – and most notably in Cape Breton Island, Nova Scotia – the language remained important for another three or four generations. This was essentially because of greater geographical remoteness; Cape Breton was an actual island until a permanent link was opened in 1955, and the community there retained a remarkable cultural cohesion. It is also the case that, after the American Revolution, most direct migration was to British North America (Newton 2001, 2003), and so most of the later emigrants to America came from or via Canada. So Canada – and Nova Scotia in particular – thus became the North American centre for the Gael, with Cape Breton Island as the new-world homeland (Newton 2005).

The major settlement of Nova Scotia by Gaelic-speaking Highlanders began in the 1770s, in a number of waves. While some 25,000 had arrived earlier, large-scale emigration to Cape Breton began after the end of the Napoleonic Wars. By mid-century, the Scots had become the biggest ethnic group in Nova Scotia, and emigration continued apace – and not only to Nova Scotia: Prebble (1969) writes, for example, that 58,000 left for Canada in 1831 and 66,000 in 1832. Even allowing for the fact that these numbers include Lowland Scots, they are very significant, given an already shrunken Highland population. By the mid-nineteenth century, Gaelic was the third language of Canada and, in Cape Breton Island, about three-quarters of the total population (of 100,000) spoke Gaelic (see Stephens 1976; Mertz 1989). Serious, if unsuccessful, arguments were made for official status for the language.

With increasing literacy and mobility, and with growing pressure from English, however, Gaelic increasingly became associated with backwardness and rurality. It was now a language of 'toil, hardship and scarcity', while English reflected 'refinement and culture' (Dunn 1953: 134). Taking the 1921 census as a starting point, MacLean (1978) claimed that Gaelic decreased by about 50 per cent every decade thereafter. Precision is unattainable, of course, but MacLeod's (1958) estimate of 30,000 Gaelic speakers in Cape Breton Island in 1931 seems corroborative. In a recent estimate, Kennedy (2002) suggested that about 500 Gaelic speakers remained in Nova Scotia, with perhaps half that number native users. Small as the figures have become, their significance shrinks further when we realise that many self-reported Gaelic speakers are far from fluent and that the numbers – whatever levels of competence they comprise – certainly do not correlate with ordinary usage patterns. Thus, when we read in the 2011 census of 1,275 Gaelic speakers (including 300 mother-tongue speakers), we should be a little wary, as we ought when enthusiastic spokesmen tell us of a Gaelic renaissance (allegedly due, in part, to the recent government establishment of a Gaelic Affairs division within the Department of Communities, Culture and Heritage) (see Taber 2014). In Gaelic, the division is called *Iomairtean na Gàidhlig*, the first word of which would be more accurately given in English as 'enterprise(s)' or even 'campaign(s)'. It is worth noting, incidentally, that the overarching government agency used to be called the 'Department of Tourism, Culture and Heritage'; the linking of the last three nouns here suggests something of contemporary bureaucratic thinking, and the slight alteration in the department's name does not indicate any sort of sea change in official impulses. The insightful work of McKay (1992, 1994) on the modern and quite conscious development of Nova Scotia 'tartanry' in the service of tourism is illustrative in this regard. (Tourism, incidentally, is now part of the government department devoted to economic and rural development.)

While Nova Scotians of Scottish ancestry comprise about 32 per cent of the region's 950,000 residents and while the very name of the province is historically revealing, it is now a predominantly Anglophone area, and has been for some time. Indeed, as Ian McKay

(Taber 2014) has pointed out, Scottish roots are more extensive in Prince Edward Island than they are in 'New Scotland'.

So far, we have overviewed the historical literature. In the following section, we turn to a number of important case studies to see what these have to tell us about the relationship between Gaelic as a minority language and Scottish identity.

Research

Gaelic in Scotland

Three large-scale research studies provide some indicators of the present state and likely prospects of Gaelic in Scotland. The first, an investigation undertaken by Alasdair MacCaluim (2002), focused upon adult learners of Gaelic. In the main section of his study, MacCaluim distributed (English-language) questionnaires to a large sample of learners, receiving completed forms back from 458 people (a response rate of 42 per cent), most of them Scottish residents. Most of the respondents were middle-aged or older, with few falling into the 'strategically important 16–25 age group' (ibid.: 323). There were disproportionate numbers of well-educated, middle-class and left-learning informants (including teachers, clerics and medical and service workers). About 20 per cent of the sample were Catholic (the latest census reveals that about 16 per cent of the general population claim Catholicism). About one-quarter of the Scottish sample had Gaelic-speaking parents and about one-third reported grand-parental competence in the language – most, that is to say, could not claim any reasonably recent ancestral involvement with Gaelic. Levels of reported competence were modest; MacCaluim writes of the predominance at the 'less advanced end of the Gaelic learning scale, due to a high drop-out rate amongst learners and the inadequacies of the Gaelic learning infrastructure' (ibid.: 237). Helping the survival of Gaelic was reported as a very important reason for learning it, considerations of identity and 'roots' also figured significantly, and a substantial proportion implied that learning Gaelic was more or less a 'hobby'. More immediately instrumental uses for the language were suggested much less frequently.

The other two studies were more official in nature. Commissioned by the BBC and Bòrd na Gàidhlig – the official governmental body with responsibility for the language – Market Research UK (2003) conducted interviews with just over a thousand respondents. This was a national sample, taken with due regard to region, age and gender. The findings revealed that, while almost 90 per cent reported no knowledge of Gaelic, about two-thirds agreed that the language was an important aspect of Scottish life. Most said that they favoured children learning Gaelic if they and their family wished, and more than half agreed that Gaelic-medium programmes should be expanded. About 30 per cent of the interviewees said that they might consider learning Gaelic in the future. Eight years later, another language-attitudes survey was officially commissioned (Scottish Government Social Research 2011). Once again, a national sample of about 1,000 respondents was drawn, 'representative of the adult population (aged 16 plus) in terms of sex, age, employment status and socioeconomic group' (ibid.: 4). As with the earlier survey, only about 10 per cent claimed some knowledge of Gaelic – but a more pointed inquiry revealed that only 2 per cent had any real degree of fluency. Most knowledge of the language was concentrated in the Highlands and Islands. Almost 60 per cent felt that Gaelic was important, or very important, for their sense of national identity. In the main, the results of the 2003 and 2011 surveys do not greatly differ. (It is worth remarking that both are stronger on data-reporting than they are on interpretation; it is also worth noting that – as with similar 'series' of surveys elsewhere – comparisons across time are sometimes hindered by inconsistency in questions asked, a point made by MacKinnon 2011.)

When we consider the findings of these three investigations – and other, smaller-scale inquiries not reported here – a pattern emerges that is familiar to all those who work in those minority-language contexts in which the use of the 'original' or 'ancestral' variety has become vanishingly small. First, apart from a small group of language activists – both within and without academia – the mass of the population no longer use or intend to use that variety. (Surveys like the ones mentioned here often suggest some slight interest in learning the language – but this is a task rarely undertaken, of course. Relatedly, programmes for language learners typically have high drop-out rates.) Second, there generally exists fairly widespread, but passive, goodwill towards the future prospects of the language. Third, individual conceptions of national allegiance often make room for the language, in what we might style a 'symbolic' sense. Fourth, there tend to exist both a rural heartland where native speakers may still be found and urban regions to which some of these speakers have migrated and in which there may also be pockets of language learners (sometimes termed 'secondary bilinguals').

Gaelic in Nova Scotia

There has been very little systematic and reliable research on Gaelic in Nova Scotia (or in the rest of North America, for that matter). Kenneth MacKinnon (1979, 1982, 1985) conducted fairly extensive fieldwork in the 1970s, focusing upon two rural communities in Cape Breton – one largely Protestant, the other mainly Catholic. His general observations: greater fluency was found among older Gaelic speakers, there was little transmission of the language to children, favourable attitudes and aspirations for the future of Gaelic were associated with fluency (and such language activism as could be found), and a broad but rather amorphous 'cultural loyalty' was much more evident than linguistic attachment. (Interestingly, MacKinnon reported that a handful of Gaelic monolinguals – women in their 80s and 90s – were still to be found in the mid-1970s).

Aside from one or two minor studies (Dembling 1991, 1997; Newton 2005) – whose findings are rather vitiated by small samples and, more importantly, by mixed and sometimes haphazard methodological procedures – we can note here the paucity of reports that have substantial research components. A Gaelic steering group commissioned, for example, the 'impact study' produced by Kennedy in 2002 – a lengthy and useful historical and contemporary overview. This report includes an insightful section on Gaelic organisations which 'have come and gone in Nova Scotia' (ibid.: 232), adding to an earlier observation that revival efforts themselves have come and gone over the years – all involving 'culture and identity, the authentic and the ersatz, right and wrong. There are clashes of ideology, egos and financial interests' (Dembling 1997: 2). Kennedy's description of organisations, of conferences and of gatherings of activists, enthusiasts and stakeholders mainly serves, however, to highlight the triumph of enthusiasm over cooler assessment. In a report commissioned by the provincial Gaelic Affairs Office, Dunbar (2008) also provides a useful overview; he goes further than Kennedy inasmuch as – drawing heavily upon the insights and opinions of Fishman (1991, 2001) – he makes some specific recommendations for language revitalisation. Like the Kennedy report, however, this later one provides no new research findings.

A more thoroughgoing investigation was reported in my own study (Edwards 1991); it involved three groups of informants, and probably remains the most detailed (relatively) recent study of Gaelic abilities, attitudes and usage in Nova Scotia. The first group ('G') – fluent and near-fluent Gaelic speakers – had already participated in a folklore project undertaken by the Celtic Studies Department of St Francis Xavier University. A list of 89 potential respondents was drawn up, of whom 50 completed questionnaires. The second group ('GS') was comprised of members of the Cape Breton Gaelic Society, and included Gaelic speakers as well as those with an interest in the language and in Scottish heritage. Drawing upon membership lists and upon meeting attendance registers over the previous five years, a total of 251 names was assembled; of this number, 30 proved impossible to contact and 132 failed to return the questionnaire. Completed forms were therefore received from 89 informants. The final group ('GL') was drawn from those members of the New Glasgow and Antigonish Highland Societies who were actively studying Gaelic – 20 in all.

The following topics were covered in the questionnaires: demographic information and Gaelic background, Gaelic competence and use, evaluations of Gaelic, the current status, transmission and survival of the language, and (for the GL group) information dealing with language learning. Respondents were encouraged to add comments, either of a general nature or relating to specific questions. Depending on the format of the question, results were assessed with chi-square and analysis-of-variance techniques. Limitations of space mean that only the most salient findings can be reported here.

The first thing to note is that, while their ages ranged from 22 to 89, most respondents were at least 60 years old. Men and women were equally represented in all three groups. The language learners were the best-educated: almost half had at least some third-level education and a number of them were teachers. Many in the G and GS groups simply described themselves as 'retired', and most were born in Cape Breton. Only three of the learners were born there, however, although all the others were mainland Nova Scotians. More than 80 per cent of all respondents knew where their forebears originated, the great majority being of Highlands and Islands ancestry. Most knew, too, when their families had emigrated (mainly between 1810 and 1830). More than half in group G were native Gaelic speakers, about 16 per cent in GS and 11 per cent among the learners (GL group).

Fluency in understanding, reading and speaking Gaelic was of course significantly greater among G informants. As well, the three groups were differentiated in terms of immediate forebears speaking Gaelic: 96 per cent of those in group G reported that their parents and most or all of their grandparents knew Gaelic, about 78 per cent in GS and 60 per cent among the GL informants. No differences across groups were found, however, with regard to the possession of Gaelic-language reading materials at home (about 70 per cent reported having such material). The linguistic superiority of the G group did not extend to writing in Gaelic: there were no group differences here, and the general level of writing ability was not great. Gaelic-language usage, as well as basic language preference, was correlated with reported linguistic ability. In no instances, however, were respondents able to report extensive or even regular daily use.

A number of questions were of course directed to opinions of the current status, the transmission and the survival of Gaelic in Nova Scotia. More than 80 per cent of all informants agreed that older people tend to see the language as more important, but it was also generally agreed that, in the future, Gaelic would continue to be an important feature of the linguistic landscape. Indeed, there appeared a very slight tendency to view Gaelic as increasing in importance. Further probing revealed that this was largely based upon hope, although many respondents mentioned various agencies, classes and programmes that they believed were active and to some degree successful in sustaining the language. When asked to list reasons that could be given to those thinking of learning Gaelic, about half mentioned its role in preserving a distinctive heritage, while another (and not unrelated) half cited enjoyment, knowledge for its own sake and the beauty of Gaelic. Fewer than one in ten argued for the use of Gaelic in conversation.

When those in the GL group were probed a little further about their current reasons for studying Gaelic, we discovered that no one mentioned actually *speaking* the language. However, when questioned about possible future use of their acquired competence, about half (again) did say that they hoped to be able to converse with other Gaelic speakers. As well, about 17 per cent mentioned learning Gaelic so as to be able to read in the language.

Here are some of the more interesting comments added by informants; in each case, they represent the views of several in each group.

> I would like to see a revival in the Gaelic language in Nova Scotia but I do not think there is enough interest among the younger people.
>
> *(Group G respondent)*

> When I attended school in 1915–20 you got a strapping with a leather strap if caught speaking Gaelic.
>
> *(Group G respondent)*

Emphasis upon the school as central to the survival of the language was commonly expressed. A frequently expressed opinion was reflected in these words from two GS group members:

> Sorry to say, but I believe that Gaelic will continue to decrease without the language being spoken in the home. I don't see much future for Gaelic even when a few short courses are taught in schools ... the home use is what counts.
>
> *(Group GS respondent 1)*

> In my youth, people speaking Gaelic were considered backward and were discouraged from speaking it.
>
> *(Group GS respondent 2)*

While several respondents seemed a little dismissive, on the grounds that the language now has only 'cultural value', some other comments on the intertwining of Gaelic with other social features were more positive. One wrote that 'in the interests of religion, music and culture, I commend the valiant efforts that are being made to preserve the Gaelic heritage'. And the long comment of another on the same matter seems worth reproducing here:

> It seems your questions are directed wholly at the Gaelic language. The continuance of Scottish culture will not be promoted or should not be promoted on Gaelic language. It is not where it is at with the prevailing interest ... Language is the living culture of a people. However, for the Scots many other aspects of their culture are near and dear to their hearts. Emphasis on the Gaelic language will I feel bring small returns. Studies in Celtic history I think are very important. Music (pipes, drums, fiddle) – all this is part of the make-up of our culture.

Discussion

While it is true that more research is desirable, on both sides of the Atlantic, the case studies presented in this chapter suggest a number of generalities that seem to apply in both contexts. These are based upon the findings that we do have, informed by historical analysis and reinforced by our knowledge of minority-language settings in other parts of the world. This chapter has been unable, of course, to do more than hint at the relevant literatures here. With appropriate caveats in mind, then, here are some rough conclusions that may reasonably be drawn.

Gaelic is a seriously threatened language, many of whose chapters – perhaps most – have already been written. While sporadic attempts have been made to teach the language, generational transmission is now very fragile. The general and, one imagines, largely sincere goodwill that is easily documented remains a passive quantity. One is reminded of what Nancy Dorian (1986: 561) – the scholar of East Sutherland Gaelic and a strong supporter of language maintenance – once pointed to: 'the deliberate non-transmission of the ancestral language to young children … a theme repeated with dreary frequency'. She has also said that parents may now sometimes be criticised by their children for not passing on the linguistic torch (see Crystal 2000: 106). In fact, regrets in this connection are commonly found in small-language communities and may be understood as a linguistic variant of the idea – popularised by Marcus Lee Hansen in his studies of immigrants in America – that 'what the son wishes to regret, the grandson wishes to remember' (Edwards 1995: 112). While 'wish' may not be quite the *mot juste* here, the pattern is familiar in both immigrant and indigenous minority-group settings.

While Gaelic may no longer be so widely dismissed as an uncultivated rural variety associated with 'toil and scarcity' and while many of its speakers – especially 'secondary bilinguals' – are now city folk, its heartland remains on the periphery. In the eyes of many, it remains on the fringe, both geographically and sociologically. While commentators in a polite Canada have not generally expressed themselves very forcefully in this matter, their transatlantic counterparts have often been blunter. Scottish journalists, among them Allan Brown (2000), Peter Clarke (1995) and Allan Massie (1998), have been regular and acerbic critics of renewed attention to the language; while I won't reproduce their intemperate remarks, titles like 'Who needs the Gaelic?' and 'From Gael force to farce' are indicative of their attitudes. While writers like these seem to have been given a rather smaller podium lately, a potent combination of ignorance and indifference continues to dog Gaelic, as indeed it does for many threatened varieties.

Even the most committed of language activists would not argue for Gaelic monolingualism: bilingual or diglossic arrangements, perfectly theoretically plausible, are the obvious ways in which an at-risk variety can be maintained without jeopardising full participation in the majority-English mainstream. However, as this and many other minority-group contexts show, 'bigger' languages often steadily eat away at the domains of 'smaller' ones: a sort of linguistic Gresham's Law is at work. An important distinction highlights what might be termed 'domains of necessity': meeting every Wednesday evening to speak German is not quite the same as having to speak it to earn a living. Many commentators have pointed out that hope always remains for minority varieties as long as they continue to predominate in the family domain. But even this most intimate of settings is susceptible to the linguistic pressures just beyond the garden gate (see Edwards 2009). So, while diglossia is certainly the norm in some situations – largely in those where neither of the languages in contact has a clear and broad dominance across domains – in many contact scenarios, it seems that people will not keep up two languages indefinitely when one comes to serve more and more across all those 'domains of necessity'.

An awareness of history coupled with close examination of contemporary trends – supplemented and reinforced by such research as exists – suggests that halting the decline of Gaelic is an unlikely proposition. Historically, languages have frequently disappeared completely, and the very existence of some is confirmed only through classical reference. Nowadays, of course, even the most threatened variety is unlikely to vanish without trace (if sufficient documentation effort can be mustered). The difficulty here rests above all on a truth which is not as universally acknowledged as it ought to be (with apologies to Jane Austen): the decline of a language is a symptom of larger social forces and, without attending to the latter, it is unlikely that much of a permanent nature can be done to shore up the latter. You don't treat measles by putting sticking plaster on the spots.

It is also the case that, on both sides of the Atlantic, revival efforts have been in the hands of a minority within a minority. Dorian (1986: 560) observed that native speakers of languages in decline often exhibit quite low levels of 'language loyalty', and she mentions a 'lightly regretful pragmatism which gives rise to general protestations about the regrettable loss of the language unaccompanied by efforts to halt that loss'. There is often a deeper, if vaguer, 'cultural loyalty'. There are obvious reasons why ordinary people are unlikely to be activists, and one is reminded, in fact, of Gellner's (1964: 1962) observations regarding nationalistic revitalisation efforts: while 'the self-image of nationalism involves the stress on folk, folklore, popular culture [and we could of course highlight the ancestral language here] ... genuine peasants or tribesmen ... do not generally make good nationalists'. Citing 'peasants and tribesmen' may not strike quite the appropriate note here, but if we bear in mind the frequent revivalist use of words like 'genuine' and 'authentic' to describe linguistically beleaguered populations, then the sense remains. It is also worth noting that the behaviour of such groups does not always support simplistic black-and-white pictures of dominance and subordination. Those same Gaelic speakers who largely acquiesced in the English education of their children in the nineteenth century were, as Withers (1988) has pointed out, strongly opposed to the imposition of catechists and ministers who knew no Gaelic. He goes on to say that 'many Highlanders actively sought English through schooling as a means "to get on in life" yet they would petition the General Assembly for Gaelic-speaking clergy and protest at any shortage' (ibid.: 165). More generally, the history of protest and agitation concerning matters of the land, of farming and of crofting again suggests the inaccuracy of many naive assessments. (I do not mean, of course, to downplay the broad-brush effects of domination but rather to point out that, while some developments provoked reactions, others did not. And these 'others' generally included language matters.)

Summary

This chapter has given an overview of the history of Gaelic in the Old World and the New, surveyed a number of case studies examining language attitudes to Gaelic in Scotland and Nova Scotia and examined the relationship of Gaelic, as a language, with Scottish identity. The history of the Gaels on both sides of the ocean suggests that language shift – and a lack of general interest in revival efforts – has come to sit quite easily with a strongly continuing sense of Scottish identity. This in turn suggests that such linguistic interest as remains is of a symbolic nature for the great majority of people. Valuing ancestry, and maintaining a sense of 'groupness' – while at the same time engaging in vernacular-language shift – is by far the most common arrangement that both indigenous and immigrant minority groups come to.

Related topics

Historical perspectives on language and identity; Identity in variationist sociolinguistics; Language and ethnic identity; Identity in post-colonial contexts; Styling and identity in a second language; The future of identity research: impact and new developments in sociolinguistics.

John Edwards

Further reading

Durkacz, V. (1983). *The decline of the Celtic languages*. Edinburgh: John Donald. (Durkacz provides an excellent historical and comparative overview that places Gaelic in the wider Celtic-language context.)

Kennedy, M. (2002). *Gaelic Nova Scotia: an economic, cultural and social impact study*. Halifax: Nova Scotia Museum (Department of Tourism and Culture). (Kennedy's study presents the Nova Scotian context in some detail.)

McKay, I. (1992). 'Tartanism triumphant: the construction of Scottishness in Nova Scotia, 1933–1954', *Acadiensis*, 21(2): 5–47. (McKay's article discusses matters from a more provocative point of view.)

Withers, C. (1984). *Gaelic in Scotland, 1698–1981: the geographical history of a language*. Edinburgh: John Donald. (This volume along with other works of Charles Withers on Gaelic in Scotland are invaluable for their depth and historical insight.)

References

Bòrd na Gàidhlig (2007). *The National Plan for Gaelic*. Inverness: Bòrd na Gàidhlig.

Brown, A. (2000). 'A tongue lashing from the Gaels', *Sunday Times*, 20 February.

Clarke, P. (1995). 'Who needs the Gaelic?', *Scotsman*, 11 March.

Crystal, D. (2000). *Language death*. Cambridge: Cambridge University Press.

Dembling, J. (1991). *Ged a tha mo Ghàidhlig gann: Cape Breton's vanishing Gàidhealtachd*. BA thesis, Hampshire College, Amherst, Massachusetts.

Dembling, J. (1997). *Joe Jimmy Alec visits the Gaelic Mod and escapes unscathed: the Nova Scotia Gaelic revivals*. MA thesis, Saint Mary's University, Halifax.

Dorian, N. (1986). Gathering language data in terminal speech communities, in J. Fishman, A. Tabouret-Keller, M. Clyne, B. Krishnamurti and M. Abdulaziz (eds) *The Fergusonian impact. Vol. 2, Sociolinguistics and the sociology of language*. Berlin: Mouton de Gruyter, pp. 555–595.

Dunbar, R. (2008). *Minority language renewal: Gaelic in Nova Scotia, and lessons from abroad*. Halifax: Department of Communities, Culture and Heritage (Gaelic Affairs Division).

Dunn, C. (1953). *Highland settler: a portrait of the Scottish Gael in Nova Scotia*. Toronto: University of Toronto Press.

Durkacz, V. (1983). *The decline of the Celtic languages*. Edinburgh: John Donald.

Edwards, J. (1991). Gaelic in Nova Scotia, in C. Williams (ed.) *Linguistic minorities, society and territory*. Clevedon: Multilingual Matters, pp. 269–297.

Edwards, J. (1995). *Multilingualism*. London: Penguin.

Edwards, J. (2009). *Language and identity*. Cambridge: Cambridge University Press.

Fishman, J. (1991). *Reversing language shift*. Clevedon: Multilingual Matters.

Fishman, J. (ed.) (2001). *Can threatened languages be saved?* Clevedon: Multilingual Matters.

Gellner, E. (1964). *Thought and change*. London: Weidenfeld and Nicolson.

Gregor, D. (1980). *Celtic: a comparative study*. Cambridge: Oleander.

Hechter, M. (1999). *Internal colonialism: the Celtic fringe in British national development*. New Brunswick, NJ: Transaction.

Kennedy, M. (2002). *Gaelic Nova Scotia: an economic, cultural and social impact study*. Halifax: Nova Scotia Museum (Department of Tourism and Culture).

MacCaluim, A. (2002). *Periphery of the periphery? Adult learners of Scottish Gaelic and reversal of language shift*. PhD thesis, University of Edinburgh.

McKay, I. (1992). 'Tartanism triumphant: the construction of Scottishness in Nova Scotia, 1933–1954', *Acadiensis*, 21(2): 5–47.

McKay, I. (1994). *The quest of the folk: antimodernism and cultural selection in twentieth-century Nova Scotia*. Montreal: McGill-Queen's University Press.

MacKinnon, K. (1979). *Gaelic language and culture in Gaelic-speaking Cape Breton communities*. Unpublished paper.

MacKinnon, K. (1982). 'Cape Breton Gaeldom in cross-cultural context: the transmission of ethnic language and culture'. Paper presented at the *Sixth Congress of the International Association of Cross-Cultural Psychology*, Aberdeen.

MacKinnon, K. (1985). 'Gaelic in Cape Breton: language maintenance and cultural loyalty in the case of a Canadian "non-official language"'. Paper presented at the *Second Biennial Conference of the Canadian Study in Wales Group*, Gregynog Hall, University of Wales.

MacKinnon, K. (2011). Public attitudes to Gaelic: a comparison of surveys undertaken in 1981, 2003 and 2011. Report to *Bòrd na Gàidhlig*. Unpublished paper.

MacLean, R. (1978). The Scots: *Hector's* cargo, in D. Campbell (ed.) *Banked fires: the ethnics of Nova Scotia*. Port Credit, Ontario: Scribblers' Press, pp. 51–72.

MacLeod, C. (1958). 'The Gaelic tradition in Nova Scotia', *Lochlann*, 1: 235–240.

McLeod, C. (2001). 'Gaelic in the new Scotland: politics, rhetoric and public discourse', *Journal on Ethnopolitics and Minority Issues in Europe*, July [Online]. Available at www.ecmi.de/publications/detail/issue-22001-208

McLeod, W. (2006). *Gaelic in contemporary Scotland: contradictions, challenges and strategies*. Edinburgh: University of Edinburgh, Department of Celtic and Scottish Studies.

Market Research UK (2003). *Attitudes to the Gaelic language*. Glasgow: MRUK.

Massie, A. (1998). 'From Gael force to farce', *Scotsman*, 21 March.

Mertz, E. (1989). Sociolinguistic creativity: Cape Breton Gaelic's linguistic 'tip', in N. Dorian (ed.) *Investigating obsolescence: studies in language death*. Cambridge: Cambridge University Press, pp. 103–116.

Mill, J.S. (1964 [1861]). *Considerations on representative government*. London: Dent.

Newton, M. (2001). *We're Indians sure enough: the legacy of the Scottish Highlanders in the United States*. Richmond, VA: Saorsa.

Newton, M. (2003). *Highland settlers: Scottish Highland immigrants in North America*. Richmond, VA: University of Richmond.

Newton, M. (2005). '"This could have been mine": Scottish Gaelic learners in North America', *e-Keltoi (Journal of Interdisciplinary Celtic Studies)*, 2: 1–54.

Paterson, L., O'Hanlon, F., Ormston, R. and Reid, S. (2014). 'Public attitudes to Gaelic and the debate about Scottish autonomy', *Regional and Federal Studies*, DOI: 10.1080/13597566.2013.877449

Prebble, J. (1969). *The Highland clearances*. London: Penguin.

Scottish Government Social Research (2011). *Attitudes towards the Gaelic language*. Edinburgh: Scottish Government.

Stephens, M. (1976). *Linguistic minorities in Western Europe*. Llandysul: Gomer.

Taber, J. (2014). 'In Nova Scotia, a decidedly muted response to Scotland's vote', *Globe and Mail* [Toronto], 14 September.

Withers, C. (1984). *Gaelic in Scotland, 1698–1981: the geographical history of a language*. Edinburgh: John Donald.

Withers, C. (1988). *Gaelic Scotland: the transformation of a culture region*. London: Routledge.

Withers, C. (1991). An essay in historical geolinguistics: Gaelic speaking in urban Lowland Scotland in 1891, in C. Williams (ed.) *Linguistic minorities, society and territory*. Clevedon: Multilingual Matters, pp. 150–172.

Withers, C. (1998). *Urban Highlanders: Highland–Lowland migration and urban Gaelic culture, 1700–1900*. Phantassie (East Linton): Tuckwell.

Withers, C. and MacKinnon, K. (1983). Gaelic speaking in Scotland: demographic history, in D. Thompson (ed.) *The companion to Gaelic Scotland*. Oxford: Blackwell, pp. 109–114.

Part V
Future directions

Intersectionality in language and identity research

David Block and Victor Corona[1]

Introduction

> ... it is impossible to develop a full and deep understanding of the discrimination and marginalisation that a 30-year-old female immigrant from Ecuador might suffer in Barcelona if one does not take into account a series of overlapping and interlinked social dimensions. These dimensions include (1) the ways that this woman is positioned in class terms in Catalan society (as a lower-class person doing low-level service jobs like cleaning); (2) her institutional and social status as an *immigrant*, that is someone who is progressively more unwelcome as the economic crisis deepens; (3) the fact that she is a person of colour, a visible minority with an Andean appearance, whose physical features are not valued in mainstream Catalan society; (4) her status as someone who is *culturally* different, someone with a world view and behaviours which are not considered 'Catalan' or even 'Spanish'; and (5) her immersion in gender regimes in her home life (with her Ecuadorian husband) and in mainstream Catalan society, which are differentiable but which in both cases work against her attempts at self-fulfilment.
>
> *(Block 2014: 69)*

The opening quotation by David Block, one of the co-authors of this chapter, sets out the dilemma faced by applied linguists who wish to explore in detail individual and collective identities in their research. In short, how can scholars in applied linguistics take on so many factors at the same time? The short answer to this question is that researchers cannot *do everything* in their research. However, applied linguists can show sensitivity, awareness and, ultimately, attentiveness to the necessarily intersectional nature of identity. In this chapter, we hope to take the reader a few steps in this direction. We begin with a discussion of the origins of intersectionality, what it means and critiques that have developed around it. This review will, by necessity, be partial, and it will, without a doubt, leave out ongoing and important areas of debate; however, our intention is modest, namely to outline what we think are the fundamentals of intersectionality as applied to language and identity research. This done, we consider how in language and identity research intersectionality has been practised in something of a default manner; seldom if ever discussed as a methodological option or in theoretical terms by researchers. We then move to an examination of data collected by Victor Corona, the other co-author of this chapter, over the past several years as part of his ongoing study of young Latinos in Barcelona. Our aim is to develop an intersectional analysis and understanding of the lives of Corona's informants, which might serve as a framework for other language and identity researchers in applied linguistics to follow. We then close the chapter with some observations.

Current issues[2]

What is intersectionality?

The increased interest in intersectionality in the social sciences and humanities in recent years (e.g. Grzanka 2014; Jackson 2014; Hill-Collins and Bilge 2015) has arisen amid several trends. First, there is a general understanding among researchers that, while research often focuses primarily on one dimension of identity, it is impossible to do this without including other dimensions. Thus, research on racial identity will necessarily include references to and an engagement with gender, nationality and other identity dimensions. Second, where researchers do deal with several identity dimensions simultaneously and do so in an overt manner, this needs to be done in conjunction with an exploration of how the different dimensions included in their analyses actually interconnect. So, in the previous example, it is not enough to say that race *and* gender are important heuristics for understanding the life of experiences of an individual; there needs to be some discussion of how they are interdependent and how they interrelate in emergent social activity. Third, and finally, there has been a paucity of research which addresses intradimensional differences and variations to a sufficient degree, that is, explorations of how labels such as 'Latino' may hide as much as they reveal if there is no acknowledgement or exploration of the differences among people classified according to these labels.

Ultimately, intersectionality is seen by researchers in the humanities and social sciences as a way to deal with issues like these, all of which point to the complexity of identity in the increasingly varied and variable circumstances of the times in which we live (call it 'late modernity', 'the new millennium' or even 'the global age'). At the same time, and again following the theme of complexity across contexts, it is worthwhile to bear in mind that 'intersectionality does not refer to a unitary framework but a range of positions, and that essentially it is a heuristic device for understanding boundaries and hierarchies of social life' (Anthias 2013: 4). In this sense, it is wise to avoid universal, overgeneralised statements about *what it is*.

Although intersectionality has arguably always been around in the humanities and social sciences (who has ever successfully isolated an identity inscription such as ethnicity in research?), any discussion of it taking place today must take on board its origins in Black Feminism (Bilge 2013),[3] the common reference being two key publications by Kimberlee Crenshaw (1989, 1991) some 25 years ago. A law scholar, feminist and anti-racist activist, Crenshaw sought a way to understand how race and gender and, to a lesser extent, class interact in the construction of inequalities in society. She noted that mainstream thinking and theorising in both feminism and anti-racism emerged in isolation from each other, based as they were in very different foundations. In addition, she noted that simply grafting race onto a feminist framework, or feminism onto a race-based framework, would not get activists very far, as experiences emanating from one's gendered positionings were very different from those emanating from one's racialised positionings. She concluded by emphasising the importance of an intersectional approach to identity, stating that '[b]ecause the intersectional experience is greater than the sum of racism and sexism, any analysis that does not take intersectionality into account cannot sufficiently address the particular manner in which Black women are subordinated' (Crenshaw 1989: 140).

At about the same time, Crenshaw's call for a greater emphasis on intersectionality was echoed by Patricia Hill-Collins (1993), who argued for the need to move away from either/ or, dichotomous thinking, whereby people are conceptualised in terms of their opposites, such as Black vs White, to 'both/and' thinking, whereby a multitude of positions, both passing and more permanent, can be included in the conversation. Hill-Collins also critiqued the tendency of some researchers to rank oppressions, posing questions such as the following: How do you feel most oppressed, as a woman or as a Black person? In bringing intersectionality to the fore in Black feminist scholarship, Crenshaw and Hill-Collins were following still earlier calls for similar thinking about identity, with three foundational sources standing out: Franz Fanon (1967 [1952]), bell hooks (1981) and the Combahee River Collective (1977), an African American feminist and lesbian association formed in 1974. Drawing on the experience of having grown up in the French colony of Martinique and several years of life in France, both during and after World War II (in which he fought), Fanon (1967 [1952]) wrote *Black skin, White masks* as a psychological treatise on the lasting negative alienating effects that colonialism had on those who experienced and endured it. In this work, he explored many issues related to race, but most important in the context of this discussion is his examination of the interrelationships between race and gender (and sexuality) in terms of 'the woman of color and the white man' (Fanon 1967: 41–62) and 'the man of color and the white woman' (ibid.: 63–82).

Some years later, and writing about North American feminism, hooks (1981) argued against the essentialisation of identity categories and how Blackness was often masculinised in discussions of race, while feminism was often framed following the interests of middle-class White women. Her book, *Ain't I a woman: Black women and feminism*, is based on the ex-slave Sigourney Truth's speech at a suffragettes' meeting in Akron, Ohio, in 1851. Truth famously interrupted the meeting, dominated by well-educated White women, with a compelling personal statement that ended with the famous question 'Ain't I a woman?' This question was posed after she made clear the differences between her experiences as a Black woman and the experiences of her fellow (White) suffragettes. Truth had worked like a man in the fields, gathering and ploughing, and she never had men to protect her from the elements or the vicissitudes of life. Meanwhile, she viewed her White counterparts as the beneficiaries of gendered regimes that, while denying them the vote, nonetheless served to protect them. Along with other early Black female activists, such as Harriet Tubman, Frances E.W. Harper, Ida B. Wells Barnett and Mary Church Terrell, Truth served as an inspiration for the Combahee River Collective, who in April 1977 issued their statement of principles. In this statement, members declared that they were 'actively committed to struggling against racial, sexual, heterosexual, and class oppression' and that their aims were to 'develop [...] integrated analysis and practice based upon the fact that the major systems of oppression are interlocking' (Combahee River Collective 1977: no page).

From this early work on intersectionality to the present, the theorisation of intersectionality has advanced considerably, such that most researchers today would accept that identity is multilayered and complex; that different dimensions of identity cannot be dealt with in isolation from one another; that intracategorical differences are often the most interesting aspect of identity research; and that to ignore intersectionality, adopting a default divide-and-analyse position, is to produce research that can only ever provide an incomplete portrayal of research informants. This consensus notwithstanding, there are, as Jennifer Nash (2008) notes, a few issues pending in discussions of intersectionality. For example, Nash queries the extent to which intersectionality is a useful component of a general theory of identity, asking if it 'actually captures the ways in which subjects experience subjectivity or strategically deploy identity' (Nash 2008: 11). In other words, do individuals live their lives intersectionally in that they are always conscious of how constraints on their activity are multilayered and never just about one single dimension? Or, do individuals self-consciously invoke different dimensions of their identity, selectively and strategically, as they go about their day-to-day activity? In the midst of these and other questions, Nash suggests that answering them 'requires intersectionality to craft a theory of agency and to grapple with the amount of leeway variously situated subjects have to deploy particular components of their identities in certain contexts' (Nash 2008: 11). It also requires a narrative-based approach to research, as there is a need to listen to the stories of individuals and collectives.

Another issue raised by Nash concerns how intersectional research is carried out. Here she cites Leslie McCall (2005), who has explored this very issue in depth. For McCall, over the years there have been three complexities that have (or have not) been dealt with by researchers working intersectionally, which she outlines as follows:

1   'Anticategorical complexity'. This means a rejection of boundaried identity categories such as race and gender, because (a) they are deemed to be overly simplistic and totalising to capture the complex lives of individuals today and (b) they strengthen the very power regimes that scholars have sought to destabilise and overturn.
2   'Intercategorical complexity'. Inequality is observed to exist between social groups, even if these are relatively difficult to define. Thus, existing analytical categories can be useful in the documentation of inequality along multiple and conflicting dimensions.
3   'Intracategorical complexity'. This angle on intersectionality is based on a suspicion of categories, as in the case of anticategorical complexity, although it is more about handling categories with care and above all about breaking them down, challenging the nature of their composition and how they are used in empirical research.

McCall frames these three types of complexity as options, as points of departure for researchers. She eschews anticategorical complexity as self-defeating, but while she is interested in intercategorical conflicts, she sees intracategorical complexity as where the most useful work remains to be done. More concretely, McCall proposes a move beyond intercategorical inequality and conflict to the examination of intracategorical inequality and conflict. It seems that until the diversity inside categories is understood, it is only with great difficulty and imprecision that they can be invoked in research examining intercategorical differences. Thus a category like Latino, apart from needing contextual clarification (are we talking about the United States or a European context?), needs to be unpacked and understood as a multilevelled marker for lived experiences before it can then be intersected with masculinities and femininities (gender), race or nationality or any other dimension of identity.

An additional issue arising with regard to intersectionality is if it is always based on a conceptual core or central dimension of identity, one that reflects the most important and significant interests of the researcher. It is fairly clear in Crenshaw's work, for example, that race is in some sense the baseline of her movements outward to examine intersections with other dimensions of identity. Meanwhile, other scholars interested in race and gender have taken different tacks. For example, hooks is far more ambiguous about the centrality of race and gender in her work (e.g. hooks 1981), sometimes seeming to devote more attention to race and other times favouring gender. In addition, in her 2000 book *Where we stand*, she situates social class as a baseline dimension of identity around which race and gender rotate continuously. Meanwhile, Mignon Moore's (2011) research examining how Black lesbians form families includes a close synthesis of race and sexuality, moving gender to a more peripheral position. We could go on citing examples, but the point is that, while intersectionality will, ideally, involve analysis across several dimensions of identity, there will usually be one particular dimension that is the baseline of the research. However, it should be noted that this kind of anchoring need not fall into the ontological isolation described by Hill-Collins, whereby 'each group identifies the type of oppression with which it feels most comfortable as being fundamental and classifies all other types as being of lesser importance' (Hill-Collins 1993: 25); rather, the idea is to engage (pro)actively with how dimensions beyond the base dimension articulate with that base dimension as well as each other.

Intersectionality in applied linguistics

In contrast to what we find in race and gender studies, in applied linguistics there is not much in the way of a developed line of discussion or debate focusing explicitly on intersectionality. This assessment applies to publications on research methodology in applied linguistics as well as the huge number of publications on language and identity which have come out in the last decade in applied linguistics journals (e.g. *Journal of Language, Identity, and Education*), as monographs (e.g. Joseph 2004; Benwell and Stokoe 2006; Omoniyi and White 2006; Block 2007; Riley 2007) and as edited collections (Pavlenko and Blackledge 2004; De Fina *et al.* 2006; Caldas-Coulthard and Iedema 2008; Lin 2008; Llamas and Watt 2010; Higgins 2012). An exception of sorts is a book chapter by Ingrid Piller and Kimie Takahashi (2010), in which the authors make explicit that intersectionality is a principle running through their research on gender, language and transnationalism: 'our concern is with the ways in which general identities are produced and maintained in transnational contexts and the ways in which they are intersected by linguistic ideologies and practices' (Piller and Takahashi 2010: 540). Of course, this is a different sort of intersection from the more common two-or-more-dimensions approach outlined above, but it is intersectionality nonetheless. In their paper, the authors manage to show how 'gendered people and gendered discourse … do not circulate in isolation from each other, nor in isolation from language ideologies and other aspects of identity' (ibid.: 549). However, what is missing throughout their discussion is a more-than-cursory presentation of what intersectionality is about and the various issues arising around it, as discussed above. In fairness to the authors, one does not normally expect explicit treatment of an approach to research in a publication that is meant to discuss content and results, and their importance.

In the absence of explicit treatments of intersectionality, one is left to observe how it actually emerges in deed if not in name; language and identity researchers, following trends in identity research in general, have long accepted as axiomatic the impossibility of isolating identity dimensions and then focusing on them individually. There is always seepage across these dimensions and in the context of migration experiences, just to cite one example; there is a confluence of ethnicity, race, gender, nationality and other dimensions of identity. Trying to isolate one of these dimensions would be fruitless. Of course, this very point is made clearly in Bonny Norton's (2013 [2000]) classic book *Identity and language learning*, in which she very effectively shows how gender and ethnicity in particular (but also, at times, nationality and social class) flow together in her analysis of the lives of five immigrant women in Canada.

Another good example of intersectionality in action in language and identity research is Carmen Fought's (2006) work on race, ethnicity and language, as she shows that one cannot really understand a dimension like race without having some notion of how it intersects with other dimensions of identity such as ethnolinguistic affiliation and social class. Fought follows up William Labov's (1972) classic research on African American Vernacular English (AAVE), which itself documented intersections between race, ethnicity, ethnolinguistic identity and class. She defines AAVE as 'a variety [of distinct non-standard English] spoken by many African-Americans in the USA which shares a set of grammatical and other linguistic features [e.g. phonological features] that distinguish it from various other American dialects' (Fought 2006: 46). Writing about contemporary American society, Fought examines how AAVE-linked racial and ethnolinguistic identities intersect with social class.

As Fought notes, early research on AAVE was based primarily on data collected from working-class informants and therefore there was a certain marginalisation of middle-class African Americans from studies. The intracategorical issue that arises here is that obviously African Americans occupy a range of class positions and that these class positions will have an impact on linguistic practices, in particular whether or not AAVE is used, how it is used and in what contexts it is used. Fought surveys research examining the linguistic practices of middle-class African Americans, contrasting their experiences with those of working-class African Americans. She argues that the latter often grow up in segregated neighbourhoods in which a very high proportion of their interactions are with working-class and poor African Americans like themselves. Meanwhile, middle-class African Americans are far more likely to grow up in desegregated neighbourhoods and to have interactions with people from a range of racial and ethnic backgrounds over the course of their lives. In addition, they are more likely to experience intensive pressure to assimilate to mainstream American middle-class culture, which tends to be identified as 'White culture'. Part and parcel of such assimilation processes is exposure to socialisation into standard varieties of English from an early age (ibid.: 62).

It is in assimilating to mainstream middle-class values and adopting middle-class American English as the dominant way of communicating that intercategorical tensions arise. In short, racial and ethnic affiliations, or the desire to maintain a recognisable and legitimised African-American identity, come into conflict with social class positions in society (Morgan 2002). This occurs, above all, because, for many African Americans, AAVE is, historically, a key marker of African American identity: as Geneva Smitherman (1977: 3) puts it, it is 'a language mixture, adapted to the conditions of slavery and discrimination, a combination of language and style interwoven with and inextricable from Afro-American culture'. However, where choices can be made as to what variety of English to employ, matters generally do not play out according to an either/or AAVE/middle-class American-English scenario; rather, there is a scale along which African Americans communicate, and middle-class African Americans insert themselves into this scale every time they speak. One interesting phenomenon that arises from this complex ethnolinguistic milieu is the fusion of middle-class grammar (in terms of morphology and syntax) with some phonological features of AAVE: just enough to identify one as African American but not enough to put off mainstream middle-class Americans (Morgan 2002).

Space does not allow further discussion of Fought's work on ethnolinguistic identity: its intercategorical intersections with other dimensions of identity and how it helps her to problematise race and ethnicity, in particular the intracategorical complexity of 'African American'. As stated above, Fought does not frame her work as intersectional, so we are once again in the realm of intersectionality in deed but not name. In the next section, we will continue along the same lines as Fought, examining intersections involving race, ethnicity, ethnolinguistic identity and class. We do so with a view to exemplifying how more explicit interactional analysis might be carried out in future research. As we have done elsewhere (Block and Corona 2014), we draw on Victor Corona's research on Latino youth in Barcelona.

Future directions

In the context of Barcelona (and by extension, Catalonia and Spain), the term *Latino* encapsulates the ways in which immigrants from Ecuador, Colombia, Bolivia, the Dominican Republic and other Latin American countries affiliate to and participate in a variety of activities (including dance, cinema and food consumption), employing semiotic resources (including language, body movement, hair styles and clothing) which index *lo Latino* (Latino-ness) as a distinctive subculture, differentiable from autochthonous Catalan and Spanish culture. Victor Corona's research on *lo Latino* in Barcelona, which began a decade ago, grew out of his interest in studying what elements were involved in the construction of this identity in the context of massive Latin American immigration to Barcelona from the early to mid-1990s onwards. In early 2005, he started an ethnographic study involving participant observation in a working-class neighbourhood in Barcelona with a high proportion of newly arrived immigrants, specifically focusing on public spaces such as parks, bars and, above all, the schools where his adolescent informants were students. The data discussed in this section come from a large corpus consisting of interviews (both group and individual) and spontaneously recorded conversations, collected between early 2005 and mid-2013. We focus on three examples from Corona's corpus which we believe show how identity dimensions – race, ethnicity, language and class – come together in the day-to-day lives of these young Latinos.

As we mentioned above, Corona's research was carried out in working-class neighbourhoods in the northern part of Barcelona. Historically, the neighbourhoods have always been predominantly low-income and working-class areas. They received a good proportion of the massive migration from other parts of Spain to Barcelona in the 1950s and 1960s, and they have received a good number of the immigrants who have come to Barcelona in recent years, with a high proportion coming from Latin American countries (Ayuso and Piñol 2010). The majority of the informants in Corona's research come from low-income families in which the parents have few or no formal qualifications and, as a result, have ended up in employment such as cleaning, construction and various manual jobs like house moving and warehouse work. In her comprehensive survey of immigration to Barcelona between 1995 and 2010, Marina Subirats notes how, for the majority of recent immigrants, 'working conditions are much more precarious than those of the autochthonous population … as a consequence of being situated in the low qualification sector' (Subirats 2012: 378; translation by David Block). And in this context, a Latino identity is very much associated with precarious work conditions and low-qualification jobs. In the interview data presented in Extract 1, Lucía, a girl from Ecuador, tells the story of her mother's plight, working as a maid in the homes of middle-class Catalan families.[4]

David Block and Victor Corona

Extract 1 Corpus 2005–2006

Participant: Lucía

Original in Spanish	English translation
mi madre también me ha contado/que cuando ella recién llegó/también tuvo que fregar pisos/en casa de españoles/pero en casa de españoles/mientras los españoles no terminaban/((xxx))/o sea sus jefes/no terminaban de comer/ella no podía comer/ no podía comer porque decían que las chachas/<u>las chachas</u>/comían después de que los jefes/entonces a mi mamá me decía también a mi/que:e/que ella vino aquí:i/y:y/ la humillaron bastante/pero ahora ya no/me dice ahora/yo humillo a los españoles/como necesitan de mi/	my mother also told me/that when she first arrived/she also had to scrub floors/in a Spanish home/but in the Spanish home/ until the Spanish had finished/((xxx))/like her bosses/until they finished eating/she couldn't eat/she couldn't eat because they said maids/<u>the maids</u>/ate after their bosses/so my mum also said to me/tha:at/that she came he:ere/and and/they humiliated her a lot/but not any more/she tells me now/I humiliate the Spanish/since they need me/

Sennett and Cobb (1972) famously wrote about the personal anguish, disappointment and shame felt by people who have not achieved as much as they might have in life in terms of material wealth, education, housing and other aspects of life that index social class, using the term 'hidden injuries of class' to capture such feelings. In Extract 1, we are allowed a glimpse at what we might call the '*unhidden* injuries of class', that is, the very overt wrongs wrought on the less powerful by the more powerful. In addition, Lucía goes on to talk about how in Ecuador her mother had worked in higher prestige jobs, certainly not as a maid, and she further reports that as soon as she was able to do so, she left the service of the Spanish family to work as a butcher in a supermarket.

One factor hindering Lucía's mother in terms of her employment conditions was her physical appearance. For the most part, Latinos in Barcelona constitute a 'visible' minority, given that many are not European in appearance (being dark-skinned and having Andean and African features), and this leads to a racialisation of their status as immigrants and ultimately how they are slotted into the existing (though ever-evolving) class system in Barcelona, Catalonia and Spain as a whole. In Extract 2, four of Corona's informants, all male Latinos, explain what their status as a visible minority actually means in practice:

Extract 2 Corpus 2013

Participants: Rony (RON) and Miguel (MIG), Ecuadorian
Sergio (SER), Colombian
Naldo (NAL), Bolivian

TN	SP	Original in Spanish	English translation
01	RON	la mayoría son racistas/aunque no lo digan/o sea/tú vas por la calle=	most of them are racists/even if they don't say so/I mean/you're walking down the street=
02	SER	=sí=	=yes=

03	RON	vamos nosotros dos/o que vayamos los cuatro/nos va a ver una señora/y si nos ve/se asusta/	and the two of us are walking/or maybe all four of us/a lady is going to see us/ and if she sees us/she's going to freak out/
04	SER	se te queda mirando/se te ve por otra calle/o se ((xxx))/	she just stands there looking at you/and she crosses the street/or she ((xxx))/
05	MIG	cuéntale cuando insultaste a la vieja/ cuéntale/	tell him about when you insulted that old lady/tell him/
06	NAL	íbamos caminando/y había una señora caminando/y yo/me crucé a otro lado para ver otra cosa/y éste ›refiriéndose a Miguel‹ se cruzó al lado/y la viejita se asustó/pensó que le íbamos a hacer algo/se ((xxx))/feo/	we were walking/and there was this lady walking/and I/I crossed the street to see something/and this one ›referring to Miguel‹ walked across with me/and the old lady freaked out/she thought we were going to do something to her/ she ((xxx))/ugly/
07	RON	ven a un latino/o a un grupo=	they see a latino/or a group=
08	NAL	=ven a un grupo de dos latinos/o más de dos latinos/y ya/	=they see a group of latinos/or more than two latinos/and that's it/

This exchange came in response to a question posed by Corona about the four boys' sense of citizenship and belonging in contemporary Catalonia. The story told here collectively is one of racial profiling as a natural part of their day-to-day lives, whereby for many older members of the local population (and perhaps for older women in particular), the mere physical presence of these young men in public spaces is framed as a threat. In this sense, being Latino is a racial positioning. However, it is also about a long list of associations marking one as different from a mainstream Catalan culture, such as the boys' tendency to be dressed in a hip-hop style (more on this below) or the fact that they are adolescent males who tend to move around the city in groups of four.

Another way that *lo Latino* gets realised is through language. Extract 3 illustrates how the pronunciations of certain phonemes serve as 'acts of identity' (LePage and Tabouret-Keller 1985) in the same way that certain linguistic features mark one as an African American in the United States (see discussion above). And the production of these features does not go unnoticed by those who self-position as Latino.

Extract 3 Corpus 2007–2008

Participants: Victor Corona (VC)
          Ángel (AG), Colombian
          Javier (JV), Ecuadorian

TN	SP	Original in Spanish	English translation
01	VC	tú que sientes/por ejemplo cuando ves un ecuatoriano por ejemplo pronunciando la +θ+ ?/	what do you feel/for instance when you see an Ecuadorian/for instance pronouncing the +θ+ ?/
02	AG	cómo?/	what?/

03	VC	por ejemplo que diga+*θine*+ ⁾cine˂/ +*coraθon*+ ⁾corazón)˂/	for instance saying +*θine*+ ⁾cinema˂/ +*coraθon*+ ⁾heart˂/
04	AG	aaa:h ⁾risas de todos˂/	aaa:h ⁾everyone laughs˂/
05	JV	se me ha españolizado/dicen/	he's become Spanish-ised/they say/
06	AG	nosotros hablamos así/pero de broma/ me entiendes?/por molestar a la gente española/sabes?/pero sí que hay gente de allá/que ya está comenzando a hablar así	we speak like that/but as a joke/you know?/to annoy Spanish people/you know?/but actually there are people from over there/that are starting to speak like that

We see here the significance of using the voiceless dental non-sibilant fricative (the *theta-θ* – typical of Spanish in much of the Iberian Peninsula) as an identity marker to be avoided if one is to be considered Latino. In effect, being Latino means talking Latino, and those who do not conform are said to have Spanish-ised, that is, sold out to local norms and culture. However, using particular vocabulary, and pronouncing it in a particular way, is not the only means by which Corona's informants position themselves as Latinos. There is the broader multimodality of communication (Jewitt 2009) to consider, whereby we take into account how communication and acts of (re)presentation are not just about language but also a whole array of modes, including dress (clothes worn), ornamentation (e.g. piercings, bracelets), body moulding (haircuts, tattoos), gestures, posture and gaze. In Extract 4, Corona is talking to five female informants and one male informant about Latinos and dress in the school context. The female informants are from a range of backgrounds: Catalan, Moroccan, Peruvian and Ecuadorian. The sole male informant, Denilson, is the son of immigrants from the Dominican Republic.

Extract 4 Corpus 2008–2009

Participants: Victor, Corona (VC)
                  Marta (MR) and Leire (LR), Catalan
                  Fatia (FT), Moroccan
                  Ana (AN), Peruvian
                  Andrea (AD), Ecuadorian
                  Denilson (DL), Dominican

TN	SP	Original in Spanish	English translation
01	VC	cómo se viste él/cómo se vis=	how does he dress/how does he dre=
02	LR	=pues se viste:e bie:en/	=he dresse:es ni:ice/
03	DL	yo primero agarro/	first I take/
04	LR	no no/	no no/
05	AD	si no estuviéramos/	if we weren't/
06	VC	chicos/hay clase/chicos/chicos (.5)	guys/there's a class/guys/guys (.5)
07	AD	EL JUAN ESTÁ MUY BUENO/⁾ risas de todas˂ (.5)	JUAN IS REALLY HOT/⁾all the girls laugh˂ (.5)
08	VC	ey/sin gritar (.5) cómo te vistes?/⁾dirigida a Denilson˂/	hey/no shouting (.5) how do you dress?/ ⁾directed at Denilson˂/

09	AD	bie:en/	ni:ice/
10	DL	primero:o/	fi:irst/
11	AD	bien (.5)	nice (.5)
12	FT	como si fuera/	like he was/
13	LR	o sea (1.5)	like (1.5)
14	DL	primero agarro la camiseta/	first I take the t-shirt/
15	LR	tiene/o sea:a/aunque vaya/aunque vaya con ropa:a/así:i ˀindicando anchura con las manos˂/ancha y eso/ pero:o/no sé/tiene glamour/	he has/li:ike/even though he goes/even though he goes around with clothe:es like tha:at ˀindicating width with her hands˂/wide and that/bu:ut/I don't know/he has glamour/
16	VC	Ey/escuchamos lo que (1.5)	eh/we are listening to what (1.5)
17	MR	y a él le pega esta ropa/	and he looks good in these clothes/
18	AD	le pega/le pega (.5) porque es moreno/	he looks good/he looks good (.5) because he is dark/
19	MR	tiene cuerpo para llevar esto/	he has the body to wear this/
20	VC	y los latinos se visten de alguna manera/	and Latinos dress in a particular way/
21	LR AN AD FT MR	sí sí sí/	yes yes yes/
22	MR	te digo una cosa/te digo una cosa	let me tell you something/let me tell you something
23	FT	no te pongas roja/	don't be embarrassed/
24	MR	yo lo he visto/hay españoles que/yo conozco uno/que intenta ser la/que intenta vestirse como latinos/pero les queda fatal/les queda fatal/no/a los españoles no les pega/a lo mejor a algunos/pero a los latinos les queda mejor la ropa así/	I've seen it/there are Spanish guys/I know one/who tries to be la/who try to dress like Latinos/but they look awful/ they look awful/no/Spanish guys don't look good/maybe some do/but Latinos look better in those clothes/

Apart from being part of the Latino group in the school, Denilson was also closely connected to the world of rap and reggaeton,[5] which acted as a shaper of his wardrobe choices. The girls evaluate his dress style favourably; they see him as cool and fashionable, and even in possession of a certain charm or 'glamour', as Leire puts it. As Andrea informs us, Denilson and other Latinos look cool wearing their clothes because they are dark-skinned (Denilson, it should be noted, is Black). What is interesting here is how Marta, Leire and Andrea relate clothing to race and ethnicity, with Marta saying that Spanish guys 'look awful' (*les queda fatal*) when they try to dress like Latinos. For these girls, not everyone can be Latino and, indeed, Spanish guys cannot even pretend to be Latino because they do not have the necessary skin colour and what Bourdieu termed *body hexis*.[6] In this context, Denilson is authentically Latino.

Summary

In this chapter we have discussed what intersectionality is about before making the point that while there would appear to be a default intersectionality at work in most language and identity research in applied linguistics, this is not made explicit. The lack of explicitness leads to the absence of any detailed and in-depth consideration of the multiple difficulties arising in the establishment of intercategorical interrelations and intracategorical divergences. We have endeavoured here to inject an explicit intersectional agenda into our discussion of young Latinos in Barcelona, all too aware that we would not be able to do justice to this population in the space allowed here. Nevertheless, we believe that by presenting and discussing the four extracts above, we have made several points about intersectionality worth carrying forward into future language and identity research.

Different individuals intervene in the four extracts, but what emerges is a set of recounted experiences that arguably are shared among those who are positioned by others and who self-position as Latinos in Barcelona. And what we see is the construction of a Latino identity as part of the larger intersection of interrelated identity dimensions embedded in McCall's (2005) 'intercategorical complexity'. In this sense we are in the realm of the intersectionality of race, ethnicity, class, gender and multimodal behaviour (which includes linguistic behaviour), even if we must be careful how we use these categories, so as not to fall into a kind of default essentialisation.

Meanwhile, the other side of the intersectional coin is 'intracategorical complexity', which is in evidence only by default. Thus, where racial phenotype is cited as an identity marker, we need only to imagine those Latin Americans who have a European phenotype (in particular, the Argentinian, Uruguayan and Chilean immigrants) to see that not all individuals potentially classified as Latinos are equal in this regard (Corona and Block in preparation). Class (see Block, this volume) also looms large here, both in terms of the informants' parents, who occupy the lower ends of the Barcelona job market, and the informants themselves, who seem to be destined to work in low-skilled jobs in the local employment market. In addition, with reference to class position, there is the dilemma faced by upwardly mobile Latinos who orient to mainstream middle-class values, a process which has an impact on speech patterns and their multimodal behaviour in general. These individuals may be positioned as disloyal to their Latino roots by other Latinos who have not moved in this direction. There are also gendered differences in evidence, particularly in the story told by the four boys in Extract 2 (would the same thing have happed if the woman in the story had come across four *Latinas* instead of four *Latinos*?), and in Extract 4, which is about *cool* masculinity and style. Indeed, there is much space for further exploration of the multiple masculinities and femininities within the category of 'Latino youth'. Of course, in the midst of this intracategorical complexity, there is also the prospect that Latino as a category may be narrowing, reserved only for those who are relatively dark-skinned, act in certain ways, work in certain sectors and so on. All of this means that intracategorical differences always depend on the demarcations and delimitations of the category in question.

Finally, we would like to return to two questions posed above in our discussion of Nash's (2008) critique of intersectionality:

- Do individuals live their lives intersectionally in that they are always conscious of how constraints on their activity are multi-layered and never just about one single dimension?
- Do individuals self-consciously invoke different dimensions of their identity, selectively and strategically, as they go about their day-to-day activity?

In the four extracts cited above, the informants do invoke different dimensions of their lived identities, and this appears to be done in a fairly self-conscious way as a means of conveying to Corona an awareness of the complexity of their lives. Lucía manifests a kind of class awareness when she retells her mother's story of the overt injuries of class in a middle-class Catalan household. In Extract 2, Rony, Miguel, Sergio and Naldo easily relate their experience of the 'old lady' crossing the street to racism in Catalan society, a racism which positions them as dangerous because they have dark skin (although mode of dress surely is an additional factor in such cases). In Extract 3, Ángel and Javier explain (and therefore show a keen awareness of) the sociolinguistic rules of the game – how speaking in certain ways situates one either as a Latino or as a sell-out. And finally, Marta, Leire, Fatia, Ana, Andrea and Denilson show an awareness of and talk candidly about the ethno-racial politics of style, inflected by a Latino/non-Latino dynamic, that reigns in secondary schools in Barcelona. In short, these young people do appear to live their lives intersectionally in that they show a degree of self-awareness as regards to how constraints on their activity are multilayered and never just about one single dimension. And they do self-consciously invoke different aspects of their identity in different contexts.

Of course, the reader may well wonder what is to be gained by making intersectionality explicit in research. After all, if most researchers are doing it without naming it, what difference does it make? In response we might point to the fact that from the earliest exemplifications of the notion, from the words of Sojourner Truth to the work of hooks (1981), Crenshaw (1989), Anthias (2013) and others, intersectionality has been linked to political activism, particularly movements demanding the civil rights of women and people of colour. We believe that a specific focus on intersectionality, in effect, makes activism more possible; it makes clear that injustice is never about just one dimension of being, and therefore is not remediable through a focus on that one dimension. In such a process, injustice is revealed as far more complex than public discourses would often have us believe. And by grasping this complexity and confronting it as such, researchers are more likely to be able to propose action on behalf of those who suffer injustice.

Related topics

Positioning language and identity: poststructuralist perspectives; Language and ethnic identity; Language, race and identity; Language and gender identities; Class in language and identity research; A linguistic ethnography of identity: adopting a heteroglossic frame; Language, gender and identities in political life: a case study from Malaysia.

Further reading

Grzanka, P.R. (ed.) (2014). *Intersectionality: a foundations and frontiers reader*. Boulder, CO: Westview Press. (This reader charts the origins and history of intersectionality in Black feminist thought via the presentation of key analytic and applied texts.)

hooks, b. (1981). *Ain't I a woman: Black women and feminism*. Boston: South End Press. (hooks examines how Black women have been oppressed throughout history by White men and Black men, albeit in different ways, and by middle-class White women as well, and in the process she lays many of the foundations of current thinking about intersectionality.)

Jackson, S. (ed.) (2014). *Routledge handbook of race, class, and gender*. London: Routledge. (This handbook consists of 21 chapters examining the intersectionality of race, class and gender from a wide range of disciplinary backgrounds.)

Notes

1 Victor Corona is grateful to the ASLAN project (ANR-10-LABX-0081) of the Université de Lyon for its financial support for his ongoing research within the programme 'Investissements d'Avenir' (ANR-11-IDEX-0007). The ASLAN project is funded by the French government, via the National Research Agency (ANR).

2 This is a reworked and expanded version of our discussion on intersectionality in Block and Corona (2014).

3 Practice varies as regards the use of capital letters when 'Black' refers to race. Here we have chosen to use capital letters, following the practice of most scholars we have read who write about race. In addition, and for the sake of consistency, we have also used 'White' with a capital W when referring to race. However, we have left intact all quoted material where either term appears in lower case.

4 It is worth noting that throughout Corona's databases informants make reference to 'the Spanish' (*los españoles*) to refer to anyone they deem to be autochthonous. This denomination does not take into account sociolinguistic differences dividing this population into Catalan-preferent and Spanish-preferent speakers, but it does go to the heart of a very real issue, namely the feeling among many Latinos that live their lives as separate from 'the Spanish'. We use 'Catalan' here because the people referred to would likely refer to themselves as 'Catalan'.

5 Reggaeton is a genre of urban music directly linked to hip-hop and rap, which also draws on Caribbean rhythms such as bomba, plena, salsa, latin pop and bachata. The specific rhythm that characterises reggaeton is referred to as 'Dem Bow'. Reggaeton is generally associated with rapping and/or singing in Spanish. It originated in Panama in the 1970s as reggae music sung in Spanish. In the 1990s, reggaeton developed and modernised in Puerto Rico and received its current name. It has since become a global phenomenon, and nowadays has a world market which spreads well beyond the geographical boundaries of Latin America.

6 Bourdieu defined *body hexis* as follows: 'Body hexis speaks directly to the motor function, in the form of a pattern of postures that is both individual and systematic, because linked to a whole system of techniques involving then body and tools, and charged with a host of social meanings and values: in all societies, children are particularly attentive to the gestures and postures which, in their eyes, express everything that goes to make an accomplished adult – a way of walking, a tilt of the head, facial expressions, ways of sitting and of using implements, always associated with a tone of voice, a style of speech, and (how could it be otherwise?) a certain subjective experience' (Bourdieu 1977: 87).

References

Anthias, F. (2013). 'Intersectional what? Social divisions, intersectionality and levels of analysis', *Ethnicities*, 13(1): 3–19.

Ayuso, A. and Piñol, G. (eds) (2010). *Inmigracion latinoamericana en España* [*Latin American immigration in Spain*]. Barcelona: Centro de Información y Documentación.

Benwell, B. and Stokoe, L. (2006). *Discourse and identity*. Edinburgh: Edinburgh University Press.

Bilge, S. (2013). 'Intersectionality undone: saving intersectionality from feminist intersectionality studies', *Du Bois Review*, 10(2): 405–424.

Block, D. (2007). *Second language identities*. London: Continuum.

Block, D. (2014). *Social class in applied linguistics*. London: Routledge.

Block, D. (this volume). Class in language and identity research, in S. Preece (ed.) *The Routledge handbook of language and identity*. London: Routledge, pp. 241–254.

Block, D. and Corona, V. (2014). 'Exploring class-based intersectionality', *Language, Culture and Curriculum*, 27(1): 27–42.

Bourdieu, P. (1977). *Outline of a theory of practice*. Cambridge: Cambridge University Press.

Caldas-Coulthard, C.R. and Iedema, R. (eds) (2008). *Identity trouble: critical discourse and contested identities*. London: Palgrave.

Combahee River Collective (1977). *The Combahee River Collective statement* [Online]. Available at www.sfu.ca/iirp/documents/Combahee%201979.pdf

Corona, V. and Block, D. (in preparation). 'The complexity of being "Latino" in Barcelona: "Latin American" is not always "Latino"'.

Crenshaw, K. (1989). 'Demarginalizing the intersection of race and sex: a Black feminist critique of antidiscrimination doctrine, feminist theory, and antiracist politics' [Online], *University of Chicago Legal Forum*, pp. 139–167. Available at http://philpapers.org/rec/CREDTI

Crenshaw, K. (1991). 'Mapping the margins: intersectionality, identity politics, and violence against women of color', *Stanford Law Review*, 43(6): 1241–1299.

De Fina, A., Schiffrin, D. and Bamberg, M. (eds) (2006). *Discourse and identity*. Cambridge: Cambridge University Press.

Fanon, F. (1967 [1952]). *Black skin, White masks*. New York: Grove Press.

Fought, C. (2006). *Language and ethnicity*. Cambridge: Cambridge University Press.

Grzanka, P.R. (ed.) (2014). *Intersectionality: a foundations and frontiers reader*. Boulder, CO: Westview Press.

Higgins, C. (ed.) (2012). *Identity formation in globalizing contexts: language learning in the new millennium*. Berlin: Mouton de Gruyter.

Hill-Collins, P. (1993). 'Toward a new vision: race, class and gender as categories of analysis and connection', *Race, Sex and Class*, 1(1): 25–45.

Hill-Collins, P. and Bilge, S. (2015). *Intersectionality*. London: Polity Press.

hooks, b. (1981). *Ain't I a woman: Black women and feminism*. Boston: South End Press.

hooks, b. (2000). *Where we stand: class matters*. London: Routledge.

Jackson, S. (ed.) (2014). *Routledge handbook of race, class, and gender*. London: Routledge.

Jewitt, C. (2009). *Handbook of multimodal analysis*. London: Routledge.

Joseph, J. (2004). *Language and identity*. London: Palgrave.

Labov, W. (1972 [1969]). The logic of nonstandard English, in P. Giglioli (ed.) *Language and social context*. Harmondsworth, UK: Penguin, pp. 179–215.

Le Page, R. and Tabouret-Keller, A. (1985). *Acts of identity: Creole-based approaches to language and ethnicity*. Cambridge: Cambridge University Press.

Lin, A. (ed.) (2008). *Problematizing identity*. Mahwah, NJ: Lawrence Erlbaum.

Llamas, C. and Watt, D. (eds) (2010). *Language and identities*. Edinburgh: Edinburgh University Press.

McCall, L. (2005). 'The complexity of intersectionality', *Signs*, 30(3): 1771–1800.

Moore, M.R. (2011). *Invisible families: gay identities, relationships and motherhood among Black women*. Berkeley: University of California Press.

Morgan, M. (2002). *Language, discourse and power in African American culture*. Cambridge: Cambridge University Press.

Nash, J. (2008). 'Re-thinking intersectionality', *Feminist Review*, 89: 1–15.

Norton, B. (2013 [2000]). *Identity and language learning: extending the conversation*. 2nd edn. Bristol, UK: Multilingual Matters.

Omoniyi, T. and White, G. (eds) (2006). *The sociolinguistics of identity*. London: Continuum.

Pavlenko, A. and Blackledge, A. (eds) (2004). *Negotiation of identities in multilingual settings*. Bristol, UK: Multilingual Matters.

Piller, I. and Takahashi, K. (2010). At the intersection of gender, language and transnationalism, in N. Coupland (ed.) *Handbook of language and globalization*. Oxford: Blackwell, pp. 540–554.

Riley, P. (2007). *Language, culture and identity: an ethnolinguistic approach*. London: Continuum.

Sennett, R. and Cobb, J. (1972). *The hidden injuries of class*. New York: Norton.

Smitherman, G. (1977). *Talkin and testifyin: the language of Black America*. Boston: Houghton Mifflin.

Subirats, M. (2012). *Barcelona: de la necesidad a la libertad* [*Barcelona: from necessity to freedom*]. Barcelona: Universitat Oberta de Catalunya.

Appendix

Transcription conventions

Slash (/) shows the end of a chunk of talk, normally paced.

A question mark (?) indicates question intonation.

Pauses are timed to the nearest with the number of seconds in brackets: (.5).

Equals sign (=) at the end of one utterance and the start of the next speaker's utterance indicates that there was no audible gap between speakers.

Phrases or words in angled brackets (< ... >) is an additional comment by the transcriber on what is happening at the time or the way in which something is said.

CAPITAL letters means a raised voice.

Underlining indicates a word or words stressed for emphasis.

Colon (:) indicates an elongated vowel (e.g. no:o).

+ + with an italicised transcription in between indicates a phonetic representation of something said.

Double brackets around 'x's shows that the speaker's utterance is inaudible or cannot be made out: ((xxx)).

33

Language and identity in the digital age

Ron Darvin

Introduction

Technology in the twenty-first century has transformed the world in multiple, exciting and unanticipated ways. Facilitating the rapid flow of information, capital and services across the globe, it has dramatically revolutionised the way we work, communicate and interact with one another. More affordable travel, mobile communication devices, social media and online connectivity have enabled new patterns of movement and forms of social participation. In this digitally connected world, people move fluidly across online and offline spaces, blurring the boundaries of time and space and transforming notions of public and private domains (Gee and Hayes 2011). The concept of space has become more embedded in people's imaginations, leading to new identifications, allegiances and relations (Warriner 2007). As technology continues to permeate all aspects of human life and transform the social order, it has impacted on language and identity in significant ways.

The digital revolution has transformed language by triggering an explosion of new vocabularies, genres and styles and by reshaping literacy practices. By developing a mode of communication where writing approximates speaking, instant messaging (IM) and texting have facilitated the production of new words and styles that bridge the interactive nature of speech and the documental capacity of writing (Warschauer and Matuchniak 2010). The constant evolution of new media has also spurred the growth of multimodal affordances, enabling people to assemble texts that integrate language with visual, aural, gestural and spatial modes. Constructing new spaces of language acquisition and socialisation (Ito *et al.* 2010; Lam 2013), social media capabilities have facilitated cross-language interaction (Luke 2003; Warschauer 2009) and fertilised transcultural and translingual practices (Canagarajah 2013). Online users are not only able to produce and share texts with greater ease, but also get immediate feedback to remediate these texts, making people active creators in a society of reflexive co-construction (Cope and Kalantzis 2010).

By transforming language, the digital also transforms identity. Weedon (1987: 21) asserts that language is 'the place where our sense of ourselves, our subjectivity is constructed'. Identity is constituted in and through language (Norton 2013), and we use language to articulate ideas and to represent ourselves and our social relations. Drawing on Weedon, Norton (ibid.: 4) defines

523

identity as 'the way a person understands his or her relationship to the world, how that relation is constructed across time and space and how the person understands possibilities for the future'. Because a person's sense of self and relation to the world continuously shifts, identity is dynamic, multiple and even contradictory. As the digital provides multiple spaces where language is used in different ways, learners are able to move across online and offline realities with greater fluidity and perform multiple identities.

As the digital reshapes language and identity, language learning also continues to evolve. Learners participate in the new spaces of socialisation afforded by the digital and continue to discover and engage in new ways of representing themselves through language and other modalities. For Norton (2013: 4), when learners speak, they not only exchange information, but also reorganise 'a sense of who they are and how they relate to the world'. As they navigate multiple contexts of power, they perform different identities and continually negotiate a legitimate space where they can claim the right to speak. At the turn of the century, Castells (2001: 3) forewarned however that the inability to participate fully in technological networks can lead to 'one of the most damaging forms of exclusion'. How learners are able to gain digital access and the literacies necessary to assert their place in an increasingly technologised world is thus an important concern for language teachers, researchers and scholars. As a social practice, learning is implicated in relations of power (Norton 2013), and the classroom, together with other learning contexts, can reproduce the inequalities of larger, institutional structures. How learners position themselves and are positioned by others shapes their investment in the language and literacy practices of these diverse contexts.

Recognising how technology has dramatically transformed language, identity and learning in the twenty-first century, this chapter aims to outline the seminal ideas and issues in language and identity research that have emerged from a perpetually shifting digital landscape. This chapter seeks to address the following questions:

- How have new linguistic structures evolved from digitally mediated communication?
- What new mindsets, literacies and strategies do learners need to develop as they navigate these spaces?
- What new means of representing and performing identities have become possible because of the digital?
- How does technology develop new modes of inclusion and exclusion for learners of different social positions?

By answering these questions, this chapter identifies the important issues and possible future directions in language and identity research for applied linguistics in the digital age.

Current issues

To understand how the digital has shaped language and identity, one has to recognise that there are different lens through which the social effects of technology have been examined. Jones and Hafner (2012) speak of a spectrum where technology is seen as beneficial to society at one end and harmful at the other. Dystopian perspectives suggest that technology destroys our ability to communicate and interact with others meaningfully and is responsible for shorter attention spans, language deterioration and erosion of privacy. On the other hand, utopian views of technology attribute progress and change to technology and regard it as something that will transform the world ultimately for the better. The limitations of these positions are that they focus solely on technology itself without examining the social contexts in which technology is used and the intentions of its users. Technological determinism views technology as ultimately controlling thought and behaviour, where language and literacy practices are determined largely because of the affordances and constraints of the digital. On the other hand, ignoring the role of technology in societal transformation and regarding it as ideologically neutral would be a grave oversight; what we need is an approach that strikes a balance between these two views.

Recognising that social contexts and ideologies shape the way languages and identities evolve across space and time, this section begins by describing how technology has contributed to the transformation of the social order and necessitated the development of new mindsets and literacies. This section then examines how language practices and the performance of identities have shifted in response to the transformations in the social order brought about by technology.

The new social order and the development of digital literacies

According to Harnard (1991: 39), technology has set off a 'fourth revolution in the means of production of knowledge' that has accelerated the processes of globalisation. Increased connectivity and the speed of communication have facilitated a shift from manufacturing to 'knowledge work' focused on information processing and knowledge creation. In this knowledge economy, the production, distribution and exchange of information are vital, and the valuing of such capital results in new jobs and modes of productivity and raises the demand for certain skills. This shift changes institutions and transforms the economic structure (Lankshear and Knobel 2011). Organisations disseminate information rapidly in order to respond to global competition and new market challenges. Service workers are expected to be able to evaluate and find patterns in large amounts of data and to create social networks where this information can be circulated. Through the efficiencies of email, video-conferencing and instant messaging, work can be distributed over large geographical distances and a greater number of people can work from multiple locations, allowing increased flexibility and productivity, but also diminishing personal interaction and visibility within organisations (Jones and Hafner 2012).

Not only has the digital facilitated the growth of the knowledge economy, by providing new opportunities for representation, it has also enabled the construction and performance of multiple identities. Cope and Kalantzis (2010) assert that digital media create affordances and constraints in four areas, namely 'agency', 'divergence', 'multimodality' and 'conceptualisation'. With regard to agency, consumers are viewed as active creators who produce their own media and differentiate themselves further through ways of speaking, seeing, thinking or acting. Audiences have become users who are able to engage more actively with media by providing real-time comments and feedback. Because of the greater capacity for creation and self-representation, users are able to take up more powerful positions as they participate in a range of diverse online communities. As these communities construct their own language practices, divergence becomes an issue as their discourses become less mutually intelligible. Multimodality – that is, the capacity to construct meaning through a variety of modes, such as images, video, sound and music – has become much easier and cheaper, allowing diverse representations of the self. Finally, the constant development and transformation of new media requires knowledge of constantly evolving social and technical architectures. Producing new media texts requires new skills of thinking not just in terms of conceptualisation, but also in how to navigate a media environment of seemingly infinite choices.

Apart from providing greater opportunities for individual agency in representing the self, digital media also enable a mobility that has become 'the ideology and utopia of the twenty-first century' (Elliott and Urry 2010: 8). As people and ideas are able to travel virtually, fluidity of movement has become the natural order to aspire to. Identities become unbounded and deterritorialised, no longer tied to fixed localities, patterns or cultural traditions. It transforms the way people work, enjoy leisure or develop intimate relationships, exerting new demands on the self, particularly as they negotiate private and public lives. This mobility also fuels a 'networked individualism', where people are connected while paradoxically controlled by scheduling, monitoring, surveillance and regulation. Blommaert (2013) characterises this state of mobility, complexity and unpredictability as 'superdiversity', where identities are differently organised and distributed over online and offline sites. Within this superdiversity, communities of interest that transcend national boundaries are able to connect and interact, shaping new global publics and forms of segmentation. While social media allows people to network, communicate and work in cyberspace with those who share interests with them, it may also encourage less social interaction in the physical space of local communities (Gee and Hayes 2011).

By facilitating new modes of productivity, representation and socialisation, technology has helped transform the stage on which language and identity is performed. The capacity of learners to participate on this stage, however, requires the development of new mindsets and literacies. Recognising how cyberspace operates on assumptions and values that are different from those of the physical world, Knobel and Lankshear (2006) speak of the need to develop a post-physical and post-industrial mindset, which views space as open, continuous and fluid, rather than enclosed in physical boundaries. For learners that are oriented to a digital mindset, learning no longer means operating in one place and doing one task at a time. Instead, it requires learners to operate in different locations online and to multitask. A digital mindset also views expertise and authority as no longer vested solely in specific experts and institutions, but distributed across social networks in which each possesses varying forms and degrees of knowledge. A greater focus on the co-construction of knowledge is demonstrated, for instance, by the collaboration of scholars in building repositories of information such as Wikipedia. With the continuous influx of available information online, there is also a greater emphasis on how to gain and structure attention, how to innovate successfully in contexts and how to break conventions and invent new rules. Because of the shared capacity to construct, redesign and disseminate information through the Internet, what is regarded as factual becomes more open to interpretation and reinvention. As Luke (2003) points out, knowledge acquisition has become even more contextual and situational, and hence learners need to develop critical literacy that will allow them to contest, deconstruct and critique the abundance of information that exists online.

As learners develop a digital mindset, they also need to develop specific literacies that can allow them to navigate this new social landscape. Jones and Hafner (2012: 13) define digital literacies as 'the practices of communicating, relating, thinking and "being" associated with digital media'. As such, they involve: the ability to operate digital media tools and to adapt their affordances and constraints in particular circumstances; the process of encoding and decoding meaning through multimodal digitally mediated texts; and the capacity to construct and maintain relationships and identities through digital practices (Snyder *et al.* 2002; Warschauer 2009; Jones and Hafner 2012). Because of the abundance of technologies and information, learners have to develop the ability not only to adapt and decide which technologies would support their purposes, but to synthesise online information effectively and appropriately. Interaction, dialogue, negotiation and contestation become intrinsic to digital media, where meaning-making is marked by simultaneous decoding, production and interaction. As learners navigate through a multiplicity of texts, they need to employ greater lateral thinking so that they may move across disciplines, genres, modalities and cultural zones and negotiate the intertextuality, transculturality and intermediality that characterise this new order (Luke 2003).

The transformation of language

By reshaping the social order and the ways we interact with one another, the digital inevitably transforms language. At the same time, language, as a way of making meaning, shapes our lived experiences. New media enables new forms of communication, which have been researched in several ways, such as by examining the linguistic features of digital communication and the identities of the users of media and their relationships with their interlocutors (Lankshear and Knobel 2011; Jones and Hafner 2012). By enabling the use of written language in ways that are similar to face-to-face oral language, digital media allow the interpretation of the written in flexible, dialogic and interactive ways. Control is less top-down than traditional modes of communication and there is a notable increase in diverse semiotic modes such as images, music, sound and visual effects. Online participation also enables cross-language interaction, where users for instance can shift between English and romanised Cantonese and assemble mixed idiomatic expressions (Warschauer 2009). Multiple studies have analysed how participants in different online spaces, such as blogs, online games or social networking sites, use language in ways that are specific to these contexts, resulting in social variations of digitally mediated discourse (Thurlow and Mroczek 2011; Barton and Lee 2013).

Shifting linguistic patterns

Because of its interactivity, text-based digital communication can be synchronous or real time, such as chat and instant messaging, or asynchronous or delayed, such as email and blogs. Some digital media also limit the number of characters allowed in one turn, resulting in a proliferation of acronyms and abbreviations. In a study of storytelling styles on Facebook, Page (2012) notes the prominence of an affective discourse style, marked by a high degree of intensification – capitalisation, repeated exclamation marks, repetition, exaggerated quantifiers, such as 'all' and 'everyone', and frequent use of boosters, such as 'very', 'really' and 'so'. The subject matter of self-reporting updates typically focuses on the minutiae of everyday events: the weather, the user's mood, travel, leisure or domestic activities. As users write about opinions, reactions and emotional responses to life experiences, this linguistic pattern of intensification suggests that users believe some form of exaggeration is needed to make their mundane stories of ordinary everyday events 'tellable' on social media.

In terms of structure, the language used in interactive media has been observed to have specific linguistic features, as can be seen in Box 33.1.

While in face-to-face communication we use facial expressions, gestures and tone to provide enough contextualisation clues in communicating meaning, digitally mediated text uses the linguistic features in Box 33.1 to convey meaning. However, this does not mean that there is a one-to-one correspondence between emoticons and facial expressions, or between nonstandard spelling and actual speech (Jones and Hafner 2012).

Diverse semiotic modes

The evolution of digital media with its shift from page to screen (Snyder 1998) intensifies the use of a multiplicity of modes, including the visual, aural, gestural and spatial, for conveying

---

Box 33.1 Linguistic features of text-based digital communication (Jones and Hafner 2012: 67)

frequent use of acronyms (e.g. 'btw', 'lol')
shortened forms (e.g. 'k' for 'okay')
less attention to standard spelling, capitalisation and punctuation
letter homophones (e.g. 'u' for 'you', 'oic' for 'oh, I see')
creative use of punctuation (e.g. multiple punctuation such as '!!!!' or ellipsis marks: '.....')
spelling based on sound, sometimes to mark a regional accent or special style of speech (e.g. 'kewl' or 'cooooool')
lexicalisation of vocal sounds (like 'umm', 'uh huh', 'haha')
emoticons and other keyboard-generated graphics (e.g. '=.=')
creative use of typographical space and layout
formulaic openings and closings (e.g. 'sup', 'bb')

---

meaning. Language loses its privileged position in the digital world as the meaning of a message is increasingly constituted by a range of modes. For Kress (2003), this requires a shift from linguistics to a theory of semiotics that accounts for gestures, speech, image, writing, 3D objects and music (see Domingo, this volume). One specific example through which learners have been able to express themselves using multiple modes is digital storytelling. Through brief personal narratives told through images, sounds and words and assembled using new media (Darvin and Norton 2014a), learners are able to identify and reflect on pivotal moments of their life and find new opportunities for creation and collaboration. By borrowing and repurposing different multimodal elements, they are able not only to claim greater authorial agency, but also employ means of expression that are not limited to language. Elsewhere, in a study of the creative process of ninth-grade students as they produce their own digital stories about an odyssey of self, Rowsell (2012) demonstrates how multimodality can be a means to represent their lived histories and how students' individual creative expression was able to effect subtle shifts in ways of thinking. Because digital stories have few constraints, they provide learners with opportunities to improvise their ideas, values and histories and reposition their identities.

By assembling different modalities to construct meaning, digital storytelling provides new opportunities for language use. In a study of second language learners producing videos for children in other countries, Toohey et al. (2012) demonstrate how digital storytelling can allow learners to draw on their rich linguistic and cultural repertoires. Because bilingual practices were legitimised, learners were able to use English to show their L2 competence and use their first language to share their linguistic and cultural knowledge. As a multimodal performance, digital storytelling, like drama, has the capacity to become a heteroglossic combination of languages, voices and accents (see Creese and Blackledge, this volume). It allows an audience to hear different languages in a heteroglossic mix and without words being made 'other' through the use of italics or parentheses in written text (Darvin 2015).

Multilingual encounters and translingual practices

Within the online world, new multilingual encounters have emerged as people are able to connect with a global network. Barton and Lee (2013) point out that an increased use of local languages among diasporic communities online has led to a multilingual Internet and enabled local and global participation that assert new identities. According to Barton and Lee, when multilingual speakers communicate online, the language they choose to use is dependent on the situated language ecology of individual users. This takes into account geographical, educational, linguistic, social and cultural backgrounds, but also considers the intended audience and the subject matter of whatever is posted. Code-switching for instance serves as a means for users to perform their ethnic identity and signal their affiliation with a specific community. At the same time, the availability of online translation tools allows people to access more information and to participate in online forums that accommodate different dialects and languages.

Through technologies such as Google Translate, which relies on bilingual text corpora to identify frequently recurring translations, online users are able to participate in a greater number of multilingual exchanges. While languages like English enjoy a high status and are widely used online, the accessibility and reach of digital media also enables the use of minority languages. In a study of language choice in online contexts among young professionals in Cairo, Warschauer *et al.* (2002) discovered the use of Romanised Egyptian Arabic, which is rarely used in offline contexts and writing, but which was revitalised and documented through online exchanges. Another example of an online bilingual project is the African Storybook Project (SAIDE 2015). Led by Norton and other scholars, this provides online open-access to digital stories, available in English and a number of African languages. By providing a library of stories for young learners in sub-Saharan Africa, the project helps develop literacy in a range of mother tongues and second languages.

While digital media enables multilingual encounters and cross-language relations, it also facilitates translingual practices. These focus on the communicative processes across different groups in the digital space rather than within a geographic speech community. As Canagarajah (2013) points out, digital communication, together with migration and transnational relations, have encouraged textual co-construction, collaborative meaning-making and different types and degrees of language mixing. While *multilingual* indicates the combination of separate languages, *translingual* signals how languages mutually influence each other and produce new hybrid meanings and grammar. The meshing of diverse languages and modalities in digital texts results in unconventional idioms and word choices. In Canagarajah's study, a Saudi Arabian student who code-meshed Arabic and English justified her creation of idioms like 'storms of thoughts stampede' as a stylistic choice that rejects a native-speaker perspective (2013: 52). Because the translingual addresses the linguistic synergy that arises during interaction, Canagarajah asserts the need for a model of negotiated rather than situated literacy. In other words, an orientation to literacy that recognises texts as co-constructed and performed in time and space rather than pre-constructed and embedded in local cultural systems.

The evolution of identities

As the digital has shaped language practices and provided dynamic ways of making meaning, it has also provided new opportunities to construct and represent online identities. Through digital affordances, learners are able to perform multiple identities, such as blogger, photographer, gamer or designer, and to document and display their lives through various modalities. This presentational culture, where multiple aspects of one's life are shared with different kinds of audiences, alters notions of private and public spaces and affects the way we perceive ourselves (Barton and Lee 2013). Because of mobile devices that are perpetually online, constant accessibility and availability leads to constant surveillance and there is little time for being idle.

Taking a picture and uploading it or posting a status update in real time has become a naturalised activity for many social media users. Through location services, geographical representations of an individual's actual position are recorded, and this displacement of the self, geographically represented in real time, blurs the boundaries between online and offline reality (Kress 2009). Because of the agency afforded by digital platforms, online users have the possibility of differentiating themselves in online interactions and postings as well as participating in a range of online discourse communities. As a tool that mediates interaction, the digital becomes an extension of ourselves and transforms what we can do and mean, how we think and relate to others and who we can be (Jones and Hafner 2012). Whether we are emailing a colleague, tweeting to the general public or posting a status update on Facebook, we adapt digital affordances to specific contexts, relations and identities.

New spaces of identity construction

Online spaces have become increasingly important arenas for the development of social identities. The networks in these spaces are constructed through technology and the imagined collectives that emerge from interacting in these spaces (boyd 2014). Within these spaces, defined by boyd as 'networked publics', learners are able to engage with others and negotiate shared values and norms of collective behaviour (Facer 2011). Online modes of socialisation provide new contexts for using and developing literacy. It may also be that the asynchronous and virtual world makes it a less threatening mode for social interaction for some learners. In a study of youth culture and social network structure in new media, Ito *et al.* (2010) classify genres of participation according to their purpose. 'Friendship-driven practices' are dominant and mainstream practices that involve everyday negotiations with friends and peers; instant messaging, social network sites and mobile phones become ways to negotiate these friendships. As Ito *et al.* point out, digital practices become a form of socialisation among peers, the equivalent of 'hanging out'. 'Interest-driven practices', on the other hand, are those where learners engage with networks that focus on specialised activities that revolve around particular interests. By focusing on interests, hobbies, career aspirations and so on, interest-driven practices allow participants to collaborate with online users of diverse ages and backgrounds.

An example of the online construction of identities can be found in Thorne and Black's (2011) study of Nanako, an English language learner, on an online fan fiction site. Thorne and Black demonstrate how composing and posting online fan fiction can provide learners with new opportunities for learning and performing identities. By appropriating and integrating popular cultural and linguistic resources to construct fan fiction texts and by interacting with a diverse group who shared a common interest in anime or Japanese animation, Nanako was able to get feedback on her writing and demonstrate her knowledge of Chinese and Japanese language and culture. This dynamic enabled her to negotiate identities of novice and expert, while affirming her Asian identity and knowledge of Asian culture as capital. To frame their analysis, Thorne and Black focus on the conditions and affordances mobilised in the digitally mediated context. These are set against three dynamics in Internet-mediated interactions: indexical linkages to macro-level categories (ethnic or nation-state affiliations); functionally defined subject positions (e.g. youth, author, expert, novice), and fluid shifts in language choice, stance and style. By analysing these interactions, they assert how language development in these online spaces is interlinked with the construction of identities. As Cope and Kalantzis (2012) point out, as developing digital literacies encourages participation, learners are able to engage with issues that interest them and bring their identities to the learning process.

Performance of multiple identities

Blommaert (2005: 207) defines identity as 'particular forms of semiotic potential, organised in a repertoire'. By assembling semiotic resources, people are able to construct 'identity repertoires' that enable a performative approach to identity (see Baxter, this volume; Jones, this volume). The range of identities available to learners are then linked to the range of available semiotic resources. Recognising how youth growing up in this mediated digital culture have a plethora of ways to represent themselves, Stornaiuolo *et al.* (2009) argue that such limitless options complexify, extend and change self-identifications. By communicating across multiple symbolic systems in the online world, individuals can imagine new identities and ways of being in the world. They are able to share these self-representations with diverse audiences, who may interpret the meanings of these representations in very different ways. Weber and Mitchell (2008) highlight how the shaping of identity online is characterised by playful and deliberate creative assembly. Because people can present different identities as they select audiences and anticipate comments and reactions, a dialectical relationship arises. People textualise themselves in social media and perform carefully managed practices of identity to project a self of their choosing (Davies and Merchant 2009).

On social media platforms, such as Facebook, requiring authentic identifiers in the form of real names and affiliations, the performance of the self is based on already established social roles. When users update their status to express their thoughts, they offer a representation of the self, based on the online socialisation they have already experienced. Even the profile picture demonstrates an identity and invites other social meanings (Ellis 2010). In social media, status updates become rhetorical performances, not transparent representations of reality, and the performance of sociality is shaped by the way the interaction is enabled and valued (Page 2012). For example, through the process of tagging, Facebook friends are able to post pictures and links and send messages to each other's Wall, contributing to the construction of an online identity. To maintain a profile that corresponds with a chosen agenda, the Facebook user must thus function as a curator, who selects what to publish and what to delete in order to compose a coherent narrative of the self.

Future directions

Recognising how the digital revolution has shaped new debates in literacy development, language use and identity construction, I outline future directions for applied linguistics research in this section. Three areas that will be increasingly significant in studies of language and identity in the digital age are identified: transforming pedagogies, designing innovative methodologies and examining digital inequalities. Focusing on these areas of teaching and research can help learners of different social positions not only develop new literacies, but also imagine new powerful identities.

Transforming pedagogies

As technology continues to provide a vast and complex digital set of information and communication possibilities, language and literacy will continue to be transformed. This presents important implications for the way language and literacies are taught. The ongoing digital revolution means that learners are likely to become more aware of hybrid linguistic systems and non-standard varieties, blurring the roles and objects of study of applied linguists (Hall *et al.* 2011). The merging of the written and the spoken in the online world requires a shift from viewing the two as dichotomous. Instead, there must be an effort to understand digitally mediated language practices as a whole, where spoken instructions are carried out on phones and computers and where talking is not necessarily to or by real people. Core units of sociolinguistics such as variation, contact and community need to be reassessed (Lankshear and Knobel 2011), and the notion of conversational turn needs to be rethought when it comes to considering the dynamics of online chat. New possibilities of linguistic organisation such as framing, animation and the hypertext link have to be integrated into the development of Internet linguistics (Crystal 2011). To understand further these shifts in the digital world of language and learning, Norton and De Costa (in press) propose new research populations and under-researched social categories that need to be explored further.

Cope and Kalantzis (2010) believe that pedagogy must adapt to the new communicative order in four dimensions, namely 'designers', 'learner differences', 'synaesthesia' and 'metacognition'. As designers, learners are able to draw on different resources such as community, environment and family to actively create experiential, conceptual, analytical and applied knowledge. Schools need to not only recognise learners as knowledge producers, but also acknowledge their diverse histories and identities and incorporate strategies of inclusion. By enabling learners to link the particularities of their life experience to the knowledge they produce, school can provide opportunities to represent the material (class), corporeal (age, race, sex and sexuality) and symbolic (culture, language, gender, etc.) differences of learners. Classrooms need to engage mode shifting, or synaesthesia, as a pedagogical device so that learners of different dispositions can find particular forms that allow them to express their identities. As digital media provides more opportunities to produce and disseminate knowledge, learners are also able to develop metacognition. Through active conceptualisation and inductive thinking, they become capable of building abstract frameworks and schemas that can cross over different disciplines.

In *Learning futures*, Facer (2011) forecasts how technological developments will continue to transform critical aspects of education and discusses how the role of schools in communities and curricula need to be reimagined as digital and physical artefacts merge and as the capacity to manage and mobilise social networks becomes more significant. Multiliterate learners will need to be able to draw from the proliferating modalities of the digital to represent and circulate knowledge from intersecting disciplines. To become critical contributors to the knowledge economy, there has to be a sharper understanding of how hardware and software structure our capacity for representation and comprehension. Recognising these new literacy needs of learners, Darvin and Norton (in press) discuss how critical pedagogies can respond to the new structures and relations of power that have emerged in digital times.

Innovative methodologies

Technology-enabled research on language and identity

Through the rapid development of new digital technologies, researchers are able to examine the individual and sociocultural dimensions of language use in new and exciting ways. Corpus technology, for instance, allows users to access corpora, principled collections of electronic texts available for qualitative and quantitative analysis (O'Keefe *et al.* 2007). By enabling the systematic examination of word frequency or key word collocations in specific corpora, this technology allows a greater understanding of the linguistic repertoires of learners and the language patterns of communities. In a study of computer-mediated communication in an academic setting, Temples and Nelson (2013) used corpus-based analysis to understand the intercultural relations among students and the ways they negotiated online discourse to construct identities and develop a sense of community. The researchers examined the 150,000-word corpus of the online forum posts of 11 Canadian, Mexican and American female graduate students on an exchange programme. By detecting patterns in the use of personal pronouns *I*, *we* and *you*, Temples and Nelson were able to draw conclusions about their level of interactivity and how they generated a discourse that crossed and merged cultural and linguistic boundaries.

In a corpus-based investigation of SMS language used by mobile phone users in Switzerland, Dürscheid and Stark (2011) were able to collect 23,988 messages from 2,627 people in Swiss-German, Standard German, French, Italian, Romansh and other mother tongues, and the demographic data of these participants. This corpus is intended for further research to examine language choice and code switching, and to detect for instance if there is a correlation between the age of texters and their choice of Standard German versus Swiss-German. By focusing on text messaging conversations, studies are also able to look into the relationship between interlocutors and to compare the linguistic strategies of the different language groups in maintaining social relationships, for instance the sending of 'good night' messages.

New methodologies

Digital literacies are interconnected with other literacy practices and aspects of material culture, and thus Leander (2008: 37) proposes a 'connective ethnography', which he defines as 'a stance or orientation to Internet related research that considers connections and relations as normative social practices and Internet social spaces as complexly connected to other social spaces'. He asserts that novel solutions are required to study this field of relations, which no longer necessarily requires a physical displacement but experiential displacement, as researchers have to move fluidly across multiple sites. For Marsh (2013: 208), 'auto-cyber-ethnography', as an ethnography that focuses on describing the experiences of the researcher in specific virtual contexts, is one dynamic way for virtual world users 'to investigate their own literacy histories in online environments over time'. Stornaiuolo *et al.* (2013), on the other hand, propose a mix of qualitative and quantitative data in studies of learners' authoring process across online and offline spaces, multiple languages and semiotic systems. The plurality of sites leads to a multiplicity of data and, because networked spaces are hybrid spaces, Stornaiuolo and Hall (2014) posit that methodological approaches have to be multidimensional, that is, they must take into account this data across contexts and over time, including the meanings digital artefacts take on long after they are created. According to Stornaiuolo and Hall (2014: 28), tracing the movements of people, texts and ideas in cross-contextual meaning is a methodological challenge in digital contexts and this asserts the need to trace 'resonances' or the 'intertextual echoing of ideas across spaces, people and texts'.

Digital inequalities

While there has been much research on how digital affordances have led to new language use and identity performance, the social and educational inequalities that emerge from technological innovation have received less attention in language and identity studies. It is important to understand that the development of digital literacies occurs in broader social, political and economic contexts. As advanced capitalist countries transition to post-industrial capitalism, where material production is replaced by information processing, being able to use technology has become 'the critical factor in generating and accessing wealth, power and knowledge'

(Castells 2010: 93). Prinsloo and Rowsell (2012) point out that, when technologies migrate particularly to the spaces in the globalised periphery, there are specific constraints that determine if and how these resources will be taken up. They are, just as Blommaert (2005: 83) views language, 'placed resources', and the specificity of place, and its material conditions and social practices, largely determine the means and ways through which these resources are activated. When digitisation is set against the wider backdrop of society, tensions and imbalances of power begin to surface. How one is able to access technology is not only dependent on one's possession of economic capital, but also contingent on government, institutions and policies that enable such access. At the same time, being able to cultivate specific digital tastes can be linked to social class (North *et al.* 2008). Recognising which digital tastes are valued as symbolic capital in school and work contexts is an area that requires greater attention in language and identity studies.

To fill this research gap, Warschauer (2009) calls for an ideological model of digital literacy to examine how power shapes the development and practice of digital literacies. An awareness of the material contexts in which online literacies develop enables a broader, situated examination of language and identity, that confronts rather than erases existing inequalities. The challenge for those who research the evolving nature of digital literacies is to not overlook the dynamics of race, class and gender that impact these shifts. More comparative studies of digital practices of different communities need to be conducted, to understand the new modes of inclusion and exclusion that emerge through the digital. By incorporating issues of power into the study of online contexts, research would be able to examine the privileging and marginalisation of languages, identities and forms of knowledge. With regard to this, Luke (2003) advocates a critical digital literacy that articulates a 'metaknowledge', or a self-reflective analysis of the sociocultural and political contexts of these technologies at local and global levels. To capture the dynamic and mobile nature of new media, language and identity research needs to develop concepts and methodologies that allow for a provisional and transformational epistemology.

A new model of investment

Responding to the need for a more critical understanding of how power operates in language and literacy practices in the digital age, I have developed a model of language learning with Norton that locates investment at the intersection of identity, capital and ideology (see Figure 33.1) (Darvin and Norton 2015). This model extends theories of identity and investment developed in Norton's earlier work (see Norton Peirce 1995; Norton 2013) and is designed to address the realities of a new world order, where labour has become more individualised and where more social processes have migrated to the virtual. As learners retreat into private, isolated spaces, navigating both online and offline worlds, the mechanisms of power become more invisible, making it increasingly difficult to recognise how specific communicative events are indexical of macrostructures of power. This model of investment aims to draw attention to how ideologies collude and compete, shaping learners' identities and positioning them in different ways, as learners move fluidly across online spaces. The value of a learner's economic, cultural or social capital shifts as it travels across time and space. It is subject to, but not completely constrained by, the ideologies of different groups that determine how the capital of learners is 'perceived and recognized as legitimate' (Bourdieu 1987: 4), and whether it is deemed worthy of being transformed into symbolic capital. How educational institutions recognise the linguistic and cultural capital of learners as symbolic capital is likely

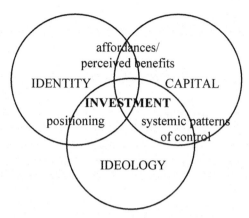

Figure 33.1 Model of investment

Source: Darvin and Norton (2015: 42).

to have an impact on the extent to which learners will invest in off and online language and literacy learning practices.

Case studies

In a comparative case study of two adolescent migrant Filipino learners, John and Ayrton, from different social class positions in Canada (Darvin and Norton 2014b), Norton and I examined how differences in economic, cultural and social capital can shape divergent digital literacies and language use. Raised solely by his mother, John struggled with learning English when he first arrived in Canada. His social network was almost entirely Filipino and his family spoke only Tagalog at home. The family shared one desktop computer, which the mother used to do Facebook and to watch Filipino soap operas. Mirroring his mother's preferences, John saw technology as an entertainment tool and used it primarily to play games. In contrast, Ayrton, who lived in a wealthy neighbourhood and spoke English almost exclusively at home, saw technology as a rich source of useful information, which could realise powerful imagined identities. Taking after his entrepreneurial father, he enrolled in an online course on currency trading, which allowed him to interact with professionals from different parts of the world. In this case, the differences in socioeconomic status and technology role models shaped their perceptions of what technology is for and the digital literacies they developed.

In a similar ethnographic study of the media engagements of two families from contrasting socioeconomic settings in South Africa, Lemphane and Prinsloo (2014) demonstrate how the use of different technologies result in different language and literacy practices. The middle-class children who had digital devices and unlimited broadband connectivity gained access to more English language resources, allowing them to develop topic-specific vocabulary and meta-awareness of language. Adapting avatars that became identity markers, they were able to experiment with different accents and become familiar with global middle-class cultural references, while developing class-specific dispositions. The working-class children, on the other hand, had only mobile phone access, and the games they were able to play on these devices provided few language development opportunities. They spoke mostly a colloquial version of isiXhosa, indexical of their working-class status and unvalued in school. In this context, the contrasting digital practices lead to different resources, tacit knowledge and habits that may or may not be bridged to school literacies. Such differences have significant implications for the educational and life trajectories of learners and their ability to exercise agency.

As applied linguists look to the future of language and identity research in the digital age, the need for an ideological model of digital literacy becomes even more crucial. How people navigate and participate as legitimate members in digital spaces requires being able to employ appropriate language registers, styles and modalities. The digital world shapes its users' identities and enables them to imagine other powerful identities, which may or may not be realisable in the physical world. Through situated and local analyses of how power operates in online spaces, research can shed light on how online identities are negotiated and how more equitable literacy development can be achieved (Warschauer 2009). Only by examining these issues through a critical lens can we ensure that the pursuit of technology redresses rather than exacerbates social divides.

Summary

This chapter examined language and identity in the digital age. It began with an overview of how technology has transformed the arenas in which communication and social participation take place. While trying to avoid the pitfalls of technological determinism, it has to be recognised that technology has been incorporated into practically every aspect of human life, domesticated and made natural, if not invisible. As discussed, not only have technological innovations led to new forms of labour and modes of productivity, they have also enabled a mobility that allows people to traverse transnational spaces and to oscillate between online and offline worlds. Through new media and connectivity, the boundaries of 'here' and 'there' are blurred, and it is this fluidity and unboundedness that mark this new social order. To participate fully in societies in which technology has become the critical factor in acquiring economic, cultural and social capital, individuals need to adopt a digital mindset that operates with different assumptions and values. As knowledge becomes broader, and more contextual and contestable, greater lateral thinking is needed to navigate through disciplines, genres, modalities and cultural specificities. The ability to assert identity becomes inextricably linked to being able to gain the attention of specific audiences and to use innovative communicative strategies. Online users consume and actively create texts by using multiple modalities and engaging with various audiences in a state of reflexive co-construction. Hence, the adoption of new literacies becomes necessary to exercise agency and to participate in the digital world.

The chapter went on to consider that when people occupy online spaces they reconstruct language in ways that match the affordances and constraints of various digital platforms. Whether communication is synchronous or asynchronous, the limitations of space and the speed in which texts can be delivered have led to the evolution of linguistic structures that merge the written and the spoken. Digital media have enabled easy access to and use of multiple modalities. Social network structures that connect people from all over the globe have provided more opportunities for multilingual encounters and translingual practices, revitalising languages and asserting new identities. Because of these new areas of socialisation that provide multiple opportunities for self-representation, identity itself has become more complex and fluid. In the digital world, online users are able to perform different identities through creative assembly, aligning themselves with different communities and imagining other identities. Participation in 'networked publics' (boyd 2014) that transcend geographical boundaries appear likely to shape affiliations, allegiances and notions of citizenship. As was argued, through this reconfiguration of relations, new modes of inclusion and exclusion develop that pose new challenges in the imagination of a just and equitable society.

Finally, the chapter considered the range of opportunities and challenges in applied linguistics research, particularly in studies of language and identity in the digital age. Technology has enabled new possibilities to understand how language is learned and used. New methodologies that reflect the fluidity of space and the imbrication of online and offline realities are beginning to emerge. These developments call for a linguistics that more adequately captures the particularities of text-based digital communication and that integrates a theory of semiotics, especially as digital texts draw significantly from multiple modalities. While early research on digital literacies may have been to a certain extent more celebratory, prescriptive or cautious, future work needs to delve deeper into the social differences of access to and use of technology and the operation of ideologies in digital spaces. By exposing the structures and relations of power that are fortified and concealed by technology, language and identity research can generate a more critical awareness of the construction of truth and the reproduction of inequality in the digital age.

Related topics

Positioning language and identity: poststructuralist perspectives; Critical discourse analysis and identity; Linguistic practices and transnational identities; Identity in post-colonial contexts; Class in language and identity research; Ethics in language and identity research; Language, gender and identities in political life: a case study from Malaysia; Straight-acting: discursive negotiations of a homomasculine identity; Language and identity research in online environments: a multimodal ethnographic perspective; Identity in language learning and teaching: research agendas for the future.

Further reading

Barton, D. and Lee, C. (2013). *Language online: investigating digital texts and practices*. Abingdon: Routledge. (This book examines how online spaces and interactions have transformed the way language is used and researched and discusses concomitant issues of identity and learning.)

Gee, J.P. and Hayes, E.R. (2011). *Language and learning in the digital age*. Abingdon: Routledge. (This book examines how technology has not only transformed modes of communication but also constructed new affinity spaces and ideas on social formation and education.)

Jones, R.H. and Hafner, C.A. (2012). *Understanding digital literacies: a practical introduction*. Abingdon: Routledge. (This book is a comprehensive and accessible overview of the major concepts, issues and debates regarding digital literacy practices.)

Lankshear, C. and Knobel, M. (2011). *New literacies: everyday practices and social learning*. 3rd edn. Maidenhead: Open University Press. (This third edition provides a timely discussion of wikis, collaborative online writing, digital remix, blogging and social networking.)

References

Barton, D. and Lee, C. (2013). *Language online: investigating digital texts and practices*. Abingdon: Routledge.

Baxter, J. (this volume). Positioning language and identity: poststructuralist perspectives, in S. Preece (ed.) *The Routledge handbook of language and identity*. Abingdon: Routledge, pp. 34–49.

Blommaert, J. (2005). *Discourse: a critical introduction*. Cambridge: Cambridge University Press.

Blommaert, J. (2013). *Ethnography, superdiversity and linguistic landscapes: chronicles of complexity*. Bristol: Multilingual Matters.

Bourdieu, P. (1987). 'What makes a social class? On the theoretical and practical existence of groups', *Berkeley Journal of Sociology*, 32: 1–17.

boyd, D. (2014). *It's complicated: the social lives of networked teens*. New Haven: Yale University Press.

Canagarajah, S. (2013). 'Negotiating translingual literacy: an enactment', *Research in the Teaching of English*, 48(1): 40–67.

Castells, M. (2001). *The Internet galaxy: reflections on the Internet, business and society*. Oxford: Oxford University Press.

Castells, M. (2010). *End of millennium*. 2nd edn. Malden, MA: Wiley and Sons.

Cope, B. and Kalantzis, M. (2010). New media, new learning, in D. Cole and D. Pullen (eds) *Multiliteracies in motion: current theory and practice*. Abingdon: Routledge, pp. 87–104.

Cope, B. and Kalantzis, M. (2012). *Literacies*. Cambridge: Cambridge University Press.

Creese, A. and Blackledge, A. (this volume). A linguistic ethnography of identity: adopting a heteroglossic frame, in S. Preece (ed.) *The Routledge handbook of language and identity*. London: Routledge, pp. 272–288.

Crystal, D. (2011). *Internet linguistics: a student guide*. Abingdon: Routledge.

Darvin, R. (2015). 'Representing the margins: multimodal performance as a tool for critical reflection and pedagogy', *TESOL Quarterly*, 49(3): 590–600.

Darvin, R. and Norton, B. (2014a). 'Transnational identity and migrant language learners: the promise of digital storytelling', *Education Matters: The Journal of Teaching and Learning*, 2(1): 55–66.

Darvin, R. and Norton, B. (2014b). 'Social class, identity and migrant students', *Journal of Language, Identity, and Education*, 13(2): 111–117.

Darvin, R. and Norton, B. (2015). 'Identity and a model of investment in applied linguistics', *Annual Review of Applied Linguistics*, 35: 36–56.

Darvin, R. and Norton, B. (in press). Identity, language learning and critical pedagogies in digital times, in J. Cenoz (ed.) *Language awareness and multilingualism. Encyclopedia of Language and Education*. 3rd edn. Vol. 6. New York: Springer.

Davies, J. and Merchant, G. (2009). *Web 2.0 for schools: learning and social participation*. New York: Peter Lang.

Domingo, M. (this volume). Language and identity research in online environments: a multimodal ethnographic perspective, in S. Preece (ed.) *The Routledge handbook of language and identity*. London: Routledge, pp. 541–557.

Dürscheid, C. and Stark, E. (2011). SMS4science: an international corpus-based texting project and the specific challenges for multilingual Switzerland, in C. Thurlow and K. Mroczek (eds) *Digital discourse: language in the new media*. Oxford: Oxford University Press, pp. 299–320.

Elliott, A. and Urry, J. (2010). *Mobile lives*. Abingdon: Routledge.

Ellis, K. (2010). 'Be who you want to be: the philosophy of Facebook and the construction of identity', *Screen Education Winter*, 58: 36–41.

Facer, K. (2011). *Learning futures: education, technology and social change*. London: Routledge.

Gee, J.P. and Hayes, E.R. (2011). *Language and learning in the digital age*. Abingdon: Routledge.

Hall, C.J., Smith, P.H. and Wicaksono, R. (2011). *Mapping applied linguistics: a guide for students and practitioners*. Abingdon: Routledge.

Harnad, S. (1991). 'Post-Gutenberg galaxy: the fourth revolution in the means of production and knowledge', *Public-Access Computer Systems Review*, 2(1): 39–53.

Ito, M., Baumer, S., Bittanti, M., Cody, R., Herr-Stephenson, B., Horst, H.A. and Tripp, L. (2010). *Hanging out, messing around and geeking out*. Cambridge, MA: MIT Press.

Jones, L. (this volume). Language and gender identities, in S. Preece (ed.) *The Routledge handbook of language and identity*. London: Routledge, pp. 210–224.

Jones, R.H. and Hafner, C.A. (2012). *Understanding digital literacies: a practical introduction*. Abingdon: Routledge.

Knobel, M. and Lankshear, C. (2006). 'Discussing new literacies', *Language Arts*, 84(1): 78–86.

Kress, G. (2003). *Literacy in the new media age*. Abingdon: Routledge.

Kress, G. (2009). *Multimodality: a social semiotic approach to contemporary communication*. Abingdon: Routledge.

Lam, W.S.E. (2013). 'Multilingual practices in transnational digital contexts', *TESOL Quarterly*, 47(4): 820–825.

Lankshear, C. and Knobel, M. (2011). *New literacies: everyday practices and social learning*. 3rd edn. Maidenhead: Open University Press.

Leander, K. (2008). 'Toward a connective ethnography of online/offline literacy networks', in J. Coiro, M. Knobel, C. Lankshear and D. Leu (eds) *Handbook of research on new literacies*, Mahwah, NJ: Erlbaum, pp. 33–65.

Lemphane, P. and Prinsloo, M. (2014). 'Children's digital literacy practices in unequal South African settings', *Journal of Multilingual and Multicultural Development*, 35(7): 738–753.

Luke, C. (2003). 'Pedagogy, connectivity, multimodality and interdisciplinarity', *Reading Research Quarterly*, 38(3): 397–403.

Marsh, J. (2013). Researching young children's literacy practices in online virtual worlds: cyber-ethnography and multi-method approaches, in P. Albers, T. Holbrook and A.S. Flint (eds) *New literacy research methods*. Abingdon: Routledge, pp. 195–209.

North, S., Snyder, I. and Bulfin, S. (2008). 'Digital tastes: social class and young people's technology use', *Information, Communication and Society*, 11(7): 895–911.

Norton, B. (2013). *Identity and language learning: extending the conversation*. 2nd edn. Bristol: Multilingual Matters.

Norton, B. and De Costa, P. (in press). 'Research tasks on identity and language education', *Language Teaching*.

Norton Peirce, B. (1995). 'Social identity, investment, and language learning', *TESOL Quarterly*, 29(1): 9–31.

O'Keefe, A., McCarthy, M. and Carter, R. (2007). *From corpus to classroom: language use and language teaching*. Oxford: Oxford University Press.

Page, R.E. (2012). *Stories and social media: identities and interaction*. Abingdon: Routledge.

Prinsloo, M. and Rowsell, J. (2012). 'Digital literacies as placed resources in the globalised periphery', *Language and Education*, 26(4): 271–277.

Rowsell, J. (2012). Artifactual English, in M. Grenfell, D. Bloome, C. Hardy, K. Pahl, J. Rowsell and B. Street (eds) *Language, ethnography and education: bridging new literacy studies and Bourdieu*. Abingdon: Routledge, pp. 195–209.

Snyder, I. (ed.) (1998). *Page to screen: taking literacy into the electronic era*. London: Routledge.

Snyder, I., Angus, L. and Sutherland-Smith, W. (2002). 'Building equitable literate futures: home and school computer-mediated literacy practices and disadvantage', *Cambridge Journal of Education*, 32(3): 367–383.

South African Institute for Distance Education (SAIDE) (2015). *Stories for multilingual literacy development* [Online]. Available at www.africanstorybook.org

Stornaiuolo, A. and Hall, M. (2014). Tracing resonance: qualitative research in a networked world, in G. Gudmundsdottir and K. Vasbø (eds) *Methodological challenges when exploring digital learning spaces in education*. Rotterdam: Sense, pp. 29–43.

Stornaiuolo, A., Higgs, J. and Hull, G. (2013). Social media as authorship: methods for studying literacies and communities online, in P. Albers, T. Holbrook and A. Flint (eds) *New literacy research methods*. Abingdon: Routledge, pp. 224–237.

Stornaiuolo, A., Hull, G. and Nelson, M.E. (2009). 'Mobile texts and migrant audiences: rethinking literacy and assessment in a new media age', *Language Arts*, 86(5): 382–392.

Temples, A. and Nelson, G. (2013). Intercultural computer-mediated communication: insights from corpus-based analysis, in D. Belcher and G. Nelson (eds) *Critical and corpus-based approaches to intercultural rhetoric*. Ann Arbor: University of Michigan Press.

Thorne, S.L. and Black, R.W. (2011). Identity and interaction in Internet-mediated contexts, in C. Higgins (ed.) *Identity formation in globalizing contexts: language learning in the new millennium*. Vol. 1. Berlin: de Gruyter, pp. 257–278.

Thurlow, C. and Mroczek, K. (eds) (2011). *Digital discourse: language in the new media.* Oxford: Oxford University Press.

Toohey, K., Dagenais, D. and Schulze, E. (2012). 'Second language learners making video in three contexts', *Language and Literacy*, 14(2): 75–96.

Warriner, D.S. (2007). 'Transnational literacies: immigration, language learning and identity', *Linguistics and Education*, 18(3): 201–214.

Warschauer, M. (2009). Digital literacy studies: progress and prospects, in M. Baynham and M. Prinsloo (eds) *The future of literacy studies.* London: Palgrave Macmillan, pp. 123–140.

Warschauer, M. and Matuchniak, T. (2010). 'New technology and digital worlds: analyzing evidence of equity in access, use and outcomes', *Review of Research in Education*, 34(1): 179–225.

Warschauer, M., Said, G. and Zohry, A. (2002). 'Language choice online: globalization and identity in Egypt', *Journal of Computer Mediated Communication*, 7(4).

Weber, S. and Mitchell, C. (2008). Imaging, keyboarding and posting identities: young people and new media technologies, in D. Buckingham (ed.) *Youth, identity and digital media.* Cambridge, MA: MIT Press, pp. 25–47.

Weedon, C. (1987). *Feminist practice and poststructuralist theory.* Oxford: Basil Blackwell.

34

Language and identity research in online environments

A multimodal ethnographic perspective

Myrrh Domingo

Introduction

This chapter sets out to explore new research opportunities and challenges for the study of language and identity in computer-mediated digital environments. The study of linguistic and social behaviours in computer-mediated communication (CmC) has been approached from a number of disciplines, including communication, media studies, applied linguistics and socio-linguistics, cultural studies and anthropology, to name a few. With the spread of Internet-based social networks from the mid-2000s, scholarly debates and emerging developments in this relatively new domain have expanded to include the multilingual and multimodal practices of young people in digitally mediated, transnational settings. Even in its brief history, the exploration of language and identity online has dealt with issues of different and, to an extent, new forms of representation made available through digital technologies and global contexts of communication. The pages of screens make visible the immense variability as well as stability in the ways that bi/multilingual youth are creating, sustaining and adapting their linguistic identities to engage with diverse communities in heteroglossic contexts. This chapter sets out to consider how multimodality and ethnography can be jointly applied to examine language and identity in online environments; and within this, consider the potentials and limitations of the combined approach for applied linguistics research.

This chapter has two main sections. The first covers key terms and concepts associated with multimodality to examine how language is used with other modes of communication, such as visuals, colours and layout, to compose in online environments. For example, what 'modes' are, and how people shape them as cultural resources, such as 'templates of identity' (Williams 2009) and 'identity texts' (Paris 2012), for communicating in digital environments. Second, it will discuss current issues with language and identity work particular to online settings and discuss the use of a combined multimodal and ethnographic perspective to explore, generate and analyse digital data that make use of 'media mixes' (Ito 2010). How are bi/multilingual individuals engaging and developing their linguistic repertoires as they relate to transnational audiences using multiple languages and modes of communication? In answering this question, case studies of online research are used, and the chapter concludes with suggestions for future research in applied linguistics.

Overview

This section will provide an introduction to the shifting functions of writing in online contexts; and within this, consider its implications for researching language and identity in digital platforms. The section will also highlight key multimodal concepts for describing and analysing the complex combination of modes often used in increasingly multilingual and multimodal online environments.

Language and identity in online composition

Online composition is often described as part of a multimodal design, which is an increasingly common feature of contemporary forms of communication (Manovich 2001; Wilson and Peterson 2002; Jørgensen *et al.* 2011). This is to say that what counts as content in online environments often includes non-linguistic forms of representation, such as layout and framing, which are often inextricably combined with language to make meaning. One consequence of this is that it is increasingly problematic to consider the use of language, both written and spoken, in isolation from the multimodal ensembles in which it is embedded (Kress and Domingo 2013). What is clear is that how content is represented, as well as the modes and platforms chosen, is a significant aspect of language and identity research in online environments.

As communication flows continue to move at rapid rates across linguistic, cultural and geographical borders, notions of authorship and composition continue to be redefined and reimagined (Boulter 2001; Kress 2009). Digital texts are moving across online spaces in unprecedented ways and, with this change, an evident shift in communication practices that principally draw on digital devices for making meaning visible to global audiences (Hull *et al.* 2013). In recent years, social media sites and online environments have started occupying a prominent position in young people's screen-based interactions and are often tied to the design of multimodal artefacts (e.g. music, videos, photographs) that make up what has been described by researchers as 'templates of identity' (Williams 2009) and 'identity texts' (Paris 2012). These sites and their potentials for shaping composition in different and often new forms of representation can be viewed as generative spaces for conducting language and identity research. For example, research in this area explores the social uses of digital technologies for developing communities and navigating belonging in the context of global and digital worlds (Dolby and Rizvi 2008; Black 2009; Ríos-Rojas 2011).

Participation in contemporary communication environments has also been described as enabling young people to draw on a range of cultural resources for shaping media and modes into 'media mixes' (Ito 2010) that allow for communication across cultures and spaces (New London Group 1996; Lam and Warriner 2012). Williams (2009) has detailed how template functions within social networking sites, such as MySpace and Facebook, enable individuals to create personal sites that allow for 'performances of identities' (p. 93) online. While he acknowledges that the templates can limit online composition to fit particular forms, he illustrates that access to multimodal design presents individuals with opportunities to think of their identities in relation to popular culture references (e.g. movies, television programmes, books) and in relation to wider, global networks. His analysis of the social media sites takes into account how online composition for youth today involves a 'culture of bricolage' (ibid.: 64) comprised of multi-modal design such as words, images, sound, animation and videos. Further, the popular culture content of individual sites can link to other pages that make the text just one collage in a wider network of constantly shifting collages. For Williams, examining social media practices is germane to the study of language and literacy in digital spaces. His work is one example of how studying composition online presents applied linguists with new opportunities and challenges for defining and identifying what counts as data in computer-mediated digital environments (see Darvin, this volume).

English and Marr (2015) have similarly taken up the study of language and identity as situated in everyday contexts, including online environments such as Facebook posts, to explore ways of analysing language and language use from a social, intercultural and multilingual perspective. In the introduction to their book, they draw on Blommaert and Jie's terminology of 'collecting rubbish' (p. 9) to describe a common practice among linguistic ethnographers to collect anything that may one day be useful for examining communicative activity. The 'rubbish' or linguistic data, that at the time of research might appear insignificant or worthless, are what they highlight as data that can offer new understandings about language, communication and social-cultural practice in day-to-day interaction. In online environments, 'rubbish' can be seen as other modes in use besides language and, as the examples in this chapter will illustrate, such modal resources are in fact integral to composition produced by young people digitally, particularly those who are multilingual and involved in collaborative work with other young people in transnational media contexts. In the latter section of this chapter, other examples will be discussed that exemplify how social media sites and digital platforms can be generative sites for studying language and identity, specifically when attention is given to the range of multi-modal artefacts rather than a primary focus on written and spoken language. First, it is significant to describe the focus on multimodality and its affordances for a linguistic ethnography of online environments.

Multimodal approaches have provided concepts, methods and a framework for the study of social interaction and environments. As an interdisciplinary approach, it has developed over the past decade to address much debated issues about changes in society, including cultural and linguistic practices as situated within and across environments (VanLeeuwen and Jewitt 2000; VanLeeuwen 2004; Kress 2009).

Three theoretical assumptions underpin the concept of multimodality:

1   All communication draws on a multiplicity of modes to make meaning;
2   Meanings realised by any mode are always interwoven with other co-present modes to produce meaning;
3   The more a set of resources (modes) has been utilised in the everyday social life of a particular community, the more fully articulated it will have become for members of that community.

(Jewitt 2009, 2012; Kress 2009)

In this chapter, these assumptions are taken up to focus on an application of multimodality in combination with ethnography to examine online composition (Jewitt 2009; Domingo *et al.* 2015), and discuss its relevance for language and identity research. In what follows, key multi-modal concepts are discussed in relation to online environments.

Modes, multimodal ensembles and texts in digital environments

Multimodality assumes that representation and communication always draw on a multiplicity of modes to articulate meaning. The term 'multimodal text' draws attention to the realisation of closely integrated meanings using a range of modes (e.g. spoken or written words; moving or still images). A blog, for example, would be considered a multimodal text just as a book would fit the same category. The book as a 'platform' would more or less be comprised of fixed and relatively linear arrangements; whereas online platforms (e.g. WordPress, YouTube) tend to be more ephemeral or increasingly modular in organisation (Domingo *et al.* 2015). This bears significance for studying language and identity. The blog platform can be seen as a 'site' of appearance of multimodal texts but also as a 'field site' for exploring traces of social and linguistic interaction among the designer, his or her imagined audience and the materialised multimodal text. From this perspective, online environments can be seen as a generative source for qualitative data (Hardey 2011).

Sites, whether online or offline, offer semiotic potentials and constraints, which have effects of a social kind: social relations of participants and kinds of social organisation such as communities of practice (see Lave and Wenger 1991). The blog[1] as an online environment offers different and to an extent a greater flexibility for shaping multimodal texts. At the same time, meaning-making is also constrained by the ways in which the designer (blogger) is provided a pre-given set of resources, which limits what modes can be shaped and in what ways they can be materialised on the page. The choice then becomes not only which modes are best used to represent meaning but also how to shape the available resources into a 'multimodal ensemble'. This is to say that how language is used in online composition is partly constrained by the technical affordance of the platform used. To analyse the written or spoken language within the digital environment should then take into account how the platform enables or constrains meaning-making.

Modal affordance, meaning potentials and multimodal orchestrations

Social characteristics of the blog platform and their formal compositional characteristics co-occur with the modes through which meaning as content appears on the site. Each mode carries specific affordances so that what is represented through image is not necessarily the same as what can be said in writing. This is illustrated in Figure 34.1, the 'About me' page of the blog *Thinly Spread* (2010). *Thinly Spread* is a UK-based parenting blog written by Chris, who is also a photographer and writer. In this blog, we see that the photograph is not merely a recount of what is expressed in words. Blog pages such as these are designed to familiarise audiences with the blogger, as well as offer a general introduction about key topics and the overall purpose of the blog.

In looking at Figure 34.1, the type of questions that would arise from a multimodal perspective include:

- What modes are available in this blog?
- What are the affordances of the modes?
- What are the affordances of the blogging platform as a communication environment?

The premise here is that modes and their historical uses have been shaped to achieve specific social purposes. Multimodality assumes that different modes carry different meaning potentials

About

I am an over stretched, thinly spread mother of 4 writing, teaching, tutoring and parenting in Somerset. My family gets first call on my time, writing is a close second, teaching brings in a bit of useful money and the housework gets neglected with glee.

This blog is about all the things I like to do. There will be the odd rant about things which get my goat and pieces about things which have caught my eye.

It will be full of all the things me and my children have enjoyed doing together over the last 16 years and the new things we are finding to do as we all get older. It is the story of all those little letting-gos as my lovely husband and I encourage our birds to spread their wings and fly.

I will be posting some of our favourite veggie family recipes, most of which can be cooked in 30 minutes or less with a toddler sitting on the work surface, an older child moaning about a grumbling stomach another one asking for homework help and yet another needing to be picked up from an after school club.

We spend a lot of time outside growing stuff and the garden has been my escape since they were tinies. I feel I am still being a good Mum while I'm planting seeds and pulling weeds accompanied by various small children digging holes, making fairy houses, climbing trees and holding tea parties. So I will be posting stuff about gardening with kids (and without) too.

I am also a freelance copywriter and photographer and an unpublished (as yet) fiction writer so I will be sticking some of my writing on here too as well as some tips and ideas which have come out of the fiction writers' workshops which I run.

I hope you enjoy sharing bits of my life with me and that you will post a comment so I know you are out there!

Figure 34.1 Chris's (2010) *Thinly Spread* 'About me' page

so that how they are taken up varies depending on the purpose and context of use. The more a set of resources (modes) has been utilised in the everyday social life of a particular community, the more fully articulated it will have become for members of that community. For example, those involved in film studies would realise different functions of an image from those involved with curating classical paintings or illustrating comics and graphic novels. Just like the meanings of words are located in social origins and change over time and across spaces, so too does the meaning potentials of modes, depending on the interests of those who make the sign in specific social contexts.

In any environment, whether online or offline, modal preference is informed not only by the interest of the sign-maker but also by the shared experiences and values of the community in which the sign-maker belongs. Interest, in this sense, can be seen as a marker of identity (see Kress 2009). While 'multimodal ensembles' name the bringing together of different modes to produce a multimodal text, 'multimodal orchestration' names the semiotic work and social action involved in the purposeful selection and arrangement of modes – which modes, for what purpose, in what order, for whom – as best suited for the environment. In Figure 34.1 we saw that what was achieved through photography is not a repeat of what was expressed in writing in the 'About me' page of Chris's blog *Thinly Spread*. From the perspective of social interaction, her modal preference reflects a certain 'politics of choice' (see discussion on 'style' in Kress 2009).

A multimodal social semiotic approach lends insight into how *Thinly Spread*'s interests are realised on the page with a certain social positing. The photograph is more conceptual (see Kress and Van Leeuwen 2006), showcasing an idealised notion of family and nature as landscape. The blogger and her son, as the subjects of the photograph, appear not to be expecting the gaze of onlookers: they are casually there to be observed and they do not engage explicitly with the audience. There are different notions of personal distance evident throughout the blog, so that the multimodal text appears at times like a professional portfolio showcasing *Thinly Spread*'s writing and the blogger's visual art (photography). This reading is supported by the blogger's account in her 'About me' page (2010), in which she states: 'I am also a freelance copywriter and photographer and an unpublished (as yet) fiction writer.' What we have here, then, is a multimodal account of *Thinly Spread*'s 'About me' page. It is at this point that theories and interests drawn from sociocultural linguistics can further extend the analysis of *Thinly Spread*'s page.

As evidenced by the case of *Thinly Spread*'s blog, the application of a multimodal framework lends itself to providing a descriptive language, a fine-grained lens for examining the various features of a text. Where applied linguists may focus primarily on writing as the main unit of analysis, multimodality broadens the notions of content to also include other modes. Further, multimodality provides a means for understanding the process involved with producing the text, and the traces of social interaction (see Kress 2009) between the blogger and the blog design as well as between the blogger and her audience in the digital community. This view can lend insight into the sociocultural understanding of language and identity work online. Notions of speech communities have become destabilised not only by the mass movement of people in the physical world, but also by the mass movement of people's multimodal texts in the virtual world – a world without borders. It seems therefore that the practices of digital communities are generative spaces for the examination of the relationship between language and identity by applied linguistics. The 'multimodal orchestration' that is materialised on the page, in this case the blog as environment or more specifically the blog platform as the site of research, makes it possible to analyse not only the multimodal text and its various features but also the process taken to produce that text (the semiotic work in designing meanings) and the social interaction (records of communicative exchanges between the blogger and her digital community through comments).

In the next section I turn to how a multimodal approach in conjunction with theories and areas of interest drawn from applied linguistics can inform research focused on language and identity in digital environments.

Current issues

In past times, applied linguistics research on language and identities viewed languages as well-defined codes spoken by particular speech communities (see Joseph, this volume). Language variation and identity processes were often linked to stable characteristics such as place, social class and gender. These premises are no longer adequate given the transformations in the social world brought about by globalisation and technological innovations. Given these transformations, applied linguistics and sociolinguistics have been concerned for some time with addressing identity within contexts of 'superdiversity' (see e.g. Blommaert and Rampton 2011; Block 2014 [2007]) and viewing the diverse linguistic repertoires of bi/multilingual individuals as resources for communication and identity work in contexts of heteroglossia (see Creese and Blackledge, this volume).

A key aim of this section is to illustrate how multimodality can be used to examine language and identity work in the virtual world and how this could complement language and identity work in the physical world undertaken in applied linguistics and sociolinguistics. The section begins with a discussion of current issues in applied linguistics research in digital environments and the implications of these issues for conducting language and identity work online. I draw on data from two research projects on blogging and video-sharing as case studies.

The issue with content and units of analysis

Multimodality focuses on people's process of meaning-making and emphasises how the choices people make, selecting one mode over another or one set of resources over another, is always embedded in a network of alternative possibilities (Halliday 1978). This is evidenced not only through the modes of writing and image but also other modes such as layout, colour and framing.

Mode is considered an organising principle of representation and communication and therefore treated as a central unit of analysis in multimodal research. This is to say that what is expressed in image is equally significant in analysis as what is stated using written words or spoken language. For example, in Figure 34.1 we may gather that the blogger draws primarily on image and writing as key modal resources for shaping the text (the 'About me' page) in her blog. Applied linguists may focus on her writing as the main unit of analysis for research. But as previously discussed, the additional modal resources used in her blog, which is comprised of a series of chronologically organised posts, can be examined to better account for how she goes about shaping the blog as reflective of her own 'template of identity' (Williams 2009: 99). A multimodal approach extends the linguistic analysis of online texts to include modal resources (the full range of representations) used for social interaction. In this way, the blog as a field site and as a site of appearance of texts can more attentively address language and identity work in digital environments.

The issue with communities

The types of questions that arise from looking at the *Thinly Spread* blog (i.e. the 'About me' page and 'Explore posts' pages) focus on the social positions and relations of participants. Specifically, these questions draw attention to the issue of communities particular to an online environment. In terms of applied linguistics research, much can be explored with regards to language identity from a multimodal perspective. The situated and often on-going interaction in a blog is reflective of online communities of practice (Lave and Wenger 1991) in which the social positions and relations of the participants can be examined by looking closely at their communication exchanges within the blog and across other spaces online. Notions of language affiliation, language expertise and language inheritance (Leung *et al.* 1997) can be explored not only within the blog platform but also by looking at the social media sites that are often linked to blogs such as Pinterest, Facebook, Instagram and YouTube. As each of these online platforms has a pre-given set of modal resources for users to shape their meanings, we find that what is largely expressed through images and tags in Instagram, for instance, might be differently explored and positioned on the platform of Facebook.[2] The latter provides users with more space for writing about the image or including writing alongside the image.

While an online environment can be categorised as a site of research, I argue that online environments can be examined as communities of practice and as sites in which identities emerge in the social orientation and online interactions afforded by the technology of specific and particular online environments. In what follows, I elaborate on these points by drawing on a case of social interaction in blogs.

The case of blogging platforms

Weblogs, or blogs as they are more commonly known, have evolved considerably since their inception in the early 1990s and have become a significant aspect of online communication (Hookway 2008). Their widespread use as an online authoring platform has been attributed in part to free, user-friendly template designs such as those offered by WordPress or Blogger. Each blog template includes a pre-given set of modal resources to design and shape meanings (e.g. columnal layout, colour scheme, social media integration) that allow bloggers to use the social and semiotic resources afforded by the template to share personal and/or professional content. For example, the Writr blog template offers a vertical orientation; drawing on the tradition of print-based platforms like a book, the blogger and his or her imagined audiences are prompted to navigate the site from top to bottom and left to right. Here the focus is the significance of writing as the primary semiotic resource, and other modes, such as colour and image, have less prominent roles in organising the content and realising meanings. In contrast, the Landscape template offers a more horizontal orientation and emphasises modularity over linearity as the organising principle. It draws from visual design to orient the reading of images (see Jewitt and Oyama 2001; Kress and VanLeeuwen 2006). The emphasis here is on the mode of image as the primary modal resource for materialising meaning on the page. In this regard, frame as a mode is a material resource that is apparent even before the blogger creates and uploads content in the blog. So what is expressed in writing and articulated through image is very much inextricably intertwined with the affordance of the platform. To realise a coherent multimodal text, all of these factors have to be addressed by the blogger. While templates can be customised (e.g. selecting number of columns, adding more images, changing the colour palette), the features of the blog design are more or less constrained to fit the designed social and technical purpose of the template (Domingo *et al.* 2014).

Thinly Spread, in using a pre-formatted blog template, can only choose from a finite number of possibilities for designing the blogger's text. Given that layout is the primary mode used by the WordPress blog platform to organise contents, the images and writing in each of *Thinly*

Spread's blog posts can only be arranged in a limited number of combinations. Formatting the size of images or adding custom layout arrangements beyond those offered for the template *Thinly Spread* selected require significant technical work and technical knowledge of programming languages used for websites.

The basis for the technical design of Wordpress blog templates is also socially, historically and culturally informed. As a contemporary digital authoring platform, widely kept and read across different social and cultural groups for a range of different purposes, Wordpress has garnered a significant following with more than 60 million blogs created by its users. Since early blogs were primarily organised chronologically, with links to other sites and a commentary by the blogger, subsequent blogs became more diary-like and offered more interaction, such as up-to-date feeds on new content generated and comments uploaded by audiences (Garden 2011). Blog uses and templates have since expanded to include categories such as professional portfolios, travel journals, photographic exhibitions, culinary displays and so on. While the introduction of free-blogging platforms is often referenced as pivotal in the widespread adoption of blogs, the general structure for integrating writing in blogs is still reliant on Western notions of composition. Top to bottom and left to right are the primary means for navigating blogs, as Figure 34.1 illustrates. This method of blog navigation is a culturally situated practice associated with reading print-bound and page-based writing in Western societies. Accessing meaning in this instance requires following a relatively linear reading path; however, when the linearity of an online page becomes less apparent, much can be explored with regards to the change in pattern. The choices in pattern can be examined for changes in modal preference and language use, and these can be used to index the identities materialised through the multimodal text. At this point, the initial questions raised above may yield more complex answers.

From a multimodal perspective, it is clear that data generated and collected in online environments is informed by its technical affordances and also its social orientation. It follows that what is analysed should also bear the platform potentials and constraints in mind. From this understanding of the blog's social and technical orientation, we can turn again to *Thinly Spread* and consider what can be said using a multimodal social semiotic approach.

Thinly Spread's blog offers itself to its readers as highly edited and reflective of a particular social positioning. Even the selection of the blogger's template is suggestive of a certain politics of choice (Kress 2009). This is evidenced through the use of 'Elegant Premium Wordpress Themes', which is not a standard, free template, but an option for purchase. As Figure 34.1 illustrates, this enables *Thinly Spread* to orchestrate multimodal ensembles – framing, layout and colour – and to draw on these modal resources to engage with the imagined audiences for the blogger's text. This enables us to see how identity may be indexed in *Thinly Spread*'s blog. The photograph on the 'About me' page functions as a conceptual image with an idealised notion of family. The gaze in the photograph does not explicitly engage with the audience and establishes personal distance, so that the blog appears like a professional portfolio showcasing the blogger's visual art (photography). This reading of the blogger's use of image and framing is supported by the writing 'I am also a freelance copywriter and photographer and an unpublished (as yet) fiction writer'.

Online communities are likely to invest considerably in developing the mode of image as a major means of communication. Yet, the specific and situated ways in which images are taken up, shaped and designed will vary largely on the preferences of each group, such as the distinctive values and interests particular to their community. This is to say that how each community will approach the multimodal orchestration of image with other modes will differ, due in large part to the social shaping and situated uses of image in their respective disciplines. In cases where members of an online community are bi/multilingual and a part of extended and other communities of practice, the interaction as materialised on the online platform becomes more complexly articulated. In the example in the following section, I elucidate this point by referring to a group of multilingual youth and their video-sharing practices on YouTube.

The case of video-sharing platforms

In the previous case, I described the social orientation and technical affordance of online platforms. Mainly, the argument detailed the need to account for the pre-given set of design resources bloggers use for meaning-making. In the case of video-sharing, I further address the potentials and constraints of online platforms with an emphasis on media use in transnational contexts.

Video-sharing websites have increased in popularity with the onset of the World Wide Web. Created in 2005, YouTube is among the top-visited websites, with millions of users and thousands of daily uploads. Adami (2009) has written about the social and semiotic affordance of YouTube as a video-sharing platform, namely its 'video-response' capability, which was introduced in 2006. YouTube is of particular interest to applied linguists interested in multimodal approaches to language and identity research given its ease of access, its widespread and worldwide use and its interactive content-sharing potential. In what follows, I discuss the use of YouTube in research that I undertook with a group of Filipino British youth,[3] who call themselves the Pinoys, focusing on their multimodal design and the affordances this created for identity work (Domingo 2012).

YouTube as a video-sharing website allows users to upload and disseminate content to a wide audience. Like the blog platform, YouTube enables comments in response to video posts and discussion threads. However, a key distinction between these two platforms is that design resources for making the video are not as extensive or readily available within the YouTube platform as in Wordpress. YouTube users, like the Pinoys, must rely on other platforms before they can upload and disseminate their videos on YouTube. It is therefore essential that YouTube users develop a level of proficiency with other digital devices beyond the video-sharing platform (e.g. using a variety of modes such as moving image, colour, speech and sound). Such practices have been referred to as a form of remix (Knobel and Lankshear 2008), whereby digitally enabled tools become cultural resources for shaping modes into creative blends through photoshopping images and layering audio. Scholars looking at these processes have theorised them in terms of hybridity (West 2008), crossing (Rampton 2005) and in-betweenness (Bhabha 2004). Current research draws from these notions to describe communication practices with media use as transnational (Madianou and Miller 2011; Lam and Warriner 2012). Research attentive to these concepts frequently examines changing notions of communities, identities and belonging in the context of globalisation (Appadurai 1996; Dolby and Rizvi 2008; Ríos-Rojas 2011).

As we will see in Figure 34.2, the Pinoys' use of YouTube demonstrates how video-sharing is linked to other digital platforms. The Pinoys employed both digitally enabled and print-based resources to compose multimodal texts. In the case of their YouTube music videos, this blending and moving across environments (both online and offline as well as across platforms) was a critical component of how they engaged with a transnational audience. This is illustrated in their rap song, 'Kapag A'koy Bumabalik' [When I return], written and performed by KidCras and KyD, key members of the Pinoys (see Appendix for the lyrics). 'Kapag A'koy Bumabalik' was first composed as written lyrics and later turned into a rap song. It was filmed and edited using a variety of digital devices, including video camera, audio recorder, mobile phone, microphone and a desktop computer, before being uploaded onto YouTube. In creating this multimodal text, KidCras and KyD collaborated with other members of their hip hop group Lirikong

Digital platforms	Social authoring utility	Multimodal design affordances
Facebook	online community-based social networking	offers profile pages, videos, images, comments/(re)posts
YouTube	online video-based social networking	offers profile pages, videos, comments, user stations
Soundclick	online music-based social networking community	offers profile pages, photos, videos, blogs, user stations for streaming and downloading music
Photoshop	digital graphics workstation	graphics editing program for photo editing and storage
Ulead	digital video workstation	video software for visual editing and processing
Cubase	digital audio workstation	audio program for effects editing and instrument processing
FL Studio (formerly FruityLoops)	digital audio workstation	audio program for effects editing and instrument processing

Figure 34.2 Inventory of the digital platforms used by the Pinoys

Supremo, both locally in London and internationally; the platform Ulead was used to edit an assemblage of video footage captured across different spaces, including iconic and historic sights, such as the Andres Bonifacio Monument in Manila and Westminster in London.

My discussion of 'Kapag A'koy Bumabalik' in this chapter draws on my three-year ethnography (Domingo 2012), in which I had the opportunity to watch the Pinoys both online and offline and observe their movement across digital and physical environments. This music video, much like other videos they created, became a generative site for an analysis of hybrid identities, transnational exchanges and global belonging. As I will show, analysis of their multimodal orchestrations made evident how their music videos were shaped both semiotically and socially, with an awareness of language as imbued with social, political and cultural narratives (Nero 2006; Brutt-Griffler 2007).

One example is that, as the Pinoys' transnational community became increasingly diverse, so too did their appropriation of digital platforms (see Figure 34.2). Additionally, they used Tagalog, British English, Spanish and other languages in online conversation with youth around the world in the various digital platforms. For example, in the case of 'Kapag A'koy Bumabalik', there were a total of 86,386 views and 119 comments for the video uploaded on YouTube. Feedback was given by youth in their group in London and also transnational audiences from a range of countries, including the United States, China, Sweden, the Philippines and Switzerland. Comments were given mostly in Tagalog and English and ranged in scope from praise of the video, affirmation of the political message and general approval of the music, to more specialised commentaries focused on the historical sites featured and their clothing design. There were also questions raised about translation of the lyrics and explanation of its meaning, as well as queries about how to download the video and music. The video garnered significant attention and communicative exchanges particular to cultural heritage, language use and the political issues the Pinoys raised in the video.

YouTube allowed the Pinoys to upload videos that encompassed their membership across communities and to reach wider social networks. The Pinoys specifically described their use of social media, digital technologies and hip hop for reaching other youth whom they may not otherwise have been able to meet in person. Using online platforms like YouTube enabled them to share their music with transnational audiences from Europe, Asia and North America and to develop a sense of belonging in local and global networks.

Unlike the digital platforms the Pinoys used (listed in Figure 34.2), YouTube is more constrained when it comes to customising a multimodal text. For example, still and moving images, written texts and audio files could be uploaded; however, the ability to manipulate their layout was very limited, as were fonts, frames and colours. For the Pinoys, this meant harnessing these limited technical orientations and finding ways to shape them to achieve their social purposes, namely to reach a wider network of transnational youth who did not always share their linguistic, cultural and social backgrounds. To do so, they used other digital platforms, such as Ulead, Photoshop, Cubase and FL Studio, to customise and personalise the videos that they uploaded on YouTube.

All of the modes used for 'Kapag A'koy Bumabalik' acted as cultural resources to signal the membership of the Pinoys across communities. For example, the Pinoys made use of colours (clothing and accessories to represent their hip hop affiliations), frames (zooming in and panning out to capture landscapes and portraits of people), rhythm (film footage corresponds to the beat of the music) and writing (visual effects of words appearing on the screen and inscription on the clothing they designed and wear for the video). Filipino and hip hop identity is indexed, for example, in the chain that KidCras wears in the video, which makes use of the Philippine flag, featuring three stars and a sun along with blue, white and red beads.

In sum, multimodal social semiotics as the sole framework would yield different understandings of identity as experienced by the Pinoys in digital environments. By combining multimodal analysis with theoretical perspectives on identity in applied linguistics, it is possible to develop notions of hybrid identities by examining the language affiliations, language expertise and language inheritance of bi/multilingual youth, such as the Pinoys, using multimodal tools that consider the interrelationship of language with other modes of communication (see Domingo 2012).

Future directions

This chapter has focused on a multimodal approach to identity research in online authoring and video-content sharing. Given their social and semiotic functions, blogs and video platforms make it possible, perhaps more so than other media sites, to look at the present state of social interaction online, and to consider how identities are indexed in these online spaces. However, there are a number of issues to which applied linguists interested in multimodal approaches need to pay attention. First and foremost, it is important to remember that content online is shaped by the potentials and constraints of the virtual environment and by the pre-given modal resources of the platform, and that these potentials and constraints impact on online identities. Additionally, writing has to be considered in its context of use in the virtual environment and as it is configured with other modes. In this regard, what is examined online, such as social interaction and text making, should also consider the social and technical affordances of a particular site.

Second, online communities are often fluid entities with less bounded communication practices. Relationships among diverse groups of people and their creative blends of multimodal texts have changed with the onset of digital innovations. Fixed notions of belonging, communities and identities are not adequate for conceptualising research on identities, as they are remixed and hybridised online. Consequently, applied linguists would need to consider how new media and digital technologies mediate the social interactions of participants, how these 'local' exchanges relate to the global and transnational and what identities are made possible in the virtual world.

Third, global and technological changes are remaking how people navigate borders to access and disseminate cultural resources (Madianou and Miller 2011; Lam and Warriner 2012). For language and identity studies in applied linguistics, the online space is a rich site for exploring changes in the social and semiotic aspects of people's interactions online. For the future, more research can be conducted that explicitly links the social, semiotic and technical affordances of platforms to examine transnational communication practices with media use and the identities that these afford.

It is evident that current social trends, alongside the innovative and creative capacities of new media, afford people with new ways of making meaning. How we see writing is changing on online platforms; what counts as text is increasingly less linear and more modular, less stable and more ephemeral – sentences, paragraphs, extended texts and narratives are not always readily available for analysis. More and more, we see a confluence of modes, a variety of layout configurations and multimodal ensembles that are remaking how we read, interact and reach imagined audiences. For applied linguists interested in language and identity, multimodality offers a means for describing and accounting for these shifts with a micro-analytic lens for examining the nuances, patterns and fluid movement of people, their texts and their cultural resources as they are made and remixed online.

Summary

New digital environments are constantly introduced and those that have existed are perpetually transforming. With these expansions in our social world, people are constantly given new semiotic tools to arrange, select and share meanings. This chapter is an attempt at illuminating some of the ways in which multimodality can begin to address these social shifts when doing language and identity studies in online environments.

To date, multimodal approaches have not often been integrated into language and identity studies in applied linguistics. This chapter demonstrated how the application of a multimodal approach can broaden notions of content in researching language and identity online. Content online increasingly integrates modes beyond writing and speech; multimodality provides a framework to analyse identity in texts and social interaction in digital environments.

The chapter also highlighted the potentials and constraints of multimodal design in digital platforms and the ways in which semiotic resources are used to shape an online identity for an imagined audience. This chapter also elucidated the key features of digital platforms, namely blogs and video-sharing websites, and their effects on writing and multimodal text making, as well as social exchanges among global and transnational audiences. Finally, this chapter provided a number of cases to illustrate how multimodality could be of assistance to applied linguists.

The two case studies offered initial findings that draw on the potentials of an interdisciplinary approach for understanding conceptualisations of language and identity in an increasingly global and digital world.

Related topics

Historical perspectives on language and identity; Language and identity in linguistic ethnography; Critical discourse analysis and identity; Linguistic practices and transnational identities; A linguistic ethnography of identity: adopting a heteroglossic frame; Challenges for language and identity researchers in the collection and transcription of spoken interaction; Straight-acting: discursive negotiations of a homomasculine identity; Language and identity in the digital age; The future of identity research: impact and new developments in sociolinguistics.

Further reading

Bezemer, J. and Jewitt, C. (2010). Multimodal analysis: key issues, in L. Litosseliti (ed.) *Research methods in linguistics*. London: Continuum, pp. 180–197. (This chapter provides an introduction to multimodal approaches to the study of linguistics, representation and communication.)

Kress, G. (2009). *Multimodality: a social semiotic approach to contemporary communication*. London: Routledge. (This book offers a comprehensive overview of multimodal social semiotics and its relevance to the study of language and communication.)

Notes

1 The chapter draws on data from a research project on food blogs and multimodal principles of composition. This research is a part of a larger project on multimodal methods for researching digital environments (MODE) (mode.ioe.ac.uk) and is funded by the ESRC.

2 Each online platform carries with it a particular social affordance. Such affordance is often described in categories associated with age, gender and class. For example, the Pew Research Internet Project (2013) identifies that 71 per cent of online adults use Facebook and only 17 per cent use Instagram. In terms of social impact, the average Facebook user has been identified as having more 'close relationships', and their distant communal ties often benefit through the social affordances of the platform for 'reviving dormant' relationships (e.g. provide newsfeed updates about daily activities and big life events such as the birth of a child or marriage). The findings from this report, while drawn from US demographics, align to a great extent with findings from other reports about social media and online behaviours. The UK-based OFCOM Report on Adults' Media Use and Attitudes (2014) also reports that Facebook remains the default service for most online adults. In both reports, distinction is made about the experiences and attitudes of users, dependent on age group. Young adults are often cited as having a more liberal approach to regulating their profiles while also being more proactive in managing their online experiences. In contrast, adults are often seen as having more conservative attitudes for protecting their identity online. This chapter departs from such bounded categorisations to attend to the more fluid movement of people and their texts within and across social media sites.

3 The discussion of the Pinoys in this chapter is drawn from a larger research project on adolescent literacy and bridging in-school and out-of-school literacy multimodal practices. It is funded by the National Academy of Education and Carnegie Corporation.

References

Adami, E. (2009). '"We/YouTube": exploring sign-making in video-interaction', *Visual Communication*, 8: 370–399.

Appadurai, A. (1996). *Modernity at large: cultural dimensions of globalization*. Minneapolis: University of Minnesota Press.

Bhabha, H. (2004). *The location of culture*. New York: Routledge.

Black, R. (2009). Online fan fiction, global identities, and imagination. *Research in the Teaching of English*, 43(4): 397–425.

Block, D. (2014 [2007]). *Second language identities*. London: Bloomsbury Academic.

Blommaert, J. and Rampton, B. (2011). 'Language and superdiversity', *Diversities*, 13(2): 3–21.

Boulter, J.D. (2001). *Writing space: computers, hypertext, and the remediation of print*. 2nd edn. Mahwah, NJ: Lawrence Erlbaum.

Brutt-Griffler, J. (2007). Bilingualism and e-learning, in R. Andrews and C. Haythornthwaite (eds) *The SAGE handbook of e-learning research*. London: SAGE, pp. 349–370.

Chris (2010). 'About me', *Thinly Spread* [Online]. Available at the British Library UK Web archive: www.webarchive.org.uk/wayback/archive/20141003085040/http://thinlyspread.co.uk//about

Creese, A. and Blackledge, A. (this volume). A linguistic ethnography of identity: adopting a heteroglossic frame, in S. Preece (ed.) *The Routledge handbook of language and identity*. London: Routledge, pp. 272–288.

Darvin, R. (this volume). Language and identity in the digital age, in S. Preece (ed.) *The Routledge handbook of language and identity*. London: Routledge, pp. 523–540.

Dolby, N. and Rizvi, F. (2008). Introduction: youth, mobility, and identity, in N. Dolby and F. Rizvi (eds) *Youth moves: identities and education in a global perspective*. New York: Routledge, pp. 1–14.

Domingo, M. (2012). 'Linguistic layering: social language development in the context of multimodal and digital technologies', *Journal of Learning, Media, and Technology*, 37(2): 177–197.

Domingo, M., Jewitt, C. and Kress, G. (2015). Multimodal social semiotics: writing in online contexts, in K. Pahl and J. Rowsell (eds) *The Routledge handbook of literacy studies*. London: Routledge, pp. 251–266.

Domingo, M., Kress, J., O'Connell, R., Elliott, H., Squire, C., Jewitt, C. and Adami, E. (2014). *Development of methodologies for researching online: the case of food blogs* [Online]. NCRM E-prints. Available at http://eprints.ncrm.ac.uk/3704

English, F. and Marr, T. (2015). *Why do linguistics? Reflective linguistics and the study of language*. London: Bloomsbury Academic.

Garden, M. (2011). 'Defining blog: a fool's errand or a necessary undertaking', *Journalism*, 13(4): 483–499.

Halliday, M. (1978). *Language as a social semiotic*. London: Edward Arnold.

Hardey, M. (2011). Ubiquitous connectivity: user-generated data and the role of the researcher, in S.N. Hesse-Biber (ed.) *Emergent technologies in social research*. Oxford: Oxford University Press, pp. 87–106.

Hookway, N. (2008). 'Entering the blogosphere: some strategies for using blogs in social research', *Qualitative Research*, 8(1): 91–113.

Hull, G.A., Stornaiuolo, A. and Sterponi, L. (2013). Imagined readers and hospitable texts: global youth connect online, in D. Alvermann, N. Unrau and R. Ruddell (eds) *Theoretical models and processes of reading*. 6th edn. Newark, DE: International Reading Association, pp. 1208–1240.

Ito, M. (2010). Mobilizing the imagination in everyday play: the case of Japanese media mixes, in S. Sonvilla-Weiss (ed.) *Mashup cultures*. Germany: Springer-Verlag/Wien, pp. 79–97.

Jewitt, C. (ed.) (2009). *The Routledge handbook of multimodal analysis*. London: Routledge.

Jewitt, C. (2012). *What is multimodality? Glossary of multimodal terms* [Online]. Available at http://multimodalityglossary.wordpress.com/multimodality

Jewitt, C. and Oyama, R. (2001). Visual meaning: a social semiotic approach, in T. VanLeeuwen and C. Jewitt (eds) *The handbook of visual analysis*. London: SAGE, pp. 134–156.

Jørgensen, J.N., Karrebæk, M.S., Madsen, L.M. and Møller, J.S. (2011). 'Polylanguaging in superdiversity', *Diversities*, 13(2): 23–37.

Joseph, J.E. (this volume). Historical perspectives on language and identity, in S. Preece (ed.) *The Routledge handbook of language and identity*. Abingdon: Routledge, pp. 19–33.

Knobel, M. and Lankshear, C. (2008). 'Remix: the art and craft of endless hybridization', *Journal of Adolescent and Adult Literacy*, 52(1): 22–33.

Kress, G. (2009). *Multimodality: a social semiotic approach to communication*. London: RoutledgeFalmer.

Kress, G. and Domingo, M. (2013). Multimodal and ethnographic semiotic analysis of digital communication environments. Paper at *MODE Summer School*, London Knowledge Lab, Institute of Education, University of London, 27 June.

Kress, G. and VanLeeuwen, T. (2006). *Reading images: the grammar of visual design*. 2nd edn. London: Routledge.

Lam, W.S.E. and Warriner, D.S. (2012). 'Transnationalism and literacy: investigating the mobility of people, languages, texts, and practices', *Reading Research Quarterly*, 47(2): 191–215.

Lave, J. and Wenger, E. (1991). *Situated learning: legitimate peripheral participation*. Cambridge: Cambridge University Press.

Leung, C., Harris, R. and Rampton, B. (1997). 'The idealised native speaker, reified ethnicities, and classroom realities', *TESOL Quarterly*, 31(3): 543–560.

Madianou, M. and Miller, D. (2011). *Migration and new media: transnational families and polymedia*. London: Routledge.

Manovich, L. (2001). *The language of new media*. Cambridge, MA: The MIT Press.

Nero, S. (ed.) (2006). *Dialects, Englishes, Creoles, and education*. New York: Lawrence Erlbaum Associates.

New London Group (1996). 'A pedagogy of multiliteracies: designing social futures', *Harvard Educational Review*, 66(1): 60–92.

OFCOM (2014). *Adults' media use and attitudes report* [Online]. Available at http://stakeholders.ofcom.org.uk/market-data-research/other/research-publications/adults/adults-media-lit-14

Paris, D. (2012). 'You rep what you're from': texting identities in multiethnic youth space, in D. Paris (ed.) *Language across difference: ethnicity, communication and youth identities in changing urban schools*. Cambridge: Cambridge University Press, pp. 126–162.

Pew Research Internet Project (2013). *Social media update* [Online]. Available at www.pewinternet.org/2013/12/30/social-media-update-2013

Rampton, B. (2005). *Crossing: language and ethnicity among adolescents*. 2nd edn. London: Routledge.

Ríos-Rojas, A. (2011). 'Beyond delinquent citizenships: immigrant youth's (re)visions of citizenship and belonging in a globalized world', *Harvard Educational Review*, 81(1): 64–94.

VanLeeuwen, T. (2004). *Introducing social semiotics*. London: Routledge.

VanLeeuwen, T. and Jewitt, C. (eds) (2000). *The handbook of visual analysis*. London: SAGE.

West, K.C. (2008). 'Weblogs and literacy response: socially situated identities and hybrid social languages in English class blogs', *Journal of Adolescent and Adult Literacy*, 51(7): 588–598.

Williams, B. (2009). *Shimmering literacies: popular culture and reading and writing online*. New York: Peter Lang Publishing.

Wilson, S.M. and Peterson, L.C. (2002). 'The anthropology of online communities', *Annual Review of Anthropology*, 31: 449–467.

Appendix

*'Kapag A'koy Bumabalik' lyrics**

Intro, KidCras:
Hey yo, this is KidCras
Back in the Philippines
Check this out, alright
Lirikong Supremo, Check it out

Chorus, KidCras and KyD:
Masarap ang pakirandam kapag a'koy bumabalik (bumabalik)
Makikita ang lugar kung saan ko nakuha ang aking katapangan
Ang loob ko ay lumalakas kapag a'koy bumabalik (bumabalik)
Daladala ko sa puso ko ang aking bansa kahit saan makarating (kahit saan makarating)
[It makes me feel good whenever I return (return)
See the place where I learned to be courageous
I get stronger within whenever I return (return)
I carry my country in my heart no matter where I go (no matter where I go)]

1st verse, KidCras:
Back in Manila from London
Jump off the plane, touch down
Kamusta ka, yeah I'm back again
With a fresh style, not one of the best style
But bet I'll still be standin on feet on the next round
Like Pacqiauo, this kid is a killa
Yea, the modern day thrilla in Manila
I set trends of my own, but don't copy it,
So many of your shirt designs are whack and that's obvious

2nd verse, KidCras:
Three stars and the sun yeah, I'm reppin it
You ain't really representin, you disrespectin it
I'm proud of my country but ain't proud of the government
The cops are corrupt and the system dysfunctionate
How can our nation not solve the situation
Survivin everyday over minimum wages
But this is my country, I will rep til the death of it
Put the flag in the air if you're proud of your heritage

Chorus, KidCras and KyD:
Masarap ang pakirandam kapag a'koy bumabalik (bumabalik)
Makikita ang lugar kung saan ko nakuha ang aking katapangan
Ang loob ko ay lumalakas kapag a'koy bumabalik (bumabalik)
Daladala ko sa puso ko ang aking bansa kahit saan makarating (kahit saan makarating)

* I take responsibility for the transcription of the lyrics from the music video and do not associate any potential errors in translation to the Pinoys.

The video can be accessed on YouTube at www.youtube.com/watch?v=mzcsKjwMSVg

Exploring neoliberal language, discourses and identities

Christian W. Chun

Introduction

The term 'neoliberalism' has been described as 'a dismal epithet ... imprecise and over-used' (Watkins 2010: 7), which has led to some confusion among the general public as well as contestations among scholars regarding its meaning. Neoliberalism will be used in this chapter as a shorthand indicator to name the complex and dynamic changes that have occurred in many countries since the 1970s that have led to political and economic rear-rangements and redistributions of power in favour of capital and governance over labour. These changes include the ever-increasing 'extension of market-based competition and commodification processes into previously insulated realms of political-economic life' (Brenner *et al.* 2010: 329) along with systematic attempts by democratically elected govern-ments acting on behalf of corporate governance to deregulate and privatise state-owned and run institutions and defund social services, such as education and health care. Efforts towards neoliberalism in the past 35 years have resulted in the massive accumulation of private capital through the concerted dispossession of public wealth (Harvey 2005). A fuller discussion of the various aspects and understandings of neoliberalism will be featured in the section 'Current issues'.

Why is neoliberalism relevant to applied linguists?

Why is neoliberalism relevant to the applied linguistics field and why should we care about it as researchers, teachers and students? Neoliberal policies and practices have attempted to remake our everyday lives so that every aspect is minutely measured, assessed and evaluated as 'outputs', in accordance with manufacturing-based standards of production, and defined as 'best practices', which is another term adopted from corporate culture now widely used in education. Those of us who work or study in applied linguistics, including TESOL and English language teaching, and/or as language teachers at primary, secondary or tertiary levels, are all affected and adversely impacted in varying ways. For example, in the case of public school K-12 teachers working in the United States, their students have been forced to take a battery of standardised tests, the results of which lead to performance-based reviews of school districts, determining who receives more or less federal funding. Teachers themselves have also been subjected to increased assessment based on their students' test scores.

In addition to these neoliberal keywords – the aforementioned 'best practices' and 'outputs', and others, such as 'flexibility' – that are shaping the way we narrate and enact our work lives, the material practices of neoliberalism in reshaping universities should also give researchers pause. In the neoliberalisation of universities, humanities courses such as Renaissance literature, Shakespeare and the nineteenth-century novel are increasingly coming under attack as insufficiently linked to the world of work and graduate employment. This can be seen in the proverbial admonition that 'studying Chaucer or Milton won't get students a job'. In this manner, academic fields and courses of particular study 'can be considered economically akin to a consumer durable which has the peculiarity of being inseparable from its owner' (Gordon 1991: 44). With many universities following government emphasis on STEM subjects (science, technology, engineering and maths), maintaining courses in the arts, social sciences and humanities has become ever more difficult even when there are healthy enrolments. With respect to our own field of applied linguistics, and in particular English language teaching, we are still struggling at many tertiary institutions to have our discipline gain recognition as a legitimate field of scholarly inquiry and practice. Another neoliberal practice has been the increasing 'adjunctification' of university faculty in many countries, which has resulted in 75 per cent of all academic tutors in the United States working as non-tenured adjunct instructors on low-paying short-term contracts (Kezar and Maxey 2013). The casualisation of the academic workforce in universities can be attributed in part to the permeation of neoliberal discourses and practices that have reconfigured the university as a site of cheap labour producing surplus value. This in part has led to the people therein to remake themselves in the true neoliberal fashion as entrepreneurs of the self as they are obliged to compete with colleagues for scarce resources.

This chapter addresses the ways in which our co-constructed identities and performed identifications (Hall 1996) have been dialogically articulated and enacted within neoliberal discursive formations that have coevolved with neoliberal policies and practices. In discussing these neoliberal identity and discursive multimodal enactments, be they through verbal and/or visual performativities, I aim not to merely describe these now not-so-new phenomena, but rather, in drawing attention to them, to also explore how we can contribute to the counter-hegemonic process of resituating and realigning our identities with community-based notions of social justice and freedom. The chapter begins with a fuller account of how neoliberalism has been understood. It then turns to the ways in which neoliberal discourses have been mediated through identity formations and agencies. I next suggest several avenues of research to explore these discursive identities, before concluding with the argument for the need to create alternatives to neoliberal discourses and identities.

Current issues

What is this thing called 'neoliberalism'?

In the past 25 years or so, the seemingly disparate academic disciplines of economics, urban geography, cultural studies, anthropology and sociology have extensively examined policies, implementations and material manifestations characterised as neoliberal in a variety of globalised and localised settings and spaces. In addition to the vast scholarly literature on neoliberalism stemming from these disciplines, there also have been an increasing number of mainstream pub-lications addressing neoliberal practices – and naming them as such – that are aimed at a wider public audience. For example, David Harvey, in his *A brief history of neoliberalism* (2005) and *Spaces of global capitalism* (2006), has analysed how urban spaces have been reconfigured around a neoliberal strategic aim of 'accumulation by dispossession' (Harvey 2005: 178). In these works, Harvey illustrates how various elite formations, comprising corporate and government interests, have undertaken and benefited from carefully planned privatisation schemes of public goods and services, such as health care, schools and transportation, as well as benefiting from the sys-temic economic crises revolving around consumer debt tied to housing mortgages and loans. Similarly, Naomi Klein, in her *The shock doctrine: the rise of disaster capitalism* (2007), documented how natural catastrophes, financial crises, environmental disasters and violent conflicts have served in the past 35 years or so as pretexts for the politically engineered dismantlement of social safety nets for the general public in the pursuit of privatised corporate profits. These texts have attempted to explain the ways in which neoliberal policies and practices in the past four dec-ades have negatively impacted on the majority of the people who are subject to various forms of neoliberal governance. Countries where neoliberalism is rife include, but are not limited to, the United States, the United Kingdom, Canada, Australia, Chile, Argentina, Spain, Greece, China, South Korea and Brazil. The negative impacts of neoliberal policies and practices can be measured in concrete ways, such as the rising rates of economic inequality, falling or stagnant wages, increasing levels of poverty, and the loss of well-paid manufacturing jobs in industrialised countries.

The aims of neoliberal principles and material practices involve and utilise a range of domains, including politics and the economy, society and cultures more generally, that 'are directed toward extending and deepening capitalist market relations in most spheres of our social lives' (Colás 2005: 70). However, it can be argued that it is not 'most spheres' that neoliberal policies and practices are targeting, but instead every sphere of our lives, so that nothing will remain untouched by the drive to monetise every imaginable and imagined private and public domain constituting and constitutive of our everyday lives. Indeed, Henri Lefebvre had already observed this in the 1960s with his *Everyday life in the modern world* (Lefebvre 1984), in which he argued that our everyday lives are now largely shaped and organised by powerful institutional decisions in which we do not participate.

Despite the prevalence and dominance of neoliberal language and discourses in our every-day lifeworlds, neoliberal ideologies, practices and identities have only recently begun to be addressed and explored in the field of applied linguistics (see e.g. Holborow 2006, 2007; Chun 2009, 2013, 2015; Gray 2010; Block *et al.* 2012). For example, in examining how students have become semantically reframed as 'customers', an important keyword in the neoliberal lexicon (Chun 2015), Holborow (2007: 61) noted that the notion and naming of customer has become 'endowed with a semi-reverential status, whose supposed needs and endless desires become the guiding light of progress and efficiency'. However, as Holborow astutely noted, students cannot be customers 'because degrees are not quite, in fact, bought and sold, and the student does not always have the last word – not because universities are authoritarian (which they may well be), but because education is not that sort of transaction' (ibid.). In another example, Gray (2010) analysed how English language teaching materials offer particular representations of English as a branded global commodity that were part of a larger constellation of commodities. These included the remaking and branding of the individual, which is a marker of neoliberal discourses. In *Neoliberalism in applied linguistics*, Block *et al.* (2012) give a critical account of how neoliberal ideologies and accompanying language have impacted on language teaching, language teacher education and language in general. They urge researchers in applied linguistics to engage more directly with issues of political economy.

My own work has focused on neoliberal discourses and the identities that neoliberal discourses afford and constrain in English language teaching (see Chun 2009, 2012, 2013, 2015). In a 2009 article addressing neoliberal discourses in English for Academic Purposes (EAP), I discussed how English language learners have been referred to as customers or clients in many intensive English language programmes in the United States. In addition, I examined how the construct of 'emotional intelligence', which was featured in an EAP textbook chapter, was framed within a neoliberal discursive formation that explicitly named a self-management technique that was claimed to provide emotional and psychological benefits for the individual worker (Foucault's (2008) notion of 'the conduct of conduct' and 'auto-correcting selves'). However, this self-management technique was in fact serving the interests of the company first and foremost, by increasing the workload, efficiency and production output of the workforce in order to bolster profits. In other publications (Chun 2012, 2013, 2015), I examined how an EAP instructor and her students in a Canadian university mediated neoliberal globalisation discourses featured in their curriculum materials, together with the subject positions that they took up and co-constructed in adopting, reproducing and/or contesting these discourses. For example, after the EAP class watched a video in which a business entrepreneur discussed worldwide trends in paper product consumption, the instructor offered her students the subject position of the global investor by asking them how they 'would profit from this information' (Chun 2015: 89). This led to an extended silence among all the students apart from one, possibly indicating a resistance on their part to inhabiting the identity of a capitalist entrepreneur in the global free market.

Although the metaphor of the market is integral to neoliberal ideological discourse, inasmuch as it is claimed to be fundamental to liberty and freedom of choice (Couldry 2010), the discourse masks the issue of what choices are offered, the limits of those choices and, importantly, who makes the decisions on which choices are available. The original proponent of neoliberalism was Friedrich A. Hayek, whose book *The road to serfdom* claimed that the most dangerous threat to individual freedom was government interference through economic and social planning. In advocating the 'free' market as the only viable and efficient instrument for social management, Hayek argued against devising 'further machinery for "guiding" and "directing"' individuals, and called for the creation of 'conditions favorable to progress rather than to "plan progress"' (1944: 240). Hayek's proposal that 'a policy of freedom for the individual is the only truly progressive policy' (ibid.: 241) is a prominent feature of the neoliberal claim that the free market is the only social mechanism capable of providing freedom and 'choice' to people. By appealing to the desire for freedom and the emotions that this evokes, neoliberal discourses propagate the idea that a hyper, ultra-competitive market can offer the best option for freedom. The fact that no market has ever been historically isolated from systemic and power-invested interests and constraints is very rarely, if ever, mentioned in neoliberal discourses.

Behind the ideological guise of declaring that individual freedom and choice is made possible only by the workings of the free market, Harvey (2005) and others have argued that neoliberal policies and practices have in fact worked to bolster the immense power of the ruling elite, coined by the Occupy Movement in the United States as the '1 per cent'. The 1 per cent have consolidated their power by re-establishing the material, political and social conditions to accumulate financial capital, through the dispossession and appropriation of public wealth via privatisation and the imposition of austerity measures that have involved actions such as destroying the social safety net and cutting budgets to public institutions, and via tax cuts to the wealthy. Not surprisingly, these policy enactments have led to a rapid increase of economic inequalities in the countries in which neoliberal policies have been enacted. They have also played a large role in the ensuing miseries stemming from chronic unemployment, underemployment and the increasing dearth of formerly well-paying jobs in the manufacturing sector in developed countries.

Different understandings of neoliberalism

While some have now observed that the term 'neoliberal' has itself become widely overused (Watkins 2010), others go even further in maintaining that it is 'an incoherent concept with no objective referent' (Barnett 2010 in Gilbert 2013: 7). However, it is still theoretically and politically useful to employ this term 'to describe the macro-economic paradigm that has pre-dominated from the end of the 1970s' (Watkins 2010: 7). Yet, although neoliberalism may be a complex 'reorganization of capitalism' (Campbell 2005: 187), and therefore just the most recent phase in the ongoing political arrangement and management of an economic system still characterised as capitalist, what are the affordances of portraying these reorganising measures as neoliberalism, rather than using the term 'capitalism' or 'globalisation' (Chun 2015)?

In following Ward and England's (2007) framework, Springer (2012: 136) details four different understandings of the ongoing neoliberal phase of capitalism. The first is to view neoliberalism as an 'ideological hegemonic project' in which 'elite actors and dominant groups organized around transnational class-based alliances have the capacity to project and circulate a coherent program of interpretations and images of the world onto others'. Springer is careful to point out that these interpretations and representations are not merely forcefully imposed against people's wills but do involve some levels and measures of both participatory active and passive consent, which will be discussed later in this chapter. The second understanding of neoliberalism is that it constitutes a formation of specific policies and programmes that have actively concentrated on the 'transfer of ownership from the state or public holdings to the private sector or corporate interests, which necessarily involves a conceptual reworking of the meaning these categories hold' (ibid.). This involves ideological work in framing and presenting the idea that public resources, such as schools, hospitals, transportation, parks and public spaces, are ineffective as constituted and thus should be reconfigured in accordance with market-based principles in the name of 'dynamic' efficiency and freedom of choice that will supposedly benefit the public. The ideological keywords of these policies and actions, ostensibly in the public interest, are the now familiar words of 'privatization, deregulation, liberalization, depoliticization, and monetarism' (ibid.). The third understanding of neoliberalism is to see it as the active transformative management of the state in its relation to a globally linked economy in which other states are similarly vying. This involves a 'quantitative axis of destruction and discreditation whereby state capacities and potentialities are "rolled back"' (ibid.: 137), as well as a 'qualitative axis of construction and consolidation, wherein reconfigured institutional mediations, economic management systems, and invasive social agendas centered on urban order, surveillance, immigration issues, and policing are "rolled out"' (ibid.). Finally, the fourth understanding of neoliberalism draws upon Foucault's (1991) notion of governmentality, in which people as neoliberal subjects can be viewed as in an endless process of 'unfolding failures and successes in the relations between peoples and their socially constructed realities as they are (re)imagined, (re)interpreted, and (re)assembled to influence forms of knowledge through "the conduct of conduct"' (Springer 2012: 137). In reducing, or in some cases abandoning, state responsibility for public well-being and welfare, neoliberal governance enmeshes individuals in the subject position of being solely responsible for their well-being and development. In other words, the onus is on the individual to find the means and resources to improve and adapt on their own and with little, if any, government-funded support. Self-improvement and learning to be 'flexible' and 'adaptable' comes about by individuals being required to invest in themselves via privatised and monetised commodities such as the for-profit charter and online schools that are now replacing many public institutions. The displacement of government in our everyday lives involves an 'ensemble of rationalities, strategies, technologies, and techniques concerning the mentality of rule that allow for the de-centering of government through the active role of auto-regulated or auto-correcting selves' (ibid.). This results in increasing self-governance that necessitates increased personal expenditure by individuals on education, health care and so on for corporate profit.

Neoliberal language, discourses and the discursive figure

Despite these four different but interconnected understandings, Gilbert (2013: 8) is still compelled to ask, 'What *kind* of a thing is "neoliberalism"?' Is it simply 'an aggregation of ideas, a discursive formation, an over-arching ideology, a governmental programme, the manifestation of a set of interests, a hegemonic project, [or] an assemblage of techniques and technologies'? In considering how all these comprise the unifying theoretical and practical stance advocating a systematic and 'deliberate intervention by government in order to encourage particular types of entrepreneurial, competitive and commercial behaviour in its citizens, ultimately arguing for the management of populations with the aim of cultivating the type of individualistic, competitive, acquisitive and entrepreneurial behaviour' (ibid.: 9), it is important to delineate how each contributes to this project of attempted cultivation and management of people in remaking themselves as neoliberal subjects. In contrast to notions of democratic and communal collectivities in shaping people's identities, the neoliberal discursive formation persistently promotes 'an individualistic conception of human selfhood and of the idea of the individual both as the ideal locus of sovereignty and the site of government intervention' (ibid.: 11).

The individualistic conception of human selfhood is what Gilbert thinks has enabled neoliberalism to endure and succeed to date. Neoliberalism is in part achieved by discourses that blame state interventions, such as unemployment benefits and welfare support for the poor and disenfranchised, for restricting the free market and, hence, freedom of choice, while omitting to mention, or obscuring, other market or state interventions that benefit private corporations. However, the complementary dimension is perhaps even more important: that of the 'management of individuals *qua* individuals' (ibid.). In what has been characterised as an increasingly fragmented, postmodern and post-ideological world of discontinuities, dislocations and hybridities, which has resulted in identities in constant flux and questioning, it is possibly the recognition of individuals and their naming as such that has social, psychological and material appeal in terms of being able to act as 'individualised selves' in an increasingly chaotic and alienating world. This narrow definition of the individualised self offered by neoliberal discourses continues to have a central and significant appeal despite the material manifestations of the narrowing of avenues available to people's agentive options that forecloses any notion of interdependent and collective agencies. The onus is on us to remake ourselves in whatever fashion in the pursuit of rewards and recognition in a highly competitive environment. This act is portrayed as allowing us to achieve an integral holistic and individualised sense of self that is independent and set apart from the rest of society. This ideological stance that 'acquisitive individualism is both an inherent feature of the human personality and the only logical basis for human civilisation' (Gilbert 2013: 14) has been made into a prevailing common-sense belief (Gramsci 1971) through repeated and sophisticated discourses in various sites, such as school, the university, the media and social media. As Hall *et al.* (2013: 13) observe, in order to legitimate itself, the neoliberal settlement, like every social settlement before it, 'is crucially founded on embedding as common sense a whole bundle of beliefs – ideas beyond question, assumptions so deep that the very fact that they *are* assumptions is only rarely brought to light'. Indeed, the successful discursive strategies that gain and win consent are 'those which root themselves in the contradictory elements of common-sense, popular life and consciousness' (Hall 2011: 713).

The neoliberal common-sense discourse has redefined the notion of individual freedom in the highly restrictive and narrow agentive options to act only in the 'capacity for self-realization and freedom from bureaucracy rather than freedom from want, with human behavior recon-ceptualized along economic lines' (Leitner *et al.* 2007: 4). The ideological discursive formation that has helped to relocate our sense of agency to the private domain of the self has resulted in what Brown (2005: 43) termed 'the neoliberal citizen'. In attempts to eliminate any sociopoliti-cal concerns that seemingly have no relevance to the 'free market', neoliberal discourses work to reduce any notions and practices of an active 'political citizenship to an unprecedented degree of passivity and political complacency' (ibid.). Indeed, it is this 'insistent belief that it is our private, personal beliefs and behaviours which define our "true" selves, whereas our public behaviour can be tolerated precisely to the extent that it is not invested with any emotional significance' (Gilbert 2013: 13). As such, neoliberal discursive formations as they are disseminated and propa-gated in various mainstream media have prominently featured 'two popular discursive figures – the "taxpayer" and the "customer"' (Hall 2011: 715). As Hall describes it, the taxpayer is the 'hard-working' person, who is continually 'over-taxed to fund the welfare "scrounger" and the "shifters" who lived on benefits as a "lifestyle" choice' (ibid.). Not coincidentally, at least in the United States, this discourse of the beleaguered taxpayer also draws upon classed and racialised discourses in that the taxpayer indexes a White middle-class person living in the suburbs and the heartland of the country. In contrast, the welfare scroungers and shifters are understood to be living in the urban areas and are members of various minority groups including recent immi-grants. These narratives have been part of the dominant discourse in both the United States and the United Kingdom – as the rise of the Tea Party and UKIP (United Kingdom Independence Party) can attest. These political movements draw on neoliberal racialised discourses aimed at White working and middle classes fearful of job loss and the growing economic inequalities engineered by neoliberal policies and practices in favour of powerful and wealthy corporations.

The customer is another significant representational figure in neoliberal discourse. This dis-cursive subject is intertwined with the taxpayer and can be seen as two sides of the same coin. As corporate enterprises in the industrialised economies in the major developed countries experi-enced falling rates of profit, partially due to the relatively well-paid and unionised jobs in sectors such as the car industry, they began to look elsewhere for new sources of profit, with many reconfiguring their organisations by shifting many of their manufacturing jobs to China, Brazil, Indonesia and India. One such enterprise is the service-based retail economy whose megastores have driven out smaller businesses from many areas. The neoliberal subject position of the customer, made to look attractive through a supposed increase in freedom of choice, has now permeated from the corporate business world into the higher education sector, with universities in countries such as the United States and the UK referring to international students as custom-ers or clients (see Holborow 2007; Chun 2009).

In fact, this discursive identity construction of English language students as customers is an apt one in light of the global marketing and selling of the English language (specifically in its

British, American, Canadian and Australian varieties) as an essential component and marker of the entrepreneur of oneself endlessly competing with others on an international scale. This commodification of the English language and the accompanying promotion of English as an integral ingredient to an identity invested in global success have important implications for English language teaching and learning (Chun 2015). For example, what might be some of the ways in which both teachers and students take up various subject positions and/or enact particular performative identities in the classroom when engaged in interacting with multimodal texts featuring neoliberal discourses tying language study with modes of remaking oneself, consumerism and global competition? These need to be explored further for not only pedagogical and learning effects, but also for how we conceive of English language learner identities both inside and outside of the classroom.

Are neoliberal language and discourses shaping new identities, and if so, how?

Neoliberal identities stem from the ideological construct that people are and can be viewed as solely comprising an 'entirety of skills that have been acquired as the result of "investments" in the corresponding stimuli' (Lemke 2001: 199), be it of schooling, job training or so-called self-improvement courses. Thus, 'the individual producer-consumer is in a novel sense not just an enterprise, but the entrepreneur of himself or herself' (Gordon 1991: 44). In the face of an increasing societal pressure to actively pursue a specific set of skills (while disregarding others that are seen as being 'impractical' or 'useless' such as studying Renaissance literature), some people now see themselves as remaking, or rather rebranding, themselves as a more marketable and, hence, more sellable and attractive commodity on the global exchange market. Indeed, as Ong (2007: 5) argued, 'neoliberalism as a technique is fundamentally about the re-management of populations' in which 'the common goal is to induce an enterprising subjectivity in elite subjects, to increase their capacity to make calculative choices'.

A central issue that has been discussed at length in various disciplines, including applied linguistics, is the tension between structure and agency. While an in-depth discussion of this complex subject is beyond the scope of this chapter, suffice to say that in addressing and articulating neoliberalism as an overarching structuring mechanism that has spread globally, there might be the risk, as Springer (2012: 135) cautions, of '[neglecting] internal constitution, local variability, and the role that "the social" and individual agency play in (re)producing, facilitating, and circulating neoliberalism'. Thus one challenge for applied linguists is to capture the dimensions and domains in which individuals reproduce, facilitate and circulate neoliberal discourses, practices and behaviours at the micro, interpersonal and interactional level through agentive acts and performances. As Gershon (2011: 539) argues, in neoliberalism's universalising aim to convince people to adopt and perform agencies that are restricted and limited to corporate-like identities, other agencies are not only 'getting pushed aside', but also there is 'a move from the liberal vision of people owning themselves as though they were property to a neoliberal vision of people owning themselves as though they were a business' (ibid.). As a result, the becoming of a 'neoliberal self' is 'produced through an engagement with a market, that is, neoliberal markets require participants to be reflexive managers of their abilities and alliances'. However, more than just their abilities and alliances are in play; other performative behaviours are expected 'through tourist performances, media forms, food, clothes, art, and so on' (ibid.: 541).

Future directions

Exploring neoliberal discursive identities

As mentioned at the beginning of this chapter, there is an increasing body of work in applied linguistics on neoliberalism. Aside from my own work (Chun 2012, 2013, 2015) that has examined how an English for Academic Purposes (EAP) instructor and her students positioned themselves in various ways while engaging with, and in, neoliberal globalisation discourses, there have been others in the field of applied linguistics and TESOL who have researched how people take on, negotiate, reproduce and/or reject neoliberal discursive identities (see e.g. Mautner 2010; Clarke and Morgan 2011; Holborow 2013; Block *et al.* 2013). One possible line of inquiry of applied linguists doing language and identity projects would be 'an interest in how material conditions shape ideologies and uses of language, including political economic approaches to language that understood it as a material form of social practice' (Shankar and Cavanaugh 2012: 356). This might involve ethnographic research into local sites in which neoliberal practices have taken hold to see how people are employing language use shaped by company policies, for example.

However, possibly more fruitful lines of research inquiries may be in the direction of how specific identities emerge through various performative acts framed within neoliberal discourse formations. If we see identity as performative sociocultural practices, and if identity 'refers to sameness' (Bucholtz and Hall 2004: 370), then what does it mean for the notion and practices of class-based politics that articulate and stress class-based identity sameness in terms of common interests and alliances across power-motivated and socially constructed differences of race, gender, sexualities, nationhood and so on? Have these dimensions of identity been co-opted by the discursive formation of a neoliberal consumer cultural and identity politics that attempts to *invent* sameness through an overarching consumer identity that downplays socially constructed differences of race, gender and sexualities? In other words, if in the case of a class-based political identity that identifies sameness as the common interest of an allied and broad-based labour movement, or, as the Occupy Movement so aptly termed it, the '99 per cent', and the necessary accompanying Other is the Capitalist, or the '1 per cent', then in the case of a neoliberal consumer identity, who is the Other? Those who do not, or cannot, consume to the same extent?

This is a point made by Jim McGuigan (2009) in his book *Cool capitalism*. He argues that prevailing neoliberal consumer identities are constructed in part from buying certain products that have cultural and symbolic purchase beyond the purchase exchange price. These products are deemed 'cool' by a combination of aggressive advertising, marketing, celebrity endorsement and audience uptake and thus acquire a cachet that bestows the veneer of 'cool' upon the buyers. But more than this, the particular angle these products take in their acquisition of being 'cool' is their seemingly oppositional stance to capitalism, the system itself. Thus, McGuigan argues that a neoliberal capitalist culture can have it both ways: producing, marketing and successfully selling significant quantities of commodity objects while making it seem to the consumer that these products are antithetical to the very system that has produced them. These material embodiments of benign disaffection or fatuous rebellion against neoliberal capitalism are on display in, for example, fashion and accessories and are visible through performative displays in public spaces. One example are T-shirts featuring either the well-known photo portrait of Che Guevara or those printed with provocative-sounding slogans such as 'Fuck Capitalism'. Consumers wearing such T-shirts view themselves as setting themselves apart from the rest who 'don't get it'. Their rebellion or oppositional stance is displaced onto the Other who is seen as buying into the system. These multimodal performances of identity enacted through sartorial performativities need to be explored further for how they construct a specific kind of neoliberal consumer identity that seemingly opposes, or at least disdains, the system, while literally embodying it.

Inasmuch as identities are constructed through the signified and articulated markings of difference and exclusion, then 'it is only through the relation to the Other, the relation to what it is not, to precisely what it lacks, to what has been called its *constitutive outside* that the "positive" meaning of any term … can be constructed' (Hall 1996: 4). This leads to several other questions. First, if identity can be seen as people's feeling or sense of belonging to particular communities, then to what extent do people primarily identify as consumers? For those who do not partake in the 'rebellious' consumer identity, do they identify as willing participants in neoliberal capitalism and do they see themselves as belonging to the capitalist system? Why might there be a need to belong to an economic system that clearly does not benefit everyone? If one identifies as belonging to capitalism, or as a 'capitalist', not in the sense of owning the means of production but merely believing that this economic system works for the most part or, at the very least, there is no viable alternative, then what is the Other in this case? The historically significant traditional Other to capitalism was communism, which in its ideological role as the *bogeyman* has largely disappeared as a bygone relic since the collapse of the Soviet Union in 1991. If communism is no longer the viable Other to capitalism, then what are people identifying against? So for those who may not be entirely content or satisfied with the economic system in which they are working, producing, purchasing, borrowing and spending most of their daily lives contributing to through the workplace, what are the possibilities of the Other? In this manner, the notion of identity as sameness in its oppositional construction to difference is problematic and worthy of further interrogation.

Another issue to explore is going beyond the linguistic constructions of neoliberal identities. While language is integral to the construction of identity, we also need to explore the social semiotic meaning-making material practices and instantiations of people engaged in acts of identity that can be characterised as part of the neoliberal remaking of oneself: branding through purchasing, performing and displaying, as in the aforementioned examples of the now ubiquitous Che Guevara T-shirts and accessories. As Hearn (2008: 195) pointed out, 'the material brand is the ultimate image-commodity: a fetish object *par excellence*, pursued and paid for by consumers who wish to become a part of its fabricated world of purloined cultural meanings'. People drawing on the practices of buying specific well-known corporate products to brand themselves as part of this imagined world of selected membership is not a new phenomenon. Displaying certain tastes and having the wealth to consume these tastes was evident in the bourgeois shoppers and passers-by walking through nineteenth-century Paris arcades, as Walter Benjamin and others have documented. However, what is new is the increased reach of brands across the globe, in that shopping malls in many developed and developing countries all feature the same stores, or at least the same well-known brands that are instantly recognisable by their logos, as these have been advertised throughout all media platforms. In this, brands, 'both as trademarked image-objects and as sets of relations and contexts for life, become the ground and comprise the tools for the creation of self and community' (Hearn 2008: 196). The relationship between brands and identity is certainly another issue for applied linguists to investigate.

These newly branded selves stem in part from 'the demise of the traditional occupations' that 'give the sense that people have choices about who and what they are; we can all, it seems, now fashion mobile reflexive identities through consumption and social mobility' (Machin and Richardson 2008: 281). The agentive acts seen in their consumer choices and purchases perhaps reflect the sense that 'we can (re)brand ourselves as successful and fashionable through what we wear and what we drink' (ibid.). Therefore, in what ways are people, especially disempowered, disenfranchised and un(der)employed youth, 'seduced by the identity markers of "affluent lifestyle"' (ibid.) that are so characteristic of neoliberal culture and how does this manifest itself in the research sites of interest in applied linguistics?

All these questions relate to how the branded neoliberal self has become its own commodity sign: 'the self as a commodity for sale in the labour market which must generate its own rhetorically persuasive packaging, its own promotional message, within the confines of the dominant corporate imaginary' (Hearn 2008: 197). Inasmuch as this branded self 'sits at the nexus of discourses of neoliberalism, flexible accumulation, radical individualism, and spectacular promotionalism' (ibid.), there needs to be further methodologies developed to examine this complex and animating nexus of discourses. Researchers and students can begin by drawing upon and expanding the work of Ron Scollon and Suzie Wong Scollon, particularly their *Discourses in place: language in the material world* (2003) and *Nexus analysis: discourse and the emerging Internet* (2004), to explore the nexus of these discourses and how people take them up at various sites and ensuing recontextualisations. And because 'identity is more a situational performance than a stable trait or a sense of subjective continuity' (Grad and Rojo 2008: 6), methodologies are needed that can trace the interactional and mediated connections and linkages contributing to situational performances in their given contexts. But it is not only these situational performances that should be investigated because, as Hall (1996: 6) astutely noted, 'the notion that an effective suturing of the subject to a subject-position requires, not only that the subject is "hailed", but that the subject invests in the position, means that the suturing has to be thought of as an *articulation*'. Thus, it is incumbent upon researchers to also explore the ways in which the neoliberal subject invests in their positioning, drawing upon multiple meaning-making resources for identity work, be they linguistic, visual or so on.

Summary

In naming the ways in which neoliberal discourse and its material manifestations have shaped our identities and practices in different contexts, this chapter has explored how the language and discourses of neoliberalism have come to prominence. I have attempted to illustrate the complex and contradictory dynamics involved in the ideologically loaded discursive constructions of the neoliberal subject. This was done with the larger aim of setting the agenda for future research directions into how we might help develop counter-hegemonic strategies of contesting neoliberal common-sense beliefs by articulating resistant identities that are aligned with notions of democratically based inclusive communities in which one's own sense of self is intimately and integrally connected to the well-being of others.

Indeed, as Gal (1989: 361) observed, 'what is called dominant discourse is itself rarely monolithic, but rather a field of competition for power among elites'. Thus, any dominant discourse has fissures. These can be made visible by identifying the practices by which dominant discourses attempt to create and impose common-sense beliefs in society and our everyday lives (Chun 2015). Neoliberal discourses and the language that helps to construct them are no exception. For applied linguistic researchers working in the critical tradition, it is imperative not only to document and challenge how these discourses work and are materially instantiated, but also to examine how particular groups of interest to applied linguists reproduce and resist these discourses in their everyday identities and lived experiences. This work is crucial for anyone interested in social justice, which has proven to be an enormous challenge inasmuch as the 'generic disposition induced by neoliberalism is an organising principle of the self, of the self's relation to the self, and of its relation to others, articulated towards the maximisation of the self in a world perceived in terms of competition' (Hilgers 2013: 83). It is my contention that applied linguistics needs to be concerned with countering neoliberal discursive identity formations that promote and encourage 'the individual to mobilise a specific reflexivity that fits into a world perceived as a competitive market where it is necessary to maximise oneself' (ibid.).

If in fact we take capitalism to be 'a massive process of ego formation, the creation of modern selves, the illusion of individual autonomy, the cultivation of distinction and preference, the idea that individuals had their own moral conscience, based on individual reason and virtue' (Grandin 2014: no page), there remains a lot of work for those of us in applied linguistics who are committed to social justice and economic democracy to address how notions of democratic community-based identities that can work for change can be reborn and embraced as the new common sense in this age of neoliberalism.

Related topics

Critical discourse analysis and identity; Class in language and identity research; The politics of researcher identities: opportunities and challenges in identities research; An identity transformation? Social class, language prejudice and the erasure of multilingual capital in higher education; Language, gender and identities in political life: a case study from Malaysia; Language and identity research in online environments: a multimodal ethnographic perspective.

Further reading

Block, D., Gray, J. and Holborow, M. (2012). *Neoliberalism and applied linguistics*. London: Routledge. (One of the first volumes in the field of applied linguistics to call for applied linguists to engage with issues in political economy in any analysis of language and its social contexts.)

Chun, C.W. (2015). *Power and meaning making in an EAP classroom: engaging with the everyday*. Bristol: Multilingual Matters. (An ethnographic English for Academic Purposes (EAP) classroom case study that examines the various identity positions the participant teacher and her students took up in their engagements with neoliberal globalisation and consumerist discourses in their curriculum materials.)

Couldry, N. (2010). *Why voice matters: culture and politics after neoliberalism*. London: SAGE. (Insightful analysis of how neoliberal discourses frame and organise the prevailing narratives in the attempt to define and limit our everyday lives and possibilities.)

Hall, S. (2011). 'The neo-liberal revolution', *Cultural Studies*, 25(6): 705–728. (From the late Stuart Hall, an excellent analysis of the historical and ongoing cultural issues associated with the advent and practices of neoliberalism.)

Harvey, D. (2005). *A brief history of neoliberalism*. New York: Oxford University Press. (An excellent historical introduction and overview of neoliberalism from one of the world's leading political geographers and theorists.)

References

Block, D., Gray, J. and Holborow, M. (2012). *Neoliberalism and applied linguistics*. London: Routledge.
Brenner, N., Peck, J. and Theodore, N. (2010). 'After neoliberalization?', *Globalizations*, 7(3): 327–345.
Brown, W. (2005). *Edgework: critical essays on knowledge and politics*. Princeton: Princeton University Press.

Bucholtz, M. and Hall, K. (2004). Language and identity, in A. Duranti (ed.) *A companion to linguistic anthropology*. Malden, MA: Blackwell, pp. 369–394.

Campbell, A. (2005). The birth of neoliberalism in the United States: a reorganisation of capitalism, in A. Saad-Fiho and D. Johnston (eds) *Neoliberalism: a critical reader*. London: Pluto Press, pp. 187–198.

Chun, C.W. (2009). 'Contesting neoliberal discourses in EAP: critical praxis in an IEP classroom', *Journal of English for Academic Purposes*, 8(2): 111–120.

Chun, C.W. (2012). 'The multimodalities of globalization: teaching a YouTube video in an EAP classroom', *Research in the Teaching of English*, 47(2): 145–170.

Chun, C.W. (2013). The 'neoliberal citizen': resemiotizing globalized identities in EAP materials, in J. Gray (ed.) *Critical perspectives on language teaching materials*. Hampshire: Palgrave Macmillan, pp. 64–87.

Chun, C.W. (2015). *Power and meaning making in an EAP classroom: engaging with the everyday*. Bristol: Multilingual Matters.

Clarke, M. and Morgan, B. (2011). Education and social justice in neoliberal times: historical and pedagogical perspectives from two postcolonial contexts, in M.R. Hawkins (ed.) *Social justice language teacher education*. Bristol: Multilingual Matters, pp. 63–85.

Colás, A. (2005). Neoliberalism, globalisation and international relations, in A. Saad-Fiho and D. Johnston (eds) *Neoliberalism: a critical reader*. London: Pluto Press, pp. 70–79.

Couldry, N. (2010). *Why voice matters: culture and politics after neoliberalism*. London: SAGE.

Foucault, M. (1991). Governmentality, in G. Burchell, C. Gordon and P. Miller (eds) *The Foucault effect: studies in governmentality*. Chicago: University of Chicago Press, pp. 87–104.

Foucault, M. (2008). *The birth of biopolitics: lectures at the Collège de France, 1978–1979*. New York: Picador.

Gal, S. (1989). 'Language and political economy', *Annual Review of Anthropology*, 18: 345–367.

Gershon, I. (2011). 'Neoliberal agency', *Current Anthropology*, 52(4): 537–555.

Gilbert, J. (2013). 'What kind of thing is neoliberalism?', *New Formations*, 80–81: 7–22.

Gordon, C. (1991). Governmental rationality: an introduction, in G. Burchell, C. Gordon and P. Miller (eds) *The Foucault effect: studies in governmentality*. Chicago: University of Chicago Press, pp. 87–104.

Grad, H. and Rojo, L.M. (2008). Identities in discourse: an integrative view, in R. Dolón and J. Todolí (eds) *Analysing identities in discourse*. Amsterdam: John Benjamins, pp. 3–28.

Gramsci, A. (1971). *Selections from the prison notebooks* [Trans. Q. Hoare and G. Nowell-Smith]. New York: International Publishers.

Grandin, G. (2014). 'Capitalism and slavery: an interview with Greg Grandin'. Available at www.jacobinmag.com/2014/08/capitalism-and-slavery-an-interview-with-greg-grandin

Gray, J. (2010). 'The branding of English and the culture of the new capitalism: representations of the world of work in English language textbooks', *Applied Linguistics*, 31(5): 714–733.

Hall, S. (1996). Who needs 'identity'?, in S. Hall and P. Du Gay (eds) *Questions of cultural identity*. London: SAGE, pp. 1–17.

Hall, S. (2011). 'The neo-liberal revolution', *Cultural Studies*, 25(6): 705–728.

Hall, S., Massey, D. and Rustin, M. (2013). 'After neoliberalism: analysing the present', *Soundings*, 53: 8–22.

Harvey, D. (2005). *A brief history of neoliberalism*. New York: Oxford University Press.

Harvey, D. (2006). *Spaces of global capitalism: towards a theory of uneven geographical development*. London: Verso.

Hayek, F.A. (1944). *The road to serfdom*. Chicago: University of Chicago Press.

Hearn, A. (2008). Variations on the branded self: theme, invention, improvisation and inventory, in D. Hesmondhalgh and J. Toynbee (eds) *The media and social theory*. London: Routledge, pp. 194–210.

Hilgers, M. (2013). 'Embodying neoliberalism: thoughts and responses to critics', *Social Anthropology*, 21(1): 75–89.

Holborow, M. (2006). Ideology and language: interconnections between neo-liberalism and English, in J. Edge (ed.) *(Re-)locating TESOL in an age of empire*. New York: Palgrave Macmillan, pp. 84–103.

Holborow, M. (2007). 'Language, ideology and neoliberalism', *Journal of Language and Politics*, 6(1): 51–73.

Holborow, M. (2013). 'Applied linguistics in the neoliberal university: ideological keywords and social agency', *Applied Linguistics Review*, 4(2): 227–255.

Kezar, A. and Maxey, D. (2013). 'The changing academic workforce', *Trusteeship Magazine*. Available at http://agb.org/trusteeship/2013/5/changing-academic-workforce

Klein, N. (2007). *The shock doctrine: the rise of disaster capitalism*. New York: Metropolitan Books.

Lefebvre, H. (1984). *Everyday life in the modern world*. New Brunswick: Transaction Publishers.

Leitner, H., Sheppard, E.S., Sziarto, K. and Maringanti, A. (2007). Contesting urban futures: decentering neoliberalism, in H. Leitner, J. Peck and E.S. Sheppard (eds) *Contesting neoliberalism: urban frontiers*. New York: The Guilford Press, pp. 1–25.

Lemke, T. (2001). '"The birth of bio-politics": Michel Foucault's lecture at the Collège de France on neo-liberal governmentality', *Economy and Society*, 30(2): 190–207.

Machin, D. and Richardson, J.E. (2008). 'Renewing an academic interest in structural inequalities', *Critical Discourse Studies*, 5(4): 281–287.

Mautner, G. (2010). *Language and the market society: critical reflections on discourse and dominance*. London: Routledge.

McGuigan, J. (2009). *Cool capitalism*. New York: Pluto Press.

Ong, A. (2007). 'Neoliberalism as a mobile technology', *Transactions of the Institute of British Geographers*, 32: 3–8.

Scollon, R. and Scollon, S.W. (2003). *Discourses in place: language in the material world*. New York: Routledge.

Scollon, R. and Scollon, S.W. (2004). *Nexus analysis: discourse and the emerging Internet*. New York: Routledge.

Shankar, S. and Cavanaugh, J.R. (2012). 'Language and materiality in global capitalism', *Annual Review of Anthropology*, 41: 355–369.

Springer, S. (2012). 'Neoliberalism as discourse: between Foucauldian political economy and Marxian poststructuralism', *Critical Discourse Studies*, 9(2): 133–147.

Ward, K. and England, K. (2007). Introduction: reading neoliberalization, in K. England and K. Ward (eds) *Neoliberalization: states, networks, peoples*. Malden, MA: Blackwell, pp. 1–22.

Watkins, S. (2010). 'Shifting sands', *New Left Review*, 61: 5–27.

The future of identity research
Impact and new developments in sociolinguistics

Bettina Beinhoff and Sebastian M. Rasinger

Introduction

This chapter discusses the impact of identity research and possible future developments it might take. Although we focus on sociolinguistics, the issues that we discuss are of relevance for applied linguists with an interest in language and identity. Brubaker and Cooper (2000: 1) were the first to highlight potential problems with the use of 'identity' as a concept in social science research, proclaiming that identity 'tends to mean too much […] too little […] or nothing at all'. Now, nearly two decades later, the concept of identity is more relevant and prominent than ever (as this volume illustrates) and it continues to gain momentum in the field. This growing interest reflects current concerns and experiences with globalisation and increasing contact between cultures on the individual and societal level. These developments are strongly influenced by factors such as migratory movements and new technologies, which have facilitated the environment for identity work.

Based on a systematic review of recent work, we propose to map the complexities of identity in the heterogeneous and interdisciplinary field of sociolinguistics and to explore the many ways in which identity research has a significant impact in a variety of societal contexts. In particular, we will address three issues that we deem are crucial for achieving theoretically and methodologically sound future work on identity: authenticity, fluidity of identities and the role of the researcher and research ethics. The first issue for discussion is *authenticity*, especially with regard to authentic data and authentic speakers or participants. We will discuss this issue with reference to the multiplicity and performative aspect of identities. The second main issue that we will address in this chapter is *fluidity of identities*. In this section we will explore how categorisation and performativity contribute to identity creation. The third main development in current identity research affects the *role of the researcher* and *research ethics* (also see Hultgren *et al.*, this volume; Giampapa, this volume). With reference to an increase in research on online communities, we will argue that the multiple identities of the researcher can have significant implications for research ethics. In particular, we will suggest that there is a significant amount of overlap between these different strands of development, sometimes so much that it is difficult to distinguish between them. For example, the issue of performativity affects all three issues; it is a means of expressing the fluidity of the multiplicity of identities available to us, which has a substantial influence on what determines authenticity in action. At the same time, researchers have (potentially) an increasing number of identities at their disposal, which they need to negotiate, coordinate and perform in specific settings, particularly in virtual environments.

While we can only give a very tentative prediction about the direction in which language and identity research is heading in sociolinguistics, we do believe that the topics discussed in this chapter need to be addressed if we are to make further progress in identity research, especially within the context of globalisation and new media.

Current issues and future directions

Authenticity and identity

Among the current issues in identity research, the concept of authenticity is one of the most central ones. Therefore, it is only appropriate that this is the first issue we address in this chapter. Traditionally, authenticity has been a central issue in linguistics – and especially in sociolinguistics – where the authenticity of the participants and the data that they provide are regarded as vital to the success of research projects. Yet, the very concept of what constitutes authentic data or authentic speakers has received relatively little attention until fairly recently. In a noteworthy paper by Bucholtz (2003) on the authentication of identity, she suggests that 'authenticity underwrites nearly every aspect of sociolinguistics' and, crucially for readers of this volume, 'sociolinguistic investment in authenticity [is] an implicit theory of identity' (p. 398). We will not reiterate her criticism here; rather, we will offer an overview of different perspectives on authenticity and how authenticity interacts and overlaps with other concepts discussed in this chapter to underline its complexity.

Authenticity is, very much like fluidity (which we will discuss later), an important and widely discussed issue in identity research both inside and outside linguistics; for example, in studies on race and ethnicity (e.g. Johnson 2003) and sex and gender (e.g. Holt and Griffin's 2003 study on authenticity in the lesbian and gay scene). These studies emphasise the influence of the global on the local (especially Holt and Griffin 2003) and the possible implications of the 'arbitrariness of authenticity', when our very beliefs of what constitutes (in)authentic behaviours impede communication and cultural exchange (Johnson 2003: 3).

In sociolinguistics we often seem to assume that our readers intuitively know what is meant by 'authenticity'. Lindholm (2008: 2), however, argues that authenticity is a combination of two overlapping modes: 'origin', which refers to the genealogical and the historical level, and 'content', which includes identity and communication. Applied to our (socio)linguistic context, the 'origin' would be the history of the observed individual or group, for example their ethnicity or regional origin, whereas 'content' might refer to the personal identities and the language patterns in whichever form of communication we choose to observe. Lindholm (2008) admits that these two modes are not always compatible and they may not always be involved in the same way depending on the situation. In fact, especially with regard to language, there is evidence that people use the content level (e.g. speech patterns) to construct alternative narratives about their origins to their actual 'authentic' personal history (or biography) in order to negotiate a new and more desirable identity.

Therefore, it seems appropriate to regard authenticity as constructed from the linguistic and paralinguistic features available to the actor to do identity work during interaction. Here the process of styling, i.e. all the strategic actions and performances that individuals use to construct their identities (Coupland 2007), gains particular relevance. Styling is part of how social identities are constructed, for example by deliberately changing the tone of voice, dialect or bodily gestures (Coupland 2001). In this way, styling 'creates social meanings around personal authenticity and inauthenticity' (Coupland 2007: 25) where 'inauthenticity' can be used as a stylistic element to portray a different identity, for example by putting on a different accent. Such changes in language use are well known from variationist sociolinguistic studies where participants have been observed to – consciously or subconsciously – adopt a more formal style in interview settings as compared to, for example, in interactions involving gossip. However, this kind of styling can also be used to cross social boundaries, for example as an expression of loyalty to the intended in-group, or as a 'denaturalizing move' to emphasise differences between groups (Bucholtz 2011: 70). To be viewed as authentic, the actor has to select the most relevant type and the 'right' amount of authenticity features in order to be convincing (termed 'enoughness' in Blommaert and Varis 2011). The notion of authenticity is well illustrated in Bucholtz's (2011) study on the use of African-American language features by European-American students. Their knowledge and use of linguistic features associated with African Americans expressed loyalty to a certain kind of lifestyle, influenced by music which developed in predominantly African-American communities (in this case, particularly rap and hip hop). Members of outgroups, such as students who did not subscribe to this lifestyle, perceived this language use as a group marker. However, on closer inspection some of the African-American language features used by these European-American students did not fully conform to the way they would normally be used in African-American English. Therefore, while their use of African-American English was convincing enough for other (outgroup) European-American students, it may well be regarded as inauthentic and 'not enough' by African-American students.

This process of constructing authenticity in communication illustrates that the issue of authenticity in identity research is closely connected to the fluidity of identities. Given the relevance of the notion of fluidity in discussions of identity and globalisation, it is no surprise that the concept of authenticity has received increased attention in discussions and research on language and globalisation. As mentioned earlier in this chapter, globalisation is generally regarded to lead to a multiplicity of identities, greater variation of identities and the idea of hybridity and uniformity in identities (see e.g. Heller 2003). At the same time, however, authenticity is relevant when global phenomena become localised and, in the process, lose some uniformity. A good example of this kind of transformation is given in Pennycook's (2007) paper on the localisation of hip hop culture where, in a first wave, hip hop rooted in African-American culture spread globally but proved to be inauthentic and hence unsuitable for many local hip hop artists in countries such as Malaysia and Korea (Pennycook 2007), Germany (Androutsopoulos 2003), China (Wang 2013) and Russia (Ivanov 2013). One major theme in all of these discussions on the localisation of hip hop is the use of language – mostly English versus local languages – and the use of code-switching. Interestingly, in this particular context, the use of English can be seen as a remnant of the global aspect of the hip hop phenomenon. This happened within a context in which there was an increasing use of the English language internationally and locally and growing bilingualism and multilingualism with English and other languages.

Many discussions of bilingualism and multilingualism rest on the assumption that the 'native speaker' is the most authentic representative of a language. This is apparent, for example, in the well-established focus on studying native speakers and in fact on only very specific groups of these native speakers in variationist sociolinguistic studies (see Bucholtz 2003 for a critique). In the domain of second language acquisition, sounding more 'native-like' is often associated with sounding authentic (e.g. Flege 1991; Bongaerts *et al.* 2000; Singleton 2001). However, it is notoriously difficult to define the concept of 'native speaker'; moreover, public perception differs greatly from scholarly definitions in sociolinguistics. In public perception, native speakers are regarded not only as the 'stakeholders' of 'their' language, but also as the people who intuitively know what is correct and what is incorrect language use (Davies 2003: 2). The native speaker concept is also closely related to the perceived cultural and national background of the speaker. For example, in one of our studies (Beinhoff 2008), first language speakers of English from the Caribbean were rated as sounding less like native speakers of English than German and Greek second language speakers of English. This study revealed that the concept of native speaker is more related to a specific model of what a native speaker should sound like. Similarly, a study by Adolphs (2005) showed that what is perceived to be a native speaker changes over time and is therefore an unstable concept even on an individual level.

No wonder then that, in discussions of the native speaker, authenticity is an important aspect. This is especially the case in sociolinguistics, where the idea of a native language is a central component of individual and social identity. However, Myhill (2003) argues that for some individuals and communities (e.g. Armenian, Jewish, Greek and Chinese communities) a native language is not necessarily a means of identification. Based on the above assumption, however, members of these communities who do not speak the communities' assumed 'native language' may – from an outsider's perspective – not count as 'authentic' members of their relevant community, which could leave them vulnerable to prejudice and discrimination (ibid.).

While we may perceive a trend towards multilingualism globally, Blommaert (2006) points out that regionally (and to some extent also nationally) monolingualism may be enforced, e.g. by prescribing the use of one particular language in official contexts. Here, language is considered to be a vehicle of authenticity and – regional or national – values, as Blommaert's (ibid.: 243) example of 'Flemish nationalism' vs 'Belgian-Francophone imperialism' illustrates. Language policies such as these can be seen as attempts at 'purifying' language and making it appear more authentic in the local context and indicate a move towards local monolingual identities. Authenticity is also a highly relevant issue in indigenous language education. The link between identity and indigenous/heritage languages is particularly strong in this area. The main concerns here are what level of knowledge constitutes a heritage language identity, i.e. to what level do the children of migrants have to be proficient in their heritage language(s)? Since the use of heritage languages is often restricted to particular environments (e.g. at home versus professional/work settings), the question is what level of use has to be achieved to pass as an 'authentic' speaker and representative of the relevant community. For example, in their study on Korean heritage language provisions in Montreal, Park and Sarkar (2007) found that Korean parents saw the main benefits of their children learning to speak Korean not only in their ability to speak with their grandparents, but also in future economic opportunities. To achieve this, a relatively high level of proficiency and a linguistic repertoire that went well beyond a single (i.e. home or professional) setting was necessary. On the other hand, heritage language learners can regard themselves as authentic members of their heritage community without high levels of proficiency in all aspects of their heritage language (Giangreco 2000 in Carreira 2004). This raises questions related to cultural and ethnic identity such as who is given access to language classes in indigenous or heritage languages and whether these are restricted to people from the specific heritage background (and whoever is included in these groups) (see Henze and Davis 1999). For example, in German schools, language classes in Turkish used to be only accessible for children of Turkish ancestry (Gogolin and Reich 2001).

So far we have introduced the wide and varied approaches to authenticity and related issues. Although it is not possible to cover the entirety of such a complex concept in this chapter, the discussion has shown how authenticity is central to identity construction and – as in the case of styling – can change identities temporarily, which will be explored in greater detail in the following section.

Fluidity and multiplicity of identities: categorisation vs performativity

The second issue to be addressed in this chapter is fluidity and multiplicity of identities. It is a well-established view that identities are not fixed but rather context-dependent (see Baxter, this volume). However, while some theories assume that an individual's identity is relatively stable (e.g. self-schema theory in Markus 1977), the idea that identity is highly variable seems to have gained more supporters in recent decades based on more compelling evidence (see e.g. Onorato and Turner 2004). This is especially the case for studies in language and identity in both socio- and applied linguistics but extends to other areas of research that inform the theoretical underpinnings of linguistic research.

These issues have become particularly relevant with the rise in the use of social media, as well as within the context of globalisation more generally, as more potential identities are made available to us, leading to the idea of a multiplicity of identities. Such multiplicity of identities, we argue, increases the likelihood that identities become more hybrid and fluid on an individual level, which needs to be considered in research design and methodologies.

One of the most widely accepted approaches to identity construction is the theory of categorisation or self-categorisation as coined by Turner (1987) following Tajfel's social identity theory (Tajfel 1978). This theory suggests that, in particular social situations, specific categories of an individual's self are more salient than others, and this saliency changes depending on the context. For example, we are conscious that our identities as members of the academic community are highly salient as we write this chapter, which is represented by the academic register we employ. In other contexts, say, when we are with our families, our identities as daughter, son or sibling will be salient and this will be indexed in our linguistic behaviour.

Closely related to categorisation is the concept of 'performativity'. Following Butler (1990), Pennycook (2004: 8) defined performativity as 'the way in which we perform acts of identity as an ongoing series of social and cultural performances rather than as the expression of a prior identity' (see Baxter, this volume). This understanding of performativity is based on the observation that salient categories of the self emerge in ongoing interactions and other embodied presentations, such as ways of dressing, walking and so on (Woodward 2002). The main idea of performativity and its relationship with identity goes back to Goffman's (1974) frame analysis, which highlights the performative aspect of social interaction; this informed Butler's (1990) groundbreaking work on the performativity of gender. Since then, the idea of performativity has permeated research on identity and informed the idea of hybridity and fluidity of identities. This has become particularly relevant in recent years, as seemingly a multiplicity of identities have become more available to us (although see Block, this volume) and modes of interaction have changed, as is evident in the growing body of research on the representation and negotiation of identity in social media (e.g. Androutsopoulos 2006; Bamman et al. 2014).

The increasing multiplicity of identities along with the notion of fluidity has received a lot of attention with regard to race as an identity inscription, where categories are seen as being socially constructed rather than as genetically endowed; this has led to an increasing blurring of racial categories, particularly in heteroglossic contexts such as the United States (Rockquemore and Arend 2002). In addition, Bucholtz (2011) emphasises that all available identity categories are constantly negotiated and navigated in social interactions, which means that 'one's assigned social category is not always the same as one's social identity' (p. 1). For example, in another of our studies, Rasinger (2012) illustrates how a Polish migrant living in the United Kingdom constructs her Polish identity while simultaneously separating herself from the local Polish community and 'everything [that] is Polish' (p. 42). However, there seem to be limits to this fluidity and multiplicity, as studies in gender and sexual identity suggest that traditional categories (as operationalised through sexuality labels like 'gay', 'lesbian' and 'bisexual') still prevail as identity categories (see Russell *et al.* 2009).

Kendall (1998) also challenges the assumption of a greater fluidity and multiplicity especially in online interactions, suggesting that people prefer not to view themselves as performed characters. Thus, there may be a discrepancy between how people view themselves and how they are seen by others. This is in line with Blommaert's (2006: 238) notion of an 'inhabited' and 'ascribed' identity, where the inhabited identity is one that people claim for themselves, whereas the ascribed identity is imposed on them by others. Such a divergence between the inhabited and ascribed identity is particularly relevant in second language acquisition contexts, where language learners are especially vulnerable to being categorised on the basis of their linguistic competence and assumed cultural background in second language environments (see e.g. Preece 2009; Block 2014 [2007]). This is illustrated in our own work in which Beinhoff (2013) found that German and Greek second language speakers of English were considered to be significantly less educated and intelligent than southern British English first language speakers based on their accents. Interestingly, and possibly in line with current stereotypes, the German speakers were rated more favourably regarding their level of education and intelligence than the Greek speakers. Such assumptions and judgements about the speaker's identity (i.e. the ascribed identity) can be a threat to the speaker's inhabited identity.

Increasing multilingualism – and resulting multiplicity of identities – challenges traditional frameworks and methods for linguistic investigation, such as social network analysis, which is based on the assumption that individuals have a first language and that this is a central part of a collective cultural identity. Lanza and Svendsen (2007) argue that multilingual communities are more complex than traditional (and often monolingual) social networks, which were originally the basis for this approach. For this reason, the social network approach may not necessarily be applicable in multilingual and multicultural communities. This is particularly the case in urban areas, characterised by superdiversity and heteroglossia, where these traditional models of communication are no longer adequate. Otsuji and Pennycook (2010), for example, have coined the term 'metrolingualism' to describe the linguistic practices of the bi/multilingual denizens of urban settings. They suggest that metrolingualism 'does not assume connections between language, culture, ethnicity, nationality or geography, but rather seeks to explore how such relations are produced, resisted, defied or rearranged; its focus is not on language systems but on languages as emergent from contexts of interaction' (ibid.: 246). This approach, then, takes as its point of departure how bi/multilingual linguistic repertoires are deployed in specific contexts and social interactions and how these index identities rather than starting with relatively fixed entities like ethnic communities, professional groups or first-language background.

Other well-established frameworks, such as the notion of motivation in second language acquisition, are also challenged by the notions of fluidity and multiplicity. For example, Dörnyei and Ushioda (2009) emphasise that motivation in second language acquisition can be strongly influenced by linguistic and sociocultural fluidity and diversity arising from globalisation. This potential for change in motivation is very much initiated by the shift of 'ownership' of the second or target language, especially in English as a global language, where the concept of integrative motivation (which relies on a target group of first language of 'native' speakers of the language; see Piller 2002) is challenged when such a target group or speakers does not exist any more, or loses its significance (for a discussion on the concept of 'ownership' in language learning see Norton 1997).

In addition, an increasing fluidity and multiplicity of identities can also affect the 'L2-self'. The L2-self has at its core the notion of the learner's 'ideal self', i.e. the 'attributes that someone would ideally like to possess' (Dörnyei and Ushioda 2009: 4). However, this ideal self may in some contexts compete with a multitude of identities. For example, within the context of English as a global language, second language learners of English may have to decide whether their ideal self is part of the global English community or whether it is more orientated towards acquiring a first language variety of English as fully as possible. Indeed, it seems that it is difficult – if not impossible – to decide between the two, which can lead to uncertainties about the desired aim in acquiring the second language (Jenkins 2007) and can result in changes in motivation (Dörnyei and Ushioda 2009).

To sum up, in this section we saw how, in social interactions, identities are constantly negotiated. Identities are fluid and may also be hybrid, and this fluidity and hybridity may affect the way individuals perform their identities in different domains. However, so far, the identities of the researchers who are conducting identity studies have not been taken into consideration. It is our view that, in identity research, the researcher's own identity can potentially shape the findings considerably; we will look at this issue in the following section.

Ethics of identity research and the role of the researcher

The first part of this chapter discussed the theoretical and methodological complexities associated with researching linguistic identities. The issues involved are considerable: on the one hand, personal identity may be, in the words of Riley (2007: 72), 'unanalysable'; on the other, social identities are constructed, or played out/performed, in social interaction. Within this context of methodological challenges linked to the empirical study of identity sits the concept of research ethics. A marked shift towards safeguarding research participants, researchers and institutions has resulted in considerable attention being paid to what constitutes 'ethical' research. At the same time, recent developments in sociolinguistics and discourse analysis have seen research increasingly moving from physical contexts to virtual or digital communities, which brings particular methodological and ethical challenges.

The concept of ethics is difficult to define, let alone to operationalise. Hammersley and Traianou (2012: 16) define the term as: 'A set of principles that embody or exemplify what is good or right, or allow us to identify what is bad or wrong.' Along similar lines, research ethics may best be defined as 'a type of applied ethics – between morality and legality' (Esposito 2012: 1); in other words, something that encompasses both the – increasingly important – aspect of legalistic research governance and judgements about what is 'right' or 'wrong' from a moral point of view.

The rise of a litigation culture in the UK over the last two decades has seen considerable efforts being made in the development of robust research ethics procedures. Professional organisations, such as the British Association for Applied Linguistics, the British Sociological Association and the British Psychological Society, publish ethical guidelines and guides for good practice. Research concordats lay out protocols that ensure research integrity and ethical principles. Legislation with regard to research ethics is complex: in the United Kingdom alone, linguistic research involves, at a minimum, the Data Protection Act (1998) and, potentially, the Mental Capacity Act (2005). In addition, universities and other research institutions have often sophisticated ethics protocols and approval processes, 'which can be both a help and a hindrance in fostering ethical practice' (Eckert 2013: 11). Within the UK, research involving the National Health Service and Social Care has to go through their separate and often lengthy approval processes, as does research that includes organisations falling under the remit of the Ministry of Justice and the Ministry of Defence. Studies involving young or vulnerable participants, or 'sensitive' research sites, are subject to researchers obtaining clearance from the Disclosure and Barring Service (DBS). The Equality Act (2010) protects people from discrimination based on age, disability, gender reassignment, marriage and civil partnership, race, religion and belief, sex and sexual orientation; libel laws offer protection to those subject to libellous behaviour. The UK Research Integrity Office's 'Code of Practice' (UKRIO 2009) stipulates seven principles researchers and research organisations ought to adhere to, among them honesty and integrity.

In the midst of what appears to be – and often is – a legal minefield is the identity researcher, attempting not only to explore the hard-to-explore, but also to do so trustworthily, that is, to conduct research that is based on a 'set of standards that demonstrates that a research study has been conducted competently and ethically' (Rallis and Rossman 2009: 264). The aim of this section is not to discuss the mechanics, let alone the intricacies, of ethics in linguistic research (see Eckert 2013 and Rasinger 2013 for overviews of key issues and procedures), but to put the emphasis firmly on what research ethics means to us as identity researchers. The role of the researcher is inextricably linked to the issues discussed in the chapter so far: linguistic fieldwork, particularly fieldwork where the researcher interacts with participants, places us in a position that requires the negotiation of multiple identities at the same time while also catering for diverse requirements. The quest for authentic linguistic data, as discussed above, takes place within a context in which we 'should do [our] utmost to ensure the accuracy of data and results' while complying 'with all legal and ethical requirements' (UKRIO 2009: 7). Data collected through interaction with participants inevitably means that the researcher's identity, or identities, becomes an integral part of the fieldwork and data-generation process; and the need for data requires us to adopt, or emphasise, identities that are performed as part of the process. Norton and Early (2011: 432), in their discussion of a digital literacy project in Uganda, provide insights into how their 'researcher identities were subject to constant negotiation and change', leading to a multiplicity of identities they adopted as part of the process. The notion of authenticity, then, does not only concern the data produced, but also those who elicit it.

Online research: multiple identities, trust and deception

In this final section, we aim at bringing together the three strands of our argument by looking in more detail at cyberspace as a context for researching identity. The rise of research on online communities in the form of digital (or virtual) ethnographies has resulted in an additional layer of complexity to be added. Rallis and Rossman (2009) draw up a set of dichotomies inherent to research ethics: privacy and confidentiality; deception and consent; and trust and betrayal. In the context of online research, these dichotomies become, potentially, intensified. Eynon *et al.* (2014) provide a thorough discussion of the ethical issues particular to online research, and highlight, in addition to the issues Rallis and Rossman raise, the specific role that researchers play in online settings. At the time of writing this chapter, a scandal involving the social networking site

Facebook has been making global headlines. As part of a research project into users' emotions, Facebook manipulated user entries to see what effect this had on users' emotions. Having failed to obtain consent from the participants involved, informed consent being at the very core of research ethics, such manipulation was highly unethical.

However, ethical issues in online research can be much more subtle. In their guidelines on ethical decision-making in Internet research, Markham and Buchanan (2012) highlight that, as Internet-based research is likely to include human participants at some point (an issue that is of course particularly prevalent in identity research), the same ethical principles apply that would be used in traditional research. As Markham and Buchanan suggest, particular emphasis needs to be paid to the contextualised nature of norms, risk and harm, as what is socially acceptable and legal in the local context of the researcher may not be acceptable in the location of the participants. In other words, despite the researcher(s) and the participants sharing virtual space, they may be physically located thousands of miles apart and subject to different legal and moral frameworks.

Driscoll and Gregg (2010) discuss how online identity – or identities – can mean different things for different people. For some, online identities can be very different from their 'real life' identity, whereas for others their online identities are an extension of their identities in work and/or home domains. This pertains to both the researcher and those being researched. In their discussion of LGBT dating websites, Driscoll and Gregg take up the issue of self-categorisation in online profiles. While identity in the physical world is constructed over time in face-to-face interaction, most online profiles allow – or force – users to self-categorise into discrete categories. Mowlabocus's (2012) study on the gay dating website Gaydar demonstrates how user identities are created by clicking ascribed categories, with templates supporting this construction. Similarly, Hughey (2008), while discussing the 'disembodied identities' in a virtual community of Black Greeks, suggests that screen names function as textual monikers to 'represent specific forms of identity' (p. 540). Identities within the community are far from static, being both dynamic and shaped by both the constraints of the online and text-based communication, as well as real-life experiences.

Static self-categorisation brings with it the problem of pre-defined perceptions of other users. For example, Baker (2005) describes how particular characteristics are openly deemed undesirable in gay men's dating ads, which he illustrates by beginning his 2008 volume with a fieldwork anecdote: 'some people get really angry about the male and female labels' (Baker 2008: 1). This element of static identity inscriptions in online sites is in stark contrast to the dynamic aspect of identity construction in the physical world.

Multiple identities and authenticity are, of course, not only a problem for researchers, but can also be tools. Both authors of this chapter are White Western Europeans and both of us have an interest in migration issues, often involving people that are not part of our own ethnic, linguistic or social group. Entering a fieldwork site in the real world poses considerable questions – issues exhaustively discussed in related research. On the surface, researching online communities, for example by means of a digital ethnography, facilitates access. Online profiles also allow each of us to be whoever we would like to – or pretend to – be. One of our colleagues, for example, has two profiles on a popular social networking site: a private one, with clear access controls, presumably only shared with close family and friends, and a public one, clearly marking her as a professional academic. Issues regarding access aside, the use of personal profiles, as opposed to professional, research-specific ones, raises the problem of the boundaries between personal and professional spaces being increasingly blurred, and in particular, in the context of social networking sites, this includes not only the researcher, but also the researcher's personal – as opposed to professional – social networks.

To an extent, this is the modern equivalent of a problem anthropologists and ethnographers have always faced: how to gain access to a site without our own, personal identity overshadowing our research interests. What is new in digital ethnographies is the 'non-presentness'. As discussed above, online communities allow users to inhabit whatever identities they choose. From a methodological point of view, this seems to be an advantage; from an ethical one, it is problematic at best.

On the one hand, research-specific online profiles may facilitate access, in particular to communities where particular characteristics are indicative for authentic membership; on the other, the use of fake or fictitious profiles by researchers violates the principles of honesty and deceives participants. This is not only a problem where researchers actively engage with online communities, for example in the form of discussion boards, but also where the role is that of an observer. If membership in an online community implies shared characteristics, pretending to be a member may trick other users into revealing information that they otherwise would keep concealed. Participant consent, if given on the wrong premise, does not solve the issue. Similarly, Duncombe and Jessops (2012) discuss the problem of the 'commodification of rapport' (p. 110) and 'faking friendships' (pp. 118 f.). Experienced fieldworkers, especially those working with qualitative methods such as interviews, are well versed in establishing a rapport with participants – a rapport that may seem personal to the participant, but may possibly be a mere, albeit valuable, skill for the researcher. The physical remoteness of research in the virtual world may exacerbate this issue, with potentially striking effects not only in terms of ethical issues but also those related to authenticity. In her study on cyber communities, Donath (1998) identifies, among others, two elements of online deception that resonate here: 'category deception' (p. 46), where online users claim to be who, in reality, they are not; and the more elaborate 'trolling' (p. 43), whereby users deliberately steer discussions through negative, often disparaging, contributions. For the researcher carrying out language and identity studies online, both categorical deceit and trolling pose significant problems. Donath (ibid.: 29) argues that 'in the disembodied world of the virtual community, identity is also ambiguous'. What may read like the contributions of an adolescent may in reality be that of an adult using a style associated with a much younger age-group, or it may be indeed that of an adolescent and hence authentic – an issue that does not arise in traditional face-to-face interaction.

A superficial scan of the readers' comments section in the online editions of the *Guardian* newspaper, traditionally on the left side of the political spectrum, finds several instances where some readers are ascribed the identities of 'trolls' by other users, a categorisation that is based on opinions voiced that are not in line with what is perceived to be that of a typical *Guardian* reader. 'Don't feed the troll' posts are aimed at discouraging other users from engaging with the troll, hence de facto excluding them from the interaction. Conversely, posts on the website of the *Telegraph* newspaper, generally pursuing a conservative agenda, identify those who post overtly 'liberal' opinions as 'Guardianistas' – the counterpart to the 'Tory troll'. The phenomenon on trolling and its perception by online communities is a fascinating one, and one that poses considerable challenges for any researcher who encounters such a community for the first time. In their discussion of trolling on a feminist Internet forum, Herring *et al.* (2002: 372) point out that trolling is generally aimed at 'luring others into pointless and time-consuming discussions' by posting deliberately provocative messages – messages that are, as Donath (1998: 45) points out, also a 'game about identity perception'. Crucially, experienced members of such a community are able to, or purport to be able to, identify trolls through non-compliance with the prevailing ideology. However, to no extent is it clear whether such non-compliant behaviour is a case of deliberately provocative trolling, or the honestly held opinion of the user posting the message.

In terms of authenticity, it is difficult to judge such posts as being authentic, or unauthentic, in order to steer the interaction. The spatial and temporal remoteness of online interaction, where users communicate asynchronously and may, at any given point in time, disengage from the interaction abruptly, exacerbates the issue. If the alleged troll only posts a single initial message, it is nearly impossible to come to any reliable conclusions about their identity.

Summary

In this chapter, we have attempted to sketch both the status quo and the future of research on identities in sociolinguistics, with particular focus on the notions of authenticity, performativity and multiplicity. What has emerged is a complex picture, where these notions, together with regulatory, legal and moral constraints, pose challenges in both theoretical and methodological terms. In this era of globalisation, an increasingly complex world with developments often subsumed under the term of 'superdiversity' (Vertovec 2007), a plethora of identity options appear to exist, although it is important to note that individuals do not have equal access to all identities. New modes of communication and the intangibility of the virtual world require identity researchers to carefully balance personal and professional identities without losing sight of the actual research aims while negotiating tensions and the needs of all those involved in the process.

Related topics

Positioning language and identity: poststructuralist perspectives; Language and gender identities; Ethics in language and identity research; The politics of researcher identities: opportunities and challenges in identities research; Straight-acting: discursive negotiations of a homomasculine identity; Styling and identity in a second language; Language and identity in the digital age.

Further reading

Benwell, B. and Stokoe, E. (2006). *Discourse and identity*. Edinburgh: Edinburgh University Press, pp. 243–279. (The chapter on virtual identities in the authors' well-known volume provides an overview of how identities are constructed in cyberspace, drawing upon multiple layers of analysis from content to graphology.)

Butler, J. (1990). *Gender trouble*. New York: Routledge. (Butler's seminal book is one of the first to emphasise the performative aspect of identity.)

Coupland, N. (2007). *Style: language variation and identity*. Cambridge: Cambridge University Press. (Drawing upon the concept of style, Coupland discusses how linguistic variation is used to create, and perform, identity in social interaction.)

Fielding, N., Lee, R.M. and Blank, G. (eds) (2008). *The SAGE handbook of online research methods*. London: SAGE. (This volume comprises a comprehensive collection of methodological issues in online research, including chapters on virtual ethnography and online ethics.)

Seargeant, P. and Tagg, C. (eds) (2013). *The language of social media: identity and community on the Internet*. Basingstoke: Palgrave Macmillan. (This edited volume brings together chapters on the construction of identity and community on the Internet, and addresses such aspects as performativity, contextualisation and 'fake' identities.)

References

Adolphs, S. (2005). 'I don't think I should learn all this' – a longitudinal view of attitudes towards 'native speaker'-English, in C. Gnutzmann and F. Intemann (eds) *The globalisation of English and the English language classroom*. Tübingen: Narr, pp. 119–132.

Androutsopoulos, J. (2003). Einleitung, in J. Androutsopoulos (ed.) *HipHop: globale kultur – lokale praktiken [Hip hop: global culture – local practices]*. Bielefeld, Germany: Transcript Verlag, pp. 9–23.

Androutsopoulos, J. (2006). 'Introduction: sociolinguistics and computer-mediated communication', *Journal of Sociolinguistics*, 10(4): 419–438.

Baker, P. (2005). *Public discourses of gay men*. London: Routledge.

Baker, P. (2008). *Sexed texts: language, gender and sexuality*. London: Equinox.

Bamman, D., Eisenstein, J. and Schnoebelen, T. (2014). 'Gender identity and lexical variation in social media', *Journal of Sociolinguistics*, 18(2): 135–160.

Baxter, J. (this volume). Positioning language and identity: poststructuralist perspectives, in S. Preece (ed.) *The Routledge handbook of language and identity*. Abingdon: Routledge, pp. 34–49.

Beinhoff, B. (2008). Looking for the 'real' native speaker: the perception of native and non-native English accents by non-native speakers of English, in E. Waniek-Klimczak (ed.) *Issues of accents in English*. Cambridge: Cambridge Scholars Publishing, pp. 120–139.

Beinhoff, B. (2013). *Perceiving identity through accent – attitudes towards non-native speakers and their accents in English*. Oxford: Peter Lang.

Block, D. (2014 [2007]). *Second language identities*. London: Bloomsbury Academic.

Block, D. (this volume). Class in language and identity research, in S. Preece (ed.) *The Routledge handbook of language and identity*. Abingdon: Routledge, pp. 241–254.

Blommaert, J. (2006). Language policy and national identity, in T. Ricento (ed.) *An introduction to language policy: theory and method*. London: Blackwell, pp. 238–254.

Blommaert, J. and Varis, P. (2011). 'Enough is enough: the heuristics of authenticity in superdiversity', *Tilburg Papers in Culture Studies*, 2.

Bongaerts, T., Mennen, S. and Slik, F.V.D. (2000). 'Authenticity of pronunciation in naturalistic second language acquisition: the case of very advanced late learners of Dutch as a second language', *Studia Linguistica*, 54(2): 298–308.

Brubaker, R. and Cooper, F. (2000). 'Beyond "identity"', *Theory and Society*, 29(1): 1–47.

Bucholtz, M. (2003). 'Sociolinguistic nostalgia and the authentication of identity', *Journal of Sociolinguistics*, 7(3): 398–416.

Bucholtz, M. (2011). *White kids: language, race, and styles of youth identity*. Cambridge: Cambridge University Press.

Butler, J. (1990). *Gender trouble*. New York: Routledge.

Carreira, M. (2004). 'Seeking explanatory adequacy: a dual approach to understanding the term "heritage language learner"', *Heritage Language Journal*, 2(1): 1–25.

Coupland, N. (2001). 'Dialect stylization in radio talk', *Language in Society*, 30(3): 345–375.

Coupland, N. (2007). *Style: language variation and identity*. Cambridge: Cambridge University Press.

Davies, A. (2003). *The native speaker: myth and reality*. Clevedon: Multilingual Matters.

Donath, J.S. (1998). Identity and deception in the virtual community, in P. Kollock and M. Smith (eds) *Communities in cyberspace*. London: Routledge, pp. 29–59.

Dörnyei, Z. and Ushioda, E. (eds) (2009). *Motivation, language identity and the L2 self*. Clevedon: Multilingual Matters.

Driscoll, C. and Gregg, M. (2010). 'My profile: the ethics of virtual ethnography', *Emotion, Space and Society*, 3(1): 15–20.

Duncombe, J. and Jessop, J. (2012). 'Doing rapport' and the ethics of 'faking friendship', in T. Miller, M. Birch, M. Mathner and J. Jessop (eds) *Ethics in qualitative research*. 2nd edn. London: SAGE, pp. 108–121.

Eckert, P. (2013). Ethics in linguistic research, in D. Sharma and R.J. Podesva (eds) *Research methods in linguistics*. Cambridge: Cambridge University Press, pp. 11–26.

Esposito, A. (2012). 'Research ethics in emerging forms of online learning: issues arising from a hypothetical study on a MOOC', *Electronic Journal of E-Learning*, 10(3): 315–325.

Eynon, C.R., Fry, J. and Schroeder, R. (2014). The ethics of Internet research, in N. Fielding, R.M. Lee and G. Blank (eds) *The SAGE handbook of online research methods*. London: SAGE, pp. 22–42.

Flege, J.E. (1991). 'Age of learning affects the authenticity of voice-onset time (VOT) in stop consonants produced in a second language', *Journal of the Acoustical Society of America*, 89(1): 395–411.

Giampapa, F. (this volume). The politics of researcher identities: opportunities and challenges in identities research, in S. Preece (ed.) *The Routledge handbook of language and identity*. Abingdon: Routledge, pp. 289–303.

Goffman, E. (1974). *Frame analysis: an essay on the organization of experience*. Harvard: Harvard University Press.

Gogolin, I. and Reich, H. (2001). Immigrant languages in federal Germany, in G. Extra and D. Gorter (eds) *The other languages of Europe: demographic, sociolinguistic, and educational perspectives*. Clevedon: Multilingual Matters, pp. 193–214.

Hammersley, M. and Traianou, A. (2012). *Ethics in qualitative research: controversies and contexts*. London: SAGE.

Heller, M. (2003). 'Globalization, the new economy, and the commodification of language and identity', *Journal of Sociolinguistics*, 7(4): 473–492.

Henze, R. and Davis, K.A. (1999). 'Authenticity and identity: lessons from indigenous language education', *Anthropology and Education Quarterly*, 30(1): 3–21.

Herring, S., Job-Sluder, K., Scheckler, R. and Barab, S. (2002). 'Searching for safety online: managing "trolling" in a feminist forum', *Information Society*, 18: 371–384.

Holt, M. and Griffin, C. (2003). 'Being gay, being straight and being yourself: local and global reflections on identity, authenticity and the lesbian and gay scene', *European Journal of Cultural Studies*, 6(3): 404–425.

Hughey, M.W. (2008). 'Virtual (br)others and (re)sisters: authentic Black fraternity and sorority identity on the Internet', *Journal of Contemporary Ethnography*, 37(5): 528–560.

Hultgren, A.K., Erling, E.J. and Chowdhury, Q.H. (this volume). Ethics in language and identity research, in S. Preece (ed.) *The Routledge handbook of language and identity*. Abingdon: Routledge, pp. 257–271.

Ivanov, S. (2013). Track 4 hip-hop in Russia: how the cultural form emerged in Russia and established a new philosophy, in S.A. Nitzsche and W. Grünzweig (eds) *Hip-hop in Europe*. Muenster: LIT Verlag, pp. 13–87.

Jenkins, J. (2007). *English as a lingua franca: attitude and identity*. Oxford: Oxford University Press.

Johnson, E.P. (2003). *Appropriating Blackness: performance and the politics of authenticity*. Durham, NC: Duke University Press.

Kendall, L. (1998). 'Meaning and identity in "cyberspace": the performance of gender, class, and race online', *Symbolic Interaction*, 21(2): 129–153.

Lanza, E. and Svendsen, B.A. (2007). 'Tell me who your friends are and I might be able to tell you what language(s) you speak: social network analysis, multilingualism, and identity', *International Journal of Bilingualism*, 11(3): 275–300.

Lindholm, C. (2008). *Culture and authenticity*. London: Wiley-Blackwell.

Markham, A. and Buchanan, E. (2012). *Ethical decision-making and Internet research: recommendations from the AoIR Ethics Working Committee* (Version 2.0) [Online]. Available at www.aoir.org/reports/ethics2.pdf

Markus, H. (1977). 'Self-schemata and processing information about the self', *Journal of Personality and Social Psychology*, 35: 63–78.

Mowlabocus, S. (2012). *Gaydar culture: gay men, technology and embodiment in the digital age*. Farnham: Ashgate.

Myhill, J. (2003). 'The native speaker, identity, and the authenticity hierarchy', *Language Sciences*, 25(1): 77–97.

Norton, B. (1997). 'Language, identity, and the ownership of English', *TESOL Quarterly*, 31(3): 409–429.

Norton, B. and Early, M. (2011). 'Researcher identity, narrative inquiry, and language teaching research', *TESOL Quarterly*, 45: 415–439.

Onorato, R.S. and Turner, J.C. (2004). 'Fluidity in the self-concept: the shift from personal to social identity', *European Journal of Social Psychology*, 34(3): 257–278.

Otsuji, E. and Pennycook, A. (2010). 'Metrolingualism: fixity, fluidity and language in flux', *International Journal of Multilingualism*, 7(3): 240–254.

Park, S.M. and Sarkar, M. (2007). 'Parents' attitudes toward heritage language maintenance for their children and their efforts to help their children maintain the heritage language: a case study of Korean-Canadian immigrants', *Language, Culture and Curriculum*, 20(3): 223–235.

Pennycook, A. (2004). 'Performativity and language studies', *Critical Inquiry in Language Studies*, 1(1): 1–19.

Pennycook, A. (2007). 'Language, localization, and the real: hip-hop and the global spread of authenticity', *Journal of Language, Identity, and Education*, 6(2): 101–115.

Piller, I. (2002). 'Passing for a native speaker: identity and success in second language learning', *Journal of Sociolinguistics*, 6(2): 179–208.

Preece, S. (2009). *Posh talk: language and identity in higher education.* Basingstoke: Palgrave Macmillan.

Rallis, S. and Rossman, G. (2009). Ethics and trustworthiness, in J. Heigham and R.A. Croker (eds) *Qualitative research in applied linguistics.* London: Palgrave Macmillan, pp. 263–287.

Rasinger, S.M. (2012). '"And everything is Polish": narrative experiences of "new" migrants', *European Journal of Applied Linguistics and TEFL*, 1(2): 33–49.

Rasinger, S.M. (2013). *Quantitative research in linguistics: an introduction.* London: Bloomsbury.

Riley, P. (2007). *Language, culture and identity: an ethnolinguistic perspective.* London: Continuum.

Rockquemore, K.A. and Arend, P. (2002). 'Opting for White: choice, fluidity and racial identity construction in post civil-rights America', *Race and Society*, 5(1): 49–64.

Russell, S.T., Clarke, T.J. and Clary, J. (2009). 'Are teens "post-gay"? Contemporary adolescents' sexual identity labels', *Journal of Youth and Adolescence*, 38(7): 884–890.

Singleton, D. (2001). 'Age and second language acquisition', *Annual Review of Applied Linguistics*, 21: 77–89.

Tajfel, H. (1978). Social categorization, social identity and social comparison, in H. Tajfel (ed.) *Differentiation between groups.* London: Blackwell, pp. 61–76.

Turner, J.C. (1987). *Rediscovering the social group: a self-categorization theory.* Oxford: Blackwell.

UK Research Integrity Office (UKRIO) (2009). *Code of practice for research: promoting good practice and preventing misconduct.* London: UK Research Integrity Office [Online]. Available at www.ukrio.org

Vertovec, S. (2007). 'Super-diversity and its implications', *Ethnic and Racial Studies*, 30(6): 1024–1054.

Wang, X. (2013). '"I am not a qualified dialect rapper": constructing hip-hop authenticity in China', *Sociolinguistic Studies*, 6(2): 333–372.

Woodward, K. (2002). *Understanding identity.* London: Arnold.

Identity in language learning and teaching
Research agendas for the future

Peter De Costa and Bonny Norton

Introduction

While cognitive approaches remain important in second language acquisition (SLA), the social turn in SLA has gained momentum since Firth and Wagner's (1997) call to consider the social aspects of language learning (Douglas Fir Group in press 2016). This timely expansion of the field has afforded a host of non-cognitive approaches such as identity, language socialisation and conversation analytic perspectives to flourish as SLA and applied linguistics researchers explore viable ways to examine language development. Of these 'alternative' approaches to SLA (Atkinson 2011), the strong interest in an identity approach has been particularly encouraging, resulting in a vast body of work on identity and language learning and teaching over the last two decades (Norton and Toohey 2011). Given this positive trend, it is daunting to consider which research agendas would most productively extend this line of research in the future. At the same time, we are excited by the opportunity to collaborate on a topic that is of much interest to both of us and to which we have dedicated many years of scholarship. In the sections that follow, we map out what we consider to be some of the most interesting research on identity in recent years, and discuss its relevance for future research. In this process, we consider not only extensions of existing research, but also new areas that have promise for the future. Our first section addresses current and future issues in relation to four broad categories: (i) theoretical developments; (ii) interdisciplinarity; (iii) research populations; and (iv) methodological innovations. These categories were selected on the basis of our interpretation of contemporary trends in identity research, which we anticipate will continue to generate robust interest in the years to come. As demonstrated in the following sections, we do not confine ourselves to one research agenda for the future, but consider a number of promising research directions, given both the breadth and depth of interest in this topic. It is important to note, however, that there is considerable overlap between the themes, directions and sections, some of which we address in the chapter. We hope this structure will help readers to navigate a complex research terrain that remains vibrant and productive.

Current issues and future directions

Theoretical developments

Globalisation

As recent identity research suggests, identity needs to be interrogated in the face of globalisation and the hybridising linguistic practices and intersecting movements of people (e.g. Heller 2011; Higgins 2011; S. Shin 2012). These processes have led to increasing multilingualism in schools and society and the production of what Higgins (2015: 373) has called 'millennium identities', to index 'the mechanisms that produce linguistic and cultural hybridity in the current era of new millennium globalization'. At the same time, the forces of neoliberalism (see Block *et al.* 2012; Duchêne and Heller 2012), which entail deregulated markets, heightened individualism and the marketisation of activities and institutions, have had concomitant effects on the identities of language learners and teachers. As Foucault (2008) notes, individuals who are required to navigate market-driven spaces are *Homo economicus*, 'an entrepreneur of one's self'. Morgan and Clarke (2011) illustrate how business ideologies have infiltrated language education, in which social actors are often described as 'stakeholders', while Piller and Cho (2013) view neoliberalism as a covert language policy mechanism driving the global spread of English.

This dynamic research will be enriched in coming years by research conducted in diverse post-colonial sites where multilingualism is the norm (e.g. Barton and Lee 2012; Kerfoot and Bello-Nonjengele 2014; Norton 2015). In this regard, two 2014 journal special issues suggest intriguing directions for future research. A special issue of the *Journal of Language, Identity, and Education* (May 2014) sought to complement the focus on urban multilingualism, characteristic of much current identity research, by highlighting the diverse ways in which indigenous peoples are affected by the conditions of late modernity. In a similar spirit, a special issue of the *Journal of Multilingual and Multicultural Development* (Norton 2014) grappled with the ways in which language learners and teachers in African communities are navigating complex identities in changing times. Two particularly active sites of research are South Africa and Uganda, where researchers are undertaking exciting research in the domains of the home (e.g. Lemphane and Prinsloo 2014) and school (e.g. Early and Norton 2014). Such research responds to calls to restore agency and professionalism in periphery communities (e.g. Bamgbose 2014) and gives due recognition to local vernacular modes of learning and teaching. Future research on identity in language learning and teaching will continue this important trajectory.

Identity and investment

The sociological construct of investment, conceptualised by Norton in the mid-1990s (Norton Peirce 1995; Norton 2013) as a complement to the psychological construct of motivation (Dörnyei and Ushioda 2009), continues to engage scholars in the field of language education and applied linguistics (Anya 2011, forthcoming; Chang 2011; Mastrella and Norton 2011; Motha and Lin 2014). In addition to asking 'Are students motivated to learn a language?' Norton suggests the following: 'Are students and teachers *invested* in the language and literacy practices of a given classroom or community?' As Kramsch (2013: 195) notes, 'In the North American context, *investment* in SLA has become synonymous with "language learning commitment" and is based on a learner's intentional choice and desire.' The construct was the subject of a special issue of the *Journal of Asian Pacific Communication* (Arkoudis and Davison 2008; Norton and Gao 2008), which examined the construct in the Chinese context. More recently, Norton and her students have been exploring the relevance of the construct to the African context, finding it helpful in explaining the relationship of Ugandan multilingual students to the affordances of digital technology (Norton *et al.* 2011; Norton and Williams 2012). While Blommaert (2010) argues that resources shift their value, meaning and function as they travel across borders, largely as a result of how they are taken up in hierarchical contexts, Norton and Williams (2012) contend that the construct of investment provides further insight into this 'uptake' given that investment indexes issues of identity and imagined futures in our increasingly digital world.

As Darvin and Norton (2015) note, however, the world has changed considerably since Norton first developed the construct of investment. In this new transnational world, characterised by technological innovation, mobility and unpredictability (Blommaert 2013), learners constantly navigate online and offline identities in fluid and complex digital spaces. To capture this changing global context, Darvin and Norton have developed an expanded model of investment, which occurs at the intersection of identity, capital and ideology. Through this critical lens, researchers and practitioners can examine more systematically how microstructures of power in communicative events are indexical of ideological structures that impact communicative practices and other social processes. By providing a multilayered and multidirectional approach, the model seeks to demonstrate how power circulates in society and constructs modes of inclusion and exclusion through and beyond language. The model was presented for debate and critique at a 2014 symposium in Lausanne, Switzerland, which was focused on the application of the construct of investment to Francophone language education contexts. Based on this symposium, a special issue of the journal *Langage et Société* is underway (Bemporad forthcoming). Such expanded conceptions of investment will prove productive for language and identity scholarship in the future.

Social categories

In the context of globalisation, the social categories of ethnicity, race, gender and class require greater research, particularly with regard to how these identity inscriptions intersect (see Block and Corona, this volume). While Feinhauer and Whiting (2012) explore the implications of community practices for the ethnic identity of Latino students, Motha's (2014) work reminds us that the teaching of English remains contested territory, inscribed by race. In a study that crosses ethnic, gender and sexuality divides, for example, Appleby (2012) found that White Australian men teaching in Japanese language schools struggled to negotiate a particularly complex contact zone, which may have limited their professional and pedagogical aspirations. Also in Japan, Kamada (2010) examined the hybrid identities of adolescent girls who were 'half' Japanese, illustrating how they struggled to negotiate desirable identities when confronted by marginalising discourses. Focusing on ethnicity in the United States, Anya (2011) found that African-American college students who wished to learn a second language were drawn by the desire to connect with and learn more about Afro-descendant speakers of their target languages. Future work on ethnicity and its intersection with other identity categories will also continue to address the long-standing native and non-native speaker distinction, which continues to be resilient in mainstream second language identity research (e.g. Trofimovich and Turuševa 2015). However, this enduring interest in ethnicity needs to be seen in relation to the neoliberal turn, which, as Pujolar and Jones (2012) show, has resulted in the marketisation of ethnolinguistic 'authenticity' to generate income.

Neoliberalism and globalisation also serve as analytical tools in new conceptions of social class, as highlighted in Block's (2014) recent work. Much of the identity work on class thus far (e.g. De Costa 2010a; Norton 2013) has drawn on Bourdieu's (1991) constructs of capital and habitus, which conceive of class as relational and emergent. However, as Block (2014) points out, an explicit discussion of class in identity research is less common. A welcome addition to this debate is a special issue on social class, edited by Kanno and Vandrick (2014), in the *Journal of Language, Identity, and Education*. The contributions in this volume provide a lens through which scholars can examine the extent to which language learning and teaching either reproduces or disrupts economic and social inequities. While recognising that the emergence of the neoliberal post-industrial work order may render traditional notions of 'middle class' and 'working class' defunct (Savage *et al.* 2013), Darvin and Norton (2014a) argue that class differences continue to impinge on the life trajectories of migrants, in visible and invisible ways. They draw on research with migrant learners in Canada to illustrate how migrants operate with a 'transnational habitus', continually negotiating their class positions (see Duff 2015 for a fuller discussion of transnationalism). While working with vulnerable migrants in educational contexts and other settings will continue to be a significant area of research in applied linguistics, we anticipate that more research will be conducted on middle and upper-class transnational learners, or what Vandrick (2011) has termed as 'the new global elite'. To date several studies (e.g. De Costa 2012; H. Shin 2012) have explored how such learners engage in identity negotiation as they traverse cultural and physical borders. Work on this group of learners and teachers promises to be significant because it highlights the material conditions of globalisation and its structures of inequality, a symptom of the overlapping contemporary trend of neoliberalism.

Towards greater interdisciplinarity

Social theory across disciplines and fields

The field of language education/applied linguistics was a latecomer to groundbreaking debates in the humanities and social sciences, beginning in the second half of the twentieth century and arising from Saussurian and post-Saussurian theories of language. What has been called the 'linguistic turn' in contemporary thought, poststructuralist theories have been influential in a wide range of disciplines associated with meaning-making. In poststructuralist theory (see Norton and Morgan 2012), language is seen as central to the circulation of discourses, which are systems of power/knowledge that define and regulate our social institutions, disciplines and practices. In poststructural terms, language is not only a linguistic system but also a social practice in which meanings are debated and identities negotiated. A recent special issue on poststructuralism in the journal *Applied Linguistics* (McNamara 2012) highlights the enduring importance of this area to the field. Future research, however, will be enriched by increased interest in theories of human agency, which is the subject of an exciting book by Miller (2014). The central argument Miller makes is that, while many scholars draw on poststructuralism to theorise learner identity in non-essentialist terms, 'agency' is often treated as an essential feature of the learner. Working with a comprehensive corpus of interview data from migrants who had become business owners in the United States, Miller theorises agency as performatively constituted in discursive practice. Such ideas are more fully developed in a 2015 co-edited volume, which focuses on interdisciplinary approaches to agency (Deters *et al.* 2015).

While poststructuralism will continue to impact future research on identity, language and learning, an interdisciplinary research agenda also arises from diverse areas within language education/applied linguistics itself. The comprehensively edited volume *Multiple perspectives on the self in SLA* (Mercer and Williams 2014) includes, for example, developmental perspectives (Ushioda 2014), neurophilosophical perspectives (Northoff 2014) and complexity perspectives (Mercer 2014). The 2015 special topic issue on identity in the *Annual Review of Applied Linguistics* (Mackey 2015) is equally interdisciplinary. An interdisciplinary research agenda can also be advanced through pairing identity with related constructs to promote a greater understanding of how identity is inextricably linked, for example, with ideology (e.g. De Costa 2011), stance (e.g. Jaffe 2009) and strategy (e.g. Cohen and Griffiths 2015). In addressing the particularly under-researched construct of affect, Kramsch (2009: 2) notes that SLA researchers have paid more attention to the processes of acquisition than to the 'flesh-and-blood individuals who are doing the learning'. Future affect-inflected identity work will go beyond examining the inner worlds of L2 learners from a psychoanalytic perspective (e.g. Granger 2004) to embrace an anthropological understanding of affect (e.g. McElhinny 2010; Benesch 2013; De Costa 2015). Identity research will also be enriched with reference to other SLA theories. For example, the Douglas Fir Group, organised by Dwight Atkinson, Heidi Byrnes and Jim Lantolf, have completed a series of workshops, beginning in 2013, which aimed to provide a transdisciplinary approach to second language acquisition. The participants in the group represent different areas of the field, and the identity approach (represented by Norton) makes an important contribution to the outcome of these deliberations (Douglas Fir Group in press 2016).

Literacy and digital literacy

Another important interdisciplinary link with identity research in applied linguistics is research on literacy. Scholars such as Moje and Luke (2009), Janks (2010) and Cope and Kalantzis (2012) have influenced much research on the relationship between literacy and learner identity. An extension of research on literacy and identity is that of multiple literacies and their relationship to language education (Prinsloo and Baynham 2008; Cummins and Early 2011) and digital literacy (Lam and Warriner 2012; Thorne *et al.* 2015; Darvin, this volume). Darvin and Norton (2014b), for example, describe the ways in which digital storytelling can expand the range of identities available to migrant language learners, creating a Third Space that acknowledges and affirms multidimensional identities. In the virtual world, the ability to construct functional selves through digital interaction is not uncommon, as Thorne *et al.* (2015) point out.

However, as informative as work on digital literacy and digital identities has been, it is not without shortcomings (Warschauer and Matuchniak 2010). As Snyder and Prinsloo (2007) note, much of the digital research on language education has focused on research in wealthier regions of the world; there is a great need for research in poorly resourced communities that can impact global debates on new technologies, identity and language learning. In this regard, the work of Toohey *et al.* (2012) is noteworthy. In an innovative video-making project with school children in India, Mexico and Canada, Toohey *et al.* found that the making of videos offered language learners opportunities for meaning-making that extended beyond their particular second language capabilities. Further, the authors argued that video-making could enhance the participants' awareness of audience, sequencing and rhetoric, leading to 'activities of critical reflection and agentive self and collective expression' (ibid.: 90). Also needed in this changing landscape are new tools to expedite future research on identity and digital literacy. To ensure analytical rigour, identity researchers could adopt more sophisticated analytical tools (see Martinec and van Leeuwen 2009; Thorne 2013) to investigate how identities are mediated along multimodal and Internet-mediated lines, a theme to be discussed more fully later in this chapter.

Scales

Also of interest to language and identity studies in applied linguistics is the construct of scales (Lemke 2000; Blommaert 2010). While Lemke (2000) has invoked the notion of timescales to illustrate how a particular event on some local timescale (e.g. fractions of a second, minutes) may simultaneously also be part of many other processes on longer timescales (e.g. days, months, years), Blommaert (2010) has shown how regularities of indexical identities and relationships to these timescales help to create power in interaction. These conceptions of scales serve as a metaphor to examine how identities develop over time and space. Both of us have long understood the value of tracing the trajectories of language learners to understand how the investments that drive language learning arise from learners' personal histories. Such longitudinal identity research will be enhanced by a scalar approach, which investigates how identity development is the result of intersecting timescales acting on an individual and the individual's movement across multiple social spaces. Such an approach to examining identity has been used by sociolinguists (e.g. Norton and Williams 2012; Canagarajah 2013), linguistic anthropologists (e.g. Wortham and Rhodes 2012; Mortimer and Wortham 2015) and SLA researchers (e.g. De Costa in press). Calling for greater attention to the level of practice, Wortham and Rhodes (2012), for example, recommend investigating identity formation through examining critical points in the activities engaged in by learners across space and time scales. Thus future identity work needs to conceptualise talk as locally constructed discursive practice, which is in line with the practice turn in applied linguistics (e.g. De Costa 2010b, 2014a; Pennycook 2010). This practice turn coincides with the growth of interest in English as a lingua franca (ELF), discussed below, a construct that Park and Wee (2011) suggest can be fine-tuned through a practice approach.

Research populations

Teacher identities

An area of identity research that is gaining momentum is that of language teacher and language teacher education (e.g. Clarke 2008; Hawkins and Norton 2009; Kanno and Stuart 2011; Norton and Early 2011; Varghese 2011; Sayer 2012; Menard-Warwick 2013; Cheung et al. 2015). As Clarke (2008) reminds us, identity researchers need to recognise the fluidity of identities and consider how identities are situated in and emerge from the local context. The importance of such a situated understanding of identity is explicated in Sayer (2012), who explored the ambiguities and tensions three Mexican EFL teachers faced while positioning themselves as legitimate language teachers and English speakers. Similarly, Kumaravadivelu (2012) has called for a reforming of teacher identities in the globalised world. Specifically, he has invoked the need for an epistemic break in the dependency on 'Western' knowledge of production and methods common in the Anglophone world. Such challenges are being taken up by emerging scholars such as Andema (2014) from Uganda and Carazzai (2013) and Sanches Silva (2013) from Brazil, who are exploring ways in which globalisation is impacting language teacher identity in tertiary language education programmes. The call to decentre and decolonise teaching is relevant in a neoliberal era that emphasises accountability and adherence to common standards. Two forthcoming journal special issues on teacher identity, in the *TESOL Quarterly* (Varghese *et al.* 2016) and the *Modern Language Journal* (De Costa and Norton forthcoming), will broaden the debate in this exciting area.

Lingua franca speakers

Lingua franca speakers are another population of interest to future identity researchers in applied linguistics. Many aspiring lingua franca languages compete for world dominance and there is growing interest in lingua franca languages (McGroarty 2006). In line with this interest in lingua franca languages is a greater exploration of non-native speaker identities (see discussion above), and a number of scholars have started to examine how non-native language learners develop and enact identities from an English as a lingua franca (ELF) perspective (Cogo and Dewey 2012; De Costa 2012; Liang 2012; Park 2012). For example, Liang (2012) examined how EFL students in Taiwan interacted with international speakers of English in the real-time, multiplayer virtual world. As observed by Clark (2013), in contrast to the teaching of English as a foreign language (EFL) or English as a second language (ESL), which positions English language learners as different from and/or deficient compared to speakers of standardised varieties of English, those working in an ELF paradigm do not view the English used by English language learners as deficient but as a flexible linguistic resource. However, ELF is not without its critics (see e.g. Prodomou 2008; Saraceni 2008; O'Regan 2014), who have raised a number of concerns regarding ELF, such as whether or not ELF can be viewed as a variety of English, which has led to a lively debate in the field. Recently, Baker and Jenkins (2015) offered a rebuttal, by asserting that more recent ELF research (e.g. Seidlhofer 2011) has focused on the processes and practices of ELF users. Despite continuing disagreement on ELF in the field, the explosive growth of contexts where English and other major languages, such as Spanish, Arabic and Chinese, are used as a lingua franca points to the scope for researchers in applied linguistics to explore identities within these contexts and to consider how linguistic practices in these settings enable language learners and teachers in periphery communities to assert their agency.

Heritage language learners

Another population of increasing interest to identity researchers is heritage language learners (see Duff 2012; Kagan and Dillon 2012; He 2014; Leeman 2015). Common in such research is a commitment to reclaim the local by venerating the languages spoken in students' home communities. For example, Leeman *et al.* (2011) describe a critical service-learning university programme that sought to build heritage language speakers' linguistic awareness through community-based opportunities to enact and strengthen identities as language experts. In their comprehensive review of second language identity, Miller and Kubota (2013) note, however, that the term 'heritage' remains slippery and contested, and needs greater clarification. To support this position, they draw on the study of Blackledge and Creese (2008), which investigated a school context in which Bengali students in the United Kingdom claimed hybrid heritage identities, rather than the essentialist heritage identities imposed by the school programmes. Miller and Kubota (2013) make the case that researchers and teachers cannot underestimate learners' agency with respect to whether and how learners identify as heritage language learners, and what implications this might have for curriculum development. The work of Rampton, Leung and Harris is helpful in this respect (see e.g. Leung *et al.* 1997; Harris 2006; Rampton 2006).

Study abroad learners

Study abroad is another promising research context, especially given the growing number of such programmes offered by universities (see Kinginger 2011; Magnan and Lafford 2012). According to Magnan and Lafford (2012), to facilitate student linguistic success abroad, candidates ought to engage in social computing networks with their future host families before arrival on site, receive extensive departure training about the target culture, live in interactive home stay situations, and participate in service learning and internships to practise the target language. Following these observations, one way in which study abroad identity research can be developed is through tracing a learner's identity transformation across the different contexts identified by Magnan and Lafford. As discussed, such a longitudinal approach would also enhance our understanding of how identities change over time and space.

Innovative methodologies

Narrative inquiry

As observed by Early and Norton (2013), narrative inquiry can illuminate how identity is negotiated, given that narratives are co-constructed and shaped by social, cultural and historical conventions (see Barkhuizen 2013). Focusing on oral narratives, De Fina and Baynham (2012) add that narratives create a space for immigrant voices, further justifying why narratives are important in the articulation of identities. Block (2010) has suggested three distinct ways of dealing with narratives: thematic analysis (focus on the content of what is said); structural analysis (focus on how narratives are produced); and dialogic/performative analysis (focus on who the utterance is directed to and the purpose of the utterance). This third analytic approach highlights the need to consider the positionings adopted by the interlocutor and to engage in rigorous analysis of the narratives. The significance of positionings is also emphasised by Talmy (2011), whose social-practice orientation of interviews focuses on how identity is performed in this particular speech event. We foresee future narrative-based identity work as continuing this recent line of methodological practice. We also anticipate a wider range of narratives being adopted, ranging from narratives of classroom life (Nelson 2011) to autoethnographies (e.g. Canagarajah 2012) and plays (Darvin 2015).

Conversation analysis

As an analytical tool, ethnomethodological conversation analysis (CA) allows researchers to explore discourse identities and social identities, thereby enhancing our understanding of how identities are ascribed through an analysis of the sequential development of talk. More recent 'applied' CA research has begun to open up new understandings of how spoken interactional practices can help sustain social identities in this way (e.g. Mori 2012). Congruent with recent studies that explore how researchers' own identities and agendas are implicated in the construction of interviewees' responses, Mori's (2012) conversation analysis of a multilingual speaker of Korean, English and Japanese revealed that the speaker co-constructed her ever-shifting identities vis-à-vis membership categories such as American, Korean or Korean-American. Such an interpretation of identities as being fluid in complexion is consistent with Bucholtz and Hall's (2005) 'interactionist approach to identity', which calls for an examination of how subjectivities emerge as individuals engage in activity of all types. As is evident from the chapters in this volume, identity studies analyse interaction in contexts beyond classroom discourse. For researchers examining the identities of second language learners/teachers or bi/multilingual students and teachers, there may be more scope for multi-site research that looks beyond the confines of the language classroom to identity work in other settings, such as in family interactions (e.g. De Fina 2012).

Corpus linguistics

While some researchers have focused on interaction data, others have adopted a corpus approach to investigate how identities are represented in written discourse (e.g. Hyland 2012). For example, Hyland (2012) explored the regularity and repetition of what is socially ratified by analysing consistent rhetorical choices associated with the constructs of proximity and positioning. Within ELF research, Cogo and Dewey (2012) have applied corpus procedures to describe the linguistic features that are characteristic of the identities associated with ELF speakers. Given the growing sophistication of concordance tools and the availability of corpora, applied linguists now have greater access to data from all around the world through websites, blogs and social networking sites (Friginal and Hardy 2014), which allow identities in the digital era to be examined in increasingly creative and rigorous ways. Importantly, such a systematic examination of how academic identities are mobilised in writing can help students become experts in the genres of their discipline (Nesi and Gardner 2012) and thus inform pedagogy and curriculum design. Given these developments, it is predicted that the application of corpora and corpus-based methods will further illuminate identity research.

Ethics

In line with the ethical turn in applied linguistics (e.g. Ortega 2012; De Costa 2016), there has also been a notable shift towards reporting on researcher reflexivity when working with language learners (e.g. Cameron et al. 1992; Tremmel and De Costa 2011; De Costa 2014b) and language teachers (e.g. Norton and Early 2011). In their work with Ugandan teachers, Norton and Early (2011) explicated the different researcher identities that were negotiated by them while working with their local counterparts. While engaging in these acts of reflexivity may not entirely erase the inequalities that exist between the researcher and the researched, it at least represents an attempt to bridge the power differentials that may exist when carrying out identity research. One way to exercise reflexivity and ethical practices in a multilingual setting as articulated by Creese et al. (2009) is to represent the multiple voices of the communities being studied. Identity research conducted in a multitude of settings would increasingly need to take into account the ethical issues associated with research and make transparent the reflexive acts of the researcher.

Summary

The world has changed considerably since the 1990s, when scholars in applied linguistics were developing theories of identity that sought to capture the complex relationship between the language learner and the social world. Identity was theorised as a site of struggle, constructing and constructed by particular language and literacy practices. Learner investment was explored with reference to learner identity and imagined but often-localised futures. Relations of power, frequently inequitable and often invisible, were the subject of much research and inquiry. Two decades on, the digital revolution has shifted our understanding of time, space and our place in the world. Using social media, transnational learners can connect the past, present and future in unprecedented ways and do not necessarily have to leave town to 'study abroad'. Both learners and teachers can explore transnational identities that were not socially imaginable two decades ago and access to conversations is now negotiable both on and off-line. While identity can be a site of struggle, the digital offers a wider range of identity options for learners and teachers. This brave new world, however, remains complex and unequal and, as we have indicated, Darvin and Norton's (2015) model of investment represents one attempt to navigate the complex relationship between identity, capital and ideology.

The transformed relationship between structure and agency, time and space, and learning and teaching invites new agendas for future research, four of which we have identified in this chapter as particularly exciting. First, we discussed how theoretical developments on identity would be enriched by changing conceptions of globalisation, investment and the identity inscriptions of race, class, ethnicity and gender. Research conducted in post-colonial sites has much to offer such advances in theory. Second, we examined how in the coming years research on identity will extend links across various disciplines and build on developments within language education, applied linguistics, the social sciences and humanities. We also argued that the interest in social theory, digital literacies and scales would continue to advance. Third, we considered how future identity research would be enriched by a focus on diverse research populations such as teachers, lingua franca speakers, heritage language learners and study abroad learners. Finally, in order for new research agendas to be mapped out, we suggested that current methodologies needed to be revised and new ones added to the methodological toolkit. We proposed that there would be increased interest in narrative inquiry, conversation analysis, corpus linguistics and ethics. In the new digital landscape, the identities of researchers themselves may possibly provide one of the most intriguing agendas for future investigation.

Related topics

Positioning language and identity: poststructuralist perspectives; Ethnomethodological and conversation analytic approaches to identity; Language and identity in linguistic ethnography; Linguistic practices and transnational identities; Identity in post-colonial contexts; Class in language and identity research; Ethics in language and identity research; Intersectionality in language and identity research; Language and identity in the digital age; Language and identity research in online environments: a multimodal ethnographic perspective.

Further reading

Cheung, Y.L., Said, S.B. and Park, K. (eds) (2015). *Advances and current trends in language teacher identity research*. Abingdon: Routledge. (Situated against a changing teacher education landscape, this volume presents contemporary research on teacher identity as understood through various theoretical orientations and methodologies.)

De Costa, P.I. and Canagarajah, S. (guest eds) (in press). 'Special issue. Scalar approaches to language teaching and learning', *Linguistics and Education*. (This collection of papers explores how our understanding of language teaching and learning can be enhanced through a scalar lens.)

Kanno, Y. and Vandrick, S. (guest eds) (2014). 'Special issue. Social class in language learning and teaching', *Journal of Language, Identity, and Education*, 13(2). (The contributors to this special issue examine how the identity category of social class can inform language learning and teaching in the age of globalisation and neoliberalism.)

Mackey, A. (ed.) (2015). 'Identity', *Annual Review of Applied Linguistics*, 35. (This issue brings together leading identity scholars who illustrate the multiple ways in which identity has been investigated in various strands of applied linguistics.)

Norton, B. (2013 [2000]). *Identity and language learning: extending the conversation*. 2nd edn. Bristol: Multilingual Matters. (The second edition of Norton's highly cited 2000 book on identity and language learning provides a comprehensive analysis of how identity research has developed in the interim years. The book concludes with an insightful Afterword by Claire Kramsch.)

References

Andema, S. (2014). *Promoting digital literacy in African education: ICT innovations in a Ugandan primary teachers' college* [Online]. PhD thesis, University of British Columbia. Available at https://open.library.ubc.ca/cIRcle/collections/ubctheses/24/items/1.0167565

Anya, U. (2011). 'Connecting with communities of learners and speakers: integrative ideals, experiences, and motivations of successful Black second language learners', *Foreign Language Annals*, 44(3): 441–466.

Anya, U. (forthcoming). *Speaking Blackness in Brazil: racialized identities in second language learning*. Abingdon: Routledge.

Appleby, R. (2012). 'Desire in translation: White masculinity and TESOL', *TESOL Quarterly*, 47(1): 122–147.

Arkoudis, S. and Davison, C. (guest eds) (2008). 'Special issue. Chinese students: perspectives on their social, cognitive, and linguistic investment in English medium interaction', *Journal of Asian Pacific Communication*, 18(1).

Atkinson, D. (2011). *Alternative approaches to second language acquisition*. Abingdon: Routledge.

Baker, W. and Jenkins, J. (2015). 'Criticising ELF', *Journal of English as a Lingua Franca*, 4(1): 191–198.

Bamgbose, A. (2014). 'The language factor in development goals', *Journal of Multilingual and Multicultural Development*, 35(7): 646–657.

Barkhuizen, G. (2013). *Narrative research in applied linguistics*. Cambridge: Cambridge University Press.

Barton, D. and Lee, C.K.M. (2012). 'Redefining vernacular literacies in the age of Web 2.0', *Applied Linguistics*, 33(3): 282–298.

Bemporad, C. (guest ed.) (forthcoming). 'Language investment, une notion majeure pour saisir les dynamiques sociales de l'appropriation langagière' [Language investment, a major construct for understanding social dynamics in language learning] *Langage et Société*.

Benesch, S. (2013). *Considering emotions in critical English language teaching: theories and praxis*. Abingdon: Routledge.

Blackledge, A. and Creese, A. (2008). 'Contesting "language" as "heritage": negotiation of identities in late modernity', *Applied Linguistics*, 29(4): 533–554.

Block, D. (2010). Researching language and identity, in B. Paltridge and A. Phakti (eds) *Continuum companion to research methods in applied linguistics*. London: Continuum, pp. 337–347.

Block, D. (2014). *Social class and applied linguistics*. Abingdon: Routledge.

Block, D. and Corona, V. (this volume). Intersectionality in language and identity research, in S. Preece (ed.) *The Routledge handbook of language and identity*. London: Routledge, pp. 507–522.

Block, D., Gray, J. and Holborow, M. (2012). *Neoliberalism and applied linguistics*. London: Routledge.

Blommaert, J. (2010). *The sociolinguistics of globalization*. Cambridge: Cambridge University Press.

Blommaert, J. (2013). *Ethnography, superdiversity and linguistic landscapes: chronicles of complexity*. Bristol: Multilingual Matters.

Bourdieu, P. (1991). *Language and symbolic power* [Trans. G. Raymond and M. Adamson]. Cambridge: Polity Press.

Bucholtz, M. and Hall, K. (2005). 'Identity and interaction: a sociocultural linguistic approach', *Discourse Studies*, 7(4–5): 585–614.

Cameron, D., Frazer, E., Harvey, P., Rampton, B. and Richardson, K. (1992). *Researching language: issues of power and method*. London: Routledge.

Canagarajah, A.S. (2012). 'Teacher development in a global profession: an autoethnography', *TESOL Quarterly*, 46(2): 258–279.

Canagarajah, A.S. (2013). *Translingual practice: global Englishes and cosmopolitan relations*. Abingdon: Routledge.

Carazzai, M.R. (2013). *The process of identity (re)construction of six Brazilian language learners: a poststructuralist ethnographic study* [Online]. PhD thesis, Universidade Federal de Santa Catarina. Available at https://repositorio.ufsc.br/handle/123456789/105150

Chang, Y.J. (2011). 'Picking one's battles: NNES doctoral students' imagined communities and selections of investment', *Journal of Language, Identity, and Education*, 10(4): 213–230.

Cheung, Y.L., Said, S.B. and Park, K. (eds) (2015). *Advances and current trends in language teacher identity research*. Abingdon: Routledge.

Clark, U. (2013). *Language and identity in Englishes*. Abingdon: Routledge.

Clarke, M. (2008). *Language teacher identities: co-constructing discourse and community*. Clevedon: Multilingual Matters.

Cogo, A. and Dewey, M. (2012). *Analyzing English as a lingua franca: a corpus-driven investigation*. London: Continuum.

Cohen, A. and Griffiths, C. (2015). 'Revisiting LLS research 40 years later', *TESOL Quarterly*, 49(2): 414–429.

Cope, B. and Kalantzis, M. (2012). *Literacies*. Cambridge: Cambridge University Press.

Creese, A., Bhatt, A. and Martin, P. (2009). Multilingual researcher identities: interpreting linguistically and culturally diverse classrooms, in J. Miller, A. Kostogriz and M. Gearon (eds) *Culturally and linguistically diverse classrooms: new dilemmas for teachers*. Bristol: Multilingual Matters, pp. 215–233.

Cummins, J. and Early, M. (2011). *Identity texts: the collaborative creation of power in multilingual schools*. Staffordshire: Trentham.

Darvin, R. (2015). 'Representing the margins: multimodal performance as a tool for critical reflection and pedagogy', *TESOL Quarterly*, 49(3): 590–600.

Darvin, R. (this volume). Language and identity in the digital age, in S. Preece (ed.) *The Routledge handbook of language and identity*. London: Routledge, pp. 523–540.

Darvin, R. and Norton, B. (2014a). 'Social class, identity, and migrant students', *Journal of Language, Identity, and Education*, 13(2): 111–117.

Darvin, R. and Norton, B. (2014b). 'Transnational identity and migrant language learners: the promise of digital storytelling', *Education Matters: Journal of Teaching and Learning*, 2(1): 55–66.

Darvin, R. and Norton, B. (2015). 'Identity and a model of investment in applied linguistics', *Annual Review of Applied Linguistics*, 35: 36–56.

De Costa, P.I. (2010a). 'From refugee to transformer: a Bourdieusian take on a Hmong learner's trajectory', *TESOL Quarterly*, 44(3): 517–541.

De Costa, P.I. (2010b). 'Let's collaborate: using developments in global English research to advance socioculturally-oriented SLA identity work', *Issues in Applied Linguistics*, 18(1): 99–124.

De Costa, P.I. (2011). 'Using language ideology and positioning to broaden the SLA learner beliefs landscape: the case of an ESL learner from China', *System*, 39(3): 347–358.

De Costa, P.I. (2012). 'Constructing SLA differently: the value of ELF and language ideology in an ASEAN case study', *International Journal of Applied Linguistics*, 22(2): 205–224.

De Costa, P.I. (2014a). 'Cosmopolitanism and English as a lingua franca: learning English in a Singapore school', *Research in the Teaching of English*, 49(1): 9–30.

De Costa, P.I. (2014b). 'Making ethical decisions in an ethnographic study', *TESOL Quarterly*, 48(2): 413–422.

De Costa, P.I. (2015). 'Re-envisioning language anxiety in the globalized classroom through a social imaginary lens', *Language Learning*, 65(3): 504–532.

De Costa, P.I. (ed.) (2016). *Ethics in applied linguistics research: language researcher narratives*. Abingdon: Routledge.

De Costa, P.I. (in press). 'Scaling emotions: insights from a scholarship student', *Linguistics and Education*.

De Costa, P.I. and Norton, B. (guest eds.) (forthcoming). 'Special issue. Transdisciplinarity and language teacher identity', *The Modern Language Journal*.

De Fina, A. (2012). 'Family interaction and engagement with the heritage language: a case study', *Multilingua*, 31(4): 349–379.

De Fina, A. and Baynham, M. (2012). Immigrant discourse, in C.A. Chapelle (ed.) *Encyclopedia of applied linguistics* [Online]. DOI: 10.1002/9781405198431.wbeal0527

Deters, P., Gao, X., Miller, E. and Vitanova, G. (eds) (2015). *Theorizing and analyzing agency in second language learning*. Clevedon: Multilingual Matters.

Dörnyei, Z. and Ushioda E. (eds) (2009). *Motivation, language identity and the L2 self*. Clevedon: Multilingual Matters.

Douglas Fir Group (in press 2016). 'A transdisciplinary framework for SLA in a multilingual world', *The Modern Language Journal*, 100.

Duchêne, A. and Heller, M. (eds) (2012). *Language in late capitalism: pride and profit*, vol. 1. Abingdon: Routledge.

Duff, P. (2012). Identity, agency, and second language acquisition, in S.M. Gass and A. Mackey (eds) *The Routledge handbook of second language acquisition*. Abingdon: Routledge, pp. 410–426.

Duff, P. (2015). 'Transnationalism, multilingualism, and identity', *Annual Review of Applied Linguistics*, 35: 57–80.

Early, M. and Norton, B. (2013). Narrative inquiry in second language teacher education in rural Uganda, in G. Barkhuizen (ed.) *Narrative research in applied linguistics*. Cambridge: Cambridge University Press, pp. 132–151.

Early, M. and Norton, B. (2014). 'Revisiting English as medium of instruction in rural African classrooms', *Journal of Multilingual and Multicultural Development*, 35(7): 674–691.

Feinauer, E. and Whiting, E.F. (2012). 'Examining the sociolinguistic context in schools and neighborhoods of pre-adolescent Latino students: implications for ethnic identity', *Journal of Language, Identity, and Education*, 11(1): 52–74.

Firth, A. and Wagner, J. (1997). 'On discourse, communication, and (some) fundamental concepts in SLA research', *The Modern Language Journal*, 81(3): 285–300.

Foucault, M. (2008). *The birth of biopolitics* [Trans. G. Burchell]. Basingstoke: Palgrave Macmillan.

Friginal, E. and Hardy, J.A. (2014). *Corpus-based sociolinguistics: a guide for students*. Abingdon: Routledge.

Granger, C.A. (2004). *Silence in second language learning*. Bristol: Multilingual Matters.

Harris, R. (2006). *New ethnicities and language use*. Basingstoke: Palgrave Macmillan.

Hawkins, M. and Norton, B. (2009). Critical language teacher education, in A. Burns and J. Richards (eds) *Cambridge guide to second language teacher education*. Cambridge: Cambridge University Press, pp. 30–39.

He, A.W. (2014). Heritage language development and identity construction throughout the life cycle, in T. Wiley, J.K. Peyton, D. Christian, S.C.K. Moore and N. Liu (eds) *Handbook of heritage, community, and Native American languages in the United States: research, policy, and educational practice*. Abingdon: Routledge, pp. 324–332.

Heller, M. (2011). *Paths to post-nationalism: a critical ethnography of language and identity*. Oxford: Oxford University Press.

Higgins, C. (ed.) (2011). *Identity formation in globalizing contexts: language learning in the new millennium*. Berlin: Mouton de Gruyter.

Higgins, C. (2015). 'Intersecting scapes and new millennium identities in language learning', *Language Teaching*, 48(3): 373–389.

Hyland, H. (2012). *Disciplinary identities: individuality and community in academic discourse*. Cambridge: Cambridge University Press.

Jaffe, A. (ed.) (2009). *Stance: sociolinguistic perspectives*. Oxford: Oxford University Press.

Janks, H. (2010). *Literacy and power*. Abingdon and London: Routledge.

Kagan, O. and Dillon, K. (2012). Heritage languages and L2 learning, in S.M. Gass and A. Mackey (eds) *The Routledge handbook of second language acquisition*. Abingdon: Routledge.

Kamada, L. (2010). *Hybrid identities and adolescent girls*. Bristol: Multilingual Matters.

Kanno, Y. and Stuart, C. (2011). 'Learning to become a second language teacher: identities-in-practice', *The Modern Language Journal*, 95(2): 236–252.

Kanno, Y. and Vandrick, S. (guest eds) (2014). 'Special issue. Social class in language learning and teaching', *Journal of Language, Identity, and Education*, 13(2).

Kerfoot, C. and Bello-Nonjengele, B. (2014). 'Game changers? Multilingual learners in a Cape Town primary school', *Applied Linguistics* [Online]. DOI: 10.1093/applin/amu044

Kinginger, C. (2011). National identity and language learning abroad: American students in the post-9/11 era, in C. Higgins (ed.) *Identity formation in globalizing contexts: language learning in the new millennium*. Berlin: Mouton de Gruyter, pp. 147–166.

Kramsch, C.J. (2009). *The multilingual subject*. Oxford: Oxford University Press.

Kramsch, C.J. (2013). Afterword, in B. Norton, *Identity and language learning: extending the conversation*. 2nd edn. Bristol: Multilingual Matters.

Kumaravadivelu, B. (2012). *Language teacher education for a global society*. Abingdon: Routledge.

Lam, W.S.E. and Warriner, D.S. (2012). 'Transnationalism and literacy: investigating the mobility of people, languages, texts, and practices in contexts of migration', *Reading Research Quarterly*, 47(2): 191–215.

Leeman, J. (2015). 'Heritage language education and identity in the United States', *Annual Review of Applied Linguistics*, 35: 100–119.

Leeman, J., Rabin, L. and Román-Mendoza, E. (2011). 'Identity and activism in heritage language education', *The Modern Language Journal*, 95: 481–495.

Lemke, J. (2000). 'Across the scales of time', *Mind, Culture, and Activity*, 7(4): 273–290.

Lemphane, P. and Prinsloo, M. (2014). 'Children's digital literacy practices in unequal South African settings', *Journal of Multilingual and Multicultural Development*, 35(7): 738–753.

Leung, C., Harris, R. and Rampton, B. (1997). 'The idealised native-speaker, reified identities and classroom realities', *TESOL Quarterly*, 31(3): 545–560.

Liang, M.Y. (2012). 'Reimagining communicative context: ELF interaction in second life to learn EFL', *Journal of Language, Identity, and Education*, 11: 16–34.

Mackey, A. (ed.) (2015). 'Identity', *Annual Review of Applied Linguistics*, 35.

Magnan, S.S. and Lafford, B. (2012). Learning through immersion during study abroad, in S.M. Gass and A. Mackey (eds) *The Routledge handbook of second language acquisition*. Abingdon: Routledge, pp. 525–540.

Martinec, R. and van Leeuwen, T.J. (2009). *The language of new media design: theory and practice*. Abingdon: Routledge.

Mastrella, M. and Norton, B. (2011). 'Querer é poder? Motivação, identidade eaprendizagem de língua estrangeira' [Is investment enough? Motivation and identity in foreign language learning], in M.R. Mastrella (ed.) *Afetividade e Emoções no ensino/aprendizagem de línguas: múltiplos olhares* [Affect and emotion in teaching and learning languages: multiple perspectives]. Pontes Editores, Campinas, pp. 89–113.

May, S. (guest ed.) (2014). 'Special issue. Deconstructing the urban–rural dichotomy in sociolinguistics: indigenous perspectives', *Journal of Language, Identity, and Education*, 13(4).

McElhinny, B. (2010). 'The audacity of affect: gender, race, and history in linguistic accounts of legitimacy and belonging', *Annual Review of Anthropology*, 39: 309–328.

McGroarty, M. (ed.) (2006). 'Lingua franca languages', *Annual Review of Applied Linguistics*, 26.

McNamara, T. (2012). 'Poststructuralism and its challenges for applied linguistics', *Applied Linguistics*, 33(5): 473–482.

Menard-Warwick, J. (2013). *English language teachers on the discursive faultlines: identities, ideologies and pedagogies*. Bristol: Multilingual Matters.

Mercer, S. (2014). The self from a complexity perspective, in S. Mercer and M. Williams (eds) *Multiple perspectives on the self in SLA*. Bristol: Multilingual Matters, pp. 160–176.

Mercer, S. and Williams, M. (eds) (2014). *Multiple perspectives on the self in SLA*. Bristol: Multilingual Matters.

Miller, E. (2014). *The language of adult immigrants: agency in the making*. Bristol: Multilingual Matters.

Miller, E. and Kubota, R. (2013). Second language identity construction, in J. Herschensohn and M. Young-Scholten (eds) *The Cambridge handbook of second language acquisition*. Cambridge: Cambridge University Press, pp. 230–250.

Moje, E.B. and Luke, A. (2009). 'Literacy and identity: examining the metaphors in history and contemporary research', *Reading Research Quarterly*, 44(4): 415–437.

Morgan, B. and Clarke, M. (2011). Identity in second language teaching and learning, in E. Hinkel (ed.) *Handbook of research in second language teaching and learning*, Vol. II. Abingdon: Routledge, pp. 817–836.

Mori, J. (2012). 'Tale of two tales: locally produced accounts and memberships during research interviews with a multilingual speaker', *The Modern Language Journal*, 96(4): 489–506.

Mortimer, K. and Wortham, S. (2015). 'Analysing language policy and social identification across heterogeneous scales', *Annual Review of Applied Linguistics*, 35: 60–72.

Motha, S. (2014). *Race, empire, and English language teaching*. New York: Teachers' College Press.

Motha, S. and Lin, A. (2014). '"Non-coercive rearrangements": theorizing desire in TESOL', *TESOL Quarterly*, 48(2): 331–359.

Nelson, C.D. (2011). 'Narratives of classroom life: changing conceptions of knowledge', *TESOL Quarterly*, 45(3): 463–485.

Nesi, H. and Gardner, S. (2012). *Genres across the disciplines: student writing in higher education*. Cambridge: Cambridge University Press.

Northoff, G. (2014). Brain and self: a neurophilosophical perspective, in S. Mercer and M. Williams (eds) *Multiple perspectives on the self in SLA*. Bristol: Multilingual Matters, pp. 142–159.

Norton, B. (2013 [2000]). *Identity and language learning: extending the conversation*. 2nd edn. Bristol: Multilingual Matters.

Norton, B. (guest ed.) (2014). 'Special issue. Multilingual literacy and social change in African communities', *Journal of Multilingual and Multicultural Development*, 35(7).

Norton, B. (2015). 'Identity, investment, and faces of English internationally', *Chinese Journal of Applied Linguistics*, 38(4): 375–391.

Norton, B. and Early, M. (2011). 'Researcher identity, narrative inquiry, and language teaching research', *TESOL Quarterly*, 45(3): 415–439.

Norton, B. and Gao, Y. (2008). 'Identity, investment, and Chinese learners of English', *Journal of Asian Pacific Communication*, 18(1): 109–120.

Norton, B., Jones, S. and Ahimbisibwe, D. (2011). 'Learning about HIV/AIDS in Uganda: digital resources and language learner identities', *Canadian Modern Language Review/La Revue canadienne des langues vivantes*, 67(4): 568–589.

Norton, B. and Morgan, B. (2012). Poststructuralism, in C. Chapelle (ed.) *Encyclopedia of applied linguistics* [Online]. DOI: 10.1002/9781405198431.wbeal0924

Norton, B. and Toohey, K. (2011). 'Identity, language learning, and social change', *Language Teaching*, 44(4): 412–446.

Norton, B. and Williams, C.J. (2012). 'Digital identities, student investments and eGranary as a placed resource', *Language and Education*, 26(4): 315–329.

Norton Peirce, B. (1995). 'Social identity, investment, and language learning', *TESOL Quarterly*, 29(1): 9–31.

O'Regan, J. (2014). 'English as a lingua franca: an immanent critique', *Applied Linguistics*, 35(5): 533–552.

Ortega, L. (2012). 'Epistemological diversity and moral ends of research in instructed SLA', *Language Teaching Research*, 16(2): 206–226.

Park, H. (2012). 'Insight into learners' identity in the Korean English as a lingua franca context', *Journal of Language, Identity, and Education*, 11: 229–246.

Park, J.S. and Wee, L. (2011). 'A practice-based critique of English as a lingua franca', *World Englishes*, 30(3): 360–374.

Pennycook, A. (2010). *Language as a local practice*. Abingdon: Routledge.

Piller, I. and Cho, J. (2013). 'Neoliberalism as language policy', *Language in Society*, 42(1): 23–44.

Prinsloo, M. and Baynham, M. (eds) (2008). *Literacies, global and local*. Philadelphia: John Benjamins.

Prodomou, L. (2008). *English as a lingua franca: a corpus-based analysis*. London: Continuum.

Pujolar, J. and Jones, K. (2012). Literary tourism: new appropriations of landscape and territory in Catalonia, in A. Duchêne and M. Heller (eds) *Language in late capitalism: pride and profit*. Abingdon: Routledge, pp. 93–115.

Rampton, B. (2006). *Language in late modernity: interaction in an urban school*. Cambridge: Cambridge University Press.

Sanches Silva, J.F. (2013). *The construction of English teacher identity in Brazil: a study in Mato Grosso do Sul* [Online]. PhD thesis, Universidade Federal de Santa Catarina. Available at https://repositorio.ufsc. br/handle/123456789/105151

Saraceni, M. (2008). 'English as a lingua franca: between form and function', *English Today*, 24: 20–26.

Savage, M., Devine, F., Cunningham, N., Taylor, M., Li, Y., Hjellbrekke, J., Le Roux, B., Friedman, S. and Miles, A. (2013). 'A new model of social class: findings from the BBC's Great British class survey experiment', *Sociology*, 47(2): 219–250.

Sayer, P. (2012). *Ambiguities and tensions in English language teaching: portraits of EFL teachers as legitimate speakers*. Abingdon: Routledge.

Seidlhofer, B. (2011). *Understanding English as a lingua franca*. Oxford: Oxford University Press.

Shin, H. (2012). 'From FOB to cool: transnational migrant students in Toronto and the styling of global linguistic capital', *Journal of Sociolinguistics*, 16(2): 184–200.

Shin, S. (2012). *Bilingualism in schools and society: language, identity, and policy*. Abingdon: Routledge.

Snyder, I.A. and Prinsloo, M. (guest eds) (2007). 'Special issue. The digital literacy practices of young people in marginal contexts', *Language and Education*, 21(3).

Talmy, S. (2011). 'The interview as collaborative achievement: interaction, identity, and ideology in a speech event', *Applied Linguistics*, 32(1): 25–42.

Thorne, S.L. (2013). Digital literacies, in M. Hawkins (ed.) *Framing languages and literacies: socially situated views and perspectives*. Abingdon: Routledge, pp. 192–218.

Thorne, S.L., Sauro, S. and Smith, B. (2015). 'Technologies, identities and expressive activity', *Annual Review of Applied Linguistics*, 35: 215–233.

Toohey, K., Dagenais, D. and Schulze, E. (2012). 'Second language learners making video in three contexts', *Language and Literacy*, 14(2): 75–96.

Tremmel, B. and De Costa, P.I. (2011). 'Exploring identity in SLA: a dialogue about methodologies', *Language Teaching*, 44(4): 540–542.

Trofimovich, P. and Turuševa, L. (2015). 'Ethnic identity and second language learning', *Annual Review of Applied Linguistics*, 35: 234–252.

Ushioda, E. (2014). Motivational perspectives on the self in SLA: a developmental view, in S. Mercer and M. Williams (eds) *Multiple perspectives on the self in SLA*. Bristol: Multilingual Matters, pp. 127–141.

Vandrick, S. (2011). 'Students of the new global elite', *TESOL Quarterly*, 45(1): 160–169.

Varghese, M. (2011). Language teacher education and teacher identity, in F.M. Hult and K.A. King (eds) *Educational linguistics in practice: applying the local globally and the global locally*. Buffalo: Multilingual Matters, pp. 16–26.

Varghese, M.M., Motha, S., Trent, J., Park, G. and Reeves, J. (2016). Language teacher identity in multilingual settings [Special issue]. *TESOL Quarterly*, 50(3).

Warschauer, M. and Matuchniak, T. (2010). 'New technology and digital worlds: analyzing evidence of equity in access, use, and outcomes', *Review of Research in Education*, 34(1): 179–225.

Wortham, S. and Rhodes, C. (2012). 'The production of relevant scales: social identification of migrants during rapid demographic change in one American town', *Applied Linguistics Review*, 3: 75–99.

Index

Page numbers in *italics* refers to a table/figure